Reconstructing Crin

Law in Context

Below is a listing of the more recent publications in the Law in Context series

Editors: William Twining (University College, London) and
Christopher McCrudden (Lincoln College, Oxford)

Ashworth: *Sentencing and Criminal Justice*
Bell: *French Legal Cultures*
Bercusson: *European Labour Law*
Birkinshaw: *European Public Law*
Birkinshaw: *Freedom of Information: The Law, the Practice and the Ideal*
Cane: *Atiyah's Accidents, Compensation and the Law*
Collins: *The Law of Contract*
Diduck: *Law's Families*
Elworthy and Holder: *Environmental Protection: Text and Materials*
Fortin: *Children's Rights and the Developing Law*
Glover-Thomas: *Reconstructing Mental Health Law and Policy*
Gobert & Punch: *Rethinking Corporate Crime*
Harlow and Rawlings: *Law and Administration: Text and Materials*
Harris: *An Introduction to Law*
Harris, Campbell and Halson: *Remedies in Contract and Tort*
Harvey: *Seeking Asylum in the UK: Problems and Prospects*
Lacey, Wells & Quick: *Reconstructing Criminal Law*
Likosky: *Transnational Legal Processes – Globalisation and Power Disparities*
Moffat: *Trusts Law – Text and Materials*
Norrie: *Crime, Reason and History*
O'Dair: *Legal Ethics Text and Materials*
Oliver and Drewry: *The Law and Parliament*
Oliver: *Common Values and the Public–Private Divide*
Palmer and Roberts: *Dispute Processes: ADR and the Primary Forms of
    Decision Making*
Reed: *Internet Law – Text and Materials*
Scott and Black: *Cranston's Consumers and the Law*
Seneviratne: *Ombudsmen: Public Services and Administrative Justice*
Turpin: *British Government and the Constitution: Text, Cases and Materials*
Twining and Miers: *How to Do Things with Rules*
Twining: *Globalisation and Legal Theory*
Ward: *A Critical Introduction to EU Law*
Ward: *Shakespeare and the Legal Imagination*
Zander: *Cases and Materials on the English Legal System*
Zander: *The Law Making Process*

Reconstructing Criminal Law

Text and Materials

Third edition

Nicola Lacey
Professor of Criminal Law, London School of Economics

Celia Wells
Professor of Law, Cardiff University

Oliver Quick
Lecturer in Law, University of Bristol

Members of the LexisNexis Group worldwide

United Kingdom	LexisNexis UK, a Division of Reed Elsevier (UK) Ltd, Halsbury House, 35 Chancery Lane, LONDON, WC2A 1EL, and 4 Hill Street, EDINBURGH EH2 3JZ
Argentina	LexisNexis Argentina, BUENOS AIRES
Australia	LexisNexis Butterworths, CHATSWOOD, New South Wales
Austria	LexisNexis Verlag ARD Orac GmbH & Co KG, VIENNA
Canada	LexisNexis Butterworths, MARKHAM, Ontario
Chile	LexisNexis Chile Ltda, SANTIAGO DE CHILE
Czech Republic	Nakladatelství Orac sro, PRAGUE
France	Editions du Juris-Classeur SA, PARIS
Germany	LexisNexis Deutschland GmbH, FRANKFURT, MUNSTER
Hong Kong	LexisNexis Butterworths, HONG KONG
Hungary	HVG-Orac, BUDAPEST
India	LexisNexis Butterworths, NEW DELHI
Ireland	Butterworths (Ireland) Ltd, DUBLIN
Italy	Giuffrè Editore, MILAN
Malaysia	Malayan Law Journal Sdn Bhd, KUALA LUMPUR
New Zealand	LexisNexis Butterworths, WELLINGTON
Poland	Wydawnictwo Prawnicze LexisNexis, WARSAW
Singapore	LexisNexis Butterworths, SINGAPORE
South Africa	LexisNexis Butterworths, DURBAN
Switzerland	Stämpfli Verlag AG, BERNE
USA	LexisNexis, DAYTON, Ohio

A CIP Catalogue record for this book is available from the British Library.

First edition 1990
Second edition 1998

ISBN 0 406 96376 2

Typeset by Columns Design Ltd, Reading, Berkshire
Printed and bound in Great Britain by Thomson Litho Ltd, East Kilbride, Scotland

Visit LexisNexis UK at www.lexisnexis.co.uk

Preface

Our first task is to introduce Dr Oliver Quick as co-author of this third edition of *Reconstructing Criminal Law*. His expertise in professional regulation, trust and medical law has brought fresh ideas to the book. Nonetheless our aims have remained constant: to provide a critical and contextual assessment of selected areas of criminal law in England and Wales, with a wide variety of readings as a basis for interdisciplinary teaching and study.

Several aspects of our work on this edition deserve particular attention. A text locating criminal law in its broader institutional and social environment cannot merely update the relevant law. Social and political changes raise new questions about, and set up new influences on, criminal law, making it necessary to reassess the interpretive framework for a contextual analysis. Since the first edition, published in 1990, the class conflicts vividly represented in the industrial disputes of the first half of the 1980s have become much less visible in the enforcement of criminal law. Although we regard issues of class, broadly speaking, as central to an adequate interpretation of criminal justice, the markers of conflict, difference and fear onto which criminal justice policies are trained have shifted in the last 15 years. Among images of threats to law, order and safety, striking miners and poll tax protesters have been replaced by paedophiles and anti-social teenagers, while the IRA and UDF have been overtaken by Al Qaeda. And what we might call psychic harms – an acknowledgment of the trauma of the experience of sexual abuse or violence, as well as a more generalised recognition of the non-tangible harms suffered by victims – have become an increasingly important focus of policy debate, if not always of legal change.

The expansion of police powers remains a consistent response to lawlessness and disorder. Procedural and technological innovations – particularly in areas such as electronic surveillance and DNA evidence – now have greater relative

salience than paramilitary policing techniques, while criminal justice increasingly aspires to the efficient management of risk and danger. Moral panics
about miscarriages of justice such as those acknowledged in the late 1980s have
been overtaken in relative importance by concerns about the capacity of the
criminal process to deliver justice to Black and Asian defendants and victims.
Yet the concerns are complicated by their juxtaposition with continuing racial
prejudices and stereotypes about the behaviour, in particular, of young Afro-
Caribbean men. These are just a few examples of the sorts of issues that have
shaped our interpretation of criminal law in this edition.

The politicisation of debate about criminal justice in England and Wales, discussed in the first two editions, has grown in intensity over the last five years. A
crude index of this politicisation is the volume of legislation passing through
Parliament. Over the last decade, at least one statute with major criminal justice
implications has been enacted in most years. While most of this legislation concerns policing, evidence, sentencing and the criminal process, much also introduces new offences. Yet, despite the best efforts of the Law Commission, sexual
offences are the only area of criminal law to receive systematic statutory restatement or reform during this period. The ill-thought-out and reactive nature of
much of this legislation makes it extremely difficult to develop a coherent
account of the trajectory of the criminal justice policy – which is such an important part of criminal law's context – beyond David Garland's 'penal populism'.
We have not explored in any detail here the causes of this undoubted cultural
shift, although we include extracts from some of the more persuasive sociological interpretations. But we have tried to map its implications for criminal law.
This, as well as our interpretation of the shifting significance of class to criminal
enforcement, has shaped our replacement of what was one chapter on public
order with two chapters focusing on contemporary concerns about, respectively, group-based and individual 'dangerousness' and risk.

From a traditional legal perspective, the passage of the Human Rights Act 1998
would doubtless be seen as the most important general development bearing on
recent criminal law and procedure. Of course we examine the actual and potential impact of this constitutional innovation, which supplements an internal critique of criminal law by placing within domestic criminal law values previously
external to it. However, the Human Rights Act is also a product of the very
complicated political environment in which contemporary criminal law operates. The policy emphasis since 1997 has undoubtedly been on the first half of
the famous 'New Labour' mantra, 'Tough on crime, tough on the causes of
crime'. Yet liberalising and repressive measures often sit side-by-side in a single
piece of legislation. This is a residue of a political equilibrium in which the
legitimation of draconian powers against the most dangerous or unpopular
offenders – international terrorists, certain groups of sex offender – is assisted
by an emphasis on human rights. Purported advances in managerial efficiency
are 'balanced' by less severe or innovative penalties and procedures for non-

dangerous or young offenders. It is no more appropriate to understand the Human Rights Act in exclusively doctrinal terms than it is to restrict ourselves to internal readings of any other legislation relevant to criminal law.

The Sexual Offences Bill – introduced in the House of Lords in February 2003 with what might be called indecent haste, following the publication in November 2002 of the White Paper *Protecting the Public* – brings a radical redesign to the architecture of sexual offences. We have incorporated, in Chapter 5, the major changes that the Act is destined to import to the structure and definitions of sexual offences (based on the Bill as sent from the Lords to the Commons in June 2003). The legislation continues the theme we have identified of increased monitoring and surveillance of sex offenders, and it extensively defines consent, via a complex set of presumptions. We can anticipate much appeal activity. We can also note the conflict between the objectives of de-gendering many sexual offences while also seeking to achieve a better conviction rate for rape (an offence that only men can commit but whose victim can be male or female). Combined with the drafting convention that the masculine form includes the feminine, the ironic outcome is that the victim of rape is referred to as 'he' or 'him'.

In preparing this edition, we have been very grateful for the assistance of a number of people: Peter Alldridge was the source of useful references and insights while Emma Hitchings, Richard Huxtable, Stephen Jones and Harry McVea also all made some extremely helpful editorial suggestions. We are indebted in particular to Declan Roche for the detailed comments he generously made on a number of chapters. Our families have tolerated, with remarkable kindness and good humour, our book-related distractions, and we are delighted to dedicate this edition to them.

Nicola Lacey, Celia Wells, Oliver Quick

June 2003

Contents

Table of statutes

References printed in **bold** type indicate where the section of an Act is set out in part or in full.

Table of cases

Page numbers in **_bold italics_** refer to extracts where the case is set out.

PAGE

PAGE

H

I

J

K

L

PAGE

PAGE

PAGE

PAGE

Approaching criminal law

I. Images of criminal law

Images of criminal law infuse our everyday lives. From newspapers and television news programmes reporting incidents or cases such as the O J Simpson trial to detective novels, films and television series such as 'The Bill', 'Law and

Order', 'Silent Witness' and 'The Sopranos', crime and the control of crime are poured into our individual and collective consciousness. The images produced are complex and contradictory: heroic detectives compete for our attention with 'bent' police; wily criminals and informers jostle with the inadequate, the psychopath, the wife-batterer and even, on occasion, the offender with whom we are invited to sympathise; the dramatic appeal of racial injustice vies with the cultural resonance of racist stereotypes.

For many people who are neither practising lawyers nor legal scholars, criminal law represents the dominant image of what it is to have a legal system. In thinking carefully about the nature of criminal law, however, this familiarity can be an intellectual barrier. Most people's image of crime is dominated by crimes of violence or serious crimes against property, proceeded against through trial by jury. But in fact violent offences in 2000 – a typical year – made up only 14% of even indictable (ie the most serious) offences. The reality of the criminal justice system is dominated by the processing of road traffic offences, health-and-safety offences and low-level property offences: these offences are largely dealt with in magistrates' courts, and since the vast majority of defendants plead guilty, the trial process is a summary affair. Yet the distortion in popular representations of criminal justice is equally marked in criminal law textbooks, whose image of criminal law is dominated by a focus on violent and sexual offences, along with the more serious offences against property, and by a preoccupation with questions of individual responsibility for serious crime. Students of criminal law are therefore rarely introduced to the more 'everyday' offences which make up the vast majority of the business of the criminal process, and even less frequently to the social context in which images of crime are produced or to the procedural context in which practices of criminal law take shape.

We have set out to produce a rather different sort of text, taking as our counterpoint the following deft caricature:

L Farmer, 'The Obsession with Definition' (1996) Social and Legal Studies 57

The Criminal Law Textbook embodies the supreme positivism of the law. The moral, political and social dimensions of the law are tantalizingly raised and dismissed in a single movement in favour of grinding technical discussions of legal minutiae. Entire chapters and many hundreds of footnotes are devoted to such arcane issues as impossible attempts or the precise meaning of 'subjective liability'. As if this weren't enough, we are continuously reminded by the authors of how uniquely enjoyable the criminal law is supposed to be to students. It alone is said to capture the rich tapestry of human life – though our experience in the classroom suggests otherwise. The standard opening chapter illustrates perfectly this uneasy relationship between the criminal law and what, for want of a better term,

might be called its moral and social context. It is, invariably, on the definition of crime – seeking to define the scope of the work and so, more or less
implicitly, the object of the criminal law. While ... it may be unfashionable
to begin law books with definitions, few seem capable of resisting. No
amount of tinkering with the order and style of presentation can alter the
fact that the authors of the average criminal-law textbook are, and perhaps
destined to remain, deeply unfashionable.

In this book, our approach to criminal law, far from devoting only a 'single
movement' to the social and political context which informs criminal law,
locates criminal laws, their development and their implementation, firmly
within a social framework.

This chapter therefore introduces the issues and ideas which form the basis for
a critical and contextual reading of criminal law. We remain, however, in
Farmer's terms, 'deeply unfashionable'. For though our starting-point is a very
broad conception of criminal law as one among several sets of practices through
which a society – in this case that of England and Wales – both defines or constructs, and responds to, 'deviance' or 'wrongdoing', we do think that it is worth
pausing to give some attention to prevailing ideas about what, if anything,
unifies or identifies criminal law as a social practice: the problem of definition.

Farmer draws attention to the link between 'the obsession with definition' and
the positivist tradition. Legal positivism asserts that law is a discrete set of rules
or norms whose validity derives from the fact that they originate from a distinctive source: they have been set down by 'the sovereign' or may be identified
through a constitutional 'rule of recognition' (Hart 1961). This positivist claim
about the nature of law is inextricably bound up with a modern, scientific conception of law and legal scholarship, in which the task of the legal scientist – and
hence of the law student – is to garner knowledge of the distinctive legal terrain
and, ideally, to produce a complete and accurate description of it. However, as
soon as one begins to think about the range of conduct covered by modern systems of criminal law – from homicide to harassment, from rape to road traffic
infringements, from paedophilia to pollution, from deception to drug dealing
(via dangerous dogs ...) – the idea that there is anything *general* to be said about
'the nature of crime' begins to look very problematic indeed. Nonetheless, the
quest for a definition or a theory of criminal law persists: and that persistence is
itself of considerable interest. We therefore want to begin by taking a closer look
at what is meant by 'the quest for a definition' and to delineate two influential
approaches to theorising – producing a general account of – criminal law.

l.a.   Theories of criminal law: history, sociology and philosophy

The first approach to theorising criminal law is located firmly within the social
sciences. This is the approach taken by sociologists of law and legal historians.

This approach seeks to answer the question of definition in relation to an analysis and interpretation of the history of criminal regulation in specific social and political contexts. This kind of criminal law theory is closely tied to the interpretation of specific areas of substantive and procedural law, and the development of such an approach will be one of the main tasks of each of the following chapters. How might an interpretive approach tackle the quest for a defining conception of criminal law?

To think about this, let us return to our broad starting-point: that of criminal law as a particular social construction of, and response to, 'deviance' or 'wrongdoing'. If we understand deviance to mean behaviour which departs from social norms enforced by criminal law, our definition is clearly circular: criminal law claims to respond to deviance, yet deviance (for the purposes of criminal law) can only be defined by looking to criminal law itself. Evidently, 'external' questions arise about the conditions under which the definitions of crime 'internal' to criminal law – what has been the positivist terrain – become socially effective. These questions include how and by whom norms of criminal law are set; the extent to which criminal laws are underpinned by social consensus at particular times and in particular places; and the relationship between criminal law and other forms of 'social control' – non-legal normative systems whose power entails that the definition and management of deviance cannot be assumed to be exclusively or even primarily the role of the state (see **section III.** below).

Let us, therefore, revise our starting-point so as to think of criminal law as a social normative system: in other words, as a system which operates within a particular social space by setting down standards of conduct, and by enforcing, in distinctive ways, those substantive standards or norms. Within this very general idea of criminal law as one normative system among many others – the religious, moral and traditional norms and institutional systems which we shall discuss in the third section of this chapter – it is important to see that there are at least two rather different ways of looking at criminal law.

In the first place, we can look at *criminal law as a moral and as a retributive system*. From this point of view, criminal law is a system of quasi-moral judgment which reflects a society's basic values; in which criminal punishment serves the retributive function of meting out to offenders their just deserts; and in which criminal law has a strongly symbolic function. This image is central to most people's stereotype of criminal law, resonating as it does with offences such as murder, crimes of violence or theft. But not everything which is regarded as wrong is criminal – and some of the things which are criminal are not regarded by everyone as wrong. So, secondly, we have to acknowledge that *criminal law has a regulatory, instrumental or utilitarian aspect*: in other words, it prohibits certain things on grounds of public health or safety, or for economic or political reasons, and sees the purpose of punishment as deterring that behaviour. This aspect of criminal law underpins offences such as health and safety offences, unwittingly serving alcohol to an underage person and a wide range of less serious road traffic offences. But it can't explain, for example, the offence of murder, which most of us would support independently of its instrumental contribution to lower rates of homicide.

This is not to say that the lines between the quasi-moral and the instrumental or regulatory aspects of criminal law are absolutely clear. Not all 'regulatory' offences are trivial: some carry severe penalties such as the loss of licences necessary to the defendant's livelihood. And many offences can be seen from both regulatory and moral points of view, with our attitudes to the boundary between 'regulatory' and 'real' crime shifting over time. For example, 20 years ago, driving under the influence of alcohol would have been seen as an essentially regulatory offence, while today it is has become heavily moralised. It is, however, crucial to a proper understanding of criminal law to see that it has these two aspects, and that the balance and interaction between them is a key to its historical development and contemporary social significance.

Not least because of these two very different aspects to contemporary criminal law, the idea that we can define 'crime' in relation to its subject matter looks implausible from an interpretive point of view. The reason is very simple: modern criminal law encompasses a quite extraordinary range of activities. In constructing its particular notions of 'deviance', 'wrongdoing' or 'harmful conduct', however, contemporary criminal law arguably does have two distinctive general features. On the one hand, it is a peculiarly institutionalised practice, structured by relatively fixed norms and procedures, and administered by official personnel. This high degree of institutionalisation is a feature of its position as a *legal* response, and to explain this aspect fully, we must reflect on the idea of law and legal regulation itself and on what, if anything, distinguishes legal from other institutional responses. The entire literature of analytical and sociological jurisprudence peers over the shoulder of the criminal lawyer as she begins her apparently straightforward task of exposition. She might well, then, turn aside to a second distinctive feature of criminal law. This is that it is distinguished among legal categories from the responses of civil law. This distinction cannot be explained merely in terms of subject matter, since many forms of behaviour are covered by both criminal and civil regulation. Here the lawyer can breathe a sigh of relief as she recognises a firm and familiar terrain; criminal law can be identified in terms of its distinctive *procedural* rules such as rules of evidence, burdens and standards of proof, special enforcement mechanisms such as public policing and prosecution, and particular tribunals and forms of trial. Criminal law can therefore be defined simply as that legal response to deviance over which the state has the dominant if not exclusive right of action; in which defendants must be proved by the prosecution to be guilty beyond reasonable doubt; and under which, if charged with an offence of a certain degree of seriousness, they are entitled to trial by jury. It is equally that area of legal regulation in which certain sorts of evidence are inadmissible, and in which the result of conviction is typically the imposition of a punitive (as opposed to compensatory) sentence executed by or on behalf of the state. Criminal law, in other words, can be identified in terms of the distinctive features of criminal procedure (Williams 1955: 123). And if anyone is sufficiently presumptuous to ask how we can tell whether criminal procedure should (legally) apply, she can be met by the simple answer, 'Whenever the law identifies itself as criminal'.

There is, of course, a sense in which this circular argument about the definition of criminal law as resting in criminal procedure represents a truth. As we have stated it, however – and as it is stated by most textbook writers – it is unilluminating, for it gives little sense of what *kind* of social practice is thus identified. But, as Farmer suggests, a careful historical interpretation can both reveal the social insight lurking within what appears a conceptual truism, and illuminate that social 'truth' as relative to a particular period in the development of criminal law. Farmer argues that both the modern bemusement about how to define criminal law and the modern tendency to resolve the problem of definition in terms of criminal procedure can best be understood in the context of the marked expansion of criminal law in the nineteenth and early twentieth centuries. This expansion was effected primarily through the creation of summary offences tried in magistrates' courts. These offences were a product of the expanding functions of the modern administrative state, for which the criminal law became an increasingly important tool for regulating the areas of social life born of industrialisation and urbanisation from the early nineteenth century onwards. They often, therefore, regulated lawful business activities, and they were punishable not by imprisonment but by fines. As a result, they infused the law with a new set of 'regulatory' standards which did not – and do not to this day – fit comfortably with the 'quasi-moral', received view of crime as genuine wrongdoing. The courts consequently grappled with the question of whether the latter were genuinely 'criminal' penalties:

L Farmer, 'The Obsession with Definition' (1996) Social and Legal Studies, 64–66

Although the answer to these problems was sought in a reference to the nature of the offence, they could not be resolved by means of the traditional categorization of crimes as 'public wrongs'. Accurate as it might once have been as a means of distinguishing between civil and criminal jurisdiction, it could no longer bear the load that was being placed on it since the issues raised by these cases largely involved minor offences arising from particular regulatory provisions with no apparent reference to larger questions of moral right and wrong. The line taken by both English and Scottish courts was thus that 'proper' criminal offences could only be distinguished by reference to the practice of the criminal courts, and in particular the matter of whether the object of the proceedings was punitive ... [C]rime was defined by the development of stricter procedural rules, the specification of criminal proceedings. This finds its clearest expression in the emergence of summary jurisdiction.

The nineteenth-century expansion in the business of the summary courts created bureaucratic demands for the administrative processing of large numbers of people, or the regulation of the administrative distribution of bodies within the criminal justice system. This demand was met by the development, among other things, of a more rigorous and systematic body of procedural law. Under this new body of law, jurisdiction was not defined primarily in terms of competence relating to a geographical space, the nature of the crime or the power of the particular court to punish – as had traditionally been the case. Instead the decisive factor was the type of procedure used … [T]he mark of the modernity of the law is less a matter of the division between civil and criminal jurisdiction than it is the emergence of this new reliance on procedural law.

This underlines a more general transformation in the legal order that occurred in the course of the nineteenth century. As the political order was secured against the threat of external domination and internal revolution, there was a movement towards the more intensive regulation or government of territory and the population of that territory. Criminal justice became a matter of administration and security, increasingly less concerned with the establishment and protection of sovereign power. So, as the substantive jurisdiction of the criminal law changed, with the increasing predominance of administrative or police offences, there was a subtle change in the way that the object of the criminal law was conceived (in relation to social order). There is … a movement away from crimes regarded as actions that offend against the community or justice, as this has been constructed through the mirror of political order (public wrong). Crimes instead come to be seen as actions that offend the community in its social interest or welfare, which is the aggregate of individual interests as this is known through the new social knowledges. That criminal law can then be defined only according to the positive criterion of whether an act is tried under criminal proceedings simply reflects the diversity of functions of law in the interventionist state. There is no single, simple moral or other purpose that is capable of holding the whole together. It cannot be that we fall back onto the definition of crime as an act that harms the community … for this is merely to reflect the same tautology (ie what harms the community – a crime) dressed up as moral or political theory. The specifically legal character of modern criminal justice cannot be so easily hidden.

The 'obsession with definition', in other words, stands in for a prevailing tension in contemporary criminal law: that between the older ideas of crime as public wrongdoing and the modern reality of criminal law as a predominantly administrative system managing enormous numbers of relatively non-serious and 'regulatory offences': between the older, quasi-moral and retributive view of criminal law and the instrumental, regulatory aspect of criminal law which has become increasingly dominant under modern and late modern conditions. This modern reality also underpins the explanatory appeal of legal positivism; since the validity of positive law derives from its source rather than its content, positivism can encompass without difficulty the expanding terrain of criminal regulation.

Interestingly, the tension between the 'quasi-moral' and 'regulatory' conceptions of criminal law also surfaces in the second, very different, approach to criminal law theory which we shall consider. This approach is essentially philosophical – Farmer's 'moral and political theory' – and consists in normative theorising: the task of producing an account of what the nature, functions and scope of criminal law *ought* to be. The most famous account of the nature and limits of criminal law is a liberal one deriving from J S Mill's 'principle of liberty' (Mill 1859) and from the associated literature which applies that principle to the limits of criminal law (Hart 1963). Mill argued from a utilitarian ethics, according to which the justifying purpose of any social rule or institution must be the maximisation of happiness. This approach leads naturally to a view of criminal law as devoted to minimising human suffering through the prevention of harmful conduct – crime – by the most efficient means possible (Gross 1979). However, the content of criminal law should be circumscribed, Mill argued, according to the principle that the coercive powers of the state should only be invoked as a means of preventing 'harm to others', and never to control harmless behaviour or to prevent the person harming herself. The 'harm principle' thus purports to accommodate the concerns of the state whilst respecting individual freedom. In the context of criminal justice, the harm principle has been refined by the liberal precept that an individual's harmful conduct should only be subject to punishment where she is genuinely responsible for it, in the sense that she had the capacity to act otherwise than she did (Hart 1968: Ch 1). Since Mill's time, this principle has informed debate about issues such as the enforcement of morality through criminal law in offences such as blasphemy, and the proper limits of 'paternalistic' legislation which aims to protect people not from the harms which are inflicted on them by others but rather from those harms which they may inflict on themselves: laws, for example, which prescribe the wearing of seat-belts or which prohibit the use of certain drugs (Hart 1963; Devlin 1965).

Yet although the harm principle captures (and indeed has been influential in shaping) some strong and widely-held intuitions about the proper limits of state power and the value of human autonomy, the test of 'harm to others' is notoriously difficult to apply. This is mainly due to the flexibility of the core notion of harm. The idea of harm is, after all, not self-defining. For example, if a large number of people find the idea of homosexuality, or prostitution, offensive, is this sufficient to justify criminalising that conduct? Does offence, in short, count as harm? And should the creation of risk – for example, by driving while intoxicated – count as 'harm'? Furthermore, the assumed opposition between individual and state interests which is central to Mill's liberal principle is not accepted by political theorists either to right or left, whose arguments, albeit in very different ways, emphasise the links between individual and social interests. These issues among others have been at the centre of a fierce philosophical debate about the acceptability of liberal utilitarian conceptions of the proper functions of criminal law (Lacey 1988).

The philosophical debate about such theories of criminal law has tried to assess their merits as normative theories: as visions of what criminal law ought to be. However, the distinction between normative, prescriptive approaches and explanatory, descriptive approaches has not always been maintained, and the theories have also been used to rationalise and explain the nature of actual criminal law (Hart 1968). In textbooks, for example, the normative theories not only act as frameworks for critical assessment of criminal law but also influence the selection of offences and aspects of legal doctrine to be discussed: hence, for example, the relative marginalisation of 'victimless' crimes which violate the harm principle or of offences of strict liability which sit unhappily with the principle of individual responsibility (Lacey 1985, 2001: see **section II.b.** below). For our purposes, the most important question is that of just how influential these theories have been in shaping both contemporary understandings and actual institutions of criminal law. In trying to assess their influence and, hence, explanatory power, it is important to distinguish between their influence on the popular image of criminal law (something which is crucial to its perceived political legitimacy) and on the content and enforcement of criminal law. For example, the harm principle has a significant place in public debate about criminal law and its limits: the idea that criminal law should be used only in response to harmful conduct has a strong common-sense appeal. Yet, at the levels of criminal law's content and enforcement, we encounter again the problem confronting any definition in terms of the law's subject matter: the vast variety of contemporary criminal laws entails that many examples can be found which appear either to exceed the harm principle (laws on conspiracy to corrupt public morals and outraging public decency are good examples here) or which fail to meet it (the exemption of rape of women by their husbands until 1991 comes to mind). Such examples suggest that the harm principle is not only indeterminate at a normative level but also incomplete at an explanatory level. They therefore imply that we should it see neither as ideal nor as explanation but rather as an ideological framework in terms of which policy debate about criminal law is expressed.

What is meant by the claim that the utilitarian conception of criminal law and its concomitant harm principle form an ideological framework? The idea that criminal law sets out in advance standards of prohibited behaviour, punishing and threatening to punish breaches of those standards, thus deterring actual and potential offenders, characterises it as a social process which is oriented to the reduction of harm. Yet empirical evidence suggests that the reductive effects of criminal processes (although extraordinarily hard to assess) are meagre, and casts doubt on the validity of characterising criminal law primarily in instrumental terms (Ashworth 2003: 17–18; von Hirsch et al 1999). Nonetheless, it may be that a widespread *belief* in the instrumental efficacy of and necessity for criminal law is something which typically underpins its existence. But if that belief lacks foundation, we need to look for the reasons sustaining a belief which is widely yet falsely held. Understood as a descriptive theory, the instrumental conception fails to consider the possibility that criminal law may have important symbolic functions in constructing social values or in upholding the prevailing structure of power relations. Understood as an ideology, the instrumental conception may itself be seen as playing a role in repressing questions about the relationship between criminal law and broader structures of social, political and economic power, and in obscuring the productive capacity of criminal law to generate norms – indeed visions of 'normality' – which have diffuse social implications. As Garland notes in relation to punishment:

David Garland, *Punishment in Modern Society* (OUP, 1990) pp 252–253

[Penality] communicates meaning not just about crime and punishment but also about power, authority, legitimacy, normality, morality, personhood, social relations, and a host of other tangential matters. Penal signs and symbols are one part of an authoritative, institutional discourse which seeks to organise our moral and political understanding and to educate our sentiments and sensibilities. They provide a continuous, repetitive set of instructions as to how we should think about good and evil, normal and pathological, legitimate and illegitimate, order and disorder. Through their judgments, condemnations and classifications, they teach us (and persuade us) how to judge, what to condemn, and how to classify, and they supply a set of languages, idioms, and vocabularies with which to do so. These signifying practices also tell us where to locate social authority, how to preserve order and community, where to look for social dangers, and how to feel about these matters ... In short, the practices, institutions and discourses all *signify* ... Penality is ... a cultural text – or perhaps, better, a cultural performance – which communicates with a variety of social audiences and conveys an extended range of meanings. ... [I]f we are to understand the social effects of punishment then we are obliged to trace this positive capacity to produce meaning and create 'normality' as well as its more negative capacity to suppress and silence deviance.

Utilitarian and other instrumental approaches are, however, not the only influential normative conceptions of criminal law. Beside them sits a different view which rests heavily on what might be called a 'moral analogy' (Devlin 1965) and which evokes the moral/retributive aspect of criminal law already mentioned.

On this view, criminal law does and should engage in a legal entrenchment of certain fundamental moral precepts. When laws are broken the offender is culpable and deserves to be punished; criminal conviction expresses an adverse social judgment of blameworthiness. Conviction is an institutionalised equivalent of the expression of moral condemnation, and criminal punishment is denunciatory and retributive: it is based on the offender's desert (Fletcher 1978) and should be commensurate with the seriousness of the offence: 'The principle of proportionality – that sanctions be proportionate in their severity to the gravity of offences – appears to be a requirement of justice' (von Hirsch 1993: 6; see also Norrie 2000). In seeking to understand what it means to have criminal law in a society like our own, retributivist ideas drawing on the analogy between criminal conviction and moral judgment are important popular attitudes. However, actual criminal laws provide many examples which sit unhappily with this conception. Obvious examples are laws which deal with relatively trivial conduct or which penalise conduct irrespective of fault. This is certainly the case with many of the 'regulatory' offences which have proliferated over the last 150 years, such as selling liquor to an intoxicated person or to someone under 18, where liability is, technically, strict (ie not based on fault). Once again, we have to consider whether the moralist theory's focus on a highly selected portion of criminal law is ideological: serving to obscure conflict and complexity by emphasising those aspects of contemporary criminal justice which command widest support. Paradoxically, the two competing normative conceptions of criminal law – utilitarian and moral-retributive – often emphasise and marginalise the same areas of law, albeit for rather different reasons (see Norrie 2001: Ch 2). Not surprisingly, an important concern of modern contributors to the philosophical debate has been to explore the extent to which the insights underlying both intrumentalist and retributive theories can be accommodated within a pluralist conception of criminal justice: a point to which we shall return when we consider the principle of criminal responsibility in the second section of this chapter (Hart 1968; Lacey 1988). Within such pluralist conceptions, however, the very different moral-retributive and utilitarian approaches remain uneasy companions.

Notwithstanding the intuitive plausibility of aspects of both instrumental and quasi-moral conceptions of criminal law, reflection on the complexity of actual criminal laws therefore prompts reservations about the possibility of a unitary conception of criminal law, and leads us back in the direction of a more historically grounded and interpretive approach. Certainly, the philosophical conceptions produce truisms; criminal law sometimes engages in condemnatory judgment analogous to moral judgment: but could we say this of conviction under all of the many 'regulatory offences' such as inadvertently failing to display a vehicle tax disc or serving an under-age customer in a pub? Criminal law often responds to serious threats to interests seen as fundamental to human well-being or social cohesion: but could this really be said of trivial breaches of the peace or offences relating to prostitution? Criminal law has some obvious instrumental functions: but could the law on conspiracy to corrupt public morals be accommodated within such a conception? It is part of the ideology of criminal law that it is used sparingly: but how is this to be reconciled with the existence of thousands of minor 'regulatory' offences and the political impulse to 'pass a law against it' whenever a social problem appears – whether it be stalking, dangerous dogs, new forms of terrorism or joy-riding? The insights generated by the philosophical conceptions are at a very high level of abstraction and, for our purposes, need to be understood not so much as 'general theories' but rather as aspects of the social meaning of criminal law. Reflection on actual criminal law suggests that the genesis of the social definition of crime is both more complicated and to a greater extent a matter of historical development, explicable in terms of the salience of particular issues at particular moments, than general theories can allow.

In particular, although the philosophical theories capture a reasonably plausible conception of a portion of actual criminal laws – what might be called 'serious' or 'conventional' crime – we can find many counter-examples among other offences which in fact make up the major part of enforced criminal laws, as measured by arrests, prosecutions and convictions. The general theories may summon up reasonably balanced images of law as applied in the Crown Court and the Appeal Courts, but at the level of the Magistrates' Court or police station they would be practically unrecognisable. This is true notwithstanding the fact that criminal justice officials' own understandings of their roles may be influenced by those images of the 'core' criminal process. We therefore need to reconceive the theories as ideologies which have been influential in shaping and legitimising legal regulation by reference to what is seen as 'real crime'. As ideologies, they have equally been influential in marginalising and obscuring empirically significant areas of criminal law which do not fit the philosophical paradigm.

The key assumption of this book is that the substance of criminalisation – how societies define deviance and determine which deviance calls for definition as criminal, and which behaviour actually meets with criminal enforcement – is of central importance to understanding criminal law. This leads inevitably to a consideration of social power relations and the political role of criminal law. Our focus will be both on economic and political power and on the power which is exercised through particular disciplinary techniques and discourses which generate their own 'truths' and 'knowledges' and which marginalise other ways of looking at the world (Foucault 1979a; Smart 1989: 4–25). Crime is a construct of particular legal and social systems, reflecting temporally and geographically specific interests, imperatives and arrangements. We must ask, then, how responsibility for crime comes to be attributed exclusively to individual offenders rather than (also) to the social, legal and political systems which define and enforce criminal law. For what reasons and under what circumstances are people drawn into the criminal process, and why it is that in our society the vast majority of crimes which are 'cleared up' are committed by young men from socio-economically and otherwise disadvantaged groups? What do patterns of criminal enforcement and the disproportionate focus, for example, on young black men tell us about our society as a whole? Without some appreciation of the answers to these questions, and of the broad vectors of power which shape patterns of criminalisation, we cannot begin to grasp the social meaning of criminal law. Yet criminal law scholarship has been even slower than has criminology to address the structural relevance of factors such as gender, race and class:

Donald Nicolson, 'Criminal Law and Feminism' in Nicolson and Lois Bibbings (eds) *Feminist Perspectives on Criminal Law* (Cavendish, 2000) pp 1–2

Crime and society's responses to it, like virtually all social phenomena, are heavily influenced by issues of gender. Gender distinctions are made in deciding what activities are criminal. Gender significantly affects who commits crimes and what crimes they commit. Those involved in enforcing the criminal law ... are influenced by gender in deciding who might have committed crimes, who ought to be prosecuted, whether they are, in fact, guilty and how they should be punished. Gender stereotypes underlie the application and even the formulation of core criminal law concepts, such as *actus reus, mens rea* and the various defences to liability.

Yet, until relatively recently, the gender dimension to crime has been ignored. Traditionally, criminal law has been analysed and taught as if its rules are gender blind and as if the gender of both the victims and perpetrators of crimes is irrelevant to the way the law is applied ...

Only in the last 30 or so years have feminists begun to uncover the 'maleness' of criminal law and the way in which it frequently discriminates against women as defendants or fails to provide adequate protection against male violence and sexual abuse. In many cases, the feminist critique of specific areas of criminal law tied in with early analyses of law and patriarchy, focusing primarily on areas of obvious concern, such as rape and prostitution ... Later, a more sophisticated critique of criminal law developed when feminists discovered that even those areas of criminal law which are not directly based on sex differentiation (like prostitution law) or deal with issues of crucial importance to women (like rape law) are premised upon assumptions about gender. As a result, even when ostensibly gender-neutral, the formulation or actual application of criminal law may, in fact, discriminate against women defendants or, even when they do not, reinforce sexist stereotypes about appropriate female and male behaviour ... Even more subtly, it was discovered that, behind the apparent gender neutrality of core criminal law concepts ... a complex process occurs whereby actors in the criminal justice system make different assumptions about female criminal behaviour. Thus, in her path-breaking book, *Justice Unbalanced*, Hilary Allen demonstrated how such actors concentrate on the external appearance of male criminal behaviour – on the assumption that it is rationally chosen – whereas with women, the focus is on their internal motivations – on the assumption that their criminality emanates from pathological states of mind ... This work showed that female criminals are generally treated by the criminal justice system (and wider social discourse) as either mad or bad. What Allen thus illustrated was that, while the denial of rational agency to female defendants frequently worked to their advantage, it dangerously reinforced stereotypes of women as inherently irrational and passive and, hence, as disqualified from fully legal and civic subjecthood.

p 25

The criminal legal subject is male. Men commit the majority of crimes and are far more likely to be charged, convicted and punished. As a result, it is their behaviour which informs the norms of criminal law and the response of actors in the criminal justice system. Equally, the law treats them as legal subjects by recognising the rationality and autonomy of their actions ... [C]riminal law tends to portray women as passive victims whose agency and autonomy is effaced by the focus on the perspective of male defendants. And, when women themselves appear as defendants, they are treated as irrational actors, borne along by psychological and external factors or, alternatively, as unfeminine monsters.

To understand these and similar issues, we have to look both at and beyond the criminal process. We must look at a range of powerful institutions and at the distinctive techniques through which they operate. We also need to set criminal law in the context of the rules and practices, the institutional goals, the aims, attitudes and professional preoccupations of the personnel at all stages of the criminal process. We need to ask how these relate to each other and to the criminal law. Does the criminal process make up one coherent whole (Packer 1968)? Or must it rather be viewed as a complex web of institutions and practices which are often pulling in different directions; as a fragmented process, fractured by divergent institutional aims and values? A general introduction to these contextual issues is provided in **section III.** of this chapter, and more detailed accounts of their relevance in specific areas are provided in each of the chapters which follow.

Yet whilst we do not adopt the formal, 'internal-legal' starting-point of most texts, we do emphasise the importance of tracing the distinctive procedural and formal logics produced within the doctrine of criminal law itself. A central aspect of the power to define 'deviance' is, after all, the distinctive power of criminal law: the way in which legal definition of certain behaviour as criminal operates as an 'objective', depoliticised construction of that behaviour as deviant or wrongful. This distinctive power is considered in the rest of this section and in **section II.** below. By juxtaposing 'external' and 'internal' analysis of criminal legal practices, we aim to develop a critical perspective whilst maintaining a sharp focus on the intricacies of criminal law conceived as a distinctive member of an interlocking set of social practices.

FURTHER READING

Box, Steven (1983) *Power, Crime and Mystification* (Tavistock).

Ellickson, Robert C (1991) *Order without Law* (Harvard University Press) Pt II.

Hart, H L A (1963), *Law, Liberty and Morality* (Oxford University Press).

Nicolson, Donald and Bibbings, Lois (eds) (2000) *Feminist Perspectives on Criminal Law.*

Smart, Carol (1989) *Feminism and the Power of Law* (Routledge) Ch 1.

I.b. Defining due process: criminal law and human rights

Our initial discussion has suggested that modern criminal law is best understood in relation to a distinctive set of procedures. This focus on 'due process' has been driven over the last 150 years both by the expansion of criminal law's scope and by liberal ideas about the rights of individuals *vis-à-vis* the state. More recently, the salience of due process has been thrown into relief by the incorporation of the European Convention on Human Rights (ECHR) into domestic law through the Human Rights Act 1998 (HRA 1998). Under this legislation, the courts must, wherever possible, interpret domestic law in a way which conforms to the standards embodied in the Convention: where they are unable to do so, they must make a declaration of incompatibility. At this point, the onus shifts to Parliament to decide how to respond.

The HRA 1998 provides a distinctive foothold for internal critique of criminal law, by introducing within criminal law standards which were previously external to it. In the other chapters of this book, we shall consider the various ways in which human rights standards may affect the substantive criminal law. In this chapter, we are concerned with the implications of the HRA 1998 for criminal procedure and for the ideals of due process which are central to the legitimation of modern criminal law. Rights such as that to a fair trial, to be presumed innocent, or not to be subject to degrading treatment have implications for prosecution procedure, trial process and punishment. In this section, we consider two of the most important doctrines which inform discussions of due process in criminal law and which have formed the objects of legal challenges on the basis of human rights standards in relation to the fairness of trials and other aspects of the criminal process: *the rule of law or principle of legality* and *the presumption of innocence*.

The most immediately relevant parts of the ECHR and the HRA 1998 from the point of view of due process are Articles 5, 6 and 7 (set out in HRA 1998, Sch 1, Pt I):

- Article 5 provides that 'Everyone has the right to liberty and security of the person. No one shall be deprived of his liberty save in the following cases and in accordance with a procedure prescribed by law'. For our purposes, the most important of 'the following cases' are 'the lawful detention of a person after conviction by a competent court' and 'the lawful arrest or detention of persons for the purposes of enforcing court orders and bringing prosecutions'. Further subsections of the Article instantiate guarantees in relation to arrest and detention, providing for example a right to be brought promptly before a court to establish the legality of detention, and to be tried within a reasonable time or released pending trial.

- Article 6 guarantees the right to a fair trial: 'a fair and public hearing within a reasonable time by an independent and impartial tribunal established by law' (publicity being however subject to exceptions justified in the interest of 'morals, public order or national security in a democratic society', or of juveniles or the protection of the private life of the parties). This Article also enshrines the presumption of innocence, providing that 'everyone charged with a criminal offence shall be presumed innocent until proved guilty according to law', and specifying a number of minimum defendants' rights in relation to adequate and timely information of the relevant charges against her, adequate time and facilities for preparing the defence, to defend herself, to examine witnesses against her, to have access to legal assistance and, where necessary, an interpreter.

- Article 7 instantiates the principle of legality: 'No one shall be held guilty of any criminal offence on account of any act or omission which did not constitute a criminal offence under national or international law at the time when it was committed. Nor shall a heavier penalty be imposed than the one that was applicable at the time the criminal offence was committed' (though the Article makes an exception to this principle of non-retroactivity for acts which are 'criminal according to the general principles of law recognised by civilised nations'). Further articles of relevance to criminal law and procedure include the guarantees of a right to respect for private and family life (Article 8); freedom of thought, conscience and religion (Article 9); freedom of expression (Article 10); the right to life 'Everyone's right to life shall be protected by law' (Article 2); the prohibition on torture or inhuman or degrading treatment or punishment (Article 3).

The ideals of the rule of law and of due process captured in Articles 5, 6 and 7 of the ECHR have a special significance for criminal law: both the legitimacy of substantive criminal laws and the fairness of the procedures through which they are enforced are seen as especially important given criminal law's distinctively coercive methods. The rule of law is generally conceived in terms of a cluster of procedural requirements: laws should be consistent, of general application, certain in their effects, clear, publicised and prospective rather than retrospective in application. These requirements are combined with the principle of equality before the law – the idea that all citizens, including the rulers or lawmakers, should be subject to law – and with the principle of legality – the idea that laws should be created in accordance with constitutional procedure. These values serve to imbue law with legitimacy and authority whilst leaving open the determination of its content. The presumption of innocence and the associated burden of proof beyond reasonable doubt are seen as necessary to the realisation of the rule of law in the field of criminal justice. Their importance is illustrated by the fact that they are the procedural features in terms of which criminal law is often defined: 'due process' seems a natural concomitant of both moral-retributive conceptions of criminal law and liberal conceptions of the citizen's rights against the state. Yet, in practice, requirements of 'due process' have to compete with the imperatives of the instrumental, regulatory conception of the criminal process which sees such procedural safeguards as costly barriers to the efficient pursuit of crime control (Packer 1968: see below). How far does criminal law in fact meet the procedural ideals which it sets for itself; to what extent do such ideals structure or confine power wielded in the name of criminal justice; and what additional safeguards have been provided by the incorporation of the European Convention?

I.b.i.   Legal ideology and the rule of law

The rule of law has long enjoyed a central place in legal ideology: it is seen as both constraining political power and legitimising legal power.

J Brewer and J Styles, *An Ungovernable People* (Hutchinson, 1980) p 14

... [T]he notion of the 'rule of law' was central to seventeenth and eighteenth century Englishmen's understanding of what was both special and laudable about their political system. It was a shibboleth of English politics that English law was the birthright of every citizen who, unlike many of his European counterparts, was subject not to the whim of a capricious individual but to a set of prescriptions that bound all members of the polity. Such a characterization of the English 'rule of law' will not, of course, pass muster as an accurate description of the *modus operandi* of the legal process, but it did serve as an idealization, a potent 'fiction' ... which commanded widespread assent from both patricians and plebeians. The purchase of this ideology of the 'rule of law' had several important consequences ... Those in authority were constrained to some extent by their obligation to act in accordance with this ideology ... Because authority derived its legitimacy from the rule of law, 'the law' was used as a standard by which to judge the just exercise of authority. Authorities therefore chose to limit themselves in order to acquire greater effectiveness: they traded unmediated power for legitimacy.

The ideal of the rule of law is therefore central to prevailing understandings of the relationship between citizen and polity in modern societies:

L Farmer, *Criminal Law, Tradition and Legal Order* (Cambridge University Press, 1997) p 6

The relationship between liberal moral and political philosophy and the criminal law would seem to be a product of the struggle against absolutism in the eighteenth century. Repressive and violent laws and institutions were attacked by reform-minded philosophers and lawyers. In Europe this led to the drawing up of the great penal codes of the Enlightenment according to new measures of restraint, certainty and humanity in punishment. Legal limits were imposed on the exercise of power in the same period as the boundaries of the modern nation state were drawn, establishing a range of both internal and external constraints on sovereignty. The demand that the criminal law respect the principle of legality, that the criminal process be subjected to rules and constraints, and that punishment be administered only in measured and determinate amounts, set the terms of the compact that was established between the criminal law and modernity. This very history, if we accept it, suggests that this is far from being a 'necessary' relationship – only that it has been perceived as fundamental to a certain characterisation of the modern state.

Though English criminal law has never been fully codified, there is a close link between the rule of law ideals of certainty, accessibility and limited government on the one hand and the ideal of a codified criminal law on the other. This link finds vivid expression in the Law Commission's arguments for codification (Law Commission 1992: 2; see Wells 1986).

In thinking about the rule of law, we need to assess both its status as a modern ideal of democratic governance *and* its role in legitimising a certain form of state power. In reflecting on the relationship between the rule of law and the perceived legitimacy of legal systems, it is worth considering the capacity of the rule of law simultaneously to structure political power and to legitimise laws whose impact is so dramatically unequal that they risk being regarded as fundamentally unjust. The delicate balance between legitimacy and power is well illustrated by the social historian, E P Thompson, in his study of the Black Act of 1723. This statute, which dealt with poaching, enacted broad offences with draconian penalties: it was a piece of legislation which, in Thompson's words (1975: 197), 'could only have been drawn up and enacted by men who had formed habits of mental distance and moral levity towards human life – or, more particularly, towards the lives of the "loose and disorderly sort of people"'. Yet Thompson's study testifies also to the sense in which the rule of law genuinely constrains political power:

E P Thompson, *Whigs and Hunters* (Penguin, 1975) pp 259–265

... [W]hat we have observed is more than the law as a pliant medium to be twisted this way and that by whichever interests already possess effective power. Eighteenth-century law was more substantial than that. Over and above its pliant, instrumental functions it existed in its own right, as ideology; as an ideology which not only served, in most respects, but which also legitimized class power. The hegemony of the eighteenth-century gentry and aristocracy was expressed, above all, not in military force, not in the mystifications of the priesthood or of the press, not even in economic coercion, but in the rituals of the study of the Justice of the Peace, in the quarter-sessions, in the pomp of the Assizes and in the Theatre of Tyburn.

Thus the law ... may be seen instrumentally as mediating and reinforcing existent class relations and, ideologically, as offering to these a legitimation. But we must press our definitions a little further. For if we say that existent class relations were mediated by the law, this is not the same thing as saying that the law was not more than those relations translated into other terms, which masked or mystified the reality. This may, quite often, be true but it is not the whole truth. For class relations were expressed, not in any way one likes, but *through the forms of law*, and the law, like other institutions which from time to time can be seen as mediating (and masking) existent class relations ... has its own characteristics, its own independent history and logic of evolution.

... It is inherent in the especial character of law, as a body of rules and procedures, that it shall apply logical criteria with reference to standards of universality and equity. It is true that certain categories of person may be excluded from this logic (as children or slaves), that other categories may be debarred from access to parts of the logic (as women, or, for many forms of eighteenth-century law, those without certain kinds of property), and that the poor may often be excluded through penury, from the law's costly procedures. All this, and more, is true. But if too much of this is true, then the consequences are plainly counterproductive. Most men have a strong sense of justice, at least with regard to their own interests. If the law is evidently partial and unjust, then it will mask nothing, legitimize nothing, contribute nothing to any class's hegemony. The essential precondition for the effectiveness of law, in its function as ideology, is that it shall display an independence from gross manipulation and shall seem to be just. It cannot seem to be so without upholding its own logic and criteria of equity; indeed, on occasion, by actually *being* just. And furthermore it is not often the case that a ruling ideology can be dismissed as a mere hypocrisy; even rulers find a need to legitimize their power; to moralize their functions, to feel themselves to be useful and just … The law may be rhetoric, but it need not be empty rhetoric.

… [T]here is a very large difference, which twentieth-century experience ought to have made clear even to the most exalted thinker, between arbitrary extra-legal power and the rule of law. And not only were the rulers … inhibited by their own force … but they also believed enough in these rules, and in their accompanying ideological rhetoric, to allow, in certain limited areas, the law itself to be a genuine forum within which certain kinds of class conflict were fought out. There were even occasions … when the Government itself retired from the courts defeated. Such occasions served, paradoxically, to consolidate power, to enhance its legitimacy, and to inhibit revolutionary movements. But, to turn the paradox around, these same occasions served to bring power even further within constitutional controls.

Thompson's reminder of the sophistication of the legal form and his warning against a crude assumption that law straightforwardly serves the interests of the ruling class are well taken. However, as we shall see in our discussion of criminal law doctrine in **section II.** of this chapter, the appeal to 'universality and equity' in the application of legal standards serves to obscure significant respects in which criminal law falls short of its own ideals of certainty and predictability. For example, as McBarnet notes in her study of criminal trials:

Doreen McBarnet, *Conviction* (Macmillan, 1981) pp 163–164

Case law is discretionary and particularistic; it does not operate at the level of general rules. What is more … it does not make law until *after* a dispute has made it into an issue. Of course there are precedents to constrain judgments. But they need only constrain the justification of the decision rather than the decision itself. Indeed, the discretion invested in judges, and the fact that the case comes before them only after dispute, only because 'informed lawyers disagree' and can make out a case for both sides, means 'a judge's decision either way will not be considered a failure to perform his judicial responsibilities'. What Hart calls the 'open texture of law' allows wide scope in the use and applications of precedent … The doctrine of precedent may thus be placed more aptly in the rhetoric rather than the actual procedure of justice. The doctrine of precedent may tell us where the ideology of the rule of law is grounded and how it is maintained, but it tells us very little about the practice of case law – not just because of judicial techniques to use and avoid precedent but because of the nature of the ideology of precedent and the post hoc discretionary particularistic form of the case law method. The result is that the law is so far from being certain as to be almost impossible to pin down …

McBarnet concludes that we should be more sceptical than Thompson about the constraining power of the rule of law. Rather, we should see it as an ideology of justice which is external to law yet which allows contradictions, gaps and uncertainties in law to be managed by representing the criminal process, and in particular the trial process, as a politically neutral one which generates 'objective' determinations of fact and law.

The positivist vision of the criminal law as a determinate body of rules which can be applied straightforwardly and even-handedly so as to generate the predictable and objective legal conclusions envisaged by the rule of law is further put into question by an understanding of the way in which facts are constructed in the criminal process. Empirical studies of courtroom practices illuminate the dynamic nature of criminal law's constitution of 'truth' through a set of processes which depend upon both the credibility and articulacy of particular witnesses and the power of cultural assumptions which shape the jury's and magistracy's interpretation of evidence. Less socially confident defendants will have greater difficulty in giving evidence, while the testimony of some classes of witness – 'sexually experienced' women giving evidence in rape cases, for example (see **Chapter 5.II.**) – are regarded with suspicion by lawyers, judges and juries.

W L Bennett and M S Feldman, *Reconstructing Reality in the Courtroom* (Tavistock, 1981) pp 32–33

It appears initially that the principles of justice introduced into formal adjudication processes such as trials are obvious. Everyone knows that adjudication procedures are designed to guarantee due process, to promote fair and impartial judgments, and to decide questions of fact in uniform and objective ways ... However, the ways in which stories represent the incidents in legal disputes produce often radical transformations of 'reality' that are hard to reconcile with commonsense understandings about objectivity. Judgments based on story construction are, in many important respects, unverifiable in terms of the reality of the situation that the story represents. Adjudicators judge the plausibility of a story according to certain structural relations among symbols in the story. Although documentary evidence may exist to support most symbolizations in a story, both the teller and the interpreter of a story *always* have some margin of control of the definition of certain key symbols. Therefore, stories are judged in terms of a combination of the documentary or 'empirical' warrants for symbols and the internal structural relations among the collection of symbols presented in the story. In other words, we judge stories according to a dual standard of 'did it happen that way?' and 'could it have happened that way?' In no case can 'empirical' standards alone produce a completely adequate judgment ...

Declan Roche, *Accountability in Restorative Justice* **(Oxford University Press, 2003) pp 115–116**

Storytelling is sometimes objected to on the basis that it is a subjective process that is inconsistent with the goal of finding the objective truth. This was one of the criticisms of the emphasis on narrative in the South African Truth and Reconciliation Commission (SATRC 1998: vol 1(5), para 35). Underlying such objections is the popular belief, questioned by restorative justice, that there is a discoverable truth about events which exists independently of people's subjective opinions. This belief is partly sustained by the adversarial formal justice system, where truth is won, in Paul Rock's words, 'dialectically and agonistically'. Trials work by reducing and reconstructing 'the indeterminacy and muddle of everyday life' into bleak choices between innocence or guilt, truth or falsehood, this or that account. In such a contest, it is usually the narratives of the least powerful which are rejected in favour of those of the dominant. Restorative justice aims to do something quite different, attempting to create a multi-layered truth reflecting people's different, and sometimes conflicting, perspectives.

pp 84–85

In many cases, communication difficulties reflect some underlying form of inequality and domination. In an abusive relationship, power imbalances may well prevent a victim of abuse speaking up and negotiating with her abuser. A long history of oppression can work to affect the communicative ability of whole groups and communities. Australian linguists and anthropologists have long observed 'the very common Aboriginal conversational pattern of agreeing with whatever is being asked, even if the speaker does not understand the question'. This pattern has been described as a strategy of accommodation (that Aboriginal people have developed) to protect themselves in their interaction with Anglo-Australians. Aborigines have found that the easiest method to deal with white people is to agree with whatever it is that the Anglo-Australians want and then to continue on with their own business.

This understanding of the trial process as involving the construction of plausible and persuasive stories, rather than the discovery of pre-existing, objective truths, suggests that we should be wary of the view that procedural safeguards are necessarily effective in ensuring the fairness of the process. What does 'equality before the law' amount to given inequalities in the story-telling and other resources of those who come to the courtroom? The release of the 'Guildford Four' in 1989 after 15 years of wrongful imprisonment marked the beginning of a series of high-profile miscarriages of justice cases. Following an extensive public campaign which included startling revelations about failures in the investigative, preparatory, forensic and indeed trial processes, the Home

Secretary had finally referred the Guildford Four case back to the Court of Appeal, at which point the DPP declined any longer to support the convictions. The Four had difficulty in telling their stories at all levels of the criminal justice system (see McKee and Franey 1988). As one of them, Carole Richardson, recalled shortly after their release:

> Then other people, important people, started saying we were innocent too. I was happy they were actually standing forward and had the guts to say, well we think this is wrong. But at the same time there was something in me that kept crying out, 'I've been saying the same thing for years'. Why should it take ex-Home Secretaries and Cardinal Hume and people like that to get something done? The truth's the truth, whoever says it.' [*New Statesman and Society*, 10 November 1989, p 15.]

The challenge in delivering real as opposed to merely formal 'equality before the law' needs to be borne in mind as we look in more detail at one of the central procedural safeguards of the criminal process.

I.b.ii.   The presumption of innocence: in search of 'the golden thread' …

The idea that people accused of criminal offences should be presumed innocent until proven guilty beyond all reasonable doubt is a core tenet of criminal law doctrine, and finds direct expression in the European Convention on Human Rights, Article 6(2) of which provides that 'everyone charged with a criminal offence shall be presumed innocent until proved guilty according to law'. Indeed, we take it so much for granted, at least until regular human rights challenges forced the question on lawyers' attention, that we have tended to ignore the fact that the concrete meaning to be attached to the presumption is very much an open question. For example, does the fact that judges can now, under certain circumstances, invite a jury to draw adverse inferences from a defendant's exercise of his or her right to remain silent offend the presumption of innocence? And what of the use of custody for suspects refused bail; the pressure on people charged to plead guilty; the imposition of 'strict' liability without proof of fault? We are also apt to forget the presumption's historical specificity. In the following passage, Allen traces the history of the presumption of innocence in English criminal law, and argues that it plays a central role in constituting popular images not only of criminal law but also, more broadly, of national culture.

C K Allen, *Legal Duties and Other Essays in Jurisprudence* (Oxford University Press, 1931) pp 253–294

If the average Englishman [sic] was asked what he considered to be the outstanding characteristic of English criminal law, or indeed of the whole legal system, he would probably answer without a moment's hesitation: 'A man is presumed to be innocent until he is proven guilty'.

... [N]othing is more remarkable in the modern criminal jurisdiction of England than the consideration which is shown to the accused. The rules of evidence have shaped themselves progressively and rapidly in his favour. The presumption of innocence and the doctrine of 'reasonable doubt' have been so constantly impressed upon juries that these principles have come to possess, as I shall endeavour to show, some of the characteristics of superstition ...

[T]here is no doubt that the theory of our law and the temper of our tribunals insist on a ... presumption of innocence. This is often thought of and spoken of as one of those primordial British institutions which have roused writers like Fortescue and Blackstone to such eloquent enthusiasm. It is the purpose of these observations to show that it is a very modern growth, not older, indeed – at all events, in the sense in which it is now understood – than the nineteenth century.

Prior to that period, the criminal law presents a curious paradox. The learning of Pleas of the Crown undoubtedly does contain what may be called the platitudes of innocence. Fortescue seems to be the first and true inventor of one of the most persistent of these commonplaces. In the twenty-seventh chapter of his *De Laudibus* he eulogizes, as a bulwark of justice, the prisoner's right of challenging the array, and Selden, in his notes to the text, adds some triumphant examples of the reversal of convictions. For the modern reader the effect is a little marred by the circumstance that most of the reversals seem to have taken place after the innocent accused had been put to death. Fortescue continues: 'Indeed, one would much rather twenty guilty persons should escape the punishment of death than that one innocent person should be condemned and suffer capitally.' I do not know whether this sentiment passed at once into a legal aphorism, but two hundred years later it reappears in a famous passage in Hale's *Pleas of the Crown*, concerning which Bentham had much to say in his *Rationale of Evidence*. ... It is not, apparently, till the beginning of the nineteenth century that our platitude is judicially described as a 'maxim' and is fixed firmly in its ratio of ten-to-one. In 1823, *R v Hobson* 1 Lew. C.C. 261, we find Holroyd J. declaring: 'it is a maxim of English law that *ten* guilty men should escape rather than that one innocent man should suffer.' And in the same case he lays down *ex cathedra* another familiar principle: 'The greater the crime the stronger is the proof required for the purpose of conviction.'

I have been unable to discover, however, that the dogma 'A man is presumed to be innocent until he is proved guilty', in the form of a brocard, anywhere occurs before the nineteenth century ...

On the whole, then, it is safe to say that before the beginning of the nineteenth century there was no explicit *presumption* of innocence, although there was a growing realization that circumstantial evidence should be regarded with caution when a man's life and property were at stake; and there was also a certain amount of pious generalization in favour of merciful acquittal rather than hasty condemnation.

... [I]t was not until the end of the nineteenth century that the prisoner obtained, amid the gravest doubts of many merciful and intelligent persons, the last privilege of giving evidence in his own behalf. These [pre-existing] disabilities of the prisoner are so well known that they need only a brief reference. He was neither able to say anything on his own behalf, nor, in cases of felony (though it was otherwise with misdemeanours), to be represented by counsel. He had no access to books, no means of knowing the exact charge which was to be brought against him, the manner in which it was to be presented, nor the witnesses who would testify to it. The evidence given against him was subject to hardly any of the rules of relevancy and admissibility which have become settled in the nineteenth century. He was always in danger of being convicted on the mere confession of an accomplice, which was regarded as particularly damning evidence. His trial was extraordinarily summary, never extending beyond a day, and execution usually following upon judgment with irreparable celerity. His inability to call sworn witnesses in capital cases was perhaps the most remarkable of these handicaps, and nothing shows more clearly the prejudice against the man who stood in conflict with the Crown; for the theory (though it was doubted) seems to have been that it was unseemly and smacked of insubordination that witnesses should be sworn against the Crown. Even complacent writers like Blackstone could not regard the rule without indignation, and it could be justified only on the most sophistical grounds ...

In sum, then, we may conclude that four hundred years ago in all criminal trials of which we have any record, the dice were loaded heavily against the accused. The presumption of innocence was not only absent from, but antagonistic to, the whole system of penal procedure. How and why have we come to hold the contrary view so strongly that it is one of the most unquestioned axioms in the whole of our law?

I believe the true explanation does not lie in ethics. It lies in the profound change which has taken place in the organization of society ...

Allen goes on to argue that the presumption was made possible by the reduced fear of lawlessness which accompanied more settled social conditions in England after 1688 – an observation which resonates with Farmer's argument cited above. These social changes facilitated the development of a systematic law of evidence which was grounded in the recognition of the rights of the individual accused. However, as Allen points out, the line between the standards of proof established as characteristic of civil and criminal cases – the balance of probabilities and beyond reasonable doubt – is far from clear:

'Probability' may mean different things. It is often loosely used to indicate mere conjecture or plausibility. Neither in civil nor in criminal cases is a

jury entitled to consider an averment established by conjecture or plausibility. But 'probability' may also mean the utmost degree of certainty or
conviction which, upon the evidence of circumstances, things and statements, can be attained by our limited powers of reasoning and observation.
That degree of certainty or conviction exists, or ought to exist, in the decision of any legal issue. It is difficult to see how men and women, called
upon to weigh evidence either in civil or criminal matters, can bring to
bear anything more than Pollock C. B. requires of them – ie 'that degree of
certainty that you would act upon in your own grave and important concerns'; for indeed they have no other means of reasoning. The principle of
'a reasonable doubt' therefore seems to be little more than a counsel of
prudence; and there is considerable judicial authority for this view. The
warning is not so frequently uttered in civil cases, because the occasion is
not so solemn; but does it follow that the same degree of care and certainty
is not as necessary, or at least as desirable, in the one case as in the other? I
apprehend that a judge who directed a jury in an action for damages, 'You
need not be as careful in arriving at your conclusions as if you were trying a
criminal case', would considerably startle the legal world and the public;
and though there is a good reason for reminding juries of the necessity for
caution in criminal cases, I know of no authority for the proposition that
their duty is any less when property, and not life or liberty, is at stake ...

  On the whole, then, historically and logically, we are led to a conclusion
which has the sanction of that great master of evidence, Wigmore –
namely, that the presumption of innocence amounts to little more than a
caution to the jury not to arrive at hasty inferences and a reminder that
affirmative allegations must be proved by those who make them, not dis-
proved by those against whom they are made ...

Nonetheless, at a rhetorical level, the English criminal process is eloquent in
declaring its conformity to the full trappings of 'due process'. This is illustrated
in *Woolmington* (1935) – a case which has become something of a legal legend.
The appellant was convicted of the murder of his wife, who had recently left
him. He claimed that he accidentally shot her when attempting to induce her to
return to him by threatening to shoot himself. In his summing-up to the jury,
Swift J said that once it was proved that he had shot his wife, this was presumed
to be murder unless Woolmington could satisfy the jury that the killing was an
accident. Woolmington was unsuccessful in his appeal to the Court of Criminal
Appeal and then appealed to the House of Lords. In a judgment whose elaboration of ancient English authorities once again illustrates the link between the
image of due process, the common law and conceptions of national culture,
Viscount Sankey allowed the appeal. He affirmed the presumption of innocence
in a striking rhetorical flourish which continues to echo through legal doctrine:

  Throughout the web of the English Criminal Law one golden thread
  is always to be seen, that it is the duty of the prosecution to prove the

prisoner's guilt subject to what I have already said as to the defence of insanity [which has to be proven by the defendant on a balance of probabilities] and subject also to any statutory exception. If, at the end of and on the whole of the case, there is a reasonable doubt, created by the evidence, given by either the prosecution or the prisoner, as to whether the prisoner killed the deceased with a malicious intention, the prosecution has not made out the case and the prisoner is entitled to an acquittal. No matter what the charge or where the trial, the principle that the prosecution must prove the guilt of the prisoner is part of the common law of England and no attempt to whittle it down can be entertained. It is not the law of England to say, as was said in the summing-up in the present case: 'if the Crown satisfy you that this woman died at the prisoner's hands then he has to show that there are circumstances to be found in the evidence which has been given from the witness-box in this case which alleviate the crime so that it is only manslaughter or which excuse the homicide altogether by showing it was a pure accident.'

The decisive terms in which the House of Lords affirmed the presumption of innocence should not blind us, however, to exceptions to it. Even restricting our view to laws of evidence, these exceptions are significant. Viscount Sankey's casual reference to 'any statutory exception' renders the 'golden thread' a thin one, and it is a thread which the legislature has not hesitated to break when instrumental concerns have militated towards less stringent procedural safeguards. For example, s 7 of the Children and Young Persons Act 1933, which creates the offence of selling cigarettes to a person under 16, provides that 'it shall be a defence for a person charged to show that he took all reasonable precautions and exercised all due diligence to avoid the commission of the offence'. And s 71(1) of the Police and Criminal Evidence Act 1984 provides that:

> In any proceedings the fact that a person other than the accused has been convicted of an offence by or before any court ... shall be admissible in evidence for the purpose of proving, where to do so is relevant to any issue in those proceedings, that that person committed that offence ...

This amounts to a reversal of the criminal burden of proof and imposes on the accused the heavy onus of proving that a conviction to which he was not a party was in fact wrong. According to s 74(2) of the same Act, once a third party's conviction is proved at the accused's trial, the third party 'shall be taken to have committed that offence unless the contrary is proved' by the accused. As the accused will have been a stranger to the events leading to that conviction, he will often be badly placed to discharge this burden. Another relevant provision is s 101 of the Magistrates' Courts Act 1980, which provides that:

> Where the defendant ... relies for his defence on any exception, exemption, proviso, excuse or qualification, whether or not it accompanies the description of the offence in the enactment creating the offence ... , the

burden of proving the exception, exemption, proviso, excuse or qualification shall be on him, and this notwithstanding that the information ...
contains an allegation negativing the exception, exemption, proviso, excuse
or qualification.

As Zuckerman notes, 'A burden as heavy as this can hardly be consistent with
the golden thread' (Zuckerman 1989: 152).

An illustration of the courts' pre-HRA 1998 approach to such statutory exceptions may be drawn from the law on unlawful drugs. In *Hunt* (1987), the appellant pleaded not guilty to an indictment charging him with possessing a Class A
controlled drug contrary to s 5(2) of the Misuse of Drugs Act 1971. Hunt told
the police that he had bought the powder which he was charged with possessing
in Shaftesbury Avenue and that it was amphetamine sulphate. The only other
evidence for the prosecution was contained in the report of an analyst which
was by agreement read out to the jury. The report showed that the powder was
not amphetamine sulphate and that it contained morphine. At the trial Hunt's
counsel submitted that there was no case to answer, because the prosecution
had called no evidence as to the proportion of morphine contained in the powder, whereas regulations made under the Act exempted certain preparations
where that proportion was not more than 0.2%. The judge ruled against the
submission, and Hunt changed his plea to guilty. The Court of Appeal held that
if the appellant wished to escape conviction the burden lay on him to prove on a
balance of probability that the preparation of morphine fell within the relevant
exception contained in the Misuse of Drugs Regulations 1973. As it was obvious
that the appellant neither intended to nor could discharge this burden of proof,
the Court of Appeal upheld the conviction.

In the House of Lords, Hunt relied on *Woolmington*, and in particular on the
passage from Viscount Sankey's judgment quoted above: he argued that in
using the phrase 'any statutory exception' Viscount Sankey was referring only
to statutory exceptions in which Parliament used express words to place the
burden of proof on the accused – a technique to be found in several other sections of the Misuse of Drugs Act 1971. Lord Griffiths rejected this general
argument, affirming that 'a statute can, on its true construction, place a burden
of proof on the defendant although it does not do so expressly', and that the
only question was the question of construction: whether Parliament had
intended to shift the burden of proof in any particular instance. In this instance,
he construed the statute not to have shifted the burden of proof onto the defendant because of the seriousness of the offence and the fact that the issue – like
that in *Woolmington* – related to the existence of an essential ingredient of the
offence. Lord Griffiths argued that in construing such statutory provisions,
the courts should be slow to interpret the burden as having been imposed on
the defendant where that burden would be difficult to discharge. He also
implied that s 101 of the Magistrates' Courts Act 1980 (quoted above) does not

necessarily apply merely because a term such as 'exemption' or 'proviso' appears in a statute. However, the House of Lords' acceptance that the principle that criminal offences must be proven beyond reasonable doubt may be derogated from *by implication* is arguably a serious fraying of the golden thread (see further Williams 1987; Mirfield 1988).

Since the passage of the HRA 1998, the question of the legality of such presumptions has, not surprisingly, been challenged. A difference of opinion between the English and European courts on the interpretation of this question provides an excellent example of the open-endedness of the principle that defendants should be presumed innocent until proven guilty. Whereas the European Court of Human Rights in Strasbourg has held that the presumption of innocence under Article 6(2) is consistent with legislative reversals of the burden of proof 'within reasonable limits which take into account the importance of what is at stake and maintain the rights of the defence' (*Salabiaku v France* 1988), the House of Lords decided in *R v Lambert* (2001) that another presumption operating against the defendant – this time under s 28 of the Misuse of Drugs Act 1971 – should be interpreted only as an evidential rather than a legal or 'persuasive' burden, and emphasised that a compelling justification would have to be made to bring reverse burdens within the scope of Article 6(2). The further impact of this decision is yet to be seen; meanwhile, it remains the case that, particularly in 'regulatory' fields, many presumptions continue to operate against the defendant, and that in summary offences, the defendant 'almost invariably has the burden of bringing himself within any defence, exemption or proviso to an offence' (Ashworth 2002: 39). Indeed, the Sexual Offences Bill 2003 contemplates a limited reversal of the burden of proof in relation to even the very serious offence of rape. Further questions arise about whether the current Criminal Justice Bill 2003's proposals to expand the admissibility of evidence of bad character and of previous convictions would be regarded as offending against human rights standards.

Andrew Ashworth, 'Criminal Proceedings After the Human Rights Act: The First Year' (2001) Criminal Law Review, 855 at 858

Article 6(2) [of the ECHR] declares that everyone charged with a criminal offence shall be presumed innocent until proved guilty. In the *Kebilene* case (2000) the House of Lords showed some enthusiasm for using the interpretative power under section 3 of the Human Rights Act so as to read a provision requiring an accused 'to prove' a certain defence as imposing merely an evidential burden. Subsequently Parliament expressly required only an evidential burden on two occasions where previously a persuasive burden would probably have been imposed on the defence (*Lambert 2001*), but the habit of imposing persuasive burdens on defendants is still evident. The House of Lords interpreted section 28 of the Misuse of Drugs Act 1971 as imposing only an evidential burden on the defendant, but the

Court of Appeal's decision that section 2 of the Homicide Act 1957 should continue to be read as imposing a persuasive burden on the defence in respect of diminished responsibility remains unaffected. In relation to confiscation of assets, legislation on drug trafficking in Scotland and in England and Wales establishes various presumptions which the offender bears the burden of disproving. The effect of these presumptions in reversing the onus of proof has been upheld both in the Privy Council and in Strasbourg (*Phillips v UK 2001*) and they are likely to reappear in the new Proceeds of Crime Bill.

p 871

In the first year of the 1998 Act's implementation, the British appellate courts have begun 'to make their own distinctive contribution to the development of human rights in Europe' (Lord Irvine LC). They have often done so by emphasising the principle of proportionality, although that is a principle with various shades of meaning. They have also shown a great attraction for the notion of 'balancing' ... There are two lines of criticism [of the balancing approach]. The first is that the notion of balancing is itself rather nebulous, unless a clear indication is given of the relative weight of the factors being balanced, and unless the notion of 'public interest' is carefully unpacked. The second criticism is that such an approach is inappropriate when dealing with such a fundamental right as that guaranteed by Article 6 of the Convention. Although one Strasbourg judgment on Article 6 – that in *Salabiaku v France* – does adopt a rather vague approach to the circumstances in which the presumption of innocence might be displaced, the prevailing authorities on most other aspects of Article 6 insist on a much more rigorous process of reasoning. Even in respect of implied rights ... the predominant Strasbourg approach is to insist that a right may only be limited if this is absolutely necessary to protect another right or for reasons such as national security; if the limitation is counter-balanced by compensating safeguards for the defence; and, where evidence is admitted as a result of applying the limitation, the conviction is not based solely or mainly on that evidence. Above all, and this requirement has been neglected in the British courts, the limitation must not be such as to impair the essence of the right ...

There is a risk, in other words, that rights may be 'balanced' out of existence. Beyond the formal laws of evidence, there are many practices in the criminal process which sit unhappily with the presumption of innocence. Practices such as remand in custody and plea-bargaining, which are seen as crucial to efficiency and crime-control, appear to contradict the presumption. What amount to criminal sanctions are on occasion imposed in response to breaches of civil orders, in contradiction of the principle of legality (for example, under anti-social behaviour orders under s 1 of the Crime and Disorder Act 1998, discussed in **Chapter 3.I.c.**; see also Ashworth 2002: 95). In recent years, notwithstanding several spectacular miscarriages of justice, the rules of evidence celebrated by Allen and by the judges in *Woolmington* have come under attack as being unduly favourable to defendants. They have begun to be modified by statute – for example, allowing adverse inferences to be drawn from the fact that an accused has exercised his or her right to silence (not to testify) in court (Criminal Justice and Public Order Act 1994, ss 34–37). Even legislation passed in the light of miscarriages of justice appears to dilute judicial formulation of the principles which should govern prosecution disclosure of material relevant to the defence (*Ward*, 1993: Criminal Procedure and Investigations Act 1996). Yet recent suggestions are that even in the earlier era which Allen would have seen as marking the height of its institutional realisation, the presumption of innocence, broadly conceived, was honoured more often in the breach than in the observance. Furthermore, the basis for this pattern lies deep in the structure of the constitution.

Andrew Ashworth and Meredith Blake, 'The Presumption of Innocence in English Criminal Law' (1996) Criminal Law Review, 306–307, 309, 314

From time to time English judges have articulated fundamental principles which they believe to underlie criminal law and procedure. In *Sang* (1980) Lord Diplock referred to ... the privilege against self-incrimination or as it was commonly known, "the right of silence". In *Brend v Wood* (1946) Lord Goddard C.J. said that "it is of the utmost importance for the protection of the liberty of the subject that a court should always bear in mind that, unless a statute, either clearly or by necessary implication, rules out *mens rea* [see **section II.** below] as a constituent part of a crime, the court should not find a man guilty of an offence against the criminal law unless he has a guilty mind". Perhaps best known is the declaration of Viscount Sankey L.C. in *Woolmington v DPP* (1935) that "throughout the web of English criminal law one golden thread is always to be seen, that it is the duty of the prosecution to prove the prisoner's guilt". Visount Sankey went on to refer to two exceptions to the general principle – the insanity defence at common law and "statutory exceptions". One way of interpreting this, and indeed Lord Goddard's statement in *Brend v Wood* , is that although a principle may be enshrined in common law Parliament can ignore it whenever it pleases and for whatever reasons, good or bad. In a system based on parliamentary supremacy, there is no arguing with that.

Developments in recent years have cast grave doubt on the existence of these "fundamental principles". Significant inroads into the privilege against self-incrimination have been made by the Criminal Justice and Public Order Act 1994. There has been a continuing flow of legislation which appears to dispense with *mens rea*, although in some instances the courts have been at least partly responsible through their interpretation of particular statutes. And Parliament has repeatedly imposed burdens of proof on defendants in statutes over the last 60 years, although, again, the interpretive role of the judiciary has played its part.

... Judges, textwriters and others sometimes seem to assume that the principles are paramount and that derogations are truly exceptional. Is this assumption borne out in practice? ... We have classified all offences recorded in the 1995 edition of *Archbold* as triable in the Crown Court ... A mere 4 per cent were common law offences, the vast majority being statutory. [Our findings] show the variety of legislative techniques which may be said to derogate, to a greater or lesser degree, from the basic principle that the prosecution should prove all elements of the case ... [W]e found 219 examples, among 540 offences triable in the Crown Court of legal burdens or presumptions operating against the defendant. As for fault, [we found] that almost exactly one half of the offences required a form of *mens rea* in respect of each element of the *actus reus*, whereas the other half had at least one element not requiring *mens rea*. About five per cent of offences triable in the Crown Court impose liability for negligence, and a further 45 per cent have an element of strict liability (of which half include some form of "due diligence" defence) ...

A central purpose of the study was to discover how frequently English criminal law departs from the presumption of innocence declared so resoundingly in *Woolmington*. Our finding, that no fewer than 40 per cent of offences triable in the Crown Court appear to violate the presumption, should prompt some searching questions. Is there anything to justify this large-scale derogation from what ought to be a basic principle? Some would seek to justify exceptions for serious offences of great public concern (eg terrorism, serious fraud, drugs, etc.), an approach which neglects the seriousness for defendants of being convicted of such offences. No less important is the apparent casualness with which Parliament has continued to add to the number of derogations. Perhaps the limited terms of Visount Sankey's speech in *Woolmington* hold the key: what he said, in effect, is that courts should invariably place the burden of proof on the prosecution, but that Parliament may do what it pleases. Article 6.2 of the European Convention on Human Rights, declaring that everyone charged with a criminal offence should be presumed innocent, has not yet been interpreted as restricting Parliament's freedom in this matter.

Since several of the proposals in the Criminal Justice Bill 2002 tend to dilute rather than to strengthen due process values, there is little reason to hope that the passage of the HRA 1998 has fundamentally changed the parliamentary freedom noted by Ashworth and Blake in 1996.

The weight attached to the presumption of innocence, like other features of due process, is closely related to the images of criminal law discussed in the first section of this chapter, and in particular to arguments about the proper functions of the criminal process. This relationship, as well as the further connection between the presumption of innocence and the rule of law, is illustrated by Packer's famous distinction between competing 'crime control' and 'due process' models of criminal justice:

Herbert Packer, *The Limits of the Criminal Sanction* (Stanford University Press, 1968) pp 150–172

The value system that underlies the Crime Control Model is based on the proposition that the repression of criminal conduct is by far the most important function to be performed by the criminal process. The failure of law enforcement to bring criminal conduct under tight control is viewed as leading to the breakdown of public order and thence to the disappearance of an important condition of human freedom ... In order to achieve this high purpose [of protecting social freedom], the Crime Control Model requires that primary attention be paid to the efficiency with which the criminal process operates to screen suspects, determine guilt, and secure appropriate dispositions of persons convicted of crime ...

The model, in order to operate successfully, must produce a high rate of apprehension and conviction, and must do so in a context where the magnitudes being dealt with are very large and the resources for dealing with them are very limited. There must then be a premium on speed and finality. Speed, in turn, depends on informality and on uniformity; finality depends on minimizing the occasions for challenge. The process must not be cluttered up with ceremonious rituals that do not advance the progress of a case ... The image that comes to mind is an assembly-line conveyor belt down which moves an endless stream of cases, never stopping, carrying the cases to workers who stand at fixed stations and who perform in each case as it comes by the same small but essential operation that brings it one step closer to being a finished product, or, to exchange the metaphor for the reality, a closed file. The criminal process, in this model, is seen as a screening process in which each successive stage – pre-arrest investigation, arrest, post-arrest investigation, preparation for trial, trial or entry of plea, conviction, disposition – involves a series of routinized operations whose success is gauged primarily by their tendency to pass the case along to a successful conclusion ...

The presumption of guilt is what makes it possible for the system to deal efficiently with large numbers, as the Crime Control Model demands. The supposition is that the screening processes operated by police and prosecutors are reliable indicators of probable guilt. Once a man [sic] has been arrested and investigated without being found to be probably innocent, or, to put it differently, once a determination has been made that there is enough evidence of guilt to permit holding him for further action, then all subsequent activity directed toward him is based on the view that he is probably guilty. The precise point at which this occurs will vary from case to case; in many cases it will occur as soon as the suspect is arrested, or even before, if the evidence of probable guilt that has come to the attention of the authorities is sufficiently strong. But in any case the presumption of guilt will begin to operate well before the 'suspect' becomes a 'defendant'.

The presumption of guilt is not, of course, a thing. Nor is it even a rule of law in the usual sense. It simply is the consequence of a complex of attitudes, a mood. If there is confidence in the reliability of informal administrative fact-finding activities that take place in the early stages of the criminal process, the remaining stages of the process can be relatively perfunctory without any loss in operating efficiency. The presumption of guilt, as it operates in the Crime Control Model, is the operational expression of that confidence.

It would be a mistake to think of the presumption of guilt as the opposite of the presumption of innocence that we are so used to thinking of as the polestar of the criminal process and that, as we shall see, occupies an important position in the Due Process Model. The presumption of innocence is not its opposite; it is irrelevant to the presumption of guilt; the two concepts are different rather than opposite ideas ...

The presumption of innocence is a direction to officials about how they are to proceed, not a prediction of outcome. The presumption of guilt, however, is purely and simply a prediction of outcome. The presumption of innocence is, then, a direction to the authorities to ignore the presumption of guilt in their eyes to what will frequently seem to be factual probabilities. The reasons why it tells them this are among the animating presuppositions of the Due Process Model. ... The pure Crime Control Model has no truck with the presumption of innocence, although its real-life emanations are ... brought into uneasy compromise with the dictates of this dominant ideological position ...

If the Crime Control Model resembles an assembly line, the Due Process Model looks very much like an obstacle course. Each of its successive stages is designed to present formidable impediments to carrying the accused any further along in the process ... The Due Process Model encounters its rival on the Crime Control Model's own ground in respect to the reliability of fact-finding processes. The Crime Control Model, as we have suggested, places heavy reliance on the ability of investigative and prosecutorial officers, acting in an informal setting in which their distinctive skills are given full sway, to elicit and reconstruct a tolerably accurate account of what actually took place in an alleged criminal event. The Due Process Model rejects this premise and substitutes for it a view of informal, non adjudicative fact-finding that stresses the possibility of error. People are notoriously poor observers of disturbing events – the more emotion-arousing the context, the greater the possibility that recollection will be incorrect; confessions and admissions by persons in police custody may be induced by physical or psychological coercion so that the police end up hearing what the suspect thinks they want to hear rather than the truth; witnesses may be animated by a bias or interest that no one would trouble to discover except one specially charged with protecting the interests of the accused (as the police are not). Considerations of this kind all lead to a rejection of informal fact-finding processes as definitive of factual guilt and to an insistence on formal, adjudicative, adversary fact-finding processes in which the factual case against the accused is publicly heard by an impartial tribunal and is evaluated only after the accused has had a full opportunity to discredit the case against him. Even then, the distrust of fact-finding processes that animates the Due Process Model is not dissipated. The possibilities of human error being what they are, further scrutiny is necessary, or at least must be available, in case facts have been overlooked or suppressed in the heat of battle. How far this subsequent scrutiny must be available is a hotly controverted issue today. In the pure Due Process Model the answer would be: at least as long as there is an allegation of factual error that has not received an adjudicative hearing in a fact-finding context. The demand for finality is thus very low in the Due Process Model ...

The most modest-seeming but potentially far-reaching mechanism by which the Due Process Model implements these anti-authoritarian values is the doctrine of legal guilt. According to this doctrine, a person is not to be held guilty of crime merely on a showing that in all probability, based upon reliable evidence, he did factually what he is said to have done. Instead, he is to be held guilty if and only if these factual determinations are made in procedurally regular fashion and by authorities acting within competences duly allocated to them. Furthermore, he is not to be held guilty, even though the factual determination is or might be adverse to him, if various rules designed to protect him and to safeguard the integrity of the process are not given effect ...

In this concept of legal guilt lies the explanation for the apparently quixotic presumption of innocence of which we spoke earlier. A man who, after police investigation, is charged with having committed a crime can hardly be said to be presumptively innocent, if what we mean is factual innocence. But if what we mean is that it has yet to be determined if any of the myriad legal doctrines that serve in one way or another the end of limiting official power through the observance of certain substantive and procedural regularities may be appropriately invoked to exculpate the accused man, it is apparent that as a matter of prediction it cannot be said with confidence that more probably than not he will be found guilty.

Beyond the question of predictability this model posits a functional reason for observing the presumption of innocence: by forcing the state to prove its case against the accused in an adjudicative context, the presumption

of innocence serves to force into play all the qualifying and disabling doctrines that limit the use of the criminal sanction against the individual,
thereby enhancing his opportunity to secure a favourable outcome ...

Note the resonance between Packer's 'crime control' and 'due process' models
and, respectively, the regulatory and moral-retributive conceptions of criminal
law canvassed in the first section of this chapter. In Packer's terms, Ashworth's
and Blake's research suggests that the English system has been moving steadily
in a 'crime control' direction. But the opposition may be less than clear.
McBarnet (1981) has argued that Packer's analysis of two competing models is
misleading in that many features of the criminal process which we think of as
elements of 'due process' in fact operate in a way which is functional to 'crime
control' (for further critical discussion of Packer, see Ashworth (1998: 24–29).
One graphic – and tragic – illustration of this lies in a number of appalling miscarriages of justice brought to light over the last 15 years (see below, and
Hickey et al 1997; Ashworth 1998: 11–18). The ultimate quashing in 1989 of
the convictions of the 'Guildford Four', convicted of murder by bombing a pub
in 1976, discussed above, and concern about the case of the 'Maguire Seven',
convicted that year of possessing explosives allegedly linked to the same bombings, gave rise to a public outcry which prompted the appointment of a Royal
Commission on Criminal Justice in 1991. In 1991, the convictions of the
'Birmingham Six' (*McIlkenny and others*, 1991) and the 'Tottenham Three'
(*Silcott, Braithwaite and Raghip*, 1991) were quashed on similar grounds of what
amounted to grave breaches of due process: the Maguires followed in 1992,
Judith Ward (*Ward*, 1993) and the 'Cardiff Three' (*Paris, Abdullahi and Miller*,
1993) followed in 1993. The last group had been convicted in 1990 of the murder of a Cardiff prostitute. Their convictions were quashed by the Court of
Appeal on the ground that the nature and length of police interviews – conducted after the safeguards of the Police and Criminal Evidence Act 1984,
which included the tape-recording of police interviews of suspects, were in
place, as had not been the case with the other miscarriages of justice – was such
that they should not have been admitted as evidence. Perhaps most startling is
that the police employed these techniques knowing that they were being filmed,
suggesting not only that they thought they were behaving properly, but that
they were working in an institutional culture which tolerated or even encouraged that belief.

In these cases, a welter of procedural and human rights issues were raised: poor
standards and failures of disclosure of evidence by forensic experts; fabrication
or falsification of evidence by police officers; oppressive police conduct during
questioning. Furthermore, the failure of most of the cases at initial appellate
hearings, as well as the difficulty of achieving a further reference back to the
Court of Appeal, revealed failings in the machinery available for investigating
possible miscarriages of justice. The genesis of the miscarriages therefore lay
not merely in individualised wrongdoing or error, but also in pervasive features

of the criminal process. These cases could not be explained away as aberrations, but prompted general questions about the conduct of contemporary criminal justice. While the main failings lay in the design and conduct of the criminal process and in rules of evidence rather than in criminal law itself, these cases also illustrate the interdependence of law and procedure in the effective establishment of the presumption of innocence. In this respect, the terms of reference of the Royal Commission are instructive:

> ... a Commission should forthwith issue to examine the effectiveness of the criminal justice system in England and Wales in *securing the conviction of those guilty of criminal offences and the acquittal of those who are innocent, having regard to the efficient use of resources* [Royal Commission on Criminal Justice, 1993, Cm 2263, p i; emphasis added].

These terms of reference represent the goals of convicting the guilty and acquitting the innocent as of equal importance, rather than according the priority to the acquittal of the innocent which 'the golden thread' would appear to dictate: furthermore, each of these goals is set up as being on a par with that of managerial efficiency. In short, the terms of reference tend towards Packer's crime control model rather than towards the due process model which one might have expected to be uppermost in the Government's thinking in the aftermath of the miscarriages of justice. Given the varying conceptions of 'due process' or 'justice' which different groups in society expect the criminal justice system to deliver, and which make it all but impossible for a legal community to acknowledge that some miscarriages of justice are an inevitable side effect of the all too human process of criminal justice, it is difficult to find a satisfactory resolution of this problem:

Richard Nobles and David Schiff, *Understanding Miscarriages of Justice* (OUP, 2000) pp 16, 37–38

The general conception of miscarriage of justice, which is shared by the diverse communities of lawyers, media, politicians and in general social communication, is not injustice *per se*, but wrongful conviction ...

The legal community generally expresses a commitment to due process as a value in addition to that of truth ... Due process provides an alternative basis to truth for deciding whether convictions are wrongful or not. Intolerance to breaches of rules, standards of procedure, and rights are presented by lawyers to themselves and to those outside the law as evidence of law's commitment to justice ...

By contrast to the legal community, the media's attachment to due process is weaker than its attachment to truth. Rights, which make no contribution to the factual correctness of a verdict, can be seen as technical and lacking merit. The media's dominant understanding of miscarriage of justice is that those who are factually innocent cannot rightfully be punished, *whatever the process which led to their conviction*. This understanding of miscarriage of justice has the ability to threaten the legitimacy of criminal justice, and to promote that perception of crisis, because it creates the possibility of putting criminal justice itself on trial … [Emphasis in original.]

In this context it is perhaps not surprising that the Royal Commission's recommendations on the reform of the criminal process were both piecemeal and relatively modest. They included the establishment of a new Criminal Cases Review Commission for the consideration and referral to the Court of Appeal of miscarriage cases; improved safeguards for defendants in the investigation and trial process, matched by greater police powers in dealing with suspects and the removal of the right to elect trial by jury in cases triable either way; and improved police training and discipline. Of these, only the first has been implemented fully (Criminal Appeal Act 1995), and the Commission's defence of the right to silence was, as we have seen, ignored by the very Government which established the Commission. It seems that the 'golden thread' must be reinterpreted as, at best, a dotted line of somewhat paler hue.

FURTHER READING

Ashworth, Andrew (2002) *Human Rights, Serious Crime and Criminal Procedure* (Sweet & Maxwell).

Collins, Hugh (1982) *Marxism and Law* (Clarendon Press) Ch 6.

Feeley, Malcom and Simon, Jonathan (1994) 'Actuarial Justice: the Emerging New Criminal Law' in Nelken, David (ed) *The Futures of Criminology* (Sage) p 173.

Hunter, Rosemary (1996) 'Gender in Evidence: Masculine Norms vs Feminist Reforms' Harvard Women's Law Journal 127.

McConville, Mike and Bridges, Lee (eds) (1994) *Criminal Justice in Crisis* (Edward Elgar).

Nobles, Richard and Schiff, David (2000) *Understanding Miscarriages of Justice* (Oxford University Press).

O'Donovan, Katherine (1989) 'Engendering Justice: Women's Perspectives and the Rule of Law' 39 University of Toronto Law Journal 127.

Wiener, Martin (1990) *Reconstructing the Criminal* (Cambridge University Press).

Williams, Glanville (1987) 'The Logic of Exceptions' Cambridge Law Journal 261.

II.   Framing criminal law

Over the last 150 years, scholars of criminal law have devoted an enormous amount of attention to the so-called 'general part' of criminal law. The 'general part' consists of the rules, principles and doctrines which apply across the whole range of specific criminal offences: the components of criminal conduct and responsibility, general defences, principles of inchoate and participatory liability. At one level, the 'general part' is an aspect of the doctrine of criminal law itself. But, as we shall try to show in this section, legal doctrines are by no means independent of the normative theories of criminal law which we considered in the last section. For criminal law doctrine contains a powerful set of assumptions – sometimes made explicit by judges and legal commentators, but sometimes left implicit – about not only the general structure of but also the rationale for criminal liability. The framework of criminal law doctrine is closely articulated with the ideal of the rule of law and with the modern conception of the legal subject as an individual invested with rights against the state. However, we shall also see in criminal law doctrine traces of the tension between instrumental and moral functions of criminal law reflected in the theories discussed in the first section of this chapter.

Our discussion will question some assumptions prevalent in both judicial discourse and standard texts. These include a pretension as to the objectivity and completeness of doctrinal analysis; a faith in the capacity of the conceptual framework to generate determinate answers to substantive questions of law; and a belief in the timeless validity of the 'general principles of criminal law'. By contrast, we aim to illuminate the openness and flexibility of doctrinal categories; the partiality of legal interpretations sailing under the banner of 'objectivity'; the historical specificity of the values embedded in doctrine; and the structural tensions lying within the doctrinal scheme. Our method here is analogous to what has been termed 'immanent' or 'internal' critique – an approach to the interpretation of legal doctrine which looks within law itself, scrutinising it closely, for examples of emergent or embedded values which are not accounted for by, or which are actually inimical to, its professed ideals. In this way, critical scholars seek to question legal doctrine *from within law as it has traditionally been understood*, exposing both its historical contingency and its relationship with a wide range of extra-legal social forces. In the following passage, Norrie gives a succinct account of the direction and motivation of this method:

Alan Norrie, *Crime, Reason and History* (Butterworths, 2001) p 8

[T]he modern criminal law was formed in a particular historical epoch and derived its characteristic 'shape' from fundamental features of the social relations of that epoch. Its principles therefore are historic and relative rather than natural and general. Furthermore these principles were established in the crucible of social and political conflict, and bear the stamp of history in the always-contradictory ways in which they are formulated. Historical analysis shows that, far from being free-standing foundations for a rational criminal law, the central principles of the law are the site of struggle and contradiction. This can only work its way through the legal rules themselves. Thus it is that the fate of law as a rationalising enterprise is tied up with the nature of law as a social, historical force.

Our first task is to describe the doctrinal model of criminal law and liability. Inevitably what we shall be producing here is a model, for we cannot hope to discuss every small point of detail. Furthermore, since commentators on criminal law themselves display some ambivalence about the status of the traditional story about 'the general principles of criminal liability' – at one moment pointing out laws' failure to meet them, yet at the next reproducing the core assumptions of the traditional principles (see further Norrie 2001: Ch 1) – any attempt to produce a critique of this method is vulnerable to the criticism that it is simply responding to a caricature. Our view is that such critique is worthwhile because, although most commentators acknowledge the incomplete realisation of general principles in criminal law, their accounts nonetheless proceed within the framework set by the 'general principles', and construe departures from them as minor irregularities which could and should be removed (cf the analysis of the presumption of innocence above). It is this view that we want to challenge. In doing so, we hope to equip the reader with the critical tools central to the detailed interpretation of particular fields of criminal law which occupy the following chapters.

The 'general part' has to do not so much with the substance as with the structure of criminal liability: it represents the conceptual building blocks out of which legal reasoning constructs arguments for and against liability. Summed up very simply, the 'general part' portrays the conditions of liability as being divided into two main elements; 'actus reus' or the 'external'/'conduct' element; and 'mens rea' or the 'mental'/'internal'/'fault' element. The paradigm of criminal liability therefore consists in a person subject to criminal law performing or causing the 'actus reus' of the offence with the requisite 'mental element', in the absence of any relevant defence.

Implicit in this paradigm is the idea of the subject as a rational agent with capacities of both cognition and self-control, and hence the idea of criminal liability as rooted in individual agency. In accordance with the precept of formal equality before the law, the legal subject is constructed as a gender-less, race-less, class-less individual abstracted – with some significant exceptions (*Morgan Smith*, 2000) – from its social situation. Linguistic convention, however, (reversed in this book) is one among many clues to its implicit masculinity, to say nothing of its ethnicity or socio-economic position (Allen 1988; MacKinnon, Kennedy 1992; Nicolson and Bibbings 2000). This abstract subject is a person of 'normal' capacities: of 'sound mind' and of sufficient age to appreciate the implications of their actions (English criminal law draws this line at age 10: Crime and Disorder Act 1998, s 34). To give a simple example, theft is defined in the Theft Act 1968, s 1, as the dishonest appropriation by a person of property belonging to another with intent permanently to deprive that other of it. Without going into detailed questions of interpretation at this stage, the appropriation of property belonging to another constitutes the 'actus reus' of this offence, whilst the dishonest intent permanently to deprive constitutes the 'mens rea'. The core assumption of doctrine is that both 'actus reus' and 'mens rea', seen as analytically separate concepts, are necessary conditions for conviction of an offence. The basic building blocks out of which criminal liability is constructed are therefore, on the face of it, very simple: in the case of a capable legal subject, 'actus reus' + 'mens rea' = offence.

This basic account has to be refined not only by the introduction of principles of excuse, justification and mitigation but also by the supplementary concepts of inchoate and participatory liability and by (what are conventionally seen as) the exceptions of 'strict' and 'vicarious' liability. To illustrate once again with the example of theft, if a defendant stole under duress such as threats to her life, her conduct may be excused. If she stole to feed a child who would otherwise have died of starvation, her conduct might (though this is controversial) be held to be justified under a doctrine of duress of circumstances. If she can prove on a balance of probabilities that she comes within the legal definition of insanity, this fundamental incapacity will also lead to her acquittal. She can be convicted of attempting or conspiring with others to commit theft, or of inciting another to do so, or for some combinations of these activities, even if she never completes or even partially performs the 'actus reus' as defined by the Theft Act 1968. And she may be convicted as an accomplice to theft even if she was not involved in the actual theft if, for example, she participated by supplying necessary equipment or giving valuable knowledge or advice, knowing that it would be used to steal. The many offences of 'strict' liability (such as driving without insurance) can be committed without any proof of 'mens rea'. And even where the person convicted has not accomplished the 'actus reus' herself but is in a relationship of authority or responsibility towards the person who has done so, the law may in certain circumstances hold her 'vicariously' liable for that other person's acts. Our preliminary equation therefore needs to be reformulated as 'actus reus' committed by a capable subject + 'mens rea' [modified by principles of inchoate, participatory, strict and vicarious liability] – defence = offence.

These elements are usually brought together under the heading 'general principles of liability'. One way of looking at these principles is as a set of interpretive postulates developed within the common law and applied by the courts to both common law and statutory offences (the latter now making up the vast bulk of criminal law). Their denomination as 'general principles' reflects the idea that the scheme is a rational, coherent and even-handed one which is both generally realised in criminal law and justified in terms of political morality. In modern, codified systems – and indeed in the Law Commission's various draft codes (Law Commission 1985, 1993) – these 'general principles' therefore tend to occupy a central position. It is important to bear in mind, however, that the quest for a 'general part' of criminal law is a specifically modern one. If we look back to one of the first systematic statements of the common law of crime – that of William Blackstone, first Vinerian Professor of English Law at Oxford in the mid-eighteenth century – we see a very different picture:

**Nicola Lacey, 'In Search of the Responsible Subject of Criminal Law'
(2001) 64 Modern Law Review, 350 at 359–360**

A structural as well as a content analysis of [of William Blackstone's
Commentaries on the Laws of England, published in the 1760s, James
Fitzjames Stephen's History of Criminal Law and his *Digest of Criminal
Law* (a Draft Criminal Code) from the 1880s and Glanville Williams'
Criminal Law, The General Part, from 1953, produces] some … striking
contrasts. Most obviously, the idea of a general part is missing from
Blackstone's text and – more significantly – exists only in sketchy form in
Stephen's; while each of them spends only about 10% of their text considering rules and principles applicable across offences (including not only the
requirements of conduct and responsibility but also defences and matters
such as the nature of penalties, inchoate offences such as attempt and
liability for secondary participation) Glanville Williams' text – which
provides the model for almost all subsequent commentaries and many
attempts at codification – almost exactly reverses the proportion. For both
Blackstone and Stephen, it is the so-called 'special part' – the criminal
offences themselves – which are, as it were, where the theoretical action is.
Their observations about general conditions of liability are focussed on the
nature of voluntary conduct and defences rather than on responsibility;
these observations are very brief, and are elaborated mainly in relation to
particular offences. Even Stephen's earlier *A General View of the Criminal
Law of England*, contrary to what today's reader might assume from its
title, has only one chapter, spanning a mere 24 of the book's nearly 500
pages, which discusses individual responsibility and which corresponds
with the 'general part' in Williams' sense.

This, I would argue, does not entail that either Blackstone's or Stephen's
account lacks rationality, coherence or system. Indeed, if we look at the
ways in which they organise their material, we perceive a perfectly systematic approach, as well as learning a great deal about how they saw their
field. Let me take just one example. For Blackstone – a great champion of
the common law, and writing as statute law was set to become an increasingly significant force – the challenge was to present the common law of
crime as rational and reasonably systematic in terms not of the arcane procedural distinctions for which common law was (in)famous but rather of
the interests it protected and the values it upheld. Blackstone therefore
presented criminal law in a way which spoke to these issues, grouping
offences not on terms of their distinctive procedural characteristics but in
terms of substantive concerns which could be seen as adding up to a coherent sense of 'public wrong': offences against God and religion, offences
against the king, offences against public order; offences against the person
and property. He then elaborated these in relation to exemplary fact
situations which spoke to the important legal issues of his time.

From the point of view of late Twentieth Century legal philosophy, Blackstone's Commentaries certainly do look a bit chaotic; there are few articulations of anything we would recognise as general principles, let alone any sustained reflection on the nature of voluntary conduct, individual responsibility or the specific excusing conditions which might undermine ascriptions of responsibility. But Blackstone's exemplary method of elaboration and analysis makes a great deal of sense in its own terms ... He is – from a late Twentieth Century perspective – spectacularly uninterested in the question, 'what makes it fair to hold an individual responsible for a crime'. But ... this should not come as any surprise when we reflect upon criminal justice institutions and socio-political conditions in mid-Eighteenth Century England.

Today, by contrast, academic and judicial discussion of criminal liability is seen as an enterprise of rational justification which focuses on the structure rather than the substance of criminal law, constantly reaching towards the ideal of presentation and development of criminal law as a certain, fair and consistent system – as opposed to *ex post facto* rationalisation of the decisions of powerful interests. For example, in Ashworth's *Principles of Criminal Law* (2003) the general part occupies over half the text: in Simester and Sullivan's *Criminal Law: Theory and Doctrine* (2000), it occupies twice as much space as the 'special part' (ie actual criminal offences). The relatively weak constitutional constraints on our 'sovereign' Parliament, though recently strengthened by the passage of the Human Rights Act 1998, might be thought to pose problems for this view of criminal law – as in the case of the inroads on the presumption of innocence discussed above. But a focus on the *structure as opposed to the content* of criminal liability as the basis for the rationalisation of criminal law doctrine – like the focus on criminal procedure rather than the substance of criminal law in the attempts at definition considered in the previous section – makes good sense in a world in which criminal law is used for a huge diversity of regulatory as well as quasi-moral purposes, and in which both the expanding terrain of criminal law and value-pluralism have undermined the kind of substantive consensus to which Blackstone could appeal in his content-based rationalisation of criminal law. The extent to which today's view of criminal law as a principled body of doctrine is defensible must ultimately be judged in the light of further discussion in chapters dealing with actual offences. It is, however, useful to look critically at each main element of criminal law doctrine in turn, so as to get a clearer idea of how the standard story fits (and fails to fit) together.

II.a.   'Actus reus'

Alan Norrie, *Crime, Reason and History* (Butterworths, 2001) p 110

Acts, omissions and causes represent the bedrock of the law of 'actus reus'. Like 'mens rea', 'actus reus' is not a tightly defined concept but rather a loose 'common denominator' which denotes the requirement that every crime requires an external element. Accordingly, it is best described negatively:

> 'All that can be said, without exception, is that a crime requires some external state of affairs that can be categorised as criminal. What goes on inside a man's head is never enough in itself to constitute a crime' (Williams 1983, 146).

This formulation indicates an immediate point of connection between the common law and the positive side of liberal values, for it is made clear that it is no crime to think criminal thoughts. Against this, it must be pointed out that the practical impact of this libertarian stance is blunted by the wide way in which the law draws certain criminal categories, such as conspiracy.

The 'actus reus' is that element of the definition of an offence which consists in the behaviour which the defendant engages in, seen from an external point of view: abstracted from its meaning or significance for the defendant herself. In some crimes, the 'actus reus' consists simply in an action or piece of behaviour – 'appropriation' of property belonging to another; hiring an '18' video to a child; having sexual intercourse with a person without their consent. But, as the last example shows, the 'actus reus' may comprehend a complex of elements which may include a 'mental state'. This may be the mental state of another person (such as lack of consent of the victim in rape) or of the defendant herself (as, arguably, in the case of careless driving, where carelessness may be at once a quality of the driving and an attitude or state of mind of the defendant). The latter example illustrates the difficulty of distinguishing between 'actus reus' and 'mens rea'; between 'external' and 'mental' elements. Should we regard 'careless' as part of the description of the quality of the *action*, and thus an aspect of the 'actus reus'? Or should it be seen as referring to an attitude of 'practical indifference', which rather represents the 'mens rea' requirement? Is it possible or necessary to classify every element as either 'mens rea' or 'actus reus'? What is the utility of doing so if the analytical clarity promised by doctrine is illusory even in the case of a simple offence such as this?

The 'actus reus' requirement of some offences consists wholly or partly in a particular result's being caused, as in the case of murder and manslaughter – causing the death of a person – or causing death by dangerous driving. These are known as 'result crimes'. Sometimes, as in the case of causing death by dangerous driving, the offence will specify the type of causal action required with some precision. In other cases, such as murder, no such precise specification is made. In yet others, an offence may be committed in alternative ways, with special legal consequences such as maximum penalties attaching to each. An example would be the Criminal Damage Act 1971 under which the 'actus reus' of general criminal damage (s 1(1)) simply consists of destroying or causing damage to property belonging to another, whereas causing such damage by means of fire (s 1(3)) constitutes the special offence of arson, and carries a greater maximum penalty. There is no general rule, therefore, as to the precision with which the 'actus reus' of an offence will be specified in its statutory formulation, let alone in the precedents which establish it where a common law offence is involved.

In the case of 'result crimes', the 'actus reus' includes a causation requirement which can itself throw up problems, both at a theoretical level and in terms of generating workable legal tests. In most actual cases, criminal law is not much exercised by problems of causation. In 'non-result' or 'conduct' crimes such as rape or possessing a prohibited drug, it hardly seems to make sense to ask if the defendant caused the offence. In 'result crimes', we are usually able to make 'common sense' judgments: if Ann shoots Bill and Bill dies, we infer that Ann caused Bill's death. If Clive sets fire to Diane's house and Eric is injured trying to put out the fire, we say that Clive's act was a cause of Eric's injury. But even this second, simple example begins to reveal one of the major problems of causation – the fact that results or events have a myriad of causes, in the sense of conditions necessary for their realisation: conditions 'but for' which the outcome would not have eventuated. In attributing legal liability, we must choose among this multiplicity, although we need not necessarily select only one cause as legally relevant. For example, if Ann shoots Bill who then receives inept medical treatment from Helen and dies, who is causally responsible for Bill's death – Ann, or Helen, or both? On what criteria should we decide? If Clive sets fire to Diane's house and John then douses the fire with petrol, who is causally responsible for Eric's injuries in trying to put out the aggravated fire? If Fred and Gill both shoot Kay simultaneously and Kay dies, which of them has caused her death?

The straightforward 'but-for' test of causation, which asks whether the result would have occurred but for the intervention of Ann, Helen, John, Fred or Gill, does not offer a satisfactory basis for selecting the legally relevant cause, for it will identify the very multiplicity of causes which is the problem. It will, for example, pick out not only Ann's shooting and Helen's negligence, but also the gun's being loaded and Bill's having been in a particular place at a particular time. Moreover, the test cannot help us to decide when an 'intervening' cause should be said to wipe out the legal effects of prior causal conduct or events: to 'break the chain' of causation. Several suggestions have been made as to possible criteria for selection; 'substantial' causes, 'efficient' causes and 'continuing' causes have all been proffered at one time or another. But these tests are difficult to apply with any precision. Hart and Honoré (1985) suggest that criminal law focuses in particular on voluntary human conduct, further selecting among human causes in terms of the unusual nature of a particular but-for cause – we select for legal liability those but-for causes which represent 'abnormal' behaviour. But this approach begs criteria of 'abnormality' and, in common with other tests, attracts the suspicion not only that policy factors in fact drive courts' decisions, but also that aspects of 'mens rea' – an attribution of fault – may creep in to the question of 'actus reus' by the back door, sullying the purity of the doctrinal structure. For one obvious way of fleshing out ideas of 'abnormality' and 'substantiality', and hence of selecting legal causes, is to do so in terms of degrees of responsibility or culpability; the person to whom we attribute causation is the person whom we regard as blameworthy. For example, in *Roberts* (1971), the defendant assaulted a woman passenger in his car. She was injured when she jumped from the moving car to escape. Despite her arguably extreme reaction, which might have been seen as interrupting the 'chain of causation' between Roberts' assault and her injury, Roberts was held liable for assault occasioning actual bodily harm. What is more, criminal law occasionally deploys a notion of causation wider than that of 'but for' cause: for example, when a person is held liable for aiding and abetting another person's crime, for example by lending a burglar a ladder, the prosecution must prove that the defendant gave assistance: the rationale for liability turns in part on the quasi-causal idea that such assistance made the commission of the offence more likely. But the prosecution is not required to prove that the offence would not have been committed but for the assistance of the ladder. In a recent civil decision which has potential relevance for criminal causation, the House of Lords has also moved beyond individualised, 'but-for' causation, holding that a person who had contracted a fatal disease as a result of exposure to risk at successive places of employment, but who could not prove which of those employers had contributed, and in what proportions, to the disease, could nonetheless recover against them (*Fairchild*, 2002). In fact (as many commentators accept) it is impossible to assert that English criminal law adheres to any coherent and consistent doctrine of causation. The question remains whether it can be as clearly categorised as an issue of 'actus reus' as traditional conceptualisation suggests.

Some offences require an 'actus reus' which consists not of 'conduct' but of a 'status' or 'condition'. This is true, for example, of the famous case of *Larsonneur* (1933). This case concerned a defendant who, being 'an alien to whom leave to land in the UK has been refused', was found in the UK (Aliens Order 1920). Such so-called 'status offences' are often portrayed as exceptional, but the difficulty of distinguishing between them and 'conduct' or 'result' offences can be demonstrated by examples such as driving with an excess of alcohol in the blood. This could be conceptualised as 'being found drunk in the process of driving' (status) or as 'doing the act of driving with an excess of alcohol' (conduct). Such examples not only show the difficulty of drawing any clear analytical distinction, but also question the significance of such a distinction, could it be drawn. Also of interest in this context is the status 'common prostitute', which can be attributed exclusively to women by the police under s 1 of the Street Offences Act 1959 (*DPP v Bull*, 1994). The criteria for this designation are obscure, and it is effectively impossible for the woman to challenge, yet it has the important legal consequence of liability to conviction for what would otherwise have been lawful behaviour (Edwards 1984: 53–77; Smart 1985).

Finally, a related complication must be added in terms of criminal law's attitude to liability for omissions. In general, doctrine affirms that liability is imposed only for acts, and not for omissions (see Ashworth 1989). The basis for this is the libertarian argument that the coercive powers of law must only be invoked in response to positive actions, or else law would become unduly burdensome and intrusive on individual freedom. Is this a strong argument? It seems unlikely that many of us would regard liability for failure to pay our taxes as more burdensome than, say, a law prohibiting us from engaging in a form of sexual conduct to which we were strongly disposed. But there is a further, technical reason why omissions liability is thought to be problematic. For it entails the possibility of multiple liability wherever there is no particular reason for attributing responsibility (or causation) to one rather than another person. For example, in a case where a person has drowned in the presence of many people in a public swimming pool, it becomes very difficult to circumscribe the ambit of liability in a manageable way: should we hold responsible everyone within sight of the incident; everyone within ten yards; every strong swimmer in the vicinity? The individualistic conceptual structure of criminal liability here creates a practical problem which is intimately linked with English law's reflection of the norms of an atomistic society which is relatively little concerned to promote mutual or collective responsibility. There is an interesting contrast here with the systems of the continent of Europe, which encompass a variety of omissions-based offences. One example is the offence with which the 'paparazzi' arrested at the scene of the fatal accident of Dodi al Fayed and the Princess of Wales in Paris in 1997 were charged: that of 'failing to assist a person in danger' (for discussion, see Cadoppi 1993).

However, English criminal law does impose liability for omissions not only in a vast range of statutory offences, many of them regulating corporate conduct, but also under the common law in two 'exceptional' types of case. The first might be called *relational*: where there is some statutory or relational basis for a duty to act, such as a parental duty of care and support for a child, or an assumed duty of care for a relative, an omission to act which results in legally recognised harm may incur liability. For example someone who assumes responsibility for an incapacitated relative and then fails to act once they become aware that the relative is in a dangerous state of health may be liable for homicide should the relative die as a result (*Stone and Dobinson*, 1977). The existence of the duty serves to defeat the presumption against curtailment of individual freedom. The second might be called *situational*: criminal liability may be imposed where an initial inadvertent action results in a dangerous or harmful situation which the defendant later knowingly fails to avert when the opportunity presents itself. A good example would be one in which the defendant has accidentally caused a fire and, on later discovering it, neither calls the fire brigade nor takes any steps to put it out (*Miller*, 1983). In such a case, liability may be imposed for the omission on the basis either of an imputed duty to act, flowing from 'responsibility' for minimising even the harms which we cause faultlessly, or on the theory that the whole sequence of events constitutes a 'continuing act' (*Fagan v MPC*, 1969).

Despite the ability of criminal law doctrine to rationalise and accommodate these cases, the general exclusion of liability for omissions continues to raise important conceptual and practical problems. This is in part because whether or not behaviour is to be regarded as an act or as an omission is often an open question, depending simply on how we choose to describe it. To take a simple example, should we regard a person holding a china vase who stops tensing her muscles so as to let the vase drop as actively breaking the vase, or as simply failing to hold it? Would our answer be different if the vase were suddenly and unexpectedly thrust into her arms? Is the switching off of a life-support machine an act which causes death or an omission to sustain life, and does it make any difference if the machine is disconnected accidentally and then deliberately left unconnected (see *Airedale NHS Trust v Bland*, 1993)? Can we make any decision about these issues purely within the framework of 'actus reus' analysis? It is apposite here to point out that all offences of negligence – careless driving, for example – are in an important sense offences of omission, in that they consist in a failure to take due care. The very large number of offences which can be committed negligently or which are of strict liability subject to a 'due diligence' defence – about 50% of offences triable in the Crown Court, on the basis of Ashworth and Blake's research (1996) – further calls into question the idea of omissions liability as exceptional.

This leads us directly to the question of what, if anything, unites the category, 'actus reus'. Even excluding, for the moment, special principles concerning participatory, inchoate and vicarious liability, it seems impossible to say anything more than that 'actus reus' consists of the legally defined elements of the offence which do not consist (exclusively) in the defendant's state of mind. This rather negative definition seems unilluminating, but does it at least have the recommendation of accuracy? Even here, a look beyond simple cases to examples such as conspiracy, where the 'actus reus' involves 'agreement', stretches the credibility of the definition. In the quest for a more substantial conception, exponents of the 'actus reus'/'mens rea' analysis have further attempted to conceptualise 'actus reus' in terms of voluntary human actions. This view coheres with a liberal theory of the limits of criminal law – a theory which is suspicious of coercive state intervention, particularly where that intervention represents any attempt to impose positive duties by means of criminal law.

The conception of 'actus reus' as voluntary action, however, immediately raises difficult questions about the boundaries between 'actus reus', 'mens rea' and defence. For, as we shall see, the concept of voluntariness is also central to one widely accepted theory of 'mens rea' and to the rationale for several defences. To take a practical example which demonstrates this problem, it is generally argued that voluntariness is a requisite feature of 'actus reus' because it is necessary even for offences of 'strict' liability which do not require proof of 'mens rea'. Someone who drives 'carelessly' whilst being attacked by a swarm of bees, or (arguably) who drives without a licence whilst in a hypnotic trance, might well be acquitted on the basis that they had not truly acted: that the event in question could not really be said to be an action of theirs. But this is neither the only nor even the most obvious analysis in all cases. If, for example, a defendant injures someone whilst in a hypnotic trance or whilst sleepwalking, we could rationalise their being excused in three ways. In the first place, we might excuse them on the basis that it was not truly their voluntary action. Secondly, we could argue that they did not have the requisite mental element of intent or recklessness as to the injury. Thirdly, we could argue for their acquittal in terms of a superimposed defence of 'automatism', where the defendant behaves without her mind being truly engaged in her actions (see below). We may be inclined to treat the trance cases as ones of automatism, and cases of sheer physical compulsion, such as reflex actions when being attacked by bees, or being physically pushed, as ones of lack of 'actus reus'. Or we might argue that the defence of automatism *amounts to* a denial of 'actus reus', conceptualising the harm as an 'event' rather than an 'action'. Nothing within the theory of 'actus reus' as presented by criminal law doctrine inclines us one way or another in determining any of these questions.

The apparently unitary category of 'actus reus', then, is difficult to rationalise in a way which is consistent with the diversity of actual criminal laws. In terms of standard doctrine, however, the core concept of 'actus reus' consists in positive, voluntary human action or omission to fulfil a positive duty, according to the definition of an offence, as extended by the principles of inchoate, participatory and vicarious liability, and excluding the elements of the offence which are solely concerned with the defendant's mental state. We shall return to the problematic borderlines between 'actus reus' and 'mens rea' and between 'actus reus' and justification below.

II.b. 'Mens rea'

Andrew Ashworth, *Principles of Criminal Law* (4th edn, Oxford University Press, 2003) pp 160–161

The essence of the principle of *mens rea* is that criminal liability should be imposed only on persons who are sufficiently aware of what they are doing, and of the consequences it might have, that they can fairly be said to have chosen the behaviour and its consequences. This approach is grounded in the principle of autonomy: individuals are regarded as autonomous persons with a general capacity to choose among alternative courses of behaviour, and respect for their autonomy means holding them liable only on the basis of their choices. The principle of *mens rea* may also be claimed to enhance the constitutional values of legality and rule of law, by reassuring citizens that they will only be liable to conviction and to the exercise of state coercion against them if they knowingly cause a prohibited harm.

The category 'mens rea' plays a perhaps yet more crucial part in traditional doctrine than does that of 'actus reus'. This is for the simple reason that the legitimacy of modern criminal law is fundamentally premised on the notion of individual responsibility. As the passage from Ashworth shows, it is relatively easy to produce a formal definition of 'mens rea', as 'the requirements stipulated in the definition of an offence as to the defendant's mental state with respect to the elements of the "actus reus"'. However, the attempt to get beyond this formal approach towards an account of what really unifies 'mens rea', whether in terms of autonomy or other conceptions of responsibility, is, as we shall see, rather more problematic than Ashworth implies. Moreover, the formal approach itself is open to criticism, given that it is sometimes unclear in criminal law doctrine whether matters pertaining to the defendant's mental attitude – a mistaken belief which is relevant to the existence of the 'actus reus', for example – should be regarded as a defence rather than as a lack of 'mens rea'. More substantially, as we shall argue below, this approach is subject to criticism on the basis that it presupposes an unrealistically dualistic approach to human behaviour, dividing physical and mental elements which cannot meaningfully be separated.

In the criminal law of England and Wales, there is held to be a presumption (one which flows directly from the liberal concern with individual freedom) that some element of 'mens rea' will be required for conviction of any offence, unless it is excluded by clear statutory wording. This common law 'principle' finds expression in many leading cases and forms a centrepiece of the Law Commission's Draft Criminal Code (Law Commission 1989: Clause 20). Exceptions are supposedly recognised by the courts only in the case of 'regulatory' offences – offences of relatively low gravity with no real stigma attaching to conviction and only moderate penalties. They usually concern areas of conduct – selling food or running a manufacturing process, for example – which are voluntarily entered into and which entail discrete risks; where the costs of obtaining proof of 'mens rea' are prohibitive or out of proportion to the moral risk of unjustly convicting an innocent defendant; and/or where the imposition of strict liability promises to afford a substantial gain in terms of deterrence and public protection. Instances of strict liability are thus marginalised as exceptional, relatively non-serious and calling for special justification.

No wonder, then, that the serious cases of strict liability which cannot be explained away have occupied a large amount of doctrinal attention. The case which has drawn most attention in this respect, that of *Prince* (1875), concerned the 'abduction' of a girl of under 16 from the possession of her father. The court construed the offence as one of (partial) strict liability in respect of the element of the girl's age, and convicted Prince in spite of his belief that the 'victim' was 16. The judges conceded, however, that had he mistakenly believed the girl not to be in her father's possession, this mistake would have precluded liability: in this respect, they construed the offence as requiring proof of 'mens rea'. This interpretation expresses the judges' view of the offence as concerned with paternal rights rather than with young women's autonomy, and reinforces the view already implicit in the existence of the offence that, in the context of sexual relations, it is men who are responsible subjects, whilst women are passive objects of criminal law's protection. Furthermore, *Prince* demonstrates that the assumption that offences are *either* of strict liability *or* requiring proof of 'mens rea' is misleading: given the fact that the 'actus reus' of most offences consists in a number of elements in relation to which 'mens rea' may or may not have to be proven, we have not so much a dichotomy between two kinds of offences (strict/'mens rea') but rather a spectrum between offences with more or less demanding 'mens rea' requirements.

A very strong version of the principle of subjective 'mens rea', and along with it an unambiguous rejection of the decision in *Prince*, has recently been reaffirmed in the House of Lords, in a case which illustrates the practical significance of the 'mens rea' requirement. *B v DPP* (2000) concerned a 15-year-old boy who had repeatedly asked a 13-year-old girl for oral sex: he was charged with inciting a child under 14 to commit an act of gross indecency. The question was whether his mistaken belief that the child was 14 meant that he should be acquitted: in other words, was a fault element of knowledge or belief about the girl being under 14 a requirement of the offence? The statute included no explicit 'mens rea' word such as 'knowledge' or 'belief', and on the basis of earlier authorities the Trial Judge ruled that the boy's mistake did not remove liability. On appeal, the Divisional Court confirmed the Trial Judge's decision. The House of Lords however overruled the Divisional Court, saying that because of the seriousness of the offence and its broad scope (in particular the fact that it could cover consensual behaviour), the courts should not find that the presumptive 'mens rea' requirement had been displaced. The statute included no express rebuttal of the presumption, and there was no rebuttal by necessary implication; nor would strict liability in relation to age further the purposes of the statute. The Law Lords argued that any implication of a reversal of the presumption must be 'compellingly clear', and drew on other recent cases to assert that the law was moving generally towards a 'subjectivist' approach which judged defendants on the basis of the facts as they believed them to be rather than on the basis of what a reasonable person would have believed in the circumstances. An honest belief that the girl was 14 would therefore suffice to remove 'mens rea', whether or not there were reasonable grounds for the belief.

The House of Lords in *B v DPP* supported the assumption that the presumption in favour of a 'mens rea' requirement can only be displaced by clear statutory words or by necessary implication, in offences pertaining to social health and public safety. The displacement would be most likely where the gains in protection or deterrence from strict liability are likely to be significant; where the offender is one of a class to whom legislation is directed and who engage in the relevant activity voluntarily and for profit; where penalties are low, and where stigma attached to conviction is low (see also *R v K*, 2001: Horder 2002). This followed up Lord Scarman's earlier statement in *Gammon v AG of Hong Kong* (1984):

> the law relevant to this appeal may be stated in the following proposition: 1) there is a presumption in law that mens rea is required before a person can be held guilty of a criminal offence; 2) the presumption is particularly strong where the offence is "truly criminal" in character; 3) the presumption applies to statutory offences, and can be displaced only if this is clearly or by necessary implication the effect of the statute; 4) the only situation in which the presumption can be displaced is where the statute is concerned with an issue of social concern; public safety is such an issue; 5) even where a statute is concerned with such an issue, the presumption of mens rea stands unless it can also be shown that the creation of strict liability will be effective to promote the objects of the statute by encouraging greater vigilance to prevent the commission of the prohibited act.

Yet, despite the resounding affirmation of the subjective 'mens rea principle' in *B v DPP*, the decision will be reversed by the Sexual Offences Act 2003 (see **Chapter 5.III.a.i.**). Moreover, since the courts have held that the right to a fair trial under Article 6 of the ECHR constitutes procedural and not substantive law, the chance of any Human Rights Act challenge to the imposition of strict liability or 'objective' 'mens rea' (see below) appears to have been ruled out (*R v G and R*, 2002).

What, then, does the presumption of a requirement of 'mens rea' amount to? A more technical way of approaching this question is to give an analytical account of the various *forms* of 'mens rea' requirement to be found in statutory offence definitions and case law. Firstly, there may be a requirement of *intention*. The clearest case of intention is 'direct' or purposive intention: a decision to bring certain consequences or states of affairs about in so far as it lies within one's powers to do so and with the aim of so doing. However, criminal law also recognises 'oblique' intention, allowing the jury to make a finding of intention when the defendant has done an act in the knowledge that a particular result will or is virtually certain to occur (*Moloney*, 1985; *R v Woollin*, 1998; see Norrie 2001: Ch3). As we shall see, criminal law doctrine purports to draw a sharp distinction between intention and motive, and holds the latter to be generally irrelevant to the attribution of criminal liability.

Secondly, there may be a requirement of *recklessness*. Recklessness divides into two subcategories: those which are 'subjective' in the sense that they judge the defendant on the basis of what she herself thought, foresaw or knew; and those which are 'objective' in the sense that they judge the defendant against the standard of what a reasonable person would have thought, foreseen or known. So a recklessness requirement may be in the '*subjective*' sense of foreseeing a risk which it is unjustifiable to take and going ahead regardless (*Cunningham*, 1957). Alternatively, recklessness may be understood as embracing not only subjective, conscious risk-taking but also 'objective' recklessness: failing to give thought to a risk in circumstances in which that (unjustifiable) risk would have been obvious, either to the defendant ('*partially subjective recklessness*') or to the 'reasonable' person ('*objective recklessness*': *Caldwell*, 1981). In some cases, the recklessness requirement has been expressed in terms of the idea of 'wilful blindness' or practical indifference: concepts which, as we shall see, blur the boundary between 'subjective' and 'objective' forms of 'mens rea' (*R v Satnam*, 1984).

Thirdly, there may be a requirement of *gross negligence* or of *negligence*, in the sense of a more or less serious deviation from a 'reasonable' standard of care or behaviour (*Andrews v DPP*, 1937). Recklessness in the second sense may also constitute negligence, but not all instances of negligence will count as instances of recklessness, as they may involve not failures to perceive risk but rather negligently mis-assessed risks which have been perceived (*Chief Constable of Avon v Shimmen*, 1986).

In addition to these forms of 'mens rea' related to consequences, *knowledge of or belief in circumstances* are forms of 'mens rea' central to conduct crimes such as rape (*DPP v Morgan*, 1976) and are often requirements in crimes which combine result and non-result aspects, such as causing criminal damage with intent to endanger life or being reckless as to life being endangered under s 1(2) of the Criminal Damage Act 1971.

The fine distinctions between result-oriented forms of 'mens rea' are best illustrated by an example. Imagine that Zoe roller-blades down a crowded slope, creating an obvious and serious risk of injury to other people. If she does so meaning to hurt someone she has a 'direct' intention, and if the slope is so crowded that she realises injury is inevitable, although her aim may be simple enjoyment and she would like to avoid the injury, she has an 'oblique' intent. If she is aware of a risk of injury (ie something less than a virtual certainty), she is 'subjectively' reckless. If she gives no thought to the possibility of the risk, and it would have been obvious to her had she done so, she is 'partially subjectively' reckless and quite possibly 'subjectively' reckless on the 'practical indifference' view of that test (see below); whereas if it would not have been obvious to her but would have been so to a 'reasonable person' she is 'objectively reckless', and also negligent if her behaviour constitutes a serious departure from 'reasonable' standards of conduct. If, finally, she considers the possibility, but, because she has an 'unreasonable' faith in her roller-blading skills, decides that there is no risk, she is negligent, but she is not reckless in any of the relevant senses.

It is worth noting that the precise way in which the 'mens rea' requirement relates to the defendant's conduct is generally left open in offence definitions. For example, it seems sensible to assume that the 'mens rea' requirement for the common-law offence of murder is 'intention to kill or cause grievous bodily harm to a person' rather than 'intention to kill or cause grievous bodily harm to a specific person'. Yet this assumption is put into doubt by the existence of a convention known as the doctrine of 'transferred malice' (*Latimer*, 1886; *Pembliton*, 1874). According to this doctrine, a particular kind of 'mens rea' vis-à-vis one object can be 'transferred' where conduct in fact has its impact on another object of the same kind. Thus a blow aimed at Amy which hits Bob will attract liability, whilst it will not necessarily attract liability if it lands on a piece of property rather than a person. If 'mens rea' requirements are not tied to specific objects, why is the doctrine of transferred malice necessary? The example also illustrates the leeway we have already noted in terms of how we describe a person's actions and attitudes: nothing in logic tells us whether Clare, who aims a gun at Denis, should be said to 'intend to kill Denis', or to 'intend to kill a person'. Interesting questions about both the doctrine of transferred malice and criminal law's conception of the objects to which it can be applied are raised by the *Attorney-General's Reference (No 3 of 1994)* (1997). In this case, a man had stabbed a woman whom he knew to be carrying his child: as a result of the attack, the child was born prematurely and died three months later. The House of Lords declined to apply the doctrine of transferred malice so as to hold the defendant liable for the child's murder, on the basis that it would be straining the doctrine to transfer the defendant's malice first from the mother to the foetus and then from the foetus to the child. This decision appears to have been driven by an understandable concern to limit the ambit of criminal liability; but it is not clear that the court's reasoning was compelled by the logic of the doctrine itself.

The openness of both actions and offence definitions to alternative descriptions allows legal doctrine to represent what are in fact contradictory positions as coherent and logical. For example, doctrinal insistence on the irrelevance of motive can be at once maintained and bypassed by conceptualising motive as an aspect of intent where this is thought by judges or commentators to achieve the 'right' result (*Court*, 1987). Two contrasting cases serve to illustrate this fundamental indeterminacy. *Steane* (1947), a British citizen, issued propaganda broadcasts for the German Government during the Second World War. He was charged with doing acts intended to assist the enemy in wartime, but the court described him as having acted not with intent to assist the German Government but rather with intent to save his family. On this basis he was acquitted. Arrowsmith (*Arrowsmith v Jenkins*, 1963), who was speaking in a public place on nuclear disarmament, was charged with 'wilful' obstruction of the highway. She was convicted on the basis that she intentionally did acts which in fact caused an obstruction, notwithstanding her 'intention' (acknowledged by the court) to try to help to keep the crowd to which she was speaking from causing an obstruction. Such manipulations are common in cases specifying the precise ambit of 'mens rea' requirements. Neither any principle of logic nor any argument internal to legal doctrine can explain why these offences were interpreted as they were, or why Arrowsmith's obstruction was constructed as (legally) wilful whereas Steane's assistance was constructed as (legally) unintentional. In each of the cases, the defendant's attitudes could have been conceptualised equally well as 'motives' or as 'intentions', just as the offence requirements could have been interpreted otherwise than they were. Hence, even where defences like duress, necessity or self-defence, which explicitly bring issues of motive into the trial, the courts have ample opportunity to take account of the motives of those with whom they sympathise at the same time as they pronounce motive legally irrelevant. As Norrie notes in the following passage, the alleged irrelevance of motive in criminal law contrasts with its central importance at the sentencing stage.

Alan Norrie, *Crime, Reason and History* (2001) 226

With the notable exception of Hall (1960), criminal lawyers have accepted the centrality of the division between intention and motive as a datum of the legal enterprise. While intention is central, motive occupies a peripheral role, scratching an existence at the edges of doctrine. Yet motive remains central to human agency and to broader moral and political claims about the nature of fault. The reason why this 'much more advanced level of ethical criticism' (Hall 1960: 83) is ignored is that motive introduces the questions of social need and right that would directly challenge the allocation of fault. The focus on intention excludes the motive of those living at the margins of society and those whose political values the existing order wishes to marginalise.

Yet motive does not go away because the law's psychological individualism tells it to, and it persists as a problem within legal doctrine. While generally excluded from the conviction process, it is admitted at the politically more 'safe' stage of sentencing, where its effects are controlled by the application of judicial discretion. It is true that admission of individual particularity at this latter stage threatens to undermine equality of treatment under the ideology of the rule of law. But the administration of such equality through formal legal categories at the conviction stage is so morally inadequate that it can only survive on the basis that individuality is allowed in through the back door of mitigation.

Furthermore, motive remains as a constant challenge to doctrine in 'dramatic' situations such as those associated with duress and necessity, and in circumstances in which the formal categories have not been tightly enough drawn to exclude disruption of the law. In relation to the former situations, the strategy is to establish certain exceptional excuses which operate above and beyond the 'normal requirements' of 'mens rea'. These permit a measure of 'special' justice, while legitimating its denial in the majority of cases ... In relation to the latter, the law can either use the distinction between motive and intention to fend off 'political' challenges to an 'apolitical' system, or seem to find some abstract formulation to neutralise the direct moral-political challenge of the disruptive or trouble-some citizen.

   These cases reveal a central element of legal practice, although one that is normally presented as peripheral. It is the political use of a depoliticised or demoralised individualism to exclude moral and political challenges to the order of things.

As in the case of intention and motive, technical arguments about forms of 'mens rea' sometimes obscure important questions. One such set of questions has to do with the assumptions and attitudes which inform the conduct of legal trials. Even in the tiny proportion of jury trials, judges, as we shall see, have considerable influence over the determination of guilt or innocence through the framing of their direction to the jury. It is therefore largely judges and mag-istrates, and hence predominantly privileged, white, middle-aged, middle-class (and in the case of judges, male) 'persons', whose judgment is decisive. Where 'subjective' tests are used, the socially skewed nature of the legal forum is important because it is likely to result in different levels of credibility for differ-ent defendants' stories and in differential inferences about what the defendant's attitude or state of mind was. Where 'reasonableness' tests are in play, doctrine veers between the application of an entirely 'objective' standard which fails to investigate who is the 'reasonable person' (Allen 1988), and modified 'objective' tests in which certain aspects of the defendant's particular characteristics are indeed taken into account (see *R v Morgan Smith*, 2000 and **Chapter 6.IV.d.ii.**). The operation of 'objective' tests in fact results in highly discre-tionary regulation. The tribunal here is effectively constructing the standard against which the defendant is judged: the legal process goes on to legitimise that standard as 'objective' and neutral.

At its most extreme, traditional doctrine represents the criminal lawyer's enter-prise as a search for a coherent conceptual scheme of neatly analytically defined instances of 'mens rea' which, if only legislatures and judges would recognise and stick to them, would clear up all ambiguities and uncertainties in criminal law and make for near-perfect clarity and predictability. But this emphasis on formal virtues – an emphasis which is firmly entrenched in the Law Commission's codification project – disguises the real basis for the hold of the 'mens rea' principle, which has to do with a (stated or unstated) normative view about the function of 'mens rea' in *justifying* the imposition of criminal liability.

This normative issue is captured by reference to 'mens rea' as 'the responsibility requirement' or, as in Ashworth's case, as based on 'the autonomy principle', and it is to this normative aspect that we now turn.

The normative function of 'mens rea' in traditional doctrine is, put simply, to ensure that responsibility for the 'actus reus' can fairly be laid at the door of the defendant – or in Fletcher's terms (Fletcher 1978) – that the act is attributable to the defendant. The 'mens rea principle' has been defended vigorously by those who take a moral-retributive approach to criminal justice. They see it primarily in terms of the expression of moral condemnation and judgments of individual blameworthiness, and they tend to discuss 'mens rea' in terms of fault, culpability and blameworthiness. 'Mens rea' has also been upheld by those who take a utilitarian or instrumentalist view of the system. They see proof of 'mens rea' as important to the deterrability of potential offenders and hence to the preventability of crime: someone who does not realise what they are doing cannot be deterred by the threat of punishment. It is also important to those who take the view that criminal justice can only be understood in terms of a combination of backward-looking and instrumentalist elements. Whichever view is taken, it cannot be doubted that 'mens rea' in liberal doctrine is the linchpin of the asserted legitimacy of coercive state intervention towards individuals in response to 'criminal' acts.

One of the most persuasive exponents of this argument for legitimacy is H L A Hart (Hart 1968). On his view, it is justifiable to hold persons accountable only for actions which they could have avoided, in the sense that they knew and understood what they were doing (including relevant circumstances and conditions) and had the capacity to control their actions. They must, in other words, have had a fair opportunity to do otherwise than they did. This notion of 'capacity-responsibility', with its cognitive (relating to understanding) and volitional (relating to self-control) aspects, is argued by Hart to underlie the 'mens rea' requirement by representing the only fair terms on which the ends of the penal system may be pursued. By responding only to genuinely voluntary human action, criminal law allows individuals the greatest possible freedom to plan their lives so as to avoid punishment. Hart's account crystallises the liberal conception of a world of free individuals whose interests are potentially in opposition to, and must be respected by, the collectivity in the form of the state. One important feature of this account is that it effects a reconciliation of the two aspects of criminal law: on the one hand, it resonates with the instrumental approach, in that it regards the overall justifying aim of the system as the reduction of criminal harms; on the other, it speaks to the quasi-moral aspect, in that it sets out stringent conditions – fair terms – on the basis of which the state's regulatory ambitions can be pursued. But, as we shall see, it gives little guidance in terms of when the value of fairness should be sacrificed for the instrumental gains to be had by imposing strict liability or fully 'objective' forms of 'mens rea' such as negligence: while, on Hart's view, it may well be fair to punish the objectively reckless or negligent person for their failure to reach a reasonable standard of care or conduct, his argument cannot justify the fully objective approach often taken in English law, which penalises the defendant irrespective of whether she was in fact *capable* of reaching this standard. A striking example would be *Eliot* (1983), who was held to be liable for criminal damage to a shed to which she set fire in spite of evidence tending to suggest that she did not have the capacity to appreciate the risk which she was running.

It is also interesting to note that Hart's analysis, in rationalising the imposition of liability for negligence, attenuates the link emphasised by doctrine between responsibility and act. If the defendant is really responsible for the failure, for example, to meet a reasonable standard of care, is not the outcome of that failure fortuitous? For instance, if a driver sets out on a journey in an absent-minded, indifferent and inattentive state, whether she has an accident or not, or is seen to be driving negligently, may well depend on chance factors such as how much traffic she encounters: the resultant 'criminal act' depends rather on such external factors than on any direct relationship with her degree of responsibility. Pursued a little further, this argument also calls into question the doctrinal insistence on the responsibility/act equation in cases of 'subjective' 'mens rea'. If, for example, you intend to steal something you desperately want and, unexpectedly, a benefactor gives it to you, you have no need to steal it. Once factors of risk and luck are accorded their place in the world of human actions, the outcome of even intentional and 'subjectively' reckless acts can be seen as, in a significant sense, fortuitous. It is hardly surprising that criminal law doctrine fails to address these issues, for they lead directly to questions about the relevance of social factors in grounding 'responsible' action, and therefore call into question the justifiability both of criminal law's focus on the abstract individual and of its claim to constitute a just and rational system.

The moral conception of 'mens rea' issues in quite naturally (although *not* necessarily) a dualistic approach to 'mens rea' and 'actus reus'. On a dualist view, 'mens rea' is cast in terms of 'subjective' mental states such as intention, foresight, knowledge and belief; these are seen both as separate from the realm of acts and as the basis on which individuals are responsible for those acts (Duff 1987; 1990: Ch 6). Much ink has therefore been spilt trying to accommodate within the dualist account the 'objective' forms of 'mens rea', such as 'objective' recklessness and negligence, which judge the defendant's responsibility in terms of failure to meet an 'objectively' determined standard rather than in terms of subjective mental states. It is difficult, after all, to conceptualise 'failure to meet a standard' as a 'state of mind'. We should notice, however, that the theory of capacity responsibility is not in fact tied to an analysis in terms of aware mental states. Hart argues that negligence liability can be accommodated on the basis that the defendant is held responsible for their failure to do something *which they could have done* (Hart 1968: 136–157). Duff, by contrast, moves beyond a dualist approach in his conceptualisation of 'objective' recklessness and negligence as the practical attitudes such as indifference and inattention. In the case of such attitudes, the offender's agency is substantially engaged: 'wilful blindness' or 'practical indifference' are 'subjective' in the sense that they judge the defendant's own attitude rather than judging her by reference to an 'objective', 'reasonable person' test. But, unlike recklessness in the sense of foresight, practical indifference is not subjective in the sense of being psychological – of representing an aware mental state. (Duff 1983; 1990: Ch 7). Whatever its attractions or drawbacks as a normative theory (Lacey 1988: Ch 2), however, it is not clear that Duff's non-dualist approach provides a persuasive rationalisation of the existing contours of criminal law (Gardner and Jung 1991). The closest English criminal law has come to adopting a 'practical indifference' test is in the offence of rape: see **Chapter 5.II.b.**

In the context of 'mens rea', then, current doctrine appears to suffer from two major shortcomings. Firstly, a combination of dualism and a narrow reading of philosophical accounts of capacity responsibility militates to designate 'subjective' 'mens rea' in the sense of intent, foresight, knowledge and belief as the paradigm forms of 'mens rea'. Negligence and 'objective' recklessness tend to be marginalised as instances of 'mens rea', just as, a fortiori, strict liability offences are marginalised as peripheral instances of crime. Yet, turning doctrine back on its own subject matter, we find that, in terms of numbers of offences, those of strict or objective liability constitute at least half of the more serious offences (those triable in the Crown Court) and the large majority of all offences. And when one takes into account patterns of the enforcement of criminal law, the preponderance of doctrinally 'non-standard' cases increases so as to invest these types of offences with overwhelming practical significance. Conversely, we must avoid making the simplistic assumption that these doctrinal categories reflect actual levels of 'fault' or 'responsibility' in law enforcement. In practice, 'subjective' recklessness can turn out to be a very thin form of 'culpability', just as many of those charged with offences of 'strict' liability are selected for prosecution precisely because some degree of fault has been involved. The 'subjective'/'objective' dichotomy itself, therefore, must be subjected to critical scrutiny (see Wells 1982).

Secondly, criminal law doctrine is unsuccessful in its attempts to construct a unitary category of 'mens rea'. In fact, it hardly gets beyond a very general statement in terms of 'mens rea' having to do with the aspects of the defendant's practical attitudes towards her actions proof of which is required for specific offences. This general statement has the normative implication that it is these requisite attitudes which render it fair to hold the defendant accountable for her actions in criminal law. This, of course, leaves open the possibility that criminal law employs a plurality of different attitudes as bases of attribution, and that the emerging patterns of these approaches as providing significant clues to both moral and instrumental aspects of criminal justice in particular periods. As we shall see in **Chapter 4**, precisely such an analysis has been developed by Fletcher, who argues that the development of criminal law is marked by shifting patterns based on 'manifest criminality', 'subjective liability' and liability for 'harmful consequences' (Fletcher 1978: Chs 1–5; see in particular p 388). These patterns articulate the relationship between 'conduct' and 'fault' elements in radically different ways.

II.c.   The 'actus reus'/'mens rea' combination

Andrew Ashworth, *Principles of Criminal Law* (4th edn, 2003) p 88

> Another implication of the principle of autonomy, and its emphasis on choice and control, is the principle of correspondence. Not only should it be established that the defendant had the required fault ... ; it should also be established that the defendant's intention, knowledge or recklessness related to the proscribed harm.

According to criminal law doctrine, it is the *coincidence* of 'actus reus' and 'mens rea' which constitutes and justifies criminal liability. This requirement has two aspects. Firstly, it implies the temporal coexistence of 'actus reus' and 'mens rea' – an 'actus reus' at one moment and 'mens rea' at another do not standardly combine to form criminal liability. If on Monday I conceive an intention to kill someone but think better of it on Tuesday, and then accidentally run that person over on Wednesday, I am not guilty of murder. Even if I still have the intention, I will not be guilty if the killing is a genuine accident. Secondly, the idea of coincidence between 'actus reus' and 'mens rea' implies that there must be a combination of external and mental elements with respect to each aspect of the offence. These implications of doctrine raise several discrete problems.

Leaving aside for the moment the offences of strict liability which doctrine treats, perversely, as exceptional, let us begin by examining the principle the 'mens rea' requirement should run to and coincide with each element of the 'actus reus'. A consideration of a range of substantive offences reveals that this is in fact the case in only a tiny proportion. In the vast majority, offence definitions fall short of this paradigm in one or both of two respects. In the first type of case, no 'mens rea' may be required as to some element or elements of the 'actus reus'. A good example here would be the offence of 'assaulting a police officer in the execution of his duty' under s 89(1) of the Police Act 1996, in which knowledge of the victim's being an officer so acting is not a requirement for conviction. In the second type of case, 'mens rea' is required as to a lesser result than that identified by the 'actus reus'. A good example here would be the offence of maliciously wounding or inflicting grievous bodily harm on a person under s 20 of the Offences Against the Person Act 1861, in which recklessness is required only as to the risk of *some* bodily harm, not as to *grievous* bodily harm (see *Parmenter*, 1991); or indeed murder, in which intent to cause grievous bodily harm, falling short of an intent to kill, will suffice. These are generally characterised as offences of 'partial "mens rea"'. Yet, as a matter of logic, they could just as well be described as offences of 'partial strict liability'. It is hard to escape the conclusion that their denomination as the former rather than the latter serves to legitimise them as firmly within the framework of the 'general principles'. Once such examples are added to those of total or substantial strict liability (not to mention those of negligence or 'objective' recklessness), the paradigm picture of criminal liability presented by doctrine begins to look insecure – indeed it begins to look marginal. As Ashworth's and Blake's research (1996) shows, a culpable practical attitude merely to some element of the offence usually suffices to ground liability in criminal law: proof of an aware, culpable mental state with respect to each element of the 'actus reus' is only exceptionally required.

Problems also arise from the requirement of a temporal coincidence between 'actus reus' and 'mens rea'. Particular difficulty is caused by cases where no such coincidence exists, but where the 'actus reus' of an offence is either preceded or succeeded by the existence of 'mens rea', perhaps accompanied by some other action or, typically, by an omission. In such cases, the paradigm of temporally fitting mental state to act is difficult to apply, and traditional doctrine has to be manipulated into a position where it can accommodate them. Two examples should suffice to illustrate the remarkable flexibility of criminal law doctrine in this respect. In the first, *R v Miller* (1983), the defendant fell asleep holding a lighted cigarette which then set light to a mattress. Shortly afterwards, he awoke to find the mattress ablaze, whereupon he left the building without taking any steps to put out the fire. In doctrinal terms, the case therefore involved two incidents: an unconscious act followed by a conscious omission. The courts considered two strategies for rationalising the imposition of liability. The first did so in terms of the existence of a situational duty to act arising where a person's unconscious omission has created a danger. The second involved interpreting the sequence of events as constituting one continuous act so as to connect 'actus reus' and 'mens rea'. The House of Lords adopted the former rationale for imposing the liability which was intuitively called for. In a second example, *Meli Thabo v R* (1954), the defendants assaulted their victim, intending to kill him: in fact they failed to do so, but later unwittingly killed him by throwing the supposed corpse off a cliff. In this case, the idea of a connected sequence of events implementing a preconceived plan was employed so as to marry 'actus reus' and 'mens rea' and allow liability.

If, in cases such as these, doctrinal analysis can be manipulated to extend the time frame on which the law focuses, why should that time frame not be extended in other cases, too (Kelman 1981)? Why should legal analysis not concern itself with *how* a defendant came to be in the situation in which she has apparently acted negligently, recklessly or intentionally, asking for example whether a person who committed theft formed the intention to steal because she was starving, or whether the person who was provoked to kill had childhood or other experiences which made her more likely to lose self-control? This might, of course, lead to significant extensions and reductions of liability, according to the circumstances of different cases. As Norrie suggests in the passage on motive quoted above, exactly these kinds of factors *do* in fact enter into legal judgments, as well as into quasi-legal judgments such as the decision to prosecute for a 'strict' liability offence. Doctrine generates no coherent account of which time frame is settled upon in which instances.

Finally, the 'actus reus'/'mens rea' framework builds into criminal law doctrine a deep commitment to philosophical dualism – the idea that a person's thoughts and her actions are separate and separable in our descriptions and analyses. On this view, we first of all describe what the defendant did, in terms of 'colourless acts', and then infer from that what was in the defendant's mind. Yet in practice we do not react to human behaviour in this way, but rather make a global judgment which encompasses act and attitude, rather than separating mental state and behaviour (Duff 1987; 1990: Ch 6). This less dualistic approach is reflected in judicial statements of offence definitions, occasional statutory examples, and the Law Commission (1989: s 18) draft code's practice of citing 'mens rea' adverbially rather than adjectivally – intentionally killing, rather than killing with intent. This emergence in law and doctrine of an alternative approach to grounding attribution casts doubt on the adequacy of the analytical framework of 'mens rea' and 'actus reus' taken as two separate but necessary components for criminal liability. At the level of practice, these arguments question the adequacy of the doctrinal account in which judges look at the act and infer the mental state in a two-stage process. They also underline the fact that legal decisions are inevitably influenced by a context richer than that acknowledged as relevant by technical rules of law. Moreover, we can quite easily cite instances where the 'actus reus'/'mens rea' distinction is extremely hard to apply. For example, in the case of conspiracy, the agreement between conspirators seems to be both 'actus reus' and 'mens rea'. This is just one among many instances of the difficulties inherent in a dualistic approach.

II.d.   Exemption, justification and excuse

George Fletcher (1978) *Rethinking Criminal Law*, p 759

The notions of justification and excuse have … become familiar figures in our structured analysis of criminal liability. Claims of justification concede that the definition of the offense is satisfied, but challenge whether the act is wrongful; claims of excuse concede that the act is wrongful, but seek to avoid the attribution of the act to the actor. A justification speaks to the rightness of the act; an excuse, to whether the actor is accountable for a concededly wrongful act. For all this apparent simplicity, the notions of justification and excuse lend themselves to considerably more refinement.

The definition of criminal liability in terms of the coincidence of 'actus reus' and 'mens rea' needs, as we have seen, to be refined by adding one further condition: absence of any exemption, justification or excuse via one of the 'general defences' (Fletcher 1978: Chs 9, 10; Norrie 2001: Pt IV). Particular illustrations of these defences will be given in the other chapters of this book; for the moment, it is the place of defences in general criminal law doctrine which will occupy our attention.

Within criminal law defences, the doctrinal importance of a distinction between exemptions, excuses and justifications is less than clear. However, we shall employ the distinction in the following analysis, because it serves to point up some of the most interesting and difficult issues which defences raise for the conceptual framework of criminal law doctrine. Exemptions, justifications and excuses may all result in acquittal, although they enter at different levels of the legal argument. The difference lies in the *rationale* of the acquittal. A plea of exemption such as insanity goes to the defendant's capacity to be addressed as a normal subject of criminal law: if a defendant's mental capacity is such that fundamental questions can be raised about her cognitive or, perhaps, volitional capacities, it might be argued that they are not even the kind of subject whom criminal law aspires to address. By contrast, a plea of justification such as self-defence goes to the 'actus reus' in the sense that it renders *the act itself* not wrongful – not within the scope of criminal law's prohibition. Since – the argument goes – we all have a right to defend ourselves, an injury caused in legitimate, genuine and reasonable self-defence does not constitute the sort of behaviour which criminal law seeks to prohibit, prevent or condemn. Excuses, on the other hand, go to 'mens rea' and are personal to the particular defendant. They represent a defect in the defendant's understanding or control, though the action is still one which criminal law seeks to prohibit. In other words, excuses excuse *actors*, whereas justifications justify *acts*. This distinction is reflected in Ashworth's treatment of justifications within the conduct element of offences and excuses as within the fault element (Ashworth 2003: Chs 4, 6 – though he, like most commentators, elides exemptions and excuses).

Prime examples of excuses are mistaken beliefs and duress, which may be held to prevent the attribution of responsibility for an 'actus reus' to the defendant. In all cases it is up to the defendant to produce evidence for the excuse; only in the cases of insanity (and diminished responsibility) – arguably an exemption rather than an excuse, but conventionally treated as an excuse – is the formal legal burden of proof, on a balance of probabilities, on the defendant. In other cases, once this evidential burden is met, it is up to the prosecution to dispel any reasonable doubts which may have been raised as to the defendant's guilt. Supplementary to the doctrines of excuse and justification there exists a category of formal mitigation. This category is exemplified by the law on provocation, diminished responsibility and suicide pacts under the Homicide Act 1957, ss 2, 3 and 4. Each of these, if made out, reduces the defendant's liability from murder to manslaughter, in recognition of some special difficulty which she met in accommodating her behaviour to criminal law standards.

The ideas of excuse and justification, like other features of doctrine, turn out to raise some very tricky questions. If, for example, the justificatory argument of self-defence genuinely removes the action from the ambit of criminal regulation, should it not rather be seen as a feature of a (refined) definition of the offence? Or, if it is (as is the practice) rather 'grafted on' to the 'actus reus', why is this so, and in what sense does it signify a removal from the real scope of criminal prohibition? Similarly in the case of excuses, conceptual neatness is unattainable because the boundary between existence of excuse and lack of 'mens rea' is very difficult to draw. The distinction often turns on how we describe both the definition of offences and the conduct in question, and, as we have seen, each process is open-ended in a way rarely confronted by traditional doctrine. Think again of the facts in *Steane* (1947), who claimed that he made the broadcasts in question because he was subjected to threats to the safety of his family. Nothing *in principle* determines whether a court should analyse these facts in terms of existence of the excuse of duress – preventing the move from action to attribution of responsibility despite the existence of 'mens rea' – or whether it should analyse them in terms of a denial of 'mens rea'. (In fact it was this latter analysis which was adopted, because of legal uncertainty as to whether the duress defence actually applied to the specific offence with which Steane was charged.) It seems unlikely that this kind of indeterminacy can be resolved by meticulous drafting, by codification, or by careful judicial reasoning.

The blurring of the line between 'mens rea' and excuse is problematic for several further reasons. First of all, the standard of liability may be 'objective' or 'subjective' depending on how we classify the issue. A good example here is the law on mistake. At one stage, the courts were inclined to hold that a genuine mistake about the existence of the elements of the offence removed 'mens rea', and hence had to be determined subjectively wherever the 'mens rea' requirement was itself a subjective one. Thus in the crime of rape, a genuine mistake as to the victim's consent entails that the defendant lacks 'mens rea', even if the mistake is based on patently unreasonable grounds. By contrast, where mistake relates not to a 'mens rea' element but rather to issues of defence (such as whether one is being attacked or threatened) courts have sometimes concluded that the mistake had to be not only genuine but also reasonable (*Tolson*, 1889). This objective approach surfaced briefly in *Albert v Lavin* (1982), but was not followed by *R v Williams* (1987) and *Beckford v R* (1987) (see, contra, *People v Goetz*, 1986). The current position appears to be that either defence or 'mens rea' may be objectively or subjectively specified according to the particular area of law in question. It remains to be seen, however, whether this issue has been decisively resolved (for a case which suggests that it has not, see *O'Grady*, 1987).

Secondly, it is impossible to generalise about how far excuse is distinct from lack of 'mens rea'. This is because some excuses, such as insanity, intoxication and mistake, arguably possess the general ability to remove or qualify 'mens rea', whilst others, such as duress, are most easily interpreted as superimposed. The mistaken rape defendant is simply not reckless as to the victim's lack of consent, and the intoxicated killer cannot plead even involuntary intoxication unless it is such as to render her incapable of forming the necessary intent, whereas the defendant who steals under duress nonetheless intends permanently to deprive. This last point is of course subject to the manipulability of the definitions of offences already mentioned. For example, if intent is conceived in terms of purpose, we could say that, by analogy with *Steane*, where a defendant is threatened with death and kills a person as a result, the defendant intended to save herself rather than to kill. But if we define intent less strictly, as encompassing necessary and envisaged means to intended ends, this argument will lead to the conclusion that the defendant intended to kill, because she intended her victim's death as a necessary means to saving herself. On this view, duress must operate as a superadded excuse and not as a removal of 'mens rea'. Because of this difference in the nature of the various excuses, it is difficult to envisage a unitary approach to excuses at anything other than a very high level of generality.

These arguments cannot be dismissed as mere academic technicalities, because the distinction between excuse and lack of 'mens rea' is sometimes of crucial practical importance. This is because particular defendants may be personally excluded from claiming an excuse. For example, voluntary membership of a gang committed to criminal activities of the type the defendant has performed will exclude her from the duress defence even if she has been threatened by a fellow gang member into committing the offence (*R v Sharp*, 1987). Lack of 'mens rea', by contrast, is available in principle to all defendants (though it is occasionally removed for policy reasons, for example where it is due to voluntary intoxication).

Also problematic for doctrinal accounts of excuse and justification is the *absence* from English law of a number of defences which would seem to be required by the principles underpinning the standard analysis. Mistake of law as an excuse and (with some recent concessions: see in particular *Re A*, 2000) necessity of circumstances as a justification constitute good examples of arguments which appear to exculpate on the basis of general doctrinal principles, yet which criminal law has been unwilling or reluctant to allow as defences (see **Chapter 4.II.f.** and **Chapter 6.IV.e.**). Although some pragmatic arguments can be given for their exclusion, these cannot convincingly be accommodated on the basis of the general normative principles to which doctrine boasts allegiance. Where defences do exist, moreover, questions can be raised about how 'general' they really are: do the terms in which they are drawn up typically make it more difficult for some kinds of defendant to make them out (Allen 1987; Nicolson and

Bibbings 2000)? For example, the requirement in the law of both provocation and self-defence that the defendant's reaction follow relatively quickly upon the provoking or threatening acts has been persuasively argued to exclude the physically less powerful – young people and women notable among them – from fair access to these defences.

Finally, we may question the line between excuse and justification itself. For example, duress is generally seen as an excuse. But it might equally be argued that where a person, succumbing to a threat of a far greater evil, commits a relatively minor offence – for example, if a person were to steal something so as to prevent someone else from carrying out a threat to kill – that conduct should fall outside the ambit of criminal law's prohibition. Indeed, just such a possibility seems to be contemplated by Lord Hailsham in *Howe* (1987). Why, conversely, should the issue of necessity generally be considered as a possible matter of justification rather than of personal excuse? And does self-defence really make the act 'right' any more than does duress? Here the line might be drawn on the basis of utilitarian considerations such as the need to discourage threats or attacks on the person: a widely available duress defence might encourage the making of threats whereas a strong right of self-defence may increase the likely costs of, and therefore discourage, assault. But it is far from clear that criminal law is consistently driven by such concerns. The distinction between act-regarding and actor-oriented defences is resonant with the moral basis of criminal law doctrine, but it is hard to apply given that actions are inevitably judged contextually, and that in assessing the 'justifiability' of an action, important parts of the context are the actor's attitude and excusing factors. Thus the neat conceptual frame may be useful as a model, but on close inspection we find that its elements shade into one another in a way that ultimatel defies the analytical clarity to which doctrine aspires.

II.e.   Participatory liability

In addition to the person who actually commits the 'actus reus' of the offence (the perpetrator), certain other categories of person who have been involved in its production may be held liable as 'principals in the second degree' to the crime and punished in the same way as the perpetrator. These parties are sometimes described as 'aiders, abettors, counsellors and procurers' (Accessories and Abettors Act 1961, s 1), and their involvement may consist in actions as diverse as providing equipment, encouragement or information, concealing evidence or giving material assistance in the actual commission of an offence. This kind of secondary liability must be distinguished from another form of extended, but primary, liability: someone who does not physically do the 'actus reus' may be liable as a perpetrator or 'principal in the first degree' if she uses another person as an instrument or 'innocent agent' for committing the crime (*Michael*, 1840). Good examples would be the use of a small child or a person under hypnosis to inflict an injury or administer a poison or to steal something. Difficult problems may arise, however, where the agent can only be described as 'semi-innocent': ie where she has some but not all of the awareness necessary for the 'mens rea' of participation (*Cogan*, 1976).

Participatory liability purports to attribute responsibility which is derivative from and dependent upon the 'actus reus' and 'mens rea' of the perpetrator. As we shall see in the next chapter, judicial interpretation has in fact moved beyond a strictly derivative approach. However, even on a strictly derivative approach, liability for participation does not necessarily depend on the principal's *liability* (she may have an excuse or claim of mitigation which does not cover the secondary party) let alone upon her conviction (she may not be apprehended). Participatory liability complicates the notion of 'actus reus', which must be extended to cover participation. It also diversifies 'mens rea', for the 'mens rea' applicable to participation is not the same as that required for perpetration (*Powell, English*, 1997). It generally consists of states of knowledge, foresight or belief about the actions of the principal: for example, knowledge of how a knife supplied will be used; foresight of a weapon being carried by one's co-assailant being used. Participatory liability thus employs a secondary and supplementary 'actus reus'/'mens rea' framework which is grafted on to the structure of primary liability.

The rationale of participatory liability is expressed by commentators and judges both in terms of the culpability of secondary parties and of the social danger presented by accessories to crime. Difficulties arise from the fact that these two rationales do not entail identical approaches to the imposition of such liability (see further **Chapter 2.IV.**).

II.f. Vicarious liability

In some areas of criminal law, one person may be held criminally liable for the actions of another. This is typically where she has some particular personal or positional responsibility for that other person in the relevant sphere of action, and where the offence in question is one of strict liability. Like strict liability, this form of liability tends to be seen as pertaining to 'less serious offences'. As a qualitative assessment, this is arguably justifiable, but it often mysteriously transposes to a quantitative assessment which is clearly unsound. The rationale of vicarious liability in criminal law is less clear than it is in civil law, where it has been seen as ensuring that there is a solvent defendant (such as an employer) and that those who profit from particular, often risky, enterprises fairly bear the costs of their pursuit. In criminal law the main suggestion put forward has also been a utilitarian one, having to do with the need to motivate those in positions of responsibility properly to supervise their employees or others in their charge. The empirical validity of the assumptions on which such arguments rest, however, is dubious. What is quite clear is that vicarious liability cannot be accommodated in the usual framework of criminal liability without its considerable extension or modification. For that framework is rooted in notions of individual responsibility. Even if we take the line suggested by Fletcher (1978) and see the *relationship* as a distinctive basis for attribution, the example pushes us towards a pluralistic account of the attributive basis of criminal liability both at a descriptive and at a normative level. This area is of particular practical significance since it impinges upon questions of corporate liability for crime which have recently caused serious difficulty for criminal law doctrine (see further **Chapter 6.II.c.**).

II.g.   Inchoate offences

A final extension of the basic framework of liability lies in the existence of inchoate offences of attempt, incitement and conspiracy. Many specific inchoate offences are created by statute, but here our focus is on the general inchoate offences which can be superimposed onto other indictable offences. For example, anyone who incites another to commit theft, who attempts to steal, or who conspires with at least one other person to commit a theft, may be convicted of the relevant inchoate offence and sentenced in the same way as someone convicted of theft itself. Unlike participatory liability, inchoate liability is not derivative but primary: it does not depend on the perpetration of the 'actus reus' of the substantive offence. In other words, inchoate offences could be analysed as discrete instances of offences with their own definitions of 'actus reus' and 'mens rea' which relate to and constitute an extension of the definitions of some other (indictable) offence. The 'mens rea' requirements for inchoate offences in law are more stringent (generally requiring 'specific intent' – intention as to consequences and knowledge of circumstances) than for the completed offence. This might be seen as an interesting, if somewhat mysterious, genre of compensation for the incompleteness of the 'actus reus'.

Several different rationales can be found for inchoate offences: the danger of completed offences posed by inchoate ones; police convenience in being able to arrest well before the completion of the offence; culpability of the defendant (especially where lack of completion is due to external, fortuitous factors). Each of these rationales implies somewhat different contours for inchoate liability. Furthermore, the lines between no liability, inchoate liability and full liability are notoriously hard to draw. For example, the definition of the 'actus reus' of attempt is that of acts 'more than merely preparatory to the commission of the offence' (Criminal Attempts Act 1981, s 1(1)). This is a point which can hardly be said to be self-defining. Does someone planning a burglary do acts 'more than merely preparatory' when she recruits accomplices, or hires the getaway car, or drives to the scene, or starts to effect entry? Criminal law simply leaves the decision to the finder of fact. These problems of indeterminacy are exacerbated where mistakes are involved: does someone who thinks they are importing heroin but who is actually importing cabbage leaves commit the offence of attempting to import a prohibited drug (*Shivpuri*, 1987)? This is just one of many possible kinds of mistake which may affect attempt and other forms of inchoate liability. Furthermore, especially in the case of conspiracy, there is an obvious overlap with participatory liability: someone who agrees to assist in a burglary has both conspired to burgle and, if the burglary takes place, acted as a principal in the second degree. This is important because it is legally possible to withdraw at a certain stage from participation in crime, thus escaping liability, whereas no such possibility exists for inchoate offences. For example, someone who has been substantially involved in planning a robbery but who has a change of heart and alerts the police to the plan before the robbery takes place will probably escape participatory liability yet be technically liable for conspiracy. The diverse forms of behaviour covered by the categories of incitement, attempt and conspiracy bring us yet further from the original, simple 'actus reus'/'mens rea' model (see further **Chapter 3.IV.** and **Chapter 4.II.c.**).

II.h.   Conclusion

The purpose of this discussion has been to describe some of the main features of criminal law doctrine, with a view to questioning some of its assumptions (an external critique) and to demonstrating its inadequacy in its own terms (an internal critique). Our internal critique has thrown up a number of ambiguities, indeterminacies and distortions in the picture presented by doctrine, especially when considered in the light of some empirical features of criminal law. The constant refinement and reshaping of the conceptual apparatus of criminal law, an important enterprise for legal doctrine, struggles to produce the rule of law ideals of certainty, coherence and clarity to which it aspires. Our analysis suggests that this situation would remain fundamentally unchanged even by a thorough codification of criminal law: for its basis lies, as Norrie noted in the passage quoted early in this section, in historical forces external to the law itself.

FURTHER READING

Dennis, Ian (1997) 'The Critical Condition of Criminal Law' *Current Legal Problems.*

Duff, Antony (1987) 'Codifying Criminal Fault', in Dennis (ed) *Criminal Law and Justice* (Sweet & Maxwell) p 93.

Gardner, John (1998) 'The Gist of Excuses' 2 Buffalo Crim LR 575.

Horder, Jeremy (1997) 'Two Histories and Four Hidden Principles of Mens Rea' 113 LQR 95.

— (2002) 'Strict Liability, Statutory Construction and the Spirit of Liberty' 118 LQR 458.

Horder, Jeremy and Mitchell, Barry (1999) 'On the Correspondence Principle' Crim LR 894.

Kelman, Mark (1981) 'Interpretive Construction in the Substantive Criminal Law' 33 Stanford Law Review, p 591.

Lacey, Nicola (1998) 'Coherence, Contingency and Conceptualism' in Antony Duff (ed) *Philosophy and the Criminal Law* (Cambridge University Press).

— (2001) 'In Search of the Responsible Subject' 64 Modern Law Review 350.

Robinson, Paul H (1997) *Structure and Function in Criminal Law* (Clarendon Press) Pts II & III.

Wells, Celia (1982) 'Swatting the Subjectivist Bug' Crim LR 209.

— (1986) 'Codification of the Criminal Law: Restatement or Reform?' Crim LR 3.

III.   Criminal laws in their social and procedural context

In this section, we explore the relationship between criminal law and the social and procedural context in which it is invoked, interpreted and enforced. We have already noted the existence of a wide array of social methods of defining and dealing with 'deviance', 'anti-social behaviour' or 'wrongdoing'. These include the total set of practices, norms and institutions which seek to shape our attitudes, producing a variety of social norms and directing our internalisation of those norms. We can therefore identify a large number of educative, preventive, coercive and reactive practices which have a relevance to and are in some respects analogous with the formal techniques of criminal law.

We begin by examining some of these broad normative systems, before focussing more specifically on the formal institutions of the criminal process within which patterns of criminalisation are shaped.

III.a.   Social norms and criminal law

Among the most important institutions in the construction and enforcement of social norms is the *education system*. In Britain, despite the existence of a substantial number of private schools and colleges, the education of children, particularly those under 16, is seen as a matter of public responsibility. This is reflected in the fact that such education is compulsory, and in the increasing extent to which the content of school education is specified and monitored by the state (Whitty and Menter 1989). The process of compulsory education involves both explicit and implicit inculcation of cultural values such as honesty, endeavour, respect for others, citizenship, cooperation and (of course) competition – although the extent to which this is so will vary from school to school. The education system constitutes a central strategy in society's practice of socialising its members and producing citizens who have internalised many of the norms embedded in criminal law. At school, children encounter an institutionalised regulatory system, in the form of school rules backed by penalties on breach, and are encouraged to have a docile attitude to this kind of disciplinary technique. From our earliest education, we begin to become accustomed to routine and surveillance which prepare us for submission to legal coercion for the rest of our lives.

Preceding, coexisting with and succeeding our experience of formal education is another fundamental social institution, the *family*. Widely regarded as a sacred 'private' sphere free from coercive state intervention, the family is in fact hedged around with legal regulation, and breaches of the standard norms and conventions of family life render family members subject to state intervention of various kinds, by children being taken into care, welfare benefits being cut, social workers' visits being imposed (Smart 1984). Notwithstanding the diversity of family forms, and the statistical 'abnormality' of the 'normal' two-biological-parent family unit, the hold of the normative stereotype remains firm, and this stereotype informs welfare and other decisions about intervention in a range of aspects of 'private life' (O'Donovan 1993; Collier 1994, 1998). Where the family is not operating as an appropriate socialiser of citizens (both through the upbringing of children and in terms of keeping adults in conventional social and gender roles), the state is not so reluctant to step in as liberal ideology would suggest. What is more, both through the development of affective ties, and through more explicitly disciplinary techniques such as parental discipline, the family itself acts as a regulatory mechanism. It also constitutes a site for the operation of other disciplinary mechanisms such as psychiatry and social work (Donzelot 1980). The direct relevance of family situation to criminal enforcement is demonstrated by reliance on information about background (and indeed school reports) in sentencing young offenders, and by feminist research which suggests that failure to occupy a conventional family role (being a single woman, a 'working' single mother, lesbian) invites a peculiarly punitive response in the criminal process (Eaton 1986; Edwards 1984; Jackson 1997). So the legal order presupposes an important control function in the family, formal and informal institutions combining to create a web of socialisation, surveillance and punishment.

Another important social factor in constructing, discouraging and responding to 'deviance' is the *welfare system*; the state system of support for those in need and those filling important social roles such as caring for children. In setting out conditions for assignment of benefits, the social welfare system in effect lays down a model of 'the right way to live'. Those who deviate from this – for example, those who have no fixed address, or who refuse to or are unable to come to a benefit office regularly and punctually, or who refuse to take up work or training – cannot claim or have difficulty in claiming benefit.

The welfare system is, of course, just one among many aspects of the *bureaucratic power* of governmental, quasi-governmental and private organisations which, through the work of officials in a wide variety of public or quasi-public bodies (factory inspectorates, the Inland Revenue, companies, local government), exerts significant influence over definitions and responses to deviance, in ways which often blur the line between criminal and non-criminal social control (Cohen 1985).

Relevant institutions also include *civil law*, which provides damages and other remedies in tort and contract and statutory claims and actions in public law for certain categories of losses and harms. The honesty, reasonableness and fair procedures of public bodies, the non-negligent, responsible behaviour of citizens, the honest and reliable dealings of contracting parties and a long list of other matters are defined and may be enforced by non-criminal norms of the legal system, and in many cases the same 'deviant' behaviour may elicit both a criminal and a civil legal response. The line between civil and criminal legal responses is, as we have seen, has varied over the course of history, and the persisting continuities in form and function between the two should not escape us. For example, civil legal regulation is ultimately underpinned by the possibility of coercive enforcement *via* penalties for contempt of court. Furthermore, civil law, like criminal law, plays some part in setting down acceptable standards of behaviour and mutual responsibilities among citizens, even if only indirectly.

Another influential source of social norms is the practice of *religion*. Many different religions are practised in England and Wales, though Christian doctrine is legally privileged in various ways. The Church of England is the established church of the state; under s 7 of the Education Reform Act 1988, collective worship in county schools must be 'wholly or mainly of a broadly Christian character'. By a last-minute political compromise, the Act was amended to allow for separate religious assemblies for non-Christian children. However, criminal laws of blasphemy apply only to Christian religions – an increasingly anomalous position in this multicultural society. The debate of 1989 about Salman Rushdie's *The Satanic Verses* – a novel regarded as blasphemous by Muslims, some groups of whom called for the book to be banned – illustrates the way in which religion can serve as the framework in which broader social questions and divisions (such as those of racism, poverty and cultural intolerance) are fought out. Yet, in spite of current fears about religious intolerance in the wake of 11 September 2001, incitement to religious – as opposed to racial – hatred is still not proscribed by criminal law. (The Anti-Terrorism, Crime and Security Act 2001 did however add religious aggravation to the existing category of racially aggravated crime: see Mazher Idriss 2002.) In many ways – through state education, in the family, through personal faith and membership of faith communities, through media coverage of the pronouncements of leading religious figures, and in terms of political symbolism (religious services on state occasions, the monarch's position as head of the Church of England) – certain key religious values are propagated, indoctrinated and more or less formally enforced. Religious practice therefore functions as a social mechanism for defining normal and acceptable behaviour and responding to deviation from it.

More intangibly, but no less importantly, we have the existence of a cluster of *conventional moralities* and prevailing *cultural assumptions.* These encompass norms concerning the proper conduct of family life, honesty, self-restraint, forbearance from violence, enterprise, effort and so on. As with religion, consensus in a society such as ours is limited by the existence of a plurality of cultures, as well as by the competing interests of groups at different positions in the structure of power relations. In many areas, however, the existence of consensus among a powerful group serves to 'legitimate' particular norms and impose them more generally; some conventional moralities, in other words, become more powerful than others. The status of this plurality of conventional moralities as means of social control and their relationship with the substance of criminal laws can hardly be doubted.

One particularly important set of cultural assumptions are those surrounding *sex and gender*, through which male and female, masculine and feminine identities are constructed in strikingly different terms. It is hard to escape the conclusion that a system in which sexual difference is so marked is directly implicated in producing one of the most striking facts about recorded crime: that over 80% of it is committed by men (Smart 1976: 1–26; Nicolson 2000; Home Office 2001b).

Ngaire Naffine, *Feminism and Criminology* (Polity Press, 1997) pp 6–7

The most consistent and prominent fact about crime is the sex of the offender. As a rule, crime is something men do, not women, so the denial of the gender question ... seems particularly perverse. Sexual difference runs right through the crime statistics – from large-scale corporate fraud to petty property crime; from major to minor crimes against the person. Crime is also something that men are expected to do, because they are men, and women are expected not to do, because we are women. Crime, men and masculinity have an intimate relationship, so intimate that we often fail to see it, and so intimate that it can seem natural. Though the vast majority of men do not enter the official criminal statistics, those individuals who do become known as criminals are usually men. ... The maleness of crime is true of the United States of America, of Britain, of Australia and indeed of all Western countries. Men are the vast majority of violent and non-violent offenders. They are virtually all of the rapists, they are responsible for the majority of other forms of assault, and they are most of the burglars. They even predominate in that area of crime which is sometimes thought to be the preserve of women: larceny. In view of this remarkable sex bias in crime, it is surprising that gender has not become *the* central preoccupation of the criminologist, rather than an after-thought ... Criminology has been developed and presented as a study of men (by men) and their relation to crime, but it is a study that is uninterested in men (as men) and that fails to recognise the consequent specificity, limitations and underlying assumptions of the discipline.

One possible explanation for the startling sex ratio of criminality is that systems of informal social control (by husbands, fathers, teachers, priests and so on) are such that women are generally too well-disciplined to breach criminal–legal norms, whereas men, who enjoy greater autonomy and power, are not so effectively informally controlled (Heidensohn 1986). The fact that it is relatively 'normal' for men to offend (and correspondingly 'abnormal' for women to do so) resonates, after all, with differences which are established very early in life, the association of boyhood with naughtiness and girlhood with compliance being reflected in the description of disobedient or independent-minded girls as 'tomboys' (Cain (ed) 1990). Another explanation has to do with women's significant involvement as positive agents of social control – notably in their continuing position as the primary socialisers of children. These arguments sidestep the spectre of women's liberation as promoting female crime, and suggest that we should shift our perspective and ask whether men's socialisation and informal control should be made more akin to that of women, and whether this would result in a reduction of male crime. But these accounts beg questions about how sex roles and controls come to be constructed and imposed in the first place. Furthermore, it seems doubtful that we would want to extend a process of informal control which is, in many ways, oppressive. The debate underlines the depth and complexity of the social processes and conditions which underpin the practice and impact of criminal justice.

Another particularly important set of cultural assumptions for criminal justice has to do with *race and ethnicity*. In the current climate, we see a starkly divided criminal justice landscape as far as race is concerned. On the one hand, the spectacular failure of the prosecutions in both the Stephen Lawrence and Damilola Taylor cases (MacPherson Report 1999), as well as growing evidence of racially motivated violence, has raised grave concerns about the capacity of the criminal process to deliver justice to members of ethnic minorities: statistics on Race and the Criminal Justice System published by the Home Office under s 95 of the Criminal Justice Act 1991 show that, during the first year of recording for the new racially aggravated offences, 21,750 offences were recorded, of which half were offences of harassment (Home Office 2000b: vi – on these offences, see further **Chapter 3.I.b.**). On the other hand, both the threat of international terrorism and political concern about illegal immigration have reinforced stereotypes about the association of criminality with certain ethnic identities. Home Office figures show a statistical over-representation of Black people at every level of the criminal justice system: while Black (as distinct from Asian) people make up 1.8% of the population, they account for 8.2% of stop-and-searches, 7.3% of arrests, 5.7% of cautions, 8.5% of prison receptions and 12.3% of the prison population (Home Office 2000b: vi). We further discuss questions of ethnicity and criminal justice in relation to policing in **section III.b.ii.** below.

The *media and popular culture* are also influential in portraying images of criminal justice, through television, newspapers, the radio, the Internet and magazines (Ericson, Baranek and Chan 1987; Sparks 1994; Reiner 2002). Norms produced and practised in other institutions such as family, church and school are publicised, underlined, exemplified in a never-ending series of morality plays (soap operas), (selective) representations of reality (the news) and many other forms of media production which themselves present competing versions of social reality. Not only are the various parts of the media important as means of conveying ideas and arguments about law reform, they also influence perceptions of how threatening crime is, what kind of crime is prevalent, and what should be done about it. Media involvement in producing social images of both perpetrators and victims of crime and of institutional responses to crime (images which are often far removed from empirical reality) has a long history. In the nineteenth century, broadsheets telling stories of notorious crimes would be circulated, rather like the modern 'True Crime' magazines; today, 'Crimewatch' and other broadcasts not only propagate images of crime but also encourage viewers to take an active role in providing information to the police. Novels, short stories, folklore, myths and other features of popular culture are also implicated in producing popular images of crime. The media is both a means of disseminating the other influences we have mentioned, and a source of power itself. Those who control the media have substantial influence over social beliefs about how much crime exists, what kind of crime it is and how seriously it should be viewed; who does it, to whom it is done, and the extent and adequacy of institutional responses to it. Who controls media channels, the extent of their accountability, and the means whereby particular parts of the media come to wield power and influence are therefore important questions for students of criminal law.

Finally, physical responses to the possibility of deviance in the form of *environmental design and technology* are an increasingly significant part of the social context in which criminal justice operates. One of the most spectacular examples of such physical embodiments of discipline is Bentham's design for the Panopticon prison, in which prisoners would be constantly open to surveillance, yet unable to tell when they were under observation (Bentham 1843: for an influential analysis, see Foucault 1979: 195–228). Such techniques reach out from the penal process and influence the design and planning of the environment: street lighting to make crime visible; housing estates with units overlooking each other and communal areas to increase visibility; similar designs applied to shopping precincts; open-plan offices; the technology of (and media campaigns for the use of) locks and strong doors and windows; surveillance cameras as an almost standard feature of supermarkets, department stores, shopping malls, stations and roads; 'spy-holes' in outer doors of domestic houses. Sociologists have reflected critically on the 'punitive city' which we have created, linking the growth of general surveillance and our tolerant attitude towards it with the criminal justice development towards both 'community corrections', the policing of 'problem populations' as opposed to particular offenders (Matthiesen 1983; Scull 1983; von Hirsch et al 2000; Pease 2002), and the development of a 'culture of control' oriented to the management of an increasingly 'exclusive society' (Garland 2001; Young 1999). Conversely, they have linked the increased emphasis on 'situational' crime prevention with an increasing governmental tendency to individualise or disperse responsibility not only for crime itself but for avoiding victimisation, drawing our attention to the implications of this political framework for those individuals or communities who cannot afford elaborate preventive technology and who risk being held responsible for their own victimisation. In the context of the criminal process, it might therefore be argued that the focus of criminal law doctrine on responsibility as founded in 'capacity' considered in the last section is being replaced by an increasing focus on criminality as founded in 'character' or social position (Lacey 2001a). These developments are assisted by other technologies such as computing, which facilitate the collection of the huge amounts of information generated by electronic surveillance and the creation of offender profiling as a tool of policing and policy construction. Some commentators have argued that the very boundaries between 'crime' and 'anti-social behaviour', between the processes of criminal justice and social control are becoming blurred in a disturbing and possibly irreversible way (Cohen 1985) – a trajectory confirmed by the invention of 'anti-social behaviour orders' under the Crime and Disorder Act 1998 (see **Chapter 3.I.c.**). These developments call into question the assumption that criminal justice is exclusively the domain of the nation-state.

These practices, systems and techniques, along with many others, combine to create a complex web of social governance. It is in these contexts, as well as those of the criminal process and of criminal law doctrine, that we must approach criminal law and its system of punishment. As Garland argues below, the relationship between these broader social and cultural factors and the concrete arrangement of the criminal process is complex, but intimate:

David Garland, *The Culture of Control* (OUP, 2001) pp x–xii.
Reprinted by permission of Oxford University Press.

My argument is that our contemporary crime control arrangements have been shaped by two underlying social forces – the distinctive social organization of late modernity, and the free market, socially conservative politics that came to dominate the USA and the UK in the 1980s ... [P]olitical actors and government agencies – police forces, prosecution agencies, courts, prisons, government departments, elected officials – were confronted with a new set of practical problems in their daily operations. Their problems chiefly flowed from the prevalence of high rates of crime and disorder in late modern society and the growing realization that modern criminal justice is limited in its capacity to control crime and deliver security ... The odd fact that punitive 'law and order' politics have co-existed, in both countries, with an entirely different strategy – of preventative partnerships, community policing and generalized crime prevention – is explained by reference to the public's ambivalence about crime and crime control: an ambivalence that gives rise to quite divergent forms of action. The sensibilities that characterize this popular culture do not stem from media representations or political rhetoric though these have a shaping effect. They originate in the collective experience of crime in everyday life and the practical adaptations to which it eventually gave rise ...

My analysis suggests that although the structures of criminal justice have changed in important ways in recent decades, the most important changes have been in the cultural assumptions that animate them ... [A] new crime control culture has emerged that embodies a reworked conception of penal-welfarism, a new criminology of control, and an economic style of decision-making. The roots of today's crime control arrangement lie in the character of contemporary social organization and the political and cultural choices that have been made in relation to it.

III.b.   Criminal laws and the criminal process

In the remainder of this chapter, we explore the relationship between criminal law and the institutions, professional groups and practices which make up the criminal process. These practices operate on the basis of more and less formal systems of norms which govern the identification, pursuit, prosecution, trial and sentence of a selection of persons who are alleged to have committed crimes as defined by criminal law. Yet many of the features thought to be crucial to and distinctive of criminal law, given its importance and coercive methods, are notoriously absent from the practice of criminal justice. These features include the (formal) burden on the state to prove guilt beyond reasonable doubt, the adoption and announcement of standards in advance, and the quest to promote certainty and curtail discretion. Conversely, issues which are systematically obscured by the abstract individualism of criminal law doctrine – issues such as ethnic, gender and socio-economic patterns of criminalisation – become glaringly obvious when we examine the operation of the criminal process.

We therefore need to step beyond the internal critique of criminal law doctrine and to set criminal law within this criminal justice context, broadly conceived, in order to develop a more sophisticated understanding of how many purportedly central criminal law principles come to be relatively marginal in the practice of criminal justice.

We should also consider the ways in which the separation of criminal law from criminal justice and criminal procedure foster the image of criminal law's principled and autonomous nature and, hence, of its legitimacy (Farmer 1997: 8–9; Norrie 2001: Ch 1). For in understanding how the political legitimacy and perceived effectiveness of criminal justice is managed in contemporary Britain, the criminal process is now, perhaps, a yet more salient focus than the substantive criminal law. Over the last 12 years, there has been a major piece of legislation reforming the criminal justice system virtually every year; the Criminal Justice Bill 2003 has 270 clauses. These pieces of legislation have restructured everything from policing to punishment. During the same period, amendments to the substance of criminal law have been interstitial and, until the sexual offences reforms of 2003, included no major systematic reform of any area of the law.

III.b.i.   Defining crimes

One possible starting-point in contextualising criminal law doctrine is to consider the way in which definitions of crime are socially produced. This approach is different from that developed in **section II.** of this chapter. It is not an internal analysis of criminal law's structure or content, but rather an external, social science analysis of the process of its creation and the groups who have the power to define and develop it.

We begin in what may appear a counter-intuitive place: with ordinary members of the public. At first sight, it might appear that private citizens have little impact on the shape of criminal law. This, however, is far from true. Both in terms of the developing definition of crime and in terms of its enforcement, the intangible phenomenon of '*public opinion*' and, perhaps more importantly, perceptions of that phenomenon, are enormously influential. The politicians who are involved in the legislative process are ultimately accountable to the populace and are therefore liable to be influenced by what they think are prevailing opinions. This fact is well-illustrated by the populist approach of both the conservative Michael Howard, Home Secretary between 1993 and 1997, and his Labour successors Jack Straw and David Blunkett, who have in their different ways exploited the popularity of tough 'law and order' policies in the face of both judicial and other expert criticism. Judges, too, often find it useful to appeal to 'public opinion' (in the form of fear, anxiety or disgust at, or sympathy for, a particular crime) to justify a particular legal outcome. This is especially so in the area of sentencing, where judges have more overtly acknowledged discretion than in many other aspects of their formal function (see **section III.b.iv.** below). Furthermore, those who apply criminal law in the vast bulk of cases are magistrates, whose amateur status is sometimes seen to invest them with the authority to embody 'public opinion' and hence with a kind of popular legitimacy, despite their unrepresentative class, ethnic and gender composition (Carlen 1976). 'Public opinion' is also at work in the fact that a jury may occasionally 'perversely' refuse to convict if the law is too far outside their common-sense conception of what is reasonable. The converse risk – that a jury may be more inclined to convict if the alleged offence is one which elicits particular revulsion – also exists, as several of the miscarriage of justice cases testify.

There is, however, a yet more fundamental sense in which the definition of crime is driven by popular opinion. The vast majority of law enforcement is initiated by public complaint and information. The views of members of the public about what is 'real' crime – crime which is worth reporting – and our very willingness to label certain behaviour a crime at all therefore directly affect patterns of enforcement and, in turn, public perceptions about the nature of the 'crime problem' (Lacey 1994a, 1995; on levels of fear of crime, see Hough 1995; Downes and Morgan 2002). The disillusionment and consequent unwillingness of sections of the public to participate in the criminal process by making complaints should also be borne in mind, for this too has its effect on the social production of crime. Key examples would be some classes of victims of crime such as those subject to rape and domestic violence and members of ethnic groups, who have a variety of reasons for placing low levels of trust in the system. A complex process of construction and reinforcement, in which news media have an important role, produces public opinion about criminal law: both public opinion and beliefs about it are in turn crucially important to criminal law's development and enforcement.

It is also important to consider the various official groups involved in the creation and interpretation of criminal law. Here the most obvious groups are the legislature, judiciary and magistracy and their clerks who define, create and apply law directly. The lawyers who select, edit and write headnotes for the small proportion of cases which come to be reported also have considerable influence over the development of the system of precedent. Even though most criminal law is now in statutory form, the judges retain significant interpretive power. This interpretive power is difficult to distinguish from the creative power the existence of which judges are generally concerned to deny; it is particularly evident in the significant fields of criminal law still governed by common law – homicide, participatory liability and the 'general part' – and in cases in which criminal law is challenged on the basis of relatively open-ended human rights standards. Beyond the judiciary, magistracy and legislature, the professional and socio-economic status of many other interest groups gives them an influence over the development of law. Among such groups are lawyers who argue in court, selecting among possible interpretations; parliamentary drafters; members of and those making representations to reform bodies such as the Law Commission; and academic commentators, both by participating in reform projects and through their published views on disputed questions of law, which are occasionally cited and adopted by judges.

As the head of the department of government responsible for running the penal system, the *Home Secretary* initiates policy review and innovation. Until recently, he also had broad powers in relation to the time in prison to be served by those given life sentences (see **section III.b.iv.** below). This blurring of judicial and executive functions has been challenged successfully on the basis of the European Convention on Human Rights (*Benjamin and Wilson v UK*, 2002; *Stafford v UK*, 2002; *R (Anderson) v Secretary of State for Home Department*, 2002). The powers of the *Attorney-General* and the *Director of Public Prosecutions* include the exclusive power to allow prosecutions to be brought in certain circumstances (for example, offences involving racial hatred under Pt III of the Public Order Act 1986 may only be prosecuted with the Attorney-General's consent), the power to stop prosecutions and to order them, and the responsibility for bringing certain prosecutions in the public interest. These powers render them an important focus in analysing the criminal process. The Attorney-General's status as a political appointee gives a special significance to his or her actions and decisions.

As head of the Criminal Courts, the *Lord Chief Justice* has responsibility for the administration of criminal trials and for judicial sentencing policy. Furthermore, the Lord Chief Justice controls any empirical research into sentencing practice which requires presence in court or the cooperation of court personnel. Lord Lane's influence in reorganising the Criminal Courts and his personal involvement in sitting regularly in Crown Courts during his term as Lord Chief Justice in the 1980s illustrates the significance of the Lord Chief Justice's position for the development and administration of criminal law. Lord Lane's activist precedent has been followed by his (very different) successors, Lords Taylor, Bingham and Woolf, all of whom have been vociferous critics of Government criminal justice policy, particularly in the field of sentencing, in the House of Lords and other public fora covered by the news media.

There are also many interest and *pressure groups* which lobby and campaign for changes in specific areas of criminal law. For example, women's groups such as Women against Rape and the Fawcett Society have argued on issues such as abortion and the redefinition of rape; organisations such as Liberty and Justice are regular advocates of criminal law reform as, more officially, are the Law Commission, Royal Commissions, the Commission for Racial Equality and public inquiries; banks and other commercial bodies have an interest in the reform of laws such as those on fraud; the police have views about matters such as extending public order laws, the scope of their own powers and rules of evidence and procedure; doctors and psychiatrists make proposals about defences such as insanity and diminished responsibility. Clearly, some of these views and groups are more influential than others, and the extent of each group's influence is itself an index of power relations in society. But they all form part of the social and political climate within which criminal law is created, applied and developed, and have a bearing on the views of those who have the final say in that application and development.

III.b.ii.   Policing and prosecuting

The *Police* play a number of roles in the enforcement of crime, and the importance of their position calls for a more extensive analysis than that devoted to the groups so far mentioned. At a general level, the police have considerable influence over the shape of detected criminality because of their ability to make managerial decisions about the style of policing, the distribution of limited resources for detection, surveillance and investigation, and the balance to be struck between investigation, conciliation, surveillance and community involvement. These decisions are circumscribed to a limited extent by principles of administrative law. But the way in which the police perceive their role in relation to prevailing 'crime problems' directly influences how they respond to information and complaints from the public, and hence what kinds of and how much crime is recorded and investigated and thus potentially prosecuted (Reiner 2000; Bowling and Foster 2002). Of course, there may be considerable local variation in police practice – and though these variations are meant to be less significant since the ultimate decisions to prosecute are now left to the Crown Prosecution Service (see below), they still affect the pattern of cases submitted to the Crown Prosecutor in the first place. Changing police attitudes to pursuing cases involving domestic violence and towards the allegations made by victims of rape and racial harassment are recent examples of how the police's perception of their role, of the characteristics of 'real' victims and 'normal' offenders, and of the nature of crime may radically affect the pattern of enforcement (Morris 1987: 181–7; Grace 1995; Cretney and Davis 1997).

Beyond these broad managerial concerns, the police make specific decisions which also affect patterns of enforcement. A brute yardstick of the breadth and significant of police discretion is given by Home Office figures on decisions taken subsequent to the recording of a crime: of the crime recorded by the police in 2001–2002 (Home Office 2002c), 25% led to a detection, 14% to a charge, 4% to a caution, 2% to the offence being taken into consideration in the context of another prosecution and 4% to no further action. On-the-street decisions about whether to arrest or question a suspect or pursue a particular investigation; decisions about whether merely to 'caution' or issue a formal warning to a suspected offender, rather than submit a case for possible prosecution; police selection and construction of 'strong cases' through vigorous efforts at collecting evidence (McConville et al 1991; Sanders and Young 2000); the conduct of interrogation of suspects and witnesses and the eliciting of confessions; decisions about whom to interview; decisions about and conduct of searches for and seizure of evidence and illegally held property; decisions to grant or refuse bail from the police station: all these factors affect the shape and content of the material – 'crime' – which the police ultimately filter for the Crown Prosecutor (Sanders 1997, 2002).

Criminological literature and government surveys speak of the 'dark figure' of true crime, far larger than the figure of reported and recorded crime, let alone than that of crime which is 'cleared up'. It is, of course, difficult to get any idea of what this 'dark figure' might be, not least because of the fact that behaviour has to be *interpreted* as coming within a criminal definition rather than merely *pre-existing* as 'criminal'. Surveys of victims of crime and self-reports of offenders such as the British Crime Survey, however, can give us supplementary pictures taken from particular vantage points (Kershaw et al 2001). The Home Office now undertakes such a survey on a regular basis, and the official criminal statistics for 2000 note that the latest British Crime Survey suggests that only 'half of all offences are reported to the police and a quarter are recorded. Reporting and recording rates vary considerably between offences' (Home Office 2001b: 17). The issue is further complicated by various practices used by the police in order to boost clear-up rates, such as getting offences 'taken into consideration' at trial, and securing 'confessions' to unsolved crimes from convicted offenders in prison. What is clear is that the police must be regarded as one of the key filters in selecting crime which becomes the subject of the criminal process and hence the focus of media and popular attention.

It is important to appreciate the institutional complexity of the police: the divergent aims of a force whose goals are as various as its powers. Important preoccupations include improving clear-up rates (particularly so as to satisfy auditing criteria set by central government); satisfying public opinion and in particular local feeling; keeping peace in the local community; presenting itself as an efficient and modern force to central government; acting as a pressure group both for more resources for policing and for law reform; and asserting directly the authority of the state by a variety of coercive techniques ranging from reactive policing through to proactive management of risks through methods such as electronic surveillance (Regulation of Investigatory Powers Act 2000: see Akdeniz et al 2001). These potentially conflicting aims are matched by tensions and complexities in the professional ethic and self-image of a body which is still expected to fulfill the role of 'friendly bobby' whilst increasingly engaging in transnational crime control and high-tech investigations on the basis of computer-assisted offender profiling (as in the recent case of paedophilia investigations) and holding itself ready to operate virtually as a paramilitary force in moments of civil unrest.

Even this brief survey suggests that it is impossible to identify organising aims and values of the police in any simple way. Questions arising from current debates about policing may usefully be divided, however, into four main issues: the organisation and style of policing, including the relationship between public and private policing; the formal legal powers of the police; the legal and political accountability of the police; and the attitudes which the police bring to the exercise of their powers.

Historically, the practice of policing has been carried out by a diversity of public and private institutions, and it was only in the nineteenth century that a national public police force was instituted. In earlier times, policing was to a significant extent the responsibility of local communities – a situation which bears an interesting resemblance to contemporary developments such as neighbourhood watch (see McConville and Shepherd 1992). Furthermore, private security has continued to be significant, and has arguably increased in importance during the course of the twentieth century, with a wide range of security firms delivering services to both companies and individuals (Johnston 1992; Bayley and Shearing 1996). In recent years, such firms have become increasingly involved in delivering security services also to the local and national state through privatisation and the contracting out of formerly publicly provided services. Hence policing, like other aspects of the process of criminalisation and punishment, is far from being exclusively the business of the state. Furthermore, public policing is not the monopoly of the national police: in areas such as customs and excise and public transport, for example, specialist police forces bear primary responsibility. In relation to criminal law, however, the national police force continues to occupy a distinctively important position, and it will therefore be our focus in the rest of this section.

One persistent theme in recent discussions of public policing concerns the ways in which specific threats of crime – particularly in relation to terrorism – have become influential in driving broader policy on police powers. Just as the industrial disputes of the 1970s and 1980s arguably encouraged a 'tooled-up', aggressive style of policing, the experience of policing Northern Ireland during the 'troubles' arguably fostered the gradual extension of general police powers: a trajectory which has been given added impetus by recent developments in international terrorism. This close relationship between developments in the style of policing and the experience of particular crime problems is illustrated by the following extract:

P Hillyard 'The Normalisation of Special Powers' in P Scraton (ed)
***Law, Order and the Authoritarian State* (Open University Press, 1987) pp 304–306**

Policing Northern Ireland and Policing Britain

The first and most important area of similarity has been in the *form* of policing. There are two dimensions to this. First, the British police, like their North of Ireland contemporaries, have become increasingly militarized both in thinking and in practice ... British police forces now have at their disposal extensive armouries which not only include lethal weapons ranging from pistols to sub-machine guns but many forces now possess guns to fire plastic bullets and CS gas – two crowd-control weapons which have been used extensively in Northern Ireland. Much of the equipment – flak jackets, steel helmets and plastic visors, leg-guards, plastic shields and batons – which is now available to police in England and Wales is similar to that used for many years in Northern Ireland ...

Increasingly, British police forces are adopting military styles of policing. As early as 1972 Sir Robert Mark had his 200-strong S[pecial] P[atrol] G[roup] trained in methods used by the RUC, including the snatch-squad method of making arrests, flying wedges to break up crowds and random stop-and-search and road-block techniques. The 1984–5 coal dispute provided the majority of police forces in Britain with the opportunity to develop military methods of policing. Every weekday morning the police organized what amounted to a military campaign against the striking miners. Every day huge convoys of police Transit vans, horse-boxes, smaller vans with dogs and their handlers, and Land Rovers with arc-lights moved into position to confront the pickets. Police tactics ranging from the extensive use of road-blocks to the specific methods of crowd-control clearly owed much to the experiences of policing in Northern Ireland. All the police documents which have become available since the strike reflect military thinking and tactics. They talk of targets, drawing fire, missiles and decoys.

This military style of policing was not some aberration during the coal dispute. As in Northern Ireland, it is now the dominant style of policing and is visible almost daily from policing inner-city incidents to industrial disputes. It also characterized the policing of the Peace Convoy travellers in the West Country during the summers of 1985 and 1986.

The other dimension concerning the *form* of policing which has parallels to Northern Ireland has been the way in which the focus of police work has increasingly been upon policing people rather than policing crime … Since 1969, this has involved a number of strands: the gathering of intelligence, monitoring and control of people in and out of Nationalist areas and the incorporation of other agencies in what has been called multi-agency policing. In Britain a similar emphasis on policing people has been emerging in recent years; particularly in relation to the black community. But it is not only the black community; many different sections of the population ranging from those who take part in industrial disputes to the travellers have been treated as suspect and subjected to surveillance and techniques of control, many of which are of dubious legality.

Developments towards greater operational autonomy have not, of course, happened in a political vacuum. An accompanying extension of the formal legal powers of the police, whilst not always directly functional or even relevant to many aspects of police actions, which may be extra-legal or illegal, nevertheless gives a clear message to the police that they have the support of the Government in the increasingly aggressive (and arguably counterproductive) pursuit of law and order. In suppressing inner city disturbances or quelling picketing, the availability of plastic bullets and riot equipment are far more important than powers of arrest; nevertheless, the society which accords extended legal powers is the same one which sanctions or acquiesces in the cruder accoutrements of police power.

The *Police and Criminal Evidence Act* (PACE) in 1984, the Criminal Justice and Public Order Act 1994, the Crime and Disorder Act 1996, the Regulation of Investigatory Powers Act 1996, the Terrorism Act 2000 and the Criminal Justice and Police Act and Anti-Terrorism, Crime and Security Act 2001 – all major pieces of legislation governing policing, among other things putting 'special' anti-terrorism powers on a permanent footing for the first time – are therefore of great significance for the enforcement of criminal law. As a whole, there is no doubt that these Acts have added significantly to the powers of the police, especially in the areas of arrest and search and – in the case of foreign nationals under the anti-terrorist legislation – detention. The balance, however, has been an interesting mixture between increasing police accountability while expanding their powers. PACE, for example, codified a substantial part of the common law framework, subjected to legal regulation several aspects of police behaviour previously either unregulated or regulated only by Judges' rules, specified for the first time maximum periods of custody before charge and the conditions under which they may be extended, provided for the first time for tape-recording of interviews, and added significantly to the bureaucratic load of the police by imposing obligations for notes and records to be kept at most stages of arrest, questioning and charge. The legislation therefore had some significant reformist aspects. Yet it could hardly be claimed as an unambiguous victory for civil rights. In the first place, it left untouched some significant common law and statutory police powers (those relating to breach of the peace and under the 'emergency' provisions relating to terrorism). And although some parts of the Act embodied liberal-sounding assertions of right and principle, it went on to specify detailed qualifications to the general standard in almost every case. As we have already seen, miscarriage of justice cases show that violation of these principles has persisted beyond the enactment of PACE, and the Royal Commission on Criminal Justice (1993) recommended amendments in relation to both police powers and police discipline. The resulting legislation, however, has made little difference to the overall power of the police.

It is worth considering a specific illustration of the degree of operational latitude which PACE gives to police officers. Section 25 provides for arrest by a constable of someone suspected of committing an otherwise 'non-arrestable' offence (ie an offence for which the maximum term of imprisonment is less than five years (PACE, s 24(1)) where the 'general arrest conditions' exist. These exist where a constable judges that service of a summons is impracticable or inappropriate because she does not know and cannot readily ascertain the person's name; where a constable has reasonable grounds for doubting the name furnished is real; where a constable judges that a satisfactory address has not been furnished or has reasonable grounds for believing the address furnished to be unsatisfactory (for example because the person will not be at it long enough for the summons to be served); where a constable has reasonable grounds for believing that arrest is necessary to prevent the person causing physical injury to herself or another, suffering injury, causing loss or damage to property, committing an offence against public decency or obstructing the highway; or where a constable has reasonable grounds for believing the arrest to be necessary to protect a child or other vulnerable person. It is not difficult to see that these general arrest conditions render vulnerable to arrest for any offence certain categories of person, notably those whose lifestyle does not, or appears to a constable not to, conform to social norms. This would include those who have no permanent address (asylum seekers come to mind) and those whose appearance or manner suggest to the constable that they may be untruthful or unable to furnish such information (a bias against the young and against young black men in particular seems almost inevitable given what we know of police attitudes – see below).

The latitude which such provisions give to the police in exercising their discretion is vast, and this latitude is endorsed by the courts' wide interpretation of concepts such as 'reasonable grounds for suspicion' on the rare occasions when police actions are challenged. And in 1994, the Criminal Justice and Public Order Act, s 60 introduced a provision whereby the police may stop and search even *without* specific grounds for suspicion, over a 24-hour period, where there is a 'general anticipation of violence'. The Criminal Justice and Police Act 2001 introduced further provisions designed to deal with various aspects of disorderly behaviour through 'on-the-spot penalties' (Pt I) and by increasing police powers on seizure (Pt II) and on arrestable offences, detention, fingerprinting and the taking of other samples (Pt III). As Wasik (2001: 931 at 946–947) sums it up:

> This is another Criminal Justice Act comprised substantially of extensions to state power. It is not in the same repressive category as the [Criminal Justice and Public Order Act 1994] ... , and a plausible case can be made for many of the incremental changes made by it but, taken together, the provisions of the Criminal Justice and Police Act represent a further significant erosion of liberty. In the case where the police have acted in breach of PACE by retaining DNA evidence which quite clearly should have been destroyed, the legislative response has been to change the law with retrospective effect so as to legitimise what was improperly done ... There is not a single example of government proposals being dropped or significantly altered in light of human rights concerns. There are, however, several instances where the government pressed ahead despite clear and strong warnings on human rights issues (travel restrictions on drug trafficking offenders, and the extension of child curfews are two examples).

In assessing the significance of policing for the conduct of trials and hence for the ultimate meaning of substantive criminal laws, it is therefore important to take into account the formal, legal powers of the police:

> If the practice of criminal justice does not live up to its rhetoric [of procedural fairness], one should not look only to the interactions and negotiations

of those who put the law into practice but to the law itself. One should not look just to how the rhetoric of justice is subverted intentionally or otherwise by policemen bending the rules, by lawyers negotiating adversariness out of existence, by out-of-touch judges or biased magistrates: one must also look at how it is subverted *in the law*. Police and court officials need not abuse the law to subvert the principles of justice; they need only use it. Deviation from the rhetoric of legality and justice is institutionalised within the law itself [McBarnet 1981: 156].

There has been a significant increase in the number of arrests since PACE was introduced, and Home Office statistics on search, arrest and prosecution suggest that the operational latitude given by its provisions has significant implications for civil liberties. Between 1986 and 1994, the number of arrests rose from 1.31 million to 1.75 million; in 2001–2002, there were 1,272,000 arrests for notifiable (ie more serious) offences. Yet in 1994, only 700,000 of those arrested were either cautioned or prosecuted for an indictable offence. In other words, about one million people who were arrested were either not proceeded against or only proceeded against for minor offences. In 1999–2000, the most recent year for which the ratio of arrests to prosecutions is available, only 60% of those arrested were prosecuted (Hillyard et al 2004). Similarly, stops and searches under PACE rose from under 100,000 in 1986 to 576,000 in 1994 and to 740,700 in 2001–2002 (Home Office 2002c). Yet in 1994 only 70,300 of those stopped – just over 12% – were arrested; and in 2001–2002 the proportion was, similarly, a mere13%. These overall figures disguise a great deal of local variation: in Nottinghamshire, 18% of stops and searches led to an arrest, while in Cleveland, where the police are operating a 'zero tolerance' policy, the figure was a mere 7%. These figures suggest that PACE mandates a large amount of unnecessary police intrusion into ordinary citizens' everyday lives. And if we look at vehicle searches in road checks mandated by the Road Traffic Act 1972 (as amended by the Criminal Justice and Public Order Act 1994), we find that in 2001–2002 there was just one arrest for every 1480 vehicles stopped (Home Office 2002c). Yet the legislative trajectory is towards an ever-greater panoply of police powers.

These police powers have particular implications for members of ethnic minorities. In London, research has shown that black (ie Afro-Caribbean) people are stopped and searched at between two and three times the rate which would be consistent with their numbers in the population (Statewatch 1995: 18–20; Hillyard and Gordon 1999). Across the country, there is strong evidence that black people are disproportionately at the receiving end of criminal justice powers (Phillips and Bowling 2002; see also Sanders 2002: 1039–1044). The findings of the MacPherson Inquiry (1999), set up to investigate policing and prosecution failures in the case of Stephen Lawrence, is of particular significance. Lawrence was a young black man stabbed to death by three white men in a racially motivated attack: the police inquiry into his killing was handled with such incompetence and insensitivity that a successful prosecution was rendered impossible (see further below). The subsequent Inquiry engaged in a general analysis of the question of race and policing in London, focusing in particular on the fact that black people (as distinct from Asians) are five times more likely to be stopped and searched than are whites – a cause of huge resentment against the police. When the fact that stops and searches are heavily directed against young men aged between 15 and 24 was taken into account, the Inquiry found that an astonishing 63% of young black men in the Metropolitan area were stopped each year (Lustgarten 2002: 605). These among other findings led the Inquiry to speak in terms of 'institutional racism' in the police service. A recent analysis has concluded not only 'that there is a strong case for a finding of indirect discrimination' but also 'that a significant proportion of street searches fail to satisfy the reasonable suspicion standard of PACE, quite apart from any issue of racial discrimination (see Lustgarten 2002: 603). The legislative and other messages sent to the police by government in this country have progressively engendered an 'ends justify means' mentality which almost certainly works counter to attempted legal safeguards. This finds its most brutal expression in the miscarriage of justice cases, which raised questions about the adequacy of controls on the police, particularly in contexts where they are under pressure to produce an offender due to public concern about a particular incident. The argument that the introduction of video-recording of interrogations is an adequate safeguard against behaviour such as that exposed in the miscarriage cases is hardly satisfactory. Quite apart from the fact that the provision does not apply in cases under terrorism legislation, no such provision can guarantee that all conversations relevant to what ends up on the tape are themselves taped or that policing norms are such as to underpin the effective implementation of existing safeguards (cf *R v Paris*, 1992).

Related to the issues of changing style and organisation of policing and growth of police powers is the concern to ensure the accountability of the police. Once again this is an area which is open to criticism. In 1984, PACE set up a new, independent Police Complaints Authority (PCA), following Lord Scarman's recognition of the importance of such independence in reducing suspicion of the police in his report on the Brixton disorders (Scarman 1982). This was a break with the tradition of purely internal investigation of complaints, but the role of the PCA is a limited, supervisory one: the investigation being conducted by police officers, albeit from a separate regional force in serious cases which have to be referred to the PCA (PACE, s 87(1); Lustgarten, 1986: 155–158). The PCA itself is not accountable to Parliament and has insufficient authority to overcome police domination of the complaints process. In 1998, 9745 complaints made to the PCA were substantiated: this constituted only 8.1% of the complaints investigated and a mere 2.3% of the complaints made (Sanders and Young 2002: 1064). The possibility of making effective complaints or indeed bringing police conduct under the scrutiny of the courts remains highly circumscribed. Moreover, political accountability to local police authorities or other elected bodies has become increasingly weak during the course of this century, so that the systematic checking and review which might be more effective than an individual-initiated, reactive and ad hoc complaints procedure, hardly exists as an alternative mode of accountability (Morgan 1987: 278–280). The Police Act 1996, consolidating the Police and Magistrates' Courts Act 1994, further attenuated local democratic accountability by reducing the proportion of elected representatives on police authorities from two-thirds to one-half (ss 3–6, Schs 2 and 3) and by providing for the appointment of a proportion of police committee members by an arcane procedure in which the Home Secretary has decisive influence. These legislative developments also serve to increase managerial accountability to central government by establishing a range of objectives and performance targets and by requiring police forces to structure their work and to account for themselves within this framework (Police Act 1996, ss 37–38). The Government's White Paper, *Policing a New Century: A Blueprint for Reform* (2001), envisaged further structural change and a renewed emphasis on co-ordination with local communities through 'warden schemes' and an 'extended police family'. After a turbulent passage through Parliament, in which the Government was accused of trying to get 'policing on the cheap' and of extending the practice of 'contracting out' without sufficient provision for accountability, the Police Reform Act 2002 duly extended the power of the Home Secretary to intervene in the individual forces and provided a framework for drawing a greater number of civilians (employed by both the police and other bodies) into a range of policing tasks (Morris 2002). Accountability to local communities is back on the agenda, in a stark symbol of both the tendency of successive police reforms to circle around a limited number of recurring issues, and of the centralising/localising tensions inherent in the varied tasks which the police are called upon to perform. While the Race Relations (Amendment) Act 2000 has opened up the criminal process to the principles of anti-discrimination law by giving individuals a right to sue the police for racial discrimination in the conduct of investigations, the implications of such individual redress are, inevitably, circumscribed within a context in which the major issues are structural rather than isolated (see Field and Roberts 2002).

Finally, negative attitudes towards certain social groups appear to characterise police work (Manning 1987). These vary as between different groups and ranks within the police (Reiner 2000), but they inevitably have a significant impact both on patterns of policing and on public attitudes towards the police. Again, this is not a new problem (see Weinberger in Hay and Snyder 1987: 174–175; Morgan 1987: 270–271). Experiences such as the policing of the miners' strike in the 1980s, poll tax disturbances and anti-war demonstrations give little reason to think that the police have become more sympathetic to, for example, left-wing or labour protests over the last half-century. However, the foremost issue concerning police prejudice has to do with racism, particularly in the context of policing inner city areas (Smith and Gray 1983; Phillips and Bowling 2002).

The case of Stephen Lawrence, in which three white youths were unsuccessfully prosecuted by the Lawrence family following the failure of the *Crown Prosecution Service* (CPS) to act, illustrates the fact that the problem of racism affects not only the conduct of police inquiries and the treatment of victims and their families but all aspects of the prosecution process. Since 1985, it has been the CPS which is responsible for deciding which of the cases referred to it by the police to prosecute, and its lawyers are responsible for the conduct of the prosecution case. The adequacy of the preparation and argument of the case, as well as the choice of charge, is obviously crucial to its success or otherwise. The CPS was set up in an attempt to ensure national consistency of prosecution policy and its more efficient pursuit on the basis of institutionally accepted criteria concerning the public interest in prosecution and the strength of the case – whether there is a 'realistic prospect of success' (Fionda 1995). The criteria for prosecution are elaborated in the Code for Crown Prosecutors and in the Annual Reports of the CPS. Without under-estimating the filtering process undertaken by the police, the Crown Prosecutor has a substantial margin of discretion both in terms of whether to proceed at all, and, if so, what charges to press and with what degree of vigour. Since its inception, the CPS has suffered from chronic under-staffing due to difficulties of recruitment; similarly, low rates of pay have led to a shortage of magistrates' clerks and to increasing reluctance on the part of solicitors to take on legal aid work. Among the consequences being felt are very long delays in the processing of cases. These factors may also bear on the persistence of high acquittal rates which have increasingly drawn criticisms of inefficiency on the CPS (for a general assessment of the work of the CPS, see the Royal Commission 1993: Ch 5; Sanders and Young 2002). Despite various changes of high-profile personnel and some structural reforms, the uneven quality of the work of the CPS remains a live political issue, surfacing from time to time in spectacular cases such as the failure of the prosecution of those accused of murdering Damilola Taylor in 2001 and the collapse of the theft trial of the late Princess of Wales' butler, Paul Burrell, in 2002.

An important part of the context within which cases are selected for prosecution is that of *plea-bargaining* – a practice only relatively recently acknowledged to exist in England and Wales. Reluctance to acknowledge the existence of plea-bargaining is hardly surprising given the threat it poses to the presumption of innocence, consistency of enforcement and the centrality of the criminal trial, all of which, as we have seen, are key parts of the prevailing ideology of criminal justice (Baldwin and McConville 1977). The public focus on contested criminal trials, particularly trials by jury, is disproportionate to their numerical significance within the criminal process. The vast majority of defendants are in fact dealt with in magistrates' courts, and the vast majority of defendants in all courts plead guilty (see Ashworth 1998: 3 and Ch 9).

By the process of plea-bargaining, a deal is made with the defendant under which she agrees to plead guilty in return for the dropping of a more serious charge or (in some cases) assurances about length of sentence. The extent of judicial involvement in plea bargaining in this country is still obscure, but the practice of offering a sentencing discount for a guilty plea has been institutionalised, as recommended by the 1993 Royal Commission, in s 48 of the Criminal Justice and Public Order Act 1994. Furthermore, it is clear that guilty pleas to reduced charges are negotiated almost as a matter of course between defendants, prosecutors and defence lawyers: the rate of guilty pleas in magistrates' courts is 94%, and in the Crown Court it is approximately 60% (Sanders and Young 2000: 396). The main rationale for plea-bargaining is, of course, managerial and pragmatic. The Crown Prosecution Service has always been under pressure due to concerns about delays, backlogs of cases and perceived efficiency, and this may have prompted an increase in the level of plea-bargaining. Plea-bargaining is thus well established as one of the most important administrative practices in the criminal process. Its existence underlines the fact that the resources which we are prepared, as a society, to devote to criminal justice are limited. Current resource levels could not sustain full enforcement procedures even for reported, cleared-up crime in which a strong case can be constructed: without plea-bargaining to hasten cases through, the whole system would collapse. Plea-bargaining is therefore not merely a matter of convenience for those working in the system, but also a matter of government interest in keeping down the costs of the criminal process.

The role of *victims* of crime in the prosecution process is also of great importance (Shapland et al 1985; Maguire and Pointing 1988; Mawby and Walklate 1994; Zedner 1997). Their position both as reporters of crime to the police and as crucial witnesses at many trials, as well as their symbolic importance even at trials from which they are absent (notably homicide trials) cannot be ignored. Moreover, they have an actual and potential role as receivers of compensation and restitution, both from the offender and from the state under the Criminal Injuries Compensation scheme (amended in 1995), as recipients of the attention of victim support schemes, and as participants in schemes of conciliation and mediation involving offenders. Most recently, pilot studies have been undertaken in 'restorative justice' – an alternative route for offenders which involves a conference with the victim and representatives of offender, victim and community, leading ideally to a negotiated settlement and formal apology. In the area of youth justice, more decisive steps were taken towards this kind of restorative and victim-integrating diversion from the formal criminal process with the creation of Youth Offender Panels under the Crime and Disorder Act 1998, which drew on several other programmes, including Scotland's Children's Hearing system and New Zealand's family group conferences for young offenders

(Crawford and Newburn 2002). Most recently, as part of a review of the Victims' Charter, the Government introduced in October 2001 a Victim Personal Statement Scheme, under which victims are given the opportunity to explain how the crime has affected them, on the understanding that their interests will be taken into account at all stages of the criminal process (Edwards 2002). As these examples show, the position of the victim lies at the crux of questions not only about the relationship between civil and criminal law but also about the relentless politicisation of criminal justice policy.

In concluding this brief assessment of the role of the pre-trial criminal process in defining crime, it is worth asking ourselves the extent to which these interlocking processes constitute a coherent 'system', as well as bearing in mind the potentially punitive effect of involvement in even the early stages of criminal enforcement.

Andrew Ashworth, *The Criminal Process: An Evaluative Study* (2nd edn, Oxford University Press, 1998) pp 22–24. Reprinted by permission of Oxford University Press.

Although many who speak and write about criminal justice tend to refer to 'the criminal justice system', it is widely agreed that it is not a 'system' in the sense of a set of co-ordinated decision-makers. … [M]any groups working within criminal justice enjoy considerable discretion, and … are relatively autonomous. Nonetheless, the inappropriateness of the term 'system' should not be allowed to obscure the practical interdependence of the various agencies. Many depend on other agencies for their case-load or for their information, and decisions taken by one agency can impinge on those taken by others. Thus, to take a few examples, the Crown Prosecution Service depends entirely on the police for its case-load, and largely on the police for information, although some information is now being supplied by the Probation Service. Decisions taken by the Crown Prosecution Service affect the case-load of the courts, and may constrain the powers of magistrates' courts and of defendants to determine mode of trial …

References to systems and interdependence are, however, very much in the managerial mode. The criminal process impinges directly on victims, suspects and defendants … A defendant who has been questioned by the police, charged, kept in police custody, remanded by the court, perhaps offered a plea bargain, and then tried in court is already likely to feel 'punished' irrespective of whether a guilty verdict and sentence follow. A person who is acquitted after such a sequence of events may well feel 'punished' by the process to which he or she has been subjected, even if relieved at the outcome. … [This] accords with the results of American research by Malcom Feeley, encapsulated in the title of his book *The Process is the Punishment* (1979). Suspects and defendants often feel that the way in which they are treated is equivalent to punishment, in the sense that it inflicts on them deprivations (of liberty, of reputation) similar to those resulting from a sentence ... For present purposes, it is sufficient to make the point that the pre-trial process is a process to which defendants are *subjected* by officials who have the power of law behind them ...

Victims are also individual citizens whose interests should be protected. There is no shortage of empirical research findings that victims have been and are being treated in the criminal process in ways that can be described as 'punishment'. In the language of victimologists, victims who report crimes are often subjected to 'secondary victimization' at the hands of police, prosecutors and courts. Whilst some steps have been taken to reduce these effects by improving techniques of police questioning and by granting anonymity to victims of certain offences, there is little doubt that some victims still suffer psychologically and socially from their involvement in the criminal process ... [T]he pre-trial process is a process to which victims of crime, too, are *subjected* by officials.

III.b.iii. Constructing crime in the trial process

We now move to the trial process itself – the stage at which criminal law doctrine is most directly invoked and yet at which many other influences are also in play.

Both *prosecution and defence lawyers* have a considerable influence over the course of the trial. This is not only through their negotiation of plea-bargains, but also through their questioning of witnesses – how hard they push particular points, their use of irony or ridicule and a whole range of rhetorical devices, especially before a jury; the quality and thoroughness of their preparation; the astuteness of the way in which they use their knowledge not only of law, but of the tribunal – of jury reactions, or those of a particular judge or magistrate. In these ways and other more subtle ones, these officials materially affect the outcome of the cases in which they are involved, in ways which do not relate directly to substantive rules or principles of criminal law.

The *judges, recorders (practising lawyers who are part-time judges) and magistrates* who hear criminal cases have diverse professional backgrounds. Judges are drawn largely from the Bar; recorders are practising lawyers; stipendiary magistrates have legal training; and magistrates (who hear the vast majority of criminal cases, including all of the less serious, summary, offences) are lay people with some basic training, acting on a voluntary basis, who are advised by a court clerk who has some legal training, and are drawn heavily from white middle-class occupations and households. But they share one important feature: their power of decision on points of law and sentence across the range of criminal cases. Quite apart from judges' interpretive power and power to set precedents, judges and magistrates have considerable powers over the conduct of the trial, which may in subtle ways affect its outcome. Their attitude to accepting guilty (often bargained) pleas; their discretionary admission or exclusion of certain forms of evidence; their conduct in letting the trial run its course or intervening to prompt or challenge witnesses; their discipline of lawyers' questioning; the framing of their direction to the jury and their power to withdraw certain issues from the jury; their manner with witnesses (sympathetic and geared to eliciting considered responses or unsympathetic, impatient and sceptical): all these may affect the outcome of the case (McBarnet 1981; Pattenden 1982, 1989). We might also mention the influence of their social prejudices and views, which tend to be relatively homogeneous given the social composition of the bench (Malleson 1998).

Judges and magistrates have diverse roles: conduct of the trial; committal for trial; decision on points of law; directions to the jury; sentencing. They also possess the important power to award or refuse bail – a decision in which they are often influenced by the views of the police and CPS. As in the case of prosecution decisions, broad statutory criteria exist under the Bail Act 1976, but leave room for the exercise of considerable discretion: recent statutory changes have reversed the presumption in favour of bail in a range of cases (Criminal Justice and Public Order Act 1994, ss 25–26) and have given the prosecution the right to appeal against an award of bail (Bail (Amendment) Act 1993). Several aspects of the bail system are currently under review because of their potential incompatibility with the Human Rights Act, and amendments are proposed in the Criminal Justice Bill 2003. Given current delays in the court system, failure to get bail is a very serious matter. This is not only because of the loss of liberty and appalling conditions in many remand centres, but also because it results in more restricted access to a lawyer and thus disadvantages a defendant's capacity to prepare for her trial and present her case credibly. The magnitude of the sums of money often demanded as surety for defendants who are offered bail prejudices those who have fewer financial resources available to them. Judges, magistrates and the police also have a discretion to specify conditions for the award of bail such as submission to various forms of treatment or monitoring.

The symbolic, ideological and instrumental significance of *juries* in the criminal process has already been touched upon in discussing popular opinion. In Crown Court trials, the jury has the power to decide, having been directed on the law, the issues of fact. The prosecution must convince the jury of the facts beyond reasonable doubt. Despite the fact that the number of jury cases is small (only about 5% even of cases eligible for jury trial are so tried), the requirement of trial by jury in the Crown Court for the most serious, indictable, offences and its availability at the defendant's option in cases which are 'triable either way' serves to legitimate the criminal process by allowing a say to non-professionals – peers of the defendant who have no vested interest either in the system itself or in any particular outcome in this case. The jury is therefore significant as an isolated instance of popular and compulsory participation in the criminal process, although juries are not representative of the general ethnic or gender composition of the population because the practice of selecting from the electoral roll systematically excludes certain groups (Baldwin and McConville 1979; Darbyshire 1991; Darbyshire et al 2001; Abramson 1994).

Until the late 1980s, public concern about 'perverse' jury verdicts tended to focus on unjustified acquittals as opposed to dubious convictions: the jury was seen as defendant-centred. A particular object of criticism was the right of lawyers to peremptory challenge of jurors. These views influenced the Criminal Justice Act 1988, s 119 of which raised the upper age limit for jury service ('senior' citizens being thought more likely to convict than young people) and s 118 of which abolished the right of peremptory challenge (the main motivation being that it could be used by the defence to 'load' the jury in the defendant's favour) (see Gobert 1989). The currency of such criticism, notwithstanding concern about miscarriages of justice, reflects an increasingly retributive public atmosphere in the context of which, notwithstanding the passage of the Human Rights Act, many of the procedural safeguards protecting defendants in the criminal process will have to be vigorously defended if they are to survive (cf the discussion of the right of silence above). The large number of defendants charged with offences triable either way who opt for jury trial reflects a continuing faith in the fairness of juries relative to magistrates, yet the Royal Commission on Criminal Justice recommended that defendants should lose the option of jury trial in such cases. The policy of reducing the number of cases in which the defendant has the right to opt for jury trial remains very much on the political agenda, as evidenced by the Auld Report (see Jackson 2002; Malleson and Roberts 2002). The Criminal Justice Bill 2003 envisages the possibility of trial by judge alone in long and complex cases (a response to the long-running debate about how best to deal with the increasingly salient issue of serious fraud trials) or those where there is a serious risk of the jury being tampered with (see Corker 2002). Finally, we should note the fact that juries are under no duty to give reasons – a conviction can only be appealed on the basis of the judge's direction or on some other point of law, and an acquittal is effectively unchallengeable. The confidentiality of jury deliberations is protected by s 8 of the Contempt of Court Act 1981, a provision which helps to preserve the jury's perceived integrity and hence its ideological functions. Cases such as that of the 'Guildford Four' and 'Cardiff Three' demonstrated the difficulty in getting proper reconsideration of a questionable conviction. Despite the inevitable backlog of cases, this situation has undoubtedly been improved by the establishment in 1997 of the Criminal Cases Review Commission, which now has the power to investigate alleged miscarriages of justice and to refer cases back to the Court of Appeal. Ironically, as a result of the Stephen Lawrence and Damilola Taylor cases, policy debate is now preoccupied with the converse problem: the difficulty of re-opening questionable acquittals. The

Criminal Justice Bill 2003 proposes to abolish the double jeopardy principle – the rule against allowing a second prosecution of someone already acquitted of a particular offence – for all offences carrying a life sentence where there is substantial and reliable new evidence which makes it 'highly probable' that a person who has been acquitted is guilty.

Apart from the various legal personnel, several different groups of *experts* are often involved in (and have views about and interests in the outcome and conduct of) the trial. Probation officers and social workers may be involved in giving evidence and/or in preparing 'pre-sentence reports' which build up a picture of the defendant's history and personality for sentencing purposes. Doctors and psychiatrists may give evidence of the defendant's current or past mental state, make prognoses of her likely future physical and mental health or make expert comment on the facts which constitute the basis of the allegation; this evidence may be relevant at conviction or sentencing stages. Forensic experts may give crucial evidence relating to the defendant's guilt or innocence: as we have seen, the work of the Forensic Science Service came under particularly adverse scrutiny in recent miscarriage of justice cases. The need for proper management of this area is pressing given that it is likely to increase in significance as developing technologies allow the production of new forms of evidence such as DNA fingerprinting. Schoolteachers, family friends, former employers may give character references going to the defendant's credibility or relevant to sentencing and may become involved in mediation or other restorative justice practices. Psychologists may give assessments of personality and level of intelligence. We could multiply this list of 'experts' with a role to play at various points in the trial process (and of course in the preparation of the case by lawyers and prosecutors). The occupational aims and values of these experts vary: they all have different professional and institutional 'axes to grind'. Thus they bring communication problems and further conflicting objectives (not to mention conflicting egos and reputations, especially where two expert witnesses in the same field are called by prosecution and defence) into the courtroom and the criminal process (Bennett and Feldman 1981).

Just as traditional thinking about criminal justice has been dogged by an artificial separation of issues of criminal law and those relating to the criminal process, so a dichotomy has tended to be assumed between rules and issues of procedure and those of substance. Hence *rules of evidence and procedure*, crucial to the practical impact of criminal law, have been termed 'adjectival' and largely excluded from studies of criminal law. These rules set out what may or may not count as evidence, whom it may be given by and about, what form it may take, who may hear it, to what standard an issue must be proved and by whom, when an issue may be withdrawn or introduced and a host of other elements crucial to the conduct of the trial (Dennis 2000). We have already considered the judge's or magistrate's role in administering these rules, and their implications for the presumption of innocence. In the current British criminal justice climate, with its renewed emphasis on the differential policing and control of particular groups, limitations on potentially prejudicial evidence such as evidence of previous convictions or 'bad character' are now being questioned, and substantial inroads on these limitations are being proposed in the Criminal Justice Bill 2003. In assessing the scope and impact of criminal law, the rules of evidence and procedure are every bit as important as those of the substantive law.

III.b.iv.   Responding to crimes

In this section, we move, finally, to the conclusion of the criminal process: the stages of sentencing and punishment. We have already noted that judges, recorders and magistrates have at least a dual role – legal decision-making relating to conviction and more discretionary, though legally structured, *sentencing*.

Andrew Ashworth, *Sentencing and Criminal Justice* (3rd edn, 2000) p 344

[S]entencing decisions are shaped and influenced by a context which runs from decisions to investigate and to prosecute, through decisions on mode of trial, remand and plea, to pre-sentence reports and speeches in mitigation, and thence to early release and decisions on fine default and breach of community orders.

One feature which distinguishes the sentencing process from most other decisions in criminal justice is that the sentence is announced publicly, after public proceedings which usually include either an investigation of the facts, or a statement of facts, and some open discussion of possible approaches to sentence ... Sentencing therefore performs a heavily symbolic function: the sentence of the court may be seen as an authoritative expression by the legal system of its response to the offence. This symbolic function will be performed by placing the sentence on a kind of conventional register of censure or disapproval, accompanied by the utterance of key words ...

In practice some of the stated justifications [for sentence] derive from patterns of reasoning required by legislation, and others derive from judicial practice ... Some have gone so far as to argue that the stated reasons are no more than verbal decorations of judgments reached on other grounds: the reasons are used as resources which judges and magistrates can call upon in order to justify conclusions which they desire for other purposes. There is no doubt an element of truth in this, in sentencing as in most other forms of decision-making, whether judicial or not. But there are also plenty of examples of courts being constrained by the terms of legislation or precedent, in the increasing areas of sentencing which are not left to unstructured discretion.

Since 1991, sentencing has been conducted within a statutory framework set by the Criminal Justice Act 1991, Pt 1 (as amended by the Criminal Justice Act 1993: see also the consolidated Powers of Criminal Courts (Sentencing) Act 2000). According to this legislation, sentences must be commensurate with the seriousness of the offence, with custodial sentences being imposed, under ss 1(2)(a) and 2(2)(a) only where an offence is sufficiently serious that neither a community nor a financial penalty is appropriate. There is an exception to this principle in cases of those already convicted of a violent or sexual offence, who under ss 1(2)(b) and 2(2)(b) may be given, where necessary for public protection, a sentence longer than that commensurate with the seriousness of the present offence. The first Blair Government's decision to implement the Crime (Sentences) Act 1997, which completed its passage through Parliament just before the General Election of that year, extended this special policy in relation to 'dangerous' offenders. It did so by adopting a modified version of the American 'three strikes and you're out' approach in the form of mandatory life sentences, other than in 'exceptional circumstances', for repeat offenders who have committed certain serious violent and sexual offences such as homicide (including attempts, incitements and conspiracies), rape, attempted rape, causing grievous bodily harm with intent and armed robbery (s 2). The Act, consolidated in the Powers of Criminal Courts (Sentencing) Act 2000, ss 109–111, also provides for a mandatory minimum sentence of seven years' imprisonment for a third class A drug trafficking offence unless this would be 'unjust in all the circumstances' (s 3) and for mandatory minimum sentences of three years for third-time domestic burglaries. This last section, implemented later than the other provisions, is likely to have a particular impact on the rapidly expanding prison population. The Criminal Justice Bill 2003, if implemented, will replace the current emphasis on proportionality in sentencing with a greater emphasis on deterrence and crime prevention: the purposes of punishment are stated to be 'punishment, public protection, crime reduction and reparation'. The Bill takes forward the Halliday Report's emphasis on a bifurcated approach of community penalties or 'custody plus' mixed penalties for less serious offenders and longer deterrent offences for more 'dangerous' sexual and violent offenders. A further complication for sentencers is their obligation to take account of Victims' Personal Statements – an obligation which may sit unhappily with the courts' recognition that sentencing should be governed by general public interest concerns which may conflict with the victim's particular perspective (Practice Direction 2001; *R v Perks*, 2000: see Edwards 2002).

The journey towards the current degree of legislative control of sentencing discretion has been a slow one. Before 1991, sentencing was constrained only by (usually very high) statutory maximum sentences, except in special cases such as young people and mentally disordered offenders, where elaborate statutory provisions have existed for some time. Even in the higher courts, the systematic reporting of sentencing cases is of relatively recent origin, and their status as precedents is still ambiguous (Ashworth 2000: Ch 2). In the 1980s, the then Lord Chief Justice, Lord Lane, instituted a practice of delivering 'guideline judgments' on important and disputed sentencing issues. This practice has persisted, but such judgments tend to cover only serious cases. Their influence over the lower courts is therefore limited. The introduction of appeals by the Attorney-General against 'lenient' sentences under s 35 of the Criminal Justice Act 1988 has made some difference to the sample of cases reaching the Court of Appeal and has given greater scope for guideline judgments, but it has not altered the basic dynamics of existing practice. Sections 80–81 of the Crime and Disorder Act 1998 gave further impetus to the systematisation of sentencing by putting the Court of Appeal under a duty to consider whether to frame guidelines or to reconsider existing guidelines in every sentencing appeal and, when the court decides to frame or revise guidelines, to notify the newly created Sentencing Advisory Panel. The Panel can formulate guidelines for certain categories of offence not only when notified by the Court of Appeal but also of its own motion and when asked to do so by the Home Secretary. The court must consider the Panel's guidelines but is not bound to adopt them. Within the generous parameters of the legislative framework, which gives no general definition of levels of offence seriousness, judicial sentencing discretion is therefore informed by a growing body of guidelines, by training through the Judicial Studies Board, by the received wisdom of an oral tradition (in sharp contrast to the formal, textual status of substantive criminal laws), and by uneven knowledge of empirical research on the past practice of sentencers.

The sentencing powers of magistrates are a good deal more limited than those of Crown Court judges; they may impose a maximum term of six months' imprisonment, or of twelve months if two offences are involved. They may, however, refer cases to the Crown Court for sentence if they feel their powers to be inadequate, and the current Criminal Justice Bill proposes to increase their powers up to a maximum of twelve months' imprisonment – another reform with significant implications for the prison population. However, the specific dynamics of magisterial justice suggest that, within their limited powers, magistrates may regard themselves as yet less constrained by legislative guidelines than do Crown Court judges:

Michael Cavadino and James Dignan, *The Penal System: An Introduction* (3rd edn, Sage, 2002) p 94

[S]tudies have shown that the chief formative influence on sentencing practice in magistrates' courts is not the law, their training or the advice they receive from other professionals, nor even the way similar cases have been decided by that particular court in the past. Instead the principal influence is the 'sentencing culture' of a particular bench, into which new recruits are gradually socialized by watching their more experienced colleagues at work. The ideology which gives substance to this culture is based on a twin belief in the uniqueness of the magisterial role itself, and also the individuality of each particular case. The latter belief explicitly rejects consistency as a virtue in its own right, while the former demands a balancing of public interests against those of the particular defendant in the light of moral judgements that only the magistrate is deemed qualified to make. Because sentencing is viewed by magistrates as a craft or mystery, whose rites are know only to initiates (as opposed to a rational enterprise dedicated to the pursuit of externally defined goals) this renders it both impervious to criticism from outside, and highly resistant to attempts at external control.

The breadth of sentencing discretion marks a significant disjuncture in the ideology of the criminal process (Lacey 1987). The values of certainty and consistency which, as we have seen, are supposed to be central to criminal law doctrine are far less evident at the sentencing stage, where they are replaced by a celebration of the judge's power to 'individualise' through finely tuned judgments of seriousness and hence to smooth out some of the wrinkles created by a rigorous application of substantive law (see Norrie 2001: Ch 10). Justice is to be done not through adherence to the rule of law, but through sentencers' discretion. The sentencer has extraordinary power over what kinds of information to solicit (for example, to decide whether a pre-sentence report is necessary) and what sort of sentence to give (for Crown Court judges, this often ranges between an absolute discharge and a substantial period of imprisonment). The Criminal Justice Act 1991 at last instituted a duty to give reasons for sentence (though only in custodial cases), and to explain these to the offender; yet a failure to do so has been held by the Court of Appeal not to constitute a breach of a legal duty (*Baverstock*, 1993 – a case in which Lord Taylor averred that the Act's provisions should not be regarded as a 'verbal tightrope' which judges had to walk: see Lacey 1994).

The sentencing aspect of the judicial role has significant executive or managerial elements. It is directly policy-oriented in that in selecting between a multiplicity of sentences, the sentencer is likely to be guided by a number of competing goals and visions of the function and justification of criminal justice, as well as by their own social attitudes. Some sentencers may be guided by a notion of desert; others by a desire to deter this and other offenders; others by a belief in the power of punishment to reform; and yet others (perhaps the majority) by a unreflective and largely unarticulated mixture of these goals and others such as denunciation, moral education, incapacitation and atonement. Though the Criminal Justice Act 1991 implicitly pins its colours to a desert or proportionality-based approach, it does so both in a relatively unconstraining way and in a manner which communicates mixed messages to the judiciary – as witnessed by the provision for longer incapacitative sentences in violent and sexual cases and the continuing relevance of rehabilitative factors to community sentences and to decisions about early release from prison. A vivid example of the Act's indeterminacy is that it has allowed the judiciary to find that the prevalence of a certain kind of offence in a particular locality affects the seriousness with which the present offence should be viewed (*Cunningham*, 1993). Indeed, the Act itself (as amended in 1993) provides that an offender's previous convictions or failure to respond to a previous sentence may be relevant to the seriousness of a later offence, and specifies that offending while on bail be regarded as an aggravating factor. These arguments appear to drive a coach and horses through the Act's establishment of a desert-based, backward-looking approach by incorporating forward-looking elements such as deterrence within the conception of seriousness – an impulse which, as we have seen, has been given further impetus and institutional accreditation by more recent legislation and would be accentuated by the current proposals. The indeterminacy of the Act has been particularly important because of the way in which that the political climate has shifted since its passage: the concern with determinate and consistent sentencing which informed the legislation has now been replaced by a far more punitive and deterrent approach in government thinking. This has been reflected in a rapid rise in the use of imprisonment from 1993 on (Lacey 1994; Cavadino and Dignan 2002: Ch 6), with the proportion of people sentenced to immediate custody for indictable offences in the Crown Court rising from 43% in 1990 to 48.9% in 1993, to 61% in 1996 and to 63% in 2000 (Home Office 2001b). In 2000, 106,200 people were received into immediate custody: the highest absolute number since 1928: looked at as a proportion, this represented 24.9% of those convicted of indictable offences – the highest percentage for over 40 years. Of those sentenced in the Crown Court, the average length of custodial sentences for males aged 21 or over was 24.2 months (Criminal Statistics 2000: 20–21). These dynamics are likely to be accentuated if the Criminal Justice Bill 2003 is passed in anything like its original form. And yet, according to Home Office statistics, England and Wales already has the second highest imprisonment rate in Western Europe: in 2000 we had 124 prisoners per 100,000 population, while Portugal had 127, Scotland 115, Germany 97, France 89 and Sweden 64 (Home Office 2000a: 3).

The inevitably purposive aspects of sentencing, along with the explicit discretion it involves, therefore make it a rather different enterprise from decision-making on questions of law, and it is generally neglected by textbook writers on criminal law. This neglect is unfortunate, since sentence is the conclusion of all trials resulting in a conviction, and since punishment is a key part of our social conception of criminal law. In many instances, the interplay between the questions of sentence and criminal law is such that the latter cannot be understood without some consideration of the former. For example, the distinction between murder and manslaughter developed and has been maintained largely because of the existence of a mandatory, fixed sentence for murder (formerly the death penalty, currently life imprisonment: see further Ashworth and Mitchell (eds) 2000). There is also a close relationship between the form of criminal law and the control of discretion at sentencing and other stages (Thomas 1978). If sentencing discretion were to be curtailed by attaching fixed sentences to particular offences, this would necessitate a refinement of offence definitions. Without such a refinement, sentencing reform could result in crudeness and effective disparity through false uniformity in the sentencing of very different cases within one broad offence definition. For example, in the case of theft, one offence definition currently covers everything from the casual theft of £1 to the planned theft of £1 billion: hence it is difficult to see how sentencing guidelines could be articulated with the legal definition of theft. If such offence definitions were to be refined, then the prosecutor would have greater discretion in choosing the charge, and a stronger lever in plea-bargaining. There would also be an increase in the jury's power to convict of one offence rather than another, through an increase in the number of 'lesser included offences' (ie less serious offences, such as manslaughter, whose elements are included in the offence charged, such as murder, and which it is therefore appropriate to leave to the jury as an alternative verdict). Disparity, uncertainty, inefficiency and injustice in sentencing have been important objects of academic and political debate over the past decade. Our perplexity about how to resolve these problems illustrates, among other things, the interrelationship between different stages of the criminal process and the danger of causing unforeseen shifts in the balance of power within the process by tinkering with one part without thinking about implications for another (Wasik and Pease 1987; Ashworth 2000: Ch 13): it is important to view criminal justice as one, albeit complex and diverse, set of processes.

A number of options are available to the sentencer: the choice among these options determines the ultimate experience of each convicted offender. The major *sentences* for adult offenders are imprisonment (sentences of imprisonment may also be suspended in exceptional circumstances); fines; community service (community punishment) orders; probation under the supervision of a probation officer (community rehabilitation orders: probation is often subject to conditions such as place of residence and may be combined with a fine or community punishment); combination orders; binding-over orders; curfew orders, which may be backed up by electronic monitoring; compensation orders; drug treatment and testing orders; and absolute and conditional discharges, which avoid most of the consequences of conviction such as a criminal record. In the cases of mentally disordered offenders and of offenders under the age of 21, a cluster of special measures and special institutions including a youth court and youth offender panels exist: in the wake of moral panics sparked by cases such as the killing of James Bulger, custody in special centres has become available for children as young as 12 (Ashworth 2000: Ch 12; Cavadino and Dignan 1997: Ch 9; Peay 2002). Sentencers are able to defer sentence where they feel material circumstances may change. The execution of sentences is administered by particular professional groups, the probation and prison services being the most important. Over the last decade, a number of pilot schemes have also operated to divert less serious offenders from the trial or sentencing process into victim-offender mediation. The current Thames Valley project selects young offenders for conferences oriented to restorative justice (Braithwaite 1989, 2002) and confronts offenders with their victims and with other community representatives. The project claims much reduced recidivism rates and commands some political support: orders aimed at restoration and reintegration are now encouraged for young offenders. Such practices of restorative justice therefore seem set to become a fully institutionalised aspect of the criminal process, operating alongside the standard sentencing system, as well as functioning to divert offenders from the criminal process altogether (Zedner 1994; Johnstone 2002).

Over the last 150 years, notwithstanding the statistical preponderance of non-custodial and financial penalties, imprisonment has however come to represent the 'paradigm' punishment in modern societies. In 2000, about 80,000 offenders were fined; 80,000 received custodial sentences, and 98,000 received some form of community sentence. But the trend, notwithstanding the criticisms of influential figures like Lord Woolf, the Lord Chief Justice, and Anne Owers, the Chief Inspector of Prisons, is towards a greater use of custody: in 2000, the average prison population was 64,600 – a slight drop from the peak of 65,300 in 1998: at the beginning of 2003, the prison population stood at 72,000. Home Office projections suggest that if sentencing practice continues in its present pattern, this will have risen to 91,400 by 2009. Given the tenor of sentencing policy already considered, this seems likely to be a relatively conservative assumption: on various alternative assumptions building in increasing sentencing severity, the Home Office projections for 2009 go as high as a staggering 109,600 (Home Office 2002d). Hidden within these global figures, their needs all too often ignored in a system in which they make up a mere twentieth of the prison population, are 4000 women prisoners – a figure which represents a 115% rise since 1993 (as compared with a 42% rise in the male prison population). As Foucault reminds us in the following passage, the birth of the prison and the shift from corporal to carceral punishments is closely tied to the emergence of the modern legal order:

Michel Foucault, *Discipline and Punish* (translation by A Sheridan, Allen Lane, 1977) pp 130–131

Broadly speaking, in monarchical law, one might say that punishment is a ceremonial of sovereignty; it uses the ritual marks of the vengeance that it applies to the body of the condemned man; and it deploys before the eyes of the spectators an effect of terror as intense as it is discontinuous, irregular and always above its own laws, the physical presence of the sovereign and of his power. The reforming jurists [of the late eighteenth century], on the other hand, saw punishment as a procedure for requalifying individuals as subjects, as juridical subjects; it uses not marks, but signs, coded sets of representations, which would be given the most rapid circulation and the most general acceptance possible by citizens witnessing the scene of punishment. Lastly, in the project for a prison institution that was then developing, punishment was seen as a technique for the coercion of individuals; it operated methods of training the body – not signs – by the traces it leaves, in the form of habits, in behaviour; and it presupposed the setting up of a specific power for the administration of the penalty. We have, then, the sovereign and his force, the social body and the administrative apparatus; mark, sign, trace; ceremony, representation, exercise; the vanquished enemy, the juridical subject in the process of requalification, the individual subjected to immediate coercion; the tortured body, the soul with its manipulated representations, the body subject to training. We have here the three series of elements that characterize the three mechanisms that face one another in the second half of the eighteenth century. They cannot be reduced to theories of law (although they overlap with such theories), nor can they be identified with apparatuses or institutions (though they are based on them), nor can they be derived from moral choices (though they find their justification in morality). They are modalities according to which the power to punish is exercised: three technologies of power.

In the recent history of sentencing theory (though not, in the last decade, of practice) there has been a growing emphasis on a move away from imprisonment through the development of alternative forms of 'community correction' such as community service. This development has been justified in more or less equal measure by humanitarian and by economic and other pragmatic considerations (Garland and Young 1983). Its more troubling ramifications in terms of the extension of surveillance and control into the community at large are only just beginning to be assessed. The introduction of electronic tagging is further stimulating debate about these implications. As Foucault observed, however, there is a strong continuity between the penal power of the prison and that of the forms of surveillance made possible both by social knowledges such as pedagogy and psychiatry and by new technologies such as electronic monitoring:

Foucault, *Discipline and Punish*, pp 227–228

The public execution was the logical culmination of a procedure governed by the Inquisition. The practice of placing individuals under 'observation' is a natural extension of a justice imbued with disciplinary methods and examination procedures. Is it surprising that the cellular prison, with its regular chronologies, forced labour, its authorities of surveillance and registration, its experts in normality, who continue and multiply the functions of the judge, should have become the modern instrument of penality? Is it surprising that prisons resemble factories, schools, barracks, hospitals, which all resemble prisons?

pp 301–302

[P]erhaps the most important effect of the carceral system and of its extension well beyond legal imprisonment is that it succeeds in making the power to punish natural and legitimate, in lowering at least the threshold of tolerance to penality.

The quest for cheaper and more humane non-custodial penalties must be set in the context of a more general malaise or even crisis in modern institutions of punishment: a sense of crisis which underpins recent swings of policy as between a focus on community-based penalties, diversion from the formal criminal process and resort to administrative penalties such as fines on the one hand, and punitive, imprisonment-oriented approaches, made economically possible by an expansion of the prison system through privatisation, on the other. In the following passage, Garland reflects on both this crisis and its relationship to the modern legal order outlined by Foucault:

David Garland, *Punishment in Modern Society* (OUP, 1990) p 4

[D]espite their institutional girding and a historical entrenchment stretching back to the early nineteenth century, a growing sense of doubt, dissatisfaction, and sheer puzzlement has now begun to emerge around our modern penal practices. The contemporary period is one in which penological optimism has given way to a persistent scepticism about the rationality and efficacy of modern penal institutions. This shift of attitude began to emerge toward the end of the 1960s when rising crime rates, growing prison unrest, and a collapse of faith in the rehabilitative ideal combined to undermine confidence in 'penal progress' and the inevitability of 'penal reform'. The new era has been one of continuing crisis and disruption in a penal system which no longer takes seriously the rehabilitative values and ideologies upon which it was originally based. Within this context it is becoming the conventional wisdom of criminologists, penologists and social scientists that contemporary methods – particularly that of imprisonment – appear increasingly to be 'irrational', 'dysfunctional' and downright counter-productive. Like the crime it is supposed to deal with, punishment is nowadays seen as a chronic social problem. It has become one of the most perplexing and perpetual 'crises' of modern social life ...

pp 7–8

Ever since the development of prisons in the early nineteenth century, and particularly since the emergence of a penological profession later in that century, there has been an implicit claim – and eventually a public expectation – that the task of punishing and controlling deviants could be handled in a positive way by a technical apparatus. It seems to me that this basic claim has now been put into question.

The question that arises today is not one of institutional adjustment and reform. It is a more basic question which asks whether the social processes and ramifications of punishment can be contained within specialist institutions of any kind. This is, in a sense, a crisis of penological modernism. It is a scepticism about a penal project that is as old as the enlightenment with its vision of punishment as one more means of engineering the good society, of organizing institutions so as to perfect mankind. After more than two centuries of rational optimism, even our 'experts' have begun to recognise the limits of social engineering and the dark side of social order. Our engineered world is facing its imperfections and is less optimistic, less confident ... Lacking a new vocabulary ... [c]ontemporary proponents of 'the justice model' or of 'general deterrence' have revived the liberal discourse of eighteenth-century jurisprudence, raising basic questions about the right to punish, the limits on state power, the responsibility and dignity of the offender, the nature of criminality, the depiction of human nature, and so on. There have also been important attempts to reintroduce questions which had previously been silenced by institutional operations, such as the role of the victim, or the responsibilities of the community in causing and preventing criminality. Notably too, there has been a re-emergence of moral arguments that claim that punitive (as opposed to correctional) measures can be a proper and defensible form of reaction to crime, a form of thinking which has been markedly absent from most twentieth-century penal discourse.

These newly revived forms of thinking about punishment are significant, not because they represent solutions to the current malaise, but because they indicate the extent of it. ...

It is not, then, only social scientists who are nowadays led to doubt the grounding and rationale of modern modes of punishment. The very staff of the criminal justice institutions are themselves increasingly perplexed as to what they are about. Consequently, it is not an idle or an 'academic' question that is being pursued when we seek to understand the foundations, forms, and effects of penal measures as they exist today. It is, on the contrary, a pressing practical issue.

Notwithstanding doubts about its proper role, imprisonment remains an important sentence even for offences of moderate seriousness, and one feature of how imprisonment is administered will serve as a graphic illustration of the tensions which Garland identifies. This is the system of *early release* (Ashworth 2000: 254–261). Most of those serving prison sentences, excluding certain categories of violent or otherwise very serious offenders, are eligible to apply for release on licence before the end of their sentences. Eligibility is governed by the Criminal Justice Act 1991, and depends on sentence length: those serving sentences of up to one year are released after one-half of their sentence has been served; those sentenced to between one and four years benefit from a presumption in favour of release after half of their sentence is served, but remain under supervision until the three-quarter point; those serving sentences of four years and more are considered for release by the Parole Board between half and two-thirds of the way through their sentences; they are subject to compulsory supervision for a period up to the three-quarter point. Decisions about these prisoners and about the release of life prisoners are made on the basis of criteria such as the likelihood of their re-offending. Under the statutory scheme, the Home Secretary had a veto over the Parole Board's decisions and the power to shape early release policies, though the former power has recently been held to breach human rights standards because of its combination of executive and judicial functions, and the power to fix the tariff to be served by life sentence prisoners and their ultimate release date has now been restored to the judiciary and the Parole Board (*ex p Anderson*, 2002). The Home Secretary has recently announced legislative proposals for a statutory framework: see **Chapter 6.IV.a.** Sections 10–13 of the Crime (Sentences) Act 1997 would have replaced this system with a significantly more restrictive scheme awarding prisoners serving sentences of two months and under two years with up to six 'early release days' a month for good behaviour, and making longer-term prisoners serving sentences of over three years eligible for release on the Parole Board's recommendation after serving five-sixths of their sentence. Happily, given the already overcrowded state of British prisons, this part of the Act was not implemented. Since 1999 all prisoners serving between three months and four years are eligible for release under curfew monitored by electronic tagging during the last two months of their sentence under the Home Detention Curfew Scheme. Early release arrangements are the object of several reform proposals under the Criminal Justice Bill 2002, but these would not affect the basic shape of the scheme.

There is a close connection between the early release system and Garland's argument. This lies in the fact that, while the system of early release has its roots in a rehabilitative belief that choosing the right moment for release from prison would increase chances of the offender's reform, its reality exists in pragmatic concerns with costs and prison overcrowding (Carlisle 1988). Early release has constituted a 'safety valve' for Government whenever the numbers of offenders sentenced to imprisonment threatens to overwhelm the prison system. Yet, notwithstanding the 1991 reforms which attempted to restore 'truth in sentencing' by establishing a more consistent framework for the relationship between articulated sentence and actual release date, early release continues to destabilise the legitimacy of law and order policy, particularly during periods in which Governments emphasise their punitive credentials. For it is a graphic illustration of the ultimate subservience of principle to pragmatism in criminal justice.

Finally, it is worth noting two disjunctures between the framework of sentencing and punishment and common understandings of criminal justice. First, debates about the relative propriety and importance of imprisonment and of community-based penalties tend to obscure the fact that the most common penalty over the last 100 years – though currently somewhat in decline – has been the fine (Bottoms 1983). It seems that the administrative nature of financial penalties sits as unhappily with the moralistic overtones of criminal justice today as it did when the nineteenth-century judges struggled with the question of whether the emerging summary offences were really 'criminal'. Secondly, although the apparent rationale of current sentences (like that of criminal law itself) appears to be individualistic – oriented to the deserts, the reform potential, the deterrence or the incapacitation of an individual offender – contemporary penality and criminalisation appear to be increasingly geared to the identification of problem populations and the control of particular groups. Some commentators have gone so far as to interpret the emergence of a 'New Penology':

> [T]he New Penology ... is actuarial. It is concerned with techniques for identifying, classifying and managing groups assorted by levels of dangerousness. It takes crime for granted. It accepts deviance as normal. It is sceptical that liberal interventionist crime control strategies do or can make a difference. Thus its aim is not to intervene in individuals' lives for the purpose of ascertaining responsibility, making the guilty 'pay for their crime' or changing them. Rather it seeks to regulate groups as a strategy of managing danger.' (Feeley and Simon 1994 p. 173: see also Rose 1999).

In the view of these American authors, the emergence of actuarial justice is closely tied to the existence of an underclass, and its distinctive marks are incapacitation and preventive detention. While these developments may be less advanced than in the United States, Britain too has recently witnessed the development of a number of policies and practices focussed upon what are constructed as 'high-risk' groups: young black men, paedophiles, 'problem families' living on housing estates; suspected terrorists. We should not let the individualism of criminal justice discourse blind us to their emergence, any more than we should allow the individualistic framework of criminal law doctrine to obscure our view of the broad structures of power which shape the implementation of criminal law and the conduct of the criminal process.

FURTHER READING

Abramson, Jeffrey (1994) *We the Jury: The Jury System and the Ideal of Democracy* (Basic Books, New York).

Baldwin, John and McConville, Michael (1979) *Jury Trials* (Clarendon Press).

Bottoms, A (1983) 'Neglected Features of Contemporary Penal Systems' in David Garland and Peter Young (eds) *The Power to Punish* (Heineman).

Bowling, Ben and Foster, Janet (2002) 'Policing and the Police' in Maguire et al (eds) *The Oxford Handbook of Criminology* (3rd edn, Oxford University Press) p 980.

Braithwaite, John (1989) *Crime, Shame and Reintegration* (Cambridge University Press).

Carlen, Pat (1976) *Magistrates' Justice* (Martin Robertson).

Cohen, Stanley (1985) *Visions of Social Control* (Polity Press).

Emsley, Clive (2002) 'The History of Crime and Crime Control Institutions' in Maguire et al (eds) *The Oxford Handbook of Criminology* (3rd edn, Oxford University Press) p 203.

Garland, David and Young, Peter (1983) *The Power to Punish* (Heinemann).

Gatrell, V A C (1994) *The Hanging Tree: Execution and the English People 1770–1868* (Oxford University Press).

Gelsthorpe, Lorraine (2002) 'Feminism and Criminology' in Maguire et al (eds) *The Oxford Handbook of Criminology* (3rd edn, Oxford University Press) p 112.

Heidensohn, Frances (2002) 'Gender and Crime' in Maguire et al (eds) *The Oxford Handbook of Criminology* (3rd edn, Oxford University Press) p 491.

Hood, Roger (1992) *Race and Sentencing* (Clarendon Press).

Jackson, John and Doran, Sean (1997) 'Judge and Jury: Towards a New Division of Labour in Criminal Trials' 60 Modern Law Review pp 759–778.

Johnstone, Gerry (2002) *Restorative Justice: Ideas, Values, Debates* (Cullompton, Devon, Willan Publishing).

Lacey, Nicola (2002) 'Legal Constructions of Crime' in Maguire et al (eds) *The Oxford Handbook of Criminology* (3rd edn, Oxford University Press) p 264.

McConville, Mike, Sanders, Andrew and Leng, Roger (1991) *The Case for the Prosecution* (Routledge).

Nelken, David (1987a) 'Criminal Law and Criminal Justice: Some Notes on Their Irrelation' in Dennis (ed) *Criminal Law and Justice* (Sweet & Maxwell).

Nobles, Richard and Schiff, David (2000) *Understanding Miscarriages of Justice* (OUP).

Peay, Jill (2002) 'Mentally Disordered Offenders, Mental Health and Crime' in Maguire et al (eds) *The Oxford Handbook of Criminology* (3rd edn, Oxford University Press) p 746.

Phillips, Coretta and Bowling, Ben (2002) 'Racism, Ethnicity, Crime and Criminal Justice' in Maguire et al (eds) *The Oxford Handbook of Criminology* (3rd edn, Oxford University Press) p 579.

Reiner, Robert (2000) *The Politics of the Police* (3rd edn, Oxford University Press).

— (2002) 'Media-made Criminality' in Maguire et al (eds) *The Oxford Handbook of Criminology* (3rd edn, Oxford University Press) p 376.

Rock, Paul (1993) *The Social World of an English Crown Court* (Clarendon Press).

Sanders, Andrew and Young, Richard (2002) 'From Suspect to Trial' in Maguire et al (eds) *The Oxford Handbook of Criminology* (3rd edn, Oxford University Press) p 1034.

Smart, Carol (1995) *Law, Crime and Sexuality* (Sage).

Zedner, Lucia (1994) 'Reparation and Retribution: Are They Reconcileable?' 56 Modern Law Review 228.

— (2002) 'Victims' in Maguire et al (eds) *The Oxford Handbook of Criminology* (3rd edn, Oxford University Press) p 419.

— (2002a) 'Dangers of Dystopia in Penal Theory' Oxford Journal of Legal Studies 341.

Chapter 2

Law and order

I.   Social and political constructions of disorder

Over the next two chapters we examine a broad range of offences and principles. We begin with public order as it is conventionally understood (riot, affray, violent disorder, breach of the peace) before moving on to look at group offending in the form of participation rules that apply to all offences (also known as aiding and abetting or complicity).

In the following chapter we continue to investigate the way criminal law, helped increasingly by advanced knowledge technologies, is used to regulate everyday life. There we focus on offences of harassment and personal violence, explore the regulation of drug and alcohol abuse, and introduce inchoate modes of liability, such as incitement and conspiracy.

The offences of affray and violent disorder are as familiar to the police as the assault and injury offences under the Offences Against the Person Act 1861 that are discussed at length in all criminal law texts. The powers of arrest that accompany public order offences are frequently used and, in conjunction with other offences, provide the police with a vital practical resource. We have argued that the doctrinal claims of many criminal commentators are overstated, even on the basis of the limited selection of offences with which they deal. Once a broader conception of criminal laws is adopted then the argument that criminal law is organised around general principles such as subjective 'mens rea' becomes strained and implausible. The frantic legislative activity in the broad area of public order in the last few years corroborates this stance. Public order offences not only affect some of our most fundamental liberties (of expression and association) but also challenge ideas about fair process with their increasing use of hybrid civil and criminal procedures (as in the Protection against Harassment Act 1997 and the Crime and Disorder Act 1998).

The method of criminalisation underpins huge areas of social regulation, including environmental pollution, health and safety at work, social security, tax, reproductive technology, road traffic, financial services and drugs. We cannot cover them all but their existence cautions us against inferring general principles from a very limited range of criminal prohibitions covering mainly indictable offences against the person and against property. There has been a proliferation of new statutory provisions dealing with the perceived social menaces of football hooliganism, possession of combat knives and other weapons, 'travellers', hunt saboteurs, stalkers and anti-social neighbours, all of which supplement (or in some cases overlap with) the existing offences of riot, violent disorder and affray, assault and battery, wounding and causing grievous bodily harm. This area has great intrinsic interest and importance, but is generally taught in law schools in the context of courses on civil liberties, thus diverting attention away from its implications for the general structure of criminal law. We seek to show how this area of criminal regulation, which impinges on some of the most contested areas of social life, illuminates our general understanding of criminal law.

Drawing on materials which adopt sociological, historical and political perspectives, we introduce some examples of the diverse social phenomena which have been understood as public disorder. Three themes can be identified in contemporary criminal justice legislation: youth, football and terrorism. Taking football as our case study, we explore the legislative scheme of public order offences, and discuss the interplay between criminal laws and criminal justice practices. We also consider an important means of extending standard modes of criminal liability which has a special significance in the public order sphere: laws on participation in crime. It is noticeable that public order has been a preoccupation of both Conservative and Labour governments in the last quarter century. The Home Office has not taken the opportunity to codify or rationalise major offence structures (with the exception of sexual offences, see **Chapter 5**). As we will see in **Chapter 3**, fatal and non fatal offences against the person, despite their seriousness, have to a large degree retained the same structure and appearance as in Victorian times (or earlier). Yet vast new legislative frameworks of specific and generic public order offences have been erected, added to, and tinkered with, in this short period.

D Garland, *The Culture of Control: Crime and Social Order in Contemporary Society* (OUP, 2001) p 1. Reprinted by permission of Oxford University Press.

We quickly grow used to the way things are. Today more than ever, it is easy to live in the immediacy of the present and to lose all sense of the historical processes out of which our current arrangements emerged. In the USA the public now seems quite accustomed to living in a nation that holds two million of its citizens in confinement on any given day, and puts criminal offenders to death at a rate of two or more per week. In much the same way, the British public no longer seems surprised by the existence of private prisons that house an increasing proportion of Britain's prisoners, and citizens go about their business hardly noticing the surveillance cameras that stare down on the streets of every major city. On both sides of the Atlantic, mandatory sentences, victims' rights, community notification laws, private policing, 'law and order' politics, and an emphatic belief that 'prison works', have become commonplace points in the crime control landscape ...

  To the moderately informed citizen who reads the papers or watches television news, these are taken-for-granted features of contemporary crime policy ... But the most striking fact about these crime policies, is that every one of them would surprise (and perhaps even shock) a historical observer viewing this landscape from the vantage point of the recent past. As recently as thirty years ago, each of these phenomena would have seemed highly improbable, even to the best-informed and most up-to-date observer.

... For at least two decades now, criminal law and penal policy have been working without clear route maps on a terrain that is largely unknown. If this field is to have any self-consciousness, and any possibility of self-criticism and self-correction, then our textbooks need to be rewritten, and our sense of how things work needs to be thoroughly revised.

I.a.   Conceptions of disorder

These headlines are taken from one day and one newspaper:
- 'Extra police sought to curb drink riots'
- 'Chief constable wants gaol sentences to deter weekend punch-ups after report on 250 "mass public disorders"'
- 'England's rural riots'
- 'Beating up on the rural bobby'
- 'Mobs shatter shire calm'
- 'Where the police tackled disturbances last year'

That these 'shock-horror' headlines appeared in *The Guardian* on a summer day, and not in one of the tabloid newspapers better-known for the high profile they give to such issues, is fitting testimony to the level of public and media pre-occupation with the issue of 'public order'. The headlines also serve to intro-duce the principal actors in the social construction of the 'law and order problem': the news media and their intended audiences; the police; and the political institutions who might be expected to provide extra police, jail sen-tences or other control mechanisms in response to the 'problem'. We are also provided with an emotive image of the offenders, depicted as 'mobs' – although, significantly, another headline declares '"White employed youth profile" puzzles theorists', acknowledging and reinforcing racist stereotypes of black unemployed youth as the standard threat to law and order. Furthermore, some of the more worrying aspects of criminal enforcement from a liberal perspective are introduced in the headline 'Gaol confessions queried'.

When we refer, as we tend to do easily and casually, to 'public order' or 'mass public disorder', what do we mean? This may seem a simplistic question, but the more thought one gives it, the more difficult it seems to be. One possible avenue would be a conceptual one. A straightforward conceptualisation of pub-lic disorder is that adopted by Gurr (1976: 9): 'manifestations of social disorder that are the objects of concerted public efforts at control'. However, this seems to beg the questions both of what constitutes 'social disorder' and of the criteria on which those efforts at control are based. If we reflect for a moment on general usage and the understandings of order and disorder which are embedded in language, we see immediately a variety of meanings, overlapping at their edges but nevertheless diverse. For example, we sometimes refer to 'the moral/social/political order', using the idea of 'order' more or less synony-mously with 'system', to mean something coherent, organised and stable: a system of power relations or norms. Used alone, the word 'order' can conjure up authority and hierarchy – order coerced by the exercise of power – but also ideas of peacefulness, tranquillity and rational organisation. We use the phrase 'law and order', which betokens not only the idea of authoritatively imposed peace, but also a certain mentality of authoritarianism. Conversely, the notion of 'disorder' conjures up a variety of images: chaos, lack of organisation, lack of coherence, system or regularity, even abnormality – perhaps corresponding to an idea of 'order ' as a 'natural' state of things.

In using the idea of *public* order or disorder, we raise the question of *whose* view of order 'public' order is. Of course, ideas of public order and disorder can be tied to descriptive meanings, for instance signifying merely 'peacefulness in places to which the public have access', or 'behaviour involving nuisance to the public or in public places', 'mass involvement in behaviour which threatens peace or tranquillity in public places', or 'behaviour causing widespread fear on the part of the public'. However, our use of the concept also typically assumes or asserts a particular, prevailing point of view about what constitutes order – for example, public order relative to institutionally accepted or imposed standards, or public disorder as threatening to the authority and stability of the state. Views differ about what constitutes order in particular contexts. Does 'public order' presuppose a consensus? Or does it rather assume the existence of (political) power to impose a particular conception of order? Who is to say whether a noisy picket line constitutes legitimate expression or an affront to public order? The problem is illustrated by research on football hooliganism:

P Marsh, E Rosser and R Harré, *The Rules of Disorder* (Routledge and Kegan Paul, 1978) pp 1–2, 28–29

The ostensible subject matter of this book is violence and disorder. Our settings are classrooms and the terraces of football grounds. Our *dramatis personae* are the people who inhabit these places and the people who speak about them in various public ways. Many people believe that there are schoolrooms and football grounds where civilized order is forever on the verge of breaking down. How have they come to believe this? Certainly not by direct experience, for few who 'know' about schoolroom or football violence have been present at its manifestations. Newspaper, radio and television reports are intimately involved in the formation of our images of the places beyond our immediate experience, and the pictures we form of the places featured in our study are no exception. Such reports suggest, often in the choice of vocabulary as much as in overt statement, that classrooms and football grounds are the settings for scenes of anarchy and disorder. But more than that, they imply a specific theory about the genesis of social violence. It is the theory that in these special places gaps widen out in the texture of order and without that order uncontrollable impulses lead to meaningless and violent behaviour.

Set against this picture and parallel to the theory that accompanies and supports it is the idea of the possibility of order as a creation of social instruments ordained for that very task, namely teachers, police, social workers, and, perhaps, in the last resort, parents.

As we will show, almost nothing of this popular conception survives a thorough examination of the day-to-day practices and explanations that are vouchsafed for them in vogue about the folk who inhabit these notorious places. Life, as it is lived in the classrooms and on the terraces, has almost none of the characteristics of anarchy and impulsiveness that are often attributed to it ...

Not only do we reveal a different interpretation of what is happening but we propose a very different psychological basis for this activity. We have come to see it through the eyes of the people who take part in it. They see their social life as a struggle for personal dignity in a general social framework that daily denies them this dignity. Far from valuing disorder, they are engaged in the genesis of significance for their lives and an order in their actions that is their own. The struggle begins when they see many of the things that seem routine to the rest of us as ways of devaluing them. The official forms of order can seem anomic to those who are systematically treated as non-persons, since, as they pursue their lives, they have no stake in the society for whose maintenance that order exists ...

Public interpretations of the 'unseemly' episodes of life in school and on the terraces are readily available in the popular press. 'Classroom chaos', and 'Fans run riot' will do to typify many hundreds of headlines. Such headlines both raise the issue of order in school and at the ground, and explicitly propose that it does not exist. Riots and chaos are essentially disorderly ...

To understand the force of these interpretations of what has been happening we must be clear as to what the contrasting but implicit concept of order is supposed to comprise. Order is associated with regularity and uniformity, that is with repetition of the same or similar elements ... In general in human contexts orderly behaviour has other features than just regularity. In particular, it seems to be required to be quiet, stable, and relatively slow ... [I]t seems also to be a taken-for-granted principle that in human affairs where there is order there is something corresponding to a rule to be looked for in the background of the actions which appear as orderly. Rule-following is the typical mode of action by which the structure of the context of the rule is reproduced in the actions of the people, though we may have to explain their aims or the acts they intend in other ways.

In their study of fans at an Oxford football ground, the authors identify 'hooligan' behaviour as itself 'ordered' in the sense of being rule-bound, involving patterns, roles and even careers, and as constituting a kind of ritualised aggression geared in particular to the assertion of masculinity.

The importance of point of view and the relativism inherent in the concept of order is further illustrated by the following philosophical reflections on the idea of authority – a notion closely linked, as we have seen, with the idea of public order. In the first passage, Steven Lukes addresses the problem of identifying relations of authority and distinguishing them from other relations:

S Lukes, 'Perspectives on Authority' in Pennock and Chapman (eds) ***Authority Revisited*, Nomos XXIX (New York University Press, 1987) pp 60–61**

What I seek to suggest ... is that such identification is an even more complex matter than is often supposed and always involves a process of interpretation. More particularly, I claim that every way of identifying authority is relative to one or more perspectives and is, indeed, inherently perspectival, and that there is no objective, in the sense of perspective-neutral, way of doing so ... Without analyzing or exploring the notion of "perspective" here, I mean it to refer to a point of view, a more or less integrated set of ways of seeing and judging matters of fact and practical questions, not excluding basic moral and political questions, and incorporating beliefs about the possibilities and necessities of social life and about how the self, its relation to society and its manner of reasoning are to be conceived. In this domain, of course, the reality upon which perspectives bear is itself in part constituted by contending perspectives. To speak thus of perspective is not in itself to embrace any deep form of relativism: some will be, for example, more perspicuous or comprehensive or consistent than others. Typically, different perspectives ... are associated with different positions within a social relation (such as an authority relation), with different social and political roles (e.g., the judicial, the bureaucrat's and the citizen's perspectives) and with different activities (e.g., the actor's, and observer's perspectives) ... I do not ... mean to suggest that any one person ever adopts only one perspective. We all engage in multiple relations, roles and activities and accordingly adopt and negotiate multiple perspectives.

Lukes goes on to distinguish between the perspectives of the exercise or holder of authority and those who are subject to it; that of the observer; the official perspective of society, definitively interpreted by judges and other state officials; unofficial and informal understandings of public rules and conventions which form various competing perspectives; the perspective emerging from social consensus, where it exists; and an impersonal, 'objective' perspective, the possibility of which Lukes calls into question. The importance of these different perspectives in understanding the complexity of the issues of social order and disorder is obvious. It also leads us directly to the question of power: who has the power to define and enforce a particular conception of order in any particular context?

M Thornton, 'Embodying the Citizen' in Thornton (ed) *Public and Private: Feminist Legal Debates* (OUP Australia, 1995) p 198

In classic definitional terms, citizenship is the status determining membership of a legally cognisable political community, although it involves more than a passive belonging. First, it includes abstract rights that are legally recognised and apply equally to all citizens, at least in a formal sense. Second, the concept includes a more subtle layer of meaning that operates to qualify the first, relating to the degree of participation within the community of citizens, although the nature of involvement differs according to the form of government, as Aristotle noted. It is apparent that variables such as gender, race, ethnicity and class are significant determinants of the extent of active participation within a particular polity ...

Marshall (E Marshall *Citizenship and Social Class and other essays*. Cambridge University Press, Cambridge 1950, p.74) terms the formal and active elements the *civil element* and the *political element*. He identifies the *social element* as a third dimension of citizenship, which comprises material rights of subsistence, together with economic and education rights associated with the welfare state ...

Citizenship, influenced by the Aristotelian tradition, has long been associated with realisation of the good life through service to the polity. More recently, this ideal has been debased as citizens have been reduced to disaffected groups of consumers, clients and bureaucratised bodies by the contemporary regulatory state.

K B Jones, 'On Authority: Or, Why Women Are Not Entitled to Speak' in Pennock and Chapman (eds) *Authority Revisited* (New York University Press, 1987) pp 152, 165

The standard analysis of authority in modern Western political theory begins with its definition as a set of rules governing political action, issued by those who are entitled to speak. Descriptions of those who act as public authorities, and of the norms and rules that they articulate, generally have excluded females and values associated with the feminine. This seems to be an unexceptional observation. After all, few women have been rulers in any political system of any epoch. But what if we argue that the very definition of authority as a set of practices designed to institutionalise social hierarchies lies at the root of the separation of women-qua-women from the process of "authorizing"? If we argue further that the dichotomy between compassion and authority contributes to the association of the authoritative with the male voice, then the implication is that the segregation of

women and the feminine from authority is internally connected to the concept of authority itself ... The dominant discourse on authority places
strict limits on the publicly expressible, and limits critical reflection about
the norms and values that structure 'private' life, and which affect the
melodies of public speech. By rejecting the ambiguities that our feelings
introduce, we reject a mode of compassionate authority.

Thornton and Jones both draw attention to the marginalisation or exclusion of
some citizens from the processes of public debate. Citizenship is only fully
realised for those individual and groups with the authority and power to be
heard. More than this, it is not merely a question of who is heard but who
makes the rules about who is heard. Those from ethnic minorities, the poor,
and the 'anti-social' are excluded from genuine participation in the social
definition of public order and authority. This issue of marginalisation also calls
into question assumptions about the extent of consensus underpinning social
conceptions of order and disorder. Can law in our society claim to represent
any conception of justice capable of reconciling these conflicting perspectives?

I.b.   Legitimate protest or moral panics?

The issues of power and perspective cannot be resolved by approaching the
identification of public order and disorder via a conceptual method. What other
approaches might we take to understanding the social phenomena in question?
If we are to grasp something of the social meaning of 'public disorder', we must
begin by moving to political history, to consider some examples of behaviour
understood as constituting public disorder, in response to which public order
law has been or could have been used. The examples which follow have been
selected principally in the light of contemporary public preoccupations with
disorder and debates about the propriety and efficacy of the use of law and
police powers to curb unrest and disorder.

Disorder associated with the existence and collective behaviour of gangs is, of
course, diverse, modern examples including fighting between British National
Party and other extreme right-wing groups and anti-racist groups, and between
rival groups of football fans. Stanley Cohen's study of societal reactions to the
'mods and rockers' in the 1960s was the first sustained development of the
concept of 'moral panic'. While 'mods and rockers' have faded (to be replaced
by other folk devils in areas such as drugs and sex offences) the term *moral panic*
has taken a firm hold in modern sociological theory.

**S Cohen, *Folk Devils and Moral Panics* (St Martin's Press, 1972)
pp 9ff, 28ff**

Societies appear to be subject, every now and then, to periods of moral
panic. A condition, episode, person or group of persons emerges to

become defined as a threat to societal values and interests; its nature is presented in a stylized and stereotypical fashion by the mass media; the moral barricades are manned by editors, bishops, politicians and other right-thinking people … Sometimes the object of the panic is quite novel and at other times it is something which has been in existence long enough, but suddenly appears in the limelight. Sometimes the panic passes over and is forgotten, except in folklore and collective memory; at other times it has more serious and long-lasting repercussions and might produce such changes as those in legal and social policy or even in the way society conceives itself.

One of the most recurrent types of moral panic in Britain since the war has been associated with the emergence of various forms of youth culture … whose behaviour is deviant or delinquent … The Teddy Boys, the Mods and Rockers, the Hell's Angels, the Skinheads and the Hippies have all been phenomena of this kind … But groups such as the Teddy Boys and the Mods and Rockers have been distinctive in being identified not just in terms of particular events (such as demonstrations) or particular disapproved forms of behaviour (such as drug-taking or violence) but as distinguishable social types. In the gallery of types that society erects to show its members which roles should be avoided and which should be emulated, these groups have occupied a constant position as folk devils; visible reminders of what we should not be …

At the beginning of the [1960s], the term 'Modernist' referred simply to a style of dress, the term 'Rocker' was hardly known outside the small groups which identified themselves this way. Five years later, a newspaper editor was to refer to the Mods and Rockers incidents as 'without parallel in English history' and troop reinforcements were rumoured to have been sent to quell possible widespread disturbances …

The scene of the first Mods and Rockers event, the one that was to set the pattern for all the others and give the phenomenon its distinctive shape, was … Clacton, a small holiday resort on the east coast of England … Easter 1964 was worse than usual. It was cold and wet, and in fact Easter Sunday was the coldest for eighty years. The shopkeepers and stall owners were irritated by the lack of business and the young people had their own boredom and irritation fanned by rumours of cafe owners and barmen refusing to serve some of them. A few groups started scuffling on the pavements and throwing stones at each other. The Mods and Rockers factions – a division initially based on clothing and life styles, later rigidified, but at that time not fully established, started separating out. Those on bikes and scooters roared up and down, windows were broken, some beach huts were wrecked and one boy fired a starting pistol in the air. The vast number of people crowding into the streets, the noise, everyone's general irritation and the actions of an unprepared and undermanned police force had the effect of making the two days unpleasant, oppressive and sometimes frightening.

I am concerned here with the way in which the situation was initially interpreted and presented by the mass media, because it is in this form that most people receive their picture of both deviance and disasters ... On the Monday morning following the initial incidents at Clacton, every national newspaper, with the exception of *The Times* ... carried a leading report on the subject. The headlines are self-descriptive: 'Day of Terror by Scooter Groups' (*Daily Telegraph*), 'Youngsters Beat Up Town – 97 Leather Jacket Arrests' (*Daily Express*) ... Straight reporting gave way to theories especially about motivation: the mob was described as 'exhilarated', and 'hell-bent for destruction' etc. Reports of the incidents themselves were followed by accounts of police and court activity and local reaction ...

Cohen goes on to describe the ways in which media reporting exaggerated and distorted the events and created expectations that they would recur, suggesting that the reporting responded to the need to produce 'newsworthy' items on a weekend which was 'particularly dull from a news point of view' (p 45). His observations about the relationship between media and public opinion are of general importance (pp 65–66):

... [There was] a striking difference ... between the mass media and the various types of public opinion. For most dimensions of this comparison, the mass media responses to the Mods and Rockers were more extreme and stereotypical than any of the sample of public opinions surveyed. This is not to say that the mass media images were not absorbed and were not the domi-nant ones to shape the reaction, but rather that the public coded these images in such a way as to tone down their more extreme implications. In this sense the public could be said to be better informed about the phenomenon than the media or the moral entrepreneurs whom the media quoted.

Cohen argues that such events tend to be followed by a spiral of 'deviance amplification' (p 18):

An initial act of deviance, or normative diversity ... is defined as being worthy of attention and is responded to punitively. The deviant or group of deviants is segregated or isolated and this operates to alienate them from conventional society. They perceive themselves as more deviant, group themselves with others in a similar position, and this leads to more deviance. This, in turn, exposes the group to further punitive sanctions and other forceful action by the conformists – and the system starts going round again ...

Cohen's conclusions about the relation between societal, media and law enforcement reaction and the development of this particular 'public order problem' give pause for thought to students of criminal law. There is also reason to question the conventional wisdom that the incidents had 'no parallel in history':

G Pearson, *Hooligan: A History of Respectable Fears* (Macmillan, 1983) pp 74, 188–189

The word 'hooligan' made an abrupt entrance into common English usage, as a term to describe gangs of rowdy youths, during the hot summer of 1898. 'Hooligans' and 'Hooliganism' were thrust into the headlines in the wake of a turbulent August Bank Holiday celebration in London which had resulted in unusually large numbers of people being brought before the courts for disorderly behaviour, drunkenness, assaults on police, street robberies and fighting. One of the more alarming aspects of these Bank Holiday disturbances was that they highlighted fierce traditions of resistance to the police in working class neighbourhoods, so that not uncommonly policemen attempting to make street arrests would be set upon by large crowds – sometimes numbering two or three hundred people – shouting 'Rescue! Rescue!' and 'Boot him!' ...

From the early 1600s the streets of London and other cities had been terrorised by a succession of organised gangs – calling themselves the Muns, Hectors, Bugles, Dead Boys, Tityre Tus, Roaring Boys, Tuquoques, Blues, Circling Boys, Bickers, Roysters, Scowrers, Bravadoes, Bawcubites and Mohocks – who found their amusement in breaking windows, demolishing taverns, assaulting the Watch, attacking wayfarers and slitting the noses of their victims with swords, rolling old ladies in barrels, and other violent frolicks. If a servant or waiter should happen to be killed in the act of wrecking a tavern, it was said to have been considered a great joke to inform the proprietor to 'Put him on the bill!'. The gangs also fought pitched battles among themselves, dressed with coloured ribbons to distinguish the different factions ...

The Nickers were said to specialise in window-breaking ... There were ... dramatic portrayals of these gangs, such as John Gay's *The Mohocks* (1712) which held up to ridicule the exaggerated fears surrounding their exploits ... and the extravagance of the rumours circulating around the Mohocks prompted some observers to question whether they existed at all, or whether they were not like the stories of hobgoblins and boggarts. But they were real enough, and what little is known about these gangs and their detailed habits suggests that they were of upper-class extraction, with some affinity to the notorious 'Hell Fire' clubs ...

Even in their barest detail these accounts of street robbers, thieves and pick-pockets, drunkenness, mob violence and the lawless antics of upper-class rowdies give the lie to simple-minded notions of an era of pre-industrial calm. The streets of Old London – which had neither an effective system of street-lighting nor a police – were perilous in the extreme. As to the allegedly quiet countryside of Merrie England, although the pattern of crime and disorder was appreciably different in ways that corresponded to the altered social landscape of the pre-industrial world, things were no better. The persistent interruption of food riots, the burning of hay-ricks and barns, smuggling offences, wrecking and coastal plunder, and crimes associated with poaching and trespass are all well documented in the eighteenth century.

The phenomena which Pearson and Cohen discuss have, of course, a variety of socio-economic and cultural roots, and they serve to remind us of the diversity as well as the historical pervasiveness of behaviour which can be constructed as a 'public order problem'. We could multiply examples of 'gang' behaviour (such as that of the Mafia and other forms of 'organised crime' syndicates (see **Chapter 4.I.c.**), not all of which are conventionally thought of as raising 'public order' issues. As we multiply our historical examples, we find the boundaries between the activities of 'street gangs', 'organised crime', 'hooliganism' and 'political demonstration' increasingly blurred:

J Bellamy, *Crime and Public Order in England in the Later Middle Ages* (Routledge and Kegan Paul, 1973) pp 70–71

The first question which needs to be asked about medieval criminal gangs concerns the size of their membership. Here we must be careful to separate the criminal himself from his hirers or maintainers, and especially those he relied on for shelter and food, his receivers. James Coterel, a gang leader who flourished around 1330 in northern Derbyshire, regularly had with him and the hard core of his band his two brothers and three or four other men of local origin. When outlawed after two or three years of misdeeds, in March 1331, the gang roved through the Peak district and northern Nottinghamshire from hide-out to hide-out. Coterel was joined as he wandered by a number of recruits, some already outlawed but most not. They must have numbered at least twenty, and with their assistance the gang leader was able to extend his criminal activities noticeably, particularly in the direction of extortion ...

There are one or two references to very large bands of criminals but they are not common. William Beckwith of Beckwith, Yorkshire, who waged a private war from 1387 to 1392 against the officials of the Duchy of Lancaster in Knaresbrough and Ockeden chases, had as the basis of his band a score of kinsfolk and friends from the Knaresborough region. In 1390, when the forces of law were closing in, he was reported to have fled to the deepest part of the forest with no fewer than 500 confederates all of them had been indicted in court.

Bellamy reminds us that social attitudes to the activities of gangs have not always taken the form of moral panic (p 82):

What impact did the activities of the criminal bands have on society at large? We may surmise that there was fear mixed with a grudging admiration. The chronicler Henry of Knighton quite approved of the murder of

Roger Bellers by the Folvilles and their allies. When he referred to the kidnapping of Sir Richard Wylughby he portrayed the villains as bold men taking reasonable revenge against the judges of trailbaston who had visited all parts of England the previous year. Richard Folville he described not as a criminal, but as a fierce, daring and impudent man. To have feuded, used violence, to have poached or pillaged, was not at this time held to debar any man from local or even national office.

Some of the assumptions underlying interpretations of events in terms of the existence of 'gangs' or 'subcultures' are noted by Thompson in his study of the eighteenth-century forest disturbances involving the 'Blacks':

E P Thompson, *Whigs and Hunters* (Penguin, 1975) pp 194–195

What twentieth-century criminologists describe as subculture eighteenth-century magistrates described as gangs. What is at issue is not whether there were any such gangs (there were) but the universality with which the authorities applied the term to any association of people, from a benefit society to a group akin to Fagin's den, which fell outside the law. This was partly self-delusion in the minds of the magistracy, and unwillingness to acknowledge the extent of disaffection with which they were faced: if after enclosure, fences were thrown down – if turnpikes were attacked – if coal-heavers besieged their sub-contractors – if threatening letters were received, it was somehow comforting to assert that these outrages were the work of 'a gang'. And the category was self-fulfilling: if an offender was then picked up, and if information was extorted as to his associates, then it confirmed that the 'gang' had been 'run to earth'. In the silence of terror which might follow their punishment, the authorities would assume further confirmation of the theory of the gang. There had been a kill and the rest of the 'gang' (if any) had 'gone to ground' ...

[These critical reflections on the indiscriminate use of the concept of 'gangs'] ... remain relevant to the question of the Blacks and the Black Act. For the category 'criminal' can be a dehumanizing one: if a group of men are described as a 'gang', then they have been described in such a way as to disallow more careful examination. They are seen ... as a threat to authority, property and order.

K Thompson, *Moral Panics* (Routledge, 1998) p 139

[T]he concept of moral panics was developed in the 1970s by British sociologists, drawing on ideas taken from American sociological theories of deviance and collective behaviour ... [Whilst the concept] became relatively neglected by British sociologists after the 1970s ... it was frequently used by other people to describe the increasingly rapid succession of scares in the mass media about risks to the social and moral order. The British sociologists who first developed the concept were interested in such phenomena as symptoms of underlying structural changes and conflicts, particularly the impact of economic changes on different sections of social classes and related ideological conflicts. In the 1980s, however, the focus of sociologists turned to the rise of the New Right economic policies and ideology, involving economic deregulation coupled with cultural and moral re-regulation. The concept of moral panic seemed less relevant because it appeared to focus on episodic and discrete events, giving too much attention to symptoms rather than focusing directly on political-economic developments and their relationship to ideological trends ... [In the 1990s] we have reintroduced the possibility of regarding moral panics as symptomatic of developments that are of wider significance, rather than viewing them simply as unrelated episodes of collective behaviour ...

Thompson concludes that moral panics are characteristic of the modern 'risk society', a term that encompasses the idea that the identification and management of risk is central to contemporary life; it is a concept we explore in more depth in **Chapter 3.I.a.** below.

I.b.i. Problem populations

Another important focus of concern about public order relates to the behaviour of groups who do not conform to contemporary conventions about lifestyle, such as Roma and other travellers for whom many local authorities do not provide sites for camping, and refugees and 'asylum seekers'. The role of criminal justice systems in controlling problem populations has been well documented. This accords with Waddington's historical review of political disorder in London. Using examples ranging from the 1910–1914 suffragette marches, through unemployment marches in the 1930s to the anti Vietnam war protests of the 1960s, he shows that violence is associated with protesters that have been castigated as 'subversive', 'unpatriotic' or communist' (1992: 29).

Earlier examples of social preoccupations with vagrancy related to similar anxieties to those which underlie more recent responses to direct action from hunt saboteurs, animal rights and environmental protesters. Each attracts different, sometimes contrasting, media and police responses. The hunt 'saboteur' contrasts with the 'respectable protester' in the Countryside March (2002). From a criminal law perspective, nothing divides these different forms of group action. It is only through the social, political and police refractions that events acquire their 'disorderly' or 'legitimate' hues.

A L Beier, *Masterless Men* (Methuen, 1985) pp 9–11, 52

The legal concept of vagabondage originated in the distinction between the able-bodied and the 'impotent' poor. The division dates from the fourteenth century, when Parliament made masterlessness an offence, but its fullest development came under the Tudors and early Stuarts. Most of the thirteen poor laws passed between 1495 and 1610 had as a first premise the discrimination between those able and unable to work ... An Act of 1531, for instance, encapsulated the three characteristics of poverty, fitness for labour, and unemployment by defining the vagabond as any man or woman being whole and mighty in body and able to labour, having no land, master, nor using any lawful merchandise, craft or mastery whereby he might get his living.

This prescription lasted until a new statute altered it slightly in 1597.

Vagrancy charges might also arise under labour legislation. The Statute of Artificers of 1563 provided that if the able-bodied poor refused to work in husbandry, or left work before their terms finished, they could be arrested and imprisoned ... the reason for regulating the unemployed was not a shortage of labour, as in the later Middle Ages. Rather it was the rising numbers of able-bodied poor that troubled officials. There the fourth and fifth characteristics of vagrants – rootlessness and disorderliness – entered the equation. Governments generally distrusted economic and social alterations and intervened to control them, although not always successfully. With vagrants, they were afraid what might happen if they were left to their own devices. The masterless man represented mutability when those in power longed for stability. He stood for poverty, which seemed to threaten their social and political dominance. Fundamentally, in prescribing that the vagrant be employed, governments were preoccupied with a problem of disorder.

The young were a special worry and were singled out in numerous statutes ... Beggars were another troublesome group, as might be expected from the learned view of them. State action again began in the fourteenth century as part of an attempt to make the able-bodied work. Tudor governments intensified the campaign, because they linked mendicancy with disorder ... The vagrancy legislation also covered a vast array of occupations: pedlars and tinkers, soldiers and mariners, many entertainers, students, unlicensed healers and even fortune-tellers ... Wizards and unlicensed healers were accused of fraud, while entertainers, military men and tinkers were thought to cause disruption ... Gypsies and the Irish were also treated as vagrants ... Both groups were accused of sedition and treason, but by the seventeenth century the Irish were considered the more dangerous. As well as being aliens, they came to England in waves of immigration caused by war and famine. To make matters worse, the native Irish were associated with popery and rebellion ... The laws were employed, finally, against disorders that were not even in the statute books under vagrancy ... Migrants were also policed under the legislation. When poor relief became law in the reign of Elizabeth I, officials began 'warning out' immigrants under threat of vagrancy charges. This was to stop them from burdening the poor rates. By law the poor were entitled to succour in their birthplaces or their last places of residence. Because anyone moving to another parish might be eligible for relief in two places it was natural, if inhumane, to query settlement rights and treat claimants as vagrants. The effect was to turn honest immigrants into vagrants by denying them residence rights ...

Vagrants were a menace to the social order because they broke with the accepted norms of family life. If the ideal was the patriarchal household, they had no part in it, and for that reason they were considered pariahs.

Such preoccupations find their modern counterpart, one might argue, in social security rules which, in effect, make the homeless ineligible for various kinds of benefit. Echoes of the practice of 'warning out' sound in policing practices such as those seen in Wiltshire in 1985, and in the Anti-Social Behaviour Orders in the Crime and Disorder Act 1998 (see **Chapter 3** below), the paedophile register first established by the Sex Offenders Act 1997 and associated injunctions. As we have already suggested, it may be tempting to distinguish between 'political' protest and (apparently) indiscriminate 'gang' or hooligan behaviour but this often proves an illusory line.

I.b.ii.   Riots

The term 'riot' has, of course, a technical legal meaning and a legal history, to which we shall return below. In popular discourse, however, the term is used more generally to refer to disturbances characterised by high degrees of disorder which are seen as verging on the uncontainable. Riot, in other words, tends to represent the ultimate threat to order and authority: an expression of anarchy, rebellion or chaos. The word has been used in the context of a variety of types of disturbance, notably industrially-related demonstrations and protests concerning fundamental social conditions, such as the price of food. Most recently, the term has been used in emotive and normative ways to characterise a number of civil disturbances in inner city areas (especially Brixton in 1980 and Bradford in 2001) and the 'poll tax' demonstrations of the early 1990s. Since both the police and protesters believe themselves to be in the right, each engages the use of force to assert the common good. 'Protesters can ... claim to be the moral equal of the police with a degree of success rarely achieved by criminals' (Waddington 2000: 157). Social reactions to these disturbances echo many of the themes (such as press exaggeration and distortion, fear of outsiders, the association of deprivation, disadvantage and class conflict with disorder) we have already encountered; they also introduce in particularly graphic and disturbing form the importance of racist attitudes in the social construction of public disorder. In each case, serious conflict with the police, fighting and damage to property followed a particular set of actions or policing strategies which confirmed local perceptions of police discrimination against a disadvantaged population. Once again, the role of the news media is implicated:

C Sumner, '"Political Hooliganism" and "Rampaging Mobs"; The national press coverage of the Toxteth "Riots"' in C Sumner (ed) *Crime, Justice and the Mass Media* (Cropwood Conference Series No 14, 1987) pp 25–28

The Scarman Report on the 'Brixton Disorders' (1982) is disappointingly quiet about the role of the media in such conflicts. It suggests timidly that the media may have given problem areas like Brixton a bad name by not paying enough attention to the good that goes on there (p.112). More strongly the Report suggests that television coverage 'escalated' the troubles by encouraging 'playing up to the cameras' and 'copy cat' riots (p.111) ...

It is my contention that examination of the immediate news coverage of the Toxteth troubles by the national press shows that the perspective of the Liverpool police chief predominated and that it treated the event as an attack on the police by black criminal hooligans; and that this partial, instant reaction of the press either at best served to justify, or at worst to precipitate, the Home Office's immediate decision to 'tool up' the police (provide them with more riot gear and weapons). Other possible interpretations of the event and definitions of the problem were either relegated to secondary spaces in the newspaper or dealt with in low-circulation newspapers ...

One way in which a powerful section of the British national press functions as propaganda for the contemporary political economy is by criminalising resistance to that social order. This function may not be produced through consciously biased reporting but through routine reliance on statements by state officials, notably the police. Its effect must inevitably be to encourage a coercive response to social dissent. All this occurred in the coverage of the Toxteth 'riots'.

Monday July 6th 1981

Mr. Oxford [Liverpool's chief constable] said: 'I have no doubt at all that this is not a racial issue as such. It is exclusively a crowd of black hooligans intent on making life unbearable and indulging in criminal activities' ...

Unfortunately, journalists lean so heavily on official sources that the Chief Constable's view of the affair dominated the day's papers. There *was* a contrary view ... One community spokesman, John Arboine, for example, saw the matter like this:

The trouble was the climax to the community's irritation over the number of police in the area. Young blacks have been constantly stopped and not treated like human beings. It has now escalated to the point where they have lost faith in the police and authority. (*Daily Mirror*, p.14)

But that view was not represented in the headlines and front-page reports, nor did it even seem to mediate or soften them: instead the police perception of the event as an orchestrated criminal attack on law and order was right to the fore. The *Mail* got the police perspective just right with the headline 'BLACK WAR ON POLICE' followed by a photograph of the police lines (from behind) captioned 'facing the fury of the mob' ...

The perspective of the community leader quoted in Sumner's article on the meaning and causes of the disorders is echoed in radical commentaries which saw them as the product of social disadvantage, racism, police malpractice, relative deprivation, political exclusion, and perceptions of injustice; see particularly J Benyon, 'Interpretations of Civil Disorder', in Benyon and Solomos (1987). It also finds some expression in the Scarman Report (1981). These arguments have important implications for the policy of 'zero tolerance' policing. The practice and structure of policing are addressed in **section III.** below.

Like other phenomena associated with public disorder, recent urban troubles are not without historical analogy:

S Field and P Southgate, *Public Disorder* (HMSO, 1982) pp 4–5

It has been widely suggested that the recent riots are quite unprecedented in scale in this century, and that in the 1930s equally high levels of unemployment were not accompanied by disorder. These views are, at best, misleading ... To counteract such amnesia it is worth cataloguing some of the major disorders which occurred before the last war and which are now beyond the living memory of many of us.

... The General Election of 1910 was accompanied by disturbances around the country, in Droitwich and High Wycombe the Riot Act was read (*Times* January 22 & 23, 1910). In the same year there was serious rioting in the Tonypandy area of the Rhondda, as a result of industrial unrest ... Troops were sent in, and there were many casualties. In 1911 Liverpool experienced its 'bloody Sunday'. Rioting broke out following a mass meeting held by trade union leaders. There were many injuries. Throughout the period 1910–1914 there were a series of disorders associated with the suffragette movement; they involved window breaking, arson of public buildings, bombings and slashing of pictures in the National Gallery ... In 1919, following demobilisation, serious rioting occurred throughout the country. In May and June there were race riots in South Wales, the East End and Liverpool when whites attacked blacks. In Cardiff three people were shot dead. In July the Peace Day celebrations were attended by riots in Wolverhampton, Salisbury, Epsom, Luton, Essex, Coventry and Swindon. In Luton the town hall was destroyed by arson.

Police and firemen were attacked with bricks, stones and bottles and there was widespread looting. On the first of August the police in Liverpool went on strike, and severe rioting and widespread looting began, continuing for four days and nights. Steel helmeted troops and tanks were sent in, there were bayonet charges and shooting. In July and August there were also riots and battles between police and youths in London: in Greenwich, Hammersmith, Tottenham, Edmonton, Wood Green, Barking and Brixton (*New Society*, 13th August 1981).

The extent to which riots are spontaneous or are planned was a vexed issue in public debate about the 'riots' of the late twentieth century, in which Conservative politicians were comforted by the thought that the disturbances might have been caused by agents provocateurs (again the theme of outsiders). The examples of direct action in relation to the community charge or 'poll tax' and, more recently, environmental and animal rights campaigns suggest that public 'disorder' does not fit either of these extremes. The following discussion of earlier riots suggests a partially structural rationale which avoids the crude instrumentalism of the provocation analysis, whilst interpreting riots as 'ordered' from a different point of view, in a way which recalls Marsh et al's discussion of football hooliganism:

J Walter, 'Grain riots and popular attitudes to the law: Maldon and the crisis of 1629' in J Brewer and J Styles, *An Ungovernable People* (Hutchinson, 1980) pp 47–48, 81–83

A complex historical reality lies imprisoned within the legal strait-jacket defining the crime of riot. Not surprisingly then, ambiguity still surrounds historians' treatment of popular disorder in early modern England. In the case of the food riot, however, it is perhaps becoming more generally accepted that the pattern of disorder was somewhat different from that suggested by the fear of the authorities, or that posited by a too simple relationship between poverty, harvest failure and a presumed popular inclination to riot ... The authoritative stereotype of the food riot as a collective form of theft with violence rarely captured the reality of such disorder. Riot was seldom, if ever, a simple and unpremeditated response to hunger and starvation. As the ultimate political weapon of the poor, the food riot was often the culmination of a preceding exchange between the poor and their governors in which the threat of popular violence had been used (unsuccessfully) to coerce authority into a constant point of reference in a more enduring relationship between rulers and ruled ...

The crowd's appearance was not designed to end its grievance unilaterally, but to do so by securing (or coercing) the necessary exercise of authority. By publicly confronting authority with its failings, the crowd attempted (more often than not successfully) to recall their governors to their self-proclaimed duty of protecting the poor. In so doing, the poor displayed a perhaps surprising knowledge of the law and an often acute awareness of its uses ...

The example of Maldon also enables us to penetrate the rhetoric of authority and to examine the nature of the magisterial response to disorder. Far from being one of proscription and punishment ... the authorities' reaction was often one which implied a recognition of the legitimacy of the complaint, if not the manner of its making. Characteristically, as in the first Maldon riot, the central government accorded the local authorities considerable autonomy in handling the aftermath of riot ... [Limitations on authority in dealing with such disorder] found their role in authorities' realization that the best way of handling disorder was not necessarily to be found in a rigorous enforcement of the law against riot. But the second Maldon riot, openly challenging authority and carrying within it the seeds of further disorder at a time of particular stress for both county and central government, revealed the latent strength of the law. It prompted an effective demonstration of the law's ability ... to meet a persistent challenge to authority ... with decisive action and exemplary punishment.

The ability to define what constituted acceptable popular action through the exercise of law was of crucial importance to the government's maintenance of social order. It is clear from the tradition of riot that a knowledge of the criminal law's scope and of the government's ability to exact the penalties it prescribed was firmly located within the popular consciousness, alongside an awareness of other laws more beneficial to the poor. If in this period grain riots did not generally conform to the government's stereotype of collective theft with violence nor spill over into a conscious attack on the social and political order, this was in part at least because popular awareness of the law of property was already sufficient to suggest that any such direct challenge would invite savage retaliation.

I.c.   Thematic summary

We have covered considerable ground in this section, exploring conceptions of order and disorder, inclusion and exclusion, from sociological, political and historical perspectives. Because public order is central to the criminal justice system, this analysis is informative for criminal law in general, not just for that part of it that is categorised as 'public order' law. Moral panics and risk society provide useful theoretical concepts when examining criminal law responses to harassment (**Chapter 3**), mugging and burglary (**Chapter 4**), sexual offences (**Chapter 5**) and corporate manslaughter (**Chapter 6**). Understanding criminal justice policies and practices as products of many interlocking forces is both useful and necessary.

The examples of 'public disorder' we have been considering are merely some of the most significant among a vast array of instances we might have chosen. For example, on a wide view of public disorder, people from different political perspectives might include soliciting for the purposes of prostitution; kerb-crawling or otherwise sexually harassing women; public drunkenness; crimes committed by the police; organised crime; joy-riding; drunken and/or dangerous driving; environmental pollution; and blasphemy. Moreover, we have scarcely touched on terrorism, which is almost universally acknowledged as a major threat to public order, and one increasingly dominating the criminal justice and due process agenda. The instances we have considered provide the necessary context in which to appreciate the operation and legitimation of institutionalised legal responses to disorder, and we now draw out some general themes from them.

First, it is clear that notions of public disorder cover an enormous variety of kinds of behaviour, in terms of participants, content, motivations and consequences. This is true even of the idea of public disorder as conventionally used. Why should an assault or street theft not be regarded as a threat to public order? In fact, such assaults, constructed as 'muggings' in the 1970s, were seen as a 'law and order problem' in an episode which had all the classic hallmarks of Cohen's moral panic (S Hall et al 1978).

This example, among others, demonstrates the malleability of the notion of disorder as a threat to state authority and the ways in which it can be appealed to reinforce punitive state reactions to forms of behaviour which, taken as individual instances, would not be seen in nearly such threatening terms. In such contexts, we can see that use of the term 'public' signifies not a particular sphere of activity (already hard to define) but rather the *conception* of order which prevails: that of the state or particular powerful groups within it. There is no logical barrier to regarding issues such as child abuse or other forms of 'domestic' violence as threatening to public order: the refusal or reluctance so to see them is political and cultural. In other words, this approach exposes the fact that in our society a husband's 'chastisement' (the conventional word is revealing) or 'battering' of his wife is still seen in some quarters as more an expression of a certain aspect of the social order (the patriarchal family) than a threat to it. A similar point could be made about attitudes to racial harassment and their relation to white supremacy. By showing the logical defensibility of a progressive extension of the application of the concept of public disorder, we can expose the contingency of the categories in terms of which the world is conventionally socially and legally constructed.

The second theme which emerges from the texts is that of the importance of 'folk devils' and 'moral' panics in understanding the social construction of public disorder. What is happening in many of the situations considered is the representation of some set of events as a serious and novel threat to the social order. Thus, public fear and anxiety are increased in a way which confirms the 'amplification of deviance' model: a combination of the labelling of certain

behaviours as 'deviant' by both the public and the participants and the legitimation of punitive state responses creates an ascending spiral. This point is well
summarised by Hall et al:

S Hall, C Critcher, T Jefferson, J Clarke and B Roberts, *Policing the*
Crisis: Mugging, the State, and Law and Order **(Macmillan, 1978) p 29**

What the agencies and the press were responding to was not a simple set of
facts but a new *definition of the situation* – a new construction of the social
reality of crime. 'Mugging' provoked an organised response, in part
because it was linked with a widespread belief about the alarming rate of
crime in general, and with a common *perception* that this rising crime was
also becoming more violent. These social aspects had entered into its
meaning ... We have entered the realm of the relation of facts to the ideological constructions of 'reality' ... We concluded from [a statistical] examination that the reaction to 'mugging' was out of all proportion to any level
of actual threat which could be reconstructed through the unreliable statistics. And since it appeared to be a response, at least in part, not to the
actual threat, it must have been a reaction by the control agencies and the
media to the *perceived* or *symbolic* threat to society – what the 'mugging'
label *represented*. But this made the social reaction to mugging now as
problematic – if not more so – than 'mugging' itself. When such discrepancies appear between threat and reaction, between what is perceived and
what that is a perception of, we have good evidence to suggest we are in
the presence of an ideological displacement. We call this displacement a
moral panic.

The pervasiveness of moral panics in the arena of public disorder suggests its
importance, both perceived and actual, to the stability and continuity of the
state and the susceptibility of our society to fears of social dissolution.

A third emerging theme is that of the historical continuity of social and public
disorder. This is accompanied by a contemporary 'amnesia' about the facts of
disorder in successive generations which is material to the construction of folk
devils and moral panics. It seems that whatever contemporary example of disorder we pick upon, we can find analogues in almost any period of history. This is
not to say, of course, that the struggles and activities of the Chartists, the
Luddites, food rioters, the 'Blacks' who roamed the eighteenth-century forests,
the garrotters, vagrants, Guy Fawkes and his associates or the suffragettes find
exact analogues in current public disorder, nor to deny that public disorder is
more widespread in some periods than in others. It is merely to identify the
persistence of disorder *perceived and interpreted as such by successive societies*. In
seeking to understand social constructions of disorder in the past, we find
certain themes emerging; factors in terms of which British society in different
ages seems to understand its incidence. These recurring themes, although not

universal, seem to be ideas of the young, 'outsiders' such as immigrants, ethnic minority members or 'agents provocateurs', of those whose lifestyle deviates from the norm, and of disadvantaged socio-economic groups as being especially implicated in public disorder or as posing a special threat of it. Fears of dissolution of the social order and of social consensus lead to the paradox that wartime is perceived as a period of public order and to the marginalisation of associated forms of disorder such as looting (Pearson 1983: 239–241). Links are drawn between explanations of disorder and anxieties about dissolution of social structures such as the family (for example, explanations of juvenile crime in terms of women working outside the home), about lack of discipline and about failures of education.

Fourth, it is impossible to ignore the role of news media in constructing moral panics and other public images of disorder. The evaluative and constructive role of the press, television and radio in selecting, filtering and presenting political, police and public reactions and in producing images of contemporary disorder is amply attested to by the most cursory perusal of reports of industrial action, 'riots' and law and order news generally (see Chibnall 1977: 226ff).

S Hall et al, *Policing the Crisis: Mugging, the State, and Law and Order* (Macmillan, 1978) p 58

... [T]wo aspects of news production – the practical pressures of constantly working against the clock and the professional demands of impartiality and objectivity – combine to produce a systematically structured *over-accessing* to the media of those in powerful and privileged institutional positions. The media thus tend, faithfully and impartially, to reproduce symbolically the existing structure of power in society's institutional order. This is what Becker has called the 'hierarchy of credibility' – the likelihood that those in powerful or high-status positions in society who offer opinions about controversial topics will have their definitions accepted, because such spokesmen are understood to have access to more accurate or more specialised information on particular topics than the majority of the population. The result of this structured preference given in the media to the opinions of the powerful is that these 'spokesmen' become what we call the *primary definers* of topics.

This extract leads us to a fifth theme – that of the importance of perspective. The idea of disorder is not simply descriptive: the notion of public order imports the idea of a state of affairs or behaviour which is ordered (ie acceptable) from a particular (powerful/legal/political) point of view. None of the instances of disorder we have discussed, nor any others we might cite, is 'disordered' in the sense of being chaotic or senseless to the participants – although they may of course be deliberately disordered in the sense of being intended as violations of the established order and authority. Whether we are dealing with intentional civil disobedience, or with peaceful demonstrations, or with football crowd behaviour ('ordered' to the point of being ritualistic), or with apparently un-ordered behaviour such as spontaneous 'riots', at one level or another we are dealing with competing definitions of order. These definitions challenge the established order and assert the legitimacy of alternative conceptions of order, behaviours or forms of life. Because of this, albeit loose, continuity, we can see that any form of behaviour which can be interpreted as a challenge to authority or consensus is susceptible of being socially constructed (whether in terms of a moral panic or not) as a 'public order problem'. Hence, although there is wide agreement that, for example, sedition, riot and mass hooliganism constitute 'public order problems', and although what is conventionally accepted as 'public order law' responds directly to these phenomena, at the margins there is always the possibility of the incorporation of other phenomena (such as 'mugging' or 'picketing'), and this flexibility, as we shall see, is matched in legal definitions and enforcement practices.

This insight about the importance of points of view is crucial, but it is obscured by a move that is central to legal discourse: the objectification of a particular point of view. In other words, institutional political reaction, including legal reaction, reflected in the media, sets up the authoritative, politically endorsed conception of order as *the* conception: public order *is* that which the state and legal institutions define it to be. A particularly clear example of the suppression of alternative interpretations and points of view can be seen in the police and media construction of events leading up to disturbances on the Broadwater Farm Estate in Tottenham, North London, in 1985, during which a police officer was killed. (This incident resulted in one of the miscarriage of justice cases discussed in **Chapter 1**.) One of the main incidents represented as foreshadowing trouble and calling forth a massive police response was a march by black people to the police station to protest over recent police action on the estate. A particular focus of protest was an incident in which a woman collapsed and died after her home had been searched without a warrant. The march was portrayed as a menacing incident; what was not explained was that such delegations were a conventional mode of peaceful protest in that community, as was well known to the police (see Gifford 1986). This kind of reporting in turn facilitates the depoliticisation of civil disobedience and other forms of disorder and their construction as 'mere lawlessness', calling for criminal law responses, which are represented as apolitical. The interpretation of moral panics as subject to legal containment and control serves symbolically to allay public anxiety and reinforce consensus notwithstanding its modest instrumental contribution to preventing and quelling disorder. The phenomenon of 'public disorder' becomes (in an apparent paradox which has a hidden logic) a site for the assertion and demonstration of the state's legitimacy and authority.

FURTHER READING

Box, Steven (1987) *Recession, Crime and Unemployment* (Macmillan) Chs 1–4.

Dahrendorf, Ralf (1985) *Law and Order* (Stevens).

Goode, Erich and Ben-Yahuda, Nachman (1994) *Moral Panics* (Blackwell).

Green, Penny and Rutherford, Andrew (eds) (2000) *Criminal Policy in Transition* (Hart Publishing).

Hillyard, Paddy and Percy-Smith, J (1988) *The Coercive State* (Fontana).

Loader, Ian and Sparks, Richard (2002) 'Contemporary Landscapes of crime, order, and control: governance, risk and globalization' in Maguire et al (eds) *The Oxford Handbook of Criminology* (Oxford University Press) p 83.

National Council for Civil Liberties (1986) *Stonehenge* (Yale Press).

Rock, Paul (2002) 'Sociological Theories of Crime' in Maguire et al (eds) *The Oxford Handbook of Criminology* (Oxford University Press) p 51.

Scarman, Lord (1982) *The Brixton Disorders* (Penguin).

Thompson, Kenneth (1998) *Moral Panics* (Routledge).

II.   Public order laws

II.a.   Football 'games'

Criminal law has the individual actor in its ideological forefront. But in the shadows, behind the doctrinal curtains, is the spectre of group liability – gangs and conspiracies, riots and crowds, youth and disorder, organised crime. We take football as a useful case study in public order law and policing. Public order laws are a mixture of generic offences (riot, violent disorder and affray, for example), and more specific provisions. Some of the specific provisions apply to all sporting fixtures (for example, alcohol restrictions), while others directly target football. One has only to pay minimal attention to contemporary news media to realise that football 'hooliganism' has become a deep national obsession, frequently calling forth a punitive response which tends to unite people of very different classes and political persuasions much more effectively than is the case with more overtly political public order issues such as demonstrations and riots. It is not a one-sided picture, however, as the reactions to the policing of football disorder outside the UK demonstrate. The line between constructing the fans as hooligans on the one hand and heroes victimised by rough 'continental' policing is a shifting and unpredictable one (witness events in Italy in 1997) underlining the essentially ambivalent attitudes in this area.

Football illustrates a number of recurring themes in this chapter and in the book as a whole:

- the multi-dimensional character of public order;
- the effect of moral panics or media-amplified concerns;
- the development of 'exclusion' as an organising theme in criminal justice policies;

- the relationship between alcohol and violence;
- the prevalence of racism;
- the political utility of an easily identified activity, providing a template for new developments in 'law and order' policing;
- the intersection of criminal law and justice and human rights.

Football hooliganism has a political significance, even stretching beyond its interpretation as an assertion and reinforcement of macho versions of masculinity:

E Moonman and P Bradley, 'Football as a Political Arena' in *Football as a Forum for Disorder* **(Centre for Contemporary Studies, 1984) p 6**

The debate as to whether football violence has been a constant factor, like the argument as to whether mugging is or is not a purely modern phenomenon, is one which has apparently no end. It seems likely that violence has always in one form or another and to varying degrees, been associated with the game. Perhaps therefore, it is the form and degree of that violence which should specially interest us – all the more so if one, albeit with due circumspection, accepts the observation that there is a close association between soccer's problems and those of society in general and that therefore soccer offers illuminating microcosmic insights into the state of the nation.

Football is a political arena, if only because it accommodates considerable numbers of people ... The National Front and the British Movement have made urgent and orchestrated attempts to recruit and stimulate young people wherever they can be found in significant numbers; at the school gate, at the rock concert, and the football ground. The last two arenas in particular offer the coveted dividend of political – and largely racist – violence.

The racism and the racist violence encountered at British soccer grounds is 'casual', in that the majority of those who express or execute it are not necessarily committed to the values they appear so aggressively to condone ... The commissioning of political hooliganism became a strategic priority for the National Front in the wake of its obliteration at the May 1979 General Election. The far right's 'politics by stealth' had abjectly failed. The Front in particular had hoped that by playing down its innate Nazism and by playing up its patriotism, by concealing its preoccupation with 'the Jewish question' and instead by exploiting white uncertainties and fears of black immigration into this country, it might begin to build for itself an image of respectable radicalism which could be converted into electoral success ... After the election, hard core Nazism and anti-Semitism with their physical complement of street violence were rapidly reinstated as the means and the end of their political argument.

The leaders of the far right were now almost convinced that the future for their cause lay not so much in convincing the middle-aged and middle-class as in enlisting the young and politically naive. The fight is on, Derek Holland wrote in 1979, 'for the control of the hearts and minds of British youth' ... The key to these strategies ... has been the perceived need on the part of the potential young recruits for 'identity'. The National Front quickly recognised that it could tap the same vein of enthusiasm and even compulsion with which football fan(atics) identify with their teams. It could offer the young 'dispossessed' and confused a set of simple remedies to a wide array of complex and apparently insoluble problems ... It could offer an essential sense of 'belonging', a common cause and a camaraderie founded on an identification of 'them and us' and supplemented by the street language of violence which, as tribal or gang violence always has, provides an essential form of both moral and physical solidarity.

The role of news media in creating public images of football hooliganism is as important as in the case of the Mods and Rockers, and disputes over alleged distortion and exaggeration in reporting of the behaviour of British fans abroad (consider the frequent fortunate coincidence of camera crew being on hand when bar brawls break out) suggest that the Press plays a role consistent with the model of 'deviance amplification'.

For a historical perspective on football hooliganism, we turn once again to Pearson:

G Pearson, *Hooligan: A History of Respectable Fears* (Macmillan, 1983) pp 29–30

There had been a rumbling discontent about misbehaviour at football matches, both on and off the field, throughout the 1920s and 1930s, which came to a head in the late 30s with renewed accusations of declining sportsmanship and crowd disorders. In 1936, the Football Association found it necessary to issue a memorandum on rough play, in an attempt to stamp out excessive violence and the 'professional foul' which is so often identified as the hallmark of the debased traditions of sportsmanship in post-war football. Indeed, after a particularly heated Derby match between Arsenal and Chelsea, *The Times* issued a curt editorial denouncing 'the cold-blooded and intentional foul' such as the Continental ankle-tap and the deliberate provocation of players known to suffer from 'temperament'. *The Times* rounded against 'the present menace to professional football'. And it was all so 'un-English': 'the shoulder-charge, the fairest and least dangerous weapon in the footballer's armoury, has declined, and in its place has arisen a regiment of mean and dangerous tricks ... What is wanted is increased firmness ... '.

Behaviour on the terraces was also thought to be deteriorating in the 1930s. Crowd incidents involving pitch invasions, attacks on referees and players, and occasional confrontations between spectators and the police were exciting the same interest. In one typical incident in November 1936, when during a match at Wolverhampton Wanderers, spectators had attacked visiting Chelsea players, there were more violent scenes after the game. *Reynold's News* described how a 'big and angry crowd' of Wolves fans estimated at 2000 people gathered outside the officials' entrance protesting at the club's policy of selling its better players. The following week police had to be called to quell disturbances at a number of grounds – including Middlesborough and Upton Park where the referee was again attacked – and *Reynold's News* (15 November 1936) thought that 'the FA will soon have to issue another "rough play" memorandum – this time to the spectators!'.

Disturbances such as these provided an intermittent focus of attention throughout the interwar years, and a number of grounds were closed because of crowd disorders ... In the early 1920s the fierce north London rivalries between Arsenal and Spurs flared into open street battles in which some of the more zealous fans were armed with iron bars and knives. Some years later, to give one final example of the kind of trouble that could break out at football games, the police found it necessary to lead a baton charge against stone-throwers during a contest between Linfield and Belfast Celtic in 1935. In the absence of any sustained historical research into football in this period, it is not possible to say how frequent or how violent these occasions were, or to arrive at a balanced comparison between football disorders in the 1920s and 1930s as against those in more recent years. Nevertheless, it is clear enough that the realities of pre-war football do not find agreement with post-war nostalgia.

Indeed, the history of football as a forum for disorder seems to go back almost as far as the commercialisation of the game in the late nineteenth century (Pearson 1983: 64–65). Or, are football matches the 'modern equivalents of medieval tournaments' (Clark 2002: 264)?

The specialist Football Intelligence Unit established in 1988 keeps records on all those arrested for football-related violence and by 1990 held the names of 6000 'hooligans'. Of these, 1500 have offences of violence recorded against their names, while offences listed against the remainder include drugs, fraud and auto crime. As Armstrong and Hobbs comment, it is a 'mystery' what these other crimes have to do with football hooliganism (1994: 222). By 2002 there were 1149 orders in force banning attendance at domestic or international matches. The vast majority of these were 'banning orders on conviction' introduced by the Football (Disorder) Act 2000 (Home Office 2002h: Table 9). This represents a high proportion of those potentially likely to travel to international matches, given that only 8000 England supporters travelled to the World Cup in 2002.

The place that football 'disorder' occupies in the modern political conscious-ness is demonstrated in the intemperate language employed by the government and judges. For example, Home Office Circular 34/2000 states:

It is less than a year since the issue of Home Office Circular 42/1999 which provided consolidated guidance on what were then all the existing legislative and administrative measures related to football hooliganism.

Sadly the shameful and utterly reprehensible behaviour of some of the followers of the England football team competing in the Euro 2000 this summer, obliged the government to introduce further legislation to deal with the particular menace of our home-grown football hooligans when abroad.

While Laws LJ painted the background to the legislation in these terms:

These cases are about statutory measures enacted ... to confront *the shame and menace* of football hooliganism ... [T]he Public Order Act 1986 ... was the first measure taken by the legislature specifically to address *the evils* of hooliganism at football matches ...

[T]he Acts of 1986 and 1989 (Football Spectators Act) ... respond to what was plainly an increasing *barbarism*. The later Act recognised the particular *evil of violence* and drunkenness by British fans abroad [in *Gough and Smith v Chief Constable of Derbyshire* [2001] EWHC Admin 554; emphasis added].

The appellants, Gough and Smith, had challenged 'banning orders' made under the Football Spectators Act 1989 on the grounds that they breached Article 7 of the European Convention on Human Rights. In a case stated, the Divisional Court held that the orders were not penalties and therefore not subject to Article 7. The Court of Appeal upheld this on appeal and the extract here gives a useful overview of the scheme:

ARTICLE 7 provides
1. No one shall be held guilty of any criminal offence on account of any act or omission which did not constitute a criminal offence under national or international law at the time when it was committed. Nor shall a heavier penalty be imposed than the one that was applicable at the time the criminal offence was committed.
2. This Article shall not prejudice the trial and punishment of any person for any act or omission which, at the time when it was committed, was criminal according to the general principles of law recognised by civilised nations.

Gough and Smith v Chief Constable of Derbyshire [2002] EWCA Civ 351

Lord Phillips MR.

The appellants ... have run foul of the statutory scheme that has been put in place to combat football hooligans. [The judge] made a banning order against each appellant under the Football (Spectators) Act 1989 as amended by the Football (Disorder) Act 2000. The banning orders prevent the appellants from attending certain football matches in England and Wales. They also prevent the appellants from leaving the country when certain football matches are taking place outside England and Wales. The appellants contend that it is not lawful to impose the latter restrictions upon them. They say that the statutory provisions under which they are imposed violate Community law in a manner which renders void those provisions. They further contend that the statutory provisions in question violate certain articles of the European Convention on Human Rights, so that the statutes are incompatible with the Convention.

...

At the beginning of his judgment Laws LJ spoke of the shame and menace of football hooliganism. As questions of proportionality are an important feature of this appeal, we propose to say a little about this phenomenon at the outset.

Football started life as an amateur sport, but professional football is now very big business. Following professional football is an activity pursued with passion by large sections of the populace in this country and abroad.

Over the last forty years the adversarial encounter on the football pitch has, in this country, been increasingly accompanied by a degree of physical conflict between certain elements of the supporters of at least some of the football clubs. For this reason, rival supporters are now segregated within the grounds. In the vicinity of the grounds where matches are played disorder has now, unhappily, become commonplace.

There is a small minority for whom the attraction of football matches is not the game itself, but the warfare that they intend shall accompany the game. To describe what takes place by the word warfare is hardly too strong. To quote from the witness statement in these proceedings of Superintendent John Wright:

> 'It has become common for groups of males to associate themselves with Football Clubs as a vehicle for them to become involved in violence and disorder. This has developed to the stage where this has become extremely organised. These groups will often make use of mobile phones and the internet to arrange fights with other like-minded individuals. These fights often involve the use of weapons, e.g., knives, bottles, and CS gas. They usually occur away from football grounds at railway stations or in or around city centre public houses.'

The behaviour of a lawless minority at matches within England and Wales has been mirrored by lawlessness on the part of a small minority of those who follow English teams in competitions abroad. Mr David Bohannan, who heads the Home Office Section responsible for tackling football related disorder provided the court with the following summary of this phenomenon:

'Disorderliness has been associated with football since the end of the nineteenth century when it became a mass spectator sport. However, it only became recognised as a major social problem in the 1960s when domestic football grounds regularly provided a venue for fights and other kinds of disorder involving many hundreds of young males. Since 1977, attention has also focussed on the behaviour of English football fans when overseas. There has been a catalogue of incidents involving English supporters, including serious outbursts of violence and disorder in Luxembourg (1977), Turin (1980), Basle (1981), Oslo (1981), Paris (1984), West Germany (1988), Italy (1990), Sweden (1992), Amsterdam (1993), Rotterdam (1993), Dublin (1995), Rome (1997), Marseilles (1998), Glasgow (1999), Copenhagen (2000), Brussels (2000) and Charleroi (2000). These incidents have mainly taken place in connection with matches played by the English national team. However, serious problems have also arisen in relation to matches played by English club sides, eg. The UEFA Cup Final in Copenhagen in 2000 between Arsenal and Galatasaray. In most cases, the disorder has occurred in streets and bars rather than in the grounds and often during the period leading up to match day. Each incident has brought shame on our national reputation and also resulted in very many arrests and expulsions of English supporters by host nations. Acts of disorder by English supporters receive wide media coverage both in the UK and abroad.'

...

The history of legislative measures introduced to address the problem of football hooliganism, ... demonstrates ... that, over the years, the legislation has not achieved the intended result of putting an end to football hooliganism and that Parliament's response has been progressively to make more stringent the circumstances in which restraints can and will be imposed on those who are believed to be liable to indulge in such behaviour ...

Under Part IV of the Public Order Act 1986 (the 1986 Act), where a court convicted a defendant of an offence of violence or drunkenness committed in connection with attendance at a football match, it was empowered to make an order excluding the defendant from attending certain prescribed football matches in this country, subject to this proviso in section 30(2):

No exclusion order may be made unless the court is satisfied that making such an order in relation to the accused would help to prevent violence or disorder at or in connection with prescribed football matches.

The Football Spectators Act 1989 provided that, in similar circumstances to those covered by the 1986 Act and subject to the same proviso, the court could place a restriction order on a defendant whereby he would be required to report to a police station during the period within which certain designated football matches were being played abroad. The object of this was to prevent the defendant from travelling to those matches.

The Football (Offences and Disorder) Act 1999 amended the relevant provisions of the earlier two Acts. Restriction orders were redefined as football banning orders, but the most significant change was in the wording of the proviso. That was, in each Act, amended to read as follows:

'It shall be the duty of the court to make a football banning order in relation to the accused if it is satisfied that there are reasonable grounds to believe that making the order would help to prevent violence or disorder at or in connection with prescribed [designated] football matches.'

The 2000 Act has amended the 1989 Act in such a way as to combine the relevant provisions of that Act and the 1986 Act. It makes provision for the making of a single banning order in relation to regulated football matches (i.e. prescribed matches) whether in England and Wales or elsewhere.

The amended Act, which we shall from now on describe simply as the 1989 Act, provides for the making of a banning order in two different circumstances. The first, under section 14A, is when a court convicts a defendant of one of the scheduled offences i.e. football related violence. The second, under section 14B, is new, and much more far reaching. The order is made on a complaint to a Magistrates' Court by the chief officer of police of the area in which the respondent resides. It must appear to the chief officer and he must prove to the court that the respondent has, within the last ten years, at any time caused or contributed to any violence or disorde in the United Kingdom or elsewhere.

By whichever of the two routes the matter comes before the court, the court must make a banning order:

(1) If the court is satisfied that there are reasonable grounds to believe that making a banning order would help to prevent violence or disorder at or in connection with any regulated football matches.

(2) An appeal lies to the Crown Court against the imposition of a banning order.

Under section 14C, violence is defined as meaning violence against persons or property and includes threatening violence and disorder has a lengthy definition which includes using threatening, abusive, or insulting words or behaviour or disorderly behaviour. There is no requirement for the violence or disorder to be football related.

The same section specifies a number of matters that the court can take into account when considering whether to make a banning order under 14B. These include conduct recorded on video or by other means.

Regulated football matches taking place outside England and Wales are prescribed by order of the Secretary of State having regard to the risk that they will be an occasion for violence and disorder on the part of English supporters. Under the current order these are matches involving the English or Welsh national teams or clubs which are members of the Football League or the Football Association Premier League.

A person subject to a banning order is not automatically affected by that order in respect of every prescribed overseas game. The Act provides for an enforcing authority ... the Football Banning Orders Authority (FBOA). Its functions include issuing individual notices to those made subject to banning orders. These set out the appropriate conditions and reporting restrictions which apply to each individual having regard to the degree of risk associated with the individual person for the individual match.

The circumstances that led to the passing of the 2000 Act, and the reasoning behind its provisions, are not in dispute ...

The 2000 Act was a response to appalling scenes of disorder at Brussels and Charleroi during the Euro 2000 tournament. In the course of that tournament 965 English citizens were arrested by the Belgian police. The English National Criminal Intelligence Service (NCIS) is an agency which dedicates a significant proportion of its time and expertise to monitoring the activities of football hooligans. Only 30 of those arrested were known to the NCIS. Only 1 of the total of 454 individuals who were subject to domestic, but not international, banning orders was among them. Mr. Straw summarised the position by stating that the disorder was prompted not by a small core of known football hooligans, but by xenophobic, racist and offensive behaviour of a significant number of drunken, white males, typically aged between 20 and 35.

The NCIS carried out an analysis of those arrested. 391 – about 40% – had previous convictions: 133 for violence, 200 for disorder, 38 for possession of an offensive weapon and 122 for criminal damage. Plainly many of these had convictions for more than one of these offences. The convictions were not, in the main, football-related.

We turn to the test to be applied when a person subject to a banning order wishes to go abroad. Before granting permission to do so the FBOA has to be satisfied that there are special circumstances which justify his being exempted from the effect of the ban and that he would not attend prescribed matches if granted an exemption. This places the onus of proof on the applicant for permission. Nor is it clear what can constitute special circumstances, or the standard of proof to be applied.

In our judgment these statutory provisions, if given their natural meaning, are capable of being applied in a manner which is harsh and disproportionate. If a low standard of proof is applied at the first stage, there is a danger of individuals being made subject to banning orders on evidence which is too slender to justify the restrictions on their freedom which these entail. The requirement to demonstrate special circumstances could also lead the FBOA, or the Magistrates' Court on appeal, to refuse to grant permission to leave the country for a purpose which, while innocuous, would not naturally be said to constitute special circumstances.

However, the question is not whether the statutory provisions are capable of being interpreted in a manner which has disproportionate effect. The question is whether they are capable of being interpreted in a manner that is proportionate. Those who have to apply them are under a duty to give them an interpretation which is compatible with the requirements of European law and of the Human Rights Convention if this can be achieved.

We have concluded that the scheme itself, if properly operated, will satisfy the requirements of proportionality. As a starting point a banning order should only be imposed where there are strong grounds for concluding that the individual subject to the order has a propensity for taking part in football hooliganism ... We believe that it is proportionate that those who have been shown to constitute a real risk of participation in football hooliganism should be required to obtain permission to travel abroad during periods when prescribed matches are taking place and to demonstrate that the purpose of doing so is other than attendance at the prescribed match or matches. We are not able to envisage a scheme which would achieve the public policy objective that involves a lesser degree of restraint. We consider that the German approach of entering restrictive endorsements in the passports of those suspected of football hooliganism would be difficult to operate in practice and would be liable to have more draconian consequences than the scheme under the 1989 Act ...

A reverse burden of proof is not incompatible with Community or Strasbourg law where the circumstances justify this ... We think it reasonable that a person subject to a banning order should be required to demonstrate that foreign travel during the period of a prescribed match is not for the purpose of attending the match. This is because the object of the foreign travel is likely to be within the exclusive knowledge of the would-be traveller, and proof of that object should not involve untoward difficulty at least if an appropriate standard of proof is applied.

It is essential that the appropriate standard of proof at both the first and the last stage of the scheme is appreciated and applied, for compliance with the principles of Community and Strasbourg law depends on this.

The standard of proof required for making a banning order

Mr Thompson contended that proceedings under section 14B are criminal proceedings and that, in consequence, the criminal standard of proof applies. Laws L.J. gave detailed consideration to the question of whether banning orders were penalties in relation to submissions made on behalf of an appellant who has not appealed to us, that Article 7 of the Convention had been violated. Laws L.J. held that banning orders were not penalties. We endorse his conclusion for the reasons that he gave. We also reject the submission that section 14B proceedings are criminal. They neither require proof that a criminal offence has been committed, nor involve the imposition of a penalty. We find that the proceedings that led to the imposition of banning orders were civil in character.

It does not follow from this that a mere balance of probabilities suffices to justify the making of an order. Banning orders under section 14(B) fall into the same category as antisocial behaviour orders and sex offenders orders. While made in civil proceedings they impose serious restraints on freedoms that the citizen normally enjoys. While technically the civil standard of proof applies, that standard is flexible and must reflect the consequences that will follow if the case for a banning order is made out. This should lead the Magistrates to apply an exacting standard of proof that will, in practice, be hard to distinguish from the criminal standard …

Thus the necessity in the individual case to impose a restriction upon a fundamental freedom must be strictly demonstrated. The first thing that has to be proved under section 14B(4)(a) is that the respondent has caused or contributed to violence or disorder in the United Kingdom or elsewhere … the standard of proof of this is practically indistinguishable from the criminal standard.

The same is true of the next requirement, that imposed by section 14(4)(b), … The court must be satisfied that there are reasonable grounds to believe that making a banning order would help to prevent violence or disorder at or in connection with any regulated football matches. In practice the reasonable grounds will almost inevitably consist of evidence of past conduct … The past conduct may or may not consist of or include the causing or contributing to violence or disorder that has to be proved under section 14B(4)(a), for that violence or disorder is not required to be football related. It must, however, be proved to the same strict standard of proof. Furthermore it must be conduct that gives rise to the likelihood that, if the respondent is not banned from attending prescribed football matches, he will attend such matches, or the environs of them, and take part in violence or disorder.

These matters are not readily susceptible of proof. We can well understand the practice that is evidenced by this case of using a football intelligence service to build up profiles of football prominents. Such a practice may well be the only way of assembling evidence sufficiently cogent to satisfy the requirements of section 14B(4)(b). Those requirements, if properly applied in the manner described above, will provide a satisfactory threshold for the making of a banning order. The banning order, in its turn, will be a satisfactory basis for the conclusion that the individual subject to it should not be permitted to go to prescribed overseas matches.

... Provided that the reason for going abroad is other than attendance at the prescribed match, there can be no justification for refusing permission. When considering whether there are special circumstances the FBOA, or on appeal the Magistrates, should do no more than satisfy themselves on balance of probabilities that this is the true position. This should not be something that is difficult to prove, for the bona fide prospective traveller is like to be in a position to produce some evidence of the proposed trip.

Happily, the approach of the FBOA to special circumstances applications appears to accord with that which we have outlined as appropriate. [T]here have been about 80 such applications and that all of them were granted. Mr Gough himself applied for and was granted permission to go abroad on holiday during the period of a prescribed match ...

The allegation that the statutory scheme is contrary to Article 6 is not made out ...

It was conceded by the Secretary of State, that a banning order might result in interference with the right to respect for private or family life [Article 8]. Whether it did would depend upon the particular facts and it certainly did not do so in the case of Mr Gough or Mr Smith. [I]f a banning order, properly made, interferes with the right to respect for private or family life, the interference is likely to prove justified under Article 8.2 on the grounds that it is necessary for the prevention of disorder.

This case is one of a number that explores the blurred line between civil and criminal proceedings which is characteristic of much recent legislation.

Now we move from the specific area of football disorder to consider generic public order provisions. The following summary underlines the intensity of legislative activity in the public order area.

Summary of public order laws

Football-specific
- Football Spectators Act 1989 (established Football Licensing Authority, introduced restriction orders)
- Football Offences Act 1991 (banned missiles, racialist etc chanting)
- Football (Offences and Disorder) Act 1999 (replaced restriction orders with domestic and international banning orders)
- Football (Disorder) Act 2000 (amendments to allow combined orders)

Sporting-specific
- Sporting Events (Control of Alcohol) Act 1985
- Fire Safety and Safety of Places of Sport Act 1987
- Criminal Justice and Public Order Act 1994, s 166(1) (banned ticket touting)

Alcohol-specific
- Confiscation of Alcohol (Young Persons) Act 1997
- Criminal Justice and Police Act 2001, ss 12–32 (alcohol in public places)

General
- Public Order Act 1986 (riot, violent disorder, affray, provoking violence, disorderly conduct trespassory assemblies)
- Criminal Justice and Public Order Act 1994 (aggravated trespass)
- Protection from Harassment Act 1997
- Crime and Disorder Act 1998 (anti-social behaviour orders (ASBOs), child curfews, racially aggravated offences)
- Criminal Justice and Police Act 2001 (fixed penalty notices)
- Police Reform Act 2002 (extends ASBOs)
- Anti-Social Behaviour Bill 2003

II.b.   Riot, violent disorder and affray

The Public Order Act 1986 (POA 1986) does not constitute a codification of public order law even narrowly conceived. It leaves untouched significant areas such as the common law relating to breach of the peace and has in any event been supplemented by numerous provisions since. Essentially the Act constituted a partial revision and updating of the common law offences of riot, affray and unlawful assembly, and the creation of two new offences of causing fear of violence and of creating harassment, alarm or distress (POA 1986, Pt I). It also revised the law relating to racial hatred (Pt III) and extended police powers to impose conditions on and ban assemblies, requiring for the first time that notice of a wide range of public gatherings be given to the police (Pt II).

Although the division is somewhat artificial we have deferred consideration of the fear of violence, harassment and racial violence offences until the next chapter. One of our themes both in this chapter and the next is the fluidity in definitions of 'public order' and 'personal violence'. A purely situation or contextual approach would mean looking at all the relevant law in relation to say football, or to environmental protest, in separate sections. But this would mean absurd amounts of overlap since most criminal laws are drafted in general terms. And even those laws passed to deal with a specific problem often end up being deployed in unpredictable directions, an example of which is the use against animal rights protesters of the Protection from Harassment Act 1997, passed to deal with stalking. Another theme is the overlap between offences such that there is often a choice of charge: causing harassment, etc (generally referred to as 'disorderly conduct') under s 5 of the POA 1986 could often be charged as an assault, for example, as could some types of stalking behaviour. The broad principle we have followed is that this chapter deals with offences that are *designed* to deal with group behaviour or public protest, while **Chapter 3** considers offences that can be committed by one person, although in reality are deployed in public order situations as well.

A tier of offences is laid out in the POA 1986 with *riot*, punishable with a maximum of 10 years, at the head, followed by *violent disorder* and *affray*. Their main distinguishing characteristics are that they do not require proof that any injury or damage actually occurred and that they allow groups of alleged offenders to be charged with the same offence.

II.b.i.   Outline of offences

Public Order Act 1986, s 1

(1) Where 12 or more persons who are present together use or threaten unlawful violence for a common purpose and the conduct of them (taken together) is such as would cause a person of reasonable firmness present at the scene to fear for his personal safety, each of the persons using unlawful violence for the common purpose is guilty of riot.

(2) It is immaterial whether or not the 12 or more use or threaten un-lawful violence simultaneously.

(3) The common purpose may be inferred from conduct.

(4) No person of reasonable firmness need actually be, or be likely to be, present at the scene.

(5) Riot may be committed in private as well as in public places.

(6) A person guilty of riot is liable on conviction on indictment to imprisonment for a term not exceeding ten years or a fine or both.

For a serious offence, s 1 is widely drawn. Subsection 1(1) sets the context in which the offence must be committed – the presence of at least 12 people present together (12 people in a shopping centre, in a bus queue, at a football match, at an airport) – who use or threaten violence (see s 8 below) for a common purpose (which can be inferred from their conduct, s 1(3)). The offence is committed when any one of those persons actually uses violence.

Since these three offences have common elements, we will outline violent disorder and affray first before giving examples of each.

The essence of *violent disorder*, the next offence in the hierarchy, punishable by a maximum of five years, is the threat or use of violence where there are at least three people present.

Public Order Act 1986, s 2

(1) Where 3 or more persons who are present together use or threaten violence and the conduct of them (taken together) is such as would

cause a person of reasonable firmness present at the scene to fear for his personal safety, each of the persons using or threatening unlawful violence is guilty of violent disorder.

(2) It is immaterial whether or not the 3 or more use or threaten unlawful violence simultaneously.

Affray, like violent disorder, is a triable either way offence, punishable on indictment with three years' imprisonment.

Public Order Act 1986, s 3

(1) A person is guilty of affray if he uses or threatens unlawful violence towards another and his conduct is such as would cause a person of reasonable firmness present at the scene to fear for his personal safety.

(2) Where 2 or more persons use or threaten the unlawful violence, it is the conduct of them taken together that must be considered for the purposes of subsection (1).

(3) For the purposes of this section a threat cannot be made by the use of words alone.

Affray needs three people (two real and one hypothetical): the person using or threatening violence, the person to whom it is directed and a third person who would have been caused to fear for her safety. Thus, threatening a police constable will not amount to affray unless a third person would have been caused such fear (*Sanchez*, 1996). Using words to command a dog to attack has been held the equivalent of using a weapon and could constitute an affray (*Dixon*, 1993). In a significant concession, however, the House of Lords held that carrying petrol bombs did not, per se, amount to affray unless there was a threat to use them directed at another person present at the scene (*I, M and H v DPP* (2001)).

II.b.ii.   Common elements

Some general comments can now be made. Despite the designation 'public' order offences, none of these offences needs to be committed in public. In each case the conduct must be such as would cause a person of reasonable firmness present at the scene to fear for his personal safety. No such person need be present, however.

'*Violence*', a key element in riot and violent disorder, is defined in the interpretation section:

Public Order Act 1986, s 8

... 'violence' means any violent conduct, so that–

(a) except in the context of affray, it includes violent conduct towards property as well as violent conduct towards persons, and

(b) it is not restricted to conduct causing or intended to cause injury or damage but includes any other violent conduct (for example, throwing at or towards a person a missile of a kind capable of causing injury which does not hit or falls short).

This almost entirely tautological definition amounts to little more than an invitation to the tribunal to define violence very broadly, and to do so in terms of their own conceptions of the concept, as constructed and influenced by images proffered by media, government and popular culture (see **Chapter 6** below). Its breadth is extraordinary – covering violence to property as well as to the person (s 8(a)) and extending to conduct capable of, but not necessarily causing, or intending to cause, damage or harm (s 8(b)).

The Act uses ordinary language to fix its 'legal definitions': violence, harassment, distress, alarm, are common words which hitherto had no technical legal meaning. Their precursors can be found in the ideas of 'threatening, abusive and insulting' conduct introduced by the Public Order Act 1936, which were taken as raising questions of fact rather than questions of law. The frequent use of such words has an important influence on the extent to which the legislation can be seen to be responding to, and thus can assuage, popular fears of disorder as constructed by government and media. The move towards 'ordinary language legislation' may be seen as an attempt to make legal definitions, at least at the level of rhetoric, correspond to popular understandings of the social problems to which law responds. The basic shape of the legislation is developed incrementally by judicial and prosecutorial discretion, but the symbolic importance of the legislative framework remains.

The offences of *riot* and *violent disorder* are inherently inchoate (the 'use' of violence needs, under s 8, amount only to conduct capable of causing damage to property) and inherently participatory (there is a requirement for a number present threatening or using violence). In *Jefferson* (1994), below, the Court of Appeal endorsed an extensive interpretation of riot and violent disorder, by dovetailing them with the normal participation rules which import liability to those who assist others to commit offences.

R v Jefferson [1994] 1 All ER 270

[*The four appellants were charged with riot, and in the alternative, violent disorder. In the absence of any specific violence by the appellants, the prosecution alleged that by their encouragement they had aided and abetted others in the use of unlawful violence. Two of them were convicted of riot (and sentenced, after a reduction on appeal in relation to one, to 21 months' imprisonment) and two of violent disorder (with sentences of 15 months and six months).*]

Auld J.

On the evening of 21 June 1990 there was serious and widespread public disorder in Bedford. It immediately followed and was occasioned by the victory by England over Egypt in a World Cup football match played that evening. The match, which had been televised, had been watched by many football fans in a number of public houses in the centre of Bedford. They spilled out onto the streets in what began as a celebration of victory but ended in widespread and sustained public disorder involving much violence and damage to property. The disorder, which eventually involved a crowd of about 300 youths, moved around the central area of Bedford. As the crowd moved about there were various individual incidents of violence and of criminal damage, and certain participants in the disorder were observed in various permutations at a number of such incidents. In the result, 30 youths were arrested and variously charged with offences under the Public Order Act 1986 and the Offences against the Person Act 1861 ...

The prosecution case against all the appellants on the counts of riot and violent disorder was that their presence at various of the specific incidents of disturbance and violence demonstrated a willing and persistent involvement in the disorder. The prosecution maintained that, although there might be no evidence of specific violence by any one of them, their presence at what took place was, and was intended by them to be, an encouragement to others to use violence. In short, the prosecution case was that each of them aided and abetted the violence of the night.

[One ground of appeal was that in relation to riot the indictment itself was defective since it referred to the defendants' using or threatening violence when the offence is committed only when violence is actually used. This might mislead the jury who have copies of the indictment before them.]

Counsel for the Crown conceded that Count 1 was badly framed. However ... he argued that, whatever the defect in the formulation of the count, the judge had directed the jury properly on the essential issues that they had to decide. In our view, counsel for the Crown is correct in his submissions. In so far as the complaint about the particulars is based on their incompleteness, it is difficult to see what further particulars of the use of 'unlawful violence' could have been given. It was plain from the way in which the prosecution put its case and from the judge's direction that the unlawful violence alleged was of a general character among a very large crowd of youths ... In so far as the complaint is based on the incorrect impression given by the wording of the count that a threat of unlawful violence alone might constitute the offence, the jury could not have been misled because it was never part of the prosecution case that any of these appellants individually threatened anyone with violence.

[As to the submission that the direction on common purpose was inadequate], the prosecution case from the outset was that the common purpose

of all those concerned in the riot, and of each appellant, was to use unlawful violence in celebrating the victory of England ... that evening ... the
jury could have been in no doubt that they could only convict any of
the appellants of riot if they were sure that he had used or was a party to
the use of violence for the overall common purpose ...

Counsel [for the two appellants convicted under s 2] submitted that the
offence of violent disorder, in common with the other offences created by
ss 1, 3, 4 and 5, is confined to the person who actually commits the actus
reus by virtue of s 6 of the Act.

Section 6, in a series of subsections, deals with the mental element
respectively required for each of the offences in ss 1 to 5. The formula in
each subsection is the same, namely that a person is guilty of the specified
offence 'only if he intends' a particular consequence appropriate to that
offence. In the case of violent disorder sub-s (2) provides that a person is
guilty of it 'only if he intends to use or threaten violence or is aware that
his conduct may be violent or threaten violence'. Counsel submitted
that the scheme of s 6, in particular the use of the term in the case of
each offence 'only if he intends', is to exclude [liability for aiding and
abetting] ...

In our judgment, the offences created by the 1986 Act may be committed by aiders and abettors as well as by principals ... In our view, s 6 is
concerned only with identifying, in statutory form, the requisite mens rea
for each of the offences ... It does not exclude or cut down in relation to
any of those offences the liability of an aider and abettor who is aware of
and party to the requisite intent of the principal offender ...

In the case of violent disorder ... the application of those principles
made them guilty under s 6(2) if they aided and abetted, by encouraging
and intending to encourage, others as described in s 2 intentionally to use
or threaten violence or, where appropriate, to use conduct that they were
aware might be violent or threaten violence. That is just how the judge put
it to the jury. For convenience, we repeat just one of the passages in the
summing up in which he put the point accurately, clearly and shortly:

> ... in order to prove that the defendant participated in this offence by
> encouraging others it is not enough to prove merely that he was
> present. It must be proved that he gave encouragement, and did so
> intending to encourage others to use unlawful violence.
> ... [after dealing with evidential grounds of appeal the judge concluded]
> Accordingly, none of the grounds of appeal against conviction having
> succeeded, each of these appeals against conviction is dismissed.

The combined effect of the inchoate and participatory nature of the offence
definitions and the derivative aiding and abetting doctrine applied in *Jefferson*
renders these widely-defined offences into ones of extraordinary breadth. No
specific 'use of violence' need be proved against the defendants.

II.b.iii.   Mental element

Public Order Act 1986, s 6
(1) A person is guilty of riot only if he intends to use violence or is aware
that his conduct may be violent.
(2) A person is guilty of violent disorder or affray only if he intends to use
or threaten violence or is aware that his conduct may be violent or
threaten violence.
[*(3) and (4) contain similar provisions in relation to the offences in ss 4 and 5.*]
(5) For the purposes of this section a person whose awareness is impaired
by intoxication shall be taken to be aware of that of which he would be
aware if not intoxicated, unless he shows either that his intoxication
was not self-induced, or that it was caused solely by the taking or
administration of a substance in the course of medical
treatment.[*Subsection (5) reverses the burden of proof but otherwise states
the general position in relation to involuntary intoxication (see **Chapter
3.III.d.**).*]
...
(7) Subsections (1) and (2) do not affect the determination for the
purposes of riot or violent disorder of the number of persons who use
or threaten violence.

We discuss the further raft of offences covering disorderly conduct (POA 1986,
ss 4, 4A and 5) and harassment (Protection From Harassment Act 1997) in
Chapter 3.

II.c.   *Trespass offences*

The Criminal Justice and Public Order Act 1994 (CJPOA 1994) restricts freedom of assembly considerably, with new powers of stop and search and removal
of trespassers from private land and provisions in relation to trespassory assemblies.

A key provision underpinning situations of perceived disorder is s 60 of the
CJPOA 1994, which introduces powers to stop and search people or vehicles
without the need for reasonable suspicion.

Criminal Justice and Public Order Act 1994, s 60

Powers to stop and search in anticipation of violence
(1) If a police officer of or above the rank of inspector reasonably
believes–
(a) that incidents involving serious violence may take place in any
locality in his police area, and that it is expedient to give an
authorisation under this section to prevent their occurrence, or

(b) that persons are carrying dangerous instruments or offensive weapons in any locality in his police area without good reason,

he may give an authorisation that the powers conferred by this section are to be exercisable at any place within that locality for a specified period not exceeding 24 hours. [This can be extended for a further 24 hours.]

...

(4) This section confers on any constable in uniform power–
   (a) to stop any pedestrian and search him or anything carried by him for offensive weapons or dangerous instruments;
   (b) to stop any vehicle and search the vehicle, its driver and any passenge for offensive weapons or dangerous instruments.

(5) A constable may, in the exercise of the powers conferred by subsection 4 above, stop any person or vehicle and make any search he thinks fit whether or not he has any grounds for suspecting that the person or vehicle is carrying weapons or articles of that kind.

(6) If in the course of a search under this section a constable discovers a dangerous instrument or an article which he has reasonable grounds for suspecting to be an offensive weapon, he may seize it.

Criminal Justice and Public Order Act 1994, s 61

Power to remove trespassers on land

(1) If the senior police officer present at the scene reasonably believes that two or more persons are trespassing on land and are present there with the common purpose of residing there for any period, that reasonable steps have been taken by or on behalf of the occupier to ask them to leave and–
   (a) that any of those persons has caused damage to the land or to property on the land or used threatening, abusive or insulting words or behaviour towards the occupier, a member of his family or an employee or agent of his, or
   (b) that those persons have between them six or more vehicles on the land,

   he may direct those persons, or any of them, to leave the land and to remove any vehicles or other property they have with them on the land.

(2) Where the persons in question are reasonably believed by the senior police officer to be persons who were not originally trespassers but have become trespassers on the land, the officer must reasonably believe that the other conditions specified in subsection (1) are satisfied after those persons became trespassers before he can exercise the power conferred by that subsection.

(3) A direction under subsection (1) above, if not communicated to the persons referred to in subsection (1) by the police officer giving

the direction, may be communicated to them by any constable at the scene.

(4) If a person knowing that a direction under subsection (1) above has been given which applies to him–

(a) fails to leave the land as soon as reasonably practicable, or

(b) having left again enters the land as a trespasser within the period of three months beginning with the day on which the direction was given,

he commits an offence and is liable on summary conviction to imprisonment for a term not exceeding three months or a fine not exceeding level 4 on the standard scale, or both.

(5) A constable in uniform who reasonably suspects that a person is committing an offence under this section may arrest him without a warrant.

(6) In proceedings for an offence under this section it is a defence for the accused to show–

(a) that he was not trespassing on the land, or

(b) that he had a reasonable excuse for failing to leave the land as soon as reasonably practicable or, as the case may be, for again entering the land as a trespasser.

As Sue Campbell explains, the trespass offences in the 1994 Act intended to deal with 'New Age Travellers', have severe implications for Gypsies:

Sue Campbell, 'Gypsies: The Criminalisation of a Way of Life?' [1995] Crim LR 28–37

[The CJPOA 1994] may soon devastate the ability of nomadic members of society to follow their traditional lifestyles. Two provisions of the Act, sections 61 and 77, have the combined result that, in the words of the Commission for Racial Equality, 'Gypsies will have two choices: either to become house dwellers or to be criminalised for following a nomadic way of life.' ...

In January 1992, the official count of Gypsy caravans revealed some 13,500 caravans in England and Wales. A majority of these (two-thirds) are legally sited whilst the remainder live under constant threat of eviction. The introduction of the Caravan Sites Act 1968 was hailed as a progressive and civilised measure. It sought to end the frequent, violent hostilities between Gypsies, the police and landowners arising from illegal occupation of land and was a recognition of Gypsies' right to a legal abode.

... Paradoxically, it might be thought that a permanent site is the last thing that a Gypsy, by definition of nomadic habit, would desire. However, successive post-war legislation had made it illegal for Gypsies to camp on their traditional sites forcing most Gypsies to concede that a sedentary life was preferable to the harassment and trauma caused by constant evictions

... With an ever increasing Gypsy population, demand for sites far exceeds supply and this seems to have contributed to the impetus for reform.

The Government has now repealed Part II of the 1968 Act on the ground that it had failed in its purpose of providing sufficient sites to keep pace with the need ...

It has been suggested that contributing to the impetus for reform, ... is the moral panic concerning the activities of large groups of travellers of non-Gypsy origin known as 'new age' travellers whose desire is to 'escape materialism, comfort and social status for a simple life in the hills and fields of rural England' ... Inevitably these two nomadic but culturally distinct groups have, in the public's perception, become entwined.

... Despite repeated ministerial assurances that the section is 'not aimed at the genuine Romany or other Gypsies', it gives considerable discretionary powers to the police in situations where the conditions necessary to trigger the offence could so readily be fulfilled by Gypsies and it is naive to suppose that powers conferred will not be powers used ...

Section 62 empowers a constable to seize and remove any vehicle after a reasonable time if he reasonably suspects that any person(s) to whom a direction to leave has been given under section 61 has failed to do so ... Thus, the decision to seize what is, in effect, a 'home' is left to the discretion of a constable. In view of the dire consequences of such action for Gypsy families in terms of homelessness and the possible break up of a family, is not a court a more appropriate forum for such a decision to be made?

Section 61 has been held compatible with Articles 3, 6 and 8 of the European Convention on Human Rights (*R (on the application of Fuller) v Chief Constable of Dorset Police* (2001)).

Sections 63 and 64 of the CJPOA 1994 deal with 'Raves', authorising superintendent police officers to issue 'dispersal' orders, entry and seizure of vehicles and sound equipment. As Smith comments (1995: 22): 'These are subject to no judicial surveillance, which is, to say the least, perturbing.' Echoes of policing the 1984 miners' strike are seen in s 65, which allows the police to stop a person believed to be travelling to a 'rave' (or 'gathering' in the 'open air' of 100 or more persons as the Act describes it) and direct them to proceed in a different direction.

Aggravated trespass under s 68, aimed at but not confined to hunt saboteurs, is another offence which seems to overlap with existing powers, in this case with the power to arrest for breach of the peace. The essence of aggravated trespass is 'trespass' (which could be a static assembly on the highway) in the open air and doing anything intended to:
- intimidate people and deter them from engaging in a lawful activity,
- obstruct a lawful activity, or
- disrupt a lawful activity.

Additionally, s 69 provides the police with power to direct people to leave the land. The senior police officer present may order people to leave if he or she believes:

- they are committing, have committed or intend to commit an offence of aggravated trespass in the open air; or
- that two or more people are trespassing and are present there with the common purpose of intimidating persons so as to deter them from or obstruct or disrupt a lawful activity.

Failure to leave or return within seven days, having been so directed, is an offence. The Divisional Court upheld the lawfulness of arrests of three protesters who were video-recording a foxhunt. Despite no evidence that there was any intimidation or intent to intimidate, it was held there was sufficient evidence to find that the police had reasonable grounds to believe there was an aggravated trespass. And the words to one, 'You either leave the land or you're arrested', were sufficient direction to all three to leave (*DPP v Capon*, 1997, discussed by Mead 1998).

The House of Lords, in *DPP v Jones*, below, took a more robust view of police powers over trespassory assemblies under s 14A of the POA 1986 (as inserted by s 70 of CJPOA 1994). Any chief officer of police may apply under this section to a local authority for an order prohibiting for a specified period all *trespassory public assemblies* in a specified area. The consent of the Home Secretary is required before s 14A can be used, and a trespassory assembly is one taking place on land to which the public has no right of access or a limited right of access (this might not cover the public highway but would encompass many shopping malls, educational institutions and other 'public' areas). Nonetheless, the section significantly broadens the effect of the original s 14 and its associated offences, which merely empowered the imposition of *conditions* on the holding of such assemblies. The offences of organising, taking part in or inciting another to take part in a trespassory assembly which has been banned, are all arrestable without warrant, punishable by three months' imprisonment, a level 4 fine and three months' imprisonment respectively (POA 1986, s 14B). This means that incitement to take part 'is an example of an incitement to commit a summary offence being subject to a higher maximum penalty than the offence itself' (Wasik and Taylor 1995: 89). An anticipatory 'stop and redirect' power, similar to that in s 65 in relation to 'raves', allows a uniformed police officer to prevent a person travelling towards a trespassory assembly (POA 1986, s 14C).

DPP v Jones [1999] 2 AC 240

Lord Irvine of Lairg, LC.

… [T]his appeal raises an issue of fundamental constitutional importance: what are the limits of the public's rights of access to the public highway?

Are these rights so restricted that they preclude in all circumstances any right of peaceful assembly on the public highway?

On 1 June 1995 at about 6.40 p.m. Police Inspector Mackie counted 21 people on the roadside verge of the southern side of the A344, adjacent to the perimeter fence of the monument at Stonehenge. ... He concluded that they constituted a "trespassory assembly" and told them so. When asked to move off, many did, but some, including the defendants, Mr. Lloyd and Dr. Jones, were determined to remain and put their rights to the test. They were arrested for taking part in a "trespassory assembly" and convicted by the Salisbury justices on 3 October 1995. Their appeals to the Salisbury Crown Court, however, succeeded. The court held that neither of the defendants, nor any member of their group, was "being destructive, violent, disorderly, threatening a breach of the peace or, on the evidence, doing anything other than reasonably using the highway."

[POA 1986, s 14A] permits a chief officer of police to apply, in certain circumstances, to the local council for an order prohibiting for a specified period "trespassory assemblies" within a specified area. An order of that kind may be obtained only in respect of land "to which the public has no right of access or only a limited right of access;" had been obtained in this case; and covered the area in which the defendants, with others, had assembled.

... The offence with which the defendants were charged is set out in section 14B(2): "A person who takes part in an assembly which he knows is prohibited by an order under section 14A is guilty of an offence."

...

The central issue in the case thus turns on two interrelated questions: (i) what are the "limits" of the public's right of access to the public highway at common law? and (ii) what is the "particular purpose" for which the public has a right to use the public highway?

... There is no suggestion in the Act of 1986 that the making of any order under section 14A(1) in itself defines the limits on the public's right of access to the highway. Rather, the conditions under which it is appropriate to make an order, and the conditions for the breach of such an order, are defined by reference to the *existing* limits upon the public's right of access. In other words, section 14A presupposes limited rights of access; it does not purport to impose such limits.

I conclude therefore the law to be that the public highway is a public place which the public may enjoy for any reasonable purpose, provided the activity in question does not amount to a public or private nuisance and does not obstruct the highway by unreasonably impeding the primary right of the public to pass and repass: within these qualifications there is a public right of peaceful assembly on the highway.

Since the law confers this public right, I deprecate any attempt artificially to restrict its scope. It must be for the magistrates in every case to decide whether the user of the highway under consideration is both reasonable in the sense defined and not inconsistent with the primary right of the public to pass and repass. In particular, there can be no principled basis for limiting the scope of the right by reference to the subjective intentions of the persons assembling. Once the right to assemble within the limitations I have defined is accepted, it is self-evident that it cannot be excluded by an intention to exercise it. Provided an assembly is reasonable and non-obstructive, taking into account its size, duration and the nature of the highway on which it takes place, it is irrelevant whether it is premeditated or spontaneous: what matters is its objective nature. To draw a distinction on the basis of anterior intention is in substance to reintroduce an incidentality requirement. For the reasons I have given, that requirement, properly applied, would make unlawful commonplace activities which are well accepted. Equally, to stipulate in the abstract any maximum size or duration for a lawful assembly would be an unwarranted restriction on the right defined. These judgments are ever ones of fact and degree for the court of trial.

Further, there can be no basis for distinguishing highways on publicly owned land and privately owned land. The nature of the public's right of use of the highway cannot depend upon whether the owner of the subsoil is a private landowner or a public authority. Any fear, however, that the rights of private landowners might be prejudiced by the right as defined are unfounded. The law of trespass will continue to protect private landowners against unreasonably large, unreasonably prolonged or unreasonably obstructive assemblies upon these highways.

Finally, I regard the conclusion at which I have arrived as desirable, because it promotes the harmonious development of two separate but related chapters in the common law. It is neither desirable in theory nor acceptable in practice for commonplace activities on the public highway not to count as breaches of the criminal law of wilful obstruction of the highway, yet to count as trespasses (even if intrinsically unlikely to be acted against in the civil law), and therefore form the basis for a finding of trespassory assembly for the purposes of the Act of 1986. A system of law sanctioning these discordant outcomes would not command respect.

However, Home Office research tends to confirm that the overall effect of the legislative flurry of the 1986 and 1994 Acts is to ensure that those charged with policing demonstrations and other gatherings can select from a splendid collection of powers.

Tom Bucke and Zoe James, *Trespass and Protest: Policing under the Criminal Justice and Public Order Act 1994* (Home Office Research Study 190, 1998) pp 33–36

Sections 68 and 69 of the CJPOA are aimed at trespassers who seek to intimidate or disrupt people engaged in a lawful activity on land.

These measures ... determine the line between two freedoms – to pursue a lawful activity and to express an opinion ... [They] were aimed primarily at the actions of hunt saboteurs and more generally at animal rights protesters seeking to disrupt or obstruct activities such as the shooting of game, horse-racing and angling (see Hansard, Vol 235, col 29) ... Their application [to environmental protesters] has in fact been one of the most important areas in which they have been applied.

... Hunt stewards seek to protect the hunt from saboteurs and other protesters and are encouraged by the British Field Sports Society. Ranging from local farmworkers to ex-soldiers and professional security guards, they may offer their services for no cost or require payment ...

Police officers' views on stewards were usually negative, since their use was viewed as leading to an escalation of the violence and disorder surrounding the hunt.

'One or two stewards were coming along who I think were worse than the sabs ... They were no more than glorified thugs.'

'They can't just be allowed to run around unchecked as vigilantes.'

'Luckily the hunt has stopped using stewards. Really they were thugs, they were bouncers.'

Table 4.1 Cautions and Court Proceedings for aggravated trespass (s 68) and failure to leave land when directed (s 69)

		Cautions	Prosecutions	Convictions
Aggravated trespass (s 68)	1995	7	111	64
	1996	14	359	211
Failure to leave land (s 69)	1995	11	15	12
	1996	0	27	11

...

Significantly, just over half of those prosecuted for aggravated trespass ... were convicted. This proportion is relatively low for magistrates' courts in which around 80 per cent of cases resulted in conviction, and reflects the extent to which well-organised groups of defendants contested their cases on the basis that the provisions had been incorrectly used. Those convicted under any of the CJPOA provisions were most likely to be given a conditional discharge or a fine.

The authors conclude that the police would have been present at the kinds of situations covered by their research irrespective of the existence of the CJPOA 1994 provisions. The Act places officers in a 'stronger legal position' to do that which they would previously have done.

II.d.   Breach of the peace

The common law power to arrest a person for breach of the peace (preserved by POA 1986, s 40(4)) can be regarded as the bottom-line in the police officer's extensive armoury. There is a breach of the peace whenever harm is actually done or is likely to be done to a person or in his presence to his property or a person is in fear of being so harmed through an assault, an affray, a riot, unlawful assembly or other disturbance (*R v Howell*, 1982; *Redmond-Bate v Director of Public Prosecutions*, 2000). Breach of the peace can take place on private land (*McConnell v Chief Constable of the Greater Manchester Police*, 1990). Arrest for breach of the peace can lead to a magistrates' court binding the person over to keep the peace or be of good behaviour (Justices of the Peace Act 1361). Over 21,000 individuals were subject to such orders in 2001. These connected powers of arrest and bind over, long taken for granted aspects of English law, have come under increasing challenge.

II.d.i.   Arrest

Arrest for breach of the peace was subjected to scrutiny by the European Court of Human Rights in *Steel v UK* (1999). The case is summarised in *McGrogan* below.

Chief Constable of Cleveland Police v Mark Anthony McGrogan [2002] EWCA Civ 86 Court of Appeal (Civil Division)

Mr. Justice Wall.

The Chief Constable of the Cleveland Constabulary (the appellant) appeals ... from an order made by His Honour Judge Bowers sitting at the Middlesbrough County Court on 10 January 2001 in which he gave judgment for Mark Anthony McGrogan (the claimant) in the sum of £1,500. He also ordered the appellant to pay 70% of the claimant's costs.

The proceedings giving rise to this appeal are an action brought by the claimant against the appellant for wrongful arrest and false imprisonment, in which he sought damages, including aggravated and exemplary damages limited to £50,000. [T]he judge "with great reluctance" came to the conclusion that part of the claimant's detention in a police station ... was unjustified. In giving permission to appeal, the judge stated that the case raised issues of law and practice of general importance regarding the continued detention by the police of a person detained for causing/being likely to cause a breach of the peace ...

[Quoting from the judge's account of the facts:]

"P.C. Greenheld attended ... in response to a complaint by a member of the public that a man ... was attacking a woman and dragging her by the hair ...

He saw the claimant and Miss M (the victim). The latter complained to him that the claimant had pulled her by the hair, dragged her to the floor and kicked her several times in the head. She appeared pale, dishevelled and in obvious pain and distress. He thought that she may have had some redness around the face.

He arrested the claimant on suspicion of assault occasioning actual bodily harm and when cautioned the claimant made no reply. He was concerned for the victim of the assault and immediately transported her to hospital and returned to the police station to which other officers had brought the claimant.

… It is accepted that the only issue for me to decide on this part of the case is whether P.C. Greenheld had reasonable cause to suspect that Miss M had suffered some actual bodily harm. Common assault is not an arrestable offence whereas assault occasioning actual bodily harm is an arrestable offence. Actual bodily harm is any hurt or injury calculated to interfere with the health and so called comfort of the victim and must be more than merely trivial or transient. Mere emotions, fear distress or panic, will not suffice.

I am quite satisfied that there were reasonable grounds to suspect that Miss M had sustained some bodily injury … [which] would be sufficient bodily harm for the purposes of the offence in law …

… [At the police station] the claimant became violent banging his head against the wall and then became extremely violent and had to be restrained by officers and put into a cell to calm down. His detention was actually authorised on the custody record at 14.56 and an entry at 15.00 describes the claimant's bizarre and violent behaviour. He was not sufficiently calm to be informed of his rights until 16.10.

… I reject the claimant's evidence of events at the Police Station … I find that the claimant was lawfully arrested and detained on suspicion of assault occasioning actual bodily harm and his continued detention was authorised on a lawful basis to enable evidence to be obtained from the victim and others and in order to question the claimant in due course."

The judge describes this part of his judgment as "the arrest and first detention". No criticism has been made before in this court either of the conduct of the police in arresting and detaining the claimant during this period or of the judge's findings in relation to it.

The judge then moved on to what he calls "the second period of detention" with which he deals as follows:

P.C. Smithson was sent to take a statement from Miss M. He had previous experience of the claimant and Miss M, and had been involved over domestic arguments between (them) during the previous six to eight months. He knew that she was addicted to heroin and believed that the claimant was also so addicted. Apart from his involvement, he was aware of regular incidents between them when other officers had attended.

He observed Miss M's fear and distress and considered that she was emotionally "stressed out" and terrified that the claimant would return to her home. She, in fact, packed all the claimant's belongings and gave them to him so that the claimant would have no reason to return ... Even though he was given the claimant's clothes and there was no need for him to return he considered that he might well return and a further breach of the peace would ensue.

He took a statement from Miss M in which she stated that she did not wish to make a complaint of assault against the claimant. P.C. Smithson considered that this was out of fear and a wish to avoid any further contact with the claimant – although the statement does not state as such.

I accept P.C. Smithson's statement and evidence. He, in my judgment, knew that the CPS would not regard the minor injury as sufficient to charge assault occasioning actual bodily harm and was correct in his assessment that if allowed his liberty it was highly probable that the claimant would return to Miss M's home and a breach of the peace would occur. He was genuinely and rightly concerned for the safety of Miss M if the claimant was released that evening.

Upon returning to the Police Station with the claimant's clothes, he and Sgt. Brock agreed that an information would be laid against the claimant for causing a breach of the peace and to detain him until he could be brought before the first available court which would be on Monday morning ...

The word "charged" is not strictly correct but is the word used in the computer handling system.

...

We thus move to the critical part of the case, namely the review which took place at 13.50 on Sunday 5 April 1998, and the decision of the police to continue the claimant's detention thereafter ...

It is plain that the concept of a breach of the peace, including the power to arrest in order to prevent it, is something of an anomaly in English law. It was, however, expressly preserved by (PACE) and has recently survived the scrutiny of the European Court of Human Rights in *Steel v UK* ...

At paragraph 55 of its judgment, the court commented:

"In this connection, the court observes that the concept of breach of the peace had been clarified by the English courts over the last two decades, to the extent that it is now sufficiently established that a breach of the peace is committed only when an individual causes harm, or appears likely to cause harm, to persons or property or acts in a manner the natural consequence of which would be to provoke others to violence. It is also clear that a person may be arrested for causing a breach of the peace or where it is reasonably apprehended that he or she is likely to cause a breach of the peace.

Accordingly, the Court considers that the relevant legal rules provided sufficient guidance and were formulated with the degree of precision required by the Convention."

Steel v UK comprised a number of cases all concerning the arrest and detention of protesters for breaches of the peace. For present purposes, the relevant Article of the European Convention on Human Rights and Fundamental Freedoms (the Convention) is Article 5, which in its material parts, provides:

Right to liberty and security
1. Everyone has the right to liberty and security of person. No one shall be deprived of his liberty save in the following cases and in accordance with a procedure prescribed by law: ... (c) the lawful arrest or detention of a person effected for the purpose of bringing him before the competent legal authority on reasonable suspicion of having committed an offence or when it is reasonably considered necessary to prevent his committing an offence or fleeing after having done so ...
2. Everyone who is arrested shall be informed promptly, in a language which he understands, of the reasons for his arrest and of any charge against him.
3. Everyone arrested or detained in accordance with the provisions of paragraph 1(c) of this Article shall be brought promptly before a judge or other officer authorised by law to exercise judicial power and shall be entitled to trial within a reasonable time or to release pending trial. Release may be conditioned by guarantees to appear for trial ...
5. Everyone who has been the victim of arrest or detention in contravention of the provisions of this Article shall have an enforceable right to compensation.

In the first case, the applicant, with 60 others, had attempted to obstruct a grouse shoot. She was arrested for breach of the peace for impeding the progress of a member of the shoot by walking in front of him as he lifted his shotgun. She was detained for a total of 44 hours before being released on conditional bail. She was charged with breach of the peace and using threatening words or behaviour contrary to section 5 of the Public Order Act 1986. [Convicted of both she appealed against the latter] but the conviction was upheld, and upon her refusal to be bound over, she was committed to prison for 28 days.

In the second case, the applicant had taken part in a protest against the building of an extension of a motorway. The protesters had repeatedly broken into a construction site and the appellant was arrested whilst standing under a digger, for conduct likely to provoke a disturbance of the peace. She was detained for approximately 17 hours. The magistrates found that the allegation of conduct likely to cause a breach of the peace was made out. She was ordered to agree to be bound over for 12 months to keep the peace in the sum of a £100, and when she refused she was imprisoned for 7 days.

In the third case, a group of three applicants had attended a "Fighter Helicopter II" conference in order to protest with others against the sale of fighter helicopters. They handed out leaflets and held up banners saying "Work for peace not war". They were arrested and taken to a Police Station where their custody record stated the "circumstances" as being that they were acting in breach of the peace. Having been detained for 7 hours they were taken before the magistrates who adjourned the hearing through lack of time. The applicants were released and when proceedings were resumed a month later the prosecution called no evidence and the magistrates dismissed the case against them.

The applicants in all three cases complained (inter alia) under Article 5 of the Convention that the concept of breach of the peace and the power to bind over were not sufficiently clearly defined for their detention to be "prescribed by law"; that their detention did not fall into any of the categories under Article 5(1) and that, because of the immunity of magistrates from civil proceedings, they had been denied a right to compensation in violation of Article 5(5).

For present purposes, it is sufficient to record that the Court concluded there had not been a violation of Article 5(1) of the Convention as regards the arrest and detention of the first two applicants. It found no reason to doubt that the police were justified in fearing that the behaviour of these applicants, if persisted in, might provoke others to violence. However, in relation to the three applicants in the third case, the court held unanimously that there had been breaches of Article 5(1), as the three individuals were conducting an entirely peaceful protest, and the Court found no indication that their behaviour was likely to cause a breach of the peace or to justify the police in fearing that a breach of the peace was likely to be caused.

...

The appellant's complaint, ... is not that the judge applied the wrong test; rather that, having formulated the correct test, he failed to apply it.

I have come to the conclusion that there is force in these criticisms ... and that their cumulative effect is sufficient to persuade me that the judge reached the wrong conclusion. I am reinforced in this view by the fact that the judge, in finding that the claimant's detention after about 13.50 on Sunday 5 April 2001 was not justified, did not appear to give any or any sufficient weight to several important factors, including: (1) the fears expressed by Miss M that the claimant would return and assault her; and (2) the fact that her accommodation remained within walking distance of the police station, and was thus likely to be the place to which the claimant would go.

... In setting out his reasons for holding the earlier period of detention lawful, the judge (perceptively in my view) had referred to the fact that the claimant was "likely to be further inflamed when he was handed his belongings upon his release". In my judgment that factor remained live at 13.50 on the afternoon of Sunday 5 April 1998.

In all these circumstances I have come to the clear conclusion that had the judge properly applied the test he formulated for himself, he would have come to the conclusion that the continuing detention of the claimant until he could be brought before the magistrates on Monday 6 April 2001 was justified.

For all these reasons, I would allow this appeal, and set aside the judgment in the claimant's favour.

[Lord Justice Mantell agreed.]

The above cases demonstrate the wide range of uses to which breach of the peace powers of arrest can be put. In addition to classic public order situations, breach of the peace is commonly employed in defusing domestic violence (see Sanders 1988). *McGrogan* also anticipates the point we make in **Chapter 3** in relation to POA 1986, s 5 offences, that the power to detain is often of more significance than determining the appropriate offence to charge.

II.d.ii.   Bind over

Closely connected with powers of arrest for breach of the peace is the corresponding magistrates' power to bind persons over to be of good behaviour or to keep the peace. This has a long and chequered history. The European Court of Human Rights has held that this may breach Article 10. The applicants in *Hashman and Harrup v United Kingdom* (2000) blew a hunting horn and engaged in hallooing with the intention of disrupting the activities of the Portman Hunt. The applicants were bound over by magistrates under the Justices of the Peace Act 1361 to keep the peace and be of good behaviour in the sum of £100 for 12 months. On appeal, the Crown Court concluded that the applicants had not committed any breach of the peace, and that their conduct had not been likely to occasion a breach of the peace. The Court however concluded that the applicants' behaviour had been a deliberate attempt to interfere with the Portman Hunt and to take hounds out of the control of the huntsman. In this respect their actions were unlawful and had exposed the hounds to danger and the applicants were likely to repeat this behaviour. The applicants' actions were *contra bonos mores* and therefore they should be bound over to keep the peace and be of good behaviour.

The ECHR held that there had been a violation of Article 10. The binding over of the applicants was an interference with the applicants' right to freedom of expression under Article 10(1) because the proceedings were brought against the applicants as a result of their protesting against hunting by disrupting the hunt. Such a protest constituted an expression of opinion within the meaning of Article 10(1). That right can be interfered with under Article 10, para 2 if the interference to be 'prescribed by law' satisfies the 'quality of law' tests developed by the court. The interference was not 'prescribed by law'. The definition of *contra bonos mores* as: 'behaviour which is wrong rather than right in the judgment of the majority of contemporary fellow citizens' was inadequate because it failed to give a clear indication of the conduct which was prohibited. One element of quality of law is certainty. The legal rule must be 'formulated with sufficient precision to enable the citizen to regulate his conduct'.

The Law Commission's recommendation that powers to bind over be abolished (1994) has been ignored. However, the Government shows every sign of retaining its various forms. While the main type is that discussed here, there are also variants such as binding over at the Crown Court and parent recognisances (Magistrates Court Act 1980; Powers of Criminal Courts (Sentencing) Act 2000, ss 1(6) and 150). In a consultation paper issued in 2003 in response to *Hashman and Harrup*, it is suggested that 'the underlying issues of *certainty* and *fairness*' can be resolved by an order that binds over an individual to do or refrain from doing specific activities, rather than 'to keep the peace' or 'to be of good behaviour' (Home Office 2003c: paras 9.4, 9.5).

II.e.   Fixed penalty notices (on-the-spot fines)

On-the-spot fines for offences such as being drunk and disorderly and making hoax 999 emergency calls, introduced in the Criminal Justice and Police Act 2001, came into force in 2003 (initially in trial areas but rapidly extended nationally by the end of the year). Fixed penalty notices of £80 and £40 will be issued if the person admits her guilt and is compliant. Offenders will not be given a criminal record unless they deny the offence and are found guilty in court. Offences covered by the £80 fine are: wasting police time, making annoying telephone calls, false calls to the emergency services and using abusive language or behaviour. People who admit being drunk and disorderly, trespassing on a railway, throwing stones at trains or throwing fireworks may be fined £40. Arrest follows if a person either fails to admit the offence or cannot produce a credit card or driving licence to prove identity. Offenders who admit their crime will be issued with a ticket, like a speeding or parking ticket, to be paid within 21 days. The Anti-Social Behaviour Bill 2003 extends the list of offences that can be discharged by fixed penalty to include parents of truanting children. It also lowers the age from 18 to 16 from which notices for disorderly behaviour may be issued.

In the pilot schemes, over half of notices were paid within 21 days and only 2% opted for a court hearing. Fines not settled within three weeks are automatically doubled, yet 44% remained unpaid. The scheme raises serious questions about due process. There is a strong incentive to pay now rather than dispute the enforcing officer's assessment of the situation. And it is not only police officers that have the power to issue notices: the Anti-Social Behaviour Bill 2003 extends the power to neighbourhood wardens and community safety officers.

M Wasik 'Legislating in the Shadow of the Human Rights Act: the Criminal Justice and Police Act 2001' [2001] Crim LR 931

Section 1 lists the offences which may lead to the issuing by the police of what is misleadingly described in the section heading as an "on the spot" penalty. Payment "on the spot" is not required, and the recipient of the notice has 21 days to pay up before proceedings for the offence can be brought. A fixed penalty provides a further way of dealing with such behaviour (aside from the existing options of informal warning, formal caution, and prosecution). ...

Section 2(1) states that where "a constable ... has reason to believe that a person aged 18 or over has committed a penalty offence [he] may give him a penalty notice in respect of the offence". Home Office guidance notes state that this subsection "has the effect of applying the scheme to adults (i.e. 18 and over)". No doubt that is how the provision will be construed, but that is arguably not what it says. As currently worded, a notice may validly be issued to a person whom the officer mistakenly believes to be 18. The purported restriction to those aged 18 or over may seem surprising in any event, since much disorder of the kinds described (e.g. playing with fireworks, or throwing stones at trains) is surely more associated with juveniles. There was discussion at Committee Stage of the Bill of practical issues such as whether the police would be able to distinguish disorderly youths aged 16 or 17 from those aged 18, and how those who gave false names might be dealt with. ... There must be other doubts over the practicality of a scheme which may often require a group of drunken people to wait around while a police officer spends several minutes making the appropriate explanations and writing out the notice(s). There is no facility in this legislation to serve notices by post, as in the case of fixed penalty traffic notices.

The penalty notice offers an opportunity to discharge any liability to be convicted of the offence, so it follows that if the person pays the penalty they acquire no formal criminal record. Unlike a formal caution, however, the penalty notice does not require the person to make an admission of guilt. There is an interesting ambiguity about fixed penalty notices. They can be seen as a decriminalising measure, in that the recipient who pays up avoids the stigma of conviction, but they could have a net-widening effect if used against those who would otherwise have been warned informally. In common with the formal caution, any victim of the offence loses the opportunity to receive compensation by way of a compensation order. Mr Clarke offered assurances during the passage of the Bill that guidance to be issued to the police on the operation on penalty notices under section 6 would deal with that point, stating that where a person could be identified as a victim of the offence, a penalty notice would not be issued. This is an important implication of the scheme, and might perhaps have been included in the legislation. Section 3 allows the Secretary of State to specify the level of penalty for each offence listed, up to a maximum of one quarter of the maximum fine for the offence. Unlike a fine, a fixed penalty carries no opportunity for adjustment to take account of the person's income.

If the recipient of a penalty notice makes payment within the prescribed period no proceedings can be brought. The person may, however, instead of paying the penalty make a "request to be tried", and then proceedings may be brought. If the recipient of the notice neither pays the penalty within the prescribed period nor makes a request to be tried, a sum equal to one and a half times the amount of the penalty may be registered as a fine and enforced against him. The "request to be tried" provides an opportunity for a person to deny commission of the offence. If the person makes a request to be tried, is prosecuted and ultimately loses, the implications of this course are not spelt out in the legislation. It would seem that there is then (i) a conviction for the offence, and consequent criminal record, and (ii) exposure to a fine greater than one and a half times the penalty or, in an appropriate case, to a community or custodial sentence. The Joint Committee commented that "in so far as a fixed penalty offence is serious enough to amount to a criminal charge within the meaning of ECHR Article 6.1, we consider the right to request trial is adequately protected".

FURTHER READING

Deards, Elspeth (2002) 'Human Rights for Football Hooligans' 27 ELR 206.
Fenwick, Helen and Phillipson, Gavin (2000) 'Public Protest, the Human Rights Act and Judicial Responses to Political Expression' Public Law 627.
Marston, John and Tain, Paul (2001) *Public Order The Criminal Law* (Callow).
Smith, A T H (1987) *Offences Against Public Order* (Sweet & Maxwell).
— (1995) 'The Criminal Justice and Public Order Act 1994: The Public Order Elements' Crim LR 19.

III. Criminal law and justice: emerging themes

It is clear by now that, more than in almost any other area, substantive law and police powers and practices in the public order sphere are intertwined. Often powers to intervene are backed by criminal offences on failure to comply, rather than criminal offences being backed by powers to arrest. Examples are the powers to ban trespassory assemblies and those in relation to aggravated trespass. Or, in the case of breach of the peace, a power to arrest and seek a bind over exists without a corresponding offence. Whereas in many areas of crime, the police are dependent on public reporting of incidents, here the police are effectively in a position to define the situation as disclosing an offence in order to justify their actions. In many cases, offences apparently designed to protect members of the public, are used by the police to protect themselves. As we will see in the next chapter, s 5 of the Public Order Act 1986 is a fine example. Home Office research concluded that in more than one in 10 s 5 arrests the police were the sole victims of the offensive behaviour (Brown and Ellis HORS 135 1994: viii).

III.a. Public order and criminal law

The offences we have discussed raise some general issues. First, to what extent do explicit 'public order' offences demonstrate any special qualities as instances of criminal law? According to Smith, this is indeed the case:

A T H Smith, *Offences Against Public Order* (Sweet & Maxwell, 1987) pp 1–3

As a general principle we employ the criminal law to prevent harm to certain social interests such as personal safety and physical integrity, and rights in property. The deliberate infliction of harm that the criminal sanction entails is justified as being designed to protect one or other of those interests, or because (to adopt a retributive justification) the offender has harmed such an interest. What is the comparable value in public order that we seek to preserve through the laws of riot, affray, violent disorder and the other, more minor, offences? Our physical integrity and safety are protected by the offences against the person, and the offences against property are designed to safeguard private property from those who would deprive us of it by stealth or violence.

By comparison with these clearly visible social needs, the interests protected by public order law are much more diffuse and indeterminate. Public order law ranges in its extent from the preservation of mere peace and tranquillity as between rowing neighbours or the prevention of unreasonable street exhibitionism – nuisance on the outer margins of criminality – to threats of an altogether different magnitude. When public order and stability are jeopardised as they are in cases of affray and violent disorder, public fear is aroused in the minds of bystanders and witnesses that the conduct impugned may lead to physical harm to persons and property. The interests to be protected are therefore, in a sense, inchoate. In cases of really serious outbreaks of public disorder amounting to riot, the constitutional stability of the country itself may seem to be threatened. There is in such situations a visible threat to the rule of law which may lead to a loss of public confidence in the ability of society to regulate itself. When the head that wore the Crown was more uneasy than it is today, the crimes of sedition and treason were employed to preserve society from (or punish after the event) widespread outbreaks of disorder. Here, we are at the borderline between riots and revolutions. But as Professor Dahrendorf [1985: 33] points out, many of these severe forms of disorder somehow defy a sanctioning process which is essentially geared to individuals and identifiable small groups. The implications of this insight were not, perhaps, fully appreciated by those responsible for framing the law that has become the Public Order Act 1986.

Historically, the offences of group disorder (riot, unlawful assembly and affray) were most unusual in English criminal jurisprudence. In principle criminal responsibility was (and is) individual and personal. Criminal liability attaches only where the individual himself brings about a proscribed harm or encourages another to do so. A person is only rarely liable for what others have done, and then only derivatively. Furthermore, mere presence at the scene of an offence is not sufficient to attract liability: proof is required of encouragement and an intention to encourage. Failure to dissociate oneself from what is happening is apt to be regarded indulgently by the common law, which is reluctant to punish omissions.

The conduct struck at by the group disorder offences is at variance with these principles, or at least places them under strain; the very essence of these offences is that the offender is one of a group of persons whose conduct together is such as to cause public fear and alarm. The law could respond to this in two quite distinct ways; it could compromise with the individualistic principles outlined, and regard presence at the scene of a disorder without more as being in itself reprehensible, but not very serious. Proof of the offender's presence at the scene would suffice. Historically, it is suggested, the common law preferred this course. Riot was regarded as a particularly heinous offence only when it became a challenge to authority after those responsible for preserving order had tried to do so, and the Riot Act had been read. Until then, it was a misdemeanour only.

Alternatively, the law could regard participation in one of the offences of group disorder as being very serious, and seek to build into the definitions of the offences the elements of individual participation of which Professor Dahrendorf speaks. It might then be justifiable to regard the commission of the offence as particularly serious. Several reasons may be offered for adopting the second course. A person who is part of a group will draw courage from the conduct of others in the group, and may well behave in ways that he would not act when alone. His chances of detection are, in the nature of things, rather lower when he can hide in the rabble. Another justification for the second alternative is that where several people are present together acting violently, their weight of numbers in itself increases the dangers to public order inherent in their conduct. A mob is not merely a collection of individuals, but a collective entity. Even though the participants cannot be proved individually to have caused any injury or damage, there is some justification in treating members of a group whose conduct causes such damage as being jointly responsible for what has happened.

The framers of the [1986] Act have adopted this second course.

This is an elegant statement of some of the major principles of traditional criminal law doctrine, and raises some important issues about the special nature of public order law. However, several of Smith's points are open to question. Whilst the argument that the harms addressed by public order law are intangible, inchoate and thus somehow marginal, has some validity, it is in stark contrast to the way in which public order aspects of particular areas of offending are sometimes used to increase their seriousness and to add to arguments for control. Sanders (1988) found that police decisions to push for prosecution in cases of domestic violence were affected in an important way by their perceptions not so much of whether a situation was domestic or not, but rather whether it threatened public order. Of course, these two may be related, in that in a sexist culture, the police are less likely to regard domestic violence against women as raising any kind of public order problem. Far from being on the 'outer margins of criminality', public order problems might be seen as constituting the very core of crime as socially constructed.

Smith is correct to draw attention to the way in which public order offences stretch traditional doctrinal principles of individual responsibility; as we shall see, this is particularly the case given the cumulation of already verging-on-the-inchoate substantive public order laws with principles of secondary liability. However, we should be cautious about accepting the validity of these traditional doctrinal claims in respect of other areas of criminal law. What is more, the extent to which the framers of the Act may genuinely be regarded as having opted for Smith's 'second course', or at least as having lived up to their choice, must be doubted in the light of the definition of riot. In the first place, the required minimum number involved is extraordinarily small, especially in view of the fact that the 'mens rea' requirement is relevant only to the individual defendant. Thus, in theory, a person could be guilty of riot even if she were the only person who could be proved to have intended or been 'subjectively' reckless as to the violence of her conduct (see *R v Mahroof*, 1989 and the succeeding note by J C Smith). Moreover, the facts that the violence or threat of it need not be simultaneous and that common purpose may be inferred from the conduct, make this allegedly very serious offence potentially applicable to an extraordinarily wide range of cases.

Riot, for example, can be committed in 'private' places (the restriction of the lesser offences to acts not committed inside dwellings confirms that the significance of the private sphere is attenuated rather than abandoned), and no 'person of reasonable firmness' need actually be present. The framing of the test in terms of the reactions of a hypothetical reasonable person acts as a positive invitation to the tribunal to interpret the situation in terms of what their own perceptions and judgment would have been. Can such a tribunal distinguish between the person who was defending herself in a disordered situation, one who was fighting with the police, or one who was simply trying to remove herself from the situation? Can a clear distinction between liability for acts and for omissions be maintained in a context where initial presence may already invoke the court's opprobrium and a willingness to interpret a defendant as having certain predispositions? Is 'subjective' 'mens rea' any real guarantee of fairness to the defendant? All these things seem dubious. Those who participate in politically oppositional events which are known occasionally to lead to disorder do so at the peril of having criminal purposes inferred and finding themselves convicted of very serious offences.

Secondly, the relationship between the Public Order Acts and instances of disorder and moral panics raises questions about the pragmatism of explicitly order-orientated legislation, its political functions, and its symbolic aspects. Public order has always been an area in which governments have been tempted to assert their authority by responding to particular events with legislation. The relationship between the Public Order Act 1936 and Fascist disturbances is well known and the 1986 legislation shares this reactive quality (Scraton 1985). This process has accelerated in the last 20 years with a battery of offences maintaining the 'peace' between the 'orderly' and the 'disorderly'. The perceived threat to public and private space by disparate (mainly youthful) groups attending 'raves' and 'acid-house parties', disrupting hunting, protesting about road-building and forming bands of 'eco-warriors' is reflected in a stream of statutes, perhaps reaching its apotheosis in the introduction of anti-social behaviour orders (Crime and Disorder Act 1998, discussed in **Chapter 3**).

What is significant about these examples of legislative opportunism and reactiveness is that they have resulted in changes which are more important symbolically than in instrumental terms. Obviously, increased police powers under the 1986 and 1994 Acts with respect to the regulation of assemblies and marches, and the extension of criminal law into the area of trespass, are important and material changes. But many other changes add very little in real terms to existing police and legal powers to deal with disorder. The political rhetoric surrounding the Acts, which had very much to do with equipping the police and the courts to deal with increasing lawlessness and threats to authority, emphasised the need for these offences. But, as the experience of the miners' strike in 1984 demonstrates, the police already had all the powers they could possibly have in legal terms, particularly in their power to arrest for actual or anticipated breaches of the peace, which is untouched by the Acts. So these new offences add little to police powers other than in providing substantive offences which mirror more closely public and media constructions of the conduct in question. In the context of spontaneous disorders such as inner-city 'riots', issues of police hardware such as water cannon and plastic bullets are far more important to quelling disorder than any kind of substantive law. Even powers to ban or impose conditions in advance are quite inapposite to the prevention or resolution of this kind of disorder. It must be concluded that the passing of the 1986 and 1994 Acts had more to do with the symbolic affirmation of a political commitment to enforcing public order, maintaining public authority and expressing support for the agencies of control than it had to do with instrumental changes in criminal law (Waddington 1991).

Thirdly, public order law is a useful area in which to consider a general feature of legal method. Whilst any criminal law relates potentially to a great variety of different kinds of behaviour in very different contexts, nevertheless, and inevitably, it constructs the world in terms of a limited number of fixed categories and conceptualisations, into which that diversity of behaviour has to be fitted. These legal categories do not necessarily match the viewpoints or self-understandings of the subjects in question – either members of the public in general, or participants in situations of disorder. Doctrinal insistence on the irrelevance of motive, although unevenly realised, is central to this feature of legal method. For example, what to the participants is a demonstration, an expression of opinion or emotion, a leisure activity or even a lifestyle will, in legal fora, become riot, violent disorder, provocation of violence, criminal trespass or obstruction. Moreover, legal categories systematically suppress the political and value-orientated aspects of the issues which come before the courts. A striking example of this is to be found in the case of *Beatty v Gillbanks* (1882), which concerned the problem of a peaceful demonstration being met by a hostile and disruptive audience. Discussions of the implications of *Beatty* in later case law (eg *Duncan v Jones*, 1936) have tended to concentrate on sophisticated legal arguments about 'mens rea' and 'causation', obscuring the fact that what is really at issue here is political judgment about weighing the values of public tranquillity against the interests of particular groups in associating and expressing themselves. This in itself is a classically liberal way of constructing the problem – yet even this straightforward human rights issue had to be read, before the Human Rights Act 1998, between the lines of English criminal law discourse.

In the area of public order law we can see clearly how this kind of legal method combines with the legitimising ideology of the rule of law to set up legal definitions as dominant, authoritative and objective. Legal categories encapsulate the authoritative view of what constitutes illegitimate disorder, and, moreover, do so in a way that is not overtly political. The traditional doctrinal story about clear and general rules that are promulgated and applied as announced allows the political sting to be taken out of the suppression of disorder. Political power is exercised with a low profile by means of wide discretionary power at all stages of the criminal process, leaving the law clean of political taint (see Norrie 2001: Ch 1).

Fourthly, some specific features of the offences which we have cited should be noted. We have already discussed the openness of the definition of riot to the discretionary interpretation of the tribunal, particularly in terms of the inference of common purpose and of 'situational' 'mens rea'. The very structure of individual responsibility and liability seems artificial in the context of public disorder situations when a person's actions can only be assessed and understood in terms of the group situation, which is itself likely to be judged on the basis of standards broader and less susceptible of scrutiny than those contained in the legal definition of riot. The use of the test of a 'person of reasonable firmness', which mirrors the use of 'objective' tests of 'reasonableness' throughout the Act, raises a further question about the ideological rather than instrumental significance of the Act's insistence on 'subjective' 'mens rea'. For although 'objective' tests are logically distinct from 'subjective' ones, and it can be argued that 'reasonableness' tests directly invite the tribunal to judge on the basis of their own personal assessments (we can hardly assume that they see themselves as unreasonable). A tribunal is bound to judge what they think the defendant *did* intend or foresee in terms of what they think she *must have* intended or foreseen, and this is in turn likely to be influenced by what they think they (as 'reasonable people' – or should we say 'reasonable men'?) would have been intended or foreseen in the circumstances. Once again, the relevance of their normative judgments about the surrounding context is only too obvious. Furthermore, the offence of riot furnishes a useful example of tensions within criminal law's construction of 'mens rea' between views of crime which stress individual responsibility and those which recognise determining causes of crime.

A Norrie, *Law, Ideology and Punishment* (Kluwer, 1991) pp 250–251

Here, I wish simply to consider a piece of reasoning which I would argue is commonplace in criminal courts, although it does not emanate from one. In his Report into the Brixton riots (Cmnd 8427), Lord Scarman details in cause and effect terms the reasons for the 1981 riots in Brixton. The causes are both general and specific, and their conjunction provides the explanation for the occurrence of riot. On the general level, the causes include unemployment, discrimination, housing, environmental conditions, etc: 'Where deprivation and frustration exist on the scale to be found among the young black people of Brixton, the probability of disorder must be strong' (p. 16). Given such a general predisposition, all that is required is a spark to set the tinder ablaze. For example:

Deeper causes undoubtedly existed, and must be probed: but the immediate cause of Saturday's events was a spontaneous combustion set off by the spark of one single incident. (p. 37)

Thus, riot is explained in terms of a complex of necessary and sufficient causes. Yet Lord Scarman at one point puts off his determinism and puts on his legal robe:

The social conditions in Brixton ... do not provide an excuse for disorder. They cannot justify attacks on the police in the streets, arson or riot. All those who in the course of the disorder in Brixton and elsewhere engaged in violence against the police were guilty of grave criminal offences, which society, if it is to survive, cannot condone. Sympathy for, and understanding of, the plight of young black people ... are no reason for releasing [them] from the responsibilities for public order which they share with the rest of us ... (p. 14)

Scarman's drift is ambiguous. In part this appears to be simply a utilitarian argument concerning what society must do if it is to survive. But equally, in part, it appears to be a retributive argument concerning the guilt and responsibility of young blacks for their actions. If this is so, however, in shifting from an account of the causes of disorder to a discussion of the individual's responsibility for that disorder, he has jumped from a discourse premised upon determinism to one premised upon individual responsibility and freewill. But he cannot have it both ways, for either the acts of young black people are free in a contra-causal sense or they are causally determined, they cannot be both, and no compatibilist compromise is ... available.

My reason for examining Lord Scarman's remarks is that it seems to me that something like this reasoning occurs day in day out in the criminal courts through the two stages of conviction and sentencing. For conviction, the individual is regarded as a free, juridical individual, unhindered by his personal or social conditions. In relation to the sentence, however, considerations of background are admitted as a means of mitigating punishment, and these normally take the form of analysis of the circumstances which led the accused into his current sorry position ...

The law's unreflective nature is not a failure of understanding alone. Rather it is a product of the fundamental nature of both the legal form and the law's function. Law is inherently concerned with individual responsibility and individual blame, and therefore it must focus on individual agency to the exclusion of its conditions of existence: law must decontextualise action if it is to attribute responsibility to individuals. If it looks behind agency to, for example, the social conditions of agency as did Lord Scarman in his analysis of urban riot, then it becomes impossible and irrelevant to blame individuals. Similarly, the function of law is to control rational individuals through their conviction, punishment and deterrence. If individuals are not seen in this abstract manner, but rather are placed in context, then this function becomes futile. Justice would entail not the conviction and deterrence of responsible individuals but the reform of anti-social and criminogenic conditions.

These arguments show that 'mens rea' is inevitably read 'situationally'; the responsibility of abstract individuals has in practice to respond to situated persons in particular contexts. Thus, the law falls between two stools: it covertly uses technically irrelevant data about factors such as circumstance and motive in applying legal tests, whilst failing fully to acknowledge the moral relevance of social conditions which the determinist views it partially recognises would dictate.

Finally, these examples drawn from the Public Order Acts confirm the political and symbolic significance of criminal laws which proclaim themselves to be concerned with public order. In constructing an authoritative conception of what counts as disorder, and by setting this up in the formal clothing of legal regulation, the law sets the scene for political and social institutions to depoliticise protest and disorder as 'mere lawlessness'. By entrenching a selection of salient 'popular images' such as 'disorder' and 'violence' in the legislation, law enforcement is enabled both to feed moral panics and to respond to popular fears in a way which is comforting and which confirms the power and authority of government. In deconstructing some examples, we hope to have exposed the political aspects of the public order law's operation.

III.b.   Institutional responses

Institutional, state-sanctioned (if not state-directed) responses to public disorder are multifarious, even though they form a relatively small part of the total array of social control of disorder. However, criminal law and, more visibly, agents of criminal justice, acting (at least avowedly) within a legal framework, do exercise a particularly important form of political control. This form is one which, as we have already seen, is crucial in affirming and maintaining the legitimacy and effectiveness of the state by constructing disorder as 'wicked lawlessness' and responding to it in the 'politically neutral' terms directed by the rule of law ideal. In this section, we direct our attention to the agencies and practices of the criminal process, many of which involve the exercise of wide discretionary powers. These are sometimes explicitly but more often implicitly accorded by law. Again, there are many instances to which we could devote attention: the roles of troops, social workers, community leaders, teachers, politicians (especially the Home Secretary and law officers), trial lawyers and judges would each form a legitimate focus of study.

D G T Williams, *Keeping the Peace* (Hutchinson, 1967) pp 16–17 (reprinted by permission of the Peters Fraser & Dunlop Group Ltd)

[A] major concern in any discussion of public order is the control of discretion. We shall find that discretionary power abounds in the preservation of public order. It is vested in prosecuting authorities, in senior police officers making decisions of policy or tactics in the control of disturbances, in police officers actually present at the scene of actual or apprehended disorder, in local authorities in such matters as the supervision of public parks and open spaces, in the central government in such matters as the regulation of assemblies in Trafalgar Square and Hyde Park, in magistrates' courts in imposing binding-over orders and in all courts in the process of sentencing. It would be misleading to generalise about such a wide sweep of discretion, and the desirable limits have to be considered in relation to particular issues and problems as they arise. Just as discretionary powers vary so do the methods of controlling or limiting discretionary powers. There are judicial controls, either through control by the courts or police of administrative action or through control by the appellate courts of the action of courts of first instance. Then there are political controls through Parliament, by virtue of the doctrine of ministerial responsibility, and through elected local authorities. Other controls include commissions or committees of inquiry, either into a general problem (such as public meetings) or into a particular event (such as the Sunday Trading Riots); provisions for the hearing of complaints against the police or against administrative authorities; private pressure groups such as the Law and Liberty League (founded in the wake of Bloody Sunday in November 1887) and the National Council for Civil Liberties (founded in the 1930s); and publicity of all kinds through the Press, television and broadcasting, and all media of communication.

We shall concentrate on three areas. The first concerns the role and practice of the police. The police have a legal responsibility to act to stop breaches of the peace, and as 'on the ground' controllers of public disorder and initiators of the criminal process occupy a position of unparalleled importance among other agencies in defining and responding to public disorder. We hope to establish some points of general importance about the role of the police as enforcers and creative interpreters of criminal law. Secondly, we advert to the existence and exercise of a wide area of discretion in deciding which cases to prosecute and what charges to bring. Finally, we shall look at the conduct of trials, the sentencing of public order offenders and the use, particularly by magistrates (given the dominance of the summary mode of trial in this as in most other areas of criminal enforcement) of the power to award or refuse bail.

III.b.i. Policing disorder

In relation to public order policing, the organisation and style of policing and the control of the hardware (such as plastic bullets and water cannon) to which the police have access are particularly important issues. While the Scarman Report into the Brixton riots criticised the Metropolitan police force for inflexibility, it recommended at the same time the expansion of public order training and the availability of specialised equipment such as water cannon, CS gas and plastic bullets (Scarman 1981: paras 5.72–5.74). However, it is important to remember that debates about styles of policing and police violence are not the only concerns. Surveillance, for example via closed circuit television, is no longer the preserve of the police. Private security firms in shopping centres and other 'private' public areas are commonplace (Pease 2002: 953). Police use of video cameras at major sporting events can produce still photographs of spectators, which may then be used in compiling files on people who have no criminal record, and the files being nationally available to the police. Surveillance in the form of telephone tapping has been given increasing statutory backing and policing is increasingly centralised (Police Act 1997 and Police Reform Act 2002). Each of these practices is of potential application to public disorder situations.

The huge variety of statutory and common law provisions in the public order area also allows the police great freedom of manoeuvre. As we have seen, the Criminal Justice and Public Order Act 1994 (CJPOA 1994) formalised many of the powers which the police had already arrogated to themselves. Arrestable offences include not only those carrying at least five years' imprisonment, or for which statutory powers exist (such as ss 4, 4A and 5 of the POA 1986) but also any listed in the Police and Criminal Evidence Act 1984, Sch 1A (as inserted by the Police Reform Act 2002, Sch 6). These latter include:

- any offences under the Football Spectators Act 1989, or under the Football (Offences) Act 1991;
- ticket touting (CJPOA 1994, s 166);
- stirring up racial or religious hatred (POA 1986, s 19);
- failing to comply with requirements imposed by a constable in relation to consumption of alcohol in a public place, and placing advertisements in relation to prostitution (Criminal Justice and Police Act 2001, ss 12(4) and 46);
- assaulting a police officer in the execution of his duty (Police Act 1996, s 89(1));
- as well as many others (listed as Sch 1A to the Police and Criminal Evidence Act 1984 by the Police Reform Act 2002, Sch 6).

In addition, the Police Reform Act 2002 gives power to uniformed police to require the name and address from any person believed to have been acting, or be acting, in an anti-social manner (s 50). As Ormerod and Roberts point out, 'The potential for abuse by officers repeatedly harassing groups of youths is obvious' (2003: 162). Police actions in low-level public order situations demonstrate a preference for arrest as the means to resolve the problem. Brown and Ellis concluded that s 5 (POA 1986) was over-used in restoring order by arrest, given the powers to arrest for breach of the peace or for being drunk and disorderly that exist. They concluded that the way public order policing is organised in some urban areas also predisposes towards confrontation and arrest when trouble arises. Officers are frequently deployed in groups of six or more in incident vans with the primary aim of responding quickly to instances of disorder. Making arrests provides a tangible measure of the impact of this strategy (1994: 51).

The relative weakness of the constraints which legal standards exert over police conduct is shown by evidence of 'over-policing' of those from ethnic minorities.

Coretta Phillips and Ben Bowling 'Racism, Ethnicity, Crime, and Criminal Justice' in Maguire et al (eds) *The Oxford Handbook of Criminology* (Oxford University Press, 2002) pp 579, 594. Reprinted by permission of Oxford University Press.

It is clear that targeting people from ethnic minorities and trawling for suspects plays a part in producing the over-representation of African/Caribbeans among those arrested by the police. They are less likely to receive the benefits of under-enforcement by the police than other ethnic groups which, alongside the ongoing targeting and heavy deployment in African/Caribbean communities, means that their offending behaviour is more likely to come to official attention than that of other ethnic groups. Hood's (1992) research in Crown Courts in the West Midlands found that 15 per cent of those dealt with for drugs offences – typically for small trades in cannabis – were black compared with only 3 per cent who were of Asian origin and 2 per cent who were whites. These offences came to official attention following proactive policing. Indeed, the most common reason given by police when searching black and Asian people was suspicion of drugs possession, even though self-report studies challenge the perception that they are more likely to use drugs than white people.

The history of police use of 'stop and search' powers provides a context for the distrust of the police felt by African/Caribbean and, increasingly, Asian communities ... Now regulated by the Police and Criminal Evidence Act (PACE 1984), a stop and search can be carried out only when there is 'reasonable suspicion' that stolen property or prohibited articles are being carried.

The national police data for 1999/2000 found, with some force variation, the number of PACE searches of black people to be five times higher than of whites. Rates for Asians were almost always higher than for whites. The same pattern has been observed in the use of other stop and search powers, including stops under s 13 of the Prevention of Terrorism Act 1989, designed specifically to combat terrorism from the IRA [now Terrorism Act 2000, s 43]. In 1997/8, 7 per cent of these stops were of African/Caribbeans and 5 per cent were of Asians, a clear example of direct discrimination ...

Fitzgerald's (1999) study in London has provided an insight into the use of stop and search in the late 1990s. It found that reasonable suspicion was frequently absent ... and that the power is often not used for the purpose of detection (as justified in PACE) but instead is used for 'intelligence gathering', 'disruption', and the 'social control' of young people. Until 1997 these practices are institutionalized by the Metropolitan Police who used stop and search as a 'performance indicator' of productivity ... In the wake of the Lawrence Inquiry, concerns were expressed about the declining use of the stop/search for ethnic minorities. However Home Office statistics show that in 1999/2000 the fall in the number of recorded stops was lower for black people in England and Wales (10 per cent) than it was for other ethnic groups (14 per cent).

We need to be aware of the institutional pressures under which the police work – the difficulties with which their institutional duty to quell disorder confronts them, and the pressure to present themselves as an efficient force via satisfactory clear-up rates and other modes of showing that they are 'tackling crime'. These pressures contribute to a situation in which the police are encouraged to engage in high-visibility actions. If we are to understand the role that the police continue to play in the construction of the 'law and order crisis' and as enforcers and interpreters of criminal law, it is important to understand all aspects of the social, institutional and political context in which the police operate.

III.b.ii. Prosecuting disorder

Discretion in the prosecution process is especially significant in situations of disorder; typically involving large numbers of people, they invite a policy of selective enforcement. (The charges brought against *Jefferson* et al, above, are good examples.) Yet the principles on which such a selection proceeds at successive stages – arrest, questioning, charge, final decision to prosecute – remain unarticulated and thus unaccountable. As we have seen, prosecutors may select among a vast array of offences, including not only the public order offences of disorder such as riot, violent disorder and affray but also general offences against the person, and many supplementary provisions covering different forms of obstruction and breaches of the peace. This diversity is not peculiar to public order, but it is especially marked in this area. While the number of *recorded* riot offences ranged from 2 to 41 between 1990 and 2000, those for violent disorder were more constant, between 1800 and 2800. The eventual number of *convictions* and cautions is less than half those numbers. Affray is included in a category of 'other public order offences' of which there are about 18,000 recorded each year of which 10,000 end up with conviction or caution (Home Office 2001b: Tables 2.21 and 5.18). Two points are worth noting: the percentage of public order offenders that are cautioned is very high (over 80%); and the gap between recorded and final result is also high. Taken together this indicates a high percentage of withdrawn charges and emphasises the deployment of these offences as policing tools for restoring or maintaining order 'on the ground'.

Inevitably, the Crown Prosecutor's broad discretion is structured by institutional pressure to ensure efficient use of court resources and hence to pick 'winnable' cases, although this would not preclude prosecution in politically salient cases which were not seen as so strong (Ashworth and Fionda 1994). However, it remains the case that the police have the major power in influencing whether a case is ultimately prosecuted, for it is their actions of surveillance, investigation, arrest, and decisions whether to charge which in a real sense 'create' the cases among which the Prosecution Service selects. This is well illustrated in studies showing that cases are not inherently 'strong' or 'weak' but become so by means of the amount of police effort devoted to building up evidence (McConville, Sanders and Leng 1993; Sanders and Young 2002). This is not to say that there are no controls on the construction of cases: charges may be dropped because of problems about police evidence or doubts about the legitimacy of undercover police investigative activities, confessions may be excluded. But police attitudes and concerns will be highly relevant in shaping the selection of cases that ultimately reach the courts. It is interesting to consider some of the features of (implicit) prosecution policy revealed by public disorder situations.

The miners' strike of 1984 furnished some disturbing examples (see Christian 1985: 121–124). The offences of riot and unlawful assembly were, in Smith's words (Smith 1987: 4), 'falling into desuetude' prior to their revival during the strike. Between 1973 and 1978 an average of 32 people a year were charged with riot; during the inner-city disturbances of 1981, this rose to 71. During the miners' strike, 137 people were charged with riot. The strike also saw 275 charges of the ancient offence of watching and besetting under the Conspiracy and Protection of Property Act 1875: these serious charges, along with riot and unlawful assembly, perhaps not surprisingly, met with relatively high acquittal rates (Percy Smith and Hillyard 1985). Such revivals are not new to contemporary disorder:

D G T Williams, *Keeping the Peace* (Hutchinson, 1967) pp 20–23

There are so many crimes relevant to public order and so many uncertainties in the definitions of particular crimes that the decision as to whether and for what to prosecute is frequently more important than the decision of a court itself. In many circumstances a court will have little option but to convict: the crucial assessment must lie with the police or any other who seeks to bring the case to court at all.

The law of public order is ... in no small part the cumulative result of a piecemeal enactment of legislation to meet particular problems. This does not mean that statutes are incapable of being adapted to meet new and different problems in later years. Consider the Statute of Northampton, which was passed in 1328 to prohibit people from going armed to the terror of the public. Counsel, in an Irish case in 1914, said that this enactment, 'in its historical occurrence, follows the turbulent times of Edward II, and was aimed at the mischief which arose at that disturbed period'. Little recourse was had to it for several centuries, but in 1903 it was suddenly invoked at Carnarvon Assizes when a chimney-sweep was charged and convicted both under the Statute of Northampton and under the law of public nuisance for going about armed and firing a revolver in a street in Bangor ...

The Incitement to Mutiny Act, also of 1797, has been used on a number of occasions in this century in circumstances far removed from those surrounding the Mutiny at the Nore. Its employment against trade union and Communist leaders has been ... especially controversial. Even common-law offences have been revived after a lengthy period of inaction to meet new problems. These include the crime of public mischief and of making an affray, the latter of which has in the last decade become one of the most important of the indictable crimes of public order ...

Where major prosecutions are contemplated it is possible that uncertainty [in the definition of the offence] can be of some assistance to those who might be prosecuted. The authorities are reluctant to undertake such cases unless they can be sure of their ground ... In very many circumstances, however, even where major prosecutions are under consideration, success in the courts is virtually certain. The real choice rests with the prosecutor. Hence, many allegations of political or other discrimination in the sphere of public order have been directed not against the courts as such – though magistrates and judges have come into their fair measure of criticism – but against the prosecutors as such. In the Chartist era, it seems, the prosecuting policy was generally very fair: a striking contrast to the policy adopted in the days of Lord Dismouth. In other eras there have been confident allegations of partiality in the process of selecting which cases to bring before the courts. This was so in the stormy years when the Salvation Army faced its hooligan opponents, the Skeleton Army, in towns throughout the land, and when – a few years later– pacifist meetings during the Boer War were attacked and broken up by loyalist mobs. Between the two wars there were many allegations of unfairness towards the Left. In 1925, for instance, the Attorney General (Sir Douglas Hogg) was asked in the

House of Commons why there had been no prosecution of Fascists who had held up a Daily Herald van in the City of London; his reply was that it had been decided that charges of larceny would not hold, but that the men responsible had been bound over in the sum of £100 each. In the 1930s there were repeated questions in Parliament about alleged discrimination.

Pearson reminds us that prosecution policy relates directly to contemporary perceptions of what counts as 'real crime' and that it determines official statistics, which in turn affect public perceptions of the nature of the 'crime problem':

G Pearson, *Hooligan: A History of Respectable Fears* (Macmillan, 1983) p 214

Between 1900 and the later 1970s ... even allowing for unknown and hypothetical alterations in the nature and scope of criminal activity, we are asked to strike comparisons between such different styles of law enforcement as to make little sense. First, in the earlier period, there were wide margins of discretion within an extremely informal mode of policing – the proverbial clip around the ear, or the dreaded flick of the Edwardian policeman's rolled cape – which has been replaced by the more likely possibility of prosecution, or the issue of a formal caution. And a formal caution ... goes into the record book as a 'known crime'. We have also seen how in earlier times people involved in acts of gross disorder would commonly be charged only with simple assault or drunkenness. Responding to a sharp increase in recorded offences in his annual report of 1899, for example, the Metropolitan Police Commissioner thought it 'satisfactory to note that arrests were mostly for offences of a trivial nature, such as drunkenness, disorderly conduct, offences against the Police Acts, common assaults etc.', and he was at pains to distinguish between these 'trivial' matters and the proper affairs of his criminal department. In other words, at a time when a quarter of London's police were assaulted each year in the course of their duties, street violence was too much of an everyday occurrence to count as a 'real' crime. There was also a tendency not to record incidents which would not be cleared up. Until the 1930s, for example, it was a routine practice for the London police to record thefts reported to them by the public as 'lost property'. When this practice was changed, recorded levels of property crime soared: but, obviously, as a consequence of changes in policing and not as a result of changes in crime.

Thus, approaches to prosecution and diversion of cases are of major importance in constructing social perceptions of public disorder as well as the pattern of legal enforcement. Nearly 20% of arrests under s 5 of the POA 1986 end in bind-overs without a finding of guilt (Brown and Ellis 1994: viii). The considerable overlap within the POA 1986 and between public order offences and other statutes, notably the Offences Against the Person Act 1861, is acknowledged in the Charging Standards for Public Order offences. Charging Standards are agreed between the Crown Prosecution Service and the police for many offences to give guidance as to the appropriate charge arising from any given factual situation. Most of the violence which comes to the attention of the police is committed in public – at weekends, outside pubs, clubs, at football and other sporting events. Many of these events could give rise to public order offences, to criminal damage offences as well as to offences such as assault. The Charging Standard for Public Order offences, issued in June 1996, acknowledges the overlapping nature of these offences, offers guidance on whether the police should proceed under public order offences, under criminal damage offences, or offences against the person ([1996] Crim LR 534). The prosecution of riot requires the consent of the Director of Public Prosecutions.

III.b.iii.   Trying disorder

Straddling the decision to prosecute and subsequent trial and sentencing is the question of bail. Blake describes the use of bail conditions in Nottinghamshire in 1984:

N Blake, 'Picketing, Justice and the Law' in Fine and Millar (eds)
***Policing the Miners' Strike* (Lawrence & Wishart, London, 1985)**
pp 114–115

It was the invariable practice in Nottinghamshire not to allow police bail but to detain those arrested until they were brought before the next sitting of the local magistrates. This was because the police had no power under the 1976 Bail Act to impose any conditions on the bail they may grant from a police station. Only the magistrates could impose conditional bail and if a person had been previously released on unconditional police bail, it would have been more difficult for the police to have decided at court on the first remand to impose conditions subsequently … Conditional bail was applied for in cases of obstruction as well as for words or behaviour likely to cause a breach of the peace … The condition which the police sought to have attached was a condition that the person should not attend at any place in the United Kingdom for the purpose of picketing or demonstrating in connection with the current dispute between the NUM and NCB save at his or her own place of work. By September 1984, 95 per cent of the 1,745 persons charged before the Mansfield Magistrates' Court had these conditions attached to their bail. The conclusion of many lawyers who dealt with these cases was that the purpose of the arrest was less to achieve a conviction and a penalty at some later date in a criminal court than to remove striking miners from the scene and prevent mass picketing by attaching these restrictive conditions to as many striking miners as possible. Frequently, when the actual case was called on before the court for hearing many months later, the police were willing to drop the charges in return for a bind-over to keep the peace.

The manner in which the magistrates' courts have upheld police applications for restrictive bail is indicative of the role these courts saw themselves playing to support the police in the dispute. As magistrates are judicial officers, who should consider the merits of each case, a challenge was mounted in the Divisional Court to the practice of the Mansfield magistrates. Evidence was presented, in the form of an affidavit by a senior probation officer, that the magistrates had determined that a general policy was to be applied to all miners' cases. The magistrates themselves denied this and the Divisional Court held that they were obliged to consider each case individually, but:

the individual circumstances of each defendant were, for the reason already stated, not material, save insofar as they showed that unless restrained, each defendant would rejoin the mass picketing operation at the first opportunity. The fact that they were men of good character and other personal considerations would not affect the likelihood of their committing public order offences on bail.

... The magistrates were unimpressed by argument of the defence lawyers that the imposition of these bail conditions effectively granted injunctions on behalf of the NCB and other employers affected by the dispute ...

This account generates some scepticism about the sincerity of official avowals of the need to reduce the number of people held on remand. A similarly depressing story is told by the National Council for Civil Liberties in relation to the peace convoy (NCCL 1986: 28–29). The use of bail conditions as a form of 'informal' punishment by the courts is thus now well established, and bail conditions were upheld in the case of the non-imprisonable offence under s 5 of the POA 1986 in *R v Bournemouth Magistrates' Court, ex p Cross* (1989). The use of 'doorstep' bail (the requirement that a defendant present herself at the doorstep during any curfew imposed when requested by a police officer) was approved in *R (on the application of CPS) v Chorley Justices* (2002 and Home Office Circular 61/2002). About a quarter of grants of bail are accompanied by conditions and the CJPOA 1994 introduced further restrictions on the use of bail (ss 25–30), curtailing the general right to bail declared by the Bail Act 1976 with two new exceptions. One concerns a person charged with homicide with a previous conviction for such offence, while the other states that a person accused of or convicted of an indictable offence which appears to have been committed while on bail 'need not' be granted bail (ss 25 and 26). The Criminal Justice Bill 2003 tightens up these provisions in the light of the Law Commission's assessment of the impact of the Human Rights Act 1998 (Law Commission 2001).

In considering the trial of public order cases it is worth emphasising that, in the vast majority of cases, we are speaking of magistrates' courts.

Practice Note: National Mode of Trial Guidelines (1990) 92 Cr App Rep 142

General Mode of Trial Considerations

Section 19 of the Magistrates' Courts Act 1980 requires magistrates to have regard to the following matters in deciding whether an offence is more suitable for summary trial or trial on indictment:

1   the nature of the case
2   whether the circumstances of the offence make the offence one of serious character
3   whether the punishment which a magistrates' court would have power to inflict would be adequate
4   any other circumstances which appear to the court to make it more suitable for the offence to be tried in one way rather than the other
5   any representations made by the prosecution or the defence ...

Public Order Act Offences

(1)   Cases of violent disorder should generally be committed for trial
(2)   Affray
1   Organised violence or use of weapons
2   Significant injury or substantial damage
3   The offence has a clear racial motivation
4   An attack on police officers, ambulance men, firemen and the like.

The combined effect of an overlapping hierarchy of offences and the availability of higher penalties on trial by indictment leaves considerable opportunities for the prosecution to determine the best combination of charge with mode of trial in any given set of circumstances. The defendant is now required to indicate his or her plea before magistrates decide whether a triable either way offence is to be tried summarily or not (Criminal Procedure and Investigations Act 1996, s 49 and Home Office Circular 45/1997).

The significance of trial by jury was underlined when a jury acquitted a group of Asian men of a charge of violent disorder, on the basis that, during the riot in Burnley in June 2001, they were legitimately carrying weapons and acting in self-defence because of the failure of the police adequately to protect them from white racists (source: www.irr.org.uk/2003/february/ak000001.html, accessed 22 February 2003):

D G T Williams, *Keeping the Peace* (Hutchinson, 1967) pp 17–19

... the vast majority of trials for crimes of public order take place before magistrates' courts. This reflects the traditional involvement of justices of the peace in the preservation of the Queen's Peace and suggests that difficult points of law rarely arise in this field. Reliance on summary trial is also to no small extent dictated by the need, after outbreaks of disorder, to deal with a large number of defendants speedily and effectively. Exemplary punishments can be awarded by magistrates' courts as well as by higher courts, and their effect is likely to be all the greater if they can be sought promptly ...

On the other hand, it is appropriate that some offences should be reserved to the higher courts for exemplary punishment. In days past, fortunately long past, the courts could show a remarkable savagery in their penalties after trial by jury. Several Luddites, for example, were sentenced to death at York Assizes in January 1813; agrarian disturbances in East Anglia in 1816 led to cruel punishments; and the agrarian troubles of 1830 also incited the judges to invoke the full severity of the law. By the second half of the nineteenth century, however, the courts no longer had the occasion, the authority or the inclination for such severity, and many of the crimes created by statute were made triable at a summary level. An example of such a crime was that of obstructing the police in the execution of their duty ... this is now provided for, still as a summary crime, in the Police Act 1964. In this century provision for summary trial only has been made in respect of several statutory crimes, including most of those set out in the POA 1936 ...

While trial on indictment opens up the possibility of heavier sentences, it also enables an accused person who distrusts any alleged bias on the part of local magistrates to seek trial before a jury. Indeed, where – subject to certain exceptions – the maximum penalty for a summary offence exceeds three months' imprisonment, a defendant is empowered by statute to demand trial by jury ... Nevertheless, despite a recent reaction against summary trial and despite the attractiveness of trial by jury to the accused in some cases, magistrates' courts still dominate the judicial enforcement of public order. Those offences which can only be tried on indictment [now only riot, under the POA 1986] ... are nowadays rarely, in some cases never, invoked. The common prosecutions are for such crimes as obstructing the police in the execution of their duty, obstructing the highway, and threatening, abusive or insulting words or behaviour ... Trials on indictment, when they do occur, are usually sought because the prosecuting authorities take a grave view of what has happened and wish to secure either an exemplary conviction or an exemplary sentence.

The fact that indictable offences seldom occur means that there are few Court of Criminal Appeal ... decisions in this field. Appeals on a point of law from magistrates' decisions go, either directly or indirectly, to the Divisional Court of the Queen's Bench Division ... Only since 1960 has there been a further appeal to the House of Lords ...

Williams's assumptions that 'difficult points of law rarely arise' and that 'indictable offences seldom occur' are open to question: it seems more likely that the specific mode of enforcement renders the raising of difficult points of law unlikely, and the behaviour which could be charged as an indictable offence tends in practice to be labelled in summary terms.

One important feature of the difference between trial by magistrates and that by higher courts has to do with sentencing powers: under the Magistrates' Courts Act 1980 these are limited to a term of six months' imprisonment or a fine of up to £5000. This is in sharp contrast to the situation with many indictable offences: riot and violent disorder respectively attract maxima of 10 and five years and/or unlimited fines; malicious wounding under s 20 of the Offences Against the Person Act 1861, and the lesser s 47 offence of assault occasioning actual bodily harm, both attract maxima of five years. In dealing with offences triable either way (all those mentioned above, with the exception of riot), magistrates have the power to commit to the Crown Court for sentence where they feel that their powers are inadequate (Powers of Criminal Courts (Sentencing) Act 2000, s 3). The relatively small number of cases which are tried on indictment have often, as Williams also notes, attracted very punitive judicial reactions in the exercise of the wide sentencing powers of the higher courts. We can be fairly confident that general predispositions of sentencers will be relevant in public order sentencing and in particular that the increasing resort to imprisonment, together with the disproportionate tendency to sentence black defendants to terms of custody, will be reflected in the public order area (Hood 1992; Phillips and Bowling 2002).

The Bradford riot in 2001 resulted in more than a hundred convictions with sentences ranging between four and six-and-a-half years. Allowing four appeals against sentence, but upholding 11 others, the Court of Appeal said that deterrent sentences were necessary. The riot had been serious: it lasted for 12 hours, involved many hundreds of people, missiles had been aimed at police officers, many of whom had been injured, and damage running to many millions of pounds had been caused. The court described as 'unfortunate' the Recorder's statement that he was 'not concerned with the origins of the violence'. If, by that, he meant that the causes of the riot were irrelevant to the court, then he was wrong, said Rose LJ. The Court of Appeal ruled that the riot was almost certainly triggered by the stabbing of an Asian man in central Bradford and that 'the Asian community was understandably concerned to defend itself against right-wing groups'. But what had begun as a spontaneous reaction became marked by premeditation. The riot then became directed at the police. Personal mitigation and good character carried comparatively little weight, as did guilty pleas since video evidence clearly identified the defendants and showed some of their actions. The appropriate sentence for any ringleader would have been around the maximum of 10 years' imprisonment; an active and persistent participant who had used petrol bombs should receive a sentence of eight to nine years after a trial; sentences of six or seven years would be appropriate for those who had participated over a number of hours and had thrown missiles which were more dangerous than stones but less dangerous than petrol bombs; those who were present for a significant period and had thrown stones should receive five years after a trial while those who had taken part to a lesser degree would receive sentences at a lower level (*Najeeb et al*, 2003). It is not clear why the one-third discount for a guilty plea should be reduced on the ground that technology delivers better evidence, nor how a riot could be both spontaneous and premeditated.

The power to remand in custody or impose conditions on bail, combined with the wide-ranging sentencing discretion and the other informal discretions of judges and magistrates in terms of their demeanour towards witnesses and lawyers, their acceptance or rejection of evidence and so on, gives them considerable scope to shape the outcome of public order (and indeed other) trials. A combination of sentencing and other powers therefore renders the courts powerfully equipped to deal severely and in a highly discretionary way with offenders. The current salience of law-and-order issues, the existence of moral panics and the temptation to single out certain categories of offender as subject to especially punitive treatment render these powers particularly significant in the public order context.

FURTHER READING

Ashworth, Andrew (1998) *The Criminal Process: An Evaluative Study* (OUP).

Bennett, W L and Feldman, M S (1981) *Reconstructing Reality in the Courtroom* (Tavistock).

Bowling, Ben and Foster, Janet (2002) 'Policing and the Police' in Maguire et al (eds) *The Oxford Handbook of Criminology* (Oxford University Press) p 980.

Evans, Roger (1994) 'Cautioning: Counting the Cost of Retrenchment' Crim LR 566.

Fionda, Julia (1995) *Public Prosecutors and Discretion* (Clarendon Press).

Hood, Roger (1992) *Race and Sentencing* (Clarendon Press).

MacPherson (1999) *The Stephen Lawrence Inquiry*, Cm 4262–1 (HMSO).

Runciman (1993) *Royal Commission on Criminal Justice and Procedure* (HMSO).

Sanders, Andrew and Young, Richard (2000) *Criminal Justice* (Butterworths).

IV. Participation in offences

While criminal law doctrine has remained uncomfortable with group liability, criminological studies have long reflected the group basis of much 'criminal' activity, the literature abounds with gangs, criminal associations, organised crime, and criminal subcultures. This chapter is concerned with the underlying 'groupness' of criminal law and practice. It is relatively easy to point to the preoccupation with individual liability and individual responsibility in traditional conceptions of criminal law. Group-based liability is uncomfortably accommodated rather than clearly embraced. Yet in practical terms its significance is hard to overstate. It is not just substantive public order offences, but aiding and abetting or participatory liability that we need to include here. Inchoate forms such as incitement and conspiracy, considered in **Chapter 3**, also assume more than one 'player'.

The legal basis for participatory liability lies at common law, but s 8 of the Accessories and Abettors Act 1861 sets out the method of charge. It provides:

> Whosoever shall aid, abet, counsel or procure the commission of any indictable offence, whether the same be an offence at common law or by virtue of any Act passed or to be passed, shall be liable to be tried, indicted, and punished as a principal offender.

The Magistrates' Court Act 1980, by s 44, makes similar provision for summary offences.

Participation in crime as a 'secondary party' can take many different forms, such as giving advice, material assistance, equipment or encouragement; it can take place before the principal offence (when it will be described as counselling or procuring) or at the same time (when it amounts to aiding and abetting); and it leads to full criminal liability for the principal offence and is punishable as severely as principal liability. The involvement of a number of parties in many situations of disorder seems to invite the application of this extended form of liability, and many appeal cases on participation concern what may be described as public order situations (see *Jefferson*, above).

The 'mens rea' requirement for participation consists in intent to assist or encourage and/or knowledge or awareness that one is doing so. The relevance of 'situational' 'mens rea', inferred from context, is clear, as is the possibility of liability being pushed back some way before the commission of substantive public order offences at the scene of disorder. The question of what level of awareness or knowledge is necessary has never been (and could not be) clearly determined, and thus the boundaries of participatory liability are always blurred. For example, is the person who helps plan the route for a demonstration, or encourages the organisers, or provides banners or posters, knowing that disorder is a possibility because of the opposition of hostile groups, liable as a participant in any disorder which subsequently transpires? The person's association with the group in question and prior participation in similar events might well be used to support inferences of a sufficient degree of knowledge, thus pushing criminal liability to extraordinarily wide margins. (For a good example of a court's failure to follow doctrine to its logical conclusions in this area see *Gillick v Wisbech Area Health Authority* (1985), discussed in **Chapter 5**.)

The problem also arises in answering the general question of the extent to which initial 'mens rea' on the part of a supplier of information, advice or equipment extends. This issue has received the attention of the House of Lords.

DPP for Northern Ireland v Maxwell [1978] 3 All ER 1140

[Maxwell was a member of the Ulster Volunteer Force, a proscribed organisation, and had led terrorists in his car to an inn, which was in fact bombed. He was charged as a principal to the offence of planting a pipe bomb: it was accepted that he had known there was to be an attack but not the precise nature of the offence which would be committed. He appealed against conviction on the ground that he must be shown to have known the type of crime intended to be committed and the kind of means of offence being carried to the scene.]

Viscount Dilhorne.

[Quoting Lowry LCJ in the Court of Criminal Appeal Northern Ireland:] The facts found here show that the appellant, as a member of an organisation which habitually perpetrates sectarian acts of violence with firearms and explosives, must, as soon as he was briefed for his role, have contemplated the bombing of the Crosskeys Inn as not the only possibility but one of the most obvious possibilities among the jobs which the principals were likely to be undertaking and in the commission of which he was intentionally assisting. He was therefore in much the same situation, so far as guilty knowledge is concerned, as a man who had been given a list of jobs and told that one of them would be carried out ...

The court certified the following point of law of general public importance:

> If the crime committed by the principal, and actually assisted by the accused, was one of a number of offences, one of which the accused knew the principal would probably commit, is the guilty mind which must be proved against an accomplice thereby proved against the accused?

The House of Lords dismissed Maxwell's appeal, with the sole proviso (on Viscount Dilhorne's part) that the particulars of the offence should in so far as possible bear a relation to the realities, and with Lord Scarman underlining the subjective nature of the test. He quoted from Lord Lowry's judgment in the Northern Ireland Court of Criminal Appeal:

> The relevant crime must be within the contemplation of the accomplice and only exceptionally would evidence be found to support the allegation that the accomplice had given the principal a completely blank check.

[and went on to say] The principle thus formulated has great merit. It directs attention to the state of mind of the accused: not what he ought to have in contemplation, but what he did have. It avoids definition and classification, while ensuring that a man will not be convicted of aiding and abetting any offence his principal may commit, but only one which is within his contemplation. He may have in contemplation only one offence, or several: and the several which he contemplates he may see as alternatives. An accessory who leaves it to his principal to choose is liable, provided always the choice is made from the range of offences from which the accessory contemplates the choice will be made.

This affirmation of the 'subjectivity' of interpretive tests is in line with traditional doctrine, but, as we have already suggested, its practical application may not be as different from that of an 'objective' test as the logical distinction suggests. Furthermore, Lord Scarman's formulation illustrates the artificial model of human thought and behaviour on which such tests proceed: not only is the 'contemplation' separated from the action, it is assumed to be a discrete, conscious and above all rational process which can then be subjected to judicial inquiry. Even leaving problems of proof aside, is it really the case that we rationally contemplate all the possible implications of our actions? And if, as we would suggest, we generally do not, does this not reveal that law is in fact engaged in constructing rather than in discovering common purposes and contemplated ends?

This kind of problem has sometimes been resolved in terms of what has been called the 'common purpose doctrine' (*Davies v DPP*, 1954), according to which liability is limited to conduct within the common purpose or joint enterprise of the parties: unexpected actions on the part of one of the participants potentially severs the link of liability. Thus, when one party to a fist fight draws out a knife which the others do not know existed, their liability will probably stop short of that for the use of the knife. But the situation is less clear if, for example, the knife is known about but is used for purposes different from those originally contemplated (*Slack*, 1989). The doctrine of 'common purpose' extends as much as it limits liability, for it is premised on the assumption that the person will be liable for unforeseen consequences of the agreed plan. If the principle of 'subjective' 'mens rea' were to be rigidly adhered to, as doctrine would prescribe, 'subjective' (and articulated? – the problems of proof are enormous) contemplation should circumscribe liability. But it seems clear that the doctrine is used inferentially, in terms of what common purpose can be 'read off' from the evidence before the court – and here factors other than 'subjective' intentions are bound to come into play. Thus, the tribunal which thinks that any 'reasonable person' should or would have foreseen the risk of the knife's use in a given way may set such use within the ascribed common purpose.

The joint enterprise doctrine was subjected to searching scrutiny in *Powell/English* below. When English's appeal was allowed, it was reported in the press as a significant shift in the archaic and restrictive aiding and abetting rules. A close reading of the case leaves us in some doubt as to whether there has been much change of substance. The general rule is still that a participant (P2) in an unlawful enterprise who realises that their accomplice (P1) might kill or cause grievous bodily harm will be liable for murder alongside P1 if P1 does kill, unless the killing was carried out with a wholly unexpected weapon. Establishing whether the use of a particular weapon was within the contemplation of the parties will always be subject to the vagaries of jury fact-finding, as Lord Hutton concedes.

In 1997 the Criminal Cases Review Commission referred to the Court of Appeal the appalling miscarriage of justice case of Derek Bentley, who was hanged in 1953, barely two months after his accomplice shot a policeman who had intercepted them while carrying out a robbery of a warehouse. Many aspects of the trial and subsequent failure to commute the capital sentence are indefensible. It is probably accurate to conclude that the joint enterprise doctrine contributed to this travesty of justice, but it was by no means the whole of it. It is important to note how much of the strict joint enterprise doctrine survives, and the case as a whole is instructive reading. While judicial training has undoubtedly improved, and the Human Rights Act has introduced a more principled basis for ensuring fair trials, it is useful to be reminded how easily courts can become swayed by the emotions of the particular case. Killings of police officers are always taken seriously, as are those of children. But the language used of football hooligans, as we saw earlier, is enough to cause us to pause before assuming that judges could never again emulate Lord Goddard's disrespect for a defendant.

R v Derek William Bentley (deceased) [1998] EWCA 2516

Lord Bingham Of Cornhill C.J.

On the evening of November 2, 1952 Police Constable Sidney Miles was shot dead in the execution of his duty on the roof of a warehouse in Croydon. Two men were charged with his murder: Christopher Craig, who was then aged 16, and Derek William Bentley, who was 19. On November 17, 1952 they were committed to stand trial on December 9 at the Central Criminal Court, where they were tried before Lord Goddard C.J. and a jury. They were convicted on December 11, in Bentley's case with a recommendation to mercy. The trial judge passed on each the only sentence permitted by law: on Craig, because of his age, that he be detained during Her Majesty's pleasure; on Bentley, sentence of death. An appeal by Bentley against conviction was dismissed by the Court of Criminal Appeal ... on January 13, 1953. He was executed on January 28.

The Criminal Cases Review Commission has referred the conviction of Derek Bentley to this Court under section 9 of the Criminal Appeal Act 1995. By section 9(2) of that Act a conviction so referred is to be treated for all purposes as an appeal against conviction under section 1 of the 1968 Act. We are accordingly required by section 2 of that Act to allow the appeal against conviction if we think that the conviction is unsafe, and otherwise to dismiss the appeal ...

On July 29, 1993 the appellant was granted a royal pardon in respect of the sentence of death passed upon him and carried out. We have no function to perform in relation to that sentence, although some of the fresh evidence reviewed in section III below has obvious relevance to that aspect of the case.

Rarely has the Court been required to review the safety of a conviction recorded over 45 years earlier. In undertaking that task we conclude:

(1) We must apply the substantive law of murder as applicable at the time, disregarding the abolition of constructive malice and the introduction of the defence of diminished responsibility by the Homicide Act 1957.

(2) The liability of a party to a joint enterprise must be determined according to the common law as now understood.

(3) The conduct of the trial and the direction of the jury must be judged according to the standards which we would now apply in any other appeal under section 1 of the 1968 Act.

(4) We must judge the safety of the conviction according to the standards which we would now apply in any other appeal under section 1 of the 1968 Act.

Where, between conviction and appeal, there have been significant changes in the common law (as opposed to changes effected by statute) or in standards of fairness, the approach indicated requires the Court to apply legal rules and procedural criteria which were not and could not reasonably have been applied at the time. This could cause difficulty in some cases but not, we conclude, in this. Where, however, this Court exercises its power to receive new evidence, it inevitably reviews a case different from that presented to the judge and the jury at the trial ...

We must first consider the case that was presented to the judge and the jury at the trial. ... Since one of the grounds of appeal ... asserts that "there are such irreconcilable inconsistencies and improbabilities in significant parts of the evidence of certain police officers as to raise a real doubt as to the reliability and truthfulness of their evidence", it will be necessary to consider parts of the evidence given at the trial in some detail.

The main thrust of the prosecution case was straightforward. Craig had deliberately and wilfully murdered P.C. Miles and the appellant had, to use prosecuting counsel's words in opening,

"incited Craig to begin the shooting and, although technically under arrest at the actual time of the killing of Miles, was party to that murder and equally responsible in law".

In order to prove the appellant's participation, the prosecution relied heavily on what counsel described as "the most important observation that Bentley made that night", namely "Let him have it, Chris". That was said to be a deliberate incitement to murder Detective Constable Fairfax, who had just arrested the appellant. It led, it was said, to Craig immediately firing at and wounding D.C. Fairfax. Counsel said in opening:

> "It was spoken to a man who he, Bentley, clearly knew had a gun. That shot began a gun fight, in the course of which Miles was killed; that incitement ... covered the whole of the shooting thereafter, even though at the time of the actual shot which killed P.C. Miles, Bentley was in custody and under arrest."

Craig's defence was that he was not guilty of murder, but guilty only of manslaughter because, although he had pulled the trigger and fired the shot, he had intended only to frighten the police officers and the killing had been an accident. Because of the doctrine of constructive malice, ... the trial judge considered that Craig had no defence to murder even if his account was believed, and he expressed that view to the jury. Notwithstanding that, he left it to the jury to consider manslaughter. In reality, the case against Craig that he had deliberately murdered P.C. Miles was very strong; and on the law as it then stood any verdict other than guilty of murder in his case would have been perverse.

The appellant's case was that he had not incited Craig to fire the gun and had at no time been party to its use. He had not known that Craig had a gun until the first shot was fired and he had not used the words "Let him have it, Chris" or any words which amounted to an incitement to use the gun. He had been standing with D.C. Fairfax for an appreciable time, making no effort to get away from him and behaving in a wholly docile manner, when Craig had fired the fatal shot. He had not participated in the murder ...

[Counsel for the appellant] submitted that the trial judge's direction to the jury, read as a whole, was unfairly adverse and prejudicial to the appellant, put unfair pressure on the jury to convict and failed adequately to put the appellant's case to the jury ...

At the outset of his summing-up the trial judge described the case as a terrible one, which on any showing it plainly was, and urged the jury in conventional terms to approach it in as calm a frame of mind as they could. He then continued:

> "Here are two lads, one of 16 and one of 19, admittedly out on a shop-breaking expedition at night, armed with a Service revolver, a dreadful weapon in the shape of a knuckle-duster, and two knives which may or may not be described as daggers – one of them I should think certainly could be – and the result is that a young policeman is shot dead while in the execution of his duty. You may think it was almost a miracle that others were not shot too. One of them, we know, Sergeant Fairfax, was wounded, but fortunately only slightly.
>
> Now let us put out of our minds in this case any question of films or comics, or literature of that sort. These things are always prayed in aid

nowadays when young persons are in the dock, but they have really very little to do with the case. These two young men, or boys, whatever you like to call them, are both of an age which makes them responsible to the law – they are over 14 – and it is surely idle to pretend in these days that a boy of 16 does not know the wickedness of taking out a revolver of that description and a pocketful of ammunition and firing it when he is on an unlawful expedition and the police are approaching him. You will remember that so far as Craig is concerned, by his own words he supplied a motive for what he was doing, for he said that he hated the police because they had got his brother 12 years – which seems to show that his brother was convicted for a very serious offence to receive a sentence of that length."

The trial judge … turning to the case of the appellant, directed the jury on the legal approach to the liability of a party to a joint enterprise …

"Now let us see what the evidence is with regard to Bentley. The first thing that you have to consider is: did Bentley know that Craig was armed? Now, you know, because I sit on the Bench and you sit in the jury-box it is not necessary that we leave our common-sense at home. The great virtue of trial by jury is that jurymen can exercise the common-sense of ordinary people. Can you suppose for a moment, especially when you have heard Craig say that why he carried a revolver was for the purpose of boasting and making himself a big man, that he would not have told his pals he was out with that he had got a revolver? Is it not almost inconceivable that Craig would not have told him, and probably shown him the revolver which he had? That is quite apart from what Bentley said afterwards. I should think you would come to the conclusion that the first thing, almost, Craig would tell him, if they were going on a shop-breaking expedition, was: 'It's all right. I've got a revolver with me.'

Then see what Bentley had on him. Where is that knuckle-duster? Apparently it was given to him by Craig, but Bentley was armed with this knuckle-duster. Have you ever seen a more horrible sort of weapon? You know, this is to hit a person in the face with who comes at you. You grasp it *here*, fingers go through – I cannot quite get mine through, I think – and you have got a dreadful heavy steel bar to strike anybody with; and you can kill a person with this, of course. Then did you ever see a more shocking thing than *that*? You have got a spike with which you could jab anybody who comes at you; if the blow with the steel is not enough, you have got this spike at the side to jab. You can have it to see, if you like, when you go to your room. It is a shocking weapon. Here was Craig armed with a revolver and that sheath knife. Hand me that sheath knife – the big one. One wonders, really what parents can be about in these days, allowing a boy of 16 – they say, perhaps, they do not know, but why do not they know? – to have a weapon like this which he takes about with him? It is not a new one, you can see; it is pretty well worn. That was the thing that Craig was taking about. Where is the other knife? Here is Bentley with a smaller knife, but you can feel it is sharp and pointed. What is he carrying that with him for in his coat, not even with a sheath on it?

Can you believe it for a moment although Bentley had said he did not know Craig had the gun? You are not bound to believe Bentley if you think the inference and common sense of the matter is over-whelming that he must have known that he had it. Now, of course, the most serious piece of evidence against Bentley is that he called out, if you believe the evidence, to Craig 'Let him have it, Chris!', and then the firing began, and the very first shot struck Sergeant Fairfax. Gentlemen, those words are sworn to by three police officers – Sergeant Fairfax, Police Constable McDonald, and Police Constable Harrison; they all swear that they heard Bentley call that out, and that then the firing started ..."

And then the judge gave the direction ... concerning the conspicuous bravery of the police officers, to which reference has already been made.

The trial judge then reminded the jury of the evidence and the alleged admissions of the appellant and at page 138A of the transcript continued:

"Then in his statement he said: 'I didn't know he was going to use the gun.' Again, if he said that, it shows that he knew it. If he knew that he had the gun, can you believe he did not know he had ammunition? Why did he have ammunition? Why did he have the gun? Why did he have the ammunition? You will remember that at one stage the offi-cers said that Craig on the roof told them that he had a .45 and lots of ammunition. I think they said something about 'blowing your head off' – 'He'll blow your head off'. Then later in his statement he said he did not know ' Chris' had a gun till he shot. That, of course, is quite inconsistent with what he said earlier in his statement. You can have the statement when you go to your room, if you like. He did say 'I didn't know he was going to use the gun', and then he said after-wards 'I didn't know Chris had one until he shot'. It does not seem very consistent, but, as I say, the real thing is, is it not, as a matter of common sense, can you believe for a moment that if Bentley had gone on that expedition with this boastful young ruffian who said he carried a gun for the purpose of making himself out bigger than he was, he would not have told Bentley he had the gun? What had he got the gun for, and what did Bentley think he had the gun for?"

The trial judge then observed that that was the whole case. He pro-ceeded to summarise Craig's defence in four sentences, and the appellant's in two:

"In the case of Bentley, Bentley's defence is: 'I didn't know he had a gun, and I deny that I said "Let him have it Chris". I never knew he was going to shoot, and I didn't think he would'."

The judge then made reference to the appellant's denial as that of a man in grievous peril …

Their Lordships realise that the judge's task in this type of trial is never an easy one. He must of course remain impartial, but at the same time the evidence may point strongly to the guilt of the defendant; the judge may often feel that he has to supplement deficiencies in the performance of the prosecution or defence, in order to maintain a proper balance between the two sides in the adversarial proceedings. It is all too easy for a court thereafter to criticise a judge who may have fallen into error for this reason. However, if the system is trial by jury then the decision must be that of the jury and not of the judge using the jury as something akin to a vehicle for his own views. Whether that is what has happened in any particular case is not likely to be an easy decision …

The killing of P.C. Miles had, very understandably, aroused widespread public sympathy for the victim and his family and a strong sense of public outrage at the circumstances of his death. This background made it more, not less, important that the jury should approach the issues in a dispassionate spirit if the defendants were to receive a fair trial, as the trial judge began by reminding them. In our judgment, however, far from encouraging the jury to approach the case in a calm frame of mind, the trial judge's summing-up, particularly in the passages we have quoted, had exactly the opposite effect. We cannot read these passages as other than a highly rhetorical and strongly worded denunciation of both defendants and of their defences. The language used was not that of a judge but of an advocate (and it contrasted strongly with the appropriately restrained language of prosecuting counsel). Such a direction by such a judge must in our view have driven the jury to conclude that they had little choice but to convict; at the lowest, it may have done so.

These complaints formed no part of the appellant's appeal against conviction. We do not know why not. We question whether, in the light of the authorities to which we have referred, this summing-up would have been thought acceptable even by the standards prevailing at the time. Complaint was made on appeal of the trial judge's failure to put the appellant's case adequately to the jury, but this ground of appeal was dismissed; the court, it seems, held that "the idea that there was a failure on the part of the Chief Justice to say anything short of what was required in putting that sort of case to the jury is entirely wrong". In his summary of the appellant's defence towards the end of his summing-up, the trial judge did indeed remind the jury of three of the essential points that he relied on: that he did not know Craig had a gun; that he did not know that Craig would shoot; and that he did not incite him to do so. But this very brief and somewhat dismissive account, coming at the very end of the summing-up and following a much longer account described as "the whole case", did not in our judgment do justice to the points which, good or bad, had been made on behalf of the appellant and which the jury should have been invited to consider. We refer to some of these (in particular those relating to the existence, scope and duration of any joint enterprise between the appellant and Craig, and the possible ambiguity of "Let him have it, Chris", if that was ever said) below. Whether the jury would have been impressed by these points if they had been dispassionately identified and laid before them we can never know. As it was, the jury were never invited by the trial judge to consider the points which had been made on the appellant's behalf. The effect was to deprive him of the protection which jury trial should have afforded.

It is with genuine diffidence that the members of this Court direct criticism towards a trial judge widely recognised as one of the outstanding criminal judges of this century. But we cannot escape the duty of decision. In our judgment, the summing-up in this case was such as to deny the appellant that fair trial which is the birthright of every British citizen.

[*His lordship then moved on to consider the doctrine of joint enterprise:*]

At the trial the Crown relied ... , on two doctrines of the common law. By the first ("constructive malice"), malice aforethought sufficient to support a charge of murder was in certain circumstances imputed to a defendant who committed an act causing death in the course of committing a felony or when resisting an officer of justice. This doctrine had obvious relevance to the Crown case against Craig. [It was abolished by the Homicide Act 1957, s. 1(1).] By the second doctrine, a participant in a joint criminal enterprise is held liable for the acts of another participant pursuant to and within the scope of the joint criminal enterprise. The application of this doctrine could make the appellant liable for what Craig did. Mr Fitzgerald argued that the trial judge's direction to the jury on constructive malice and joint enterprise, so far as it related to the appellant, was wrong in law.

[T]he trial judge directed the jury in these terms:

"Well, now I turn to Bentley. Members of the jury, these two youths are tried together, and they are both tried for the murder of the policeman. It is quite unnecessary, where two or more persons are engaged together in an unlawful criminal act, to show that the hand of both of them committed the act ... where two people are engaged on a felonious enterprise – and warehouse-breaking is a felony – and one knows that the other is carrying a weapon, and there is agreement to use such violence as may be necessary to avoid arrest, and this leads to the killing of a person or results in the killing of a person, both are guilty of murder, and it is no answer for one to say 'I did not think my companion would go as far as he did'.

Now you can only judge whether there is an agreement to use such violence as may be necessary by looking at what happened and all the circumstances of the case, but I do remind you that it is no excuse and no defence to say 'I knew he was carrying a loaded revolver' – if you find he was – 'that he was carrying a loaded revolver, or a revolver, but I didn't think he would use it'. If one is carrying a revolver and the other knows that he intends to use some degree of violence, it is no answer, if that violence results in death to say 'Well, I didn't think he would go as far as that'. What you have to consider is: is there evidence from which you can properly infer that these two youths went out with a common purpose not merely to warehouse-break but to resist apprehension, even by violence if necessary? That is all. It is, as I repeat, no answer, if you come to that conclusion, for one to say: "Yes, but I didn't think he would go as far as he did"."

[T]he trial judge added:

"Then in the car first of all he said: 'I knew he had a gun' – that is sworn to by three officers – 'I knew he had a gun, but I did not think he'd use it'. As I have told you, if he knew he had a gun, and knew he was taking the gun for protection in their common unlawful enterprise, or to prevent arrest by violence, Bentley is as guilty as Craig; he is as guilty in law as Craig."

It seems to us, in the light of those authorities binding on the trial judge, that his direction to the jury was in accordance with the law as it then stood and was, if anything, favourable to the appellant. But it was argued that later developments in the law governing the liability of secondary parties to joint criminal enterprises, in particular the recent decision of the House of Lords in R. v. Powell and R. v. English [below] rendered his direction unsound. The relevant law is in our judgment summarised with sufficient accuracy for present purposes in the following propositions advanced on behalf of the Crown:

"(i) Where two parties embark on a joint enterprise to commit a crime and one party foresees that in the course of the enterprise the other party may carry out, with the requisite *mens rea*, an act constituting another crime, the former is liable for that crime if committed by the latter in the course of the enterprise ...

(ii) Where the principal kills with a deadly weapon, which the secondary party did not know that he had and of which he therefore did not foresee use by the principal, the secondary party is not guilty of murder.

(iii) If the weapon used by the primary party is different to but as dangerous as the weapon which the secondary party contemplated he might use, the secondary party should not escape liability for murder because of the difference in the weapon, for example if he foresaw that the primary party might use a gun to kill and the latter used a knife to kill or vice versa (R. v. English, above at 286DE and 30GH, *per* Lord Hutton).

(iv) The secondary party is subject to criminal liability if he contemplated the act causing the death as a possible incident of the joint venture unless the risk was so remote that the jury take the view that the secondary party genuinely dismissed it as altogether negligible ...)."

Even if we undertake the anachronistic exercise of applying those principles to the trial judge's direction to the jury in 1952, the soundness of that direction is not in our view invalidated. Nothing in his direction suggested that the appellant could be liable if he did not know that Craig had a gun, nor did he suggest that the appellant could be liable if he did not foresee the use of the gun. His direction was founded on the premise of an agreement between the appellant and Craig to use such violence as might be necessary to avoid arrest: this would plainly embrace use of the gun, even if the appellant did not intend that the gun should be fired, or fired so as to cause injury, and did not expect the gun to be fired unless the firing was regarded by the appellant as a wholly remote possibility. On the basis of the law of constructive malice as it then stood, and the law of joint enterprise as it now stands, the trial judge's direction in the passages we have quoted was in our judgment correct.

That is not, however, the end of the matter. [T]his was a case calling for a very careful direction and review of the evidence relevant to, first, the existence and nature of any agreement or understanding between Craig and the appellant; secondly, the scope and purpose of such agreement or understanding; and, thirdly, the duration and possible termination of any such agreement or understanding. This last matter was of particular importance, since the appellant's defence at the trial rested strongly on the contention that if, contrary to his assertion, there had ever been any joint agreement to resist arrest by violence, he had dissociated himself from it. Reliance was placed on a number of facts already mentioned above: the absence of any struggle or resistance or attempt to escape by the appellant following his seizure by Detective Constable Fairfax; his compliant surrender of the weapons on his person; the fact that he was under arrest for a significant period, perhaps 15 minutes, before Police Constable Miles was shot; and the number of observations attributed to the appellant by the police officers: "That's all I've got guv'nor; I haven't got a gun"; "He'll shoot you"; He's got a .45 Colt and plenty of bloody ammunition too"; "I told the silly bugger not to use it"; "You want to look out; he'll blow your heads off"; "Look out, Chris; they're taking me down", and, of course, the important but possibly ambiguous statement (if made): "Let him have it, Chris."

The circumstances in which a party to a joint enterprise may claim to have abandoned or withdrawn from that enterprise was the subject of consideration by Sloan J.A., sitting in the Court of Appeal of British Columbia, in Whitehouse [1941] 1 D.L.R. 683 at 685 where he said:

"... After a crime has been committed and before a prior abandonment of the common enterprise may be found by a jury there must be, in my view, in the absence of exceptional circumstances, something more than a mere mental change of intention and physical change of place by those associates who wish to dissociate themselves from the consequences attendant upon their willing assistance up to the moment of the actual commission of that crime ... [I]t seems to me that one essential element ought to be established in a case of this kind: where practicable and reasonable there must be timely communication of the intention to abandon the common purpose from those who wish to dissociate themselves from the contemplated crime to those who desire to continue in it. What is 'timely communication' must be determined by the facts of each case but where practicable and reasonable it ought to be such communication, verbal or otherwise, that will serve unequivocal notice upon the other party to the common unlawful cause that if he proceeds upon it he does so without the further aid and assistance of those who withdraw. The unlawful purpose of him who continues alone is then his own and not one in common with those who are no longer parties to it nor liable to its full and final consequences."

... Whether, properly directed, the jury would have found that the appellant had done enough to withdraw and signify his withdrawal from the enterprise which they must have found to exist between him and Craig we cannot know. But this was an important limb of the appellant's defence, and it is in our view clear that the trial judge should have given the jury a careful direction on it. He gave none.

... The Crown case throughout was that the appellant was under arrest (or "technically under arrest", which must be the same thing) at the time when Police Constable Miles was shot; and it is very difficult to see how any answer given by the appellant could have any bearing on the legal question whether he was under arrest or not. In any event, when asked in cross-examination whether he was not under arrest at the time, he simply answered "I was standing there, sir". It is quite true that for much of the time after his initial seizure he was not physically held, and he agreed that he had been free to run away if he had wanted to, but this was in itself evidence of potential significance supporting the suggestion that, for him, the criminal enterprise was over. We feel bound to say that, in our judgment, the Court of Criminal Appeal failed to grapple with this ground of appeal, which should have succeeded.

For all the reasons given in this section of the judgment we think that the conviction of the appellant was unsafe. We accordingly allow the appeal and quash his conviction. It must be a matter of profound and continuing regret that this mistrial occurred and that the defects we have found were not recognised at the time.

The doctrine of joint enterprise was reconfigured in *Powell and English*, below.

R v Powell, R v English [1997] 4 All ER 545

[All the judges concurred with the speech of Lord Hutton. Extracts from the additional comments made by Lords Mustill and Steyn are also included below.]

Lord Hutton.

… [T]he appeals before your Lordships' House relate to the liability of a participant in a joint criminal enterprise when another participant in that enterprise is guilty of a crime, the commission of which was not the purpose of the enterprise.

In the case of Powell and Daniels the purpose of the joint enterprise was to purchase drugs from a drug dealer. Three men, including the two appellants, Powell and Daniels, went to purchase drugs from a drug dealer, but having gone to his house for that purpose, the drug dealer was shot dead when he came to the door. The Crown was unable to prove which of the three men fired the gun which killed the drug dealer, but it was the Crown case that if the third man fired the gun, the two appellants were guilty of murder because they knew that the third man was armed with a gun and realised that he might use it to kill or cause really serious injury to the drug dealer.

In the course of summing up to the jury at the trial the Recorder of London said:

> If B or C realised, without agreeing to such conduct being used, that A may kill or intentionally inflict serious injury and they nevertheless continue to participate with A in the venture, that will amount to a sufficient mental element for B or C to be guilty of murder if A with the requisite intent kills in the course of the venture. In those circumstances B and C have lent themselves to the enterprise and by so doing have given assistance and encouragement to A in carrying out an enterprise which they realised may involve murder. These are general principles which must be applied to the facts of this case.

Powell and Daniels were convicted of murder and their appeals were rejected by the Court of Appeal, and the question certified for the opinion of your Lordships' House is:

> Is it sufficient to found a conviction for murder for a secondary party to a killing to have realised that the primary party might kill with

intent to do so or must the secondary party have held such intention himself?

In the case of English the purpose of the joint enterprise in which he and another young man, Weddle, took part was to attack and cause injury with wooden posts to a police officer, Sergeant Forth, and in the course of the attack Weddle used a knife with which he stabbed Sergeant Forth to death. It was a reasonable possibility that English had no knowledge that Weddle was carrying a knife, and on this basis the learned trial judge, Owen J, stated in his summing up to the jury:

> If he did not know of the knife then you have to consider whether nevertheless he knew that there was a substantial risk that Weddle might cause some really serious injury with the wooden post which was used in the manner which you find it to have been used. So there is the question; 'Has the Prosecution proved' – and this is an alternative, of course – 'that English joined in an unlawful attack on the sergeant realising at that time that there was a substantial risk that in that attack Weddle might kill or at least cause some really serious injury to the sergeant? If no, not guilty'.

The judge then, in effect, directed the jury that if they answered that question in the affirmative they should find English guilty of murder.

Weddle and English were convicted of murder and their appeals were rejected by the Court of Appeal. English now appeals to your Lordships' House and the two questions certified for the opinion of the House are as follows:

(i) Is it sufficient to found a conviction for murder for a secondary party to a killing to have realised that the primary party might kill with intent to do so or with intent to cause grievous bodily harm or must the secondary party have held such an intention himself?

(ii) Is it sufficient for murder that the secondary party intends or foresees that the primary party would or may act with intent to cause grievous bodily harm, if the lethal act carried out by the primary party is fundamentally different from the acts foreseen or intended by the secondary party?

The question certified in the appeals of Powell and Daniels and the first question certified in the appeal of English raise the issue whether foresight of a criminal act which was not the purpose of the joint enterprise (in the case of Powell and Daniels the use of a gun, and in the case of English the use of a knife) is sufficient to impose criminal liability for murder on the secondary party in the event that the jury find that the primary party used the weapon with intent to kill or cause really serious harm.

... I would answer the certified question of law in the appeals of Powell and Daniels and the first certified question in the appeal of English by stating that (subject to the observations which I make in relation to the second certified question in the case of English) it is sufficient to found a conviction for murder for a secondary party to have realised that in the course of the joint enterprise the primary party might kill with intent to do so or with intent to cause grievous bodily harm. Accordingly I would dismiss the appeals of Powell and Daniels.

[The argument for the Crown in respect of English is that where the infliction of grievous bodily harm came within the contemplation of the accomplices, they cannot argue that murder was a different crime from the attack which they contemplated and escape liability for murder on the ground that it was outside the common design.]

...

[*After discussing Gamble [1989] NI 268, Lord Hutton continued:*] In my opinion, this decision was correct in that a secondary party who foresees grievous bodily harm caused by kneecapping with a gun should not be guilty of murder where, in an action unforeseen by the secondary party, another party to the criminal enterprise kills the victim by cutting his throat with a knife. The issue (which is one of fact ...) ... whether a secondary party who foresees the use of a gun to kneecap, and death is then caused by the deliberate firing of the gun into the head or body of the victim, is guilty of murder is more debatable.

... [In English's case] ... the direction of the judge was defective ... because in accordance with the principle in *Anderson and Morris* ... he did not qualify his direction on foresight of really serious injury by stating that if the jury considered the use of the knife by Weddle was the use of a weapon ... which English did not foresee as a possibility, then English should not have been convicted of murder. As the unforeseen use of the knife would take the killing outside the scope of the joint venture the jury should also have been directed ... that English should not be found guilty of manslaughter.

... I think it undesirable to seek to formulate a more precise answer ... [to the second certified question] in case such an answer might appear to prescribe too rigid a formula for trial judges. However, I would wish to make this observation: if the weapon used by the primary party is different to, but as dangerous as, the weapon which the secondary party contemplated he might use, the secondary party should not escape liability for murder ... for example, if he foresaw that the primary party might use a gun to kill and the latter used a knife to kill, or vice versa.

... [T]he secondary party is subject to criminal liability if he contemplated the act causing the incident as a possible incident of the joint venture, unless the risk was so remote that the jury take the view that the secondary party genuinely dismissed it as altogether negligible.

... [I]n directing the jury, the judge need not adopt a set of fixed formulae ... I consider that the test of foresight is a simpler and more practicable test for a jury to apply than the test of whether the act causing the death goes beyond what was tacitly agreed as part of the joint enterprise. Therefore, in cases where an issue arises as to whether an action was within the scope of the joint venture, I would suggest that it might be preferable for a trial judge ... to base his direction on the test of foresight rather than on the test set ... in *Anderson and Morris* ... But in a case where, although the secondary party may have foreseen grievous bodily harm, he may not have foreseen the use of the weapon employed ... or the manner in which the primary party acted, the trial judge should qualify the test of foresight ...

[T]here will be cases giving rise to a fine distinction as to whether or not the unforeseen use of a particular weapon or the manner in which a particular weapon is used will take a killing outside the scope of the joint venture, but the issue will be one of fact for the common sense of the jury to decide.

Lord Mustill.

I concurred without hesitation in the orders made by the House on 17 July 1997. Even as regards the case of English, which is much the more difficult of the appeals, I felt and continue to feel that neither on the authorities nor in plain justice could it be right to sustain the conviction once it was very properly conceded on behalf of the respondent that the appellant might have been unaware that the knife ultimately used by Weddle was even in the latter's possession. So much is to my mind clear. Much less clear is the proper analysis of the law in a situation where the secondary party foresees that the principal offender may commit a more serious crime than the one which the two set out to commit, and nevertheless decides to go ahead with the plan.

My own reasoning was, in summary, as follows:

Throughout the modern history of the law on secondary criminal liability (at least of the type with which this appeal is concerned) the responsibility of the secondary defendant has been founded on his participation in a joint enterprise of which the commission of the crime by the principal offender formed part. Any doubts on this score were set at rest by *R v Anderson; R v Morris* [1966] 2 All ER 644 by reference to which countless juries have been directed over the years. As it seemed to me the House should not depart from this long-established principle without the strongest of reasons. The problem is to accommodate in the principle the foresight of the secondary party about what the main offender might do. Two aspects of this problem are simple. If S did not foresee what was actually done by P he is not liable for it, since it could not have been part of any joint enterprise. This is what the court decided in *R v Anderson; R v Morris*. Conversely, if S did foresee P's act this would always, as a matter of common sense, be relevant to the jury's decision on whether it formed part of a course of action to which both S and P agreed, albeit often on the basis that the action would be taken if particular circumstances should arise.

Intellectually, there are problems with the concept of a joint venture, but they do not detract from its general practical worth, which has proved itself over many years. In one particular situation there is, however, a problem which this time-honoured solution cannot solve. Namely, where S foresees that P may go too far; sincerely wishes that he will not, and makes this plain to P; and yet goes ahead, either because he hopes for the best, or because P is an overbearing character, or for some other reason. Many would say, and I agree, that the conduct of S is culpable, although usually at a lower level than the culpability of the principal who actually does the deed. Yet try as I may, I cannot accommodate this culpability within a concept of joint enterprise. How can a jury be directed at the same time that S is guilty only if he was party to an express or tacit agreement to do the act in question, and that he is guilty if he not only disagreed with it, but made his disagreement perfectly clear to P? Are not the two assertions incompatible?

What the trial judge needs is a clear and comprehensible statement of a workable principle, which he or she will find in the speech of my noble and learned friend, Lord Hutton; and the judge's task will not be helped in any way by a long exposition of a theory which might have prevailed, but in the event has not. This being so I am entirely willing to concur in the reasoning to which the remainder of your Lordships subscribe. This will, I suspect, require some judges to look again at the terms in which they have customarily directed juries, but the task should not be at all difficult to perform.

Lord Steyn.

There are two separate but complementary legal concepts at stake. The first is the mental element sufficient for murder, ie an intention to kill or to cause really serious bodily injury. Only if this element is proved in respect of the primary offender, and if the other ingredients of murder are proved, does the second concept arise for consideration, viz the criminal liability of accessories to a joint criminal enterprise. Under the accessory principle criminal liability is dependent on proof of subjective foresight on the part of a participant in the criminal enterprise that the primary offender might commit a greater offence, that being in these cases foresight that the primary offender might commit murder as defined in law.

The thrust of both appeals was to challenge the existing law and practice regarding the second concept. The appeals under consideration relate to charges of murder. But there is no special rule regarding the criminal liability of accessories in cases of murder. The principle governing the criminal liability of accessories applies across the spectrum of most criminal offences. Any alteration in the accessory principle, as presently understood, would have to apply to most criminal offences. That does not mean that the arguments advanced on behalf of the appellants are unsound. But it underlines the sweeping impact of the changes to the existing law and practice necessarily involved in an acceptance of the submissions made on behalf of the appellants in these appeals.

The established principle is that a secondary party to a criminal enterprise may be criminally liable for a greater criminal offence committed by the primary offender of a type which the former foresaw but did not necessarily intend. The criminal culpability lies in participating in the criminal enterprise with that foresight. Foresight and intention are not synonymous terms. But foresight is a necessary and sufficient ground of the liability of accessories. That is how the law has been stated in two carefully reasoned decisions of the Privy Council: see *Chan Wing-Sui v R* [1984] 3 All ER 877 and *Hui Chi-ming v R* [1991] 3 All ER 897 ... And Lord Hutton has demonstrated in his comprehensive review of the case law that the law is as stated in the two Privy Council decisions. That does not mean that the established principle cannot be re-examined and, if found to be flawed, re-formulated. But the existing law and practice forms the starting point.

Counsel for the appellants argued that the secondary party to a criminal enterprise should only be guilty of a murder committed by the primary offender if the secondary party has the full mens rea sufficient for murder, ie an intent to kill or to cause real bodily harm ... I would reject the argument that the accessory principle as such imposes a form of constructive liability. The accessory principle requires proof of a subjective state of mind on the part of a participant in a criminal enterprise, viz foresight that the primary offender might commit a different and more serious offence ... Nevertheless, as the critics point out it is enough that the accessory is reckless, whereas, in the case of the principal, intention must be proved. Recklessness whether death be caused is a sufficient mens rea for a principal offender in manslaughter, but not murder. The accessory to murder, however, must be proved to have been reckless, not merely whether death might be caused, but whether murder might be committed: *he must have been aware, not merely that death or grievous bodily harm might be caused, but that it might be caused intentionally, by a person whom he was assisting or encouraging to commit a crime.* Recklessness whether murder be committed is different from, and more serious than, recklessness whether death be caused by an accident. (My emphasis.)

The foresight of the secondary party must be directed to a real possibility of the commission by the primary offender in the course of the criminal enterprise of the greater offence. The liability is imposed because the secondary party is assisting in and encouraging a criminal enterprise which he is aware might result in the commission of a greater offence. The liability of an accessory is predicated on his culpability in respect of the greater offence as defined in law. It is undoubtedly a lesser form of mens rea. But it is unrealistic to say that the accessory principle as such imposes constructive criminal liability.

At first glance there is substance in the ... argument that it is anomalous that a lesser form of culpability is required in the case of a secondary party, viz. foresight of the possible commission of the greater offence, whereas in the case of the primary offender the law insists on proof of the specific intention which is an ingredient of the offence. This general argument leads, in the present case, to the particular argument that it is anomalous that the secondary party can be guilty of murder if he foresees the possibility of such a crime being committed while the primary can only be guilty if he has an intent to kill or cause really serious injury. Recklessness may suffice in the case of the secondary party but it does not in the case of the primary offender. The answer to this supposed anomaly, and other similar cases across the spectrum of criminal law, is to be found in practical and policy considerations. If the law required proof of the specific intention on the part of a secondary party, the utility of the accessory principle would be gravely undermined. It is just that a secondary party who foresees that the primary offender might kill with the intent sufficient for murder, and assists and encourages the primary offender in the criminal enterprise on this basis, should be guilty of murder. He ought to be criminally liable for harm which he foresaw and which in fact resulted from the crime he assisted and encouraged. But it would in practice almost invariably be impossible for a jury to say that the secondary party wanted death to be caused or that he regarded it as virtually certain. In the real world proof of an intention sufficient for murder would be well nigh impossible in the vast majority of joint enterprise cases. Moreover, the proposed change in the law must be put in context. The criminal justice system exists to control crime. A prime function of that system must be to deal justly but effectively with those who join with others in criminal enterprises. Experience has shown that joint criminal enterprises only too readily escalate into the commission of greater offences. In order to deal with this important social problem the accessory principle is needed and cannot be abolished or relaxed. For these reasons I would reject the arguments advanced in favour of the revision of the accessory principle.

The benefits accruing to the appellant, English, from this restatement of the law of joint enterprise may prove elusive at the trial stage. The threshold for secondary liability in these circumstances remains at the 'foresight as possible' level; juries will have the opportunity to apply the 'fine distinction' to which Lord Hutton refers between a foresight (which will lead to liability), and one which exonerates, that is, where the weapon or the act fundamentally differs from that person's contemplation. An example of the latter is *Uddin* (1999).

The 'actus reus' requirements of participation, too, conduce to breadth and flexibility. Two particular issues stand out for consideration in the public order context. In the first place, doctrinal insistence on liability only for acts and not for omissions becomes, in participation, the injunction that mere presence is insufficient for liability; some active involvement or encouragement is necessary. Yet the distinction between presence and encouragement is exceedingly difficult to draw. The relevance of the issue to public order contexts is illustrated in the old case of *Coney* (1882), in which a spectator at a prize fight was charged with aiding and abetting the assaults involved. The issue was considered more recently in the case of *R v Allan* (1963). The appellants had been convicted of affray and appealed on the basis of the judge's direction that a person is a party to an affray where, without any prior agreement, 'he unlawfully joins in a fight [between two or more people in a public street that is likely to terrify passers-by or residents] or, being present, chose to remain present, either (a) knowing that his continued presence encouraged the fight, or (b) intending to join in the fight if his help was needed by his side'. Edmund Davies J expressed the opinion of the Court of Appeal in concluding:

> The jury were in terms told that a man who chooses to remain at a fight, nursing the secret intention to help if the need arose, but doing nothing to evince that intention, must in law be held to be a principal in the second degree and that, on these facts being proved, the jury would have no alternative but to convict him. In our judgment, that was a misdirection. As Cave J said in *Coney*, 'Where presence is prima facie not accidental it is evidence, but no more than evidence, for the jury', and it remains no more than evidence for the jury even when one adds to presence at an affray a secret intention to help.

This is a robust affirmation of some basic doctrinal principles; but how clearly would they apply in the public order context where initial presence at the event may be interpreted by the court as evincing a prior intention or willingness to participate in an offence? It is all very well to draw clear conceptual distinctions between evidential and legal questions, but in practice everything will turn on the making of those evidential inferences. The preconceptions which tribunals and courts are likely to have in doing so in the public order area are such that the safeguards prized by doctrine and avowed by the courts may turn out to be worth a great deal less than their face value.

The second issue in relation to 'actus reus' which merits attention is the possibility of withdrawal from participation. Criminal law allows that secondary parties may escape liability by making an effective withdrawal – but what constitutes an effective withdrawal inevitably relates to the nature of the participation in question. Thus, the giver of encouragement may have to attempt dissuasion; the aider at the scene must not only withdraw her help but make a timely communication of that withdrawal (*R v Becerra*, 1975). The very idea of withdrawal renders it inappropriate to certain kinds of participants – for example, the procurer or provider of information and advice which cannot be withdrawn or removed, in which case the only possible kind of withdrawal, if indeed there is any, would seem to be physical obstruction or notification to the police. These limitations on the possibility of withdrawal are of particular relevance to those who are marginally involved in situations of public disorder. The person who has been involved at the planning stage may find it impossible to make any satisfactory withdrawal given the effective completion of her participation, and the person present at the scene of disorder may well find it impossible to communicate withdrawal at the time – indeed, the very ideas of 'common purpose', 'contemplation' and 'communication of withdrawal of support' seem inapposite and artificial in the context of disorders involving large numbers of people.

R v Rook [1993] 2 All ER 955, CA

[*The appellant and two others agreed with MA to kill MA's wife for £20,000. The appellant did not turn up at the agreed site of the killing and it was carried out by the two others. All four were jointly charged with the murder of MA's wife. The two others pleaded guilty but the appellant and MA stood trial. The appellant's defence was that he never intended the killing to take place and he thought the other two would not go ahead without him. His appeal against conviction was dismissed.*]

Lloyd LJ.

… [T]he position, on his own evidence, was that he took a leading part in the planning of the murder. He foresaw that the murder would, or at least might, take place. For a time he stalled the others. But he did nothing to stop them, and apart from his absence on the [day of the murder], he did nothing to indicate to them that he had changed his mind.

… [Counsel for the Crown] submits that where a person has given assistance, for example by providing a gun, in circumstances which would render him liable as a secondary party if he does not withdraw, then in order to escape liability he must 'neutralise' his assistance. He must … break the chain of causation between his act of assistance, and the subsequent crime, by recovering the gun, or by warning the victim to stay away, or by going to the police. [Counsel for the appellant] submits, on the other hand, that the Crown must prove that the defendant continued ready to help until the moment the crime is committed; and if there is doubt as to the defendant's state of mind on the day in question, or his willingness to provide further help if required, then the jury must acquit.

As between these two extreme views, we have no hesitation in rejecting the latter.

… In the present case the appellant never told the others that he was not going ahead with the crime. His absence on the day could not possibly amount to 'unequivocal communication' of his withdrawal.

... If the summing-up had been confined to the oral directions given by the judge, the appellant would have had little to complain about. But the judge went on to put his directions in writing ... [which] bear the imprint of many minds. Simplicity and clarity have suffered in the process. The directions are as follows:

Q.2 If the answer to Q.1 is Yes, then has the prosecution proved that R's absence alone from the enterprise was not capable of neutralising and did not in fact neutralise the assistance and/or encouragement he had previously given. If Yes, then guilty of murder. If No, then go to Q.3.

Q.3 If the answer to Q.2 is No, has the prosecution proved that by that absence he did not intend to neutralise the effect of what he had previously said and done. If Yes, then guilty of murder. If No, then not guilty.

[T]hese directions were at best confusing and at worst misleading ... We are driven to the conclusion that questions 2 and 3 are a misdirection.

But, having said that, a clearer case for the proviso would be hard to conceive. If the jury had been properly directed in accordance with *Becerra* there can be no doubt whatever that the verdict would have been the same, for there was never any suggestion that the appellant had communicated his intention to the other parties, so as to make his withdrawal effective. Accordingly we would dismiss the appeal.

Similarly in *Mitchell* (1999) the Court of Appeal suggested that withdrawal from pre-planned violence requires, where reasonable and practicable, communication to the other party. And the joint enterprise rules survived a challenge of unfairness under Article 6 of the European Convention on Human Rights in *Concannon* (2002). The defendant went with his co-accused to the flat of a man dealing in drugs; he admitted that he suggested to the co-accused that they should rob this man. When they arrived at the flat the door was open and they went in. The defendant asked the man for money and drugs and then punched him. The co-accused subsequently stabbed the man to death but the defendant said he was not present at the time and that he had not known that his co-accused had a knife. The judge, directing the jury on joint enterprise in accordance with *Powell and English*, explained that it was sufficient if they were sure that the defendant foresaw a reasonable possibility that, in pursuit of the common purpose, the co-accused would stab the victim with murderous intent. Both the defendant and his co-accused were convicted of murder. The defendant applied for leave to appeal against conviction on the grounds that it was not fair, within the meaning of Article 6 of the European Convention on Human Rights, that the defendant who did not personally inflict the fatal wounds on the deceased should be convicted of murder when it was not necessary under domestic law for him personally to have intended that the victim should die or suffer really serious injury. The application was refused; these were arguments about substantive law. Provided the criminality established against a defendant equated with the legally prescribed criteria for murder, then he was guilty of murder, and if he was convicted after a fair trial the sentence was prescribed by law. The criteria for and the consequences of conviction were not susceptible to change by reference to Article 6.

Participatory liability extends 'subjective' doctrinal principles of personal responsibility to cover a range of activities at various degrees of distance from the perpetration of the 'actus reus' of criminal offences. The cumulation of secondary liability with the group offences of riot, affray and violent disorder under the POA 1986 increases the flexibility of an already broad and inclusive area of criminal regulation. Serious questions can be raised as to whether the full extent of participatory liability can be justified either as necessary to reduce social danger or as responding to culpable conduct. The further cumulation with inchoate offences makes possible applications of criminal law which are of staggering breadth. As we shall see, the crime of conspiracy has been strongly associated with the regulation of public disorder (**Chapter 3.IV.**).

The Law Commission proposed in its Consultation Paper *Assisting and Encouraging Crime* (CP 131, 1993) that liability for the full offence should be replaced by two new inchoate offences of assisting crime and encouraging crime. These proposed offences would then mirror that of assisting an offender with intent to impede his or her apprehension or prosecution after the commission of an offence (Criminal Law Act 1967, s 4(1)). Although the Law Commission's proposal would overcome some of the due process objections to the present law, which labels a person who merely discussed a murder as guilty of murder (see *Rook*, above), no doubt a whole branch of new questions would arise as to the line between a joint principal and a person encouraging or assisting an offence (see Smith 1994).

We have mainly concentrated on group disorder in this chapter. Groups are always composed of individuals and criminal law and justice, except when it deals with corporate entities, deals through individuals. Our next chapter continues the themes of disorder, risk, violence and deviance.

FURTHER READING

Norrie, Alan (2001) *Crime, Reason and History* (2nd edn, Butterworths) Chs 2 and 3.
Smith, K J M (1991) *A Modern Treatise on the Law of Complicity* (Clarendon Press).
— (1994) 'The Law Commission Consultation Paper on Complicity: A Blueprint for Rationalism' Crim LR 239.
— (2001) 'Withdrawal in Complicity: A Restatement of Principles' Crim LR 769.
Sullivan, G R (1994) 'Fault Elements and Joint Enterprise' Crim LR 252.
Wells, Celia (2000) 'Girls, Gangs and Fears' in and Nicolson and Bibbings, *Feminist Perspectives on Criminal Law* (Cavendish Publishing) p 123.

Risk and danger

I.   Home and away: inclusion and exclusion

I.a.   Space, knowledge and technology

We build in this chapter on the foundations laid in **Chapter 2**. In many cases, disorder offences dovetail with offences of harassment and of personal violence (assault, wounding and so on) under the Offences Against the Person Act 1861. Arguments about the regulation of drug and alcohol use, including the construction of the dangerous deviant and the doctrinal relevance of intoxication to criminal liability, are canvassed in **section III.** Certain features of these areas are thrown into sharp relief against the backcloth of public order contexts; they help to illustrate the continuity between the narrow, 'literal' conception of public order and the broad, political and 'metaphysical' conception with which we would argue law is equally concerned. We conclude with an introduction to inchoate modes of liability. In the same way that complicity, or aiding and abetting, considerably broadens the circle of liability when an offence is committed, inchoate modes such as conspiracy and attempt allow liability even though an offence is not completed.

While the separation between private and public spheres of activity was never as simple as it sounded, we have recently witnessed a rapid decline in the availability of public space, and increasing modes of surveillance (CCTV) both in public streets and in 'private' public areas such as shopping malls and leisure facilities. The idea of surveillance and controlling citizens' activities is one that continues in our discussion of the array of harassment offences and of regulatory techniques such as the anti-social behaviour order and child curfews. There is then a blurred line between 'public order' in the traditional sense of groups on the streets (which may or may not be pursuing political aims), and 'keeping streets orderly' (which informs much recent legislation) through control of those thought to threaten the peace and quiet of the community. That this is an artificial division is exacerbated by the tendency for laws passed for one purpose to be appropriated for another. The use of the Protection from Harassment Act 1997 against animal rights protesters is one example, while the application of anti-social behaviour orders to prostitutes is another.

Noting that 'The crime control future is the present we now inhabit', Garland (2001) suggests 12 major shifts in criminal justice policies in the last 30 years:
(1) the decline of the rehabilitative ideal;
(2) the re-emergence of punitive sanctions and expressive justice;
(3) changes in emotional tone (fear of crime has replaced the penal-welfare tone of rationalisation);
(4) the return of the victim;
(5) protecting the public (protection from the state replaced by protection by the state);
(6) politicisation and new populism (crime policy no longer for 'experts');
(7) reinvention of the prison (imprisonment rose 500% in the US between 1973 and 1997, and doubled in the UK);
(8) transformation of criminological thought (control theories replaced deprivation theories);
(9) expansion of crime prevention and community safety infrastructure;

(10) civil society and commercialisation of crime control (public and private lines blurred);

(11) new management styles (managerialism affecting all criminal justice agencies); and

(12) a perpetual sense of crisis.

These themes are reflected in the following extract in which Drakeford and Vanstone place criminal justice policy in the broader context of social (and political) changes in the last 30 years.

Drakeford, M and M Vanstone, 'Social Exclusion and the Politics of Criminal Justice: A Tale of Two Administrations' (2000) 39 Howard Journal 369–381

[P]olicies in the criminal justice area can only be fully understood and judged within the context of social policy as a whole ... The myth that criminal justice services, by themselves, can tackle crime and protect the public is one which has both made the realisation of those essential goals less attainable and caused substantial harm to those services themselves, subverting traditional aims and purposes and substituting ambitions which are unrealisable at both individual and corporate levels ...

Our contention that criminal justice policy has to be understood through a consideration of wider social policy developments means that we need to begin by suggesting three themes which, in our view, dominated the neo-liberal agenda between 1979 and 1997: the thoroughgoing privileging of the private over the public; the organisation and delivery of services through market relations; and the application of coercive rather than co-operative approaches to those individuals unable or unwilling to fulfil their social obligations within the new arrangements ...

Where markets produce winners, they inevitably provide losers ... [C]ertain individuals emerge, in market relations, as actors who are not only unable to maximise their own interests, but whose activities appear to damage the interests of others. During the 18 years of Conservative government, the approach adopted towards these individuals and their families represented one of the sharpest breaks with the ideology which informed the post-1945 welfare state. In the T.H. Marshall analysis, the welfare state had provided its citizens with a set of social rights to complement those of earlier political settlements. These rights could only be denied in exceptional circumstances and could be qualified only in degree, rather than as a whole ... Under the [1979–1997 Conservative] governments, these basic tenets were altered. Across the range of social welfare policy areas, those who failed to prosper within the market framework were subjected to far more draconian forms of discipline, including deliberate exclusion. Individuals excluded from school, patients removed from doctors' lists, homeless people denied re-housing ... Such individuals were to be made as responsible for their own futures as, it was argued, their past behaviour had been responsible for their present predicament. In no policy area such arguments more stridently advanced than in the case of criminal justice ...

In criminal justice itself the Conservative Administration's principal legacy was the dismantling of ... the modernist project, characterised by notions of citizenship through social equality; social justice through State intervention; general acceptance of social order; the bulk of deviance determined by psychological and environmental factors; and the assimilative state in which attempts were made to re-include the deviant. It accelerated the shift from the inclusive to the exclusive society ...

Two features in particular distinguished the criminal justice system bequeathed to the new Labour administration: it was no longer based on the post-war consensus that deviant behaviour had social causes that should be addressed by criminal justice and social policy; and it posited prison as a sentence of first resort thus rejecting the need to exhaust the use of constructive community penalties which were perceived as ineffective in reforming the individual and protecting the public ...

In the mid-term of the Labour government, it is now possible to draw out some of the underlying themes in its approach to this area of policy making. In relation to the three key characteristics of social policy developed under the Conservatives, the first two, at least, have undergone major changes in emphasis. In the third area, however, previous policies have been more re-invigorated than reformed ... [T]he coexistence of a welfare and a disciplinary state, [is] sustained by the fiction that a criminal minority pose a constant threat to the decent majority. New Labour's ... capacity for dividing the social world into those who are worthy of assistance and those who are in need of restraint ... marks one of the major boundaries between this and earlier Labour governments.

Finer Jones (Finer Jones C 'The new social policy in Britain' 1997 31 Social Policy and Administration 154–70) provides a useful analysis of these changes in terms of the stakeholding vocabulary which new Labour politicians have appropriated ... Governments are responsible for creating the conditions in which each citizen is able to receive a fair chance of making something of her or his life. The responsibility for taking that chance, however, lies with the individual. Those who don't will have demonstrated their lack of suitability for further State investment. Three subdivisions of individuals may be found amongst this group of non-deservers, each of which has relevance to the interaction between social and criminal policy, at a practical and ideological level.

The first category ... [the non stakeholders] ... are the economic migrants and suspect asylum seekers of Fortress Europe ... The second are the passive resisters of stakeholding, those, for example who fail to work actively enough to satisfy the new enforcers of the New Deal or the Job Seekers Allowance requirements ... Thirdly, there are the anti-stakeholders, the cheats and the frauds of the benefit system, the neighbours-from-hell of the Crime and Disorder Act 1998 and the persistent burglars and muggers of the criminal justice system. Lying outside New Labour's embrace, these last groups represent the point at which the administration has shown itself willing to employ directly criminal justice sanctions to deal with the social problems which non-stakeholders bring in their wake.

...

We wish to be clear that, within the administration's approach to criminal justice policy, a series of positive initiatives are taking place ... Labour's struggle is to find a way of reducing the prison population, without appearing to do so – or of doing good by stealth. This is in itself complicated by other policy trends within the same administration that are likely to add to prison numbers.

The single most striking example of such a strategy lies in the Crime and Disorder Act 1998 in which the Anti-Social Behaviour Order – available for children as young as ten years – will be available on the basis of a civil standard of proof, but where breach will be a criminal offence, punishable with a term of imprisonment of up to two years ...

A more specific example of overtly exclusionary strands in existing policy, in which there is an interesting paradox, is that relating to men who have been convicted of sexual offences against children ... The combination of the Register of Sex Offenders, negative local council housing policies and evictions forced by popular pressure has led to a situation in which convicted sex offenders have to disappear or 'go underground' in order to be included in society. This is a potent example of official attempts to protect the vulnerable producing exactly the opposite effect because of the accreted message about exclusion. Unsupervised paedophiles determined to avoid the consequences of social exposure present considerably more danger to children ...

It is ironic, in this context, to note that New Labour's general willingness to employ what Hall (1998, p. 13 – 'The Great Moving Nowhere Show' Marxism Today, Nov Dec. 9–14) describes as 'low-flying authoritarianism' is especially pronounced in relation to children and young people ...

[O]ur central conclusion is that the purpose which Conservative policies displayed in relation to exclusion from social and civil society is mirrored in Labour's approach to those who cannot, or will not, act in accordance with the new responsibilities. The use of criminal justice sanctions to deal with essentially social problems has become the hallmark of the administration in this critical part of the policy-making agenda. Rather than pursue criminal justice outcomes through social policy measures, the government is in danger of reaching always for the criminal justice solutions to problems which more appropriately lie in the civic space in which the benefits of an education, an income and a place to live are distributed.

... We view social exclusion as more than exclusion from the labour market; rather it is detachment from the resources needed to survive legitimately in the community and draw upon what might be described as the normal rights of citizenship.

David Feldman, *Civil Liberties and Human Rights in England and Wales* (OUP, 2002) p 1016

More worrying, however, than the slowness of the development towards judicial recognition of rights of public access and expression is a movement in the opposite direction in the legislature. Since the early 1990s, Parliament has enacted legislation which has sought to exclude people – individuals or groups – from public areas. Sometimes this is done as a public-order measure, as in the case of several restrictions on freedom of access under the Criminal Justice and Public Order Act 1994. At other times is said to be to protect children from coming to harm in dangerous places at night or to combat rowdy behaviour in public (as in the case of child curfew orders under the Crime and Disorder Act 1998 and powers to combat public drinking under the Criminal Justice and Police Act 2001), or to protect sections of the community against alleged troublemakers (for example by making anti-social behaviour orders under the Crime and Disorder Act 1998). The overall effect is to exclude people from making use of the relatively few genuinely public places still available, and to discourage or prohibit the exercise of freedom of assembly.

The 'anti-social behaviour' bandwagon appears to be on an unstoppable roll. The White Paper *Respect and Responsibility – Taking a Stand against Anti-Social Behaviour* published in 2003 sets out the Government's vision for dealing with 'low-level' criminality. Amongst other measures, the Anti-Social Behaviour Bill 2003 (the fifteenth dealing with crime and disorder since 1997) includes: an extension of on-the-spot fines to street beggars and to 16- and 17-year-olds; fines and residential parenting classes for parents of disorderly children; and a tier of community courts.

It is clear that the new forms of public order law that we discuss in this chapter rely on the gathering of information not only by the police but by other public institutions as well. Anti-social behaviour orders are a particularly good example of partnership between the police and local authorities for example. Multi-agency cooperation is now enshrined in the Police Reform Act 2002.

Celia Wells, 'I Blame the Parents: Fitting New Genes in Old Criminal Laws' (1998) 61 Modern Law Review 724–739

A powerful theme in recent theorising about criminal law draws on Ulrich Beck's 'risk society' thesis which provides insights into the role and focus of blame in contemporary society. Risk itself is about external danger: disaster, technological breakdown, and human misbehaviour are all examples. Knowledge about risk has been assisted by the twin developments of statistical analysis and the technology to communicate the results of that analysis. Concern with risk is not merely to do with knowledge of probability, it is to do with cultural attitudes to the acceptability of different hazards. ... Much of the risk society literature is couched in complex and sophisticated terms but at bottom there is a simple argument about our transition from localised self-sufficiency through industrial paternalistic societies to the emergence of societies where risk is privatised and a matter for individual judgement. However, individual situations are also institutional, Beck argues, because 'the liberated individual is dependent on a series of secondary agencies and institutions'. Risk society thus raises issues of trust, accountability and personal responsibility. The social institutions associated with law – of which the criminal justice system is emblematic – themselves play a significant role in risk management and the production of risk knowledge. How then do these arguments apply specifically to the risks, dangers or hazards of 'crime'.

...

In their study of the police as knowledge workers, Ericson and Haggerty describe how the police supply risk information to a web of institutions – insurance companies, regulatory agencies, financial institutions, amongst others. Criminologists 'know' that the popular image of policing as portrayed in TV and film, and even as reflected in news reporting, is wildly biased in favour of action, detection and contact with 'criminals'. Arresting suspects is a relatively rare event for most police officers, even detectives spend almost half their time in the office recording investigative work rather than engaging in it. Much of this recording, this production of knowledge, is for internal purposes. If you haven't arrested someone you can at least produce a paper trail explaining what you have been doing. If you have arrested someone, then preparation of papers in relation to custody decisions, in relation to interrogation, or in preparation for prosecution, is necessary. The provision of information to a complex web of other institutions is a major function of police work. Other social institutions, such as education and health, are similarly engaged in the production and communication of risk knowledge. 'Institutionalized communications systems form the foundation of contemporary society and provide the governing basis of social life'. The information is used to establish and monitor, amongst other things, identities: achieved identities such as careers are monitored through record-keeping (in relation to offenders and victims) and through licensing (gun ownership for example), while ascribed identities (age, race, gender etc) are maintained and constructed through the use of categories into which people are fitted. Often these categories of identity are determined externally and the police mould the individual to fit the pre determined boxes. Youth is one obvious identity here. Police interaction with agencies such as schools takes a number of forms but is characterised by systems of risk selection (which areas, which schools, which pupils). Here the interplay between institutions is apparent with knowledge exchanged between schools, social services, individual parents and the police.

Ericson and Haggerty, *Policing the Risk Society* (OUP, 1997) pp 17, 18

It is our contention that the risk logics of external institutions, and the classification schemes and knowledge requirements they entail, fundamentally influence the police. The framework through which police officers think and act is determined not only by formal legal rules, administrative rules, and the informal rules of the occupational culture but also by the risk communication rules, formats, and technologies of external institutions. In other words, it is the structure of institutional communications more than the legal, administrative, or informal rule-structures that circumscribes the discretion of police officers. The legal and administrative rules do have a bearing on risk classifications, but it is these classifications that in turn shape and direct police officer autonomy ...

In risk society the traditional police focus on deviance, control and order is displaced in favour of a focus on risk, surveillance and security. The concern is less with the labelling of deviants as outsiders and more on developing a risk-profile knowledge of individuals to ascertain and manage their place in institutions.

Policing in 'the risk society' has developed into a complex web of knowledge production amongst various public agencies. Ericson and Haggerty suggest that things only become mobilised as police work if they fit the risk knowledge requirements of external institutions such as Inland Revenue, or education or social services. In place of deviance, control and order are risk, surveillance and security (Akdenis, Taylor and Walker 2001).

I.b. Harassment offences

I.b.i. Public Order Act 1986

Sections 4, 4A and 5 of the Public Order Act 1986 contain overlapping arrestable offences. We summarise them first before setting out s 5 in full.

(a) **Section 4: Fear or provocation of violence**
  (i) *Conduct:* Uses towards **another person** threatening, abusive or insulting words or behaviour, or distributes etc **to another person** any writing, etc which is threatening, etc.
  (ii) *Circumstances:* In public or private unless both inside a dwelling.
  (iii) *Mental element:* **With intent to cause that person to believe that immediate unlawful violence** will be used against him or another by any person, or **to provoke the immediate use of unlawful violence ... ,** or **whereby that person is likely to believe** that such violence will be used or it is likely that such violence will be provoked.
  (iv) *Penalty:* 6 months or level 5 fine.

(b) **Section 4A: Causing intentional harassment, alarm or distress**
  (i) *Conduct:* Uses threatening, etc words or behaviour, or distributes etc which is threatening, abusive or insulting, thereby causing that or another person harassment, alarm or distress.
  (ii) *Circumstances:* In public or private unless both inside a dwelling. Defence to show inside dwelling and no reason to believe conduct would be perceived by person outside or that conduct reasonable.
  (iii) *Mental element:* **With intent to cause a person harassment, alarm or distress.**
  (iv) *Penalty:* 6 months or level 5 fine.

(c) **Section 5: Disorderly conduct**
  (i) *Conduct:* As for s 4.
  (ii) *Circumstance:* Within the hearing or sight of a person likely to be caused harassment, alarm or distress thereby.
  (iii) *Mental element:* Intends his words etc to be threatening, abusive or insulting, **or is aware that it may be threatening,** etc or intends or **is aware that it may be** disorderly.
  (iv) *Penalty:* Level 3 fine.

The main feature to note about s 4 is the extraordinarily broad scope of the offence, which might easily be read as covering heated exchanges between irritated drivers or exuberant behaviour of sports fans in circumstances which most people would think of as falling far short of justifying a criminal response. This underlines the enormous discretion that such offences give to the police and prosecuting authorities in making arrests, framing charges and bargaining guilty pleas. The relatively mild nature of the maximum penalty and the arrest power, although out of all proportion to the seriousness of the offence, can hardly be accounted instrumentally significant, given the pre-existing powers of arrest for subjectively perceived breaches of the peace and the possibility of binding-over orders. However, s 4 has proved useful as a 'catch-all' lesser offence, conviction for which can be substituted where the prosecution is unable to discharge its burden of proof for one of the more serious offences (*Mahroof*, 1989).

Intentional harassment under s 4A, carrying the same maximum penalty as s 4, was inserted by the Criminal Justice and Public Order Act 1994. Its introduction was prompted by a reported increase in incidents of racial violence and harassment but in its final form it covers a much wider field. While s 4 requires proof of an intention to cause fear or to provoke violence, intention to cause harassment, alarm or distress is sufficient under s 4A. In addition, s 4A demands that harassment, alarm or distress was actually caused.

But it is s 5 of the POA 1986 that touches the depths (or breadths) of this series of offences dealing with behaviour that might cause alarm or distress:

Public Order Act 1986, s 5
(1) A person is guilty of an offence if he–
  (a) uses threatening, abusive or insulting words or behaviour, or disorderly behaviour, or
  (b) displays any writing, sign or other visible representation which is threatening, abusive or insulting,
  within the hearing or sight of a person likely to be caused harassment, alarm or distress thereby.
(2) An offence under this section may be committed in a public or a private place, except that no offence is committed where the words or behaviour are used, or the writing, sign or other visible representation is displayed, by a person inside a dwelling and the other person is also inside that or another dwelling.
(3) It is a defence for the accused to prove–
  (a) that he had no reason to believe that there was any person within hearing or sight who was likely to be caused harassment, alarm or distress, or
  (b) that he was inside a dwelling and had no reason to believe that the words or behaviour used, or the writing, sign or other visible representation displayed, would be heard or seen by a person outside that or any other dwelling, or
  (c) that his conduct was reasonable.
(4) A constable may arrest a person without warrant if–
  (a) he engages in offensive conduct which a constable warns him to stop, and
  (b) he engages in further offensive conduct immediately or shortly after the warning.
(5) In subsection (4) 'offensive conduct' means conduct the constable reasonably suspects to constitute an offence under this section, and the conduct mentioned in paragraph (a) and the further conduct need not be of the same nature.
(6) A person guilty of an offence under this section is liable on summary conviction to a fine not exceeding level 3 on the standard scale.

Section 5 does not require proof of intent (recklessness is sufficient under s 6(4)) or consequence. Its most notable features are the breadth of conduct potentially covered and the use of language open to subjective interpretation. This point is emphasised by the explicit introduction of a defence that the conduct was reasonable – probably a recognition of the fact that the bare offence definition could easily cover forms of behaviour (such as sexual harassment) which many people do not think should constitute a crime. Again, the exclusion of actions entirely within, or reasonably thought to be confined to, dwellings, confirms the existence of a limited private sphere into which the law purports not to intrude. It extends to public bars, as a Newcastle landlady discovered. She was fined £400 after displaying in her bar a black and white scarf (Newcastle United's colours) with the words 'Sunderland are Shite'. The scarf was forfeited as a threatening, abusive or insulting sign likely to cause harassment, alarm or distress (*The Guardian*, 3 May 2002).

The power of arrest is qualified by the need for a warning. This seems of dubious protection given the practical impossibility of giving effective warnings in the context of public disorder (the very situations to which this section was addressed), the fact that the 'further offensive conduct' which must follow the warning need not be the same as the original conduct, and the supplementary power to arrest for anticipated breach of the peace (*DPP v Orum*, 1988). So a vigorous response to a constable's warning might in itself render the offence arrestable if the constable decided it was threatening, abusive or insulting and felt likely to be caused harassment, alarm or distress thereby. It seems too much to hope that all police officers enjoy such psychological equilibrium that their reactions to abuse would be so temperate as to deny themselves a power of arrest. The trivial nature of the offence, which need not even be directed against another person (*R v Ball*, 1989) underlines the explosion of criminal law into almost any area where the police perceive any kind of threat to authority or 'law and order'. This is reflected in a maximum penalty which is low even as compared with the already existing power to bind over. The flexibility and manipulability of public order law perhaps reaches its zenith in this section which, in effect, asks the police and the courts to respond ad hoc to any behaviour which they perceive as disorderly, distasteful or inconvenient.

D Brown and T Ellis, *Policing Low Level Disorder: Police Use of section 5 of the Public Order Act 1986* (Home Office Research Study No 135, 1994) p 49

It was found that the level of use varied considerably and that, while in some areas it was clear that section 5 was being employed in preference to other provisions that covered similar misconduct, elsewhere the new offence was not extensively used. The most frequent use of section 5 was to deal with a broad spectrum of abusive or threatening behaviour in public places, although there was also some use to deal with violent or potentially violent situations. Section 5 was also sometimes called in to play to deal with domestic disputes, indecency and football-related disorder … [M]any incidents amounted to alcohol related disorder in and around entertainment centres.

… An important finding was that, in a substantial minority of incidents, police officers were treated as the victims of offensive conduct – a situation that is not precluded by the legislation although it may not have been anticipated. It is for consideration whether the conduct used to justify arrest was always sufficient to alarm or distress police officers. Furthermore, in a third of cases in which members of the public were apparently viewed as victims, there were doubts about whether any real alarm was caused. Police actions in arresting for section 5 offences were not always backed up by action taken later by the Crown Prosecution Service or the courts …

The extent to which section 5 is used in some areas and the circumstances in which arrests are made raise important questions about whether this provision … is being used appropriately …

It is arguable whether in some section 5 cases any useful purpose is served by arresting … When arrest does eventually occur, following the typical spiral of warning/abuse/arrest, it is uncertain whether the reasoning the police use to justify their action can always be sustained. First, in the circumstances in which many incidents occur there are grounds for questioning whether members of the public in the vicinity are genuinely likely to be alarmed or distressed. City centre disorder when licensed premises close at the weekend is a commonplace … Secondly, while much of the bad language and abuse directed at the police themselves may be grossly insulting, it is doubtful whether it is generally such as would be likely to cause alarm or distress except to unduly sensitive officers … Thirdly, if the underlying reason for arresting is to instil respect for the police, it is very doubtful whether this object is achieved.

Section 5 is not susceptible however to an on the spot fine (fixed penalty notice, see **Chapter 2.II.e.**). As Wasik (2001: 933) explains:

The [Criminal Justice and Police] Bill had also listed criminal damage, and threatening, abusive or insulting words or behaviour under section 5 of the Public Order Act 1986. These offences were removed after opposition in the Commons (which was resisted) and the Lords (accepted at the last minute to allow the Bill to become law), on the grounds that these were inherently more serious offences …

This view of the seriousness of s 5 contrasts with the comment of Metropolitan police deputy assistant commissioner, Steve House, when on the spot fines were first announced:

These are the lowest level of public order offences. As an example, it could be used when someone is messing around in a public place, standing in the doorway of [a restaurant] at 11pm giving lip to people going in and out, being warned and not going away … The whole point of this is to keep people out of the criminal justice system and to save police time. [*The Guardian*, 22 March 2002.]

Section 5 is commonly used to restrain political protest. For example, *in Chambers and Edwards v DPP* (1995), the appellant M11 motorway protesters were warned by the police that holding their hands in front of a measuring instrument which was operated by the surveyor was disorderly and caused harassment. Convictions under s 5 of the 1986 Act were upheld on the grounds that the surveyor had been inconvenienced by the behaviour. The Divisional Court held that whether any behaviour was to be characterised as disorderly was a question of fact for the trial court to determine. The words 'disorderly behaviour' should be given their ordinary meaning and in causing 'harassment', no element of apprehension about one's safety was required, nor was any element of violence, present or threatened required.

The deployment of s 5 against those involved in political protest has been challenged under the Human Rights Act 1998.

Percy v DPP ([2001] EWHC Admin 1125, Queen's Bench Division, Divisional Court, 21 December 2001)

[*This was an appeal against conviction for a s 5 offence arising from the appellant's behaviour at an American air base.*]

Mrs Justice Hallett.

The appellant is a co-ordinator of an organisation called the "Campaign for Accountability of American Bases" and has experience over many years of protesting against the use of weapons of mass destruction and against American military policy, including the Star Wars National Missile Defence System. She believed that the base … would have a part to play in such a system. She defaced the American flag by putting a stripe across the stars and by writing the words "Stop Star Wars" across the stripes. She stepped in front of a vehicle and she placed the flag down in front of it and stood upon it. Those affected by her behaviour were mostly American service personnel or their families, five of whom gave evidence of their distress to varying degrees. They regarded her acts as a desecration of their national flag to which they attach considerable importance. The District Judge rejected the appellant's evidence that she was unaware of the effect of her conduct upon those present … The court concluded from her failure to offer any explanation save that "it was a spontaneous protest" to place the flag on the floor and stand upon it, that her actions were calculated to offend. The court found that the appellant's behaviour with the flag was insulting to American citizens at whom it was directed.

The appellant did, however, satisfy the court that her behaviour was motivated by strongly held beliefs that the "Star Wars" project was misguided, posed a danger to international stability and was not in the best interests of the United Kingdom.

She failed to persuade the court that her conduct on the balance of probabilities was reasonable ... [T]he District Judge ... He acknowledged that Article 10 applied and that it protected an individual's right to express views which are unpopular and offensive to others. He highlighted, however, that under Article 10(2) the right is not unqualified. The exercise of the right to freedom of expression carries attendant duties and responsibilities and so may be restricted and made subject to penalties, provided that they are prescribed by law and are necessary in a democratic society (for example, for the prevention of disorder, or for the protection of the rights of others). The court considered in this case the risk of disorder and criminal offences by others to be slight. His only concern, therefore, was as to the protection of the rights of others. So far so good. No one takes exception to his approach to this point.

The District Judge went on to consider, however:

"The need to protect the rights of American service personnel and their families occupying the base to be free from gratuitously insulting behaviour in the ordinary course of their professional and private lives and their right to have their national flag, of significant symbolic importance to them, protected from disrespectful treatment."

...

He accordingly held that there would be no violation of the appellant's right under Article 10 in convicting her of an offence under section 5.

The questions posed for this court in the case stated are:

(i) Was the appellant's conviction under section 5 of the Public Order Act 1986 compatible with Article 10 of the European Convention on Human Rights and Fundamental Freedoms?

(ii) If the answer to question (i) is "No", should the appellant's conviction under section 5 of the Public Order Act be quashed?

The provisions under Article 10 and section 5 so far as relevant to these proceedings are as follows:

"*Article 10*

(1) Everyone has the right to freedom of expression. This right shall include freedom to hold opinions and to receive and impart information and ideas without interference by public authority and regardless of frontiers ...

(2) The exercise of these freedoms, since it carries with it duties and responsibilities, may be subject to such formalities, conditions,

restrictions or penalties as are prescribed by law and are necessary
in a democratic society ... for the prevention of disorder or crime
... for the protection of the reputation or rights of others ..."

...

The right to freedom of expression was well established in the United
Kingdom before the incorporation of the Convention. Peaceful protest
was not outlawed by section 5 of the Public Order Act. Behaviour which is
an affront to other people, or is disrespectful or contemptuous of them, is
not prohibited: see *Brutus v Cozens* (1973) AC 854. A peaceful protest will
only come within the terms of section 5 and constitute an offence where
the conduct goes beyond legitimate protest and moves into the realms of
threatening, abusive or insulting behaviour, which is calculated to insult
either intentionally or recklessly, and which is unreasonable.

It is significant in my view that sections 5(3)(c) and section 6(4) of the
Public Order Act specifically provide for there to be proof of mens rea and
for the defence of reasonableness. Even where a court finds that conduct
has been calculated to insult and has, in fact, caused alarm or distress, the
accused may still establish on the balance of probabilities that his or her
conduct was reasonable.

The question of reasonableness must be a question of fact for the
tribunal concerned taking into account all the circumstances.

Where the right to freedom of expression under Article 10 is engaged, as
in my view is undoubtedly the case here, it is clear from the European
authorities put before us that the justification for any interference with that
right must be convincingly established. Article 10(1) protects in substance
and in form a right to freedom of expression which others may find insulting. Restrictions under Article 10(2) must be narrowly construed. In this
case, therefore, the court had to presume that the appellant's conduct in
relation to the American flag was protected by Article 10 unless and until it
was established that a restriction on her freedom of expression was strictly
necessary.

I have no difficulty in principle with the concept that there will be circumstances in which citizens of this country and visiting foreign nationals
should be protected from intentionally and gratuitously insulting
behaviour, causing them alarm or distress. There may well be a pressing
social need to protect people from such behaviour. It is, therefore, in my
view, a legitimate aim, provided of course that any restrictions on the
rights of peaceful protesters are proportionate to the mischief at which
they are aimed. Some people will be more robust than others. What one
persons finds insulting and distressing may be water off a duck's back to
another. A civilised society must strike an appropriate balance between the
competing rights of those who may be insulted by a particular course of
conduct and those who wish to register their protest on an important
matter of public interest.

The problem comes in striking that balance, giving due weight to the presumption in the accused's favour of the right to freedom of expression.

I turn to the way in which the District Judge approached the task confronted him in this case. I remind myself that Ms Percy attended RAF Feltwell intending to protest against the "Star Wars" project, a matter of legitimate public debate. The message she wished to convey, namely "Stop Star Wars" was a perfectly lawful, political message. It only became insulting because of the manner in which she chose to convey the message. That manner was only insulting because she chose to use a national flag of symbolic importance to some of her target audience.

In carrying out the balancing exercise, the District Judge first found that there is a pressing social need in a multi-cultural society to prevent the denigration of objects of veneration and symbolic importance for one cultural group.

For my part, I am prepared to accept that he was entitled to find that such protection was a legitimate aim. The next stage of his task was to assess whether or not interference with the accused's right to free expression by criminal prosecution for using her own property to convey a lawful message in an insulting way was a proportionate response to that aim. The only aspect of the case referred to by the District Judge in this respect was the fact that the appellant's "conduct was not the unavoidable consequence of a peaceful protest against the 'Star Wars' project, which was her stated intention, but arose from the particular manner in which she chose to make her protest."

The fact that the appellant could have demonstrated her message in a way which did not involve the use of a national flag of symbolic significance to her target audience was undoubtedly a factor to be taken into account when determining the overall reasonableness and proportionality of her behaviour and the state's response to it. But, in my view, it was only one factor.

Relevant factors in a case such as this, depending on the court's findings, might include the fact that the accused's behaviour went beyond legitimate protest; that the behaviour had not formed part of an open expression of opinion on a matter of public interest, but had become disproportionate and unreasonable; that an accused knew full well the likely effect of their conduct upon witnesses; that the accused deliberately chose to desecrate the national flag of those witnesses, a symbol of very considerable importance to many, particularly those who are in the armed forces; the fact that an accused targeted such people, for whom it became a very personal matter; the fact that an accused was well aware of the likely effect of their conduct; the fact that an accused's use of a flag had nothing, in effect, to do with conveying a message or the expression of opinion; that it amounted to a gratuitous and calculated insult, which a number people at whom it was directed found deeply distressing.

In my judgment, at the crucial stage of a balancing exercise under Article 10 the learned District Judge appears to have placed either sole or too much reliance on just the one factor, namely that the appellant's insulting behaviour could have been avoided. This seems to me to give insufficient weight to the presumption in the appellant's favour, to which I have already referred. ... Merely stating that interference is proportionate is not sufficient. It is not clear to me from the District Judge's reasons, given in relation to his findings under Article 10, that he has in fact applied the appropriate test. . ... I am driven to the conclusion, therefore, that this conviction is incompatible with the appellant's rights under the European Convention on Human Rights and I would answer the first question posed in the case stated: "No".

... the appropriate course, therefore, is simply to quash the convictions.

Percy gives protesters a limited protection and does not address at a more fundamental level the restriction that s 5 places on the freedom to protest. As the research study on aggravated trespass discussed in **Chapter 2.II.c.** makes clear, those against whom the protests are made – those who are protected by these laws – are often in a position to employ their own security officers, some of whom can be likened to bouncers (Bucke and James 1998). The 'battle' is then enjoined between the security officers and the protesters with the police holding some kind of peace line. Behaviour or language that could well be offensive to a passer-by is not particularly novel or alarming to either the staff or the police. Section 5 gives a default power that can be invoked at any stage. There is no guarantee that a person arrested and charged will be able to obtain legal advice about a potential breach of human rights and, in any case, the offence becomes the excuse to exercise the power of arrest rather than the other way round.

It might be asked why the trio of offences in ss 4, 4A and 5 is needed to deal with the relatively minor harm of causing alarm or distress, especially when other offences deal with related behaviour, such as inciting racial hatred under s 18, or the offence of common assault or (since 1998) racially aggravated assault.

I.b.ii.   Protection From Harassment Act 1997

A further offence of harassment was introduced to deal with stalking by the Protection from Harassment Act 1997. Stalking provides yet another example of the moral panic thesis discussed in **Chapter 2**. Stalking, like shoplifting, hooliganism and vandalism, is a description rather than a legal category. Before the passage of the 1997 Act, there was no offence directed at stalking, nor does the Act use the term 'stalking' as such. The Act, based on the proposals in the Home Office consultation paper 'Stalking – the Solutions', provides two criminal offences of harassment and a civil tort. This underlines the increasingly blurred line between civil and criminal forms of redress. The higher-level offence under s 4, which carries a maximum penalty of five years in prison, is committed where the harasser's behaviour is so threatening that the victims fear violence against them. The lower-level offence of harassment under s 1, with a six-month maximum penalty, does not require proof of fear of violence. The conduct has to occur at least twice (ss 4(1) and 7(3)). For neither offence is it necessary to prove an intention to cause fear of violence or a sense of harassment; proof that the conduct took place in circumstances where a reasonable person would realise that its effect would be a fear of violence or sense of harassment is sufficient. Under s 7(3)(a):

> a person's conduct on any occasion shall be taken, if aided, abetted, counselled or procured by another, (a) to be conduct on that occasion of the other (as well as conduct of the person whose conduct it is); and (b) to be conduct in relation to which the other's knowledge and purpose, and what he ought to have known, are the same as they were in relation to what was contemplated or reasonably foreseeable at the time of the aiding, abetting, counselling or procuring [as inserted by Criminal Justice and Police Act 2001].

In addition to the penalties on conviction, a restraint order can be obtained, breach of which is itself an offence punishable with five years' imprisonment (s 3(9)). Both offences are arrestable without warrant and a power to search the suspect's property is also included.

The broad scope of the offence definitions, together with the provision for access to the civil courts, makes harassment available well beyond the social problem of stalking. For an early example, an injunction under the Act was served on Newcastle Animal Rights coalition following a peaceful demonstration at a mink farm, banning the group from writing letters, telephoning or demonstrating near the farm (SchNews, www.cbuzz.co.uk, 15 August 1997).

D Thomas 'Right of peaceful Protest Preserved' (1998) Legal Action (April) 10

The Act began life as a private member's bill aimed specifically at the problem of stalking. The ... government then adopted it ... and extending [its] ambit to cover other anti-social behaviour, such as racial harassment and nuisance by neighbours ...

'Harassment' is only partially defined to '*include* alarming the person or causing the person distress.' ... Perhaps the most significant feature about harassment is that it will usually involve conduct which would otherwise be held to be perfectly lawful ...

Over recent months, a number of companies using animals for commercial purposes and proponents of fox-hunting have obtained injunctions against protesters under the Act. Some of the injunctions have been in very broad terms and have prohibited conduct such as communicating with the plaintiffs and using roads in the vicinity of their premises ... In addition, they have extended to law-abiding organisations and to 'any person holding himself out to be an animal rights activist.'

One of the injunctions was obtained by Huntingdon Life Sciences Ltd, the largest contract animal-testing laboratory in the UK, against the British Union for the Abolition of Vivisection ...

[*The BUAV successfully applied to have the injunction discharged on the argument that it had nothing to do with any illegal activities: Huntingdon Life Sciences and Another v Curtin (1997).*]

Huntingdon Life Sciences obtained, in 2003, a wide-ranging interim injunction preventing protesters from coming within 50 yards of employees' homes and allowing only one demonstration, by a maximum of 25 people, every 30 days outside the company's sites. Protesters are banned from 'assaulting, molesting, harassing, pestering, threatening or otherwise interfering with' those named in the high court injunction, 'directly or indirectly'. The list of those protected includes the company itself, employees and 'their families, servants or agents' and any person 'setting out to visit them' (*The Guardian*, 16 April 2003).

Inclusion of the company as a potential victim raises an interesting point of interpretation. In *Dziurzynski* (2002), the defendant was charged with pursuing a course of conduct which amounted to the harassment of the employees of B&K Universal Group Ltd. In an obiter dictum, Rose LJ said:

I accept of course that the word "person", unless the contrary intention is shown, is ... to be understood, by virtue of the Interpretation Act 1987, as including a body of persons corporate or incorporate. But that said, it seems to me that the legislative history to which, in my view, reference can properly be made when construing what is meant by the word "person" in section 1 of the Act, points against person here meaning a corporation.

... As it seems to me, as a matter of statutory construction, this Act was not intended by Parliament to embrace, within the ambit of a criminal offence, conduct amounting to harassment directed to a limited company rather than to an individual human being.

The combined effect of the range of harassment offences in the 1986 and 1997 Acts is to introduce a vast discretionary range to prosecutors; to erode further the presumption of innocence by frequent deployment of reverse-onus of proof defences; and to invite fact-finders (magistrates and juries) to interpret terms such as 'threatening', 'abusive', 'insulting', 'harassment', 'alarm' and 'distress' in accordance with their 'ordinary' meaning (see *Chambers and Edwards v DPP* (1995) above, following *Brutus v Cozens* (1973)). The offences are rarely limited to 'public' spaces and, where the offences call for a third party to be harassed, alarmed or distressed (or likely to be), this can be a hypothetical bystander represented by the arresting officer (*DPP v Orum*, 1989).

l.c.   Anti-social behaviour orders

As we have noted, 'anti-social behaviour' is the catchword of the moment in the Home Office's crime strategy. Anti-social behaviour orders (ASBOs) were introduced by the Crime and Disorder Act 1998 to deal with severe persistent, disorderly conduct. Of 678 applications made in the first two years, 24 were refused. Such orders have been used against prostitutes (Jones and Sagar 2001) and the effect has been to widen the explicit reach of the criminal law by creating 'a personalised criminal law for the defendant for a minimum period of two years, breach of which is a criminal offence carrying imprisonment for up to five years' (Cooper 2003). The agency applying for an ASBO does not have to prove an intention on the part of the defendant to cause harassment, alarm or distress. 'In a desperate attempt to make the ill fated ASBO work' (Ormerod and Roberts 2003: 162) the Police Reform Act 2002 extended the original provisions in a number of directions. The local basis of the ASBO was removed so that an order can effectively travel with the person to whom it applies. Magistrates and country courts can now make interim orders (Crime and Disorder Act 1998, s 1C). ASBOs are now available as a sentencing option on conviction for a criminal offence involving anti-social behaviour, or a county court can make one where dealing with an eviction notice (Crime and Disorder Act 1998, s 1C). Authorised parties can apply for such an order, but significantly the court itself may also take the initiative in making an ASBO. The Police Reform Act 2002 also introduces powers for uniformed officers to stop and seize vehicles used in a manner causing alarm, distress or annoyance (s 59).

Crime and Disorder Act 1998

1(1) An application for an order under this section may be made by a relevant authority if it appears to the authority that the following conditions are fulfilled with respect to any person aged 10 or over, namely–

(a) that the person has acted, since the commencement date, in an anti-social manner, that is to say, in a manner that caused or was likely to cause harassment, alarm or distress to one or more persons not of the same household as himself; and

(b) that such an order is necessary to protect relevant persons from further anti-social acts by him.

[(1A) 'Relevant authority' includes local authorities, chief officer of any police force, the chief constable of the British Transport Police Force, and 'registered social landlords'.]

...

(3) Such an application shall be made by complaint to the magistrates' court whose commission area includes the local government area or police area concerned.

(4) If, on such an application, it is proved that the conditions mentioned in subsection (1) above are fulfilled, the magistrates' court may make an order under this section (an "anti-social behaviour order") which prohibits the defendant from doing anything described in the order.

(5) For the purpose of determining whether the condition mentioned in subsection (1)(a) above is fulfilled, the court shall disregard any act of the defendant which he shows was reasonable in the circumstances.

(6) The prohibitions that may be imposed by an anti-social behaviour order are those necessary for the purpose of protecting persons (whether relevant persons or persons elsewhere in England and Wales) from further anti-social acts by the defendant.

(7) An anti-social behaviour order shall have effect for a period (not less than two years) specified in the order or until further order.

(8) Subject to subsection (9) below, the applicant or the defendant may apply by complaint to the court which made an anti-social behaviour order for it to be varied or discharged by a further order.

(9) Except with the consent of both parties, no anti-social behaviour order shall be discharged before the end of the period of two years beginning with the date of service of the order.

(10) If without reasonable excuse a person does anything which he is prohibited from doing by an anti-social behaviour order, he is guilty of an offence and liable–

    (a) on summary conviction, to imprisonment for a term not exceeding six months or to a fine not exceeding the statutory maximum, or to both; or

    (b) on conviction on indictment, to imprisonment for a term not exceeding five years or to a fine, or to both.

(11) Where a person is convicted of an offence under subsection (10) above, it shall not be open to the court by or before which he is so convicted to make [a conditional discharge] in respect of the offence.

The House of Lords has held that an ASBO made under s 1 of the Crime and Disorder Act 1998 was made in civil proceedings rather than in criminal proceedings, and that its nature was not penal as its purpose was not punitive:

***Clingham (formerly C) (a minor) v Royal Borough of Kensington and Chelsea; R (McCann) v Crown Court at Manchester* [2002] UKHL 39**

Lord Steyn.

… There are two appeals before the House. They are unrelated but raise overlapping issues. Both cases involve the power of the magistrates court under section 1 of the Act, upon being satisfied of statutory requirements, to make an anti-social behaviour order prohibiting a defendant from doing prescribed things. Breach of such an order may give rise to criminal liability. That stage has, however, not been reached in either case.

...

It is common ground that proceedings taken for breach of an anti-social behaviour order are criminal in character under domestic law and fall within the autonomous concept "a criminal charge" under article 6 of the European Convention for the Protection of Human Rights and Fundamental Freedoms, as scheduled to the Human Rights Act 1998. The principal general and common questions are:

(a) whether as a matter of domestic classification proceedings leading to the making of an anti-social behaviour order are criminal in nature; and

(b) whether under article 6 of the European Convention such proceedings involve "a criminal charge".

... Article 6 of the European Convention provides as follows:

1   In the determination of his civil rights and obligations or of any criminal charge against him, everyone is entitled to a fair and public hearing within a reasonable time by an independent and impartial tribunal established by law. Judgment shall be pronounced publicly but the press and public may be excluded from all or part of the trial in the interest of morals, public order or national security in a democratic society, where the interests of juveniles or the protection of the private life of the parties so require, or to the extent strictly necessary in the opinion of the court in special circumstances where publicity would prejudice the interests of justice.

2   Everyone charged with a criminal offence shall be presumed innocent until proved guilty according to law.

3   Everyone charged with a criminal offence has the following minimum rights:

(a) to be informed promptly, in a language which he understands and in detail, of the nature and cause of the accusation against him;

(b) to have adequate time and facilities for the preparation of his defence;

(c) to defend himself in person or through legal assistance of his own choosing or, if he has not sufficient means to pay for legal assistance, to be given it free when the interests of justice so require;

(d) to examine or have examined witnesses against him and to obtain the attendance and examination of witnesses on his behalf under the same conditions as witnesses against him;

(e) to have the free assistance of an interpreter if he cannot understand or speak the language used in court.

....

In late February 2000, the Royal Borough of Kensington and Chelsea
received a report by a housing trust about the behaviour of the defendant,
then aged 16, who lived on an estate within the Borough. After detailed
investigations the Borough resolved to apply to the magistrates' court for
an anti-social behaviour order. The complaint was supported by witness
statements containing some first hand evidence of the defendant's
behaviour. The application was, however, primarily based on hearsay
evidence contained in records of complaints received by the trust and in
crime reports compiled by the police.

...

The allegations revealed a high level of serious and persistent anti-social
behaviour. The material from the records of the trust and the police fell
into three categories:
(i)   anonymous complaints where the source was never known;
(ii) complaints where the source was known but was not disclosed;
(iii) computerised reports made by police officers in the course of their
      duties, where the source of the complaint was either unknown or not
      disclosed.
... Between May and September 1999 the Chief Constable of
Manchester collected evidence with a view to seeking anti-social behaviour
orders against the three McCann brothers who were then respectively aged
13, 15 and 16. They had been accused by various members of the public of
criminal activity and other anti-social behaviour including burglary, theft,
threatening and abusive behaviour, and criminal damage ... The applications sought various prohibitions against them including orders excluding
them from Beswick. The seriousness and persistence of their alleged
anti-social behaviour is clearly described by Lord Hope of Craighead. The
evidence against them consisted of oral evidence of eye witnesses, as well as
hearsay evidence consisting of a number of witness statements, and police
evidence of what had been reported to them by complainants.

...

Before the issues can be directly addressed it is necessary to sketch the
social problem which led to the enactment of section 1(1) and the technique which underlies the first part of section 1. It is well known that in
some urban areas, notably urban housing estates and deprived inner city
areas, young persons, and groups of young persons, cause fear, distress and
misery to law-abiding and innocent people by outrageous anti-social
behaviour. It takes many forms. It includes behaviour which is criminal
such as assaults and threats, particularly against old people and children,
criminal damage to individual property and amenities of the community,
burglary, theft, and so forth. Sometimes the conduct falls short of

cognisable criminal offences. The culprits are mostly, but not exclusively, male. Usually they are relatively young, ranging particularly from about 10 to 18 years of age. Often people in the neighbourhood are in fear of such young culprits. In many cases, and probably in most, people will only report matters to the police anonymously or on the strict understanding that they will not directly or indirectly be identified. In recent years this phenomenon became a serious social problem. There appeared to be a gap in the law. The criminal law offered insufficient protection to communities. Public confidence in the rule of law was undermined by a not unreasonable view in some communities that the law failed them. This was the social problem which section 1 was designed to address.

The aim of the criminal law is not punishment for its own sake but to permit everyone to go about their daily lives without fear of harm to person or property. Unfortunately, by intimidating people the culprits, usually small in number, sometimes effectively silenced communities. Fear of the consequences of complaining to the police dominated the thoughts of people: reporting incidents to the police entailed a serious risk of reprisals. The criminal law by itself offered inadequate protection to them.

... There is no doubt that Parliament intended to adopt the model of a civil remedy of an injunction, backed up by criminal penalties, when it enacted section 1 of the Crime and Disorder Act 1998. The view was taken that the proceedings for an anti-social behaviour order would be civil and would not attract the rigour of the inflexible and sometimes absurdly technical hearsay rule which applies in criminal cases. If this supposition was wrong, in the sense that Parliament did not objectively achieve its aim, it would inevitably follow that the procedure for obtaining anti-social behaviour orders is completely or virtually unworkable and useless. If that is what the law decrees, so be it. My starting point is, however, an initial scepticism of an outcome which would deprive communities of *their* fundamental rights ...

[*Lord Steyn concluded that proceedings to obtain an anti-social behaviour order are civil proceedings under domestic law.*]

... [T]he making of an anti-social behaviour order is not a conviction or condemnation that the person is guilty of an offence. It results in no penalty whatever. It cannot be entered on a defendant's record as a conviction. It is also not a recordable offence for the purpose of taking fingerprints ...

...

In my view an application for an anti-social behaviour order does not involve the determination of a criminal charge.

...

Having concluded that the relevant proceedings are civil, in principle it follows that the standard of proof ordinarily applicable in civil proceedings, namely the balance of probabilities, should apply. However, I agree that, given the seriousness of matters involved … Lord Bingham of Cornhill has observed that the heightened civil standard and the criminal standard are virtually indistinguishable. I do not disagree with any of these views. But in my view pragmatism dictates that the task of magistrates should be made more straightforward by ruling that they must in all cases under section 1 apply the criminal standard. If the House takes this view it will be sufficient for the magistrates, when applying section 1(1)(a) *to be sure* that the defendant has acted in an anti-social manner, that is to say, in a manner that caused or was likely to cause harassment, alarm or distress to one or more persons not of the same household as himself. The inquiry under section 1(1)(b), namely that such an order is necessary to protect persons from further anti-social acts by him, does not involve a standard of proof: it is an exercise of judgment or evaluation. This approach should facilitate correct decision-making and should ensure consistency and predictability in this corner of the law. In coming to this conclusion I bear in mind that the use of hearsay evidence will often be of crucial importance. For my part, hearsay evidence depending on its logical probativeness is quite capable of satisfying the requirements of section 1(1).

I.d.   The (ir)responsible child

The Crime and Disorder Act 1998 largely focused on youth offenders (Piper 1999). It abolished the rebuttable presumption that a child over 10 is *doli inca-pax* (s 34), and introduced child safety orders and child curfews (s 14). Because of the low take-up, the upper age-limit for curfew orders was increased from 10 to 16 in 2001. The police as well as local authorities can apply. The law, according to the Home Office, is designed to 'defend communities from anti-social behaviour and to protect children'. The extended curfew orders can cover the hours between 9pm and 6am, last up to 90 days, after which they can be renewed, and there is no criminal penalty for breaking them. The Act also introduced a number of provisions in relation to the structure and delivery of youth justice including the establishment of the national Youth Justice Board.

As Piper argues, an Act addressing 'Crime and Disorder' which concentrates so much on children and young persons 'is clearly endorsing those political and social ideas which emphasise the "danger" of young people's behaviour – the perceived threat from children "out of control" and the potential threat to society if children are not guided into responsible and law-abiding adulthood'.

Christine Piper, 'The Crime and Disorder Act 1998: Child Community Safety' (1999) 62 MLR 397, 398

Such fears are, of course, not new: they have justified state intervention in factories and families since the early 19th century with a focus on one or both of those two categories of children labelled by the Victorians as the 'depraved' and the 'deprived.' They have, however, currently been amplified by a particular 'politicisation' of law and order whereby ... 'popular resentment' about crime has been exploited by both right and centre left political parties and governments in successfully 'garnering political support' ... The fears engendered have increasingly focused on the young in the 1990s, despite unclear statistics about juvenile offending trends and despite the fact that the death of James Bulger in 1993 – which intensified concerns and led to calls for tougher penalties for young offenders – was unrepresentative of youth crime ...

What has emerged ... is a particular image of the young offender which concentrates on the personal responsibility of the child or young person for his or her offending ...

The 'no-excuse' culture and the constitutions of children and young people as sufficiently responsible and mature to be held to account has also allowed restorative justice to re-emerge as a legitimate option in relation to offending by minors ...

These current dominant images of the minor who offends or engages in 'deviant' behaviour, though by no means novel, are in contrast to other images which have underpinned legislative provisions in the past ... [T]here has at times been an image of the child whose offending is viewed as an indicator of need – whether that need is in relation to social and economic conditions or personal behaviour difficulties ... The dominant image of the young offender is also in contrast to images of children underpinning recent legislation relating to the family. For example the Family Law Act 1996 relies on an image of a vulnerable child harmed by parental conflict and violence and who needs protection from divorcing or abusive parents by state encouragement of mediation and remedies to remove abuses from the family home.

... The proclaimed commitment of the ... Government to a two-pronged strategy in relation to young offenders is well known: 'Both research and common sense indicate that there are links between social conditions and crime ... As well as tackling these underlying causes of offending, immediate action can be taken at a local level to reduce crime.' It would be a pity if the immediate action in the provisions of the Crime and Disorder Act 1998 set the tone for professional and magisterial responses to children who offend. Terms such as risk, harm and safety are now ubiquitous concepts deployed in different policy areas but with different meanings and outcomes in each. There is a danger that the Act will contribute to the dominance of particular meanings whereby children's rights and welfare are subsumed in community safety.

There was a 16% increase in the number of 18-year-olds in prison from 2002 to 2003. As of 17 January 2003, there were 2615 under-18-year-olds in prisons in England and Wales (Prison Reform Trust, 5 February 2003). Magistrates can imprison children charged with medium-level offences of vandalism, car-crime and non-domestic burglary (Criminal Justice and Police Act 2001, s 130).

FURTHER READING

Budd, Tracey and Mattinson, Joanna (2000) *The Extent and Nature of Stalking: Findings from the 1998 British Crime Survey* (Home Office Research Study 210).

Campbell, Siobhan (2002) *A Review of Anti-social Behaviour Orders* (Home Office Research Study 236).

Finch, Emily (2002) 'Stalking the Perfect Stalking Law: An Evaluation of the Efficacy of the Protection from Harassment Act 1997' Crim LR 703.

Harris, Jessica (2000) *An Evaluation of the Use and Effectiveness of the Protection From Harassment Act 1997* (Home Office Research Study 203).

Hunter, Caroline and Nixon, Judy (2001) 'Taking the Blame and Losing the Home: Women and Anti-Social Behaviour' 23 JSWFL 395.

Loader, Ian and Sparks, Richard (2002) 'Contemporary Landscapes of Crime, Order and Control' in Maguire et al (eds) *The Oxford Handbook of Criminology* (Oxford University Press) p 83.

Mullen, Paul E and Pathe, Michele (2002) 'Stalking' in Tonry M (ed) *Crime and Justice: A Review of Research* (vol 29, University of Chicago Press) 273.

Nellis, Mike (2003) 'News Media, Popular Culture and the Electronic Monitoring of Offenders in England and Wales' 42 Howard Journal 1.

Newburn, Tim (2002) 'Young People, Crime, and Youth Justice' in Maguire et al (eds) *The Oxford Handbook of Criminology* (Oxford University Press) p 531.

Uglow, Steve (2002) *Criminal Justice* (Sweet & Maxwell) Ch 3.

Young, Jock (2002) 'Crime and Social Exclusion' in Maguire et al (eds) *The Oxford Handbook of Criminology* (Oxford University Press) p 457.

Zedner, Lucia (2003) 'The Concept of Security: an Agenda for Comparative Analysis' 23 Legal Studies 153.

II.   Offences against the person

Offences of personal violence have a wide potential relevance in the public order area and beyond. We focus here on assault and battery, and the three main general offences under the Offences Against the Person Act 1861. The somewhat imperfect hierarchy of the Act reflects both differences in the seriousness of injury or harm and in the mental element. The Government has endorsed the codified set of offences based on the Law Commission's proposals in Report No 218 (1993) but as yet no legislation has been introduced (Home Office 1998).

II.a.   The general scheme

Assault and battery are not statutorily defined. They are separate summary offences leading on conviction to a maximum penalty of imprisonment of six months or a fine not exceeding level five (Criminal Justice Act 1988, s 39). They are not arrestable offences, unlike assault occasioning actual bodily harm (by virtue of its maximum penalty) and assaulting a police officer in the execution of his or her duty (which became arrestable under the Police Reform Act 2002).

Assault occasioning actual bodily harm is found in s 47 of the Offences against the Person Act 1861 (OAPA 1861). Moving up the hierarchy, we reach *malicious wounding* in s 20. The offences under ss 47 and 20 are triable summarily as well as on indictment. Finally, the most serious general offence, *wounding or causing grievous bodily harm with intent*, is contained in s 18. Consent will often, but not always, be a defence to assault and injury offences. It is generally not possible to consent to serious injury (*Brown*, 1993).

II.b.   Assault and battery

Assault can be broadly defined as putting a person in fear of the application of immediate personal violence, while *battery* is the application of force to the person (*DPP v K*, 1990). These basic concepts apply to assault occasioning actual bodily harm (OAPA 1861, s 47), and to the offence of assaulting a police officer in the execution of his or her duty (Police Act 1996, s 89(1)). Once the offence ingredients of assault or battery have been proved, no further mental element is required for the 'aggravated' assaults (see *Savage and Parmenter*, in **section II.c.** below).

What are the 'mens rea' requirements of assault and battery? For assault and battery at common law, only knowledge or awareness as to the fact of the assault or battery is required, and this is true also of assault occasioning actual bodily harm. No mental element as to the actual bodily harm is required.

These offences constitute a good example of the way in which criminal law often fails to fulfil its own doctrinal ideals. Arguments for the justice of 'subjective' responsibility are premised at least implicitly on that responsibility existing as to the full extent of the 'actus reus'. This restricted 'mens rea' requirement must also be seen in the light of arguments about how courts can be expected to 'find' subjective mental elements. It will be difficult for them to avoid a form of reasoning based on what they think must have been in the defendant's mind, which is influenced by what they think should have been, and therefore by what they think would have been in their own minds in the circumstances. The way in which 'mens rea' is inferred is well illustrated by a case which affirmed the subjective principle whilst exemplifying its flexibility. Note that the word 'assault' is frequently and confusingly used to embrace both technical assault (causing apprehension of violence) and battery (physical touching). The following case contains a classic definition of assault:

R v Venna [1975] 3 All ER 788, CA

[*Venna and others were creating a disturbance in a public street. The police were sent for and during a scuffle which ensued as the police sought to arrest him the appellant kicked out with his feet. In so doing he struck the hand of an officer and caused a fracture. He was convicted of an assault occasioning actual bodily harm.*]

James LJ.

… [T]he judge directed the jury in these terms … :

> … Counsel on behalf of Venna says, 'Well, he is not guilty of an assault because it was neither intentional nor reckless. It was a pure accident that he happened to hit the officer', and this is quite right. If you hit somebody accidentally, it cannot be a criminal offence. So you have got to ask yourselves, 'Was this deliberate, or was it reckless?' If it was, then he is guilty. To do an act deliberately hardly needs explanation. If you see somebody in front of you and you deliberately kick him on the knee, that is a deliberate act and, no two ways about it, that is an assault but it can equally well be an assault if you are lashing out, knowing that there are people in the neighbourhood or that there are likely to be people in the neighbourhood and, in this case, it is suggested that he had two people by his arms and he knew that he was being restrained so as to lead to arrest. If he lashed out with his feet, knowing that there are officers about him and knowing that by lashing out he will probably or is likely to kick somebody or hurt his hand by banging his heel down on it, then he is equally guilty of the offence. Venna can therefore be guilty of the offence in … the indictment if he deliberately brought his foot down on Police Constable Spencer's hand or if he lashed out simply reckless as to who was there, not caring an iota as to whether he kicked somebody or brought his heel down on his hands.

Counsel for the appellant argued that the direction is wrong in law because it states that the mental element of recklessness is enough, when coupled with the actus reus of physical contact, to constitute the battery involved in assault occasioning actual bodily harm. Recklessness, it is argued, is not enough …

On the evidence of the appellant himself, one would have thought that the inescapable inference was that the appellant intended to make physical contact with whoever might try to restrain him. Be that as it may, in the light of the direction given, the verdict may have been arrived at on the basis of 'recklessness'.

... In our view the element of mens rea in the offence of battery is satisfied by proof that the defendant intentionally or recklessly applied force to the person of another. If it were otherwise, the strange consequence would be that an offence of unlawful wounding contrary to s 20 of the Offences Against the Person Act 1861 could be established by proof that the defendant wounded the victim either intentionally or recklessly, but if the victim's skin was not broken and the offence was therefore laid as an assault occasioning actual bodily harm contrary to s 47 of the 1861 Act, it would be necessary to prove that the physical force was intentionally applied.

We see no reason in logic or in law why a person who recklessly applies physical force to the person of another should be outside the criminal law of assault. In many cases the dividing line between intention and recklessness is barely distinguishable ...

The relatively clear facts in this case should not blind us to the way in which the trial judge's direction effectively gives with one hand (by stating a general, liberal principle favourable to the accused) and takes away with the other (by drawing inferences rendering that principle inapplicable in the context in question). This approach is continued in the more serious offences of personal violence in the OAPA 1861.

II.c.   Occasioning actual bodily harm, wounding and grievous bodily harm

OAPA 1861, s 47

Whosoever shall be convicted upon an indictment of any assault occasioning actual bodily harm shall be liable ... to [imprisonment for five years].

The essence of the s 47 offence is that the assault 'occasions' (that is, causes) 'actual bodily harm'. Hobhouse LJ said in *Chan-Fook* (1994) that this phrase could 'in the ordinary course' be left undefined: 'The word "harm" is a synonym for injury. The word "actual" indicates that the injury (although there is no need for it to be permanent) should not be so trivial as to be wholly insignificant.'

OAPA 1861, s 20

Whosoever shall unlawfully and maliciously wound or inflict any grievous bodily harm upon any other person, either with or without any weapon or instrument, shall be guilty of [an offence], and being convicted thereof shall be liable ... to [a term of imprisonment not exceeding five years].

OAPA 1861, s 18

Whosoever shall unlawfully and maliciously by any means whatsoever wound or cause any grievous bodily harm to any person ... with intent ...

to do some grievous bodily harm to any person, or with intent to resist or prevent the lawful apprehension or detainer of any person, shall be guilty of an offence, and being convicted thereof shall be liable … to [imprisonment] for life.

'Malicious wounding' under s 20 and 'wounding with intent' under s 18 of the OAPA 1861, both require proof of wounding (breaking of the skin) or of grievous bodily harm (really serious injury).

Before turning to consider whether 'harm' in all three offences includes psychiatric injury (*Burstow*, below), we continue our exploration of 'mens rea'. In the following case, the House of Lords considered the relationship between the offences of assault and battery, assault occasioning actual bodily harm and malicious wounding (OAPA 1861, s 20).

R v Savage, DPP v Parmenter [1992] 1 AC 699

Lord Ackner.

… [T]hese two appeals have been heard together, because they each raise the issue of the mental element which the prosecution have to establish in relation to offences under two sections of the Offences Against the Person Act 1861, viz s 20, unlawfully and maliciously wounding or inflicting grievous bodily harm, and s 47, assault occasioning actual bodily harm.

… [S was convicted of unlawful wounding under s 20. She had thrown a glass of beer at another woman with the result that the woman's wrist was cut by the glass] …

The material words of s 20 read: 'Whosoever shall unlawfully and maliciously wound or inflict any grievous bodily Harm upon any other Person … '

In the course of his summing up the recorder said:

It is alleged that on 31 March Mrs Savage unlawfully and maliciously wounded Tracey Beal. What does this mean? First of all it means that you must find Susan Savage did some unlawful action, unlawful in the sense that it was not in self-defence and it was not a mere accident; malicious in the sense that it was deliberate and aimed against Tracey Beal and that as a result of that unlawful, deliberate act aimed against Tracey Beal, Tracey Beal suffered a wound … She went up to her … and threw deliberately the contents of a pint glass at her. That is an assault, that is an unlawful action aimed deliberately against Tracey Beal. Mrs. Savage admitted it … If you were sure that in throwing the liquid from the glass she let go of the glass and it struck Miss Beal, then that is a consequence of her unlawful act. If a wound resulted from it then that is unlawful wounding.

In the Court of Appeal reference was made to *R v Mowatt* [1967] 3 All ER 47 and to the following statement of Diplock LJ, giving the judgment of the court:

> In the offence under s 20 ... the word 'maliciously' does import on the part of the person who unlawfully inflicts the wound or grievous bodily harm an awareness that his act may have the consequence of causing some physical harm to some other person ... It is quite unnecessary that the accused should have foreseen that his unlawful act might cause physical harm of the gravity described in the section, i.e., a wound or serious physical injury. It is enough that he should have foreseen that some physical harm to some person, albeit of a minor character, might result ...

The Court of Appeal observed that, despite doubts which had been expressed about the above statement of the law, it was binding on the court and that the test imported by the word 'maliciously' is a subjective and not an objective one. In the opinion of the Court of Appeal, it accordingly followed that the recorder was wrong to direct the jury that 'malicious' meant deliberate and aimed at Tracey Beal with the result that wound occurred. The recorder omitted to direct the jury that they had to find that Mrs Savage foresaw that some physical harm would follow as a result of what she did. The question as to whether she foresaw that her act was likely to cause some harm, other than wetting Miss Beal with the beer, was a question they should have been asked to consider. In view of this misdirection, the Court of Appeal quashed the verdict and then went on to consider whether they should substitute another verdict.

[The Court of Appeal decided that a verdict of guilty of assault occasioning actual bodily harm, contrary to s 47 of the 1861 Act should be substituted, and then] gave leave to appeal, certifying the following points of law to be of general public importance:

1. Whether a verdict of guilty occasioning actual bodily harm is a permissible alternative verdict on a Count alleging unlawful wounding contrary to section 20 of the Offences Against the Person Act, 1861?
2. Whether a verdict of guilty of assault occasioning actual bodily harm can be returned upon proof of an assault and of the fact that actual bodily harm was occasioned by the assault?
3. If it is proved that an assault has been committed and that actual bodily harm has resulted from that assault, whether a verdict of assault occasioning actual bodily harm may be returned in the absence of proof that the Defendant intended to cause some actual bodily harm or was reckless as to whether such harm would be caused ...

[*Parmenter was convicted of four offences under s 20 for causing injury to his baby son. The trial judge directed the jury as to the meaning of 'maliciously' by quoting from the case of Mowatt. The Court of Appeal noted that the judge had 'inadvertently imparted a fundamental change to the principle laid down in Mowatt' by asking the jury 'Are we sure that he should have foreseen that some physical harm, albeit of a minor character might result?' Although Diplock LJ uses this phrase in Mowatt, the Court of Appeal held that using it out of context would lead the jury to believe they were being asked 'not whether the defendant* actually *foresaw that his acts would cause injury, but whether he* ought to have *foreseen it' (emphasis in original). The Court of Appeal quashed the convictions under s 20 and then considered whether to substitute convictions under s 47. It discovered that the Court of Appeal had delivered two judgments on the necessary intent for s 47 on the same day – Savage being one and Spratt [1991] 2 All ER 210 the other – and had reached opposite conclusions as to whether foresight is required as to the consequences of the assault.*]

[T]he Court of Appeal … certified the following points of law to be of general public importance:

1(a) Whether in order to establish an offence under Section 20 of the Offences Against the Person Act 1861 (the Act) the prosecution must prove that the defendant actually foresaw that his act would cause the particular kind of harm which was in fact caused, or whether it is sufficient to prove that (objectively) he ought so to have foreseen.

(b) The like question in relation to section 47 of the Act.

2(a) For the purposes of the answer to Question 1(a), whether the particular kind of harm to be foreseen may be any physical harm, or harm of (i) the nature, or (ii) the degree, or (iii) the nature and the degree of the harm which actually occurred.

(b) The like question in relation to section 47 of the Act.

It will be observed that some of the certified questions in *R v Parmenter* overlap with those in *R v Savage*.

[I. *Ireland/Burstow*, below, supercedes this case in relation to the first question]

II. Can a verdict of assault occasioning actual bodily harm be returned upon proof of an assault together with proof of the fact that actual bodily harm was occasioned by the assault, or must the prosecution also prove that the defendant intended to cause some actual bodily harm or was reckless as to whether such harm would be caused?

Your Lordships are concerned with the mental element of a particular kind of assault, an assault 'occasioning actual bodily harm'. It is common ground that the mental element of assault is an intention to cause the victim to apprehend immediate and unlawful violence or recklessness whether such apprehension be caused (see *R v Venna* [above]). It is of course common ground that Mrs. Savage committed an assault upon Miss Beal when she threw the contents of her glass of beer over her. It is also common ground that however the glass came to be broken and Miss Beal's wrist thereby cut, it was, on the finding of the jury, Mrs. Savage's handling of the glass which caused Miss Beal 'actual bodily harm'. Was the offence thus established or is there a further mental state that has to be established in relation to the bodily harm element of the offence? Clearly the section, by its terms, expressly imposes no such a requirement. Does it do so by necessary implication? It uses neither the word 'intentionally' nor the word 'maliciously'. The words 'occasioning actual bodily harm' are descriptive of the word 'assault', by reference to a particular kind of consequence.

[In *R v Roberts* (1972) 56 Cr App 95, CA] … Roberts was tried on an indictment which alleged that he indecently assaulted a young woman. He was acquitted on that charge, but convicted of assault occasioning actual bodily harm to her. The girl's complaint was that while travelling in the defendant's car he sought to make advances towards her and then tried to take her coat off. This was the last straw and, although the car was travelling at some speed, she jumped out and sustained injuries. The defendant denied he had touched the girl. He had had an argument with her and in the course of that argument she suddenly opened the door and jumped out. In his direction to the jury the chairman of quarter sessions stated:

If you are satisfied that he tried to pull off her coat and as a result she jumped out of the moving car then your verdict is guilty.

It was contended on behalf of the appellant that this direction was wrong since the chairman had failed to tell the jury that they must be satisfied that the appellant foresaw that she might jump out of the car as a result of his touching her before they could convict. The court rejected that submission …

Accordingly, no fault was found in the following direction of the chairman to the jury (at 103):

If you accept the evidence of the girl in preference to that of the man, that means that there was an assault occasioning actual bodily harm, that means that she did jump out as a direct result of what he was threatening her with, and what he was doing to her, holding her coat, telling her that he had beaten up girls who had refused his advances, and that means that through his acts he was in law and in fact responsible for the injuries which were caused to her by her decision, if it can be called that, to get away from his violence, his threats, by jumping out of the car.

Thus, once the assault was established, the only remaining question was whether the victim's conduct was the natural consequence of that assault. The words 'occasioning' raised solely a question of causation, an objective question which does not involve inquiring into the accused's state of mind.

My Lords, in my respectful view, the Court of Appeal in *R v Parmenter* was wrong in preferring the decision in *R v Spratt*. The decision in *R v Roberts* (1972) 56 Cr App R 95 was correct. The verdict of assault occasioning actual bodily harm may be returned upon proof of an assault together with proof of the fact that actual bodily harm was occasioned by the assault. The prosecution are not obliged to prove that the defendant intended to cause some actual bodily harm or was reckless as to whether such harm would be caused.

III. In order to establish an offence under s 20 of the 1861 Act, must the prosecution prove that the defendant actually foresaw that his act would cause harm, or is it sufficient to prove that he ought so to have foreseen?

Although your Lordships' attention has been invited to a plethora of decided cases, the issue is a narrow one. Is the decision of the Court of Criminal Appeal in *R v Cunningham* [1957] 2 All ER 412, [1957] 2 QB 396 still good law, subject only to a gloss placed upon it by the Court of Appeal, Criminal Division in *R v Mowatt* [1967] 3 All ER 47, [1968] 1 QB 421, or does the later decision of your Lordships' House in *R v Caldwell* [1981] 1 All ER 961, [1982] AC 341 provide the answer to this question?

... [Counsel for Parmenter] submitted that in *R v Caldwell* your Lordships' House could have followed either of two possible paths to its conclusion as to the meaning of 'recklessly' in the 1971 Act. These were: (a) to hold that *R v Cunningham* (and *R v Mowatt*) were wrongly decided and to introduce a single test, wherever recklessness was an issue; or (b) to accept that *R v Cunningham* (subject to the *R v Mowatt* 'gloss' to which no reference was made) correctly states the law in relation to the Offences Against the Person Act 1861, because the word 'maliciously' in that statute was a term of legal art which imported into the concept of recklessness a special restricted meaning, thus distinguishing it from 'reckless' or 'recklessly' in modern 'revising' statutes then before the House, where those words bore their then popular or dictionary meaning.

I agree with [counsel] that manifestly it was the latter course which the House followed. Therefore in order to establish an offence under s 20 the prosecution must prove either that the defendant intended or that he actually foresaw that his act would cause harm.

IV. In order to establish an offence under s 20 is it sufficient to prove that the defendant intended or foresaw the risk of some physical harm or must he intend or foresee either wounding or grievous bodily harm?

It is convenient to set out once again the relevant part of the judgment of Diplock LJ in *R v Mowatt* [1967] 3 All ER 47 at 50, [1968] 1 QB at 426 [when he said:]

> In the offence under s 20 ... for ... which [no] specific intent is required – the word 'maliciously' does import ... an awareness that his act may have the consequence of causing some physical harm to some

other person ... *It is enough that he should have foreseen that some physical harm to some person, albeit of a minor character, might result.* (My emphasis.)

[Counsel] submits that ... the section requires foresight of a wounding or grievous bodily harm ... and that a person should not be criminally liable for consequences of his conduct unless he foresaw a consequence falling into the same category as that set out in the indictment.

Such a general principle runs contrary to the decision in *R v Roberts* (1972) 56 Cr App R 95, which I have already stated to be, in my opinion, correct. The contention is apparently based on the proposition that, as the actus reus of a s 20 offence is the wounding or the infliction of grievous bodily harm, the mens rea must consist of foreseeing such wounding or grievous bodily harm. But there is no such hard and fast principle. To take but two examples, the actus reus of murder is the killing of the victim, but foresight of grievous bodily harm is sufficient and, indeed, such bodily harm need not be such as to be dangerous to life. Again, in the case of manslaughter death is frequently the unforeseen consequence of the violence used.

The argument that, as ss 20 and 47 have both the same penalty, this somehow supports the proposition that the foreseen consequences must coincide with the harm actually done, overlooks the oft-repeated statement that this is the irrational result of this piecemeal legislation. The Act 'is a rag-bag of offences brought together from a wide variety of sources with no attempt, as the draftsman frankly acknowledged, to introduce consistency as to substance or as to form' (see Professor J C Smith ... ([1991] Crim LR 43)).

If s 20 was to be limited to cases where the accused does not desire but does foresee wounding or grievous bodily harm, it would have a very limited scope. The mens rea in a s 20 crime is comprised in the word 'maliciously'. As was pointed out by Lord Lane CJ, giving the judgment of the Court of Appeal in *R v Sullivan* [1981] Crim LR 46, the 'particular kind of harm' in the citation from Professor Kenny was directed to 'harm to the person' as opposed to 'harm to property'. Thus is was not concerned with the degree of the harm foreseen. It is accordingly in my judgment wrong to look upon the decision in *R v Mowatt* ... as being in any way inconsistent with the decision in *R v Cunningham* ...

My Lords, I am satisfied that the decision in *R v Mowatt* was correct and that it is quite unnecessary that the accused should either have intended or have foreseen that his unlawful act might cause physical harm of the gravity described in s 20, i.e. a wound or serious physical injury. It is enough that he should have foreseen that some physical harm to some person, albeit of a minor character, might result.

In the result I would dismiss the appeal in *Savage*'s case but allow the appeal in *Parmenter*'s case, but only to the extent of substituting, in accordance with the provisions of s 3(2) of the Criminal Appeal Act 1968, verdicts of guilty of assault occasioning actual bodily harm contrary to s 47 of the 1861 Act for the four s 20 offences of which he was convicted.

[*Appeal in R v Savage dismissed; appeal in R v Parmenter allowed in part and conviction of assault occasioning actual bodily harm substituted.*]

Thus, at a minimum, s 47 requires a subjectively *reckless* assault or battery that *in fact* causes actual bodily harm. No mental element or 'mens rea' is required in relation to the actual bodily harm. 'Malicious wounding' under s 20 requires that the wound or grievous bodily harm be accompanied by foresight of some (not necessarily serious) harm.

The stricter 'mens rea' requirement in s 18, wounding or causing grievous bodily harm with intent, may not be as constraining as might be thought. The intention requirement can be satisfied either by an intention to cause grievous bodily harm or by the alternative possibility of an intention to resist or prevent lawful apprehension. This could have special relevance in public order cases. Imagine a chaotic situation in which a demonstration has become disorderly and the police respond vigorously. It is not impossible to imagine a court inferring intention to resist arrest where a defendant has caused a wound or grievous bodily harm, even though the injury itself was negligent or even accidental in the heat of the moment. The possible disjuncture between defendants' own understandings of their actions and courts' interpretation in applying the law is very clear even in the case of an offence with a stringent 'mens rea' requirement.

The stalking cases involving harassment through silent telephone calls and other non-verbal behaviour have raised the question whether such conduct amounts to an assault, that is, does it cause an apprehension of immediate violence? The House of Lords cut through the technical interpretation of 'assault' and 'inflict' (the use of this latter word in s 20 had been thought to imply a technical assault had to accompany the injury) to achieve a more modern understanding of the range of harms covered by these offences. A further question arose in these appeals: whether 'harm' in ss 47, 20 and 18, covers both psychiatric as well as physical injury. Again, the House of Lords agreed that it should. However, the ease with which appellate courts move from blind adherence to anachronistic statutory forms to blatantly ignoring them does little for confidence in the observance of the principle that criminal statutes should be interpreted strictly in favour of defendants.

R v Ireland, R v Burstow [1997] 4 All ER 225, HL

Lord Steyn.

... It is easy to understand the terrifying effect of a campaign of telephone calls at night by a silent caller to a woman living on her own. It would be natural for the victim to regard the calls as menacing. What may heighten her fear is that she will not know what the caller may do next. The spectre of the caller arriving at her doorstep bent on inflicting personal violence on her may come to dominate her thinking. After all, as a matter of common sense, what else would she be terrified about? The victim may suffer psychiatric illness such as anxiety neurosis or acute depression. That the criminal law should be able to deal with this problem, and so far as is practicable, afford effective protection to victims is self evident.

From the point of view, however, of the general policy of our law towards the imposition of criminal responsibility, three specific features of the problem must be faced squarely. First, the medium used by the caller is the telephone: arguably it differs qualitatively from a face to face offer of violence to a sufficient extent to make a difference. Secondly, ex hypothesi the caller remains silent: arguably a caller may avoid the reach of criminal law by remaining silent however menacing the context may be. Thirdly, it is arguable that the criminal law does not take into account 'mere' psychiatric illnesses.

At first glance it may seem that the legislature has satisfactorily dealt with such objections by s 43(1) of the Telecommunications Act 1984 which makes it an offence persistently to make use of a public telecommunications system for the purpose of causing annoyance, inconvenience or needless anxiety to another. The maximum custodial penalty is six months' imprisonment. This penalty may be inadequate to reflect a culpability of a persistent offender who causes serious psychiatric illness to another. For the future there will be for consideration the provisions of ss 1 and 2 of the Protection from Harassment Act 1997 [not then in force, see above], which creates the offence pursuing a course of conduct which amounts to harassment of another and which he knows or ought to know amounts to harassment of the other. The maximum custodial penalty is six months' imprisonment. This penalty may also be inadequate to deal with persistent offenders who cause serious psychiatric injury to victims. Section 4(1) of the 1997 Act which creates the offence of putting people in fear of violence seems more appropriate. It provides for maximum custodial penalty upon conviction on indictment of five years' imprisonment. On the other hand, s 4 only applies when as a result of a course of conduct the victim has cause to fear, on at least two occasions, that violence will be used against her. It may be difficult to secure a conviction in respect of a silent caller: the victim in such cases may have cause to fear that violence may be used against her but no more. In my view, therefore, the provisions of these two statutes are not ideally suited to deal with the significant problem which I have described. One must therefore look elsewhere. It is to the provisions of the Offences Against the Person Act 1861 that one must turn to examine whether our law provides effective criminal sanctions for this type of case.

Making a due allowance for the incongruities in these provisions [ss 18, 20 and 47] can be described as 'a ladder of offences graded in terms of relative seriousness': ... An ingredient of each of the offences is 'bodily harm' to a person. In respect of each section the threshold question is therefore whether a psychiatric illness, as testified to by a psychiatrist, can amount to 'bodily harm'. If the answer to this question is no, it will follow that the Act of 1861 cannot be used to prosecute in the class of cases which I have described. On the other hand, if the answer to the question is yes, it will be necessary to consider whether the persistent silent caller, who terrifies his victim and causes her to suffer a psychiatric illness, can be criminally liable under any of these sections. Given that the caller uses the medium of the telephone and silence to terrify his victim, is he beyond the reach of these sections?

Similar problems arise in the case of the so called stalker, who pursues a campaign of harassment by more diffuse means. He may intend to terrify the woman and succeed in doing so, by relentlessly following her, by unnecessarily appearing at her home and place of work, photographing her, and so forth. Is he beyond the trilogy of sections in the 1861 Act?

... There are two appeals before the House. In *Ireland* the appellant was convicted on his plea of guilty of three counts of assault occasioning actual bodily harm, contrary to s 47 of the 1861 Act ... The case against Ireland was that during a period of three months in 1994 covered by the indictment he harassed three women by making repeated phone calls to them during which he remained silent. Sometimes, he resorted to heavy breathing. The calls were mostly at night. The case against him, which was accepted by the judge and the Court of Appeal, was that he caused his victim to suffer psychiatric illness. *Ireland* had a substantial record of making offensive phone calls to women. The judge sentenced him to a total of three years' imprisonment.

Before the Court of Appeal there were two principal issues. The first was whether psychiatric illness may amount to bodily harm within the meaning of s 47 of the Act of 1861. Relying on a decision of the Court of Appeal in *R v Chan-Fook* [1994] 1 WLR 689 the Court of Appeal in *Ireland*'s case concluded that psychiatric injury may amount to bodily harm under s 47 of the 1861 Act. The second issue was whether Ireland's conduct was capable of amounting to an assault. In giving the judgment of the court in *Ireland*'s case Swinton Thomas LJ said (at p 119):

It has been recognised for many centuries that putting a person in fear may amount to an assault. The early cases predate the invention of the telephone. We must apply the law to the conditions as they are in the 20th century.

The court concluded that repeated telephone calls of a menacing nature may cause victims to apprehend immediate and unlawful violence. Given these conclusions of law and Ireland's guilty plea, the Court of Appeal dismissed the appeal. The Court of Appeal certified the following question as being of general public importance, namely 'As to whether making a series of silent telephone calls can amount in law to an assault'. But it will also be necessary to consider the question whether psychiatric illness may in law amount to bodily harm under s 47 of the 1861 Act. Those are the issues of law before the House in the appeal of *Ireland*.

In *R v Burstow* the appellant was indicted on one count of unlawfully and maliciously inflicting grievous bodily harm, contrary to s 20 of the 1861 Act ... Burstow had a social relationship with a woman. She broke it off. He could not accept her decision. He proceeded to harass her in various ways over a lengthy period. His conduct led to several convictions and periods of imprisonment. During an eight month period in 1995 covered by the indictment he continued the campaign of harassment. He made some silent telephone calls to her. He also made some abusive calls to her ... The victim was badly affected by this campaign of harassment. It preyed on her mind. She was fearful of personal violence. A consultant psychiatrist stated that she was suffering from a severe depressive illness. In the Crown Court counsel asked for a ruling whether an offence of unlawfully and maliciously inflicting grievous bodily harm contrary to s 20 may be committed where no physical violence has been applied directly or indirectly to the body of the victim. The judge answered this question in the affirmative. Burstow thereupon changed his plea to guilty. The judge sentenced him to three years' imprisonment.

Burstow applied for leave to appeal against conviction ... Two questions of law were canvassed before the Court of Appeal. First, there was the question whether psychiatric injury may amount to bodily harm under s 20. The Court of Appeal regarded itself as bound by the affirmative decision in *Reg v Chan-Fook* (1994). The second issue was whether in the absence of physical violence applied directly or indirectly to the body of the victim an offence under s 20 may be committed. The Court of Appeal concluded that this question must be answered in the affirmative ... It will be noted that in neither appeal is there an issue on mens rea: the appeals focus on questions of law regarding the actus reus.

... It will now be convenient to consider the question which is common to the two appeals, namely whether psychiatric illness is capable of amounting to bodily harm in the terms of ss 18, 20 and 47 of the 1861 Act. The answer must be the same for the three sections.

> The only abiding thing about the processes of the human mind, and the causes of its disorders and disturbances, is that there will never be a complete explanation. Psychiatry is and will always remain an imperfectly understood branch of medical science ...

But there has been progress since 1861. And courts of law can only act on the best scientific understanding of the day. Some elementary distinctions can be made. The appeals under consideration do not involve structural injuries to the brain such as might require the intervention of a neurologist. One is also not considering either psychotic illness or personality disorders. The victims in the two appeals suffered from no such conditions. As a result of the behaviour of the appellants they did not develop psychotic or psychoneurotic conditions. The case was that they developed mental disturbances of a lesser order, namely neurotic disorders.

The civil law has for a long time taken into account the fact that there is no rigid distinction between body and mind. The criminal law has been slow to follow this path ... Counsel for the appellants in both appeals submitted that bodily harm in Victorian legislation cannot include psychiatric injury. For this reason they argued that *Chan-Fook* was wrongly decided. They relied on the following observation of Lord Bingham of Cornhill CJ in *Burstow* [1997] 1 Cr App R 144, 148:

> Were the question free from authority, we should entertain some doubt whether the Victorian draftsman of the 1861 Act intended to embrace psychiatric injury within the expressions 'grievous bodily harm' and 'actual bodily harm'.

Nevertheless, the Lord Chief Justice observed that it is now accepted that in the relevant context the distinction between physical and mental injury is by no means clear cut. He welcomed the ruling in *Chan-Fook* ... I would go further and point out that, although out of considerations of piety we frequently refer to the actual intention of the draftsman, the correct approach is simply to consider whether the words of the 1861 Act considered in the light of contemporary knowledge cover a recognisable psychiatric injury. It is undoubtedly true that there are statutes where the correct approach is to construe the legislation 'as if one were interpreting it the day after it was passed': *The Longford* (1889) 14 PD 34 ... Bearing in mind that statutes are usually intended to operate for many years it would be most inconvenient if courts could never rely in difficult cases on the current meaning of statutes.

Recognising the problem Lord Thring, the great Victorian draftsman of the second half of the last century, exhorted draftsmen to draft so that 'An Act of Parliament should be deemed to be always speaking' ... In cases where the problem arises it is a matter of interpretation whether a court must search for the historical original meaning of a statute or whether it is free to apply the current meaning of the statute to present day conditions. Statutes dealing with a particular grievance or problem may sometimes require to be historically interpreted. But the drafting technique of Lord Thring and his successors have brought about the situation that statutes will generally be found to be of 'always speaking' variety ...

The proposition that the Victorian legislator when enacting ss 18, 20 and 47 of the 1861 Act, would not have had in mind psychiatric illness is no doubt correct. Psychiatry was in its infancy in 1861. But the subjective intention of the draftsman is immaterial. The only relevant enquiry is as to the sense of the words in the context in which they are used. Moreover, the 1861 Act is a statute of the 'always speaking' type: the statute must be interpreted in the light of the best current scientific appreciation of the link between the body and the psychiatric injury.

For these reasons I would, therefore, reject the challenge to the correctness of *Chan-Fook* [1994] 1 WLR 689. In my view the ruling in that case was based on principled and cogent reasoning and it marked a sound and essential clarification of the law. I would hold that 'bodily harm' in ss 18, 20 and 47 must be interpreted so as to include recognisable psychiatric illness.

R v Burstow: the meaning of 'inflict' in s 20

The decision in *Chan-Fook* opened up the possibility of applying ss 18, 20 and 47 in new circumstances. The appeal of Burstow lies in respect of his conviction under s 20. It was conceded that in principle the wording of s 18, and in particular the words 'cause any grievous bodily harm to any person' do not preclude a prosecution in cases where the actus reus is the causing of psychiatric injury. But counsel laid stress on the difference between 'causing' grievous bodily harm in s 18 and 'inflicting' grievous harm in s 20. Counsel argued that the difference in wording reveals a difference in legislative intent: inflict is a narrower concept than cause ...

...

The problem is one of construction. The question is whether as a matter of current usage the contextual interpretation of 'inflict' can embrace the idea of one person inflicting psychiatric injury on another. One can without straining the language in any way answer that question in the affirmative. I am not saying that the words cause and inflict are exactly synonymous. They are not. What I am saying is that in the context of the Act of 1861 one can nowadays quite naturally speak of inflicting psychiatric injury. Moreover, there is internal contextual support in the statute for this view. It would be absurd to differentiate between sections 18 and 20 in the way argued on behalf of Burstow ... [T]his should be a very practical area of the law. The interpretation and approach should so far as possible be adopted which treats the ladder of offences as a coherent body of law. Once the decision in *Chan-Fook* ... is accepted the realistic possibility is opened up of prosecuting under section 20 in cases of the type which I described in the introduction to this judgment.

For the reasons I have given I would answer the certified question in *Burstow* in the affirmative.

R v Ireland: was there an assault?

There has been substantial academic criticism of the conclusion and reasoning in *Ireland* ... Counsel's arguments, broadly speaking, challenged the decision in *Ireland* on very similar lines. Having carefully considered the literature and counsel's arguments, I have come to the conclusion that the appeal ought to be dismissed.

The starting point must be that an assault is an ingredient of the offence under section 47. It is necessary to consider the two forms which an assault may take. The first is battery, which involves the unlawful application of force by the defendant upon the victim. Usually, section 47 is used to prosecute in cases of this kind. The second form of assault is an act causing the victim to apprehend an imminent application of force upon her ...

It is to assault in the form of an act causing the victim to fear an immediate application of force to her that I must turn. Counsel argued that as a matter of law an assault can never be committed by words alone and therefore it cannot be committed by silence ... The proposition that a gesture may amount to an assault, but that words can never suffice, is unrealistic and indefensible. A thing said is also a thing done. There is no reason why something said should be incapable of causing an apprehension of immediate personal violence, e.g. a man accosting a woman in a dark alley saying 'come with me or I will stab you'. I would, therefore, reject the proposition that an assault can never be committed by words.

That brings me to the critical question whether a silent caller may be guilty of an assault. The answer to this question seems to me to be 'yes, depending on the facts'. It involves questions of fact within the province of the jury. After all, there is no reason why a telephone caller who says to a woman in a menacing way 'I will be at your door in a minute or two' may not be guilty of an assault if he causes the victim to apprehend immediate personal violence. Take now the case of the silent caller. He intends by his silence to cause fear and he is so understood. The victim is assailed by uncertainty about his intentions. Fear may dominate her emotions, and it may be the fear that the caller's arrival at her door may be imminent. She may fear the possibility of immediate personal violence. As a matter of law the caller may be guilty of an assault: whether he is or not will depend on the circumstance and in particular on the impact of the caller's potentially menacing call or calls on the victim. Such a prosecution case under section 47 may be fit to leave to the jury.

[The appeals were dismissed.]

Lord Steyn pointed out that liability for an intentional campaign of harassment that does not necessarily cause recognisable psychiatric injury will now be covered by offences under the Protection from Harassment Act 1997. Expert evidence is still required even where the fear and anxiety caused by stalking is clearly manifested in physical symptoms (*Morris*, 1998).

To summarise, the offences under the OAPA 1861 have, for the most part, received extraordinarily wide definitions from the courts. Actual bodily harm under s 47 comprises any harm whatsoever, however slight; and grievous bodily harm has been defined as 'really serious injury', the example given being that of a broken limb (*DPP v Smith*, 1961). A wound (the alternative 'actus reus' in both ss 18 and 20) means merely a break in the skin (*C v Eisenhower*, 1984). Thus, these very serious offences against the person could in principle be proven in circumstances that anyone outside a legal context would probably interpret as relatively minor or trivial. This is important in the public order context because, although the more serious offences against the person are in fact only rarely charged, their potential application is a powerful police and prosecution threat in the plea-bargaining and prosecution processes. In situations involving crowds, for example, the 'actus reus' of these offences may easily be caused in a way which the defendant regards as involuntary (as in a crush or stampede), yet which to the eye of the court seems to have involved intent or recklessness. The choice to charge a general offence rather than a public order offence may, of course, aid the process of depoliticisation of politically motivated disorder by constructing it as 'ordinary crime'. The importance of the Charging Standards (see **section II.e.** below) becomes ever clearer.

This area also illustrates the flexibility of some of the basic doctrinal principles regarding 'actus reus'. One example is the liberal principle that criminal regulation should cover actions rather than omissions, out of respect for the freedom of the individual. *Fagan v Metropolitan Police Comr* (1969) clearly demonstrates the ultimate flexibility of this distinction: the common-sense omission to remove the car from the police officer's foot was constructed as an action, on the basis of its interpretation as part of a continuing course of conduct. Hence, criminal law's usual focus only on the isolated, momentary actions of the abstract individual can always be broadened out to include reference to past actions and context when this facilitates the law's coercive functions. As Kelman puts it, legal discourse switches between momentary and non-momentary time frames and between broad and narrow views of the defendant. It does so in a pragmatic way which is obscured by legal doctrine (Kelman 1981).

II.d. Racial hatred, racial and religious aggravation

The most obvious hate crimes in England, specifically defined in terms of criminalising racial hatred, are those concerning incitement to racial hatred, now found in Pt III (ss 17–29) of the *Public Order Act 1986*. Criminal liability ensues where a person uses or publishes words or behaviour or written material that is threatening, abusive or insulting where, having regard to all the circumstances, racial hatred was likely to be stirred up or the person intended to stir up racial hatred. There are also the crimes of possessing racially inflammatory material with a view to publication, and of inciting to racial hatred by the distribution, showing or playing of films, videos, sound recordings and other media, including, generally, broadcasting. The definition of 'racial hatred' means hatred against a group of persons in Great Britain defined by reference to colour, race, nationality (including citizenship) or ethnic or national origins. Neither religion nor sexual orientation is included in the definition. Nonetheless, given the wide interpretation of 'ethnic group' by case law, an attack on Jews, for example, would be regarded as an attack against an ethnic group.

Legislation has also been introduced to protect racial groups in the context of football hooliganism. Section 3(1) of the *Football (Offences) Act 1991* makes it an offence to take part in chanting of an indecent or racialist nature at a designated football match.

The Crime and Disorder Act 1998 introduced a new raft of racially aggravated offences that build on existing provisions, as explained in the following extract:

E Burney, 'Using the Law on Racially Aggravated Offences' [2003] Crim LR 28

In the Crime and Disorder Act 1998 the Labour Government fulfilled its pledge to legislate against racially motivated crime. This was done by creating a new category of racially aggravated criminal offences (ss.28–32). The general principle that offences displaying racial aggravation should attract more severe punishment was also codified (s.82). Subsequently, in the aftermath of the events of September 11, 2001, religion was added to race (Anti-Terrorism, Crime and Security Act 2001, s.39) but this aspect will not be discussed here, although there is clearly a considerable overlap between the two groups. Section 28(4) defines "racial group" in the same terms as anti-discrimination law: that is "race, colour, nationality (including citizenship) or ethnic or national origins"; and section 28(2) also protects people victimised by association.

    The statute follows common American practice in structuring the law by means of penalty enhancement. … [R]ather than creating either a general law against racial violence, or discrete race-directed crimes (such as exist in little-used public order legislation with regard to the dissemination of race-hatred) the statute relies on existing categories of crime which have to be proved alongside the evidence required to classify the offence as racially aggravated and therefore liable for a higher penalty. Nine new offences of violence, public order, harassment and criminal damage, based on pre-existing offences, are thus created in sections 29–32, with new maximum sentences. Several summary-only offences, including common assault, thus become triable by the Crown Court in the aggravated form. Section 82 (now s.153 of the Powers of Criminal Courts (Sentencing) Act 2000) covers any offence not included in the list of nine specific offences, where racial aggravation is present, as defined in the statute. It must be stated in open court that the offence was so aggravated. For example crimes of violence carrying a maximum of life are sentenced under this general procedure, because there is no scope for enhancement of their maximum sentence, but the sentence imposed should reflect the seriousness of the aggravation.

The "piggy-backed" structure of racially aggravated offences (RAOs) gives rise to a number of procedural problems, highlighted in the Home Office research, which are discussed below. In addition, the definition of racial aggravation is all important. It goes considerably wider than American prototypes, creating conceptual problems for prosecutors and sentencers ...

Thus it is not essential to prove a racial motive in order for an offence to be racially aggravated; the two-pronged definition was deemed necessary because of the difficulty of proving motive ...

How to treat the nuances of racial hostility was of concern to many of the criminal justice practitioners interviewed, although a great range of opinion was expressed. Within the same court opinions differed: one stipendiary remarked to a researcher:

"Black bastard is everyday language on the streets of London: it must be seen in context".

But one of his colleagues, when interviewed, said:

"Words can hurt ... this sort of language is so common that you should review the case very carefully before deciding to drop the charge."

Many people said that there was an essential difference between the deliberate targeting of somebody on racial grounds and the use of racial language in the course of an unrelated confrontation. Others pointed out that there was no legal difference, merely a different degree of seriousness which should be reflected in the sentence.

This type of dichotomy was found at all levels amongst all agencies ...

The courts have hardly been overwhelmed by racially aggravated cases. In the year 2000/2001 there were 25,103 RAOs recorded by police, or 1.8 per cent of all recorded offences. During the year 2000, 493 people were cautioned and 4,048 prosecuted for such offences: the cautioning rate is low in comparison to equivalent "basic" offences: 9 per cent compared with 21 per cent. In the same year a mere 1,737 defendants were actually convicted and sentenced for racially aggravated offences (excluding a small number dealt with under the s.82 CDA98 / s.153 PCC(S)A 2000 procedure). The reasons for the high attrition rate of prosecuted cases are examined below.

Set against these figures are the far larger numbers of "racist incidents" recorded by the police. In 1999–2000 these shot up to 47,814, nearly three times the level recorded two years earlier, as reporting increased and police recording systems became more sensitive and responded to the definition prescribed by the Stephen Lawrence Inquiry report, that a racist incident is "any incident which is perceived to be racist by the victim or any other person". Many such incidents are not crimes or cannot be verified as such, but among the biggest factors affecting whether a "racist incident" becomes a recorded RAO are the greatly varying focus and practice of different police forces and individual police officers, as the research found ...

A different perspective is supplied by the British Crime Survey, which asked a sample of crime victims whether they believe that the perpetrator was racially motivated. In 1999, 0.3 per cent of white victims, 2 per cent of black, and 4 per cent of Indian, Pakistani and Bangladeshi victims said yes. But the overall perception of racist crime by both groups had shrunk dramatically, down by 30 per cent since the same survey in 1995, a larger decrease than the 22 per cent drop in crime generally. Even so, minority ethnic victims seemingly still reported many more racist incidents than appear in police statistics. It remains to be seen whether, following the events of September 11, 2001, this experience worsened significantly . ...

Criticisms (especially from the police) voiced to the Home Office researchers that prosecutors downgrade RAOs too easily, or sometimes overlook the possibility of an RAO charge, or, once in court, respond too readily to pleas to the basic offence, appear to be upheld by the findings of the CPS inspectors' thematic review which scrutinised a sample of cases. They report that " ... our evidence suggests that in a significant proportion of racist incident cases, the charges selected and pursued by the CPS do not reflect the seriousness of the offending or give courts adequate sentencing powers". Charge-reduction at pre-trial stage was judged inappropriate in 28.1 per cent of cases so reduced. Moreover in cases where pleas were accepted, this was "inappropriate" in 18.7 per cent of racist incident cases, compared with 8.5 per cent in a general sample.

In order to understand the pressures on the CPS in this type of case we must return to the structure of the RAO legislation. Magistrates cannot return alternative verdicts, so the prosecution has to decide whether to proceed on the RAO charge alone, and risk losing the case altogether even where there is good evidence that the assault, threat or whatever took place with or without any racist addition; or they must offer an alternative, basic, charge, in case the racial aggravation is not proved. It is not permissible to prosecute a basic offence and then introduce evidence of racism; if the ingredients of an RAO are present, that must be the charge. Sentencers sometimes express frustration at the presence of racist evidence which cannot be used in sentencing because the charge is not an RAO.

... In the Crown Court in 1999 83 per cent of RAOs were contested compared with 47 per cent of the equivalent basic variants. In London – where over half of all Crown Court RAO cases were tried – the not guilty proportion rose to an astonishing 92 per cent, compared with 65 per cent for the non-racial alternatives. It is the high proportion of contested cases, rather than a higher rate of jury acquittals, that causes Crown Court RAOs to have less than half the conviction rate of basic equivalent offences.

Not only do defendants who contest the charges wish to avoid the higher penalty involved, but many have a strong objection to the "racist" label attached. The researchers were told of people who admitted racial abuse but vehemently denied racism. Friends and relatives from ethnic minorities are often deployed as character witnesses. According to one defence solicitor in London, "No-one will plead to a racially aggravated variant of any offence. They just won't have it" ...

Most appeals in this field are, not surprisingly, about the length of sentences. Since sentence length is the core of the legislation, the subject requires close consideration ... Court staff and others sometimes remarked that magistrates had not noticeably increased sentences in cases involving racial aggravation prior to the legislation.

The analysis of specially supplied Home Office figures showed that this has changed. Comparison of magistrates' courts sentencing of RAOs with that of the equivalent basic offences displayed significant sentence enhancement. Adults are more than twice as likely to receive custody and fines are twice as high. Youth court sentences, pro rata, are even more severe. The Crown Court, on the other hand, showed almost no statistical evidence of sentence increase, although comparisons are more difficult due to the generally more severe nature of the ordinary offences dealt with, or the underlying offences in RAO cases. Moreover the year in question, 1999, was the first full year of the statute's operation, and only 151 RAOs had been sentenced in the Crown Court. By 2000 this figure had risen to 293, against 811 committed for trial or sentence. The influence of the charge reduction process described above (denied by the CPS to be "plea-bargaining") is surely apparent ...

What of the wider principle? The main justification for specific laws against racially aggravated crime is based on social cohesion. Attacking somebody (verbally or physically) because of their racial identity harms not only the victim but wider circles of people who share that identity, and threatens the stability of mixed communities and the development of a tolerant society. It may be asked how far the criminal law can really be expected to exert a corrective influence on dissonant social relations; at least it offers a symbol of civilised norms, which is not without value. Fortunately, the extreme unbridled racism expressed by some defendants (who often appear mentally unbalanced) dealt with in published cases is not shared by the majority of the public, and on the whole sentences reflect decent revulsion, although they may not do much to change the behaviour in question. Most appellants already have a string of convictions for violent and abusive behaviour. The general deterrence provided by heavier sentences is also open to question.

Denunciation is the strongest element in this law, reflected back in the powerful sense of stigma said to be felt by many defendants. But leaving court feeling predominantly stigmatised is not helpful. Research connects stigma with anger, alienation, and rejection of the tribunal's ethical position. It is likely to encourage recidivism, unless there is some process to resolve the shame.

II.e.   Reforming offences against the person

As we have seen, offence definitions – ie 'the law' – do not necessarily match up with the actual practices of criminal justice. Nor do official statistics represent actual levels of offending. The Home Office conducts regular British Crime Surveys. These involve questioning in depth a cross-section of the population asking them to report their own offending and their victimisation.

Home Office, *Crime in England and Wales 2001/2* (2002), Ch 6

The BCS estimates that there were 2,891,000 violent incidents experienced by adults in England and Wales … The BCS violence estimate has fallen 17 per cent since 1999 and by 22 per cent since 1997, both falls being statistically significant. There were 812,954 violent crimes recorded by the police in 2001/02, an increase of 11 per cent since 2000/01. The numbers of recorded violence against the person offences increased by eight per cent … The increase in violent crime recorded by the police, in contrast to the estimates from the BCS, appears to be largely due to increased recording by police forces. Taking into account recording changes, the real trend in violence against the person in 2001/02 is estimated to have been a reduction of around five per cent … Both police recorded crime and the BCS cover a wide range of violent offences, of varying levels of seriousness. Common assaults, that involve at most minimal injury, account for 62 per cent of BCS violence but only 32 per cent of police recorded violence. This reflects the relatively low recording and reporting rates for common assault. Police recorded violence also covers a generally wider category of offences including the most serious crimes, such as murder, but also many less serious offences …

The category of violent crime covers a wide range of different types of incidents, which generally have in common only that they involve actual violence or the threat of violence. The degree of violence will vary considerably, even between incidents within the same crime classification. It is important to remember that the large majority of the incidents categorised as violent crimes do not actually involve any significant injury to the victim, although many of the crimes not resulting in injury are still traumatic for their victims.

It has been estimated that only around a quarter of injuries from assaults result in attendance at hospital Accident and Emergency Departments (Shepherd and Lisles, 1998). However, incidents reported to the BCS in 2001/02 indicate that:

Fourteen per cent of BCS violent incidents result in medical attention from a doctor, with this percentage rising to 39 per cent of victims of wounding and 19 per cent for robbery victims. Two per cent of victims of common assault were seen by a doctor.

A survey by Clarkson et al (1994) examined not only the general attrition level for assaults, but also the relationship between the 'culpability' of the offender and the eventual punishment. They found that the main points of 'drop out' were: failure to inform police in the first place; no 'formal' complaint; failure to identify assailant and failure on the part of victims to sustain interest in the prosecution. What their study showed was that there was little relationship between the seriousness of the attack and the eventual criminalisation.

The three key stages are: (1) reporting (which is largely in the hands of the victim), (2) the police and CPS response and (3) any court proceedings. Reasons for victims' not reporting were that they believed the assailant could not be traced; they were 'marginalised' through drug use or homelessness and were accustomed to victimisation; they were reluctant to have their own conduct scrutinised; or the social costs were too high (ie they knew the assailant). As far as the police response goes, the more serious their perception of the offence, the more likely the police are to arrest; they assess the victim's credibility as a witness; and they determine whether it is a 'public' or 'private' matter. Lastly, aspects of the court process itself may contribute to the collapse of the case: for example, delays in bringing the case to court, the burden of the trial process on witnesses and the difficulty in discharging the burden of proof all contribute to lowering the conviction rate.

The role of the victim in the system is not straightforward:

A Cretney and G Davis, 'Prosecuting Domestic Assault: Victims Failing Courts, or Courts Failing Victims?' (1997) 36 Howard Journal of Criminal Justice 146

Normative accounts of the criminal justice process rest on the classic conception of crime as an offence against the sovereign authority, with the crime victim as the servant of the criminal justice process rather than its master. These normative accounts cannot be easily reconciled with the burdens placed upon assault victims at every stage of criminal prosecution burdens which the police implicitly recognise in that they respond not to violent conduct *per* se but to a 'complaint' from an 'aggrieved'. This may not matter greatly where victim and assailant are strangers to one another ... But most assaults involve people who are known to one another –

neighbours, customers of the same pub, regulars at the same night shelter, members of the same drugs scene ... assault victims are permitted to exercise a power of veto over the prosecution; and as far as domestic assault is concerned, so much so the police anticipate that this power will in due course be exercised that they give every opportunity to victims to withdraw their co-operation at the outset. [*See **Chapter 6** further on domestic violence.*]

An important element of discretion, as we have already suggested in relation to public order offences, concerns the choice of charge. Stalking is a good example. A number of different criminal laws could have been invoked in a case such as *Burstow*, including improper use of a public telecommunications system, malicious communication and public nuisance. None of these captures the seriousness of the harm caused in those cases where the victim develops a psychiatrically recognised condition. As a result, charges for assault occasioning actual bodily harm and maliciously inflicting grievous bodily harm under the 1861 Act have become increasingly common. The Charging Standards for Offences against the Person issued in 1994 are more enlightening than the offences themselves in distinguishing between different injuries. They encourage bottom-slicing so that assaults which could theoretically sustain a charge under s 47 (assault occasioning actual bodily harm) are charged in fact as common assault. The standards raise serious questions about the legitimacy of 'law' (in the form of legislation and case law), and formally acknowledge the broad discretions available at many stages of the criminal justice process.

Editorial 'Charging Standards: Offences against the Person' [1994] Crim LR 777

The purposes of the standards are twofold: to improve fairness to defendants, through greater uniformity of approach to charging, and to reduce administrative burdens in the criminal justice system by ensuring that appropriate charges are laid at the outset ...

The potential importance of the standards is quickly established when they tackle the borderline between common assault/battery and assault occasioning actual bodily harm: 'Although any injury can be classified as actual bodily harm, the appropriate charge will be contrary to section 39 [battery] where injuries amount to no more than the following – grazes, scratches, abrasions, minor bruising, swellings, reddening of the skin, superficial cuts, a black eye.'

... After dealing with assaults on the police, the standards then turn to assault occasioning actual bodily harm, contrary to section 47. Examples of the types of injury that fall appropriately under section 47 are given: loss or breaking of tooth; temporary loss of sensory functions; extensive or multiple bruising; displaced broken nose; minor fractures; minor cuts; psychiatric injury which is more than fear, distress or panic.

... In relation to sections 20 and 47, the standards give the following examples of grievous bodily harm: injury resulting in permanent disability or permanent loss of sensory function; injury which results in more than minor permanent, visible disfigurement; broken or displaced limbs or bones ... ; injuries which cause substantial loss of blood ... ; injuries resulting in lengthy treatment or incapacity.

In the case of psychiatric injury, expert evidence is required.

The mode of trial is important too. Many of those charged and tried on indictment end up with basic common assault convictions (see Table 1 in Home Office Research Bulletin No 37, 1995, p 67). The National Mode of Trial Guidelines (discussed above) suggest the following criteria for trial on indictment for ss 20 and 47 offences:

1. The use of weapons of a kind likely to cause serious injury.
2. A weapon is used and serious injury is caused.
3. More than minor injury is caused by kicking, head butting or similar forms of assault.
4. Serious violence is caused to those whose work has to be done in contact with the public eg police officers, bus drivers, taxi drivers, publicans and shopkeepers.
5. Violence to vulnerable people eg the elderly and infirm.

The same considerations apply to cases of domestic violence.

The implementation of these guidelines has led to a decrease in the number of wounding and assault offences tried on indictment (Home Office 1996: 28).

Adopting the Law Commission's recommendation for a neater tier of offences (Report No 218, 1993), the Home Office published a draft Bill in 1998.

Home Office, *Violence – Reforming the Offences Against the Person Act 1861* (Consultation Paper, 1998)

Draft Offences Against the Person Bill

Injury and assault

1(1) A person is guilty of an offence if he intentionally causes serious injury to another.
(2) A person is guilty of an offence if he omits to do an act which he has a duty to do at common law, the omission results in serious injury to another, and he intends the omission to have that result.
(3) An offence under this section is committed notwithstanding that the injury occurs outside England and Wales if the act causing injury is done in England and Wales or the omission resulting in injury is made there.

(4) A person guilty of an offence under this section is liable on conviction on indictment to imprisonment for life.

2(1) A person is guilty of an offence if he recklessly causes serious injury to another.

(2) An offence under this section is committed notwithstanding that the injury occurs outside England and Wales if the act causing injury is done in England and Wales.

(3) A person guilty of an offence under this section is liable–

    (a) on conviction on indictment, to imprisonment for a term not exceeding 7 years;

    (b) on summary conviction, to imprisonment for a term not exceeding 6 months or a fine not exceeding the statutory maximum or both.

3(1) A person is guilty of an offence if he intentionally or recklessly causes injury to another.

(2) An offence under this section is committed notwithstanding that the injury occurs outside England and Wales if the act causing injury is done in England and Wales.

(3) A person guilty of an offence under this section is liable–

    (a) on conviction on indictment, to imprisonment for a term not exceeding 5 years;

    (b) on summary conviction, to imprisonment for a term not exceeding 6 months or a fine not exceeding the statutory maximum or both.

4(1) A person is guilty of an offence if–

    (a) he intentionally or recklessly applies force to or causes an impact on the body of another, or

    (b) he intentionally or recklessly causes the other to believe that any such force or impact is imminent.

(2) No such offence is committed if the force or impact, not being intended or likely to cause injury, is in the circumstances such as is generally acceptable in the ordinary conduct of daily life and the defendant does not know or believe that it is in fact unacceptable to the other person.

(3) A person guilty of an offence under this section is liable on summary conviction to imprisonment for a term not exceeding 6 months or a fine not exceeding level 5 on the standard scale or both.

5(1) A person is guilty of an offence if he assaults–

    (a) a constable acting in the execution of his duty, or

    (b) a person assisting a constable acting in the execution of his duty.

(2) For the purposes of this section a person assaults if he commits the offence under section 4.

(3) A reference in this section to a constable acting in the execution of his duty includes a reference to a constable who is a member of a police

force maintained in Scotland or Northern Ireland when he is executing a warrant, or otherwise acting in England and Wales, by virtue of an enactment conferring powers on him in England and Wales.

...

(5) A person guilty of an offence under this section is liable on summary conviction to imprisonment for a term not exceeding 6 months or a fine not exceeding level 5 on the standard scale or both.

6(1) A person is guilty of an offence under this section if he causes serious injury to another intending to resist, prevent or terminate the lawful arrest or detention of himself or a third person.

(2) The question whether the defendant believes the arrest or detention is lawful must be determined according to the circumstances as he believes them to be.

(3) A person guilty of an offence under this section is liable on conviction on indictment to imprisonment for life.

7(1) A person is guilty of an offence if he assaults another intending to resist, prevent or terminate the lawful arrest or detention of himself or a third person.

(2) The question whether the defendant believes the arrest or detention is lawful must be determined according to the circumstances as he believes them to be.

(3) For the purposes of this section a person assaults if he commits the offence under section 4.

(4) A person guilty of an offence under this section is liable–
   (a) on conviction on indictment, to imprisonment for a term not exceeding 2 years;
   (b) on summary conviction, to imprisonment for a term not exceeding 6 months or a fine not exceeding the statutory maximum or both.

Meaning of fault terms and of injury

14(1) A person acts intentionally with respect to a result if–
   (a) it is his purpose to cause it, or
   (b) although it is not his purpose to cause it, he knows that it would occur in the ordinary course of events if he were to succeed in his purpose of causing some other result.

(2) A person acts recklessly with respect to a result if he is aware of a risk that it will occur and it is unreasonable to take that risk having regard to the circumstances as he knows or believes them to be.

(3) A person intends an omission to have a result if–
   (a) it is his purpose that the result will occur, or
   (b) although it is not his purpose that the result will occur, he knows that it would occur in the ordinary course of events if he were to succeed in his purpose that some other result will occur.

(4) A person is reckless whether an omission will have a result if he is aware of a risk that the result will occur and it is unreasonable to take that risk having regard to the circumstances as he knows or believes them to be.

(5) Related expressions must be construed accordingly.

(6) This section has effect for the purposes of this Act.

15(1) In this Act "injury" means–
   (a) physical injury, or
   (b) mental injury.

(2) Physical injury does not include anything caused by disease but (subject to that) it includes pain, unconsciousness and any other impairment of a person's physical condition.

(3) Mental injury does not include anything caused by disease but (subject to that) it includes any impairment of a person's mental health.

(4) In its application to section 1 this section applies without the exceptions relating to things caused by disease.

Although this scheme is undoubtedly neater and more rational than the 1861 Act, it nonetheless attempts the same basic equation, reflecting both seriousness of the injury caused and the culpability in terms of intention or recklessness accompanying that injury. 'Injury' is widely defined which may leave the same need for Charging Standards to ensure that injuries at the bottom end of the band are charged as assaults rather than one of the injury offences. Horder has mounted a strong attack on the proposed scheme as 'morally sterilized' in conflating such a wide range of possible injuries into such a small range of offences (Horder 1994). In tidying up the house, the Law Commission and the Home Office may have left a skeleton or two in the cupboards.

FURTHER READING

Burney, Elizabeth and Rose, Gerry (2002) *Racist Offences – how is the law working?* (Home Office Research Study 244).

Genders, Elaine (1999) 'Reform of the Offences against the Person Act: Lessons from the Law in Action' Crim LR 689.

Horder, Jeremy (1994) 'Rethinking Non-fatal Offences Against the Person' 14 OJLS 335.

— (1998) 'Reconsidering Psychic Assault' Crim LR 392.

Maguire, Mike (2002) 'Crime Statistics, The "Data Explosion" and Its Implications' in Maguire et al (eds) *The Oxford Handbook of Criminology* (Oxford University Press) p 322.

Malik, Michale (1999) '"Racist crime": Racially Aggravated Offences in the Crime and Disorder Act 1998 Part II' 62 Modern Law Review 409.

Phillips, Coretta and Bowling, Ben (2002) 'Racism, Ethnicity, and Criminal Justice' in Maguire et al (eds) *The Oxford Handbook of Criminology* (Oxford University Press) p 679.

III. Drugs and alcohol: legal constructions of a social problem

III.a. Drug and alcohol control

The legal regulation of drugs and alcohol is instructive as an example of the legal response to, and construction of, a 'social problem'. This particular 'social problem' periodically generates moral panics which result in, and rely upon, the representation of offenders as 'dangerous' and of the relevant activities as presenting a *general* threat to crime control and to 'law and order'. A number of specific questions can be raised about the criminal regulation of drugs and alcohol. Notable among these are the uneven 'mens rea' requirements under the Misuse of Drugs Act 1971, and in particular the arbitrary distinction between alcohol and other drugs. This division is especially contestable given the facts that alcohol has greater addictive qualities than some of the proscribed drugs under the Misuse of Drugs Act 1971, and is arguably more strongly associated with health and social problems in the UK than is, for example, cannabis (Husak 2002).

The Home Office's Updated Drug Strategy places the emphasis on discouraging the supply and use of Class A drugs such as heroin, crack, cocaine and ecstasy. The investigation and confiscation powers in the Proceeds of Crime Act 2002 (building on the Drug Trafficking Act 1994), the establishment of the Recovered Assets Fund, and the focus on international trafficking all point to the need to look beyond the enforcement of offences in the 1971 Act if we are to have a balanced view of drug regulation in Britain.

III.a.i. The nature of the problem

Drug and alcohol (ab)use is currently regarded, in the UK and beyond, as a severe social problem. Alcohol is associated, as we have seen with football hooliganism, youth disorder and violence. It is estimated that 40% of violent crime, 78% of assaults and 88% of criminal damage cases are committed while the offender is under the influence of alcohol (South 2002; Home Office 2003b). There are many specific offences associated with alcohol and drug use. While alcohol is lawfully available but regulated, the possession of many drugs is prohibited. A large number of people come into the criminal justice system through alcohol-specific offences, for example being drunk and disorderly in public, and offences against the licensing laws, such as selling or serving alcohol to under-age drinkers. In the case of illegal drugs, in addition to criminalisation through offences of possession and supply, drug use is financed through theft, robbery, burglary and other offences.

The number of people in prison for drugs offences has multiplied rapidly in the last 20 years. Between 1991 and 2001 alone the number more than tripled, from 2850 to 9050. Of these, 3000 were for unlawful supply, 2450 for possession with intent to supply, 2700 for unlawful import or export and 600 for posses-sion. The rate of increase for female offenders has been even more marked: the 1132 women in prison for drug offences in 2001 showed a 20% increase on the previous year (Home Office 2003a: Table 1.7A). Of all women in prison, 30% are there for drugs offences; of female foreign nationals in prison, that propor-tion increases to 81%. At 19%, the proportion of the female prison population who are foreign nationals and mostly 'drug mules' shows no signs of easing (Home Office 2003a: Ch 6). Prison itself produces yet more drug offenders: it has been estimated that a total 525,870 days were added to prison sentences as the result of positive mandatory drugs tests (Simmons 2002: 6).

There are three main strands to the 'drugs debate'. One is that it is morally wrong to use them; the second is that their use is harmful; and the third that there is an association between drug or alcohol abuse and criminal behaviour. In relation to each of these strands, some differentiation between hard and soft drugs is often made.

The proper role of criminal law in enforcing *moral values* has always generated a lively debate. To what extent should criminal law attempt to reflect moral values or to influence moral attitudes? How effectively can it enforce contested moral views? And should punishment be reserved for those who are 'blame-worthy'?

The moral argument may be difficult to sustain in the light of increasing evidence that drug use is normal rather than 'deviant'. Some argue a thesis of 'normalisation', ie that there are now very few groups of young people who are anti drug use. Over a quarter of 16- to 24-year-olds reported that they had used cannabis in the last year, while those who report use of ecstasy (6.8%), amphetamines (5%) or Class A drugs in general (8.8%) is significantly lower (Aust et al 2002).

Arguments about the *harm* of drugs are also difficult to sustain, especially in the light of the availability of alcohol, which is harmful in excess, and tobacco, which is harmful in itself. Increasingly, the argument for legalising cannabis is made on medical grounds, that it is a drug which, far from being harmful, should be available for some treatments. Although medical use does not necessarily equate with safe recreational use, official attitudes have softened towards it in the last decade. This leads to the third strand of the debate, that drug use leads to crime. The association with crime is complex.

Nigel South 'Drugs, Alcohol and Crime' in Maguire et al (eds) *The Oxford Handbook of Criminology* (Oxford University Press, 2002) p 933

Debate about the drugs/crime relationship generally follow one or other of the following propositions: 'criminal lifestyles may facilitate involvement with drugs'; or 'dependence on drugs then leads to criminal activity to pay for further drug use' ... Typically drug-related crime is non-violent and acquisitive, involving theft, shop-lifting, forgery, burglary, or prostitution. More serious drug-related crimes of violence, murder, large-scale trafficking and money-laundering have been increasing in Britain ...

Some studies provide evidence that heroin or other serious drug users would already have been involved in delinquent or criminal activities before they started using these drugs ...

Of course, other studies argue that there *is* a *causal* link, and that drug use (particularly of heroin) causes crime ... The simple resolution of this debate is to agree with Nurco et al (1985), who sensibly argue that 'the long and continuing controversy over whether narcotic addicts commit crimes primarily to support their habits, or whether addictions are merely one more manifestation of a deviant and criminal life-style seems pointless in view of the fact that addicts cannot be regarded as a homogeneous group.'

[I]t is alcohol rather than illegal drugs that tends to be linked to aggression and violent crimes ... Nonetheless it remains the common conclusion of such research that the existence of a causal relationship between alcohol and violent crime is difficult to substantiate ... Research findings suggest that a variety of co-factors may play a significant role in alcohol-related aggression. As with illegal drug consumption, *belief* about how alcohol is 'supposed' to affect behaviour, *coupled* with the influences of immediate social context and wider culture are as important for the behavioural outcome as the amount of alcohol consumed.

A further element in the debate is the alleged *pathway* from soft to hard drug use:

H Parker, 'Adolescent Drugs Pathways in the 1990s' in J Braggins, *Tackling Drugs Together: One Year On* (ISTD, 1997) p 19

There is no relationship whatsoever, other than breaking the Misuse of Drugs Act, between youthful drug use and crime [and the government in the 1995 White Paper *Tackling Drugs Together* has confused] heroin use and crime in the 80s with recreational drug use and young people in the 90s.

... [W]hat are the key drug arenas at the moment? Of course there are several million alcohol, tobacco and cannabis users, but the scene I am talking about today is 'adolescent recreational drug use'. Then at the end, because the cohort study I will talk about are 18 years old this year, they are moving into the young adult, rave party, university, staying out all night, not telling your parents where you are, scene, I think we ought to look at the young adult drug scene as well. Obviously Ecstasy (MDMA) is prominent here, though I will suggest that cocaine is now slipping into this arena. There are also the 80s/90s heavy heroin lifestyles. That is where the drug/crime connection is strongest. And I think there is another issue about poly-drug use, led on by crack or rock cocaine. What we found in our study was that the crack cocaine users ... were poly-drug users, and whilst they used crack cocaine as their primary drug, they used heroin to manage the come-down effect.

We conducted a five-year study of 550 young people from the age of 14 ... There are four very clear groups. There are *current drug users [22%]*, most of whom have been using drugs for two or three years; a lovely little group called *ex-users [10%]*, who tried experimenting or using drugs at 14 or 15, and have now decided drugs are not for them ... ; a group that we call *in transition [33%]*, which is a large group: they may or may not have tried drugs but they do not regard themselves as drug-users, they do not use drugs regularly; and there are some who have not used drugs, but what they have in common is that they think that they will use drugs in the future ... the fourth group is *abstainers [35%]*, who have never tried an illicit drug and do not expect to in the future ...

Normalisation does not mean that it is normal for all young people to take drugs. It means that those who do not take drugs accept those who do, and accept that drugs are around and do not call the police or tell the teachers ...

My conclusion is that while a lot of recreational drug users will get drugs to fit into the rhythms of their life, a minority will turn out to be problem users. The problems will be greater because more drugs are available and because their expectations of what these drugs can do are much greater ... The drinks industry might not like this but if you are looking for a gateway drug to drug use it is alcohol.

A recent Home Office study is also sceptical about the pathway from recreational soft drugs use to hard drug addiction (Pudney 2002). It concludes that the proposed reclassification of cannabis from Class B to Class C under the Misuse of Drugs Act is unlikely to lead more young people to progress to more harmful drugs. The origins of anti-drug legislation lie in pragmatism and social policy rather than in moral zeal (Ward and Dobinson 1988; Duster 1970). The history of criminal regulation of drugs in the UK suggests an intimate, if complex, relationship between law and social morality.

III.a.ii. Prohibition and regulation

A wide range of criminal laws and processes impinges upon the use of alcohol and drugs. Criminal laws regulate the way in which specified drugs they may be sold, imported or supplied. Licensing regulations control when, where, by whom and for what purposes alcohol may be consumed or supplied.

The Misuse of Drugs Act 1971 contains the main provisions on the possession and supply of controlled drugs. 'Controlled drugs' are divided into three classes: Class A includes cocaine, LSD, mescaline and opium; included in Class B are amphetamine and codeine, while Class C includes benzphetamine and pemoline.

Section 5 contains the offence of possession. Under s 4 a number of modes of misuse are detailed: producing, supplying or offering to supply. The maximum penalty for production or supply of Class A drugs is now life imprisonment, which brings it into line with the penalty for importing drugs (Customs and Excise Management Act 1979, s 170). It is also an offence under s 8 for a person knowingly to allow their premises to be used for the production, supply or consumption of controlled drugs.

As explained in *Carrera*, below, there has been a fundamental reconsideration of these offences in the light of the Human Rights Act 1998. In *Lambert* (2001), the House of Lords held that s 28 should no longer be interpreted as placing upon the defendant the burden of proving that she did not know suspect nor have reason to suspect that she was in possession of a controlled drug.

R v Carrera [or *Lozano*] [2002] EWCA Crim 2527

Lord Justice Pill.

[T]he appellant ... was convicted ... of an offence of possessing a class B controlled drug (cannabis resin) with intent to supply [and] sentenced to five years' imprisonment. He appeals against conviction ... [He] is a Spanish national who earned his living as a self- employed haulier renting and driving his own lorry. He came to Britain from Spain once a week delivering goods and returned to Spain with goods supplied in this country by regular agents and contacts. [The police] discovered nine boxes containing 162 kilogrammes of cannabis resin with a street value of almost £1 million.

...

The jury found the appellant not guilty on the count alleging importation. The judge also directed the jury as to count 2. ..."That says that the defendant, on 3rd December 1999, had in his possession a controlled drug of class B, namely cannabis resin, with intent to supply it to a person or persons unknown, in contravention of section 4(1) of the Misuse of Drugs Act 1971". The judge then stated the ingredients of the charge, namely possession and intention to supply. He continued his direction:

> "So far as possession is concerned, firstly, the initial burden of proving that the defendant had and knew that he had boxes in his control in his lorry and that the boxes contained something is upon the prosecution. That establishes the necessary possession. The prosecution must also prove that the boxes contained cannabis resin.

Secondly, if these matters are proved then it is for the defence, for the defendant, to prove that he neither knew of nor suspected, nor had reason to suspect that cannabis resin was in the boxes. The law is that that is a matter for him to prove on all the evidence.

Whenever the law requires a defendant to prove something he does not have to make you sure of it. He has to show that it is probably, which means he is more likely than not, that he did not know or suspect he was carrying cannabis resin. If you decide he did not know or suspect he was carrying cannabis resin you find him not guilty.

If you decide he did know or suspect he was carrying cannabis resin, then providing the prosecution has made you sure of what it has to prove, you must find him guilty."

Since the trial, in the case of *Lambert* [2001] 3 WLR 206, the House of Lords has held that in the light of the Human Rights Act 1998 the law as to burden of proof is not in this context as it had previously been understood to be. That in this context is the combined effect of sections 4, 5 and 28 of the Misuse of Drugs Act 1971. Section 28(2) provides:

"Subject to subsection (3) below, in any proceedings for an offence to which the section applies it shall be a defence for the accused to prove that he neither knew of nor suspected nor had reason to suspect the existence of some fact alleged by the prosecution which it is necessary for the prosecution to prove if he is to be convicted of the offence charged.

(3) Where in any proceedings for an offence to which this section applies it is necessary, if the accused is to be convicted of the offence charged, for the prosecution to prove that some substance or product involved in the alleged offence was the controlled drug which the prosecution alleges it to have been, and it is proved that the substance or product in question was that controlled drug, the accused–

(a) shall not be acquitted of the offence charged by reason only of proving that he neither knew nor suspected nor had reason to suspect that the substance or product in question was the particular controlled drug alleged; but

(b) shall be acquitted thereof– (i) if he proves that he neither believed nor suspected nor had reason to suspect that the substance or product in question was a controlled drug; or (ii) if he proves that he believed the substance or product in question to be a controlled drug, or a controlled drug of a description, such that, if it had in fact been that controlled drug or a controlled drug of that description, he would not at the material time have been committing any offence to which this section applies."

In *Lambert* Lord Hope stated at paragraph 94:

"I would therefore read the words 'to prove' in section 28(2) as if the words used in the subsection were 'to give sufficient evidence', and I would give the same meaning to the words 'if he proves' in section 28(3). The effect which is to be given to this meaning is that the burden of proof remains on the prosecution throughout. If sufficient evidence is adduced to raise the issue, it will be for the prosecution to show beyond reasonable doubt that the defence is not made out by the evidence. ..."

As to the burden of proof, [Lord Clyde] also referred, at paragraph 157, to the test laid down in the House of Lords in *Warner* [1969] 2 AC 256 and referred to its undue harshness. He added:

"It seems to me that the proper way by which that harshness should be alleviated is to recognise that the accused should have the opportunity to raise the issue of his knowledge but to leave the persuasive burden of proof throughout on the prosecution. Respect for the 'golden thread' of the presumption of innocence deserves no less."

At paragraph 43 Lord Steyn stated:

"... this is a case of an accused found in possession of two kilograms of cocaine worth over £140,000. It must be comparatively rare for a drug dealer to entrust such a valuable parcel of drugs to an innocent. In any event the appellant's detailed story stretches judicial credibility beyond breaking-point. Even if the judge had directed the jury in accordance with law as I have held it to be the appellant's conviction would have been a foregone conclusion."

The detailed story is not set out in the speeches, understandably as they were concerned with the important legal point which had been raised, and it is impossible to make a comparison of the detailed story in the present case with that in *Lambert*. In any event, each case must turn on its particular facts and the importance of the direction on the burden of proof considered in that context. We would however begin with the proposition that the burden of proof is a matter of fundamental importance. That appears from Article 6(2) of the Convention:

"Everyone charged with a criminal offence shall be presumed innocent until proved guilty according to law."

It follows from that, in our view, that a lawful direction to a jury upon the burden of proof is a matter of fundamental importance. In two cases since *Lambert* this court has rejected the submission which succeeded in *Lambert* that the conviction was a foregone conclusion and that the appeal could be dismissed on that ground ...

There is no doubt that the appellant in his evidence raised the question of his knowledge so that, in accordance with the decision of the House of Lords, the burden of proof was upon the prosecution with respect to the appellant's knowledge. Having considered the evidence and submissions, we are not satisfied that the jury would inevitably have reached the same conclusion as they did on count 2. We see the force of the prosecution case and its strength but, having regard to the fundamental importance of the burden of proof, as highlighted by their Lordships, a verdict adverse to the appellant upon a proper direction was not inevitable.

We bear in mind that the appellant was a regular carrier of goods. This was not a case where boxes were found in a vehicle or at a place where boxes would not be expected to be. The jury were entitled to consider his evidence on the basis of the presumption of innocence. Moreover the primary case for the prosecution was that the appellant had imported the drugs. Since the drugs came from Morocco, and Spain is between Morocco and the United Kingdom, it is not surprising that the case was put on that basis. If there was guilty knowledge then a court would certainly start on the assumption that the goods were being brought into this country from Spain. However, on count 1 the appellant was acquitted. The obvious explanation, if there was guilty knowledge, was rejected by them. They must, in our view, have given some credibility to his denial that he had imported the drugs. They went on to convict on the alternative basis, although not put as an alternative, nor need it have been, that he took possession of the Moroccan drugs in the United Kingdom with the intent either of supplying them here or back in Spain where there is no doubt he was intending to go.

The question where the burden of proof was may well have determined, or at least there is a real possibility that it would have determined, on the particular facts, the verdict of the jury on count 2. Had they been given a proper direction, the possibility that they would have acquitted cannot, in our view, properly be excluded. We only add that following *Lambert* there may well be further debate as to the extent of the burden on the prosecution given the wording of section 28(2) and (3), but it is not necessary or appropriate to conduct that debate in order to resolve this appeal.

For the reasons we have given and as indicated at the close of the hearing last evening, the appeal is allowed and the conviction quashed. [A request for a retrial was not granted.]

Penalties are on a sliding scale depending on the classification (A, B or C) of the drug in question. The Government proposes to reclassify cannabis from B to C in 2003, but has rejected a recommendation that ecstasy be reduced from A to B (Advisory Council on the Misuse of Drugs 2002).

A Ashworth, *Sentencing and Criminal Justice* (Butterworths, 2000) p 107

Offences involving the importation or supply of prohibited drugs rank high in the current English scale of ordinal proportionality. They were the subject of the first of Lord Lane's guideline judgments in *Aramah* (1982). Since then, Parliament has increased the maximum penalty under the Misuse of Drugs Act 1971 from 14 years, to life imprisonment, and the *Aramah* guidelines have been revised and progressively replaced by specific guidelines on different types of drugs ... The general approach in sentencing is to distinguish between importation, supply and mere possession, and to distinguish between drugs in classes A, B, and C.

Aroyewumi (1994) deals with trafficking Class A drugs such as heroin and cocaine and recommends 10 years for 500g and 14 years for 5kg. Guidelines for ecstasy are found in *Warren and Beeley* (1996) and for cannabis in *Ronchetti* (1998). The suggested sentence for 100kg of cannabis is seven to eight years, and 10 for 500kg. Under the 'three strikes' law introduced in 1997, a minimum sentence of seven years' imprisonment is mandatory on the third conviction for a Class A drug trafficking offence (Powers of Criminal Courts and Sentencing Act 2000, s 110). However, this is not any more than is indicated in the guidelines.

Although alcohol is legally available, its distribution and consumption is nonetheless subject to extensive regulation. Some laws concern use in general; many others regulate use in specific contexts – for instance, while driving (Road Traffic Act 1988), while attending sporting events (Sporting Events (Control of Alcohol) Act 1985) or when under 18. The Licensing (Young Persons) Act 2000 made it an offence for any person to sell alcohol to an under-18 on licensed premises, or knowingly to allow another person to do so. And it creates the offence of buying, or attempting to buy, alcohol on licensed premises on behalf of an under-18. The Confiscation of Alcohol (Young Persons) Act 1997 gave police powers to confiscate alcohol from under-age drinkers in public places. We can note in passing the use of an ASBO to ban a man from buying or consuming alcohol anywhere in England and Wales for three years (*The Guardian*, 24 December 2002). Building on the provisions in the Criminal Justice and Police Act 2001, the Home office has identified a number of strategies to 'tackle alcohol-related' crime (2003b). Penalty notices (on-the-spot fines) were introduced in 2003. The scheme is targeted at low-level anti-social behaviour which typically occurs late at night at weekends, which is often drink-related and is applicable to those aged 18 or over.

III.b.   Intoxication and criminal responsibility

Another area of great significance is criminal law's response to defendants who seek to excuse themselves from liability on the basis of intoxication, whether from alcohol or other drugs. As a question of 'general principle', orthodox doctrine would seem to indicate that intoxication should remove liability whenever it prevents the formation of 'mens rea'; that is, where it has meant that the defendant did not have the requisite intention, foresight, knowledge or belief. However, 'self-induced' intoxication may not be pleaded in this way in most cases.

The judicial history of this rule affords a classic illustration of the malleability of doctrinal principles:

Director of Public Prosecutions v Majewski [1977] AC 443, HL

Lord Elwyn-Jones LC.

... Robert Stefan Majewski appeals against his conviction on 7 November 1973, at Chelmsford Crown Court on three counts of assault occasioning actual bodily harm and three counts of assault on a police constable in the execution of his duty. He was bound over to come up for judgment when called upon. On 5 December 1973, he was placed on probation for three years. Later he committed a further offence for which he was given an additional sentence of six months' imprisonment for the original offences.

The appellant's case was that when the assaults were committed he was acting under the influence of a combination of drugs (not medically prescribed) and alcohol, to such an extent that he did not know what he was doing and that he remembered nothing of the incidents that had occurred. After medical evidence had been called by the defence as to the effect of the drugs and drink the appellant had taken, the learned judge, in the absence of the jury, ruled that he would direct the jury that on the charges of assault or assault occasioning actual bodily harm, the question of whether he had taken drink or drugs was immaterial. The learned judge directed the jury that in relation to an offence not requiring a specific intent, the fact that a man has induced in himself a state in which he is under the influence of drink and drugs, is no defence. Since the counts for assault did not require proof of any specific intent the fact that the accused might have taken drink or drugs was irrelevant, provided the jury was satisfied that the state which he was in as a result of drink and drugs or a combination of both was self-induced. He concluded ' ... upon my direction in law you can ignore the subject of drink and drugs as being in any way a defence to any or more of the counts in this indictment.' In dealing with assault, he directed that it meant some blow or kick, 'not something which is purely accidental' ...

The Court of Appeal dismissed the appeal against conviction but granted leave to appeal to your Lordships' House certifying that the following point of law of general public importance was involved:

> Whether a defendant may properly be convicted of assault notwithstanding that, by reason of his self-induced intoxication, he did not intend to do the act alleged to constitute the assault ...

Self-induced alcoholic intoxication has been a factor in crimes of violence, like assault, throughout the history of crime in this country. But voluntary drug taking with the potential and actual dangers to others it may cause has added a new dimension to the old problem with which the courts have had to deal in their endeavour to maintain order and to keep public and private violence under control. To achieve this is the prime purpose of the criminal law ...

[The] case for the appellant was that there was no such substantive rule of law and that if there was, it did violence to logic and ethics and to fundamental principles of the criminal law which had been evolved to determine when and where criminal responsibility should arise. His main propositions were as follows:

1. No man is guilty of a crime (save in relation to offences of strict liability) unless he has a guilty mind.
2. A man who, though not insane, commits what would in ordinary circumstances be a crime when he is in such a mental state (whether it is called 'automatism' or 'pathological intoxication' or anything else) that he does not know what he is doing, lacks a guilty mind and is not criminally culpable for his actions.
3. This is so whether the charge involves a specific (or 'ulterior') intent or one involving only a general (or 'basic') intent.
4. The same principle applies whether the automatism was the result of causes beyond the control of the accused or was self-induced by the voluntary taking of drugs or drink.
5. Assaults being crimes involving a guilty mind, a man who in a state of automatism unlawfully assaults another must be regarded as free from blame and be entitled to acquittal.
6. It is logically and ethically indefensible to convict a man of assault; it also contravenes s 8 of the Criminal Justice Act 1967.
7. There was accordingly a fatal misdirection ...

What then is the mental element required in our law to be established in assault? This question has been most helpfully answered in the speech of Lord Simon of Glaisdale in *R v Morgan* (1976) at 216:

By 'crimes of basic intent' I mean those crimes whose definition expresses (or, more often, implies) a mens rea which does not go beyond the actus reus. The actus reus generally consists of an act and some consequence. The consequence may be very closely connected with the act or more remotely connected with it: but with a crime of basic intent the mens rea does not extend beyond the act and its consequence, however remote, as defined in the actus reus. I take assault as an example of a crime of basic intent where the consequence is very closely connected with the act. The actus reus of assault is an act which causes another person to apprehend immediate and unlawful violence. The mens rea corresponds exactly. The prosecution must prove that the accused foresaw that his act would probably cause another person to have apprehension of immediate and unlawful violence, or would possibly have that consequence, such being the purpose of the act, or that he was reckless as to whether or not his act caused such apprehension. This foresight (the term of art is "intention") or recklessness is the mens rea in assault. For an example of a crime of basic intent where the consequence of the act involved in the actus reus as defined in the crime is less immediate, I take the crime of unlawful wounding. The act is, say, the squeezing of a trigger. A number of consequences (mechanical, chemical, ballistic and physiological) intervene before the final consequence involved in the defined actus reus – namely, the wounding of another person in circumstances unjustified by law. But again here the mens rea corresponds closely to the actus reus. The prosecution must prove that the accused foresaw that some physical harm would ensue to another person in circumstances unjustified by law as a probable (or possible and desired) consequence of his act, or that he was reckless as to whether or not such consequence ensued.

How does the fact of self-induced intoxication fit into that analysis? If a man consciously and deliberately takes alcohol and drugs not on medical prescription, but in order to escape from reality, to go 'on a trip', to become hallucinated, whatever the description may be and thereby disables himself from taking the care he might otherwise take and as a result by his subsequent actions causes injury to another – does our criminal law enable him to say that because he did not know what he was doing he lacked both intention and recklessness and accordingly is entitled to an acquittal?

Originally the common law would not and did not recognise self-induced intoxication as an excuse. Lawton LJ [in the Court of Appeal] spoke of the 'merciful relaxation' to that rule which was introduced by the judges during the 19th century, and he added, at p. 411:

> Although there was much reforming zeal and activity in the 19th century, Parliament never once considered whether self-induced intoxication should be a defence generally to a criminal charge. It would have been a strange result if the merciful relaxation of a strict rule of law had ended, without any Parliamentary intervention, by whittling it away to such an extent that the more drunk a man became, provided he stopped short of making himself insane, the better chance he had of an acquittal ... The common law rule still applied but there were exceptions to it which Lord Birkenhead LC tried to define by reference to specific intent. ([1975] 3 WLR 401)

There are, however, decisions of eminent judges in a number of Commonwealth cases in Australia and New Zealand, (but generally not in

Canada nor in the United States) as well as impressive academic comment in this country, to which we have been referred, supporting the view that it is illogical and inconsistent with legal principle to treat a person who of his own choice and volition has taken drugs and drink, even though he thereby creates a state in which he is not conscious of what he is doing, any differently from a person suffering from the various medical conditions like epilepsy or diabetic coma and who is regarded by the law as free from fault. However our courts have for a very long time regarded in quite another light the state of self-induced intoxication. The authority which for the last half-century has been relied upon in this context has been the speech of the Earl of Birkenhead LC in *DPP v Beard* (1920) who stated, at 494:

> Under the law of England as it prevailed until early in the 19th century voluntary drunkenness was never an excuse for criminal misconduct; and indeed the classic authorities broadly assert that voluntary drunkenness must be considered rather an aggravation than a defence. This view was in terms based upon the principle that a man who by his own voluntary act debauches and destroys his will power shall be no better situated in regard to criminal acts than a sober man.
>
> ... I do not for my part regard that general principle as either unethical or contrary to the principles of natural justice. If a man of his own volition takes a substance which causes him to cast off the restraints of reason and conscience, no wrong is done to him by holding him answerable criminally for any injury he may do while in that condition. His course of conduct in reducing himself by drugs and drink to that condition in my view supplies the evidence of mens rea, of guilty mind certainly sufficient for crimes of basic intent. It is a reckless course of conduct and recklessness is enough to constitute the necessary mens rea in assault cases: see *R v Venna* (1976) per James LJ at 429 [*see section II.b. above*]. The drunkenness is itself an intrinsic, an integral part of the crime, the other part being the evidence of the unlawful use of force against the victim. Together they add up to criminal recklessness ...

This approach is in line with the American Model Penal Code (s.208(2)):

> When recklessness establishes an element of the offence, if the actor, due to self-induced intoxication, is unaware of a risk of which he would have been aware had he been sober, such unawareness is immaterial.

Acceptance generally of intoxication as a defence (as distinct from the exceptional cases where some additional mental element above that of ordinary mens rea has to be proved) would in my view undermine the criminal law and I do not think that it is enough to say, as did Mr Tucker, that we can rely on the good sense of the jury or of magistrates to ensure that the guilty are convicted ...

Lord Edmund-Davies.

The criticism by the academics of the law presently administered in this country is of a two-fold nature: (1) It is illogical and therefore inconsistent with legal principle to treat a person who of his own volition has taken drink or drugs any differently from a man suffering from some bodily or mental disorder of the kind earlier mentioned or whose beverage had, without his connivance, been 'laced' with intoxicants; (2) it is unethical to convict a man of a crime requiring a guilty state of mind when ex hypothesi, he lacked it. I seek to say something about each of these two criticisms.

(1) *Illogicality*

... The undeviating application of logic leads inexorably to the conclusion that a man behaving even as Lipman [1969] unquestionably did must be completely discharged from all criminal liability for the dreadful consequences of his conduct. It was, as I recall, submissions of this startling character which led my noble and learned friend, Lord Simon of Glaisdale, to comment trenchantly to appellant's counsel: 'it is all right to say "Let justice be done though the heavens fall." But you ask us to say "Let logic be done even though public order be threatened," which is something very different.'

Are the claims of logic, then, so compelling that a man behaving as the Crown witnesses testified the appellant did must be cleared of criminal responsibility? As to this, Lawton LJ said [at 411]:

> Although there was much reforming zeal and activity in the 19th century, Parliament never once considered whether self-induced intoxication should be a defence generally to a criminal charge. It would have been a strange result if the merciful relaxation of a strict rule of law had ended, without any Parliamentary intervention, by whittling it away to such an extent that the more drunk a man became, provided he stopped short of making himself insane, the better chance he had of an acquittal.

If such be the inescapable result of the strict application of logic in this branch of the law, it is indeed not surprising that illogicality has long reigned, and the prospect of its dethronement must be regarded as alarming.

(2) *Lack of Ethics*

It is sometimes said in such cases as the present that it is morally wrong to convict of a crime involving a certain state of mind even where it be established that the charge is based on a man's behaviour when he lacked that guilty mind. Rightly or wrongly, Coke was not of that view, for although he asserted that 'Actus non facit reum nisi mens sit rea' he also said that, so far from gross intoxication excusing crime, it aggravated the culpability.

Your Lordships are presently concerned with a public-house brawl, which is said to have been due to the ingestion of drugs rather than drink. Such a plea is becoming much more common, and those acting judicially or who have otherwise acquired any knowledge of addiction are familiar with such parlance of the drug scene as 'going on a trip' or 'blowing the mind', the avowed intention of the taker of hallucinatory drugs being to lose contact with reality. Irrationality is in truth the very essence of drug-induced phantasies.

Illogical though the present law may be, it represents a compromise between the imposition of liability upon inebriates in complete disregard of their condition (on the alleged ground that it was brought on voluntarily), and the total exculpation required by the defendant's actual state of mind at the time he committed the harm in issue. It is at this point pertinent to pause to consider why legal systems exist. The universal object of a system of law is obvious – the establishment and maintenance of order ...

For these reasons, I concur in holding that 'Yes' is the proper answer to the certified question and that, there having been no misdirection, the appeal should be dismissed. [Lord Diplock and Lord Kilbrandon concurred with the Lord Chancellor. Lord Russell of Killowen and Lord Salmon delivered separate judgments dismissing the appeal. The appeal was dismissed.]

In the case of voluntarily intoxicated defendants, therefore, the usual principles of responsibility do not apply. No link between 'actus reus' and 'mens rea' need be proven; the 'recklessness' in getting intoxicated is magically linked to the subsequent action in a way which defies doctrinal strictures. The significance of *Majewski* in effectively subjecting voluntarily intoxicated defendants to strict liability was noted and criticised by the High Court of Australia in *R v O'Connor* (1970). However, there has been a gradual reversion to the *Majewski* rule (via the Criminal Code Act 1995 which applies to Commonwealth offences and encourages model principles across the different Australian State jurisdictions). In his powerful 'internal' critique of *Majewski* in *O'Connor* Barwick CJ favoured the creation of an offence of reducing oneself to a non-responsible state. Since this would seem to constitute both an (allegedly 'exceptional') 'status' offence and to be an offence of strict liability to which the presumption of innocence would have scarcely more application than under the *Majewski* approach, this preferred solution was no more consistent with doctrinal values.

The lack of any clear rationale for the distinction between offences of basic and specific intent was acknowledged by the Court of Appeal in *O'Grady* below, in a context that extended rather than restricted the *Majewski* doctrine. Lord Lane suggested that voluntary intoxication may supply not only recklessness but also, where a defence is at issue, intent:

R v O'Grady [1987] 3 All ER 420, CA

[*The appellant was charged with murder but convicted by the jury of manslaughter. He had killed one of his friends during the night following a day in which they had both been drinking heavily. He claimed that he had woken to find his friend attacking him with a piece of glass and had responded in self-defence.*]

Lord Lane CJ.

... [The judge] gave the classic direction on self-defence. He made no mention of the possibility that the appellant might by reason of intoxication have been mistaken as to the threat posed to him ... This was no doubt because no-one had taken the point. Counsel for the prosecution ... saw fit to invite the judge to remedy what he plainly regarded as this lacuna in the charge to the jury ... The judge then gave this further direction:

> It might be a view that you take, I know not, that this defendant thought he was under attack from the other man mistakenly and made a mistake in thinking that he was under attack because of the drink that was in him. If he made such a mistake in drink he would nevertheless be entitled to defend himself even though he mistakenly believed that he was under attack. He would be entitled in those circumstances to defend himself. But if in taking defensive measures, then he went beyond what is reasonable either because his mind being affected by drink or for any other reason, then the defence of self-defence would not avail him because, as I told you earlier on, you are entitled to defend yourself if it is necessary to do so, but the defensive measures that you take must be reasonable ones and not go beyond what is reasonable.

... How should the jury be invited to approach the problem? One starts with the decision in *Williams* (1983), namely that where the defendant might have been labouring under a mistake as to the facts he must be judged according to that mistaken view, whether the mistake was reasonable or not. It is then for the jury to decide whether the defendant's reaction to the threat (real or imaginary) was a reasonable one. The court was not in that case considering what the situation might be where the mistake was due to voluntary intoxication by alcohol or some other drug.

[W]here the jury are satisfied that the defendant was mistaken in his belief that any force or the force which he in fact used was necessary to defend himself, and are further satisfied that the mistake was caused by voluntarily induced intoxication, the defence must fail. We do not consider that any distinction should be drawn on this aspect of the matter between offences involving what is called specific intent, such as murder, and offences of so-called basic intent, such as manslaughter. Quite apart from the problem of directing a jury in a case such as the present where manslaughter is an alternative verdict to murder, the question of mistake can and ought to be considered separately from the question of intent. A sober man who mistakenly believes he is in danger of immediate death at the hands of an attacker is entitled to be acquitted of both murder and manslaughter if his reaction in killing his supposed assailant was a reasonable one. What his intent may have been seems to us to be irrelevant to the problem of self-defence or no ...

This brings us to the question of public order. There are two competing interests. On the one hand the interest of the defendant who has only acted according to what he believed to be necessary to protect himself, and on the other hand that of the public in general and the victim in particular who, probably through no fault of his own, has been injured or perhaps killed because of the defendant's drunken mistake. Reason recoils from the conclusion that in such circumstances a defendant is entitled to leave the court without a stain on his character.

[The appeal was dismissed.]

It should be noted that the impact of *Majewski* in removing voluntary intoxication from the ambit of 'normal' principles of responsibility is diminished in offences which require proof of an 'objective' form of recklessness or negligence, as illustrated by the decision of the House of Lords in *Caldwell*:

R v Caldwell [1981] 1 All ER 961, HL

[*The respondent set fire to a hotel in pursuit of a grievance he had against its proprietor. There were 10 residents there at the time. The fire was discovered before any serious damage was done. He was charged, inter alia, with an offence under s 1(2) of the Criminal Damage Act 1971, which provides:*

A person who without lawful excuse destroys or damages any property, whether belonging to himself or another ...
(a) intending to destroy or damage any property or being reckless as to whether any property would be destroyed or damaged; and
(b) intending by the destruction or damage to endanger the life of another or being reckless as to whether the life of another would be thereby endangered;
shall be guilty of an offence.

The Court of Appeal certified the following point of appeal: whether evidence of self-induced intoxication can be relevant to the following questions – (a) whether the defendant intended to endanger the life of another; and (b) whether the defendant was reckless as to whether the life of another would be endangered, within the meaning of s 1(2)(b) of the Criminal Damage Act 1971.]

Lord Diplock.

… 'Reckless' as used in the new statutory definition of the mens rea of these offences is an ordinary English word. It had not by 1971 become a term of legal art with some more limited esoteric meaning than that which it bore in ordinary speech – a meaning which surely includes not only deciding to ignore a risk of harmful consequences resulting from one's acts that one has recognised as existing, but also failing to give any thought to whether or not there is any such risk in circumstances where, if any thought were given to the matter, it would be obvious that there was.

If one is attaching labels, the latter state of mind is neither more nor less 'subjective' than the first. But the label solves nothing. It is a statement of the obvious; mens rea is, by definition, a state of mind of the accused himself at the time he did the physical act that constitutes the actus reus of the offence; it cannot be the mental state of some non-existent, hypothetical person.

Nevertheless, to decide whether someone has been 'reckless' as to whether harmful consequences of a particular kind will result from his act, as distinguished from his actually intending such harmful consequences to follow, does call for some consideration of how the mind of the ordinary prudent individual would have reacted to a similar situation. If there were nothing in the circumstances that ought to have drawn the attention of an ordinary prudent individual to the possibility of that kind of harmful consequence, the accused would not be described as 'reckless' in the natural meaning of that word for failing to address his mind to the possibility; nor, if the risk of the harmful consequences was so slight that the ordinary prudent individual upon due consideration of the risk would not be deterred from treating it as negligible, could the accused be described as 'reckless' in its ordinary sense if, having considered the risk, he decided to ignore it. (In this connection the gravity of the possible harmful consequences would be an important factor. To endanger life must be one of the most grave.) So to this extent, even if one ascribes to 'reckless' only the restricted meaning, adopted by the Court of Appeal in *R v Stephenson* (1979) and *R v Briggs* (Note) (1977), of foreseeing that a particular kind of harm might happen and yet going on to take the risk of it, it involves a test that would be described in part as 'objective' in current legal jargon. Questions of criminal liability are seldom solved by simply asking whether the test is subjective or objective.

In my opinion, a person charged with an offence under s 1(1) of the Criminal Damage Act 1971 is 'reckless as to whether any such property would be destroyed or damaged' if (1) he does an act which in fact creates an obvious risk that property will be destroyed or damaged and (2) when he does the act he either has not given any thought to the possibility of there being any such risk or has recognised that there was some risk involved and has nonetheless gone on to do it. That would be a proper direction to the jury; cases in the Court of Appeal which held otherwise should be regarded as overruled ...

As respects the charge under section 1(2) the prosecution did not rely upon an actual intent of the respondent to endanger the lives of the residents but relied upon his having been reckless whether the lives of any of them would be endangered. His act of setting fire to it was one which the jury were entitled to think created an obvious risk that the lives of the residents would be endangered; and the only defence with which your Lordships are concerned is that the respondent had made himself so drunk as to render him oblivious of that risk.

If the only mental state capable of constituting the necessary mens rea for an offence under s 1(2) were expressed in the words 'intending by the destruction or damage to endanger the life of another', it would have been necessary to consider whether the offence was to be classified as one of 'specific' intent for the purposes of the rule of law which this House affirmed in *R v Majewski* (1977), and this it plainly is. But this is not, in my view, a relevant inquiry where 'being reckless as to whether the life of another would be thereby endangered' is an alternative mental state that is capable of constituting the necessary mens rea of the offence ...

The speech of the Lord Chancellor in *Majewski* ... is authority that self-induced intoxication is no defence to a crime in which recklessness is enough to constitute the mens rea ...

Reducing oneself by drink or drugs to a condition in which the restraints of reason and conscience are cast off was held to be a reckless course of conduct and an integral part of the crime ...

So ... the fact that the respondent was unaware of the risk of endangering the lives of the residents in the hotel owing to his self-induced intoxication, would be no defence if that risk would have been obvious to him had he been sober ...

[T]he Court of Appeal ... regarded the case as turning upon whether the offence under s 1(2) was one of 'specific' intent or 'basic' intent. Following a recent decision of the Court of Appeal by which they were bound, *Orpin* (1980), they held that the contrast to the offence under s 1(2) was one of 'specific' intent in contrast to the offence under s 1(1) which was of basic intent. This would be right if the only mens rea capable of constituting the offence were an actual intention to endanger the life of another. For the reasons I have given, however, classification into offences of 'specific' and 'basic' intent is irrelevant where being reckless as to whether a particular harmful consequence will result from one's act is a sufficient alternative mens rea. I would give the following answers to the certified questions:

(a) If the charge of an offence under s 1(2) of the Criminal Damage Act 1971 is framed so as to charge the defendant only with 'intending by the destruction or damage [of the property] to endanger the life of another' evidence of self-induced intoxication can be relevant to his defence.

(b) If the charge is, or includes, a reference to his 'being reckless as to whether the life of another would thereby be endangered', evidence of self-induced intoxication is not relevant.

[Lord Keith of Kinkel and Lord Roskill agreed with Lord Diplock. Lord Wilberforce agreed with the following speech by Lord Edmund-Davies:]

Lord Edmund-Davies.

... My respectful view is that *Majewski* ... supplies no support for the proposition that, in relation to crimes of specific intent (such as s 2(1)(b) of the 1971 Act) incapacity to appreciate the degree and nature of the risk created by his action which is attributable to the defendant's self-intoxication is an irrelevance. The Lord Chancellor was dealing simply with crimes of basic intent, and in my judgment it was strictly within that framework that he adopted the view expressed in the American Model Penal Code and recklessness as an element in crimes of specific intent was, I am convinced, never within his contemplation ... Having revealed in *Majewski* my personal conviction that, on grounds of public policy, a plea of drunkenness cannot exculpate crimes of basic intent and so exercise unlimited sway in the criminal law, I am nevertheless unable to concur that your Lordships' decision should now become the law of the land. For, as Eveleigh LJ said in *Orpin* (1980 at 324):

> ... there is nothing inconsistent in treating it as irrelevant when considering the liability of a person who has willed himself to do that which the law forbids (for example, to do something which wounds another), and yet to make it relevant when a further mental state is postulated as an aggravating circumstance making the offence even more serious.

... [Appeal dismissed.]

The 'objective' conception of recklessness (which applies to the offence of criminal damage but not to offences against the person or public order offences) in effect renders the question of intoxication irrelevant: the 'reasonable person' to whom the risk would have been obvious is, by definition, sober. But, despite the difference in the reasoning, this leads to much the same result as the *Majewski* rule. There, in basic intent offences such as assault, assault occasioning actual bodily harm and malicious wounding, evidence of intoxication is inadmissible, leaving defendants with nowhere to go in denying the mental element. It is useful to recall, however, that cases such as *Venna* (1975) and *Savage and Parmenter* (1992) hardly suggest that proving the mental element presents a tremendous challenge to the prosecution. Coupled with the fact that most defendants plead guilty, the number of defendants who are seriously affected by the intoxication rules is probably not huge. This is borne out by the discovery that the level of convictions did not vastly decrease in the common-law states of Australia, South Africa and Canada when they abandoned the *Majewski* rule (Orchard 1993). The most that can be said about judicial activity in this area is that it shows signs of the severe strain involved in rationalising the irreconcilable. The Court of Appeal in *Hardie* (1984) did make an exception for 'legitimate' drug users:

R v Hardie [1984] 3 All ER 848, CA

[*The defendant set fire to a wardrobe in the flat where he had been living with his girlfriend. Their relationship had recently broken down and because he was upset had taken that day a number of tranquilliser tablets which she had previously obtained on a lawful prescription. He argued that the effects of the drug prevented him forming the 'mens rea' for an offence under s 1(2) of the Criminal Damage Act 1971. The jury were directed by the judge to ignore evidence about the drug because it was self-administered.*]

Parker LJ.

... The appellant's evidence was that he had never taken valium before, that he took one at about 12 noon to calm him down, for he was in a distressed state, that it did not have much effect, that he and [his girlfriend] had then gone shopping, that he had taken two more in front of her and she had said, 'Take as many as you like, they are old stock and will do you no harm,' that he had taken two more shortly afterwards, that he may have taken two of the other [diuretic] tablets also, and that shortly thereafter on return to the house he had fallen into a deep sleep and could thereafter remember only periods ...

The defence was that the appellant was so affected by the valium that he could remember nothing about the fire and had not the necessary mens rea to constitute either of the offences charged. On the basis no doubt of *Majewski* (1977) and *Caldwell* (1981), the judge directed the jury in effect that, as the valium was voluntarily self-administered, it was irrelevant as a defence and its effects could not negative mens rea ...

It is clear from *Caldwell* that self-induced intoxication can be a defence where the charge is only one of specific intention. It is equally clear that it cannot be a defence where, as here, the charge included recklessness. Hence, if there was self-intoxication in this case the judge's direction was correct. The problem is whether, assuming that the effect of the valium was to deprive the appellant of any appreciation of what he was doing, it should properly be regarded as self-induced intoxication and thus no answer ...

Majewski was a case of drunkenness resulting from alcoholic consumption by the accused whilst under the influence of non-medically-prescribed drugs. *Caldwell* was a case of plain drunkenness. There can be no doubt that the same rule applies both to self-intoxication by alcohol and to intoxication by hallucinatory drugs, but this is because the effects of both are well known and there is therefore an element of recklessness in the self-administration of the drug. *Lipman* (1969) is an example of such a case.

'Intoxication' or similar symptoms may, however, arise in other circumstances. In *Bailey* (1983) this court had to consider a case where a diabetic had failed to take sufficient food after taking a normal dose of insulin and struck the victim over the head with an iron bar. The judge directed the jury that the defence of automatism, i.e. that the mind did not go with the act, was not available because the incapacity was self-induced. It was held that this was wrong on two grounds: (a) because on the basis of *Majewski* it was clearly available to the offence embodying specific intent and (b) because although self-induced by the omission to take food it was also available to negative the other offence which was of basic intent only.

[Parker LJ then quoted what Griffiths LJ said in *Bailey* [1983] 2 All ER 503 at 507]:

> [I]t seems to us that there may be material distinctions between a man who consumes alcohol or takes dangerous drugs and one who fails to take sufficient food after insulin to avert hypoglycaemia. It is common knowledge that those who take alcohol to excess or certain sorts of drugs may become aggressive or do dangerous or unpredictable things; they may be able to foresee the risks of causing harm to others, but nevertheless persist in their conduct. But the same cannot be said, without more, of a man who fails to take sufficient food after an insulin injection. If he does appreciate that such a failure may lead to aggressive, unpredictable and uncontrollable conduct and he nevertheless deliberately runs the risk or otherwise disregards it, this will amount to recklessness ... In our judgment, self-induced automatism, other than that due to intoxication from alcohol or drugs, may provide a defence to crimes of basic intent ...

In the present instance the defence was that the valium was taken for the purpose of calming the nerves only, that it was old stock and that the appellant was told that it would do him no harm. There was no evidence that it was known to the appellant or even generally known that the taking of valium in the quantity taken would be liable to render a person aggressive or incapable of appreciating risks to others or have other side effects such that its self-administration would itself have an element of recklessness. It is true that valium is a drug and it is true that it was taken deliberately and not taken on medical prescription, but the drug is, in our view, wholly different in kind from drugs which are liable to cause unpredictability or aggressiveness ...

[The jury] should have been directed that if they came to the conclusion that, as a result of the valium, the appellant was, at the time, unable to appreciate the risks to property and persons of his actions they should then consider whether the taking of the valium was itself reckless ...

[The appeal was allowed and the conviction quashed.]

The House of Lords was not in the mood for generosity in the following case in which the defendant argued that *involuntary* intoxication had led to the commission of the offence:

R v Kingston [1994] 3 All ER 353

[*The defendant was convicted of indecent assault. He claimed that, unknown to him, his co-defendant had administered sedative drugs to him which meant that he did not realise what he was doing. The Court of Appeal, upholding a defence of involuntary intoxication, quashed the conviction. The prosecution appealed to the House of Lords with a certified point of law of general public importance: (a) whether, if it was proved that the necessary intent was present when the necessary act was done by him, a defendant has open to him a defence of involuntary intoxication; (b) if so, on whom does the burden of proof lie?*]

Lord Mustill.

... In academic circles the decision under appeal has not been favourably received ... [It has been] characterised ... as surprising, dangerous and contrary to principle. On the other hand there is an instinctive attraction in the proposition that a retributory system of justice should not visit penal consequences on acts which are the ultimate consequence of an event outside the volition of an actor, and that it is not sufficient to acknowledge the special circumstances by mitigating the penalty which would otherwise be appropriate ... This divergence of opinion reflects a general issue of fundamental importance as well as a more technical question on the law of intoxication. Since the matter is also of increasing practical significance, given the availability of hallucinogenic drugs whose ingestion in very small quantities can lead to behaviour which is bizarre, unpredictable and violent, it must be considered in some detail ...

The general nature of the case is clear enough. In ordinary circumstances the respondent's paedophiliac tendencies would have been kept under control, even in the presence of the sleeping or unconscious boy on the bed. The ingestion of the drug (whatever it was) brought about a temporary change in the mentality or personality of the respondent which lowered his ability to resist temptation so far that his desires overrode his ability to control them. Thus we are concerned here with a case of disinhibition. The drug is not alleged to have created the desire to which the respondent gave way, but rather to have enabled it to be released ...

On these facts there are three grounds on which the respondent might be held free from criminal responsibility. First, that his immunity flows from general principles of the criminal law. Secondly, that this immunity is already established by a solid line of authority. Finally, that the court should, when faced with a new problem acknowledge the justice of the case and boldly create a new common law defence.

It is clear ... that the Court of Appeal adopted the first approach ... that if blame is absent the necessary mens rea must also be absent.

My Lords, with every respect I must suggest that no such principle exists or, until the present case, had ever in modern times been thought to exist.

[*After concluding that there was no authority for the existence of a defence of involuntary intoxication, he continued:*]

To recognise a new defence of this type would be a bold step. The common law defences of duress and necessity (if it exists) and the limited common law defence of provocation are all very old ... I suspect that the recognition of a new general defence at common law has not happened in modern times. Nevertheless, the criminal law must not stand still, and if it is both practical and just to take this step, and if judicial decision rather than legislation is the proper medium, then the courts should not be deterred simply by the novelty of it. So one must turn to consider just what defence is now to be created. The judgment under appeal implies five characteristics.

(1) The defence applies to all other offences, except perhaps to absolute offences. It therefore differs from other defences such as provocation and diminished responsibility.

(2) The defence is a complete answer to a criminal charge. If not rebutted it leads to an outright acquittal, and unlike provocation and diminished responsibility leaves no room for conviction and punishment for a lesser offence. The underlying assumption must be that the defendant is entirely free from culpability.

(3) It may be that the defence applies only where the intoxication is due to the wrongful act of another and therefore affords no excuse when, in circumstances of no greater culpability, the defendant has intoxicated himself by mistake (such as by short-sightedly taking the wrong drug). I say that this may be so, because it is not clear whether, since the doctrine was founded in part on the dictum of Park J, the 'fraud or stratagem of another' is an essential element, or whether this was taken as an example of a wider principle.

(4) The burden of disproving the defence is on the prosecution.

(5) The defence is subjective in nature. Whereas provocation and self-defence are judged by the reactions of the reasonable person in the situation of the defendant, here the only question is whether this particular defendant's inhibitions were overcome by the effect of the drug. The more susceptible the defendant to the kind of temptation presented, the easier the defence is to establish.

... [S]ince the existence or otherwise of the defence has been treated in argument at all stages as a matter of existing law the Court of Appeal had no occasion to consider the practical and theoretical implications of recognising this new defence at common law, and we do not have the benefit of its views. In their absence, I can only say that the defence appears to run into difficulties at every turn.

[T]he fact that a new doctrine may require adjustment of existing principles to accommodate it, and may require those involved in criminal trials to learn new techniques, is not of course a ground for refusing to adopt it, if that is what the interests of justice require. Here, however, justice makes no such demands, for the interplay between the wrong done to the victim, the individual characteristics and frailties of the defendant, and the pharmacological effects of whatever drug may be potentially involved can be far better recognised by a tailored choice from the continuum of sentences available to the judge than by the application of a single yea-or-nay jury decision. To this, there is one exception. The mandatory life sentence for murder, at least as presently administered, leaves no room for the trial judge to put into practice an informed and sympathetic assessment of the kind just described. It is for this reason alone that I have felt any hesitation about rejecting the argument for the respondent. In the end however I have concluded that this is not a sufficient reason to force on the theory and practice of the criminal law an exception which would otherwise be unjustified ... For many years mandatory sentences have impelled juries to return merciful but false verdicts, and have stimulated the creation of partial defences such as has made them hard to apply in practice. I do not think it right that the law should be further distorted simply because of this anomalous relic of the history of the criminal law.

All this being said, I suggest to your Lordships that the existing work of the Law Commission in the field of intoxication could usefully be enlarged to comprise questions of the type raised by this appeal, and to see whether by a statute a merciful, realistic and intellectually sustainable statutory solution could be newly created. For the present, however, I consider that no such regime now exists, and that the common law is not a suitable vehicle for creating one. For these reasons I consider that both the ruling and the direction of the learned judge were correct. Accordingly I would answer the first certified question in the negative and would allow the appeal.

Note that Kingston's (rejected) argument that mens rea in the absence of blame should equal no liability, was the mirror of that accepted in *Majewski*, that blame in the absence of (conventional) 'mens rea' equals liability. Kingston was held responsible, despite the involuntariness of his intoxication, because he was a sex offender. This underlines the shift from individual responsibility for each offence to the labelling 'character' liability inherent in much contemporary regulation of sex offenders.

The Law Commission, when it first considered this question, concluded that the present law was illogical and out of step with the requirement that the prosecution should prove all elements of the offence. A number of reform options were advanced, of which the Commission particularly favoured two: abolish the *Majewski* distinction and allow intoxication as evidence in all offences, or replace the present rule with a separate offence of causing harm while intoxicated (LCCP 127 1993). However, the Law Commission finally recommended (Report 229, 1995) that the status quo should remain, although the law should be placed on a statutory footing.

In the next extract, Gardner presents a theoretical basis for the *Majewski* rule:

S Gardner, 'The Importance of *Majewski*' (1994) 14 OJLS 279

The argument of 'logic' or 'principle' against *Majewski* takes the following lines. *Majewski* applies, essentially, to crimes where mens rea is subjective recklessness. Conviction for such a crime requires that the accused adverted to at least the possibility of the actus reus occurring. When the accused was so intoxicated that he lacked such advertence, it is therefore illogical, or contrary to principle, to convict him.

In examining this argument, we must, of course, begin by agreeing that in the crimes in question, the law has adopted advertence as inculpatory. But then the questions begin. For the fact that the law adopts advertence as inculpatory does not necessarily entail that the absence of advertence must be exculpatory. The law could without contradiction adopt a second inculpatory state, such as intoxication. So the argument of logic or principle must depend on the supposition that the crime may indeed be committed *only* when advertence is present. Is this supposition in fact true?

On the face of it, of course, the supposition is clearly untrue. As things stand, a full statement of the crime in question would have to refer to inculpation for intoxication as well as to inculpation for advertence ... The fact that a crime has advertence as a basis for liability thus provides no ground for the supposition that advertence *must* be its exclusive basis for liability, leaving no room for intoxication.

Gardner goes on to argue that the gulf between subjective recklessness in offences against the person and objective *Caldwell* recklessness in criminal damage offences is more apparent than real, partly because it is mediated by the intoxication rules. While agreeing with this, it is important to emphasise the insistence in cases such as *B v DPP* (2000) on the importance of proving subjective mental states. This appears deliberately to ignore the significant qualifications introduced by the intoxication rules, and in different ways by the participation rules. What you get is not what you see. The Law Commission is committed to making the criminal law accessible, clear and consistent, but it can only do that effectively if it abandons its assumption that advertence is the only blameworthy state recognised in criminal law. This the Commission belatedly acknowledged when it came to consider manslaughter, which presents a major deviation from the so-called general principle of subjectivism (see **Chapter 6.IV.c.**).

Incidentally, the Law Commission rejected on two grounds Lord Mustill's invitation to consider the *Kingston* involuntary defence question: first, that 'it was simply too late' to incorporate it within the project, especially as there had been no consultation on it; and second, that it raised too broad an issue relating to the relationship between matters going to liability and those going to mitigation (Report 229: paras 1.7–1.8). Neither of these reasons is convincing. Few of the Commission's proposals in the criminal law field are immediately legislated (and this area is no exception); a delay in reporting while this question was considered would have had little practical effect. The Commission is engaged in a gradual process of codification of criminal law, including general principles, and it is desirable that the interface between each of its areas of investigation is fully considered. It begs the question to say that the issues raised by the inculpatory effects of intoxication (with which the report does deal) are different from those of exculpation.

The proposals for reform of the OAPA 1861 address the problem of intoxication and recklessness as follows:

Home Office, *Violence: Reforming the Offences against the Person Act 1861* (Consultation Paper, 1998)

Draft Offences Against the Person Bill 1998

19(1) For the purposes of this Act a person who was voluntarily intoxicated at any material time must be treated–
  (a) as having been aware of any risk of which he would have been aware had he not been intoxicated, and
  (b) as having known or believed in any circumstances which he would have known or believed in had he not been intoxicated.
  ...
 (3) A person is voluntarily intoxicated if–
  (a) he takes an intoxicant otherwise than properly for a medicinal purpose,
  (b) he is aware that it is or may be an intoxicant, and
  (c) he takes it in such a quantity as impairs his awareness or understanding.
  ...
 (5) Intoxication must be presumed to have been voluntary unless there is adduced such evidence as might lead the court or jury to conclude that there is a reasonable possibility that the intoxication was involuntary.

(6) An intoxicant is any alcohol, drug or other thing which, when taken into the body, may impair the awareness or understanding of the person taking it.

(7) A person must be treated as taking an intoxicant if he permits it to be administered to him.

FURTHER READING

Braggins, J (1997) *Tackling Drugs Together: One Year On* (ISTD).

Clarkson, C, Cretney, A, Davis, G and Shephard, J (1994) 'Assaults, the Relationship between Seriousness, Criminalisation and Punishment' Crim LR 4.

Hobbs, Dick (1997) 'Criminal Collaboration: Youth Gangs, Subcultures, Professional Criminals, and Organized Crime' in Maguire et al (eds) *The Oxford Handbook of Criminology* (Oxford University Press) p 801.

Parker, Howard (1999) 'Illegal Leisure: Alcohol, Drugs and the Regulation of Modern Youth' in Carlen, P and Morgan, R (eds) *Crime Unlimited? Questions for the 21st Century* (MacMillian Press) 144.

Perri 6 (1997) *Young People and Drugs* (Joseph Rowntree Foundation).

Smith, K J M (1991) *A Modern Treatise on the Law of Complicity* (Clarendon Press).

South, Nigel (2002) 'Drugs Alcohol and Crime' in Maguire et al (eds) *The Oxford Handbook of Criminology* (Oxford University Press) p 914.

Valverde, Mariana (1998) *Diseases of the Will* (Cambridge University Press).

IV.   Conspiracy

Those who attempt or conspire to commit crimes (Criminal Attempts Act 1981; Criminal Law Act 1977) or who incite others to do so are themselves criminally liable. This general rule is supplemented by many statutory inchoate offences, where no harm or result need be proved. Possession of controlled drugs is one such example. There are other more obviously 'inchoate' statutory offences such as possessing articles for use in burglary, theft or cheat (Theft Act 1968, s 25). The concern to impose inchoate liability in general, and conspiracy liability in particular, discloses a pervasive anxiety about the risk of harm. Indeed, the legislative fashion is to provide conspiracy mode liability within specific statutes. So for example, under the Proceeds of Crime Act 2002 a person commits an offence 'if he enters into or becomes concerned in an arrangement which he knows or suspects facilitates ... the acquisition etc of criminal property' (s 328). This is probably wider than a conspiracy charge. The incomplete nature of the 'actus reus' of inchoate offences, 'compensated' by a stringent 'mens rea' requirement, is suggestive of a strongly subjective conception of criminality. This is particularly noticeable in attempts, which we discuss in detail in **Chapter 4.II.c.ii.** The debate about liability for 'impossible' incitements, conspiracies and attempts reflects, as we show there, a concern with manifestly criminal conduct.

Incitement is still regulated by common law and consists in the use of persuasion, pressure, threats or encouragement with intention that the person so pressured or persuaded should commit the offence in question, and with knowledge of all the relevant circumstances. Incitements to commit indictable offences are themselves triable on indictment, and in theory are subject to unlimited punishment at the discretion of the court. Incitements to commit summary offences are triable only summarily, and can result only in the maximum penalties for the completed offence (Magistrates' Courts Act 1980, s 45). Many of the most interesting issues about incitement arise also in relation to other forms of inchoate liability, and the analogies and contrasts between these different forms will be dealt with in the course of our more extensive treatment of conspiracy and attempt.

The crime of conspiracy consists, broadly speaking, in an agreement to pursue an unlawful object. What is the underlying rationale for this form of liability?

R Hazell, *Conspiracy and Civil Liberties* (NCCL, Cobden Trust, 1974) pp 86–88, 93

In America it is traditional to divide the justifications for having a crime of conspiracy into the 'specific object' rationale and the 'general danger' rationale. The former rationale provides a straightforward explanation of conspiracy as an inchoate offence. Conspiracy attacks potentially criminal conduct, but at an earlier stage than attempt; the conspiratorial agreement derives its criminal character purely from the criminal conduct that is the object of the agreement. Under this rationale the agreement is logically punishable only if the conspiratorial objective is a crime.

The 'general danger' rationale is much broader, and provides a justification for punishing not only combinations with criminal objectives but also combinations whose aims are merely considered to be socially undesirable. The argument rests at bottom on the greater threat from the numbers involved in a conspiracy.

The ambiguity between these two rationales underpins the long and unglorious political history of conspiracy law, in which the boundaries of liability have extended well beyond the contours apparently determined by legal doctrine:

G Robertson, *Whose Conspiracy?* (NCCL, 1974) pp 13–18

The crime of conspiracy entered the law of England in 1304, in the form of an act to punish malicious prosecutions ... Several centuries elapsed before the political potential of the conspiracy charge was, in the words of one eminent legal historian, 'emphasised by the Star Chamber, which recognised its possibilities as an engine of government and moulded it into a substantive offence of wide scope, whose attractions were such that its principles were gradually adopted by the common law courts ... ' Before its abolition in 1641, the Star Chamber had established that the essence of the crime of conspiracy is the actual agreement, and hence no overt actions need be proved by the prosecution to obtain a conviction. Moreover, conspiracy ... extended to agreements to commit all crimes, however trivial. These two cardinal principles are still being applied by the courts, 300 years later, to situations that Star Chamber judges would never have envisaged ...

The most devastating extension of the conspiracy law since the Star Chamber days was to punish, as though they were serious crimes, agreements to do acts which themselves entailed only civil liability for damages at the complaint of an injured party. The encroachment of this doctrine was stealthy at first, beginning with cases of 'conspiracy to defraud' by not paying a civil debt. But in 1832 one judge caught these straws in the wind and wove them into the fabric of the criminal law, in a pattern which has had a baleful influence on judicial thinking ever since. Lord Denman defined a conspiracy as 'an agreement to do an unlawful act, or a lawful act by unlawful means'. 'Unlawful' included actions giving rise merely to civil damages.

The immediate casualties of this formula were the incipient trade unions, whose every strike or picket was elevated into a criminal conspiracy. A conspiracy conviction exiled the Tolpuddle Martyrs, while 'conspiracy to obstruct an employer and interfere with his lawful freedom of action', and 'conspiracy to annoy and interfere with the masters in the conduct of their business' abound in other nineteenth century industrial cases ... Finally political pressure forced Disraeli to pass the Conspiracy, and Protection of Property Act 1875, which abolished conspiracy charges in respect of trade disputes ... but left a loophole which almost a century later was relentlessly exploited by another Tory government to prosecute building workers whose picketing activities ... were alleged to be conspiracies to intimidate [under s 7 of the Act] ...

To the 'bitter legacy' bequeathed by use of conspiracy charges to oppress the working class has been added another twentieth century codicil designed to persecute political minorities whose activities amount to no more than innocuous trespass. In 1973 Lord Hailsham decreed that an agreement to commit a trespass – a mere temporary presence on another's property without permission – constitutes a serious criminal offence if the public interest is deemed to be at stake; a conclusive presumption if the property belongs to those he chooses to term 'the authorities' ... Lord Hailsham approved conspiracy prosecutions of the parties to an agreement [to occupy the Sierra Leone High Commission] which would, if carried out, give an aggrieved individual the right to sue for more than nominal damages ... or where execution of the agreement 'invades the domain of the public'. The Sierra Leone Embassy decision, delivered in June 1973, will have a chilling effect on political protest ...

How has modern criminal law doctrine rationalised the imposition of criminal liability for conspiracies to do things which would not in themselves constitute offences, and the possibility of punishments more stringent than those available for completed offences? The following extract from the case to which Robertson refers illustrates the way in which legal reasoning can accommodate even problematic cases such as criminal conspiracy to commit civil wrongs within the ideological framework of the rule of law:

Kamara v DPP [1973] 2 All ER 1242

Lord Hailsham.

If combinations involving tortious conduct are not all indictable, is there any rational principle on which those which are indictable can be separated from those which cannot?

In my view, there is such a principle, and in my view, the rational principle can be deduced from the nature of the considerations which have led courts over the centuries to decide that they must protect certain wrongs to individuals from acts done by a number which, had they been done by a single wrongdoer, would have given rise to a civil remedy only ...

... [A] combination the execution of which has as its object not merely a tort or other actionable wrong, but also either the invasion of the public domain, or the intention to inflict on its victim injury and damage which goes beyond the field of the nominal is indictable, whether the object be achieved by trespass to land, goods or person, by ruin of the reputation through the defamation of character, by the commission of private nuisance, by some contrivance of fraud, by the imposition of force, or by any other means which is tortious. This is in fact the thread which has run through the law from Hawkins *Pleas of the Crown* to Lord Simon LC's speech in the *Harris Tweed* case (1942), although I do not necessarily indorse the view perhaps implicit in that speech that a combination to injure is necessarily indictable without some element involved in its execution otherwise inherently unlawful ... Trespass or any other form of tort can, if intended, form the element of illegality necessary in conspiracy. But in my view, more is needed. Either (1) execution of the combination must invade the domain of the public as, for instance, when the trespass involves the invasion of a building such as the embassy of a friendly country or a publicly owned building, or (of course) where it infringes the criminal law as by breaching the Statutes of Forcible Entry and Detainer, the Criminal Damage Act 1971 or the laws affecting criminal assaults to the person. Alternatively, (2) a combination to trespass becomes indictable if the execution of the combination necessarily involves and is known and intended to involve the infliction on its victim of something more than purely nominal damage. This must necessarily be the case where the intention is to occupy the premises to the exclusion of the owner's right ...

Note Lord Hailsham's emphasis on the common law as developing historically in a coherent way; his accommodation of conspiracy law within the liberal 'harm principle'; and his assumption that the commission of any crime 'of course' brings us within a public order arena in which criminal penalties, however dubiously arrived at, can be justified.

The offence of conspiracy in England and Wales is now regulated by a statutory framework: this framework addresses criticism of the common law offence by curtailing its breadth:

Criminal Law Act 1977, s 1

1. The offence of conspiracy
(1) Subject to the following provisions of this Part of this Act, if a person agrees with any other person or persons that a course of conduct shall be pursued which, if the agreement is carried out in accordance with their intentions, either–
  (a) will necessarily amount to or involve the commission of any offence or offences by one or more of the parties to the agreement, or
  (b) would do so but for the existence of facts which render the commission of the offence or any of the offences impossible,
  he is guilty of conspiracy to commit the offence or offences in question.
  ...
(2) Where liability for any offence may be incurred without knowledge on the part of the person committing it of any particular fact or circumstance necessary for the commission of the offence, a person shall nevertheless not be guilty of conspiracy to commit that offence by virtue of subsection (1) above unless he and at least one other party to the agreement intend or know that that fact or circumstance shall or will exist at the time when the conduct constituting the offence is to take place.
  ...
(4) In this Part of this Act "offence" means an offence triable in England and Wales.

The Act seeks to locate conspiracy within the 'general principles' of criminal law doctrine by limiting it to agreements to forms of conduct which are themselves offences, and by limiting the degree of punishment to that which could be imposed for the completed offence. Subsection 3 excludes acts done in contemplation or furtherance of a trade dispute provided that they constitute only a summary offence not punishable with imprisonment. Section 2 excludes liability for intended victims of conspiracy offences and certain other categories such as spouses and persons under the age of criminal responsibility. Section 4 provides that the consent of the DPP (or sometimes the Attorney-General) shall be necessary for conspiracy prosecutions where the substantive offence is a summary one.

Section 5 proceeds to abolish the common law crime of conspiracy. It does so, however, with two significant exceptions: conspiracy to defraud and conspiracies to engage in conduct which tends to corrupt public morals or outrages public decency are retained as distinct offences. Remarkably, in relation to the latter forms of conspiracy, the saving is drafted in conditional terms: s 5(3) provides that 'Subsection 1 above shall not affect the offence of conspiracy at common law *if and in so far as* it may be committed by entering into an agreement to engage in conduct which tends to corrupt public morals or outrage public decency' but would not amount to the commission of an offence if carried out by a single person (emphasis added). This odd wording reflects the legislature's lack of certainty about the state of the common law in this area. Section 5(3) nonetheless preserves the effect of the notorious case of *Shaw*, in which the judiciary asserted its general power to define and uphold social order:

Shaw v DPP [1961] 2 All ER 446, HL

[*Shaw had published a booklet entitled 'The Ladies' Directory', which printed the names and addresses of prostitutes and advertisements for the types of conduct in which they engaged, and for which the women paid. He was convicted of living on the earnings of prostitution and of publishing an obscene article. One might have thought that these charges would suffice, but he was also charged with and convicted of conspiracy to corrupt public morals. The court held that conduct calculated and intended to corrupt public morals was an indictable misdemeanour at common law and that it followed that an agreement to do so was a conspiracy. Viscount Simonds expresses the values underlying the decision:*]

... [I]t is said that it is not possible in the twentieth century for the court to create a new head of public policy ... In the sphere of criminal law, I entertain no doubt that there remains in the courts of law a residual power to enforce the supreme and fundamental purpose of the law, to conserve not only the safety and order but also the moral welfare of the state, and that it is their duty to guard it against attacks which may be the more insidious because they are novel and unprepared for ... When Lord Mansfield, speaking long after the Star Chamber had been abolished, said ... that the Court of King's Bench was the *custos morum* of the people and had the superintendence of offences *contra bonos mores* he was asserting, as I now assert, that there is in that court a residual power, where no statute has yet intervened to supersede the common law, to superintend those offences which are prejudicial to the public welfare. Such occasions will be rare, for Parliament has not been slow to legislate when attention has been sufficiently aroused. But gaps remain and will always remain since no one can foresee every way in which the wickedness of man may disrupt the order of society.

Lord Reid's famous dissent, in which he asserted that 'where Parliament fears to tread, it is not for the courts to rush in', should be seen in the light of his judgment in the later case of *Knuller* – a case in which the homophobic attitudes of the judiciary, as well as the power of conspiracy charges to convert lawful actions into illegal ones, are all too evident:

Knuller Ltd v DPP [1972] 2 All ER 898, HL

[*Knullers published a magazine which contained on inner pages advertisements inserted by homosexuals for the purposes of attracting sexual partners. The magazine had a circulation of over 30,000, and many copies were read by young students and schoolboys. Knullers was convicted of conspiracies both to corrupt public morals and to outrage public decency. Lord Reid expressed concern that a parliamentary assurance by the 'Solicitor General that conspiracy to corrupt public morals would not be charged so as to circumvent the statutory defence in s 4 of the Obscene Publications Act' to obscenity charges had not been communicated to the legal profession, but continued:*]

Although I would not support reconsidering *Shaw*'s case, I think that we ought to clarify one or two matters. In the first place conspiracy to corrupt public morals is something of a misnomer. It really means to corrupt the morals of such members of the public as may be influenced by the matter published by the accused ...

I can now turn to the appellants' second argument. They say that homosexual acts between adult males in private are now lawful so it is unreasonable and cannot be the law that other persons are guilty of an offence if they merely put in touch with one another two males who wish to indulge in such acts. But there is a material difference between merely exempting certain conduct from criminal penalties and making it lawful in the full sense. Prostitution and gaming afford examples of this difference. So we must examine the provisions of the Sexual Offences Act 1967 to see just how far it altered the old law. It enacts subject to limitation that a homosexual act in private shall not be an offence but it goes no further than that. Section 4 shows that procuring is still a serious offence and it would seem that some of the facts in this case might have supported a charge under that section.

I find nothing in the Act to indicate that Parliament thought or intended to lay down that indulgence in these practices is not corrupting ... So if one accepts *Shaw*'s case as rightly decided it must be left to each jury to decide in the circumstances of each case whether people were likely to be corrupted. In this case the jury were properly directed and it is impossible to say that they reached a wrong conclusion ...

The second count is conspiracy to outrage public decency ... The crucial question here is whether in this generalised form this is an offence known to the law. There are a number of particular offences well known to the law which involve indecency in various ways but none of them covers the facts of this case. We were informed that charges of this character have never been brought with regard to printed matter on sale to the public. The recognised offences with regard to such matter are based on its being obscene ... The basis of the new offence, if it is one, is quite different. It is that ordinary decent-minded people who are not likely to become corrupted or depraved will be outraged or utterly disgusted by what they read. To my mind questions of public policy of the utmost importance are at stake here.

I think that the objections to the creation of this generalised offence are similar in character to but even greater than the objections to the gener-alised offence of conspiracy to corrupt public morals. In upholding the decision in *Shaw's case* we are, in my view, in no way affirming or lending any support to the doctrine that the courts still have some general or resid-ual power either to create new offences or so to widen existing offences as to make punishable conduct of a type hitherto not subject to punishment. Apart from some statutory offences of limited application, there appears to be neither precedent nor authority of any kind for punishing the publication of written or printed matter on the ground that it is indecent as distinct from being obscene.

[*Lord Reid enumerates the existing offences involving indecency and rejects any analogy with the proposed new offence:*]

I must now consider what the effect would be if this new generalised crime were held to exist. If there were in any book, new or old, a few pages or even a few sentences which any jury could find to be outrageously inde-cent, those who took part in its publication and sale would risk conviction. I can see no way of denying to juries the free hand which *Shaw's* case gives them in cases of conspiracy to corrupt public morals ... It may be said that no prosecution would ever be brought except in a very bad case. But I have expressed on previous occasions my opinion that bad law is not defensible on the ground that it will be judiciously administered. To recognise this new crime would go contrary to the whole trend of public policy followed by parliament in recent times. I have no hesitation in saying that the conviction of the appellants on the second count must be quashed.

On criminal law's approach to homosexuality and to obscenity, see further **Chapter 5.III.a.ii.** and **III.c.**

Lord Reid's limited rebellion against judicial originality was, however, unsuc-cessful, in that three of the Lords accepted that the offence already existed, albeit that its elements were not satisfied in the present case. *Knuller* provides an excellent example of the capacity of legal doctrine to accommodate and rationalise even parts of institutional history which are radically at odds with its basic tenets. As Robertson comments:

> Punishing a man [sic] for merely *agreeing* to commit a criminal offence can be unfair; punishing him for acquiescing in conduct which only entails civil liability is positively unjust; but what are we to say of the third category of conspiracy, which punishes agreement to do actions which of themselves involve no liability whatsoever? [Robertson 1974: 18.]

Moving to statutory conspiracies under the 1977 Act, several further critical observations may be made. Statutory conspiracy – conspiracy, for example, to steal – raises a wide range of doctrinal complexities. For example, the definition of the 'actus reus' in terms of 'agreement' means that it is difficult to separate 'mens rea' and 'actus reus' requirements: evidence of either is bound to tend to proof of both. Furthermore, if read literally, the statutory definition would exclude almost all liability, since practically no agreement would *necessarily* lead to the commission of an offence. The ambiguity about this phrase also renders problematic the purported stringency of the 'mens rea' requirement: in the case of parties who agree to pursue a course of conduct which they realise is likely to lead to the commission of an offence, it will be difficult to distinguish between intention and recklessness. There has also been uncertainty about whether a party to a conspiracy must intend to play an active part in the agreed course of conduct herself (*Anderson* (1986), imaginatively interpreted in *Siracusa* (1989)). Although an 'intended victim' is immune from a conspiracy charge (s 2(1)), the person to whom drugs are supplied is (for these purposes) not a victim and can be indicted for conspiracy (*Drew*, 2000). These features of conspiracy law mean that it remains among the most uncertain and discretionary areas of substantive criminal law. In particular, the consistency of conspiracy law with rule of law values is called into question by its implications for evidence and procedure:

R Spicer, *Conspiracy: Law, Class and Society* (Lawrence & Wishart, London, 1981) pp 127–129

A major criticism of conspiracy law is that, when the charge is brought, the rules of the game change in favour of the prosecution. Over the centuries a body of special rules of evidence has been built up, which are peculiar to conspiracy trials. The Irish and Chartist cases demonstrate the extent to which political trials, heard at a time when judges were prepared to admit that trials could be political, have contributed a special body of evidential and procedural rules to the present system. In Pritt's view:

> The proof of conspiracy is made easier by the provision of the law of evidence … that so long as there is any evidence, however tenuous, from which the agreement might be inferred, the acts and words of

any of the alleged conspirators, alleged to have been done or spoken in pursuance of the conspiracy, are admissible in evidence against all the others, on the footing that they are all agents of one another (although, at the time when the evidence is admitted, the jury has not found that there was an agreement – and so some agency – as alleged).

The rule against hearsay, described by Glanville Williams as 'one of the best known rules of law as well as one of its most intricate professional mysteries', is all but abandoned in conspiracy trials. An early example is ... the Monmouthshire Chartists ... [case] where evidence of someone other than the accused having told people to go to a meeting was admitted against the accused on the basis that all the acts in question were part of one transaction ...

It is extremely difficult for the prosecution to prove conspiracy according to the normal rules of evidence, because direct evidence of an agreement is rarely available. This has led to the development of the doctrine of inference. The judges have repeatedly declared that, so far as proof goes, conspiracy is generally to be inferred from the acts of the parties carried out in pursuance of their agreement. Prosecution strategy is generally aimed at establishing that the accused acted in a certain way and in asserting that such behaviour could only have arisen as the result of a plan of action. In this way, proof of conspiracy is actually easier than proof of other offences. One example is *Hunt*, where Mr. Justice Bayley directed the jury that if ' ... the circumstances were such that they could not have occurred except in pursuance of a previous plan between the parties', then that implied that there must have been such a plan, and would warrant the conclusion of conspiracy. In this way, standards of proof have been relaxed to such an extent that it has been said that a conspiracy is easier to prove than a normal commercial contract ...

The Law Commission was silent on this point. In fact, the only comment relevant to rules of evidence was the view stated in its 76th report (Law Commission, 1976) that the reason for retaining the offence of conspiracy is to enable the criminal law to intervene at an early stage before a contemplated crime has actually been committed. The Commissioners felt that the necessity for proof of an agreement was a sufficient safeguard against the danger of punishing conduct too far removed from an actual crime ... Their statements take no account of the fact that most conspiracy charges, far from enabling the law to intervene at an early stage and nip criminal organisations in the bud, are normally preferred *after* the agreed offence has been committed ... One of the great myths of English law, comparable with the myths of judicial neutrality, the separation of powers and an unarmed police force, is the fictional assertion that conspiracy has an essentially 'preventive' nature. As a general rule, and certainly in the great majority of cases decided since 1960, conspiracy counts have been tacked on by the prosecution because the relaxation of rules of evidence makes a conviction more likely and increases judicial sentencing power.

Spicer's argument alerts us to the way in which enforcement practice shapes the meaning of criminal law itself. Though a harm or risk-based pattern of criminality may serve to rationalise the formal law on conspiracy, the implementation of the law appears to describe a pragmatic (and often politically marked) pattern which sits uneasily with any coherent theory of criminality.

Extraterritoriality is a notable feature of the modern law of conspiracy. Section 1A, inserted by s 5 of the Criminal Justice (Terrorism and Conspiracy) Act 1998 reversed the earlier rule that conspiring to perform abroad acts which are illegal elsewhere, and would be illegal in the UK, is not criminal. The origins of this provision lie in concerns about 'sex tourism', overlaid with a reaction to the Omagh bombing in Northern Ireland in 1998 (Alldridge 2000: 152). It replaces the limited exception to territoriality in the Sexual Offences (Conspiracy and Incitement) Act 1996 which introduced extraterritorial liability only in respect of listed offences. As Alldridge comments: 'The discourse of terrorism has provided one of the most important foci for internationalisation of criminal law' (2000: 151).

Criminal Law Act 1977, s 1A

1A. Conspiracy to commit offences outside the United Kingdom
(1) Where each of the following conditions is satisfied in the case of an agreement, this Part of this Act has effect in relation to the agreement as it has effect in relation to an agreement falling within section 1(1) above.
(2) The first condition is that the pursuit of the agreed course of conduct would at some stage involve–
  (a) an act by one or more of the parties, or
  (b) the happening of some other event,
  intended to take place in a country or territory outside the United Kingdom.
(3) The second condition is that that act or other event constitutes an offence under the law in force in that country or territory.
(4) The third condition is that the agreement would fall within section 1(1) above as an agreement relating to the commission of an offence but for the fact that the offence would not be an offence triable in England and Wales if committed in accordance with the parties' intentions.
(5) The fourth condition is that–
  (a) a party to the agreement, or a party's agent, did anything in England and Wales in relation to the agreement before its formation, or

(b) a party to the agreement became a party in England and Wales (by joining it either in person or through an agent), or

(c) a party to the agreement, or a party's agent, did or omitted anything in England and Wales in pursuance of the agreement.

(6) In the application of this Part of this Act to an agreement in the case of which each of the above conditions is satisfied, a reference to an offence is to be read as a reference to what would be the offence in question but for the fact that it is not an offence triable in England and Wales.

(7) Conduct punishable under the law in force in any country or territory is an offence under that law for the purposes of this section, however it is described in that law.

...

(11) Any act done by means of a message (however communicated) is to be treated for the purposes of the fourth condition as done in England and Wales if the message is sent or received in England and Wales.

(12) In any proceedings in respect of an offence triable by virtue of this section, it is immaterial to guilt whether or not the accused was a British citizen at the time of any act or other event proof of which is required for conviction of the offence.

There may be difficulties in the interpretation of the 'second condition', that the conduct 'amounts to an offence under the law in that country'. However, there is a presumption that the 'second condition' is satisfied unless the defence serves notice that it disputes this (s 1A(8)).

We have covered in the last two chapters a broad sweep of offences and principles of liability. Terms such as harassment, breach of the peace, anti-social behaviour, assault, bodily harm, aiding and abetting, inchoate and more, all have specific meanings and applications in criminal law. In the next three chapters we examine the ways in which criminal law protects property rights, how it seeks to regulate sexual behaviour and bodily integrity, and finally how it constructs violent deaths.

Property and propriety

I. Defining and defending private property
   a. Conceptions of property in social and political thought
   b. Shoplifting
   c. Occupational and 'white collar' crime and conceptions of fraud
   d. Burglary
II. Constructing property in criminal law
   a. Theft
      i. The history of theft
      ii. Contemporary conceptions of theft: ordinary language through the looking glass ...
   b. Offences of deception
   c. Conspiracy to defraud and attempts
      i. Conspiracy to defraud
      ii. Attempts
      iii. Inchoate liability, impossibility and patterns of criminality
   d. Burglary
   e. Criminal damage
   f. Duress, necessity and property
   g. Respect for property?
III. Property rights and criminal enforcement
   a. 'Situational' crime prevention
   b. Diversifying and privatising control
   c. 'Real' crime and selective enforcement
   d. 'Intangible' property crime and the criminal process

I.   Defining and defending private property

In this chapter, we examine criminal law's regulation of property. Both the importance of the social institution of property and the prevalence of property offences, which constitute more than three-quarters of recorded crime (Home Office 2002g: 7), make this a highly significant field. It is also a vast field, encompassing many different kinds of terrain, and even a partial survey such as that offered here can be disorienting. In what follows, therefore, we focus upon a number of specific themes which may help to illuminate the landscape.

First, following on from the theme of the last two chapters, much of our discussion is concerned to examine the relationship between property crime and perceived risk or threats to the prevailing social order. In this context, patterns of enforcement of property offences vary as between offences which are seen as more or less threatening to social order, closer or more distant from our ideas of 'real' crime – for example, tax evasion or corporate fraud on the one hand versus shoplifting or social security fraud on the other. These varying levels of enforcement are facilitated by wide discretion at the enforcement stage; they illustrate both the blurred boundaries between property and public order offences and the potency of legal conceptions of 'real' crime.

Second, the field of property offences illustrates the fragility of social consensus about the lines to be drawn between 'criminal' and 'non-criminal' behaviour. Particularly in commercial arenas, the boundary between 'entrepreneurialism' and 'sharp practice' is an obscure one. Throughout the chapter, we shall see how criminal law's reliance on partially defined concepts such as 'dishonesty', and its delegation of decisions about the existence of dishonesty to magistrates and juries, both proceed from and serve to obscure social ambivalence about what counts as property crime. Similar ambivalence is exemplified by the uneasy relationship between criminal and civil regulation of property which surfaces at a number of points in the following pages.

Third, we shall explore the ways in which widely recognised social influences on property offending – notably economic conditions and the prevailing distribution of wealth – raise difficulties for criminal law's individualistic framework, and prompt questions about how responsibility for property crime should be attributed. If it is mainly the relatively poor who commit 'real' property crime such as theft or burglary, should this unsettle the law's focus on responsibility as solely individual and not also social? Should poverty or injustice be held 'responsible' for property crime? The illustration of this third theme is assisted by the inclusion of an analysis of the defences of duress and necessity – defences which are relatively rarely applied to property crimes, yet whose underlying rationale raises difficulties for prevailing conceptions of individual criminal responsibility in the property area.

Finally, we shall use the field of property offences to explore shifting doctrinal patterns in the attribution of criminal liability over the last 250 years. Drawing on Fletcher's conception of different 'patterns of criminality' (Fletcher 1978), we shall consider the contemporary balance between manifest, subjective and harm or risk-based conceptions of the basis for criminal liability. Our focus on this theme, which arises with particular force from an analysis of the history of theft, will be sharpened by including in the chapter a discussion of the inchoate offence of attempt – an offence whose history and current contours serve to illustrate the different patterns of criminality which co-exist in systems of criminal law.

I.a.   Conceptions of property in social and political thought

The institutions of private property and the 'free market' through which it is exchanged are core components of modern Western societies. In liberal thought, the model of individual property rights underpins the general conception of personal rights; the 'ultimate' human right is often seen as one of self-ownership, and the paradigm of the free individual is the actor in the market. The protection of private property rights is therefore an important concern of criminal regulation, and the perceived success of the criminal justice system in this respect is central to judgments about its efficacy and legitimacy. Criminal law's regulation of property takes place within a framework of civil law, which sets up property rights in laws relating to land tenure, ownership of personal goods and transfers of ownership by contract, gift or succession: criminalisation of property crime is therefore just one among a range of legal arrangements which underpin the conditions of trust and security of expectations which allow a market economy to flourish.

The allocation and organisation of resources is a pressing issue for any society, and the question of property is accordingly a prominent theme in the history of political thought. Theories of private property are, in particular, a central feature of the liberal conceptions of political order which developed in Western countries during the eighteenth century. For liberals, individual entitlements to property have been seen as of both instrumental and intrinsic value. Instrumentally, private property is often argued to conduce to the efficient management of resources and even to the greatest human happiness. There are various approaches to the ethical justification for private holdings in property: some liberals have argued that rights in property derive from original appropriations in a state of nature when nothing is owned, followed by just (typically market) transfers since (see Nozick 1974), while others have argued that private ownership constitutes an essential aspect of the expression and realisation of human personality (see Waldron 1988; MacPherson 1978).

The emergence of these liberal ideas marked a move away from an explicitly hierarchical era in which property relations were seen as matching a status-based social order. In this era the 'lower' classes enjoyed only minor acquisitions of property: most private wealth inhered in the landed aristocracy (and later in an emerging bourgeois class), while a limited amount of land was recognised as subject to common use. Since the eighteenth century, a different conception of the social role of private property has developed, notably in the area of commerce and the market. For the modern liberal, each and every individual has an equal capacity to hold property rights, to enter the market as a contracting party. Yet in assessing their justice, liberalism continues to focus on the processes whereby property rights are created and transferred: it is less concerned with the substantive patterns of property rights which result from those processes of creation and exchange. Although social democratic liberals have begun to develop 'patterned' theories of social justice which do attend to the substantive distribution of property (see, for example, Rawls 1972; Dworkin 1981) even those who come closest to defending some substantive conception of distributive justice or equality are committed to the market. The correction of inequalities and injustices emerging from market processes is thus a persistent preoccupation for liberals and social democrats who espouse a commitment both to the market economy and to social justice.

There is a link between these debates about substantive versus procedural conceptions of justice in property and the ideology of the rule of law considered in **Chapter 1.I.b.i.** The notion of formal equality in the capacity to hold property rights is mirrored in the discourse of legal rights and in the conception of equality of subjects, abstracted from their social circumstances, before the law. This ideology contrasts with critical approaches, which search beneath the rhetoric of liberal equality to scrutinise the actual operation and distribution of legal rights. One particularly influential critical analysis of the implications of distributions of property rights in different societies is that of classical Marxism. In capitalist society, according to Marxist analysis, private property, and in particular the ownership of the means of production, becomes the means whereby the ruling classes maintain their dominant position by exploiting the labour power of the proletariat. While Marxist theory has been extensively criticised, it nonetheless serves to illuminate the ways in which institutions of property shape some of the most fundamental dynamics of political, economic and social systems. It is not surprising, therefore, that there is a link between property crime and macro-economic factors: Home Office research demonstrates that in times of low or negative economic growth, property crime rises at a faster rate (Barclay (ed) 1995: 5; see also Box 1987). In considering criminal law's regulation of property, therefore, one has to be alive to the significance of property not only as an individual entitlement which may be violated by property crime but also as an institution which is a defining feature of contemporary social order. As we shall see, the history of criminal law's development has accordingly been marked by concerns about the law's capacity to facilitate the efficient conduct of commerce. Equally, the justice of criminal law has been questioned in the light of the radically inegalitarian distribution of property and by the difficulty of drawing in a capitalist culture a clear moral line between legitimate and illegitimate dealings with property. These tensions surface in a particularly obvious way in criminal law's difficulty in delineating the concept of dishonesty (see **section II.a.ii.** below), as well as in its uncertainty about the proper scope of defences such as necessity (see **section II.f.** below).

The preoccupation with private property is a particular feature of modern Western political thought and social structure rather than a universal phenomenon: the organisation of other cultures reminds us that private property does not have to be central to social life. Different forms of property holdings have characterised the social organisation of other cultures. The Mohegan Indians, for example, held fast to their system of collective property even when their expropriation by the white immigrants to America made it almost impossible to survive without resorting to the dominant conception of proprietorship as the 'cultivation' of individual parcels of land (Thompson 1989). It is in the nature of particular conceptions of property that they marginalise alternative conceptions and, with them, ways of life. Laws – both criminal and civil – are centrally involved in this process of marginalisation, as is well illustrated by the history of the expropriation of indigenous peoples and debates about its rectification in countries such as Australia (*Mabo No 2*, 1992: see Ivison et al 2000). Liberal theory has come to acknowledge the existence of certain forms of collective ownership and contracting, but it does so by analogy with individual ownership and by creating complex legal entities such as 'companies' which are themselves often referred to as 'fictions'. The dominant position of private property and of market economies, as well as globalisation and the internationalisation of markets, since the late twentieth century is such that it has become difficult for any society to maintain a totally different system – as witnessed by the 'capitalisation' of China, one of the few remaining state socialist societies.

Within the dominant idea of private property, different conceptions of proprietary interest abound, and these, too, pose a number of challenges for the legal framework. It has been argued, for example, that the development of the 'welfare state' in liberal capitalist democracies has issued in a conception of 'new property', consisting in entitlements to welfare and other social benefits provided by the state (Reich 1964). The position of this last form of property in terms of legal recognition as a property-type right is tenuous, and seems currently to be undergoing redefinition not so much as an entitlement but as a privilege reminiscent of older conceptions of charity. The flexibility and importance of law in setting up different kinds of property is well-illustrated in a vast range of private law provisions having to do with, for example, 'choses in action'; 'trusts' splitting 'legal' and 'equitable' interests in property; freeholds, leases and licences; life interests; bailments; covenants and easements. Our idea of property and criminal law's regulation of it must also go beyond the common-sense image of property as tangible goods and resources to include a wide range of intangible interests with indistinct boundaries. The incorporation into law of 'intellectual properties' such as copyrights and patents has gradually been established; but should laws of criminal libel be seen as a form of property law, protecting a group's right to 'cultural capital' in its reputation? Laws prohibiting unauthorised telephone tapping could be seen as protecting a property right in the private and uninterfered with use of a telephone line, and laws regulating pollution or even road traffic as protecting collective property rights in a clean or safe environment. As we shall see in **Chapter 5**, even sexual offences have sometimes been interpreted as protecting a proprietary interest in controlling sexual access to the body. The variety and breadth of legal and social regulations which can be interpreted as recognising property-type rights is therefore vast. Much the same is true of non-legal systems of norms: one has only to think of some of the most basic elements of children's socialisation and education, or of the domestic rules of clubs, schools and societies, to see how many of those regulations relate to property. Central notions of conventional morality such as honesty and enterprise relate intimately to the social value attached to respect for property. The role of law in constructing property relations and thereby facilitating and legitimising certain uses of resources and powers, and impeding and delegitimising others, is therefore of the first social importance.

A review of social histories of crime through the ages bears witness both to the pervasiveness and variety of property offences, and to the public anxiety and soul-searching to which offending against property gives rise.

J Bellamy, *Crime and Public Order in England in the Later Middle Ages* (Routledge and Kegan Paul, 1973) pp 6–8

… The chronicler Henry Knighton, under the year 1364, described a wave of theft, pointing out how many churches were entered and robbed … In the fifteenth century the first evidence that law and order were in serious jeopardy came not at the time of the rebellions of 1403 or 1405–8 but in Henry IV's last three or four years as king, when recurrent sickness had sapped his physical vitality. In Norfolk, secret societies were reported to be extorting money by threats, particularly from abbots and priors, and there were widespread riots and feuding in the north midlands and Yorkshire. In Staffordshire, at least, the years were noteworthy for the giving of livery to retainers illegally …

When the child king Henry VI had ascended the throne, complaint started again. In October 1426 the government admitted there were open and notorious robberies and misdeeds being committed in divers parts of the realm, and made special provision for the proclamation in public places of those statutes which concerned the safeguarding of the peace most vitally. Three years later the king, or rather his ministers, claimed to have reliable information from many sources that in every county a great number of robberies had lately been committed by thieves in criminal bands, 'more than used to be in times past'. He was especially unhappy, he said, because ordinary citizens were doing little to capture the miscreants ... A petition in parliament in 1429 referred to the daily occurrence of forcible entries into other men's property and claimed that the land so acquired was often being granted away to the locally powerful in order to have their maintenance.

This passage suggests one persistent theme in official preoccupations with property offences. This is that they are potentially undermining to political authority in that those who have little or no property may perceive the enforcement of property laws as a form of social injustice: in an unequally propertied society, the consensus underpinning property laws is likely to be vulnerable and will often be perceived by propertied classes to be so.

The following passage confirms the pervasiveness of social preoccupations about property crime and shows that it was seen as linked with socio-economic factors as long ago as the sixteenth century:

J S Cockburn, 'The Nature and Incidence of Crime in England 1559–1625: A Preliminary Survey' in Cockburn (ed) *Crime and Society in England 1550–1800* (Methuen, 1977) pp 60–61

Almost all contemporary complaints that crime was increasing focused upon offences against property. To some extent this merely reflected the obvious fact that trials for theft traditionally dominated criminal court proceedings. Throughout this period the vast majority of indictments laid at assizes were for theft of some sort: of 7544 persons indicted in the three counties under review, 5493 (almost 73 per cent) were accused of larceny, burglary or robbery. For those wishing to moralize or to urge more severe penalties for offences against property, the consistently high proportion of thieves appearing on gaol calendars constituted an undeniably powerful argument.

In seeking to explain this feature, most contemporaries embraced the view that theft was a socio-economic phenomenon. Pamphleteers occasionally noticed that the lower classes did not enjoy a monopoly of theft and violent crime. But rarely did they go on to draw the direct connection between crime and childhood training advanced by the pediatrician John Jones in 1579. Crime in the 1570s was due, he claimed, to 'nothing so much ... as to the manner of bring up in liberty, void of the fear of God's justice, terror of the Prince's laws, knowledge of themselves, and exercise in youth how to attain lawfully their living and maintenance in age ... '. Privy Councillors, M.P.s and grand jurymen alike regarded thieves, vagrant solders, rogues, paupers and the idle as associated, or even indistinguishable categories. Poverty and roguery were cut from the same quarry; ale – and gaming-houses were both resorts for the idle and 'nurseries of naughtiness'; 'the cause of great misdemeanours and outrages'; 'the very stock and stay of our false thieves and vagabonds'. An anonymous pamphleteer in 1595 summed up popular thinking: 'such is the reward of riot; where no regard is had of spending above the course of lawful getting necessity must needs follow; games, wantonness and ease are not continued without excessive cost'. In noting the connection between scarcity and crime and the more permanent dislocating effects of urban life, contemporary writers commonly associated offences against property with those sectors of society thought to have been most affected by the economic and social dislocation of the late sixteenth and early seventeenth centuries – rural labourers driven from the land, unemployed craftsmen, discharged and deserted soldiers. Nor did the more general point that crime may be seen as an indicator of social tensions and instability entirely escape them. 'England had never so much work for a chronicle', mused a commentator on the shooting of a Chancery master in 1616, 'never such turnings, tossings and mutabilities in the lives of men and women and the streams of their fortunes'.

Much of the indictment evidence tends to support those generalizations which sought to explain property crime in socio-economic terms. However, the social classification of criminals in this period poses serious problems. Traditional legal definitions – 'labourer', 'husbandman', 'yeoman' – reflected by this time only the broadest social grouping; court clerks used the terms loosely, and it is not uncommon to find the same man described as a 'labourer' in one indictment and as a craftsman of some sort in another. It is therefore impossible to give statistical definition to contemporary generalizations attributing theft to particular social groups.

On the other hand, individual indictments occasionally confirm the connection between crime and economic misfortune. 'Weavers' occupation is a dead science nowadays', declared a Colchester weaver in 1566. 'We can get no work', said another, nor we have no money; and if we should steal we should be hanged, and if we should ask no man would give us; but we will have a remedy one of these days or else we will lose all.

Cockburn concludes from a study of the available evidence, including the relationship between prices and property crime, that 'in the early seventeenth century theft was to a perceptible degree motivated by economic necessity' (p 70).

As we might expect given the relationship between property crime and fears of public disorder, further historical evidence suggests that property crime was often associated with 'moral panics' (see **Chapter 2.I.b.**). Beattie, for example (1977: 155ff), tells of the arousal of high public anxiety about robbery in the eighteenth century. Nor were robbery and theft the only property crimes which preoccupied our ancestors: counterfeiting and the more subtle property offences now associated with fraud also have a long history (see, for example, MacFarlane 1981: 186ff). The diversity of kinds of and motivations underlying even standard property offences such as theft continues to puzzle criminologists who seek to explain property offending – whether as an act of political protest stemming from social injustice or as an instrumental and calculated action which participates in the values of the very capitalist system whose norms it violates.

Hay's research on the enforcement of property offences in the eighteenth century calls into question any simple assumptions about the law's instrumental functions, and reveals the varying attitudes to criminal law evinced by those with different stakes in the system of property:

D Hay, 'Property, Authority and the Criminal Law' in D Hay, P Linebaugh and E P Thompson, *Albion's Fatal Tree* (Penguin, 1975) p 17 at pp 59–60

... Romilly and the rest of the reformers were undoubtedly right that convictions in the courts were uncertain, and that the occasional terror of the gallows would always be less effective than sure detection of crime and moderate punishments. Yet the argument had little weight with the gentry and aristocracy. In the first place they had large numbers of personal servants to guard their plate and their wives. Their problem was not attack from without but disloyalty within their houses. No code of laws or police force would protect them there. Their own judgment of character and the fair treatment of servants within the family were the only real guarantees they could have. Nor did the technicalities of the law bother country gentlemen when they did come to try pilferers of their woods and gardens. For as MPs they passed a mass of legislation that allowed them, as JPs, to convict offenders without the trouble of legalistic indictments or tender-minded juries. In cases involving grain, wood, trees, garden produce, fruit, turnips, dogs, cattle, horses, the hedges of parks and game, summary proceedings usually yielded a speedy and simple conviction. The other crime from which the gentry commonly suffered was sabotage: arson, cattle-maiming, the destruction of trees. Although all these offences were punished by death, few offenders were ever caught. Here too gentlemen knew that a reform of the capital statutes would not increase the certainty of the conviction. Moreover, sabotage was primarily an attack on their authority rather than their property. Their greatest protection against such assaults was acquiescence in their right to rule: the belief in their neighbourhoods that they were kind and just landlords and magistrates. In one area alone were they exposed to the danger of great financial loss from theft. Their largest possession was land. The only way it could be taken from them illegally was by forgery – and it is significant that forgery was punished with unmitigated severity throughout the century, by death.

Lower down the social scale, the property of men in trade and manufacturing and farming was much less secure. In the eighteenth century very few of the offences from which such men suffered were punishable on summary conviction. Instead, to recover embezzled banknotes or shoplifted calico or stolen sheep, it was necessary to go to the expense and trouble of a full criminal trial. Its outcome was always uncertain: the technicalities of indictment or the misplaced sympathies of juries allowed many thieves to escape. After the trial came the misplaced sympathies of petitioners for pardons. Martin Madan, anxious to see property secured by a more rigorous execution of the laws, argued that 'the outside influences of great supporters' had too great effect on the prerogative of mercy. The result was that the great indulged their humanity at the expense of lesser men's property.

There was, therefore, a division of interest among propertied Englishmen about the purpose of the criminal law. The reformers' campaign spoke to humanitarians of all classes, men revolted by the public agonies of the condemned at the gallows. But their argument that capital punishment should be replaced by a more certain protection of property appealed mostly to that great body of 'middling men', almost half the nation, who earned from £25 to £150 a year at mid-century, and created more than half of England's wealth. Although they could use the discretionary elements of the law to a limited degree, their property was the prey of thieves undeterred by terror. Their complaints did not impress a tiny but powerful ruling class, whose immense personal property in land was secure, who could afford to protect their other goods without public support, and who in any case were most concerned with the law as an instrument of authority.

Hay's research also illustrates the way in which the discretionary application of criminal law may serve to maintain a delicate balance between the efficacy and legitimacy of criminal law: the capital penalties which he discusses were frequently commuted, and the exercise of the prerogative of mercy acted, paradoxically, as a means whereby the legitimacy of state authority could be strengthened (cf Thompson 1975, discussed in **Chapter 1.I.b.i.**).

In the early nineteenth century, anxieties about poaching and about riots and criminal damage in protest at land enclosure once again illustrate the continuity between property and public order issues and the way in which changes in the form of property holdings, imposed by those with political power, radically affect the conditions of life of ordinary people and hence on occasion generate protest-related crime (see Rudé 1985: 21, 30–31, 81ff). In this era, too, larceny was the dominant form of property crime, although forgery of banknotes and bills of exchange was also prevalent. The conclusions of another historian underline the difficulty of constructing any overarching explanation of property offending:

G Rudé, *Criminal and Victim: Crime and Society in Early Nineteenth-Century England* (Clarendon Press, 1985) pp 117–119

But does this tendency of criminal and victims to belong to different, if not opposing classes in this confrontation mean that, through crime and the combating of crime, they were engaged in a form of class war? To some commentators and to some historians of crime this has appeared as a reasonable proposition; for does not the criminal, as an evident reject from society, attempt, through crimes committed against those most socially favoured, to restore the balance or to climb his way back into his own? It seems a logical and an apparently attractive theory; but … the premiss is a false one. Most conspicuously so in the case of those I have called the 'acquisitive' type of criminal, who, far from turning his back on the norms of the society he lives in, is the one (in my view) who exploits these norms, including the competition for property and profit, in order to enrich himself and become more securely entrenched in a form of society that he patently admires and wishes to belong to. Nor does the proposition hold in the case of those to whom I have attached the label 'survival', those who have generally confessed to or been found guilty of stealing clothing, food-stuffs, fowls, bed-linen, or small amounts of money and who, as so many prisoners appearing at the Old Bailey in certain years have testified, have been 'impelled to steal, rob, and burgle by economic 'distress" … such crimes tend to respond directly to short-term economic factors such as a rise in prices or a fall in wages whereas the more serious and more violent crimes, or those more susceptible to capital punishment, were not so responsive to economic motivation … [C]rimes committed for survival, whoever the victim, do not betoken a class war. In fact, from the records we have examined, the only suggestion of a class war was that engaged in by certain participants in unlawful protest …

The inclination to regard property crime as a symptom of class conflict and a threat to social order is itself relative to the stability and self-confidence of that order. As Wiener argues, changing attitudes to crime are associated not only with changing patterns of offending but also with shifting understandings of criminal responsibility. Wiener's analysis shows how the early Victorian conception of the rational and self-governing individual who is responsible for crime was gradually displaced by a more deterministic approach which had very different implications for criminal policy:

Martin Wiener, *Reconstructing the Criminal* (Cambridge University Press, 1990) p 12

Although fears of both social and personal disorder were steadily allayed by the success of Victorian efforts at control, this very success, taking place while both scientific and social thinking were profoundly altering, nurtured [a] new anxiety. As technology and economic advances kept extending the scale and complexity of life, and as the natural sciences put forth new deterministic models of understanding the human world, the Victorian image of the individual weakened. Reflective persons were coming to feel dwarfed by their natural and social environment ...

... At the same time that upper-middle-class individuals began to feel less autonomous and less vital, they began to perceive criminal offenders as less threatening and less responsible for their behaviour and instead saw them as social wreckage and stepchildren of nature, rather than willful enemies of society. As self-realization began to replace self-discipline as the organizing theme of middle-class lives, the prison and its impersonal disciplinary regime appeared ever less a satisfactory answer to crime. Criminals appeared now to require direct therapeutic intervention rather than deterrence or discipline. Consequently, the link between liability to criminal sanctions and moral blame was loosened, while these sanctions were made less punitive and more welfarist ...

pp 279–281

In the diminishing insistence upon personal responsibility, the treatment of theft [in the late nineteenth century] paralleled that for most forms of homicide. As with the latter, the statistics showed that the amount of traditional theft was in decline; the proportion of trials to population began to fall in the mid-1860s and continued to do so down to World War 1. With a relaxation of fear of crime and the spread in the 1880s of social conscience, the responsibility of society was increasingly stressed. The argument was made by criminals as well as by social reformers. Michael Davitt recounted to the 1895 Departmental Committee on Prisons a conversation he had had with a Dartmoor burglar. "Put yourself in my position", the convict had told him.

> "I never knew my father or my mother. My first recollection is of being turned out of a workhouse. I fell among thieves. I got educated in crime. I learned to read and write in prison. Unlike you I have had no moral training. I hold that man is naturally a thief. Take for instance a child in its mother's arms; anything that excites its fancy it wants to get, and if that natural feeling is not corrected by parental training and moral influence and education it gets stronger as the child grows older. I am such a product of your civilisation. You allowed me to grow up with these animal instincts uncorrected, and then you send me to prison when I exercise them."

Toward a related form of misappropriation of property – that of debt default, both elite and popular – the law ... was gradually adopting a less punitive attitude. Bankruptcy was losing its harsh stigma and nonwillful debt default had been relieved in 1869 of penal liability. The continued imprisonment, as willful defaultors, of substantial numbers of small debtors after 1869 began to draw increasing fire, and though the courts resisted formal change in the law the length of time such persons spent in jail steadily fell.

... Street criminals were rarely now being described as dangerous beasts or self-willed villains, but rather as almost pathetic incompetents. In this context, current sentencing practices seemed misdirected and, for the first time since the abolition of capital sanctions for property crime, official interest reappeared in realigning penalties for offenses against the person and offenses against property. From 1880 on, the Liberal M.P. D.H. Macfarlane kept before the public eye the lack of seriousness with which the courts treated assaults against women and children as compared to offenses against property; he called for both greater judicial protection of the helpless and more lenient sentencing of petty property offenders ...

Underneath this divergence in concern about these two categories of objectionable offenses lay several broad developments: the increasingly successful control of street crime, which relaxed fears; the spread of material prosperity (and the appearance of insurance against theft), which lessened the economic importance of the offenses; a growth of democratic sensitivities, which raised concern for the weaker members of society, disproportionately the victims of violence more than of theft (as Macfarlane pointed out, all had a person but only a minority had significant property); and, not unconnected with democratization, a weakening belief in the chosen, willed character of deviant behaviour.

Wiener's account of the 'reconstruction of the criminal' in the late nineteenth century is directly relevant to our analysis of contemporary property crime. For, as we shall see, debates about social versus individual responsibility continue to flourish, bringing with them implications for both the structure of criminal liability and the nature of punishment.

In considering contemporary concerns with criminal threats to property, we could focus on a wide variety of conduct. Vandalism; housebreaking; illicit reproduction of copyright materials; insider dealing; pollution; tax evasion; theft associated with vehicles (which, despite a drop in 2000, still constituted 19% of the offences recorded by the police in 2000–2001: Home Office 2001b): these constitute just a few of the diverse phenomena which are daily reported in newspapers and by other news media. In setting the context for our discussion of the history and contemporary framework of criminal offences against property, we have selected some particular areas for detailed study. They have been selected because they illustrate both the flexibility of legal categories and, conversely, the extent to which conventional images of property offences, reflected in legal definitions, focus on particular kinds of behaviour which do not necessarily represent either the most prevalent or the most serious threats to established property interests. Hence, like Wiener, we shall try to identify the nature of the images of the property offender which practices of criminalisation produce. We shall also examine the toleration of forms of property offending such as tax evasion and other forms of 'white collar crime' which are technically within legal definitions but which are not seen as particularly threatening to the legal and social order.

I.b.   Shoplifting

Among the many forms of property offence, theft probably occupies the central position in popular conceptions of property crime:

K Bottomley and K Pease, *Crime and Punishment: Interpreting the Data* (Open University Press, 1986) pp 8–10

Offences of theft (including 'handling stolen goods' or 'receiving' as it used to be known) have always constituted a majority of all notifiable crime recorded by the police. In 1983 more than half of all notifiable [mostly indictable] offences were in this category; in 1963 two-thirds of all indictable offences were theft or receiving stolen property. The rate of increase in these offences has been slightly lower than that for all notifiable offences; between 1978 and 1983 the annual average rate of increase was only 3%, compared with an average of 7% a year between 1973 and 1978. In 1983 almost half of all the offences in this group involved either theft from or unauthorized taking of a motor vehicle, but in 1963 the comparable figure (including the then non-indictable offence of taking a motor vehicle without the owner's consent) was only 27%. Other social and technological changes are reflected in the drop in the proportion of thefts from automatic machines and pre-payment meters to only 2% of the total in 1983 (compared with 8% in 1963) and the increase in recorded thefts from shops, which in 1983 constituted almost 1 in 7 of all thefts, compared with only 1 in 12 in 1963. Despite inflation, the face value of property stolen in the majority of thefts remains surprisingly low; thus, in 1983 more than a third of recorded offences involved theft of property worth less than £25, and in a further quarter the value was from £25 up to but not including £100.

In 2000, over 2,100,000 theft and handling offences were recorded by the police – 24% of recorded notifiable offences (Home Office 2001b). At the other end of the criminal process, theft and handling made up 41% of convictions or cautions for indictable offences. The disparity between this and the official figure illustrates, as we saw in **Chapter 1.III.b.**, there are many filters between behaviour which might be regarded as criminal and the recording of crime, let alone the ultimate conviction of an offender. But the filters work in different ways with different types of offence, producing varying 'clear-up' rates. In 2000 thefts from shops constituted a huge 62% of theft convictions. This high clear-up rate is almost certainly due to the fact that large shops employ security staff and only tend to report to the police if they have identified a suspect. Such figures, of course, do not represent anything like the total amount of theft: the *British Crime Surveys* (BCS: see Kershaw et al 2001; Home Office 2002g), based on victimisation surveys and self-report studies, indicate that the actual level of thefts of and from motor vehicles and from the person are about three and seven times more common, respectively, than official statistics suggest: the 2001–2002 British Crime Survey estimated that there were 3,939,000 thefts, excluding vehicle thefts, in England and Wales (Home Office 2002g: 36; see further Maguire 2002; on the British Crime Surveys, see **Chapter 1.III.b.ii.**).

Among forms of theft, shoplifting is of particular interest because of the vivid way in which it relates to changing cultures of consumption in capitalist economies. The BCS does not cover shoplifting, but it seems likely that this kind of theft very often goes unreported, either because of lack of detection or because informal measures such as warnings are judged to be appropriate. Official figures are influenced by the extent to which members of the public are likely to *interpret* a particular incident as criminal and hence to report it; the importance of social attitudes in shaping such perceptions is vividly illustrated by the case of shoplifting. Shoplifting is often thought of as a typically female crime. While it is true that theft and handling as a whole constitute a far higher proportion of female (60%) as opposed to male (36%) indictable cautions or convictions, the total number of men convicted or cautioned for theft or handling (137,800) is over double that of women (52,700) (figures taken from Home Office 2000c: 4, 8). Yet although the specific instance of shoplifting does indeed represent one of the few areas where women's offending approaches the level of men's (at least as judged by the official statistics), the figures do not bear out the stereotype of shoplifting as a female-dominated crime:

A Morris, *Women, Crime and Criminal Justice* (Blackwell, 1987) pp 29–31

The offence most commonly attributed to women, especially to girls, is shoplifting. In 1985, half of the women sentenced for indictable offences in the magistrates' courts were shoplifters compared with 16 per cent of men. The percentages for juveniles were similar: for 10- to 14-year-olds it was 53 per cent of girls compared with 20 per cent of boys, and for 14- to 17-year-olds it was 44 per cent and 14 per cent respectively ... Such figures have led researchers to link women's crime to women's traditional role, that is, to describe such offences as role-expressive. Put simply, the argument is that women shop and so shoplifting is an extension of their normal role ...

... [I]t is questionable how helpful it is to categorize such offence as predominantly 'masculine' or 'feminine' ... [S]hoplifting is not numerically more common amongst women and girls than men and boys, even in the criminal statistics [for example, 33,892 women and 46,562 men were cautioned by the police or dealt with in the magistrates' or Crown Courts for thefts from shops in 1985], and, if we take into consideration the sex of those who use stores, there is even less reason to call shoplifting a woman's crime. The claim that shoplifting is an offence committed mainly by women is a myth, but one which persists.

Research also suggests that women may be over-represented in the recorded offences of shoplifting ... This raises the issue that women may figure to a great extent in shoplifting statistics because store detectives, sales-persons and the like expect women to shoplift because of preconceived notions of 'menopausal' or 'kleptomaniac' women, and thus they observe women more carefully. This obviously increases women's chances of detection.

Another important feature of shoplifting is a popular ambivalence about its causes: the social perception of shoplifting as wrongful is tempered by a recognition of the temptations inherent in a society organised to ever-greater degrees around the logic of consumption. This recognition introduces a determinism at odds with the usual notions of individual responsibility in terms of which crime is constructed. The very label 'shoplifting', as opposed to the more moralistic 'theft', is significant in this respect. Nonetheless, severe legal sanctions remain available for cases which the public and the courts do interpret as 'mainstream' theft, and stereotypes are doubtless influential. Sensational reporting of large-scale shoplifting in London by women from overseas contrasts, for example, with press reaction to the conviction in the US of actress Winona Ryder: while the latter explained Ryder's offence in terms of psychological problems, the former has all the marks of a moral panic raised against those who can be classified as 'outsiders'. Murphy reminds us that legal responses to shoplifting have on occasion been draconian:

D J I Murphy, *Customers and Thieves, An Ethnography of Shoplifting* (Gower, 1986) pp 85–86

Despite the recent concern about shoplifting, it is not a new world of activity. Reference to 'The Lifting Law' was made in 1597, and the modern usage of the term, specifying theft from shops, dates from the seventeenth century when shoplifting became an established feature of everyday life ...

The offence was officially recognised in the preamble to the 1698 Act 10 of Parliament, William III, c. 12: 'The Crime of stealing goods privately out of Shops and Warehouses commonly called shoplifting ... ' Under the Act, shoplifting was a capital offence, and it was not until 1820 that Sir James Mackintosh succeeded in abolishing the death penalty for the offence of 'stealing five shillings from a shop'. Edwards ... records that

'In the Summer of the year 1726, shoplifters became so common and so detrimental to the shopkeepers, that they made application to the Government for assistance in apprehending the offenders; and in order thereto, offered a reward and a pardon for any who would discover their associates in such a practice.'

This amnesty to informers led to the downfall of the notorious Jonathan Wild who had built up an empire of 'fencing', partly on the proceeds of shoplifters ...

Until his death, Wild operated an ingenious system by which he controlled much of London's underworld; acting as an agent through whom victims of crime could recover their stolen property, which Wild had bought from the thieves, at a price. For example, if a gold watch were stolen from a prosperous gentleman, Wild would let it be known, either directly to the victim or through advertising, that the watch could be recovered for a fee, and the arrangement was duly completed.

Wild's career raises not only the continuing spectre of 'professional' or 'organised' crime in the context of shoplifting, but also the way in which the fine line between enterprise and crime is mediated in capitalist culture by moral and legal notions of property and honesty. Shoplifting also provides a good example of the way in which forms of offending develop in response to changing social conditions:

D P Walsh, *Shoplifting: Controlling a Major Crime* (Macmillan, 1978) p 3

The process of translation, whereby fairs became markets with stalls, which became covered markets or permanent shops, took time, and it was never complete. There are still covered markets and for that matter fairs, as well as thousands of open market stalls. Judging by contemporary legislation, it seems highly likely that before and during this transition shop theft was rife. The harsh lessons learnt in the market-place were not forgotten when it came to constructing and using permanent shop-houses. For example, the same conventions relating to the 'counter' or boundary between customer and shopkeeper were still observed, unlike shops in other cultures where buyer and seller sit and talk in comfort in the back of the shop before bargaining with each other ... The shop was organised around its stock and the protection of it ...

In medieval times the businessmen who were most alert to theft were of course those who had most to lose, that is the jewellers, the goldsmiths and the silversmiths, who always kept their most valuable wares concealed from the view of the ordinary shopper to make it harder for the impromptu thief ... Such (justified) apprehension about theft has always meant that jewellers and the like have been quick to take advantage of any new security devices which have become available, from early iron bars on shop windows and heavy iron-studded oak doors to modern photo-electric alarm systems and radar sentries ... The earliest shops and stalls of course had no glass windows, and this made it very easy for people to steal by just reaching in and grabbing articles ...

p 6

... The nineteenth century shop had reached a pinnacle of development and perfection with regard both to selling and to controlling shop theft.

Very little substantive change in the shape, structure and selling techniques adopted by shops occurred from then on to the end of the Second World War. Such change as did occur was chiefly in the variety and appearance of the goods, and how they were prepared for sale ... The most significant changes in shop organisation were the introduction of voluntary wholesale chains and retail buying groups, and new merchandising techniques, especially important being self-service and self-selection. Self-service was first developed in America as a sales technique and its proposed introduction into England was initially regarded with horror by established, experienced, shop managers. Their view was that at the cost of a great deal of time, effort and ingenuity, they had finally reduced the theft problem to manageable proportions, and now the suggestion was that after all the customers should be allowed to help themselves! This would set at nought all the practical lessons of selling which had been so hardly won ... In 1950 there were less than 500 self-service grocery shops in England, ten years later there were 6,500. Despite all the adverse criticism and the comments that the idea of self-service had attracted, there were compelling reasons for accepting it ultimately in many retail areas. Customers liked it for a start, but the main pressure to change to self-service was the growing cost of shop labour ...

pp 16–17

In large department stores and supermarkets shoplifting can occur for hundreds of separate reasons, and can be seen as illustrating selfishness, human greed, or virtually anything else along similar lines, but to shop managers the most important aspect of this is not shoplifting alone, but the final rate of 'shrinkage'. Shrinkage as a term represents total stock-loss, and it includes stock lost through damage or decay, as well as through theft, by delivery-men, shop staff and shoplifting by customers ... It is indeed interesting to consider how such shop managers are able to combine their initial moral indifference to the problem of shoplifting with the moral indignation which they display when it starts to present itself in a fashion which cannot be ignored, and how they manage to resolve this psychologically.

Walsh relates the modern increases in levels of (recorded) shoplifting (a four-fold increase from 1939 to 1964, and a further twofold increase between then and 1972, rising by another nearly 50% by 1976 – p 29) to the developments of increased opportunities provided by the self-service system. He also recognises the diversity of motivations for and types of shoplifting, ranging from the casual and opportunistic to (less frequent) organised offences.

This discussion of shoplifting exposes competing ideologies informing our interpretation of property offences – ideologies which reflect, respectively, a commitment to the individualistic and social conceptions of criminal responsibility identified by Wiener. These competing ideologies are reflected in the ways in which property crime is talked about: the language of dishonesty and culpability can quickly replace acknowledgement of temptation accompanied by tolerance and indifference. The criteria for the shift are not legal but cultural and political. The significance of those criteria are further illustrated by our next example.

I.c.   Occupational and 'white collar' crime and conceptions of fraud

As we shall see in **Chapter 6.II.c.**, the crimes of corporate offenders tend to be marginalised by criminal regulation despite the fact that corporations frequently conduct themselves in ways which can be seen as harmful and even violent. Corporate offenders also engage in conduct which causes economic and material loss. Research has drawn together some of the actual examples of corporate crime which have caused serious material, psychological and financial harm (Box, 1983: 25ff). Examples of corporate crime by fraud, price-fixing and insider dealing are in sharp contrast to the popular image of property offenders – the young 'mugger', the masked burglar, the menopausal or 'foreign' shoplifter, the working-class 'fence'. Yet the serious impact of corporate crime cannot be doubted. In this section, we consider both corporate crime and individual offending in the corporate and employment contexts – what has been called 'white collar crime' and 'occupational crime' such as 'pilfering' and 'fiddling'.

The classic conceptualisation of white collar crime is to be found in the pioneering work of American criminologist Edwin Sutherland:

E Sutherland, _White Collar Crime_, 1949 (Yale University Press, 1983) pp 7–8

Persons who violate laws regarding restraint of trade, advertising, pure food and drugs and similar business practices are not arrested by uniformed policemen, are not tried in criminal courts, and are not committed to prisons: their illegal behaviour receives the attention of administrative commissions and of courts operating under civil or equity jurisdiction. For this reason such violations of law are not included in the criminal statistics nor are individual cases brought to the attention of the scholars who write the theories of criminal behaviour. The sample of criminal behaviour on which the theories are founded is biased as to socio-economic status, since it excludes these business and professional men ...

The thesis of this book, stated positively, is that persons of the upper socio-economic class engage in much criminal behaviour; that this criminal behaviour differs from the criminal behaviour of the lower socio-economic class principally in the administrative procedures which are used in dealing with the offenders; and that variations in administrative procedures are not significant from the point of view of causation of crime ...

These violations of law by persons in the upper socio-economic class are, for convenience, called "white collar crimes". This concept is not intended to be definitive, but merely to call attention to crimes which are not ordinarily included within the scope of criminology. White collar crime may be defined approximately as a crime committed by a person of respectability and high social status in the course of his occupation ...

Although Sutherland's arguments about white collar crime were innovative and were for some time not accepted by other criminologists, the phenomenon itself was hardly new:

W G Carson, 'White-collar crime and the institutionalisation of ambiguity: the case of the early Factory Acts', in G Geis and E Stotland (eds) *White-collar Crime* (Sage Publications, 1980) p 142

The factory crime of ... [the mid-nineteenth century] was calculated and, as occasion demanded, pervasive. As Leonard Horner, one of the first and arguably the most important Inspector in this period, ruefully reflected after more than fifteen years' experience, "We unfortunately know too well that all mill-owners are not to be trusted: that many of them have a very loose kind of morality in regard to evasions of the factory law". Despite open admissions of the grounds on which they might violate, however, employers were frequently none too willing to assume personal responsibility for the law having been broken. More often than not, juvenile labour was hired directly by the skilled adult operatives themselves, the industry's employment structure again intruding, this time to lend superficial credibility to claims that the master was not the really culpable party. Moreover, as the law was framed at the point when Inspectors were first appointed and some measure of real control became a possibility for the first time, it was legally permissible to shift responsibility from the mill-occupier to the employee, where the magistrates were satisfied that the offence had been committed without personal consent, concurrence or knowledge of the master ...

Displacement of responsibility onto others was not, however, the only strategy used by employers in this period to deny any real criminal guilt on their own part, while continuing to profit from factory crime. Some, of course, deemed it sufficient to follow the letter of the law even though its spirit was grossly abused – Ashworth, for example, maintained that even if a child was actually and patently under the permitted age, once an employer had paid sixpence for a certificate of age, however false, he had a licence to work the child. Others contended that although they might indeed be in breach of the law, their delinquencies were merely formal or even technical offences involving no substance of moral responsibility commensurate with conviction on a criminal charge.

This passage illustrates the fluidity of conceptions of property crime: the use of child labour to maximise profit might not normally be seen as property crime, but can certainly be represented as such. We shall return below to the strategies used to 'neutralise' guilt and responsibility by white collar offenders. Pearce, in his study of violations of anti-trust laws in the United States, reminds us both of the enormous value of white collar crime and sets out the factors which favour its marginalisation as a category of crime:

F Pearce, *Crimes of the Powerful; Marxism, Crime and Deviance* (Pluto Press, 1978) p 79

Using the [US] government's own criteria of the cost of crime to the community, burglary, an 'index crime' for the FBI, is surprisingly insignificant. The $284 million worth of goods stolen in 1965 represents only 3 per cent the annual estimated profits of 'organised crime' (conventionally defined), and only 3 per cent of the money gained by the tax frauds of the wealthiest 1 per cent in 1957.

This alone calls into question the justifications given for the mode and distribution of police enforcement activity and for the severity of sanctions imposed by the court. Bourgeois ideologues would answer this by talking of the 'common' good, yet the most economically significant crimes, those of the wealthy, are the least publicised, investigated and, if punished, there is little stigma attached to the known offenders.

p 81

[The concentration of criminal justice agencies on lower-class criminals] ... is functional in maintaining the American class system. Firstly, it strengthens the dominant individualistic ideology. If the criminals are also the social failures (those at the bottom of an open, competitive, hierarchical class system, where any man can succeed), then their criminality is caused by their inadequacies (lack of determination, moral weakness, etc.) and the major social institutions are not exposed to critical assessment. Secondly, by defining such individuals as non-citizens with no rights to employment, education, etc. the system's failure to provide these for them (independently of their criminality) is obscured. Finally, by criminal-ising them and treating them as social and amoral, their potential for developing an ideologically sophisticated understanding of their situation is neutralised, and by incarcerating them it is made difficult for them to organise to realise their ideas. American class society would be threatened by the development of an ideologically sophisticated lower-class political movement.

Furthermore not all white-collar crimes are equally immune to prosecution. If for, example, embezzlement was left unprosecuted and there was a large increase in such activity, capitalism might well collapse; for the financial transactions essential to this kind of economy inevitably involve trust but cannot take place in a manner which gives fool-proof protection from violations of it. It is necessary to investigate the social effects of these crimes. Thus, in the Second World War it was imperative that the state should succeed in stopping those black market offences that undermined the American war effort, since American capitalism depended on military success, in order to gain control of crucial Asian markets. Immediate easy profit was in this case opposed to long-term interests. On the other hand, violations of the anti-trust laws (involving monopolistic control of certain markets) do not pose a threat to the social structure of American capitalism and can, therefore, be tolerated.

Levi's study of the regulation of fraud in Britain confirms the significance of this kind of crime, whilst reminding us that its social functions and official attitudes towards it are more complex than Marxian critics such as Pearce assume. Levi's arguments are of special interest in the context of public concern over city fraud in general and 'insider dealing' in particular:

M Levi, *Regulating Fraud: White-collar crime and the criminal process* (Tavistock, 1987) p 4

The twentieth century has witnessed a vast expansion in recorded fraud and in the number of offenders who are officially dealt with for fraud. This is a trend that fraud shares with other forms of crime ... There has been an increase not only in the absolute but also in the relative importance of fraud, which was a mere 0.5 per cent of indictable crime in 1898 but had risen to become 4.6 per cent of indictable crime by 1968 before falling to 3.8 per cent of 'notifiable offences' in 1985 [in 2000/1 the figure for fraud and forgery was 6%] ... The number of recorded offences of fraud quadrupled between 1938 and 1968. Since then, the fraud figures have stabilized, although some of this stability may be more apparent than real, due to the 'crime-deflating', effects of changes in recording procedures in 1980, when the Home Office, in an attempt to improve consistency, directed that 'continuing offences' should be recorded as one offence rather than as a multiplicity of offences.

Levi notes that in 1985, 37 frauds by company directors, etc, 1823 cases of false accounting and 120,758 other frauds were recorded, and reminds us of the high costs of fraud as a form of crime, both in economic and other terms:

pp 22–23

Those data that are available show that in purely financial terms, losses from fraud dwarf all other types of property crime. During 1985, the Metropolitan Police section of the Metropolitan and City Police Company Fraud Branch undertook 791 new enquiries. The 446 cases still under investigation at the end of 1985 involved £867 million 'at risk'. At the end of 1985, the City of London Police had 109 cases under investigation, involving £446.2 million in sterling, plus overseas frauds totalling £452.4 million: an increase of 59.6% over 1984. If we include those investigations that were completed before the year's end, the new enquiries undertaken by the City of London Police Company Fraud Department totalled £541.7 million. (Additionally, the Cheque Fraud Squad dealt with £1 million of fraud, plus one attempted deception of £9.2 million.) ...

The costs of fraud do fluctuate, but ... they have almost tripled since 1980 and have quintupled since 1974 when the cost of fraud in London was £223 million ... Even if calculating the costs of 'fraud currently under investigation' on an 'at risk' basis is an inaccurate reflection of fraud in any given year, this does not cast doubt upon the fact that fraud consistently recorded on this basis has grown dramatically. We should note that these figures exclude the costs of public-sector corruption cases, which are not collated either centrally or by individual forces ...

In short, in 1985, commercial fraud recorded by the Metropolitan and City Police Commercial Fraud Department represented four times the total cost of all other property crimes in London ... To this picture, we should add £814.4 million, which is the total for fraud and corruption recorded by Fraud Squads outside London, compared with £757.2 million of theft, burglary, and robbery outside London. This gives a total of £1084 million for theft, burglary and robbery combined, and a total of £2113 million for Fraud Squad recorded fraud (including attempts). Further work is needed on the validity of the fraud cost statistic, but it appears that the total cost of police-recorded fraud in England and Wales is approximately twice that of theft, burglary and robbery.

p 46

Another important dimension of fraud is more difficult to quantify: its impact upon social values and sense of well-being. Certainly, this has economic ramifications. All commerce, and even the acceptability of a national currency, depends upon some degree of trust and confidence. An early example of the consequences of such a collapse of confidence was the Wall Street Crash of 1929 ... In the case of fraud affecting financial institutions, or the diversion of funds from governmental or non-governmental aid agencies, the effects are measurable, but may well extend far beyond the money stolen, to the death of thousands from malnutrition, for example ...

This last point is brought home with particular intensity by the 2001 Enron scandal, in which the sudden collapse of America's seventh largest company revealed that the apparent success of this giant energy corporation had been manufactured by systematic lies about its profits and debts, the latter concealed so that they did not show in its accounts. It further emerged that Arthur Andersen, Enron's auditors, had destroyed evidence of its relationship with the company. Enron employees lost billions of dollars because their pensions scheme was heavily invested in Enron's own stock. As the Securities and Exchange Commission, the FBI, Congress and the Justice Department proceed with investigations, with a view to prosecution of a number of executives for fraud, conspiracy and false accounting offences, other companies are having to reconsider the use of so-called 'aggressive accounting practices' which are vulnerable to definition as criminal yet which have apparently been accepted as normal practice in vast areas of commerce. Furthermore, questions are being asked about the influence of business on national energy policy and the role of business funds in US political campaigning: Enron was a substantial contributor to the Republican presidential campaign.

As compared with theft, official statistics suggest that serious fraud is relatively infrequent: for every fraud or forgery recorded in the 2000–2001 statistics, there are about seven thefts. But Levi's discussion of the value of serious frauds reminds us that, even leaving aside the question of under-recording, the social impact of fraud cannot be properly estimated merely in terms of its frequency. Levi also underlines the relationship between levels of reported fraud and media interest in it:

M Levi, *Regulating Fraud: White-collar crime and the criminal process* (Tavistock, 1987) pp 10–13

Although there is much dispute about the importance of the media in influencing legislation, policing and public perceptions of and attitudes towards crime, there can be little doubt that press, television and radio interest does play some role in defining (and thereby moulding) 'the crime problem'. Media interest in business crime has increased considerably since the 1960s. Despite the dominance of 'pro-business' Conservative governments and the absence of a strong popular radical press in most western countries, there has been – particularly since Watergate – a cult of expose machismo in media circles that favours the making of programmes on abuse of power by businesspeople or politicians ...

Upperworld malpractices do not receive high coverage in all countries ... However, the British and American television viewer or the reader of the 'quality' or even 'tabloid' national press might find ample daily evidence to refute the assertion – still repeated in many key criminological texts (Box, 1983) – that because of the 24 hour news cycle and the fact that they are owned by 'big business', white-collar crime receives little or no attention in the media ...

In liberal democracies, the perceived public acceptability of business, governmental, and police malpractice stories can change over time. It may be that until the Iranian arms deals, under Reagan – though not in 1985 or 1986 under Thatcher – the revival of patriotism and support for business as central cultural themes made exposê less popular among the media. However, unless the scandal concerns the direct owner or editor of the newspaper or television station ... , or unless his actual or prospective business partners are affected, the general relative media neglect of business crime compared with other forms of crime is explicable more by laziness, investigative cost, the invisible nature of the crime and the deviousness of its progenitors, and by the difficulty of presenting it simply in the human terms expected by mass audiences, than by any elite conspiracy to suppress it.

Another important feature of corporate fraud and white collar crime is their relationship with developing technology and in particular with the use of computers and the Internet, which have generated means of conducting frauds and thefts which are very hard to detect. These new technologies have increased the scope for behaviour threatening 'intellectual', intangible property such as information and programmes. They have also facilitated the commission of a wide range of property offences including theft, deception, forgery and breaches of trust, and have given rise to new offences such as those under the Computer Misuse Act 1990 (OECD 1986). New technologies increase the ability to cause high losses and reduce chances of detection, though they also provide the criminal justice system with new tools of detection and surveillance.

Some important ambiguities in the definition of white collar crime are already emerging from this discussion (see also Nelken 2002). On the one hand, Sutherland's focus is primarily on the status of the offender. Pearce, too, attaches importance to this, but also develops a macro-economic and political approach to the marginalisation of certain kinds of crime. A different and in some ways complementary perspective concentrates rather on the kinds of actions in question – forms of corruption, cheating and straightforward norm-infraction (such as the evasion of factory legislation) which have an important impact on proprietary interests but which do not conform to stereotyped images of 'real' property crime. The offenders in question are not necessarily those on whom Sutherland focused, but their position is analogous in that the conduct in question, whilst clearly illegal, becomes legitimised within a particular subculture. These areas may therefore usefully be examined in the context of 'white collar crime'. One example is the practice of work-related, 'part-time' crime (Ditton 1977). Once again, this is a practice which has a history far longer than that acknowledged by criminology:

Clive Emsley, *Crime and Society in England, 1750–1900* (2nd edn, Longman, New York, 1996) pp 122–126

Workplace crime or 'fiddles' come under a variety of alternative headings, most of which are not neutral words but are those employed by employers or, more commonly, agents of the law concerned with repression. Perquisites or 'perks' can be tolerated by an employer; they can also be the objects of periodic clamp-downs. Generally a 'perk' is regarded by the workforce as an entitlement, though it can sometimes be abused to the extent that few employees could, or would seek to, justify. It is a hazy line that separates perks from pilferage or small-scale theft from the workplace. Pilferage can be practised by virtually an entire workforce at a particular workplace or in a particular job; in a few instances it might shade into more organised and more large-scale theft. A third kind of workplace crime can come under the heading of fraud ... Examples of all of these crimes, or 'fiddles', abound throughout the eighteenth and nineteenth centuries.

The largest single employment sector in Britain during the eighteenth, and for much of the nineteenth century, was agriculture. Various labourers and agricultural communities claimed a whole series of allowances or perks which were gradually whittled down or subjected to greater control and supervision. Gleaning was the best known allowance whereby, after the harvest had been gathered, women and children entered the fields and collected the scattered grain which the harvesters had missed. Corn or beans collected in this way could form a significant percentage of the poor rural family's diet or wage. The custom had biblical authority, though it was clearly practised differently from place to place. During the eighteenth century it was known for individuals to object violently to anyone from outside the community seeking to glean in local fields, and farmers who tried to prevent gleaning, or who turned hogs or cattle out to graze on stubble and thus denied access to the poor, were the objects of popular odium and even assault ...

In 1788 the Court of Common Pleas gave judgment in the case of *Steel v Houghton and Uxor*; the judges declared that there was no specific right in common law permitting anyone to glean without the authority of the farmer who owned the land. 'Though [the farmer's] conscience may direct him to leave something for the poor', added one judge, 'the law does not oblige him to leave anything' ... Here was a vigorous defence of property against what many considered as a custom: such a defence was typical of the eighteenth century. Yet it was not necessarily acted upon in such a way in the courts. In Essex a group of farmers set out to put a stop to gleaning on the basis of this ruling; the magistrates refused to convict at summary level, and the one case indicted at the quarter sessions was thrown out by the grand jury ...

... Farmers did not use the 1788 judgment as the opportunity for a blanket assault on gleaning; the gleaners' case continued to be underpinned by humanitarian and scriptural arguments, and such prosecutions as there were seem to have depended rather more on local farming practice than on a new determination to preserve property rights ...

As the nineteenth century wore on communities regulated gleaning themselves with the use of gleaning bells which rang to start and finish daily operations ... Gleaning gradually disappeared partly as a result of technological change in the shape of mechanical binders and reapers which were introduced towards the end of the nineteenth century and which transformed harvesting, but probably rather more because a rise in real wages reduced the incentives.

Long after the 1788 ruling by the Court of Common Pleas gleaning continued to be justified in terms of customary rights; the taking of other produce from the land was not open to such justification, though some may have considered that their labour in the fields entitled them to some such 'perks'. Some farmers probably tolerated such behaviour, providing it was only occasional and limited; and, of course, such 'perks' or pilfer-age were difficult to prove unless a man was caught in the act, or with the produce on him ... It would, of course, be folly to suppose that every incidence of the appropriation of growing produce was prompted by a labourer's need to feed a starving family or by a belief that his sweat and effort justified a 'perk'. Growing crops could only be taken at certain times of the year; there was a peak of summary indictments in the late summer and autumn when such crops were plentiful but also when there was a peak of agricultural employment. Furthermore, on occasion growing crops were taken by organised gangs. In 1822 eight bushels of apples were stolen from farmer John Burr's land on the outskirts of Bedford. Five men armed with bludgeons cowed his night watchmen and took the apples away in a cart.

In this passage, Emsley illustrates the relationship between crime and socio-economic change, the blurred boundaries between lawful and unlawful property-related conduct, and the interaction between legal and informal regulation of property relations which we shall see reproduced in many parts of this chapter. Work-related crime has attracted some measure of public attention over the last two decades, particularly in the context of concern about a 'hidden economy' whose implications for the 'open economy' become salient in times of recession:

S Henry, *The Hidden Economy* (Martin Robertson, 1978) pp 6–7

In spite of the considerable attention it has been given in the last two years, the hidden economy is not new. Its history can be traced back to the thirteenth century, when it appears to have been much the same as it is today. According to Jerome Hall, (Hall, 1952) fiddles of 'office' are probably the oldest property crimes in history. Aristotle spoke of the embezzlement of funds by road commissioners and other officials, and in thirteenth-century England, the Articles of Edward I provided for the investigation of 'overseers of works' who, by adjusting the accounts, acquired 'stone or timber which should have gone into public construction' (Hall, 1952: 36) ... These offences can be seen as direct forerunners of tax dodging, evasion or avoidance ...

The activity of fiddling accounts 'by the highest officials' was considerable in the fourteenth century ... By 1589, Queen Elizabeth I had a statute directed against 'persons who embezzled munitions of war which had been entrusted to them' (Act 31 Eliz c.4) and a statute of James I's made it criminal for any person in the wool industry to 'imbezil any Wool or Yarn delivered to him to be wrought' (Act 7 Jac I.7) ... Pilfering by people in honest jobs was also prevalent and was known as 'Larceny by Servant'. Hall says that this was recognised as a problem as early as 1339, but was disregarded in the 1344–5 Statutes of Edward III (Hall p.7). However, in 1529 Henry VIII had made it a felony for a servant to take his master's goods (Act 21 Hen. VIII c.7) ...

p 10

By the nineteenth century, instances of pilfering, fiddling and dealing were reported to have occurred in almost every occupation and, importantly within legitimate jobs. John Tobias has said, for example, that among young people in Birmingham, 'the most prevalent crime was larceny from their masters or from ships, committed by youngsters who had an honest job' ... One of the important aspects of this on-the-side trading was that, having taken the opportunity, the employee could rely on an understanding of what he was doing on the part of other tradesmen whom he could trust not to betray him ...

pp 12–13

The matter of explaining the hidden economy is ... complicated by the historical treatment of this kind of illegal activity. Until the last few years, no one had been prepared to see hidden-economy activities as phenomena in their own right. The belief was widely held that people were either completely honest or completely dishonest and anyone who persistently, even if only occasionally, committed an illegal offence, was dishonest. As a consequence of this assumption, no attempt was made to conduct a detailed examination of part-time property crime and its wider implications. It was preferred, instead, to concentrate upon the professional criminal and his stereotypical world. But the stereotype of the property criminal is an ill-fitting explanation for hidden-economy crime. Assuming, as it does, that property crimes are committed for the pursuit of economic gain, the dishonest criminal theory cannot account for the 'part-timeness' of hidden-economy crime. Thus, while almost all the activities comprising the hidden economy involve an illegal transfer of money, goods and services ... they are not the province of 'criminals', but an everyday feature of ordinary people's lives. The artificial distinction between 'honest' and 'dishonest' masks the fact that the hidden economy is the on-the-side, illegal activity of 'honest' people who have conventional jobs and who would never admit to being dishonest. More importantly, the distinction fails to accommodate the finding ... that although money may be involved in the hidden economy, a multiplicity of other factors are often more significant, not least of these being the nature of the social relationship between all those taking part in hidden-economy crime ...

A graphic example of the widespread existence and 'normalisation' of workplace crime was reported in *Le Monde* (10 September 1988) in an article describing disciplinary proceedings against police officers in a region of Paris who admitted to having systematically removed items such as radios from stolen cars before returning the cars to their owners. The defendants confounded the tribunal by not only freely admitting the practice but defending themselves vigorously on the basis that this constituted an 'institution', utterly accepted by the whole brigade (and apparently well known by the local community). The analysis of the cultural ambivalence which characterises attitudes to occupational crime is taken further by Mars, who opens his own study in the following way:

G Mars, *Cheats at Work: An Anthropology of Workplace Crime* (Unwin Paperbacks, 1982) pp 1–2

This is a book about crime at work. It is not, however, about crime in the normal sense. First, most of the 'criminals' do not regard what they are doing as remotely blameworthy and secondly, they appear in all respects to be no different from other people. And nor are they – since self-report studies show that between 75 and 92 per cent of us regularly add to our incomes in ways that are technically against the law.

More recent studies have argued that occupational crime is characteristic of a whole range of occupations, while intensive studies of particular occupations have confirmed the findings of earlier self-reports ... [T]he extent and variety of these activities are astonishing. The range of description alone indicates their extent. In England one speaks of 'pilfering' and 'the fiddle', in the USA it is called 'skimming' or 'gypping', in France 'le travail noir' and in the Soviet Union it is known as 'rabotat nalyevo', which means 'on the left'. These terms are not exact synonyms. Indeed, the complexity of these activities is such that no one word or phrase can convey the scope and ingenuity they involve. In English there are also words such as 'moonlighting', 'tax evasion' and 'perks'. Although almost everyone is aware of them, and although the majority of us fiddle in one way or another, fiddling is still considered a trivial activity without serious implication. This view needs to be challenged ...

Mars goes on to develop a typology of 'fiddling' which is related to the structure of particular jobs, which provide specific roles and opportunities which relate directly to the kinds of fiddling which go on. He argues:

p 3

The fiddled benefits obtained (unlisted in audits and unmentioned in official statistics on incomes), far from being the exceptional activity of the minority, are an integral aspect of all the occupations they include. They are indeed the shadow side of conventional economic transactions.

... [S]ome occupations are so fiddle-prone, for instance, that the workings of whole sectors of the economy cannot be understood unless these aspects of reward are taken into account. It is impossible to explain industrial relations in much of the personal services sector, for example, or to understand the real reasons behind some strikes, or why technical changes are blocked, or why some trade unions make no headway, when orthodox theories of strike-proneness or of trade union growth are all we have to depend on.

These examples not only extend our conception of the scope of 'white collar crime', but also force us to re-examine our understanding of the ways in which white collar or occupational offenders (ie most of us) adopt points of view which allow us to interpret our own actions as not 'really criminal' whilst upholding our general attitudes of support for criminal law. Building on Sutherland's early insights, a wide range of neutralisation strategies has been identified by students of occupational crime:

S Henry, *The Hidden Economy* (Martin Robertson, 1978) pp 76–77

Three fundamental distinctions are made by members of the hidden economy by which they contrast their own 'insignificant' behaviour with the 'really villainous' activity of the professional criminal. It is argued, for example, that whereas 'criminals' behave in a predatory way, ordinary people, in contrast, need only accept things that 'come their way'. A number of the people I interviewed made a sharp distinction between 'going out and doing something' and accepting 'good fortune' that might come their way ...

A further distinction made between hidden economy and full-time crime in the minds of ordinary people is the scale of operation. In the course of conducting interviews ... I was continually told that the activity of the person I was interviewing was only 'small-time stuff' and not a fraction of what some people were doing. More than once I was told to 'go to where it's really at' ... However, the most significant contrast made between the public stereotype of full-time crime and the hidden economy, is the fact that real crime provides the basic source of income for those involved. It is this, rather than any other aspect of the criminal stereotype, that renders a person morally free to commit part-time crime.

The relationship between the 'neutralisation' of occupational crime and institutional culture was suggested by Cressey in his early study of violations of trust in America:

D R Cressey, *Other People's Money: A Study in the Social Psychology of Embezzlement* (1953, Patterson Smith (1973 reprint)) pp 136–137

The rationalisations which are used by trust violators are necessary and essential to criminal violation of trust. They are not merely ex post facto justifications for conduct which already has been enacted, but are pertinent and real "reasons" which the person has for acting ... Each trusted person does not invent a new rationalisation for his violation of trust, but instead he applies to his own situation a verbalisation which has been made available to him by virtue of his having come into contact with a culture in which such verbalisations are present. Cultural ideologies which sanction trust violation are in basic contradiction to ideologies which hold non-violation as the norm, and in trust violation the trusted person applies a general rule to his specific case ... A large majority of the independent businessmen and trusted employees who take funds over a period of time apply ... the rationalisation that they are merely borrowing the funds ... Frequently it is necessary for an individual to abandon the rationalisations which he has been using, and when this occurs he looks upon himself as a criminal ...

pp 140–142

Among the violators interviewed, the accountants, bankers, business executives and independent businessmen all reported that the possibility of stealing or robbing to obtain the needed funds never occurred to them, although many objective opportunities for such crimes were present. Even a man who had been convicted of fraud or embezzlement as many as three times stated that crime of any other kind is repulsive ...

Also, trust violators usually consider the conditions under which they violated their own positions of trust as the only "justifiable" conditions, just as they consider their own trust violation to be more justified than a crime such as robbery or burglary. The individual who embezzles by "borrowing because I needed the money", looks with some contempt upon an embezzler whom he thinks embezzled "in order to try to make a killing" … just as he looks with some contempt upon burglars.

The ambiguities in individuals' views of the moral status of their actions find a counterpart in society's attitudes to crime:

G Mars, *Cheats at Work: An Anthropology of Workplace Crime* (Unwin Paperbacks, 1982) pp 163–165

[S]ociety has an ambiguous attitude towards the actions of its 'big men'. In a perverse way, the corrupt means such men employ to achieve success and power is seen as part of their achieving-style: to have succeeded, the individual must have 'fixed' things for himself. On the other hand, society's view of the actions of 'little men' is unambiguous. The supermarket cashier who rings short is seen as nothing more or less than dishonest.

It is tempting to explain this distinction purely in terms of class … The class argument is based upon the view that opinions are moulded and social agencies activated by the most powerful elements in society in their own interest. There is a lot in this argument, and yet … individuals, as far as their fiddling goes, are not so much simply the victims of a class system as the victims of its mediation through occupational structures which determine the nature, type and scale of fiddles that are practised …

The basis of the different views society takes of different offences can be seen in the different words it uses to describe them. Throughout this book I have tended to use the word 'fiddle' rather than pilferage or theft. The word is not used lightly, but it is a 'light' word: morally it is relatively neutral … It allows us to look at part-time crime not so much with complaisance as with empathy. Using the word 'fiddle', we can more readily appreciate the world-view or cosmology of the fiddler … If, on the other hand, we use the word 'theft', we stand outside the fiddler's view of his own actions.

pp 166–167

[I]f we accept that there are different methods of transaction, even within the relatively 'straight' operation of market exchange, we can see that fiddling is not necessarily the 'wrong' way of doing something but rather that it is another way of doing something. And we can now appreciate that the use of 'heavy' words like 'theft' and 'crime' by people who are outside the operating quadrant excludes (because it has to if these terms are to have meaning) the possibility of there being such alternative methods of transaction. It effectively prejudges because it recategorises the acts that are being discussed. Therefore when I use the word 'fiddle' I do so not to condone theft, but to allow for the possibility of other systems of dealing which 'theft' does not adequately describe.

It is because people are in a sense 'trapped' in their own cosmologies that they do not have the ability to split up the image of what they see. Their view of fiddles is determined by where they stand, since a specific cosmology not only orders the world, it also precludes alternative orderings. The use of words to describe what is seen suggests that different viewpoints need different words to describe the same view ... When a 'perk' is classed as fraud, perhaps because it oversteps acceptable limits and becomes the subject of prosecution, it is prosecuted as a fraud and the charge has to be answered in these terms. Generally there is no answer ... The transaction has broken the rules of 'normal' dealing and it is for this that punishment is appropriate and recategorisation becomes a necessity.

Moreover, the existence of alternative systems of exchange, cosmologies and categories produces problems for the fiddler, as Mars also explains:

p 170

This squaring of the working self with the fiddling self is often achieved, as we have seen, through group support. When Ditton's (Ditton, 1977) bread salesman was shown the ropes by an experienced salesman or supervisor, he was also shown certain truths about the job. He was shown how to balance his books and then shown, in the course of learning, that the books would never balance; that he would always be down at the end of the day. He was gradually led to realise that only through fiddling could he stay on top of the job. He then adopted the cosmology of the group of bread salesmen, in which fiddling is intrinsic not extrinsic to the job. In the same way the docker's world-view is also pressed home by the group – that because managements are perceived as inherently untrustworthy, the group itself is the only secure defender of members' interest. It is the group worker's acceptance and absorption of group assumptions that allows him to square his straight self with his sinful self. The two are insulated at one level but coalesce at another and thus ambiguity is resolved. Without group support, however, ambiguity remains unresolved. In jobs where the worker is isolated, there is an individual but not a group view. Hence the personal 'sinning' self threatens to overwhelm the working self.

These group norms, argues Mars, generate controls on the extent and type of fiddling, and these contribute to its status not so much as an anarchic, individualistic activity but as 'one of the factors that contribute to equilibrium in normal economic activity' (p 171). The fiddler thinks (perhaps not at a conscious level) that he or she will have society's support for his or her actions because of the continuity between their underlying ideology and that of capitalism – an assumption which turns out to be radically misplaced once Mars's 'heavy' criminal definitions are applied to recategorise fiddling as theft.

Another question which underlies many discussions of 'white collar' and occupational property crime is the extent to which it is 'organised' or 'professional'. As we have seen, the part-time nature of much occupational crime has supported its marginalisation as criminal – but criminal violations of property which are systematic and justify the definition 'organised' may be marginalised in their turn. Naturally, 'organised' crime does not have its impact only on property interests: as the activities of groups such as the Mafia show, it can have serious implications in terms of public order and often involves violence. Our image of organised crime is dominated by the Mafia, 'gangs' and similar organisations of a 'criminal underworld' which operate unambiguously outside the law, and tends to disregard the many areas in which legitimate and illegitimate activities are closely intertwined. Yet it would be perfectly appropriate to expand our perspective so as to apply the label 'organised' or 'professional' crime to the apparently 'respectable' activities of corporations and individuals who systematically violate environmental laws, take calculated risks in terms of the safety of their products in order to increase their profits, or systematically under-report their earnings on their tax returns. For the line between legitimate and illegitimate profit-oriented activity turns out to be exceedingly fine. The suggestion that we should conceptualise much white collar crime as organised crime was made by Sutherland:

E Sutherland, *White Collar Crime*, 1949 (Yale University Press, 1983) pp 256–257

Evidence has been presented … that crimes of businesses are organized crimes. This evidence includes references not only to gentlemen's agreements, pools, trade associations, patent agreements, cartels, conferences and other informal understandings, but also to the tentacles which business throws out into the government and the public for the control of those portions of the society. The definition of specified acts as illegal is a prerequisite to white collar crime, and to that extent the political society is necessarily organized against white collar crime. The statutes, however, have little importance in the control of business behavior unless they are supported by an administration which is intent on stopping the illegal behavior. In turn the political administration has little force in stopping such behavior unless it is supported by a public which is intent on the enforcement of the law. This calls for a clear-cut opposition between the public and the government, on the one side, and the businessmen who violate the law, on the other. This clear-cut opposition does not exist and the absence of this opposition is evidence of the lack of organization against white collar crime. What is, in theory, a war loses much of its conflict because of the fraternization between the two forces. White collar crimes continue because of this lack of organization on the part of the public.

Far from public institutions organising against such crime, Chambliss's undercover study of networks of crime and corruption in public and corporate life the United States suggests that the fabric of capitalist society actually supports it:

W J Chambliss, *On the Take: From Petty Crooks to Presidents* (Indiana University Press, 1978) pp 178–183

Kickbacks, bribes, collusion, and corruption are as much a part of corporate business as they are a part of crime networks everywhere. So too are public lies and disclaimers of business men and politicians caught in the act. In 1967 and 1968 the top executives and accountants of Lockheed Aircraft, with the complicity of high-ranking officers of the Air Force, falsified public reports of the cost of overruns on the C-5A airplane. Complicity of the Pentagon was purchased by the favors Lockheed does for the high-ranking officers, including, perhaps most significantly, the prospect of high-paying jobs in the aircraft industry upon retirement from the service ... Investigative agencies such as the FBI and IRS are co-opted in similar if not identical ways. Retired FBI agents become "special investigators" or are employed by banks, corporations, or state governments at high-paying jobs ...

We could of course go on indefinitely with such examples but the point would be the same: there is an inherent tendency of business, law enforcement, and politics to engage systematically in criminal behavior. This is so not because there are too many laws but rather because criminal behavior is good business, it makes sense, it is by far the best, most efficient, most profitable way to organize the activities and operations of political offices, businesses, law-enforcement agencies and trade unions in a capitalist democracy ...

By now it should be clear that the logic of capitalism is a logic within which the emergence of crime networks is inevitable. Capitalism is based on the private ownership of property. Property is acquired by selling products, providing services, or selling one's labor. By law most of the products and services which can be exchanged for money at a profit are legal ... At one time in American history most of the products and services which support the crime industry were legal ... In time some commodities and services came to be defined as illegal. But the demand for these things did not disappear with their transference from legality to illegality. Indeed, in some cases the profits increased as a consequence of their newly established illegality ... Through it all the crime network becomes an institutionalized, fixed and permanent link in the chain of a nation's political economy ...

These studies of white collar and occupational crime provide us with a complex picture of the variety of property-violating behaviour in which a range of systems of property relations and exchanges co-exist with competing definitions of what is and is not honest or legitimate. This complexity relates both to the motivations and self-understandings of property offenders and to society's attitudes to particular forms of conduct and the application of criminal definitions thereto. The idea of organised crime is open to reconstruction in the light of evidence about existing forms of criminal behaviour in just the same way as work on 'white collar crime' has challenged perceptions of 'real' property crime in general. It is instructive to consider how the individualistic and moralistic definitions of legal offences such as theft (see below **section II.a.ii.**) would apply to the systematic and normalised behaviour discussed by Sutherland and Chambliss.

I.d.   Burglary

For our final example, we return to the well-charted waters of 'real' crime, to consider the crime of burglary – an offence which is central both to popular images of property crime and to popular anxieties about crime in general. Burglary also serves to illustrate the blurred boundaries between property and other crime: the sense of invasion of privacy and fear of violence are clearly important factors in determining the high level of social anxiety about this form of crime. It is this feature of burglary, as well as concern about its prevalence, that underpinned the decision to implement the Crime (Sentences) Act's provisions on mandatory minimum sentences for repeat burglars (see **Chapter 1.III.b.iv.** and, for further discussion of the sentencing issues, Tyrer 2003).

In 2000–2001, residential and non-residential burglary represented 16% of notifiable crime recorded by the police (Home Office 2001b). In 2000, 409,000 residential burglaries were recorded by the police, whereas the British Crime Survey estimated that 1,063,000 had occurred (Kershaw et al 2001). According to the 1992 British Crime Survey, which examined trends in residential burglary since 1972, relatively few burglaries involve either violence or very high losses. Only 3% of burglaries involved a violent or threatening confrontation between offender and victim. One-fifth of burglaries involved initial losses of less than £100, and the average initial loss was £1320. Mainly as a result of insurance (held by over half of those surveyed), a majority of burglaries involved *net* losses of less than £50. The average net loss was £370; the aggregate losses to victims of burglary were estimated as being in the region of £500 million (Mayhew et al 1993: 59–60). By 2000–2001, this had risen to £1,883 million (Home Office 2002g: 33). This latest British Crime Survey estimates that there were 991,000 burglaries in England and Wales in 2001–2002: a 23% fall since 1999 (contrasting with a rise in the recorded level of burglary, which the BCS attributed to changed reporting procedures). Of these, less than half – 406,000 – involved the loss of property: the rest were either attempted entry or entry without loss (Home Office 2002g: 29–30).

The British Crime Survey also suggests that burglary is predominantly a feature of urban life, burglaries in inner-city areas being about twice as frequent as those in rural areas (Kershaw et al 2001). The first British Crime Survey revealed fears about burglary among a wide range of people, many of whom were concerned about violation of their territory and sense of order rather than with material loss (Hough and Mayhew 1983: 24–27): in the 2001–2002 British Crime Survey, 81% of interviewees reported that they had been emotionally affected by being burgled, with the most common emotions being anger, shock, fear, feelings of vulnerability and difficulty with sleeping (Home Office 2002g: 34). Further data about patterns of burglary and popular attitudes to it emerged from the first Islington Crime Survey. Jones et al (Jones, Maclean and Young 1986: 20ff; 42ff; see also Crawford et al 1990) found a similar rate to that of the British Crime Survey. Their evidence suggested, contrary to popular belief, that burglary is neither opportunistic nor professional, but often involves amateurs who break into a certain dwelling over and over again because they have found it an easy target in the past.

Crime Surveys also show that there is a marked variation in reporting rates for different kinds of burglaries: this variation relates to the extent of loss, the existence of insurance, perceptions of 'real' and 'unreal' burglaries and to victims blaming themselves (for example, for failing to lock their home adequately). The Islington Survey showed that burglaries involving breaking and entering were reported to the police in 82% of cases, while of those not involving an actual break-in only 54% were brought to the attention of the police. The British Crime Survey indicated that by 1991, 94% of burglaries involving loss were being reported to the police – a significant rise from the 1972 rate of 78%, and one which is almost certainly related to increasing levels of insurance (Mayhew et al 1993: 42). In 2001–2002, the British Crime Survey found that just over 60% of burglaries were reported to the police: of burglaries involving loss, 84% were reported. It also found that young households, single-parent households and those in areas of 'high physical disorder' were particularly at risk, though these high-risk households had shared in an overall reduction of burglary by 17% between 1999 and 2000. Households where the head of household is between 16 and 24 and single-parent households were at particular risk (Home Office 2002g: 31).

There exists a wide variety of opinion about the motivation for the 'typical' burglary among commentators who persist in the belief that such a thing exists. One approach is that adopted by economic analysts of the Chicago school:

M Sesnowitz, 'The Returns to Burglary' in R Andreano and J Siegfried (eds) *The Economics of Crime* **(John Wiley and Sons, 1980) pp 181–183**

Burglary is a risky activity, since the individual's return depends upon whether or not he is apprehended and convicted. Accordingly, the monetary return is an expected value and can be expressed as

$$R = (1 - p) S + p (S - D)$$

where p is the probability that the individual is caught and penalized; S is the monetary component of the income from the act – or simply the amount stolen – and D is the dollar equivalent of the penalty imposed on those apprehended ... In 1967 the average market value of stolen property yielded by a burglary in Pennsylvania was $288. However, the gain to the burglar generally falls short of this amount since he is unable to dispose of his non-monetary ill-gotten gains at their market value ... To compute the probability of conviction, the number of adult convictions for burglary in Pennsylvania is divided by twice the number of reported adult burglaries ... This method of computation yields a probability of conviction of .058.

Calculation of the dollar value of the penalty will include only those direct costs resulting from incarceration and the confiscation of stolen property ... The measure of the value of the burglar's time while incarcerated will be his net foregone earnings, less the value of his consumption and earnings, if any, while in prison. The personal discomfort associated with prison life is a subjective element which will be negative for most, if not all, inmates. No attempt will be made to measure this factor ... The measure of foregone earning will be the present value of the average after-tax earning of individuals with characteristics similar to those of burglars ... [On this calculation], [w]hile the burglar forgoes $4,321 per year while in prison, he is provided with consumption goods and may be paid for work he performs ... The expected yearly value of consumption, then, to a burglar sentenced to prison is $567.

The net result of this complex calculation is that the expected cost of imprisonment to the burglar is approximately $316. This approach, with its strong assumptions about the rationally calculated nature of criminal behaviour, has informed some significant developments in crime control – notably the situational approach to crime prevention (see below **section III.a.**). It contrasts sharply with research methods which aspire to shed light on the actual social phenomenon of burglary:

M Maguire and T Bennett, *Burglary in a Dwelling* **(Heinemann, 1982) pp 164–170**

Burglary of private houses conjures up many frightening and disturbing images – of violent strangers in the night, ransacked rooms, fouling of property and sexual assault ... We have confirmed that about one-quarter of those who actually become victims are, temporarily at least, badly shaken by the experience. Moreover, a small minority, mainly women, suffer long-lasting effects including fear, sleeplessness and a deep distrust of others.

Analysis of the actual circumstances of the offence has revealed that, although it is an all-too-common crime, burglary is rarely as objectively serious as people imagine. Confrontations between victim and offender are unusual, and physical contact or violence result in only a tiny proportion of cases. Research leaves us in no doubt that, generally speaking, people who engage in burglary are 'sneak' thieves who will do what they can to avoid coming into contact with residents and, if disturbed, their first reaction is to run away ...

Deliberate violence to property, apart from force used to effect entry, is also less common than widely believed. Only five of the 322 victims we interviewed reported any gratuitous acts of vandalism and only one had the experience of finding a pile of faeces. Untidy searches were more common ... but in the majority of cases very little had been moved.

The value of property stolen is often low. In 1979, over one-quarter of recorded burglaries in England and Wales resulted in a loss of under £5, and 65 per cent in under £100. Cash is the prime target, and is stolen in well over one third of all cases. Roughly one in five cases involve pre-payment meters ... Otherwise, burglars steal mainly electrical goods, silverware, jewellery, cigarettes, food and alcohol. However, there has in recent years been a rapid increase in the number of burglaries involving very valuable property, particularly high-quality jewellery and antiques.

The distribution of burglaries both across the country and within smaller areas displays very uneven patterns ... The burglar's selection of a specific house rather than others nearby is determined by a number of complex factors and is difficult to analyse precisely. The evidence suggests that both small and large detached houses are generally more vulnerable than semi-detached or terraced houses ... Occupancy is also a very important factor ... On the other hand, it is not certain that either care in locking up or the fitting of good locks and bolts greatly influences burglars' choice of targets. If the house offers sufficient rewards and the entry-point is not easily visible from the road or from other buildings, offenders are both capable of and willing to spend time in defeating all but the most sophisticated crime-prevention devices ...

Data on known offenders suggest that on the whole they operate relatively close to home ... The major exception to these patterns is the kind of burglary that occurs frequently in Gerrards Cross. Very wealthy areas attract the most ambitious thieves who are prepared to travel much greater distances, and are interested mainly in silver, jewellery and antiques ... These are not necessarily all sophisticated 'professional' criminals –

older teenagers with ambitions to move into the world of serious crime sometimes try their hand at wealthy properties despite the difficulty in selling items profitably afterwards – but almost certainly form only a small proportion of all those who become involved in burglary ... [A]lthough there is a widespread tendency to think of thieves as falling into one of two categories – 'professional' or 'amateur' – the majority of frequent offenders are best thought of as 'middle-range' thieves, people who have before them an image of successful professional crime but who fail to display the caution, self-discipline and organisation that this requires. Many take a short-sighted view of criminal behaviour, taking risks which virtually ensure their arrest at least once every one or two years ... Despite periods in which they may make a considerable amount of money, very few could be described as having 'made crime pay' over the long term ...

As most researchers have discovered, burglary in a dwelling remains one of the most intractable crime problems of all. It is a crime which, despite heavy penalties, has flourished for many centuries; which is extremely difficult to detect or prevent; and which is committed by the most persistent adult criminals as well as by an exceptionally high proportion of children.

In assessing the importance of burglary, Maguire and Bennett emphasise its impact on the psychological rather than the pecuniary interests of victims. Their study demonstrates that it is difficult to generalise about any aspect of 'property crime', let alone property crime in general.

The examples selected in this section have demonstrated the diversity of behaviour which threatens established interests in property as defined by criminal law. They have also thrown light on the social construction of 'real crime': the way in which both public perception and enforcement practice, themselves influenced by the media and other social institutions, distinguish between behaviours equally subject in principle to criminal law. More generally, among those behaviours having an adverse impact on property interests, the boundaries between those which are and which are not regarded as legitimate are blurred. Commercial and governmental policies (not to mention market operations) which are legal and widely perceived as legitimate may raise prices, devalue certain commodities or cut welfare benefits in ways which affect interests in property far more radically than does property crime. Not all interests in property which are or could be recognised socially come within the scope of legal protection.

Within the area of illegal property-affecting behaviours, we saw how common practices are tolerated, acquiesced in or rationalised by the operation of a variety of strategies which 'neutralise' criminality and illegitimacy. From social, official and offenders' points of view, competing definitions and interpretations of behaviour affecting property interests are constructed. The intervention of the criminal process into this area is relatively infrequent. However, criminal law affirms certain conceptions of property as legitimate and deserving of protection and as such makes a symbolic as well as an instrumental contribution to the social definition of property, theft and related concepts. In the next two sections, therefore, we turn to the substantive law and its implementation.

FURTHER READING

Ditton, Jason (1977) *Part Time Crime: An Ethnology of Fiddling and Pilfering* (Macmillan).

Geis, G and Meier, R F (1977) *White-Collar Crime* (Free Press).

Levi, Michael (2002) 'The Organisation of Serious Crimes' in Maguire et al (eds) *The Oxford Handbook of Criminology* (Oxford University Press) 878.

MacPherson, C B (1978) *Property: Mainstream and Critical Positions* (University of Toronto Press).

II.   Constructing property in criminal law

We now move to the legal context to consider how criminal laws themselves construct property interests and threats to property. Just as many 'offences against the person' have public order or property-affecting aspects, so many 'property offences' have public order or person-affecting repercussions. Taking one important source of property crimes, the Theft Acts of 1968 and 1978, the relative seriousness of the offences enacted – theft, handling stolen goods, burglary and aggravated burglary, robbery, taking a conveyance without authority, abstracting electricity, going equipped for stealing, blackmail, making off without payment and a variety of offences of deception – relates not only to the extent to which they threaten property rights but also to violations of trust and the threats to social order, authority and the person which they pose. Robbery and aggravated burglary attract maximum sentences of life imprisonment largely on the latter ground, and the fact that there is a higher statutory maximum for handling than for theft is perhaps to be explained not just by the argument that thieves could not survive without handlers and thus that handling is an important focus for punishment and prevention (after all, the converse is equally true) but in terms of the idea that handling systematically supports the institution of theft in a way which potentially undermines the system of property entitlements more thoroughly than does theft.

In considering criminal law's construction of property offences, we should not, however, confine our view to the Theft Acts. We need to bear in mind the laws relating to criminal damage, computer misuse, conspiracy to defraud, offences relating to forgery and counterfeiting, criminal nuisances or trespasses (see **Chapter 2.II.c.**) and indeed offences relating to terrorism and hijacking, which may have considerable implications for property holdings. Many 'regulatory' offences such as those relating to pollution and safety precautions are also relevant, as are laws relating to 'intellectual property' and the protection of copyrights, computer software and data and performing rights. These may not always have come squarely within conventional social and legal conceptions of property, but they have called for accommodation in law as social conceptions have developed. The protection of these forms of property interest, along with regulatory arrangements to do with revenue, licensing and the like, lie at the muddy junction between criminal and civil regulation: between a system geared to prevention, blame and punishment and a system geared to promoting security of expectations and providing compensation. They are not seen as being a core part of criminal law, yet they have similar functions and some criminal law aspects.

We cannot deal with more than a small selection of property offences, and we have chosen a sample to illustrate some of the most interesting points which arise in this area. Our focus will be on theft, deception and criminal damage. We shall also use the context of property offences to consider the contours of certain features of inchoate liability, considering conspiracy to defraud and the law of attempts, which serves further to illustrate the shifting patterns of criminality illuminated by our discussion of the historical development of theft. Finally, we shall examine the defences of duress and necessity, which raise important questions about the location of responsibility for property crime.

II.a. Theft

II.a.i. The history of theft

William Blackstone's *Commentaries*, written in the middle of the eighteenth century, represent one of the first systematic expositions of the common law. His volume on criminal offences included a substantial section on 'offences against private property':

William Blackstone, *Commentaries on the Laws of England 1765*, Vol IV (University of Chicago Press, 1979) p 230

Simple larciny then is the 'felonious taking, and carrying away, of the personal goods of another'. This offence certainly commenced then, whenever it was, that the bounds of property, or laws of meum and tuum, were established. How far such an offence can exist in a state of nature, where all things are held to be common, is a question that may be solved with very little difficulty. The disturbance of any individual, in the occupation of what he has seised to his present use, seems to be the only offence of this kind incident to such a state. But, unquestionably, in social communities, when property is established, the necessity whereof we have formerly seen, any violation of that property is subject to be punished by the laws of society: though how far that punishment should extend, is matter of considerable doubt.

In the next few pages, we shall examine the development of conceptions of theft since Blackstone's time, so as to provide a historical context in which to consider the contemporary law of theft. The history of theft produces a striking illustration of the way in which distinctive logics of legal argumentation may persist notwithstanding legal and social change, whilst also exemplifying a significant shift in the very basis of attributing criminal responsibility. Yet, despite the extensive legislative codification of property offences, many of the problems thrown up by the history of larceny reproduce themselves in a curious way in the modern law of theft. These traces serve to cast doubt on the extent to which older forms of viewing crime have been entirely displaced by modern conceptions of responsibility and wrongdoing.

Laws against theft (or 'larceny') count among the most historically and geographically pervasive forms of criminal law, yet the form of the offence is bound to be culturally specific: it reflects prevailing ideas of property (Fletcher 1978: 1–122). Blackstone's comment neatly captures not only the interaction between prevailing social formations and the form of criminal offences against property, but also the persistent controversy about the shape of those forms within any particular polity. From the seventeenth century on, there was in England a growing body of statutory law which specified many different instances of larceny, grading them as grand or petit, and distributing penalties accordingly. For example, horse theft, sheep and cattle theft, theft from bleaching grounds, theft from houses and ships, shoplifting and picking pockets were all categories singled out as grand larcenies, reflecting socio-economic structures, the demands of local economies, and (closely related) popular perceptions of the relative seriousness of different kinds of theft (Beattie 1986). Among these distinctions, places or locations, and specific objects, are of particular importance, suggesting a conception of larceny as essentially about the transgression of commonly recognised boundaries. But as the integrity of these boundaries gradually dissolved in more mobile and fragmented modern societies, criminal law increasingly struggled to articulate a determinate conception of theft.

In his extensive analysis of the development of the modern law of theft, Fletcher (1978) distinguishes between three basic kinds of property crime: larceny, embezzlement and false pretences. Larceny, as defined by Blackstone, consists in a felonious taking and carrying away of the personal goods of another: it must be felonious in the sense of being done with an 'animus furandi' – theftous spirit or intent (though, as we shall see, this is not really equivalent to contemporary 'mens rea'/intent); and it is essentially a crime against possession – hence physical taking – which entails that those in possession could not be guilty of larceny. Embezzlement, by contrast, consists in appropriating goods entrusted to the defendant's possession to her or his own use; and false pretences, deception or fraud in getting possession of goods by means of some pretence or cheating. If you snatch my wallet and run off with it, you commit theft; if you falsely tell me you are starving so as to persuade me to give it to you, you commit false pretences; if I put my wallet in your hands for safekeeping, but you then decide to abscond with it, you commit embezzlement. Embezzlement and false pretences tend to develop in modern systems as statutory innovations coming much later than larceny. As Fletcher explains, the difference between these three kinds of offence has centrally to do with the nature of the victim's participation: in larceny, the victim in no way voluntarily participates: in embezzlement the victim agrees to the initial taking but not to the later appropriation; in false pretences, the victim agrees to the transfer, but only because he or she is the victim of a deception. This illustrates the variety of interests or wrongs which criminal laws on property can express: whilst larceny is fundamentally concerned with possession, embezzlement is concerned rather with trust.

Fletcher's argument is that in the development towards contemporary law, the distinction between these three forms of separate property violation became blurred, and that this blurring not only produced the modern concept of theft, but also expressed a deeper change in the underlying conception of criminality – a change from 'manifest' to 'subjective' patterns of liability. Whilst the accounts provided by writers such as Quinney and Hall (see below) represent these changes as driven by social and economic factors, Fletcher's explanation is rooted in the logic of legal forms themselves. Fletcher rejects both the idea that the development of theft is a question of historical accident and the idea that it is a matter of historical determinism – primarily a product of social and economic conditions. These factors certainly have a place in his story, but his account shows how those broader influences are filtered through a set of legal forms which have their own internal logic. To explore these competing legal and social explanations, and their implications for modern criminal law, it is worth examining the law of larceny in a little more detail.

In Blackstone's time, as we have seen, the essence of larceny was a taking. In other words, the consent of the owner had to be wanting; and there had to be a taking from possession – someone legally in possession could thus not be a thief. This meant that uncertainties in the law of possession, and in particular about the line between possession and mere use or custody, were of central importance in the law of larceny. For example, was a domestic servant in possession of cutlery or linen, or did she only have 'care and oversight'? If the latter, she could be guilty of larceny if she took the goods away; if the former, she could not – it was merely a private or civil matter. Further difficult doctrinal issues had to do with what constituted a carrying away. Blackstone cites the case of a guest stealing goods from an inn, and being caught on his way out: this was thought to be a sufficient taking away.

Of particular interest to modern eyes is the summary way in which Blackstone deals with 'animus furandi' – what looks to us like the 'mens rea' of larceny. He simply observes that, apart from its role in 'excusing those who labour under incapacities of mind or will', it 'indemnifies also mere trespassers and other petty offenders'. He explains that the paradigm example of 'animus furandi' is that of the person found taking 'clandestinely' – though he goes on to say, not entirely helpfully, that 'this is by no means the only criterion of criminality: for in cases that may amount to larciny the variety of circumstances is so great, and the complications thereof so mingled, that it is impossible to recount all those, which may evidence a felonious intent, or animum furandi; wherefore they must be left to the due and attentive consideration of the court and jury' (Blackstone 1765: 232). As we shall see, the contrast between the eighteenth-century conception of 'animus furandi' and contemporary conceptions of 'mens rea' plays a central role in grounding Fletcher's argument that the early common law's conception of larceny was based on a very different pattern of criminality from the modern law of theft.

Fletcher points out that the basic idea of larceny as a felonious taking from possession created a number of problem cases which arose regularly but which were outside the definition: examples include the person who comes into possession with a felonious purpose unknown to the owner; the person who finds goods which he later appropriates; the person to whom goods are mistakenly delivered, and who then appropriates them; and the person to whom goods are delivered by a third party and who appropriates them rather than passing them on to the owner. Each of these cases posed a problem for common law larceny, because each encountered the barrier of possessorial immunity: ie in each case the putative thief has got possession, and hence cannot become a thief by his or her later appropriation. As Quinney observes in the following passage, these problems began to be resolved in *Carrier's Case* (Star Chamber 1473):

R Quinney, *The Social Reality of Crime* (Little, Brown & Company, 1970) pp 70–73

The creation of a particular criminal law must have its conception in some concrete setting of time and place. The development of the law of theft demonstrates that necessity. For prior to the fifteenth century there was no legal conception of theft as we know it today. It was during the fifteenth century in England that the modern law of theft was officially formulated into criminal law. The law of theft was shaped by changing social conditions, and especially by pressing social interests of the time. The definition of theft as a crime was a solution to a legal problem that arose within a particular social framework.

The decision that resulted in the legal concept of theft occurred in England in 1473, in what is known as the *Carrier's Case*. The case has been documented and interpreted by Jerome Hall in his book Theft, Law and Society (Hall, 1952). The facts of the case are these: the defendant was hired to carry bales to Southampton. Instead of fulfilling his obligation, he carried the goods to another place, broke open the bales, and took the contents. The man was apprehended and charged with felony.

The most illustrious judges of the time discussed the case at length. While the defendant was finally held guilty by a majority of the judges, a legal problem of considerable portent developed during the proceedings. Before the case arose, the common law recognized no criminality in a person who came legally into possession and converted it to his own use. The reasoning of the common law had been that the owner of transported goods was responsible for protecting himself by employing trustworthy persons ...

Until the *Carrier's Case* it had been agreed that while trespass (the taking of property from one who is in possession of it) was an essential element of larceny, a person in possession of property could not commit a trespass upon that property. Therefore, since a bailee (an employee who is trusted with property) had possession, larceny could not technically be committed by such an employee. The judges, however, departed from precedent by introducing a new concept which could neither be found among the existing legal rules nor logically derived from them. For the judges held that "breaking bulk" terminated the bailment, that such property at once reverted to the possession of the bailor, and that the removal of it from the bales supplied the trespass. Hall thus observes: "By this refinement the door was opened to admit into the law of larceny a whole series of acts which had up to that time been purely civil wrongs." (Hall 1952 p.10) ...

An important question arises as to the forces that were active in the creation of a new legal concept. In his analysis of the case, Hall outlines the changes that were occurring in fifteenth century England. These changes coupled with the social conditions and institutions of the period made convenient a change in the law of theft. To begin with, in the political realm, the courts were subservient to the wishes of Edward IV. This meant that the special interests of the Crown were protected by the courts. Among the interests of the king that received the favour of the courts were the royal commercial activities, including trade with merchants on the Continent. Edward himself was a merchant who carried on many private ventures.

The economic conditions of the period were especially important for the decision reached in the *Carrier's Case*. During this phase of the Renaissance a commercial revolution was taking place in England and Europe. The old feudal structure resting on an agricultural economy was giving way to a new order based on industry and trade ... Hall ... argues that the complainant was a foreign merchant ... whose trade was desired by the Crown. Such foreign merchants were subject to special risks: there was naturally hostility by local merchants toward foreign trade. Moreover, foreign merchants were handicapped in the transport of goods because of the uncertainty of finding trustworthy carriers who would not abscond with the goods. The king attempted to relieve the situation somewhat, issuing covenants of safe conduct through the country … The merchandise taken by the bailee of the *Carrier's Case* was probably wool or cloth, or both. Such goods were usually transported in bales … All these deductions mean that "the interests of the most important industry in England were involved in the case." (Hall 1952 p.31)

…

The *Carrier's Case* of 1473 vividly demonstrates the way in which changing social conditions and emerging social interests may bring about the formulation of a criminal law. The decision of the *Carrier's Case* provided the framework for the further development of the law of theft. Eventually, with the growth in banking and the use of paper currency, the law was expanded to include the act of embezzlement by clerks, officers and the like. A Whig Parliament in the eighteenth century passed an embezzlement statute in order to protect mercantile interests. The legal protection of property has always been to the interest of the propertied segments of society.

Through the ingenious means of Lord Chokke's argument that the carrier's 'breaking bulk' constituted a trespass, and that there was therefore a felony, the *Carrier's Case* therefore overcame the barrier presented by the doctrine of possessorial immunity. This idea of breaking bulk remained the major exception to that doctrine until the mid-nineteenth century. By this time, fraud and embezzlement had encompassed such behaviour, and the common law had developed an array of other techniques for avoiding the doctrine's effect – for example by arguing that certain kinds of bailees did not get possession in the first place.

What explains the decision in the *Carrier's Case*? On the face of it, the rule about possessorial immunity may seem an obscure technicality, and the argument about breaking bulk a clever judicial fiction designed to get around it. But this explanation of the case begs the question of why the judges would have wanted to get round it from the late fifteenth century on. As Quinney notes, Jerome Hall argued that the decision was driven by the imperatives of commerce and the desire in particular to protect foreign merchants so as to encourage trade. Fletcher points out, however, that this is not a convincing argument, because the contrary decision on the point would have protected the merchant just as well: the merchant's difficulty in recovering the goods actually derived from the fact they were argued to have reverted to the King, through the law of waif, as being the products of a felony. Thus the Star Chamber's decision that the bulk-breaking did indeed constitute a felony necessitated the further innovation, to protect merchants, that the ordinary law of waif would not apply to goods of foreign merchants. But even if Hall's explanation were convincing, it begs a further question: what was the rationale for the original rule, and why did this apparently rather technical modification of it – along with the other ways the common law found around problem cases – survive for so long?

Fletcher's argument is that the original form of larceny reflected a framework of 'manifest' criminality – the idea that criminal liability should be based on actions manifestly dangerous to the community – and that the subsequent modifications were designed (though with increasing dilution) to retain the law of larceny within that framework:

George Fletcher, *Rethinking Criminal Law* (1978) pp 115–120

The metamorphosis of larceny permits us to abstract two general patterns of criminality that find expression in a variety of crimes in addition to larceny. The common law of larceny up to the time of Blackstone reflected what we may call the pattern of manifest criminality; the modern law of larceny, emerging in the late eighteenth century, stands for a pattern of subjective criminality ... The tension between the pattern of manifest criminality and the pattern of subjective criminality is one that pervades a wide field of the criminal law ...

The critical feature of [the manifest] pattern of liability is that the commission of the crime be objectively discernible at the time that it occurs. The assumption is that a neutral third-party observer could recognize the activity as criminal even if he had no special knowledge about the offender's intention ...

Two important features of crimes follow from this distinguishing mark of manifest criminality. First there is a sense in which the crime itself crystallizes as the product of community experience, rather than being imposed on the community by an act of legislative will. The contours of what we perceive to be larceny spring from a shared experience with thieves. It is incorporated in our language as well as our legal judgments ... There is no doubt that this way of looking at crime and criminals is foreign to the modern view that the criminal law is imposed on the community by the courts or the legislature ...

The second feature born of the principle of manifest criminality is the subsidiary position of intent in the analysis of liability. The issue of non-intent arises primarily as a challenge to the authenticity of appearances, rather than as a basis for inculpating the actor. It is only after the manifestly criminal quality of the act is established that intent can conceivably become an issue. In this way of thinking the required intent is linked conceptually to the commission of certain acts. It is not thought of as some mysterious inner dimension of experience that exists independently from acting in the external world.

The pattern of manifest criminality may be understood as a theory about the appropriate jurisdiction of the criminal courts. The premise is that the courts should stay their hand until the actor manifests discernible danger to the community. Thus the criteria for judicial intervention resemble the ground for the private execution of thieves in ancient legal systems ...

The contrasting [subjective] pattern of liability begins with the radically different assumption that the core of criminal conduct is the intention to violate a legally protected interest. A crime in this pattern may presuppose the occurrence of a particular event, such as the "taking from possession" required by larceny. But this result is often not incriminating, as indicated by the cases of finders and those who receive a chattel by mistaken delivery. The function of the criminal act is to demonstrate the firmness rather than the content of the actor's intent ...

This pattern of liability presupposes a notion of intending that treats intent as a dimension of experience totally distinct from external behaviour. Intending is conceived as an event of consciousness, known to the person with the intent but not to others. Thus the relationship of intending to action is dualistic rather than monistic. The intent exists in the realm of the mind, the act in the realm of the body.

This dualistic way of thinking about intent has undergone philosophical criticism in recent years [see **Chapter 1.II.b. and II.c.**]; yet it retains a powerful grip on the way lawyers think about the criminal law. Its power derives in part from its dovetailing with an appealing theory of criminality. The criminal law should begin, this theory holds, by identifying interests that are worthy of protection. The next step should be preventing conduct that threatens those interests. The reasons that humans sometimes threaten those interests is either that they intend to do so or that they take risks that subject the protected interests to danger. Therefore the purpose of the criminal law should be to prevent people from embarking on courses of behaviour that threaten these worthy interests ... The only reason we require that offenders act on their intention is to make sure that the intention is firm and not merely fantasy ...

One key concept in understanding the difference between the patterns of manifest and subjective criminality is the distinction between substantive and evidentiary rules. Manifest criminality requires, as a substantive rule of law, that the act betoken danger to the community. The subjective criminality of intending harm invites a variety of means of proving the required intent, and one of these may be an act manifesting danger. In a particular case of manifestly criminal, punishable conduct, it may be impossible to determine whether the fact fulfills a substantive requirement or whether it functions merely as evidence of intent. The distinction has a concrete impact only in cases where the conduct of the accused is outwardly unincriminating. If manifest criminality is a substantive requirement, no surrogate proof of intent will suffice; if, in contrast, it fulfills an evidentiary function, the absence of manifestly criminal conduct may be corrected with surrogate proof of a criminal intent.

Thus the difference between the two patterns may be simply stated as turning on whether a manifestly criminal act is a substantive requirement.

In the pattern of manifest criminality it is; in the theory of subjective criminality, it is not.

These two patterns of liability – the manifest and the subjective – interweave in contemporary thinking about criminal law. Yet they remain camouflaged by a common stock of legal maxims that create an image of unity in criminal theory. It is generally said that criminal liability presupposes (1) an act, (2) an intent, (3) a union of act and intent. In addition, it might be asserted that (4) danger to the community, and (5) an intrusion upon the public sphere are general features of criminal conduct. Though the requirement of these elements is nominally common to both patterns of criminality, the concepts of act, intention, union, danger and public sphere acquire different meanings and significance, as they are interpreted in one pattern of liability or the other.

Fletcher's account denies that the common law of larceny was merely chaotic and beset by procedural technicalities. His argument allows us to perceive criteria of order and coherence which related to the specific social conditions of the time. Essentially, Fletcher diagnoses in the early common law of larceny a throwback to early conceptions of *furtum manifestum* from Roman law, under which manifest theft – catching a thief red-handed, as it were – entailed the immediate right of justified killing on the part of the discoverer. This contrasted sharply with non-manifest theft, which was treated as a matter pertaining to compensation. Fletcher suggests that the doctrine of possessorial immunity in common law was doing much the same thing: it was identifying the line between those relationships which were properly within the ambit of the criminal as opposed to the civil courts. Domestic servants' appropriations were not criminal, unless manifest, even after the *Carrier's Case*, because they took place within the ambit of ongoing relationships which provided a framework of social control in relation to property: it was up to a master to see that his servants did not misappropriate his property. Commercial relationships between strangers, by contrast, were gradually moved into the public sphere and regulated by criminal as well as civil law.

What Fletcher identifies here is therefore a particular conception of the nature of the private and of the proper line to be drawn between criminal and civil law. The assumption of the pattern of manifest criminality is that criminal law should not intervene until there is an unequivocal manifestation of danger to the community. This gradually gave way to a subjective pattern, in which the essence of crime was individual intent or responsibility. Fletcher does not elaborate any general explanation of the shift from the manifest pattern to a subjective pattern, but it seems plausible that this had to do with changing conceptions of the nature of human agency, and of the relationship between the individual and the state. In the relatively static social order of the early common law, the idea of crime as something immediately identifiable as threatening to community interests made sense. But as society became more fragmented, the criminal law more extensive, and criminal law's functions more diverse, the emerging conception of individual, subjective responsibility began to replace the increasingly untenable conception of crime as manifest, generally identifiable wrongdoing (cf Farmer 1996, quoted in **Chapter 1.I.a.**).

Within the framework of manifest criminality, 'animus furandi' does not operate to underpin the need for social protection or to justify the ascription of culpability, as intent or 'mens rea' within a subjective framework would. Rather, in so far as 'states of mind' are relevant to manifest criminality, they function merely as evidence, bolstering the interpretation of an equivocally criminal act as indeed criminal (see Lacey 2001b and **Chapter 1.II.b.**). Unlike the modern, dualistic analysis, the pattern of manifest criminality engaged in an integrated reading of an action as one which could be recognised by any observer as a crime. Hence 'animus furandi' spoke to the perceived limits of criminal law and the nature of crime. By contrast, in the emerging subjective pattern, the intent of the offender to violate a legally established and socially recognised interest is the foundation for the attribution of liability, and this brings with it a focus on the conceptual distinction between 'mens rea' and 'actus reus', an elaboration of excuses, and a movement towards inchoate offences such as attempt (see **section II.c.ii.–iii.** below). In the specific area of property law, it entails the gradual blurring of the boundaries between the later offences of embezzlement and false pretences and the original conception of larceny – a blurring which was already evident in the Larceny Act 1916, and which, as we shall see, reaches its zenith in the Theft Act 1968. We shall now move on to consider the modern law of theft and to examine the ways in which it replays the technical problems identified by Fletcher and, in doing so, echoes conceptions of criminality often regarded as having been transcended by modern, subjectivist criminal law doctrine.

II.a.ii.   Contemporary conceptions of theft: ordinary language through the looking glass ...

Although the common law of theft was subjected to a significant degree of rationalisation in 1916, the Larceny Act of that year still encompassed a wide range of different offences. Following a consideration of the area by the Criminal Law Revision Committee, the passage of the Theft Act 1968 represented an attempt to engage in a systematic codification of theft. This project of codification was informed by rule of law values such as clarity, comprehensiveness, coherence and consistency, and in particular by the idea that the criminal law should be accessible to the citizen and that its technicality should be reduced. In pursuit of these goals, the drafters of the Theft Act 1968 aspired to frame it in 'ordinary language'. This aspiration had two aspects: that the definition of theft should capture common sense conceptions of stealing and that the Theft Act should be comprehensible to citizens without legal training.

Theft therefore provides an occasion to consider both the practice of statutory interpretation and the extent to which ideals of codification are capable of being realised. It is interesting in particular to assess the extent to which the law of theft reflects ordinary conceptions of stealing and remains relatively 'untechnical' after 35 years of judicial interpretation.

Theft Act 1968

1(1)A person is guilty of theft if he dishonestly appropriates property belonging to another with the intention of permanently depriving the other of it; and "thief" and "steal" shall be construed accordingly.

(2) It is immaterial whether the appropriation is made with a view to gain, or is made for the thief's own benefit.

This one basic definition is to be applied to the whole gamut of stealing, from one-off and opportunistic shoplifting through pocket-picking and small-scale workplace theft to systematic, 'professional' or organised thefts of large values of goods or money. The important task of distinguishing between the relative seriousness of thefts is deferred to magistrates' and judges' sentencing function, in which they have a broad discretion (see **Chapter 1.III.b.iv.**). Theft is triable either way, and the maximum penalty on trial on indictment is seven years' imprisonment.

Despite its grounding in the philosophy of 'ordinary language' whose meaning should be accessible to the lay person, the Act further defines the terms of the basic definition, and does so in ways which often stretch the meanings of the original words far beyond what any lay person could be expected to anticipate. Several features of this extended definition and of the courts' interpretations of it call for special comment. The statutory definition reflects very clearly the 'actus reus/mens rea' dualism typical of the subjective pattern of liability. We may therefore begin by considering the 'mens rea' requirement – a dishonest intention permanently to deprive.

Theft Act 1968

Dishonesty

2(1)A person's appropriation of property belonging to another is not to be regarded as dishonest–

(a) if he appropriates the property in the belief that he has in law the right to deprive the other of it, on behalf of himself or of a third person; or

(b) if he appropriates the property in the belief that he would have the other's consent if the other knew of the appropriation and the circumstances of it; or

(c) (except where the property came to him as trustee or personal representative) if he appropriates the property in the belief that

the person to whom the property belongs cannot be discovered
by taking reasonable steps.

(2) A person's appropriation of property belonging to another may be
dishonest notwithstanding that he is willing to pay for the property.

The framing of theft in the moralistic terms of 'dishonesty' is interesting,
particularly given the absence of such 'loaded' terms from legislation dealing
with what might be thought to be more serious crimes (eg aggravated criminal
damage under s 1(2) of the Criminal Damage Act 1971: see **section II.e.**
below). Dishonesty is an idea about which there is incomplete social consensus.
Yet s 2 of the Act offers only a partial definition. After some prevarication, the
higher courts have now settled on a partial definition which effectively
delegates the task of further interpretation and application to the fact-finding
bodies: ie magistrates and juries:

R v Ghosh [1982] 2 All ER 689, CA

[*The appellant had been charged with several offences of attempting to obtain and
obtaining money by deception by falsely representing that he had carried out
abortion operations which had in fact been carried out by someone else or under
NHS provisions. His defence was to deny dishonesty and deception on the basis that
the sums paid were legitimately payable under the regulations. Lord Lane,
delivering the judgment of the court, engaged in a lengthy analysis of the case law
on dishonesty from a variety of fields and concluded:*]

In determining whether the prosecution has proved that the defendant
was acting dishonestly, a jury must first of all decide whether according to
the ordinary standards of reasonable and honest people what was done was
dishonest. If it was dishonest by those standards, then the jury must consider whether the defendant himself must have realised that what he was
doing was by those standards dishonest. In most cases, where the actions
are obviously dishonest by ordinary standards, there will be no doubt about
it. It will be obvious that the defendant himself knew that he was acting
dishonestly. It is dishonest for a defendant to act in a way which he knows
ordinary people consider to be dishonest, even if he asserts or genuinely
believes that he is morally justified in acting as he did. For example, Robin
Hood or those ardent anti-vivisectionists who remove animals from vivisection laboratories are acting dishonestly, even though they may consider
themselves to be morally justified in doing what they do, because they
know that ordinary people would consider these actions to be dishonest.

In this passage, Lord Lane simultaneously affirms the central doctrinal value of
'subjectivity' in 'mens rea' whilst appealing to an assumed social consensus
about dishonesty. He also underlines with an example a particular view of
behaviour which should not be accounted honest, because it is asserted that it is
not morally justifiable. Both the concept of dishonesty and the institution of

jury are being asked to do considerable work here. The founding of dishonesty in what 'ordinary people' think may well facilitate the differential treatment of certain classes of defendant, such as the white collar defendant whose actions are seen as only 'marginally' dishonest, or the defendant whose conduct has coincided with a 'moral panic' about a particular form of property crime (these two categories occasionally overlap, as illustrated by the extract from Halpin below). Furthermore, the approach assumes that it is appropriate for magistrates and juries to make 'at large' moral judgments under the guise of applying determinate legal standards. But it is easy to think of examples which many 'ordinary people' might not see as lending themselves to assessment in terms of honesty or dishonesty. The anti-vivisectionists seem a good example here, as does the neighbour who refuses to allow the retrieval of a ball which has landed in her garden. Do these situations really fall squarely within some unproblematic social conception of honesty versus dishonesty which a jury may easily apply? While it might be possible to agree that the conduct of the animal activists is anti-authoritarian, or the response of the neighbour uncharitable, it seems odd to ask whether they are dishonest. These problems, as well as the way in which the judiciary is nonetheless able to shape the construction of dishonesty by means of its directions to the jury and through appellate cases, are identified by Halpin in relation to cases of city fraud:

Andrew Halpin, 'The Test for Dishonesty' (1996) Crim LR pp 286–292

The appeal of the *Ghosh* test is precisely that it appears to strike an effective compromise. Upon further examination, however, we find within it not a stable compromise but a continuing tension between the subjective and objective approaches, concealed by the great assumption of the *Ghosh* test that there exists a set of ordinary standards of dishonesty ...

Although the *Ghosh* test firmly places the issue of dishonesty in the hands of the jury, juries have to be directed, and judges' directions come to be scrutinised by appellate courts. The course that the test has taken in appeal cases provides some insight into its practice. It also demonstrates that the test has undergone significant modification.

The simplest modification occurs when the test is not properly applied in the trial judge's directions, but the verdict is nevertheless upheld on appeal by applying the proviso to section 1 of the Criminal Appeal Act 1968 [available where the Court of Appeal is satisfied that no injustice has been done because no reasonable, properly directed jury could have failed to convict]. This effectively substitutes the appellate court's determination for the jury's, by an evidential presumption, whilst still following the form of the test ...

... Notwithstanding the technical authority of *Ghosh*, the courts have taken a hard line by holding particular circumstances to amount to absolute dishonesty, thus permitting 'objective' standards to be imposed by the courts ... The implications are twofold. First, the subjective element, which could operate in the *Ghosh* test at least partially to resolve the uncertainties over dishonesty in the defendant's favour, can be excluded in a case of obvious dishonesty. Secondly, the clash of different standards of dishonesty may reappear in determining what is a case of obvious dishonesty ...

Ernest Saunders allowed several million pounds of the assets of Guinness to be used for an illegal share support scheme without standing to gain a penny for himself. Thomas Ward accepted several million pounds of the assets of Guinness for himself in contravention of the company's articles of association. Why was Saunders convicted of theft and Ward acquitted? In both cases the guilt of the defendant turned on dishonesty.

The £5.2 million success fee paid on the takeover of Distillers to Ward, an American corporate lawyer, had been agreed by a committee of Guinness directors (one of them Ward himself) rather than by the full board as the company articles required. On this basis summary judgment for the return of the money to Guinness was upheld by the House of Lords, where Lord Templeman criticised Ward's conduct in allowing personal interests to conflict with his duties as a director.

In these circumstances, it might have been anticipated that dishonesty would be established at the criminal trial, but Ward was acquitted. It is impossible to know what influenced the jurors, but one part of the evidence may have proved crucial. In describing the negotiation and size of his success fee, Ward informed the court that it was agreed in the manner in which he was used to operating in America. It is quite possible that this convinced the jury of Ward's honesty – honest by the standards of ordinary American corporate lawyers ...

Saunders was convicted of theft of the money used for the illegal share support scheme. Comments made by the trial judge, subsequently approved by Neill L.J. in the first failed appeal to the Court of Appeal, indicate that Saunders had made no personal gain, and had behaved properly and honestly until he had "got sucked into dishonesty by the ethos of the bitterly fought contested takeover".

The clear implication is that the dishonesty of Saunders consisted solely in the fact that he was involved in breaching section 15 of the Companies Act 1985, even though perhaps not dishonest by the standards of ordinary company directors. The convicted Guinness defendants were widely reported in the media at the time as expressing astonishment that their practices should be regarded as dishonest. And one of the grounds of the second appeal was that evidence of similar practices in the City, which had been withheld by the prosecution, substantiated this viewpoint.

The Court of Appeal accepted that the material should have been disclosed but nevertheless upheld the convictions, since there was "ample evidence of a dishonest scheme". Although the Court elaborated on the "scheme" as involving not merely a breach of section 151 but also indemnities, false invoices and huge success fees, the impact of the two failed Guinness appeals is to establish the possibility of constructive liability [i.e. liability which is assumed, as a matter of law, on the basis of certain facts] for theft whereby the infringement of company (or other) regulations may lead to a holding of "obvious dishonesty".

The idea of obvious dishonesty can relate to the *Ghosh* test in two ways. In the first case the full rigour of the test is not required because there exists a moral consensus in society over the conduct in question, such that even the rogue is aware that he is acting dishonestly. This does not operate as a qualification on the *Ghosh* test itself, but rather on the procedure for applying the test: there is no need to apply the second limb in asking whether the defendant was aware that his conduct would be regarded as dishonest, since it is a foregone conclusion that he was.

In the second case, the test is modified. It is assumed as a matter of law that there exists a consensus. So, for example we assume that all reasonable honest people would consider Robin Hood's conduct as being dishonest (and that all unreasonable dishonest people would realise this). The crucial distinction consists in the fact that we have moved to a purely objective test. The defendant is now precluded from asserting that he himself thought that his behaviour would be regarded as honest even where he did.

Halpin argues that these tensions can be resolved only by reverting to a subjective approach or by enacting a statutory definition of dishonesty. His analysis illustrates a final feature of the test enunciated in *Ghosh*. Particularly when interpreted in the 'constructive' way exemplified by Saunders' case, it does not in substance fit the 'actus reus/mens rea' dualism, for it is as easily seen as inviting the jury to consider the *quality of the defendant's action* as *the state of her mind*. As we shall see below, the preservation of a clear line between questions of 'dishonesty' and of 'appropriation' has in practice caused considerable difficulty in the interpretation of the Theft Act.

Theft Act 1968

Section 6 Intention permanently to deprive

(1) A person appropriating property belonging to another without meaning the other permanently to lose the thing itself is nevertheless to be regarded as having the intention of permanently depriving the other of it if his intention is to treat the thing as his own to dispose of regardless of the other's rights: and a borrowing or lending of it may amount to so treating it if, but only if, the borrowing or lending is for a period and in circumstances making it equivalent to an outright taking or disposal.

(2) Without prejudice to the generality of subsection (1) above, where a person, having possession or control (lawfully or not) of property

belonging to another, parts with property under a condition as to its return which he may not be able to perform, this (if done for purposes of his own and without the other's authority) amounts to treating the property as his own to dispose of regardless of the other's rights.

The double-think underlying 'ordinary language legislation' is vividly illustrated by this extended definition of 'intention permanently to deprive', which turns out to mean no such thing. Under the terms of s 6, 'intention permanently to deprive' appears to encompass both recklessness and certain forms of temporary deprivation. Subsection (1) provides that someone who does not mean the other permanently to lose the thing itself has nevertheless such an intention if she intends 'to treat the thing as [her] own to dispose of regardless of the other's rights'. A specific example is given: that of borrowing or lending in circumstances in which this is 'equivalent to an outright taking or disposal'. This might seem obvious and reasonable in the case of property such as a ticket which loses its value after a certain time, but marginal cases can easily be imagined. How are we to categorise the person who hides someone else's property believing there is a 40% chance she will find it? Would it make a difference if she assessed the chances as 60%? This extended definition of 'mens rea' is in part an attempt to side-step the difficult issue of just what 'property' is being appropriated in such cases. For example, the courts have decided that there is no intention permanently to deprive under s 6 where someone 'borrows', say, a season ticket and returns it before the end of the season: where some value remains, there has been no 'equivalence to an outright taking or disposal' (*Lloyd*, 1985; *Arnold*, 1997). If the ticket is returned after the end of the season, however, this may constitute a theft. In such a case, what, precisely, is stolen? What the defendant intends to deprive the other of is not the ticket but its value: yet it is not at all apparent either that this can naturally said to be what is 'appropriated' or that the 'value' or 'rights of an owner' which are appropriated come within the definition of 'property' given by s 4.

Further issues arise in relation to s 6(2). This subsection includes within the definition of 'intention permanently to deprive' the attitude of someone who parts with property under a condition with which she may not be able to comply wherever this amounts to 'treating the property as [her] own to dispose of regardless of the other's rights'. This provision appears to allow for theft by recklessness – for example where one pawns something knowing that there is a chance that one will not be able to redeem it. Yet the provision simultaneously allows the surface of the law to proclaim the need for 'specific intent', and thus to reflect what is perceived as the 'ordinary' person's conception of theft. The strategy also suppresses the question of whether such recklessness should be interpreted 'subjectively' or 'objectively': while the definition of theft in terms of 'intent' suggests a 'subjective' test, the framing of s 6(2) moves in a significantly 'objective' direction. Indeed, it does so to the extent of imposing 'constructive' liability similar to that identified by Halpin in relation to dishonesty: it states that parting with property in the given circumstances '*shall be regarded*' as an intention permanently to deprive. This approach of taking 'mens rea' as proven by the existence of an external situation is fundamentally at odds with the ideology of modern criminal law doctrine, and is one of the practices which the modern law claims generally to avoid. The 'mens rea' requirement for theft therefore constitutes a good example of criminal law proclaiming strict safeguards for the defendant whilst in fact introducing broad, uncertain and potentially objective standards.

Similar points can be made about the elaborated definition of the 'actus reus' of theft.

Theft Act 1968

Section 3 Appropriation
(1) Any assumption by a person of the rights of an owner amounts to an appropriation, and this includes, where he has come by the property (innocently or not) without stealing it, any later assumption of a right to it by keeping or dealing with it as owner.
(2) Where property or a right or interest in property is or purports to be transferred for value to a person acting in good faith, no later assumption by him of rights which he believed himself to be acquiring shall, by reason of any defect in the transferor's title, amount to theft of the property.

The use of the concept of 'appropriation' was intended to broaden the notion of 'taking' so as to be able to encompass a wider range of situations and objects. But the statutory definition in terms of 'any assumption … of the rights of an owner', including later assumptions of rights after an initially non-theftous acquisition (although excluding the purchaser in good faith), threatens to take on such a wide meaning as effectively to undermine its status as a genuine requirement of or restriction on the definition of theft. Given that an assumption of any of the rights of the owner suffices (*Morris*, 1983), a broad reading could support the view that *any* dealing with goods accompanied by the requisite 'mens rea' already constitutes theft. On this view, the dishonest shopper who has placed some food in her supermarket trolley intending to hide it at the checkout to avoid paying has already stolen – a view which raises the question of what could possibly constitute attempted theft (see **section II.c.ii.** below). On a narrower reading, by contrast, an assumption of the owner's rights would only count as an appropriation where it was inherently adverse to those rights; this would exclude the action of placing food in a supermarket trolley. The competition between these two, broader and narrower, approaches to appropriation is of particular interest because it evokes some of the difficulties arising within the common law about the relationship between larceny, embezzlement and false pretences. On the narrow view, the modern notion of theft as appropriation seeks to preserve a notion of stealing as distinct from deception, embezzlement or false pretences. Until 1993, this narrow interpretation found favour with the House of Lords:

R v Morris, Anderton v Burnside [1983] 3 All ER 288

[*The defendants in this case had dishonestly switched the price tags of goods and put the goods bearing the lower price into a supermarket trolley. These circumstances raised neatly the issue of just when an appropriation had taken place, especially given that Burnside, unlike Morris, had been arrested before he had paid the lower price. Lord Roskill adopted a narrowed conception of appropriation which sought to avoid the absurdities of a literal reading of the Act:*]

My Lords, counsel for the prosecution sought to argue that any removal from the shelves of the supermarket, even if unaccompanied by label-switching, was without more an appropriation. In one passage in his judgment in Morris's case, Lord Lane CJ appears to have accepted the submission, for he said:

' ... It seems to us that in taking the article from the shelf the customer is indeed assuming one of the rights of the owner, the right to move the article from its position on the shelf to carry it to the check-out ...'

With the utmost respect, I cannot accept this statement as correct. If one postulates an honest customer taking goods from a shelf to put in his or her trolley to take to the check-point there to pay the proper price, I am unable to see that any of these actions involves any assumption by the shopper of the rights of the supermarket. In the context of s3(1), the concept of appropriation in my view involves not an act expressly or impliedly authorised by the owner but an act by way of adverse interference with or usurpation of those rights. When the honest shopper acts as I have just described, he or she is acting with the implied authority of the owner of the supermarket to take the goods from the shelf, put them in the trolley, take them to the check-point and there to pay the correct price, at which moment the property in the goods will pass to the shopper for the first time. It is with the consent of the owners of the supermarket, be that consent express or implied, that the shopper does these acts and thus obtained at least control if not actual possession of the goods preparatory, at a later stage, to obtaining property in them on payment of the proper amount at the check-point. I do not think that s 3(1) envisages any such act as an 'appropriation', whatever may be the meaning of that word in other fields such as contract or sale of goods law.

However, in 1993, the House of Lords reverted to the broad view of appropriation taken in the earlier case of *Lawrence v MPC* (1971):

R v Gomez [1993] 1 All ER p 1

The respondent, who was employed as the assistant manager of an electrical goods shop, was approached by B, who asked to be supplied with quantities of electrical goods from the shop in exchange for two stolen building society cheques which were worthless. The respondent agreed and asked the shop manager to authorise the supply of the goods against the cheques. The manager told him to find out from the bank whether the cheques were acceptable and the respondent later pretended to have done so and told him that the cheques were 'as good as cash'. The cheques were then used for the purchase of goods to the value of over £16,000 and were later dishonoured on presentation. The respondent was jointly charged with B and another with theft. At his trial, it was submitted that there was no case to answer, on the ground that the electrical goods were sold to B pursuant to a contract of sale between B and the shop (the owner of the goods) and although it was conceded that the contract had been induced by the fraudulent misrepresentation of the respondent and that the manager would not have agreed to the removal of the goods had he known the truth, the manager had expressly authorised the goods to be removed and therefore there had been no 'appropriation' within s1(1) of the Theft Act 1968. The judge rejected that submission and the respondent then pleaded guilty. He appealed on the grounds that the judge's ruling was wrong. The Court of Appeal held that there had been no appropriation and accordingly it allowed the respondent's appeal and quashed his conviction. The Crown appealed to the House of Lords.

The House of Lords (Lord Lowry dissenting) held that an appropriation could exist:

> 'if the owner of the goods was induced by fraud, deception or a false representation to consent to or authorise the taking of the goods, since it was the actual taking of the goods, whether with or without the consent of the owner, in circumstances where it was intended to assume the rights of the owner that amounted to the 'appropriation' and the fraud, deception or false representation practised on the owner made the appropriation dishonest. It was irrelevant that the taking of goods in such circumstances could also constitute the offence of obtaining property by deception under s.15 (1) of the 1968 Act.'

The respondent's conviction was accordingly restored.

Lord Keith, p 4

The court [of Appeal] granted a certificate under s 33(2) of the Criminal Appeal Act 1968 that a point of law of general public importance was involved in the decision, namely:

'When theft is alleged and that which is alleged to be stolen passes to the defendant with the consent of the owner, but that consent has been obtained by a false representation, has a) an appropriation within the meaning of s.1(1) of the Theft Act 1968 taken place, or, b) must such a passing of property necessarily involve an element of adverse 'interference' with or usurpation of some right of the owner?' ...

pp 5–6

The facts in *Lawrence v Cmr of Police for the Metropolis* (1971) as set out in the speech of Viscount Dilhorne, were these:

' ... the appellant was convicted on 2nd December 1969 of theft contrary to s.1(1) of the Theft Act 1968. On 1st September 1969 a Mr. Occhi, an Italian who spoke little English, arrived at Victoria Station on his first visit to this country. He went up to a taxi driver, the appellant, and showed him a piece of paper on which an address in Ladbroke Grove was written. The appellant said that it was very far and very expensive. Mr. Occhi got into the taxi, took £1 out of his wallet and gave it to the appellant who then, the wallet being still open, took a further £6 out of it. He then drove Mr. Occhi to Ladbroke Grove. The correct lawful fare for the journey was in the region of 10s.6d. The appellant was charged and convicted of the theft of the £6.'

The conviction was upheld by the Court of Appeal, Criminal Division, which in granting leave to appeal to your Lordships' House certified the following questions as involving a point of law of general public importance:

'(1) Whether Section 1(1) of the Theft Act, 1968, is to be construed as though it contained the words "without the consent of the owner" or words to that effect.

(2) Whether the provisions of Section 15(1) and Section 1(1) of the Theft Act 1968 are mutually exclusive in the sense that if the facts proved would justify a conviction under Section 15 (1) there cannot lawfully be a conviction under Section 1(1) on those facts.'

Viscount Dilhorne, whose speech was concurred in by Lord Donovan, Lord Pearson, Lord Diplock and Lord Cross of Chelsea, after stating the facts, and expressing some doubts as to what Mr Occhi had meant when he said that he 'permitted' the taxi driver to take the £6, continued:

'The main contention of the appellant ... was that Mr. Occhi had consented to the taking of the £6 and that, consequently, his conviction could not stand. In my opinion, the facts of this case to which I have referred fall far short of establishing that Mr. Occhi had so consented. Prior to the passage of the Theft Act 1968 ... it was necessary to prove that the property alleged to have been stolen was taken "without the consent of the owner" (Larceny Act 1916 s1(1). These words are not included in s 1(1) of the Theft Act 1968, but the appellant contended that the subsection should be construed as if they ... appeared after the word 'appropriates' ... I see no ground for concluding that the omission of the words 'without the consent of the owner' was inadvertent and not deliberate, and to read the subsection as it they were included is, in my opinion, wholly unwarranted. Parliament by the omission of these words has relieved the prosecution of the burden of establishing that the taking was without the owner's consent. That is no longer an ingredient of the offence ... Belief or the absence of belief that the owner had with [full knowledge of the circumstances] consented to the appropriation is relevant to the issue of dishonesty, not to the question of whether or not there has been an appropriation ... '

pp 9–13

In the civil case of *Dobson v General Accident Fire and Life Insurance Corp plc* (1989) ... [the Court of Appeal] considered the apparent conflict between *Lawrence*'s case and *R v Morris* and applied the former decision. The facts were that the plaintiff had insured property with the defendant company against, inter alia, 'loss or damage caused by theft'. He advertised for sale a watch and ring at the total price of £5,950. A rogue telephoned expressing an interest in buying the articles and the plaintiff provisionally agreed with him that the payment would be by a building society cheque in the plaintiff's favour. The rogue called on the plaintiff the next day and the watch and ring were handed over to him in exchange for a building society cheque for the agreed amount. The plaintiff paid the cheque into his bank, which informed him that it was stolen and worthless. The defendant company denied liability under its policy of insurance on the ground that the loss of the watch and ring was not caused by theft within the meaning of the 1968 Act ... One of the arguments for the defendants was that there had been no theft because the plaintiff had agreed to the transaction with the rogue and reliance was placed on Lord Roskill's statement in *R v Morris* that appropriation 'involves not an act expressly or impliedly authorised by the owner but an act by way of adverse interference with or usurpation of those rights'.

[*Having noted Parker LJ's rejection of Lord Roskill's assertion that the House of Lords in Lawrence had not considered the precise meaning of 'appropriation', Lord Keith went on to quote further aspects of his critique of Morris from the judgment in Dobson:*]

In the first passage Lord Roskill, as it seems to me, impliedly envisages that mere label-switching could be an appropriation and that this is so is confirmed by the answer to the certified question which specifically used the words 'either by that act alone'. What then is it which would make label-switching alone something which adversely affects or usurps the right of the owner? In that passage it appears to be envisaged that it will depend on the question whether the label-switching was dishonest and coupled with the other elements of the offence of theft or was due to a perverted sense of humour. This, however appears to run together the elements of dishonesty and appropriation when it is clear from *Lawrence*'s case that they are separate. That the two elements were indeed, at any rate to some extent, run together is plain from the fact that the answer to the certified question begins with the words 'there is a dishonest appropriation'. Moreover, on general principles, it would in my judgement be plain interference with or usurpation of an owner's rights by the customer if he were to remove a label which the owner had placed on goods or put another label on. It would be a trespass to goods and it would be usurping the owner's rights, for only he would have any right to do such an act and no one could contend that there was any implied consent or authority to a customer to do any such thing. There would thus be an appropriation. In the case of the customer with a perverted sense of humour there would however be no theft for there would probably be no dishonesty and certainly no intent permanently to deprive the owner of the goods themselves. The case of the customer who simply removes goods from the shelves is of course different because the basis on which a supermarket is run is that customers certainly have the consent of the owner to take goods from the shelves and take them to the checkout point, there to pay the proper price for them. Suppose, however, that there were no such consent in, for example, a shop where goods on display were to be taken from the shelves only by the attendant. In such a case a customer who took from the shelves would clearly be usurping the right of the owner. Indeed he would be doing so if he did no more than move an item from one place on a shelf to another. The only difference appears to be that in the one case there is consent and in the other there is not. Since, however, it was held in *Lawrence*'s case that consent is not relevant to appropriation there must, one would have supposed, be no difference between the two cases on that aspect of the offence. There are further matters in *R v Morris* in which I find difficulty. I mention only two. The first is the observation made on *R v McPherson* (1973). That was a case in which the defendant took two bottles of whisky from the shelves and put them in her shopping bag. The sole question in issue was whether there had been an appropriation. It was held in the Court of Appeal that there had been. As to this Lord Roskill said (p.294): 'That was not, of course, a label-switching case, but it is a plain case of appropriation effected by the combination of the acts of removing the goods from the shelf and of concealing them in the shopping bag ... ' Reference to the transcript of the judgment in that case however reveals that the decision did not turn on concealment in the shopping bag but was expressly on the ground that the goods were appropriated when they were taken from the shelves ... After anxious consideration I have reached the conclusion that whatever *R v Morris* did decide it cannot be regarded as having overruled the very plain decision in *Lawrence*'s case that appropriation can occur even if the owner consents and that *R v Morris* itself makes it plain that it is no defence to say that the property passed under a voidable contract.

On this ground Parker LJ dismissed the appeal ...

It was argued for the respondent in the present appeal that *Dobson*'s case was wrongly decided. I disagree, and on the contrary find myself in full agreement with those parts of the judgment of Parker LJ to which I have referred ... The actual decision in *R v Morris* was correct, but it was erroneous, in addition to being unnecessary for the decision to indicate that an act expressly or impliedly authorised by the owner could never amount to an appropriation. There is no material distinction between the facts in *Dobson*'s case and those in the present case. In each case the owner of the goods was induced by fraud to part with them to the rogue. *Lawrence*'s case makes it clear that consent to or authorisation by the owner of the taking by the rogue is irrelevant. The taking amounted to an appropriation within the meaning of s 1(1) of the 1968 Act. *Lawrence*'s case also makes it clear that it is no less irrelevant that what happened may also have constituted the offence of obtaining property by deception under s 15 (1) of the 1968 Act ...

My Lords, for the reasons which I have given I would answer branch (a) of the certified question in the affirmative and branch (b) in the negative, and allow the appeal.

Gomez therefore firmly endorsed the broad view of appropriation (see also *Atakpu*, 1993). Yet the decision left several important issues unresolved. In the first place, the line between 'appropriation' and 'dishonesty' remained blurred. Though Lord Keith's analysis envisaged that an appropriation might take place even in the absence of any fraud which casts doubt on the reality of the owner's consent – arguing that such fraud relates to dishonesty rather than appropriation – the certified question was framed narrowly. Hence the decision in the case might be read strictly, as covering only cases in which some form of fraud is involved. In view of these factors, and of Lord Lowry's strongly argued dissent, it was therefore not surprising that the issue of appropriation found its way to the House of Lords once again relatively quickly, and this time in a form which forced the judges to confront the ambiguities left in place by *Gomez*.

In *Hinks*, the defendant had received property and large transfers of money from a vulnerable low-IQ man who was more or less in her care. She had been convicted of theft and her appeal to the Court of Appeal was dismissed. On appeal to the House of Lords, the certified question was whether an appropriation could take place notwithstanding the fact that a valid gift had taken place and that, hence, Hinks had acquired an 'indefeasible title to the property'. The House of Lords decided by a majority of 3 to 2 that on the basis of *Lawrence* and *Gomez* appropriation could indeed take place under such circumstances. The question of whether the gift was void or voidable due to undue influence or coercion was irrelevant to appropriation under the Theft Act: these factors were, as the trial judge had directed, merely questions relevant to dishonesty. While recognising the criticism that this interpretation stretches the offence of theft very wide, Lord Steyn, with whom Lords Slynn and Jauncey concurred, argued that prosecution discretion and the contours of dishonesty under s 2 would be adequate to keep the law of theft in reasonable bounds:

R v Hinks [2000] 4 All ER 833 at 841, 843–844

Lord Steyn

[After quoting from Lord Browne-Wilkinson's speech in *Gomez*] [I]t is immaterial whether the act was done with the owner's consent or authority. It is true of course that the certified question in *R v Gomez* referred to the situation where consent had been obtained by fraud. But the majority judgments do not differentiate between cases of consent induced by fraud and consent given in any other circumstances. The ratio involves a proposition of general application. *R v Gomez* therefore gives effect to s3(1) of the 1968 Act by treating 'appropriation' as a neutral word comprehending 'any assumption by a person of the rights of an owner'. If the law is as held in *R v Gomez*, it destroys the argument advanced on the present appeal, namely that an indefeasible gift of property cannot amount to an appropriation.

...

Counsel for the appellant ... pointed out that the law as stated in *Lawrence*'s case and in *R v Gomez* creates a tension between the civil and the criminal law. In other words, conduct which is not wrongful in a civil law sense may constitute the crime of theft. Undoubtedly, this is so ... The question whether the civil claim to a title by a convicted thief, who committed no civil wrong, may be defeated by the principle that nobody may benefit from his own civil *or* criminal wrong does not arise for decision. Nevertheless there is a more general point, namely that the interaction between criminal law and civil law can cause problems: compare Beatson and Simester (1999) ... The purposes of the civil law and the criminal law are somewhat different. In theory the two systems should be in perfect harmony. In a practical world there will sometimes be some disharmony between the two systems. In any event, it would be wrong to assume on a priori grounds that the criminal law rather than the civil law is defective. Given the jury's conclusions, one is entitled to observe that the appellant's conduct *should* constitute theft, the only available charge. The tension between the civil and the criminal law is therefore not in my view a factor which justifies a departure from the law as stated in *Lawrence*'s case and *R v Gomez*. Moreover these decisions of the House have a marked beneficial consequence. While in some contexts of the law of theft a judge cannot avoid explaining civil law concepts to a jury ... , the decisions of the House of Lords eliminate the need for such explanations in respect of appropriation. That is a great advantage in an overly complex corner of the law.

My Lords, if it had been demonstrated that in practice *Lawrence*'s case and *R v Gomez* were calculated to produce injustice that would have been a compelling reason to revisit the merits of the holdings in those decisions. That is however not the case. In practice the mental requirements of theft are an adequate protection against injustice. In these circumstances I would not be willing to depart from the clear decisions of the House in *Lawrence*'s case and *R v Gomez*. This brings me back to counsel's principal submission, namely that a person does not appropriate property unless the other (the owner) retains, beyond the instant of the alleged theft, some proprietary interest or the right to resume or recover some proprietary interest. This submission is directly contrary to the holdings in *Lawrence*'s case and in *R v Gomez*. It must be rejected. The alternative submission is that the word 'appropriates' should be interpreted as if the word 'unlawfully' preceded it so that only an act which is unlawful under the general law can be an appropriation. This submission is an invitation to interpolate a word in the carefully crafted language of the 1968 Act. It runs counter to the decisions in *Lawrence*'s case and in *R v Gomez* and must also be rejected. It follows that the certified question must be answered in the affirmative.

Does this broad conception of appropriation leave that concept any distinct role in defining and hence limiting the scope of theft? Or does it collapse theft back onto dishonesty, hence conflating 'actus reus' and 'mens rea' and implying that more or less any dishonest behaviour around property will satisfy the appropriation condition? Commentators have differed both on these questions and in their attitude to the fact that, on the broad view of appropriation, criminal law conceptions of property rights do not track civil law conceptions (see Beatson and Simester 1999; Shute 2002). By allowing a valid civil law transfer to count as an appropriation, the law now relies on dishonesty to do virtually all the work in drawing the line between theft and lawful behaviour. This, in effect, allows the line between crime and non-crime to depend on the jury's view of the moral status of the offender's behaviour. Quite apart from generating an over-extensive concept of theft, we could ask whether, given areas of social disagreement about the concept of dishonesty, this meets the standards of certainty and predictability which a commitment to human rights would dictate. On the other side of the debate, the actual wording of the Theft Act and the differing social functions of civil and criminal law – securing expectations and providing compensation as opposed to setting standards and imposing punishment – have been cited in support of the *Gomez/Hinks* approach. The difference of opinion is not confined to academic commentaries. In *Morris*, Lord Roskill, like Lord Steyn in *Hinks* and Lord Keith in *Gomez* argued strongly against aligning criminal and civil law questions: 'I respectfully suggest that it is on any view wrong to introduce into this branch of the criminal law questions whether particular contracts are void or voidable on the ground of mistake or fraud or whether any mistake is sufficiently fundamental to vitiate a contract. These difficult questions should so far as possible be confined to those fields of law to which they are immediately relevant, and I do not regard them as relevant questions under the 1968 Act.' But in a passionately argued dissent in *Hinks*, Lord Hobhouse argued for a narrow reading of *Gomez* and a closer articulation of the civil and criminal law of property – a position also implicit in Lord Hutton's dissenting view that 'it appears contrary to common sense that a person who receives money or property as a gift could be said to act dishonestly no matter how much ordinary and decent people would think it morally reprehensible for that person to accept the gift'.

R v Hinks [2000] 4 All ER 833 at pp 852–853

Lord Hobhouse.

Another aspect of the Court of Appeal's reasoning which also has to be examined is the relationship of that proposition [that a gift may be evidence of appropriation] to the concept of dishonesty. It is explicit in the Court of Appeal judgment that the relevant definition of the crime of theft is to be found in the element of dishonesty and *R v Ghosh* ... and that this is to receive no greater definition than consciously falling below the standards of an ordinary and decent persona and may include anything which such a person would think was morally reprehensible. It may be no more than a moral judgment.

The reasoning of the Court of Appeal therefore depends upon the disturbing acceptance that a criminal conviction and the imposition of custodial sanctions may be based upon conduct which involved no inherent illegality and may only be capable of being criticised on grounds of lack of morality. This approach itself raises fundamental questions. An essential function of the criminal law is to define the boundary between what conduct is criminal and what merely immoral. Both are the subject of the disapprobation of ordinary right-thinking citizens and the distinction is liable to be arbitrary or at least strongly influenced by considerations subjective to the individual members of the tribunal. To treat otherwise lawful conduct as criminal merely because it is open to such disapprobation would be contrary to principle and open to the objection that it fails to achieve the objective and transparent certainty required of the criminal law by the principles basic to human rights.

Three further points arise on the interpretation of appropriation under the Theft Act. First, the continuing difficulty of establishing the line between appropriation and dishonesty undermines the doctrinal assumption, clearly reflected in the structure of the Theft Act, that it is possible completely to define an offence in terms of a number of discrete 'actus reus' and 'mens rea' requirements, and suggests once again that criteria legally proclaimed to be analytically distinct run together in the practical interpretation of cases. In many theft cases, it is the concept of 'dishonesty', delineated by the magistrates or jury, which is the crucial factor in determining liability. Though the centrality of intent to the modern definition of theft places it firmly within Fletcher's subjective pattern, the definition of dishonesty in terms of popular standards echoes the pattern of 'manifest criminality' in which crime is conceived in terms of actions recognised as wrongful by the community.

Second, there is an indeterminacy both in *Morris* and in *Gomez/Hinks* as to just what is being appropriated. For example, on facts such as those in *Morris*, is it the whole of the property whose label has been switched (as reflected in the framing of actual charges of theft), or the difference in price, or the supermarket's right to fix the price? If it is the last of these, is this property within the definition in s 4, with its reference to 'things in action and other intangible property'?

Third, the cases on appropriation leave the relationship between theft and obtaining property by deception in a peculiar position (see **section II.b.** below). For the broad, *Gomez/Hinks* view entails that every case of obtaining property by deception will also be a case of theft. In this context, one wonders about the rationale for having two separate offences. The extent of the overlap also illustrates the degree to which, as Fletcher argues, the modern conception of theft has come to swallow up the distinct ideas of embezzlement and false pretences.

Theft Act 1968

Section 4 Property
(1) "Property" includes money and all other property, real or personal, including things in action and other intangible property.
(2) A person cannot steal land, or things forming part of land and severed from it by him or by his directions, except in the following cases, that it to say–
  (a) when he is a trustee or personal representative, or is authorised by power of attorney, or as liquidator of a company or otherwise, to sell or dispose of land belonging to another and he appropriates the land or anything forming part of it by dealing with it in breach of the confidence reposed in him; or

(b) when he is not in possession of the land and appropriates anything forming part of the land by severing it or causing it to be severed, or after it has been severed; or

(c) when, being in possession of the land under a tenancy, he appropriates the whole or part of any fixture or structure let to be used with the land.

For purposes of this subsection "land" does not include incorporeal hereditaments; "tenancy" means a tenancy for years or any less period and includes an agreement for such a tenancy, but a person who after the end of a tenancy remains in possession as statutory tenant or otherwise is to be treated as having possession under the tenancy, and "let" shall be construed accordingly.

(3) A person who picks mushrooms growing wild on any land, or who picks flowers, fruit or foliage from a plant growing wild on any land, does not (although not in possession of the land) steal what he picks, unless he does it for reward or for sale or other commercial purpose.

For purposes of this subsection "mushroom" includes any fungus, and "plant" includes any shrub or tree.

(4) Wild creatures, tamed or untamed, shall be regarded as property; but a person cannot steal a wild creature not tamed nor ordinarily kept in captivity, or the carcass of any such creature unless either it has been reduced into possession by or on behalf of another person and possession of it has not since been lost or abandoned, or another person is in course of reducing it into possession.

We have already noted legal uncertainty about just what 'property' is concerned in cases in which the extended definitions of appropriation or intention permanently to deprive are in play. The definition of 'property' under s 4 is itself very wide. Given this breadth, it is perhaps odd to find the continued exclusion, subject to some exceptions, of land from the definition of property, for there is no doubt that some kinds of interference with interests in land could without difficulty be brought within the extended definition of appropriation. This suggests the perceived importance of preserving a popular image of theft as the dishonest taking of goods – a conception which resonates with the old idea of 'taking and carrying away'. Indeed, the genius of the 1968 definition lies in the fact that the basic definition resoundingly echoes a 'common-sense' conception of theft, thus serving to legitimise the law, whilst the extended definitions allow its application to a vast range of situations. Notwithstanding the breadth of s 4, however, it appears to exclude certain forms of intangible phenomena which occupy an important place in contemporary conceptions of property (Firth 1995). The most obvious example is that of information:

OECD, *Computer-Related Crime* (1986) 24–26

Information is clearly coming to be considered more and more as a tradable economic asset. This raises the question of who is entitled to hold the asset and what is the scope of that right supposing, that is, there is such a right ... [T]he issue of whether information can count as a good ... [comes up] ... in relation to the legal definition of theft. Although the description of the offence of theft differs from one country to another, it seems worthwhile to reproduce the Canadian thinking on this matter: the unauthorized acquisition or disclosure of representations of information is colloquially called "theft of information", but the description is a misnomer. While information can be acquired without permission, it is questionable whether information can be stolen in the legal sense or ever be included within traditional concepts of "theft". Section 283 of the Canadian Criminal Code describes the general offence of theft:

"Everyone commits theft who fraudulently and without colour of right takes, or fraudulently and without colour of right converts to his use or to the use of another person, anything, whether animate or inanimate, with intent to deprive, temporarily or absolutely, the owner of it or a person who has a special property or interest in it ...".

A closer examination of the definition is required in order to understand the meaning of the concepts used ... "Property" is a very difficult and technical term to attempt to describe. "Property" can loosely be described as something of which one has the *exclusive right*, as against the world at large, to possess, to do with or to do as one wills, and to prevent all other persons from doing anything in relation to that thing which they are not specifically authorized to do. Accordingly, information, knowledge or ideas have traditionally not been recognised as constituting "property" for the purposes of the criminal law. Even the civil law has been reluctant to grant a general property status to information, knowledge or ideas, preferring instead to merely clothe particular types of information, knowledge or ideas with some of the attributes of a general property status. For example, statutes such as the Copyright Act and the Patent Act can, if certain conditions are met, grant exclusive rights to an individual to use particular types or forms of representations of information, knowledge or ideas, but even these Acts do not transform that which is patented or copyrighted into a form of traditional property ...

Regardless of whether information can be considered as "property" for the purposes of the Criminal Code, there are a number of other problems that arise when one attempts to apply the law of theft to a variety of abuses that can occur in relation to computers. While one can "take" (i.e. physically move) a disk, tape or print-out, there are some things which it is difficult to conceive of as being "taken". Just as one can take, and thereby steal, a ticket to a theatrical performance, once can take a magnetic tape, disk or sheet of computer print-out paper containing representations of information. However, the viewing of the theatrical performance has not been "taken", and it can be argued that neither has the information ...

The ... situation concerning the copying of information also raises another problem with respect to the law of theft; the issue of deprivation. There must be an intention to "deprive" the victim, either permanently or temporarily of that which was taken or converted. However, it can be argued in this situation that there has been no intention to deprive. The victim still retains his data bank intact, and there may have never existed the intention to deny such retention, but only to become apprised of the contents and nature of the data bank.

We have seen how the extended definitions of 'intent' and 'appropriation' in the Theft Act 1968 have sought to overcome some of these difficulties. In its working paper on computer misuse (Law Commission 1988), the Law Commission acknowledged the flexibility of existing law in concluding that the vast majority of computer abuse which calls for criminal as opposed to civil law regulation can be charged as theft or as conspiracy to defraud (see below **section II.c.i.**). It accordingly suggested that the only changes necessary were an amendment of the definition of deception in the Theft Acts (see below **section II.b.**) to include 'inducing a machine to respond to false representations', and the introduction of a specific offence to deal with 'hacking' – obtaining unauthorised access to a computer. In the event, the Computer Misuse Act 1990 enacted three offences of unlawfully entering another's computer system with dishonest intent (Wasik 1991). The Act was passed following the House of Lords' refusal to extend the law of forgery to cover cases of 'hacking' (*Gold and Schifreen*, 1988). English law has stopped short of recognising confidential information as intangible property within the meaning of the Theft Acts (*Oxford v Moss*, 1979). The potential complexities which arise from intangible phenomena such as information would be matched by an even larger area of potential uncertainty were it ever to be argued that aspects of what has been called the 'New Property' – welfare rights against the state – should be incorporated as potential subjects for criminal regulation through laws of theft or deception.

Theft Act 1968

Section 5 Belonging to another
(1) Property shall be regarded as belonging to any person having possession or control of it, or having in it any proprietary right or interest (not being an equitable interest arising only from an agreement to transfer or grant an interest).
(2) Where property is subject to a trust, the persons to whom it belongs shall be regarded as including any person having a right to enforce the trust, and an intention to defeat the trust shall be regarded accordingly as an intention to deprive of the property any person having that right.

(3) Where a person receives property from or on account of another, and is under an obligation to the other to retain and deal with the property or its proceeds in a particular way, the property or proceeds shall be regarded (as against him) as belonging to the other.

(4) Where a person gets property by another's mistake, and is under an obligation to make restoration (in whole or in part) of the property or its proceeds or of the value thereof, then to the extent of that obligation the property or proceeds shall be regarded (as against him) as belonging to the person entitled to restoration, and an intention not to make restoration shall be regarded accordingly as an intention to deprive that person of the property or proceeds.

(5) Property of a corporation sole shall be regarded as belonging to the corporation notwithstanding a vacancy in the corporation.

The extended definitions reach what is perhaps their furthest point of departure from popular images of theft in s 5's conception of 'belonging to another', which encompasses not only possession, control or practically any other non-equitable proprietary right or interest but also a range of other situations. The section has generated copious case law concerning issues such as whether the obligations envisaged by s 5(3) and (4) to deal in a particular way with or to restore property must be legal or need only be social; exactly when such obligations exist (see, for example *R v Hall* (1972), *R v Meech* (1973), *R v Arnold* (1997)); and the effects of various kinds of mistakes. In allowing for the conviction of someone who takes advantage of another's mistake (as in the case, for example, of overpayment of salary: *A-G's Reference (No 1 of 1983)* 1983), s 5(4) in effect creates an offence of theft by omission – again, subtly stretching doctrinal margins. The breadth of the section is illustrated by the fact that it enables the conviction of someone for theft of their own property (where another has possession and control, as in the case of a defendant who takes his car from the garage without having paid for the repairs – *R v Turner (No 2)* (1971)). Thus theft law operates with a relative rather than an absolute conception of property (property 'as against him'), and one which, notwithstanding deployment of concepts drawn from company law, contract, trusts and the law of restitution, departs substantially from civil law conceptions. As we have seen, the criminal courts have been reluctant to engage in civil law analysis, and both the Law Commission and the legislature have supported this posture by engaging in piecemeal reform where difficulties have arisen as a result of this separated approach.

Legal regulation of theft, then, illustrates the flexibility of legal definitions even in the context of a modern statute explicitly drafted on the basis of 'ordinary language' philosophy. What is more, the openness of the legal definition of theft, and in particular the scope for magistrates' and juries' interpretations of dishonesty, illustrate once again the potential relevance of competing perspectives, definitions and points of view in the construction of criminal liability. The existence of competing conceptions of what 'ordinary people' regard as dishonest gives rise to the possibility of applications of the law which discriminate along particular lines – for example in favour of 'white collar' offenders as compared with shoplifters. Similarly, the plausibility of defences such as belief in consent or claim of right will depend to a large extent on technically legally irrelevant criteria affecting the defendant's credibility as a witness and on jury views about the nature of 'real crime'. The combination of a basic definition which reflects popular images of 'real crime' and technical extended definitions which go well beyond it renders the law of theft a flexible and effective tool of social control, and one which is, not surprisingly, widely and selectively used in our society. This combination marks the persisting relevance of both manifest and subjective patterns of liability in modern criminal law. It is worth returning, therefore, to reconsider Fletcher's analysis in the light of our discussion of the contemporary law of theft.

Does the modern law of theft exemplify a consistent expression of the subjective pattern of liability, and what, precisely, explains modern law's development towards the subjective pattern? The problematic cases of larceny which Fletcher discusses – mistaken delivery, appropriation by a possessor – are explicitly covered by the modern law of theft: the doctrine of appropriation requires no taking from possession, and the decisions in *Gomez* and *Hinks* effectively elide false pretences with theft. Thus s 1 of the Theft Act 1968, in Fletcher's terms, covers larceny, embezzlement and false pretences. But have the problematic cases really gone away? Does the ongoing disagreement about the meaning of appropriation in fact echo the older concern with manifest criminality? Is this what underlies Lord Roskill's idea that appropriation requires 'usurpation' of the owner's rights? This view is rejected in *Gomez* and *Hinks*, but it is fascinating to perceive such echoes even in contemporary law. The modern law is comfortable neither with the view that crime consists in manifestly wrongful acts, with malice or intent playing a merely evidentiary role, nor with the view that crime inheres in subjective responsibility, with conduct playing a merely evidentiary role. The idea that current law is exclusively based on a subjective pattern is also rendered problematic by the way in which s 6 encompasses a form of constructive intent, objectifying that which is purportedly subjective so as to convert temporary taking into permanent deprivation. There are traces here of Fletcher's third pattern of criminality, distilled from the law of homicide: a pattern based on harm or risk, which complements and even displaces the subjective focus on intent. While the subjective pattern which locates liability within mental states such as intent may resonate strongly with modern conceptions of individual agency and of the relationship between citizen and polity, it is far from clear that it completely dominates other patterns, either in positive law or as a basis for critique of that law. As Fletcher observes, rather than a unitary set of 'general principles', a variety of approaches to criminal liability co-exist in modern criminal law.

Nor are these traces of non-subjective patterns of criminal liability confined to the offence of theft. As we shall see in the following sections, similar questions arise in relation to several other offences both within and beyond the Theft Act. For example, one might speculate that a concern with manifest criminality – overtly wrongful or dangerous acts as the core of criminality – underlies objections to the idea that offences of deception can be committed by silence. Like the broad view of appropriation, the idea of deception by silence seems to minimise the conduct requirement of the offence to an extent which expresses a very pure form of subjective criminality. It is on precisely this basis that it has been subject to criticism (see **section II.b.** below). Moreover, the debate about the interpretation of the law of deception as covering cases such as *Charles* and *Lambie* (see below) harks back to the ancient preoccupation of where the line should be drawn between civil and criminal law: critique of these cases might be thought to be grounded in a continuing sense of the importance of 'manifest' criminality. The uncertainty in the modern law of burglary about whether the trespassory quality of an entry is exclusively a subjective question might also be argued to echo a concern with both 'manifest' and 'harm-based' criminality (see **section II.d.** below). The debate about 'impossible attempts', too, turns to an important extent upon the question of whether or not a 'manifest' criminal wrong is properly required for conviction (see **section II.c.iii.** below). The idea of manifest criminality depends on a notion which seems inapposite to the modern, pluralistic age: that all members of a community can *recognise* criminality. But is this not, in effect, what the modern law assumes in leaving the determination of dishonesty to magistrates or juries? Against this, one could ask whether the problems of operationalising a conception of manifest theftous criminality have become overwhelming in a capitalist culture in which the underlying values informing 'theft' and 'enterprise' are not necessarily easy to distinguish, and in which the more fluid notions of risk or harm are more apposite. Yet the delegation of the core element of theft – dishonesty – to the finder of fact sustains an image of manifest criminality by creating the aura of social consensus – an aura which is sustained by the fact that jury deliberations are secret and not supported by reasons.

II.b.   Offences of deception

Criminal law's general regulation of fraud and deception is catered for by ss 15 and 16 of the Theft Act 1968, which institute offences of dishonestly obtaining, respectively, property belonging to another or a pecuniary advantage by deception. A good example of deception was recently reported in *The Guardian* (8 April 2003) where:

'[An] army major, his wife and a college lecturer were found guilty ... of attempting to cheat on the game show Who Wants to be a Millionaire? Major Charles Ingram and his wife Diana, both 39, were convicted by majority verdicts along with a college lecturer, Tecwen Whittock, 53, after the three came up with a scheme to defraud the quiz show of £1m. As the army officer sat in the hotseat on the show, the lecturer was 10ft behind him and coughed to steer him towards the right answers. The major's wife, who rang Whittock repeatedly in the run-up to the recording, was the point of contact between the two. The major was given a cheque for £1m but it was stopped after the show's makers, Celador, became suspicious and contacted police. All three were spared prison because the Ingrams have young children, but they received hefty fines.

Not all prosecutions for deception are so straightforward. The unhappy experience of s 16(2)(a), the most generally framed of s 16's subsections, in the courts, led in 1978 to its repeal and replacement by the offences of dishonestly obtaining services by deception and evading liability by deception (Theft Act 1978, ss 1 and 2). The 1978 Act further created an offence of dishonestly making off without payment (a less serious offence which does not require proof of deception: s 3). Further 'gaps' in the scope of deception offences have been plugged by the Theft (Amendment) Act 1996, which enacts offences of obtaining a money transfer by deception (s 1, enacted as s 15A of the 1968 Act) and dishonestly retaining a wrongful credit (s 2, enacted as s 24A of the 1968 Act). This further piecemeal amendment of the 'codified' law of property offences was prompted by the practical need to reverse the case of *Preddy* (1996). This case held that a person who obtained a mortgage advance by deception did not commit an offence of obtaining by deception under s 15 because no 'property belonging to another' was obtained – the nature of the banking transaction being rather to extinguish one 'thing in action' (a credit) and to create another, different one (a debt). (On the restricted scope of *Preddy*, see *Nathan* (1997) and *Williams* (2001), in which the Court of Appeal confirmed that the presentation of a cheque which caused a diminution of the victim's credit balance in his bank account could amount to an appropriation of property.)

The judicial history of the deception offences again provides some good illustrations of the malleable nature of criminal law doctrine. The basic structure of the offence under s 15 is close to that of theft: not only dishonesty but also an intention permanently to deprive are required. The maximum sentence on trial on indictment is 10 years' imprisonment. The other offences have, variously, lower maxima and different intent requirements: what binds them together is the requirement of deception and its causal operation. Section 15, whose definition of deception extends to all the other offences, has a wide ambit: deception is to cover 'any deception (whether deliberate or reckless) by words or conduct as to fact or as to law, including a deception as to the present intentions of the person using the deception or any other person'. Apart from technical brainteasers concerning issues such as whether a machine can be deceived, the main difficulty which tends to arise in deception cases has to do with the causal effect of the deception: was the property, service or other advantage obtained by the deception? It is this area which provides our first illustration of the logical gymnastics which the legal definition has prompted.

First, let us consider the early case of *DPP v Ray* (1974), in which the defendant left a restaurant without paying the bill during the waiter's absence from the dining-room. The defendant was convicted of obtaining a pecuniary advantage by deception under the original s 16(2)(a) of the Theft Act 1968. The reasoning was that his conduct as an honest customer constituted a continuing representation of his intention to pay, which lulled the waiter into a false sense of security and meant that he felt free to leave the room. This may seem a sensible outcome, but can it be said strictly to accord with the legal definition? Is it really appropriate to say that the deception caused the waiter to leave the room and that the obtaining was thus gained *by means of* the deception? Even if we are content to go so far, what if the customer originally orders the meal with honest intent, but changes her mind – unlike the defendant in *Ray* – during the waiter's absence from the room? In his dissenting judgment, Lord Reid accepted without question, as did the majority, that this would preclude liability, but went further in asking just the question which common sense seems to dictate: 'Why does his sitting still for a short time in the presence of the waiter make all the difference?'. In arguing that Ray's conduct was insufficiently positive to amount to a deception, Lord Reid was clearly exercised by the way in which the majority's decision in effect imposed liability for an omission. The legally decisive implications of the fine distinction accepted by majority lay behind the enactment of the offence of making off without payment (see below).

We are entitled to ask just how the House of Lords would have reacted had there been evidence that Ray had made his dishonest decision during the waiter's absence. In other cases decided under the Theft Act 1968 the courts have been unwilling to pass up the chance of what they saw as justifiable convictions on the basis of 'technical' arguments of this kind. Two relevant examples of judicial willingness to engage in interpretive gymnastics are *Metropolitan Police Commr v Charles* (1976) and *R v Lambie* (1981). In the latter, the defendant was charged with obtaining a pecuniary advantage by evasion of a debt under s 16(1) of the 1968 Act. She had bought goods from a branch of Mothercare using her Barclaycard after having been required (and having agreed) to return the card due to her account being well in excess of her credit limit. This was charged as amounting to the dishonest obtaining of a pecuniary advantage 'namely, the evasion of a debt for which she then made herself liable by deception, namely, by false representations that she was authorised to use a Barclaycard'. Lord Roskill delivered the judgment of the House of Lords, restoring the conviction quashed by the Court of Appeal:

R v Lambie (1981) 1 All ER 332

... [I]n . ... [*Metropolitan Police Commissioner v Charles*, 1976] this House was concerned with the dishonest use, not as in the present appeal of a credit card, but of a cheque card. The appellant defendant was charged and convicted on two counts of obtaining a pecuniary advantage by deception, contrary to s 16 of the Theft Act 1968. The Court of Appeal, Criminal Division, and your Lordships' House both upheld those convictions. Your Lordships unanimously held that where a drawer of a cheque which is accepted in return for goods, services or cash, uses a cheque card he represents to the payee that he has the actual authority of the bank to enter on its behalf into the contract expressed on the card that it would honour the cheque on presentation for payment.

My Lords, I venture to quote in their entirety three paragraphs from the speech of my noble and learned friend Lord Diplock which, as I venture to think, encapsulate the reasoning of all those members of your Lordships' House who delivered speeches:

> "When a cheque card is brought into the transaction, it still remains the fact that all the payee is concerned with is that the cheque should be honoured by the bank. I do not think that the fact that a cheque card is used necessarily displaces the representation to be implied from the act of drawing the cheque which has just been mentioned. It is, however, likely to displace that representation at any rate as the main inducement to the payee to take the cheque, since the use of the cheque card in connection with the transaction give to the payee a direct contractual right against the bank itself to payment on presentment, provided that the use of the card by the drawer to bind to pay the cheque was within the actual or ostensible authority conferred on him by the bank.
>
> "By exhibiting to the payee a cheque card containing the undertaking by the bank to honour cheques drawn in compliance with the conditions endorsed on the back and drawing the cheque accordingly, the drawer represents to the payee that he has actual authority from the bank to make a contract with the payee on the bank's behalf that it will honour the cheque on presentment for payment.
>
> "It was submitted on behalf of the accused that there is no need to imply a representation that the drawer's authority to bind the bank was actual and not merely ostensible, since ostensible authority alone would suffice to create a contract with the payee that was binding on the bank: and the drawer's possession of the cheque card and the cheque book with the bank's consent would be enough to constitute his ostensible authority. So, the submission goes, the only representation needed to give business efficacy to the transaction would be true. This argument stands the doctrine of ostensible authority on its head. What creates ostensible authority in a person who purports to enter into a contract as agent for a principal is a representation made to the other party that he has the actual authority of the principal for whom

he claims to be acting to enter into the contract on that person's behalf. If (1) the other party has believed the representation and on the faith of that belief has acted on it and (2) the person represented to be his principal has so conducted himself towards that other party as to be estopped from denying the truth of the representation, then, and only then, is he bound by the contract purportedly made on his behalf. The whole foundation of liability under the doctrine of ostensible authority is a representation, believed by the person to whom it is made, that the person claiming to contract as agent for a principal has the actual authority of the principal to enter into the contract on his behalf."

If one substitutes in the passage the words 'to honour the voucher' for the words 'to pay the cheque', it is not easy to see why mutatis mutandis the entire passages are not equally applicable to the dishonest misuse of credit cards as to the dishonest misuse of cheque cards.

Lord Roskill went on to reject any distinction between the situations in *Charles* and *Lambie* and to argue that the relevant representation related not to Lambie's credit standing but to whether she had actual authority to make the contract with Mothercare on the bank's behalf. This enabled him to treat as irrelevant the shop assistant's evidence that she never adverted to the question of whether Lambie's account was in credit. Lord Roskill could therefore infer an operative deception by relying on the hypothesis that if the assistant had known Lambie was acting dishonestly, she would not have completed the transaction. His approach also allowed him to affirm the propriety of convicting on the basis of inferred, hypothetical inducements: this, he argued, was justified because of the evidential difficulties presented by the fact that those allegedly deceived rarely remember the particular transactions in question. It is instructive to note in this context Lord Roskill's ready acceptance of the relevance of technical arguments from civil law of contract – just the arguments whose relevance he denied in the later case of *Morris* (see **section II.a.ii.** above). Those arguments might usefully have been applied to the basic issue of how Lambie could be said to have 'evaded a debt' which was certainly still in existence as a matter of civil law. Ultimately it seems to be a policy argument about the need to address credit card fraud which wins the day. In the process, an awkward but doctrinally relevant fact – that most shop assistants and others in similar situations do not advert to questions of real authority or credit, but simply follow the mechanics of a procedure with the aim of ensuring that their employer is paid – is lost from view. Indeed, this fact is demonstrated by the shop assistant's assertion that 'We will honour the card if the conditions are satisfied whether the bearer has authority to use it or not'.

In *Nabina* (2000) the Court of Appeal accepted the logic of this argument, allowing the appeal of a defendant who had obtained a number of credit cards by giving false personal information and who had then gone on to use the cards to obtain property. Distinguishing *Lambie* on the basis that there was no 'actual authority' to use the card in that case, the Court of Appeal:

> had the gravest possible doubt about whether a jury could properly [have inferred that the defendant had falsely represented himself to be the legitimate holder of the card]: suppliers of goods were generally concerned to ensure that they would receive payment when a credit card was used, but there was room to doubt whether they were interested in how the holder got the card, provided that the transaction would be honoured. It appeared that the defendant did have actual authority to warran that the transactions would be honoured by the issuers.

This reasoning seems to apply with equal force to the facts in *Lambie*, and it is hard to escape the conclusion that *Nabina* casts serious doubt on the authority of the earlier case. In its recent report on *Fraud*, however, the Law Commission assumes that *Lambie* establishes the proposition that those who use a credit card invariably make an implicit representation that they have authority to use it for the transaction in question. Under the Commission's proposal to replace the deception offences with an offence based on misrepresentation, the causal link between deception and obtaining, and with it the further problem of the *effect* of the representation on the shop assistant encountered in *Lambie*, would disappear (Law Commission 2002: 60; see further **section II.c.i.** below).

The cases of *Ray* and *Lambie* illustrate the ways in which the courts can both take refuge in an extreme application of the logic of legal definitions and, at the next moment, simply ignore that logic on policy grounds. This means that even the most precise of statutory formulations are bound to be less than determinate. It is also worth reflecting on the implications of *Lambie* for the boundaries between civil and criminal legal controls. We may have little sympathy for defendants who deliberately abuse the credit card system, although the well-documented difficulties of many people in resisting overuse of such cards and the aggressive marketing of them renders even this problematic. But we should remember that the possibility of reckless deception and the lack of need for intent of permanent deprivation under, for example, the offence of obtaining services by deception (Theft Act 1978, s 1(1)) opens the way for the conviction of people (most of us?) who are merely careless or ignorant about the state of their bank or credit card accounts and who enter into transactions which they realise may exceed their authority, with the intent of sorting the problem out with the bank at a later stage. Once again, it will be the overworked concept of 'dishonesty' as interpreted by magistrates and juries which will be used to draw the line between cases which result in serious criminal convictions and those which lead only to civil redress. This critical argument, as well as the ultimate reliance on dishonesty, suggests that we remain uncomfortable with purely subjective attribution of liability, and continue to regard some element of manifest criminality as more than a merely evidentiary requirement.

Section 16(2)(a) has been replaced by ss 1 and 2 of the Theft Act 1978, which create offences of obtaining services and evading liability by deception, punishable with up to five years' imprisonment. However, the drafting of s 2 of the new Act provides the second focus for critical appraisal in this area, this time with respect to the legislature's approach to deception. Whilst the apparently straightforward wording of the repealed s 16(2)(a) created difficulties in practice, s 2 presents the converse problem: it is a piece of drafting which is so clearly concerned to cover every eventuality that its meaning and the distinctions between its subsections range from the opaque to the impenetrable. The section creates three offences of dishonest evasion of liability by deception: securing the remission of the whole or part of an existing liability to pay; inducing a creditor or other to wait for or forgo payment with intent to make permanent default in whole or in part; and obtaining exemption from or abatement of liability to pay. How do these three offences relate to one another? The examples of the applicability of the subsections given in the Criminal Law Revision Committee's Thirteenth Report on the draft legislation clarify the situation somewhat, yet it is not difficult to produce examples to which it is hard to see which subsection should apply. For example, does the dishonest holder of a forged season ticket count as securing the remission of an existing liability or an exemption from liability? Plausible arguments can be constructed for either interpretation, or indeed for the conclusion that neither offence is committed because, as a matter of civil law, the relevant fares are still owed, and liability hence neither remitted nor exempted. The lack of case law on the section over the last decade suggests that prosecutors are wary of the technical pitfalls presented by charges under s 2. Remarkably, neither this section nor s 1 does anything to resolve the basic difficulty encountered in *Charles* and *Lambie*. The 'straightforward' offence of making off without payment under s 3 of the 1978 Act (*R v Vincent*, 2001), which does not require proof of any deception, was enacted precisely in response to the potential problems posed by cases such as *Ray*. Yet the 'straightforwardness' of the offence has been compromised by the fact that it has been interpreted as requiring proof of intent never to pay (*R v Allen*, 1985). This decision, whatever its merits, seems likely to present considerable problems of proof. In the light of this interpretation, the significantly less serious view of the offence (a maximum punishment of two as opposed to five to 10 years for theft and deception offences) seems odd. Even after two major legislative initiatives in the space of a decade, it seems that criminal law still lacks a rational, complete and practicable scheme of regulating deception – an assessment which has recently led the Law Commission to propose that the deception offences should be abolished and replaced by a more limited set of fraud offences (see **section II.c.i.** below).

II.c. Conspiracy to defraud and attempts

Those who attempt or conspire to commit crimes are, as we have seen (**Chapter 1.II.g.**; **Chapter 3.IV.**), themselves criminally liable. This general rule is supplemented by many statutory inchoate offences, of which the form of burglary enacted by s 9(1)(a) of the Theft Act 1968 (see **section II.d.** below) may be regarded as one example. The field of property offences provides a useful context in which to consider some specific questions about the operation of inchoate liability, not least because Fletcher's patterns of manifest, subjective and harm-based criminality also illuminate debates about the rationale of this area of criminal law. The incomplete nature of the 'actus reus' of inchoate offences, 'compensated' by a stringent 'mens rea' requirement, is suggestive of a strongly subjective conception of criminality. Yet the debate about liability for 'impossible' conspiracies and attempts reflects, as we shall see, a concern with manifestly criminal conduct, while the concern to impose inchoate liability in general, and conspiracy liability in particular, also discloses a pervasive anxiety about the risk of harm.

II.c.i. Conspiracy to defraud

While conspiracy in general was put on a statutory footing in 1977 (see **Chapter 3.IV.**), the property crime of conspiracy to defraud survives as a common law offence. Conspiracy to defraud is broadly defined as an agreement between two or more persons by dishonesty to deprive another person of something to which he or she is or may be entitled, or to injure some proprietary right of that person, with intent to cause economic loss: if the person conspired against is a public official, the prohibited agreement may also be one by dishonesty to cause the official to act contrary to his or her public duty (*Scott v Metropolitan Police Commr*, 1975). It therefore criminalises conduct which would not be criminal if one person did it when two or more people agree to engage in it. The Criminal Justice Act 1987, s 12 provided that conspiracy to defraud and statutory conspiracy should not be regarded as mutually exclusive, allowing the prosecution a free choice between the two charges where a conspiracy to defraud may also constitute a statutory conspiracy. It is worth considering conspiracy to defraud in some detail, for its anomalous survival reveals some general features of the structure of statutory property offences. The generally accepted rationale for its continued existence – that it fills an important gap in criminal regulation of property interests – seems odd in an area so fully legislated on, and poses a challenge to some basic doctrinal values.

Notwithstanding the Law Commission's longstanding acknowledgment that the breadth of the current definition of conspiracy to defraud is objectionable (Law Commission 1987, 2002), the Commission postponed recommendations for reform pending its full review of offences of dishonesty (Law Commission

1994, 1999: see Ormerod 1999). Proposals for the reform of conspiracy to defraud have therefore been remarkably slow in coming, during a period which has seen legislation on other areas of criminal law relating to property such as deception and computer misuse. It is difficult to reconcile this delay with doctrinal values such as the key doctrinal principle of legality. For 20 years the Law Commission has wavered between two options. The first is the detailed reform of criminal law to provide a range of new substantive offences covering areas such as deceiving machines, fraudulent trading, temporary deprivation, taking land, commercial and gambling swindles, dishonest failure to pay where there is no intent to make permanent default, commercial counterfeiting, fraudulent acquisition of confidential information and some non-economic frauds. The second is the creation of a general fraud offence. On either of these approaches, the general law of statutory conspiracy could be applied in the usual way. In 2002, the Commission finally settled on the second option, recommending the abolition of the eight offences of deception created by the Theft Acts 1968–1996 and of the common law offence of conspiracy to defraud, and their replacement by two statutory offences: one of fraud, and one of obtaining services dishonestly. The offence of fraud would be committed where a person made a false representation, or failed to disclose information which she was under a legal duty to disclose or which the other person actually and reasonably trusts her to disclose, or secretly abused a position of trust in which she is expected to safeguard the financial interests of another person, in each case dishonestly and with an intent to make a gain or to cause loss or to expose another to the risk of loss. The offence of obtaining services dishonestly would be committed where a person obtained services by any dishonest act with intent to avoid payment when payment is required. The Commission's hope is that this reform would make the law more comprehensible to juries, particularly in serious fraud trials; would streamline the preparation of a prosecution case; and would dramatically simplify the law of fraud while leaving an adequate margin of definitional flexibility to accommodate the very varied forms of fraudulent behaviour, particularly in the light of rapidly developing technologies. In the following passage, the background to the Commission's thinking is set out, and the continuing power of the philosophy of ordinary language legislation revealed:

Law Commission, *Fraud* (Report No 276, 2002) pp 57–59

We now believe that what is needed is a fresh approach, involving a middle course between ... two extremes [ie a general offence criminalising all dishonest conduct and piecemeal reform specifying particular instances of criminal dishonesty]. We think it is possible to devise a general fraud offence which, without relying too heavily on the concept of dishonesty, would nevertheless be sufficiently broad and flexible to catch nearly every case that would today be likely to be charged as a conspiracy to defraud.

Conspiracy to defraud would then be virtually redundant (in practice if not in theory), and could safely be abolished.

In our view, the key to defining such an offence ought to be the ordinary (non-legal) usage of the word "fraud". At present, the criminality or other-wise of a fraudulent act depends whether it falls within one of a multitude of offences of varying degrees of specificity. The fact that it is fraudulent will not necessarily mean that it is an offence. Most non-lawyers would think this an extraordinary state of affairs ...

The difficulty that we have encountered in seeking to formulate a satisfactory fraud offence, we believe, results largely from the fact that the concept of fraud developed by the criminal courts has in some respects parted company from the word's ordinary meaning ... This divergence between the ordinary and legal meanings of fraud has laid a trap for law reformers ... To render conspiracy to defraud dispensable, a new fraud offence needs *only* to catch those kinds of dishonest conduct that an ordinary person would call fraud. The question is: what are the hallmarks of such conduct ...

After setting out the elements of James Fitzjames Stephen's 'classic' statement of fraud as consisting in the dual elements of actual or intended deceit plus actual, possible or intended injury, the Commission concludes:

We note first that Stephen did not say these two elements are *sufficient* to constitute fraud: he said that they *at least* are essential ... [W]e are now persuaded, contrary to the view we provisionally expressed in Consultation Paper No 155, that the element of *dishonesty* should be essential to (thought not sufficient for) criminal liability for fraud. With the addition of this element, Stephen's definition requires

1) deceit, intention to deceive or secrecy, *and*
2) *either*
   a) actual or possible injury to another *or*
   b) an intent thereby to cause injury to another or to expose another to a risk of possible injury,
3) *and* dishonesty.

We have adopted this analysis as our starting point.

In framing its proposals, the Law Commission was particularly exercised by the question of whether there should be a general offence of dishonesty, and by the implications of the use of the broad Theft Act /*Ghosh* conception of dishonesty to characterise criminal behaviour (see Law Commission 2002: Pt V, pp 39–49). Reflecting some of the human rights and other concerns expressed by the dissenting judges in *Gomez* and *Hinks*, discussed in **section II.a.ii.** above, the Commission stopped short of recommending a general dishonesty offence. However, it regarded the possibility of undue variance in jury interpretations of dishonesty as merely a 'theoretical risk' and, in the light of the widespread use of the *Ghosh* test in the criminal law and the consequently wide implications of rejecting it, decided to retain *Ghosh* dishonesty as a necessary though not a sufficient condition the new offence of fraud. This would mean that the scope for the boundaries of criminal law to be determined by juries' moral evaluations would remain wide, even though the specification of the four broad kinds of fraudulent conduct makes some contribution to certainty and precise labelling of the relevant wrong. While the Commission's rejection of the Crown Prosecution Service's call for a general offence of dishonesty is to be applauded, and while its proposals would certainly dispense with the arcane technicalities of the 1978 Theft Act considered in **section II.b.**, we may nonetheless ask whether the *Fraud* report remains unduly ready to assume that the expense and inconvenience of civil enforcement militate towards a wide reach for criminal law. Criminal enforcement is, after all, likely to be equally expensive and just as unreliable from the point of view of the victim's chances of recovery. It is also significant that debates about possible decriminalisation and greater use of civil regulation have tended to be in areas of 'white-collar' crime such as business and tax fraud and unfair trading (see Levi 1987: 105–109).

II.c.ii. Attempts

Attempts are defined by the Criminal Attempts Act 1981:
    1(1) If, with intent to commit an offence to which this section applies, a person does an act which is more than merely preparatory to the commission of the offence, he is guilty of attempting to commit the offence.

    (2) A person may be guilty of attempting to commit an offence to which this section applies even though the facts are such that the commission of the offence is impossible.

    (3) In any case where–
      (a) apart from this subsection a person's intention would not be regarded as having amounted to an intent to commit an offence; but
      (b) if the facts of the case had been as he believed them to be, his intention would be so regarded,
    then, for the purposes of subsection (1) above, he shall be regarded as having had an intent to commit that offence.

Subsection (4) provides that 'attempt', as defined, applies to all indictable offences other than conspiracy and offences of aiding, abetting, counselling, procuring, suborning or assisting. Section 4 provides that the maximum penalties for attempts tried on indictment shall be the same as for the completed offences, and that attempts to commit offences triable either way which are tried summarily shall be subject to the maximum for the completed offence on summary conviction. Section 6 abolishes the offence of attempt at common law.

Whilst the statutory definition of attempt is less problematic than is that of conspiracy, the determinacy of the central concept of a 'more than merely preparatory' act may be questioned: significantly, this is left to the magistrates or jury, who may well be influenced in their interpretation by ideas of manifest criminality (see below).

As we noted in **Chapter 1.II.g.**, the preliminary nature of the conduct element in inchoate offences is counterbalanced by a stringent 'mens rea' requirement of specific intent. This requirement, however, does not extend to circumstances, which may be the object merely of recklessness: hence in the crime of rape, for example, a defendant may be convicted of attempt if he intentionally does acts more than merely preparatory to intercourse being reckless as to the victim's consent (*Khan*, 1990). Furthermore, a question has arisen about whether a 'conditional intent' may in certain circumstances suffice. The way in which this issue has been resolved provides a good illustration of the interaction between doctrinal elements and prosecution discretion in the operation of criminal law:

The Law Commission, *Attempt and Impossibility in Relation to Attempt, Conspiracy and Incitement* **(No 102, 1980, Appendix E)**

Theft-related offences, such as attempted theft, burglary, attempted burglary, assault with intent to rob, going equipped for burglary or theft … form a large part of the cases being tried every day in the magistrates' courts and Crown Court …

They all have two features in common–
 (i)   each requires proof that the accused 'intended to steal' at the time when he committed the 'actus reus' of the offence;
 (ii) none requires proof that anything has in fact been stolen,

In delivering the judgment of the Court of Appeal in the attempted theft case of *R v Husseyn* (1978), Lord Scarman stated (p.132) that 'it cannot be said that one who has it in mind to steal only if what he finds is worth stealing has a present intention to steal.'

This simple statement, taken by itself and out of context, was the origin of the difficulties. It gave rise to the doctrine that 'conditional intent' in the sense of 'intending to steal whatever one might find of value or worth stealing' was not a sufficient mental element in these theft-related offences; the prosecution must aver and prove that at the time of attempting, entering as a trespasser, etc., the accused had a settled intention to steal some particular and specified object existing or believed by him to exist in his target area.

In such a form, the doctrine was obviously capable of mischievous results. In particular, it excluded from criminal liability the large majority of sneak thieves and burglars who conduct their operations 'on spec'. Without knowing what a handbag, a package left in a car, or a house contains, they nevertheless proceed in the hope or expectation that they will find something of value or worth stealing there, and intend, in that event, to steal it ...

... [W]ithin a few months of the decision in *R v Husseyn*, submissions that 'conditional intent is not enough' were being accepted by magistrates and Crown Court judges in all these theft-related offences, causing frustration and perplexity to prosecuting authorities and bringing the criminal law into disrepute.

Study of the relevant indictments and transcripts convinced us that ... the matter could be put right without recourse to legislation, and that the appropriate way to proceed was by way of Attorney General's References to the Court of Appeal under section 36 of the Criminal Justice Act 1972.

The two References were decided by the Court of Appeal as *Attorney General's References (Nos. 1 and 2 of 1979)* and ... restore clarity and common sense to the law. Where the accused's state of mind is that of intending to steal whatever he may find worth stealing in his target area, there is no need to charge him with attempting to steal specific objects. In appropriate cases of attempted theft a charge of attempting to steal some or all of the contents of (for example) a car or a handbag will suffice. In cases where the substantive offence does not require anything to be stolen, it is not necessary to allege more than 'with intent to steal'. The important point is that the indictment should correctly reflect that which it is alleged the accused did and that the accused should know with adequate detail what he is alleged to have done.

Property offences also serve, finally, to illustrate the potential breadth of the boundaries of attempts liability. The statutory definition of the 'actus reus' of attempt exemplifies the practical difficulty of achieving the law's doctrinal ideals of clarity and certainty: the interpretation of 'more than merely preparatory' will inevitably be influenced by the vagaries of particular cases. Despite the best efforts of the courts, who have spoken in terms of acts which demonstrate an 'unequivocal' intention to complete the offence (*Geddes*, 1996; *Nash*, 1999) it would be very difficult to produce principles to constrain tribunal discretion in such an area. Given the very broad conception of appropriation established in *Gomez* and *Hinks*, which itself covers conduct which would formerly have amounted to attempt, what would constitute an attempted theft in the context of a label-switching incident? An attempted burglary under s 9(1)(a), furthermore, institutes what could be seen as a form of doubly inchoate liability (see further **section II.d.** below).

II.c.iii.   Inchoate liability, impossibility and patterns of criminality

Inchoate offences therefore provide some intriguing examples of the difficulty which criminal law encounters in meeting the requirements of its professed 'general principles' and, in particular, of generating determinate and limited bounds within which citizens may reasonably be expected to confine their behaviour. The primary nature of inchoate liability means that there is no possibility of withdrawal once the 'actus reus' is complete. Indeed, s 5 of the Criminal Law Act 1977 provides that the acquittal of the only other alleged parties to a conspiracy does not necessarily justify quashing the conviction of the remaining defendant. As we have already seen, the scope of criminal liability is further broadened by the possibility of cumulation between these forms of inchoate liability themselves and between them and participatory liability (see **Chapter 1.II.e.; Chapter 2.IV.; Chapter 3.IV.**). The Criminal Law Act (s 5(7)) excludes the possibility of incitements to commit conspiracies, and the Criminal Attempts Act 1981 (s 1(4)) excludes attempts to conspire or to aid and abet. It also appears that it is impossible to incite or to conspire to participate in an offence. However, one can clearly aid and abet an incitement or an attempt, or counsel an attempt, whereas the aiding and abetting of a conspiracy would probably in any case amount to primary liability for conspiracy. Incitement to attempt would seem to be possible in some cases, as would an incitement to incite and a conspiracy to incite. Clearly, wherever cumulation is possible, the ambit of criminal liability reaches into areas very remote from primary liability for the completed offence.

Particularly difficult questions about the rationale of inchoate liability arise out of the extension of liability to cover attempts and statutory conspiracies to do the impossible. These questions are illustrated by an episode in which the House of Lords changed its mind within a year about the construction of the 1981 Act. The debate about 'impossible attempts' constitutes a particularly instructive example of the tension in modern criminal law between manifest, harm-based and subjective conceptions of criminality:

Anderton v Ryan (1985) AC 560

[*The defendant had bought a video which, as she confessed to the police, she had believed to be stolen. There was, however, no evidence that it had been stolen, and the court therefore had to treat it as if it had not. She was convicted of dishonestly attempting to handle a stolen video recorder.*]

Lord Bridge.

Does section 1 of the Act of 1981 create a new offence of attempt where a person embarks on and completes a course of conduct which is objectively innocent, solely on the ground that the person mistakenly believes facts which, if true, would make that course of conduct a complete crime?

If the question must be answered affirmatively it requires convictions in a number of surprising cases: the classic case ... of the man who takes away his own umbrella from a stand, believing it not to be his own and with intent to steal it; the case of the man who has consensual intercourse with a girl over 16 believing her to be under that age; the case of the art dealer who sells a picture which he represents to be and which is in fact a genuine Picasso, but which the dealer mistakenly believes to be a fake.

The common feature of all these cases, including that under appeal, is that the mind alone is guilty, the act is innocent. I should find it surprising that Parliament, if intending to make this purely subjective guilt criminally punishable, should have done so by anything less than the clearest express language, and, in particular, should have done so in a section aimed specifically at inchoate offences ...

It is sufficient to say of subsection (2) that it is plainly intended to reverse the law ... that the pickpocket who puts his hand in an empty pocket commits no offence. Putting the hand in the pocket is the guilty act, the intent to steal is the guilty mind, the offence is appropriately dealt with as an attempt, and the impossibility of committing the full offence for want of anything in the pocket to steal is declared by the subsection to be no obstacle to conviction ...

It seems to me that subsections (2) and (3) are in a sense complementary to each other. Subsection (2) covers the case of a person acting in a criminal way with a general intent to commit a crime in circumstances where no crime is possible. Subsection (3) covers the case of a person acting in a criminal way with a specific intent to commit a particular crime which he erroneously believes to be, but which is not in fact, possible. Given the criminal action, the appropriate subsection allows the actor's guilty intention to be supplied by his subjective but mistaken state of mind, notwithstanding that on the true facts that intention is incapable of fulfilment. But if the action is throughout innocent and the actor has done everything he intended to do, I can find nothing in either subsection which requires me to hold that his erroneous belief in fact which, if true, would have made the action a crime makes him guilty of an attempt to commit that crime.

The defendant was therefore to be regarded not as having attempted to handle a stolen video recorder but simply as having handled a non-stolen video recorder, and hence was to be acquitted. This 'objective' view of criminality (which has something in common with the older 'manifest' pattern) is one in which the absence of a manifestly or objectively criminal act cannot be 'compensated' by a subjective intent:

George Fletcher, *Rethinking Criminal Law* (1978) pp 138–139

From the perspective of the major movements that sweep across the terrain of criminal law, there is a close connection between the two doctrinal problems in defining criminal attempts – distinguishing attempts from preparation and impossibility. The critical question that unites them is the elementary issue whether the act of attempting is a distinct and discernible element of the crime of attempting. To say that the act is a distinct element is to require that the act conform to objective criteria defined in advance. The act must evidence attributes subject to determination independently of the actor's intent. In short, there must be features of the attempt as palpable as the death of the victim in homicide or a trespassory taking in larceny. We shall refer to the set of arguments favoring this approach as the 'objectivist' theory of attempts. Though the term 'objective' may have a different connotation in some contexts, we shall use the term to mean a legal standard for assessing conduct that does not presuppose a prior determination of the actor's intent.

The opposing school is appropriately called 'subjectivist', for it dispenses with the objective criteria of attempting. The act of execution is important so far as it verifies the firmness of the intent. No act of specific contours is necessary to constitute the attempt, for any act will suffice to demonstrate the actor's commitment to carry out his criminal plan.

... [O]bjectivists tend to favour a minimalist approach, and subjectivists, a maximalist approach to liability ... This means that objectivists tend to draw the line of liability as close as possible to consummation of the offense and tend, further, to be sympathetic to claims of impossibility as a bar to liability ... Subjectivists, in contrast, tend to push back the threshold of attempting and reject the relevance of impossibility – a stance that yields a maximalist net of liability.

These 'minimalist' and 'maximalist' approaches relate in turn to whether criminal law is seen as reflecting common judgments about wrongdoing, minimising objective 'dangers' or harms, deterring responsible actors, or punishing subjective fault (Ashworth 2003: 445–450). Fletcher's passage demonstrates that the subjectivist position which is so central to liberal conceptions of the proper limits of criminal law can, paradoxically, rationalise a very wide scope for state intervention. This is demonstrated by the current law on impossible attempts, in which the decision in *Anderton* was reversed in favour of a maximalist, subjective approach:

R v Shivpuri, [1986] 2 All ER 334, House of Lords

[*Shivpuri was charged with attempting to commit the offence of being knowingly concerned in dealing with and harbouring prohibited drugs under s 170(1)(b) of the Customs and Excise Management Act 1979. He had been found in possession of a suitcase which he admitted he believed to contain prohibited drugs, but which in fact contained harmless vegetable matter. He appealed against his conviction on the basis that he had not done a 'more than merely preparatory' act, given that commission of the offence charged was impossible.*]

Lord Bridge

The certified question depends on the true construction of the Criminal Attempts Act 1981 ... It was considered by your Lordships' House last year in *Anderton v Ryan* [1985] 2 AER 355 ... That might seem an appropriate starting point from which to examine the issues arising in this appeal. But your Lordships have been invited to exercise the power under the 1966 Practice Statement to depart from the reasoning in that decision ... I propose to approach the issue in the first place as an exercise in statutory construction, applying the language of the Act to the facts of the case, as if the matter were *res integra* ...

... [T]he first question to be asked is whether the appellant intended to commit the offences of being knowingly concerned in dealing with and harbouring drugs of class A or class B with intent to evade the prohibition on their importation. Translated into more homely language the question may be rephrased, without in any way altering its legal significance, in the following terms: did the appellant intend to receive and store (harbour) and in due course pass on to third parties (deal with) packages of heroin or cannabis ... The answer is plainly Yes, he did. Next, did he, in relation to each offence, do an act which was more than merely preparatory to the commission of the offence? ... In each case the act was clearly more than preparatory to the commission of the *intended* offence; it was not and could not be more than merely preparatory to the commission of the *actual* offence, because the facts were such that the commission of the actual offence was impossible. Here then is the nub of the matter. Does the 'act which is more than merely preparatory to the commission of the offence' in s1(1) of the 1981 Act ... require any more than an act which is more than merely preparatory to the commission of the offence which the defendant intended to commit? Section 1(2) must surely indicate a negative answer; if it were otherwise, whenever the facts were such that the commission of the actual offence was impossible, it would be impossible to prove an act more than merely preparatory to the commission of that offence and sub'ss (1) and (2) would contradict each other.

This very simple, perhaps over-simple, analysis leads me to the provisional conclusion that the appellant was rightly convicted of the two offences of attempt with which he was charged. But can this conclusion stand with *Anderton v Ryan*? The appellant in that case was charged with an attempt to handle stolen goods. She bought a video recorder believing it to be stolen. On the facts as they were to be assumed it was not stolen. By a majority the House decided that she was entitled to be acquitted. I have re-examined the case with care. If I could extract from the speech of Lord Roskill or from my own speech a clear and coherent principle distinguishing those cases of attempting the impossible which amount to offences under the statute from those which do not, I should have to consider carefully on which side of the line the instant case fell. But I have to confess that I can find no such principle ...

If we fell into error, it is clear that our concern was to avoid convictions in situations which most people, as a matter of common sense, would not regard as involving criminality ... [T]he distinction between acts which are 'objectively innocent' and those which are not is an essential element in the reasoning in *Anderton v Ryan* ... I am satisfied on further consideration that the concept of 'objective innocence' is incapable of sensible application in relation to the law of criminal attempts. The reason for this is that any attempt to commit an offence which involved 'an act which is more than merely preparatory to the commission of the offence' but which for any reason fails, so that in the event no offence is committed, must *ex hypothesi*, from the point of view of the criminal law, be 'objectively innocent'. What turns what would otherwise, from the point of view of the criminal law, be an innocent act into a crime is the intent of the actor to commit an offence ...

Another conceivable ground of distinction ... would make guilt or innocence of the crime of attempt in a case of mistaken belief dependent on what, for want of a better phrase, I will call the defendant's dominant intention. According to the theory necessary to sustain this distinction, the appellant's dominant intention in *Anderton v Ryan* was to buy a cheap video recorder; her belief that it was stolen was merely incidental ... By contrast, in the instant case the appellant's dominant intention was to receive and distribute illegally imported heroin or cannabis.

While I see the superficial attraction of this suggested ground of distinction, I also see formidable practical difficulties in its application. By what test is a jury to be told that the defendant's dominant intention is to be recognised and distinguished from his incidental but mistaken belief? But there is perhaps a more formidable theoretical difficulty. If this ground of distinction is relied on to support the acquittal of the appellant in *Anderton v Ryan*, it can only do so on the basis that her mistaken belief that the video recorder was stolen played no significant part in her decision to buy it ... But this line of reasoning runs into head-on collision with s 1(3) of the 1981 Act ... This seems to me fatal to the dominant intention theory.

Lord Bridge concludes with a rationalisation of the decision to overrule such a recent case. Assumptions about the values of rationality and coherence underlie his argument, which skilfully weaves together technical analysis and appeals to 'common sense', creating the impression that what might be seen as an extraordinary episode in the court's history is in fact explicable on sound, logical grounds. The integrity of the doctrinal arguments employed are, however, open to question. We should note, for example, the implications of Lord Bridge's argument about the difficulty of reconciling the notion of 'objective innocence' with the law on defences such as mistake, and hence for the distinction between justification and excuse (pp 343–344; see **Chapter 1.II.d.**

and **section II.f.** below). The critique of the 'dominant intention' theory also
seems puzzling given its application to the case of *R v Steane* (1947) (see
Chapter 1.II.b.), later cited with approval by Lord Bridge himself in *R v
Moloney* (1985) (see **Chapter 6.IV.b.**).

The rationalisation of doctrinal 'principles' illustrated in our extract suggests
that the House of Lords' ultimate decision that mistakes such as Ryan's and
Shivpuri's do generate the kind of impossibility envisaged by the 1981 Act owes
more to policy than to legal logic and statutory interpretation. Although
Shivpuri to some extent clarifies that law as far as conspiracy and attempt
are concerned, the anomalous continued existence of some common law
conspiracies and of incitement at common law means that this area is still
covered by earlier case law excluding liability in situations of impossibility (*DPP
v Nock*, 1978; *R v Fitzmaurice*, 1983).

II.d. Burglary

The distinctive wrong of transgressing the boundaries of buildings is recognised in s 9 of the Theft Act 1968, which creates two offences of burglary.
Section 9(1)(a) enacts what we might call 'pure' burglary: this offence is committed where someone enters any building or part of a building as a trespasser
and with intent to steal within the building or to inflict grievous bodily harm on
or rape anyone within it or to commit unlawful damage to the building. One
might regard this as an inchoate offence or as an aggravated trespass. Section
9(1)(b), by contrast, enacts what we might call 'completed' burglary: it is
committed where someone, having entered as a trespasser, goes on to commit
theft or to inflict grievous bodily harm or attempts to commit either of those
offences within the building. Since 1991 (Criminal Justice Act, s 26(2)),
burglary of a dwelling has been further differentiated as a more serious offence,
with a 14-year, as opposed to a 10-year, maximum penalty; since the implementation of the Crime (Sentences) Act 1997, third-time burglars receive a
mandatory minimum three-year sentence absent exceptional circumstances
(**Chapter 1.III.b.iv.**). The elements of burglary serve once again to illustrate
some discontinuities between civil and criminal law, as well as tensions between
different approaches to attributing criminal responsibility. Each of these can be
demonstrated in relation to the issue of trespass, canvassed in the unforgettable
case of *Collins*:

R v Collins [1973] QB 100

Edmund-Davies LJ.

... Let me relate the facts. Were they put into a novel or portrayed on the
stage, they would be regarded as being so improbable as to be unworthy of

serious consideration and as verging at times on farce. At about 2 o'clock in the early morning of Saturday, July 24, 1971, a young lady of 18 went to bed at her mother's home in Colchester. She had spent the evening with her boyfriend. She had taken a certain amount of drink, and it may be that this fact affords some explanation of her inability to answer satisfactorily certain crucial questions put to her at the trial.

She has the habit of sleeping without wearing night apparel in a bed which is very near the lattice-type window of her room ... At about 3.30 or 4 o'clock she awoke and she then saw in the moonlight a vague form crouched in the open window. She was unable to remember, and this is important, whether the form was on the outside of the window sill or on that part of the sill which was inside the room, and for reasons which will later become clear, that seemingly narrow point is of crucial importance.

The young lady then realised several things: first of all that the form in the window was that of a male; secondly that he was a naked male; and thirdly that he was a naked male with an erect penis. She also saw in the moonlight that his hair was blond. She thereupon leapt to the conclusion that her boyfriend, with whom for some time she had been on terms of regular and frequent sexual intimacy, was paying her an ardent nocturnal visit. She promptly sat up in bed, and the man descended from the sill and joined her in bed and they had full sexual intercourse. But there was something about him which made her think that things were not as they usually were between her and her boyfriend. The length of his hair, his voice as they had exchanged what was described as 'love talk', and other features led her to the conclusion that somehow there was something different. So she turned on the bed-side light, saw that he companion was not her boyfriend, and slapped the face of the intruder, who was none other than the defendant ...

The complainant said that she would not have agreed to intercourse if she had known that the person entering her room was not her boyfriend. But there was no suggestion of any force having been used upon her, and the intercourse which took place was undoubtedly effected with no resistance on her part.

The defendant was seen by the police ... the next morning ... He was very lustful the previous night. He had taken a lot of drink ... On this occasion, desiring sexual intercourse – and according to the police evidence, he added that he was determined to have a girl, by force if necessary, although that part of the police evidence he challenged – he went on to say that he walked around the house, saw a light in an upstairs bedroom, and he knew that this was the girl's bedroom. He found a step ladder, leaned it against the wall and climbed up and looked into the bedroom. He could see through the wide-open window a girl who was naked and asleep. So he descended the ladder and stripped off all his clothes, with the exception of his socks, because apparently he took the view that if the girl's mother entered the bedroom it would be easier to effect a rapid escape if he had his socks on than if he was in his bare feet. That is a matter about which we are not called upon to express any view, and would in any event find ourselves unable to express one.

Having undressed, he then climbed the ladder and pulled himself up on to the window sill. His version of the matter is that he was pulling himself in when she awoke. She then got up and knelt on the bed, she put her arms around his neck and body, and she seemed to pull him into the bed ...

Now, one feature of the case which remained at the conclusion of the evidence in great obscurity is where exactly Collins was at the moment when, according to him, the girl manifested that she was welcoming him. Was he kneeling on the sill outside the window or was he already inside the room, having climbed through the window frame, and kneeling upon the inner sill? ...

The second ingredient of the offence [of burglary under s 9(1)(a)] – entry as a trespasser – is one which has not, to the best of our knowledge, been previously canvassed in the courts.

The matter has been dealt with by Professor Griew, who in paragraph 4–05 of his work *The Theft Act 1968* has this passage: 'What if D wrongly believes that he is not trespassing? His belief may rest on facts which, if true, would mean that he was not trespassing: for instance, he may enter a building by mistake, thinking that it is the one he has been invited to enter. Or his belief may be based on a false view of the legal effect of the known facts: for instance, he may misunderstand the effect of a contract granting him a right of passage through a building. Neither kind of mistake will protect him from tort liability for trespass. In either case, then, D satisfies the literal terms of section 9(1): he 'enters as a trespasser'. But for the purposes of criminal liability a man should be judged on the basis of the facts as he believed them to be, and this should include making allowance for a mistake as to rights under the civil law. This is another way of saying that a serious offence like burglary should by held to require 'mens rea' in the fullest sense of the phrase: D should be liable for burglary only if he knowingly trespasses or is reckless as to whether he trespasses or not.

[*Edmund Davies LJ endorses this approach to trespass, and continues:*]

Having so held, the pivotal point of this appeal is whether the Crown established that this defendant at the moment that he entered the bedroom knew perfectly well that he was not welcome there or, being reckless as to whether he was welcome or not, was nevertheless determined to enter. That in turn involves consideration as to where he was at the time that the complainant indicated that she was welcoming him into her bedroom ... Unless the jury were entirely satisfied that the defendant made an effective and substantial entry into the bedroom without the complainant doing or saying anything to cause him to believe that she was consenting to his entering it, he ought not to be convicted of the offence charged ... We have to say that his appeal must be allowed on the basis that the jury were never invited to consider [this] vital question ...

Collins's liability therefore turned on whether he was already inside the house when the woman beckoned him in: if so, he was a trespasser; if not, her invitation negatived trespass and hence burglary. This approach to liability is, however, in marked contrast to the approach taken in the later case of *Jones and Smith* (1976). The case involved two young men who had stolen a television set from the house of the father of one of them. Notwithstanding the fact that the father gave evidence that his son 'would never be a trespasser in my house', the court held that the intent to steal itself established the trespass. In this decision, trespass as a distinct requirement of burglary shrinks to almost nothing, being simply inferred from the 'mens rea' for the further offence contemplated at the time of entry. On this approach, Collins should have been convicted whatever side of the window he was on, on the basis that he intended (if necessary) to rape.

II.e.   Criminal damage

Even a selective review of criminal laws relating to property would be lacking without some reference to the area of criminal damage. Here we are no longer in the sphere of dishonesty but rather at the margins of maintenance of public order and protection of the person. The basic offence of criminal damage, defined as the intentional or reckless destruction or damaging of another's property without lawful excuse (Criminal Damage Act 1971, s 1(1)), is punishable by up to 10 years' imprisonment. This offence most obviously relates to the social phenomenon of 'vandalism', but the Act also creates two aggravated forms of the offence. Where property has been intentionally or recklessly damaged or destroyed with intent or recklessness as to endangering life (s 1(2)), or where the means used is fire (s 1(3)), the offence carries a maximum penalty of life imprisonment.

For our purposes, two important issues can be raised about the scope and interpretation of the basic offence of criminal damage. As we have seen, in the criminal damage case of *R v Caldwell* (1981), Lord Diplock gave an 'objective' interpretation to the statutory term 'reckless'; in other words, a person is reckless not only where they are aware of a relevant risk but also where they fail to advert to a risk which would have been obvious to a reasonable person (see **Chapter 1.II.b.**). This was confirmed as a wholly 'objective' test in *Elliott v C* (1983). This extends a particularly clear invitation to the tribunal of fact (magistrate or jury) to infer 'mens rea' where the conduct in question is regarded as 'unreasonable' even where some specific explanation exists as to why the defendant did not share the perceptions and judgment of a 'reasonable person'. What should we make of the fact that this novel interpretation of recklessness

occurred in the context of criminal damage – an area in which the recommendations on which the legislation was based clearly envisaged a subjective
conception of recklessness? The objective conception was immediately applied
also to reckless driving (*Lawrence*, 1981). But, significantly, its extension into
the interpretation of sexual offences of recklessness and non-fatal offences
against the person has been resisted by the courts. Moreover, the contrast
between the apparent stringency of the 'mens rea' requirement for criminal
damage and that for theft-related property offences suggests that the development has an ideological significance which outweighs its relatively limited
instrumental importance.

The decision in *Caldwell* is a testimony to judicial power. It sits unhappily with
the proposals of the Law Commission, whose recommendation that the old
offence of 'malicious' damage be replaced by an offence framed in terms of
'recklessness' clearly envisaged an updating of statutory language rather than a
change in meaning of the 'mens rea' requirement. It is also apparently at odds
with the Act's own definition of 'lawful excuse' (s 5), which is drawn in explicitly
'subjective' terms. The latter section has even been used by the courts to accord
a defence to a voluntarily intoxicated defendant who mistakenly thought she
had the owner's consent to enter his property by breaking a window (*Jaggard v
Dickinson*, 1980) – a decision which contrasts with criminal law's usual reluctance to accept defences based on voluntary intoxication (see **Chapter 3.III.d.**).
However, the rigorously subjective approach directed by the wording of s 5 has
not been pursued consistently by the courts. For example, it has been rejected
in cases involving attempts to damage the perimeter fences of nuclear bases. In
R v Ashford and Smith (1988) the defendants sought to rely on a s 5 defence on
the basis that they had an honest belief that they were acting 'in order to
protect property belonging to [themselves] or another ... and at the time of the
act or acts alleged to constitute the offence [they] believed ... that the property
right or interest was in immediate need of protection and ... that the means of
protection adopted or proposed to be adopted were or would be reasonable
having regard to all the circumstances'. The Court of Appeal held that the
question of whether the defendant was acting 'in order to protect property
belonging to another' must be judged objectively. In *R v Hill and Hall* (1989),
the Court of Appeal squared a circle by affirming that the initial question to be
determined was the subjective one of what the defendant actually thought, yet
asserting that the question of whether, on the basis of the facts as believed by
her, her acts were capable of amounting to something done to protect property
in immediate need of protection was to be determined objectively. These cases
do violence to the apparent intention of s 5 and add contradiction within the
interpretation of a single section to that already noted between interpretations
of different sections of the Act. Attempts to invoke a human rights challenge
to the *Caldwell* test based on Article 6 of the ECHR have, however, been
unsuccessful (*R v G and R*, 2002: see **Chapter 1.II.b.**).

In Lord Diplock's argument for his reading of 'recklessness' in *Caldwell*, policy arguments about the need to secure convictions are interwoven with arguments about the culpability of 'objectively' reckless defendants and about the impracticality of drawing fine distinctions between subjective and objective conceptions. The policy arguments may have been particularly appealing in the area of criminal damage, given the importance of images of vandalism in constructing popular fears about social disorder. Criminal damage, perhaps, is seen by the judiciary to represent lawlessness and rejection of authority in a more blatant way than theft and deception, which may often be read as acts which, albeit in a 'deviant' way, participate in the values of the capitalist system. At a symbolic level, it expresses rejection of the value of property and is therefore liable to be interpreted as nihilistic.

Secondly, the definition of criminal damage in the 1971 Act makes it unsuitable for dealing with many 'white collar' offenders. This is because the Act does not follow the relatively broad definition of property adopted in the Theft Act, extending only to 'property of a tangible nature' (although going further than the Theft Act in including land). Thus the image of criminal damage which the Act reproduces is the image of the destruction of tangible goods – the smashed bus shelter, the indelible inner city graffiti, the vandalised car, the trampled field. The polluted air or river, like the deleted or spoilt computer file, are apparently excluded from the definition of criminal damage. However, the last of these cases has been the subject of a piece of judicial ingenuity which was gratefully seized upon by the Law Commission in its Working Paper on computer misuse (1988), as Wasik explains:

M Wasik, 'Law Reform Proposals on Computer Misuse', (1989) Crim LR 257: 266–268

… Sometimes manipulation or destruction of data has been the objective of unauthorised access by remote terminal, and the deliberate "infection" of computer systems by computer viruses is a present-day reality. While there can be no conviction for destruction or damage of computer programs or data as such, since intangible property lies outside the scope of the Criminal Damage Act 1971, *Cox v Riley* (1986) "gave the quite emphatic answer" that D could be convicted of damage to a "plastic printed circuit card" which operated a computerised saw … where D deliberately blanked the programs from the card by repeated operation of the program cancellation facility.

Exactly what was damaged in this case? First, the court rejected defence counsel's argument that the intangible programs had been damaged by erasure. Secondly, the court could have held that the machine, the saw itself, was damaged … [but] Stephen Brown L.J. made it clear that damage to the card was the ground for dismissing the appeal. Now, thirdly, if the card is regarded as a receptacle for receipt of programs it is clear that there was in fact no damage done to the card when the programs were erased. So, fourthly, the true basis for the decision must be that the card containing the programs was an item of property distinct from and in a sense greater than the sum of its constituent parts ...

The immediate implication of *Cox v Riley* is that it is no longer the case that damage must be tangible to qualify under the Act. This is unobjectionable, since it has probably always been the law that, for instance, food can be damaged within the meaning of the Act by invisible contamination. The more general significance of the case and the Law Commission's reliance upon it to cover all cases of damage or destruction of data or programs is, however, open to doubt. The Law Commission suggest that the case decides that "any interference with the operation of a computer or its software which causes loss or inconvenience to its legitimate users can probably now be charged as criminal damage". On the face of it, this goes very wide, encompassing what may be described as "criminal mischief" as well as "criminal damage". The Law Commission's interpretation would include a case where D, who has the only key to the computer room, locks it and hides away the key. This is certainly mischievous, ... but it would be remarkable if it fell within the scope of the Criminal Damage Act. It is submitted that the case does not go so far, being limited to cases of physical interference with tangible property which brings about some deleterious change in that property, which costs time and effort to repair ... [I]t was possible to obtain a conviction in *Cox v Riley* because there was tangible property which had been impaired by the deletion of the programs. This will not always be so. Suppose that a hacker manages to damage or destroy data which is housed in the memory of a computer, or data which is in the process of being transferred from one medium to another. It seems that such damage, with no impact upon a storage medium such as a disc or tape, would not come within the decision ... Legislative change is appropriate in this area, and the present writer would advocate the extension of the definition of "property" within the Criminal Damage Act 1971 to include "data or programs," as has already been done in other jurisdictions, notably Canada.

As we have seen, 'hacking' and other such interference with computers is now covered by the Computer Misuse Act 1990, which created three offences of dishonestly and unlawfully entering another's computer system (Wasik 1991; see **section II.a.ii.** above).

It should be noted, finally, that the relatively narrow conception of property is not mirrored by the other definitional elements of criminal damage. For example, the idea of 'belonging to another' is construed broadly, as under the Theft Act, to include custody, control and a variety of other proprietary rights short of ownership. Furthermore, the scope of the aggravated form of criminal damage endangering life is enormously extended by the fact that there is no requirement that the property damaged belong to another. It is hence possible for the owner of property or someone who damages property with the owner's authorisation to be convicted of this very serious offence even if the risk is created for a short period and the defendant takes immediate steps to eliminate it (*Merrick*, 1995). This, like several other features of the law relating to criminal damage, suggests the increasing influence of a risk-based pattern of criminality in contemporary criminal law.

II.f. Duress, necessity and property

One of the themes explored in the first section of this chapter was the instability of criminal law's individualisation of responsibility for property crime given the connection between property offending and social patterns such as the unequal distribution of wealth or employment. From the perspective of criminal law doctrine, this means that individuals may be under economic or other forms of pressure when they commit property offences, and raises the question whether such pressure can ever excuse or even justify an offence. So although duress and necessity are more often pleaded in relation to offences against the person, the field of property crime is an interesting one in which to consider the contours of these defences.

It is a well-established 'principle' of English criminal law that acts (other than intentional killing and attempted killing and possibly treason) committed under duress consisting in threats of death or serious personal injury to or imprisonment of the accused or her immediate family do not attract criminal liability (see **Chapter 1.II.d.**). Yet, although a person who offends in the course of protecting their own property may well have a defence under s 3 of the Criminal Law Act 1967 on the basis that they were acting with reasonable force in the prevention of crime, and despite the high value attached to property rights in our society, threats to property interests alone do not ground the duress defence. Duress is, however, available to a defendant accused of property crimes. The potential application of duress in the field of property offences helps to illustrate not only the fragility of criminal law's construction of individual responsibility but also ambiguities in the rationale of duress and the related defence of necessity.

Some of the philosophical and political issues at stake are canvassed in the following extract:

L Vandervort, 'Social Justice in the Modern Regulatory State; Duress, Necessity and the Consensual Model in Law' 6 Law and Philosophy 1987, 205 at 217–219

... [I]t has been argued that within the consensual model [the model of criminal liability based on free choice and responsibility] findings of voluntariness or involuntariness and reasonableness or unreasonableness are policy based determinations and only superficially findings of legal fact. In case after case, policy masquerades as fact. The concepts of choice, waiver, consent, etc., the key operative concepts in the consensual model, are highly subject to conscious and unconscious manipulation, explicit or overt, to achieve the results deemed desirable by a particular decision-maker on policy grounds. Decision-makers, including judges, often must "make" law in order to dispose of a particular case, and their decisions invariably contain a normative component where the consensual model is relied on. Where the manipulation of the operative legal concepts is perceived to be apt or appropriate, the result will be regarded as just. The community and the defendant or applicant will regard the determination of legal guilt or acquittal, liability or non-liability, entitlement or non-entitlement, as a reflection of the moral "desert" of the individual.

... [T]he consensual model, through the use of the concept of "free choice" to determine moral "desert", can operate as an effective subterfuge to conceal the policy aspects of formal decisions that apply positive law to individual cases ... There is no question but that the legal system makes routine use of such subterfuges to allocate liability and entitlement, and, in effect, choose victors and victims, and at the same time conceal or deny societal responsibility for structuring key social determinants of the outcome for which the individual alone is held liable – all in the name of impartial justice under a system of formal positive law.

General recognition that legal criteria for legal responsibility and "desert" are shaped by policy considerations would not only eliminate the duplicity now often entailed in the use of the consensual model by judges and other decision-makers, but at the same time would direct increased attention and criticism towards the formation of public policy in the political forum. Overtly political first order determinations – involving fundamental issues of social justice and affecting great numbers of persons – would receive greater scrutiny. Judicial decisions about individual legal responsibility would more frequently be seen to be concerned not with individual choice alone, but rather with the consequences of social policy mediated by individual choice.

pp 220–223

Once it is agreed that the conditions of life ... of persons in the contemporary state are significantly shaped by political decisions, and that those conditions constitute the context within which individuals make choices, it follows that the traditional legal concepts of necessity (choice dictated by life-threatening circumstances [in American law]) and duress (choice dictated by an agent) must be re-interpreted. Re-interpretation of these concepts is required to adapt the consensual model to accommodate contemporary social realities. It must be recognized that choices made by individuals are often influenced and sometimes "dictated" by socio-economic factors that are themselves the product of collective societal decisions. For the individual who must make a choice, factors comprising the context in which the choice is made are not less "real" simply because some of the conditions that constitute the immediate threat to life and well-being and generate the pressure or impetus to act have an "institutional" source and cannot be uniquely attributed to any specific human agent or to fortuitous natural causes.

Decisions about the allocation of resources (distribution) can be distinguished from decisions to impose sanctions (retribution). But the most difficult and politically significant decisions of both types are those that are concerned with scarce but essential commodities and direct or indirect threats to life and well-being. In retributive judgments social vindictiveness would be deflected where societal conditions for which there is a collective responsibility, even if only as a consequence of non-feasance, were seen to have had significant influence as determinants of individual choice. Reference to social factors in mitigation is familiar from sentencing law. Sentencing law is relevant, however, only if a conviction has been entered. At issue here instead is the prior question of whether socio-economic duress and necessity, arising from socio-economic causes for which there is collective responsibility, may not sometime "excuse" or "justify" acts that would be "criminal" but for the excuse or justification. Such arguments have been rejected in the past to protect "social order". But the query raised here is: is such a negative response consistent with the exceptions to the principles of legal responsibility recognized within the traditional consensual model? Is it not instead the case that the source of the threat to life and well-being that provides the justification or excuse is irrelevant to the determination of individual legal responsibility? If so, we must acquit where the other prerequisites of excuse or justification are present. And if the concern with social order and the values it is said to protect is more than rhetoric, presumably the underlying and collectively created conditions that justify or excuse order threatening behavior must be changed. This requires re-examination of distributive practices and principles.

Vandervort shows that what appear to be relatively limited doctrinal issues about the definition and scope of a particular set of defences in fact raise wide-ranging questions about the legitimacy of criminal law and, in particular, about its capacity effectively to individualise and depoliticise the attribution of responsibility. These issues have been played out in cases dealing with the conditions under which the defences may be pleaded and, notably, in judicial reluctance to acknowledge the defence of necessity, or 'duress of circumstances'.

The test for the availability of the defence of duress, as stated in *R v Graham* (1982: 806), contains both 'subjective' and 'objective' elements, asking:

Was [the accused], or may he have been, impelled to act as he did because, as a result of what he reasonably believed [X] had said or done, he had good cause to fear that if he did not so act [X] would kill him or … cause him serious physical injury? If so, have the prosecution made the jury sure that a sober person of reasonable firmness, sharing the characteristics of [the accused], would not have responded to whatever he reasonably believed [X] said or did by taking part in the killing?

The fragile balance between objective and subjective aspects of the test is well-illustrated by the case of *Bowen* (1996). In this case, the defendant pleaded duress in his defence against the allegation of obtaining services by deception. His case was that two men had threatened to petrol-bomb him and his family if he did not obtain goods for them and told him that if he went to the police his family would be attacked. Despite the fact that witnesses testified that Bowen was a 'simple man who had difficulty reading and writing' and that a psychologist testified that he was abnormally suggestible, vulnerable and with a very low IQ, the judge simply directed the jury to consider whether the words and conduct alleged would have driven a person of reasonable firmness of the same sex and age and in the same circumstances as the accused to have committed the offences. Bowen appealed against conviction on the grounds that his low intelligence was a relevant characteristic which should have been put to the jury. His appeal was dismissed by the Court of Appeal on the basis that a low IQ short of mental impairment could not be said to be a characteristic which made those who had it less courageous and less able to withstand threats and pressure than an ordinary person. Quite how this squares with the psychologist's evidence is unclear from the report.

Interpretive issues arising in duress cases include the question of how immediate the threat has to be and how far avenues of escape must be explored (*R v Hudson*, 1971); the exclusion from the ambit of the defence of an accused who is voluntarily a member of an organisation which she knew might exert pressure to commit an offence (*R v Fitzpatrick*, 1977); and the unavailability of the defence in respect of actions in response to threats to property (*R v M'Growther*, 1746). Each of these reveals ambiguities about the basis for the defence in criminal law doctrine. However, these ambiguities are perhaps best revealed by judicial debate about the applicability of the duress defence to murder. The House of Lords, contrary to its earlier decision in *DPP for Northern Ireland v Lynch* (1975), has decided in *R v Howe* (1987) that the defence of duress is not available to any party, principal or secondary, to a completed murder and the House of Lords has also ruled out the duress defence in cases of attempted murder (see *R v Gotts*, 1992). Two competing arguments about the basis for the duress defence are very clearly illustrated by the reasoning in *Howe*. The first, which sees duress in terms of excuse, interprets the coercive threat as rendering it unfair or inappropriate to attribute responsibility to the defendant. The second, which regards duress rather in terms of justification, bases the defence on the accused's decision to take the lesser of two evil courses, implying that duress takes the 'actus reus' itself outside the scope of wrongs criminal law seeks to prevent and deter. Clear evidence of both approaches, and lack of awareness of any tension between them, is to be found in the judgment of Lord Hailsham in *Howe* (1987). Lord Hailsham begins by construing the defence as a species of excuse:

R v Howe (1987) 1 All ER 771; 775

... [T]he definition of duress, whether applicable to murder or not, was correctly stated by both trial judges to contain an objective element on the lines of their respective directions and thus must involve a threat of such a degree of violence that 'a person of reasonable firmness' with the characteristics and in the situation of the defendant could not have been expected to resist. No doubt there are subjective elements as well ...

In similar vein, Lord Hailsham quoted approvingly from Lord Kilbrandon's judgment in *Lynch*:

... 'the decision of the threatened man [sic] whose constancy is overborne so that he yields to the threat, is a calculated decision to do what he knows to be wrong, and is therefore that of a man with, perhaps to some exceptionally limited extent, a "guilty mind". But he is at the same time a man whose mind is less guilty than is his who acts as he does but under no such constraint' [777].

Lord Hailsham proceeded to assert that he did:

not at all accept in relation to the defence of duress that it is either good morals, good policy or good law to suggest, as did the majority in *Lynch*'s case and the minority in *Abbot v R* (1977) that the ordinary man of reasonable fortitude is not to be supposed to be capable of heroism if he is asked to take an innocent life rather than sacrifice his own [779–780].

He went on to admit that:

Consistency and logic, though inherently desirable, are not always prime characteristics of a penal code based like the common law on custom and precedent [780].

He then (unconsciously) illustrated this point by gradually shifting into the discourse of justification in denying the appropriateness of allowing duress as a defence to murder:

In such a case [one of assault] the 'concession to human frailty' is no more than to say that in such circumstances a reasonable man of average courage is entitled to embrace as a matter of choice the alternative which a reasonable man could regard as the lesser of two evils. Other considerations necessarily arise where the choice is between the threat of death or a fortiori of serious injury and deliberately taking an innocent life. In such a case a reasonable man might reflect that one innocent human life is at least as valuable as his own or that of his loved one. In such a case a man cannot claim that he is choosing the lesser of two evils. Instead, he is embracing the cognate but morally disreputable principle that the end justifies the means.

This interweaving of arguments of excuse and justification continues through the rest of Lord Hailsham's judgment, which appears at once to claim that duress operates to excuse the actor's 'human frailty', and that it is inapplicable in murder cases because choosing one's own life above another's is never a justifiable action. Note also the gender-specific images of the normal subject: the duress defence is designed to excuse people invested with characteristics which are strongly marked as masculine in our society.

Given the difficulties which the rationale for duress poses for criminal law doctrine, it is hardly surprising that in this area judges have often been willing to opt for pragmatic solutions legitimised by appeals to 'common sense'. One such strategy has been for judges to comfort themselves that potential injustice wreaked by the denial of the duress defence in murder cases can be mitigated despite the mandatory life sentence by the exercise of executive discretion to release the person convicted on licence at an early stage – a good example of the interplay between issues of substantive law, sentence and post-trial discretion. However, as the following extract suggests, the 'common sense' mode of argument presents its own problems:

P Alldridge and C Belsey, 'Murder under Duress: Terrorism and the Criminal Law' (1989) International Journal for the Semiotics of Law 223 at 234–235

It was Lord Wilberforce who pointed to the legal crisis precipitated by Lynch's story, [*Lynch was threatened with a gun into driving some IRA members to a garage where they shot a person dead*] when he said, 'A law, which requires innocent victims … to be tried … and convicted … is an unjust law.' This oxymoron, an injustice in the system of criminal justice, a blindness in the authorities which constituted the guarantee of their own legal authority, was the problem which exercised all five of the Law Lords in *Lynch*. Though their verdicts differ, their judgments have this in common, that the law must be made to *make sense* again. The sliding signifiers, put into process by the case of an action which is simultaneously voluntary and involuntary, are to be arrested in their headlong course. The law must be 'restated', either by the judges or by Parliament, in order to reconstitute the legitimacy of an institution which derives its sovereignty from the conviction that it administers justice.

The inconsistency resides in the legal code itself: the signifying slippage is in the (authorising) texts, the authorities. The Lords therefore invoke a supplement, something from outside the criminal code itself which will make the law *work* again. Lord Morris enlists normal standards of rationality. His decision is based on what 'any rational system of law *should* take into account' … 'The law must, I think, take a common sense view.' If it does, it cannot find Lynch guilty. It is not right that the law should demand more than can 'reasonably' be expected. 'The law would be censorious and inhumane which did not recognise the appalling plight of a person who perhaps suddenly finds his life in jeopardy unless he submits and obeys.' To demand that law should *understand* how ordinary people behave when they are threatened 'is not to make the law weak but to make it just.'

In psychoanalytic theory negation represents unconscious affirmation. The unprompted insistence that a specific event is not important or that a state of affairs is not the case unconsciously provides the analyst with an indication of what matters most. Is there, perhaps, a hint of unconscious anxiety in Lord Morris's final assertion? To bring the law into line with common sense is *not* to make it weak, he insists. What is the statement that is being made here on behalf of the legal institution? That it would be a mistake to suppose that to exonerate Lynch would weaken the law? Probably. But also, perhaps, at another level of meaning, that the invocation of supplementary standards of what is reasonable threatens to reveal a weakness in the institution of the law, by acknowledging its inadequacy in the present case. Because if common sense could determine what ought to be done, what need would there be of courts and judges, of the House of Lords as the court of final appeal, or indeed of the entire institution which endows Lord Morris himself with the authority to participate in the process of determining the fate of Lynch and so many others?

The duress defence illustrates a tension in criminal law doctrine between a world-view based on assumptions about defendants' freedom of will and one which assumes rather that human actions are, wholly or largely, causally determined. This tension is of particular relevance to property crime, where 'situational' pressures to offend are widely acknowledged (not least in the field of crime prevention: see **section III.a.** below). In the following passage, Kelman identifies the slippage between intentionalist and determinist interpretive frames in legal discourse, touching on themes already raised by Vandervort and by Alldridge and Belsey:

M Kelman, 'Interpretive Construction in the Substantive Criminal Law' (1981) Stanford Law Review 591: 642–644

Anglo-American courts and commentators assert that our criminal justice system is based on the supposition of "free will" or intentionalistic conduct. Of course, though, in a number of areas we allow determinist excusing conceptions of the defendant to be considered. This residual determinism negates the simplest claims justifying the generally asserted intentionalism, i.e. that a determinist discourse is somehow technically infeasible or methodologically inapplicable to legal contexts. The standard methodological objections to a more general determinism are twofold: first, a simple skepticism about the necessity of any effect following from any cause, and second, a distrust of our capacity to account for the roots of particular decisions that explain the precise conduct that the actor ultimately engaged in. Yet, these objections apply as well to the uses of determinism that we do tolerate ...

Ordinarily, we judge criminal liability at the moment the crime occurs. A defendant is guilty if he performs a harmful act in a blameworthy fashion. The origin of a decision to act criminally is ordinarily of no concern.

At times, though, we open the time frame to look at earlier events in the defendant's experience and construct deterministic accounts of the intentional wrongdoing. For instance, a defendant may perjure himself after being threatened. At the moment the defendant is perjuring himself, he is intentionally telling a lie. But the decision to lie under duress may seem normal, expectable, and therefore blameless.

... The duress defence represents a severe threat to ordinary criminal law discourse and is strictly confined, in terms of both time and the pressures that may influence the reasonable defendant. For the most part, we accept only discrete incidents as forming the basis of a duress plea, and we demand that these incidents occur close in time to the arguably criminal incident. Furthermore, the pressures must be attributable to a single human agent or group of agents that focuses his or their efforts on inducing the defendant to commit the crime. This second restriction maintains the illusion of an intentionalist discourse, but the relevant will is now that of the source of the duress, not that of the defendant. Of course, though, from the vantage point of the defendant on trial, we have shifted to a determinist mode. What is odd is that the "substitution of wills" metaphor implies that the defendant is acting involuntarily, or at least without exercising normal rational facilities, when he commits the crime. In fact his conduct may be as voluntary and sensible as any behaviour we can imagine, given the background conditions, The defendant is not rendered will-less; it is simply that the content of the expressions of his will, in the typically relevant broader time perspective we are suddenly using, is deemed to be determined.

The co-existence of responsibility-oriented and deterministic arguments in relation to duress is clear. What is also significant is that on *either* of these approaches, a thorough pursuit of the appropriate rationale for the defence would dictate a considerable extension of its scope and of that of other related defences. If we are to regard duress as an excusing condition within a voluntarist or subjective framework, why should restrictions based on the 'reasonableness' of the defendant's response be introduced? A person who is particularly anxious or fearful – Bowen, for example – is so through no fault of their own, yet the operation of the 'objective' test renders them liable even when their will may have been thoroughly 'overborne'. Similarly, such a person may be 'unreasonably' timorous in taking advantage of possible avenues of escape, hence excluding the application of the defence. If, conversely, we were to take a more deterministic approach, the framing of the defence would be concerned with motivating and justifying the taking of the lesser of evil courses, and a far wider scope would be appropriate. For example, if the basis of the duress defence is the justified taking of the least harmful course, why not allow the defence in the case of threats to property to which the accused has submitted by committing a property offence less harmful than the conduct threatened? The argument from justification seems to apply: the accused does no wrong in taking the lesser of two evil courses.

In pointing out these ambiguities in legal approaches to duress, we hope to show the importance of recognising the choices being made and the underlying issues which are involved. The results of failure to do so are well illustrated by the chaotic development of law on the application of duress to murder cases in *Lynch* (1975), *Abbott* (1977) and *Howe* (1987). Arguments from voluntariness and responsibility have constantly competed with arguments from lesser evil and social policy in motivating acceptable behaviour: the outcome of these arguments in particular cases has been spectacularly unpredictable. Yet criminal law's continued insistence on (purportedly principled) limitations to the duress defence provides important clues not just to competing world-views underlying doctrine but also to a pragmatic concern with preserving the authority of law and the perceived reality of its threats. It is perhaps this fundamental concern which dictates that criminal law resist the full force of the arguments which follow from any of the suggested rationales for the duress defence.

For example, on a view of duress or necessity as excuses, the voluntariness and 'subjective' responsibility of especially anxious or impetuous defendants may be radically affected by threats to their property or remote threats to their person. But criminal law sees a danger that its authority will be undermined by consistent adherence to a 'subjective' approach through recognition of the defence, and demands instead a baseline of 'reasonableness' beyond which its inquiries into 'subjectivity' will not go. Similarly, the recognition that an individual's situation – extreme poverty, for instance – might attenuate the basis for holding her fully responsible for an offence is threatening to the abstract method of legal doctrine. Conversely, although trivial property offences might be regarded as justifiable – the lesser evil – if done in response to much more serious threats to property, a consistent acceptance of the argument opens up the worrying possibility of its generalisation beyond the area of threats and its use by any defendant who claims that their offence was committed to avoid a greater evil (see also the discussion of self-defence in **Chapter 6.IV.e.**). This argument is threatening to the very core of criminal law's method, which is to denominate certain forms of behaviour absolutely unacceptable subject only to limited excusing arguments – a method of asserting authority which would also be undermined by recognition, for example, of a general defence of superior orders. The idea of defence from lesser evil opens up the possibility of endless debates in court about the relative merits of particular courses of action, thus sacrificing criminal law's promised certainty and the efficacy of its threats, as well as undermining law's supposed autonomy by introducing moral and political argument, explicitly, within the legal arena.

These arguments explain the courts' ambivalence about any general defence of necessity. Recently, however (*Re A*, 2000), the courts have taken a further, tentative step towards recognising the defence, albeit in the very particular circumstances presented by the case of conjoined twins. To appreciate the significance of this new development it is instructive first to consider the history of judicial resistance to a necessity defence.

The most famous judicial discussion is to be found in the case of *R v Dudley & Stephens* (1884), in which the defence was denied to two shipwrecked sailors who had killed and eaten a cabin boy in order to survive. The fact that the case concerned murder and that no lots had been drawn before the killing of the weakest party narrows the general applicability of the decision, and it can be questioned whether it stands for the general denial of a necessity defence which it has been taken by later cases to establish (*Buckoke v GLC*, 1971). However, it is worth quoting Lord Coleridge's splendid rhetoric, which combines an exaggerated equation of duty and supererogation with expression of fears about either defendant or judge being put in the position of having to choose which should be regarded as the lesser of evils:

R v Dudley and Stephens (1884)

Lord Coleridge.

To preserve one's life is generally speaking, a duty, but it may be the plainest and highest duty to sacrifice it. War is full of instances in which it is a man's duty not to live, but to die … It is not correct, therefore, to say that there is any absolute and unqualified necessity to preserve one's life … It is enough in a Christian country to remind ourselves of the Great Example which we profess to follow.

It is not needful to point out the awful danger of admitting the principle which had been contended for. Who is to be the judge of this sort of necessity? By what measure is the comparative value of lives to be measured? Is it to be strength, or intellect, or what? It is plain that the principle leaves to him who is to profit by it to determine the necessity which will justify him in deliberately taking another's life to save his own. Was it more necessary to kill him than one of the grown men? The answer be, No ...

Where, it might be asked, would the authority of criminal law be if defendants could come to court and plead not just illicit pressure or threats, or even exceptional circumstances such as shipwreck, flood or famine, but also crushing poverty and overwhelming need as defences to crime? Would this not threaten the entire basis of the property system? Just such a fear was later expressed by Lord Denning:

> ... if hunger were once allowed to be an excuse for stealing, it would open a door through which all kinds of lawlessness and disorder would pass ... If homelessness were once admitted as a defence to trespass, no one's house could be safe. Necessity would open a door which no man could shut [*Southwark London Borough v Williams*, 1971: 179].

Similar preoccupations led Edmund Davies LJ to make the following assertion in the same case:

> ... the law regards with the deepest suspicion any remedies of self-help, and permits these remedies to be resorted to only in very special circumstances. The reason for such circumspection is clear – necessity can very easily become simply a mask for anarchy [p 181].

These defences potentially challenge the basic doctrinal precept of criminal liability as based on individual responsibility. For they introduce arguments of social context which may well lead to a reading of crime as proceeding not just from individual decision and action but from action situated in an influential environment for which the individual herself is largely not responsible. As Vandervort envisages, it raises the possibility of laying, in whole or in part, the 'responsibility' for crime at the door of government, state or social structure. This is particularly true of the defence of necessity in which there is no possibility of simply shifting law's focus onto the actions of another individual – a strategy which, as Kelman rightly observes, is crucial to the limitation of the duress defence.

It was therefore a pleasant surprise (especially given that the point was not at issue) that the House of Lords in *Howe* expressed the view that no relevant distinction could be drawn between duress and necessity. However, anxieties about the implications of the defence are reflected in the cautious tendency to conceptualise this defence, now applied by the Court of Appeal, as 'duress of circumstances':

R v Conway (1988) 3 All ER 1025; 1029

[*Conway had been charged with reckless driving: his defence of necessity of circumstances (based on the need to escape a supposed attack on his passenger) had been rejected by the court of first instance but was accepted on appeal.*]

Woolf L.J.

We conclude that necessity can only be a defence to a charge of reckless driving where the facts establish 'duress of circumstances', as in R v Willer, i.e. where the defendant was constrained by circumstances to drive as he did to avoid death or serious bodily harm to himself or some other person.

As the learned editors point out in Smith and Hogan Criminal Law (6th edn, 1988) p225, to admit a defence of 'duress of circumstances' is a logical consequence of the existence of the defence of duress as that term is ordinarily understood, i.e. 'do this or else'. This approach does no more than recognise that duress is an example of necessity. Whether 'duress of circumstances' is called 'duress' or 'necessity' does not matter. What is important is that, whatever it is called, it is subject to the same limitations as the 'do this or else' species of duress. As Lord Hailsham LC said in his speech in R v Howe (1987: 777):

> 'There is, of course, an obvious distinction between duress and necessity as potential defences: duress arises from the wrongful threats of violence of another human being and necessity arises from any other objective dangers threatening the accused. This, however, is, in my view, a distinction without a relevant difference, since on this view duress is only that species of the genus of necessity which is caused by wrongful threats. I cannot see that there is any way in which a person of ordinary fortitude can be excused from the one type of pressure on his will rather than the other'.
> No wider defence to reckless driving is recognised.

Lord Justice Woolf's denial of the significance of whether the defence is called duress or necessity calls to mind Alldridge and Belsey's argument about negation. In *R v Martin* (1989), the Court of Appeal followed *Conway* in accepting the applicability of a plea of necessity to a charge of driving whilst disqualified. The defendant had done so after his wife had threatened to commit suicide if he did not drive her son to work. Simon Brown J, whilst acknowledging a general defence of 'necessity in extreme circumstances', was quick to insist that the defence 'most commonly ... arises as duress' (p 653). And in what was, before *Re A*, the most serious case in which the defence was invoked – a case in which the defendants were charged with hijacking a plane, their defence being that they were acting under the extreme pressure created by the fact that their families had been tortured and killed and that they faced a similar threat – the courts once again conceptualised this as a potential defence of duress of circumstances (*R v Abdul-Hussain*, 1999).

The field of duress was considered by the Law Commission in its consultation paper on the general principles which should inform a criminal code (1992). The Commission's recommendations, which reproduce the designation 'duress of circumstances' (see also Law Commission 1989: s 43), supported the uneasy division between duress by threats and duress by circumstances which has emerged from the cases just considered. As Padfield notes in the following passage, neither the legal nor the moral basis for this division, or for the continued exclusion of a justification of necessity, is convincing:

Nicola Padfield, 'Duress, Necessity and the Law Commission' (1992) Crim LR 778 at pp 786–789

Why separate duress by threats from duress of circumstances? The [Commission's Draft] Code acknowledges that '[t]he impact of some situations of imminent peril upon persons affected by them is hardly different from that of threats such as give rise to the defence of duress.' If it is hardly different, the two forms of duress should be seen as one defence, combined in one clause. In that way, the accused would establish the defence of duress by proving either that he could not reasonably be expected to resist the pressure of the threat or of the circumstances. This would have the merit not only of avoiding a clumsy phrase which has little meaning in ordinary English [duress of circumstances], but would also avoid unnecessary distinctions ...

If the two forms were but one defence, the way would be left open for the Law Commission at this stage to incorporate into its Bill a defence of necessity. The Law Commission's 1977 report suggested that the principal difference between duress and necessity lies in the source of the threatened harm. This ignores the vital point that generally speaking duress excuses, whereas necessity justifies behaviour. It is certainly odd that what might be seen as the stronger defence (justified behaviour) will, under the [Draft Code] Bill, be left to the common law, while Parliament will prescribe what defences may excuse. The importance of separating excusing defences from justificatory ones appears to be much better understood in the American literature than it is in England. However, it is increasingly recognised in this country that there are important reasons for recognising the differences.

p 788

A model which the Law Commission should re-examine is the American Model [Penal] Code, drafted by the American Law Institute between 1952 and 1962. Approximately one-half of the States have recognised the choice-of-evil defence in the Model Code:

Section 3.02 Justification Generally – Choice of Evils
(1) Conduct which the actor believes to be necessary to avoid harm or evil to himself or to another is justifiable, provided that:
   (a) the harm or evil sought to be avoided by such conduct is greater than that sought to be prevented by the law defining the offence charged; and

(b) neither the Code or other law defining the offence provides exceptions or defences dealing with the specific situation involved; and

(c) a legislative purpose to exclude the justification claimed does not otherwise plainly appear.

(2) When the actor was reckless or negligent in bringing about the situation requiring a choice of harms or evils in appraising the necessity for his conduct, the justification afforded by this Section is unavailable in a prosecution for any offence for which recklessness or negligence, as the case may be, suffices to establish culpability.

This version has the merit of making explicit the difference between this defence and that of duress. It is a 'residual justification' defence: that is, it legitimises technically wrongful conduct that common sense, fairness, or utilitarian concerns convince us is justified, but which does not fall within any other recognised justification defence ... Without the defence a system of criminal laws is neither rational nor just' (Dressler 1987: 249) ...

p 789

English common law has tumbled upon a term for necessity-as-excuse, and this has been developed by the Law Commission into clause 27 of the current draft Bill. The Law Commission now needs to reject its fear of bogus defences and to recognise the defence of necessity-as-justification.

The judgment of Robert Walker LJ in *Re A* comes close to taking such an approach. In this case (also discussed in **Chapter 6.III.a.** and **IV.e.**), a hospital applied to the courts for a ruling on the legality of an operation to separate con-joined twins. One of the twins was judged to be capable of survival if separated from her weaker twin sister, but the separation operation would be certain to kill the latter. In his analysis of the issues, Robert Walker LJ described duress of circumstances, along with duress by threats and private defence, as 'a residual category of necessity' (p 1064) which might apply in such circumstances (though he rejected the idea that there was any significance in a distinction between excuses and justification). The full implications of the case are difficult to judge, not only because of its very particular facts but also because it reached only the Court of Appeal, where the judges, though agreeing that the operation would not amount to murder of the weaker twin, took rather different routes to this conclusion. The judges were at pains to emphasise the special facts of the case, 'In truth there is no helpful analogy or parallel to the situation which the court has to consider in this case' (per Robert Walker LJ at p 1066), which involved a conflict not merely between moral but between legal duties. Nonetheless, the case offered an opportunity for an extensive review of the authorities on the necessity defence, drawing in particular on Wilson J's judg-ment in the Canadian case of *Perka v R* (1984), which argued for a necessity defence as 'the justification of a wrongful act ... premised on the need to fulfil a legal duty which was in conflict with the duty which the accused was charged with having breached' (per Brooke LJ at p 1048). In the course of this review, *Re A* also provided a significant reassessment of the decision in *Dudley and Stephens*:

Re A [2000] 4 All ER 961 at p 1051

Brooke LJ

I have considered very carefully the policy reasons for the decision in R v Dudley and Stephens, supported as it was by the House of Lords in R v Howe. These are, in short, that there were two insuperable objections to the proposition that necessity might be available as a defence for the ... sailors ... [W]ho is to be the judge of this sort of necessity? By what measure is the comparative value of lives to be measured? The second objection was that to permit such a defence would mark an absolute divorce of law from morality. In my judgement, neither of these objections are dispositive of the present case.

Implicit in this reassessment is the acknowledgment that the necessity defence is likely to continue to develop: '[I]n the absence of Parliamentary intervention the law as to the defence of necessity is going to have to develop on a case by case basis' (per Robert Walker LJ at p 1067, following Rose LJ in *Abdul-Hussain*). The special facts of *Re A* render it of limited relevance in the property area or elsewhere. But the courts may yet be confronted with a case which forces upon their attention the fact that the logic which dictated an extension of existing defences to cover duress of circumstances also militates towards a general focus on social conditions in attributing criminal responsibility. We can therefore look forward to displays of judicial ingenuity in preserving the fragile barriers which protect the doctrinal integrity of criminal law and the appearance of the legitimacy of offences against property in the context of a radically unequally propertied society.

II.g. Respect for property?

In its delineation of offences against property and the application of general 'principles' of liability and excuse, criminal law helps to construct a particular social conception of legitimate interests in property and a particular image of illegitimate threats to those interests. Thus criminal law's focus on a relatively 'conventional' conception of property excludes many forms of 'intangible property' and fails to accommodate the interests in welfare and social security provision which have been dubbed the 'new property'. Images of property offending which are thought of as 'real crime' remain salient, despite the existence of hundreds of statutory offences relating to property in fields such as taxation and company law. Criminal law constructs property offending as an issue of individual responsibility which abstracts the defendant from her social context and thus from potentially embarrassing contextual conditions such as poverty, discrimination and radical inequalities of wealth. In this way, the legal institution is enabled not only to protect property rights but to express and reinforce the legitimacy of the property system. This process is supported by the construction of many property offences in the moralistic terms of dishonesty, which is applied dispositively, so as to represent the subjects of the legal process as either dishonest or honest, either guilty or innocent. Moreover, the delegation of the definition of dishonesty to the magistrates or the jury serves to paper over cracks in social consensus about the legitimacy of a variety of dealings in property.

However, as we discovered in our consideration of some instances of property offending, the dispositive, either/or approach suppresses deep ambiguities in societal attitudes to respect for property. For whilst our public discourse supports the simple moral judgments expressed in criminal law, our private practice is replete with examples of deviations from those standards – deviations which we rationalise in a complex combination of world-views. With the help of institutional and group support, we seek to neutralise our guilt by speaking from different perspectives and distinguishing our actions – whether 'part-time', 'white collar' or other crime – from the 'real' crime of other people. The occasional 'moral panic' about particular activities generally marginalised as crime, such as the current preoccupation with business fraud, can be argued merely to reinforce the power of these distinctions by focusing attention on those who have overstepped the informal, institutional limits and whose actions have taken them beyond the scope of the relevant institutional support. Their conviction serves to affirm the majestic impartiality of 'the law'. These distinctions and vocabularies are not to be found in law or in most scholarly discussions of it, but they are essential to our understanding of the social meaning, functions and operation of criminal law.

FURTHER READING

Beatson, Jack and Simester, Andrew (1999) 'Stealing One's Own Property' 115 Law Quarterly Review 115.

Duff, R A (1996) *Criminal Attempts* (Clarendon Press).

Elliot, D W (1991) 'Directors' Thefts and Dishonesty' Crim LR 732.

Firth, Alison (1995) 'The Criminalisation of Offences against Intellectual Property', in Loveland, I (ed) *Frontiers of Criminality* (Sweet & Maxwell) p 149.

Hall, Jerome (1952) *Theft, Law and Society* (2nd edn, Bobbs-Merrill).

Law Commission (1989) *A Criminal Code for England and Wales* (No 177), Chs III and IV.

Ormerod, David (1999) 'A Bit of a Con? The Law Commission's Consultation Paper on Fraud' Crim LR 789.

Shute, Stephen (2002) 'Appropriation and the Law of Theft' Crim LR 445.
Smith, Keith (1989) 'Must Heroes Behave Heroically?' Crim LR 622.
Wasik, Martin (1991) *Crime and the Computer* (Oxford University Press).

III.   Property rights and criminal enforcement

In the area of offences against property, as in other contexts, we cannot achieve real insight into the nature of criminal law without examining how it is enforced. As we shall see in this section, the relative frequency of property crime has bred a diversification of enforcement practices, ranging from the formal to the informal, the publicly scrutinised to the privately controlled, the civil to the criminal. This diversity reflects the complexity of our responses to threats to property: it also raises a number of important political issues concerning accountability in and selectivity of enforcement. In particular, the eminently movable boundaries between formal and informal and between civil and criminal enforcement render discretion and discrimination important issues in the area of protection of interests in property.

Both historical and contemporary evidence reveal an important interaction between enforcement practice and the meaning of the criminal law. Blackstone berated the common law for its unjust severity in relation to grand larceny and notes the 'pious perjury' on the part of juries which this engendered: juries would find the value of the goods to be a shilling or less in order to avoid the death penalty. Similarly, Beattie's evidence suggests that grand larcenies were rather rarely prosecuted, particularly from the late eighteenth century when popular confidence in the jury system was waning and distaste for the draconian punishments was growing. Presumably victims initiating prosecutions, too, would manipulate the value of the goods, and Beattie's evidence from the late eighteenth century suggests that among grand larcenies, only horse theft was still tried with any regularity; the vast majority of property crime was petty larceny, with the most prevalent serious offences being burglary and robbery. There is a further link here with Hay's account of the way in which draconian penalties provided for by eighteenth-century law were often commuted by the authorities – a practice which fostered a sense of their munificent clemency (Hay 1975: see **section I.a.** above). This was ideologically more useful than a reputation for even-handed enforcement – something which becomes a much more insistent demand from the late eighteenth century on.

Because of the way in which crimes against property still dominate the officially recorded statistics of crime, much of the time and resources of the various agencies of the criminal process are devoted to 'tackling' crimes against property, and much public debate focuses on ways in which property crime should be addressed and, if possible, reduced. In this part of the chapter, we focus on four issues of criminal enforcement which have arisen out of this debate. Our discussion adds to the emerging picture of the social and political nature of criminal enforcement and suggests that some incipient developments are peculiarly related to social concerns about property crime.

III.a. 'Situational' crime prevention

In recent years, public fears about increases in crimes such as burglary, 'mugging' and 'vandalism' have generated a shift in focus from the offender towards a debate about how we might change the environment in which such offences occur so as to prevent or inhibit their commission. This 'situational' approach may be contrasted with 'social crime prevention', which attempts more directly to address the conditions which generate offending behaviour. The contrast between situational and social approaches therefore raises once again the question of where responsibility for property crime is assumed to lie.

R V G Clarke and P Mayhew, *Designing Out Crime* (Home Office Research Unit, HMSO, 1980) pp 5–12

In defining the 'situational' approach, opportunity is ... a key concept ... The term criminal opportunity has several shades of meaning. First it can refer simply to the material conditions in which a potential offender is competent or able to commit a crime. And, of course, for those crimes which are the result of impulse or temptation, the opportunity for crime consists simultaneously in the material conditions and the inducement: a car with a key in the ignition provides both conditions and inducement. But it has a still broader meaning which includes the element of chance – criminal opportunities exist not only where the material conditions are present but where benefits can be gained at low risk ...

Situational measures are exemplified below under eight headings. The first three groups comprise measures which reduce opportunity by making crime physically harder to commit. The remainder involve the manipulation of the costs and benefits, as well as the material conditions, of offending in ways which are considerably more complex.

Target hardening

The most obvious way of reducing criminal opportunities is to obstruct or 'target harden' – to increase the physical security of targets of theft through the use of locks, reinforced materials and immobilising devices, to protect against vandalism by installing unbreakable and paint-resistant materials, and by placing vulnerable objects behind grills or meshes ... In this country, the Post Office have succeeded in virtually eliminating theft from telephone kiosks by the wholesale replacement of vulnerable aluminium coin boxes with stronger steel ones.

Target removal

A second group of measures consists in the removal of targets of crime from the environment. Thus the opportunities for wage-snatches are reduced if employers are encouraged to pay their staff by cheque rather than cash ... A further variant of target removal is to be found in measures which disguise the opportunities for crime or make temptations less blatant, even if in these cases the target is only removed from the subjective world of potential offenders. For example, the rapid repair of vandalism damage may prevent further attacks.

Removing the means to crime

Some sorts of crime have been dramatically reduced by removing the means to commit them. For example the incidence of aircraft 'skyjacking' has been reduced from an annual average of about 70 in the early seventies to the present rate of about 15 a year by screening passengers and baggage to detect weapons and bombs ... [C]hildren can be denied the opportunities for some sorts of vandalism if, for example, they are not allowed to buy aerosol paint sprays ...

Reducing the pay-off

Some preventive measures are designed to reduce the incentives to crime, or the pay-off accruing to successful offenders. Most of these are applicable only to property crime and rest on making stolen goods less valuable to people who acquire them illegitimately. One example is to be found in the 'Operation Identification' schemes now popular in North America whereby households are encouraged to mark valuable possessions with indelible codes which render the goods uniquely identifiable and thus of less value to the thief ...

Formal surveillance

Formal surveillance refers to the activities of those whose sole or primary function is to provide a threat of apprehension sufficient to deter potential offenders. The police, of course, are the main agency to provide formal surveillance, but ... there seem to be few realistic policies open to them which would achieve any further substantial impact on crime. Under certain circumstances, however, it may be worthwhile for public authorities or private organisations to provide themselves with formal surveillance for high risk targets. Some local authorities have set up special patrols to protect their parks, for example, and the private sector is making increasing use of private security services ...

Natural surveillance

The 'natural' surveillance afforded by people going about their everyday affairs can afford a source of (free) protection against crime, the potential of which can be exploited by intelligent design. 'Planning' solutions of this kind are associated most with Jane Jacobs, who argued that increased population densities and 'mixed' land use (shared between housing, schools, recreational facilities and so on) would lead to a stronger sense of community and higher levels of street activity – conditions which she thought would provide considerable informal surveillance ...

The 'architectural' solutions of Oscar Newman have centred on the design of housing estates to give residents a better view of vulnerable areas and an increased sense of responsibility for the areas surrounding their homes. These have had particular appeal in combining solutions to the problem of crime with the promise of more attractive and less alienating environments. Both here and abroad 'action' projects to build or modify housing complexes along defensible space lines have been initiated as well as a number of empirical studies relating levels of crime and vandalism to defensible space features ... Other 'natural' surveillance measures aim to increase the visibility of crime by upgrading the quality of street lighting and designing out features such as pedestrian tunnels, which are susceptible to very little surveillance. Evidence as to the effectiveness of these measures is mixed ...

Surveillance by employees

If formal surveillance encounters problems of cost and natural surveillance is of limited effectiveness, there is rather more promise in exploiting the surveillance role of certain sorts of employee such as caretakers in schools and on housing estates, doormen, shop assistants, bus conductors and so on. Research in North America has shown that apartment blocks with doormen are less vulnerable to burglary ...

Environmental management

A final group of situational measures can be loosely identified under the heading of environmental management. These measures have some but not all the characteristics of the situational approach, and some are oppor-tunity-reducing only in an extended sense. Insofar as a distinction can be drawn between the social and physical environment, this group tends to involve manipulation of the former. Perhaps the best example is to be found in the organisation of events such as football matches. Good liaison between the police, two football clubs and supporters' clubs can reduce the opportunities and temptations for vandalism and violence; arrival and departure of supporters can be better managed so as to avoid long periods of delay; within the grounds routes of access to stands and occupation of stands can be co-ordinated so as to minimise contact between rival supporters; sale of alcohol can be controlled within, and possibly around, the grounds ... Housing allocation policies can be pursued which avoid high concentrations of children on certain sorts of estate ...

The objection most often raised to opportunity-reducing measures is that they are subject to 'displacement' – either in causing offenders to choose their time carefully; shift their attention to other places where there are unprotected targets; employ a different method of committing crime; or turn instead to some completely different form of illegal activity. To the extent that displacement occurs, then, situational measure might be effective only in protecting individual targets, leaving overall crime levels intact. There are reasons for thinking, however, that the problem of displacement has been overestimated. The dispositional bias in theory has tended to reinforce popular beliefs in the inevitability of displacement ('bad will out'). People find it hard to accept that actions with often momentous consequences for both victim and offender can turn on apparently trivial situational contingencies. But shifts in opportunities do affect levels of behaviour such as suicide, which not unlike many forms of crime is usually thought to be the result of deep-seated motivation ...

It is also clear ... that there is an enormous number of people whose engagement in crime is marginal and who would be seen by very few people as 'real' criminals; these people, as almost all of us know from personal experience, commit offences which are defined by themselves as relatively trivial, are easy to commit and have a low probability of detection. There are very few people, according to self-report studies, who have not at some time or other committed offences such as shoplifting, theft from their employers or vandalism. A sizeable proportion of the population regularly evades income tax, drives whilst drunk, or commits drugs offences. It is unlikely that reducing the opportunities for these sorts of offences will displace energies to other illegal activities ... A certain amount of displacement does not vitiate a preventive measure; so long as the benefits accruing from a reduction in crime exceed the social cost of a measure, it can be regarded as a success not only by the individuals receiving the protection but also by those who have a responsibility for crime control.

This last paragraph illustrates the extent to which cost–benefit analysis pervades policy discussions in criminal justice – particularly in relation to property crime. We should also note the assumptions about the links between environment and behaviour which underlie some of the strategies: can these assumptions of 'architectural determinism' be justified? The authors go on to explain that the realisation of situational strategies is not without its difficulties:

p 17

Problems of implementation include cost, difficulties in persuading people to take and co-ordinate action, and resistance arising out of a general distaste for what can be seen as mechanistic and illiberal solutions to complex social problems. These objections are neither specific to the situational approach nor sufficient to invalidate it. Like any form of social control, the situational approach is open to both use and abuse. Assessed in context – in the light of the costliness, unwieldiness and doubtful effectiveness of our existing criminal justice system – it is clear that it merits a great deal more support.

The book from which this passage is taken reports a variety of studies concerning attempts to control crime situationally, including surveillance on buses and the London Underground and car security campaigns. These studies and subsequent research give mixed messages about the effectiveness of situational measures (Gilling 1997, though see Clarke (ed) 1997), in particular about the potential for situational measures to displace crime from one area to another rather than to prevent it altogether. Several implications of any serious attempt to espouse a generally situational approach do, however, emerge. In the first place, since it is people and their property who are the 'targets' of crime, the implication of situational prevention is that they should change their behaviour, for example by staying off the streets at night or not going out alone. Such implications are not necessarily reconcilable with people's sense of the importance of their choices about their own behaviour and the quality of their lives. Moreover, the situational approach can become associated with a tendency to 'blame' the victims of crime for their victimisation: if we all have a social responsibility to act so as to reduce the chances of our being victimised by crime, the natural result may be the judge's censure of the rape victim who took a lift – or indeed of the burglary victim who left her window unbolted (cf Maguire and Bennett's research cited in **section I.d.** above) – or again of the person who has no elaborate security locks or alarms, perhaps because she could not afford them. Moreover, the situational approach raises important issues not only about where responsibility for crime lies but also about the implications of crime prevention strategies for social justice and political culture:

R A Duff and S E Marshall, 'Benefits, Burdens and Responsibilities: Some Ethical Dimensions of Situational Crime Prevention' p 17 in von Hirsch et al (eds), *Ethical and Social Perspectives on Situational Crime Prevention* (Oxford, Hart Publishing, 2000) at pp 21–22

Discussions of 'the ethics of SCP [situational crime prevention] often (rightly) focus on the *impacts* of such measures: the benefits they bring by reducing crime; the burdens they impose in material costs, in limiting freedom or in infringing privacy. We should also attend, however, to their *meanings*: to the attitudes, the conceptions of citizens and their mutual relationships, that they manifest. Two examples will illustrate this point.

The first concerns trust. It is commonplace that civil society depends on our ability to trust each other not to attack or harm us in various ways … SCP measures typically manifest a lack or loss of trust: they are (seen as) necessary because we do not trust people not to commit the crimes that they aim to prevent … Suppose that I take to locking my wallet away when I leave my office with colleagues or students in it, to make sure that they don't steal from me. Apart from questions about whether such a measure is cost-effective, we might question the attitude it displays: we might say that I *insult* my colleagues and students by taking such mistrustful precautions …

The second example concerns inclusion and exclusion, in relation to fellow-citizenship. Consider … a policy of excluding certain groups from a shopping mall; or a housing estate whose streets used to be a public space open to all, which is turned into a private estate that admits only residents and 'legitimate' visitors. 'Public' space is space to which all citizens have access, in which they can coexist and interact: to exclude some groups from such space (as from a mall) is to refuse to treat them as fellow citizens …

pp 28–30

The impact of simple target-hardening measures like locking one's house is focused only on actual or would-be offenders … Other kinds of SCP measures, however, are focused on *potential* rather than actual or would-be offenders, and have a larger impact than this.

Suppose that the owners of a shopping mall aim to reduce thefts in the mall by excluding those who can be identified as potential thieves. Such a measure does not just make it hard or impossible for *would-be* thieves, who have already formed and are acting on the intention to steal … it deprives *potential* thieves, who have as yet formed no such intention, of opportunities to form or act on such intentions; and it also deprives them of other opportunities and goods by excluding them from the benefits of the mall …

The possible criteria of *potential* criminality are of two kinds. The first kind concerns the person's own prior and relevant criminal conduct … The second kind concerns the possession of other characteristics, whether behavioural or non-behavioural, which are supposedly correlated with the commission of the relevant kind of crime: that this person … is a young, unemployed male, that he is dressed like a tramp or a gypsy – and that there is a correlation between the possession of these characteristics and the commission of the relevant kinds of crime … *No* such criteria, we suggest, can provide legitimate grounds for exclusion: for exclusions based on such criteria fail to treat, or to trust, those excluded as responsible fellow citizens … What … of the first kind of criterion for exclusion, based on the person's own relevant criminal conduct? This seems a more appropriate kind of criterion, since we can now say that those excluded have defined themselves as untrustworthy by their own criminal conduct ... Even here, however, there are serious questions to be asked: questions about proof ... and questions about the length of exclusion that could be justified ... The requirement that such exclusions be justified by reference to the person's own past criminal conduct subjects them to demands of due process and proportionality which will radically constrain their use.

The emphasis on situational crime prevention may be connected with governmental attempts to diffuse responsibility for crime control in response to the perceived crisis of the state criminal justice system (see Garland 1990, quoted in **Chapter 1.III.b.iv.** above): in the context of these sorts of political and economic imperatives, ethical issues such as those raised by Duff and Marshall are all too easily forgotten.

It is also interesting to note the resonance of the situational approach with a utilitarian view of criminal behaviour. Situational approaches assume a theory of deterrence which has tenuous empirical support (von Hirsch et al 1999): they also assume the centrality of an economistic, cost–benefit analysis of crime which arguably ignores some of the most important social and political issues raised by criminality. In doing so, situational crime prevention encounters all the general 'pros' and 'cons' of utilitarian analysis. Utilitarian approaches to crime, whatever their real plausibility, promise some accommodation of social factors in determining crime, rather than seeing it as purely the result of individual transgression and wickedness. This is an important feature of the environmental approach – as reflected in the headline 'When design is the real criminal' (*The Guardian*, 9 March 1988: 23). But the situational approach, when wholeheartedly pursued, is potentially equally continuous with an explanation of crime in terms of the individual dispositions of offenders. For example, we might interpret the imprisonment of those who have committed serious offences against the person or property as a situational approach to crime prevention: it changes the environment by removing those who are likely to commit crimes. As such, it resonates with the 'new penology' canvassed by Feeley and Simon (1994: see **Chapter 1.III.b.iv.**). The situational approach runs the risk of legitimising both the blaming of victims *and* the selection of some kinds of offenders as 'real' criminals who must be removed from the environment. Particularly in the context of 'zero tolerance' policing policies, questions about the displacement of crime problems and the zoning of 'dangerous populations' into the poorest areas cannot be ignored.

The situational approach, however, with its potential for suggesting a re-distribution of responsibility for crime and its prevention, has clear attractions for governments which are unable to match their tough rhetoric on law and order with substantial reductions in crime. It is therefore not surprising that a persistent theme in contemporary criminal justice policy is an emphasis on police-community liaison and arrangements such as neighbourhood watch schemes, property marking schemes and the latest wardenship schemes under the Police Reform Act 2002 (see **Chapter 1.III.b.ii.**). The implications of such schemes in terms of increased and unaccountable surveillance and their potential social divisiveness given limited trust of the police in many urban areas raise, however, serious ethical questions. Some sociologists have pointed out that movements such as 'situational' crime prevention and 'community corrections' for offenders (such as community penalties, widely used for property offenders) have the adverse side-effect of generating ever-higher levels of surveillance in the community (see Cohen 1985; Garland and Young 1983: see also Welsh and Farrington's systematic review of the – inconclusive – preventive effects of closed circuit TV: Welsh and Farrington 2002). The impact of situational strategies needs to be assessed not only in narrow, cost–benefit terms but also in terms of their broader social implications. We increasingly take for granted the existence of video equipment in shops and other public places such as sports stadia, stations and roads. Should we be worried about the extent to which our society is intent on equipping itself with the paraphernalia of 1984-type surveillance (see **Chapter 1.III.b.iv.**)? These developments, furthermore, have importance in terms of the trial process: the poor quality of much video evidence (for example of the identity of those accused of shop robbery or theft) render its use controversial. If it is the case that current standards of evidence would rule out reliance on many security videos in court, will it be the use of the videos or the standards of evidence which will be adapted?

A final question about situational crime prevention relates to its commercial aspects. One has only to read and watch the media to witness the extent of advertising of crime prevention devices such as burglar alarms. Their production is now a large-scale and highly profitable business – one which plays cleverly on popular anxieties about crime. The fact that many insurance companies now make household cover dependent on the use of alarms and elaborate locks broadens the implication of this development. The differential availability of such preventive hardware to the more and less propertied members of society raises issues of social justice and illustrates the inequitable consequences of holding potential victims at least partially responsible for avoiding victimisation. Moreover, some commentators suggest that preventive controls can actually be counter-productive:

S Henry, *The Hidden Economy* (1978) pp 145–148

At a conference on major property crime held at Edinburgh University in 1975, the question was raised of whether the cost of crime was high enough to justify the expenditure of so much money and effort on crime prevention. More precisely, it was argued that there is little or no evidence to show that security is really cost-effective ...

Clearly, a crucial dilemma for the economic or cost-effective analysis of controlling hidden-economy activity is what is taken to be 'loss'. If all activities which detracted from profits were taken as 'loss', then employees would be expected to work for nothing. Fortunately, this is not how wage-earning is seen by most companies. Wages and salaries are taken into account as part of the economic 'costs' of production. The problem occurs with activities such as pilfering, fiddling and trading. These are considered by some employers as part of the costs of production. But employers are increasingly being urged to see these costs as unnecessary losses and that further costs (of security and crime prevention) are necessary in order to cut these losses. Thus, in retail business, for example, the Group 4 Total Security Company claim that a retailer who spends £1 on their services should save at least £2 on his losses in staff theft and customer shoplifting. As a rule of thumb, the company says, shopkeepers should be prepared to devote 0.1 per cent to 0.5 per cent of their turnover to security. In London's Oxford Street shops are spending around £5m per year on security to combat an estimated £10m worth of losses. This is without the additional cost of £20 for each case that is brought to court ...

Of course, it will always be argued, especially by private security companies, that without controls the situation would be much worse ... However, I contend that in the case of hidden-economy controls, expenditure on security actually represents an economic loss. The assumption made, notably by security companies, is that pilfering, fiddling and dealing start suddenly at the instigation of either the odd, morally defective individual who is unable to resist temptation, or of the criminally dishonest person who has planned to steal. It is argued that these 'bad apples' will affect the rest of the work force if they are not stopped in their prime. Furthermore, it is felt that by not taking security precautions, managements encourage employee theft ... I take a contrasting view to this. I have tried to show ... that hidden-economy activity is not something that suddenly grows. Rather it is, and always has been, a part of the costs of production. Like wages, it provides another set of satisfactions, in this case to do with the personalised nature of work and the relationship between labour and property ownership ... In other words, hidden-economy activity is ... a natural, ever-present feature of human work. The implications of this for controlling the hidden economy are considerable. By paying for security, employers are creating an additional, unnecessary loss which, in turn, may be multiplied by lost production through strikes. But there is an even more ironic consequence of the employment of external security of policing agencies. This concerns the natural control that already exists within the hidden economy ... By removing the responsibility for self-control from the hidden economy, the introduction of external control policies may actually exacerbate the activity ... Employers' private justice is arbitrary, unfair and wide open to abuse, and private security is politically and economically dubious.

The rapid development of situational approaches to the prevention of property and other crime over the last two decades therefore raises important issues. These include the relevance of cost–benefit analysis and utilitarian models of crime and punishment and their relation to criminal law's doctrinal insistence on individual responsibility for crime; the allocation of responsibility for crime and its prevention; and the extension of surveillance and control in the community. These themes are often insufficiently explored by proponents of the approach. The attractions of situational crime prevention are, however, manifest: for the alternative 'social' approach is liable to raise the intractable issues about social rather than individual responsibility for crime. These issues threaten the individualist basis of criminal law and, as we have seen, the judiciary has been assiduous in framing areas such as the necessity defence in terms which keep them firmly out of the courtroom (see above, **section II.f.**).

III.b.   Diversifying and privatising control

Linked to moves towards situational crime control is the issue of the range and nature of the institutions and agencies involved in the criminal process. Situational approaches, particularly to property crime, are implemented by a greater and greater diversity of agencies at the margins of, or clearly beyond, the bounds of the formal criminal process. They are also generating a diversity of forms of sanction (such as adverse publicity in the contrasting cases of corporations and paedophiles) which draw on the offender's susceptibility to community or peer pressure. The prevalence of property crime, its costs and the gap between the resources of the police and the extent of the problem, have contributed to the generation of not only a wide range of private and state-sanctioned preventive initiatives but also new institutions which supplement formal criminal justice controls. Thus, for example, residents on housing estates are encouraged to cooperate with the police in implementing 'community crime prevention' schemes including neighbourhood watch; members of the public may be involved in mediation or 'restorative justice' schemes which divert offenders from the formal criminal process and require them to negotiate reparations with their victims and members of the local community (Braithwaite 1989; Zedner 1994; Roche 2003); shops, employers and places of public entertainment such as cinemas, theatres and malls increasingly pay for private detectives and security workers to engage in surveillance of customers and employees (Johnston 1992: Chs 4 and 5; Bayley and Shearing 1996: see **Chapter 1.III.b.ii.**).

Among these diverse phenomena, that of restorative justice deserves particular attention. This is not only because of its growing importance in policy terms but also because, as Braithwaite explains in the extract below, it illustrates the way in which forms of regulation developed in a particular field may be used as imaginative resources for the construction of more general policy development:

**John Braithwaite, *Restorative Justice and Responsive Regulation*
(Oxford University Press, 2002) pp 10, 12, 16**

Restorative justice is most commonly defined by what it is an alternative to. Juvenile justice, for example, is seen as seesawing back and forth during the past century between a justice and a welfare model, between retribution and rehabilitation. Restorative justice is touted as a long-overdue third model ...

The process idea of restorative justice as a method of bringing together all stake-holders in an undominated dialogue about the consequences of an injustice and what is to be done to put them right is important. But so is the idea of restorative justice as an alternative that has a very different values framing than punitive justice. A perfect restorative process in which all stakeholders have their say can result in an undominated democratic decision ... to impose an extremely punitive outcome. An approach that is impoverished from the perspective of a process definition of restorative justice ... might result in a richer result in terms of restorative values such as apology, repairing of harm, forgiveness, and reconciliation. In evaluating how restorative a program is, we need to analyze both the restorativeness of its processes and its values ...

Most restorative justice advocates came to the approach through juvenile crime as a result of evidence of the failures of the welfare and justice models. The path that led me and a number of my colleagues who are experts in corporate crime to restorative justice is quite different and instructive. Many young criminologists began to study white-collar crime after Watergate to resurrect Edwin Sutherland's project [*see **section I.c.** above*]. We wanted to document systematically how the crimes of the powerful were unpunished. What we found, in effect, was that the regulation of corporate crime in most countries was rather restorative. The reasons for this were far from ennobling, being about corporate capture combined with the high costs of complex corporate crime investigations that states were unwilling to pay. Nevertheless, some of us began to wonder whether we were wrong to see our mission as making corporate crime enforcement more like street crime enforcement through tougher sanctions. Instead we began to wonder whether street crime enforcement might be more effective it if it were more like corporate criminal enforcement.

In England, schemes exploring the possibility of mediation leading to some form of reparation after conviction but before sentence, and schemes which aim to divert offenders from the criminal justice system altogether, have both been piloted for juveniles and, more recently, for adults. As Cavadino and Dignan (2002: 135) argue, this second type of restorative justice:

offers a way of combining diversion from prosecution with constructive reparation for victims, thereby ensuring that their interest are not sacrificed in the pursuit of cost savings of administrative convenience. Indeed, experience elsewhere (notably in New Zealand and Australia) gives ground for cautious optimism that this kind of approach might assist in the development of a more restorative system of criminal justice in general.

In the area of fraud, the Inland Revenue, HM Customs and Excise, the Department of Trade and Industry and the Serious Fraud Office (see below) have investigative functions just as important as those of the police, and disciplinary proceedings by professional bodies such as Lloyd's and by Self-Regulatory Organisations can lead to severe financial penalties (Johnston 1992: Ch 6). In these regulatory contexts, warnings and other informal – sometimes 'restorative' – sanctions are very often used so as to divert offenders seen as trivial or deterrable from the formal criminal process (Weait 1995). While the framework of self-regulation resonates to some degree with the situational emphasis on victim-responsibility, it raises important questions about the extent, openness and accountability of the power which regulatory institutions wield. This power is, at least in theory, circumscribed by law – for example, administrative law and laws on unfair dismissal – but it is unlikely that someone in the vulnerable position of having been accused of an offence will turn to the legal process to protect themselves against abuse of private power. Though the general move to privatisation, occasioned by both economic and ideological arguments, over the last twenty years has doubtless increased the involvement of non-state bodies in what amounts to law enforcement, the involvement of alternative institutions has a long history. Braithwaite has even claimed that, 'Restorative justice has been the dominant model of criminal justice throughout most of human history for perhaps all the world's peoples' (Braithwaite 2002: 5; for critical discussion of this claim, see Daly 2002); and even within the framework of a criminal justice system dominated by a punitive ethos, a diversity of social institutions are involved in what might broadly be called criminal enforcement:

G Rudé, *Criminal and Victim* (Clarendon Press, 1985) pp 92–93

... [T]here was no systematic method of detecting crime in London until the Whig reformers, following Peel, created the first professional detective force in 1842. In the meantime, detection was left to the plain-clothes police, directed from the Police Offices, who called to their aid the resources of a familiar but thoroughly unprofessional institution. This was the pawnbroker's shop, later supplemented, or succeeded, by the marine-store shop, which dealt in second-hand goods. The pawnshop performed a useful, dual, function. On the one hand it provided the thief with a convenient means of exchange for his ill-gotten gains ... On the other hand the pawnbroker's shop, precisely because it offered such ready opportunities for thieves, was under close police surveillance, and the pawnbroker was expected to report all suspicious transactions and to attend at court in order to bring committed persons to justice. In fact, in the Proceedings for March 1830 we find the case of a pawnbrokers' refusal to attend a police hearing inconvenient to themselves – much to the indignation of the prosecutor who charged that the pawnbrokers, by not attending at the proper time, '[had] done everything they could to prevent this prosecution'.

One area of contemporary property crime in which 'informal' control institutions are used is that of shoplifting. Here, despite the fact that their technical legal powers are no more than those of ordinary citizens, the initial enforcement stage lies in the hands of store detectives:

D J Murphy, *Customers and Thieves* (1986) pp 237–238

Among other things, what emerged [from the empirical study of shops' responses to shoplifting] was that most stores viewed store detectives as the best means of controlling shoplifting and so their training was investigated. It was apparent that the intensity of training, both formal and on the shopfloor, varied enormously between retailers.

… Three models of store detective activity were outlined: the 'law-enforcer', the 'peace-keeper' and the 'moral entrepreneur'. It was argued that the law-enforcer model corresponded closely to the traditional conception of police activity. The first stage of this model was 'exclusion': potential troublemakers were not permitted entry – a policy which was only minimally pursued. The next step was 'screening' – the ways in which store detectives selected suspects for investigation. How store detectives apprehended suspects and the problems they had to overcome in doing so was the third stage of the model. Next came the interview with the suspect … Finally, came 'disposal', which usually entailed police referral unless the suspect fell into one of the categories where leniency was exercised.

The peace-keeping model followed the first two stages of the law-enforcement model ('exclusion' and 'screening'); the arrest stage, however, was eschewed in favour of 'manipulation' whereby the would-be thief was converted into a legitimate 'customer'. The peace-keeping role might be adopted by the law-enforcers where the apprehension of the suspect would be inappropriate or undesirable; and only a minority of retailers followed the peace-keeping model by preference, arresting suspects when all else had failed.

Store detectives also act as 'moral entrepreneurs', particularly when dealing with adolescents and gangs of children. More usually, this model was adopted in conjunction with the law-enforcer or peace-keeping model, and was especially used to reinforce the anxiety of apprehension when the police were not called. Critically, these three roles were not mutually exclusive; the store detective might adopt one in preference to another as the circumstances changed.

The activities of store detectives not only constitute a filter through which the impact of criminal law is mediated but also have implications for the role of the formal control agencies:

> ... Shoplifting is a significant offence for the police not least because it has a considerable positive effect on the 'clear-up' rate of offences detected, even though police involvement in detecting shoplifters is minimal, their role generally being that of 'processers'.

The diversification of enforcement processes has involved debate about the possibility of decriminalising shoplifting altogether or at least providing for private, civil enforcement as an alternative. There has also been discussion of the merits of police cautioning rather than prosecution: at one moment it is accepted that this is an appropriate standard procedure for first offenders; at others, this is seen as going 'soft on crime'. This debate raises an issue which is never far below the surface of the debate about property crime: the question of the appropriate line between civil and criminal enforcement and the co-existence of the two. The enforcement of criminal law relating to property raises criminological issues about how far it is accurate to envisage property offenders as rational calculators who may regard moderate criminal penalties as modest price tags or taxes attaching to their activities (a recurring spectre in accounts of property crime). It also raises moral issues about how far offenders should effectively be able to buy the right to offend by paying fines, which are the predominant mode of sanction in this area. The latter concern has emerged clearly in debate about compensation for victims of crime, the recovery of the profits of crime, and the relationship between these practices and pecuniary criminal penalties in the form of fines. The deliberations of the Hodgson Committee reflected these concerns, and provided a useful summary of the different possible forms of compensatory or profit-stripping provision:

D Hodgson, *Profits of Crime and Their Recovery* (Report of a Committee for the Howard League) (Heinemann, 1984) pp 3–5

In the summer of 1978 a case which came to be known as the 'Operation Julie' case ... was tried in the Crown Court at Bristol. Those convicted at the trial had over a number of years, and on a vast scale, manufactured and sold the hallucinogenic drug ... LSD ... The offenders were sentenced to long terms of imprisonment. In addition, the Judge made an order, confirmed by the Court of Appeal, for the forfeiture of certain assets in their hands purportedly exercising a power given by sect. 27(1) of the Misuse of Drugs Act 1971. Huge profits had been made, and the prosecution was able to trace some 750,000 of those profits to assets in the criminals' hands ... The power given to the Court under the Act was to 'order anything shown to the satisfaction of the Court to relate to the offence to be forfeited'.

A further appeal was made to the House of Lords against the orders for forfeiture and the House 'with considerable regret' found itself compelled to allow the appeals. Among the reasons given for allowing the appeal the House held that Parliament had never intended orders of forfeiture to 'serve as a means of stripping the drug traffickers of the total profits of their unlawful enterprises'. The power could only be used where it was 'possible to identify something tangible that can fairly be said to relate to any such transaction such as the drugs involved, apparatus for making them, vehicles used for transporting them or cash ready to be or having just been handed over for them' (*R. v Cuthbertson* [1981] AC 470). The House also held that an English court has no jurisdiction to make orders for the transfer of property situated abroad ...

The apparent inability of the Court effectively to deprive an offender of the profits of his offending caused substantial public concern, particularly when it was realised that there were many other criminal activities where huge profits were made and the Court's powers were similarly restricted. Nor, it was realised, were the courts in any better position where the offences committed were of less glaring criminality. Large profits can result from the contravention of regulatory provisions, and the power of the Court to impose monetary penalties is often wholly insufficient substantially to touch them ... A great deal more could, and we believe should, be done to help the victims of crime ...

The committee went on to define the forms of recovery which they consider:

p 5

By forfeiture we mean the power of the court to take property that is immediately connected with an offence. Spread throughout our law there are very many specific powers of forfeiture such as the one unsuccessfully sought to be exercised in the Operation Julie case. There is also a general power contained in sect. 43 of the Powers of Criminal Courts Act 1973.

We use compensation to refer to financial reparation to a victim by an offender for loss, injury, suffering or damage resulting from an offence. Sects. 35 to 38 of the 1973 Act contain the principal powers of the criminal courts to award compensation.

Restitution is used to mean the return of property or its monetary equivalent to the person from whom it was unlawfully taken. The power to order restitution is found in Section 28 of the Theft Act 1968 and is given to magistrates by the Police (Property) Act 1897.

Finally confiscation is taken to mean the depriving of an offender of the proceeds or the profits of crime. It was the inability of the courts to order confiscation in this sense which was highlighted by the Operation Julie case.

Each of these practices raises, as the Committee recognised, important issues about the role of the victim in the criminal process and about bias in criminal enforcement:

pp 8–10

[The argument] ... that the victim can always bring a civil action against the defendant for the recovery of the loss resulting from a criminal act, ignores the financial inability and the lack of litigious stamina of the majority of victims to sustain a civil suit. At present criminal justice is administered principally for the protection of the whole of society. Its concern for the individual victim should not be merely incidental to that purpose; such concern is central to society's need in order that the collective purpose may be served.

Excluding crimes of violence where containment in prison may be the only way in which society can be protected, there are three broad categories of illegal conduct from which substantial gains can be made. There are 'victim' crimes, the paradigms of which are fraud and theft; there are 'non-victim' crimes, for example the drug and pornography rackets, unlawful gaming, the transportation of illegal immigrants and the corruption of officials; and there are those regulatory offences that involve less obvious criminality [!]; for example the property developer who enormously increases the value of his land by demolishing a listed building or cutting down protected trees ... The profits made out of this last method of transgressing the law can be enormous and the fines imposed are frequently derisory in comparison; the fine which can be imposed is often a very cheap price to pay for the profit made.

An attempt was made to deal with serious victim-crime by the introduction ... of the Criminal Bankruptcy Order. Unfortunately this addition to the armoury of the criminal courts has proved almost wholly ineffective and is infrequently used ... With one exception, no serious attempt is made to redress the harm done and profit made by the second and third category of offending. The exception is the procedures adopted by the Inland Revenue and Customs and Excise which provide in effect for the confiscation of the gains of offenders guilty of offences of immediately recognisable criminality. While the effectiveness of these procedures may point a way forward to the more general use of comparable procedures in the criminal law their present unique position is socially significant because it reflects a disturbing discrimination between classes of offenders. By the payment of penalties the fraudulent evader of taxes escapes the obloquy of a criminal conviction, a privilege denied to the shoplifter or the embezzler. If society is content that a tax fraudster should escape conviction by the payment of a penalty, why not also the porn merchant, the corrupter of officials and the transporter of illegal immigrants, not to mention the type of petty offender referred to above.

If redress is seen as having greater importance in our criminal process and the victims of crime as having an essential role to play there are implications throughout the whole of that process; investigation, prosecution and disposal ...

Another aspect of victim-support which we have had at the front of our mind during our work is the danger that increasing the powers of the Court to redress the results of serious or profitable crime may have unintended consequences in relation to low income offenders. The ability of an offender to pay a monetary penalty, whether by way of fine, compensation or confiscation is something which we believe is of great importance if the infliction of the penalty is not to have the effect of driving the offender into further offending or of imposing undue hardship on his or her innocent family.

Notwithstanding these difficulties, the Hodgson Committee ultimately recommended the extended recognition within the criminal justice system of victims' interests and the greater accommodation of compensation and profit-stripping. The report met with a positive institutional response in the Criminal Justice Act 1988, which provided for forfeiture and the confiscation of proceeds of offences (ss 69–89), and made changes in the provision for compensation of victims by offenders (ss 104–107: see Miers 1989), notably in extending the range of compensable injuries to include death and imposing a duty on courts to give reasons why they have not made an order in any case in which they have power to do so. The 1988 Act also provided for the Criminal Injuries Compensation scheme to be placed on a statutory footing (ss 108–117); however, this part of the Act was not brought into force, and it was not until the Criminal Injuries Compensation Act 1995 that a statutory basis was established – a long-delayed achievement given the rhetorical commitment to 'victims' rights' encapsulated in the *Victims' Charter*. Compensation paid directly to victims by offenders is, conversely, an increasingly significant practice, at least at the level of official endorsement. It is mandated by ss 130–134 of the Powers of Criminal Courts (Sentencing) Act 2000. In 1998, over half of offenders convicted at Magistrates' Courts of indictable offences of criminal damage were ordered to pay compensation; in the case of those convicted of offences of violence, 44% and 19% in Magistrates' and Crown Courts respectively were the subject of compensation orders (Ashworth 2000: 3). However, between 1990 and 1999 – a period during which unemployment levels were falling – the proportionate use of compensation orders fell in both Magistrates' and Crown Courts, apparently as a result of sentencers' reluctance to impose such orders on those who lack the means to pay (Cavadino and Dignan 2002: 133). Moreover, the larger questions of social justice and about the functions and priorities of the criminal process raised by Hodgson have yet to be addressed.

III.c.   'Real' crime and selective enforcement

The importance of perceptions of what constitutes 'real' property crime in criminal enforcement has always been considerable: recognition of this fact is the counterpart of recognising that white collar crime has been marginalised. Law-makers have, on occasion, prescribed draconian penalties for certain forms of property offending which could be seen as forms of protest and thus as threatening to the social order (Thompson 1975). However, their execution has not always matched the original intention, as is illustrated by Hay's discussion of the use of the prerogative of mercy in the eighteenth century (Hay 1975: 40–49). Hay argues that the existence of wide discretion to pardon acted to legitimate a system which is fundamentally loaded against the interests of the propertiless. Such examples reveal the significance of law's ideological functions, and the limits on its perceived legitimacy, reflected in middle-class juries' frequent refusals to convict as property laws became unduly brutal towards the end of the eighteenth century (see Rudé 1985: Ch 7). The extraordinary degree of discretion in both prosecution and sentencing of criminal cases still enables enforcement agencies to treat with special severity property offences which sit squarely within the social ideas of 'real crime' propagated by state and media (Cook 1989). In the following extract, Levi comments on the particular (often 'privatised' and deferential) modes of enforcement developed around white collar crime and the political implications of these developments:

M Levi, *Regulating Fraud* (1987) pp 354–357

Post-industrial society is characterized by a desperate search on the part of government to find responsible non-governmental bodies to carry out key regulatory functions. The inspection of factories in the nineteenth century was a comparatively easy task; hours of work, and health and safety provisions were visible, even if they were not vigorously enforced. But technological changes and increasing consumerism mean that it becomes harder and harder to tell whether or not a rule is being violated. How do we know if food sold to the public contains contaminated and/or banned substances? This, at least, is a problem that can be resolved by forensic analysis, if anyone reports it or if government or commercial compliance officers inspect it. But how can we tell if insurance or securities are being sold by an unauthorized person? Or if a director or professional is engaged in insider dealing? For tasks like this, social control must be dispersed and, at least in part, privatized. To borrow from Foucault (Foucault, 1977), a new 'carceral archipelago' – i.e. a new area of imprisonment – must be created within the metaphorical 'punitive city'. Thus, 'responsible corporations' – those with a comparatively good track record of violations – are permitted to police their own health and safety violations, leaving (reduced) resources to be focused upon the higher risk firms; S[elf] R[egulating] O[rganizations]s, set up alongside the established professional bodies, police their members who in turn have their own corporate compliance officers: upperworld community policing, with as few state police officers as possible to upset the delicate mechanisms of control.

For the remainder of society, however, this sort of strategy is labelled in advance as being doomed to failure. It is a common misunderstanding in some circles that large numbers of police and extensive police powers are positively desired to police the working-class city. This is foolish: self-policing is always preferable. But the family defects and the other pathologies of the poor give them (and us) inadequate protection against the forces of greed. Their crimes are highly visible; their police are already in place; there are all too few responsible bodies – schools, churches, youth clubs, football supporters' clubs (for the 'true' soccer-lovers) – to do the control work that is necessary. Fortunately, there are other regulatory factors, – work prospects for some; social-security benefits for others; leisure activities (or, in the case of television and video, inactivities); narcotics; and even, perhaps, the 'black economy' – which serve to counteract the risk of revolt that is 'caused' by the ineffectiveness of family, school, and religion. We see now why we need the police: even in Japan, with its increasing geographical mobility and recently privatized families, social disorganization is rife. So Foucault's punitive city was designed to regulate the workers and the unemployed, because they were the dangerous classes from whom 'social problems' … originated. Or so it was said.

But now we have a different set of disciplinary problems, created by people who live, not in the slums or even the suburbs of the punitive city, but in leafy Oxfordshire villages, … from which their Porsches zoom forth at 5 am en route for the City … They work hard, sustained by adrenalin … as they play on the great financial casinos of the world with other people's money. What if they break the law? Well, with a bit of luck, nobody will notice, and 'everybody knows' that there are strong economic reasons why insider dealing is actually beneficial to the markets, though governments are forced to act tough because the public are ignorant and might misunderstand what was going on. But as for corporate embezzlement, computer fraud, commercial credit fraud, etc., there is general agreement that something must be done … Thus we see the intensification of surveillance within the commercial City …

This shape of regulatory things to come is naturally overdrawn: for to stop the embezzlers and the money-launderers completely would make life too uncomfortable for the money-makers, and in a fast-changing global market in which, once behind, we may never catch up, we all depend upon the money-makers … So although we may try to develop our upperworld equivalent of the punitive city, we cannot try too hard: for whether they are market-makers, first class chefs or Presidential advisers, those who are socially useful and create our wealth have to be allowed the occasional peccadillo. The ironic circle is complete: to fund the punitive city for those who are too young or too old or too ill-equipped to join the ever-shrinking ranks of the merchants, or the labouring poor, or the 'middling people', we must give the City the latitude to police itself, even if this means that the striving for prosperity triumphs over law. Persistent offenders who steal £1 go to prison; persistent insider dealers who steal £10 million pay back the money – perhaps in addition to a substantial fine – on the rare occasions that they are caught. De maximis non curat lex: for the greatest things, the law provides no remedy.

The specific issues of discrimination in favour of white collar crime in prosecution and sentencing are difficult to address, in that the data available are susceptible of many different interpretations. For example, do statistics which on the face of it suggest a fairly lenient treatment of 'white collar' fraudsters relative to the value of frauds as opposed, say, to thefts, reflect a special openness to some arguments from mitigation, the skill of the lawyers engaged by middle-class defendants, the shorter criminal records of fraud defendants (which may itself reflect differential patterns of enforcement) or other factors? Cook's research, however, reveals important contradictions in official responses to tax and social security fraud:

D Cook, *Rich Law, Poor Law: Different Responses to Tax and Supplementary Benefit Fraud* (Open University Press, 1989) p 160

In 1983, 268 Social Security offenders were imprisoned compared to 32 tax law offenders, and this despite the Revenue's aim of seeking harsh deterrent punishments for its most severe fraudsters. But is should also be stressed that over 8,000 benefit fraudsters also acquired criminal records in that year. Even though significant numbers of tax defaulters are dealt with through the imposition of compounded financial penalties, this does not involve the publicity and effective criminalization suffered by benefit fraudsters, who are far more likely to undergo court proceedings.

pp 165–168

There is a common assumption that the differential treatment of tax and benefit fraud derives from disparities in the offenders' relative 'ability to pay' ... It is often asserted that this explains both the high rate of prosecution of poorer fraudsters by the DHSS and the comparably low rates of prosecution (coupled with emphasis of financial settlement) by the Inland Revenue where richer fraudsters are concerned. However, this argument ignores that fact that the poorest members of society do pay for their fiddles, both in reparation to the DHSS through deductions from benefit, and in reparation to society through the courts, where in 1983 62% of benefit fraudsters were also ordered to pay fines ...

... Until 1980 [DHSS] practice followed the rule that any deductions from benefit made in respect of overpayments should not reduce the claimant's income to below the basic supplementary benefit level, regarded as the 'poverty line'. But current regulations enable up to £6.80 to be deducted from the weekly benefit of ... claimants admitting fraud ... [I]t is difficult to see how benefit fraud is deterred by the use of recovery methods which can reduce a claimant's income to £6.80 below the poverty line and, if criminal proceedings ensue, possibly involve a fine imposed by the courts in addition: under such circumstances fiddling benefits or other crimes may ironically become the only means of financial survival.

Taxpayers are almost by definition better able to pay financial penalties than benefit claimants ... [Yet] the taxpayers' ability to repay tax lost and to pay additional compounded penalties (if appropriate) is used as a justification for 'sparing the taxpayer's feelings' and for the adoption of an essentially non-prosecution policy ... Officials were particularly aware of the relatively extensive publicity which 'scrounging' attracts in comparison to tax evasion. But publicity is inextricably linked to the reporting of criminal proceedings in the courts, and if tax fraud cases do not reach the courts, then public awareness of the extent and costs of the problem will be minimal ... [The] rationale for the relatively 'quiet' treatment of the tax fraudster is closely linked to the mitigation offered in court ... , that social disgrace is in itself sufficient punishment for tax evaders. The notion that a fraudster has 'suffered enough' merely through the public exposure of his/her crimes is one which is not applied to supplementary benefit fraudsters. Indeed, the media treatment of them suggests just the opposite! It seems that in order to 'pay' for one's crimes through personal suffering and disgrace, one has to have some social standing to lose: hence these discourses are not available to justify lenience towards benefit fraudsters ...

... [A]lthough the DHSS at present officially operates a policy designed to reduce numbers of prosecutions and seek 'benefit savings', effectively it still prosecutes over 8,000 supplementary benefit claimants per year; this is in stark contrast to the official 'selective' approach to Revenue prosecutions which effectively resulted in only 459 prosecutions in 1986–7 ... Moreover, the justificatory rationale behind both policies – deterrence – is not applied equally to tax and benefit fraudsters.

Judicial responses (and sentencing practice) towards tax and supplementary fraud are based on entirely different premises: the analysis of discourses used in court demonstrated crucial differences in the assumptions being made about claimant and taxpayer. In some cases it seemed that tax evaders were presumed to be victims – either of the ethos of the business and corporate world, or victims of the disgrace of their fellow citizens – as a result of Revenue prosecution. According to magistrates observed in this study, in cases of supplementary benefit fraud the victim is the taxpayer (who was seen to finance benefit payments), not the benefit fraudster. The tax fraudster is represented as at best folk-hero, at worst a victim of the taxman.

At the heart of the contradictions in policy and in practice ... is the ideological representation of the taxpayer as a 'giver' to the state and the supplementary benefit claimant as a 'taker' from the state (and thus, ultimately, from the compliant taxpayer).

Despite the election of a Labour Government in May 1997, there is little evidence to suggest that the balance of political concern as between these two forms of fraud has fundamentally changed.

III.d.   'Intangible' property crime and the criminal process

Finally, the fact that certain sorts of property crime present special problems of detection and proof is often at issue in the development of the enforcement process. The following extracts present a variety of examples related to this issue:

H Edelhertz and C Rogovin, *A National Strategy for Containing White Collar Crime* (Lexington Books, 1980) pp 4, 30–31

The problem of dealing with white-collar crime is further compounded by the fact that there is no clear separation between criminal, civil, and regulatory responses. Precisely the same behaviour may be, and often is, subject to the same remedies. For example, the decision to prosecute a securities fraud criminally or a banking violation criminally will depend relatively more on the prosecutor's evaluation of the evidence than on the inherent characteristics of the behaviour being assessed. Unlike street crime or conventional property theft where the questions for law-enforcement authorities are what happened and who was responsible, in this area the question is whether there is sufficient proof of wrongful intent to warrant criminal prosecution even where what happened and who caused it to happen are not in dispute. In white-collar cases there are usually noncriminal alternatives available that make it easier to decline criminal prosecution, for example civil action, regulatory agency action, administration measures, and private litigation. Such actions can be undertaken by victims if they have personal resources to launch the efforts or can make it attractive for private counsel to enlist in their causes on a contingent-fee basis. [*Note the assumption that these options are not also available in relation to 'blue collar' property crime! Also note that contingency fees were until recently contrary to professional rules of practice in this country, and can now only be arranged under limited circumstances (which include insolvency cases).*]

Anybody who has a vivid sense of the limited capabilities of the criminal justice system [will worry that] arrayed against the vast agenda of white-collar offenses, the criminal-justice system seems too small, too clumsy and too fragile. It is inconceivable that the criminal-justice system could deal with any substantial portion of the individual incidents of fraud, embezzlement, graft, and abuses of authority that could occur in a society as large and complex and as wedded to the principle of caveat emptor as ours. Part of the problem is the sheer number of offenses that are likely to occur. But another part of the problem arises from the enormous expense of preparing cases of this type of prosecution.

Moreover ... one does not need too much experience with the actual operations of the criminal-justice system to understand that the men [sic] who work that system face acute personal dilemmas and risks in attacking institutions that represent significant economic, governmental or political power. In enforcing environmental laws against a firm that threatens to close down if they are prosecuted, the criminal-justice official feels that he is dealing with a larger policy choice than he would like to deal with ... The blade of the criminal law is simply apt to shatter when it is brought into contact with powerful political and economic institutions.

Organisation for Economic Co-operation and Development (OECD), *Computer-Related Crime* (OECD Publications, 1986) p 8

One of the factors inherent in information and telecommunications technologies is that their misuse can leave no trace; but law is traditionally based on texts and material evidence of acts which, for computer-related crime, are often unavailable. This makes it difficult to assess the scale of and to detect and prosecute computer-related crime. The amendment of laws on the admissibility of evidence to take the supporting technology into account, could thus assist in prosecuting offences ... The victim may be no clearer than the offender of his rights and obligations and may not be prepared to divulge information if the consequence could be to threaten a market position or commercial credibility. Many victims feel that they have not taken all the necessary measures to protect their new computer based asset, on cost–benefit grounds ... Quantifying the damage suffered can often be difficult, which again raises the issue of the 'new economic values' that are now being created.

A Bequai, *White Collar Crime* (Lexington Books, 1978) p 171

The cost of litigation in this country [the USA] exceeds the annual gross national product of many small nations. Litigation of every kind has become extremely expensive. The prosecution of one antiwar figure ran over $3 million. White-collar crimes have proven, more than other forms of litigation, to be extremely costly and time consuming. Voluminous pages of documents, numerous witnesses, and armies of attorneys are usually involved. At present, few prosecutorial offices have the funds and manpower to handle these costly and time-consuming cases. A complex fraud case could easily bankrupt a local prosecutorial office. Unless the cost of litigation is brought down, white-collar felons may thwart the law by simply making it too costly to prosecute them ...

Our entire penal model was designed to deal with traditional criminals, those of the lower classes who were involved in common-law crimes. For example, in deciding on whether to place an individual on probation, a judge looks at such things as the offender's emotional maturity; use of drugs, alcohol, or other dangerous substances; his family status and stability; and the neighborhood from which he comes or intends to live in. The judge also considers such things as the offender's employment plans. When applying this criterion to a convicted white-collar felon, it becomes meaningless; it is not a true yardstick of whether he continues to pose a threat to society. A more realistic yardstick is needed; the penal model itself needs to be reviewed ... If we are to curb white-collar crime, it is not enough to simply modernize the investigatory and prosecutorial machineries. We need to also look at the judiciary and at the many laws that we presently have on our books. Many of these are antiquated and create environments in which frauds flourish ...

In this country, the Law Commission's Working Paper and subsequent report on Computer Misuse (Law Commission 1988, 1989) showed a remarkable lack of concern with issues of process and proof. However, the particular procedural problems raised by fraud trials have been scrutinised by a special inquiry chaired by Lord Roskill:

Roskill, *Report of the Fraud Trials Committee* (HMSO, 1986) pp 140–143

... [Fraudsters] exercise great skill in conducting their operations, and may use companies or bank accounts overseas through which funds are channelled. These skills are used to conceal the substance of dishonest transactions by shrouding them in a form which makes them appear convincing to a layman. There is often a network of companies in which the identities of the beneficial owners are impossible to discover. There may be an elaborate structure of agencies, contracts and accounts which make it difficult to discover whether it is a legal and honest framework designed to cope with complex trading and fiscal circumstances or a labyrinth designed to conceal deceit ...

When the case eventually comes to trial the juror is faced with many difficulties. He is initially likely to be unfamiliar with the procedure. There may be many defendants, and multiple charges against each ... The background against which frauds are alleged to have been committed – the sophisticated world of high finance and international trading – is probably a mystery to most or all of the jurors ... A knowledge of accountancy or book-keeping may be essential to an understanding of the case. If any juror has such knowledge, it is by chance ... The evidence before the jury may run to hundreds, or even thousands, of documents ... Little attempt may have been made to summarise or simplify the evidence. In the largest cases the photocopying bill alone may run to thousands of pounds ...

Fraud trials often involve exceedingly lengthy hearings of weeks and months, and they form a substantial proportion of the longest trials. A survey carried out for the Committee showed that in the five years from 1979 to 1983 there was a yearly average of 26 fraud trials each lasting for longer than 20 working days ... The longest single fraud trial lasted 137 working days, which was the retrial of a case of similar length ... The disruption to the life of a juror as a result of a lengthy trial is serious but is not however, the major issue. The problem of maintaining an adequate degree of concentration for long periods, and consequently of understanding the issues is profound ...

There is another factor to which we attach great importance. We made enquiries whether prosecuting authorities refrained from prosecuting in some cases because of the difficulty of presenting them to juries selected at random in a way which the juries would be able to comprehend. We were told that this was rarely the sole reason, but that it was sometimes a major contributory factor in deciding not to proceed with a prosecution. We also had evidence that the difficulty of presenting a complex case often resulted in a decision to opt for less serious charges than the facts warranted.

... [I]n this report we recommend improvement in the investigation and preparation of cases; changes in the remuneration structure for the Bar designed to favour proper case preparation; an alternative procedure designed to bring cases more quickly to the Crown Court pending the Government's decision on the abolition of committal proceedings; further development of the pre-trial review designed to simplify cases and isolate the real grounds of difference; the abolition of the right of peremptory challenge [of jurors]; substantial changes in the rules of evidence; a higher standard of presentation at the hearing; the use of visual aids; the selection of judges with special experience. In sum, these proposals represent a fundamental overhaul of the court-room process, which most of our witnesses regard as long overdue.

Several of Lord Roskill's recommendations have been implemented. The Criminal Justice Act 1987 (CJA 1987), Pt 1 set up a Serious Fraud Office consisting of lawyers, accountants and police officers. The Office is intended to generate greater confidence in the City of London by investigating more effectively than can the police serious frauds which call for an expert and integrated approach, and by raising the level of successful prosecutions by preparing cases more imaginatively for presentation to juries (Wood 1989). The CJA 1987 also provided for the immediate transfer of serious and complex fraud cases to the Crown Court's management (s 4) and for preparatory hearings to facilitate the presentation of such cases to the jury (ss 7, 9). The Criminal Justice Act 1988 (CJA 1988) modified evidential rules (Pts II and III), notably by allowing for the presentation of evidence by video link (s 32), and abolished the right of peremptory challenge of jurors (s 118). The widely publicised failure of many high-profile serious fraud cases through the 1990s, and in particular the dismissal of a number of cases because of procedural complexities which made it impossible to put the issues fairly or comprehensibly to the jury suggests, however, that the difficulties identified by Lord Roskill are far from being resolved. Debate continues about the proper framework for serious fraud trials, while the Serious Fraud Office's special powers in relation to collecting evidence have drawn widespread criticism from a civil libertarian direction. Such debates raise a number of issues about the wisdom of framing reforms *ad hoc* to deal with difficulties of enforcement in particular areas. On the one hand, it is widely accepted that fraud trials (and particularly those complex trials which often do involve 'white collar' defendants) pose special problems of proof. On the other hand, the relaxing of procedural safeguards such as the right to silence (Criminal Justice and Public Order Act 1994, ss 34–37), the abolition of peremptory challenge and modifications to rules of evidence (CJA 1988, Pt II), may be thought to present a risk of a general lowering of the level of such safeguards in the process as a whole. Should a lack of understanding of psychology and psychiatry undermine the jury's role in a murder trial where the defendant pleads diminished responsibility, for example? One wonders whether the major barriers to the successful prosecution of these cases lie primarily in technical procedural factors rather than in underlying factors having to do with the construction of 'real crime' and the lack of social consensus about the key legal concept of dishonesty (cf **section II.a.ii.** above). As we saw in **Chapter 1.I.b.** and **III.b.** the Criminal Justice Bill 2003 once again places this issue on the immediate political agenda, since it proposes to dispense with jury trials in long and complex cases. Levi's analysis of the implications of Lord Roskill's recommendation that jury trial be abolished remains instructive:

M Levi, *Regulating Fraud* (1987) pp 301–311

Most controversially of all, the Committee – Walter Merricks dissenting – recommended that in 'complex fraud cases' – whose precise definition is regarded as impossible – there should be no right to jury trial and that either prosecution or defence counsel should be entitled to apply to a High Court judge for the accused to be tried before a Fraud Trials Tribunal consisting of a specially chosen judge ... and two 'lay members' who shall be 'selected from a panel of persons who have skill and expertise in business generally and experience of complex business transactions' (147) ... The verdicts of this Tribunal would be by majority vote – so the judge could be outvoted – but no dissenting opinions would be stated or acknowledged (151) ...

If implemented – as is not government policy at present – this might have a dramatic effect upon the current temptations for trial judges to direct acquittals. This is not to deny there are many legal issues which arise in fraud cases upon which expert judges may reasonably disagree, but given the caustic comments by the Court of Appeal on some judicial summings-up, inexperienced trial judges may find it less traumatic to take the view that there is 'no case to answer' than to proceed to sum up with a full jury decision. Though there is no hard evidence as to the relative importance of these factors, it has been suggested that this, combined with prosecutorial misjudgments and witness disillusion (or threats or bribery) may account for my research finding (Levi, 1987:Ch.6) that most complex cases ending in acquittal were thrown out by the judge rather than by the jury. Unfortunately, it is not clear what would count as adequate reasoning on the part of the Fraud Trials Tribunal ...

We are asked to make a leap of faith to agree that the specially selected judges and 'lay members' will unquestionably have the 'proper understanding' which jurors are alleged to lack. Moreover, unless we are to move towards the position where dishonesty becomes a matter of law ... rather than of fact ... there remains the difficulty of how we are to know what ordinary people regard as dishonest if we do not have ordinary people making the judgement but instead have a judge and members of professional elites making it. In other words, the Fraud Trials Tribunal may be better at applying legal rules to the facts of the case ... but however independent-minded and impartial their members may be their views about dishonesty may be open to criticism. This indeed is the moral and political danger of the proposal, just as it is in self-regulation by the City. If there is an acquittal, it may look as if this is an elite-group 'fix' ...

There remain ways of making fraud trials better without abolishing the jury. The least contentious changes in the trial of fraud are the proposed provision of glossaries and the increased use of audio-visual aids to assist juror understanding ... Another approach – not suggested by Roskill – is to allow jurors to play a more active role in court, instead of being discouraged from asking questions by lawyers who regard them as a nuisance or as children who should speak only when spoken to ...

It may be argued that the procedural safeguards which are threatened are them-selves of little instrumental value to defendants and serve rather the ideological function of legitimising a criminal process which is already loaded towards conviction, particularly in certain sorts of cases (see McBarnet 1981). If Bennett and Feldman (1981) are right that the structure of criminal trials is similar to that of story-telling, and that the outcome depends primarily on the relative plausibility of prosecution and defence accounts as judged by the tribunal in the light of cultural norms, expectations and frames of meaning, the articulate middle-class defendant may always be at an advantage no matter what the technical details of procedural safeguards (see further **Chapter 1.I.b.**).

These are just some of the important issues which arise from a consideration of the practices of the criminal process in responding to threats to property interests. Just as the boundaries between property offences and other offences are blurred, the issues we have identified in this section also arise in other areas of enforcement. Nevertheless, the interwoven features of situational prevention, the diversification of institutions of control, the class and other divisions in enforcement practices and in political responses to the difficulties in addressing certain forms of property crime serve to raise issues of fundamental importance for the system as a whole. These have to do with the nature and site of responsibility for crime, the role of victims, the relation between civil and criminal law and the effect of socio-economic and cultural differences in the criminal process.

Our reflections on the protection of property again lead us away from a simple view of criminal law as even-handedly protecting a conception of valued interests underpinned by social consensus. Rather, our study suggests a broader and subtler set of functions for criminal law, encompassing the expression and underpinning of the perceived social legitimacy of a particular conception of the interests which it serves. Criminal law defends not property at large, but certain kinds of – highly unevenly distributed – property. It thereby defends not only property, but the power of certain interests and the authority of the social order.

FURTHER READING

Carlen, Pat and Cook, Dee (eds) (1989) *Paying for Crime* (Open University Press).

Clarke, Ronald V (ed) (1997) *Situational Crime Prevention* (2nd edn, Perpetuity Press).

Fisse, Brent and Braithwaite, John (1983) *The Impact of Publicity on Corporate Offenders* (State University of New York Press).

Heal, K and Laycock, G (eds) (1986) *Situational Crime Prevention* (HMSO).

Justice (Report) (1984), *Fraud Trials*, London.

Lacey, Nicola and Zedner, Lucia (1995) 'Discourses of Community in Criminal Justice', Journal of Law and Society, p 301.

Nelken, David (2002) 'White-Collar Crime' in Maguire et al (eds) *The Oxford Handbook of Criminology* (3rd edn, Oxford University Press) p 844.

Pease, Ken (2002) 'Crime Reduction' in Maguire et al (eds) *The Oxford Handbook of Criminology* (3rd edn, Oxford University Press) p 947.

Sieh, E H (1987) 'Garment Workers: Perceptions of Inequality and Employee Theft' 27 British Journal of Criminology, p 174

Taylor, Ian (1997) 'The Political Economy of Crime' in Maguire et al (eds) *The Oxford Handbook of Criminology* (2nd edn, Oxford University Press) p 265.

von Hirsch, Andrew, Bottoms, A E, Burney, E and Wikstrom, P-O (1999) *Criminal Deterrence: an analysis of recent research* (Oxford, Hart Publishing).

von Hirsch, Andrew, Garland, David and Wakefield, Alison (2000) *Ethical and Social Perspectives on Situational Crime Prevention* (Oxford, Hart Publishing).

Chapter 5

Constructions of sexuality and bodily autonomy: trust and integrity

V.   Euthanasia
   a.   Respect for life and death
   b.   Consent and necessity

I.   The social construction of sexuality and bodily autonomy

The state, through law, exercises a significant influence over bodily autonomy in general and the construction of sexuality in particular. Laws regulate, for example, the age of consent to sexual intercourse, and the nature of consent required for medical examinations, cosmetic and ritual procedures such as tattooing and circumcision, and for procedures in relation to childbirth and reproduction. Criminal laws embody norms of sexual practice and regulate the right of citizens to engage in sexual activity which is not consistent with those norms. Legal interventions in these areas inevitably confront the blurred social boundaries between 'legitimate' and 'illegitimate', 'normal' and 'abnormal' conduct, and raise in a particularly vivid way questions about the proper scope of criminal law.

Steven Box, *Power, Crime and Mystification* (Tavistock, 1983) p 121

Nearly one hundred years ago, Durkheim wrote that suicide is 'merely the exaggerated form of common practices' and that it 'appears quite another matter once its unbroken connection is recognised with acts, on the one hand of courage and devotion, on the other of imprudence and clear neglect'. This relatively simple, but radical idea – that there is considerable overlap between deviance and convention, rather than the former being distinctly different and opposite to the latter – inspired later generations of sociologists ... [A] similar lesson can be obtained from considering how 'normal' sexual encounters merge imperceptibly into sexual assaults of which rape is the most serious, and how the former provide the ingredients out of which the latter can emerge.

The categorisation of many of the issues dealt with in this chapter presents difficult decisions. Should rape, sexual assault and the sexual transmission of disease be thought of not as specifically sexual offences but as crimes of violence, and hence included in **Chapter 6**? Clearly, the latter offences may be regarded as involving violence, though they are equally clearly connected with cultural images of male and female sexuality and of bodily autonomy. The non-consensual element of rape and many forms of sexual assault might be thought to separate them, in turn, from regulation of areas such as prostitution and pornography, which have symbolic and public order dimensions. We have grouped these offences together in this chapter because each of them raises issues about bodily autonomy and, in particular, about consent and the conditions under which consent can be said to be 'valid'. Consent becomes a

key concept when we look at the extent to which the state regulates our autonomy. Can we choose to exercise control over our bodies, even to the extent of
choosing to die? Suicide is no longer itself an offence, but aiding and abetting a
suicide is, and euthanasia is not formally condoned. The notion of *autonomy* is
the theme that binds together the wide-ranging discussion contained in this
chapter. This is not, of course, to imply that the offences considered here are
the only ones in which considerations of autonomy are important. Similar
issues arise in relation to many other areas of criminal law, and notably that of
drugs – tobacco and alcohol are not regulated to the same degree as other, in
some cases less harmful, drugs: see **Chapter 3.III.a.**

It may seem easier to explain why societies develop ways of enforcing property
rights, maintaining public order and controlling violence than it is to
understand the development of systems controlling the forms of behaviour
considered below. However, it is often possible to detect in these areas of state-
regulated conduct an underlying concern with property, public order or
violence. The regulation of sexuality plays an important role in maintaining the
institution of the family, which is of economic as well as social significance.
Nonconformity is threatening and displays of culturally inappropriate behaviour
are often controlled through the use of public order mechanisms, such as the
power to bind a person over to be of good behaviour, and anti-social behaviour
orders (**Chapter 2.II.d.** and **Chapter 3.I.c.**) or through mental health
procedures. Gender difference plays an important role in the maintenance of
prevailing social and economic institutions; this is reflected in the law of rape
and its enforcement. Laws do not always support women who do not consent to
sexual intercourse. Through lifestyles such as prostitution – and, until recently,
through marriage – they effectively lose that choice. Criminal law has often
reflected an image of rape which arguably demonstrates a concern with maintaining the sexual status quo rather than with asserting the right of women to
autonomy in sexual and other matters.

Similar tensions are played out in the areas of prostitution and pornography.
The ideologies of a free-market economy and of free expression are allowed to
obscure the exploitation inherent in these activities. Some of the most difficult
moral questions arise here. They make us pause to think about the underlying
justification for using criminal law as a coercive form. At the same time it is
noticeable that much of the moral debate ignores the dimension of gender,
obscuring the fact that these apparently consensual activities may be particularly
damaging to women.

The regulation of reproduction contributes to the construction of sexuality as
well as limiting bodily autonomy more generally. Contraception and abortion
are not the only relevant issues. Criminal laws are invoked to prohibit the
commercialisation of surrogacy arrangements. Fear of an 'attack of the clones'
has also led to the banning of reproductive cloning (Human Reproductive

Cloning Act 2001). There are interesting contrasts here between the perceived need to prevent the exploitation of surrogate mothers and the prevailing view that pornography and prostitution need be controlled only in so far as they offend the public gaze, or have public order implications.

In the last section of this chapter we move to the broader aspect of bodily autonomy involved in the question of euthanasia. This connects closely with the issue of medical non-treatment (**Chapter 6.III.b.**), and illustrates how the issues raised by criminal regulation are not clear-cut: categorisation itself plays a significant role in the construction of crime. Whereas in **Chapter 6** non-treatment is used as a basis for considering criminal law's construction of violence, in this chapter our focus is on what it tells us about the law's (ambivalent) attitude to the role of human autonomy in circumscribing the limits of the criminal sanction.

The concept of autonomy running through each of the sections is a broad one which pulls in two directions. Bodily autonomy can demand protection in two senses: first, protection of one's own choices and, second, protection against interference by others. Protection of one's own choices can include freedom to engage in (possibly) 'self-harming' activities, such as prostitution, surrogacy and euthanasia. Protection against interference by others would mean prevention of rape, as well as sexual and other forms of assault. Although these two senses of protection are two sides of the same coin, it is useful to conceive of them as different tensions within debates about criminal regulation of bodily autonomy. If, for example, we are considering euthanasia, the initial protection we might seek is the freedom to make one's own decision about death. But in order to achieve that freedom, we would also be saying that a person is entitled not to be subject to medical or other interference which could prolong life. We are not here pre-judging the debate, but rather pointing to the different conceptions of autonomy which might be invoked.

Another important aspect of human autonomy consists in having the means to exercise a formally protected right or freedom. Contraception and abortion, for example, are dependent on the priorities of medical research and on the availability and accessibility of services. The capacity effectively to consent or to withhold consent may depend on information (as in medical contexts) or power (as in sexual contexts). Yet many debates canvassed in this chapter – particularly in legal literature – obscure vital questions about the positive conditions necessary for the effective exercise of autonomy.

Finally, the idea of autonomy raises questions about the extent to which consent or voluntariness do, or should, operate to delimit criminal regulation. Though in the law of rape, consent marks the limits of criminal law, this is not the case in many other areas considered in this chapter. The Surrogacy Arrangements Act 1985 is one example (see **section IV.b.** below); another is the courts' response to sado-masochistic practices (see **section II.a.ii.** below).

Autonomy is closely connected to the notion of trust. Given the centrality of trust to social interaction and our perceptions of individuals and institutions, it is surprising that it has escaped the same level of scrutiny that autonomy has attracted. Trust is a complex multi-dimensional concept, but may be broadly classified as two-fold: interpersonal and social trust. *Interpersonal trust* revolves around interaction between individuals, for example, the intimate and emotional ties of family and friends. *Social trust*, on the other hand, involves the ways and extent that we trust institutions such as the criminal justice system. Giddens and Beck have written about the increasing scepticism towards experts, expert knowledge and expert institutions in a 'risk society' (Giddens 1990; Beck 1992). Despite different theories, there is something of a consensus that there has been a shift in attitudes towards and perceptions of experts, the system they work within, and the institutions which regulate them. As Onora O'Neill reminds us, discussion of declining trust is something of a cliché of our times (O'Neill 2002). Given that in one sense we have no choice but to trust, this phenomenon may more properly be described as a culture of suspicion.

It is perhaps unsurprising that suspicion sits comfortably in criminal justice systems, particularly those driven by crime control concerns. However, the sense of a breakdown of trust has gathered momentum in recent years. The sheer volume of criminal justice legislation is itself a commentary on this, and on one level, most of this book revolves around questions of trust. However, it seems particularly pertinent to think about trust in a chapter on bodily integrity. Reforms in the Sexual Offences Bill 2003 reflect increased suspicion at both individual and social levels. In terms of individuals, suspicion underlies the new offence of sexual grooming and explicitly so in relation to breach of trust offences for those in positions of authority. The reforms are also an attempt to restore broken trust in the system. Continued criticism of the low conviction rate for rape, as well as the negative experiences of rape victims, provides the background to the (belated) proposed structured scheme of consent and the partial reversal of the burden of proof. Such controversial changes are an admission of declining faith in the system, and reflect a (sometimes misplaced) form of paternalism.

Similarly, abortion and euthanasia may also be framed in terms of trust. Do we trust individuals to make decisions at the edges of life? In addition, reflex legislation such as the Human Organs Transplants Act 1989 and the Human Reproductive Cloning Act 2001 are striking examples of suspicion of money and markets in body parts and of biomedical advances. Prostitution and pornography are generally viewed as issues of autonomy, but may equally be framed in terms of how far we trust certain types of behaviour.

Trust appears in another final sense: how far should we trust that the reforms will deliver? To what extent will they meet the liberal and radical feminist arguments set out in **section I.b.** of this chapter? Will they increase the trust of such victims in the criminal justice system? Without pre-judging the debate, there is room for legitimate suspicion. For example, substantive reforms to the law of rape may be undermined by prejudicial attitudes held about rape that persist at a number of different layers in the system. Recent history of law reform, particularly surrounding sexual history evidence, permits such pessimism.

I.a.   Attitudes to sexuality and autonomy

Before investigating these areas in more depth, it is useful to have an overview of contemporary social attitudes both to sexuality and regulation of the body. These attitudes are, of course, themselves socially constructed. Responses to all surveys are mediated by the setting in which the questions are asked, the type of questions, the presence of others during the questioning and so on. A classic example of this was the first British Crime Survey (Hough and Mayhew 1983), in which very little unreported sexual violence was disclosed to interviewers. Subsequent surveys have revealed far higher rates of such violence through the use of different interviewing techniques. As with all 'facts and figures', a cautionary note has to be entered. Within the framework of the caution, however, the social attitudes described below give us an insight into how bodily autonomy is constructed socially, as well as identifying some of the broad factors influencing attitudes to sexual and bodily autonomy over the last decade.

R Jowell et al, *British Social Attitudes, 9th Report* (Dartmouth, 1992) pp 123–124

As a number of previous reports in this series have shown, attitudes towards homosexuals became more censorious in the 1980s as public concern about AIDS mounted. As Brook has suggested, 'Our data cannot ... prove the link but they certainly imply a clear connection. Either that, or we are witnessing a selective return to more puritanical values, coincidentally on just those issues that are connected strongly in the public mind with AIDS'.

We do not as yet have a long enough series of questions on AIDS to explore attitude change, but a question on homosexuality has been asked regularly since the inception of the British Social Attitudes series. It forms part of the following set of questions on social relations:

If a man and a woman have sexual relations before marriage, what would your general opinion be?

What about a married person having sexual relations with someone other than his or her partner?

What about sexual relations between two adults of the same sex?

... [I]increased censoriousness towards homosexuality (and ... towards adultery and premarital sex) peaked in 1987, having risen from 50 per cent in 1983 to 64 per cent during the four year period when the initial impact of the arrival of AIDS was at its greatest. Since then attitudes have partially swung back, although not to their 1983 level.

...

In contrast, not only was the 1987 increase in censoriousness towards heterosexual sex outside marriage smaller in magnitude than that towards homosexuality, but the subsequent fall was also steeper. The net change, then, in sexual attitudes over the period was in a more permissive direction ...

Even more striking trends in a liberal direction are apparent in attitudes towards abortion. As with AIDS there has been considerable publicity, particularly over the Human Fertilisation and Embryology [Act] 1990 which specified time limits for the stage of a pregnancy at which abortions could legally be performed.

The British Social Attitudes surveys have regularly asked questions about seven different circumstances in which abortion might or might not be allowed, ranging from circumstances such as 'the woman might become pregnant as a result of rape', and 'the woman's health is seriously endangered by the pregnancy', to reasons of preference such as 'the couple agree they do not wish to have a child' and 'the woman decides on her own she does not wish to have a child'. Almost identical trends over time are revealed on all the items ...

Here we see net increases of 16 and 18 points in the proportions saying that abortion should be allowed by law. In this respect at least society certainly seems to have become more permissive.

In the 1996 social attitudes survey (Jowell et al, 11th Report, 1996), an attempt was made to relate patterns of permissive and censorious attitudes to demo-graphic and other social factors. Perhaps not surprisingly, the factors with by far the strongest impact on attitudes to both homo- and hetero-sexuality are a person's age and their underlying (authoritarian or libertarian) values and beliefs, with education, church attendance, gender and parental responsibility also significant (pp 34–40). The 2002/2003 survey revealed a continuing tolerance of homosexual sex perhaps as educational campaigns have gradually weakened the popular association of AIDS with male homosexuality. In 2000, 33% of respondents saw 'nothing wrong' with homosexuality, compared with 13% in 1985 (19th Report, 2002: 218). The social attitudes surveys demonstrate the fact that attitudes to sexual and bodily autonomy may shift significantly over relatively short periods of time. Although these attitudes do not tell us anything about whether particular legal regulations are justifiable, they do affect the context in which relevant legal frameworks operate. As attitudes to both abortion and homosexuality show, it would be naive to assume that attitudinal changes are directly or immediately influenced by legal changes: conversely, however, attitudes at variance with legal arrangements may on occasion make particular aspects of law difficult or even impossible to enforce.

I.b. Sexual freedom and sexual discipline

Any debate about the regulation of forms of behaviour presupposes a common understanding of the relevant phenomenon. As Foucault argues (1976: 49), it is a mistake to assume either that such social understanding is uncontested or that law is the only disciplinary mechanism in the production and control of sexuality:

> We must ... abandon the hypothesis that modern industrial societies ushered in an age of increased sexual repression. We have not only witnessed a visible explosion of unorthodox sexualities; but ... a deployment quite different from the law ... has ensured ... the proliferation of specific pleasures and the multiplication of disparate sexualities.

In a society which thinks of itself as liberal, the legal regulation of sexuality poses a number of distinctive issues: how can law justifiably be invoked to sanction apparently 'harmless' activities, and how far, if at all, may law be used to enforce conventional moral standards? The following extracts present a liberal approach to these issues and they form the background to the feminist approaches which follow (see also **Chapter 1.I.a.**).

P J Fitzgerald, *Criminal Law and Punishment* (Clarendon Press, 1962) pp 78–81

With regard to other classes of crimes ... it is not hard to find agreement as to the justification for their existence in law. Few could deny that a man has the right to defend himself against physical attack and to defend his property likewise against attack ... Nuisance is perhaps less easy to justify as a crime, but here again most people would accept the proposition that a person is entitled to protect himself to some extent against offensive activities; he has a right to demand that others do not, by producing unpleasant fumes, noise, and so on, render his life intolerably unpleasant. Offences against public decency are in the same case. People have a right to demand that certain behaviour which disgusts or nauseates them should not take place in public. With regard to nuisance and indecency, however, the offence to the person affronted has to be weighed against the hardship involved in preventing the person committing the offence from continuing the activity in question. The justification of the existence of all these types of crimes is based on the right of the individual to protect himself against certain types of harm; his private right is supplemented and to some extent supplanted by state prevention of these activities.

The punishment by law of offences of immorality can sometimes be justified on similar grounds. Some of these offences, like rape, involve physical assaults, and here the justification is the same as for ordinary offences of violence. Others, while free from violence, involve a measure of corruption, where one of the parties is young, inexperienced, or economically dependent on the other. The justification for punishing corruption is that even if it were admitted that everyone should be free to choose his own way of life, nevertheless the young and inexperienced should be protected against their own immaturity until they are old enough to appreciate what is involved in this choice. Sometimes the punishment of these offences can be supported on the ground that they are committed in such circumstances as to offend against public decency. This still leaves the case of those offences whose commission involves neither violence nor corruption nor indecency, viz. homosexual behaviour between consenting adults in private. [*This was written before the Sexual Offences Act 1967 partially legalised homosexual conduct; see **section III.a.ii.** below.*]

Such offences differ in one very important respect from ordinary crimes, in that it is only those who commit them that are obviously and directly affected. Such conduct is not other-regarding as is violence or dishonesty. No clear and direct attack is made on third parties by such behaviour. In order, therefore, to defend the imposition of penalties on those who behave in this way, it must either be shown that it is somehow good in itself to prevent people from so behaving or that their conduct does in reality affect other people, who consequently have a right to be protected against the harm caused by it. Not many champions are to be found in the first of these views. Enforced conformity to a moral code merely for the sake of such conformity would not generally be thought in these days to be in itself of any value. To force a person by fear and threat of punishment to act according to certain moral standards is not to make him act morally, though it could of course be argued that a man who was forced by law not to give way to certain sexual passions might end up resisting them purely for moral reasons. Today, however, the imposition by force of moral standards for their own sake is not generally accepted as defensible. Most people would agree with the Wolfenden Committee that the function of the law in this context is to preserve public order and decency, to protect the citizen against what is offensive and injurious, and to provide safeguards against corruption and exploitation. The committee concluded that private immorality should not be the concern of the law and recommended that homosexual behaviour between consenting adults in private should no longer be an offence.

Many people, however, while accepting the premise as to the proper function of the criminal law, would refuse to draw the same conclusion as the committee as to this particular problem. Such refusal is based on the view that such conduct, though not directly injurious to the citizen, is indirectly so. It has been argued that those who indulge in such practices with consenting adult partners may later extend their activities to corruption of the young. The Wolfenden Committee concluded here, however, that factual evidence did not support this proposition.

A different attempt to show that such behaviour is not self-regarding but is in fact injurious to others has been made by Lord Devlin, who denies the validity of the distinction between public and private morality. His main argument is that the established morality of a society is as necessary to its continued existence as are the institutions of government and that just as a society is justified in defending itself against subversive activities resulting in the overthrow of its government, so it is entitled to protect itself against the disintegration which would follow from the loosening of moral bonds resulting from failure to observe the rules of the established morality ...

[T]his analogy between sexual immorality and treason has been challenged, notably by Professor H. L. A. Hart, who points out that the argument rests on several unproved assumptions. In the first place there seems little evidence that failure to enforce sexual morality in the past has led to the disintegration of societies. Secondly, it is by no means established that the failure by some members of a society to observe certain rules of a moral code will lead to the abandonment of all the rules of the code by all the members of the society. Thirdly, mere failure to conform to a moral rule or standard is a quite different matter from a direct attack on an institution of the state; a closer parallel would be an attack on the moral standards made by a person advocating a change of attitude. This brings us to the next unproved assumption, viz. that a society is justified in resisting change, a view which would seem to entail that it is defensible to use the law to stifle criticism and reform and block the way of all peaceful change of the constitution and of all alteration of moral attitudes. Yet moral codes and political constitutions change without effecting the disintegration of society. Finally it is by no means clear that there in fact exists such unanimous moral agreement in our society on this matter as Devlin assumes; the established morality may well on closer inspection be found to be more like the Established Church, accepted in practice only by a minority of the citizen body.

Gilbert Geis, *Not the Law's Business* (National Institute of Mental Health, Washington, 1972) pp 4, 252

Some consensus is evident among the more preeminent thinkers who have concentrated upon issues such as homosexuality, gambling, prostitution, narcotics use, and abortion regarding the ground rules under which debate shall be conducted. Official action may legitimately be taken against a behaviour, they appear to agree, if some substantial harm can be demonstrated to result from it, either to a victim, seen as an involuntary party, or to the society and its legitimate interests. The classic statement of this position is that of John Stuart Mill:

> The sole aim for which mankind are warranted, individually or collectively, in interfering with the liberty of action of any of their number, is self-protection ... The only purpose for which power can rightfully be exercised over any member of a civilized community, against his will, is to prevent harm to others. His own good, either physical or moral, is not a warrant.

Mill's statement, for all its clarion stress on individual liberty, is more tantalizing than definitive when the attempt is made to employ it as a guide to social policy. The terms 'self-protection' and 'to prevent harm to others' admit of numerous interpretations, so that honest persons may strongly disagree when confronted by the same facts ...

A definition is offered by Packer of the kinds of behaviour that ought to be looked at very closely in terms of their proper place in the criminal law apparatus. These are 'offences which do not result in anyone's feeling that he has been injured so as to impel him to bring the offence to the attention of the authorities.' Three conditions ought to be assessed – the gravity, proximity, and probability of the harm – in regard to each offence, Packer notes, if it is alleged that the behaviour threatens social life and ought to be condemned by use of the criminal law. Packer further identifies six conditions that should be present before criminal sanctions are invoked against disapproved conduct ...

1. The conduct must be regarded by most people as socially threatening and must not be condoned by any significant segment of society.
2. Subjecting the conduct to criminal penalties must not be inconsistent with the goals of punishment.
3. Suppressing it will not inhibit socially desirable conduct.
4. It can be dealt with through evenhanded and nondiscriminatory law enforcement.
5. Controlling it through the criminal process will not expose that process to severe qualitative or quantitative strains.
6. No reasonable alternatives to the criminal sanction exist for dealing with it. [Packer, 1968.]

The legal and philosophical liberalism represented in the previous extracts has been criticised for being blind to issues of gender and power. Feminist scholars have argued that, far from being a politically neutral framework, criminal laws and criminal processes 'consolidate and reproduce aspects of social relations at a formal institutional level'; they need to be 'understood in the context of a network of actions, structures and ideologies which reinforce and reveal the nature of patriarchal relations between men and women' (Fishwick 1988: 170).

Debate about two dichotomies is particularly noticeable in recent feminist writing. One is the distinction between public and private spheres, on which much liberal discourse has relied; the second is that between sexual violence as violence and sexual violence as sex.

The delineation of a 'private' realm is one way of looking at the liberal guarantee of autonomy: the liberal state leaves its citizens free from interference in spheres such as sexual morality which are, in Wolfenden's famous phrase, 'not the law's business'. Feminist writers have pointed out that, for example, placing the family in the private sphere has allowed certain forms of male domination to remain outwith public regulation. 'Domestic' violence and, until recently, rape within marriage serve as graphic examples. The analytical as well as the political integrity of the public–private distinction has also been questioned. These debates are discussed in the extracts by O'Donovan and Zedner below:

Katherine O'Donovan, *Sexual Divisions in Law* (Weidenfeld & Nicholson, 1985) p 99

Questions of regulating sexuality bring into focus the liberal view of a world split between public and private. The dilemma is whether to place practices such as prostitution, incest, sexual intercourse with children and homosexuality on the public or private side of the divide. Since ... the boundary between these two areas of life shifts over time and according to dominant beliefs, the dilemma constantly presents itself. The form of presentation is that of an exercise of line-drawing; the source is the belief that life can be so divided. Once it has been decided where to draw the line the problem does not end. The means of regulation must be incorporated in the law. This latter decision is not merely technical, for the choice of means affects the perception of the dichotomy ...

   Regulation of sexuality takes various forms. Behaviour unregulated in private may be prohibited, controlled or regulated in public. Much of the discussion on decriminalisation of sexual behaviour fails to specify whether it is boundary-shifting which is being advocated, and if so what form public control of sexual behaviour should take. The notion of public in discussions of sexuality often seems to be equated with prohibition and control and to have territorial connotations. Private is then equated with freedom.

Lucia Zedner, 'Regulating Sexual Offences within the Home' in I Loveland (ed) *Frontiers of Criminality* (Sweet & Maxwell, 1995) pp 73–175

In traditional, liberal discourse, notions of the 'private' were conflated with the 'family'. Accordingly, sexual offences committed within the family home were deemed to be outwith the legitimate ambit of the law. This was never entirely matched by the realities of regulation and more recently, feminist legal theorists, among others, have advanced a different view; that the division between public and private is not a well-delineated boundary but little more than a line drawn in sand, constantly shifting in response to political and other pressures ... The private sphere, far from occupying some tangible space on the social map, becomes little more than a justificatory device for legal non-intervention.

However, we would be mistaken in concluding that an absence of formal law represents an absence of regulation. Instead, the lack of law may reflect the greater strength of other quasi or non-legal regulatory mechanisms of social control which operate outside the legal context and state bureau-cracy. In the field of sexuality we would do well to heed the maxim that 'analysis of law is the wrong place to start if one wishes to understand regulatory strategies.' [Rose 1987: 61.] It would be precipitous, therefore, to assume that the historical reluctance to criminalise sexual relations within the family home implies lack of concern or interest by the state. Rather, the means of regulation are differentiated. The coercive powers of the criminal law in the public sphere are supplanted in the private sphere by the more subtle but no less powerful dominion of the family. Seen this way, the family is not beyond the purview of the state, but is itself an important means of regulating sexual morality.

The legal framework which surrounds and shapes the family recog-nises it as the site of procreation and of motherhood. Before the advent of effective contraception, and even since then, sexuality was inseparable from its reproductive consequences. In order to protect both patriarchy and property, the family was constituted as the sole site in which sexual relations might be legitimately pursued. Reflecting on this, Smart argues that 'the law on sexual behaviour, although defined as part of the criminal law and subject to a very different mode of enforcement to civil law, is analytically much closer to family law' [Smart 1981: 45]. Yet one might go further and question whether any branch of doctrinal law represents the most important means of regulating sexual behaviour. In exploring the regulatory powers of the family ... where the range of the law is most limited, other ideological and social institutions may play a more determinative part in policing the sanctioning of aberrant sexuality.

... A brief incursion into the historical development of the family reveals high expectations of its capacity for self-regulation. However, and this is where the liberal account really fails, when these expectations were not met, intervention at a myriad of levels quickly followed. The mythology of the Victorian family home as a site enjoying privileged status, free from the state's disciplinary gaze, seems to rely on a deliberate misreading of the past.

The second dichotomy which structures feminist debate relates to the interpretation of sexual violence: is it best understood as a form of violence on a par with other assaults, or rather as an expression of the prevailing sexual order? These competing interpretations are discussed in the extracts by MacKinnon and Vega below:

Catharine MacKinnon, *Feminism Unmodified* (Harvard, 1987) p 160

Calling rape and pornography violent, not sexual, the banner of much antirape and antipornography organizing, is an attempt to protest that women do not find rape pleasurable or pornography stimulating while avoiding this rejection as women's point of view. The concession to the objective stance, the attempt to achieve credibility by covering up the specificity of one's viewpoint, not only abstracts from our experience, it lies about it. Women and men know men find rape sexual and pornography erotic. It therefore is. We also know that sexuality is commonly violent without being any the less sexual. To deny this sets up the situation so that when women are aroused by sexual violation, meaning we experience it as our sexuality, the feminist analysis is seen to be contradicted. But it is not contradicted, it is proved ... To reject forced sex in the name of women's point of view requires an account of women's experience of being violated by the same acts both sexes have learned as natural and fulfilling and erotic, since no critique, no alternatives, and few transgressions have been permitted.

Judith Vega, 'Coercion and Consent: Classic Liberal Concepts in Texts on Sexual Violence' (1988) 16 International Journal of Sociology of Law 75, 76

In contrast to the legal and psychiatric notions, in which rape is seen as a violent sexual incident and a matter of individual deviance, the feminist approach to sexual violence is characterized by the emphasis on the structural, social character of sexual violence, and the view of sexual violence as an expression of the power relations between men and women.

... Is consent an ideological farce and merely constitutive of situations of coercion, or can consent be isolated as a moment in itself viz a viz coercion?

Representatives of these two positions are Catharine MacKinnon and Susan Brownmiller. Brownmiller published her book *Against Our Will* in 1975 and the book can be seen as a widely-read first statement on sexual violence. MacKinnon gave her views on the violence of men against women in two articles in *Signs*, in 1982 and 1983. Both authors base their views on certain structural and power-political notions of sexual violence. Their texts might be placed in a specific tradition of political theory: the liberal, rationalist theory of natural right ...

In Brownmiller's work, the image of the structural character of sexual violence is created through the description of detailed accounts of the repetitive history of actual violence. She describes rape as a universal, terrifying, omnipresent instrument of male power which can be used against all women in order to keep them in a constant state of fear and intimidation ...

With her approach Brownmiller actually sketches a setting of the battle between the sexes, which can, like Hobbes's state of nature, be observed: the violence of everyone against everyone else, however, changes into the violence of men against women ... Mention is made of a continuous physical threat which forms the social control mechanism of women. It works both through actual rape and through the image of it, which women have internalized as a warning ... While rape represents a highly effective means of control when seen in this light (direct or indirect it always works), Brownmiller nevertheless has remarkably little difficulty delineating the area of coercion ... The consent of the woman marks the difference between 'sexuality' and 'coercion'.

Brownmiller criticizes the legal practice which is in fact based on a Lockean concept of 'tacit consent'. Women are assumed to have consented to sexual activities, unless there has been clear proof of resistance or unless the offender used an insurmountable degree of physical violence. In legal practice many forms of obligingness can be constructed as tacit consent, the circumstances notwithstanding.

... Brownmiller seeks to relinquish this concept and proposes the new criterion of explicit consent for every sexual act ... Although her explicit consent seems to be a rather sympathetic improvement, she thereby automatically accepts the male female relationship as natural and self-evident. In other words, she accepts heterosexuality as such as if it were free from power. The only sort of coercion she recognizes is physical force or the threat of force that violates 'natural' rights ...

For MacKinnon 'sexuality' is the form and content of power. Sexuality is the form of sex inequality itself, and she calls sexual objectification 'the primary process of the subjection of women' ... MacKinnon criticizes Brownmiller for seeing rape as violence instead of sexuality and thus as distinguishable from situations of real consent. MacKinnon tries to erase this distinction between rape and sexuality in various places.

Here the victim's perspective grasps what liberalism applied to women denies: that forced sex as sexuality is not exceptional in relations between the sexes but constitutes the social meaning of gender.

Her criticism of Brownmiller's solution to consent bears witness to some evolution in feminist thinking about sexual violence: she makes the sexual autonomy of women the problem, rather than seeking it as simply the alternative. But that does not mean that MacKinnon's analysis brings us any closer to a real understanding of the problem. The solution becomes rather more problematic. MacKinnon does not take the actual reality of consent of women into account. She 'solves' the problem of consent by denying its existence ... The female perspective is that of the victim and apparently all women are and will be victims at all times.

MacKinnon's account also seems to imply that law itself is irreducibly 'male':

Catharine MacKinnon, 'Feminism, Marxism, Method and the State: an Agenda for Theory' (1983) 7 Signs: Journal of Women in Culture and Society 635

As a beginning I propose that the state is male in the feminist sense. The law sees and treats women the way men see and treat women. The liberal state coercively and authoritatively constitutes the social order in the interest of men as a gender, through its legitimizing norms, relation to society, and substantive policies. It achieves this through embodying and ensuring male control over women's sexuality at every level, occasionally cushioning, qualifying, or de jure prohibiting its excesses when necessary to its normalization ... the state, in part through law, institutionalizes male power.

Such a view appears to entail that criminal law is incapable of recognising women's autonomy. Like Vega, Smart suggests that the relationship between law, the state and the construction of sexuality is more complex than either the liberal or the radical feminist approach reveals:

Carol Smart, 'Feminism and Law: Some Problems of Analysis and Strategy' (1986) 14 International Journal of Sociology of Law 109–123, 117

There is no simple relationship between law and the economic structure of society ... law has an autonomy from the state, and law itself is not a unified entity, indivisible in terms of structure and effects. Neither can legal changes be regarded as 'causing' economic or social change, although legislation may, in some instances, provide the means to achieve change.

The idea of the uneven development of law is an important one. It allows for an analysis of the law that recognises the distinctions between law-as-legislation and the effects of law, or law-in-practice. It rejects completely any concept of law as a unity which simply progresses, regresses or reappears as a cycle of history to repeat itself ... Law both facilitates change and is an obstacle to change ... Legislation in the areas of pornography and reproductive rights provides an illuminating example of this uneven development. The decade of the 1960s is commonly regarded as an era of permissive legislation in the UK. Hence legislation introducing legalised abortion for non-medical reasons, and legislation reducing censorship on theatrical displays (and ultimately books and magazines) are linked together under the permissive banner. For some the legislation represents the triumph of liberalism over Victorian hypocrisy and repression. For others it symbolises the moral decline of the nation. Both schools of thought can be seen as treating legislation as indivisible, a unity that represents either progress or regress. From the position of a feminist analysis of law, neither position is correct. The lack of control over pornographic material is analysed as an instance of the exercise of power by others over women's bodies. The availability of abortion on the other hand, represents a limited extension of power over reproduction, and hence women's bodies, to women themselves. This is an oversimplification of the feminist position, but it serves to identify an instance of one dimension of what is meant by the uneven development of law.

To follow the example one stage further, the legislation on abortion is not itself an unambiguously positive development. While extending self-determination to some women, it also gives to the medical profession the power to withhold or to extend the surgical procedure. Although the technology of abortion is becoming increasingly simple, its control rests with doctors as opposed to nurses or women themselves. To this extent doctors can decide who should, and who should not, have an abortion. In the exercise of their discretion, the ethnic origin, the class background, or the marital status of a woman may become exceedingly important. The law-in-practice does not therefore operate simply to give women greater self-determination over biological reproduction.

Yet, notwithstanding the complex relationship between law and broader social forces, gender is a remarkably consistent influence on both legal practice and subjects' experiences of criminal law. In the following extract, Smart offers a framework within which questions about 'the sex of law' might be assessed:

Carol Smart, 'Law's Truth/Women's Experience' in R Graycar (ed) *Dissenting Opinions* (Allen and Unwin, 1990) pp 7–9

[W]here women resort to law, their status is always already imbued with specific meaning arising out of their gender. They go to law as mothers, wives, sexual objects, pregnant women, deserted mothers, single mothers and so on ... In going to law women carry with them cultural meanings about pregnancy, heterosexuality, sexual bodies ... [L]aws that deal with the private sphere operate on fully gendered subjects ...

Phallogocentrism is a neologism constructed from phallocentric and logocentric ... [F]eminism has begun to reveal the multifaceted nature of gender oppression. It reveals that gender difference (and hence oppression) exists in the language we use, it shows that the way knowledge is constructed is gendered, it suggests that sexual desire is not a matter of false consciousness but a deep psychic process which cannot be easily undone.

Logos means literally the father's spoken word. It is used to invoke a system of thought or ideas which cannot be said to be neutral, but rather constructed under conditions of patriarchy ...

Phallocentric is ... deployed to refer to a culture which is structured to meet the needs of the masculine imperative. However, it is a term which is meant to imply more than the surface appearance of male dominance and to invoke the subconscious and questions of desire and sexuality. The term phallocentric attempts to give some insight into how patriarchy is part of women's (as well as men's) subconscious, not merely a system imposed from outside and kept in place by threat and force ...

Within this conceptual framework, we can begin to understand how it is that, while the sexual offence of rape formally penalises men, the enforcement of rape law often reinforces male domination over women, to the extent that one empirical study of rape cases concludes that the criminal process in fact 'condones' rape (Lees 1996: 262). By focusing on rape as a crime committed by strangers who are deviant, the reality of 'intimate' rape is obscured (Estrich 1987). We can also start to subject to critical analysis the conception of valuable sexuality which the sexual offences purport to protect. For some, this appears to mean only economic value. Applied to rape this can lead to a chilling presentation of sexual favours as a scarce market commodity:

Richard Posner, *The Economic Structure of Tort Law* (Harvard University Press, 1987) p 157

If we tie the idea of value to the voluntary processes of the market, there is no increase in value in the rape case because it is not the kind of coercive act that improves the operation of the market, as the theft [of food] from [a deserted cabin] does. In any event, it is understandable why the legal system would not undertake to compare the hypothetical offer price of the rapist with the hypothetical demand price of his victim. The measurement problems are overwhelmingly difficult and hardly worth undertaking to identify the rare rape that may in some sense be thought to increase social wealth. Also, there are market substitutes for coercive sexual acts – substitutes presumptively more efficient than using the legal system to direct the allocation of resources to sex.

The reforms in the Sexual Offences Bill 2003 evidence an increased commitment to dealing with sexual crime. The Government, preparing the ground for reform, recognised the disempowerment of women in the rape trial that lies at the heart of Smart's thesis.

Home Office, 'Setting the Boundaries: Reforming the Law on Sex Offences' (2000)

Why did the law need reviewing? It is a patchwork quilt of provisions ancient and modern that works because people make it do so, not because there is a coherence and structure. Some is quite new – the definition of rape for example was last changed in 1994. But much is old, dating from nineteenth century laws that codified the common law of the time, and reflected the social attitudes and roles of men and women of the time. With the advent of a new century and the incorporation of the European Convention of Human Rights into our law, the time was right to take a fresh look at the law to see that it meets the need of the country today.

...

The law on sex offences is the part of the criminal law which deals with the most private and intimate part of life – sexual relationships – when they are non-consensual, inappropriate or wrong. As such it embodies society's view of what is right and wrong in sexual relations. Our guiding principle was that this judgement on what is right and wrong should be based on an assessment of the harm done to the individual (and through the individual to society as a whole). In considering what was harmful we took account of the views of victims/survivors and of academic research. The victims of sexual violence and coercion are mainly women. They must be offered protection and redress and the law must ensure that male victims/survivors are protected too. The law must make special provision for those who are too young or otherwise not able to look after themselves, and offer greater protection to children and vulnerable people within the looser structures of modern families. In order to deliver effective protection to all, the law needs to be framed on the basis that offenders and victims can be of either sex. We have recommended offences that are gender neutral in their application, unless there was good reason to do otherwise.

We explore the criminalisation of sexual violence in detail in the next section.

FURTHER READING

Barrett, Michele and McIntosh, Mary (1982) *The Anti-Social Family* (Verso).

Foucault, Michel (1976) *The History of Sexuality: An Introduction* (Peregrine translation).

Frigon, Sylvie (1995) 'A Genealogy of Women's Madness' in Dobash, R Emerson; Dobash, Russell; and Noaks, Lesley (1995) *Gender and Crime* (University of Wales Press).

Kennedy, Helena (1992) *Eve Was Framed* (London, Chatto & Windus) Chs 5 and 6.

MacKinnon, Catharine (1983) 'Feminism, Marxism, Method and the State: An Agenda for Theory' 7 Signs: Journal of Women in Culture and Society 635.

Smart, Carol (1995) *Law, Crime and Sexuality* (Sage).

Smith, Roger (1981) *Trial by Medicine* (Edinburgh University Press).

Weeks, Jeffrey (1985) *Sexuality and its Discontents: Meanings, Myths and Modern Sexualities* (Routledge & Kegan Paul).

II.   Sexual violence

II.a.   Sexual violence and the criminal process

Home Office, *Protecting the Public: Strengthening Protection Against Sex Offenders and Reforming the Law on Sexual Offences* **(Cmnd 5668) (HMSO, 2002) p 9**

The law on sex offences, as it stands, is archaic, incoherent and discriminatory. Much of it is contained in the Sexual Offences Act 1956, and most of that was simply a consolidation of nineteenth-century law. It does not reflect the changes in society and social attitudes that have taken place since the Act became law and it is widely considered to be inadequate and out of date.

While some piecemeal reform has taken place over the years, we have now undertaken a comprehensive review of the law so that it can meet the needs of today's society. The law on sex offences needs to set out what is unacceptable behaviour and must provide penalties that reflect the seriousness of the crimes committed. Some behaviour that should be covered by the criminal law is not at present. We know far more now about the insidious ways in which sexual abuse takes place and we have listened to the voices of victims about the profound and long-lasting effects of abuse. Our new framework of offences will plug existing gaps and seek to protect society from rape and sexual assault at one end of the spectrum and from voyeurism at the other. A special emphasis must be placed on the protection of children and the most vulnerable.

The conviction rate for rape is very low and has been falling in recent years. The number of persons found guilty of rape in comparison to the total number of offences reported has fallen from 25% in 1985 to 7% in 2000. Much of this is due to the change in the nature of the cases coming to trial, with many more instances of date or acquaintance rape being reported than before. These cases, which often rely on one person's word against that of another, make the decision of juries much harder than in cases of stranger rape. The recent HMIC / CPSI report on rape set out the issues that need to be addressed at all stages of the criminal justice system to reverse this trend, from the thoroughness of police investigations, through the preparation of cases for trial, to the role of the prosecutor and the cross-examination of victims in court. In July 2002 we published an action plan of practical measures to implement the report's recommendations and make improvements across the whole of the criminal justice system. Through these improvements, we want to give victims of rape more confidence in the system and encourage them to report offences of rape. We also aim to send a strong message to perpetrators that this crime will not be tolerated and the law will be enforced.

We believe that there should be greater clarity in the law as it relates to consent. We intend to specify, in legislation, certain circumstances where, even if the victim had the capacity to consent, it is highly unlikely that consent would have been given; for example where the victim was abducted or subjected to force. Once the prosecution has proved beyond reasonable doubt that sexual activity has taken place in one of these limited circumstances, it will be for the defendant to establish on the balance of probabilities whether consent had in fact been given.

In addition, we plan to change the law on consent to help juries decide whether a defendant, who claims that he believed the other person consented, acted reasonably in the circumstances [*discussed below at section II.b.iv.*].

II.a.i.   A continuum of violence

Ken Plumer, *Telling Sexual Stories: Power, Change and Social Worlds* (Routledge, 1995) pp 77–78

The 'story of rape' that was given its voice by the women's movement in the early 1970s has now moved out beyond this into much wider communities, creating a rich mine of new, but linked, narratives. A crucial new language has been created through which lives are being lived and transformed. The story is now of a 'continuum of sexual violence' towards women which moves all the way from the 'lust murders' that receive prominent (maybe too prominent) coverage as sensational stories in the media through a myriad cluster of abusive acts newly named or reidentified: *wife-beating, incest, child sexual abuse, daughter-rape, date rape, acquaintance rape, marital rape, indecent exposure, sexual harassment*; on to a range of 'little rapes' *wolf whistles, lookism* and *voyeurism*; and through to a general climate of *sexual fear*. A network of new sufferings, new stories and new groups ripples outwards: *nursery crimes, child sex rings, Satanic abuse, fraternity gang rapes* and *children who molest children*. Such stories become criss-crossed with race: black women speak out about incest, Latinos tell of wife-battering. And eventually it is not just a continuum of violence for women but for men too: *male rape, male sexual harassment, abused boys, male-battering*. And not just heterosexual victims but gays and lesbians too: *lesbian and gay battered partners, same sex-sexual harassment, same sex-rape* and *hate crimes*. Twenty years ago almost none of this had found its voice, and much of it is still silent. All these acts of coercion use sexuality as a means to abuse, pollute and desecrate: they generate enormous sexual suffering. Unsolicited and undesired, sexuality becomes the tool to defile and a source of danger.

The language of sexual danger defilement is now enormous. Shades of such language existed in the nineteenth-century women's evangelical movement, but it was then a much muter story (as all sexual stories were). Today, however, a multitude of dangers and defilements bring their own biographies, their own chat-show presentations, their own docudramas, their own research programmes. The story is told. And the stories are fed by social worlds and into social worlds to shift along the understanding and experience of sexual suffering as sexual danger. Of course all these experiences are very different – a 'lust murder' is not a 'wolf-whistle', and each unique experience brings its own unique pain. But the power of stories here can clearly be seen. For although the story of another person's sexual danger may not be exactly our story, it provides signs and cues for us to make sense of our pains. As always, sexual stories aid in the creation of a past, a present and an anticipated future marking out histories, differences, unities and agendas for action.

However, as we will see, such emerging narratives have not readily translated into law reform, or at least into any meaningful change. The social practice of criminalisation assumes, by definition, the exceptional or 'abnormal' character of that which it proscribes. However, just as Durkheim noted the continuity between suicide and 'normal' behaviour, some feminist writers have suggested that sexual violence is far from exceptional in our society. Indeed, its very 'normality' turns out to be one of the factors which give rise to difficulties of enforcing this area of criminal law.

Liz Kelly, *Surviving Sexual Violence* (Polity, 1988) pp 74, 95

As I transcribed and analysed the interviews [on which the research was based], it became clear that most women had experienced sexual violence in their lives. It was also clear that the range of men's behaviour that women defined as abusive was neither reflected in legal codes nor in the analytic categories used in previous research. In order to reflect this complexity I began to use the term 'continuum' to describe both the extent and range of sexual violence recorded in the interviews ...

Feminist services for abused women as well as recent research have demonstrated that the incidence of sexual violence is far higher than recorded in the official statistics. Furthermore, many incidents which women experience as abusive are not defined legally as crimes. Official statistics and victimisation studies are, therefore, of limited use in measuring the prevalence of sexual violence.

Table 4.1   The Continuum of Prevalence

Form of Violence	Number of Women	% of Sample
Threat of violence	60	100
Sexual harassment	56	93
Pressure to have sex	50	83

Sexual assault	42	70
Obscene phone calls	25	68
Coercive sex	38	63
Domestic violence	32	53
Sexual abuse	30	50
Flashing	30	50
Rape	30	50
Incest	13	22

... As this sample is self-selected and at least 50 per cent of women partici-pated on the basis that they had had experience of rape, incest or domestic violence, it would be inappropriate to over-generalise on the basis of these findings. The figures do, however, show clearly that the vast majority of this sample experienced the more common forms of sexual violence; the threat of violence, sexual harassment, and pressure to have sex. These forms of sexual violence were extremely common in women's lives, both in the sense that they occurred to most women and that they occurred on multiple occasions.

Deborah Cameron and Elizabeth Frazer, *The Lust to Kill* (Polity, 1987) p 164

Male violence against women is defined broadly by feminists to include not just the obvious abuses – rape, wife-battering and incest for instance – but also and importantly, a range of male behaviours that have often been dismissed as mere routine minor nuisances, like flashing, stealing under-wear and making obscene phone calls. Feminist analysis puts these things together for two reasons.

First, they all enact very similar assumptions about male sexuality and women's relation to it. They say that men need and feel entitled to have unrestricted sexual access to women, even – sometimes especially – against women's will. They say that men's sexuality is aggressive and predatory. Superficially, flashing is quite different from rape, yet from the point of view of their function they are surprisingly similar: both are acts which men do to reassure themselves of their power and potency; both include, as a crucial factor in that reassurance, the fear and humiliation of the female victims.

Secondly, the myriad manifestations of male violence collectively function as a threat to women's autonomy. They undermine our self-esteem and limit our freedom of action – not only must we all live with the fear of sexual violence, society makes it our own responsibility to prevent it. If the worst does happen we may be blamed, not protected; our suffering will be trivialized, questioned or ignored. Thus a powerful incentive exists for us to police our own behaviour and acquiesce in the idea that men's sexuality is 'naturally' predatory, only to be contained by female circumspection.

These facts have led feminists to locate male violence against women in the realm of the political. It expresses not purely individual anger and frustration but a collective, culturally sanctioned misogyny which is important in maintaining the collective power of men ... There is more to sexual killing than misogyny and terror ... From the start ... we have had to take seriously the existence of killers whose victims are men ... [and] we found that men who murdered other men or boys were quite strikingly similar to those who murdered women.

[W]hat we need is a 'common denominator' which connects sexual killings of women and of men. Instead of focusing on the gender of the victim, we must look at what does not vary – the gender of the killer. The common denominator is not misogyny, it is a shared construction of masculine sexuality, or even more broadly, masculinity in general. It is under the banner of masculinity that all the main themes of sexual killing come together: misogyny, transcendence, sadistic sexuality, the basic ingredients of the lust to kill.

Sandra McNeill, 'Flashing: Its Effect on Women' in J Hanmer and M Maynard (eds) *Women, Violence and Social Control* (Macmillan, 1987) p 93

While there are no laws explicitly denying women free access to public places at all times, in practice their freedom is curtailed by men who attack them, men who threaten to attack them, insufficient law enforcement against these men, and a tendency for the media to trivialise all incidents except the most serious ones – and these they sensationalise. It is against this background that flashing is examined – the most minor and most common sexual offence against women, classified as a criminal offence ...

Flashing has two histories, one as a criminal offence, the other as a medical condition. Section 4 of the Vagrancy Act, 1824 makes it an offence for a person 'wilfully, openly, lewdly and obscenely, to expose his person with intent to insult any female'. 'Person' was subsequently clarified to mean the penis ... Rooth [1971] ... tells us, 'Contemporary accounts in Hansard suggest that the measure was introduced in response to an epidemic of flashing in London parks' ... Although suspected of being vastly under-reported, flashing is the commonest sexual offence ...

The study consisted of interviews with 100 women. The sample comprised twenty-five students (occupants of a resident block), twenty-five women attending a woman's liberation conference and fifty women from a door-to-door survey in Leeds.

The first finding is that out of 100 women interviewed, sixty-three recalled having seen a flasher and forty-three had done so more than once. Out of 233 incidents only 14 were reported to the police, by eleven of the sixty-three women, three women reporting twice. In general, those who reported were treated sympathetically, but were given the impression that the police did not really take the offence seriously ... The main reason given for non-reporting was that the women did not believe that the police would treat them seriously ...

Using the interviewees' own words the first emotional reactions to the incidents were tabulated. Fear, shock and disgust were the most common reactions, followed by (if taken together) giggles/funny/amusement. Anger and outrage mentioned alone came next – but where interviewees mentioned 'mixed' reactions, anger frequently rated as the second, for example 'fear and anger' or 'shock and anger'. Some women felt guilt/shame/humiliation. And three women reported no reaction, for example, 'I just ignored it'.

... The original question I set out to answer was 'what do women fear?' and the answer was a surprise. Every researcher has hidden or conscious expectations, which a survey can confirm or confound. Before this survey began I assumed that the fear would be fear of rape, and indeed in general discussion of flashing in the second part of the interview, many women linked it in some way with rape. But at the time of the incidents women don't fear rape: women fear death.

The sexual invasion aspect of 'flashing' is reinforced in the Sexual Offences Bill 2003, clause 68 of which prohibits the intentional exposure of genitalia by an individual who 'knows or intends that someone will see them, and be caused alarm or distress'. This contrasts with the public order focus of the Town Police Clauses Act 1847, s 28, that it replaces.

II.a.ii.   Investigating and prosecuting sexual violence

Official crime statistics suggest that serious sexual violence is a relatively infrequent occurrence: in 2001, 9008 rapes and 21,765 indecent assaults on women were recorded (Home Office 2003f). Sexual offences constitute just 10% of all offences of violence, which in turn constitute only 6% of recorded (notifiable) crime. However, these statistics paint only a partial picture of the social phenomenon of sexual violence and the disparities tell us more about reporting and recording practices than about sexual violence per se. Sexual violence against women in general and rape in particular are among the least reported and most under-enforced crimes. Official statistics belie the true toll of rape. Clearly, estimating the 'true' extent of sexual violence is very difficult, but the findings of crime surveys confirm that the reporting rate is far lower than that for burglary or non-sexual assaults. The Rape Crisis Federation of England and Wales for example, suggests that only 12% of the 50,000 women who contacted their services in 1998 reported the crime of rape to the police (HMCPSI 2002: para 13.3).

Based on the 2000 British Crime Survey figures, Myhill and Allen estimated that 61,000 rapes were committed in 1999, suggesting that 1 in 20 women between the ages of 16 and 59 have been raped. The percentage of rapes committed by partners (45%) was higher than that by strangers (8%). The findings in relation to victim perception of sexual attacks may also partly explain the low reporting of rape: fewer than 60% were willing to classify their experience as 'rape'. Women subjected to sexual attacks from partners or dates were even less likely to consider the incident criminal.

Myhill and Allen, *Rape and Sexual Assault of Women: The Extent and Nature of the Problem* (Home Office Research Study 237) (Home Office 2002) pp 53–68)

It is extremely interesting to see what proportion of the incidents classified as rape using the follow-up questions in the self-completion modules were classified as rape by the victims themselves. Only three-fifths of victims whose most recent incident could be classified as a rape using the follow-up questions actually self-classified the incident as 'rape'. A further fifth of victims whose most recent incident could be classified as rape avoided self-classifying into any of the legal categories offered. It is also interesting to note that 18 sexual assault victims (3%) self-classified themselves as having experienced a rape, despite answering 'no' to the question about having been forced to have penetrative sex.

...

Koss' controversial (1987) study on the sexual victimisation of college students was heavily criticised for the majority of its victims not regarding themselves as having been raped ... However, these findings can be seen to provide further evidence to support the notion that the concept of 'rape' carries with it a specific set of meanings, assumptions and stereotypes that victims may not wish to associate themselves with – the notion of rape as a stigmatised and degraded status. It must also be remembered that the concept of 'the rapist' is also heavily stereotyped. Soothill and Walby (1991) conducted an analysis of media reporting of rape and found that 'the popular imagery of rape ... typically involves strangers, madmen, multiple attacks and reckless women, some of whom brought it on themselves' (cited in Walby and Myhill, 2001: 514). It may be more difficult for women raped by somebody they know, perhaps even somebody they liked or loved, to label this person a rapist. As we have seen, a relatively small proportion of incidents picked up by the self-completion modules fit the stereotypical 'stranger attack'. It is also likely that some victims have to overcome the shock of being attacked before they can admit, even to themselves, that they have been raped.

As you would perhaps expect, the vast majority (91%) of women who classified themselves as having been raped also considered the incident to be a crime. However, this still means that 9 per cent of women that considered themselves a victim of rape did not consider the incident to be a criminal offence. It is possible that this is a similar phenomenon to some women not wanting to be seen as having been raped. Perhaps some women would rather not view themselves as a 'victim', or their partner or ex-partner, for example, as a rapist. These figures are more pronounced for the other offence categories. Only 70 per cent of women who self-classified their most recent victimisation as 'attempted rape' also classified it as a crime; the figure for 'indecent assault' is just over two-thirds (67%). It must also be remembered, though, that rape within marriage was only made a criminal offence relatively recently (1994 [eds: *in fact it changed after R v R (1991)*]) and that these figures refer to incidents 'ever' experienced. It is likely, though, that some women do not easily reconcile the concepts of sex and criminality, particularly when the perpetrator is a partner or close relative ... It is possible that women from traditional, patriarchal back-grounds would view victimisation in a domestic, or even 'date' scenario as 'just something that happens', despite the wide changes of attitudes in society as a whole over the last few decades.

The effect of perpetrator identity on victim perceptions was also marked (at p 68):

> Victims of stranger attacks are, not surprisingly, the most likely to define their experiences as criminal, with almost three-quarters of stranger victims saying they believed their last incident of sexual victimisation to be a crime. Under half of attacks by dates were defined by the victim as criminal. Further to this, around a fifth of women victimised by a 'date' considered the incident to be 'just something that happens'.

Many factors contribute to the low reporting rate for sexual offences. Complainants often fear that they will be treated unsympathetically at police stations. In response to these fears, the police have begun to develop special procedures for handling rape victims, and, perhaps as a result, the total number of rapes reported to the police has risen significantly. However, despite improvements, Temkin's study of rape reporting in Sussex in the 1990s found that 'old practices and attitudes, widely assumed to have vanished, are still in evidence and continue to cause victims pain and trauma' (Temkin 1997: 527). Similar findings from a replication of Temkin's study in New Zealand suggest a cross-cultural problem (Jordan 2001). Both studies suggest a small rather than seismic shift in victims' experiences of the rape reporting process. For Jordan, the tension between victims' needs and police responsibilities places them 'worlds apart'.

J Jordan 'Worlds Apart? Women, Rape and the Police Reporting Process', British Journal of Criminology (2001) 41, 679–706 at p 703

The victim is trying to manage the effects of trauma and regain a sense of personal equilibrium at the same time as the police are making excessive demands on her stamina and seeking to establish her veracity as a complainant. Attempts to resolve this inherent conflict can begin only with an acknowledgement of its existence. The police focus is likely to be on the identification and apprehension of the offender, which may or may not be a goal she shares. What she is likely to need most is to have a sense of safety restored and to be able to heal and re-establish control of her life, something that the police are not trained to provide and which some of their procedures may even work against. The police role is not designed to assist in healing – this role rightly belongs to support workers and therapists, whose involvement can assist both police and victims alike. The police occupational culture, built as it is around the crime-fighting role, can in fact reinforce and emphasize qualities in police officers that may be anathema to the needs of rape victims ... Even when police officers and rape victims desire similar outcomes, their respective journeys towards this goal may traverse different terrain. This is apparent from the initial police contact onwards, established as it is against a backdrop of police power and authority coupled with victim vulnerability and disempowerment ... As long as police officers and rape victims continue to exist as if they were worlds apart from each other, the police will bear the brunt of public criticism and victims will continue to express dissatisfaction with the police response.

No such changes, however, have taken place in the conduct of trials. While there has been a huge rise in the number of reported and therefore recorded rapes (from 1842 cases recorded in 1985 to 8593 cases in 2000 (Home Office 2001b)), the proportion of cases which ultimately result in a conviction has fallen from 24.4% in 1985 to 7% in 2000 (Home Office 2002a). Only one in five reported cases currently reaches the trial stage. This 'attrition' in the prosecution and trial process meant that, notwithstanding increased reporting, the actual number of men convicted of or cautioned for rape was more or less the same in 1994 as in 1985. As the table below indicates, the total number of convictions has crept up from 450 to 631; this represents only 8% of recorded offences.

Myhill and Allen, 2002, HORS 237

Table E.1   Trends in official rape statistics

Year	Total number of offences recorded by the police as rape (N. %)		Total offenders cautioned or found guilty of rape (N. %)	
1985	1,842	100	450	24
1986	2,288	100	415	18
1987	2,471	100	453	18
1988	2,855	100	540	19

1989	3,305	100	613	19
1990	3,391	100	561	17
1991	4,045	100	559	14
1992	4,142	100	529	13
1993	4,589	100	482	10
1994	5,032	100	460	9
1995	4,986	100	578	12
1996	5,759	100	573	10
1997	6,281	100	599	9
1998	7,139	100	656	9
1999	7,809	100	631	8
1988	2,855	100	540	19
1989	3,305	100	613	19
1990	3,391	100	561	17
1991	4,045	100	559	14
1992	4,142	100	529	13
1993	4,589	100	482	10
1994	5,032	100	460	9
1995	4,986	100	578	12
1996	5,759	100	573	10
1997	6,281	100	599	9
1998	7,139	100	656	9
1999	7,809	100	631	8

The number convicted or cautioned fell below 600 in both 2000 and 2001. Of the 559 total in 2001, 37 were cautioned, rather than formally convicted (Home Office 2002j: Table 5.12). An investigation of 1741 crime reports by the Crown Prosecution Service Inspectorate revealed a charge/summons or caution rate of 28.3%. Nearly 60% resulted in no charge. Of the 230 cases in the police file sample, 42.2% proceeded to court. Prosecuted cases resulted in a conviction rate of 60.8% (including guilty pleas). Cases that proceeded to trial resulted in an acquittal of 70.4% (HMCPSI 2002: para 3.35).

The array of statistics can be baffling. To some extent this reflects the multi-dimensional character of the criminal justice 'system'. Whether the measure is of recorded rapes, or of charges, cautions or convictions, the overall picture is consistent. What is interesting is the gradual official recognition of the attrition rate in rape cases and that this is a matter that should be addressed. It is generally accepted that there are four key stages in the attrition process: (1) the decision to report; (2) during investigation; (3) when the CPS drops a case; and (4) acquittals after trial (HMCPSI 2002: para 13.1). Each of these is affected by policies, procedures and practices in the criminal justice system. Even if everyone were free of stereotyped prejudicial attitudes, there would still be the need to gain the confidence of women who are raped or sexually assaulted. There is a clear momentum for change and a commitment by the Home Office to reduce the attrition rate. It is too soon to assess the combined impact, if any, of the reforms in the Sexual Offences Bill 2003, and the Home Office's Action Plan on implementation of the recommendations of the HMCPSI Report (Home Office 2002i). It may never be possible to chart these accurately because of general changes in crime recording practices introduced in 2002 (Maguire 2002: 346).

Problems of proof in sexual offences (see **section II.b.v.** below) have undoubtedly helped to reinforce police and CPS views that only the most blatant cases can be successfully prosecuted. Evidential rules and official attitudes to complainants are symbiotically related and have at their base some very outdated ideas about women: their tendency to make false reports ('women are born liars'), and their complicity in the offence ('she asked for it'). Significantly, such prejudicial attitudes appear to creep into the practice of sections of the medical and legal professions that come into contact with rape victims. Defence barristers use a range of strategies designed to discredit the victim in front of the jury, such as maligning the victim's clothes at the time of the alleged incident. Thus one of the barristers interviewed by Temkin remarked that:

> This girl has gone into a bikers' pub wearing a mini-skirt and a see-through shirt. That's part of the story. I don't think they (young girls) realise the effect of their appearance on men. Guys get turned on if they can see through the women's clothes. Dress *is* significant [Temkin, 2000, p 233].

More surprising is the discovery of similar sentiments amongst doctors carrying out the forensic medical examination:

> [I]f people are dressed in an alluring way, they are inadvertently giving out overt messages. So if someone is wearing a black, slinky dress and red lipstick and has a lovely, curvaceous figure they are saying yes without saying yes. The man is receiving messages because he lacks the judgment to know what is and isn't a message [Temkin, 1998, p 842].

The risk that such assumptions from medical professionals will perpetuate existing police prejudices is obvious. Many of the legal arrangements considered in the next section continue to disclose the stereotype that sexual violence is committed by strangers.

II.b.   The offence of rape

Criminal law includes a large number of different, and often overlapping, sexual offences. We deal here with the offence of rape. Child sexual abuse and other adult sexual activities are considered in **section III.** below.

The Sexual Offences Bill 2003 repeals and replaces most of the Sexual Offences Act 1956. Clause 1 widens the definition of rape to include penile penetration of the vagina, anus or mouth. It applies for the first time to surgically reconstructed male and female genitalia. However, its real significance lies in issues in proving consent and the mental element; in particular, the rejection of the 'defence' of honest belief in consent, and its replacement with a test based on reasonableness.

Sexual Offences Bill 2003 [as amended by the House of Lords, June 2003]

Clause 1   Rape
(1) A person (A) commits an offence if–
    (a) he intentionally penetrates the vagina, anus or mouth of another person (B) with his penis,
    (b) B does not consent to the penetration, and
    (c) A does not reasonably believe that B consents.
(2) Whether a belief is reasonable is to be determined having regard to all the circumstances, including any steps A has taken to ascertain whether B consents.
(3) Sections 76 and 77 apply to an offence under this section.
(4) A person guilty of an offence under this section is liable, on conviction on indictment, to imprisonment for life.

The definition of rape is controversial in a number of ways. It concentrates on a specific form of sexual violation: penetration by a penis. Although rape has included anal intercourse since 1994, the new offence continues to exclude vaginal or anal penetration with other objects. However, it does now extend to forced oral sex. (An insight into official attitudes to the latter was recently provided by a judge who compared it with 'a trip to the dentist' (*The Guardian*, 14 November 1997).)

The legal construction of the wrong of rape hinges on lack of consent. As we have already seen, the concept of consent is problematic, and these difficulties are reflected in the trial process. 'Consent' is statutorily defined for the first time in the 2003 Bill. The wider definition is reinforced by the use of presumptions, set out in clauses 76 and 77 (see **section II.b.iv.** below). These definitional changes, along with the evidential issues relevant to the treatment of rape victims and questions about sentencing practice, are discussed in the following sections. Throughout the discussion, we try to throw light on the images of ('normal') femininity and masculinity, of sexuality and sexual relations, which are embodied in law, as well as consider criminal law's conception of the value of sexuality or sexual autonomy and of the nature of sexual wrongs. We shall also consider the extent to which law can (or should) succeed in meeting the liberal ideal of gender-neutrality in an area in which – unusually – gender-specific subject positions remain written onto the surface of legal rules.

II.b.i. Penile penetration

Steven Box, Power, *Crime and Mystification* (Tavistock, 1983) p 121

Students of rape are immediately confronted by a definitional problem. Does the legal definition, both in principle and juridical practice, refer to a reasonably inclusive category of behaviour? Or does it exclude behaviour which is very similar to that which it includes? ... Although there are minor variations amongst legislatures in western countries, there is a broad agreement that rape constitutes a particular act of sexual access, namely the penis penetrating the vagina, gained without the consent of the female concerned. This legal definition and its embodiment in legal practice has been criticized by feminists and other writers on at least three counts: it contains a suppressed and unjustified major 'exclusion' clause; it reflects a male fetish with one female orifice and one instrument for its violation; its notion of consent places an unfair burden of proof on the victim, and because it is premised on the idea of a voluntary actor, it fails to include a consideration for coerced consent or submission other than under physical duress.

The Criminal Justice and Public Order Act 1994 met one of these objections by extending the definition of rape to non-consensual anal intercourse, hence mitigating the law's heterosexual norm. In 2001/2002, 735 rapes of men were recorded (Home Office 2003f). The new offence of rape remains gender-specific: the perpetrator will be male. However, this is accompanied by the offence of 'Causing a person to engage in sexual activity without consent' (Sexual Offences Bill, clause 5), to penalise a woman who forces a man to penetrate her without his consent and so to compensate for the gender-specificity of rape. However, the other criticisms enumerated by Box remain applicable: the definition of rape reflects an essentially masculine image of sexuality, and poses formidable difficulties of proof for the prosecution. Naffine suggests that although the legal definition of rape has been adapted in a more 'sexually democratic' direction, even in Australian jurisdictions where the definition is now gender-neutral, its underlying view of male and female sexuality remains unchanged:

Ngaire Naffine, 'Possession: Erotic Love in the Law of Rape' (1994) 57 MLR 10, 24–25

The sexual being still implicit in the law of rape has a rich history. Depictions of the strong, possessing male, mainly of a laudatory kind, are to be found in the Romantic and philosophical literature of the eighteenth and nineteenth century. In legal writing, he can be traced back at least until the time of Hale who specifically approved of sexual relations between strong men and capitulating women ... [A] traditional possessive heterosexual form of 'erotic love' still ... pervades the law of those Australian jurisdictions which have ... instituted ostensibly dramatic changes to the meaning of rape.

In many parts of Australia, rape or its equivalent is now a crime which can be committed by and against either sex in a wide variety of ways. And yet we find that little has changed in substance. Though the crime has been sexually democratised on the statute books, faith has been kept with a simple, reductive and orthodox view of sexual relations ...

In the modern Australian law of rape, women are now formal equal subjects (and objects). Each is now recognised to have the ability to rape the other and the law will intervene to stop it happening ... Women have been granted equal rights with a vengeance. We have been given precisely the same rights formerly possessed only by men and we now have imposed upon us precisely the same prohibitions. The classic liberal solution has been achieved, that of granting equality (that is, the same) rights to women. In modern rape law it is this formal reciprocal capacity to rape and be raped which represents sexual equality. We now have two Cartesian or Kantian selves, not one, represented in the law of rape: two unities of subjective being – two abstract individuals.

But Australian feminists still feel a profound unease. Whatever the law says about it, we know that it is still men who are raping and women who are being raped. Hale and Blackstone knew this to be true, that rape was a crime of men against women; and yet this persistent fact – that it is men who rape women – seems to have escaped the modern Australian jurist. Rape laws may now be gender-neutral, but the behaviour is not. We sense also that there is something deeply wrong with the ideal of sexuality implicit in modern rape law. Ostensibly, then, there has been a rejection of the possessive form of heterosexual love in which men exclusively are the ravishers, women the ravished. Now it works both ways. Man can still take and possess woman but now woman can possess man. Australian rape law tells us that women can oblige men to surrender themselves to us utterly, and women can use force to achieve it when the man refuses to submit ...

... Though the traditional Kantian idea of subjectivity has now, by necessary implication, been recognised reciprocally in Australian women, no attempt has been made to consider whether this idea makes sense to women (or at all). There has been no exploration of new sexual terrains in order to discover what sexual subjectivity to women might mean. Faith has been kept with the old ways. Though ostensibly dramatic in the changes it has effected, liberal rape law reform has not extended to the development of new meanings of male and female sexuality. The old dream of symmetry implicit in the traditional form of 'erotic love' remains: the dream is that one part (the man) possesses another (a woman), who wishes only to be possessed.

Modern Australian rape laws have simply inverted this possessive relation, without considering whether it is appropriate to regard the sex protected by such law as possession. The reciprocity of sex implicit in the new laws is a curiously mechanical thing, one which fails to convince.

Naffine's argument that gender-neutral definitions obscure the actual nature of the social phenomenon of rape raises an intractable difficulty. Can the law of rape create a framework which recognises the current asymmetry of sexual power without perpetuating a disempowering, victimised image of female sexuality?

Although the definition of rape in terms of penile penetration means that only men can perpetrate rape, women can be convicted as secondary parties, even where it is not clear that the perpetrator had full legal capacity (*R v Cogan and Leak*, 1976; *DPP v K and C*, 1997). The irrebuttable presumption that a male under the age of 14 could not commit offences involving sexual intercourse was abolished in 1993.

Jennifer Temkin, *Rape and the Legal Process* (Oxford University Press, 2002) p 56

In their study of 115 rape victims, Holmstrom and Burgess found that vaginal penetration by the penis had been accompanied by forced fellatio in 22 per cent of cases, cunnilingus in 5 per cent, anal intercourse in 5 per cent, urination on the victim or her clothes in 4 per cent, and insertion into the vagina of an object in 1 per cent of cases respectively. Wright and West, in a study of all incidents recorded by the police as genuine rapes or attempted rapes in six English counties over a five-year period from 1972 to 1976, found that of a total of 297 cases, fellatio was attempted or demanded in 30 incidents, cunnilingus in 13, buggery in 12 and other sexual acts usually involving masturbation in 38. Forced fellatio was particularly common where the assailant had been drinking and was unable to sustain an erection or reach orgasm. Holmstrom and Burgess found that forced fellatio was twice as common in multiple assailant rape whereas cunnilingus only featured in single assailant rape, but these differences do not appear in Wright and West's larger sample.

II.b.ii.   Rape and marriage

Janet Radcliffe Richards argues that men have overcome their natural problem of being unable to produce children which are identifiable as their own by taking control of women, and insisting on their sexual fidelity (1982: 252). Until 1991, the marital rape immunity in England and Wales gave this power an institutional legitimacy. The marital rape exemption commanded a remarkable degree of official support until relatively recently. For example, the Criminal

Law Revision Committee, in its 1984 Report on Sexual Offences, concluded that there were circumstances in which marital rape should not be an offence:

> The majority of us ... believe that rape cannot be considered in the abstract as merely 'sexual intercourse without consent'. The circumstances of rape may be peculiarly grave. This feature is not present in the case of a husband and wife cohabiting with each other when an act of sexual intercourse occurs without the wife's consent. They may well have had sexual intercourse regularly before the act in question and, because a sexual relationship may involve a degree of compromise, she may sometimes have agreed only with some reluctance to such intercourse. Should he go further and force her to have sexual intercourse without her consent, this may evidence a failure of the marital relationship. But it is far from being the 'unique' and 'grave' offence described earlier. Where the husband goes so far as to cause injury, there are available a number of offences against the person with which he may be charged, but the gravamen of the husband's conduct is the injury he has caused not the sexual intercourse he has forced [1984, para 2.66].

The Committee thought that the institution of marriage would be under threat if the marital immunity were removed altogether.

> Violence occurs in some marriages but the wives do not always wish the marital tie to be severed ... Once, however, a wife placed the facts of an alleged rape by her husband before the police she might not be able to stop the investigative process if she wanted to ... The effect of the intervention of the police might well be to drive couples further apart in cases where a reconciliation might have occurred. All of this, more likely than not, would be detrimental to the interests of any children of the family.
>
> ... Moreover, a prosecution for rape might necessitate a complicated and unedifying investigation of the marital history ... Some of us consider that the criminal law should keep out of marital relationships between cohabiting partners – especially the marriage bed – except where injury arises, when there are other offences which can be charged [para 2.69].

The Committee perpetuated, of course, the commonly-held stereotype of the 'real' rapist as a stranger. The idea that rape by a non-stranger is not really grave unless actual injury is caused of course begs many questions about what is meant by injury. Acknowledging that many rape victims are known to their assailants does not itself displace the frequently-held view that stranger rapes are more serious or threatening. Just five years after the CLRC report, however, the High Court of Justiciary in Scotland took a very different view, and decided that the marital immunity, along with its extraordinary vision of the asymmetrical marital relationship as central to social order, was no longer appropriate (*S v HM Advocate*, 1989). Soon afterwards the exemption came under renewed and ultimately successful attack in the English courts:

R v R [1991] 4 All ER 481

[*The defendant was charged with raping his wife. His wife had left him; he forced his way into her parents' home and attempted to have intercourse with her against her will. The trial judge overruled the defence's submission of marital immunity, and R changed his plea to guilty of attempted rape. His appeal against conviction was dismissed by the Court of Appeal. This decision was upheld by the House of Lords, which took a rather different view of the strength of the common law authorities supporting the exemption than that taken in Steele:*]

Lord Keith.

... For over 150 years after the publication of Hale's work there appears to have been no reported case in which judicial consideration was given to his proposition ... It may be taken that the proposition was generally regarded as an accurate statement of the common law of England. The common law is, however, capable of evolving in the light of changing social, economic and cultural developments. Hale's proposition reflected the state of affairs in these respects at the time it was enunciated. Since then, the status of women, and particularly married women, has changed out of all recognition in various ways which are very familiar and upon which it is unnecessary to go into detail. Apart from property matters and the availability of matrimonial remedies, one of the most important changes is that marriage is in modern times regarded as a partnership of equals, and no longer one in which the wife must be the subservient chattel of the husband. Hale's proposition involves that by marriage a wife gives her irrevocable consent to sexual intercourse with her husband under all circumstances and irrespective of the state of her health or how she happens to be feeling at the time. In modern times any reasonable person must regard that conception as unacceptable.

... The position then is that part of Hale's proposition which asserts that a wife cannot retract the consent to sexual intercourse which she gives on marriage has been departed from in a series of decided cases. On grounds of principle there is no good reason why the whole proposition should not be held inapplicable in modern times. The only question is whether section 1(1) of the [Sexual Offences (Amendment) Act 1976] [which defined rape as 'unlawful' sexual intercourse] presents an insuperable obstacle to that sensible course. The argument is that 'unlawful' in the subsection means outside the bond of marriage. That is not the most natural meaning of the word, which normally describes something which is contrary to some law or enactment or is done without lawful justification or excuse. Certainly in modern times sexual intercourse outside marriage would not ordinarily be described as unlawful. If the subsection proceeds on the basis that a woman on marriage gives a general consent to sexual intercourse, there can never be any question of intercourse with her by her husband being without her consent. There would thus be no point in enacting that only intercourse without consent outside marriage is to constitute rape ...

...

The fact is that it is clearly unlawful to have sexual intercourse with any woman without her consent, and that the use of the word in the subsection adds nothing. In my opinion there are no rational grounds for putting the suggested gloss on the word, and it should be treated as being mere surplusage in this enactment ...

Lord Keith's speech is driven by social considerations: he found legal reasons for following his social instincts. In doing so, he swept away one of the major formal injustices of modern criminal law. But he also adopted – notwithstanding the technical niceties in which he framed his argument – a quasi-legislative role. Lord Keith was conscious of this, and justified it by the argument that it was not the creation of a new offence, rather 'the removal of a common law fiction which has become anachronistic and offensive'. Yet the decision is one which expands rather than contracts the criminal law, and applies it (retrospectively) to a particular defendant. For this reason, some commentators who welcomed the substance of the decision nonetheless questioned its implications for the principle of legality and the proper relationship between courts and legislature (Giles 1992). 'R' appealed to the European Court of Human Rights on the ground that his conviction was in violation of Article 7 on retrospective punishment (*CR and SW v UK*, 1996). The terms in which the court dismissed his appeal imply that criminal law has an immanent capacity to adapt itself to prevailing social standards: the argument draws on an idea of 'manifestly' wrongful acts reminiscent of Fletcher's account of ideas of criminality underpinning the early common law (see **Chapter 4.II.a.i.**).

Stephanie Palmer, 'Rape in Marriage and the European Convention on Human Rights' (V Feminist Legal Studies, 1997) 91 at 95–96

The Court stressed the importance of the guarantee enshrined in Article 7 and stated that it should be construed 'to provide effective safeguards against arbitrary prosecution, conviction and punishment.' But clearly the object and purpose of this essential guarantee should not be interpreted at the expense of other objectives of the Convention itself. The Court seemed to acknowledge this by stating that '[t]he essentially debasing character of rape is so manifest that the result of the decision [of the English appellate courts] cannot be said to be at variance with the object and purpose of Article 7 of the Convention'. The Court then added that the abandonment of the 'unacceptable idea' of the marital rape exemption conformed not only with a 'civilised concept of marriage but also, and above all, with the fundamental objectives of the Convention', namely human dignity and freedom.

In 1994, the legislature took the opportunity of the Criminal Justice and Public Order Act to endorse the House of Lords' decision by removing the word 'unlawfully' from the statutory definition of rape.

While the symbolic importance of these developments in the law of rape can hardly be underestimated, their practical significance is likely to be moderate. The general factors weighing against the reporting and successful prosecution of rape cases are particularly strong in marital cases, and courts take a more lenient view of relationship rates than of other cases (see **section II.b.vi.** below; and on 'domestic' violence, see **Chapter 6.I.b.**).

II.b.iii.   Consent, belief and mistake – the background

As we have seen, the essence of the conduct element of rape lies in the lack of the victim's consent (Sexual Offences Bill 2003, clause 1). The capacity of consent to remove conduct from the ambit of criminal regulation in rape is in marked contrast to its incapacity to do so in the field of sado-masochist (homosexual) sexual practice (*Brown*, 1993; see **section III.a.ii.** below). Two broad questions arise in relation to consent. First, how is consent to be defined and established, and what clues does this give us to the value attached to the autonomy of different sexual subjects? Second, what view of the wrong of rape, and of the meaning of sexual relationships, is implicit in the crime's definition in terms of non-consent? Intimately connected with the issue of consent is that of the defendant's belief in consent. Rape cases hinge on these two crucial issues: on the *fact of non consent* on the part of the victim and on *the defendant's state of mind or belief* about whether the victim was consenting. The 2003 Bill takes a radical step in partially defining the meaning of consent, and in setting out presumptions about consent and mistaken belief (2003 Bill, clauses 75–77). In order to understand the Bill's approach, it is helpful first to rehearse some of the previous judicial attempts to nail the elusive flag of consent to a clear mast and to reconcile traditional principles of criminal responsibility with the complex area of human relations that comprises unwanted sexual activity.

Consent

R v Olugboja [1981] 3 All ER 443, CA

Dunn LJ.

We do not think that the issue of consent should be left to a jury without some further direction. What this should be will depend on the circumstances of each case ... They should be directed that consent, or the absence of it, is to be given its ordinary meaning and if need be, by way of example, that there is a difference between consent and submission; every consent involves a submission, but it by no means follows that a mere submission involves consent ...

The following passage suggests that this common-sense summing up may obscure the assumptions on which inferences of consent are based:

Carol Smart, 'Law's Truth/Women's Experience' in R Graycar (ed) *Dissenting Opinions* (Allen and Unwin, 1990) pp 9, 10, 14, 16, 17–18

The central concerns of the rape trial are consent and pleasure. Although the law is framed around mens rea and consent, the issue of mens rea only becomes relevant if consent/pleasure cannot be established. The man's intentions are therefore not a priority, the whole focus is on the woman, her intentions and her pleasure ... The law in seeking to find innocence or guilt cannot accommodate the supposed ambiguity of a submission to a sexual assault. Either a woman does not consent or she consents. If the former cannot be established the latter must have occurred. Hence, in law's domain the more that non-consent can be made to look like submission, the more it will be treated like consent ... It is important also to consider the sexual map onto which the idea of a woman's consent or non-consent is projected. I have argued above that in a phallocentric culture women's sexuality becomes mysterious – to themselves, it is argued, as much as to men. Women's rejection of sex is therefore always ambiguous. Submission is already a part of 'normal' heterosexual relations.

[I]n spite of feminist challenges to the sexual status quo, sexuality is comprehended as the pleasures of the phallus ... the penis is constructed as the organising principle of the sex act. Female pleasure remains a mystery. One has only to consider the debate starting with Freud and continuing into the 1980s about the mystery of the site of the female orgasm, and whether it should be situated in one place or another ... [T]he presumption in favour of the pleasure/intercourse linkage makes it virtually impossible for women to establish that it was not pleasurable when there is a contested account such as in the rape trial ...

The concept of phallogocentrism is one which allows us ... to understand how the construction of femininity and masculinity, and the values attributed to these constructs, are part of our world view and identity. They are also part of law ...

In the rape trial a woman's denial of pleasure must be taken in the context of layers of cultural contradictions over what this pleasure might be. Her denial of consent must be taken in the context of a woman's No meaning Yes. But the trial process itself adds another dimension, this is the process by which the trial becomes a pornographic vignette ... The more an account of a rape has resonances with the standard pornographic genre, the less it will be regarded as rape. There are a number of narrative conventions within pornography. One is the vignette in which the woman says no, but her resistance is overcome and she becomes sexually voracious. Another is the woman who is ready for sexual adventure, will take on lots of men, and even surprises men with how willing and forward she is.

... [T]he story that the woman must tell ... is the same story that gives pleasure in the tabloid newspaper or soft porn magazine. She cannot dissociate herself from her body, the body on which the assault was carried out. As MacKinnon has argued in relation to sexual harassment, for a woman to appear in person to complain of sexual abuse, is to lose the sympathy of the court. This is because they can see her and sexualise her ... We cannot ignore that accounts of rape are sexually arousing – tabloid newspapers thrive on this fact ... The process of the rape trial can be described as a specific sexualisation of a woman's body which has already been sexualised within the confines of a phallocentric culture.

As well as the hazy line between submission and consent, there was an (apparently) difficult question about consent obtained through fraud. The courts severely limited criminal law's protection of women's sexual integrity by developing a distinction between fraud as to the nature of the act and other fraud.

Papadimitropoulos v R (1957) 98 CLR 249, High Court of Australia

[*The defendant appealed against a conviction for rape. He had misled a Greek woman who could not speak English into thinking that he had married her when in fact all he had done was give notice at the registry office of intention to marry. The intercourse took place during the 'honeymoon'. What follows is taken from the court's written judgment.*]

Dixon CJ, McTiernan, Webb, Kitto and Taylor JJ.

... There has been some judicial resistance to the idea that an actual consent to an act of sexual intercourse can be no consent because it is vitiated by fraud or mistake. The key to the difficulty may perhaps be found in a brief sentence of Cussen J in *Lambert* (1919 at 212): 'Now, carnal knowledge is merely the physical fact of penetration though, of course, there cannot be consent even to that without some perception of what is about to take place ... '

[*After reciting a number of nineteenth-century cases concerning impersonation and fraud, the judgment continues:*]

... At this point a declaration of law was made by statute. Section 4 of the Criminal Law Amendment Act 1885, after reciting that doubts had been entertained whether a man who induces a married woman to permit him to have connection with her by personating her husband is or is not guilty of rape, enacted and declared that every such offender should be deemed guilty of rape.

The next judicial step was taken in the case of *Clarence* (1888). The decision was simply that a husband who infects his wife with venereal disease is not thereby guilty of inflicting grievous bodily harm. But this led to the judges giving much consideration to what was involved in the wife's consent, ignorant as she was of her husband's condition. The judgments contain many observations which are pertinent to the distinction upon which this case turns ... 'Take, for example, [said Wills J] the case of a man without a single good quality, a gaol-bird, heartless, mean and cruel, without the smallest intention of doing anything but possessing himself of the person of his victim, but successfully representing himself as man of good family and connections prevented by some temporary obstacle from contracting an immediate marriage, and with conscious hypocrisy acting the part of a devoted lover, and in this fashion, or perhaps under the guise of affected religious fervour, effecting the ruin of his victim' (1888: 29, 30). The conception which Wills J had of what sufficed to vitiate consent is expressed as follows: 'The essence of rape is, to my mind, the penetration of the woman's person without her consent. In other words it is, roughly speaking, where the woman does not intend that the sexual act shall be done upon her either at all, or, what is pretty much the same thing, by the particular individual doing it, and an assault which includes penetration does not seem to me to be anything but rape.' (1888: 34) ...

In *Williams* (1923) a new version of the 'medical treatment' cases was dealt with by the Court of Criminal Appeal. This time it was a singing master and the pretence was that the treatment was for breathing. Possibly the case went a little further than *Case* (1850) and *Flattery* (1887) but, if so, that is only with reference to the complexion the facts were given. The materiality of the case lies only in a broad statement which Lord Hewart C J quoted from a text book. 'A consent or submission obtained by fraud is, it would seem, not a defence to rape or cognate offences' (1923). It is interesting to notice that this statement is contradictory of that of Sir James Fitzjames Stephen in his note in his Digest of the Criminal Law, 3rd ed (1883) at p. 185, in which he describes the principle to be 'that where consent is obtained by fraud the act does not amount to rape'. It is contradictory too of that made by Bovill C J in *Barrow* (1868). From what has been said already, however, it should be clear that the truth lies between the two opposing generalisations.

In the language of a note to the Canadian decision of *Harms* (1944), fraud in the inducement does not destroy the reality of the apparent consent; fraud in the factum does. The note distinguishes 'between the type of fraud which induces a consent that would not otherwise have been obtained but which is none the less a valid consent and the type of fraud which prevents any real consent from existing ...

It must be noted that in considering whether an apparent consent is unreal it is a mistake or misapprehension that makes it so. It is not the fraud producing the mistake which is material so much as the mistake itself ... the identity of the man and the character of the physical act that is done or proposed seem now clearly to be regarded as forming part of the nature and character of the act to which the woman's consent is directed ...

In the present case the decision of the majority of the Full Court extends this conception beyond the identity of the physical act and the immediate conditions affecting its nature to an antecedent cause – the existence of a valid marriage. In the history of bigamy that has never been done. The most heartless bigamist has not been considered guilty of rape ... Rape, as a capital felony, was defined with exactness, and although there has been some extension over the centuries in the ambit of the crime, it is quite wrong to bring within its operation forms of evil conduct because they bear some analogy to aspects of the crime and deserve punishment. The judgment of the Full Court of the Supreme Court goes upon the moral differences between marital intercourse and sexual relations without marriage. The difference was indeed so radical that it is apt to draw the mind away from the real question which is carnal knowledge without consent. It may well be true that the woman in the present case never intended to consent to the latter relationship. But, as was said before, the key to such a case as the present lies in remembering that it is only the penetration of the woman's body without her consent to such penetration that makes the felony. The capital felony was not directed to fraudulent conduct inducing her consent. Frauds of that kind must be punished under other heads of the criminal law or not at all; they are not rape ... To return to the central point; rape is carnal knowledge of a woman without her consent: carnal knowledge is the physical fact of penetration; it is the consent to that which is in question; such a consent demands a perception as to what is about to take place, as to the identity of the man and the character of what he is doing ... the appeal should be allowed and the conviction quashed.

In the court's analysis, consent has become refracted and distorted. If the question were asked in many of the cases cited in *Papadimitropoulos*, 'did the woman consent to sexual intercourse in these circumstances?' the answer could only be 'no, she did not'. But the question which the courts have required to be put is 'did she mistake the nature of the act?'. Hence, for example, a woman who agrees to have intercourse with a man in exchange for money is not raped if he refuses to pay (*Linekar*, 1995). Similarly, a woman who agrees to sexual intercourse in ignorance of the fact that she is thereby likely to be infected with a serious disease is not a victim of rape (*Clarence*, 1888).

The context in which consent to sex takes place brings us to our second question: the vision of sexuality, and of sexual abuses, implicit in criminal law's conception of rape as non-consensual intercourse. One way of looking at the wrong of rape is that it infringes a woman's right to the autonomous control over access to a rather curious form of property – her body (Dripps 1992). Such a reading, which constructs rape as a form of property offence, has a clear resonance with early conceptions of rape as protecting a husband or father's proprietary right to control sexual access to a wife or daughter. But, in focusing on a proprietary conception of sexuality, the wrong of rape is commodified in a way which sits uneasily with modern conceptions of the affective dimension – and value – of sexuality (Lacey 1998a). Moreover, it might be argued that the construction of rape in terms of non-consent itself expresses the possessory view of erotic love identified by Naffine: by definition, the defendant – and hence, in English law, a man – is the active party, to whom the victim – a woman or a man 'feminised' by penetration – responds by granting or withholding consent. Moving on from this analysis, feminist commentators have tried to reconstruct the notion of consent in more substantive and reciprocal terms. Box, for example, suggests that rape could be defined as 'sexual access gained by any means where the female's overt genuine consent is absent' (1983: 125); and Lees goes further in calling for a definition of rape which would embody a 'communicative view of sexuality':

Sue Lees, *Carnal Knowledge: Rape on Trial* (Hamish Hamilton, 1996) p 260

The main reason why the rape law is so unsatisfactory in all advanced countries is the failure of judges to adopt a modern communicative model of sexuality which implies that there must be some positive responses by both parties ... [a] concept of sexuality as mutually negotiated. As Naffine proposes, judges should be aware that women who do not actively resist, or say nothing, do not necessarily want to have sex, but may acquiesce because they see no alternative. This has already become law in Australia, where in 1992 the Victoria Parliament passed an amendment to its Crimes Act which requires a judge, in relevant circumstances, to direct the jury that 'the fact that a person did not say or do anything to indicate free agreement to a sexual act is normally enough to show that the act took place without the person's free agreement'. The South Australian Supreme Court has endorsed a similar model of communicative sexuality by indicating that where a man has received signals of non-consent, he can no longer assume that the woman is consenting. He must inquire. For such reforms to become acceptable requires dramatic changes in the attitudes and composition of the judiciary in England and Wales.

As we have seen, Naffine is sceptical about the capacity of gender-neutral reforms to achieve substantive justice. Conversely, it might be argued that the emphasis on positive signs of consent is unrealistic in the intimate context of sexual encounters. Nonetheless, in different ways these Australian and UK reforms embody a recognition of the way in which contextual factors such as unequal power relations may affect the 'reality' of consent, and respond both to this asymmetry and to the potential damage caused by mistakes about consent by somewhat easing the prosecution's burden of proof. In doing so, they take a small but significant step towards constructing sexuality as involving reciprocal responsibilities. The definition of consent in the Sexual Offences Bill 2003 reflects a commitment to a communicative model of sexuality. However, it remains to be seen how such reforms will take root in a legal system that permits prejudicial cultural attitudes to persist.

This move towards the communicative model of sexuality has been questioned from opposing directions. On the one hand, Shute suggests that the Law Commission overplayed the specificity of the rape context, with the result that it proposed a change whose underlying logic would dictate a more general move to objective standards; yet the Commission failed to consider the implications of such a general change (see below). Conversely, one might question how far these changes will modify the practice of rape law. For it must be borne in mind that a jury's interpretation of what would have been 'obvious' to a 'reasonable man' will itself be shaped by prevailing cultural assumptions about masculine and feminine sexuality. To the degree, therefore, that these are misogynistic, the move from a subjective to an objective test may make only a limited difference. A woman's 'no' is often regarded as 'yes': one influential commentator in the mid-1980s introduced his discussion of sexual offences with a verse expressing precisely this sentiment (Williams 1983: 238) and judges have been known to echo such views.

Belief and mistake

It is again instructive to survey the legal picture in the period immediately before the 2003 reforms. In 1976 statute declared:

> If at a trial for a rape offence the jury has to consider whether a man believed that a woman or man was consenting to sexual intercourse, the presence or absence of reasonable grounds for such a belief is a matter to which the jury is entitled to have regard, in conjunction with any other matters, in considering whether he so believed [Sexual Offences (Amendment) Act, s 1].

The background was the decision of the House of Lords in *DPP v Morgan* (1976). The appellant invited three friends to have intercourse with his wife, telling them that her signs of resistance were not to be interpreted as lack of consent: she enjoyed it better that way. The friends were charged with rape, the appellant with aiding and abetting. They appealed against the direction of the trial judge that, if they were to be acquitted on the basis of their mistake, their belief in her consent must have been reasonable. The House of Lords decided by a 3:2 majority that it was irrelevant whether the defendants had reasonable grounds for their belief that she was consenting. The proviso to s 2(1) of the Criminal Appeal Act 1968 was, however, applied on the grounds that no jury would have failed to convict even if it had been given the right direction. In construing the 'defence' of mistaken belief as going to 'mens rea', Lord Hailsham found the logic of subjectivist criminal law doctrine compelling ([1976] AC 182 at 214):

> Once one has accepted, what seems to me abundantly clear, that the prohibited act in rape is non-consensual sexual intercourse, and that the guilty state of mind is an intention to commit it, it seems to me to follow as a matter of inexorable logic that there is no room either for a 'defence' of honest belief or mistake, or of a defence of honest and reasonable belief and mistake. Either the prosecution proves that the accused had the requisite intent, or it does not. In the former case it succeeds, and in the latter it fails. Since honest belief clearly negatives intent, the reasonableness or otherwise of that belief can only be evidence for or against the view that the belief and therefore the intent was actually held ...

If, as Lord Hailsham suggested, the definition of rape was so 'abundantly clear', it seems strange that it was necessary for the case to be appealed to the House of Lords which only decided the issue on a majority. What he failed to acknowledge was that the issue had previously been fudged, in that, although there was support for the view that rape consisted of intentional intercourse without consent, there were equally cases suggesting that mistakes had to be reasonable in order to exculpate. Lord Hailsham was right that those two propositions were irreconcilable. But there was nothing indicating which one would have to yield. What is particularly noticeable about Lord Hailsham's speech is that he hardly alluded to the actual issue before him, which was whether a man who believes without reasonable grounds that the woman is consenting should be guilty of rape. He referred neither to the prevalence of rape nor to the role of the criminal law in its control.

The question of how far the subjective approach could accommodate 'thoughtless' or 'inconsiderate' rape continued to trouble both commentators and the courts (Gardner 1991). The Law Commission suggested in 1995 – in marked contrast to its previous position (Law Commission 1994: see Leng 1994) – that the subjectivist approach to mistaken belief in the context of rape should be reconsidered:

Stephen Shute, 'Something Old, Something New, Something Borrowed' [1996] Crim LR 687–688

[M]any of the Commission's conclusions will come as a shock to dyed-in-the-wool subjectivists. For, in sharp contrast to the approach taken by the Heilbron Committee, the Draft Criminal Code and *Morgan*, the Commission now accepts that there are good grounds for saying that a man who engages in sexual intercourse should be required both to consider beforehand whether his partner is consenting and to take care that any beliefs he forms about consent are accurate. If he does not, the Commission argues, he violates his partner's rights because he 'fails to give proper value to her existence as a human being' (LC para. 7.18).

The force of this new-found objectivism is illustrated by the Commission by dint of two compelling examples, in each of which a man crassly concludes that his sexual partner is consenting when it would have been obvious to any reasonable person in the same situation that she was not. The first example, based on facts very similar to those in *DPP v Morgan*, describes a man whose mistaken belief in consent derives solely from the fact that a third party has told him that signs of resistance should be taken as an indication of consent. In such circumstances, the Commission claims, there is a 'respectable case' for saying that because the man's conduct involves a 'denial' of his partner's autonomy and a 'lack of respect for her status as an individual with a will of her own', he must take the consequences of his actions. The second example concerns a man whose belief in consent derives from his firmly-held view that when women say 'no' they mean 'yes'. Once again, the Commission considers that there is a 'respectable case' for saying that this man ought to be liable for rape. However, the Commission wisely recommends in both these examples that the prosecution should be required to prove that the woman's lack of consent would have been 'obvious' to a reasonable man, not just perceptible, and that the defendant had the capacity to understand that the woman did not consent. Otherwise ... rape liability would be imposed for negligence *per se*.

These examples nicely illustrate the Commission's point that there can be good grounds for imposing criminal liability on those who indulge in sexual intercourse on the basis of crass mistakes concerning their partners' consent. What the Law Commission overlooks, however, is that sexual intercourse is not unique in this respect. Other harmful or potentially harmful activities undertaken on the basis of mistaken beliefs are also strong candidates for criminalisation. The fact is that our mutual interdependence and social interaction spawn a wide range of moral duties which are designed to prevent us from imposing excessive and unreasonable risks of harm on our fellow citizens; and, far from diffusing moral responsibility, grossly mistaken beliefs may actually aggravate our culpability when these duties are breached. Yet the Commission seems unwilling to accept that this is a consequence of its position.

The question of mistaken belief affords another opportunity for defence barristers to appeal to jury perceptions and prejudices. This was evident in the recent acquittal of Quinten Hann, an Australian snooker player charged with rape, where his counsel remarked that:

> sometimes in the heat of passion when a woman says no, she doesn't necessarily mean no. You can say 'no' a thousand times, but if you show by your actions that you don't mean it, it doesn't necessarily mean that consent is withdrawn [*The Guardian*, 4 July 2002].

The need to counter this type of comment partly explains clause 1 of the Sexual Offences Bill 2003 which replaces the *Morgan* 'defence' of honest belief with one based on reasonableness.

II.b.iv.   Consent, belief and mistake – the 2003 reforms

Reflecting the widespread concern with the low conviction rate for rape, the Home Office made the argument for a more structured approach to consent in the White Paper preceding the Sexual Offences Bill 2003:

Home Office, *Protecting The Public: Strengthening Protection Against Sex Offenders and Reforming the Law on Sexual Offences* (Cmnd 5668) (HMSO, 2002)

Human beings have devised a complex set of messages to convey agreement or lack of it. Agreement or lack of agreement is not necessarily verbal, but both parties should understand it. Each must respect the right of the other to demonstrate or say "no" and mean it. We do not of course wish to formalise such understanding into an unnecessary or semi-contractual agreement; it is not the role of Government or the law to prescribe how consent should be sought and given. It is, however, the role of the law to make it unambiguously clear that intimate sexual acts should only take place with the agreement of both parties.

The proposed offence of rape, as we have seen above, has three components:
(a)   intentional penile penetration of B by A;
(b)   B's lack of consent; and
(c)   that A does not reasonably believe that B consents.

Subclause (c) introduces an objective element in contrast with the fully subjective approach that has applied since *Morgan*. The Bill as originally introduced in Parliament went to the other extreme by measuring the defendant's conduct against a reasonable person. If that 'reasonable person' would 'in all the circumstances' have doubted whether B consented, the defendant would then have been expected to act in way that the reasonable person would consider sufficient to resolve such doubts. The 'reasonable belief' standard now contained in the Bill is more a half-way house for it may allow the defendant's reasonableness to be measured in relation to his own perception of the circumstances.

Sexual Offences Bill 2003

Clause 75   Consent

For the purposes of this Part, a person consents if he agrees by choice, and has the freedom and capacity to make that choice.

Clause 76   Presumptions about the absence of belief in consent

(1) If in proceedings for an offence to which this section applies it is proved–
    (a) that the defendant did the relevant act,
    (b) that any of the circumstances specified in subsection (2) existed, and
    (c) that the defendant knew that those circumstances existed,
the complainant is to be taken not to have consented to the relevant act unless sufficient evidence is adduced to raise an issue as to whether he consented, and the defendant is to be taken not to have reasonably believed that the complainant consented unless sufficient evidence is adduced to raise an issue as to whether he reasonably believed it.

(2) The circumstances are that–
    (a) any person was, at the time of the relevant act or immediately before it began, using violence against the complainant or causing the complainant to fear that immediate violence would be used against him;
    (b) any person was, at the time of the relevant act or immediately before it began, causing the complainant to fear that violence was being used, or that immediate violence would be used, against another person;
    (c) the complainant was, and the defendant was not, unlawfully detained at the time of the relevant act;
    (d) the complainant was asleep or otherwise unconscious at the time of the relevant act;
    (e) because of the complainant's physical disability, the complainant would not have been able at the time of the relevant act to communicate to the defendant whether the complainant consented.

(3) In subsection (2)(a) and (b), the reference to the time immediately before the relevant act began is, in the case of an act which is one of a continuous series of sexual activities, a reference to the time immediately before the first sexual activity began.

Clause 76 applies to both the issue of consent and that of the defendant's reasonable belief in consent. In each case it creates a rebuttable presumption that there was no consent or no reasonable belief in consent where: violence was used or threatened; the victim was unlawfully detained; was asleep or unconscious, or otherwise incapable of communicating consent. The presumption that the victim did not consent where one of these circumstances is proved can be rebutted only if the defendant raises sufficient evidence for the issue to be considered. This is known as an evidential burden. Normally it is for the prosecution to raise evidence and prove each element of an offence. Here, however, the prosecution is relieved of that evidential burden. Without some evidence from the defence, it will be assumed, on proof by the prosecution of one of the circumstances outlined in clause 76(2), that there was no consent. If that evidence is produced then the prosecution will have the usual burden of proving beyond reasonable doubt that the victim did not consent.

Partial reversals of evidential burdens, though not altogether uncommon, have never been free from controversy. Although Ashworth and Blake have suggested that around 40% of indictable offences partially reverse the burden (1996: 306) this is especially significant in terms of serious sexual offences such as rape. It is rare for a serious offence to place an evidential burden on the defendant. The Bill in its original form went even further and required the defendant to satisfy the probative as well as the evidential burden in relation to belief in consent. This might have been incompatible with the fair trial provisions of Article 6 of the ECHR which states that 'Everyone charged with a criminal offence shall be presumed innocent until proved guilty according to law'. Recent appellate activity, albeit in other criminal contexts, confirms that beyond attempting to clarify the distinction between legal and evidential burdens, the courts have been reluctant to embrace reverse onus burdens within Article 6(2): see *Kebilene* (2000), *Lambert* (2001), *Daniel* (2003). The reasoning in *Attorney-General's Reference No 4 of 2002* (2003) suggests that the Government's original formulation could have been challenged on this point. And it remains to be seen how the courts will respond not only to the evidential burdens the clause imposes but also to the substance of the clause itself, with its use of terms such as 'immediately before the relevant act' (clause 76(1)(3)).

Under the Sexual Offences Act 1956 there were separate offences of procuring a woman to have unlawful sexual intercourse by threats or intimidation (s 2), by false pretences or false representations (s 3) and of administering drugs to overpower her in order to have unlawful sexual intercourse with her (s 4). Between 2001 and 2002 there were only 130 recorded offences of procuration (Home Office 2002j). The existence of these fall-back offences was therefore of very limited practical significance, and obscured criminal law's restrictive conception of sexual autonomy. Their accommodation within clause 76 of the Sexual Offences Bill 2003, as presumptions against consent, is therefore to be welcomed.

Clause 77 restates the current law on vitiation of consent, creating a conclusive presumption of no consent where the defendant either intentionally deceived the complainant as to the nature or purpose of the act, or induced consent by impersonating someone known personally to the complainant.

Our next section sheds further light on the culture which shapes the interpretation of rape law in the courts.

II.b.v.   Evidence and the rape trial

Laws of criminal evidence have a widespread impact on criminal trials. In the case of sexual offences, legislation introduced in 1976 attempted to control the extent to which a complainant is questioned about her past sexual experience – questioning which would generally be allowed under common law rules. The reform did not prevent cross-examination on or other evidence of her sexual past *with the defendant*, and judges were often willing to use their discretion to allow evidence of past sexual experience with other men (Adler 1987). In addition, until 1994, sexual offences, whether committed by men or women, formed one of the categories for which a corroboration warning was required.

Zsuzsanna Adler, *Rape on Trial* (Routledge, 1987) pp 50–53, 73–77

The victim in a rape trial is the chief prosecution witness: without her evidence, the case against the defendant collapses. In fact, a fairly substantial number of men are acquitted if she is unwilling or unable to attend court, however legitimate the reasons for her absence ...

Once a woman gets into the witness box, she can expect to spend anything from one hour to several working days there – the average is somewhere between three and four hours. Most of that time will be spent in cross-examination ... It is often asserted that in most criminal cases, the credibility of the event is not an issue because of the unambiguous visible signs which indicate that a crime has taken place. When it comes to homicide, there is usually a body; burglary is usually accompanied by signs of forcible entry, malicious damage, and the disappearance of property. However, for many rapes all we have is signs of intercourse, possibly accompanied by some minor bruising, and a woman who says that she did not consent to the intercourse ...

The defence of rape trials uses a number of strands of attack to undermine the woman's evidence and to shake her story, all of which would be considered totally unacceptable if she had reported, say, a serious non-sexual assault. First, there is continual questioning about the details of the rape, with suggestions that she was in the defendant's company willingly, that any protests she made were not genuine, that the intercourse was with her consent, and any injuries, the result of loveplay. A second strand is to probe her prior relationship, however vague or distant, with the accused, and on the strength of that, to suggest that she must have known what to expect when she accepted a lift, invited him in for a drink, allowed him to read the gas meter etc. A real trump card for the defence is a previous sexual relationship between her and the accused: once that is established, it will be practically impossible to convince the jury that the incident in question was anything other than one in a long series of consensual acts. In addition, her general character and reputation are probed in great detail: the list of less than 100 per cent 'respectable' women is almost endless, and includes Greenham Common supporters, single mothers, mothers with children in care, girls with punk hairstyles, women with a criminal record, or anyone living in a commune. This line of questioning is based on the assumption that such women are unlikely to be genuine victims of rape; or worse, that even if they are raped, it does not matter all that much.

Lastly, the woman's previous sexual experiences with persons other than the defendant is used to suggest that because she has consented to intercourse with one or several men in the past, she is that much more likely to have agreed to the defendant too ...

Applications for permission to introduce evidence of the woman's previous sexual experience were made in [40 per cent] of contested trials ... They were most common in trials involving several defendants: ... The reason for this is probably that it becomes imperative to attack the woman's sexual morality when she is said to have agreed to intercourse with several men – the jury is unlikely to believe that of just anybody. Although in these cases, applications were not always made on behalf of all defendants, the introduction of evidence about the woman's sexual past has a halo effect, which affords some benefit to all concerned ...

Predictably, the overwhelming majority of applications were made by defendants whose case involved the question of consent: nearly 60 per cent of these men wanted to bring in some evidence of the woman's sexual past. Applications under section 2, although not universal, are certainly a good deal less exceptional than the Heilbron group or Parliament intended. Furthermore, at 75 per cent, their success rate is considerable ...

[T]he findings of this study suggest that judges' decision-making in this area continues to reflect the principles of case-law established in the nineteenth century. The basic assumption that a victim's prior sexual experience is relevant in establishing consent has not been substantially altered by a procedural change in the law.

When a judge 'wrongly' allowed such questioning there could be no appeal, since the mistake benefits the defendant (although the Criminal Justice Bill 2003 introduces the possibility of retrial following acquittal: clauses 62–66). This explains the relatively small number of appellate decisions on the 1976 Act. In *Viola* (1982), the defendant was refused permission to cross-examine the complainant as to whether she had made sexual advances to two casual visitors only a few hours before the alleged rape, and whether a few hours after it she had entertained a naked man in her house. In allowing the appeal, Lord Lane said it was clear that the section was 'aimed primarily at protecting complainants from cross-examination as to credit, from questions which went merely to credit and no more' (at 77). He contrasted this with questions which were 'relevant to an issue in the trial in the light of the way the case is being run, for instance relevant to the issue of consent, as opposed merely to credit'. Such questions 'are likely to be admitted, because to exclude a relevant question on an issue in the trial ... will usually mean that the jury are being prevented from hearing something which, if they did hear it, might cause them to change their minds about the evidence given by the complainant'. The difficulty with this approach is, of course, that the section would have had no purpose if it did not result in some questions being excluded on the ground that to allow them would cause the jury to change its mind. In other words, the section was of limited utility if its purpose was merely to prevent questions being asked rather than also to try to prevent the jury reaching unwarranted conclusions from this sort of evidence. The distinction between credit and issue can be a fine, or misleading, one (Zuckerman 1989: 102). Part of the problem seems to be a failure to recognise that concepts such as 'relevance' and 'probative usefulness' are themselves open to interpretation. In *Viola*, for example, it is not self-evident why the contested questions were relevant to issue or probatively use-ful-. Their admissibility seems to rest on the assumption that having consented once, a woman is to be regarded with suspicion when she denies having consented subsequently. Why is it assumed that previous sexual experience tells us anything about a woman's veracity in relation to an alleged rape?

Inevitably, where sexual history evidence is admitted, the focus of the trial shifts from questions about the legality of the defendant's acts to those about the propriety of the victim's behaviour. Temkin's study of the operation of s 2 identifies a 'Catch-22' situation for rape victims: where they represent them-selves as sexually inexperienced or 'chaste', hence seeking to benefit from stereotypes of feminine virtue (and, hence, veracity), evidence of *any* sexual experience will be likely to undermine their credibility. Conversely, if they admit sexual experience, they are almost routinely assumed to have been more likely to have consented to sex with the defendant on this occasion. Where the trial turns on the issue of consent, the defendant can attack the woman in this way without risking having any of his own past conduct brought in. Consent is seen as a separate issue: it is not assumed that a man's sexual history is relevant to whether he imposed non-consensual sex on the woman on this occasion. So the risks of raising questions about sexual history are – like contemporary discourses of sexuality – entirely asymmetrical. Temkin's research revealed that, where judges refused to exercise their discretion to allow sexual history evidence under s 2, defendants were often successful in their appeals, on the basis that the verdict might have been different had the evidence been admitted (see, for example *Barnes*, 1994; *Walker*, 1994; *Redguard*, 1991; *R v C*, 1992; on sexual history evidence, see also Brown et al 1993; Lees 1996). The guarantee of anonymity accorded to rape victims by s 4 of the 1976 Act (and extended to victims of other sexual offences in 1992) is poor compensation for the damaging experience which the (non-)operation of s 2 inflicted upon them at trial. The lengthy and gruelling cross-examination of rape victims by defendants-in-person led to the removal of this 'right' in 1999 (Youth Justice and Criminal Evidence Act 1999, s 34).

This was an early indication of the Labour government's promise to improve the plight of victims in the criminal justice system. A more structured approach to sexual evidence in rape trials was introduced by s 41 of the Youth Justice and Criminal Evidence Act 1999. This prohibited evidence about the victim's sexual history except in circumstances defined in subsections (3) and (5), which are set out below.

Youth Justice and Criminal Evidence Act 1999

Section 41 Restriction on evidence or questions about complainant's sexual history
(1) If at a trial a person is charged with a sexual offence, then, except with the leave of the court–
  (a) no evidence may be adduced, and
  (b) no question may be asked in cross-examination,
  by or on behalf of any accused at the trial, about any sexual behaviour of the complainant.
(2) The court may give leave in relation to any evidence or question only on an application made by or on behalf of an accused, and may not give such leave unless it is satisfied–
  (a) that subsection (3) or (5) applies, and
  (b) that a refusal of leave might have the result of rendering unsafe a conclusion of the jury or (as the case may be) the court on any relevant issue in the case.
(3) This subsection applies if the evidence or question relates to a relevant issue in the case and either–
  (a) that issue is not an issue of consent; or
  (b) it is an issue of consent and the sexual behaviour of the complainant to which the evidence or question relates is alleged to have taken place at or about the same time as the event which is the subject matter of the charge against the accused; or
  (c) it is an issue of consent and the sexual behaviour of the complainant to which the evidence or question relates is alleged to have been, in any respect, so similar–
  (i) to any sexual behaviour of the complainant which (according to evidence adduced or to be adduced by or on behalf of the accused) took place as part of the event which is the subject matter of the charge against the accused, or
  (ii) to any other sexual behaviour of the complainant which (according to such evidence) took place at or about the same time as that event, that the similarity cannot reasonably be explained as a coincidence.

(4) For the purposes of subsection (3) no evidence or question shall be regarded as relating to a relevant issue in the case if it appears to the court to be reasonable to assume that the purpose (or main purpose) for which it would be adduced or asked is to establish or elicit material for impugning the credibility of the complainant as a witness.

(5) This subsection applies if the evidence or question–

   (a) relates to any evidence adduced by the prosecution about any sexual behaviour of the complainant; and

   (b) in the opinion of the court, would go no further than is necessary to enable the evidence adduced by the prosecution to be rebutted or explained by or on behalf of the accused.

Section 41 extends the ban to evidence about the victim's sexual history with the defendant, unless the previous occasion was 'at or about the same time' as the alleged incident (s 41(3)(b)). However, any hope that s 41 represented a breakthrough in terms of victims' rights was dealt a blow by the House of Lords in *R v A (No 2)* (2001). The accused alleged that the woman had consented to intercourse, or if not, that he had believed she had. At trial, the judge refused to allow cross-examination of the victim about a previous consensual sexual relationship they shared. The Court of Appeal allowed his appeal on the basis that such evidence was admissible on the issue of the defendant's *belief* in consent (s 41(3)(a)). The question for the House was whether the evidence was also admissible on the issue of *whether she had in fact consented*. Section 41 appeared to say no – but how would this stand in light of the fair trial provisions of Article 6? Using the new canon of interpretation under s 3 of the Human Rights Act 1998, s 41(3)(c) was construed in order to ensure the right to fair trial of the defendant. Lord Steyn, although accepting the prejudices surrounding rape and the legal process, refused to accept a blanket ban on the use of sexual history evidence between the victim and the accused:

R v A (No 2) [2001] 2 WLR 1546

Following the 1939–45 war the general principle of the equality of men and women in all spheres of life has gradually become established. In the aftermath of the sexual revolution of the sixties the autonomy and independence of women in sexual matters has become an accepted norm. It was this change in thinking about women and sex which made possible the decision of the House of Lords in *R v R (rape: marital exemption)* [1991] 4 All ER 481, [1992] 1 AC 599 that the offence of rape may be committed by a husband upon his wife. It was a dramatic reversal of old-fashioned beliefs. Discriminatory stereotypes which depict women as sexually available have been exposed as an affront to their fundamental rights. Nevertheless, it has to be acknowledged that in the criminal courts of our country, as in others, outmoded beliefs about women and sexual matters lingered on. In recent Canadian jurisprudence they have been described as the discredited twin myths, viz 'that unchaste women were more likely to consent to intercourse and in any event, were less worthy of belief' (see *R v Seaboyer, R v Gayme* [1991] 2 SCR 577 at 604, 630 per McLachlin J). Such generalised, stereotyped and unfounded prejudices ought to have no place in our legal system. But even in the very recent past such defensive strategies were habitually employed. It resulted in an absurdly low conviction rate in rape cases. It also inflicted unacceptable humiliation on complainants in rape cases.

...

As a matter of common sense, a prior sexual relationship between the complainant and the accused may, depending on the circumstances, be relevant to the issue of consent. It is a species of prospectant evidence which may throw light on the complainant's state of mind. It cannot, of course, prove that she consented on the occasion in question. Relevance and sufficiency of proof are different things. The fact that the accused a week before an alleged murder threatened to kill the deceased does not prove an intent to kill on the day in question. But it is logically relevant to that issue. After all, to be relevant the evidence need merely have some tendency in logic and common sense to advance the proposition in issue. It is true that each decision to engage in sexual activity is always made afresh. On the other hand, the mind does not usually blot out all memories. What one has been engaged on in the past may influence what choice one makes on a future occasion. Accordingly, a prior relationship between a complainant and an accused may sometimes be relevant to what decision was made on a particular occasion.

[*With the unanimous support of the full house, Lord Steyn concluded that (at p 1564):*]

The effect of the decision today is that under section 41(3)(C) of the 1999 Act, construed where necessary by applying the interpretive obligation under section 3 of the Human Rights Act, and due regard always being paid to the importance of seeking to protect the complainant from indignity and from humiliating questions, the test of admissibility is whether the evidence (and questioning in relation to it) is nevertheless so relevant to the issue of consent that to exclude it would endanger the fairness of the trial under article 6 of the convention.

Much debate has surrounded s 41. However, whilst some have questioned the confines of its categories approach, Temkin reminds us of the potential prejudicial effect that knowledge of previous sexual behaviour with the accused may have:

Jennifer Temkin, 'Sexual History Evidence – Beware the Backlash' Crim LR [2003] 217 at 233

The previous sexual behaviour could have taken place in circumstances which would be highly likely to excite the prejudice of the jury as where the complainant was involved in "swinging", a "one-night stand", adultery or infidelity. But even if none of these circumstances apply, the jury will undoubtedly be invited to buy in to the myth that rape of a previous partner is most unlikely to have occurred and, if it did, does not deserve to be categorised as true rape. Myths and prejudicial assumptions can unfairly distort the outcome of trials.

Temkin also questions whether the analysis of s 41(3)(c) in *R v A* will continue to be confined to cases of previous sexual relationships with the accused. Past practice suggests that it is unlikely that defence barristers will be shy in seeking to stretch the strict limits of the decision.

Until the passage of the Criminal Justice and Public Order Act 1994, s 32, an evidential rule applying to all sexual offences required the judge to warn the jury that it may not be safe to convict the defendant on the uncorroborated evidence of the victim. As Temkin (2002: 256) notes, the rationale for such warnings 'rested on the alleged proclivities and weaknesses of women. Women, it was said, might fabricate sexual assault out of jealousy, spite, revenge, or because of a tendency to tell lies and fantasize'. Given that the victim's evidence is likely to be the principal basis for the prosecution case, the effect of the judge's opening his or her direction to the jury with such a warning was bound to have a significant impact on conviction rates. It was on this basis, as well as on the basis of a rejection of the assumptions about feminine unreliability which it embodied, that the Government abolished the requirement. It is interesting (and somewhat painful) to reflect that the need for children's evidence to be corroborated was abolished by the Criminal Justice Act 1988 – six years before the abolition of the corroboration warning in sexual cases: see **section III.a.iii.** below. In the intervening years, the law of evidence treated children as more reliable than adult witnesses in sexual cases, the vast majority of whom were women. Since it is still open to judges to give a corroboration warning, it cannot be assumed that the sexual stereotypes which underpinned the old requirement are now irrelevant to the conduct of trials.

Although the abolition of the mandatory corroboration warning was a significant advance from a feminist point of view, Temkin notes the need for research into the compliance of trial judges. Research in New South Wales, which abolished the need for a corroboration warning in 1981, found that such warnings were given in 80% of trials in a sample of 92 cases (see Temkin 2002: 266). More generally, the laws of evidence are still far from consistent. A trial judge dismissed a case of indecent assault against a woman suffering from multiple sclerosis on the basis that she could not be cross-examined (the woman had given evidence to the police using an alphabet board, and was eager to appear in court; see *The Times*, 20 August 1997, p 3), confirming the impression that criminal procedure is all too often bound by outdated and inflexible assumptions about the capacities of participants in the criminal process.

In this section, we have concentrated, for obvious reasons, on the influence of stereotypes of female sexuality on the construction of evidence in rape trials. Also relevant to the law of rape are assumptions which may mark non-white, and in particular Afro-Caribbean, defendants and 'complainants' as less credible witnesses because of stereotypes about black sexuality – an issue which is especially troubling because of the role of accusations of rape in the history of racial oppression. This analysis is, therefore, only one instance of the general power of cultural assumptions to shape the interpretation of testimony in criminal cases.

II.b.vi.   Punishing rape

Sentencing in rape cases is structured by guidance set out by the Court of Appeal (on sentencing guideline judgments, see **Chapter 1.III.d.**):

Billam [1986] 1 All ER 985

Lord Lane CJ.

We have had listed before us today a number of cases where there has been a conviction for rape or attempted rape, in order to give us an opportunity to restate principles which in our judgment should guide judges on sentencing in this difficult and sensitive area of the criminal law.

In the unhappy experience of this court, whether or not the number of convictions for rape has increased over the years, the nastiness of the cases has certainly increased, and what would ten years ago have been considered incredible perversions have now become commonplace. This is no occasion to explore the reasons for that phenomenon, however obvious they may be ...

This court emphasised in *Roberts* (1982) ... that rape is always a serious crime which calls for an immediate custodial sentence other than in wholly exceptional circumstances. The sort of exceptional circumstances in which a non-custodial sentence may be appropriate are illustrated by the decision in *Taylor* (1983) [in which a mentally retarded man raped a woman of 19 with Down's Syndrome]. Although on the facts that offence amounted to rape in the legal sense, the court observed that it did not do so in ordinary understanding.

Judges of the Crown Court need no reminder of the necessity for custodial sentences in cases of rape. The criminal statistics for 1984 show that 95% of all defendants who were sentenced in the Crown Court for offences of rape received immediate custodial sentences in one form or another. But the same statistics suggest that judges may need reminding about what length of sentence is appropriate.

Of the 95% who received custodial sentences in 1984, 28% received sentences of two years or less; 23% over two and up to three years; 18%

over three and up to four years; 18% over four and up to five years and 8% over five years (including 2% receiving life) ... Although it is important to preserve a sense of proportion in relation to other grave offences such as some forms of manslaughter, these statistics show an approach to sentences for rape which in the judgment of this court are too low ... There are, however, many reported decisions of the court which give an indication of what current practice ought to be and it may be useful to summarise their general effect.

For rape committed by an adult without any aggravating or mitigating features, a figure of five years should be taken as the starting point in a contested case. Where a rape is committed by two or more men acting together, or by a man who has broken into or otherwise gained access to a place where the victim is living, or by a person who is in a position of responsibility towards the victim, or by a person who abducts the victim and holds her captive, the starting point should be eight years.

At the top of the scale comes the defendant who has carried out what might be described as a campaign of rape, committing the crime on a number of different women or girls. He represents a more than ordinary danger and a sentence of 15 years or more may be appropriate.

Where the defendant's behaviour has manifested perverted or psychopathic tendencies or gross personality disorder, and where he is likely, if at large, to remain a danger to women for an indefinite time, a life sentence will not be inappropriate.

The crime should in any event be treated as aggravated by any of the following factors: (1) violence is used over and above the force necessary to commit the rape; (2) a weapon is used to frighten or wound the victim; (3) the rape is repeated; (4) the rape has been carefully planned; (5) the defendant has previous convictions for rape or other serious offences of a violent or sexual kind; (6) the victim is subjected to further sexual indignities or perversions; (7) the victim is either very old or very young; (8) the effect on the victim whether physical or mental, is of special seriousness. Where any one or more of the aggravating features are present, the sentence should be substantially higher than the figure suggested as the starting point.

The extra distress which giving evidence can cause to a victim means that a plea of guilty, perhaps more so than in other cases, should normally result in some reduction from what would otherwise be the appropriate sentence ...

The fact that the victim may be considered to have exposed herself to danger by acting imprudently (for instance by accepting a lift in a car from a stranger) is not a mitigating factor; and the victim's previous sexual experience is equally irrelevant. But if the victim has behaved in a manner which was calculated to lead the defendant to believe that she would consent to sexual intercourse, then there should be some mitigation of the sentence. Previous good character is only of minor relevance.

The *Billam* guidelines have been followed consistently in subsequent appellate cases (see *Cawthray*, 1994; for discussion see Henham 1994). Government emphasis on severe punishments for violence and sexual crimes since the decision in *Billam* has given further impetus both to the re-evaluation of the seriousness of rape and to public and judicial perceptions of the 'dangerousness' of repeat sex offenders. The Criminal Justice Act 1991, s 1(2)(b) provided for persons convicted of violent or sexual offences to be given custodial sentences longer than would be commensurate with the seriousness of the present offence on the ground of public protection, and the handing down of life sentences to such offenders is no longer exceptional (see *Hann*, 1995). 'Two strikes' laws, first introduced in 1997, mean an automatic life sentence for individuals committing a second serious offence, including those who repeat rape or attempted rape, unless there are exceptional circumstances (now Powers of Criminal Courts (Sentencing) Act 2000, ss 94 and 109). Early release policies are similarly organised around a principle of public protection which has a special impact on those serving long sentences for sexual offences.

The Criminal Justice Act 1988, ss 35 and 36, gave the Attorney-General power to refer to the Court of Appeal sentences which are considered to be 'unduly lenient': in 1995, rape cases made up 11% of these references (*The Times*, 26 November 1996). Custodial sentences are the norm for those (few) men convicted of rape. Sentences of 12 years or more are considered appropriate where the victim is either very young or very old (Ashworth 2000: 114).

There was already evidence before the *Billam* guidelines that, in the small sample of cases reaching the conviction stage, sentencing for rape was becoming more severe (*Lloyd and Walmsley*, 1989). The distribution of long sentences reflects the kinds of criteria mentioned in *Billam*: that is, sentences are longer where there has been additional violence, additional sexual acts or longer periods of coercion. But stranger rapists receive a much larger proportion of sentences of over five years than non-strangers. Lloyd and Walmsley's study concludes that the increase in severity in sentencing has been greater for rapes with aggravating features than for those without. So it is clear that at all stages of the criminal process stranger rape is the paradigm for serious or 'real' rape (see also **section II.a.** above). For example, in *Berry* (1988), in reducing the sentence of a man convicted of raping his former girlfriend from six to four years, Lord Mustill said that 'in some instances the violation of the person and defilement that are inevitable features where a stranger rapes a woman are not always present to the same degree when the offender and the victim had previously had a long standing relationship' (at p 15).

This discrimination is also graphically reflected in one of the first appellate cases dealing with a husband convicted of raping his wife, in which the defendant's appeal against a sentence of five years was rejected. What is interesting about the case is that the five-year term – the *Billam* 'standard' sentence – was given notwithstanding the existence of serious aggravating factors on the *Billam* criteria: the defendant had wielded a knife and threatened to kill his wife. The Court of Appeal's reference to these factors as 'overwhelming the fact of marriage' suggest strongly that it regarded marriage as a mitigating factor (*R v W*, 1992).

In *Millberry* (2003), the Court of Appeal broadly accepted revisions to the *Billam* guidelines proposed by the Sentencing Advisory Panel. This first major revision in 16 years was driven by changes in both the type and understanding of rape cases. However, Lord Woolf CJ's judgment reflects the continued reluctance of the judiciary to embrace the notion of 'rape as rape':

R v Millberry [2003] 1 Cr App R 25

Lord Woolf CJ.

All the circumstances of the particular offence, including the circumstances relating to the particular victim and the particular offender are relevant. Clearly, there can be mitigating circumstances as the Panel recognises. Where, for example, the offender is the husband of the victim there can, but not necessarily, be mitigating features that clearly cannot apply to a rape by a stranger. On the other hand, as the advice from the Panel points out, as is confirmed by the research commissioned by the Panel, because of the existence of a relationship the victim can feel particularly bitter about an offence of rape, regarding it as a breach of trust. This may, in a particular case, mean that looking at the offence from the victim's point of view, the offence is as bad as a 'stranger rape'. The court has the task of balancing any circumstances of mitigation against the aggravating circumstances. In drawing the balance it is not to be overlooked, when considering 'stranger rape', the victim's fear can be increased because her assailant is an unknown quantity. Is he a murderer as well as a rapist? In addition, there is the fact (not referred to specifically by the Panel) that when a rape is committed by a stranger in a public place, not only is the offence horrific to the victim it can also frighten other members of the public. This element is less likely to be a factor that is particularly important in a case of marital rape where the parties to the marriage are living together.

One might expect recognition of rape as an extreme breach of trust in the context of supposedly loving relationships, and to the (not unreasonable) fear amongst marital rape victims of repeat attacks. Recent Home Office research confirms that women are most likely to experience multiple attacks by their partners (62%) (2002e). However, Lord Woolf stopped short of endorsing the panel's view of regarding non-stranger rape as seriously as stranger rape (para 26 of the advice):

There can be situations where the offender and victim are sharing the said same bed on a regular basis and prior to retiring to bed both had been out drinking and because of the drink that the offender consumed he failed to show the restraint he should have. It would be contrary to common sense to treat such a category of rape as equivalent to stranger rape as on one interpretation of the research material, the Panel could appear to be suggesting.

Lord Woolf's concern with common sense is not supported by research into rape trauma, which suggests that the psychological effects of relationship rape is sometimes greater than stranger rape. As Rumney has demonstrated, the post *R v R* position has not heralded equality in rape sentencing. His analysis of the majority of rape sentencing appeals in the Court of Appeal between 1986 and 1997, shows the sentence discrepancy between different types of rapes:

- stranger (9.7 years);
- acquaintance (8.2 years);
- marital rape (non-cohabitee) (6.3 years);
- relationship rape (5.0 years); and
- marital rape (cohabitee) (3.8 years).

Strikingly, the average sentence for attempted rape (5.7 years) is significantly higher than that for 'cohabiting' marital rape (3.8 years). The average sentence in all cases was 7.4 years (p 260). Such apparent leniency is compounded by the fact that most rape is non-stranger rape. As the extracts from Rumney and Lees below suggest, the judiciary's conception of rape continues to lag behind reality.

Philip N S Rumney, 'When Rape Isn't Rape: Court of Appeal Sentencing Practice in Cases of Marital and Relationship Rape' (1999) Oxford Journal of Legal Studies 243–269, 253

The main distinguishing feature of the method adopted by MacKinnon and that adopted by the judiciary in their discussions of rape is that women's actual experiences are central to MacKinnon's (and feminists') understanding of what rape is, its impact, and wider societal significance. In contrast, judicial pronouncements on the trauma of non-stranger rape take no account of women's experiences. As a consequence while MacKinnon and others argue that some forms of 'consensual' sex contain elements of coercion and might be more appropriately labelled rape, the judiciary works from the perspective that some forms of rape are more akin to sex and therefore should not be subject to the same level of criminal sanction as 'real' (stranger) rape. The willingness of the judiciary to equate rape and sex is the product of an approach to understanding rape which takes no account of the available research evidence on rape trauma.

**S Lees, *Ruling Passions: Sexual Violence, Reputation and the Law*
(Open University Press, 1997) p 120**

The vestiges of patriarchal rights lead judges to take the view that marital
rape is less serious than rape by a stranger or acquaintance on the grounds
that a husband has certain sexual rights over his wife. The notion that rape
is merely an extension of the sexual relationship reflects the myth, strongly
contested by survivors and researchers, that rape is an expression of sexual
desire rather than sexual power and violence. Judicial condoning of marital
rape is due to their reluctance to interfere with the privacy of the family
where traditionally 'a man's home is his castle'.

Judicial leniency may also be an attempt to reflect the (misconceived) attitude of
the general public that relationship rape is not really rape.

Rape law is both a product of the social construction of sexuality and a means
by which that construction is reinforced. Thus, any reform of law alone is
unlikely to have more than symbolic impact, and even that impact will be
largely enfeebled if there is not an accompanying move towards a reconcep-
tion of women as other than sexually attributed beings. In some jurisdictions,
New South Wales, Michigan and Canada for example, reform moves have
aimed to replace the separate offence of rape with a graded scheme of types of
sexual assault. The Canadian Criminal Code (s 246) goes so far as to remove
the distinction between penetrative and other forms of sexual assault. These
schemes are discussed in detail by Temkin (2002: Ch 3) (see also Bronitt
1992, 1996).

Our discussion has shown that the legal definition of rape interacts with aspects
of trial procedure and evidence to provide a very hostile climate for rape
complainants. Whilst the revised definition of consent in the Sexual Offences
Bill 2003 offers some hope of protecting the personal and sexual autonomy of
rape victims, the operation of rules of evidence, as well as negative 'official'
attitudes throughout the legal process may serve to undermine them.

FURTHER READING
Bronitt, Simon (1992) 'Rape and Lack of Consent' 16 Crim LJ 289.
Brown, Beverley, Burman, Michele and Jamieson, Lynn (1993) *Sex Crimes on
    Trial* (Edinburgh University Press).
Clark, Anna (1987) *Women's Silence, Men's Violence: Sexual Assault in England
    1770–1845* (Pandora Press).
Davies, Margaret and Naffine, Ngaire (2001) *Are Persons Property? Legal Debates
    about Property and Personality* (Ashgate) Ch 4.
Home Office (1999) 'A Question of Evidence? Investigating and Prosecuting
    Rape in the 1990s' (Jessica Harris and Sharon Grace, HORS 196).
— (2002) 'Protecting the Public: Strengthening Protection Against Sex
    Offenders and Reforming the Law on Sexual Offences' (Cmnd 5668).

Lacey, Nicola (1998) 'Unspeakable Subjects, Impossible Rights: Integrity, Sexuality and Criminal Law' Canadian Journal of Jurisprudence, reprinted in N Lacey, *Unspeakable Subjects* (Hart Publishing).

— (2001c) 'Beset By Boundaries: The Home Office Review of Sex Offences' Crim LR 3.

Lees, Sue (1996) *Carnal Knowledge: Rape on Trial* (Hamish Hamilton).

Schulhofer, Stephen (1998) *Unwanted Sex: The Culture of Intimidation and the Failure of Law* (Harvard University Press).

Smart, Carol (1989) *Feminism and the Power of Law* (Routledge) Ch 2.

Temkin, Jennifer (2000) 'Criminal Procedure Prosecuting and Defending Rape: Perspectives from the Bar' 27 J Law & Soc 219.

— (2002) *Rape and the Legal Process* (2nd edn, Oxford University Press).

III.   Regulating sexuality

The orthodox separation of sexual offences into consensual and non-consensual offences significantly shapes legal images of sexuality. Yet, as we have seen, the question of consent in adult sexual relationships is a contested one. Duncan notes that:

> the power of the criminal law in respect of physical and sexual violence is not merely or even mainly juridical, but, more importantly, disciplinary. As a disciplinary power, these aspects of the law's text demarcate the boundary between the normal and the abnormal and, in doing so, they define the normal around the notion of the heterosexual male subject in two principal ways: first, by a concept of consent which is very differently constructed as between offences and, secondly, by a subtext of visibility which privileges visible physical violence over (often) invisible sexual violence. The law disciplines bodies differentially as between different genders and different sexual orientations [Duncan, 1995, p 326].

The extraordinary number of different offences, albeit most now gathered in the Sexual Offences Bill 2003, testifies to the confusions besetting what are regarded as appropriate legal and social responses in this area. What is the connection between sexual activity between two 15-year-olds and the persistent sexual abuse of a small child by a relative? Is child sexual abuse an abuse of sexual autonomy, or of trust, or of physical security, or all three? What does criminal law's construction of child abuse, along with what we know about domestic violence and about sexual aggression, tell us about the place that families possess in our culture? It would be foolish to attempt to answer these questions but it would be myopic to ignore them.

In this section we look at ages of consent, consensual violence, child sexual abuse and incest, before moving on to discuss the regulation of prostitution and pornography.

III.a.   Forbidden degrees

III.a.i.   Ages of consent

The varying levels and relevance of ages of consent provide important clues to how criminal law constructs different sexual subjects and different forms of sexuality. For most sexual activities the age of consent is 16, including male homosexual activity and heterosexual buggery, which was lowered from 18 when the Sexual Offences (Amendment) Act 2000 stuttered its way through Parliament.

A preoccupation with the sexual vulnerability of young girls (along with a consonant image of men as sexually predatory) is reflected in a number of specific offences. The pattern of offences in the Sexual Offences Bill 2003 divides children into two classes of vulnerability. Consent is completely irrelevant for children under 13, with offences of assault by penetration and sexual assault below this age (clauses 7, 8). Sexual conduct involving children between 13 and 15 will be caught by two new offences: sexual activity with a child (clause 10) and causing or inciting a child to engage in sexual activity (clause 11). These offences are broader than their 1956 predecessors: beyond their gender-neutrality, sex has shifted to 'sexual activity', which includes touching or other activity that reasonable people would consider sexual (clause 79). Furthermore, the 'young man's defence' has become the 'reasonable person's defence' (ie the offence requires an unreasonable belief that the child is 16 or over). See **section IV.a.** below for discussion of the age of consent in relation to contraception; see also the discussion of *Prince* in **Chapter 1.II.b.** The Bill also includes offences of sexual activity in the presence of a child (clause 12) and causing a child to watch a sexual act (clause 13).

Reflecting an underlying paternalism, the Bill also criminalises *consensual* sexual activity between minors:

Sexual Offences Bill 2003

Clause 14   Child sex offences committed by children or young persons
(1) A person under 18 commits an offence if he does anything which would be an offence under any of sections 10 to 13 if he were aged 18.
(2) A person guilty of an offence under this section is liable–
    (a) on summary conviction, to imprisonment for a term not exceeding 6 months or a fine not exceeding the statutory maximum or both;
    (b) on conviction on indictment, to imprisonment for a term not exceeding 5 years.

The prohibition of adolescent sexual autonomy here, for example the early sexual experimentation of 17 and 15 year olds, appears to be a striking example of over-criminalisation. The maximum penalty of five years' imprisonment still seems steep in this context. Again such a provision is driven by a sense of manipulation, in which the older child appears to occupy the position of trust. Doubts that this does indeed overstep the mark are even evident in the White Paper, and are hardly reassured by its assertion that any over-zealousness in terms of criminalisation may be weeded out through the exercise of prosecutorial discretion.

Indecent assault is replaced by two gender-neutral offences: assault by penetration (clause 3) and sexual assault (clause 5), the former carrying a maximum sentence of life imprisonment. Because at one stage indecent assault was construed by the courts to require a touching of the victim by the defendant, the Indecency with Children Act 1960 was passed to cover the situation where a child is asked to touch the defendant. It provided that an offence is committed when any person commits 'an act of gross indecency with or towards a child under the age of 14, or who incites a child under that age to such an act with him or another'. In *B v DPP* (2000), the House of Lords held that the offence required absence of honest belief that the child was 14 or over. The 2003 Bill signals clearly when the defendant's belief is relevant, and when reasonable belief is relevant. It leaves no room for an 'honest' but unreasonable mistake. There is repeated use in the Bill of the phrase 'Does not reasonably believe that B is 16':

Sexual Offences Bill 2003

Clause 10   Sexual activity with a child
(1) A person aged 18 or over (A) commits an offence if–
    (a) he intentionally touches another person (B),
    (b) the touching is sexual,
    (c) B is under 16, and
    (d) A does not reasonably believe that B is 16 or over.

This formulation is also found in clause 11 (causing or inciting a child to engage in sexual activity). There is a variant in the offence of engaging in sexual activity in the presence of a child (clause 12).

Clause 11   Causing or inciting a child to engage in sexual activity
(1) A person aged 18 or over (A) commits an offence if–
    (a) he intentionally causes or incites another person (B) to engage in an activity,
    (b) the activity is sexual, and
    (c) either–
    (i) B is under 16 and A does not reasonably believe that B is 16 or over, or
    (ii) B is under 13.

The Protection of Children Act 1978 creates offences of taking, permitting to be taken, possessing or publishing indecent photographs of persons under 16. Reflecting greater concern for the vulnerable, this has been increased to 18 under the 2003 Bill, although no offence will be committed where the child over 16 consents to being photographed (clause 47).

III.a.ii.   Homosexuality

The age of consent for homosexual activities was lowered from 18 to 16 following the decision of the European Commission of Human Rights in *Sutherland v UK* (1997). However, the formal expression of this was not straightforward. The House of Lords resisted its initial appearance as an amendment to the Crime and Disorder Bill 1998, and only with the aid of the Parliament Acts 1911 and 1949 did it re-appear and become enacted as s 1 of the Sexual Offences (Amendment) Act 2000. The move to non-discrimination in the Sexual Offences Bill 2003 in abolishing the homophobic offences of the past – buggery, gross indecency and soliciting by men – is to be welcomed. Nonetheless this remains a site for conflict. The Sexual Offences Bill originally contained an offence targeting couples who have sex in public, including gay men in public toilets. However, the Government announced during the course of the Bill's passage that it would be removed. Instead the existing common law offence of outraging public decency is to be amended (*The Guardian*, 16 April 2003).

Richard Collier *Law, Masculinity and the Family* (Routledge, 1995) pp 91–95

On one level the law can be understood to serve as a barometer of social reactions to homosexuality. 'Repressive' or 'liberal' laws may be taken to be indicators of the degree to which homosexuality is tolerated in a certain society at a particular time. However ... the law has a significance other than simply as the indicator of fewer or greater freedoms which are somehow granted by the liberal state. Law has been important in its capacity as a significant social source of stigmatisation of non-heterosexual behaviour.

What status has the law accorded homosexuality? The criminal law is concerned with homosexual relations in a number of different ways. The object of legal intervention has not tended to be homosexual desire as such so much as the carrying out of a specific range of homosexual acts. However, if the law has not been concerned to prosecute those men who are simply attracted to their own sex, then this is not to say that the law can be seen to approve of homosexuality or to condone homosexual activity. The law is not concerned, at least formally, with individuals who believe themselves to be homosexual. It is concerned with the denial of the legitimacy of homosexual relations as viable alternatives to the heterosexual norm (Weeks, 1991).

A variety of political, social, economic, legal and religious considerations have historically informed the negation of the legitimacy of homosexuality. We know that social and historical variations in the regulation of homosexuality are well established in histories of homosexuality, frequent reference being made to ancient Greece and Rome where pedagogic homosexual relations were accepted as part of the societal sexual mores. Yet the avowedly Christian-Judaic taboos against homosexuality which have influenced the moral regulation of homosexuality in the UK have not been reflected in any consistent level of legal sanction. Rather, the western tradition has witnessed, and continues to witness, considerable variation in the criminal law's treatment of homosexuality. More generally, different countries continue to vary considerably in setting an age of consent for homosexual acts ... Even though other European countries have now seen fit to equalise the age of consent at which heterosexual and homosexual sex can take place, in Britain the distinction remains.

Until the Criminal Law Amendment Act 1885 the law concerning homosexual behaviour had been constructed in terms of the offence of sodomy, a definition of which may be found in Chief Justice Coke's 'Institutions of the Laws of England' as

> A detestable and abominable sin, amongst Christians not to be named, committed by carnal knowledge against the ordinance of the creator, and order of nature, by mankind with mankind, or with brute beast or by womankind with brute beast.

Significantly, this definition omits references to carnal knowledge of 'womankind with women' and does not actually name the sin to which it is referring. One effect of such a silence has been to cultivate an official and popular ignorance as to just what the sinful sexual acts are in the first place ...

Sodomy in law involves intercourse when one man's penis enters the anus of another man or woman. It is not sex specific in this sense. Buggery, in contrast, seems to be a wider offence covering both sodomy and intercourse with an animal. Until 1861 buggery (sodomy or bestiality) remained punishable by execution ... Various attempts had been made to repeal the death penalty ... and, though it was not applied in practice after the 1830s, it was not to be until the Offences Against the Person Act 1861 that the death penalty was eventually replaced with sentences of between ten years and life imprisonment.

Before the statutory codification, therefore, the law was directed 'against a series of sexual acts, not a particular type of person, although in practice most people prosecuted under the buggery laws were probably prosecuted for homosexual behaviour (sodomy)' (Weeks 1981: 99). Part of the significance of the 1885 Criminal Law Amendment Act, very much the product of the social, economic and political climate of the mid- to late nineteenth century, lies in how it shifted the definition of the homosexual offence in law. The Labouchère Amendment to the Act brought all forms of homosexual activity within the criminal law and, at a stroke, the Act widened the range of offences covered by statute by bringing into the gaze of the law the new (though uncertain) category of 'gross indecency'. The law thus, in effect, made male masturbation as an intersubjective act a matter for the criminal law. Subsequent legislation, notably the Sexual Offences Act 1967, did not abolish the offences of the 1885 Act as such; they merely exclude consenting adult males in private from the operation of the law ... It would be misleading to state that [the Act] 'legalised' homosexuality ...

In law, any act which involves contact with the genitals of another man (unless justified by some good reason, for example, a medical examination) constitutes an act of 'gross indecency'. What this means is that masturbation in the presence of another man, even without contact taking place, might count as gross indecency (*Hunt*, 1950). A succession of cases have subsequently sought to define gross indecency. Yet these discussions remain bound up with the parameters of a moralistic condemnation of homosexuality ... Although the law is now to be changed so as to reduce the homosexual age of consent to 18, a differential age of consent is to continue. Equality before the law, it would seem, is as elusive as ever. In a sense, therefore, homosexuality is similar to prostitution – not a crime, but clearly undesirable and contrary to public morality. [*Knuller, 1973; Shaw, 1962: see further **Chapter 3.IV**.*]

What is the law saying about the male body here? It is explicitly concerned with sex, desire and male genital interaction. The parameters of this concern are marked by a discourse premised on the naturalness of heterosexuality; the very moralistic language of the law is archaic and, in a sense, pre-sexual. It will be 'gross' and 'indecent' for two men to kiss in public or to act with clear sexual overtones ... This is clearly not the case for heterosexuality, where 'public' displays of sexuality (though within certain limits) are accepted if not encouraged. Even a 'preliminary homosexual act' has constituted an offence in law, though what this might be is not clear (a glance, a stare, a touch or a kiss?). Procuring homosexual acts and soliciting or importuning in a public place for 'immoral purposes' are each subject to legal sanction ... It appears to be the *visibility* of homosexuality which is the object of legal intervention ...

Police officers have sought to entrap gay men with a variety of techniques ... Ultimately ... public displays of homosexual attraction involve a threat to no less than public order itself. In 1989, with an estimated 5,000 gay men convicted for consenting homosexual relations, laws as diverse as the 1986 Public Order Act and the Justices of the Peace Act 1361 had been used to push the number of convictions of consenting male adults in England and Wales to the highest level since the mid-1950s.

The policing of male homosexuality by invoking criminal laws well beyond the ambit of the sexual offences is spectacularly exemplified by the case of *Brown*. This decision both underlined the perceived public order dimension of homosexuality and illustrated the inconsistent way in which consent enters into the delineation of criminal liability:

R v Brown [1993] 2 All ER 75, HL

*[The appellants belonged to a group of homosexual men who, over a 10-year period from 1978, willingly participated in the commission of sado-masochistic acts in relation to one another. These acts, which the law report describes as 'genital torture', were in each case consented to and resulted in no permanent injury. The conduct took place in private in the homes of members of the group and was recorded on video tapes which were then copied and distributed to members of the group. The appellants pleaded guilty to offences of assault and wounding under the Offences Against the Person Act 1861, ss 47 and 20 (see **Chapter 3.II.c.**), having changed their pleas to guilty following the trial judge's ruling that consent of the victim afforded no defence to these charges. Both the Court of Appeal and the House of Lords (by a 3–2 majority) dismissed their appeals against this ruling. The appellants took their case to the European Court of Human Rights, arguing that the ruling breached Article 8 of the European Convention, which states that 'Everyone has a right to his private and family life, his home and his correspondence'. The European Court dismissed the case on the basis that the denial of the consent defence was capable of falling within Article 8(2). This subsection allows public authorities to limit the right of privacy 'in accordance with the law and [as] necessary in a democratic society in the interests of national security, public safety or the economic well-being of the country, for the prevention of disorder or crime, for the protection of health or morals, or for the protection of the rights and freedoms of others'.*

Having reviewed the authorities on the defence of consent, which are taken to establish that consent cannot exculpate in charges of causing actual or grievous bodily harm or wounding in the course of an 'unlawful activity' (Coney, 1882; A-G's Ref (No 6 of 1980), 1981; Lord Templeman continued (at 81):]

By the 1967 Act Parliament recognised and accepted the practice of homosexuality. Subject to exceptions not here relevant, sexual activities conducted in private between not more than two consenting adults of the same sex or different sexes are now lawful. Homosexual activities performed in circumstances which do not fall within s 1(1) of the 1967 Act remain unlawful. Subject to the respect for private life embodied in the 1967 Act, Parliament has retained criminal sanctions against the practice, dissemination and encouragement of homosexual activities.

My Lords, the authorities dealing with the intentional infliction of bodily harm do not establish that consent is a defence to a charge under the 1861 Act. They establish that the courts have accepted that consent is a defence to the infliction of bodily harm in the course of some lawful activities. The question is whether the defence should be extended to the infliction of bodily harm in the course of sado-masochistic encounters. The Wolfenden Committee did not make any recommendations about sado-masochism and Parliament did not deal with violence in 1967. The 1967 Act is of no assistance for present purposes because the present problem was not under consideration.

The question whether the defence of consent should be extended to the consequences of sado-masochistic encounters can only be decided by considerations of policy and public interest. Parliament can call on the advice of doctors, psychiatrists, criminologists, sociologists and other experts and can also sound and take into account public opinion. But the question must at this stage be decided by this House in its judicial capacity in order to determine whether the convictions of the appellants should be upheld or quashed.

Counsel for some of the appellants argued that the defence of consent should be extended to the offence of occasioning actual bodily harm under s 47 of the 1861 Act but should not be available to charges of serious wounding and the infliction of serious bodily harm under s 20. I do not consider that this solution is practicable. Sado-masochistic participants have no way of foretelling the degree of bodily harm which will result from their encounters. The differences between actual bodily harm and serious bodily harm cannot be satisfactorily applied by a jury in order to determine acquittal or conviction.

Counsel for the appellants argued that consent should provide a defence to charges under both ss 20 and 47 because, it was said, every person has a right to deal with his body as he pleases. I do not consider that this slogan provides a sufficient guide to the policy decision which must now be made. It is an offence for a person to abuse his own body and mind by taking drugs. Although the law is often broken, the criminal law restrains a practice which is regarded as dangerous and injurious to individuals and which if allowed and extended is harmful to society generally. In any event the appellants in this case did not mutilate their own bodies. They inflicted bodily harm on willing victims. Suicide is no longer an offence but a person who assists another to commit suicide is guilty of murder or manslaughter.

The assertion was made on behalf of the appellants that the sexual appetites of sadists and masochists can only be satisfied by the infliction of bodily harm and that the law should not punish the consensual achievement of sexual satisfaction. There was no evidence to support the assertion that sado-masochistic activities are essential to the happiness of the appellants or any other participants but the argument would be acceptable if sado-masochism were only concerned with sex, as the appellants contend. In my opinion sado-masochism is not only concerned with sex.

Sado-masochism is also concerned with violence. The evidence discloses that the practices of the appellants were unpredictably dangerous and degrading to body and mind and were developed with increasing barbarity and taught to persons whose consents were dubious or worthless.

A sadist draws pleasure from inflicting or watching cruelty. A masochist derives pleasure from his own pain or humiliation. The appellants are middle-aged men. The victims were youths some of whom were introduced to sado-masochism before they attained the age of 21. In his judgment in the Court of Appeal, Lord Lane CJ said that two members of the group of which the appellants formed part, namely one Cadman and the appellant Laskey –

> were responsible in part for the corruption of a youth 'K' ... It is some comfort at least to be told, as we were, that 'K' has now it seems settled into a normal heterosexual relationship. Cadman had befriended 'K' when the boy was 15 years old. He met him in a cafeteria and, so he says, found out that the boy was interested in homosexual activities. He introduced and encouraged 'K' in 'bondage' affairs. He was interested in viewing and recording on video tape 'K' and other teenage boys in homosexual scenes ... One cannot overlook the danger that the gravity of the assaults and injuries in this type of case may escalate to even more unacceptable heights.

The evidence disclosed that drink and drugs were employed to obtain consent and increase enthusiasm. The victim was usually manacled so that the sadist could enjoy the thrill of power and the victim could enjoy the thrill of helplessness. The victim had no control over the harm which the sadist, also stimulated by drink and drugs, might inflict. In one case a victim was branded twice on the thigh and there was some doubt as to whether he consented to or protested against the second branding. The dangers involved in administering violence must have been appreciated by the appellants because, so it was said by their counsel, each victim was given a code word which he could pronounce when excessive harm or pain was caused. The efficiency of this precaution, when taken, depends on the circumstances and on the personalities involved. No one can feel the pain of another. The charges against the appellants were based on genital torture and violence to the buttocks, anus, penis, testicles and nipples. The victims were degraded and humiliated, sometimes beaten, sometimes wounded with instruments and sometimes branded. Bloodletting and the smearing of human blood produced excitement. There were obvious dangers of serious personal injury and blood infection. Prosecuting counsel informed the trial judge against the protests of defence counsel that, although the appellants had not contracted AIDS, two members of the group had died from AIDS and one other had contracted an HIV infection although not necessarily from the practices of the group. Some activities involved excrement. The assertion that the instruments employed by the sadists were clean and sterilised could not have removed the danger of infection, and the assertion that care was taken demonstrates the possibility of infection ...

In principle there is a difference between violence which is incidental and violence which is inflicted for the indulgence of cruelty. The violence of sado-masochistic encounters involves the indulgence of cruelty by sadists and the degradation of victims. Such violence is injurious to the participants and unpredictably dangerous. I am not prepared to invent a defence of consent to sado-masochistic encounters which breed and glorify cruelty and result in offences under ss 47 and 20 of the 1861 Act.

It would be hard to imagine a more comprehensive condemnation of a certain sexuality: both homosexual conduct and homosexuals themselves are constructed as dangerous, as threatening public order, in language which consistently evokes metaphors of disease and contamination. Doubt is repeatedly cast on the 'reality' of the 'victim's' consent – a question which would, of course, have had to be determined by the jury had the consent defence been allowed. Even the dissenting speeches are informed by a marked distaste:

R v Brown [1993] at 101

Lord Mustill.

My Lords, this is a case about the criminal law of violence. In my opinion it should be a case about the criminal law of private sexual relations, if about anything at all ... The speeches already delivered contain summaries of the conduct giving rise to the charges ... Fortunately for the reader my Lords have not gone on to describe other aspects of the appellants' behaviour of a similar but more extreme kind which was not the subject of any charge on the indictment. It is sufficient to say that whatever the outsider might feel about the subject matter of the prosecutions – perhaps horror, amazement or incomprehension, perhaps sadness – very few could read even a summary of the other activities without disgust. The House has been spared the video tapes, which must have been horrible.

In his dissent, Lord Mustill drew on the European Convention to argue for a reconsideration of the existing case law. Lord Mustill argued that willing consent should be regarded as legitimating actual bodily harm inflicted in private for the (non-commercial) gratification of sexual desire. His argument was that the appellants' conduct fell within a sphere of 'private morality' (at 115), and was not properly charged under the 1861 Act, which 'was clearly intended to penalise conduct of a quite different nature' (at 116). His conclusion, however, appears to associate sado-masochism with danger of crime more generally:

[P]lain humanity demands that a court addressing the criminality of conduct such as that of the present should recognise and respond to the profound dismay which all members of the community share about the apparent increase of cruel and senseless crimes against the defenceless.

It is interesting to compare this with Lord Mustill's judgment in *Kingston* (1994, **Chapter 3.III.d.**) in which the defendant's 'paedophiliac tendencies', 'disinhibited' by alcohol, combine to conjure up an image of dangerousness inherent in his 'disposition' and hence a 'status-based' idea of responsibility which sits unhappily with criminal law doctrine's purported values.

As Lord Mustill's speech emphasises, the decision in *Brown* was very far from being determined by the logic of legal doctrine. Indeed, as Bibbings and Alldridge note, the case in fact has some striking doctrinal implications:

Lois Bibbings and Peter Alldridge, 'Sexual Expression, Body Alteration and the Defence of Consent' (1993) Journal of Law and Society 356 at 364–365

As a consequence of Operation Spanner, twenty-six people were cautioned for the (alleged) offence of aiding and abetting offences against themselves. This is not without difficulty. The principle in *R v Tyrell* is that a victim cannot be an accomplice. If it is correct that the passive participants in *Brown* were not covered by this principle, the participant in sado-masochism seems to be getting the worst of all worlds. When it comes to criminal injuries, civil actions or participation in crime, s/he is not a victim, and consequently loses whatever benefits may accrue from being a victim. When it comes to the criminal liability of the perpetrators s/he *is* a victim, and so all participants are criminal. [*On participation, see* **Chapter 2.IV.**]

At the Jim Rose circus, in addition to acts of self-mutilation, there are acts which may fall within the scope of the decision in *Brown*. For example, darts are thrown into the back of one of the participants by another performer, and members of the audience are invited to stand on the performer whilst he lies first on a 'bed of nails' and later, face down on freshly broken glass. If such activities are covered by the decision in the case, then any person attending is criminally liable as it is clear from *R v Coney* that paying to watch an unlawful event can incur liability as an accomplice.

The decision in *Brown* seems to render unlawful sado-masochist parties where there are consensual whippings, beatings or spankings ... which can sometimes result in injury. The legality of literature describing techniques or advertising equipment falls into question. The existence of offences also triggers police powers of surveillance and intervention in sado-masochist parties, and seizure of sado-masochistic equipment with consequent dangers of discriminatory enforcement. It has been suggested that it is significant that the first case to consider fully the legality of sado-masochist activities involved not a heterosexual couple but, rather, a group of gay men ...

Brown suggests that sexual expression is limited and that the defendants' fears of a 'bedroom police' were justified. But, in the light of the Lords' decision, are we really to assume that householders hearing suspicious noises from their neighbours could telephone the police who may decide to investigate the situation? If such action is to be undertaken by the police in cases involving men 'dominating' women, this would contrast with past policing practices in relation to non-consensual 'domestic' incidents. [*See further* **Chapter 6.I.b.** *below.*]

How do we explain a decision that not only contradicts the liberal value of privacy but also engenders such doctrinal complications? Two important issues underlying the judgment in *Brown* are the criminal law's investment in a certain image of bodily integrity and its need to assert an exclusive jurisdiction over the determination of meaning and the infliction of pain:

Matthew Weait, 'Fleshing it Out' in Lionel Bentley and Leo Flynn (eds) *Law and The Senses* (Pluto Press, 1996) pp 169–172

By drawing blood and allowing it to be drawn to gain pleasure we are abusing a body that should be entire and intact. The waste is gratuitous and ultimately extravagant. Similarly, faeces and urine should be flushed away. To enjoy their sensual possibilities is to reverse their accepted status and meaning as by-products without utility ...

What these men did to each other might indeed be interpreted, as it was, as violence to the person. The legitimacy of the House of Lords' decision could, as it was, be based on the risk which their activities posed to the bodies concerned and to society in general, and the decision may be understood in these terms. However, it can perhaps be better understood by the threat which their conduct was seen to represent to the state and to state law. These men created an alternative rule-system – organised, ritualised and elaborate. They had code words: 'No' and 'Stop' did not have their accepted meaning in the context of their activities. It is a central aspect of the courts' function that they have the authority to decide what words mean, and yet these men were reserving that right to themselves. More importantly, for present purposes, they were parodying punishment and torture. They were doing to each other for pleasure what the criminal courts had formerly done in order to manifest the authority of law. If there is to be humiliation and submission, let it be in the pillory – in public – in order that it serve the law's purposes; if corporal injury be inflicted such that blood is shed, let that be on the streets at the 'cart's tail' so that it may invoke terror rather than sensual exhilaration. For if it is possible to derive pleasure from pain, which the law has assumed people wish at all costs to avoid, what is left for law to use? The only legitimate dominant/submissive relationship is that which exists between the law and the legal subject ...

It is one of the most notable features of contemporary criminal justice in this, and most other Western countries, that we have all but abandoned institutionalised corporal punishment. The body which once was whipped, birched, burnt and dismembered is now disciplined in other ways. Where once state punishment was characterised by the direct infliction of force on a body which might then go free, its paradigm is now the withdrawal of freedom from a body which is left physically unmarked. The scars which the criminal law once left on the body are now left in the mind ... We have become much more subtle. We are more civilised ... However, as Foucault has so persuasively argued, we should be wary of any assumption that because we have stopped hitting bodies and inflicting pain directly, we have renounced violence towards them or that pain and corporal manipulation are no longer integral to state punishment. While penal policy and practice may have changed their emphasis in line with party politics or in response to empirical research ... the body is still a *locus* of control. The pain inflicted upon it may be less direct, the mark it makes and the traces it leaves less visible; but the exercise of coercive discipline over the body and a recognition of the anguish which it is capable of experiencing are still at the heart of punishment ...

What may be important ... is that it is in the law's own interest that this corporal violence, manipulation and discipline be disguised.

... Our criminal law is now, or so we are led to believe, rational, just and fair. It is the product of the age of reason. It has general principles. We should respect it because it respects us, assuming responsibility, carefully assessing fault, calculating appropriate responses. Like the institutions it feeds, its problems are peripheral and remediable – reverse a decision here, issue a guideline there, censure a judge somewhere else. However, the Common Law has a memory, is, indeed, a system of memory, and sometimes it is reminded of its violent foundations. In *Brown* the judges were graphically confronted with the images of a past they would have us forget. It is not so long ago that they were directly responsible for the mutilation, branding and scarring of the people who came before them, for their pain, suffering and humiliation. Of course, the conduct of the defendants in *Brown* must be outlawed; we, the judges, must not – cannot – be seen to sanction the kind of violence for which we were once responsible, and which we have been so successful at disguising.

Ngaire Naffine, 'The Body Bag' in N Naffine and R Owens (eds)
***Sexing the Subject of Law* (Law Book Co, 1997) pp 83–84, 90–91**
[This material has been reproduced with the express permission of LBC Information Services]

... Mill, like Kant, regarded embodied persons as essentially separate and distinct, as bodies whose dignity depended on a respect for the physical integrity of the self and the integrity of others.

A further common feature of the body written about by Kant and by Mill is that it is taken to be already constituted, a self-evident thing in itself; it is theorised as material suitable for the application of liberal rights and duties. Implicit in their theories is the idea that the body is by nature discrete and self-contained (once it has achieved adulthood). Certainly it needs tending and respect accorded by not indulging in inappropriate animal pleasures. But the body has its own nature and that nature is a self-enclosed and bounded one. This bounded nature is not a creation of liberal theory, but is instead a natural feature of physical being with which liberal theory must deal.

It is this bounded autonomous body of liberal theory which I wish to suggest has been incorporated into criminal law and still resides within it. The implicit sexing and sexualising of this bounded body, most evident in the writing of Kant, has I believe also been carried over into criminal law. In common with the liberal theory from which it derives, criminal law treats its behaviour to the body as simply a response to the body's own nature. In other words, implicit in our criminal law is the idea that law never legislates the nature of the body. It only ever responds to the body's own intrinsic character, which is by nature bounded ... Law's purpose is to ensure that the person as flesh is treated with proper regard, the sort of regard which ensures human dignity ...

My reply to this criminal legal orthodoxy is that law's approach is always, and inevitably, constitutive rather than simply reactive. Criminal law is always assigning qualities to the body, seeing the body in terms of some things and not others, seeing some bodies in certain ways and other bodies in others. By examining criminal law's reaction to bodies coming into contact with one another, we can see that law is always interpreting and creating the meaning of bodies. Thus we will discover that a pierced body can be regarded as either whole or as invaded. A body can be enclosed by the body of another and yet still be regarded as separate and distinct, that is, as a suitably autonomous body. A body which encloses that of another can be regarded as pierced ... It all depends on how law legislates the body.

... The central concern of law is (to police the boundaries of) the bounded heterosexual male body. Bodies which are not like this, or are not allowed to be like this, are somehow deviant and undeserving bodies. They are 'unnatural', even 'loathsome', because they have apparently lost their clear definition ...

Despite the consistent modern trend towards liberalisation of laws against homosexuality, there are still ample contemporary legal statements to be found about the unnaturalness and inappropriateness of men having sex with men. [Naffine goes on to cite *Brown*] ... The ongoing reluctance of the British to part with the idea of the bounded masculine body is also apparent in the *Local Government Act 1988* which now proscribes the promotion of homosexuality by local authorities. In Australia the legal attitude to homosexuality remains mixed ...

While the injury incurred on the sporting field often only does the man good, the consensual and loving penetration of a man by a man is highly corrosive to sovereignty (conceived as bounded status) and so has consistently been condemned by the criminal law as inappropriate human contact ...

For a man to have sex with a man is to jeopardise his very autonomy and sovereignty. The man who reveals his cavity/vulnerability, who opens his body boundaries in a manner which is seen to resemble or mimic the female mode of opening, becomes a woman as non-bounded subject. To be entered sexually is to be feminised. Law, therefore, outlaws the incomplete man. It prohibits the violation of the male sovereign self and simultaneously, in the same act, constructs the incomplete female self. By necessary implication, laws against homosexuality have made penetrative sex of a woman the correct form of sex, the sexual norm.

Naffine's identification of the heterosexual dynamics of criminal law's conception of physical integrity is confirmed by the contrast between the decision in *Brown* and that in a case of heterosexual 'violence' decided not long afterwards. In *Wilson* (1996), a man who had branded his initials on his wife's buttocks with a hot knife was charged with an offence under s 47 of the Offences Against the Person Act 1861. He claimed that this had been done 'for love' and not only with his wife's consent but 'at her instigation'. On the basis of *Brown*, the trial judge directed the jury to convict. Overturning this on appeal it was held that: *Brown* was not authority for the proposition that consent was not a defence to s 47 in all circumstances where actual bodily harm was deliberately inflicted; there was no logical difference between this type of branding and tattooing, which was a lawful activity; and it was not in the public interest that such consensual activity between husband and wife in the privacy of the matrimonial home should be the object of criminal sanctions. The two cases illustrate not only the 'differential discipline' described by Duncan (above) but also a deep confusion about the relative importance of autonomy and of certain conceptions of order and morality in legal constructions of sexuality. They also offer a glimpse of judicial attitudes: the repugnance towards the conduct in *Brown* was reserved for the decision of the authorities for even bringing a prosecution in *Wilson*. The status of *Brown* as a precedent was further undermined by *Emmett* (1999). The defendant was charged under s 47 after his partner sustained injuries during their consensual (although unusual) sexual activity. She suffered partial asphyxiation, after a plastic bag was placed over her head and tied at the neck, and burns after lighter fluid was lit on her breasts. In upholding his conviction, the Court of Appeal was unwilling to permit the private expression of bodily autonomy to go unchecked. Injuries that were more than transient or trivial, even in the heterosexual domestic setting, fell on the wrong side of consent's Maginot line.

As the Law Commission's report on consent in the criminal law reveals (Law Commission 1995), this confusion about the scope and meaning of autonomy extends well beyond the sexual field. It encompasses, for example, the validity of consent to practices such as tattooing and cosmetic surgery, circumcision, euthanasia, violence on the sports field and a range of medical interventions such as sterilisation, organ transplants and sexual reassignment operations. While affirming the 'general principle that a person with capacity should be able to give a legally effective consent to any injury up to a level which we will be describing as "seriously disabling injury"' (Law Commission 1995: para 2.19), the Commission argues that this general standard needs to be raised and lowered in certain special situations, and that in certain fields formal age limits should continue to define the existence of capacity. The conduct which was the object of prosecution in *Brown* would be removed from the ambit of criminal law on this approach, subject to an 18-year age-limit: 'Consent by a person under 18 to injuries intentionally caused for sexual, religious or spiritual purposes should not be treated as a valid consent' (Law Commission 1995: para 10.55). Ormerod and Gunn note some of the difficulties with such an approach:

D C Ormerod and M J Gunn, 'Consent – a Second Bash' [1996] Crim LR 694 at 703

The Commission proposes that in the course of tattooing, circumcision, branding, scarring, dangerous exhibitions, and undisciplined horseplay, injury, *but not serious disabling injury*, will be permitted. Unfortunately, there is inadequate definition of these various activities. This casts doubt on whether they amount to serious disabling injury ... For example is male circumcision a permanent disfigurement which causes serious distress when performed? If it is a serious disabling injury then perhaps it can be justified in some circumstances as medical treatment, although there is a great deal of conflicting medical evidence as to the benefits. The illogicalities when this activity is compared with sexual reassignment surgery or cosmetic surgery [areas in which the Commission proposes that people should be allowed to consent to seriously disabling injury] or female circumcision (outlawed [under the Prohibition of Female Circumcision Act 1985]) are obvious. As far as male circumcision goes, whether it is a serious disabling injury or not, the question of ritual circumcision must be faced. Why should it be limited to specific religious groups? Is it limited to children? Can it be said to be in the best interests of the child?

Several of these areas in which the relationship between autonomy and order – and hence the proper role of consent – continue to puzzle criminal law are considered in the later sections of this chapter.

III.a.iii.   Abusing positions of trust

The Sexual Offences Bill 2003 re-enacts and extends provisions first contained in the Sexual Offences (Amendment) Act 2000. The 2003 Bill contains four breach of trust offences: sexual activity with a child; causing and inciting a child to engage in such activity; sexual activity in the presence of a child; and causing a child to watch a sexual act (clauses 18–21). Furthermore, clause 23 extends 'positions of trust' to include personal advisers and those who 'care for, advise, supervise or train young people in the community'. Provision for allowing the Secretary of State to extend this further suggests that there is some doubt as to whether this goes far enough. However, whilst clearly seeking to protect those at risk from sexual predators on the one hand, how far do such provisions also shift criminal law towards the edges of excessive paternalism? One thinks of the consensual conduct between a 22-year-old college lecturer and her 17-year-old student which would be caught by such offences.

III.a.iv.   Child sexual abuse

Sexual abuse of children might be thought to be an area in which dimensions of violence and the exploitation of sexual power combine with considerations of public order and 'decency' to over-determine criminalisation. However, as the following passages show, the criminalisation of child abuse has, historically, been patchy, and sexual abuse of children continues to pose distinctive problems for the criminal process:

Liz Kelly, *Surviving Sexual Violence* (Polity, 1988) pp 54–59

The literature on child sexual abuse, particularly incest, has a much longer history than that on other forms of sexual violence. This is partly accounted for by the interest of psychoanalysts and anthropologists in 'incest taboos'. These early influences are reflected in the emergence, and shifting of dominant theoretical frameworks within which research findings are placed. A further contrast with research on rape and domestic violence is that there has been little development in the major themes of research although there has been some increase in studies of incidence and the long-term effects of abuse ...

The research on offenders who abuse children follows a similar pattern to the study of rapists. The medical/psychological model again results in person-ality characteristics and/or individual life experiences being cited as causes of abuse. The most common explanation is 'psychosexual immaturity'; the most recent a version of the cycle-of-violence theory whereby abuse in childhood is seen to account for abusive behaviour in adulthood. The behaviour of wives is frequently seen as a determining factor, particularly where the offence is incest. However, as adult sex with children is defined as deviant, most researchers argue that offenders against children represent a specific deviant psychopathology ... The major problem with all the research to date is that, once again, samples are limited to convicted offenders. Convicted child abusers are likely to be the more compulsive and blatant offenders and/or those who have committed more 'extreme' offences (murder, rape or use of excessive force) ... Many investigators maintain child abusers use far less physical violence than other groups of sex offenders. One study cross-checked offenders' self-reports with court medical reports and found that 75 per cent seriously underestimated the violence that they had used ...

The participation of children in abuse was a central theme in many of the articles published in the 1950s and 1960s. One of the most revealing papers offers an explicit statement of how 'participation' is defined – more than one incident of abuse! Thus, 60 per cent of the children are described as 'full participants'. Nineteen other studies transform the inability of children to stop abuse into participation and complicity ...

The view that court appearances are damaging to the child is inextricably linked to the insistence that the long-term impact of the abuse itself is minimal; only four research reports are ever quoted to support this latter argument. With the exception of [one] study, they contain very small samples and make no distinctions between the impact of flashing and that of rape or prolonged incestuous abuse. Despite the fact that recent research on rape and incest consistently reports serious negative effects both at the time and over time ... some experts still hold this view and still fail to distinguish between forms of sexual abuse:

> The minimal damage attributable to most sexual encounters does not justify extreme reactions ... In particular, police questioning, appearances in court, family dissension and eventually perhaps the imprisonment of a parent, friend or relative to whom the child is strongly attached are likely to be far more traumatic than the sexual incidents themselves [West, 1984].

... No study has been done on the effects of criminal investigation on children and little attention has been given, until recently, to making court procedures less distressing. The only study to specifically address the impact of prosecution for incest found no differences in the percentage of family break-ups between two US counties with radically different prosecution policies.

A 1954 study of 11 children referred by the court for psychological assessment produced further themes that have informed research to the present day. Family dynamics are presented as the causal mechanism in incest; fear of separation unites the whole family in complicity. The mother is depicted as 'dependent and infantile', sexually rejecting her husband and 'unconsciously participating' in the abuse. Abusive fathers have had 'emotionally deprived and chaotic childhoods' ...

The dominance of the family-dynamics model in the study of incest has been extremely influential in the recent development of treatment strategies. If the cause of incest is family dysfunction, in which all members are implicated, then criminal prosecution is an inappropriate response. A 'humanistic' treatment model based on family therapy ... is now the predominant response throughout the USA and has powerful support in the UK ... Jon Conte, an academic who is also connected to a centre providing services for abused women and girls, maintains that there is still no evidence of its effectiveness ... Findings from several projects that the abused girls may not want the family reunited and get little benefit from family therapy have been ignored.

Lucia Zedner, 'Regulating Sexual Offences within the Home' in I Loveland (ed) *Frontiers of Criminality* (Sweet & Maxwell, 1995) pp 187–189

The re-politicisation of the family in the 1980s and the bright light thrown on sexual offences, their incidence and impact, collided on two distinct areas of criminal activity: the sexual abuse of children and the immunity of husbands from rape within marriage. The 'moral panic' over child sexual abuse which absorbed so much media and political attention in the latter years of the 1980s is instructive in our bid to understand how the 'frontiers of criminality' are constructed. We are accustomed to recognising that the boundaries of criminality relating to fraud, to environmental offences, or public safety are determined as much by the politics of regulation as by changes in the criminal law. We are less ready to recognise the importance of enforcement policies in respect of 'real crimes' (activities which entail culpable individuals perpetrating moral wrongs which inflict grave harms on identifiable victims). Yet, the response to child abuse during the so-called 'Cleveland Crisis' in 1987 is one, above all, of the vagaries of regulation. Sexual abuse or assault on children, whether carried out by a member of the household, other relatives, family friends or outsiders, is covered by a number of statutory offences. Until the past decade, however, it only rarely came to light, mainly because, except in the most violent cases, it generally leaves little tangible evidence of its occurrence. Its victims rarely have the means to instigate prosecution and too often become entangled in a familial conspiracy of silence. Bringing these crimes to light relies, therefore, on active intervention by an array of agencies, from family G.P.s, social workers, voluntary agencies or the police. Intervention is thus scattered across a range of professional bodies each with its own operational philosophy, its own definition of the problem it seeks to tackle and of the child's best interests. The tensions created by this dispersal of responsibility, of judgement and of aim combined in an explosive cocktail in Cleveland in the spring of 1987. Impelled by growing evidence that far greater numbers of children were being sexually abused than had been previously known, key professionals in Cleveland identified more than 100 cases of sexual abuse in 5 months (March to July) compared with only 2 in the whole of the previous year. The children were taken immediately into local authority care following a series of dramatic dawn raids.

If the story stopped at this point we might conclude that here was an example of heavy-handed intrusion on the part of an all-powerful state intent on undermining the sanctity of the home. Instead, what emerged was evidence of an extraordinary fragmentation of authority. There was an absence of agreed diagnostic guidelines, disagreement over the implementation of place of safety orders and of criminal proceedings, and conflict among medical, welfare, and criminal justice agencies each seeking to stake out their territory against the intrusions of the others. Even within areas of expertise, disagreement raged; for example, medical opinion differed about the reliability of techniques for determining whether abuse had taken place (in particular in respect of the highly controversial reflex anal dilatation test). Paradoxically, the very politicians whose endorsement of family values had done so much to expose abuse to the public gaze now supported parents trying to secure the return of their children through a series of distressing court battles. The courtroom became an arena, in the full glare of national media attention, in which rival medical, welfare and legal expertise competed for ascendancy.

The Cleveland affair prompted a major inquiry by Lord [as she was then termed, now Lady] Justice Butler-Sloss which, in turn, made sweeping recommendations for managerial and regulatory, but significantly not legal, change. It prompted, too, the proliferation of preventative initiatives, help-lines, and innovations in the workings of welfare and criminal justice agencies. Yet, pressures for a more proactive role by police and prosecutors clashed irreconcilably with equally insistent demands for the protection of the family from state interference. Even those of us who demanded that 'the criminal law should not stop at the door of the family home' were obliged to concede that criminal proceedings and penal sanctions are far from being an unproblematic solution to the sexual abuse of children.

The 'discovery' of child sexual abuse followed closely on the heels of the 'baby battering syndrome', which itself followed the emergence of 'wife battering'. Yet during the last decade, notwithstanding a doubling of the numbers of offences recorded by the police, the number of people cautioned for or convicted of 'gross indecency with a child' has fallen. The problems of pursuing criminal enforcement of sexual violence discussed earlier in this chapter, as well as those of enforcing criminal law in the field of 'domestic' violence (see **Chapter 6.I.b.**), flow from a number of distinct although interrelated factors, including police and social attitudes as well as formal evidential restrictions at trial. The change in the rules of evidence relating to child witnesses must be viewed against this background. The Criminal Justice Act 1988, s 34, abolished the corroboration requirements for a child's sworn or unsworn evidence. The Act also authorised evidence by video link (s 32).

More recently, and partly in response to further revelations about systematic sexual abuse in institutions such as children's homes, legislative developments have moved towards the construction of sexual offenders against children – 'paedophiles' – as a dangerous group from whom society requires special protection. In 1996 criminal law's jurisdiction was extended to incitements and conspiracies to engage in conduct abroad which is criminal where performed and which, had it been committed in England, would have grounded a conspiracy or incitement offence (see **Chapter 3.IV.**). One significant feature of the legislation is that the 'condition' that the conduct be criminal where performed is 'taken to be satisfied if the defence fails to serve a notice denying it' – a pragmatic reversal of the presumption of innocence (see **Chapter 1.I.b.ii.**). This legislation originated in a Private Member's Bill prompted by the organisation in England of 'sex tourism' based on child prostitution in countries such as Thailand and the Philippines (Alldridge 1997). The Sex Offenders Act 1997 further extended criminal law's jurisdiction in this area by making it an offence for a UK resident to commit sexual offences against children abroad.

This provision, and the major institution of the Sex Offenders Register (Cobley 1997), are replicated and reinforced in the Sexual Offences Bill 2003. Under these provisions, anyone who has been convicted of a sexual offence against children must tell the police where they live or if they change home. The period for doing this has been shortened from 14 to 3 days (clause 84). Failure to do so makes the person liable to a maximum penalty of five years' imprisonment (a hefty increase from the original six-month term). The registration requirement is not subject to appeal or review. Anyone imprisoned for 30 months or more will be required to register for the rest of their life; those imprisoned for between six and 30 months will have to register for 10 years. In terms reminiscent of Feeley and Simon's 'new penology' (1994) (see **Chapter 1.III.iv.**), the police will be able in exceptional cases to pass on details of registration to third parties in accordance with the degree of risk an individual is judged to pose. The Home Office has estimated that about 6000 offenders were liable to immediate registration, and that this figure would grow by up to 3500 each year. The register, referred to by some commentators as a form of 'criminal apartheid' (Soothill and Francis 1997: 1285), groups together a large and very diverse range of offenders within a new legal status, and extends the effects of criminal conviction well beyond the scope of 'deserved' punishment and the time limits after which convictions are normally 'spent'. The fact that this includes men convicted of having consensual sex with 16- or 17-year-olds before equalisation of the age of consent in 2000 somewhat undermines the attempt to abolish such homophobic discrimination (*The Guardian*, 27 January 2003). Furthermore, continuing concerns about child sex abuse are reflected in the new offences of sexual activity with children in the 2003 Bill (see above), and in the strengthened notification requirements so that offenders spending more than seven days at another address per year must inform the police. The range of offences subject to notification is also extended and includes for example the offence of meeting a child following 'sexual grooming'.

Sexual Offences Bill 2003

Clause 17   Meeting a child following sexual grooming etc
(1) A person aged 18 or over (A) commits an offence if–
    (a) having met or communicated with another person (B) on at least two earlier occasions, he–
    (i)   intentionally meets B, or
    (ii) travels with the intention of meeting B in any part of the world,
    (b) at the time, he intends to do anything to or in respect of B, during or after the meeting and in any part of the world, which if done will involve the commission by A of a relevant offence,
    (c) B is under 16, and
    (d) A does not reasonably believe that B is 16 or over.
(2) In subsection (1)–
    (a) the reference to A having met or communicated with B is a reference to A having met B in any part of the world or having communicated with B by any means from, to or in any part of the world.

The offence will be accompanied by a civil preventive order where an adult has displayed inappropriate sexual behaviour prior to committing an offence. The explanatory notes accompanying the Bill offer a striking insight into the breathtaking reach of this provision:

Sexual Offences Bill 2003

Explanatory Notes, para 21

The course of conduct prior to the meeting may have an explicitly sexual content, such as the defendant entering into conversations with the child about the sexual acts he wants to engage her in when they meet or sending images of adult pornography. *However, the meetings or communication need not have an explicitly sexual content and could for example simply be A giving the child swimming lessons or meeting her incidentally through a friend.* The offence will be complete either when A meets the child or when he travels to the pre-arranged meeting with the intent to commit a relevant offence against the child. *The planned offence does not have to take place.* The evidence of the intent may be drawn from the communications between A and the child before the meeting or may be drawn from other circumstances, for example A travels to the meeting with ropes, condoms and lubricants.

Subsection (2)(a) provides that A's previous meetings or communications with the child can have taken place in or across any part of the world. This would cover for example A emailing the child from abroad, A and the child speaking on the telephone in Thailand or A meeting the child in Portugal. The meeting itself must take place (or be arranged to take place in relation to the 'travelling to' limb of the offence) in England or Wales or Northern Ireland. [Emphasis added.]

This provision responds to fears of sexual contact initiated by new forms of electronic engagement, such as Internet chat rooms. However, it clearly extends the reach of criminal law to policing 'thought crimes' and raises obvious civil liberty concerns for those at risk of being labelled 'sexual groomers'. It also further undermines the notion of public space referred to in **Chapter 3.I.a.**, casting a shadow of distrust over healthy adult–child relationships. Notwithstanding society's legitimate concern about sexual abuse of children, serious questions arise both about civil liberties and about the costs and potential effectiveness of what appears to be a very cumbersome system.

III.a.v.   Incest

Moral panics about practices such as organised and ritual abuse continue to pose both practical and ethical problems for the criminal justice system, not least because of the way in which they reflect society's perplexity about the capacities and sexuality of children and about the integrity of the family. This perplexity is perhaps even more evident in debates surrounding the law of incest. At the level of official enforcement, incest is a rare phenomenon: fewer than 50 convictions have occurred each year since 1998 (Home Office 2002j: Table 5.12). Public perception of the 'dangerousness' of incest, however, has been accentuated not only by the debates about child abuse discussed above but also by the appalling case of Frederick and Rosemary West, whose killing of a number of young women, including one of Frederick West's daughters, was committed within a 'family home' in which incest and sexual abuse appear to have been integral to family relationships.

Reflecting the make-up of modern families and the pivotal concept of trust, the Sexual Offences Bill 2003 extends incest involving children beyond the confines of blood ties, to include adoptive relationships (clause 29). The thinking behind this extension is explained in the White Paper:

Home Office, 'Protecting the Public: Strengthening Protection Against Sex Offenders and Reforming the Law on Sexual Offences' (Cmnd 5668) (HMSO, 2002), p 29, para 58

It is recognised that the balance of power within the family and the close trusting relationships that exist make children particularly vulnerable to abuse within its environment. The offence will therefore be designed to protect children up to the age of 18 from any form of activity that a person would consider sexual or indecent. The offence will be drawn widely to capture all those individuals of any age who have a "familial" relationship with a child by virtue not only of blood-ties, adoption, fostering, marriage or quasi-marital relationship but also by virtue of living within the same household as the child and assuming a position of trust or authority in relation to the child. The offender may be either an adult or another child who falls entirely within the clearly defined scope of the offence.

Sexual Offences Bill 2003

Clause 27   Sexual activity with a child family member
(1) A person (A) commits an offence if–
    (a) he intentionally touches another person (B),
    (b) the touching is sexual,
    (c) the relation of A to B is within section 29,
    (d) A knows or could reasonably be expected to know that his relation to B is of a description falling within that section, and
    (e) either–
        (i) B is under 18 and A does not reasonably believe that B is 18 or over, or
        (ii) B is under 13.
(2) Where in proceedings for an offence under this section it is proved that the other person was under 18, the defendant is to be taken not to have reasonably believed that that person was 18 or over unless sufficient evidence is adduced to raise an issue as to whether he reasonably believed it.
(3) Where in proceedings for an offence under this section it is proved that the relation of the defendant to the other person was of a description falling within section 29, it is to be taken that the defendant knew or could reasonably have been expected to know that his relation to the other person was of that description unless sufficient evidence is adduced to raise an issue as to whether he knew or could reasonably have been expected to know that it was.

The penalty is a maximum of 14 years' imprisonment for offenders over 18 at the time of the offence, otherwise the maximum is 5 years.

However, sexual activity involving adults in the family unit continues to be confined to blood relatives (parent, grandparent, child, grandchild, brother, sister, half-brother or half-sister) and to acts of penetration (clauses 65, 66). The prosecution power of appeal against sentence introduced in the Criminal Justice Act 1988 (s 36) was first used in an incest case. The case provided an opportunity for Lord Lane to offer some guidelines for sentencing in incest cases:

Re A-G's Reference (No 1 of 1989) **[1989] 3 All ER 571**

At one end of the scale is incest committed by a father with a daughter in her late teens or older who is a willing participant and indeed may be the instigator of the offences. In such a case, the court usually need do little more than mark the fact that there has been a breach of the law and little if anything is required in the way of punishment. The next class of case is that where the girl has achieved the age of 13, which in most cases will mean that she has achieved puberty. This of course is the demarcation line chosen in the Sexual Offences Act … Sentences in this area seem to vary between about 2 years to 4 or 5 years on a plea of guilty, depending on the mitigating or aggravating factors … The last and much the most difficult area is that involving girls under the age of 13. As in the case of those between 13 and 16, sexual intercourse is an offence, quite apart from the parental relationship. For victims under the age of 13, however, a further factor comes into play. Although the girl may 'consent' to the act of intercourse in such a way as to render a charge of rape inappropriate, the girl is from the very relationship in a particularly vulnerable position, which the father is in a position to exploit due to her dependence and inexperience and possibly fear of disrupting relations between mother and father if she lets it be known what is happening, or fear of her father if she refuses to comply with his demands. In those circumstances, the crime although falling far short of rape, has some of the unpleasant aspects of that particular crime …

[*On the basis of a plea of not guilty, the following sentence levels were recommended:*]

(1) Where the girl is over 16. Generally speaking a range from 3 years' imprisonment down to a nominal penalty will be appropriate depending in particular on the one hand on whether force was used, and upon the degree of harm, if any, to the girl, and on the other the desirability where it exists of keeping family disruption to the minimum. The older the girl the greater the possibility that she may have been willing or even the instigating party to the liaison, a factor which will be reflected in the sentence. In other words, the lower the degree of corruption, the lower the penalty.

(2) Where the girl is aged from 13 to 16. Here a sentence between about 5 years and 3 years seems … appropriate. Much the same principles will apply as in the case of a girl over 16, though the likelihood of corruption increases in inverse proportion to the age of the girl …

(3) Where the girl is under 13. It is here that the widest range of sentence is likely to be found. If one can properly describe any type of incest as the 'ordinary' type of case, it will be one where the sexual relationship between husband and wife has broken down;

the father has probably resorted to excessive drinking and the eldest daughter is gradually, by way of familiarities, indecent acts and suggestions made the object of the father's frustrated sexual inclinations. If the girl is not far short of her thirteenth birthday and there are no particularly adverse or favourable features on a not guilty plea, a term of about 6 years on the authorities would seem to be appropriate ...

Other aggravating factors, whatever the age of the girl may be (inter alia) as follows. (1) If there is evidence that the girl has suffered physically or psychologically from the incest. (2) If the incest has continued at frequent intervals over a long period of time. (3) If the girl has been threatened or treated violently by or was terrified of the father. (4) If the incest has been accompanied by perversions abhorrent to the girl, eg buggery or fellatio. (5) If the girl has become pregnant by reason of the father failing to take contraceptive measures. (6) If the defendant has committed similar offences against more than one girl.

Possible mitigating features are ... the following. (1) A plea of guilty ... (2) If it seems that there was a genuine affection on the part of the defendant rather than an intention to use the girl simply as an outlet for his sexual inclinations. (3) Where the girl has had previous sexual experience. (4) Where the girl has made deliberate attempts at seduction. (5) Where, as very occasionally is the case, a shorter term of imprisonment for the father may be of benefit to the victim and the family.

Lord Lane seems to introduce a presumption that girls over 16 collude in incest and that in other cases sexual abuse by fathers of their daughters can be understood in terms of their failure to maintain a satisfactory sexual relationship with their wife. It would not be a very big step from this to the proposition that the wife is to blame for the incest. The list of mitigating features perpetuates the idea that 'nice girls don't get raped'. If the girl has sexual experience this somehow provides an element of excuse for the father's abuse. There has been no attempt to disentangle the complex dynamics of family emotional life. Who is to say that the girl's sexual precocity is not attributable to her upbringing? The guidelines seem to assume that incest can be an unfortunate aberration. Even if it can be, it is inherently unlikely that such a case would ever be reported let alone prosecuted. The guidelines seem to assume throughout that the man is not necessarily responsible for his own actions, and conversely, that the women in his life get what they ask for.

FURTHER READING
Campbell, Beatrix (1988) *Unofficial Secrets, Child Sexual Abuse: The Cleveland Case* (Virago).
Duncan, Sheila (1995) 'Law's Sexual Discipline: Visibility, Violence and Consent' 22 Journal of Law and Society 326.

King, Michael and Piper, Christine (1995) *How the Law Thinks about Children* (2nd edn, Arena).

Lacey, Nicola (2001) 'Beset by Boundaries: The Home Office Review of Sex Offences' Criminal Law Review 3.

Law Commission (1995) *Consent in the Criminal Law* (Consultation Paper 139, HMSO).

Moran, Leslie J (1995) 'Violence and the Law: The Case of Sado-Masochism' 2 Social and Legal Studies 225.

— (1996) *The Homosexual(ity) of Law* (Routledge).

Morgan, Jane and Zedner, Lucia (1992) *Child Victims: Crime, Impact and Criminal Justice* (OUP).

Smith, K J M (1991) 'Sexual Etiquette, Public Interest and the Criminal Law' 42 Northern Ireland Legal Quarterly 309.

Soothill, Keith and Francis, Brian (1997) 'Sexual Reconvictions and the Sex Offenders Act 1997' 147 NLJ 1285, 1324.

Stychin, Carl (1996) *Law's Desire: Sexuality and the Limits of Justice* (Routledge).

Sullivan, Kathleen M and Field, Martha A (1988) 'AIDS and the Coercive Power of the State' 23 Harvard Civil Rights – Civil Liberties Law Review 139.

Wolfram, Sybil (1983) 'Eugenics and the Punishment of Incest Act 1908' Crim LR 308.

III.b.   Prostitution

The Report of the Wolfenden Committee (1957) considered the 'proper role' of law in relation to homosexuality and prostitution. It often passes without comment that these two topics were thought to present sufficiently similar problems to be considered together. Perhaps if the report had been entitled 'Homosexuality and Heterosexuality', the oddity would have been at once removed and highlighted; because, of course, heterosexuality in the 'right place', ie amongst married couples, was not 'a problem'. Or the report could have been more accurately entitled 'Offensive Public Manifestations of Sexuality'. As is well known, the report adopted a liberal approach based on Mill's 'harm principle', and led to the Street Offences Act 1959, which outlawed public soliciting.

Like other areas of sexual conduct, prostitution poses questions both about the relative value to be accorded to autonomy and about how sexual autonomy should be conceived. Are women who engage in prostitution 'victims' of a patriarchal sexual order, or competent subjects exercising their sexual autonomy and making rational choices about their lifestyle, or both? How far should we trust individuals to do as they wish with their own bodies? Before examining the legal regulation of prostitution, we consider some provocative analyses of the phenomenon of prostitution.

Kate Millett, *The Prostitution Papers* (Ballantine Books, 1976) p 93

... [P]rostitution is ... the very core of the female's social condition. It not only declares her subjection right in the open, with the cash nexus between the sexes announced in currency, rather than through the subtlety of a marriage contract (which still recognises the principle of sex in return for commodities and historically has insisted upon it), but the very act of prostitution is itself a declaration of our value, our reification.

Carole Pateman, *The Sexual Contract* (Polity, 1988) p 189

Prostitution is an integral part of patriarchal capitalism ... Prostitutes are readily available at all levels of the market for any man who can afford one and they are frequently provided as part of business, political and diplomatic transactions. Yet the public character of prostitution is less obvious than it might be. Like other forms of capitalist enterprise, prostitution is seen as private enterprise, and the contract between client and prostitute is seen as a private arrangement between a buyer and seller. Moreover, prostitution is shrouded in secrecy despite the scale of the industry. In Birmingham, a ... city of about one million people, some 800 women work either as street prostitutes, or from their homes or hotels, from 'saunas', 'massage parlours', or 'escort agencies'. Nearly 14,000 men each week buy their services, i.e., about 17 men for each prostitute. A similar level of demand has been recorded in the United States, and the total number of customers each week across the country has been conservatively estimated at 1,500,000 men. One estimate is that $40 million per day is spent on prostitution in the United States. The secrecy exists in part because, where the act of prostitution is not itself illegal, associated activities such as soliciting often are. The criminal character of much of the business of prostitution is not, however, the only reason for secrecy. Not all men wish it generally to be known that they buy this commodity. To be discovered consorting with prostitutes can, for example, still be the downfall of politicians. The empirical evidence also indicates that three-quarters of the clients of prostitutes are married men. Certainly, the prostitutes in Birmingham find that trade slackens during holiday periods when men are away from the city with their wives and children.

The sexual subjection of women has never lacked defenders, but until very recently an unqualified defence of prostitution has been hard to find ... A radical change has now taken place in arguments about prostitution. Prostitution is unequivocally defended by contractarians ... Many recent feminist discussions have argued that prostitution is merely a job of work and the prostitute is a worker, like any other wage labourer ... Contractarians argue that a prostitute contracts out a certain form of labour power for a given period in exchange for money ... A prostitute does not sell herself, as is commonly alleged, or even sell her sexual parts, but contracts out use of sexual services ...

Defenders of prostitution admit that some reforms are necessary in the industry as it exists at present in order for a properly free market in sexual services to operate. Nevertheless, they insist that 'sound prostitution' is possible ... A universal defence of prostitution entails that a prostitute can be of either sex. Women should have the same opportunity as men to buy sexual services in the market ... A moment's contemplation of the story of the sexual contract suggests that there is a major difficulty in any attempt to universalize prostitution ... The story of the sexual contract reveals that there is good reason why 'the prostitute' is a female figure ...

Contractarians who defend an ostensibly sexually neutral, universal, sound prostitution have not, as far as I am aware, taken the logic of their arguments to its conclusion. The final defeat of status and the victory of contract should lead to the elimination of marriage in favour of the economical arrangement of universal prostitution, in which all individuals enter into brief contracts of sexual use when required.

Any discussion of prostitution is replete with difficulties. Although contractarians now deny any political significance to the fact that (most) prostitutes are women, one major difficulty is that, in other discussions, prostitution is invariably seen as a problem about the prostitute, as a problem about women ... To argue that there is something wrong with prostitution does not necessarily imply any adverse judgement on the women who engage in the work ... [T]he patriarchal assumption that prostitution is a problem about women ensures that the other participant in the prostitution contract escapes scrutiny. Once the story of the sexual contract has been told, prostitution can be seen as a problem about men. The problem of prostitution then becomes encapsulated in the question why men demand that women's bodies are sold as commodities in the capitalist market. The story of the sexual contract also supplies the answer; prostitution is part of the exercise of the law of male sex-right, one of the ways in which men are ensured access to women's bodies.

However we view this general interpretation of prostitution, the influence of prevailing ideas of 'normal' femininity on the treatment of prostitute women is well established:

Kathryn Chadwick and Catherine Little, 'The Criminalization of Women' in Scraton (ed) *Law, Order and the Authoritarian State* (Open University Press, 1987) pp 254, 264

Women's respectability is judged largely by their sexuality and, placed along a continuum, women are either 'good' or 'bad', virgins or whores. The ideological construction of the prostitute serves to divide and separate women into different categories. Sheila Jeffreys considers some of the reasons for this separation:

It is in the interests of men that women are divided into groups whose interest are apparently opposed. 'Good' women have been encouraged to turn their anxiety at their precarious position into anger at prostitutes who can appear to threaten the married woman's security and home, to undermine her efforts to control her man and his sexual demands. Or we are told that prostitution is necessary to protect the married woman's security. Neither is true ... It is vital to male supremacy that women be divided into the 'pure' and the 'fallen' so we may not pool our knowledge and engage in the fight against male sexuality as the social control of women.

... These divisions serve to undermine any shared class or gender interests and lay the foundations for the process of criminalization.

Traditional explanations for the occurrence of prostitution invariably are biological and focus on the abnormal sexuality of women. In these portrayals women are seen to lack any moral fibre; they are promiscuous, sex-crazed or simply men-haters who wish to use prostitution to exercise their power over men. Coupled with this they are seen to be lazy, and in search of easy work, hence easy money. They are predators on men's sexual needs ...

In reality prostitution is far from easy work or a comfortable style of living. Prostitutes are alienated from the rest of society, they are subjected to personal degradation and social stigma, they work long and unsociable hours, and run the constant risks of attacks or murder. Many women, as a result of the processes of the labour market ... find themselves economically marginalized, so that prostitution becomes an economic necessity. Poverty and lack of real employment opportunities often leaves many women with little choice. The commonly held view that prostitutes choose this form of employment because they 'like it' is strongly rejected by prostitutes ...

It is important to notice the relevance of class relations within prostitution. Those who work on the streets tend to be working-class women, while 'escort' or 'agency' workers are not only involved at a different economic level, but also are less likely to come into contact with the law. The 'street-walkers' are the most vulnerable and exposed of all prostitutes and they are likely to come into most regular contact with the police.

One of the difficulties with accounts such as that of Pateman is that they might be taken to represent prostitute women as mere 'dupes' of an oppressive social order rather than as responsible agents making choices within an (unfair) set of circumstances. Ironically, the law on prostitution is one of the few areas of sexual offences in which the images of women produced by criminal law involve positive agency rather than passive victimisation. Nonetheless, it can hardly be doubted that the phenomenon of prostitution reflects prevailing –

differentiated – sexual relations. To the extent, therefore, that prostitution is consonant with the values and demands of a patriarchal social order, what could be the rationale for proscribing it? The following extracts return us to the public/private distinction, and to criminal law's preoccupation with the visibility of 'deviant' sexualities:

Katherine O'Donovan, *Sexual Divisions in Law* (Weidenfeld & Nicholson, 1985) p 100

The regulation of prostitution, since the enactment of the Street Offences Act 1959, depends on the distinction between public and private. According to the Wolfenden Report the criminal law should not concern itself with matters of private morality but should 'aim to protect the citizen from what is offensive or injurious'. This expression of liberal philosophy has come to dominate thinking about control of sexuality. The result was a recasting of legal provisions whereby prostitution itself is not illegal but any public manifestation such as soliciting, advertising or making agreements with clients, is. Street offences, since 1959, are punished more severely than previously because: 'both loitering and importuning for the purpose of prostitution are so self-evidently public nuisances that the law ought to deal with them, as it deals with other self-evident public nuisances, without calling on individual citizens to show that they were annoyed'. To safeguard citizens from having to prove their annoyance the law uses the notion of the 'common prostitute' as part of the mechanism of control of prostitutes' behaviour in public.

... The use of the term 'common prostitute' dates back to the Contagious Diseases Acts in force from 1864 to 1886, when state control of prostitution was established in certain military and naval towns. By 1869 there were eighteen such districts in which any woman could be arrested on suspicion of being a common prostitute. Unless she could prove other-wise to the police, or in court, she was registered a common prostitute and had to submit to fortnightly medical examinations. Refusal to be examined meant imprisonment. If found to be suffering from venereal disease she would be interned in a lock hospital for up to nine months.

The object of the measures was to protect military men from disease, but the legislation contained assumptions about male and female sexuality which continue to inform law-making today. Sex was considered essential for the fighting men of the empire and no effort was directed at preventing them from visiting prostitutes. But the women were criminalised and con-trolled. A social identity, which had not previously existed, the prostitute, was constructed. What had been for many poor women a transitional stage in their working lives became, through criminalisation, the only means of livelihood. Prostitutes as sexually active women were separated from virtuous and passive models of femininity.

Josephine Butler led the successful campaign against the Acts, which were seen as a threat to all women. Feminist repealers stressed the double standard implied in the legislation, which punished women but not their clients. This double standard, so prevalent in Victorian beliefs and morality, remains part of prostitution law. The middle-class women who belonged to the Ladies' National Association, the repeal organisation, had quite different views of morality from those enshrined in the law of today. They subscribed to an ideology of separate spheres for women and men that stressed women's purity, moral supremacy and domestic virtue. They were indignant when confronted by a prostitute who adhered to her way of life. Their public discourse was a condemnation of male sexual licence and it was proposed that the standards of domestic purity and fidelity replace the double standard.

In their criticism of the double standard reformers were confronted not only with differential standards for female and male behaviour, but also with Victorian hypocrisy in which public pronouncements were not matched with private behaviour. The separation, in bourgeois ideology, of public and private morality was complex. On the one hand family, home and domesticity constituted the private place in which those female virtues of chastity and moral purity were upheld and respected. On the other hand the private sphere was that of male sexual licence ... In the public sphere politicians laid down high standards of public morality; the public was also the place of prostitution, vice on the streets, crime. The resolution of this was to be the imposition of those private, domestic, womanly values on all, in both private and public, through the social purity movement. Later liberal reforms which imply that private behaviour is personal and no concern of the law, but that what is done in public is what matters, are the direct antithesis of the moral purity reforms.

Clearly, prostitution raises questions relating to human rights. But is the major human rights issue the violation of women's bodies or state repression which continues to marginalise prostitutes?

Priscilla Alexander, 'Feminism, Sex Workers, and Human Rights' in J Nagle (ed) *Whores and Other Feminists* (Routledge, 1997) p 86

Prostitutes' human rights have long been violated by agencies – police and public health – charged with protecting people from harm. The desire to isolate the prostitute, to wall her off from the rest of society, goes back almost to the origins of what we call "civilization". Early Sumerian texts, written around 4,000 years ago, described prostitutes as wise women, able to educate, civilize and tame men. But as men took over the early city states, they separated harlots – often poets, teachers, musicians, dancers, and priestesses – from other women. One of the oldest sumptuary laws, written around 1250 B.C.E., required "wives" to walk veiled in the street.

Although Sumerian law-makers permitted concubines to veil themselves if they lived with a man and his family, they prohibited the independent prostitute from doing so, threatening to take all her clothes, pour pitch on her head, and punish any man who knowingly walked with her. In medieval France, an endless series of laws prescribed prostitutes' dress, or symbols on their dress, to distinguish them from the good women, whom they admonished not to dress like whores. Medieval lawmakers also allowed prostitutes on one street for a while, then forced them to move to another. Sometimes these streets were inside, sometimes outside the city wall. Sometimes authorities required women to work alone, one woman to a house, while at other times they made them work in groups with a manager. Whenever laws have become more repressive, the management of prostitution has moved from the hands of women to the hands of men, and vice versa, down through the ages to our own time.

Occasionally governments wrote laws designed to protect prostitutes from exploitation and abuse by madams and other managers, but the overwhelming weight of the law has pressed on the prostitutes, routinely described as "disorderly", "vagrant", "parasitic", "dirty", "dangerous", and "diseased".

Alexander concludes that (p 92):

There are some days when I feel overwhelmed by the woman-hatred that shores up these policies and practices. In every century, on every continent, in every country, societies use such measures to control women who dare to step outside of the normative role of virgin daughter / chaste wife. Although the stigma and repression have been greater in some times and places than others, they have never been absent. I have trouble understanding why – in the face of all the documentation provided by individual sex workers and sex workers' rights organizations to show the enormous cost to them, and to society, of the continued enforcement of laws prohibiting prostitution – anti-*prostitution* activists are calling for greater enforcement of those laws. I can only conclude that they, like most of society, are anti-*prostitute*.

Cate Haste, *Rules of Desire: Sex in Britain, World War I to the Present* (Pimlico, 1992) p 262

The rights of prostitutes began to be scrutinized mainly because the women began to organize to publicize their case. They exposed their vulnerability under the law, but also the anomalous position of women in the new sexual ethic. Since the earliest days of emancipation, women had challenged the marriage contract as one in which men agreed to support women for life in return for sexual favours. There had been no shortage of people who pointed out the basic contract was not dissimilar to the bargain of prostitution, the main difference being that one was culturally and morally respectable and protected by the law and the other was not. The continuing economic disadvantage of women and their cultural subordination served to perpetuate this bargain. The aims of nineteenth-century emancipationists and twentieth-century feminists had been to transform those power relations in the name of equality, freedom and justice. They had continually come up against the dual obstacles of the double sexual standard, and the continuing economic disadvantages of women, chiefly low pay, limited occupational opportunities, the undervaluation of women's work and their expendability in a job market which tended to see women as a reserve labor force, all of which narrow women's choices.

The so-called oldest profession remains young in terms of collective trade organisation. The creation of the International Union of Sex Workers (IUSW) in 2000 represents the most notable development since the formation of the English Collective of Prostitutes (ECP) in 1975. The Union's determination to move sex work from the margins to mainstream is reflected in its decision to affiliate with the GMB (*The Guardian*, 8 March 2002). The shift of language from the morally maligned *prostitute* to the neutral *sex worker* selling services in the sex industry may also be significant. As such language gains cultural recognition it may become harder to resist calls for regulation. Reflecting this, in 2000 the Netherlands legalised voluntary prostitution, seeking to regulate sex work as any other business, and thus bringing with it the promise of legal and employment rights and reduced stigma (Kilvington et al 2001). In the UK, a symposium of sex workers, police officers, judicial personnel and academics, brought together as part of Channel 4 television series on prostitution, have recently demanded a 'national enquiry into the sex industry and existing laws chaired by an independent national figure' (Dispatches, Sex on the Street, 16 September 2002). However, IUSW membership is very low (around 200) out of around 90,000 prostitutes. Furthermore, as O'Connell Davidson suggests below, any meaningful transformation in the status of the prostitute may require far more substantial changes:

Julia O'Connell Davidson, *Prostitution, Power and Freedom* (Polity, 1998) pp 190–191

Prostitution, like both wage and labour slavery, is an institution through which certain powers of command over the person are transferred from one individual to another. It is not fully distinguished from either slavery or wage labour ...

It is also important to note that both wage labour and slavery, like prostitution, are institutions which involve more than just *economic* oppression of human subjects. However, in terms of possibilities for collective political action implicit in these institutions, it seems to me that prostitution *is* distinguished by the fact that the contradictions implicit in the relationship between prostitute and clients, both as individuals and collective groups, does not generate an immediate or straightforward dialectic for change.

... Certainly clients are often just as much interested in exploiting willing and co-operative prostitutes as employers are in exploiting willing workers ... but clients have no direct *economic* interest in securing prostitutes' co-operation – it is not necessary for clients, as a collective group, to accumulate sexual value, or to socialize prostitution, or then to deal with prostitutes as a collective group. From the client's point of view the prostitute contract involves a relation of consumption, not production. Negotiations over the prices and terms of prostitution contracts are thus highly atomized. They represent an individualized form of haggling over an existing exchange value, not a struggle over how much sexual 'value' is collectively produced and retained by prostitutes, and this seriously limits the potential for collective resistance by prostitutes.

Street Offences Act 1959, s 1(1)

It shall be an offence for a common prostitute *(whether male or female)* to loiter or solicit in a street or public place for the purpose of prostitution. [Words in italics proposed in Sexual Offences Bill 2003, Sch 1, cl 2.]

The designation 'common prostitute' had applied only to women (*DPP v Bull*, 1994); men could not be convicted under this section. 'Common prostitution' for the purposes of s 1 is proven by police evidence that the person persisted in conduct for which she has previously been cautioned by a constable. The Home Office approves a system whereby the police do not charge a woman unless she has been formally cautioned on two occasions and the cautions have been formally recorded. (Status offences and the tension between the operation of the category 'common prostitute' and the presumption of innocence are also discussed in **Chapter 1.I.a.ii.** and **II.a.**) About 4000 women are found guilty of soliciting each year, and the conviction rate is well over 90% (Home Office 2002j: Table 5.20). When the option of imprisonment for this offence was removed by the Criminal Justice Act 1982, s 71, magistrates were effectively left with a penalty choice between probation and fine. The number of women imprisoned for fine default has decreased substantially from 1370 in 1995 to 70 in 2001 (Home Office 2002m: 33). However, as we saw in **Chapters 2** and **3**, there are large numbers of provisions that can be used to regulate prostitutes and others whose lifestyles are perceived as inappropriate. In particular, anti-social behaviour orders (ASBOs) under the Crime and Disorder Act 1998 are widely used for these purposes. A civil order accompanied by criminal penalties for breach, an ASBO may be made if a person 'has acted ... in an anti-social manner ... that caused or was likely to cause harassment, alarm or distress' (s 1). Prostitution accounts for around 5% of ASBOs (Campbell 2002), and in the first two years since they were introduced, at least 14 prostitutes have been imprisoned for between three and six months for breaching the terms of their ASBOs (see Crim LR [2001] 873).

The implications of the current legal regime for women working as prostitutes are discussed in the following extracts:

Susan Atkins and Brenda Hoggett, *Women and the Law* (Blackwell, 1984) p 79

In theory the law prohibits almost all methods of contacting clients. The prostitute cannot solicit in the open, or even in view of the open, or through a directory or contact magazine. The former offend against the Street Offences Act and the latter against the common law offence of conspiracy to corrupt public morals discovered by the House of Lords only shortly afterwards [*Shaw v DPP, 1962: see **Chapter 3.IV.**] ... In theory the law also makes it difficult for a prostitute to find premises. If she shares with another, they may be prosecuted for running a brothel, and their landlord will also be at risk. If she rents a place on her own, she runs no risk herself, but her landlord does so if he lets the room for that purpose or charges her an inflated rent, and in either event he may not be entitled to recover the rent by legal process. It is well known that debts which cannot be recovered by legal process are often collected in less orthodox ways. Together these provisions prevent two or three prostitutes from sharing for mutual comfort and protection, as many would wish to do. The Criminal Law Revision Committee (CLRC) [1982: paras 3.44–3.46] would keep the offences of managing, letting or permitting premises to be used for prostitution, except where they are used as both a home and a business by only one or two prostitutes. This is certainly a step in the right direction, although it would create a new offence of letting business premises to a single prostitute and would encourage others to work from home in residential areas. There is every reason to believe that this is what many of them do already. In theory the law also makes it virtually impossible for the prostitute to carry on any sort of normal life outside working hours or to establish more conventional relationships if she wishes. Any man who lives with or is habitually seen with her is presumed to be living on immoral earnings. The CLRC would like to see this presumption go, but it is undoubtedly the only way to earn a good living in a man's world while retaining their independence.

Susan Edwards, *Women on Trial* (Manchester University Press, 1984) pp 68–70

The application of the term 'common prostitute' in criminal proceedings has had a much greater and more profound influence on the criminal justice system than to be merely discriminatory, to challenge ... self-definitions of women or to disadvantage their case before presiding magistrates. The belief that the application of the term 'common prostitute' is regarded as an acquired status and biases their case before it is heard is a fact which influences both the defendants' choice as to plea, and magistrates' conviction and sentence.

It has been stated elsewhere in more general terms that a defendant's decision as to plea is the single most important aspect of decision-making in the penal process. Whilst any efficiency in the administration of criminal justice would cease if all defendants in exercising this right pleaded not guilty, it is perhaps of some significance that any prostitute challenges the system and pleads not guilty at all ...

Carol Smart, 'Legal Subjects and Sexual Objects: Ideology, Law and Female Sexuality' in J Brophy and C Smart (eds) *Women in Law: Explorations in Law, Family and Sexuality* (Routledge, 1985) p 50

Our current laws on soliciting and loitering ... [are] a prime example of straightforward legal sexual discrimination because only women can be defined as common prostitutes and so only women become subject to the particularly repressive regime of regulation that follows from this definition. It is not, however, these visible and well-documented features of law relating to prostitution that I wish to explore here. Rather I wish to examine the ideological content of the views of judicial actors, who routinely adjudicate in cases of soliciting and related offences ... Although I would argue that legislation does identify a special class of women (in this case common prostitutes) and therefore constructs some women as specific 'legal subjects' with fewer rights than other citizens, I would also like to argue that it is legislation and legal practice informed by specific ideologies of female sexuality which serves to construct prostitute women as mere 'sexual objects'. In turn this sexual objectification of prostitute women reinforces their special status as denigrated legal subjects and helps to preserve legislation which, by most standards, must be regarded as unusually harsh and repressive.

That there is great resistance to changing the law in this area is evidenced by the number of fruitless attempts to introduce reforms in recent years. There have been five private members bills in the House of Lords since 1967 and two in the Commons in 1979 and 1981. Moreover, since the Wolfenden Report of 1957, which provided the basis for the subsequent rationalisation of legislation on prostitution, there have been two important Government reports: one produced in 1974 by the Home Office, entitled Working Party on Vagrancy and Street Offences Working Paper, and the other produced by the Criminal Law Revision Committee in 1982, entitled Working Paper on Offences Relating to Prostitution and Allied Offences ... Yet, in spite of all these efforts and documents, the law remains basically unchanged and the major criticism of the law which was expressed over fifty years ago (Report of the Street Offences Committee, 1928) is still valid today, namely that the law constructs a specific category of women called common prostitutes which it then subjects to a unique form of prosecution and regulation ...

When discussing women's sexuality it is important to recognise that it is extremely difficult to avoid talking at the same time about marriage, love, the family and children ... Women and girls who have sex outside marriage are still regarded as promiscuous ... unmarried mothers are still unable to legitimize their children without getting married. So unless we concentrate solely on the physiology of sex, discussions of female sexuality almost always invoke the determining context of marriage and the family. Consequently, most discussions of prostitution also invoke the cultural ideals of heterosexual love, monogamous marriage and the sanctity of the family ...

Smart tape-recorded interviews with 25 randomly-selected magistrates, 14 men and 11 women, who were sitting regularly in the Sheffield Magistrates' Courts in the winter of 1981:

It would be a mistake ... to assume that all magistrates spoke from a unified position or set of values. Although all shared the view that some coercive intervention into the lives of prostitute women was necessary ... the nature of that intervention varied according to the magistrates' perceptions of the problem. [This] tended to fall into three main categories or ideological positions which were influenced by three different discourses on sexuality. These discourses I have identified as liberal/permissive (the largest category), puritan/authoritarian (the second largest) and welfarist ...

(a) The liberal/permissive discourse

This discourse was probably most clearly articulated in the Wolfenden Report (1957) which argued that what consenting adults did in private should not be the concern of the criminal law. The magistrates who adopted this view ... like Wolfenden, argued that prostitution was only a matter for the criminal law when it became visible on the streets. The solution, they tended to argue, was a pragmatic recognition of the need for licensed brothels where people could get on with it without causing a nuisance.

(b) The puritan/authoritarian discourse

This category of magistrates were concerned to control not just prostitution but also prostitutes; they tended to be in favour of imprisoning women, felt the police 'did a good job' and saw no reason to reform the laws on soliciting ... The puritan/authoritarian discourse relied significantly upon three main axes: a Christian morality which sees prostitution as immoral and undermining of the value of family and social life; a puritan ethic which condemns prostitution because it is assumed (mistakenly) to be a way of making easy money without really working for it; and an exaggerated concern over disease ...

(c)   The welfarist discourse

This third discourse ... is based on vague psychoanalytic theories of child development which are much influenced by a melange of welfare concerns and a good deal of 'common sense'. This constituted the smallest category and was made up almost exclusively of women magistrates. Basically this position held or presumed that there was something psychologically amiss with prostitute women, and this was frequently explained in terms of childhood development. Prostitution was not usually seen as resulting directly from economic need or greed as with the two previous categories. Rather it was perceived as the result of some unresolved personality problem ...

[A] disenchantment with current legislation did not lead the magistrates to the view that the problems inherent in the law arose from its aim to extensively control the lives of prostitutes who work outside the invisible networks of saunas, hotels and escort agencies. Instead their discontent led to proposals for more rational systems of regulation and surveillance, namely legalised brothels ...

Very few of the magistrates considered the desirability of legalised brothels from the point of view of the prostitute women involved ... The plan for legalised brothels does not therefore reflect any change in the common perception of prostitute women: on the contrary, it simply reflects a different dimension of the same view, namely that prostitutes are sexual objects which constitute a health hazard unless properly regulated.

Criminal law also encompasses a variety of offences aimed at those (men and women) who profit from and exploit prostitute women, but the number of prosecutions is relatively low:

Before 1985, it could have been argued that the disparity in the numbers prosecuted for procuration etc, compared with those for soliciting under the Street Offences Act 1959, was a result of easier police access to evidence of public loitering. Although the Sexual Offences Act 1956 provided in s 32 for persistently soliciting or importuning in a public place for immoral purposes, courts refused to sanction the use of this offence to control kerb crawling (*Crook v Edmondson*, 1966). The only exception was where the object of the crawler's attention was under 16 (*R v Dodd*, 1977: cf *Kirkup*, 1993 in relation to homosexuality). This implicitly endorsed the view that women out on the street are fair game for sexual harassment. Police in some areas sought to avoid this by using binding-over powers under the Justices of the Peace Act 1361 or, in London, by the use of the Metropolitan Police Act 1839, which allows the control of 'insulting behaviour'.

The Sexual Offences Act 1985 specifically made kerb-crawling an offence. In its first year of operation there were 189 prosecutions under this section, with 161 convictions. By 1987 the number of convictions had risen to 275, with a further 225 men cautioned, and in 1995, 1270 men were convicted of or cautioned for kerb-crawling. This is still a modest number compared with that of women held liable for prostitution-related offences. The wording of the Act creates some interpretative difficulties, but it seems unlikely that this is the sole reason for the low number of prosecutions. The Sexual Offences Bill 2003 proposes to remove the gender specificity of these offences (Sch 1, clauses 3, 4 and 5) [*changes in square brackets*]:

Sexual Offences Act 1985, ss 1, 2(1), 4(3)

[Soliciting for the purpose of prostitution]
1   A *man [person]*commits an offence if he solicits *a woman [another person]* (or different *women [persons]*) for the purpose of prostitution–
   (a)   from a motor vehicle while it is in a street or public place; or
   (b)   in a street or public place while in the immediate vicinity of a motor vehicle that he has just got out of or off, persistently or, subject to section 5(6) below, in such manner or in such circumstances as to be likely to cause annoyance to the *woman [person]* (or any of the *women [persons]*) solicited, or nuisance to other persons in the neighbourhood.

[Persistent soliciting]
2(1)A *man [person]* commits an offence if in a street or public place he persistently solicits a *woman [another person]* (or different *women [persons]*) for the purpose of prostitution.
4(3)*Paragraphs (a) and (b) of section 6 of the Interpretation Act 1978 (words importing the masculine gender to include the feminine) do not apply to this Act. [Section omitted.]*

The plight of prostitutes as victims of crime is often overlooked. A survey of 110 street prostitutes across 18 locations in the UK found that 72% claimed to have been attacked by clients, while 60% claimed to have been badly beaten up or raped during the previous 12 months (Dispatches, Sex on the Street, 16 September 2002). Such risks have, some argue, been exacerbated by the extension of police powers of arrest, detention, and to take DNA samples from kerb-crawlers in the Criminal Justice and Police Act 2001. Section 71 makes kerb-crawling an arrestable offence by amending s 24(2) of the Police and Criminal Evidence Act 1984. The rationale is that this will deter kerb-crawlers and further 'clean up the streets'. The reality is that sex will be bought in more desolate and dangerous places. Furthermore, s 46 of the 2001 Act reflects the law's continued rejection of prostitution by making it an offence to place in a public telephone advertisements in relation to prostitution.

The Sexual Offences Bill 2003 partly consolidates this array of prostitution-related offences by criminalising commercial sexual exploitation (ie replacing those from the Sexual Offences Act 1956). There are separate offences for those found 'causing or inciting prostitution for gain' (clause 54) and those 'controlling prostitution for gain' (clause 55). These are accompanied by the offence of trafficking people for commercial sexual exploitation, which carries a maximum penalty of 14 years' imprisonment (clauses 58–60). In addition, as we have noted, the existing prostitution offences under the Street Offences Acts of 1956 and 1985 will become gender-neutral (clause 57).

It is therefore quite misleading to talk of the regulation of prostitution, because what we have had, prior to the 2003 reforms, are laws which specifically discriminate against prostitute women. Not only are women singled out in terms of enforcement, but the very structure of the offence of soliciting labels and condemns them in advance. Furthermore, notwithstanding Pateman's analysis, she is denied the status of contracting subject: 'public policy' dictates that prostitution contracts are unenforceable as being for 'immoral purposes'. The image of women as either chaste or impure on which the control of soliciting depends and which it reinforces can be seen in many other areas. The idea that women with previous sexual experience might lie about rape is one example (see **section II.b.v.** above); another is judicial guidance on sentencing in incest cases (see **section III.a.v.** above).

FURTHER READING

Bland, Lucy (1985) 'In the Name of Protection: the Policing of Women in the First World War' in Julia Brophy and Carol Smart (eds) *Women in Law* (Routledge).

Christina, Diana and Carlen, Pat (1985) 'Christina: In Her Own Time' in Pat Carlen et al *Criminal Women* (Polity) p 59.

Criminal Law Revision Committee (1984) Sixteenth Report *Prostitution in the Street* (Cmnd 9329, HMSO).

— (1985) Seventeenth Report *Prostitution: Off-Street Activities* (Cmnd 9688, HMSO).

Mathews, Roger and O'Neill, Maggie (eds) (2003) *Prostitution* (Ashgate).

Scambler, Graham and Scambler, Annette (eds) (1997) *Rethinking Prostitution: Purchasing Sex in the 1990s* (Routledge).

Walkowitz, Judith (1980) *Prostitution in Victorian Society* (Cambridge University Press).

III.c.   Pornography

III.c.i.   Pornography, obscenity and freedom of speech

As we move from serious sexual offences through the regulation of homosexuality and prostitution to pornography, we find ourselves in areas in which the consensus about the proper role of criminal law is increasingly fragmented. Should pornography be regulated by criminal laws at all? Is it a manifestation and cornerstone of patriarchal power, an offensive and possibly dangerous social practice, or a valuable form of sexual expression, experimentation and fantasy? Should the legal regulation of pornography be regarded as an illiberal violation of free expression, a manifestation of concern for public order and decency, or an attempt to eliminate sex discrimination? Before turning to the actual criminal regulation of obscenity, we consider some of these deeply contested questions.

Joel Feinberg, *Offense to Others* (© 1985 Oxford University Press, Inc) pp 127, 142 [Used by permission of Oxford University Press, Inc]

There is no more unfortunate mistake in the discussion of obscenity than simply to identify that concept, either in meaning or in scope of designation, with pornography. To call something obscene, in the standard uses of that term, is to condemn that thing as shockingly vulgar or blatantly disgusting, for the word 'obscene', like the word 'funny', is used to claim that a given response (in this case repugnance, in the other amusement) is likely to be the general one and/or to endorse that response as appropriate. The corresponding term 'pornographic', on the other hand, is a purely descriptive word referring to sexually explicit writing and pictures designed entirely and plausibly to induce sexual excitement in the reader or observer. To use the terms 'obscene' and 'pornographic' interchangeably, then, as if they referred to precisely the same things, is to beg the essentially controversial question of whether any or all (or only) pornographic materials really are obscene. Surely, to those thousands or millions of persons who delight in pornographic books, pictures, and films, the objects of their attachment do not seem disgusting or obscene. If these materials are nevertheless 'truly obscene', they are not so merely by virtue of the definitions of the terms 'obscene' and 'pornographic' but rather by virtue of their blatant violation of some relevant standards, and to establish their obscenity requires serious argument and persuasion. In short, whether any given acknowledged bit of pornography is really obscene is a logically open question to be settled by argument, not by definitional fiat ...

In the absence of convincing evidence of its causal tie to social harms, pornography ought to be prohibited by law only when it is obscene and then precisely because it is obscene. But obscenity (extreme offensiveness) is only a necessary condition, not a sufficient condition, for rightful prohibition. In addition, the offending conduct must not be reasonably avoidable, and the risk of offence must not have been voluntarily assumed by the beholders.

It is not clear what Feinberg hopes to achieve by this strongly put argument that 'pornography' should be reserved for descriptive purposes only. Can his approach help to advance the debate as to whether material, whether obscene in his terms or not, portraying women as objects for sexual gratification is properly proscribed? In criticising the use of a 'definitional fiat' in relation to the word obscenity, Feinberg may be open to the same criticism in relation to 'pornography'. In arguing for a clear distinction between the concepts of obscenity and pornography, he ignores the advantages of a prescriptive use of the term 'pornography', as well as its potential usefulness as an expression in other situations, such as 'the pornography of the rape trial' (cf Smart, above).

Catharine MacKinnon, *Feminism Unmodified* (Harvard, 1987) p 147

This inquiry is part of a larger project that attempts to account for gender inequality in the socially constructed relationship between power – the political – on the one hand and the knowledge of truth and reality – the epistemological – on the other. For example, the candid description Justice Stewart once offered of his obscenity standard, 'I know it when I see it', becomes even more revealing than it is usually understood to be if it is taken as a statement that connects epistemology with power. If I ask, from the point of view of women's experience, does he know what I know when I see what I see, I find that I doubt it, given what's on the newsstands. How does his point of view keep what is there, there? To liberal critics, his admission exposed the obscenity standard's relativity, its partiality, its insufficient abstractedness ... [T]he obscenity standard – in this it is not unique – is built on what the male standpoint sees. My point is: so is pornography. In this way the law of obscenity reproduces the pornographic point of view on women on the level of Constitutional jurisprudence.

It may be useful, before considering more fully arguments for and against the control of pornography, to examine current legal responses. Control of pornography in the UK has been ad hoc, deploying a range of public order offences such as 'conspiracy to corrupt public morals' (see **Chapter 3.IV.**). But it often relies in particular on the concept of obscenity. The major legislation is the Obscene Publications Act 1959, subsequently amended to cover a broader range of activities by the Cinemas Act 1985, the Broadcasting Act 1990, and the Criminal Justice and Public Order Act 1994, Pt VII. The 1959 Act adopted the common law test under which obscenity is defined in terms of its tendency to 'deprave and corrupt' (*Hicklin*, 1868).

Obscene Publications Act 1959, ss 1, 4

1   [An article is obscene if] its effect or (where the article comprises two or more distinct items) the effect of any one of its items is, if taken as a whole, such as to tend to deprave and corrupt persons who are likely, having regard to all relevant circumstances, to read, see or hear the matter contained as embodied in it.

4   [No conviction should follow] if it is proved that publication of the article in question is justified as being for the public good on the grounds that it is in the interests of science, literature, art or learning or of other objects of general concern.

The Act creates offences of publishing, whether for gain or not, an obscene article and having an obscene article for publication or gain. 'Publish' is defined to include all forms of distribution, including giving and lending, and offering to sell or rent. The word 'article' is defined to include written and pictorial material, sound recordings, objects and films. Section 3 authorises the issue of warrants entitling police officers to seize material believed to be obscene. A jury must consider the effect on a significant proportion of the likely readers (*R v Calder and Boyars Ltd*, 1969). A 'significant proportion' may be much less than half of the relevant group and the jury may find that the article tends to deprave if it encourages private sexual fantasies even without overt sexual activity (*DPP v Whyte*, 1972). Articles encouraging drug abuse or violence have also been found obscene under this definition (*John Calder Publications v Powell*, 1965 and *Calder and Boyars Ltd*, 1969). The 'deprave and corrupt' definition is therefore capable of wide interpretation by judge and jury alike. There is also a plethora of legislation dealing with the import and export of obscene material, with films, with the use of child models and with indecent public displays (Broadcasting Act 1990; Customs Consolidation Act 1876; Cinema Act 1985; Video Recordings Act 1984; Protection of Children Act 1978; and Indecent Displays (Control) Act 1981). The Local Government (Miscellaneous Provisions) Act 1982 gives local authorities broad powers over 'sex establishments', including the power to exclude such businesses entirely from certain areas and districts. The City of Westminster has used its powers to exclude sex establishments from a large number of areas within London and to set a maximum for the number of licences it will grant. Most of these were allocated to Soho. In 1982 the Act was extended to cover exhibitions of moving pictures.

None of this has, however, been taken to interfere with common law offences of blasphemy and outraging public decency (*R v Lemon*, 1978; *Knuller (Publishing etc) Ltd v DPP*, 1973). In January 1989 an artist and a gallery owner were convicted of the common law offence of outrage to public decency. They were fined £500 and £350 respectively. (The level of fine could be compared with those for breaches of health and safety regulations following injuries or deaths to workers; see **Chapter 6.II.a.ii.** and **II.c.**) The prosecutions followed the exhibition of a sculpture of a mannequin's head with two freeze-dried human foetuses as earrings. The judge directed an acquittal on charges of public nuisance. The defendants failed in their arguments that their cases should be dealt with under the Obscene Publications Act 1959 so that they could invoke a defence of artistic merit. Judge Brian Smedley told the jury that: 'In any civilised society, there has to be a constraint on freedom to act in a way which has an adverse effect on other members of the society in which we live' (*Independent*, 10 February 1989). As Rosalind Coward commented:

> The charges presume a shared morality, outraged by this apparent trivialisation of human death. But equating an embalmed foetus with a dead person carries as a logical concomitant the idea that abortion is murder, which is currently neither law nor a point of shared morality [*New Statesman and Society*, 27 January 1989].

The defendants' appeal was dismissed on the basis that common law charges were only ruled out by s 2(4) of the Obscene Publications Act 1959 where the essence of the offence was a tendency to corrupt public morals. It followed that the common law offence had properly been charged in this case, where the essence of the allegation was outraging public decency (*Gibson*, 1991). Furthermore, the Court of Appeal confirmed that no intention or recklessness as to outraging public decency had to be proved: the Crown needed merely to show that the defendants had intentionally done something which in fact outraged public decency (on this point the decision mirrors the position in the law of blasphemy: *Lemon*, 1978; see further Brown 1998, Robertson 1993: 247–254). The Court of Appeal similarly endorsed the use of the common law outrage to decency charge in place of an available statutory alternative in *May* (1990), notwithstanding that the facts would also have supported an offence under s 1(1) of the Indecency with Children Act 1960 (replaced by Sexual Offences Bill 2003, clauses 18–21). The latter, unlike the common law offence, carries a maximum sentence of two years' imprisonment. In the following passage, Robertson considers the statutory concept of obscenity and its specific implications for pornography:

Geoffrey Robertson, *Freedom, the Individual and the Law* (7th edn, Penguin, 1993) pp 227–230

The enforcement of obscenity laws is now directed largely at 'hard-core pornography'. This has no legal definition, although juries are often told that 'pornography is like an elephant. You cannot define it, but you know it when you see it.' [*Cf MacKinnon's comment above.*] ...

Any material which combines violence with sexual explicitness is a candidate for prosecution. Yet there are many gradations between a friendly slap and a stake through the heart, and most 'spanking' books and articles escape indictment. 'Video nasties', however, which combine

pornography with powerful scenes of rape and terror have been successfully prosecuted …

The very existence of a law against literature which 'tends to deprave
and corrupt' offers a temptation to prosecutors to 'have a go' at publications they – and most of the community – find obnoxious …

The Obscene Publications Act gives a broad discretion to prosecuting
authorities to take action against any publication which a jury might consider to 'deprave and corrupt'. In order to achieve some national consistency in prosecution targets, decisions are referred to the DPP, who has
been reluctant since the acquittal of Inside Linda Lovelace to prosecute the
publisher of books and films which have any claim to merit. But the law
allows two ways of avoiding a major 'test case' trial. One way is to prosecute
the shop-owner who stocks the book or the video, rather than its publisher.
The shop-owner will not have the commitment or the resources to mount
full-blooded opposition, and will probably rely on a special defence that he
had not examined the article and had no reason to believe it obscene. In
1983 the DPP sanctioned a large number of obscenity prosecutions against
video shops for stocking so-called 'video nasties' – the results were chaotic,
as juries in different parts of the country reached different decisions in
respect of the same video title, and major distributors were powerless to
intervene to defend their works as they would have wished. In an effort
to reduce confusion, the DPP issued an index of some sixty titles which he
regarded as candidates for prosecution. Some of these films had claims to
merit, but shopkeepers took fright and refused to stock them. The distributors once again were powerless to protest against this back-door state
censorship: the DPP was reluctant to prosecute them, but sought to have
their films withdrawn from sale by a form of intimidation. The particular
problem was resolved by the Video Recordings Act, which requires every
video to be submitted to the British Board of Film Classification, and it is to
be hoped that law-enforcement authorities never again succumb to the
temptation of imposing censorship by threat rather than by prosecution.

The other deficiency in the 1959 legislation is that it permits police to
avoid jury trial entirely by seizing books and magazines from local stores
and applying for 'forfeiture orders' at local magistrates' courts. This
procedure, under section 3 of the Act, is used in some areas to destroy
material which the police are well aware would never be convicted by a
jury. Local Justices are less broadminded, and can generally be relied upon
to make forfeiture orders against 'adult' magazines on national sale.

Section 3 may well have been appropriate to meet the situation where
a bookshop or street-stall proprietor stocks only a few obscene books,
perhaps inadvertently, and does not deserve to be convicted of a criminal
offence. But the forfeiture power has been exploited in a number of cases
for the wholly objectionable purpose of depriving publishers of their right
to trial by jury.

In 2000, tension between freedom of expression and prevention of harm surfaced around the interpretation of s 4 of the Video Recordings Act 1984. The
Act allows the British Board of Film Classification (BBFC) to issue certificates
in relation to video works. Appeals against refusals to certify videos are heard
by the Board's Video Appeals Committee. The Board's more liberal approach
of awarding R18 certificates to hardcore videos, which enabled their sale in
licensed sex shops, set the scene for political and judicial attention to the issue,
the background to which Travis describes below:

Alan Travis, *Bound and Gagged, A Secret History of Obscenity in Britain* (Profile, 2000)

In late 1996, with calls for the sacking of the "feeble censors" ringing in
his ears, Lord Birkett, vice-president of the British Board of Film
Classification, defended the decision not to ban the film Crash by arguing
that it had to cause lasting harm, and not just offence, to prove unacceptable. He felt the sight of Holly Hunter taking her clothes off in a damaged
car was simply not a good enough reason to ban it. This liberal view
shocked the new home secretary, Jack Straw, to such an extent that in
November 1998 he secretly blocked Birkett becoming president of the
BBFC. Instead he installed Andreas Whittam Smith, former editor of
the Independent. The fight was sparked by the BBFC's decision to allow
hardcore videos to be sold in licensed sex shops under the adult-only R18
category. Those licensed featured explicit scenes, including oral sex and
buggery, as long as they were non-violent and appeared consensual. Birkett
and BBFC director James Ferman argued that the thriving black market
traded in degrading material including torture, bestiality and violence. The
80 or so licensed sex shops were failing because, as Tory Home Office
minister Tom Sackville informally suggested, they were not allowed to sell
anything the punters wanted to see. So, without parliamentary approval or
debate, the sex shops stocked up with videos such as Makin' Whoopee!,
which included erect penises and consensual sex.

... Straw said the BBFC had failed to consult the Home Office, the
police, customs and the crown prosecution service and was now licensing
videos that were being seized by the enforcement authorities ...

... The BBFC withdrew the R18 certificates, and Birkett was replaced by
Whittam Smith. A new director, Robin Duval, was also appointed and the
new regime made its mark by permitting the release of such long-banned
videos as The Exorcist and Driller Killer. Their liberal approach did not
extend to R18 videos. However, the companies that had produced the
videos, Sheptonhurst and Prime Time (Shifnal), went to the independent
Video Appeals Committee (VAC). The VAC, applying the "harm test" set
out in the 1984 video-nasties legislation, allowed Makin' Whoopee!
through. The companies did not stop there. They argued that since

Makin' Whoopee! had been let through, seven similar videos should also be classified R18. Whittam Smith and Duval said no and refused the certificates. They argued the VAC did not have the legal power to make such a judgment and if allowed to stand it would have implications for all the BBFC's decisions. It was left to the high court to sort out this shambles. In a ruling that left Straw fuming, Mr Justice Hooper said the VAC had acted within its powers and said the seven videos, including Horny Catbabe, Nympho Nurse Nancy and Office Tarts, should be given R18 certificates. The judge said the risk of the videos being viewed by and causing devastating harm to young people was "on the present evidence insignificant".

The High Court's rejection of the Board's application for judicial review of the *VAC* decision enabled the legal purchase of certain hardcore porn films (*R v Video Appeals Committee of the BBFC ex p The BBFC* (2000). The Home Office swiftly responded by issuing a consultation paper on the regulation of R18 videos. This included a proposal for creating new criminal offences under the 1984 Act including 'failing to take reasonable care to prevent a child from watching R18 videos' (Home Office 2000f). There has been a strange silence on the matter since.

III.c.ii.   Beyond the liberal approach?

Debates about the regulation of pornography highlight the tension between liberal conceptions of freedom, particularly freedom of speech, and feminist concerns about the sexual objectification of women. The view that the publication and distribution of pornographic and/or obscene material should be allowed is usually defended on grounds of freedom of speech:

Eric Barendt, *Freedom of Speech* (Clarendon Press, 1985, by permission of Oxford University Press) pp 30–31, 272

(i)   Great Britain

The absence of any constitutional or legislative statement of a freedom of speech means that the liberty is largely residual. In other words the freedom exists where statute or common law rules do not restrict it … [C]ourts now frequently invoke a common law principle of freedom of speech (or of the press) to limit the scope of other common law rules which inhibit the freedom … It is, however, very unusual for British judges to discuss the philosophical justifications for recognizing a free speech principle or interest. But owing to the absence of a constitutional right and the (probably consequent) reluctance of British courts to allow arguments of political and moral philosophy to influence their decisions, the United Kingdom contribution to the difficult questions posed by adherence to a free speech principle has been small …

(ii) The United States of America

It will be helpful to set out the relevant part of the First Amendment: 'Congress shall make no law ... abridging the freedom of speech, or of the press, or the right of the people peaceably to assemble, and to petition the Government for a redress of grievances' ...

Most liberals find the idea of banning pornography on the grounds that it may cause particular individual harm to its readers or that it undermines the moral fabric of society wholly unacceptable. But they find more tolerable the proposition that the display of some types of pornography may be controlled in so far as it offends reasonable people. The exhibition of pornographic magazines would therefore be regulated as a public nuisance ... The key point is that while the availability of obscene material may be restricted by this method of control, it is not entirely suppressed. But it may not always be easy to distinguish these two types of control.

... In so far as some, if not all, pornography is to be regarded as 'speech', it is entitled to the same degree of constitutional protection as other types of communication. And, in Britain, where freedom of speech is only one value to be taken into account by the legislature and the courts, it is as relevant in determining the restrictions that may be placed on obscenity as it is in defining the limits of political debate. Yet the Williams Committee (1979) was prepared to recommend restrictions on the availability of pornography which would not be countenanced for other types of publication. Can this be justified because much sexually explicit material offends reasonable people? It is commonplace that speech which offends the majority is the type which most needs the law's protection. One argument for the offensiveness principle which surely does not work is that the display of pornographic material on street bookstalls and hoardings invades a right of privacy which people somehow carry around with them when they are shopping or go for a Sunday promenade. (There is almost certainly a right of privacy not to have obscene material sent to one's home, but this is incidental to the main argument.) Moreover, the public nuisance argument proves too much. Most people probably object to the appearance of skinheads, but nobody suggests this is any basis for legislation confining their movements to certain areas. And it would clearly not be acceptable for the local authority in a predominantly Conservative area to outlaw political advertising or leafleting by a left-wing minority, on the ground that this is offensive or a nuisance.

A number of problems are immediately apparent with this argument. Barendt assumes that the right to privacy is inherently territorial or spatial. To suggest that protection from being circulated with obscene material in one's home is justifiable, whereas being confronted with it on the street corner is not, appears to give unequal protection to the agoraphobic amongst us. Barendt also regards as comparable a restriction of obscene material on grounds of offensiveness and a restriction of the movement of 'skinheads'. The argument against the restriction of obscene material is based on freedom of speech. It seems strange to infer further that obscene material should attract the protection of freedom of movement and access to public places. Few people would argue that freedom of speech exists in order to protect pornography. However, many would hold that political freedoms can be effectively safeguarded by allowing only the most cogently argued exceptions to a principle of freedom of speech. So it is odd to use an example of political freedom par excellence, ie the leaflet example, in order to argue against the regulation of offensiveness and obscenity.

The Williams Committee on Obscenity and Film Censorship (1979) recommended that material should be restricted if it is offensive to reasonable people by reason of the manner in which it portrays or deals with violence, sexual functions or the genital organs:

Eric Barendt, *Freedom of Speech* (Clarendon Press, 1985, by permission of Oxford University Press) pp 64–66

This confines the control to pornography and ensures that the law does not interfere with the availability of political speech. But the formula begs the question whether there is more reason for protecting the public from offence by sexually explicit material than from distress occasioned by other phenomena. The Committee offered two reasons for distinguishing restrictions on pornography from those that might be imposed on other types of speech: first, the restriction is not directed against the advocacy of any opinion, and second, it does not defeat the publisher's aims if pornography is only available to willing customers. Both points seem to be rather obliquely asserting that pornography is not really 'speech' ...

[T]here is a difference between the total suppression of material and its restriction to separate premises which adults would only enter after due warning of the wares displayed there and from which children would be totally excluded. This second approach may be equally hard to justify in terms of free speech principles, but there are probably enough practical arguments to support it. It enables addicts to satisfy their craving, while a cynic might add that society thereby is able to combine muted moral disapproval with a measure of tolerance. A law based on the offensiveness principle is also probably easier to justify than a total ban, the imposition of which encourages an underground market.

A W B Simpson, *Pornography and Politics: The Williams Committee in Retrospect* (Waterlow Publishers, 1983) p 19

The Report of the Williams Committee (1979) characterised the period preceding its appointment as being marked by the retreat of the law, a retreat culminating in the failure of the attempt, in 1976, to prosecute Johannes Hanau, the publisher of Inside Linda Lovelace. This book first became generally available in England in 1974, and was a pornographic work particularly concerned with oral and anal sexual intercourse, and with the use of vibrators, contraptions now becoming readily available and selling, one is told, briskly. To an older generation, it seemed quite incredible that such a book could be lawfully sold – the judge who tried the case at the Central Criminal Court whose experience of such matters was obviously limited put it thus:

If this book is not obscene within the definition of the [Obscene Publications Act 1959] it might well be difficult to imagine anything that would fall within that category.

... But perhaps as significant as the retreat of the law has been the discrediting of the law, both in the eyes of those who seek stronger controls over pornography and those who would prefer the controls to be weakened or abolished.

Robertson points out that, before the trial, only a few thousand copies of *Inside Linda Lovelace* had been sold, whereas after the trial the sales leapt to 600,000. This confirms his observation that '[t]he history of obscenity provides a rich and comic tapestry about the futility of legal attempts to control sexual imagination' (Robertson 1993: 213). The resultant change in prosecution policy is described by Robertson above. The Williams Committee attempted to satisfy critics from a variety of directions by tempering its liberal approach with a deft deployment of the public–private distinction. The Committee (whose proposals have not been implemented) endorsed the liberal principle that complete censorship of pornographic material could only be justified if it caused harm. If the only complaint was that the material was offensive, this could, however, be dealt with by restricting its public availability and display. In other words, offensiveness could not justify depriving those who were not offended by pornography from obtaining it. As a result, the Committee proposed a tripartite approach of non-restricted, restricted and prohibited material.

Restrictions would apply to matter (other than the printed word) and to a performance whose unrestricted availability is offensive to reasonable people by reason of the manner in which it portrays violence, cruelty or horror, or sexual, faecal or urinary functions or genital organs (paras 9.36 and 11.8). Restriction would consist in a ban on the display or sale of such material other than by way of postal delivery or, in the case of performance, other than in premises to which persons under 18 are not admitted and to which access involves passing a prominent warning notice (paras 9.15 and 11.8). No material or performance would be exempt from these restrictions on the ground of any intrinsic merit it might possess (para 9.41). Breach of the restrictive scheme would amount to a relatively minor offence, triable by magistrates and punishable, except in cases of wanton persistence, by a fine.

Prohibition would apply to photographs and films whose production appears to the court to have involved the exploitation for sexual purposes of any person where either:

(a) that person appears to have been under the age of 16; or
(b) the material gives reason to believe that actual physical harm was inflicted on that person (para 10.6).

A live performance would be prohibited if:

(a) it involves actual sexual activity of a kind which would be offensive to reasonable people; or
(b) it involves the sexual exploitation of any person under the age of 16 (para 11.15).

It would be an offence to present, organise or take part in a performance which contravenes the prohibition (para 11.16).

Some critics have questioned whether the Williams Committee went far enough in its analysis. If pornography is seen, as Williams sees it, and as Wolfenden saw prostitution, as essentially a problem of offensiveness, then the type of control proposed will rely on a distinction between private and public display. The Williams proposals accepted that pornography could be harmful, and therefore justifiably banned, only if the models used in its production caused actual physical harm or were under 16. But many commentators now see pornography in a very different light. Two sorts of arguments have been deployed. The first moves the focus from that of the viewer to that of the viewed. Here the emphasis shifts from seeking to protect those who are the witting or unwitting consumers of pornography to examining its effect on the image of women generally, and on those, mainly women, who participate in its production. This argument seeks to undermine the liberal case for free pornographic expression by pointing out that, to the extent that pornography 'silences' women – for example by changing the meaning of their speech by constantly portraying them as sexualised – non-regulation in fact protects the speech of pornographers at the expense of women's speech. This first argument also asserts the need to understand freedom not merely negatively – as the absence of constraint in the form of regulation – but also positively – as the provision of facilities such as a public culture in which all subjects have the chance not only to speak, but to be heard (Lacey 1993). The second argument turns on the question of harm. Here it is sought to demonstrate that pornography and the representations which it portrays are a contributory cause not only of the social degradation of women but also of violence against women (see **Chapter 6.I.b.**).

Susanne Kappeler, *The Pornography of Representation* (Polity Press, 1986) pp 21, 29, 32–33

[W]omen, who are at the centre of pornographic representations, and who experience pornography not only as a nuisance, but as a direct assault upon their image, their dignity and their self-perception, are not part of the censorship committee's concern. The [Williams] Committee's concern is with the 'processes of law' in the 'bourgeois community' [1983: 23], that is to say, with the public image of our society rather than with the image of women in our society. Instead, we hear a great deal about 'environmental oppression', 'the question of nuisance, the obtrusive effect of publicly displayed pornography' ... In the nineteenth century there was much similar concern about the nuisance and obtrusiveness of prostitution ...

The present law's most crucial operative is the 'test' of whether pornography has a 'tendency to deprave and corrupt' the spectator. This poses the question of why he is watching in the first place. The Williams report, which recommends the abolition of this test and redefines 'harms', makes a distinction between a voluntary and an involuntary audience, relevant in particular to the display of visual pornography in our city streets which forces itself on a large involuntary audience. But as concerns the voluntary spectator, there is as much eagerness to protect his freedom of consumption as there is to protect the pornographer's freedom of expression. Just as the latter shall express himself as freely as possible, so the voluntary consumer of pornography shall consume as freely as possible. Only if we wish to save him from corruption and depravity, that is, from getting into trouble with the law, should such a cause-and-effect relationship be established. He is protected, in other words, for his own sake, and perhaps for the sake of the moral health of the nation, rather than for the sake of any identifiable potential victims. The suggestion that those potentially so corrupted and depraved might have a tendency to assault and degrade, let alone view a particular class of potential victims, that is, real women, along the lines of pornographic representation, is disregarded by committees, experts and laymen ...

... Pornography, like much other public imaging, is constructed for male viewing ... Representations are not just a matter of certain objects – books, images, films etc. The structure of representation extends to 'perceptions' and self-images, the anxious pose of the bourgeois community in front of the camera of public opinion, the self-representation through 'high culture' of a dominant social minority ...

The public debate about obscenity and censorship is, in fact, a little internal quibble between sections of the bourgeois community ... This dilemma between the desire to guard Culture and regulate non-culture (popular culture) on the one hand and the fear of Mary Whitehouse-ism ... on the other is negotiated by the liberal cultural establishment by a reinforcement and defence of the boundaries of high culture (the literary, the artistic) in preference over an outright attack on (censure of) the 'bad' culture.

Some American feminists have attempted to turn the liberal argument about free expression on its head. Drawing an analogy with hate speech, they have argued that instead of invoking the Constitution to protect pornography, the law should provide a civil remedy against producers of pornography precisely on grounds of its violation of civil rights:

Catharine MacKinnon, *Feminism Unmodified* (Harvard University Press, 1987) pp 156, 148, 140, 175, 200, 201, 177

First Amendment logic, like nearly all legal reasoning, has difficulty grasping harm that is not linearly caused in the 'John hit Mary' sense. The idea is that words or pictures can be harmful only if they produce harm in a form that is considered an action. Words work in the province of attitudes, actions in the realm of behaviour. Words cannot constitute harm in themselves – never mind libel, invasion of privacy, blackmail, bribery, conspiracy or most sexual harassment. But which is saying 'kill' to a trained guard dog; a word or an act? Which is its training? How about a sign that reads 'Whites only'? Is that the idea or the practice of segregation? Is a woman raped by an attitude or a behaviour? Which is sexual arousal? ... The trouble with this individuated, atomistic, linear, isolated, tort like – in a word, positivistic – conception of injury is that the way pornography targets and defines women for abuse and discrimination does not work like this. It does hurt individuals, not as individuals in a one-at-a-time sense, but as members of the group 'women' ...

Pornography, in the feminist view, is a form of forced sex, a practice of sexual politics, an institution of gender inequality. In this perspective, pornography is not harmless fantasy or a corrupt and confused misrepresentation of an otherwise natural and healthy sexuality. Along with the rape and prostitution in which it participates, pornography institutionalizes the sexuality of male supremacy, which fuses the erotization [sic] of dominance and submission with the social construction of male and female. Gender is sexual. Pornography constitutes the meaning of that sexuality. Men treat women as who they see women as being. Pornography constructs who that is. Men's power over women means that the way men see women defines who women can be. Pornography is that way ...

The First Amendment absolutist position ... supposes that we all have an equal interest in the marketplace of ideas it supposedly guarantees. This is not the case for women. First of all, the marketplace of ideas is literal: those with the most money can buy the most speech, and women are poor. Second, protecting pornographers, as the First Amendment now does, does not promote the freedom of speech of women ... Understanding how speech also exists within a substantive system of power relations is a feminist position ...

Based on the observation and analysis that everything is not just fine, Andrea Dworkin and I considered pornography to be a violation of civil rights – the civil rights of women and children primarily, but of everyone who is hurt by it on the basis of their sex.

At the request of the city of Minneapolis, Andrea Dworkin and I conceived and designed a local human rights ordinance in accordance with our approach to the pornography issue. We define pornography as a practice of sex discrimination, a violation of women's civil rights, the opposite of sexual equality. Its point is to hold those who profit from the benefit from that injury accountable to those who are injured. It means that women's injury – our damage, our pain, our enforced inferiority – should outweigh their pleasures and their profits, or sex equality is meaningless.

We define pornography as the graphic sexually explicit subordination of women through pictures or words that also includes women dehumanized as sexual objects, things, or commodities; enjoying pain or humiliation or rape; being tied up, cut up, mutilated, bruised, or physically hurt; in postures of sexual submission or servility or display; reduced to body parts, penetrated by objects or animals, or presented in scenarios of degradation, injury, torture; shown as filthy or inferior; bleeding, bruised or hurt in a context that makes these conditions sexual. Erotica, defined by distinction as not this, might be sexually explicit materials premised on equality. We also provide that the use of men, children, or transsexuals in the place of women is pornography. The definition is substantive in that it is sex-specific, but it covers everyone in a sex-specific way, so is gender neutral in overall design.

There is a buried issue within sex discrimination law about what sex, meaning gender, is. If sex is a difference, social or biological, one looks to see if a challenged practice occurs along the same lines; if it does, or if it is done to both sexes, the practice is not discrimination, not inequality. If, by contrast, sex has been a matter of dominance, the issue is not the gender difference but the difference gender makes. In this more substantive, less abstract approach, the concern with inequality is whether a practice subordinates the basis of sex. The first approach implies that marginal correction is needed; the second requires social change ... Although it is consonant with both approaches, our anti-pornography statute emerges largely from an analysis of the problem under the second approach ...

The definition does not include all sexually explicit depictions of the subordination of women. That is not what it says. It says, this which does that: the sexually explicit that subordinates women. To these active terms to capture what the pornography does, the definition adds a list of what it must also contain. This list, from our analysis, is an exhaustive description of what must be in the pornography for it to do what it does behaviourally. Each item in the definition is supported by experimental, testimonial, social, and clinical evidence ...

Our civil rights law allows victims of four activities, and four activities only – coercion, force, assault, and trafficking – to sue civilly those who hurt them through pornography.

To focus what our law is, I will say what it is not. It is not a prior restraint. It does not go to possession. It does not turn on offensiveness. It is not a ban, unless relief for a proven injury is a 'ban' on doing that injury again. Its principal enforcement mechanism is the civil rights commission, although it contains an option for direct access to court as well as de novo judicial review of administrative determinations, to ensure that no case will escape full judicial scrutiny and full due process.

Although the Minneapolis City Council passed the ordinance in 1983 and in 1984, the Mayor twice vetoed it. The Indianapolis City Council also passed the ordinance but it was struck down as unconstitutional on First Amendment grounds by the Indiana State Supreme Court in 1984. That decision was upheld by the US Supreme Court in *American Booksellers Association Inc v Hudnut* 475 US 1132 (1986). This affirmed the result of the state decision, but the reasons are open to debate in any subsequent case (MacKinnon 1989: 213). Meanwhile, a similar approach has been accepted in Canada – a country in which the idea of pornography as sex discrimination has also received constitutional recognition (*Butler*, 1992; on pornography as hate speech, see further Butler 1997; Matsuda et al 1993):

Geoffrey Robertson, *Freedom, the Individual and the Law* (7th edn, Penguin, 1993) pp 233–234

The feminist case has been accepted to some extent in Canada, where a recent Royal Commission recommended that material depicting violence against women or female submissiveness should be banned. It argued for a distinction between 'good clean pornography' which would be publicly available as 'erotica', and 'bad dirty pornography' which should be punished by heavy prison sentences. This distinction is being applied, with some difficulty and at enormous expense, by an army of customs censors who carefully scan every work of rubbishy US magazines for innuendoes derogatory to women. It remains to be seen how effectively this well-intentioned censorship works in practice – there is something unedifying and prurient in obliging state officials to decide which sexual fantasies are to be 'authorized' and which are to be turned back at the border. Ultimately, perhaps, it makes the mistake of taking pornography too seriously ...

In the following extract, Sunstein encapsulates the arguments central to the American debate about the legitimacy of MacKinnon and Dworkin's anti-pornography ordinance:

Cass Sunstein, 'Pornography, Sex Discrimination, and Free Speech' in L Gostin (ed) *Civil Liberties in Conflict* (Routledge, 1988) pp 152, 154, 160, 166

Only recently has pornography come to be regarded as posing any problem at all in terms of concrete harm – and that approach remains controversial in some circles. Constitutional consideration of the pornography problem has almost always been obscured by the gender-neutral term 'obscenity' ... An approach directed at pornography differs in important respects from one directed at obscenity. The term 'obscenity' refers to indecency and filth; the term 'pornography' – derived from the Greek word for 'writing about whores' – refers to materials that focus on the role of women in providing sexual pleasure to men ... In contrast to the vague basis of the obscenity doctrine, the reasoning behind antipornography legislation is found in three categories of concrete, gender-related harms: harms to those who participate in the production of pornography; harms to the victims of sex crimes that would not have been committed in the absence of pornography; and harms to society through social conditioning that fosters discrimination and other unlawful activities.

First, pornography harms those women who are coerced into and brutalized by the process of producing pornography. Evidence of these harms is only beginning to come to light. But in many cases, women, mostly very young and often the victims of sexual abuse as children, are forced into pornography and brutally mistreated thereafter ...

The second harmful effect that pornography produces is a general increase in sexual violence against women, violence that would not have occurred but for the massive circulation of pornography. To say that there is such a connection is hardly to say that pornography lies at the root of most sexual violence. Nor is it to say that most or even a significant percentage of men will perpetrate acts of sexual violence as a result of exposure to pornography. But it is to say that the existence of pornography increases the aggregate level of sexual violence. Pornography is at least as much a symptom as a cause; but it is a cause as well ... [E]vidence shows an association between the growth of pornography in particular areas with increases in rape and other forms of sexual violence ... The liberalization of pornography laws in the United States, Britain, Australia, and the Scandinavian countries has been accompanied by a rise in reported rape rates ... In countries where pornography laws have not been liberalized, there has been a less steep rise in reported rapes ... And in countries where restrictions have been adopted, reported rapes have decreased. The increase in reported rapes, where it has occurred, has not been matched by an increase in serious nonsexual offences. Furthermore, there appears to be a temporal relationship between changes in pornography regulation and changes in the level of reported rapes. Finally, recent studies have found a correlation between pornography and sexual violence even when controls are instituted for possible confounding variables, such as police practices, propensity to report rape, and so forth ...

...

But again, these comparisons alone do not clearly establish the causal link. The simultaneous rise of pornography and sexual violence may stem from some external factor ...

A third harmful effect of pornography stems from the role it plays as a conditioning factor in the lives of both men and women. Pornography acts as a filter through which men and women perceive gender roles and relationships between the sexes. Of course, pornography is only one of a number of conditioning factors, and others are of greater importance ...

[I]t would be difficult to imagine a sensible system of free expression that did not distinguish among categories of speech in accordance with their importance to the underlying purposes of the free speech guarantee ... There is thus a two-stage argument for the regulation of pornography. First, pornography is entitled to only a lower level of protection. Under any standard, pornography is far afield from the kind of speech conventionally protected by freedom of expression. The effect and intent of pornography are to produce sexual arousal, not to affect self-government. Though comprised of words and pictures, pornography has few of the qualities that single out speech for special protection; it is more akin to a sexual aid than a communicative expression ... Second, the harms produced by pornographic materials are sufficient to justify regulation.

Some of the most powerful objections to anti-pornography legislation concern vagueness. Even if a definition of pornography identifies the specific class of materials with which one is most concerned, there remains the problem of over-inclusion – regulating materials that have some social value and that are unlikely to produce the relevant harm. Three limiting strategies, therefore, might be helpful.

First, it might be desirable to limit anti-pornography legislation so that at the very least it protects 'isolated passages' in longer works. Some materials that have pornographic components may on the whole generate little of the relevant harm. Second, as under current obscenity law, the regulation could be limited to material devoid of serious social value. Third, it may be desirable to limit regulation to motion pictures and photography, and to exclude purely written materials. The evidence suggests that motion pictures and photography do the most to generate sexual violence; the data are more obscure with respect to written material. Moreover, the harm to women participating in the production of pornography is, of course, limited to motion pictures and photography.

Some have taken the 'pornography as harm' thesis a stage further by claiming that it causes rape (Russell 1998). Unsurprisingly, this has been criticised as somewhat crude and simplistic. In particular, it fails to account for the opposing argument that pornography may help reduce sexual crimes. Others have linked the more liberal stance towards pornography in Japan and Scandinavia with their relatively low rates of sexual crime.

More fundamentally, as the extracts below reveal, some have called for the concept of objectification to be reconsidered, whilst others criticise anti-pornography feminism as unwittingly contributing to the plight of sex workers:

Martha Nussbaum, *Sex and Social Justice* (Oxford University Press, 1999) pp 213–215 (originally published in Philosophy and Public Affairs 24 (1995) 249–291)

Sexual objectification is a familiar concept. Once a relatively technical term in feminist theory, associated in particular with the work of Catharine MacKinnon and Andrea Dworkin, the word "objectification" has by now passed into many people's daily lives. It is common to hear it used to criticize advertisements, films, and other presentations and also to express skepticism about the attitudes and intentions of one person or another, or of oneself to someone else. Generally it is used as a pejorative term, connoting a way of speaking, thinking, and acting that the speaker finds morally or socially objectionable, usually, though not always, in the sexual realm. Thus, Catharine MacKinnon writes of pornography, "Admiration of natural physical beauty becomes objectification. Harmlessness becomes harm." The portrayal of women "dehumanized as sexual objects, things, or commodities" is, in fact, the first category of pornographic material made actionable under MacKinnon and Dworkin's proposed Minneapolis ordinance. The same sort of pejorative use is common in ordinary social discussions of people and events.

Feminist thought, moreover, has typically represented men's sexual objectification of women as not a trivial but a central problem in women's lives, and the opposition to it as at the very heart of feminist politics. For Catharine MacKinnon, "women's intimate experience of sexual objectification … is definitive of and synonymous with women's lives as gender female." It is said to yield an existence in which women "can grasp self only as thing." Moreover, this baneful experience is, in MacKinnon's view, unavoidable. In a most striking metaphor, she states that "[a]ll women live in sexual objectification in the way fish live in water" – meaning by this, presumably, not only that objectification surrounds women but also that they have become such that they derive their very nourishment and sustenance from it. But women are not fish, and for MacKinnon objectification is bad because it cuts women off from full self-expression and self-determination from, in effect, their humanity.

But the term "objectification" can also be used, somewhat confusingly, in a more positive spirit. Indeed, one can find both of these apparently conflicting uses in the writings of some feminist authors, for example, legal theorist Cass Sunstein, who has been generally supportive of MacKinnon's critique of sexuality. Throughout his earlier writings in pornography, Sunstein speaks of the treatment of women as objects for the use and control of men as the central thing that is bad in pornographic representation. On the other hand, in a recent, mostly negative, review of a book by Nadine Strossen defending pornography, Susstein writes the following:

> People's imaginations are unruly … It may be possible to argue, as
> some people do, that objectification and a form of use are substantial

parts of sexual life, or wonderful parts of sexual life, or ineradicable parts of sexual life. Within a context of equality, respect and consent, objectification – not at all an easy concept to define – may not be so troublesome.

To be sure, Sunstein expresses himself very cautiously, speaking only of an argument that might be made and not indicating his own support for such an argument. Nonetheless, to MacKinnon and Dworkin, who have typically represented opposition to objectification as at the heart of feminism, this paragraph might well seem puzzling. They might well wish to ask: What does Sunstein wish to defend? Why should "objectification and a form of use" ever been seen as "wonderful" or even as "ineradicable" parts of sexual life? Wouldn't it always be bad to use a "someone" as a "something"? And why should we suppose that it is at all possible to combine objectification with "equality, respect, and consent"? Isn't this precisely the combination we have shown to be impossible? My hunch, which I shall pursue, is that such confusions can arise because we have not clarified the concept of objectification to ourselves, and that once we do so we will find out that it is not only a slippery but also a multiple concept. Indeed, I shall argue that there are at least seven distinct ways of behaving introduced by the term, none of which implies any of the others, though there are many complex connections among them. Under some specifications, objectification, I shall argue, is always morally problematic. Under other specifications, objectification has features that may be either good or bad, depending on the overall context. (Sunstein was certainly right to emphasize the importance of context, and I shall dwell on that issue.) Some features of objectification, furthermore, I shall argue, may in fact in some circumstances, as Sunstein suggests, be either necessary or even wonderful features of sexual life. Seeing this requires, among other things, seeing how the allegedly impossible combination between (a form of) objectification and "equality, respect, and consent" might after all be possible.

Lynne Segal and Mary McIntosh, *Sex Exposed: Sexuality and the Pornography Debate* (Rutgers University Press, 1993), pp 9–10

But of course most sex workers are not looking for feminist salvation. On the contrary, they complain bitterly about the stigmatization of women who work in the sex industry by anti-pornography feminists. Speaking for themselves, both individually and collectively, some sex workers have described why they choose the work they do and the type of control they feel it gives them over their lives, as well as their feelings of victimization caused not so much by how they are treated at work as by their fears of arrest, low pay, poor working conditions, inadequate health care and social stigmatization. These are all dangers they see *exacerbated* by state censorship and criminalization of their work. Sex workers provide an important corrective to feminist debates around pornography by suggesting that it is the privileges of largely white and middle-class anti-pornography feminists, who are not as exploited or oppressed as many other women, which enable them self-centredly to present the issue of women's sexual objectification by men as *the* source of oppression of all women.

Brod picks up Sunstein's argument that pornography can also be seen as harmful to men:

Harry Brod, 'Pornography and the Alienation of Male Sexuality' (1988) 14 Soc Theory and Practice 265

My primary focus is to examine pornography's model of male sexuality ...

I shall be claiming that pornography has a negative impact on men's own sexuality. This is a claim that an aspect of an oppressive system, patriarchy, operates, at least in part, to the disadvantage of the group it privileges, men. This claim does not deny that the overall effect of the system is to operate in men's advantage, nor does it deny that the same aspect of the system under consideration, that is, male sexuality and pornography under patriarchy, might not also contribute to the expansion and maintenance of male power even as it also works to men's disadvantage ...

In terms of both its manifest image and its effects on male sexuality ... pornography restricts male sensuality in favour of a genital, performance-oriented male sexuality. Men become sexual acrobats endowed with over-sized and overused organs ... using penile performance as an indication of male strength and potency directly contradicts biological facts ... All social mythology aside, the male erection is nothing more than localized high blood pressure. Yet this particular form of hypertension has acquired mythic significance ...

The predominant image of women in pornography presents women as always sexually ready, willing, able, and eager. The necessary corollary to pornography's myth of female perpetual availability is its myth of male perpetual readiness. Just as the former fuels male misogyny when real-life women fail to perform to pornographic standards, so do men's failures to similarly perform fuel male insecurities. Furthermore, I would argue that this diminishes pleasure.

A thoroughgoing critique of pornography does not, however, entail that its legal proscription is either justifiable or wise (Lacey 1993). The argument for legal regulation of pornography is accordingly a matter of deep controversy even among feminists, and has been criticised both for overplaying the power of pornography and for reproducing the very assumptions about gender to which it objects:

Drucilla Cornell, *The Imaginary Domain: Abortion, Pornography and Sexual Harassment* (Routledge, 1995) pp 95–96, 99

The pornography debate portrays its contestants within sex and gender stereotypes, its contending figures drawn in the broad outlines of a Harlequin romance. Rapacious men with libidos of mythological proportions heartlessly brutalize innocent women as the hopeless victims of their lust, while the anti-pornography feminist poses herself as the sacrificial victim, the barrier to a tide of male sexuality that threatens violence. Bold freedom fighters ride out, drawing their lances against the oppressive feminists, the purported enemy of these brave warriors.

Meanwhile, there thrives an eight to thirteen billion dollar a year industry, churning out hundreds of low-budget videos every month. If pornography was once a powerful political tool, produced in secret places by revolutionary groups, it is now also big business.

How can a feminist approach to pornography that challenges rather than replicates gender stereotypes be developed? How can we both recognize the nitty-gritty of the industry and the suffering it can impose upon its workers at the same time that we affirm the need for women to freely explore their own sexuality? The first step in answering these questions is to insist on an important distinction. Feminists need to separate political action from legal action in the sphere of pornography. I advocate an alliance with two forms of representational politics currently being undertaken by women pornographers and porn workers that are challenging the terms of production in the mainstream heterosexual porn industry. Political action, not legal action, should be the main mode of intervention in the *production* of pornography. In accordance with this distinction between the political and the legal a second distinction must be made, one which can help us clarify what kind of legal action should be taken – and at what point it should be taken – in the area of pornography.

We need to separate legal action to be taken in the *production* of pornography from action addressed specifically to the *distribution* of pornography. I insist on these distinctions primarily to serve the feminist purpose of treating women, including porn workers, as selves individuated enough to have undertaken the project of becoming persons. To treat women in the industry as reducible to hapless victims unworthy of solidarity refuses them that basic respect.

The alternative to such solidarity has been an attempt to correct for the abuse in the production of pornography through indirect, primarily legal means that focus on curtailing the distribution of pornography. This approach treats the women in the industry as if they were incapable of asserting their own personhood and, in this way, assumes that others need to act on their behalf. The wealthy woman as moral rescuer has a long history in both the United States and England. The prostitute, in particular, has always been a favorite candidate for rescue. By remaining 'other', the epitome of victimization, she stands in for the degradation of all women. Her life is then reduced to that figuration of her. Now, porn workers have become the ultimate figuration of the victim who needs to be rescued. But this is certainly not how most porn workers see themselves ...

I am suspicious of overreliance on law in the regulation of pornography for two specifically feminist reasons. The first is that we must not entrench stereotypes of femininity as the basis of discrimination law. We do not, in other words, want law to endorse the culturally encoded femininity that, in the work of Catharine MacKinnon, reduces woman to the 'fuckee', or the victim, and demands her protection as such. Thus I reject MacKinnon and Andrea Dworkin's civil rights ordinance as an appropriate legal means to regulate pornography.

Second, law is, at least in part, a force for accommodation to current social norms, even if it also provides us with a critical edge in its normative concepts such as equality. But feminism expresses an aspiration to struggle beyond accommodation, beyond those symbolic forms that have been deeply inscribed in and by the structures of gender. Feminism, particularly in the complex area of sexuality, demands that we live with the paradox that we are trying to break the bonds of the meanings that have made us who we are as women.

Cornell's conclusion touches upon a general question about the use of criminal law reform: can a system which is marked by certain structures of power itself be used to reshape those structures? This general question is highly relevant to the issues discussed in our next section.

FURTHER READING

Brown, Beverley (1998) *Legal Spectacles* (Athlone Press).

Butler, Judith (1997) *Excitable Speech* (Routledge).

Downs, Alexander (1990) *The New Politics of Pornography* (University of Chicago Press).

Dworkin, Andrea (1981) *Pornography: Men Possessing Women* (Women's Press).

Easton, Susan (1994) *The Problem of Pornography: Regulation and the Right of Free Speech* (Routledge).

Eckersley, Robyn (1987) 'Whither the Feminist Campaign?: An Evaluation of Feminist Critiques of Pornography' 15 Int Jnl Soc of Law 149.

Everywoman (1988) *Pornography and Sexual Violence, Evidence of the Links* (Everywoman).

Grace, Sharon (1996) *Testing Obscenity: An International Comparison of Laws and Controls in Relation to Obscene Material* (Home Office Research Study 157).

Itzin, Catherine (ed) (1992) *Pornography: Women, Violence and Civil Liberties* (Oxford University Press).

Lacey, Nicola (1993) 'Theory into Practice? Pornography and the Public/Private Dichotomy' 20 Journal of Law and Society 93.

MacKinnon, Catharine (1989) *Toward a Feminist Theory of the State* (Harvard University Press) ch 11.

— (1993) *Only Words* (Harvard University Press).

Matsuda, Mari J; Lawrence III, Charles R; Delgado, Richard; Williams Crenshaw, Kimberlé (1993) *Words that Wound: Critical Race Theory, Assaultive Words and the First Amendment* (Westview Press).

Robertson, Geoffrey (2002) *Media Law* (Penguin Books).

Smart, Carol (1989) *Feminism and the Power of Law* (Routledge) Ch 6.

IV. Regulating maternity

IV.a. Contraception and abortion

Female sexuality is constructed and regulated through a wide variety of social practices. Significant among these are medical practice and laws on various aspects of reproduction: contraception, abortion, sterilisation and surrogacy arrangements. The use of criminal law as opposed to other forms of regulation appears to be unpredictable, if not arbitrary. Abortion is the clearest and historically best established example of control through criminal powers. Historical evidence shows that abortion has existed in practically all societies (Petchesky 1986). Notwithstanding its gradual (and partial) legalisation in the late twentieth century (see Lewis 1984, below), the dangers of poorly carried out abortions continue to provide a rationale for regulation. Regulatory power is divided, however, between law and medicine: the Abortion Act 1967 established a certification scheme exclusively within the control of doctors.

Petchesky, in the first extract below, places the abortion debate firmly in the context of the broader struggle by women for control of their bodies, and distinguishes the biological from the social and economic imperatives of reproduction:

Rosalind Pollack Petchesky, *Abortion and Woman's Choice* (Verso, 1986) pp 3–6

The principle that grounds women's reproductive freedom in a 'right to bodily self-determination', or 'control over one's body', has three distinct but related bases: liberalism, neo-Marxism, and biological contingency. Its liberal roots may be traced to the Puritan revolution in seventeenth-century England. In that period, the Leveller idea of a 'property in one's own person' was linked explicitly to nature and paralleled the idea of a 'natural right' to property in goods ... A person, to be a person, must have control over himself or herself, in body as well as in mind. This Leveller notion of individual selfhood, although phrased in masculine terms, had specific applications to the conditions of women in the seventeenth century: the enactment of the Puritan idea of marriage as a contract, restrictions against wife-beating, and the liberalization of divorce. It had other applications that affected men and women: ... above all, a resistance to the idea of selling, or alienating, one's body to another through wage labour. Thus, the original notion of 'property in one's person' was not only an assertion of individualism in an abstract sense but had a particular radical edge that rejected the commoditization of bodies through an emergent labour market. The Levellers were saying: My body is not property; it is not transferable; it belongs only to me.

While the liberal origins of the 'bodily integrity' principle are clear, its radical implications should not be forgotten ... Control over one's body is an essential part of being an individual with needs and rights, a concept that is the most powerful legacy of the liberal political tradition ...

A certain idea of individuality is also not antithetical to a Marxist tradition, which distinguishes between the idea of individual human beings as historically determined, concrete, and particular in their needs and the ideology of 'individualism' (i.e. 'the individual' conceived as isolated, atomized, exclusive in his possessions, disconnected from larger social fabrics) ...

Similarly Marcuse argues in favour of restoring a sense of individual 'happiness' to a revolutionary ethic ('general happiness apart from the happiness of individuals is a meaningless phrase'). Through his analysis of contemporary forms of domination and repression that alienate individuals from a sense of connectedness with their own bodies and thus with the physical and social world, Marcuse arrives at a hedonism containing a liberatory element. That element is a sense of 'complete immediacy', of sensuality, which is a necessary precondition for the 'development of personality' and the participation of individuals in social life. The link between eroticism and politics is a 'receptivity that is open and that opens itself [to experience]'. Control over one's body is a fundamental aspect of this immediacy, this 'receptivity', a requirement of being a person and engaging in conscious activity. Understood thus, it is a principle of radical ethics that should never be abandoned.

The direct connection between 'control over one's body' and feminist claims regarding women's control over reproduction seemed obvious to early birth control advocates ... This connection is as real today. Because pregnancies occur in women's bodies, the continued possibility of an 'unwanted' pregnancy affects women in a very specific sense, not only as potential bearers of fetuses, but also in their capacity to enjoy sexuality and maintain their health. A woman's right to decide on abortion when her health and her sexual self-determination are at stake is 'nearly allied to her right to be'.

Reproduction affects women as women; it transcends class divisions and penetrates everything – work, political and community involvements, sexuality, creativity, dreams ... As long as women's bodies remain the medium for pregnancies, the connection between women's reproductive freedom and control over their bodies represents not only a moral and political claim but also, on some level, a material necessity ...

[W]omen's control over their bodies is not like preindustrial workers' control over their tools; it cannot be wrested away through changes in technology or legal prohibitions and repression – which is why no modern society has succeeded for long in outlawing abortion or birth control, only in driving it 'underground'.

It is important, however, to keep in mind that woman's reproductive situation is never the result of biology alone, but of biology mediated by social and cultural organization. That is, it is not inevitable that women, and not men, should bear the main consequences of unintended pregnancy and thus that their sexual expression be inhibited by it. Rather, it is the result of the socially ascribed primacy of motherhood in women's lives ...

The principle of 'control over our bodies', then, has a material as well as a moral and a political basis. The 'liberal', the 'radical' or 'neo Marxist', and the 'biological' elements of this principle should not be seen as alternatives to one another but as different levels of meaning that give the principle its force and complexity. Sorting out these levels should make it easier for us to distinguish between situations when we are describing 'control over our bodies' as a material fact, when we are asserting it as a right, and when we are defining it as part of a larger set of socially determined human needs.

In similar vein, Cornell traces the relationship between the right to abortion and women's status as full legal subjects:

Drucilla Cornell, *The Imaginary Domain: Abortion, Pornography and Sexual Harassment* (Routledge, 1995) p 53

Abortion should be protected as a right necessary for the establishment of the minimum conditions of individuation for women, which must include the protection of the individual's projection of bodily integrity. I stress the word 'individual' here to reiterate ... that what the feminine within sexual difference 'is' has been defined by the masculine imaginary, and then resymbolized in law so that women are not representable as fully individu- ated beings with their own imaginary. The move from the objectification of the feminine within sexual difference as a 'what', as a container for a fetus in the case of abortion, and to a 'who', a sexual being with her own imaginary, is precisely what my own re-articulation of the right to abortion seeks to effectuate.

The right to abortion should not be understood as the right to choose an abortion, but as the right to realize the legitimacy of the individual woman's projections of her own bodily integrity, consistent with her imagination of herself at the time that she chooses to terminate her pregnancy ...

As we imagine women re-imagining themselves, our captivity by a discourse that has told us what we are as women is also challenged. Recognizing the right to abortion challenges the discourse which legitimizes our social status as objects to be manipulated, since it insists that it is women who must be empowered to define and re-imagine what maternity means to them.

The idea that abortion is best thought of in terms of individual rights has, however, been called into question. Rights discourse can equally be invoked in relation to the foetus, hence constructing a 'competitive' relation between woman and foetus. Furthermore, cases in both England and Scotland, in which men have attempted to persuade courts to grant injunctions preventing their partners from having abortions, illustrate the fact that rights discourse is potentially capable of accommodating the interests of fathers, too (see, for example, *Kelly v Kelly*, 1997). The paternal interest argument did not ultimately prevail, but the possibility of a legal change in this direction cannot be ruled out. In the following extract, De Gama explores the way in which a rights analysis may set up competitive and ultimately indeterminate arguments, and draws analogies between legal and medical/scientific regimes of regulation:

Katherine De Gama, 'A Brave New World? Rights Discourse and the Politics of Reproductive Autonomy' (1993) 20 Journal of Law and Society 114–116

New medico-legal technologies, from *in vitro* fertilisation to ultrasound, are redrawing the boundaries between the biological and the social. As such, they are located at the centre of struggles over sexuality and gender relations. Medicine has long been used to subject women to a centralized, panoptic mode of containment reducing them to the status of objects of reproduction. However, in recent years, an anti-feminist New Right ideology emerging in Europe and North America has sought to construct rights discourses within law which redefine the interests of foetuses and fathers in the reproductive process. Attempts have been made to attribute to the foetus the status of personhood and patient, thereby asserting control over the bodies and lives of women. Similarly, the quest for genetic parenthood which informs and underpins all new reproductive technologies has found expression in an extension of the legal concept of paternity. In this context, it is hardly surprising that the practice of surrogacy and the possibility of 'virgin births' have attracted great disapprobation. In a patriarchal, phallo-centric society the resistance to autonomous motherhood reveals most graphically the problematic, politicized nature of reproduction.

Headlines proclaimed the birth fourteen years ago of Louise Brown, the world's first test-tube baby, as a 'miracle of science'. In the years that have followed terms such as *in vitro* fertilisation, egg donation, and surrogacy have become incorporated into our vocabularies. The elaboration of new reproductive technologies cannot but evoke the apocalyptic nightmare of Aldous Huxley's *Brave New World*. First published in 1932, his fable remains one of the most enduring of anti-utopias in that its chilling prophecy retains a capacity to prefigure current concerns and crises. Huxley offers a vision of a new world order secured by a sophisticated technological apparatus of discipline and control. Mass production and scientific management are Huxley's metaphors for debasement and de-humanization. The logic of Fordism is, of course, applied not only to production but also to reproduction. Embryos are gestated in bottles, decanted in hatcheries, and carried on conveyor belts to conditioning centres where hypnosis and behaviourism are used to ascribe to them the fixed identities required by a rigid, hierarchical, scientific/biological caste system. In the brave new panoptic world, science and technology are employed to create docile minds and bodies. Order is bought at the price of a de-humanized, mechanical existence in which diversity and creativity are unthinkable and all emotion is reified and conventionalized.

Brave New World throws out a challenge to science's claim to rationality, objectivity and moral neutrality remarkably similar to feminism's challenge to law and legal ideology. Huxley questions science's triumphant status as the 'father of progress'. He recognizes the relativity of science's claim to truth and, as part of a politics embracing feminism, ecology, and much more besides, scorns its emancipatory potential. Interestingly, his concerns have much in common with feminist critiques of the Enlightenment which start with the insight that science has from its very beginnings embraced a highly partial view of objectivity. Contesting the assumption that science is committed to the ungendered, objective pursuit of the truth, feminism has sought to distinguish the parochial from the universal ...

The same critique of objectivity [applied by feminism to science] has been applied to law. Its shiny ideological adjuncts of equality, neutrality, and universalism are just as vulnerable to charges of epistemological oppres-sion. With its emphasis on rules, rights, and their enforcement, law fosters and privileges a historically and culturally specific form of ordering the world. Rights discourse, its ideological underpinning, speaks of an individu-alizing, competitive system of values in which the individual is abstracted from her or his social context. Connectedness, mutuality, and reciprocity are systematically effaced. The detached, mechanistic, deterministic view of the world, which is reflected, reinforced, and reproduced by both law and science, in the words of Shulamith Firestone, 'duplicates and exaggerates the catalogue of male vices' (*The Dialectic of Sex* 1970). Both discourses are of crucial importance to feminism because they are instruments employed to silence and disempower. By denying the experience of their subject, law and science deny and degrade women's experiences.

This is symbolically revealed in the politics of 'foetal rights'. Law and science are yoked together to produce a chillingly Hobbesian representation of *man* as isolated, atomistic and egotistical. The technology of ultrasound, for example, allows a visual image of the foetus to be presented which appears free-floating and unconnected. As such, it accords it both the appearance of an objective reality and obscures the contingent nature of its existence. In this reification of pre-natal life, the status of the pregnant woman is reduced to that of reproductive object while the foetus is presented as the personification of abstract individualism. Pro-natalists have juxtaposed images of the rights-bearing foetus with representations of conflict, competition, and distrust appropriate to the battlefield or marketplace. Keyserlingk, for example, seeks to persuade us that 'unless armed with juridical personality as the basis of *his* right to care and protection', the foetus would be 'unable to compete on a more of less equal basis with other parties with whom *his* needs and rights may be in conflict' because they would be legal persons and '*he* [the foetus] would remain more or less at the mercy of their ethics, whims or compassion.'

A similar rights discourse, buttressed by the institutions and ideologies of science, has been appropriated by a coalition of right-wing doctors and lawyers in the United States to promote campaigns for curbs on abortion and restrictions on the activities of all pregnant women. 'Foetal rights', backed by sanction of criminal and civil penalties for 'foetal abuse', have become an emotive rallying cry. Pregnant women in the United States have been compulsorily hospitalised, subjected to non-consensual surgical interventions and even jailed for disregarding medical advice. Most prominent in this context is the issue of abortion. Mass protests outside clinics, challenges mounted in the Supreme Court, and the drafting of new restrictive legislation all too often evidence an increasing concern for the rights of the foetus at the expense of women's physical and emotional integrity.

Contraception competes with abortion as the major area of contention with regard to criminal regulation of reproductive control (see *Smeaton*, 2002 below).

Rosalind Pollack Petchesky, *Abortion and Woman's Choice* (Verso, 1986) p 7

... [T]he idea of 'a woman's right to choose' as the main principle of reproductive freedom is insufficient and problematic at the same time as it is politically compelling. For one thing, this principle evades moral questions about when, under what conditions, and for what purposes reproductive decisions should be made.

Feminists writing on abortion usually have not claimed that a pregnant woman 'owns' the fetus or that it is part of her body. On the contrary, feminists have generally characterized an unwanted pregnancy as a kind of bodily 'invasion'. Recognizing a real conflict between the survival of the fetus and the needs of the woman and those dependent on her, the feminist position says merely that women must decide because it is their bodies that are involved, and because they have primary responsibility for the care and development of any children born.

But determining who should decide – the political question – does not tell us anything about the moral and social values women ought to bring to this decision.

The extract below gives an interesting philosophical perspective on the perennial debate about the status of the foetus:

Bassen, Paul, 'Present Stakes and Future Prospects: The Status of Early Abortion' (1982) 11 Philosophy and Public Affairs 34 © 1982 by Princeton University Press [Reprinted by permission of Princeton University Press]

Many different charges have been brought against abortion: that it erodes respect for human life, diminishes the standard of parental responsibility, abets sexual promiscuity. But the main and most familiar charge against it, the one which chiefly animates debate about this topic, is that of murder. It is disconcerting that the primary antiabortion claim is framed so crudely, for murder is not a translucent or a simple concept. There are degrees or varieties of it, and near relatives to it; moral facts which are reflected and defined in the law. People who participate in abortion are liable not to see the act as prolifers do, which is morally enough to vitiate the murder charge. But despite all this something important is expressed by calling abortion murder, something to which prochoice thinking often seems unresponsive: the idea that abortion has a victim, and that the fundamental injury done to this victim is the same as is done to the victim of a very early murder. And it is true: if the fetus is a victim, the injury is catastrophic, for it consists in total deprivation of the span of human time through which it would have lived had it not been aborted.

The murder charge also has a legal aspect. It implies that, in justice, the law should protect the fetus from abortion. Fixing on this aspect, prochoice advocates reply that such a law would do an injustice to the pregnant woman. But there is more to the problem of abortion than enters into the dispute about law. Whatever the law should require, no conscientious person who sees the aborted fetus as the object, or even possibly the subject, of such a severe misfortune can undertake abortion without serious conflict of mind. This remains true whether or not abortion wrongs the victim, or violates its rights. However cogent the prochoiceposition may be on the level of law, it leaves unresolved a very nasty problem on the level of personal choice.

The recent literature on abortion has been dominated by the question of personhood. This is a natural consequence of the murder charge, since murder is (minimally) the killing of a person, or at least the killing of something with the same natural right to life that a person is thought to have ... But the first question we need to ask is not whether the fetus is a person, or whether it has a person's right to such a life span, but whether it is victimized by abortion at all; whether it is the sort of thing that can be a victim. For if the fetus cannot be a victim, abortion does not victimize it, and the question of personhood simply need not arise.

Fetal development makes a difference here. A late fetus is essentially a baby, and a baby can be victimized. But an early fetus, an embryo, is not like a baby at all. To take a vivid example, consider the blastula. This is a ball of cells that forms about a week after conception. Later it will be more, but it is not more yet: for the time being it is nothing but a ball of cells. And a mere ball of cells cannot be a victim. This is an intuitive remark, which must be enlarged and defended ...

There is no limit to the variety of things that can be harmed, injured, damaged, hurt. Harm can befall living things, artifacts, any thing which benefits a person or an animal, and other things as well. The fact that an action causes (or will or may cause) harm of any kind to any thing can count as a reason not to perform it. But in some cases such a fact is by itself a reason not to perform the action, while in other cases this is not so.

Suppose you find your young daughter preparing to chop at her baby doll with a hatchet. Among the many possible reasons for her not to do this is the fact that chopping would damage the doll. But in order for this to be a reason there must be a further reason, which explains why damage to the doll matters. A familiar explanation of this sort is one which traces the damage beyond the doll to someone whose interests or rights would be affected by damage to the doll. But if there is no further reason, the damage to the doll does not provide a reason, either for the girl not to chop or for you to prevent her.

On the other hand suppose you find your daughter preparing to swing the hatchet at her baby brother. Here it is not necessary to trace the injury beyond its recipient in order to give reasons why the act should not be done. The (primary) reason to refrain is not, for instance, that someone else has an interest in the brother's wellbeing. Rather, it is that chopping would injure him. Unlike the doll, the brother is a possible victim ...

A possible victim is a being (prospective) harm to which by itself gives reason to prevent an action.

Bassen then discusses the argument that all living things, including plants, should be protected from injury and harm:

The nonvictimizability of plants bears on the status of the embryo. This comparison is particularly useful against the background of the familiar antiabortionist point that the embryo 'has life'. Of course the embryo has life. But this only means that the biological life processes go on in it. The cells of the embryo respire, ingest, assimilate, excrete, reproduce. The embryo has exactly the kind of life that a plant has. This is the kind of life that does not ground victimizability.

The antiabortionist point about life belongs to a repertoire of similar points, all of which have a superficial ring of pertinence but no real bearing on the abortion issue. It does not matter whether what the embryo has is human life. It does not matter whether the embryo is the same individual as the later person. It does not even matter whether the embryo should be called a 'person'.

To see all this it is useful to draw upon another comparison, that between the embryo and a human body in forebrain death. This is a condition in which many bodily processes continue (including breathing and heartbeat), but the prospect of sentient capacity has been destroyed. It is increasingly recognized that a decision to disconnect a person or body in this condition – a 'neomort' – is not a 'quality of life' decision. Confusingly, this is often expressed by claiming that a neomort is dead. It would be better to call a neomort the living body of a dead person. But none of this matters. Whatever a neomort is, it does not have the kind of life that counts …

[J]ust as the neomort is not victimizable any longer, the embryo is not victimizable yet. Injury to itself-now may well constitute victimization of itself later. But for this to be so there must eventually be such a thing as itself-later. If the embryo is aborted there will not be such a thing. That is exactly what early abortion accomplishes: it prevents the embryo from becoming victimizable … Thus, early abortion is like contraception: it lacks a victim. So there is no ground for serious moral scruples about it; no basis whatever for an assimilation to murder …

And so we arrive at the crux of the dispute about early abortion: the question whether the human embryo receives victimizability from its potential …

The prospects of the embryo play a dual role in antiabortion argumentation. First, they are said to constitute a retroactive source of victimizability. This retroactivity is eccentric … Secondly, the embryo is said to have an interest in the realization of these prospects. The claim is that since (as we assume) a span of human years is a good, depriving the embryo of this span visits an evil upon it …

The idea of retroactive victimizability is something altogether new. It does not appear anywhere else, or resemble anything else, or follow from anything else in our moral thinking. Even regarding abortion, there is no tradition or belief in it. It contradicts the well-founded principle that something which is neither a subject nor an agent cannot be a victim. Its implications are grossly counterintuitive. All this, taken together, shows that the retroactivity or potentiality defense of the embryo must be unsound. And here we should recall that if this defense does not succeed, nothing does.

Two consequences follow. The first is that so long as the developing embryo is clearly a vegetative object, the assimilation of abortion to murder is utterly baseless. The second is that at whatever point this ceases to be clear, the absolute difference between abortion and murder becomes compromised.

This is one among many philosophical views. It is surprising how few philosophical accounts of abortion are by women (for exceptions, see Thompson 1971; Whitbeck 1983). Whitbeck suggests that this may be because women find it difficult to defend something which at best is only ever what she calls a 'grim option': no one wants abortion for its own sake, and if a woman opts for abortion it is because the other choices she has are considered to be worse. Also, as Petchesky (1986) notes, arguments for a right to choose abortion take place against a backdrop of socially ascribed roles and responsibilities in relation to motherhood. These arguments are vividly put by Rich:

Adrienne Rich, *Of Woman Born: Motherhood as Experience and Institution* (Norton, 1976) pp 273–274

No free woman, with 100 percent effective, non-harmful, birth control readily available, would 'choose' abortion. At present, it is certainly likely that a woman can – through many causes – become so demoralized as to use abortion as a form of violence against the ecology of guilt and victimization in which so many women grow up. In a society where women entered sexual intercourse willingly, where adequate contraception was a genuine social priority, there would be no 'abortion issue'. And in such a society there would be a vast diminishment of female self-hatred – a psychic source of many unwanted pregnancies.

Abortion is violence: a deep desperate violence inflicted by a woman upon, first of all, herself. It is the offspring, and will continue to be the accuser, of a more pervasive and prevalent violence, the violence of rapism.

Laws relating to the destruction of a foetus are based on the Offences Against the Person Act 1861, the Infant Life (Preservation) Act 1929 and the Abortion Act 1967 (as amended by the Human Fertilisation and Embryology Act 1990):

Offences Against the Person Act 1861, s 58

Every woman being with child who, with intent to procure her own miscarriage, shall unlawfully administer to herself any poison or other noxious thing, or shall unlawfully use any instrument or other means whatsoever with the like intent, and, whosoever, with intent to procure the miscarriage of any woman, whether she be or be not with child, shall unlawfully administer to her or cause to be taken by her any poison or other noxious thing, or shall unlawfully use any instrument or other means whatsoever with the like intent, shall be guilty of felony.

The maximum penalty is life imprisonment.

Offences Against the Person Act 1861, s 59

Whosoever shall unlawfully supply or procure any poison or other noxious thing, or any instrument or thing whatsoever, knowing that the same is intended to be unlawfully used or employed with intent to procure the miscarriage of any woman, whether she be or be not with child, shall be guilty of a misdemeanour.

The maximum penalty is five years' imprisonment.

Recently, the Society for the Protection of Unborn Children (SPUC) sought to argue (by way of judicial review) that the prescription, supply and use of the morning-after pill was contrary to ss 58 and 59 of the 1861 Act. Although on one level Mr Justice Munby had little difficulty dismissing the application, reasoning that since the pill prevented implantation there could be no (mis)carriage, the wider implications of the case led to a detailed history of abortion law, and provides a good insight into statutory interpretation. Whilst remarking that the meaning of 'miscarriage' did not hinge on shifting social mores, Mr Justice Munby clearly supported the increasing trend for an 'always speaking' approach to statutory interpretation (see also *Ireland/Burstow*, 1997; **Chapter 3.II.c.**):

R (John Smeaton on Behalf of the Society for the Protection of Unborn Children) v The Secretary of State for Health [2002] FLR 146

Munby J.

A poet famously suggested that "Sexual intercourse began / In nineteen sixty-three". That caustic comment, which Larkin mordantly related to what he called "the end of the *Chatterley* ban", conceals an important truth. The simple fact is that, as in so many other matters sexual, so far as concerns contraception, in both its technological and its social aspects, the modern world – our world – is a world which has come into being during the lifetime of many of us alive today. It is a development of the 1960s – whether 1963, the poet's Annus Mirabilis, or 1967, Parliament's year of activity, matters not for present purposes.

But that does not mean that a judge can simply re-write the 1861 Act in the light of all these medical, social and cultural changes. On the contrary, the very fact that the world of 1861 is almost irrecoverable to us – "there lies a gulf of mystery which the prose of the historian will never adequately

bridge. They cannot come to us, and our imagination can but feebly penetrate to them" – makes it all the more important, as it seems to me, to
resolve the issue at hand *not* by conducting the debate either on some
assumption, almost certainly erroneous, as to how the wider debate was
being conducted in 1861, or in the modern terms in which it is currently
so often pursued, but rather, strictly and faithfully, within the narrow
parameters of the debate which is enjoined on us by the language in which
in 1861 Parliament chose to legislate.

I must explain in a moment why in my judgment SPUC's case is wrong
both in fact and in law. In summary, however, SPUC is wrong in law in
seeking to tie the meaning of the word "miscarriage" to the sense in which
it was understood in 1861 (whatever that was) and in the limited effect it
allows to the principle of updating construction. There is nothing in the
1861 Act to demonstrate a Parliamentary intention to protect "life" from
the point of fertilisation. The construction for which the defendants
contend does not involve any alteration in the conceptual reach of the
1861 Act. Parliament's intention in 1861 was to criminalise the procuring
of "miscarriages". The content of that Parliamentary intention has, as a
matter of law, to be assessed by reference to current – not nineteenth
century – understanding of what the word means.

There are, in my judgment, a number of separate reasons why SPUC is
wrong and why, as I have concluded,

i)   the word "miscarriage" when used in sections 58 and 59 of the 1861
     Act presupposes that the fertilised ovum has become implanted in the
     endometrium of the uterus; and

ii) accordingly there is nothing in sections 58 and 59 of the Act which in
     any way criminalises, makes unlawful, or otherwise prohibits or
     inhibits the prescription, supply, administration or use of the pill, the
     mini-pill or the morning-after pill (or, so far as the evidence before
     me bears on this aspect of the case, of IUDs).

Although no one sought to raise human rights arguments in relation to the
right to life of the fertilised ovum, Munby J considered that the use of contraception fell within the respect for private and family life under Article 8:

> No one has addressed me on any aspect of either the Human Rights Act
> 1998 or the European Convention for the Protection of Human Rights
> and Fundamental Freedoms. Thus Mr Gordon has not sought to argue
> that the fertilised ovum has a right to life under Article 2: cf *Paton v United
> Kingdom* (1981) 3 EHRR 408, *H v Norway* (1992) 73 DR 155, *Open Door
> Counselling and Dublin Well Woman v Ireland* (1992) 15 EHRR 244. Nor,
> on the other hand did Mr Parker or any of the others seek to argue that the
> right to respect for private and family life protected by Article 8 extends to
> confer the kind of privacy interest protected right to distribute and use
> contraceptives ...

...

Decisions on such intensely private and personal matters as whether or not to use contraceptives, or particular types of contraceptives, are surely matters which ought to be left to the free choice of the individual. And, whilst acknowledging that I have had no argument on the point, I cannot help thinking that personal choice in matters of contraception is part of that "respect for private and family life" protected by Article 8 of the Convention.

Infant Life (Preservation) Act 1929, s 1

(1) ... any person who, with intent to destroy the life of a child capable of being born alive, by any wilful act causes a child to die before it has an existence independent of its mother, shall be guilty of felony, to wit, of child destruction, and shall be liable [to life imprisonment]: Provided that no person shall be found guilty of an offence under this section unless it is proved that the act which caused the death of the child was not done in good faith for the purpose only of preserving the life of the mother.

(2) For the purposes of this Act, evidence that a woman had at any material time been pregnant for a period of twenty-eight weeks or more shall be prima facie proof that she was at that time pregnant of a child capable of being born alive.

Section 2 provides that on a charge of murder or manslaughter of a child, or of infanticide, or an offence under s 58 of the Offences Against the Person Act 1861, the jury can give an alternative verdict of child destruction.

Abortion Act 1967, s 1 [as amended by the Human Fertilisation and Embryology Act 1990, s 37]

(1) Subject to the provisions of this section, a person shall not be guilty of an offence under the law relating to abortion when a pregnancy is terminated by a registered medical practitioner if two registered medical practitioners are of the opinion formed in good faith–

(a) that the pregnancy has not exceeded its twenty-fourth week and that the continuance of the pregnancy would involve risk, greater than if the pregnancy were terminated, of injury to the physical or mental health of the pregnant woman or to any existing children of her family; or

(b) that the termination is necessary to prevent grave permanent injury to the physical or mental health of the pregnant woman; or

(c) that the continuance of the pregnancy would involve risk to the life of the pregnant woman, greater than if the pregnancy were terminated; or

(d) that there is a substantial risk that if the child were born it would suffer from such physical or mental abnormalities as to be seriously handicapped.

The 1990 Act also amended s 5, uncoupling the Abortion Act from the Infant Life Preservation Act by providing that no offence under the 1929 Act 'shall be committed by a registered medical practitioner who terminates a pregnancy in accordance with the provisions of' the 1967 Act. Until 1990, the relationship between child destruction under the 1929 Act and the Abortion Act had been the subject of much debate. In *C v S* (1987) the Court of Appeal held that a child was not capable of being born alive unless it had the capacity to breathe. This supported the view that the 1929 Act is concerned with viability rather than with any fleeting sign of life (see Tunkel 1985). Under the amended Act, there remains uncertainty as to the time limits to be applied in cases other than those falling under subsection (a). The 1929 Act now covers non-consensual killing other than in the course of an abortion. For example, in 1987 a man who had attacked his girlfriend and caused the death of the foetus she was carrying was convicted of child destruction and sentenced to life imprisonment (*The Guardian*, 26 September 1987). If the foetus had been born alive and subsequently died, the defendant would have been liable for murder or manslaughter (see Temkin 1986; *McCluskey v HM Advocate*, 1993; and **Chapter 6.III.e.**). A threat to kill a foetus is not, however, covered by s 16 of the Offences Against the Person Act 1861 (see *Tait*, 1989). The reasoning given in that case illustrates well the confusion which arises when issues relating to the protection of both the interests of the foetus and those of the pregnant woman are insufficiently articulated. The interests of the woman may, as in *Tait*, be concerned with protecting her foetus or, as in abortion, be concerned with her ability to control her reproduction. The legality of the practice in fertility clinics of selectively reducing multiple foetuses and the problematic issues in relation to the general regulation of the health of the foetus are discussed by Price (1988) and by Grubb (1991). For discussion of liability for deaths caused by pre-natal injuries and of the (non-)status of the foetus as an object of homicide, see **Chapter 6.III.e.** and *A-G's Reference (No 3 of 1994)* (1997). In the rest of this section, we consider first, the background to the 1967 Act and, secondly, the control it invests in the medical profession.

John Keown, *Abortion, Doctors and the Law* (Cambridge University Press, 1988) p 159

It appears that a central (though not exclusive) concern of the [medical] profession in both the restriction of the law in the nineteenth century and its relaxation in 1967 has been self-interest ... [T]wo central concerns of the profession are freedom from control and the prevention of encroachment upon its sphere of influence by the medically unqualified. This book provides some evidence that both of these concerns have been prominent in the development and operation of the laws relating to abortion from 1803 to 1982. In 1967, the profession supported the passage of an Act whose central declared aim was the abolition of 'back-street' abortion – an aim which was to be achieved by granting registered medical practitioners a legal monopoly on the induction of abortion. It also supported the restriction of the abortion law in the nineteenth century – a reform which may also have served the interests of the profession by penalising the performance of abortion by irregular practitioners.

Jane Lewis, *Women in England 1870–1950* (Wheatsheaf Books, 1984) pp 17–18

[I]t is also important to remember that working class women viewed abortion as a natural and permissible strategy. As late as 1938, a government Inter-Departmental Committee on Abortion found that 'many mothers seemed not to understand that self-induced abortion was illegal. They assumed it was legal before the third month [before quickening], and only outside the law when procured by another person'. Abortion decisions and practices were very much a part of a female culture and to some extent must be considered apart from, rather than as an alternative to, other methods of birth control. For example, it cannot be argued that poor women resorted to abortion because doctors withheld information about other birth control methods. Such women went to doctors but rarely on their own account, largely because they could not afford to do so. However, there is evidence to suggest that some women distrusted other methods of birth control, and particularly that of male withdrawal ...

It is difficult to assess the incidence of abortion. The British Medical Association estimated that 20 per cent of abortions were criminal and using that figure David Glass estimated that a total of 68,000 criminal abortions took place in 1935. However, a practising midwife in a small colliery village during the 1930s believed that of 227 miscarriages amongst 122 women over a period of seven years, few were accidental. Prosecutions for abortion doubled between 1900 and 1910 and doubled again during the next twenty years, but this may merely indicate more vigilance on the part of the authorities rather than increasing incidence ...

Sally Sheldon, *Beyond Control: Medical Power and Abortion Law* (Pluto, 1997) pp 24–25

The Abortion Act is fundamentally underpinned by the idea that reproduction is an area for medical control and expertise and that the doctor is the most appropriate expert to deal with abortion. This reflects not merely a belief in his technical expertise, but also the notion that the doctor is in the best position to observe the woman, assess her needs and interests, and take charge of her situation. The doctor is here seen as taking on many of the pastoral functions which have in previous times been associated with the priest: he is guardian of the social body and a bastion of moral values.

... The casting of abortion as a matter for medicine has had a particular effect in the way abortion has come to be viewed. Science – and especially medicine – has a special role in justifying a particular type of power, and making its exercise seem logical and neutral. Scientific knowledges can legitimate and depoliticise, providing grounds for making what might otherwise be seen as an inherently political decision seem neutral or commonsensical.

Sheldon continues (p 52):

Reproduction is the most important area where doctors operate control over women's lives. Birth, an event long controlled by women with help from friends, older women and midwives, has gradually fallen under hegemonic medical control ... Whatever benefits the medicalisation of reproduction may have brought in the way of safety (and these are not undisputed), it has also led to considerable erosion of women's autonomy. As reproduction has become more and more technologised, reproductive knowledge has become increasingly privatised, available only to the medically trained. This has provided the rationale for all sorts of reproductive decisions traditionally made by women (regarding pregnancy, contraception, infertility and abortion) to be made instead by – or at best in conjunction with – doctors.

John Keown, *Abortion, Doctors and the Law* (Cambridge University Press, 1988) p 116

In 1970 a paper published in the British Medical Journal described a series of 400 abortions performed by vacuum aspiration. The indications for these operations were classified according to the main indication and not the categories on the notification form, and read as follows:

Obstetric	4	(1%)
'At risk' foetus	11	(2.75%)
Medical	15	(3.75%)
Psychiatric	56	(14%)
Psychiatric-Social	150	(37.5%)
Social	164	(41%)

Similarly, the following year, a larger series consisting of 1000 terminations performed by this method was presented. The authors noted that in the months since the advent of the Abortion Act, referral of patients was becoming more common 'for less well defined – that is, social – reasons' ...

Obstetric	10	(1%)
Medical	21	(2.1%)
'At risk' foetus	14	(1.4%)
Psychiatric	85	(8.5%)
Psychiatric-Social	297	(29.7%)
Social	573	(57.3%)

In these series, it appears that the 'social' indication refers to operations performed not on account of the patient's existing children but because, possibly for environmental or personal reasons, the pregnancy was unwanted. If these reasons, and not the health of either the woman or her existing children, were the grounds for these abortions, then the operations were unlawful. Moreover, if representative, these series suggest that a sizeable proportion of abortions performed, even in the N.H.S., are illegal ...

However, there is an argument to the effect that the Act allows just this [abortion on request]. The argument runs that, as the risk to the woman's life is, statistically, greater if she goes to term than if she has her pregnancy terminated before the fourteenth week, the Act always allows abortion before that time. Glanville Williams states that a doctor can adopt this 'statistical argument' provided that it is not rendered inapplicable in an individual case by either the risk of morbidity or the patient's condition. It is submitted that this is an accurate statement of the law. Consequently, the Act is not, as has been claimed, 'very precise and restrictive' but is, as Lane concluded, 'imprecise and can be widely interpreted'.

To what extent is the exercise of this broad, though not unlimited, discretion supervised by the courts? Hitherto, the courts have shown a marked reluctance to interfere. In *R v Smith* (1974), Scarman L.J. in the Court of Appeal observed that the Act placed 'a great social responsibility' on the shoulders of the medical profession, though he did point out that, if a case was brought to trial which concerned the good faith of a doctor, the decision rested with the jury and not with the medical profession. This comment must, however, be read in the light of the court's ruling that a verdict against a doctor will often be likely to be unsafe in the absence of evidence as to professional practice and medical probabilities.

An even greater judicial reluctance to interfere with clinical freedom was evident in *Paton v Trustees of B.P.A.S. and another* (1978) where a husband unsuccessfully sought an injunction to prevent his wife from having an abortion without his consent. Counsel for the plaintiff contended that if the two doctors did not hold their certified opinions, or had reached them in bad faith, his client might be granted an injunction. This was disputed by counsel for the trustees of the nursing home involved, and the judge declined to decide the question. Nevertheless, he did indicate the reluctance of the courts to question the exercise of medical discretion. Citing Scarman L.J.'s dictum that the law placed the great social responsibility on the medical profession, Baker P. said it would be quite impossible in his view for the courts to supervise its operation. He observed that in the case before him the two doctors had given a certificate, and he went on to remark: 'It is not and cannot be suggested that the certificate was given in other than good faith and it seems to me that there is the end of the matter in English law.' Although this statement should be viewed in the light of Baker P.'s earlier refusal to decide the question, his comments as a whole betray an unwillingness to interfere with the exercise of medical discretion in relation to an abortion performed, at least ostensibly, in compliance with the terms of the 1967 Act.

It is interesting to speculate on the messages which these laws bear. What do they tell us about the status of the foetus, or about women and men as reproductive beings? The persistence of a moralistic 'maternal ideology' (Fegan 1996) in which women who opt for abortions are constructed as selfish (if not downright homicidal), is often evident in scholarly analyses:

Andrew Grubb, 'The New Law of Abortion: Clarification or Ambiguity?' [1991] Crim LR 659

The 'maternal medical' ground, either alone or in conjunction with the 'familial medical' ground, has been the basis for the majority of terminations of pregnancy. Many of these terminations involve what have become known as 'social abortions' performed because the pregnancy is unwanted and an *inconvenience* to the mother and her family. Distress and pressure generated by the unwanted pregnancy are *only too readily* seen as creating a risk to the 'mental health' of the woman. [Emphasis added.]

Discussions of contraception and abortion centre on body ownership and control, with the added complication of the status of the 'foetus'. Stychin below summarises the shifting sands of the reproductive autonomy debates, and the eclipsing of body ownership with the rise of the 'free-floating' identifiable foetus.

Carl Stychin, 'Body-Talk: Rethinking Autonomy, Commodification and the Embodied Legal Self' in Sheldon S and Thomson M, *Feminist Perspectives on Health Care Law* (Cavendish Publishing, 1998) 211, pp 223–224

Although this discourse continues to resonate strongly, advances in biomedical technology have rendered the rhetoric of body ownership problematic. Reproduction increasingly is not relegated to the 'private realm.' Instead, the maternal, reproductive body has become intensified as an object of knowledge, regulation and control by legal and medical discourses … [A]utonomy-based arguments are being deployed, through the use of medical knowledges, not to bolster women's rights of control and ownership of the body, but instead, so as to facilitate the construction of the foetus as a separate rights-holding 'being'. Thus, the foetus is being discursively abstracted from the woman's body (it becomes 'free-floating'), and the doctor is constituted as best placed to protect its autonomy interest. The foetus becomes a patient, 'an entity requiring a separate physician and often an separate legal advocate.' This construction, which has been facilitated by advances in medicine, exemplifies ... the male fantasy of autonomy as the transcendence of the maternal body. As the foetus is made into an autonomous being, the female body is erased from the picture. It becomes simply the container holding the rights-bearing foetus.

In addition, the principle of control over one's body (and over reproductive choice) immediately raises the question of when it begins. Are we born with it? Can others – parents, doctors, spouses, friends – control it on our behalf? If so, do they do so as an exercise of paternalism or as a form of substituted judgment? Paternalism involves determination of another's best interests while substituted judgment requires the decision-maker to try to decide what the person themselves would have decided (see also *F v West Berkshire Health Authority*; and **section V.b.** below). The notion of parental authority is so well entrenched that it is only relatively recently that these issues have been confronted in a legal forum. It was so confronted, however, in *Gillick v West Norfolk and Wisbech Area Health Authority* (1985). In 1980 the DHSS issued a Health Service Notice which outlined arrangements for the organisation and development of NHS Family Planning Services. It was accompanied by a Memorandum of Guidance which suggested that a doctor was entitled in exceptional circumstances to prescribe contraception for girls under 16 without consulting their parents. Mrs Gillick sought two declarations: (1) that the Health Service Notice (HN(80)46) had no authority in law since it gave advice which was unlawful in both contravening parental rights and duties and encouraging doctors to aid and abet unlawful sexual intercourse; and (2) that no doctor or other professional within the Family Planning Services would be permitted to give contraceptive advice or treatment to any child of Mrs Gillick below the age of 16 without Mrs Gillick's consent.

Strictly speaking, the declarations should have been sought in the alternative. If, as Mrs Gillick claimed, the advice would be unlawful, then presumably parental consent would not make it lawful. 'The debate in the courts was phrased in terms of parental rights versus those of the medical profession, but the subject of the debate was in fact the control of female sexuality and the role of mothers' (Lewis and Cannell 1986: 328). Their Lordships' arguments in *Gillick* are summarised by Kennedy below:

Ian Kennedy, *Treat Me Right* (Oxford University Press, 1988) pp 90, 96 [by permission of Oxford University Press]

The issue before the House was, of course, the criteria to be applied in law to determine the capacity of a child below the age of 16 to consent to contraceptive treatment ... The criterion of capacity to consent in law, they decided, is not a matter of age, but of the ability of the person to understand what is involved in any particular transaction or procedure, which in turn involves a combination of maturity, intelligence, and understanding. The age of discretion, resurrected, or exhumed, by the Court of Appeal as the correct legal criterion of capacity, was returned to the shadows or laid to rest again, for the last time, it is to be hoped.

In applying these legal principles to the specific issue at hand, Lord Scarman held that a girl below the age of 16 could give valid consent to receive contraceptive and other medical treatment. Conscious, however, of the great sensitivity of the issue, he was at pains to emphasize that the determination of a girl's competence by a doctor was a matter of great responsibility, particularly in the context of contraception. Before she could be regarded as entitled to make her own decisions and, consequently, as free of parental control, Lord Scarman made it clear that:

> [I]t is not enough that she should understand the nature of the advice which is being given: she must also have a sufficient maturity to understand what is involved. There are moral and family questions, especially her relationship with her parents; long-term problems associated with the emotional impact of pregnancy and its termination; and there are the risks to health of sexual intercourse at her age, risks which contraception may diminish but cannot eliminate.

Lord Fraser expressed the criterion of capacity somewhat differently at different stages during his speech. First, he spoke of the girl being 'capable of understanding what is proposed'. Later, he spoke of the necessity of the girl to have 'sufficient understanding and intelligence'. Later still, however, he made it a requirement 'that the girl (although under 16 years of age) will understand his [the doctor's] advice'. Lord Fraser was equally anxious, however, to emphasize the great care which must be taken in translating the principle of legal capacity into practice in the case of any particular young girl. To this end he laid down five requirements on which the doctor must be satisfied if he is to be entitled to act upon the girl's consent and treat her without involving others. They are:

> (1) that the girl ... will understand [the doctor's] advice; (2) that he cannot persuade her to inform her parents or to allow him to inform the parents that she is seeking contraceptive advice; (3) that she is very likely to begin or to continue having sexual intercourse with or without contraceptive treatment; (4) that unless she receives contraceptive advice or treatment her physical or mental health or both are likely to suffer; (5) that her best interests require him to give her contraceptive advice, treatment or both without the parental consent.

It is these five requirements which have come to be regarded as the principal ruling in the case, even though Lord Scarman makes no mention of them and may ... have contradicted at least one of them. The importance they have acquired can be gauged by the fact that they form the central part of the redrafted Memorandum issued by the DHSS in the light of the case [Appendix HC (86) 1] ...

The argument that the doctor, by following the advice contained in the Memorandum, is an accessory to a crime under the Sexual Offences Act 1956, which was largely ignored by the Court of Appeal, was advanced with renewed vigour before the House of Lords. Lords Fraser, Scarman, and Bridge were unpersuaded ... Lord Scarman summed up the majority's position somewhat pithily. 'It would depend ... on the doctor's intention, a conclusion hardly to be wondered at in the field of the criminal law'.

Lord Templeman, although in dissent, appears also to have adopted the view of the majority ... in this regard. To him too, it is a matter of the doctor's intention. Where contraceptive treatment is given because the girl cannot be deterred from sexual intercourse or it is otherwise judged to be in her best interests, Lord Templeman takes the view that it is provided 'not for the purpose of aiding and abetting an offence under s.6 but for the purpose of avoiding the consequences, principally pregnancy, which the girl may suffer from illegal sexual intercourse' ...

Lord Brandon's view is as follows:

> On the footing that the having of sexual intercourse by a man with a girl under 16 is an unlawful act, it follows necessarily that for any person to promote, encourage or facilitate the commission of such an act may itself be a criminal offence, and must, in any event, be contrary to public policy. The question again arises whether the three activities to which I referred earlier should properly be regarded as, directly or indirectly, promoting, encouraging or facilitating the having, contrary to public policy, of sexual intercourse between a man and a girl under 16. In my opinion there can be only one answer to this question, namely that to give such a girl advice about contraception, to examine her with a view to her using one or more forms of protection and finally to prescribe contraceptive treatment for her, necessarily involves promoting, encouraging or facilitating the having of sexual intercourse, contrary to public policy, by that girl with a man.

(Aiding and abetting is considered further in **Chapter 2.IV.** and in the extract from Bibbings and Alldridge (1993) in **section III.a.ii.** above.)

In their use of the term 'intention', the majority in *Gillick* seem to be subscribing to a narrow 'purpose' construction. There is therefore a suggestion of motive being a relevant consideration: something which conventional doctrinal analysis strenuously denies (see **Chapter 1.II.b.** and **Chapter 6.IV.b.**). The interconnection between sexuality and reproduction is illustrated well by the *Gillick* case.

IV.b.   Surrogacy arrangements

The responses to commercial surrogacy arrangements, which first became a matter of public cognisance in 1984, provides a somewhat different instance of criminal law's role in the regulation of reproduction. Unlike abortion and many other aspects of reproductive control, surrogacy has not been 'medicalised'. Yet the surrogacy debate raises similar questions to those about abortion. Evidence that reproduction has appeared increasingly on the legislative agenda can be seen not only in the Human Fertilisation and Embryology Act 1990 but also in the Surrogacy Arrangements Act 1985, which criminalised commercial surrogacy agreements.

Derek Morgan, 'Who to Be or Not to Be: The Surrogacy Story' (1986) 49 MLR 358, 363

The Act has been defined in such a way as to catch anything in which there is the underlying possibility of payment, extending to a 'promise or understanding that payment will or may be made to the [surrogate mother] or for her benefit ... ' (s.1(4)). However, the Act does not deal with 'altruistic' or family arrangements, nor those in which the offices of a charitable organisation have assisted the establishment of the contract. To underline the fact that the thrust of this legislation is directed towards commercial agencies, the surrogate herself is exempted from the prohibitions of section 2(1), which encompass the initiation or participation in prearrangement negotiations, an offer or undertaking to negotiate such an agreement, or even the compilation of 'any information' with a view to using it in making or negotiating surrogacy agreements. A similar dispensation is given in section 2(2)(b) for somebody who commissions a surrogate to carry a foetus 'for him'. The expressed reasoning behind these exemptions is to avoid the birth of a child whose mother or family are 'subject to the taint of criminality'.

The Surrogacy Arrangements Act 1985 was based on the recommendations of the Warnock Report (1984), which adopted a 'moralistic, paternalistic' position (Freeman 1989: 166). The Report recommended regulating only the commercial aspects, not because it approved of non-commercial surrogacy, but on grounds of practicality and the need to avoid labelling the surrogate as a criminal. As Dame Mary Warnock herself explained it (Warnock 1985: vii):

Not only was the wrongness of surrogacy compounded by its being exploited for money, but also a law against agencies would not be intrusive into the private lives of those who were actually engaged in setting up a family.

This is a position towards one extreme on a continuum which includes a number of options: total opposition to surrogacy plus total prohibition; through total opposition but favouring commercial prohibition (the Warnock position); commercial opposition/commercial prohibition; commercial opposition/no regulation; to no opposition/no regulation. Surrogacy arrangements may be seen as a pivot around which turn many of the arguments about sexual autonomy which we have already discussed. On one side lie arguments that regulation of women's reproductive choices is paternalistic, and on the other arguments that surrogacy (either in its commercial form or in all forms) is exploitative. On the paternalism side it can be said that controlling or regulating surrogacy would be based on the 'very rationales that feminists have fought against in the contexts of abortion, contraception, non-traditional families and employment' (Andrews 1988: 73). These rationales include the ideas that surrogacy is demeaning to society since it involves baby-selling and that it is potentially harmful to women and children. The baby-selling point can be countered by comparing surrogacy with the sale of sperm for AID (artificial insemination by donor). The analogy may be inexact – AID is closer to egg donation. But, conceptually, AID and surrogacy can both be seen as 'pre-conception termination' of parental rights (Andrews 1988: 74).

The 'harm to women' point rests on the view that surrogacy is exploitative. Exploitation assumes a form of coercion – that women would not enter such arrangements if they had alternative means of earning money. In answer to this the proponents of surrogacy argue that women do not act as surrogates purely for money but also because they enjoy the status which pregnancy brings and regard themselves as being altruistic (Steinbock 1988: 48). In other words, it enhances their self-worth. Is it significant that the suggestion that an activity should be done for altruism rather than money relates to an activity undertaken exclusively by women (Andrews 1988: 76)?

As Brazier explains below, the prevailing wish of the majority of the Warnock report, that the problem of surrogacy would subside, led to an Act that fails properly to regulate surrogacy, ie through a licensing authority.

Margaret Brazier, 'Regulating the Reproduction Business?' Medical Law Review (1999) 166–193 at 180

Surrogacy did not wither on the vine. At least two non-profit making groups, COTS and SPC, established themselves as 'agencies' who introduced surrogates and couples, and advised and assisted with surrogacy arrangements. A number of infertility clinics actively started to engage themselves in helping to establish surrogate pregnancies. Reported payments to surrogates reached, in some instances, levels of £10K to £15K. Despite some favourable media attention, a number of high profile cases emerged where surrogacy had gone disastrously wrong. In July 1997, the British government decided to institute a review of certain aspects of the law pertaining to surrogacy. Essentially, government concern focused

on whether some additional degree of regulation of surrogacy was
desirable and whether payments to surrogate mothers should be allowed.

The Brazier review (*Surrogacy: Review for Health Ministers of Current
Arrangements for Payments and Regulation* (1998) (Cm4068)) rejected the 'medicalisation' or 'professionalisation' of surrogacy in favour of a more specialised
solution:

Margaret Brazier, 'Regulating the Reproduction Business?' Medical Law Review (1999) 166–193 at 182–183

Thus two variants of professionalisation arrive on the agenda. We could
develop and regulate *medical* surrogacy services, or, endorse and regulate
professional surrogacy. The first option was rejected by the review team
because most of the aspects of surrogacy which make it 'special', which
raise social and ethical questions absent in relation to other fertility
services, are not *medical* questions. The professional expertise required to
advise and assist those contemplating surrogacy is not a clinical expertise
... The second 'solution', *professional* surrogacy, radically challenges both
our perceptions of fertility services as an essential clinical and scientific
endeavour, and, society's understanding of motherhood.

To endorse the latter solution, in effect to create a regulated market in
motherhood, would take Britain in a markedly different direction from its
European partners and well down the road of express recognition of a
reproduction business. The proposals made to the government in the
Surrogacy Review Report seek to develop *special* solutions for the *special*
problems of surrogacy. Regulation should be implemented by requiring all
agencies involved in assisting in surrogacy to be registered with the
Department of Health and subject to a Code of Practice. That Code,
binding on all agencies, would also operate as an advisory document for all
surrogacy arrangements, a manual of good practice. Given that the Review
also rejects overt payment for a surrogate's services, the number of
surrogacy arrangements would be unlikely to grow. Were the Review's
proposals to be accepted, a policy of 'containment' might best describe the
legal response to surrogacy.

On the other side of the exploitation debate are those who argue that the 'free'
choice of women to become surrogate mothers is an ideological myth. Dworkin
argues that the current social, economic and political situation is such that the
sale by women of sexual or reproductive capacities are essential to their survival
(1983: 180–188). According to this argument, in protecting a woman's choice
we are engaging in a fiction. 'Women, by definition, are condemned to a
predetermined status, role, and function' (Dworkin 1983: 182). The analogy
being drawn here between surrogacy and prostitution (and indeed between
these institutions and marriage) relates to the discussion by Carole Pateman

(1988) quoted at **section III.b.** above). Is there a relevant difference between prostitution and surrogacy? Should surrogacy be left unregulated while prostitution is condemned? Whatever the answer to that question, it is important to recall that the present regulation of prostitution is highly discriminatory. However appealing are arguments which derive from a realism about the social and economic position of women, they confront the objection that regulating on the basis of anything other than choice involves an exercise of paternalism by (largely) male legislatures. Arguing for deregulation, in this as in other areas such as pornography, does not necessarily amount to arguing that the activity is itself an unqualified good.

FURTHER READING

Brazier, Margaret (1998) *Surrogacy: Review for Health Ministers of Current Arrangements for Payments and Regulation* (Cm 4068).

Cusine, Douglas (1988) *New Reproductive Techniques: A Legal Perspective* (Gower).

Fegan, Eileen V (1996) 'Father's Foetuses and Abortion Decision-making: The Reproduction of Maternal Ideology in Canadian Judicial Discourse', 5 Social and Legal Studies 75.

Freeman, M D A (1989) 'Is Surrogacy Exploitative?' in McLean (ed) *Legal Issues in Human Reproduction* (Gower) p 164.

Glendon, Mary Ann (1987) *Abortion and Divorce in Western Law* (Harvard University Press).

Grubb, Andrew (1991) 'The New Law of Abortion: clarification or ambiguity' Crim LR 659.

Lee, R G and Morgan, Derek (1989) 'A Lesser Sacrifice: Sterilisation and Mental Handicap' in R G Lee and Derek Morgan (eds) *Birthrights: Law and Ethics at the Beginnings of Life* (Routledge).

Norrie, Kenneth McK (1985) 'Abortion in Great Britain: One Act, Two Laws' Crim LR 475.

Seymour, John (2000) *Childbirth and the Law* (Oxford University Press).

Thomson, Judith Jarvis (1971) 'A Defense of Abortion' Philosophy and Public Affairs 47.

Whitbeck, Caroline (1983) 'The Moral Implications of Regarding Women as People: New Perspectives on Pregnancy and Personhood' in Bondeson et al, *Abortion and the Status of the Fetus* (Reidel).

V.   Euthanasia

V.a.   Respect for life and death

Our final example illustrates perhaps most vividly of all the issues discussed in this chapter the complexity of social attitudes towards bodily autonomy, and the difficulties which this poses for criminal law. It also tells us something about how far we trust individuals to make end of life decisions. First though, how can we explain this increasing desire to engage in death talk?

Margaret Somerville, *Death Talk: The Case Against Euthanasia and Physician-Assisted Suicide* (McGill–Queen's University Press, 2001) pp 111–112

... [O]urs is a death-denying, death obsessed society. Those who no longer adhere to the practice of institutionalised religion, at any rate, have lost their main forum for engaging in death talk ... Arguably, our extensive discussion of euthanasia in the mass media is an example of contemporary death talk. Instead of being confined to an identifiable location and an hour a week, it has spilled out into our lives in general. This exposure makes it more difficult to maintain the denial of death, because it makes the fear of death more present and "real." One way to deal with this fear is to believe that we have death under control. The availability of euthanasia could support that belief. Euthanasia moves us from chance to choice concerning death ... Although we cannot make death optional, we can create an illusion that it is by making its timing, and the conditions and ways in which it occurs, a matter of choice.

We are frightened not only as individuals, however, but also as a society. Collectively, we express the fear of crime in our streets. But that fear, although factually based, might also be a manifestation of a powerful and free-floating fear of death in general. Calling for the legalization of euthanasia could be a way of symbolically taming and civilizing death – reducing our fear of its random infliction through crime. If euthanasia were experienced as a way of converting death by chance to death by choice, it would offer a feeling of increased control over death, and, therefore, decreased fear. We tend to use law as a response to fear, often in the misguided belief that the law will increase control over the things that frighten us and so augment our safety ...

Matters such as euthanasia, which would once have been the topic of moral or religious discourse, are now explored in courts and legislatures, especially through concepts of individual human rights, civil rights, and constitutional rights. Man-made law (legal positivism), as compared with divinely ordained law or natural law, has a very dominant role in establishing the values and symbols of a secular society. In the euthanasia debate, it does so through the judgments and legislation that result from "death talk" that takes place in the "secular cathedrals" – courts and legislatures.

David Lamb, *Death, Brain Death and Ethics* (Croom Helm, 1985) p 1

The concept of death, unlike that of disease, has a significance that extends beyond scientific knowledge and clinical practice. It is central to most of the great religions and is given a special role in ethical discourse. In many cultures death is seen as a natural and inevitable end to life. When the time of death approaches, the traditional task of the physician is to render comfort and assistance to the patient in his or her remaining hours. But in the West death is increasingly seen as an enemy to be combatted. This is a consequence of the influence of scientific medicine and is a relatively recent phenomenon. Whereas physicians formerly accepted death as natural but strove to eliminate disease, in recent years the very idea of death has come to resemble a disease to be eliminated. This change of attitudes has led to a shift of emphasis in theoretical and practical questions associated with death. For the Greeks and early Chinese the acceptance of death as a natural event meant that questions could be posed regarding the possibility of some kind of life after death. In a more secular age we are more concerned with the mechanics of death, its postponement and possibly reversal.

(See also Bassen, quoted in **section IV.a.** above.)

Jowell et al (eds), *The British Social Attitudes Survey*, **Thirteenth Report (1996–1997) pp 168–169**

There is evidence from previous British Social Attitudes Surveys of widespread and increasing support for the legalisation of euthanasia in certain circumstances. Thus, in the decade between 1984 and 1994 there was a seven percentage point increase in the proportion thinking that doctors should be able to end the life of someone with a painful incurable disease. By 1994, more than eight out of ten people thought that euthanasia should be an option in these circumstances. We asked:

Suppose a person has a painful incurable disease. Do you think that doctors should be allowed by law to end the patient's life, if the patient requests it?

	1984	1989	1994
Yes, the law should allow it –%	75	79	82
No, the law should not allow it –%	24	20	15
Base	1562	1274	1000

In 1995, the BSA survey was able to focus on the issue of euthanasia in more depth than before, allowing us to address many of the issues central to informed debate. These include the degree of the subject's dependency, their level of pain, their likelihood of recovery and whether they are capable of speaking for themselves. As we shall see, these sorts of issues are crucial when it comes to people's attitudes towards euthanasia.

We constructed seven scenarios and asked respondents whether in these circumstances a doctor should *ever* be allowed by law to end a patient's life or not. These scenarios, and people's responses to them, are shown in the next table.

*% who think euthanasia should 'definitely' or 'probably' be allowed
by law for a person:*

... who has an incurable illness which leaves them unable to make a decision about their own future, for instance, imagine a person in a coma on a life support machine who is never expected to regain consciousness (if their relatives agree)	86
... who has an incurable and painful illness from which they will die, for example, someone dying of cancer	80
... in a coma, never expected to regain consciousness, but who is not on a life support machine (if their relatives agree)	58
... who is not in much pain, nor in danger of death, but becomes permanently and completely dependent on relatives for all their needs, for example, someone who cannot feed, wash or go to the toilet by themselves	51
... with an incurable illness from which they will die, but which is not very painful, as might be the case for someone dying from leukemia	44
... with an incurable and painful illness from which they will not die, for example, someone with severe arthritis	42
... someone who is not ill or close to death, but who is simply tired of living and wishes to die – for example someone who is extremely lonely and no longer enjoys life	12

Base: 1234

This shows that there are varying levels of support for euthanasia, and that these depend on the particular circumstances involved. For instance, support for euthanasia is generally higher when the case involves someone never expected to regain consciousness than it is when the case involves a conscious patient. People do not, therefore, regard euthanasia, and decisions about its legalisation, as a one-dimensional issue.

These social and cultural attitudes provide the context within which legal arrangements have to operate and command legitimacy. But how, if at all, do they affect the moral case for euthanasia?

Ronald Dworkin, *Life's Dominion: An Argument about Abortion and Euthanasia* (HarperCollins, 1993) pp 215–217

Anyone who believes in the sanctity of human life believes that once a human life has begun it matters, intrinsically, that that life go well, that the investment it represents be realized rather than frustrated. Someone's convictions about his own critical interests are opinions about what it means for his *own* human life to go well, and these convictions can therefore best be understood as a special application of his general commitment to the sanctity of life. He [sic] is eager to make something of his own life, not simply to enjoy it; he treats his own life as something sacred for which *he* is responsible, something *he* must not waste. He thinks it intrinsically important that he live well, and with integrity ...

Someone who thinks his own life would go worse if he lingered near death on a dozen machines for weeks or stayed biologically alive for years as a vegetable believes that he is showing more respect for the human contribution to the sanctity of his life if he makes arrangements in advance to avoid that, and that others show more respect for his life if they avoid it for him. We cannot sensibly argue that he must sacrifice his own interests out of respect for the inviolability of human life. That begs the question, because he thinks dying is the best way to respect that value. So the appeal to the sanctity of life raises here the same crucial political and constitutional issue that it raises about abortion ... [T]he critical question is whether a decent society will choose coercion or responsibility, whether it will seek to impose a collective judgment on matters of the most profound spiritual character on everyone, or whether it will allow and ask its citizens to make the most central, personality-defining judgments about their own lives for themselves.

... [T]he public discussion [of euthanasia] ... centres on difficult and important administrative questions ... But much of it concerns moral and ethical issues, and that part of the debate has been seriously compromised by two misunderstandings ...

The first is a confusion about the character of the interests people have in when and how they die. Many arguments against euthanasia presuppose that patients who are not suffering great pain, including patients who are permanently unconscious, cannot be significantly harmed by being kept alive. That assumption underlies ... the procedural claim that relatives urging that an unconscious patient would have wanted to die must meet an especially severe standard of proof, the 'slippery slope' argument that the law should license no euthanasia because it may end by licensing too much, and the claim that doctors will be corrupted and their sense of humanity dulled if they are asked and allowed to kill. When we understand how and why people care about their deaths, we see that the assumption on which each of these arguments depends is fallacious and dangerous.

The second misunderstanding arises from a misapprehension about ... the sanctity of life. It is widely supposed that active euthanasia – doctors killing patients who beg to die – is always offensive to that value, and should be prohibited for that reason. But the question posed by euthanasia is not whether the sanctity of life should yield to some other value, like humanity or compassion, but how life's sanctity should be understood and respected. The great moral issues of abortion and euthanasia, which bracket life in earnest, have a similar structure. Each involves decisions not just about the rights and interests of particular people, but about the intrinsic, cosmic importance of human life itself. In each case, opinions divide not because some people have contempt for values that others cherish, but, on the contrary, because the values in question are at the center of everyone's lives, and no one can treat them as trivial enough to accept other people's orders about what they mean. Making someone die in a way that others approve, but he believes a horrifying contradiction of his life, is a devastating, odious form of tyranny.

How do these moral and cultural issues affect the legal regulation of medical treatment?

Ian Kennedy, *Treat Me Right* (OUP, 1988) pp 321, 331, 340 [by permission of Oxford University Press]

Perhaps the most fundamental precept of the common law is respect for the liberty of the individual. In a medical-legal context this means that a person's right to self-determination, to deal with his body as he sees fit, is protected by law. The doctor's first duty is to protect this right. This applies as much to the terminally ill patient as to any other ... Thus, if a patient who is aware of the nature of his condition and competent to make a decision refuses further treatment from his doctor, then continued treatment is unlawful, as constituting a battery or a criminal assault. This is so notwithstanding the fact that the doctor may find the patient's decision as wrong or ill-advised. To abide by the refusal may be difficult for the doctor; but it is required by law, the principle of self-determination overruling any notion that 'the doctor knows best' or some vague notion of there being a public policy in favour of preserving life ...

[R]espect for life is a cardinal principle of English law. It follows that the taking of a patient's life by some conduct deliberately designed with the primary intention of bringing about his death is unlawful, whether it be at the patient's request or without his knowledge or consent. This is homicide ...

Medical treatment which involves any touching of a patient is still analysed generally in law as lawful because the patient has consented to what would otherwise have been an assault. There are two key concepts involved in such an analysis. The first, which will not concern us here, is that of 'treatment'

... The second concept, and the one we are concerned with here, is consent.

If consent makes a touching lawful, then it must follow that if a patient withholds consent, if he refuses to be touched by a doctor, any further touching will be unlawful, and will give rise to civil and criminal liability ...

The general principle contemplates a model of a patient of an age recognized as endowing him with the competence to exercise a valid choice, and who is lucid in the sense not only that he regards himself as being in control of his mental faculties, but also that he is recognized to be so by others. There are, therefore, two key features: first, that the patient is of an age the law regards as proper, and second, that he is of sound mind. This latter feature has two distinct negative qualities: first, that the patient must not be someone categorized as chronically mentally unfit, and second, that he must not be someone who is regarded as suffering from temporary unsoundness of mind. The philosophical premise which underlies the general principle is the right of self-determination. My submission is that the identification and analysis of the two key features mentioned above indicate that it is a right which is far from being the general bulwark it purports to be ... Indeed, there exists an equally strong, and in this context often contradictory, philosophical premise, that of paternalism. Clearly, the basis of paternalism – that decisions concerning a particular person's fate are better made for him than by him, because others wiser than he are more keenly aware of his best interests than he can be – conflicts with the notion of a right to self-determination, whereby a person is deemed entitled to make his own decisions concerning himself, within tolerable limits, free from the interference of others.

Paternalism, however, makes its demands which have to be met. Indeed, it is the purpose of this article to suggest that what was alleged at the outset to be the general principle, that of self-determination, is in fact the exception. I shall suggest that the dominant philosophy in practice is paternalism ... Because we are dealing with what purport to be exceptions to a general principle, it is sometimes argued that there is no single legal principle of justification, merely a number of disparate responses to the specific factual and legal details of a particular case. Alternatively, a general principle of justification is advanced and given the name of 'necessity' or 'privilege' or some kind of 'comprehensive justification in relation to medical procedures'. Or it is merely called 'public policy' ... if it is necessary for my argument, I am prepared to say that there is, as regards the particular situation under review, a general legal justification, and I will call it 'necessity' ...

Everything turns on the capacity of the patient and, just as important, who makes the final determination as to that capacity. My position is that the law is so constructed that in all probability, only the lucid, self-assertive patient who has a sympathetic, understanding doctor is able in most circumstances to have his way and be left alone, free from other interference, to die. All other patients run the risk of having their wishes flouted. Consent is represented as the critical feature of the law which ensures the patient's right to self-determination, whereas, in fact, it is referred to and manipulated so as to produce the opposite result.

A number of legal and extra-legal factors combine to produce this result. First, the determination of capacity to consent or to withhold consent is not made by the patient, but by those treating him ... Second, the presumption made by the healthy is that no one really wants to die. When these two factors are put together, it is readily understandable that a request that treatment should cease should be seen as not really meant, but as merely the response to either a passing mood or a loss of mental fitness. Thus – and this is a critical point – refusal of consent is seen not as an assertion of will, but rather as a symptom of unsoundness of mind ... Once a patient is deemed incapable ... his powers of self-determination are taken from him. The law, as ever in these areas, is unclear. Some state categorically that the fact that a patient is judged mentally unfit does not mean that he can therefore have treatment forced upon him against his will and despite his express refusal ... The real problem here, because of the nature of the legal framework, is not so much a legal one as one of evidence. For it is the doctor who makes the determination that the view expressed by the patient is unreliable and that the particular treatment is called for. Once this determination has been made, two consequences follow. First, the way is made clear to invoke the plea of necessity; and, in the majority of cases, such a determination is, as a practical matter, virtually impossible to overturn. Second, the patient's right to self-determination, in other words, becomes not a matter of legal principle, but rather a consequence of the degree of paternalism exercised by the doctor, supported by societal attitudes which reinforce such paternalism ...

Confirmation of Kennedy's conclusion that consent may be a rather limited device in the protection of autonomy can be found in the House of Lords' decision in *F v West Berkshire Health Authority* (1989) (see below). Significantly, euthanasia receives only very brief treatment in the Law Commission's discussion of consent in criminal law (Law Commission 1995: paras 2.11, 3.28–3.32; Appendix C, paras 54–57; the Commission's 1994 Report on Consent and Offences Against the Person made no mention of euthanasia whatsoever). In the above extract, Kennedy isolates a tension in the legal framework within which medical decisions, including those which might be seen as forms of euthanasia, are made. This tension is a refracted image of the conflict which confronts those who care for others, either by profession or nature or both, between respect for the autonomy of others and the desire to act in what is seen to be their best interests. Cases where women refuse to have Caesarean sections illustrate this well: see *St Georges NHS Trust v S* (1999) (see Wells 1998). The conflict or tension is at its height when a person expresses a wish to die. The reasons for this are not difficult to see. Punishment for death wrongfully caused is the symbolic jewel in the criminal law's crown, although the legal construction of unlawful homicide draws rather artificial boundaries, as we shall see in **Chapter 6.III.** and **IV.** Because death at the hand of another is usually seen as the worst harm which can befall a person, the notion of allowing that person to choose death is very threatening. Kennedy suggests that the paternalism which allows medical treatment to be given without the patient's consent may be legally justified through a defence of necessity.

V.b.   Consent and necessity

Refusal of medical treatment is one way in which a person might ensure their own death (see *Re B*, 2002, below). The case below considers the circumstances in which treatment can be given without consent:

F v West Berkshire Health Authority [1989] 2 All ER 545

[*F, a 36-year-old mentally handicapped woman, sought, through her mother as next friend, a declaration that the absence of her consent would not render unlawful an operation to sterilise her. The judge granted the declaration, which was approved by the Court of Appeal and the House of Lords.*]

Lord Goff.

... [I]t is well established that, as a general rule, the performance of a medical operation on a person without his or her consent is unlawful, as constituting both the crime of battery and the tort of trespass. Furthermore, before Scott Baker J. and the Court of Appeal, it was common ground between the parties that there was no power in the court to give consent on behalf of F ... or to dispense with the need for her consent ... I for my part have become convinced that the concessions made below on these points were rightly made ... It follows that ... if the operation on F is to be justified, it can only be justified on the applicable principles of common law. The argument of counsel revealed the startling fact that there is no English authority on the question whether as a matter of common law (and if so in what circumstances) medical treatment can lawfully be given to a person who is disabled by mental capacity from consenting to it. Indeed the matter goes further, for a comparable problem can arise in relation to persons of sound mind who are, for example, rendered unconscious in an accident or rendered speechless by a catastrophic stroke. All such persons may require medical treatment and in some cases, surgical operations ... It is necessary first to ascertain the applicable common law principles and then to consider the question of sterilisation against the background of those principles ...

I start with the fundamental principle, now long established, that every person's body is inviolate ... of course, as a general rule physical interference with another person's body is lawful if he consents to it; though in certain limited circumstances the public interest may require that his consent is not capable of rendering the act lawful. There are also specific cases where physical interference without consent may not be unlawful: chastisement of children, lawful arrest, self-defence, the prevention of crime and so on. As I pointed out in *Collins v Wilcock* [1984] at 374, a broader exception has been created to allow for the exigencies of everyday life: jostling in the street or some other crowded place, social contact at parties and such like. This exception has been said to be founded on implied consent ... Today this rationalisation can be regarded as artificial ... I consider it more appropriate to regard such cases as falling within a general exception embracing all physical contact which is generally acceptable in the ordinary conduct of everyday life ...

... [I]n the case of medical treatment, we have to bear well in mind the libertarian principle of self-determination which, to adopt the words of Cardozo J. (in *Schloendorff v Society of New York Hospital* 211 NY 125 (1914) at 126), recognizes that –

> Every human being of adult years and sound mind has a right to determine what shall be done with his own body; and a surgeon who performs an operation without his patient's consent, commits an assault ...
>
> [*After rejecting the argument that the treatment of mentally disabled people could be brought within the exception for everyday events, Lord Goff continued:*]

On what principle can medical treatment be justified when given without consent? We are searching for a principle on which, in limited circumstances, recognition may be given to a need in the interests of the patient, that treatment should be given to him in circumstances where he is (temporarily or permanently) disabled from consenting to it. It is this criterion of a need which points to the principle of necessity as providing justification.

That there exists at common law a principle of necessity which may justify action which would otherwise be unlawful is not in doubt. But historically the principle has been seen to be restricted to two groups of cases, which have been called public necessity and private necessity ... There is, however, a third group of cases ... concerned with action taken as a matter of necessity to assist another person without his consent. To give a simple example, a man seizes another and forcibly drags him from the path of an oncoming vehicle, thereby saving him from injury or even death, commits no wrong ... we are concerned here with action taken to preserve the life, health or well-being of another who is unable to consent to it ... Doubtless, in the case of a person of sound mind, there will ordinarily have to be an emergency before such action taken without consent can be lawful; for otherwise there would be opportunity to communicate with the assisted person and to seek his consent. But this is not always so ... Emergency ... is simply a frequent origin of the necessity which impels intervention. The principle is one of necessity, not of emergency.

... [T]he basic requirements, applicable in these cases of necessity [are] that to fall within the principle, not only (1) must there be a necessity to act when it is not practicable to communicate with the assisted person, but also (2) the action must be such as a reasonable person would in all the circumstances take, acting in the best interests of the assisted person.

... The distinction I have drawn between cases of emergency and cases where the state of affairs is (more or less) permanent is relevant in another respect. We are here concerned with medical treatment, and I limit myself to cases of that kind. Where, for example, a surgeon performs an operation without his consent on a patient temporarily rendered unconscious in an accident, he should do no more than is reasonably required, in the best interests of the patient before he recovers consciousness ... But where the state of affairs is permanent or semi-permanent, as may be so in the case of a mentally disordered person, there is no point in waiting to obtain the patient's consent. The need to care for him is obvious; and the doctor must then act in the best interests of his patient, just as if he had received the patient's consent so to do. Were this not so, much useful treatment and care could, in theory at least, be denied to the unfortunate ...

I have said that the doctor has to act in the best interests of the assisted person. In the case of routine treatment of mentally disordered persons, there should be little difficulty in applying this principle. In the case of more serious treatment ... the doctor must act in accordance with a responsible and competent body of relevant professional opinion on the principles set down in *Bolam v Friern Hospital Management Committee* (1957). No doubt in practice, a decision may involve others besides the doctor. It must surely be good practice to consult relatives and others who are concerned with the care of the patient ... It is very difficult, and would be unwise for the court, to do more than to stress that, for those who are involved in these ... decisions, the overriding consideration is that they should act in the best interests of the person who suffers from the misfortune of being prevented by incapacity from deciding for himself what should be done to his own body in his own best interests.

Although Lord Goff suggests that necessity has always been recognised as a criminal law defence, it has in fact only recently been accepted outside the specific areas of self-defence and prevention of crime (see **Chapter 4.II.f.**). *Re A (Conjoined Twins)* 2000, discussed in **Chapter 6.IV.** is another example of its revival. The decision in *F v West Berkshire Health Authority* implied that a patient who is not competent to make decisions would not be able to resist treatment which would prolong life. However, in recent cases the appellate courts have moved some distance towards recognising the legitimacy of ending the lives of those in a 'persistent vegetative condition' who have no chance of recovery and whose relatives are in favour of 'allowing' the person to die. In the widely discussed case of Anthony Bland, a young man reduced to a persistent vegetative state as a result of being crushed by crowds at the Hillsborough Stadium football disaster, the House of Lords confirmed the legality of withdrawal of treatment (*Airedale NHS Trust v Bland*, 1993; see further **Chapter 6.III.b.**). However, the grounds specified as a legitimate basis for doing so were narrowly drawn, and rested on a tenuous distinction between acts and omissions (see **Chapter 1.II.a.**). The House of Lords explicitly distanced itself from the more wide-ranging judgment of Hoffmann LJ in the Court of Appeal. Lord Justice Hoffmann had argued that the case should be recognised as posing a moral rather than a legal dilemma, and – echoing Dworkin's argument above – that although a belief in the sanctity of human life and its corollary, the inviolability of human life, requires that the criminal law be invoked to punish those who kill others even with consent, there might be cases in which a proper recognition of the mortal nature of human life requires that the duty to provide care and assistance should cease. In another case, a prisoner on hunger-strike was recognised as having a right to self-determination which took precedence over any countervailing interest of the state in preserving life and preventing suicide (*Secretary of State for the Home Department v Robb*, 1995).

Recently, the principle of autonomy has been pitched against the sanctity of life in two high-profile cases involving women wanting to end their lives. In *Re B* (2002), a 43-year-old woman paralysed from the neck down and sustained by artificial ventilation was allowed to end her life by refusing further ventilation. In the same year, Dianne Pretty, terminally ill with motor neurone disease, failed in her attempt to secure death on her own terms. In particular, she sought an undertaking from the Director of Public Prosecutions not to prosecute her husband who was willing to assist with her suicide. In dismissing her appeal against the refusal of such prosecutorial immunity (*Pretty v DPP*, 2002), respect for bodily autonomy appears incomplete and inconsistent:

Peter Singer, 'Ms B and Diane Pretty: a commentary' (2002) 28 Journal of Medical Ethics 234

To a lay observer, there seems to be an inconsistency in the way in which these two cases were decided. Ms B, a paralysed competent adult, was allowed to end her life; Mrs Pretty, another paralysed competent adult, was not. How can this make sense? To a lawyer, on the other hand, there is no inconsistency. Indeed, both decisions were entirely predictable. It is a well established principle of law that a competent adult has the right to refuse medical treatment ... On the other hand, courts in Canada, the United States, the United Kingdom and elsewhere have held that laws prohibiting assisted suicide prevent anyone assisting a person to die, even if that person is paralysed and unable to bring about their own death. So putting these two principles together, we get a right to refuse medical treatment, even if that means you will die, but no right for someone else to assist you to die, if the mere withdrawal of medical treatment will not bring about that end, or will not bring it about in an acceptable manner. Technically, the lawyers are correct. The two cases can be reconciled. They are not inconsistent, in the strict meaning of that term. But in a deeper ethical sense, the lay observers are right. We have arrived at the absurd situation where a paralysed woman can choose to die when she wants if her condition means that she needs some form of medical treatment to survive; whereas another paralysed woman cannot choose to die when or in the manner she wants, because there is no medical treatment keeping her alive in such a way that, if it were withdrawn, she would have a humane and dignified death. What we have done is build legal doctrines based on two separate rules of law, and thereby we have reached a situation that makes no ethical sense at all.

As Singer remarks, on one level the decisions in *Re B* and *Pretty* were predictable. The assessment that Ms B was competent freed her to refuse any treatment. In this sense the decision continues the commitment to autonomy and the departure from a rigid adherence to sanctity of life (seen also in *Bland* (1993) and *Re A (Conjoined twins)* (2001) see **Chapter 6.III.a.**). Nevertheless, the absurdity to which Singer refers is arguably exacerbated by the fact that whilst Dianne Pretty would die within a matter of months, Ms B would have lived for years (albeit a life she had no wish for). Are there other clues to help understand what appears to be a confused and selective use of autonomy? Do such apparent inconsistencies reflect the extent to which we trust particular individuals to make the 'right' decision? For instance, was it significant that Ms B was regarded as a 'most impressive witness' and previously worked as a social worker in the NHS? Of course, it cannot be said that such cases hinge on such factors, but to what extent do they creep into judicial decisions, for instance the assessment that Ms B was competent?

The margin of bodily autonomy respected by the law at the 'limits of life' is therefore a narrow one. Suicide is a lawful option open to a person who is physically capable of carrying out the act of killing herself. But for those like Dianne Pretty requiring assistance, any person so helping her may commit an offence under s 2 of the Suicide Act 1961 (or of murder or attempted murder, see *Hough* below):

Suicide Act 1961, ss 1, 2

1   The rule of law whereby it is a crime for a person to commit suicide is hereby abrogated.

2(1) A person who aids, abets, counsels or procures the suicide of another, or an attempt by another to commit suicide, shall be liable on indictment to imprisonment for a term not exceeding fourteen years.

(2) If on the trial of an indictment for murder or manslaughter it is proved that the accused aided, abetted, counselled or procured the suicide of the person in question, the jury may find him guilty of that offence.

Dianne Pretty challenged the refusal to grant her husband immunity from prosecution, claiming it violated various rights of the European Convention. In particular, she argued that: the right to life in Article 2 extended to the right to end life; her situation involved inhuman or degrading treatment contrary to

Article 3, a failure to respect her private and family life under Article 8, her freedom of thought under Article 9; and that it was discriminatory contrary to Article 14. In unanimously dismissing her appeal, the House of Lords revealed the tension between individual autonomy and societal concerns underpinning human rights:

R (on the application of Pretty) v DPP [2002] 1 All ER 1

Lord Steyn.

[T]his is the first occasion on which the House of Lords has been asked to consider the question of assisted suicide by a terminally ill individual. She suffers from motor neurone disease and she has not long to live. The specific question before the House is whether the appellant is entitled to a declaration that the Director of Public Prosecutions (the Director) is obliged to undertake in advance that, if she is assisted by her husband in committing suicide, he will not be prosecuted under s 2(1) of the Suicide Act 1961. If Mrs Pretty is entitled to this relief, it follows that it may have to be granted to other terminally ill patients or patients suffering excruciating pain as a result of an incurable illness, who want to commit assisted suicide. Her case is squarely founded on the Human Rights Act 1998, which incorporated the European Convention for the Protection of Human Rights and Fundamental Freedoms (Rome, 4 November 1950; TS 71 (1953); Cmd 8969) (as set out in Sch 1 to that Act) into English law. For her to succeed it is not enough to show that the convention allows member states to legalise assisted suicide. She must establish that at least that part of s 2(1) of the 1961 Act which makes aiding or abetting suicide a crime is in conflict with her convention rights. In other words, she must persuade the House that the convention compels member states of the Council of Europe to legalise assisted suicide.

Counsel for Mrs Pretty argued that art 2 and in particular its first sentence acknowledges that it is for the individual to choose whether to live or die and that it protects her right of self-determination in relation to issues of life and death. This interpretation is not sustainable. The purpose of art 2(1) is clear. It enunciates the principle of the sanctity of life and provides a guarantee that no individual 'shall be deprived of life' by means of intentional human intervention. The interpretation now put forward is the exact opposite, viz a right of Mrs Pretty to end her life by means of intentional human intervention. Nothing in the article or the jurisprudence of the European Court of Human Rights can assist Mrs Pretty's case on this article.

...

Article 3 provides: 'No one shall be subjected to torture or to inhuman or degrading treatment or punishment.' The core of counsel's argument is that under art 3 the state's obligations are to take effective steps to ensure that no one shall be subjected to inhuman or degrading treatment. For my part art 3 is not engaged. The word 'treatment' must take its colour from the context in which it appears. While I would not wish to give a narrow interpretation to what may constitute degrading treatment, the concept appears singularly inapt to convey the idea that the state must guarantee to individuals a right to die with the deliberate assistance of third parties. So radical a step, infringing the sanctity of life principle, would have required far more explicit wording. But counsel argues that there is support for his argument to be found in the jurisprudence of the European Court of Human Rights on the 'positive obligations' of a state to render effective the protection of art 3. For this proposition he cites the decision of the European Court of Human Rights in *D v UK* (1997) 2 BHRC 273. The case concerned the intended deportation of an individual in the final stages of an incurable disease to St Kitts where there would not be adequate treatment for the disease. The European Court of Human Rights held that in the exceptional circumstances of the case the implementation of the decision to remove the individual to St Kitts would amount to inhuman treatment by the United Kingdom. Unlike *D v UK* the present case does not involve any positive action (comparable to the intended deportation) nor is there any risk of a failure to treat her properly. Instead the complaint is that the state is guilty of a failure to repeal s 2(1) of the 1961 Act. The present case plainly does not involve 'inhuman or degrading *treatment*'.

Counsel submitted that ... [Article 8] ... explicitly recognises the principle of the personal autonomy of every individual. He argues that this principle necessarily involves a guarantee as against the state of the right to choose when and how to die. None of the decisions cited in regard to art 8 assist this argument. It must fail on the ground that the guarantee under art 8 prohibits interference with the way in which an individual leads his life and it does not relate to the manner in which he wishes to die.

If I had been of the view that art 8 was engaged, I would have held (in agreement with the Divisional Court) that the interference with the guarantee was justified. There was a submission to the contrary based on the argument that the scope of s 2(1) is disproportionate to its aim. This contention was founded on the supposition that Mrs Pretty and others in her position are not vulnerable. It is a sufficient answer that there is a broad class of persons presently protected by s 2 who are vulnerable. It was therefore well within the range of discretion of Parliament to strike the balance between the interests of the community and the rights of individuals in the way reflected in s 2(1).

Counsel submitted that Mrs Pretty is entitled to manifest her belief in assisted suicide by committing it. This cannot be right. This article was never intended to give individuals a right to perform any acts in pursuance of whatever beliefs they may hold, eg to attack places where experiments are conducted on animals. The article does not yield support for the specific proposition for which it is invoked. In any event, for the reasons already discussed, s 2 is a legitimate, rational and proportionate response to the wider problem of vulnerable people who would otherwise feel compelled to commit suicide.

Counsel submits that Mrs Pretty is in effect treated less favourably than those who are physically capable of ending their lives. The Divisional Court held that art 14 is not engaged. The alleged discrimination can only be established if the facts of the case fall within arts 2, 3, 8 or 9 (*Botta v Italy* (1998) 4 BHRC 81 at 90 (para 39)). They do not. This is a sufficient reason to reject this argument. But there is a more fundamental reason. The condition of terminally ill individuals, like Mrs Pretty, will vary. The majority will be vulnerable. It is the vulnerability of the class of persons which provides the rationale for making the aiding and abetting of suicide an offence under s 2(1) of the 1961 Act. A class of individuals is protected by s 2(1) because they are in need of protection. The statutory provision does not therefore treat individuals in a discriminatory manner. There is no unequal treatment before the law. In any event, for reasons already given, s 2(1) is fully justified.

Although Dianne Pretty's appeal to the European Court of Human Rights was dismissed (Application No 2346/02 *Pretty v UK*, 2002), the Court held that Article 8 was engaged. Following her failure lawfully to secure death on her own terms, others have sought assisted death outside the UK. In January 2003, motor neurone disease sufferer Ivor Crewe flew to Switzerland to receive the help of Dignitas, an assisted suicide group in Zurich. An investigation was launched into whether his wife would be prosecuted for aiding and abetting an assisted suicide, although no charges were brought (*The Guardian*, 15 April 2002). The unedifying prospect of such 'death trips' has prompted renewed attention to a statutory framework for regulating assisted dying (see below).

Assisted suicide overlaps with attempted murder, as the following case shows.

R v Hough (1984) 6 Cr App R(S) 404

[*The defendant pleaded guilty to attempted murder. She assisted an elderly blind and deaf woman to commit suicide by supply of sodium amytal and use of a plastic bag.*]

Lord Lane LCJ.

What she did ... fell to a great extent within the terms of the Suicide Act 1961, s.2 ... The maximum sentence for that offence is 14 years' imprisonment ... It is clear from that that Parliament had in mind the potential scope for disaster and malpractice in circumstances where elderly, infirm and easily suggestible people are sometimes minded to wish themselves dead. It is a crime, whether you pigeon-hole it under attempted murder or assisting in suicide. In terms of gravity it can vary from the borders of cold blooded murder down to the shadowy area of mercy killing or common humanity. [Nine months' sentence confirmed.]

Criminal law, then, takes significant steps to hinder a person from choosing their own death. At the level of enforcement (and given the understandable paucity of empirical research on the actual extent of assisted death), we can only assume that the operation of criminal law is, to say the least, both patchy and arbitrary. Euthanasia also provides yet another instance of criminal law's apparent reliance on motive rather than (as asserted by doctrine) on intention (see **Chapter 1.II.b.** and **Chapter 6.III.b.** and **IV.b.**). As Otlowski suggests, euthanasia exposes criminal law's pretence to consistency in principle and enforcement and reveals discrepancies between theory and practice:

Margaret Otlowski, *Voluntary Euthanasia and the Common Law* (1997, Clarendon Press) pp 148–150

Although questions of motive are strictly speaking irrelevant for the purposes of establishing criminal liability, in practice, they will often be decisive in determining the outcome of cases of active euthanasia and doctor-assisted suicide. Without disputing that such cases ought to be dealt with leniently ... there are certain fundamental problems with the present legal position which tolerates serious inconsistencies between legal principles and the law in practice. First, there is the concern that because the administration of the law depends to such a large extent on intangible considerations of sympathy, there is no guaranteed consistency of application, thus raising serious questions regarding justice and equality before the law. The second problem is that the enormous discrepancies between the law in theory and the law in practice threaten to undermine the public confidence in the law and bring it into disrepute. Further, there is the problem that the present ad hoc approach fails to establish any legal precedent by which medical decisions in the context of terminal patients can be made and evaluated. A related concern is that there is a very real risk that the illegality and secrecy associated with the practice of active voluntary euthanasia tends to undermine the rights of patients.

Furthermore, as Kennedy argues, the medical application of the principle of self-determination is fraught with contradiction. The same contradiction can be seen in legal rules. The defendant in *Blaue* (1975) was convicted of manslaughter after the woman he stabbed refused a life-saving blood transfusion because she was a Jehovah's Witness. The medical evidence was that she would not have died had she accepted the transfusion. The decision was predicated on her refusal to have life-saving treatment being respected by those treating her. Why was she 'allowed' the self-determination or autonomy denied to those with painful, terminal illness? Should the defendant have had to bear responsibility for his victim's exercise of the right to self-determination? This transfer of responsibility effectively qualifies that right. This aspect of the case is consistent with the decision in *Stone and Dobinson* (1977). The defendants were convicted of the manslaughter of Stone's sister who suffered from anorexia nervosa. She starved to death while living as a lodger in the house which the defendants shared. The case is troubling because the evidence indicated that the defendants' mental capacities were such that they would have found it difficult to care for the sister, or to summon help. But even if they had been better endowed with mental, social and financial resources, it is not clear why they should have been regarded as responsible for the sister's own decisions in relation to her health. It is argued, however, that to allow a person to be helped or assisted in their decision to neglect themselves or to die or both, albeit thus respecting their autonomy, is too dangerous a principle to be formally legalised. In the following passage, Rachels argues against this position. The distinction between active and passive euthanasia which he discusses is one on which medico-legal discourse often implicitly relies (cf the distinction between acts and omissions distinction applied in *Bland*):

James Rachels, 'Euthanasia' in Regan et al (eds) *Matters of Life and Death* (Random House, 1986) pp 38, 49, 62

The phrase 'active euthanasia' is used to refer to cases in which the patient is killed – for example, by being given a lethal injection. The phrase 'passive euthanasia' refers to cases in which the patient is not killed but merely allowed to die. In passive euthanasia we simply refrain from doing anything to keep the patient alive – for example, we may refuse to perform surgery, administer medication, give a heart massage, or use a respirator – and let the person die of whatever ills are already present. It is important to note this distinction because many people believe that, although active euthanasia is immoral, passive euthanasia is morally all right ... In addition ... it is important to bear in mind the difference between voluntary, non-voluntary, and involuntary euthanasia. Voluntary euthanasia occurs whenever the patient requests death ... Non-voluntary euthanasia occurs when the patient is unable to form a judgement or voice a wish in the matter and, therefore, expresses no desire whatever ... Finally involuntary euthanasia occurs when the patient says that he or she does not want to die but is nevertheless killed or allowed to die ... I shall not be concerned with involuntary euthanasia. My view is that it is simply murder and that it is not justified. If a person wants to live on, even in great pain and even with the certainty of a horrible end, that is the individual's right ...

What are we to understand by the word 'euthanasia'? Primarily it means killing someone – or letting someone die – who is going to die soon anyway, at the person's own request, as an act of kindness ...

The single most powerful argument in support of euthanasia is the argument from mercy ... Terminally ill patients sometimes suffer pain so horrible that it is beyond the comprehension of those who have not actually experienced it ... The argument for mercy says euthanasia is justified because it provides an end to that ... In connection with this argument, the utilitarians should be mentioned ... They argued that actions and social policies should be judged right or wrong exclusively according to whether they cause happiness or misery; and they argued that when judged by this standard, euthanasia turns out to be morally acceptable. The utilitarian argument may be elaborated as follows:

1. Any action or social policy is morally right if it serves to increase the amount of happiness in the world or to decrease the amount of misery. Conversely, an action or social policy is morally wrong if it serves to decrease happiness or to increase misery.

2. The policy of killing, at their own request, hopelessly ill patients who are suffering great pain would decrease the amount of misery in the world ...

3. Therefore, such a policy would be morally right ...

Although the foregoing utilitarian argument is faulty, it is nevertheless based on a sound idea. For even if the promotion of happiness and the avoidance of misery are not the only morally important things, they are still very important. So, when an action or a social policy would decrease misery, that is a very strong reason in its favour. In the cases of voluntary euthanasia ... great suffering is eliminated, and since the patient requests it, there is no question of violating individual rights ... I believe that the following argument is sound and proves that active euthanasia can be justified:

1. If an action promotes the best interests of everyone concerned and violates no one's right, then that action is morally acceptable.

2. In at least some cases, active euthanasia promotes the best interests of everyone concerned and violates no one's rights.

3. Therefore, in at least some cases, active euthanasia is morally acceptable ...

There has been one famous case in which the question of nonvoluntary passive euthanasia was put before the courts. In April 1975, a twenty-one-year-old woman named Karen Ann Quinlan, for reasons that were never made clear, ceased breathing for at least two fifteen-minute periods. As a result, she suffered severe brain damage, and, in the words of the attending physicians, was reduced to 'a chronic persistent vegetative state' in which she 'no longer had any cognitive function'. Accepting the doctors' judgement that there was no hope of recovery, her parents sought permission from the courts to disconnect the respirator that was keeping her alive in the intensive-care unit of a New Jersey hospital. The Quinlans are Roman Catholics, and they made this request only after consulting with their priest, who assured them that there would be no moral or religious objection if Karen were allowed to die.

Various medical experts testified in support of the Quinlans' request ... The trial court, and then the Supreme Court of New Jersey, agreed that the respirator could be removed and Karen Quinlan allowed to die in peace. The respirator was disconnected. However, the nuns in charge of her care in the Catholic hospital opposed this decision, and anticipating it, had begun to wean Karen from the respirator so that by the time it was disconnected she could remain alive without it ... So Karen lingered on in her 'persistent vegetative state', emaciated and with deformed limbs and with no hope of ever awakening, but still alive in the biological sense. Finally, she died in June 1985.

Rachels goes on to propose a simple statute binding on criminal courts and declaring that a plea of mercy-killing would be acceptable as a defence to a murder charge in the same way that a plea of self-defence is. The defence would need to prove (a) that the deceased was suffering from a painful terminal illness and (b) that she had 'requested death'.

The House of Lords Select Committee on Medical Ethics decided unanimously in 1994, primarily on the basis of the 'slippery slope' argument criticised by Dworkin, that there should be no change in the substantive law on euthanasia, mercy killing or complicity in suicide (Report of the Select Committee, 1993–94). The Committee did, however, endorse case law which recognises that an adult person of sound mind should be entitled to refuse invasive medical treatment, either on a contemporary basis or in anticipation of future incapacity (eg see *Re B* (2002) above).

However, in a judicial capacity, the House of Lords has repeated its earlier call in *Bland* for parliamentary attention to law reform:

R (on the application of Pretty) v DPP [2002] 1 All ER 1

Lord Steyn.

If s 2 of the 1961 Act is held to be incompatible with the convention, a right to commit assisted suicide would not be doctor-assisted and would not be subject to safeguards introduced in the Netherlands. In a valuable essay Professor Michael Freeman trenchantly observed: 'A repeal of *Section 2* of the Suicide Act 1961, without more, would not be rational policy-making. We would need a "Death with Dignity" Act to fill the lacuna.' (See 'Death, Dying and the *Human Rights Act 1998*' (1999) 52 CLP 218 at 237.) That must be right. In our parliamentary democracy, and I appre-hend in many member states of the Council of Europe, such a fundamental change cannot be brought about by judicial creativity. If it is to be considered at all, it requires a detailed and effective regulatory proposal. In these circumstances it is difficult to see how a process of interpretation of convention rights can yield a result with all the necessary in-built protections. Essentially, it must be a matter for democratic debate and decision-making by legislatures.

...

The logic of the convention does not justify the conclusion that the House must rule that a state is obliged to legalise assisted suicide. It does not require the state to repeal a provision such as s 2(1) of the 1961 Act. On the other hand, it is open to a democratic legislature to introduce such a measure. Our Parliament, if so minded, may therefore repeal s 2(1) and put in its place a regulated system for assisted suicide (presumably doctor-assisted) with appropriate safeguards.

Lord Joffe proposed an Assisted Dying Bill in 2003. Although it had no chance of becoming law, we can note that it would have allowed competent adults suffering from a terminal diseases or a serious, incurable physical illness to request medical assistance to die. The slippery slope would be safeguarded by the confirmation of diagnosis by two doctors and consideration of all the alternatives to assisted suicide, including hospice and palliative care. A patient would have to make a written statement declaring their wish to die, witnessed by a solicitor who was satisfied of the patient's mental competence to understand their decision (*The Guardian*, 16 April 2003).

Some limited legislative developments towards the legalisation of euthanasia have appeared in other jurisdictions, an example is the California Natural Death Act 1976, adopted in a large number of states. Notwithstanding its affirmation of human autonomy in relation to medical treatment, the scheme instituted by the California Act is, however, a restrictive one: it employs the distinction between passive and active euthanasia and reaffirms legal prohibition of the latter. A survey of physicians' understanding of the Act indicated that only approximately 17% of dying patients receive artificial life support and so qualify to opt for a natural death (Note (1979) 31 Stan L Rev 913). Even the Netherlands, often regarded as at the forefront of legalising euthanasia, only formally reformed the law in 2001 by passing the Termination of Life on Request and Assisted Suicide (Review Procedures) Act, after previously providing doctors with an immunity from prosecution on satisfying certain conditions. In the same year, Belgium followed by legalising euthanasia. Legislation legitimating euthanasia in the Northern Territory of Australia proved deeply controversial, not least on the grounds that it might be used for racist and eugenic purposes, and was annulled by the Federal Euthanasia Law Act in 1997.

In this chapter we have examined a number of criminal laws organised around the concept of bodily autonomy. Like public order, bodily autonomy can be seen both as a specific area of criminal law and as an underlying concern of criminal law in general. Our principal focus has been on sexuality and on the extent to which people in general, and women in particular, are able to use their bodies in ways in which they wish. Criminal law does not explicitly recognise the concept of bodily autonomy, and this provides a partial explanation of the varied legal responses to social practices and situations that put in issue the proper scope for decision-making about physical integrity. Both the understanding of bodily autonomy and its regulation are markedly gendered, and gendered in entirely asymmetrical ways: this is shown both in the law's historical construction of sexual violence and in its regulation of prostitution and pornography. Our analysis of relevant aspects of criminal law has further revealed the extent to which the operation of the law interacts with and depends upon the practices of other institutions and professional groups. This is particularly clear in relation to the medical profession – a powerful interest group influencing and regulating a diverse range of choices in the fields of contraception, abortion and euthanasia.

FURTHER READING

Diamantides, Marinos (1995) 'Ethics in Law: Death Marks on a Still Life: A Vision of Judgment as Vegetating' VI Law and Critique 209.

Dworkin, Gerald (1972) 'Paternalism' The Monist 56.

European Commission (1996) *Euthanasia and Assisted Suicide in the Netherlands and in Europe* (Directorate-General XII: Luxembourg OOPEC).

Freeman, Michael (2002) 'Denying Death its Dominion: Thoughts on the Dianne Pretty Case' 10 Medical Law Rev 245.

House of Lords, *Report of the Select Committee on Medical Ethics* (1993–1994).

Kennedy, Ian (1988) *Treat Me Right* (OUP).

Keown, John (2002) *Euthanasia, Ethics and Public Policy: An Argument Against Legalisation* (Cambridge University Press).

Magnusson, Roger (2002) *Angels of Death: Exploring the Euthanasia Underground* (Melbourne University Press).

Otlowski, Margaret (1997) *Voluntary Euthanasia and the Common Law* (Clarendon, Oxford).

Smith, K J M (1983) 'Assisting in Suicide – The Attorney-General and the Voluntary Euthanasia Society' Crim LR 579.

Tur, Richard (2003) 'Legislative Technique and Human Rights: The Sad Case of Assisted Suicide' Crim LR 3.

Veatch, Robert M (1976) *Death, Dying, and the Biological Revolution* (Yale University Press).

Williams, Glanville (1958) *The Sanctity of Life and the Criminal Law* (Stevens).

Making a killing: conceptions of violence

      i.   Diminished responsibility
      ii. Provocation
  e. Self-defence

I.   The social construction of violence and personal harm

I.a.   Conceptions of violence

In this chapter we explore the relationship between behaviour which is regarded as violent by the formal processes of the criminal justice system (that is, police investigation, prosecution and trial), and that which is condoned or seen as appropriately controlled by other means. In each of the first three sections we take a specific context in which violence occurs and use it to demonstrate different ways in which the line between acceptable and unacceptable killing is socially constructed. We show that the criminal law definitions of unlawful homicide (murder, manslaughter and infanticide) cannot on their own explain the ways in which deaths are culturally understood as acceptable or not acceptable. At the same time, we seek to emphasise the argument that criminal regulation has an uneven and contested relationship with other forms of social control. In **section I.**, we discuss conceptions of violence using as our context domestic violence. **Section II.** takes the broader context of regulation of safety, while in **section III.** we examine attitudes to death in relation to medical non-treatment or withdrawal of treatment. These sections prepare the ground for **section IV.**, in which we examine the distinction between murder and manslaughter as understood in legal doctrine, and we end with a gendered analysis of defences to homicide.

The term 'violence' is rarely found in statutory definitions, although, as we saw in our exploration of violence in the public order context, the Public Order Act 1986 provides an exception (see **Chapter 2.II.b.ii.**). Violence, however, is a concept which informs and underlies the practice of criminal law. For example, robbery is treated more seriously than theft because it involves the use of direct force. Violence is hidden in other ways. Road traffic offences exist in part to protect people from injury, yet until the emergence of 'road rage' they were never perceived as being connected with the stereotype of violent behaviour; academic studies of criminal law routinely ignore road traffic offences. This academic sidelining, as though the issues raised were inherently less interesting than the intellectual challenge of theft of a wild anemone or criminal damage of a greenhouse, reflects their wider marginalisation from issues of serious concern.

As the next two extracts emphasise, violence has to be viewed as historically, culturally and situationally contingent: it does not define itself. As Cotta argues, ideas and images of violence are contested and changing. Perceptions of violence are affected by changes in 'space, time and field'. We live in an era of intensive communication and increased mobility, which has rendered 'space' less fixed. Into this continuous and continuing space, the concept of 'time' has become compressed so that news is conveyed almost contemporaneously. One of the effects of this immediacy is to expand the conceptual 'field' of concepts such as violence. The word 'violence' is no longer confined to interpersonal physical harms: it is used for all kinds of unjust behaviour and wrongful acts (Cotta 1985: 9–11).

In the first extract, Beattie places current preoccupations in an historical context. This is followed by a more philosophically centred discussion by Harris:

J M Beattie, *Crime and the Courts in England, 1660–1800* (Clarendon Press, 1986) p 74

Violent physical conflict brought men and women to court charged with a wide variety of offenses against the person that had differed in the violence employed and in their motives and consequences, and that differed in the way they were regarded by society and the courts. Prosecutions that arose from some form of personal violence have some common characteristics, for usually a real victim suffered some harm. But murder, manslaughter, infanticide, rape, assault, and riot were so fundamentally different that they simply do not form themselves into a neat and coherent subject. A more serious difficulty arises from the fact that the view of violence from the courts is inevitably very limited. Most confrontations in which physical force or intimidation was used in the resolution of conflicts did not give rise to legal actions, and it is clear that the character and the full extent of violence in society cannot be adequately judged from the small number of prosecutions that were undertaken. There is good reason to think that violent physical conflict and physical abuse were commonly experienced in seventeenth and eighteenth century society. The family was the scene of much of it, for family discipline was commonly maintained by physical force … Physical intimidation within the household was matched and sustained by a broader acceptance of violence in society, and by the expectation that disagreements among men might reasonably be solved by physical means, or an insult redressed by fighting. On the whole such matters would have been regarded as private, not something that would normally engage the attention of the authorities … revealing of the general attitude toward violence and of the violent temper of the society is the use of terror and physical intimidation by the State in combating crime.

John Harris, *Violence and Responsibility* (Routledge and Kegan Paul, 1980) p 11

Despite its pervasive interest, there is surprisingly little agreement on the question of what violence in fact is, and what is in fact violence.

By far the most significant role in the generation of disputes about violence is played by a consideration which perhaps best accounts for their extreme intractability. This is the fact that definitions of violence have been propounded, and theories of violence advanced, by men who have had very different sorts of contrast in mind. Ghandi, with whom modern thinking about the morality of violence begins, contrasted violence with a rather complicated notion of non-violence of which love was an essential ingredient and of which the purpose, inevitably, included a seeking after truth. Ghandi's ideas of non-violence embodied a code for conducting one's life, deviation from which would be likely to involve violence to others. Marxist thinkers have developed a conception of violence which sees society as acting violently towards those of its members whom it exploits or otherwise injures by unjust treatment, or by forcing them to live in degrading conditions and perform alienating tasks for which they are inadequately compensated. The Marxists have in mind a picture of human life as it might be and they see a social order which prevents men from living this life as doing them great violence. Among the many theories of violence that have recently been advanced is one which contrasts violence with an ideal of peace on earth. Included in this definition of violence are those man-made features of the world which would have to be eliminated before the ideal of peace on earth could be said to have been achieved.

Some philosophers have felt that the most important feature of violence is that it involves violation of person's dignity or of his rights and have adopted conceptions of violence that give these features central place. In contrast to these rather broad conceptions of violence and perhaps as a reaction to them, other philosophers have produced very strict conceptions of violence. Their preoccupation is with law and order, and violence is contrasted with this to yield a narrow definition designed to capture the twin monsters of civil disorder and criminal assault. Other thinkers, impressed by political violence, have further limited the conception of violence by confining its application to acts directed towards political change ...

What can and what can't be called an act of violence? Are some people who use the word violence in the grip of a linguistic compulsion to which clear and decisive objections can be made, or must we perhaps accept a wide and all-embracing definition? ... A concept of violence must enable us to distinguish violent methods of dealing with people from methods that are not violent, it must make clear the difference between acts of violence and acts which are not acts of violence. Such a concept may capture what we might call the rape, murder, fire-and-sword paradigm; it will outline a concept which preserves the fearful associations with which we have loaded the notion of violence, it will be such as to include the violent events of history, and finally this concept will show why almost everyone insists on a moral distinction between violent methods and methods which do not involve violence.

The first thing to note is a distinction between violent acts and acts of violence. 'Violent' is an adjective, and a violent act, an act appropriately qualified by that adjective. An act of violence, on the other hand, is an act belonging to a particular category or class of actions not co-extensive with violent acts ... [S]ome acts, while not themselves violent in character, may result in the sort of harm which we would unhesitatingly classify as an act of violence if deliberately inflicted by human agency. For example, if a gangster throws acid in the face of a policeman we would call it an act of violence. If the same gangster were to creep into the same policeman's house at dead of night and pour the acid over his face we would, I think, still be inclined to classify it as an act of violence. But perhaps this is because the burning action of acid is itself in a sense violent. A death can, after all, be a violent death even if not brought about by a violent act ...

An act of violence occurs when injury or suffering is inflicted upon a person or persons by an agent who knows (or ought reasonably to have known) that his actions would result in the harm in question.

I.b.   Domestic violence

We turn now to violence against women – an area which causes difficulties in terms of categorisation. In conventional criminal law texts, sexual offences are usually treated sui generis and placed adjacent to, rather than within, the section on offences against the person. This tends to reinforce the widespread notion that sexual offences are more about sex than about violence, when in reality they are about both (Clark and Lewis 1977: 128–129; and see **Chapter 5.I. and II.**). While not all sexual offences are committed against women, most of them are, and 98% of defendants tried at Crown Courts for sexual offences are male. Women are subjected to violent sexual abuse both inside and out of the home. The existence and enforcement of sexual offences contribute to the way in which sexuality is regulated, and for that reason we considered them in **Chapter 5**. Women are also subjected to 'non-sexual' domestic violence, which we discuss in this chapter. The division between domestic violence and sexual offences is clearly artificial. By drawing it, we do not mean to suggest that there are any fundamental differences between the violence to which women are subjected in the form of beatings and killings and that which comes in the form of rape and other varieties of sexual assault. Both have to be understood in the context of the institutions and ideologies which nurture patriarchal relations between men and women.

The social control exercised through law is often that of last resort after the processing effect of many other systems of example or discipline. The family, school, work, neighbours, friends, doctors, all exert forms of social, moral, religious and medical control (see **Chapter 1.III.**). Social control has diversified, with the result that it is less obvious. While it is pervasive it is not always perceptible (Cohen 1985: 63). Community control has developed alongside, and in many cases replaced, the formal institutions such as psychiatric hospitals. However, the decarceration movement has not necessarily resulted in an absolute reduction in the use of traditional custody. The length of sentences for offences of violence has significantly increased since 1993. Not only has the last decade witnessed the success of 'law and order' conservatives in maintaining the prison as an observable institution of social control, but even when the relative proportions between community and custodial control change, the system overall 'expands relentlessly' (Cohen 1985: 49). The net result is a vast increase in the reach of the state into everyday life.

New professional groups have been established to police norms of conduct: 'The paradox of decarceration is that it was founded on a principle of removing the state from many areas of activity, of limiting its agency, yet it has led to a vastly increased and pervasive mechanism for state regulation' (Garton 1987: 328). This can be observed in the increasing role of social workers in policing family life. Child abuse scandals, cuts in resources and the increasing demands from rising unemployment have forced social workers back onto their statutory responsibilities (see also the discussion of child abuse in **Chapter 5.III.a.iv.**).

The role of the family itself as a form of control is one of the most interesting because of its characterisation as a private institution. This tends to reinforce the false idea that violence largely takes place between strangers rather than amongst relatives or acquaintances. The tendency to characterise crime as happening outside the family and outside known circles is particularly distorting in relation to violence; homicide is overwhelmingly domestic and rape amongst spouses, cohabitants and acquaintances is not in the least uncommon. Violence in families, whether explicitly sexual or not, is frequent, and to call it 'domestic' makes it sound cosy. But in many ways it is far more alarming than stranger violence, not least because of the opportunity for it to be repeated continually against the same person. The family is ideologically portrayed as safe for its members from the outside world (in the words of Lasch (1977), 'a haven in a heartless world'), as well as being a locus of discipline, a standard-setter for its members in their relations with non-family. If it is in the family itself that people are vulnerable, then that rhetoric is more than inappropriate; it serves an ideological purpose of obfuscation.

The people who are most at risk in this family 'haven' are women and children. Although it would be wrong to suggest that these groups are not recognised at all as 'victims', the interaction between the institutions of the family and those of criminal justice is inevitably complex. The family is perceived as a strong and vital mediator between individuals and society, which renders recognition that it also harbours appalling levels of violence and abuse more difficult. The reality of much violence should, as the extract below suggests, be a source of discomfort:

Rebecca Dobash and Russell Dobash, 'Violent Men and Violent Contexts' in Dobash and Dobash (eds) *Rethinking Violence Against Women* **(Sage, 1998) pp 141–168**

Popular conceptions of violent acts and those who commit them often reflect the notion that this is mindless, incomprehensible, unpredictable, and unpatterned behavior enacted by the alcoholic, the mentally unstable, or the socially desperate. Such notions are less uncomfortable and less challenging than the notion that violence might be functional, intentional, and patterned. If violence is a form of random deviance rather than a reflection of recurring social relations, then one need not worry about the shape and form of everyday social life but only about deviations from it. The concern about violence and its attending circumstances can thereby be removed from the concerns of those who have had no direct experience of it and expect none. It is the problem of others, the behavior of others, and an issue for others. If, however, violence is seen as intentional acts undertaken in order to achieve ends that are deeply embedded in the circumstances of daily life, it becomes an issue for us all, may affect anyone, and is about daily life. This conception requires a detailed account of violent actions and the circumstances and contexts in which they occur. Locating violence in the midst of daily life demands a focus on the mundane, the ordinary rather than extraordinary, the conflicts of interest embedded in daily life, and the rationales and justifications of perpetrators as well as the reactions and responses of victims …

The term 'domestic violence' has been criticised on a number of grounds. First, it does not specify that it is mainly women who are victims, although a further dimension to the whole debate is the extent to which violence by women has been suppressed (Heidensohn 2002: 499). Use of the term 'victim' is open to the criticism that it obscures 'the real nature of the violence; that it is violence committed by men against the women they live with' (Maguire 1988: 34). The tendency to marginalise women as crime victims is further emphasised in the choice of the term 'battered wives' rather than 'violent husbands'. Historically, English common law clearly articulated the rights of husbands over their wives' property and of control of their daily affairs. This included the right to use reasonable force to chastise them. Thus, physical force (albeit reasonable!) was legitimate, both socially and legally.

All this adds up to huge difficulties in the quest to capture the essence or estimate the extent of domestic violence. There are no separate figures in the annual Criminal Statistics for domestic violence. Techniques used for gathering data have a marked effect on the statistics found. In 1996, the use of a self-completion questionnaire for the British Crime Survey suggested that there were 6.6 million incidents of domestic physical assault in 1995, significantly higher than previous estimates based on face-to-face interviewing. As with domestic sexual assaults, women were reluctant to consider themselves as victims of crime, with only 17% of incidents meeting the legal definition of assault perceived as crimes (Mirrlees-Black 1999). The significant decline of domestic violence noted in the most recent British Crime Survey is partly attributed to the use of face-to-face interviewing, where respondents are less likely to divulge such information (Home Office 2002g: Table 3.01).

The growth of mass and local victim surveys has produced much conflicting data. Despite methodological problems and disparities produced from differing perceptions of what counts as violence, these studies all tend to indicate low levels of *reporting* of domestic violence (Zedner 1997: 582). In a survey of 1000 married women, Painter and Farrington (1998) found that 24% of married and 59% of divorced/separated women had been hit by a husband or ex-husband. Studies based on women in refuges have, not surprisingly, disclosed the highest figures. For example, Pahl (1985) found that 71% of women who had resorted to a refuge had reported the violence which had driven them there. A survey in *Woman* magazine (1984) disclosed that one in four women who reported experience of violence had told no one. Of those who had, only 28% told the police. Not all these reports will be recorded: Edwards (1986) found that only 12% of reported cases were made the subject of a crime report and, of these, four-fifths were later 'no crimed'. Despite the fact that a considerable proportion of all requests for assistance to the police involve 'domestic disturbances', non-intervention is not an uncommon police response.

One result is that victims of domestic violence are far less likely to receive compensation. The Criminal Injuries Compensation Scheme originally excluded victims of domestic violence, underlining the view that these were not worthy victims. The bar was removed in 1979, but one condition for claiming is that offences should be prosecuted unless there are practical, technical or 'other good reasons' why a prosecution has not been brought. It is not always easy to comply with this condition. Awards are also unlikely if there continues to be a link between the offender and victim, given the risk that this could benefit the offender (Criminal Injuries Compensation Authority 2001).

Over the last 20 years, there has undoubtedly developed a greater awareness of the prevalence of domestic violence and police forces have developed initiatives to handle complaints of both sexual and domestic assault more sensitively and to reduce the attrition rate. However, as the next extract suggests, some re-thinking of the premises underlying such changes might be needed:

Antonia Cretney and Gwynn Davis, 'Prosecuting "Domestic" Assault' (1996) Crim LR 162

The law no longer recognises a private realm in which a man is free to beat his wife, nor makes the assumption that it is otiose to expect a wife to give evidence against a husband alleged to have assaulted her. Domestic violence is now recognised as a social evil as well as a private misfortune which may eventually have fatal results; it also constitutes a considerable part of the workload of police, prosecutors and the courts. Few would claim that the criminal law alone can solve the problem of domestic violence, but it is nonetheless legitimate to ask what the task of the criminal law should be in this sphere and to examine how far it is currently successful in carrying out that task.

In the past the police and courts have been accused of failing to protect women because they followed a policy of non-intervention which led to the trivialisation of serious injury ... Where there has been intervention this has been criticised as imposing secondary victimisation on the woman, as trivialising the harm done to her, and as offering little symbolic support in the form of severe penalties for offenders. With the development of a feminist critique of police and court responses to domestic violence we have seen the introduction in North America and other jurisdictions of 'pro-arrest' or even mandatory arrest policies under which the police response is no longer based upon their assessment of the victim's commitment to the prosecution enterprise. Coupled with this there has been a more co-ordinated response to the problem, involving the provision of support networks for victims. In the wake of North American reforms have come developments in the police response in England and Wales. Home Office Circular 60/90 prompted the introduction of special units intended to handle the large volume of domestic violence cases confronting the police. It also encouraged the presumption that assailants would be arrested.

Are victims of domestic violence willing partners in these pro-arrest policies? In an inter-agency report on domestic violence it was observed that 'very many cases are withdrawn from prosecution on the grounds that the woman either withdraws her allegations or is unwilling to act as a witness'. So what is going on? Are the present policies operating to the benefit of assault victims? It is one thing to get from the woman, as a footnote to her statement, the written assurance that she will support a prosecution and is prepared to give evidence in court if necessary; it is another to ensure that she has thought through the implications of this and has the necessary firmness of purpose and access to continuing support to enable her to sustain that commitment. The presumption that a man who assaults his partner should be arrested and charged like any other assailant – although of course police officers exercise discretion in *all* cases – may, *as far as the police are concerned*, demonstrate that they are taking domestic violence seriously. But it is possible that it pushes the problem further up the line rather than solves it ...

The public interest is seen to demand the prosecution of 'domestic' assailants. But the interest of the victim may be much harder to discern, her wishes in the matter distinctly equivocal. She may turn to the police for rescue, only to find herself expected to sustain a prosecution against a partner to whom she still has strong emotional ties. She may believe that the involvement of the police and the *threat* of prosecution has been enough to prevent further violence. She may decide that the stigma of a criminal conviction is too high a price for her partner to pay. She may suspect that invoking the criminal law will serve to terminate a relationship which she does not in fact want to end. Also to be weighed in the balance is the burden of the trial process, involving public exposure as well as much anxiety and inconvenience. Once cannot assume that a 'successful' outcome, that is to say conviction and sentence, is in the woman's interests.

Faced with such potential conflicts and ambiguities prosecutors have to decide what weight to give to the *wishes* of the victim and also how to interpret her *interests*. For the most part they appear to accept that considerations pertaining to 'the relationship' should have priority and that when a woman comes to court and expresses a wish to withdraw her complaint, it is indeed 'relationship' considerations which motivate her action. This is despite the fact that there is now a presumption of prosecution in domestic violence cases ...

At the same time it should be recognised that from the victim's point of view a discontinued case need not be a 'failure' at all: the experience of arrest and the threat of conviction may be enough to deter some men from further violence. The threatened end of the relationship may deter others. This is not to say that there might not be less confused or less costly ways of achieving those same ends. Indeed some will argue that prosecution, whether 'successful' or not, is an irrelevance as far as the victim is concerned.

Of course, there are some cases – a minority, we believe – in which there is no clash between the public and the private interest. Where a relationship has ended and the victim is financially and emotionally independent; where she wants to see her assailant publicly denounced; where she is seeking compensation and sees conviction as a means to that end; or where she has the support of her family or a new partner, then her support for the prosecution may be unequivocal. The fact is, however, that most domestic violence prosecutions involve a complainant whose commitment to the enterprise is in some doubt. Perhaps the real task is to convince women who wish to withdraw their support that it is in their interests not to do so. But this is unlikely as long as victims perceive that they are tools of the prosecution – that is to say, mere witnesses, having no special standing in the eyes of the court ...

Over the past 10 years criminal justice agencies have endeavoured to construct a firm response to violence against women in the home. In the same period we have seen a potentially significant change in the substantive law relating to domestic violence, namely the extension of the compellability provision to married partners – section 80(3) of the Police and Criminal Evidence Act 1984. The police have addressed the issue by making certain organisational changes and by encouraging a change in attitude amongst officers; the CPS has made public its guidelines for prosecutors in domestic violence cases. It now appears that offenders are being arrested and charged where once they would only have been 'advised', and that in general women who seek police help are receiving a better service, both in terms of the immediate response and in the support which they receive during the prosecution process.

We would suggest that further thought now be given to the management of those cases in which the woman indicates that she no longer wishes to proceed. It does not seem to us that the issue of intimidation and pressure has been effectively addressed. Much that police, prosecutors and courts currently do to ensure that a retraction is properly made appears designed to protect the prosecuting authorities rather than to uncover coercion. The fact that coercion is seldom if ever revealed by these means forces this conclusion. We would suggest therefore that the courts and the CPS abandon the practice of requiring withdrawal from the witness-box. Instead, the emphasis should be on facilitating private consultation between victim and prosecutor, a policy which we recognise does present certain difficulties for the CPS although it is managed well enough by some prosecutors. A second issue which we would identify is the tendency to blame the woman. It has been part of police culture to regard victims of domestic violence as vacillating women who in the end deserve what they get because they are unable to make a break with their abuser. With an apparent increase in the number of domestic violence cases coming before the courts there is a tendency to regard the woman who withdraws at this stage as failing all those (police, CPS and court) who have put themselves out on her behalf. It should be evident by now that we consider there to be very good reasons why some women withdraw, whether this withdrawal be early or late. Furthermore, withdrawal does not necessarily denote failure on anyone's part.

Others have paused to question the merits of the pro-arrest and pro-charge strategy. As the extract below discusses, the symbolic strength of such messages may be undermined by the reality of sentencing.

Carolyn Hoyle, *Negotiating Domestic Violence: Police, Criminal Justice, and Victims* (Clarendon, 1998) pp 191–192

Women who want their partners to be treated harshly are likely to be disappointed. As Edwards has argued, sentences in the domestic context, compared with the non-domestic context, have tended to be derisory. Buchanan and Edwards' study of sentencing in London in 1990 found that in cases of assault the more typical sentence of the court was a fine, and even in the case of assault occasioning grievous bodily harm, very few offenders were committed to prison. Only 3 per cent of Thames Valley incidents originally attended by officers resulted in a suspect being convicted of a criminal offence. And conditional discharges, community service orders, and fines were the usual sentences imposed by the courts.

The Family Law Act 1996 introduced civil remedies for domestic violence victims in the form of protective orders (see Pt IV of the Act). Any use or threat of violence brings with it the presumption of powers of arrest (s 47(2)). In the recent criminal justice White Paper (Home Office 2002b) the Government suggest criminalising breach of non-molestation orders, following in the footsteps of other hybrid provisions such as anti-social behaviour orders. However, it has been suggested that in focusing on the disregard for state authority, such penalties often lose sight of the conduct in question and the protection of the victim (see Burton 2003: 301). More detailed proposals in relation to domestic violence, including the introduction of a register of offenders, are outlined in a Government Consultation Paper issued in June 2003 (Home Office 2003g).

This discussion of violence against women underlines the need for gender sensitivity in our analysis of trends in crime and of criminal law doctrine. It is often assumed that the statistics for homicide are more reliable than those for many other offences. However, crime surveys have only recently presented figures on the relationship between victims and suspects (see **section IV.d.ii.** below).

Children under 12 months are four times more likely to be the victims of homicide than adults aged 30 to 50 (Home Office 2003f: Table 1.07). Child abuse engenders extreme reactions. On the one hand, those who attempt to protect vulnerable children are seen as interfering with the privacy of family life, while on the other, social workers are frequently criticised for failing to prevent deaths from child battering (see **Chapter 5.III.a.iv.**). Once such a death, or child abuse, has been acknowledged to have occurred, people do not doubt that it is properly a matter for criminal law. The contradictions it raises are more about perceptions of the sort of family an abuser is likely to come from and conflicts of interest between different members of the family.

But there are other circumstances of death and injury about which we do have doubts – we do not seem to know whether to classify them as wrongdoing. We will be examining some of these in the following sections – road traffic deaths and deaths at work (**section II.**), and deaths from medical non-treatment (**section III.**).

FURTHER READING
Davis, Nanette J (1988) 'Battered Women: Implications for Social Control', Contemporary Crises 345.
Dobash, R E and Dobash, R P (1992) *Women, Violence and Social Change* (Routledge).

Glover, Jonathan (1977) *Causing Death and Saving Lives* (Penguin).

Grace, Sharon (1995) *Policing Domestic Violence in the 1990s* (Home Office Research Study No 139).

Hoyle, Carolyn (1998) *Negotiating Domestic Violence: Police, Criminal Justice and Victims* (Oxford University Press).

Hoyle, Carolyn and Sanders, A (2000) 'Police response to Domestic Violence: From Victim Choice to Victim Empowerment' BJ Crim 40.

Kelly, Liz (1999) *Domestic Violence Matters* (Home Office Research Study No 193, HMSO).

Mirrlees-Black, C (1999) *Domestic Violence: Findings from a new British Crime Survey self-completion questionnaire* (Home Office Research Study No 191, HMSO).

Sanders, Andrew (1988) 'Personal Violence and Public Order: The Prosecution of "Domestic" Violence in England and Wales' 16 IJSL 359.

II.   The criminal regulation of public safety

II.a.   Regulation in context

In this section we consider the wider context of serious injuries and deaths: those caused in road traffic accidents and at work. Both are marginalised from the mainstream of criminal law by the provision of separate offences, by differential enforcement and, in the case of workplace deaths, by the provision of a separate regulatory scheme. The marginalisation both results from and reinforces the notion that some criminal offences are neither 'really' criminal nor violent, despite causing death or serious injury.

One way of looking at criminal law and criminal regulation is in terms of the different conceptions which have arisen of 'real' crime and 'quasi' crime. 'Quasi' crime is a term used to describe offences committed largely by white collar criminals pursuing their business interests and those committing road traffic offences. We do not mean, by using these terms, to endorse that distinction. To do so would be to suggest that environmental pollution or injuries resulting from breaches of health and safety regulations are conceptually different from assaults or thefts. This is difficult to justify. It is the existence of the distinction in the ideology of criminal law that we emphasise. Although it has been thought necessary to subject much business activity to a form of regulation and, frequently, to back this up with a criminal sanction, completely separate enforcement agencies have developed with distinctive styles of operation. So, whereas the police generally adopt a 'them and us' approach to criminal law breaking, the dominant mode for many regulatory agencies is negotiation and compliance. However, the example of road traffic indicates that the difference cannot be explained merely by the different agendas of the police and of regulatory agencies.

II.a.i. Road traffic

More than 3500 people die in UK road traffic accidents each year, yet few of these result in manslaughter prosecutions. And few are prosecuted for non-fatal offences against the person in respect of the 40,000 who suffer serious injuries. This 'tolerance' of vehicle accidents is not new. Dangers arose in early modern Britain from the very large numbers of horses in circulation. London accounted for 8000 private and public coaches in the middle of the eighteenth century, which suggests many thousands of horses. The earliest reliable survey suggests 1000 deaths from accidents involving horses and carriages in the year 1840 (Hair 1971: 5–24). Then, as now, very few of the homicide cases before the courts arose from death caused by transport accidents. Juries tended to find a verdict of death by 'misfortune' and to acquit the accused entirely when faced with homicide charges arising from accidents with horses, coaches or wagons (Beattie 1986: 86). Causing death by dangerous driving is less well tolerated nowadays. As a result of safety campaigns, and improved car and road design, the number of fatal accidents has decreased by nearly 40% in the last 20 years.

The choice of charge (if any) following road traffic deaths is between manslaughter or one of the offences under the Road Traffic Act (RTA) 1988 (as inserted by RTA 1991). These include causing death by dangerous driving (s 1); causing death by careless driving when under the influence of drink or drugs (s 3A); or dangerous driving (s 2). Causing death by dangerous driving now attracts more serious sentences (the average is three years in prison), but nonetheless its survival as a separate offence marks it out from the generic manslaughter offence.

There are annually about 200 convictions for the various driving-death offences, excluding manslaughter. This can be compared with the 500 or so convictions for unlawful homicide from all other causes (469 in 2001/2002 – Home Office 2003e: Table 1.10). The death-driving offences are recorded separately, thus confirming their distance from the 'real' criminality of homicide. The maximum penalty for the causing death offences was increased to 10 years' imprisonment in 1993. Of the 161 people convicted of causing death by dangerous driving in 2001, 104 received immediate sentences of imprisonment; of the 32 convicted of causing death by careless driving under the influence, 26 were so sentenced (Home Office 2003f: Table 7). Males comprise 94% of those found guilty of causing death by dangerous driving. Where a death arises from aggravated vehicle-taking, the penalty is five years (Theft Act 1968, s 12A as inserted by the Aggravated Vehicle Taking Act 1992). The introduction of the aggravated offence of temporary vehicle-taking to deal with the social problem of 'joyriding' is a good illustration of the use of labels to stigmatise certain types of offender (young, inner-city rebels) for mimicking the widely accepted macho styles of driving which attract far less opprobrium. It also illustrates the thesis that legal solutions to perceived social problems are often superfluous, given the range of other offences. There were only seven convictions for this offence in 2001. There is a discernible shift in mood in relation to road deaths and custodial penalties are more likely to be imposed than in the past. The power to refer lenient sentences to the Court of Appeal under s 36 of the Criminal Justice Act 1988 has provided a useful focus for victim groups such as the Campaign against Drinking and Driving (Shute 1994: 749), with the result that 12% of such references are for driving-death cases (Shute 1999: 608). As a result, a number of sentences have been increased. The tone was set early on when, in the first year after the introduction of the procedure, the Court of Appeal imposed custodial sentences on two people convicted of causing death by reckless driving in place of the non-custodial sentences they had received at trial (*A-G's Reference (Nos 3 and 5 of 1989)*, 1989). Over 70% of these offenders receive custodial penalties, but a significant proportion are fined or placed on community service orders, sentences rarely deployed for those convicted of manslaughter.

There is some correlation between serious traffic offenders and more general criminal behaviour.

Gerry Rose, *The Criminal Histories of Road Traffic Offenders*, Research Study No 206 (Home Office, 2000) Executive Summary

Serious traffic offenders were of a similar age profile to mainstream offenders with the exception of drink drivers, many of whom were older (48% of the ... sample were aged over 33). For disqualified drivers, dangerous drivers, and mainstream offenders, between 60 per cent and 75 per cent of convicted offenders were in the age-range 18 to 32. The prevalence of traffic offending was higher for young white people than for those from other ethnic groups. . ...

Analysis of criminal histories ... concentrated on the links between serious traffic offending, 'mainstream' criminal offending and vehicle theft. ... Clear differences were found between the three serious traffic offender groups, especially in comparison with mainstream offenders.

Drink drivers were about twice as likely to have previous convictions as would be expected in the general population. Although 40 per cent of drink drivers had a criminal history, this was less extensive than any other group of offenders examined in this study and the average time since a last conviction was eight years. Drink drivers usually appeared in court for only that offence, rather than a number of offences (as was the case with other offender groups). Drink driving was not closely associated with criminal offending.

Disqualified drivers had criminal histories similar to those of mainstream offenders (79% had a criminal record as compared with 72% of mainstream offenders). They had a similar number of previous convictions, and their likelihood of subsequent conviction within a year was the same (at 37%). The reconviction patterns of this group showed some tendency to repeat disqualified driving but within a more generalised context of offending.

Dangerous drivers showed less involvement with crime than disqualified drivers but more than drink drivers. Approximately 50 per cent had a previous conviction and a quarter was reconvicted within a year. The research suggested there may be two groups of dangerous drivers: about a third had previous convictions that included car theft, and were otherwise similar to recidivist mainstream offenders and disqualified drivers; the other two-thirds showed criminal histories more similar to those of drink drivers.

Although road traffic offences are enforced by the police, in other respects the system by which they are regulated shares many of the characteristics of business and corporate regulation. In particular, there is a set of specialised offences, many of which are strict liability, and enforcement practices differ from those used for 'mainstream' violence offences. The notion that these offences are not quite the same sort of crime as burglary or drunken brawls is reinforced through such substantive and procedural differences. The interactive process between the social reception and the legal response to driving offenders means that even where people use a vehicle as a weapon of deliberate harm, they are treated surprisingly gently.

J R Spencer, 'Motor Vehicles as Weapons of Offence' (1985) Crim LR 29

There were three heart-warming items in the newspapers recently. The first was the happy news that although compulsory seatbelts had dramatically reduced the number of fatalities in cars, 'the number of organs available for transplant has not been affected because most come from pedestrians or cyclists involved in accidents.' The second was that a driver who turned his car round and drove for 40 yards on the wrong side of the road at a cyclist who had annoyed him, killing him instantly, had received a sentence of six months' imprisonment. And the third was a claim by a cycling organisation that where cyclists are killed or injured by even the most terribly bad driving, derisory sentences are often imposed. These prompt the question: has society in general, and have the criminal courts in particular, got their moral values mixed up when it comes to damage done to pedestrians and cyclists by motor vehicles? In an attempt to answer it, I tried to make a little study of the usual legal consequences of the worst conceivable case: where a driver deliberately turns his vehicle on a pedestrian or cyclist, using it against him as a weapon of offence.

It shows how common this behaviour is that I had no difficulty in collecting over 30 such cases. A few were old, but most were modern: 17 from the 1980s, and six were from the late 1970s. In most of them the prosecution case was that the driver drove straight at his victim, usually intending to scare him, but in some instances he did so intending to cause him serious harm. In three cases, the driver accidentally or deliberately impaled his victim on the front of his car, and then zigzagged at speed in order to throw him off ... I fear the evidence strongly suggests that the answer to this question is 'yes'. Drivers who behave in this fashion, although usually guilty of serious offences against the person, often seem to be treated as mere motoring offenders, and to escape lightly.

We would expect to find the motorist who drives at a pedestrian or cyclist in serious trouble. If he kills he is usually guilty of murder. This is obviously so if he runs his victim down intending to kill or maim. As the law stands, however, he is equally guilty of murder if he so kills without any premeditated intention to kill or maim ... The penalty for murder is mandatory imprisonment for life. Where a person gets convicted of the lesser offence of manslaughter for killing a pedestrian or cyclist by deliberately running him down with a car, we would expect him also to receive a fairly severe prison sentence. The 'tariff' for manslaughter resulting from an attack on another with a gun, axe, knife or broken bottle is around the five-year mark, and the same should surely apply to the manslaughterer who chooses the bluntest of all blunt instruments, a car.

Even where he does not kill, one would expect the motorist who runs someone down on purpose to be in serious trouble. To run someone down intending to kill him is attempted murder; to do so intending serious injury is causing grievous bodily harm with intent, contrary to the Offences Against the Person Act 1861, s.18, or an attempt if the intended victim jumps clear. In any of these cases the maximum penalty is life imprisonment. The tariff for a section 18 offence is in the region of three to five years' imprisonment, towards the upper end if a lethal weapon was used, and as a car is obviously a very lethal weapon this is therefore the sort of sentence one would expect a motorist to receive for this offence ...

...

[T]he use of a motor vehicle as a weapon of offence is often treated with remarkable lenity. First, in fatal cases murder charges are usually not pressed where they could be. Murder charges have occasionally been pressed against motorists who ran over with premeditated intention to kill or injure ... but where they have killed ... by driving at them to frighten them, or have done so by driving at them in a blind rage, they usually seem to be charged with manslaughter at the most. Thus, if a man, exasperated by a noisy party, shoots a gun at random into the house and kills, he gets prosecuted for murder; but if he kills by driving straight at a group of cyclists, one of whom has offended him by giving a rude sign, he will almost certainly be prosecuted for manslaughter only. In *Stratton* (1983), for example, a driver shot some traffic lights at red, impaled a pedestrian on the front of his car, and drove off at top speed swerving violently to throw him off. The pedestrian, a 14-year-old-boy, was killed when his head struck the pavement. The similarity with *D.P.P. v Smith* (1961) is obvious: yet the driver was prosecuted for manslaughter only, and at the trial the prosecution and the judge agreed to the manslaughter charge being dropped in return for a plea of guilty to causing death by reckless driving ... The only cases I have discovered where the prosecution have pressed a murder charge against a risk-taking driver are *D.P.P. v Smith*, where the victim was a policeman, *Hedley* (1945), where the driver was an escaping robber and *Key* (1983), where the driver deliberately drove at a senior citizen who rebuked him for kerb-crawling ...

Secondly, accepting that manslaughter rather than murder is the proper charge where the driver kills, and accepting the scale of sentences approved by the Court of Appeal, there are many cases where the court of trial has imposed sentences which were amazingly light. For crushing her lover, the driver in *English* (1981) was conditionally discharged and disqualified from driving for 12 months. Perhaps this can be dismissed as a crime passionnel by a woman with genuine medical problems, but the same can hardly be said of *Leonard* (1983) and *Haste* (1983), where young men used their cars to kill total strangers who had temporarily offended them. Each of these defendants received sentences of only six months ...

[B]ehind all the practical explanations for lenity in this sort of case there probably lurk psychological factors related to public attitudes to the motor-car ... [T]he motor vehicle is firmly linked in everyone's mind with accidental death, and in the minds of lawyers with the criminal offences associated with carelessness rather than intentional injury.

The concern, or moral panic, about 'road rage' has not translated into prosecutions for more serious offences and more severe sentencing. According to the criminal statistics, the number of homicides (murders and manslaughters) where a vehicle was used as the method of killing has been increasing gradually from seven in 1991 to an average of 12 over the last five years (Home Office 2003f: Table 1.03). Any road traffic deaths recorded as offences of death caused by dangerous driving or careless driving under the influence of drink or drugs are not categorised as homicides in the official statistics. This separation both contributes to, and reflects, the way these offences are perceived.

II.a.ii.   Work hazards

Box (1983: 29) estimated that, adjusting for the population at risk, seven times as many people die from occupational accidents or disease than from homicide. Few of those deaths result in any form of prosecution. When charges are brought they are nearly always pursued as health and safety offences rather than the more serious manslaughter offence.

Celia Wells, *Corporations and Criminal Responsibility* (OUP, 2001) p 121

Between 1996 and 1998, 510 people died and 47,803 suffered major injuries from work-related accidents. In some industrial sectors the number of major injuries has increased in the last two decades ... 3,555 people have lost their lives at work in the last ten years. Many of these deaths were preventable according to the HSE which concluded that 75% of maintenance accidents in the chemical industry were either partly or wholly the result of site management's failure to take reasonably practicable precautions. Studies of other industries reveal similar startlingly high rates of both regulatory violations and reckless endangerment of workers' lives. ... Between 1981 and 1985 there were 739 deaths in the construction industry 70% of which (over 500) could have been avoided by 'positive action by management'. Yet there have only been a handful of prosecutions of company directors for manslaughter following a workplace death and these resulted in only two convictions. Prosecutions of companies are also rare. Workplace deaths are automatically investigated by the HSE who do not have the power to bring manslaughter prosecutions and have only since 1998 agreed a protocol with the police and the Crown Prosecution Service for co-ordinating investigations in such cases ... [O]f 59 cases referred to the CPS by the HSE in the period 1992–1998, only 18 prosecutions for manslaughter were brought, most against individuals. Prosecutions under the Health and Safety at Work Act are brought in only 20% of workplace deaths and after 1% of reported major injuries. Between 1996–1998, the HSE did not prosecute any managers or directors in relation to over 500 workplace deaths and 47,000 major injuries reported to it.

Centre for Corporate Accountability, 'The Health and Safety Executive's Memorandum to the House of Commons', Environment Subcommittee of the Select Committee on Environment, Transport and Regional Affairs HC 828 (HMSO 1999)

It is important to clarify the law. In relation to workplace safety, there are two types of offences that may be committed by companies and their senior officers:

- a health and safety offence, or
- a conventional offence of violence, like manslaughter, or inflicting grievous bodily harm. These offences can only apply after a major injury or death.

... Every workplace death is subjected to an HSE investigation; the issue of major concern is HSE's prosecution policies. 18.8% of deaths in 1996–8 resulted in a prosecution for health and safety offences. All of the prosecutions that did take place were against companies: none were against directors or managers. There was a big differential between one region and another. ...

72% of these prosecution took place in the magistrates' court (where the maximum fine available is £20,000). The average fine per death was £18,032. The prosecution of companies for only 19% of deaths is an extraordinary low figure considering all the evidence that indicates that the majority of deaths result from management failure.

... One of the reasons for the low fines imposed upon companies – even when a death has taken place –is directly related to HSE's failure to ensure that more cases are heard in the Crown Court which have the power to impose unlimited fines. Compare for example, the average fine in the North West (£9,000) where all the cases were heard in the magistrates' court to the fines imposed in the Home Counties (£26,000) where 40% took place in the Crown Court.

There have been some notably large fines and each year the previous maximum appears to be exceeded. Fines in excess of a million have been known but these are rare. For example, Balfour Beatty were fined £1.7 million following the collapse of a tunnel they were building for the Heathrow express link (15 February 1999) and GWT were fined £1.5 million after the Southall rail crash in 1997 (Wells 2000). The appellate courts have begun to show concern at the low level of fines imposed and described as 'derisory' the fine of £100 handed out to British Steel for a breach of safety regulations which led to a worker's death (*British Steel*, 1995). Even the very large exemplary fines in the Crown Court often represent a tiny fraction of the company's turnover. Gobert (1994a) points out that the £750,000 fine on BP in 1987 amounted to 0.05% of the company's after-tax profits.

The sentencing guidance in health and safety offences recently provided by the Court of Appeal may herald a new era of more punitive sentencing (*Howe*, 1999). The court outlined as aggravating features: causing death, failure to heed warnings and taking risks to maximise profits. Mitigating factors include prompt admission of responsibility, timely guilty plea, evidence of having taken steps to remedy the deficiency and a good safety record. Because the objective is to achieve a safe working environment, fines need to be large enough, the court said, to bring home the message not only to managers but also to shareholders. The fine should not be so large as to imperil earnings of employees, but there may be cases where the offence was so serious that the defendant ought not to be in business. Mr Justice Scott Baker added:

> As to the level of fines imposed generally for offences of this nature, it is the view of each member of this court that they are too low and therefore not an appropriate yardstick for determining the level of fine in the present case.

Under the Criminal Justice Act 1991, any fine should reflect not only the gravity of the offence but also the means of the offender, and this applies just as much to corporate defendants as to any other (s 18(3)). The judge added that magistrates should always think carefully before accepting jurisdiction in health and safety at work cases, where it is arguable that the fine may exceed the limit of their jurisdiction or where death or serious injury has resulted from the offence.

Sanctions for health and safety deaths inevitably fall far short of those imposed for murder or manslaughter, since custodial sentences are rare and, where the defendant is a corporation, there is no custodial equivalent. But there seems little doubt that a prosecution under health and safety legislation for a work-related death is not taken as seriously as the equivalent causing dangerous driving or manslaughter case. For example, the owner of a painting and decorating firm was fined £200 when his nephew, who was working for him, fell from an unsupported scaffold (Health and Safety at Work, March 2003: 8). See **section II.c.** below for a discussion of corporate accountability.

II.b.   Characteristics of regulatory offences

The three main characteristics of the regulatory model are, first, that the form in which the offences are defined often omits any mention of the consequential harm; secondly, that liability is technically 'strict'; and thirdly, that the model of enforcement is based on a consultative, us-and-us, rather than them-and-us, conception of the regulated employer or company. We now explore these characteristics in more detail.

II.b.i.   Offence labels

Although breaches of health and safety offences often cause serious injury and sometimes death, any conviction under the Health and Safety at Work etc Act 1974 will not reflect that result. Instead of being held criminally liable 'for the death of x', the employer will be convicted (if at all) of a breach of the duty to provide for the safety of her workers.

A contemporary example which illustrates the sanitising effect of the separate systems of both road traffic and health and safety regulation is that of a driver who failed to secure the arm of a mechanical digger he was transporting by lorry. Having driven 500 miles and worked a 16-hour day, this slip cost the lives of five motorists whose roofs were peeled off as they drove at night into the unlit digger arm straddling their side of the road. Neither the driver nor the company which had contracted him to deliver the digger was charged with manslaughter. The driver was charged with causing death by dangerous driving, which at least reflected in its offence label the fact that death had resulted. The company which had contracted him was prosecuted for an offence under s 3 of the Health and Safety at Work etc Act 1974 (see below). The company was fined half a million pounds, which reflects a level of culpability beyond the baseline for the offence (*Independent*, 11 October 1997). This still leaves the question why a culpable death is not routinely prosecuted as manslaughter. As our discussion of involuntary manslaughter will disclose, Saturday night brawls frequently result in manslaughter prosecutions based on relatively low culpability.

Health and Safety at Work etc Act 1974, ss 2, 3

2. It is the duty of every employer to ensure, so far as is reasonably practicable, the health, safety and welfare at work of all his employees.
3. It shall be the duty of every employer to conduct his undertaking in such a way as to ensure, so far as is reasonably practicable, that persons not in his employment who may be affected thereby are not thereby exposed to risks to their health and safety.

Section 33(1) states that it is an offence for an employer not to discharge these duties. The employer can be an individual or a company. Under s 37, company directors can be additionally charged where the offence has been committed with their 'consent or connivance ... or is attributable to any neglect on their part'. Most of their prosecutions are against companies, but in 2001/2002 the Health and Safety Executive prosecuted individuals on 55 separate charges, of which 40 led to conviction. This included 31 charges against directors and managers, of which 23 led to conviction. The overall average fine for offences by directors and managers was £3098. As well as fines, the courts also have the power to imprison individuals convicted of certain health and safety offences, in particular for failure to comply with improvement and prohibition notices. Five people have been sent to prison for health and safety offences since January 1996, although none in the last two years. Under the Company Directors' Disqualification Act 1986, the courts may also disqualify directors who have been found guilty of health and safety offences. A total of eight directors have been disqualified for health and safety offences, although again, none in the last two years (HSE 2003).

II.b.ii.   The prevalence of strict liability

Strict liability is a key feature of regulatory offences. Where strict liability is imposed, a person can be convicted of an offence without proof of a mental element such as intention or knowledge, or with the possibility of a reverse-onus defence of due diligence, or reasonable practicability.

David Janway Davies v Health and Safety Executive, Court of Appeal (Criminal Division) [2003] IRLR 170

[*The appellant ran a plant hire firm. One of his employees was killed when a JCB reversed into him. The appellant was convicted under ss 3 and 33, and fined £15,000, following a ruling by the trial judge that s 40 was compatible with the ECHR and therefore there was a legal (persuasive) burden on the appellant to prove (on the balance of probability) that it was not reasonably practicable for him to do more than he had in fact done. The appellant contended that s 40 was only compatible if read down so as to impose an evidential burden.*]

Tuckey LJ.

Once again this court has to consider whether a reverse burden of proof provision in a statute creating offences is compatible with the presumption of innocence enshrined in Article 6 (2) of the ECHR. The statute in question is the Health and Safety at Work Act 1974. The combined effect of sections 3(1) and 33 of the Act make it an offence for an employer to fail to discharge the duty to conduct his undertaking in such a way as to ensure, so far as is reasonably practicable, that persons not in his employment who may be affected thereby are not thereby exposed to risks to their health or safety.

Section 40 says that in any proceedings for an offence consisting of a failure to comply with a duty ... to do something ... so far as is reasonably practicable ... it shall be for the accused to prove ... that it was not reasonably practicable to do more than was in fact done to satisfy the duty ...

... A Health and Safety Executive witness produced a leaflet entitled "Reversing Vehicles". This said that nearly a quarter of all deaths involving vehicles at work occur while the vehicle is reversing and that most happen at low speeds and could be prevented by taking some simple safety precautions. These included the use of a banksman to ensure safe reversing.

In some cases where a statute provides for a reverse burden of proof the court first has to consider as a matter of construction whether the burden is legal (persuasive) or merely evidential. No such issue arises in this case. The language of the statute, "it shall be for the accused to prove", clearly imposes a legal burden.

Equally the authorities show that if it is necessary to achieve compatibility by reading such clear language down so as to provide simply for an evidential burden, the court should do so.

The only issue of construction in this case is whether the section 40 defence relates to an ingredient of the offence created by sections 3 and 33. If it does not, some cases suggest that there is no infringement of the presumption of innocence ...

The duty cast on the defendant is a "duty ... to ensure as far as is reasonably practicable". It is a breach of this qualified duty which gives rise to the offence. [Counsel for the Crown] had to concede that but for section 40 it would be for the Crown to negative reasonable practicability. This makes the point against him.

This construction of the statute means that section 40 does make some inroad into the presumption of innocence. It does not follow however that it is incompatible with the Convention. As the ECHR said in *Salabiaku v France* (1988) 13 EHRR 379 at para. 28

Presumptions of fact or law operate in every legal system. Clearly the Convention does not prohibit such presumptions in principle. It does however require the contracting States to remain within certain limits in this respect as regards criminal law ... Article 6 (2) does not therefore regard presumptions of fact or law provided for in the criminal law with indifference. It requires States to confine them within reasonable limits which take into account the importance of what is at stake and maintain the rights of the defence.

It is worth adding at this point that in the field of health and safety the E.E.C. accept that it is possible to impose absolute duties on employers. Thus Article 5.1 of Council Directive 89/391/EEC requires member states to provide that:

The employer shall have a duty to ensure the safety and health of workers in every aspect related to the work.
Member states may, but are not required:

... to provide for the exclusion or the limitation of employers responsibility where occurrences are due to unusual and unforeseeable circumstances beyond the employers' control, or to exceptional events, the consequences of which could not have been avoided despite the exercise of all due care.

... The first point to be noted about the legislation is that it is regulatory rather than prescriptive. This is important in the balancing exercise. A strict responsibility may be acceptable in the case of statutory offences which are concerned to regulate the conduct of some particular activity in the public interest. The requirement to have a licence in order to carry on certain kinds of activity is an obvious example. The promotion of health and safety and the avoidance of pollution are among the purposes to be served by such controls. These kinds of cases may properly be seen as not truly criminal. Many may be relatively trivial and only involve a monetary penalty. Many may carry with them no real social disgrace or infamy.

The reasons for the distinction between truly criminal and regulatory offences were spelt out cogently by Cory J in the Canadian Supreme Court in *R v Wholesale Travel Group* (1991) 3 SCR 154. He expressed the rationale for the distinction as follows:

The objective of regulatory legislation is to protect the public or broad segments of the public (such as employees, common consumers and motorists to name but a few) from the potentially adverse affects of otherwise lawful activity. Regulatory legislation involves the shift of emphasis from the protection of individual interests and the deterrence and punishment of acts involving moral fault to the protection of public and societal interests. While criminal offences are usually designed to condemn and punish past, inherently wrongful conduct, regulatory measures are generally directed to the prevention of future harm through the enforcement of minimum standards of conduct and care.

It follows that regulatory offences and crimes embody different concepts of fault. Since regulatory offences are directed primarily not to conduct itself but to the consequences of conduct, conviction of a regulatory offence may be thought to import a significantly lesser degree of culpability than conviction of a true crime. The concept of fault in regulatory offences is based upon a reasonable care standard and, as such, does not imply moral blameworthiness in the same manner as criminal fault. Conviction for breach of a regulatory offence suggests nothing more than that the defendant has failed to meet a prescribed standard of care.

... We have concluded that the imposition of a legal burden of proof in section 40 of the Act is justified, necessary and proportionate for the reasons which we set out below which take account of the various points we have discussed above.

First the Act is regulatory and its purpose is to protect the health and safety of those affected by the activities referred to in sections 2 to 6. The need for such regulation is amply demonstrated by the statistics with which we have been supplied. These show that fatal injuries reported to the U.K. enforcing authorities by industry are running at an average of about 700 a year and non-fatal major injuries at nearly 200,000 a year. Following a survey in 1995/6 the Office of Statistics put the financial costs of accidents at work in the U.K. at between £14.5 and £18.1 billion. The Act's purpose is therefore both social and economic.

The reversal of the burden of proof takes into account the fact that duty holders are persons who have chosen to engage in work or commercial activity (probably for gain) and are in charge of it. They are not therefore unengaged or disinterested members of the public and in choosing to operate in a regulated sphere of activity they must be taken to have accepted the regulatory controls that go with it. This regulatory regime imposes a continuing duty to ensure a state of affairs, a safety standard. Where the enforcing authority can show that this has not been achieved it is not unjustifiable or unfair to ask the duty holder who has either created or is in control of the risk to show that it was not reasonably practicable for him to have done more than he did to prevent or avoid it.

Before any question of reverse onus arises the prosecution must prove that the defendant owes the duty ... and that the safety standard ... has been breached. Proof of these matters is not a formality. There may be real issues about whether the defendant owes the relevant duty or whether in fact the safety standard has been breached, for example where the cause of an accident is unknown or debateable. But once the prosecution have proved these matters the defence has to be raised and established by the defendant. The defence itself is flexible because it does not restrict the way in which the defendant can show that he has done what is reasonably practicable.

… The facts relied on in support of the defence should not be difficult to prove because they will be within the knowledge of the defendant. Whether the defendant should have done more will be judged objectively.

If all the defendant had to do was raise the defence to require the prosecution to disprove it, the focus of the statutory scheme would be changed. The trial would become focused on what it was the enforcing authority was saying should have been done rather than on what the defendant had done or ought to have done which is what Parliament intended.

In complicated, and therefore potentially the most serious cases, the prosecution might face considerable difficulties in assuming this burden of proof where the only relevant expertise was with the defendant or even its state of the art supplier or licensor abroad. In such cases therefore enforcement might become impossible if the defendant only had an evidential burden.

Last but not least the defendant in cases where the reverse burden of proof applies does not face imprisonment. The offence involves failure to comply with an objective standard. The consequences of such failure may be newsworthy in some cases but the moral obloquy is not the same as that involved in truly criminal offences. …

For these reasons we think the judge reached the right conclusion in this case. The reverse legal burden of proof contained in section 40 of the Act is compatible with the ECHR. The appellant's conviction on this basis was not therefore unsafe.

This judgment is a clear demonstration of the double thinking that regulatory crime induces. It is consistent with a number of cases, such as *British Steel* (1995) and *Howe* (1999), in which the Court of Appeal has shown a much tougher attitude towards health and safety offences. Yet the argument appears to be both that these are serious offences (witness the need for regulation mentioned by Tuckey LJ) and that they are not very serious (witness the lack of the imprisonment as a possible penalty to which he later refers). As the following extracts show, this kind of reasoning has bedevilled this area of criminal regulation. Strict liability (or reverse onus offences) supply a multi-edged sword. It might make prosecution easier, but it undermines the seriousness of the offence, especially where enforcement practice is to prosecute only where fault is manifest.

David Nelken 'Criminal Law and Criminal Justice: Some Notes on Their Irrelation' in I H Dennis (ed) *Criminal Law and Justice* (Sweet & Maxwell, 1987) p 139

It is now many years since Carson showed how strict liability rules governing factory safety were enforced in such a way that the only offenders prosecuted were those who deliberately ignored repeated warnings and advice as to their breach of the rules (in addition to those prosecuted after incidents of serious injury and death). The same pattern has been shown to exist in the enforcement of laws dealing with other regulatory offences involving business and industry. Offenders against these criminal provisions therefore benefit from the reduced stigma attaching to what are seen as merely 'regulatory' or 'quasi-crimes' whilst in actuality they often may possess more than the usual requirements of intentional mens rea. Whilst not all strict liability offences are enforced in this way it is nonetheless strange to see textbooks continue to agonize over the justifications of strict liability without building on this work. The importance of law in context studies for problems of institutional design in the criminal law should not need further to be demonstrated.

But this strategy is not without its weaknesses. The division of labour between the concerns and methods of doctrinal scholarship and those who specialize in the description of the criminal process (reproduced in the distinction between 'law in books' and 'law in action') is too neat. It makes it too easy for criminal law scholars to minimize the importance of these contextual findings. They may treat them as unrepresentative or idiosyncratic reports of particular institutional settings or local practices. They may deny that there is anything problematic about any given use of law, or, even if some deviation is acknowledged, may insist that it is the nature of normative standards that they be distorted or broken without detracting from their significance. Some doctrinal scholars even give the impression that they see themselves as providing a framework which is important in its own right, as something which can appeal directly to citizens over the heads, as it were, of the legal actors (not excluding the judges!) who operate the criminal process in such a way as to confuse their counsels.

As the following passage suggests, this is not to imply that the distinction between offences of strict liability and those requiring 'mens rea' is of no practical or social importance:

Leslie Sebba, 'Is Mens Rea a Component of Perceived Offense Seriousness?' (1980) 71 Journal of Criminal Law and Criminology 124, 127–135

The first and main hypothesis of this study was that respondents will attribute greater seriousness to prohibited acts committed with a higher level of mental element than to the same acts committed with a lower level of mental element ... Yet it is indisputable that the degree of harm actually inflicted, whether or not foreseen by the offender, traditionally has played a significant role in the criminal law, and it seems probable that public attitudes to some degree, would reflect such 'objective' concepts of seriousness. Therefore, it will be hypothesized that, in addition to the significance of the mental element, the seriousness of the physical act constitutes an independent component in the judgment of offense seriousness ...

The empirical investigation reported here ... found: (i) that the form of mental element accompanying the offense, controlling for the degree of harm inflicted, has a significant effect on the estimation of offense seriousness; (ii) that where no mental element is specified in an offense definition respondents generally are attributing intentionality to the perpetrator of the offense, if it be of a traditional 'street-crime' nature, they may be attributing only recklessness or negligence where regulatory offenses are concerned ... ; and (iii) that the degree of harm inflicted, controlling for the mental element, has a significant effect on the estimation of offense seriousness ...

One further topic requires consideration: the problem of the weight to be attributed to unforeseen harm resulting from the commission of the offense. While the criminal law traditionally has inflicted heavier penalties where greater harm is caused even though such harm was not anticipated, the classical example being the felony-murder doctrine, this approach has been strongly criticized on grounds of morality and efficacy ... On the other hand, the present study indicates that the public (at least as represented by student respondents) in fact attributed seriousness weighting to resulting harm, even where unforeseen ...

The implication of studies of the measurement of offense seriousness have become acutely relevant in contemporary criminal policy in light of the trend away from rehabilitation toward a retributive justice model of sentencing, with its emphasis on proportionality between the gravity of the offense and the severity of the sentence.

The precise orientation of such a model may take different forms. In particular, in determining the gravity of the offense, emphasis may be laid either on the seriousness of the harm inflicted, following the ancient concept of 'talio', or on the moral gravity of the act, as reflected in the term 'just desert'. Insofar as this new penal philosophy is to reflect public attitudes, it seems that both these concepts have a role to play: for in determining the seriousness of a criminal offense, respondents relate to both the mental element which accompanied it and its harmful consequences.

This suggests, therefore, that the harm versus culpability equation is complex, and that how seriously we view different types of conducts cannot be addressed simply through a comparison of strict liability versus 'mens rea':

Genevra Richardson, 'Strict Liability for Regulatory Crime: the Empirical Research' [1987] Crim LR 295

Strict liability, it is claimed, provides an improper basis for the imposition of criminal sanctions since it can lead to the punishment of the 'faultless'. Such an outcome is said to be both unacceptable of itself and damaging to the criminal law. In response several arguments have been advanced. For some the demotion of fault is welcome since it signifies a move away from the punitive concept of the criminal law. Alternatively it can be argued that the strict liability regulatory offender is not a 'blameless innocent'. By indulging in the regulated activity she has voluntarily adopted the risks of regulatory infraction and her supposed 'innocence' flows from the law's traditional tendency to view the criminal act 'only in the context of its immediate past'.

Most frequently the case for strict liability in the regulatory context is put in utilitarian terms. Government regulation is required to protect the public from specific harms and the criminal sanction is frequently provided as a device for achieving compliance with such regulations. The primary role of the regulation is preventive rather than retributive and the criminal law is employed in order to deter non-compliance. In such a context, it is said, regulatory infraction is not criminal in any real sense and, provided the penalties imposed are low, strict liability is justified in so far as it furthers deterrence and aids the enforcement of the regulatory requirements.

That strict liability does in fact increase the deterrent impact of the regulations is open to question but, on the assumption that it does, some claim that the presence of strict liability also serves to deter welcome activities, the selling of meat, for example, when all reasonable steps have been taken to ensure that it is uncontaminated. The imposition of liability for negligence, it is argued, would adequately protect the public. In response it can be claimed that most regulatory offences, including those of strict liability, do in fact incorporate a notion of culpability 'akin to certain kinds of negligence'. Further, it is now widely recognised that the specialised agencies commonly entrusted with the enforcement of regulatory codes apply notions of fault when exercising their prosecutorial discretion and rarely proceed in the absence of 'negligence' at the very least. However, while this de facto introduction of fault may go some way to meeting the claim that strict liability over-prohibits, it is itself open to the charge both that it removes crucial questions of culpability from the courts and that it delegates too much to the 'uncontrolled' discretion of the enforcement agency.

Thus, the debate surrounding strict liability remains obstinately un-resolved and it might plausibly be argued that it will remain so as long as it is based on the questionable assumption that the existing fault-based principles of criminal law successfully avoid penalising the innocent. Indeed, some argue that the outcry surrounding the condemnation of the innocent by way of strict liability plays an important role in reinforcing the im-pression that the rest of the criminal law is concerned exclusively with condemning the morally blameworthy. Further it is alleged that the presence of strict liability favours the regulated since it serves to marginalise their non-compliance and to distinguish it from real crime ...

In the first place, there is evidence that enforcement personnel to some extent share the widespread belief that many regulatory offences are not real crime ...

Secondly, it is clear that, whether or not the regulatory prohibitions are part of the true criminal law, enforcement personnel are concerned with their legitimacy [The legitimacy of a regulation refers to the extent to which it appears justified and thus obligatory. It will flow not only from the substance of the regulation but also from its form and the manner of its enforcement] and that that concern extends beyond the question of blameworthiness.

... Much protective regulation creates offences which may be regarded as morally neutral in the sense that the conduct prohibited can closely resemble acceptable business practice. In such circumstances officers are concerned about the precise definition of the prohibited conduct. They are particularly influenced both by the relationship between the prohibited event and the threatened harm and by the degree of liability attaching, and will reflect in their enforcement practice any dissatisfaction they feel.

... Whether or not regulatory offences constitute 'real' crime, the majority can be readily distinguished from the mass of traditional street crime as currently regarded ...

Legislative schemes regulating corporate conduct are primarily designed to prevent particular harms and are certainly seen in that light by those responsible for their enforcement ... With regard to traditional offences the prevention of harm as the justification for criminal punishment has been severely challenged. In relation to regulatory offences, however, the argument may carry less weight. In the first place corporate offending is often regarded as less intractable than traditional criminality: the application of criminal sanctions might successfully deter, incapacitate, or even rehabilitate. Secondly, with regard to the problem of inequality of treatment, which is often linked to the preventative use of criminal sanctions, Braithwaite has argued that complete equality for regulatory offenders is beyond the scope of any criminal justice system and that the need to prevent serious harm, Thalidomide or Bhopal, for example, should take priority over strict equality of treatment. Finally, the rearrangement of a company's practices and procedures in order to ensure that it operates without causing harm is not open to the same moral objections as the coerced rearranging of a psyche.

Richardson here usefully summarises a number of strands in the debate about the regulation of business activities. However, how true is it that business crime is inherently distinguishable from the 'ordinary crime'? While the two 'types' of crime are certainly *perceived* differently, that is not quite the same as saying that they *are* different, and some people have argued that *all crime* at its margins closely resembles legitimate practice (see Box 1983).

II.b.iii.   Enforcement models

The following extract indicates that the regulatory model is part of, but distinct from, the criminal justice system as we conventionally understand it.

Jeremy Rowan-Robinson, Paul Q Watchman and C R Barker, 'Crime and Regulation' (1988) Crim LR 211

One of the characteristics of legislative development in Britain during the last century has been the enormous growth in the number of codes of regulation and the extent to which government has sought to regulate areas of social, economic and commercial activity by the creation of a plethora of criminal offences. Indeed, so rapid has been the growth of regulation that 'there is no readily available measure of the number of regulations, but these run into thousands of pages of statutes' ...

The purpose of this article is to make some assessment of the role of the criminal law as an instrument for enforcing such codes. The value of such an exercise is underlined by the distinction which is sometimes drawn between the high level of non-compliance with regulatory codes and the extremely low level of prosecution initiated by the majority of regulatory agencies. Lidstone records, to give just one example, that the wages inspectorate discovered about 40,000 offences under the Wages Council Act in 1976; but not one of these offences was prosecuted.

[T]here are two groups of factors which bear on the role of the criminal law in this field. These factors, which we refer to as 'legislative factors' and 'operational factors', are now considered in turn.

... There is no doubt that the way in which a code of regulation is framed can have a bearing on the role of the criminal law in its enforcement. This manifests itself in several ways. First of all, the point at which anti-social conduct becomes criminal varies from regulation to regulation. Unlawful conduct may, for example, be a straightforward matter of omission or commission. A person may have deposited litter on open land to which the public has access, which is prohibited. Although the use of straightforward obligations and prohibitions has been criticised for inflexibility it makes employment of the criminal law relatively straightforward.

Alternatively, and commonly, the legislature may prescribe, generally by statutory instrument, the exact level of performance which must be attained (for example, building standards) or which must not be exceeded (for example, preservatives in food). Such precise standards give clear guidance to the potentially deviant population, they make detection of offences relatively straightforward and they encourage uniformity in enforcement. On the other hand, detailed regulations may suffer from multiplicity, complexity and, on occasion, obsolescence. And they give rise to 'over-inclusion' (in the sense that an offence is committed whether the standard is breached by an infinitesimal amount or by a large amount) and 'under-inclusion' (in the sense that by specifying exactly what is required and what is not permitted, there is a risk that damaging practices or products may be left unregulated).

Because of the inherent defects of detailed rules, the legislature sometimes opts for imposing standards in more general terms. 'Unwholesome', 'best practical means', 'reasonable care' are examples. Such general standards allow for a degree of flexibility and responsiveness; their use discourages routine and mechanical prosecution and allows enforcement officers to take account of a variety of factors in deciding whether an offence has been committed; they also avoid the obvious problems of over- and under-inclusion and obsolescence which beset detailed standards. However, the use of general standards also has disadvantages. It can be difficult for traders, manufacturers, employers etc., to know with certainty whether they are complying with the law; it makes enforcement problematic and there is scope for disagreement about whether an offence has been committed; and it can result in a lack of uniformity in enforcement practice.

The second way in which the framing of the code of regulation may have a bearing on the role of the criminal law is through a requirement to establish criminal intent or mens rea ...

The third way in which the framing of the code of regulation may bear on the role of the criminal law is through the provision of alternative sanctions. For example, failure to secure regular attendance of a child at school in Scotland may be the subject of an attendance order, referral to a children's hearing, a prosecution or a combination of these. And the use of prohibition and improvement notices by the Health and Safety Executive may be regarded as an alternative to prosecution as criminal liability arises irrespective of notification of an infraction ... Finally provision in the legislation for a severe financial penalty for infringement may be taken to indicate society's marked disapproval of particular conduct ... For example, the Prevention of Oil Pollution Act 1971 introduced a maximum fine of £50,000 upon summary conviction for discharging oil into United Kingdom waters ...

... Our research confirms the findings of other research into discrete codes of regulation that the employment of the criminal law is influenced in practice, not only by the form of legislation, but also by a range of external matters ... There are numerous such factors including, for example, the perception by the regulatory agency of its functions, the level and nature of accountability of the agency, the method of discovering and detecting offences, the nature of the client group, and the availability of alternative sanctions ...

Perhaps the most important institutional pressure which structures the way in which regulatory agencies seek to attain legislative goals is the regulatory agency's own policy of enforcement ... Formal statements of enforcement policy providing an explicit 'top down' approach tend ... to be exceptional. With most agencies, enforcement policy seems to emerge from the 'bottom up'. Policy in such cases is not articulated but evolves as the sum of day to day practice ...

A further operational factor ... is the allocation of resources. As the resources of any regulatory agency are finite, it is necessary for each agency to identify priorities and to allocate resources accordingly ...

It is time to consider in more detail the different enforcement models which may be employed in responding to various kinds of offending conduct. In the next extract, which is based on a case study of road safety regulation, Friedland identifies two models of enforcement, one relying on prosecution, and the other on non-coercive methods for achieving compliance. The former, characterised by sanctioning and deterrence, has a clear symbolic role and he quotes Thurman Arnold's observation that: 'There are two very distinct problems of criminal administration: first, the keeping of order in the community; and, second, the dramatization of the moral notions of the community' (*The Symbols of Government* (1935) in Friedland 1990: 4).

M L Friedland (ed), *Securing Compliance: Seven Case Studies* (University of Toronto Press, 1990) p 165

... [M]ost of the effort to control accidents has concentrated on changing driver behaviour ... Police surveillance and prosecution have dominated control strategies. But one looks in vain for studies that compare the cost-effectiveness of policing with, for example, road maintenance or specific safety features in cars ... Nevertheless, after reviewing the traffic safety literature, our strong impression is that we have concentrated and continue to concentrate our resources too heavily on changing driver behaviour. Switching some of the resources now devoted to policing and prosecutions to improving car and road design and to curtailing activity levels of high-risk classes of drivers would, we believe, improve road safety ...

There has been a fairly uniform decrease in fatality rates in many ... countries over the years. The OECD ... notes: 'It is remarkable that this uniformity exists in spite of the diversity of legislation, governmental structures, safety programmes, and their management.'

... Personal injury and accident rates, per million kilometres driven, have fallen much less dramatically than fatality rates ... The divergence between fatalities and injuries might permit at least two explanations: first, while accident frequency has not declined, accident severity has done so, perhaps reflecting safer vehicles; second, medical science continues to make advances so that many auto-related personal injuries that would once have been fatalities are now non-terminal. Possibly both factors (safer vehicles and improved health care) are at work ...

A variety of legal interventions were used to regulate the automobile when it was introduced ... From the start, traffic regulation focused on control of driver behaviour through the threat of sanctions. The prevalence of deterrence strategies of controlling traffic can in part be explained by the automobile's introduction at about the same time as the culmination of a shift in emphasis in methods of policing. [This involved a strategic shift from compliance systems based on inspection and prevention to deterrence systems.] ... If the automobile had been introduced earlier and had not been rapidly popularised, its regulation perhaps might have followed the pattern of the regulation of ships and railways, which do not rely primarily on the deterrent effect of criminal prosecutions. If traffic safety regulation had originally been oriented toward compliance as opposed to deterrence, regulation through civil liability and insurance, licensing, informal systems of sanctions and rewards, and education might have played a larger role than they have done.

... In a traditional legal framework, much energy is devoted to isolating and punishing blameworthy behaviour, whereas in the epidemiological framework, attention is devoted to whatever source will be most effective in reducing injuries and their harmful consequences ... We accept that there will be some adaptive behaviour in drivers to safety features ...

An important factor that has brought the use of the criminal law back onto centre stage over the past decade is the increasing political activity of pressure groups concerned with victims of drunk driving and the sensitivity of politicians, police and prosecutors to these groups. This is part of a growing trend toward concern for victims of crime, coupled with a move away from rehabilitation toward 'just deserts' in criminal justice. Whereas in the 1960s collective responsibility for traffic safety was stressed through epidemiological vision, the 1980s has witnessed a resurgence of attention to the role of driving behaviour and individual responsibility for traffic accidents.

Friedland draws attention to the contingency in regulating human behaviour through the sanctioning process of police-enforced criminal laws. While concern for safety is taken as axiomatic, it is clear that regulation through criminal law is often too blunt an instrument to achieve a reduction in accident levels. Yet its appeal as a mechanism of symbolic condemnation would seem to be on the increase, despite its demonstrable ineffectiveness and costliness as an instrument in reducing accident rates.

It is particularly interesting to compare the regulatory solutions which have developed in various safety contexts. Health and safety at work, and environmental control, have tended to follow the compliance model. As Gunningham argues, this involves elements of negotiation rather than conflict or sanction.

Neil Gunningham, 'Negotiated Non-Compliance: A Case Study of Regulatory Failure' (1987) 9 Law and Policy 69

In determining what approach to take in enforcing regulation, an agency must choose between (or incorporate some mixture of) two enforcement styles or strategies: those of deterrence and compliance. The deterrence strategy emphasizes a confrontational style of enforcement and the sanctioning of rule-breaking behaviour. It assumes that those regulated are rational actors capable of responding to incentives, and that if offenders are detected with sufficient frequency and punished with sufficient severity, then they and other potential violators will be deterred from violations in the future. The deterrence strategy is accusatory and adversarial. Energy is devoted to detecting violations, establishing guilt and penalizing violators for past wrongdoing.

In contrast, a compliance strategy emphasises co-operation rather than confrontation, conciliation rather than coercion. As described by Hawkins:

> Compliance strategy seeks to prevent a harm rather than punish an evil. Its conception of enforcement centres upon the attainment of the broad aims of legislation, rather than sanctioning its breach. Recourse to the legal process here is rare, a matter of last resort, since compliance strategy is concerned with repair and results, not retribution. And for compliance to be effected, some positive accomplishment is often required, rather than simply refraining from an act. [1984: 4]

Bargaining and negotiation characterize a compliance strategy. The threat of enforcement remains, so far as possible, in the background. It is there to be employed mainly as a tactic, as a bluff, only to be actually invoked where all else fails, in extreme cases where the regulated remains uncooperative and intransigent.

These two enforcement strategies are ideal types, hypothetical constructs unlikely to be found in their pure form. They can best be regarded as polar extremes on a continuum. Any enforcement agency is likely to employ some mixture of both.

This leads us to an enduring problem in considering regulation: what role should criminal law have in relation to corporations?

II.c. Corporate liability for crime

For Carson (1982) there was little doubt that the lack of safety enforcement in the North Sea oilfields contributed to the high death and injury toll. By the middle of the 1970s the rate of accidental death in the oil industry was 11 times that for construction, nine times that for mining and six times that for quarrying. Carson's evidence suggests that the accidents arose not from the difficulties of working 'on the frontiers of technology', but from 'mundane design faults, human error and unsafe working conditions'. Not only were regulations often ignored but for five years the safety inspectors had no statutory regulations to enforce. Time and tide certainly waited for no law. The parallels with the development of factory legislation in the last century are close:

W G Carson, 'White-collar Crime and the Enforcement of Factory Legislation' (1970) 10 BJ Crim 383

In that era, as in the present, there were immutable laws of capital which rendered it 'imperative' that regulation should be minimised. Then, as now, it was constantly threatened that capital would flee if subjected to any more constraints. In the nineteenth century too, it was held that those who had no practical acquaintance with the advanced technology of an industry upon which the nation's new-found wealth depended could not possibly purport to ordain how far its labour practices should be ordered.

The reduced reliance on labour-intensive heavy industry has not led to a concomitant reduction in accident levels. The ways in which business crimes are marginalised by the legal process have already been rehearsed. The use of separate regulatory agencies enforcing separate regulatory law allows the exclusion of conventional criminal labelling and processing. This encourages the dichotomy between 'real' crime and 'quasi' crime. Another mechanism in the legal construction of business crime is the frequent use of strict liability offences. We have noted that strict liability is also used in some offences enforced by the police, such as traffic offences. But wherever it is used, the real crime/quasi crime division can be seen as either its cause or effect. Imposition of strict liability in the first place is seen as justified because the prohibited activity is not thought to be 'real crime'. At the same time, the fact that an offence has been interpreted as one of strict liability is used as evidence that the prohibited activity cannot be all that serious and therefore is not 'real crime'.

Laureen Snider, 'Towards a Political Economy of Reform, Regulation and Corporate Crime' (1987) 9 Law and Policy 37

The older established view on the nature, form, and intention of government regulation is that advanced by the consensus/pluralist school. Its adherents argue that it is the role of the polity, those who are responsible for the decision-making in the public sector … to carry out the wishes of the majority in the electorate. Policies are formulated by governments to reconcile diverse interests and prevent conflict. This may mean interfering with the power and privileges of the rich and powerful to benefit the poor and the powerless. One version of this, the public interest model, asserts that a neutral state responds to problems in the interests of all. More sophisticated pluralists do not assume that all the diverse groups are equally effective in making their voices heard, or that some groups are not more powerful or 'strategic' than others, but in general they argue that any group of people, if they feel strongly enough about an issue and if there are enough of them, can be effective. For them, then, no one group dominates the political process in a fashion that is either permanent or overwhelming.

Thus, they would expect governments, when properly alerted, to respond to the social wrongs caused by corporate crime ...

The conflict/Marxist theorists see government regulation and law creation quite differently. The instrumentalist school starts from the premise that the state exists ultimately to defend and further the interests of the ruling class, and sees government regulation as a tool which serves to preserve the (very unequal) status quo ... Laws which seem to benefit the working or lower classes, or which aim to restrict the power or privileges of the ruling class (such as those on corporate crime), will prescribe the minimum reform necessary to pacify the loudest and most disruptive interests, in order to reinforce the fiction that all citizens are protected by law from socially harmful acts (the universalistic myth) ...

The initial stage of law creation is public agitation, often accompanied by a crisis in which large numbers of people are defrauded, injured or killed. The state has historically been very reluctant to get involved. For example, Paulus details the painful progress from 1851 to 1878, of securing effective laws to give the government in Britain the power to ensure that foodstuffs offered for sale were safe. It took several wholesale poisoning episodes (including one in 1858 in which 200 people were injured and 17 died from eating adulterated lozenges) and nearly forty years before effective controls were instituted. The progression went from unsuccessful attempts at control through adverse publicity (publishing the names of offenders), to allowing local authorities to issue summonses to sellers, but requiring them still to prove the adulteration was intended, to providing inspectors, public analysts, and strict liability legislation, the stage at which the legislation became effective.

Shover tells us how small eastern and large western mine operators hysterically opposed the efforts of environmentalists in the late 1960s to restrict strip mining. Heaping scorn on the claims of consumer/environmentalist groups and promoting local rather than federal laws as adequate and desirable, they defeated initial attempts to ban strip mining, attributing environmental harm (which could not be denied) to small fly-by-night operators who had since left the business ...

Carson [1970] reviews the history of British laws on the factory from 1819 to 1853, the period during which laws were passed to limit the length of the working day, the hours of women and children, the number of breaks workers had to have, rudimentary provisions for ventilation, etc. The resistance to all these provisions was massive, as the need for cheap labour in this stage of laissez-faire capitalism was extreme. The owners felt pressed to make an ever higher return on their investment, which meant that overworking their human capital was an economically rational thing to do. Such laws also were opposed because they interposed the power of the (still rudimentary) state between the worker and the factory owner, and necessitated much internal bureaucracy for record-keeping.

Nor is such resistance restricted to the 19th century. More recent studies showed a similar resistance to the passage of effective controls over ... North Sea Oil rigs. A major disaster on December 27 1965 which killed 18 people was necessary before the state even examined the question of safety laws, and it took another six years before any were actually passed ...

[I]f the pressure for reform continues (on policy-makers, in the media, among pressure groups, etc) this blind and total resistance changes. Typically, certain segments of the industry begin to define a limited and modified version of the legislation as being in their interests ... Thus, Paulus says that by 1875, segments of the business community in Britain, particularly the more powerful businesses, were coming to see the pure food laws, in a limited form, as being in their own interests. They would increase public trust in their products, many of the increased inspection and production costs could ultimately be passed down to the consumer, and the higher costs of manufacturing might drive some of the smaller and weaker competitors out of business ...

Thus the legislative initiative typically progresses from total resistance to partial sponsorship of the laws by the most powerful segment of the target industry or group. A law is passed, usually a weaker law than its proponents wished but a stronger law than its opponents originally envisaged. Sometimes the new law is totally without teeth (a fact which promotes a Marxist conspiracy view of the process), but is gradually made stronger over the years (a fact which fortifies the pluralists).

II.c.i. The rise of corporate manslaughter

Enforcement of health and safety offences is often taken against the corporate body, for the simple reason that the 1974 Act is addressed to 'employers' and many of those are companies. One argument that emerges from the ensuing discussion is whether the harms caused by health and safety breaches should not also be prosecuted under 'conventional' criminal laws, in particular, for manslaughter. Where death or injury is caused by corporate activity, the company itself is, in theory, vulnerable to prosecution for manslaughter or for an offence against the person. But far more likely would be a prosecution for a regulatory offence. But, as we have seen, this is by no means the most likely outcome of a breach even where it has led to serious injury. A process of double marginalisation takes place, therefore. Industry crime is not brought within conventional definitions of crime (murder, manslaughter, etc) and where specific offences are drawn, such as pollution and health and safety laws, they are policed separately and set apart from 'ordinary' crime by their own system of regulation.

The creation and enforcement of regulatory schemes tends to decriminalise the harmful activities of businesses and thus of corporations. It is not always easy to say which comes first – the reluctance to use criminal law leading to specific regulation, or the existence of special regulation diverting attention from the possibility of prosecution for offences such as manslaughter, murder or assault. Either way, there is no doubt that many deaths caused by corporations could be prosecuted as potential manslaughters but that few are. However, the debate about corporate criminality in general and corporate manslaughter in particular has become considerably more focused over the last 20 years. As a result, the Health and Safety Executive belatedly published guidelines on corporate manslaughter for its inspectors (HSE Document OC 165/5, 1993). David Bergman explains:

David Bergman, 'Weak on crime – weak on the causes of crime' (1997) 147 NLJ 1652

[Until 1993, the] idea that companies could commit a crime other than a technical breach of health and safety law was just not within its legal vision. If the HSE ever referred a case to the police it was because it suspected 'horseplay' by workers or a road traffic offence. Investigations carried out by inspectors were therefore never concerned with finding evidence of gross negligence or, if they did, never resulted in anything other than a prosecution under health and safety law. [Since the guidelines were published] there have been 1452 workplace deaths but the HSE have only referred 48 of these to the police or the Crown Prosecution Service (CPS), that is a rate of 3%.

The HSE argues that the low rate simply reflects the lack of culpability on the part of the companies. There was a time when the HSE could get away with this argument – but no longer. Three years ago the West Midlands Health and Safety Advice Centre undertook its own detailed investigations into the region's 28 workplace deaths occurring between 1988 and 1992. One of the country's most senior QCs looked at the evidence and concluded that four of the deaths should have resulted in manslaughter prosecutions and another seven should have been referred to the police ... If these figures reflect what is happening in the rest of the country ... in the last five years there should have been 217 manslaughter prosecutions ...

Why do those empowered to enforce criminal law perceive it as concerned with individual actors rather than with corporations? Why are harms caused by corporate disregard for safety not conceived as criminal wrongs despite their greater impact in terms of deaths and injuries? How are certain forms of behaviour perceived? How does crime come to be perceived as such? How seriously are crimes perceived relative to each other? These questions are of vital interest to those involved in the study of criminal law. People fear crime. Their fear is often quite disproportionate to their victimisation. But what is the process that leads some events to be seen as 'criminal' and others as 'accidents'?

The criminal offences of homicide and assault conjure up a three-dimensional image. The picture contains a particular kind of injury arising from a particular range of causes, committed by a particular type of offender, involving a particular type of victim: 'Crime is not inherent in behaviour but it is a judgment made by some about the actions and characteristics of others' (Quinney 1970: 16).

Generally, it seems that corporations have been immune from such judgment, but increasingly that immunity is under threat. The sinking of the *Herald of Free Enterprise* in 1987 focused the debate in the UK. Although the prosecution of P&O for manslaughter was ultimately unsuccessful and few companies have been convicted of manslaughter, people are now familiar with the idea of corporate manslaughter: it has acquired a place in popular vocabulary; it has achieved cultural recognition.

Whatever the theoretical hurdles or practical difficulties in mounting such prosecutions, it is clear that events which earlier might have passed as ghastly accidents, or unavoidable misfortune, now attract a demand for blame, for a formal allocation of responsibility. In many cases, the focus of those campaigns is a business enterprise, and/or those in positions of managerial power within those organisations. To understand the background to this change, we need to pay attention to the cultural relativity of attitudes to risk. The cultural shift towards blaming corporations can be traced to a number of historical developments.

First, technological advance has meant greater mobility, and mass transport introduces an increased likelihood of collisions and explosions of near universal threat. The associated media transmission and publicity mean that we are more aware of the threat. A good recent example of this is the possibility of manslaughter charges being brought against airlines for failing adequately to warn of the risks of deep vein thrombosis (DVT) (*Independent*, 2 April 2003). Secondly, the way we go about attributing cause has changed. Previously, the causes and consequences of death were explained through the discourses of magic or religion. Now we are more likely to see the human hand in events. From these two major changes – different hazards, different cultural background – flow a number of connected points.

In late modern societies, more events are seen as having a human cause. This leads to the boundaries between natural and human causes being questioned. Not only are there more human-caused events as technology grows, but technology also affects the previously 'natural' – flooding is the best example here. What looks like a natural disaster is often attributable to some human industrial or agricultural activity further upstream. Then there is the illusion of control – people will take and therefore accept greater risks if they believe they are in control and if they believe the activity is voluntary (eg skiing or roller-coastering). Advanced transport systems, and industrial development mean that more and more areas of life are perceived as not within individual control and therefore blaming others becomes necessary.

Finally, pre-existing hostility is relevant. Hostility can arise from the imposition of authority in the form of institutions of government, or reliance on the expertise of groups such as scientists, or industrialists. So what has changed is not the need to attribute responsibility but the form and focus of that attribution. The more that we believe a disaster is a result of human action the more likely we are to believe it is avoidable.

However, there is a terrible paradox in all this. While individuals seek to direct blame for untoward events on to outsiders, society is engaged in the opposite direction, making individuals responsible for their own misfortunes. They have had the risk information and they have made the choices. Anthony Giddens calls this the 'privatization of risk' (1991: 111). Whereas, in earlier ages, religion led to a degree of fatalism, contemporary understanding pulls paradoxically towards an acceptance of risk but away from a tolerance of results when they occur.

It would, however, be a mistake to think that turning to the possibility of a manslaughter charge is an exclusively modern phenomenon. Cory Brothers were prosecuted in 1927 following the electrocution of an unemployed miner on an electrified fence during the coal strike of 1926; the judge held that a corporation could not be indicted for an offence against the person (*R v Cory Bros*, 1927). And, 75 years earlier, an inquest jury in Yorkshire expressed regret that a water board could not be prosecuted for manslaughter following 78 deaths when a reservoir burst (Simpson 1984: 221). Conditions were not yet in place to facilitate the translation of such expressions into a legal form. Gradually, over the course of this century, courts became more familiar with the concept of a corporate defendant. At first, this was manifested in regulatory schemes directly addressing business enterprises, such as those concerned with consumer protection, health and safety and environmental control. These introduced, as we have seen, mainly strict liability offences and companies were potentially liable whenever their employees committed the conduct element of the offence, whether it was the supply of adulterated milk, or the breach of the factories legislation. The development of liability for offences outside the regulatory sphere, and therefore for offences more likely to have a mental element, came later.

II.c.ii.   Vicarious and direct liability

A dual system of liability has developed, and corporations can be liable for criminal offences either vicariously or directly. Vicarious liability generally depends on the relevant offence being construed as one of strict liability or with a reverse-onus defence. As we have seen, most regulatory schemes use such offences, rather than require proof of 'mens rea'. In doctrinal terms, it is thus relatively easy to pursue a prosecution against a corporation for a regulatory offence. Vicarious liability means that the company is liable whenever any of its employees commits an offence in the course of their work.

Direct liability applies to traditional, 'mens rea' offences. It renders the company liable only when a director or senior officer of the company has the appropriate knowledge to satisfy the mental element of the offence. In the case of manslaughter, gross negligence will satisfy the mental element.

The circumstances in which a corporation will be liable for 'mens rea' offences were spelled out in detail by the House of Lords in the case of *Tesco v Nattrass* [1972] AC 153. Lord Reid pointed out (at 170) the difference between the two forms of liability when he said that a corporation:

> must act through living persons, though not always one and the same person. Then the person who acts is not speaking or acting for the company. He is acting as the company and his mind which directs his acts is the mind of the company. There is no question of the company being vicariously liable. He is not acting as a servant, representative, agent or delegate ... if it is a guilty mind then that guilt is the guilt of the company.

In the first piece of litigation arising from the *Herald* disaster, when various rulings by the inquest coroner were challenged, Bingham LJ explained the distinction in this way (*R v HM Coroner for East Kent*, 1987):

> A company may be vicariously liable for the negligent acts and omissions of its servants and agents, but for a company to be criminally liable for manslaughter ... it is required that the mens rea and actus reus of manslaughter should be established not against those who acted for or in the name of the company but against those who were to be identified as the embodiment of the company itself.

Only a narrow group of persons within a corporation is recognised as being identified with the company in this philosophically challenging theory, which raises questions about how we appropriately conceive a collective group such as a company – is it an aggregation, is it more than the sum of its parts, is it metaphysically separate? The controlling officers, those whose thoughts and actions are regarded as those of the company are 'the board of directors, the managing director and perhaps superior officers of a company [who] carry out the functions of the management and speak and act as the company' (Lord Reid in *Tesco v Nattrass* at 170).

In a series of cases since the 1990s, the House of Lords and the Privy Council began to move away from the narrowness of the *Tesco v Nattrass* conception of corporate liability and also applied vicarious liability to a wider range of offences (see *R v Associated Octel*, 1996; *Meridian Global Funds Management Asia Ltd v Securities Commission*, 1995). However, in relation to liability for an offence such as manslaughter, the underlying principle of direct liability, even in expanded form, has proved difficult to apply to large, diffusely managed companies. As the next two sections reveal, many people attribute the failure of the P&O prosecution to the unsuitability of the *Tesco* doctrine and as a result the Law Commission has proposed a completely separate offence of corporate killing (see **section II.c.iv.** below).

II.c.iii.   The *Herald of Free Enterprise* story

The *Herald* story can be told through a series of cases, beginning with the challenge to the coroner's ruling:

R v HM Coroner for East Kent (1987) 88 Cr App Rep 10 at 16

[*The applicants sought leave to move for judicial review by way of declaration as to the law, on the grounds that the coroner, at the inquest in October 1987, made an incorrect ruling, inter alia, that a company could not be indicted for manslaughter.*]

Bingham LJ.

The inquest arises from the capsize of the vehicle ferry 'Herald of Free Enterprise' off Zeebrugge on March 6, 1987 and the huge loss of life, both of passengers and crew, to which that tragic disaster gave rise. Nearly 200 lives were lost, causing widespread grief, and the facts of the disaster are etched not only on the recollections of all who were involved, directly or indirectly, but on the consciousness of the nation as a whole.

Very shortly after the disaster the Secretary of State for Trade ordered a formal investigation under s.55 of the Merchant Shipping Act 1970. Sheen J, sitting with assessors, was appointed to conduct it. There was a long, comprehensive and well publicized investigation culminating in a full report and recommendations published in July [1987].

The investigation found that the immediate cause of the vessel's loss was that she sailed with her bow doors open trimmed by the head, ie. with her nose down. The manoeuvre in which she engaged led to the entry of water into the vehicle deck, the heavy listing of the vessel and her speedy capsize.

Sheen J criticised a number of the individuals who had failed to perform their duty, in particular those responsible for failing to close the bow doors, failing to see that the doors were closed and sailing without knowing that the doors were closed. He expressed his criticisms in strong terms. The vessel was owned and operated by Townsend Car Ferries Limited, and that company also was the subject of severe criticism.

In para 14.1 of his report [Sheen J] said this:

At first sight the faults which led to this disaster were the aforesaid errors of omission on the part of the Master, the Chief Officer and the assistant bosun, and also the failure by Captain Kirby to issue and enforce clear orders. But a full investigation into the circumstances of the disaster leads inexorably to the conclusion that the underlying or cardinal faults lay higher up in the company.

The Board of Directors did not appreciate their responsibility for the safe management of their ships. They did not apply their minds to the question: What orders should be given for the safety of our ships? The directors did not have any proper comprehension of what their duties were. There appears to have been a lack of thought about the way in which The Herald ought to have been organised for the Dover/Zeebrugge run. All concerned in management, from the members of the Board of Directors down to the junior superintendents, were guilty of fault in that all must be regarded as sharing responsibility for the failure of management. From top to bottom the body corporate was infected with the disease of sloppiness ... The failure on the part of shore management to give proper and clear directions was a contributory cause of the disaster ...

The report then goes into very considerable detail and in the course of the present hearing three points are relied on as being particularly relevant. First, it is pointed out that the company and its representatives failed to give serious consideration to a proposal that lights should be fitted on the bridge of the vessel which would inform the Master whether the bow doors and, for that matter, the stern doors were closed or not ...

Secondly, attention is drawn to the failure of the company and its representatives to report and collate information relating to previous incidents when vessels had sailed with their doors open. It appears that there were five such incidents between October of 1983 and February of 1987. Had knowledge of these repeated incidents been appreciated it should have alerted the officers of the company to the risk of disaster, but it appears that there was no person within the company who ever knew of all the incidents.

Thirdly, attention was drawn to the lack of any proper system within the company to ensure that the vessels were operated in accordance with the highest standards of safety. It is rightly urged upon us that where the result of an unsafe system is liable to be so grave, the onus on a company to ensure safe operation is correspondingly high.

At the very end of his report, Sheen J answered the questions posed for the investigation by the Secretary of State. Question 3 was in these terms: 'Was the capsize of the "Herald of Free Enterprise" caused or contributed to by the fault of any person or persons and, if so, in what respect?'

The answer given to that question was: 'Yes, by the faults of the following', and three individuals are listed. Then:

4. Townsend Car Ferries Limited at all levels from the Board of Directors through the managers of the Marine Department down to the Junior Superintendents. As to the respects in which each of the above-named was guilty of causative fault, see report.

... [The coroner] said this:

Another potential verdict you will have to consider in due course, and perhaps most controversially, is the verdict of unlawful killing ... [A]lthough it is possible for several persons to be guilty individually of manslaughter, it is not permissible to aggregate several acts of neglect by different persons, so as to have gross negligence by a process of aggregation ...

... The learned coroner reached four conclusions. First, he expressed his opinion that there was no arguable case of manslaughter against the five named individuals. Secondly, he expressed the opinion that a company cannot in law be indicted for manslaughter. Thirdly, he ruled that there was no evidence of conduct which would found a charge of manslaughter against the company even if such a crime could be committed by a company. Fourthly, he ruled that a charge of manslaughter cannot be founded on the aggregation of individual acts which do not individually constitute gross negligence.

The case [of *R v Northern Strip Mining Company Ltd*, Glamorgan Assizes, February 1965] having been drawn to the coroner's attention ... he replied:

I am very grateful to you for drawing my attention to the case ... It is not clear whether the question of corporate liability was argued. However, as I said in my ruling ... the acts of the company would have to be those of an individual (and I should have said an individual director) who was himself guilty of unlawful killing ... Had the facts been, as in the Glamorgan Assizes case (where the instruction alleged, which had been given by the Managing Director, was to demolish a bridge starting in the middle), that the company brains had given instructions to go out to sea with the bow doors open, at full speed, when trimmed by the head, that would be a wholly different set of facts ...

The first question is whether a corporation can be indicted for manslaughter ... [W]e indicated at an early stage that we were prepared to assume for the purposes of this hearing that it could. As a result the question has not been fully argued and I have not found it necessary to reach a final conclusion. I am, however, tentatively of the opinion that on appropriate facts the mens rea required for manslaughter can be established against a corporation. I see no reason in principle why such a charge should not be established. I am therefore ... of opinion that the coroner's original ruling was wrong, and indeed I would need considerable persuasion to reach the conclusion that it was correct.

... The coroner made it clear that he was of the opinion that the evidence ... was not capable of supporting the conclusion that those who represented the directing mind and will of the company and controlled what it did had been guilty of conduct amounting to manslaughter.

I am not persuaded that this is a conclusion which is or may be wrong ... It is important to bear in mind an important distinction. A company may be vicariously liable for the negligent acts and omissions of its servants and agents, but for a company to be criminally liable for manslaughter ... requires that the mens rea and the actus reus of manslaughter should be established not against those who acted for or in the name of the company itself but against those who were to be identified as the embodiment of the company itself ... I would add that I see no sustainable case in manslaughter against the Directors who are named either.

I do not think the aggregation argument assists the applicants ... The case against a corporation can only be made by evidence properly addressed to showing guilt on the part of the corporation as such. On the main substance of his ruling I am not persuaded that the coroner erred. [Mann and Kennedy JJ agreed.]

The jury, having been instructed that there were no grounds for basing their verdict on corporate manslaughter, nevertheless returned verdicts of unlawful death. Eighteen months after the inquest, and two-and-a-half years after the capsize, P&O (which had taken over Townsend) was charged with manslaughter in respect of the deaths at Zeebrugge. Seven employees of the company, including the assistant bosun, the captain and directors, were also charged. The trials took place at the beginning of 1990. However, the trial judge concluded before the end of the prosecution evidence that there was insufficient basis for a jury to convict. Having heard evidence exclusively from employees and ex-employees of P&O, the judge was not convinced that one sufficiently senior member of the company's management could have been said to have been reckless as to the risk of the ferry's sailing with open doors.

The prosecution was nonetheless highly significant. It confirmed that a company could commit manslaughter. The judge's ruling on this point of law is found in *R v P&O European Ferries (Dover) Ltd*:

R v P&O European Ferries (Dover) Ltd (1990) 93 Cr App Rep 72

Turner J.

... Since the 19th century there has been a huge increase in the numbers and activities of corporations whether nationalised, municipal or commercial, which enter the private lives of all or most 'men and subjects' in a diversity of ways. A clear case can be made for imputing to such corporations social duties including the duty not to offend all relevant parts of the criminal law ... [O]ver the period of the last 150 years it can be seen how, first tentatively and finally confidently, the courts have been able to ascribe to corporations a 'mind' ... Once a state of mind could be effectively attributed to a corporation, all that remained was to determine the means by which that state of mind could be ascertained and imputed to a non-natural person. That done, the obstacle to the acceptance of general criminal liability of a corporation was overcome ... I find unpersuasive the argument of the company that the old definitions of homicide positively exclude the liability of a non-natural person to conviction for an offence of manslaughter.

Converting this ruling into the first successful corporate manslaughter conviction in England and Wales in 1994 was made easier by a coincidental change in the law of manslaughter (see **section IV.c.** below). But OLL Ltd's conviction for the manslaughter of three children in a sea canoeing trip underlined the limitations of the *Tesco* doctrine of direct liability (*Kite and others*, 1994). Effectively a one-man company, it was not difficult to 'identify' the company with the actions or omissions of the managing director. The Southall rail crash in 1997 became the next high-profile corporate manslaughter case. A Great Western train en route from Swansea to London ran through red lights and collided with a goods unit on the last leg of its journey, while the driver was allegedly packing his bag ready for arrival at Paddington. GWT's procedures had allowed a high-speed train with a malfunctioning Automatic Warning System to be driven by one person. The new Automatic Train Protection system was not in use because this particular driver had not been trained to operate it. Seven passengers were killed. The company pleaded guilty to a charge under s 3(1) of the Health and Safety at Work Act 1974. The evidence disclosed that the company encouraged drivers to depart on time even if safety devices were not working. The company was fined a record £1.5 million pounds for what was described by the trial judge as 'a serious fault of senior management'. But the manslaughter prosecution proved to be much more difficult.

As described earlier the courts had begun to broaden its approach to corporate liability. The first stage was the sidelining of the *Tesco v Nattrass* identification doctrine in relation to some regulatory offences. Secondly, the Privy Council laid the foundations for a broader conception of the 'directing mind' in offences still subject to the identification rules (*Meridian Global Management*, 1995). The prosecution sought to exploit these changes arguing that it was unnecessary to pursue an individual director of GWT. Instead, the company's liability should be established by proving that the company's *management policies* had resulted in the failure to have a proper warning system which led directly to the crash. This attempt to forge a route to liability independent of an individual director's negligence was rejected by the trial judge, who ruled that a non-human defendant could only be convicted via the guilt of a human being with whom it could be identified. It was a condition precedent to a conviction for manslaughter by gross negligence for a guilty (human) mind to be proved. The case therefore collapsed. The Attorney-General referred the question to the Court of Appeal for a ruling on whether this was correct. This would not have affected the outcome in this particular case but would have clarified the law.

Attorney-General's Reference (No 2 of 1999) [2000] QB 796

Rose LJ.

The court's opinion is sought in relation to two questions referred by the Attorney-General under section 36 of the Criminal Justice Act 1972. (1) Can a defendant be properly convicted of manslaughter by gross negligence in the absence of evidence as to that defendant's state of mind? (2) Can a non-human defendant be convicted of the crime of manslaughter by gross negligence in the absence of evidence establishing the guilt of an identified human individual for the same crime?

The case for the prosecution was that the cause of the collision was, first, the driver's failure to see or heed the double yellow and single yellow signals warning of impending red and, secondly, the defendant's manner of operating the H.S.T. The case against the defendant was that it owed a duty to take reasonable care for the safety of its passengers, of which it was in grossly negligent breach. Three signals were passed because the A.W.S. and A.T.P. were switched off and there was only one man in the cab. The defendant should not have permitted such a train to operate in such circumstances.

[Q]uestion 1 must be answered "Yes." Although there may be cases where the defendant's state of mind is relevant to the jury's consideration when assessing the grossness and criminality of his conduct, evidence of his state of mind is not a prerequisite to a conviction for manslaughter by gross negligence. ...

... There is, as it seems to us, no sound basis for suggesting that, by their recent decisions, the courts have started a process of moving from identification to personal liability as a basis for corporate liability for manslaughter ... [C]orporate liability was not mentioned anywhere in the submissions of counsel or their Lordship's speeches in *Adomako*]. In any event, the identification principle is in our judgment just as relevant to the actus reus as to mens rea. In *Tesco v Nattrass* Lord Reid said:

> "the judge must direct the jury that if they find certain facts proved then as a matter of law they must find that the criminal act of the officer, servant or agent including his state of mind, intention, knowledge or belief is the act of the company."
>
> ...

In our judgment, unless an identified individual's conduct, characterisable as gross criminal negligence, can be attributed to the company, the company is not, in the present state of the common law, liable for manslaughter.

...

This approach is entirely consonant with the Law Commission's analysis of the present state of the law and the terms of their proposals for reform in their report on Legislating the Criminal Code: Involuntary Manslaughter (Law Com. No. 237). ... We agree with the [trial] judge that the Law Commission have not missed the point and ... the identification principle remains the only basis in common law for corporate liability for gross negligence manslaughter.

It follows that, in our opinion, the answer to question 2 is "No."

In July 2003, charges of manslaughter were brought against Railtrack's successors, Network Rail, contractors Balfour Beatty and a number of senior executives of each company, in relation to the Hatfield train crash in which four people died in 2001 (*The Guardian*, 8 July 2003). The case alleges that senior managers in both companies had known for nine months that a broken rail needed to be replaced. As we saw earlier (section **II.a.ii**), Balfour Beatty already has a poor safety record having been fined a record penalty of £1.5 million for health and safety offences during construction of the Heathrow Express line in 1994. The prosecution in that case claimed that this 'raises many issues from which lessons need to be learned. The level of the fines sends a clear message to all in the industry, including clients, designers, consultants, contractors and subcontractors that they must ensure the safety of the public and workers'. But a month later the same company was fined £500,000 after a derailment of a goods train in 1997. At the time this was the highest ever for a railway accident and it was eclipsed only when GWT were fined £1.5 million after Southall (an accident that incidentally occurred a few days after the derailment). Whether any lessons were learned must remain a moot point.

II.c.iv.   Corporate killing – the new offence

The Law Commission's Report on Involuntary Manslaughter recommended that a separate offence of corporate killing should be introduced, in addition to those offences committable by individuals (Report 237, 1996).

Shortly after the Southall rail crash in 1997, in which seven passengers died, the Government announced its intention to legislate the Law Commission's proposed offence. The consultation paper was not however published until May 2000; this coincided with the failure of the manslaughter charges against Great Western Trains (see **section II.c.iii.** above). The Paddington (Ladbroke Grove) crash in October 1999, in which 31 people died, served as an additional reminder that the promise to legislate had not been fulfilled. A draft Bill is promised in late 2003.

The Commission believed that the new offence would overcome the difficulties in securing a conviction in cases similar to that of P&O.

Home Office, *Reforming the Law of Involuntary Manslaughter: The Government's Proposals: Involuntary Homicide Bill 2000* (HMSO, 2000)

Clause 4
(1) A corporation is guilty of corporate killing if–
   (a) a management failure by the corporation is the cause or one of the causes of a person's death; and
   (b) that failure constitutes conduct falling far below what can reasonably be expected of the corporation in the circumstances.
(2) For the purposes of subsection (1) above–
   (a) There is a management failure by the company if the way in which its activities are managed or organised fails to ensure the health and safety of persons employed in or affected by those activities; and
   (b) Such a failure may be regarded as a cause of a person's death notwithstanding that the immediate cause is the act or omission of an individual.

The key element here is that culpability rests in the concept of 'management' rather than deriving from the failings of individual directors. The draft Bill goes on to specify that 'such failure may be regarded as a cause of a person's death notwithstanding that the immediate cause is the act or omission of an individual'. How would this new test for corporate liability assist in a case such as that brought against P&O? The key difficulty in the P&O trial, states the report, was that:

> There was insufficient prosecution evidence to justify a finding that the risk of the vessel putting to sea with her bow doors open was "obvious" to a "hypothetically prudent master or mariner or whosoever would have perceived it as obvious and serious".

It would appear from this passage that the source of the difficulty was the culpability test for *manslaughter* as it applied to corporations rather than the *identification* rule of corporate liability itself. (It should be noted, incidentally, that the culpability test for manslaughter, based on the *Caldwell/Lawrence* definition of recklessness, which applied at the time of the trial was replaced by 'gross negligence': *Adomako*, 1995, **section IV.c.** below.)

The Law Commission Report quoted Turner J's reason for bringing the trial to a halt before the end of the prosecution's case. Evidence had been heard from P&O's own employees that no one had thought that there might be a risk of the ferry sailing with an open door. Discussing the yet-to-be-heard evidence from non-P&O mariners, the judge said this:

> I do not understand that the statements of any of these witnesses condescend to criticism of the system employed by the defendants in this

case as one which created an obvious and serious risk, *except to the extent that any legitimate deduction may be made from the fact that they took precautions other than those employed by any of these defendants.* [Emphasis added.]

The Law Commission accepted the conventional wisdom that this was a convincing reason for abandoning the trial and that a different route to corporate liability based on 'management failure' would overcome this. The report argued that, if the P&O case occurred again:

it would probably be open to a jury to conclude that, even if the immediate cause of the deaths was the conduct of the assistant bosun, the Chief Officer or both, another of the causes was the failure of the company to devise a safe system for the operation of the ferries; and that that failure fell far below what could reasonably have been expected.

Can that claim be reconciled, however, with the earlier assertion that the P&O trial was bound to fail because there was no obvious and serious risk perceptible to a prudent master that the ferry might sail with its doors open? Are these not two different ways of putting the same question? We can either say 'the company's failure to provide a safe system fell far below what was reasonably expected' or 'the company [ie the directors] failed to realise that there was an obvious risk that a ship might sail with its doors open'. If the risk were not obvious, as the judge concluded, why should we expect the company to devise a safe system to prevent it? It is the judge's conclusion which is perplexing: long before the trial, the Sheen inquiry had concluded that all concerned in the company's management shared responsibility for the failure in their safety system.

Another question left unclear by these recommendations is the relationship between the liability of a corporation itself and of individuals within it. Should it be either or, or both? Some of the relatives of those who drowned at Zeebrugge were concerned at the time of the inquest that the blame should not be borne by the officers who operated the ship but by the company who managed both them and the ship. But the experience of the Health and Safety Executive suggests that corporate liability allows companies to evade rather than to take responsibility.

How do we reconcile these two arguments – that corporations should be pursued more often, and that, where they are prosecuted, the individual directors generally escape responsibility? The answer lies partly in the nature of the offences concerned and partly in differentiating between directors and more lowly employees. The relatives at Zeebrugge did not want ship-level operatives to take the blame for management failure, while the Health and Safety Executive is concerned that management does not hide behind the corporation which, as the 'employer' is the most obvious defendant in prosecutions under the 1974 Act. The niceties of corporate versus individual responsibility may not have mattered to the Zeebrugge relatives so long as the right individuals were pursued.

While corporations may commit any of the three offences proposed by the Law Commission (reckless killing, killing by gross carelessness and corporate killing), individuals are not liable for prosecution as secondary parties to the new offence of corporate killing. The assumption that the liability of individuals would be more appropriately dealt with via the two general offences ignores the vagaries of prosecution policy. It does not seem very likely that a prosecutor will pursue, in relation to any one corporate incident, the corporation under one offence, and also proceed against individual directors or others under another. Similarly, even where there is evidence to bring the corporation under the individual offences on the identification route (which would automatically bring to attention individual culpability of senior company officers as well), we might expect most prosecutors to be led to the custom-made offence of corporate killing. In other words, despite the potential areas of overlap, both individual directors and corporations may benefit as a result of the introduction of the separate corporate offence. A strategy of extending corporate liability generally, by adding a third route based on an organisational or systems model, such as that contained in the Australian Criminal Code Act 1995 would overcome this particular objection. The Act legislates general principles of criminal responsibility and the section dealing with corporate liability provides that for offences of intention, knowledge or recklessness 'that fault element must be attributed to a body corporate that expressly, tacitly or impliedly authorised or permitted the commission of the offence' (Criminal Code Act 1995 (Cth), s 12.3). Authorisation or permission can be shown in one of three ways – the first echoes the *Tesco v Nattrass* version of identification liability, and the second extends the net wider to 'high managerial agents'. It is the third which represents a clear endorsement of an organisational or systems model, based on the idea of 'corporate culture'. This is defined in much more detail than is the Commission's 'management failure' provision. 'Corporate culture' can be found in an attitude, policy, rule, course of conduct or practice within the corporate body generally or in the part of the body corporate where the offence occurred. Evidence may be led that the company's unwritten rules tacitly authorised non-compliance or failed to create a culture of compliance. The President of the Australian Law Reform Commission summarises the proposals thus (Rose 1995):

> This approach quite clearly seeks to address the significant criticisms of the 1972 *Tesco* decision, which restricted corporate criminal liability to the conduct or fault of high-level managers or a delegate with full discretion to act independently of in-house instructions, an approach ironically appropriate to the small and medium-sized business, with which large national and multi-national corporation [sic] have almost nothing in common.

It is important to realise, however, that this covers only Commonwealth (federal) offences. Homicide law is a matter for the individual states and they continue to follow the identification rule.

FURTHER READING

Box, Steven (1983) *Power, Crime and Mystification* (Tavistock).

Carson, W G (1979) 'The Conventionalization of Early Factory Crime' 1 International Journal of Sociology of Law 37–60.

Cunningham, Sally (2001) 'The Reality of Vehicular Homicides: Convictions for Murder, Manslaughter and Causing Death by Dangerous Driving' Crim LR 679.

Gobert, James and Punch, Maurice (2003) *Rethinking Corporate Crime* (Butterworths).

Gunningham, Neil and Johnstone, Richard (1999) *Regulating Workplace Safety: Systems and Sanctions* (OUP).

Hawkins, Keith (2002) *Law as Last Resort: Prosecution Decision-Making in a Regulatory Agency* (OUP).

Nelken, David (2002) 'White-Collar Crime' in Maguire et al *Oxford Handbook of Criminology* (Oxford University Press) 844.

Shute, Stephen (1999) 'Who Passes Unduly Lenient Sentences? A Survey of Attorney-General's Reference Cases, 1989–97' Crim LR 603.

Sullivan, G R (1996) 'The Attribution of Culpability to Limited Companies' CLJ 515.

Wells, Celia (2001) *Corporations and Criminal Responsibility* (Clarendon Press).

III. Homicide

In the remainder of this chapter we concentrate on criminal laws which directly address those who cause death unlawfully. We have already examined many of the areas of legal regulation which touch upon and help to construct the broader social meaning of violence. In **Chapters 2** and **3** we saw how public order laws invoke a wide conception of violence, and how they interact with non-fatal offences against the person. In **Chapter 5** we looked at sexual violence in the context of personal autonomy. This chapter has built up a picture from many facets, ranging from domestic violence to safety on the roads and at work. In relation to each, what might otherwise be regarded as examples of unlawful violence are subjected to systems of enforcement and, in the case of road traffic and workplace deaths, a system of substantive law, which runs parallel with that of traditional homicide offences. Even when we turn to unlawful homicide, this process of construction continues, as can be seen when medical practitioners make decisions not to treat or to withdraw treatment. Before turning to the law of homicide, a basic question needs to be asked – is killing wrong?

III.a.   Is killing wrong?

Many people would claim that the principle of sanctity of life is absolute. Sorell, below, gives a general introduction to some of the difficulties of holding such a position (cf Dworkin 1993, quoted in **Chapter 5.V.a.**). The question of the morality of deliberate killing infuses all aspects of the law of homicide, although it is perhaps found in its starkest form in relation to capital punishment. Although this was restricted by the Homicide Act 1957 and abolished in 1965, and replaced by the mandatory life sentence, the desirability of its reintroduction is voiced regularly in political debate (see **section IV.a.** below). Moral responses to killing clearly affect both the borderline between murder, which carries the mandatory penalty, and manslaughter, which does not, and help demarcate those killings which are regarded as unlawful and those which are not. Moral reactions also influence the different legal responses to what might be seen as similar phenomena. Why, for example, is poisoning someone by breaking a domestic gas pipe charged as homicide, while poisoning by the unlawful emission of industrial fumes is charged as a regulatory offence (see **section II.b.** above)? Why is killing a baby sometimes seen as a particularly abhorrent murder and at other times as 'passive killing' and even good medical practice?

George Orwell, 'Decline of the English Murder' in *The Collected Essays, Journalism and Letters of George Orwell* Vol IV (Penguin, 1970) p 124

Our great period in murder, our Elizabethan period, so to speak, seems to have been roughly between 1850 and 1925 ... It is difficult to believe that any recent English crime will be remembered so long and so intimately [as the notorious murders of that period], and not only because the violence of external events has made murder seem unimportant, but because the prevalent type of crime seems to be changing ... [O]ne can construct what would be, from a News of the World reader's point of view, the 'perfect' murder. The murderer would be a little man of the professional class – a solicitor or a dentist, say – living an intensely respectable life somewhere in the suburbs, and preferably in a semi-detached house, which will allow the neighbours to hear suspicious sounds through the wall. He should be either chairman of the local Conservative Party branch, or a leading Non-conformist and strong Temperance advocate. He should go astray through cherishing a guilty passion for his secretary or the wife of a rival professional man, and should only bring himself to the point of murder after long and terrible wrestles with his conscience. Having decided on murder, he should plan it all with the utmost cunning, and only slip up over some tiny, unforeseeable detail. The means chosen should, of course, be poison.

To contrast with the paradigm of murder so aptly captured by Orwell, the following extracts point to the difficulty of placing boundaries around 'right' and 'wrong' violence and killing:

Tom Sorell, *Moral Theory and Capital Punishment* (Blackwell, 1987) pp 1–3

If the loss of human life is always unfortunate, must it not be more than unfortunate – evil – for human life to be taken deliberately? It is often thought to be evil. Yet is it so evil that it must be avoided at all costs? If so, then suicide must be avoided at all costs. Euthanasia and capital punishment must be avoided at all costs. Abortion, war, and the assassination of a Hitler or an Amin must be avoided at all costs. The sweeping consequences of an absolute prohibition may make us think twice. Is it true that one must avoid taking human life no matter what? Or may there, in certain circumstances, be good reasons for killing that make it morally permissible in spite of what is otherwise wrong with taking human life?

These questions have more than theoretical interest, because many people have experience of situations in which taking life seems a real, even a reasonable, option. Unwanted pregnancies are not uncommon, and the fact that a pregnancy is unwanted gives a reason, though perhaps not a decisive reason, for having an abortion. Wars and military adventures are not uncommon. When they are in a cause people can agree to be good, the cause seems to justify the taking of life. People who lack direct experience of unwanted pregnancy or military service in wartime can often imagine themselves in such situations, and can confront vicariously the questions they raise. And they can put themselves in other circumstances calling for life and death decisions as well. For example, many generally stable people suffer depressions that make suicide thinkable, however occasionally or fleetingly.

Again, many people have jobs that can lead them to consider either taking life or doing nothing to prevent it ending. Nurses, police officers, doctors, lawyers and judges may be attracted in theory to the idea that killing is never right and yet they may be faced with situations that seem to demand or permit the taking of human life, situations that require them to act. Since it is important for people to be able to justify to themselves and to other people what they are prepared to do, and since standards of justification are likely to be particularly exacting when lives are in the balance, it should matter particularly to people in law or medicine or allied fields whether taking life is always or only sometimes wrong. It should also matter to the rest of us who have to be able to justify to ourselves and to other people what we are prepared to stand back and see done. Everyone, it seems, has a stake in the question of whether killing people is always wrong. So much for the question. The answer appears to be that it is not always wrong, that the prohibition on killing people has exceptions. Take, for example, killing in self-defence, or killing in a case where not to do so would mean a lingering, painful death for someone whose life cannot be saved anyway. These cases seem to tell against an absolute prohibition.

They seem to show that taking human life is not always but perhaps only usually wrong. But if killing people is permissible in some cases but not in others, which cases are which? Is it possible to qualify the principle that killing people is always wrong and still be left with a principle that tells us when it is wrong?

If we are looking for a single qualified principle to take the place of an absolute prohibition on killing, one that is merely the conjunction of a lot of different principles, then we are likely to be in for a disappointment. This is because different exceptions to the absolute prohibition recommend themselves for different reasons, which a revised principle cannot unify all at once. For example, killing a dying person who is in unrelievable agony may be permissible, because the quality of the rest of his life may be so bad as to make him better off dead. Killing in self-defence may be all right, because in doing so one is reacting against the evil of a life-threatening attack, not just saving one's own skin at the expense of someone else's. These grounds for allowable killing are not easy to put together. Consequently, it may be unreasonable to hope for a principle that says simply and directly when killing is permitted and when it is not. It may be that general moral guidance about allowable killing must take the form of a plurality of principles.

The ethics of killing arose again in the case of conjoined twins, Mary and Jodie. Mary lacked heart and lung function and relied on a common artery by which Jodie's heart and lungs were able to keep her alive. Without treatment both would die, whilst an operation to separate would kill Mary but probably save Jodie. After the parents refused to 'choose' between the two and consent to separation, preferring instead to leave it to 'the will of God', the hospital sought a declaration that the procedure could be lawfully performed. The declaration was granted and the parents' appeal placed the court 'on the horns of such a terrible dilemma', reflected by its decision to allow written submissions by the Archbishop of Westminster and the Pro-Life Alliance. The conclusion that separation amounted to the murder of Mary called for some creative analysis of defences to homicide, notably self-defence and necessity (see below at **section IV.** and above at **Chapter 4.II.f.**). For now, it is worth reflecting on how the court confronted the conflict between its decision to allow separation and the sanctity of life.

Re A (children) (conjoined twins: surgical separation) [2000] 4 All ER 961, 1016–7

Lord Justice Ward.

What are the doctors to do if the law imposes upon them a duty which they cannot perform without being in breach of Mary's right to life if at the same time the respecting of her right puts them in breach of the equally serious duty of respecting Jodie's right to life? A resort to a sanctity of life argument does not enable both rights to receive the equal protection the doctrine is supposed to provide each of them equally. In those circumstances it seems to me that the law must allow an escape through choosing the lesser of the two evils. The law cannot say, 'heads I win, tails you lose'. Faced as they are with an apparently irreconcilable conflict, the doctors should be in no different position from that in which the court itself was placed in the performance of its duty to give paramount consideration to the welfare of each child. The doctors must be given the same freedom of choice as the court has given itself and the doctors must make that choice along the same lines as the court has done, giving the sanctity of life principle its place in the balancing exercise that has to be undertaken. The respect the law must have for the right to life of each must go in the scales and weigh equally but other factors have to go in the scales as well. For the same reasons that led to my concluding that consent should be given to operate so the conclusion has to be that the carrying out of the operation will be justified as the lesser evil and no unlawful act would be committed.

I should emphasise that the doctors do not cease to owe Mary a duty of care; they must continue to furnish such treatment and nursing care as may be appropriate to ensure that she suffers the least pain and distress and retains the greatest dignity until her life comes to an end.

The second reason why the right of choice should be given to the doctors is that the proposed operation would not in any event offend the sanctity of life principle. That principle may be expressed in different ways but they all amount to the same thing. Some might say that it demands that each life is to be protected from *unjust attack*. Some might say as the joint statement by the Anglican and Roman Catholic bishops did in the aftermath of the *Bland* judgment that because human life is a gift from God to be preserved and cherished, the deliberate taking of human life is pro-hibited *except in self-defence or the legitimate defence of others*. The Archbishop defines it in terms that human life is sacred, that is inviolable, so that one should never aim to cause an *innocent* person's death by act or omission. I have added the emphases. The reality here – harsh as it is to state it, and unnatural as it is that it should be happening – is that Mary is killing Jodie. That is the effect of the incontrovertible medical evidence and it is common ground in the case. Mary uses Jodie's heart and lungs to receive and use Jodie's oxygenated blood. This will cause Jodie's heart to fail and cause Jodie's death as surely as a slow drip of poison. How can it be just that Jodie should be required to tolerate that state of affairs? One does not need to label Mary with the American terminology which would paint her to be 'an unjust aggressor', which I feel is wholly inappropriate language for the sad and helpless position in which Mary finds herself. I have no difficulty in agreeing that this unique happening cannot be said to be unlawful

The Court of Appeal concluded that separation represented the least detrimental option, and would be lawful. Although manoeuvring around homicide with reference to the different justifications of self-defence (Ward LJ), necessity (Brooke LJ) and to recourse to the doctrine of double effect and best interests (Walker LJ), the Court of Appeal were united in arriving at the conclusion that they were not setting any kind of precedent. However, to what extent is such a conclusion supportable?

Richard Huxtable, 'Logical Separation? Conjoined twins, Slippery Slopes and Resource Allocation' (2001) Journal of Social Welfare and Family Law 23(4) 459, at 460–461

Ward LJ is most emphatic ... that *Re A* does not set a precedent. Formulating the 'unique circumstances' into a narrow *ratio*, he reiterates, 'this is a very unique case'. Quite simply, as law students are instructed early in their studies, English law apparently does not operate in the manner that Ward suggests. It is doubtful whether there can exist degrees of uniqueness. Certainly, the facts of the case were uncommon and unprecedented ... however, having issued its ruling, the Court of Appeal must have set a precedent available to other judges in, for example, cases analogous to the present 'unique' case.

This contention is bolstered by mere reference to the declaratory nature of the proceedings. Legally problematic, the declaration purportedly involves a statement of the existing, applicable legal principles. We might, of course, question whether this is truth involves 'creating' rather than 'stating' law. But if we take the party line, the Court of Appeal ought to concede that the principles utilized were 'out there' ... [and] must be available in other cases.

Medical lawyers are familiar with at least one other attempt at minimization, in *Airedale NHS Trust v Bland* [1993] 2 WLR 316. But that case must have set a precedent: the court of appeal in *Re A* noted that *Bland* was 'binding on this court and accordingly cited the Lords' opinion on, for example, the sanctity of life doctrine. Although the court might not like the fact, *Re A*, like *Bland*, must have set a precedent beyond its facts, on points of principle ... Centrally, the reasoning relating to the sanctity of life, a patient's 'best interests' and the defences to murder might have potentially wide ramifications.

The status of *Re A* as a precedent has already been confirmed by the Supreme Court of Queensland in *Nolan* [2001] QSC 174 (see Grubb 2002). In authorising the procedure, the court relied on the troubling minority reasoning of Walker LJ that separation would be in each of the twin's best interests, in not depriving the weaker twin of her bodily integrity. Huxtable further suggests that, in allowing the active and intentional killing of Mary, the decision is radically inconsistent with the sanctity principle. To what extent does it also logically point to the proposition that Y may be actively killed in order that X might benefit from resources devoted to Y? Similar trends evident in the 'passive killings' that follow from medical decisions not to treat may lend further support to this.

III.b. Medical non-treatment

Medical practices in relation to the non-treatment of neonates (ie newly born infants), and the extent to which doctors can use pain-killing drugs to hasten death, illustrate the general point that systems of control and regulation, even over matters as crucial as life and death, are determined by social and professional mores as much as by criminal law. In particular, they indicate the difficulties in perceiving questions of this kind pathologically either in terms of the 'actor' or in terms of the 'victim'. The fact that the decision to resuscitate a handicapped neonate is an individual one, for both the medical staff and the parents, involves a double delegation. It also signifies an unwillingness on the part of the legal system, here represented by criminal enforcement processes, to determine the legality of certain areas of medical management. The *Bland* case exposes the uneasy alliance between law and medicine (see below, and also **Chapter 5.V.**). The medical profession's traditional reluctance to give guidelines as to the appropriate criteria to apply tended to leave many of the questions to the individual practitioner. The 'doctor's dilemma' is gradually giving way to professional guidelines which reflect, but more often lead, the legal response in these areas. We take first the example of the non-treatment of neonates.

Infanticide has acquired, in legal discourse at any rate, a specific and limited meaning; it is something which unbalanced mothers do. The construction of female criminality as the product of madness, as well as madness and irrationality themselves being seen as peculiarly female, are topics which we explore further in **section IV.**

The medicalisation of pregnancy and childbirth has led to a re-ordering of the respective roles of women and professionals in making decisions about survival of new-born infants.

Jacques Donzelot, *The Policing of Families* (Hutchinson, 1980) p 19

Up to the middle of the eighteenth century, medicine took little interest in children and women. Considered simply as reproducing machines, women had their own medicine, scorned by the School of Medicine and forming a tradition whose trace remains in the expression 'old wives' remedies'. Child-birth, the maladies of women giving birth, and children's illnesses were the responsibility of the 'old wives', a corporation that was on the same footing as the servants and nursemaids who partook of its knowledge and put it into practice. The conquest of this market by the medical profession therefore implied the destruction of the dominant influence of the old wives, a long struggle against their practices, which were deemed worthless and pernicious. The main points of confrontation were, of course, maternal breast-feeding and the clothing of children. The works of the eighteenth and nineteenth centuries repeat the same praises of maternal nursing, lavish the same pieces of advice on the choice of a good nursemaid, and tirelessly denounce the practice of swaddling babies and the use of corsets ... [W]ith the mother's help, the doctor prevailed against the stubborn hegemony of that popular medicine of the old wives; and on the other hand, owing to the increased importance of maternal functions, he conceded a new power to the bourgeois woman in the domestic sphere. It became evident as early as the end of the eighteenth century that this alliance was capable of shaking paternal authority. In 1875, the Academy of Berlin offered the following questions for competitive discussion: (1) In a state of nature, what are the foundations and limits of paternal authority? (2) Is there a difference between the rights of the mother and those of the father? (3) To what degree can the laws extend or restrict this authority? Among the award winning replies, that of Peuchet, the author of the *Encyclopedie methodique*, took a position clearly in favour of a revaluation of the powers of the mother: 'If the grounds for the power that parents hold with respect to their children during their age of weakness and ignorance reside for the most part in the obligation they are under to attend to the welfare and preservation of these fragile beings, there is no question that the extent of this power grows in proportion to the duties one has to fulfill in their behalf. Owing to her position as mother, nurse and protectress, the woman is prescribed duties that are unknown to men, and consequently she has a more positive right to obedience. The best reason for asserting that the mother has a more genuine right to the submission of her children is that she has the greater need of it.'

By augmenting the civil authority of the mother, the doctor furnished her with a social status. It was this promotion of the woman as mother, educator, and medical auxiliary that was to serve as a point of support for the main feminist currents of the nineteenth century.

Medicalisation has taken over the sphere marked out as within the control of women as experts in managing pregnancy and childbirth: here we shift from the image of the woman in labour assisted by professional midwives, to the 'special baby care unit', to high technology 'saving' ever-more premature and low-birthweight babies. This has, in fact, been a two-stage process. Where once it was the woman herself to whom the medical profession needed to pay most attention, the significant reduction in the risks of dying in childbirth has led to more focus on the survival of low-birthweight or handicapped neonates. The development of infant paediatrics, exploiting the developments in life-saving and life-maintaining technologies, began to give rise to a number of troubling questions. Once kept alive, are there circumstances in which it is legitimate to let go of a low-birthweight baby, and if so, how does this affect the contours of unlawful homicide? These are debates at the edges of life, at the edges of ethics and at the edges of law. Yet, as Weir explains below, these questions are not in essence new ones. What has changed are the forms in which they arise resulting from developments in medical technology, and the medicalisation of pregnancy and childbirth:

Robert F Weir, *Selective Nontreatment of Handicapped Newborns: Moral Dilemmas in Neonatal Medicine* (Oxford University Press, 1985) pp 3, 12, 20 [used by permission of Oxford University Press, Inc]

The contemporary practice of selective non-treatment of handicapped newborns is, in many aspects, a continuation of historical practices of infanticide. The settings and circumstances vary from historical patterns, but infant deaths brought about in neonatal intensive care units often provide parallels to acts of infanticide in earlier times and places. Although dealing with life-and-death decisions in a sophisticated technological context that earlier generations could not have imagined, current debates about selective non-treatment retrace familiar ground when they focus on the attitudes of parents toward anomalous newborns, the rights and limits of parental discretion, the appropriate roles of physicians in neonatal cases, the proper function of the law in cases of infant homicides, and the morality of terminating the lives of some infants with serious congenital anomalies ...

To modern minds the word 'infanticide' suggests an easily performed, despicable act of killing once tolerated by developing societies but rarely practised in the contemporary world. In many respects this general understanding of infanticide is correct. Infanticide has traditionally been an easy act of killing to perform, given the obviously helpless condition of infants and small children when the destructive impulses of adults turned in their direction. Infanticide has also been tolerated by the great majority if not all of the world's societies, for reasons ranging from the need of population control in times of scarcity to the sheer inability of governments to prevent parents from killing their defenceless babies. Moreover, infanticide has come to be regarded, given modern perspectives on the value of children, as a homicidal act bordering on the unthinkable. Yet the practice persists and, in the age of neonatal medicine, takes on new forms ...

A second general feature of infanticide is the diversity of means used to bring about the deaths of young children ... Children have been killed through starvation, drowning, strangulation, burning, smothering (often by 'accidental' overlaying in the parent's bed), poisoning, exposure, and a variety of lethal weapons. With the advances of medical technology and the establishment of NICUs over the years since the early 1960s, new means of killing neonates – or at least hastening their dying – can be added to the list: lethal injections, overdoses of sedatives, and 'accidental' coughs or sneezes over neonates highly susceptible to infection.

A third general feature of the practice of infanticide is that, as with abortion, governments have often displayed considerable uncertainty in dealing with it. Is the killing of infants by their parents to be legally acceptable and possibly even promoted for eugenic reasons, or are such homicidal acts to be legally prohibited and the killers actively prosecuted and punished? In earlier centuries many governments appear to have been indifferent toward infanticide, and some of them (e.g., Sparta in Ancient Greece) even required the killing of weak and deformed infants. Since the Enlightenment, virtually all governments in developed societies have moved toward the current consensus on infanticide: regard it as an illegal act, but have uncertain punishment for those who actually commit the crime ...

Tribal societies in various parts of the world have practised infanticide for centuries. The ancient Hebrews, for instance, accepted the killing of firstborn children as religious offerings and signs of religious obedience, as suggested by the biblical story of Abraham and Isaac (Genesis 22) ...

The customs of some tribal groups regarding the destruction of infants have changed only in the modern era. The Eskimos have only in recent years begun to move away from their traditional practice of setting infants out on the ice to freeze whenever the father or tribal elder decided that the tribe could not support them ...

In addition to these traditional tribal practices, major civilizations have permitted and sometimes encouraged the destruction of infants thought to have little value. In the ancient cultures of China and India, such infants have generally been females. For the Chinese, whose traditional culture was largely shaped by the Confucian tradition, female infanticide was not only a means of controlling population growth but also a way of reflecting their belief in the basic inferiority of females ...

India's version of female infanticide has traditionally served other purposes in addition to population control. The practice of offering female infants (and occasionally firstborn males) as a sacrifice to the gods was widely accepted among some Hindus until the nineteenth century. For other Hindus, the destruction of female infants was merely an easy way of lessening a family's liabilities ...

England was no exception to the infanticidal practices common to Europe in the eighteenth century ... Victims of parental destruction traditionally were neonates, bastards, and/or infants thought to be defective in some manner. As in other European countries, some of the anomalous infants were believed to be 'changelings'. English parents tried to rid themselves of these children as soon as possible, lest they be regarded as accomplices of the devil. Physically deformed and mentally retarded infants were also regarded as subhuman parasites who, if fed, sucked 'whitened blood' (milk) from the mother's breasts at every feeding ...

Although all kinds of children have been killed by their parents, most victims of infanticide have been singled out in a selective manner. In virtually every society, the chances of an infant's surviving to experience adolescence and adulthood have been significantly improved when the infant was male, legitimate according to societal standards, a member of the racial and religious majority, several weeks or months (or even years) old, and apparently normal according to physical appearance and mental performance.

Donzelot and Weir thus provide a useful reminder that ideas about child-rearing roles and the practice of infanticide have both historical continuity and cultural specificity.

Many people seem unaware of the extent to which non-treatment is, or has been until recently, practised in neonatal intensive-care units. It is only in the last 30 years that the implications of the increased production of damaged children for contemporary practices in neonatal care have begun to be discussed openly, even in medical journals. What has emerged since two paediatricians broke 'the public and professional silence on a major social taboo' (Duff and Campbell 1973) is much less diversity of approach between different hospitals or on international comparisons than might have been expected. There are dissentient voices, of course, both within and between hospitals, but the main impression is that the most forceful opposition to non-treatment comes from those who have the least contact with neonatal units. Two dilemmas face paediatricians in neonatal units: whether to use high-technology life-support machines to prolong the lives of infants with profound neurological or other physical abnormalities, and whether to resuscitate extremely low-birthweight babies. A report from the Hammersmith Hospital suggested that non-treatment was considered for 75 cases over a four-year period. In 68% the medical staff agreed that there was either no chance of a meaningful life or near certainty of death. The parents agreed in 92% of these to withdrawal of treatment (Whitelaw 1986). These acute dilemmas arise in only a tiny proportion of live births; babies born at 27 weeks' gestation or earlier represent 0.05% of live births, genetic disorders occur in less than 5% of live births and chromosomal disorders in less than 0.5%. The mortality rate for extremely premature babies of under 25 weeks' gestation and weighing less than 1000 grams can be as high as 90%, with or without intensive care. Babies who manage between 1000 and 1500 grams at birth benefit in terms of lower mortality rates from intensive intervention but not in terms of morbidity.

The non-treatment of neonates has infrequently attracted criminal law attention, although increasingly civil courts are asked to determine the lawfulness of proposed non-treatment decisions (Kennedy and Grubb 2000: 2155). The perceived moral distinction between killing and letting die was relied upon in the trial of Dr Leonard Arthur, one of the few occasions when non-treatment has been considered a matter for criminal law:

J C Smith and M J Gunn, '*Arthur*'s Case and the Right to Life of a Down's Syndrome Child' [1985] Crim LR 705

John Pearson was born suffering from Down's syndrome at 7.55 a.m. on Saturday, June 28, 1980. He died at 5.10 a.m. on Monday, July 1, 1980. Dr Leonard Arthur, a highly respected consultant paediatrician, was charged with the murder of John Pearson and, after a trial at which the charge was reduced to attempted murder, acquitted ... Since it resulted in an acquittal and there was no reference by the Attorney-General [under s 36 of the Criminal Justice Act 1972] there was no authoritative ruling by an appeal court ... When John Pearson was born it was immediately recognised that he was suffering from Down's syndrome. When the mother was informed she rejected the baby. Dr Arthur saw her and her husband for the first time at noon. There was a discussion as to whether or not the mother should keep the child. As a result of that discussion Dr Arthur wrote in the case notes, 'Parents do not wish the baby to survive. Nursing care only.' He entered on the treatment chart a prescription for a drug, dihydrocodeine (DF 118), to be given 'as required' in doses of 5mg at four-hourly intervals by the nurse in charge. The baby died 57 and a quarter hours after birth, the cause of death being stated to be broncho-pneumonia as a result of Down's syndrome ...

At the trial before Farquharson J ... it was alleged by the prosecution, on the basis of the evidence of the pathologist, Dr Usher, that the cause of death was lung stasis produced by DF 118 poisoning; and that the poisoning was the result of a decision by Dr Arthur to cause the death of the child.

Doubt was cast on the evidence of Dr Usher by Professor Emery for the defence who established that the child was suffering from certain defects before birth. Since the child may have died of these inherent defects and not as a result of anything done after his birth, Farquharson J. directed that the murder charge be dropped and replaced by one of attempted murder ... The judge treated the distinction between act and omission as crucial. It was for the jury to say whether ' ... there was an act properly so-called on the part of Dr Arthur, as distinct from simply allowing the child to die.'

The distinction between actively killing the child and 'allowing nature to take its course' is constantly stressed. Thus if a doctor were to give a severely handicapped child a drug in such an excessive amount as to cause its death it would be open to the jury to decide that he was guilty of murder.

'However serious the case may be; however much the disadvantage of a mongol, indeed any other handicapped child, no doctor has the right to kill it.' On the other hand the judge advised the jury, no-one could say that a surgeon was committing an act of murder by declining to operate on a mongol child with duodenal atresia [a condition readily corrected by surgery] and so allowing the child to die.

The distinction between acts and omissions is of course well established in the law of homicide. There is no general duty to take any steps to preserve the life of others. It is equally well established, however, that certain persons do owe such a duty and these include the parents of the child and the doctor who has undertaken its care ...

The duty which everyone has not to kill another by any act is the same whether that other be an abnormal child or anyone else. The duty to do acts to preserve the life of a child is owed by only a limited class of persons. It appears that the duty owed by this limited class of persons to an abnormal newly-born child is different from and of a lower order than that owed to a normal child. This was certainly assumed in *Arthur*, and at least in part, appears to be supported by *Re B (a minor)* (1981). The parents in that case were informed that the child would die if she did not have an operation to remove an intestinal blockage. They refused their consent to the operation. The child was made a ward of court and the judge, Ewbank J., directed that the operation be carried out. The surgeon who was to do the operation declined when he learned of the parental objection. The matter was referred back to the judge who concluded that the wishes of the parents should be respected and revoked that part of his order authorising surgery. The Court of Appeal allowed an appeal, holding that it was in the child's best interests that the operation should take place.

Though the court decided that Baby B. should undergo the operation, Dunn L.J. said that the decision of the parents to allow the child to die was one which everyone accepted as 'entirely responsible.' It is difficult to suppose that a decision in which a judge of the High Court is willing to concur, and which the Court of Appeal think to be entirely responsible, is a decision to commit murder. The conclusion seems to be that the parents have a discretion in the matter ... The decision in *Re B* related to that particular operation on that particular child. Templeman L.J. recognised that 'There may be cases, I know not, of severe proved damage where the future is so uncertain that the court may be driven to a different conclusion.' He contemplates the possibility that the court itself might say: Do not operate. Let the child die ...

On the facts as they appeared to Dr Arthur at the time of his decision and, indeed, up to the time of the child's death, John Pearson's circumstances were, if anything, better than Baby B.'s. If those responsible for Baby B. owed a duty to keep her alive, there must have been at least an equal duty on those responsible for John Pearson. Probably, however, *Re B* decided no more than that, on the facts of the case, the parents did have a discretion to decide whether the child should live. If the parents decided that the child should live, steps would have to be taken to preserve the life of the child. The court, in loco parentis, had so decided.

The acquittal may have been attributable to the conflict in evidence on whether 'nursing care only' would be interpreted as an instruction not to feed, or because of jury sympathy with a respected doctor as to whose motives no question was raised. The trial judge distinguished between murder and the 'setting of conditions' in which death is allowed to occur. The line between murder and the proper practice of medicine appeared to depend on something akin to the distinction between act and omission. The examples which the judge used in *Arthur*'s case allowed that neither an omission to treat a Down's syndrome baby with an intestinal obstruction nor the failure to give antibiotics to a handicapped baby with pneumonia would be said by a jury to be murder. But to give pain-killing drugs to a baby who was not otherwise going to die might be so regarded.

Reliance on acts and omissions, as a moral determinant, was exposed as a 'distinction without a difference' in *Re A* (2000) (Ward LJ at 1015) and prior to this in the landmark case of *Airedale NHS Trust v Bland* (1993), which took the debate beyond neonates to adults (see **Chapter 1.II.a.**). Nor can the raw application of principles of legal causation and responsibility help in making the fine moral distinctions which medical treatment decisions demand. Thus, although legal texts expound the view that any acceleration of death is sufficient for causation in homicide, subject to a doctor's freedom to give pain-killing drugs where necessary, its application to medical treatment is of singularly little help. Nor is it only medical decisions involving painkillers for the terminally ill which challenge the capacity of the principles of the law of murder to make adequate moral differentiations. If that law does not protect a handicapped baby who 'providentially' develops pneumonia, then there is no reason why it should protect that same baby from being actively killed (painlessly). It makes little sense for a less handicapped baby to 'be allowed to die' while enforcing the continued existence of one with severe handicaps who fails to attract the intervention of providence. If the jury in Arthur's trial thought pain-killing drugs had been given in lethal amounts with intent to cause death, it was open to them to convict of attempted murder. The moral distinction needs to be based on something less crude.

One approach asks whether there are any relevant features distinguishing a new-born baby from other persons, such that conduct which would be regarded as unacceptable in relation to the latter is not so regarded in relation to the former. This involves rejecting the 'sanctity of life' doctrine as a reason for disapproving all non-treatment. The principle of absolute sanctity of life ignores the fact that the concept of life is an historical event, an object of economic and political decision-making. So, if all human life is not of equal worth, what criteria can be used to distinguish those lives which are deserving of the protection of life support (in its broadest sense) and those which are not?

The concept of personhood may be useful here. But at what stage does an embryo or foetus become a person? We have seen in **Chapter 5.IV.a.** how law begins to answer this question in relation to abortion. Some writers suggest that personhood is arrived at after 12 weeks' gestation, others not until a baby is three months old. These are both based on physiological arguments about the acquisition of capacities such as the capacity to feel pain through to the capacity to have a knowledge of oneself. Aside from the physiological there is also the social concept of personhood – the point at which a neonate shifts from being of biological to social significance. It may be justifiable to distinguish in some circumstances between a being which has the capacity to be aware of self and one that does not. How does this avoid the legitimation of the indiscriminate killing of all neonates? The answer there is that the potential of a baby for reaching personhood should not be compromised unless there are other pressing reasons. One of those might be used in an argument for abortion, which is the right of the mother on whom the baby is dependent for existence. Another might be the desire to avoid pain and suffering – a quality of life argument. This can be used to justify the practice of non-treatment. Neonates are non-autonomous beings. This both allows their killing but also introduces reasons for their greater protection. Their killing is justifiable because they do not have an awareness of self, but only where their prognosis is such that their lives are going to be severely restricted mentally or physically or through pain.

Kuhse and Singer (1985: 172) argue that:

> Decisions about severely handicapped infants should not be based on the idea that all life is of equal value, nor on any other version of the principle of the sanctity of human life ... There is therefore no obligation to do everything possible to keep severely handicapped infants alive in all possible circumstances. Instead, decisions to keep them alive – or not to do so – should take account of the interests of the infant, the family, the "next child", and the community as a whole.

An opinion poll at the time of the *Arthur* trial revealed that four-fifths of the respondents believed that doctors should not be guilty of murder in such circumstances, a view both reflected in the jury's verdict and in the developing jurisprudence in relation to withdrawal of treatment in cases such as *Re B* (1981) and *Re J* (1990). The passive killing of terminally ill children through withholding treatment has also been held to be compatible with the right to life under Article 2 of the European Convention on Human Rights (*A NHS Trust v D*, 2000).

The Royal College of Paediatrics has issued guidelines as to the circumstances when non-treatment or withdrawal of treatment to children (not just neonates) might be considered (1997). The guidelines suggest that withdrawal or withholding of treatment might be considered in the following situations: Where:

(a) the child is brain dead (see the following section on definitions of death);

(b) the child is in persistent vegetative state (PVS);

(c) the child has such severe disease that life sustaining treatment simply delays deaths without significant alleviation of suffering (the 'No Chance Situation');

(d) the degree of physical or mental impairment which would accompany survival is unreasonable (the 'No Purpose Situation');

(e) the child and/or family felt that further treatment in the face of progressive and irreversible illness cannot be borne (the 'Unbearable Situation') (Irwin and Glasson 1997).

In the US, by contrast, these kind of questions have been out in the open for much longer and the legislative tendency is towards accounting for decisions not to treat rather than setting out the circumstances when withdrawal or non-treatment is appropriate. Under amendments to the federal Child Abuse Prevention and Treatment Act, which came into force in 1984, states have been required to develop procedures for responding to reports of cases of 'medically indicated treatment' being withheld. Such treatment is indicated unless: (i) the infant is irreversibly comatose; or (ii) it would merely prolong dying; or (iii) where it would not be effective in correcting all of the infant's life-threatening conditions.

The right-to-life tenor of these rules is qualified only by the final provision that treatment is not mandatory where it would be virtually futile in terms of the survival of the infant, and the treatment itself under such circumstances would be inhumane.

This brings us to the next question – how does criminal law mediate relations between terminally ill adults and their medical or other helpers? (This has been addressed as an issue relating to autonomy in **Chapter 5.V.**, which dealt with the situation where the patient positively requests death-hastening treatment, or requests the withdrawal of treatment.)

In the same way that non-treatment of neonates is practised in a legal vacuum, so also the acceleration of death through the medical administration of pain-killing drugs lies in something of a no-man's land. What happens where doctors take this decision themselves and administer pain-relieving drugs in doses which will surely kill? Dr Adams was tried on a specimen charge of murder in 1957 after, it was alleged, a number of his wealthy, elderly patients had died shortly after altering their wills in his favour. He was acquitted. There are both similarities and differences between the cases of Dr Arthur and Dr Adams. These cases are both unusual, in that prosecutions of doctors in relation to their medical practice are rare (although less so than they were). The reasons for the prosecutions were very different. That against Dr Arthur was brought because there was concern amongst members of the LIFE organisation about the general practice of non-treatment. Dr Adams, on the other hand, was suspected of hastening the deaths of his elderly patients through the administration of dependence-producing painkillers in order the sooner to relieve them of their money. Adams regarded what he was doing as 'easing the passing':

> Easing the passing of a dying person is not all that wicked. She wanted to die. That cannot be murder. It is impossible to accuse a doctor [Dr Adams in 'conversation' with Detective-Superintendent Hannam, quoted by Devlin 1985: 7].

Adams was tried before Mr Justice (later Lord) Devlin, who later wrote about the trial:

Patrick Devlin, *Easing the Passing* (Bodley Head, © Timothy and Matthew Devlin Trustees 1985) pp 171–172

[All punctuation in the original. The inverted commas surround direct quotations from the summing-up. The rest of the passage is Devlin's paraphrase.]

Murder is the cutting short of life, whether by years, months or weeks. It does not matter that Mrs Morrell's days were numbered. 'But that does not mean that a doctor who is aiding the sick and the dying has to calculate in minutes or even in hours, and perhaps not in days and weeks, the effect upon a patient's life of the medicines which he administers or else be in peril of a charge of murder. If the first purpose of medicine, the restoration of health, can no longer be achieved, there is still much for a doctor to do, and he is entitled to do all that is proper and necessary to relieve pain and suffering, even if the measure he takes may incidentally shorten life.' This is not because there is a special defence for medical men [sic] but because no act is murder which does not cause death. We are not dealing here with the philosophical or technical cause, but with the commonsense cause. The cause of death is the illness or the injury, 'and the proper medical treatment that is administered and that has an incidental effect on determining the exact moment of death is not the cause of death in any sensible use of the term. But ... no doctor, nor any man, has the right deliberately to cut the thread of life.' It is not contended by the defence that Dr Adams had any right to make that determination.

As contemporary accounts of the trial indicate, the prosecution case was not very strongly presented. If Adams had been convicted it would have been because his motive rather than his deeds were doubted. Yet, as we show in the discussion of murder and manslaughter below, the significance of motive is consistently denied by criminal law. The *Adams* case therefore has dual interest. It confirms, by its very unusualness, the reluctance of the processes of criminal law to regulate the activities of doctors and it casts doubt on the irrelevance of motive asserted by criminal law doctrine.

The following is a case which straddles those of *Arthur* and *Adams*. Cox gave an admittedly lethal dose of a painkiller to his patient and was convicted of attempted murder. There had been a distinct shift in attitudes in the 30 years since Adams's trial: while doctors themselves were no longer practically immune from criticism, faith in modern medicine had probably increased.

R v Cox (1992) 12 BMLR 38, Winchester CC

Ognall J.

... If it is proved that Dr Cox injected [the victim] with potassium chloride in circumstances which make you sure that by that act he intended to kill her, then he is guilty of the offence of attempted murder ... [F]rom the earliest stage, it has been admitted that he did indeed inject her intravenously with two ampoules of undiluted potassium chloride ... Is it proved that in giving that injection Dr Cox intended thereby to kill his patient? ... We all appreciate ... that some medical treatment, whether of a positive, therapeutic character or solely of an analgesic kind, by which I mean designed solely to alleviate pain and suffering, carries with it a serious risk to the health or even the life of the patient. Doctors ... have to make up their minds as to whether the risk, even to the life of their patient ... is or is not medically justified. Of course, if a doctor genuinely believes that a certain course is beneficial to his patient ... even though he recognises that that course carries with it a risk to life, he is fully entitled, nonetheless, to pursue it. If sadly, and in those circumstances the patient dies, nobody could possibly suggest that ... the doctor was guilty of murder or attempted murder ... And the problem ... is particularly acute in the case of those who are terminally ill and in considerable pain, if not agony. Such was the case [here]. It was plainly Dr Cox's duty to do all that was medically possible to alleviate her pain and suffering even if the course adopted carried with it an obvious risk that as a side effect ... of that treatment her death would be rendered likely or even certain ... what can never be lawful is the use of drugs with the primary purpose of hastening the moment of death.

This approach was confirmed when the House of Lords considered the case of Anthony Bland (*Airedale NHS Trust v Bland*, 1993 – see **Chapter 5.V.**). The case was different in a number of respects. It concerned a person who was neither competent nor were his prior wishes known. The question to be determined was the lawfulness of withdrawal of treatment in order to hasten death, not with the giving of treatment for that purpose. It was an action for judicial review, not a trial. The case makes important statements about many issues connected with medical treatment but the core issue was the status of a person in persistent vegetative state (PVS). The procedure on withdrawal which the House of Lords approved applies only to a person in such a state and thus, on one analysis, their Lordships have redefined the 'person' to whom the protection of homicide laws apply (see **section III.e.** below). Although *Bland* deals only with the highly specific case of a person in PVS, it nonetheless represents a hugely significant step in the development of homicide law. Causing death in the circumstances specified in *Bland*, that is through withdrawal of treatment to a person in PVS, is rendered lawful.

This creates an exception or qualification to the law of murder. As we will see, the offence of murder is committed when a person (unlawfully) causes the death of another with intention to do so (or to cause grievous bodily harm). Doctors are under a duty to their patients such that, in the normal course of events, an omission to treat will be as culpable as a positive act to kill. In respect of a person satisfying the conditions laid down in *Bland*, that duty is removed. However, it would still be murder if the doctors actively killed him with an injection – see *Cox*, and *Adams* above. Other examples of lawful killing would be killing in self-defence, in the prevention of crime or under the principle of necessity. In *Re A (Conjoined Twins)* (2000) the Court of Appeal utilised these defences in creating another qualification to murder, albeit denying that they were setting any precedent (see **sections III.a.** above and **IV.e.** below). *Bland* also acknowledges changes in the medical definition of death, to which we now turn.

III.c.   Definitions of death

One of the questions which has to be confronted in homicide is when is a person to be regarded as *dead*: if a person is to be accused of causing the death of another, we have to know when life departed and death began. In the past, death was a simple state to identify – the person would stop breathing or her heart would stop beating. Advances in our understanding of biochemistry and physiology, and advances in medical techniques and technology have called these simple definitions into question. With developments in resuscitation and life support it is now possible to keep the heart and respiratory functions going even when there is little likelihood of an individual recovering consciousness. In open heart surgery, conversely, there is deliberate cardiac arrest. Resuscitation following spontaneous cardiac arrest is also commonplace.

In addition to the traditional acceptance of cardio-respiratory death, the medical profession agrees that 'brain stem death' (irreversible loss of brain function) constitutes an alternative criterion of the end of life. Brain stem death was endorsed by the House of Lords in *Bland*. In the words of Lord Keith:

Anthony Bland has for over three years been in the condition known as persistent vegetative state … It arises from the destruction, through prolonged deprivation of oxygen, of the cerebral cortex, which has resolved into a watery mass. The cortex is that part of the brain which is the seat of cognitive function and sensory capacity. Anthony Bland cannot see, hear or feel anything. He cannot communicate in any way. The consciousness which is the central feature of individual personality has departed forever. On the other hand the brain stem, which controls the reflexive functions of the body, in particular heartbeat, breathing and digestion, continues to operate. In the eyes of the medical world and of the law a person is not clinically dead so long as the brain stem retains its function.

III.d.   Causing death

Before a person can be found guilty of murder or manslaughter it must be shown that they *caused* the death of the victim. Many factors contribute to an event, and since death is inevitable for all of us, law has to decide which causal factors are of relevance. Generally, proof of factual causation is straightforward – the defendant need have done no more than contribute to the death by her actions (or omission where she is under a duty to act). Legal causation will not always follow from this. If the connection between the defendant's contribution and the death is in some way too remote, then causation may not be established. The old 'year and a day' rule was an example of a rigid, and therefore certain, cut-off point which provided that no prosecution for homicide could be brought if more than a year and a day elapsed between the injury causing the death and the death itself. The Law Reform (Year and a Day Rule) Act 1996 abolished the rule (s 1). The Act also provides that proceedings brought more than three years after the initial injury or where a person has already been convicted of an offence committed in circumstances connected with the offence (for example, an offence of causing grievous bodily harm) can only be brought with the consent of the Attorney-General (s 2). The rule had begun to make little sense in the face of modern medical techniques and knowledge. Victims of serious woundings might well be maintained for more than a year and tracing the cause of death to the original wounding might be less of a challenge.

James Fitzjames Stephen, *A History of the Criminal Law of England* (Burt Franklin NY, 1973; text reprint of 1883 edition) Ch XXVI

In order that a man may be killed by an act the connection between the act and the death must be direct and distinct, and though not necessarily immediate it must not be too remote. These conditions are not fulfilled (1) if the nature of the connection between the act and the death is in itself obscure, or (2) if it is obscured by the action of concurrent causes, or (3) if the connection is broken by the intervention of subsequent causes, or (4) if the interval of time between the death and the act which causes it is too long. Whether in particular cases these conditions are or are not fulfilled is always a question of degree dependent on the circumstances. The principle may be illustrated in a variety of ways but no precise and completely definite statement of it can be made.

Killing by an act which causes death in a common well recognised way either immediately or after an interval of time insufficient to disguise or complicate the connection between the cause and effect is the typical and normal case ...

The wrongful intervention of a third party may break the chain of causation. Once again, medical practice dominates the development of legal doctrine. Medical treatment is not always competent. When should incompetent treatment be regarded as 'taking over' as the cause of death? One argument would be that a defendant who put the victim in need of medical treatment should be liable, however bad that treatment turned out to be. This would be consistent with the principle that 'you take your victim as you find her'. However, as the case below demonstrates, a less rigorous principle applies in relation to poor medical treatment, albeit one that gives little hope to defendants who have placed their victims at the peril of the medical profession.

R v Cheshire [1991] 3 All ER 670

[*The appellant was convicted of murder. During an altercation in a fish and chip shop, C fired at the deceased, wounding him in the leg and stomach. One bullet entered the deceased's thigh and a second entered his stomach. After about six weeks' hospital treatment he began to show improvement. However, during his time in intensive care the deceased suffered lung congestion problems.*]

Beldam LJ.

... On 8 February he again complained of difficulty in breathing ... Whilst in intensive care the deceased had on several occasions shown signs of anxiety and a tentative diagnosis was made that the intermittent problem with his breathing of which he complained after 8 February was due to attacks of anxiety. He was seen by several doctors of differing experience during the ensuing week. Later, on the evening of 14 February, he complained of further difficulty with breathing and was attended by a house surgeon ... She was worried about the deceased's condition ... The deceased's condition deteriorated and the medical registrar was called. Urgent resuscitation, including cardiac massage, was given but the deceased died shortly after midnight.

At post-mortem it was found that the deceased's windpipe had become obstructed due to narrowing near the site of the tracheotomy scar. Such a condition is a rare but not unknown complication of intubation of the windpipe. The deceased's windpipe had become so narrowed that even a small amount of mucus could block it and cause asphyxiation.

The experienced pathologist who conducted the post-mortem gave evidence that the immediate cause of death was cardio-respiratory arrest –

due to a condition which was produced as a result of treatment to provide an artificial airway in the treatment of gunshot wounds of the abdomen and leg.

And he said:

In other words, I give as the cause of death cardio-respiratory arrest due to gunshot wounds of the abdomen and leg.

For the appellant it was conceded that the sequence of events which had led to the deceased's death was that described by the pathologist but a consultant surgeon, Mr. Eadie, gave it as his opinion that by 8 February 1988 the wounds of the thigh and the abdomen no longer threatened the life of the deceased and his chances of survival were good.

One question for the jury at trial therefore was whether the Crown had proved, so that they were sure, that the shots fired by the appellant had caused the deceased's death.

In this appeal it has been argued that the judge misdirected the jury on this issue. The appellant complains of a passage in which the judge said:

… [I]f the treatment could have been better, if it is no more than that, then the bullets caused the death, even if the treatment was incompetent, negligent. The bullets caused the death. For you to find that the chain was broken, the medical treatment or lack of medical treatment must be reckless … Mere carelessness or mere negligence are not recklessness. Reckless conduct is where somebody could not care less. He acts or he fails to act careless of the consequences, careless of the comfort and safety of another person … You are looking for recklessness.

In this paragraph it is said that the judge virtually withdrew from the jury consideration of the doctor's failure to diagnose the deceased's clinical condition as the cause of his death because no juror would be likely to accept that a doctor treating a patient was reckless in the sense that he could not care less whether the patient lived or died …

In the criminal law, and in particular in the law of homicide, whether the death of a deceased was the result of the accused's criminal act is a question of fact for the jury, but it is a question of fact to be decided in accordance with legal principles explained to the jury by the judge. We think the matter cannot be better put than it was by Robert Goff LJ in *R v Pagett* (1983) Cr App R 279 at 288, where he said:

In cases of homicide, it is rarely necessary to give the jury any direction on causation as such. Of course, a necessary ingredient of the crimes of murder and manslaughter is that the accused has by his act caused the victim's death. But how the victim came by his death is usually not in dispute. What is in dispute is more likely to be some other matter: for example, the identity of the person who committed the act which indisputably caused the victim's death or whether the accused had the necessary intent; or whether the accused acted in self-defence, or was provoked. Even where it is necessary to direct the jury's minds to the question of causation, it is usually enough to direct them simply that in law the accused's act need not be the sole cause, or even the main cause, of the victim's death, it being enough that his act contributed significantly to that result. It is right to observe in passing, however, that even this simple direction is a direction of law relating to causation, on the basis of which the jury are bound to act in concluding whether the prosecution has established, as a matter of fact, that the accused's act did in this sense cause the victim's death. Occasionally, however, a specific issue of causation may arise. One such case is where, although an act of the accused constitutes a causa sine qua non of (or necessary condition for) the death of the victim, nevertheless the intervention of a third person may be regarded as the sole cause of the victim's death, thereby relieving the accused of criminal responsibility. Such intervention, if it has an effect, has often been described by lawyers as a novus actus interveniens. We are aware that this time-honoured Latin term has been the subject of criticism. We are also aware that attempts have been made to translate it into English; though no simple translation has proved satisfactory, really because the Latin term has become a term of art which conveys to lawyers the crucial feature that there has not merely been an intervening act of another person, but that that act was so independent of the act of the accused that it should be regarded in law as the cause of the victim's death, to the exclusion of the act of the accused. At the risk of scholarly criticism, we shall for the purposes of this judgment continue to use the Latin term.

[There are] difficulties in formulating and explaining a general concept of causation but what we think does emerge from [the] cases is that when the victim of a criminal attack is treated for wounds or injuries by doctors or other medical staff attempting to repair the harm done, it will only be in the most extraordinary and unusual case that such treatment can be said to be so independent of the acts of the accused that it could be regarded in law as the cause of the victim's death to the exclusion of the accused's acts.

Where the law requires proof of the relationship between an act and its consequences as an element of responsibility, a simple and sufficient explanation of the basis of such a relationship has proved notoriously elusive.

In a case in which the jury have to consider whether negligence in the treatment of injuries inflicted by the accused was the cause of death we think it is sufficient for the judge to tell the jury that they must be satisfied that the Crown have proved that the acts of the accused caused the death of the deceased, adding that the accused's acts need not be the sole cause or even the main cause of death, it being sufficient that his acts contributed significantly to that result. Even though negligence in the treatment of the victim was the immediate cause of his death, the jury should not regard it as excluding the responsibility of the accused unless the negligent treatment was so independent of his acts, and in itself so potent in causing death, that they regard the contribution made by his acts as insignificant.

It is not the function of the jury to evaluate competing causes or to choose which is dominant provided they are satisfied that the accused's acts can fairly be said to have made a significant contribution to the victim's death. We think the word 'significant' conveys the necessary substance of a contribution made to the death which is more than negligible.

Although for reasons we have stated we think that the judge erred when he invited the jury to consider the degree of fault in the medical treatment rather than its consequences, we consider that no miscarriage of justice has actually occurred. Even if more experienced doctors than those who attended the deceased would have recognised the rare complication in time to have prevented the deceased's death, that complication was a direct consequence of the appellant's acts, which remained a significant cause of his death. We cannot conceive that, on the evidence given, any jury would have found otherwise.

Accordingly, we dismiss the appeal.

Cheshire is consistent with the relatively tough stance taken when the victim contributes to her own demise. This can be at the time of the death-causing injury – for example, where the victim takes evasive action in fleeing from an attack and injures herself in the process. Only a 'daft' reaction – one beyond the foreseeable range of consequences – would break the chain of causation (*Corbett*, 1996). It is not clear how daftness is to be measured, whether in relation to the gravity of the actual attack, or in relation to the risks of the evasive action. Jumping out of a moving car to escape unwanted sexual attention was not regarded as daft or unforeseeable in *Roberts* (1971). Once the injury has been inflicted, it seems that the victim can act as 'irrationally' as she likes without the chain of causation being broken. Where the victim chooses to forgo treatment that would save her life (for example, a Jehovah's Witness refusing a blood transfusion), the defendant has been held responsible for the death (*Blaue*, 1975); or where victims contribute in other ways to their failure to recover, this will not avail the defendant (*Dear*, 1996).

Questions of causation also arise in the context of deaths following drug abuse. In *Cato* (1976), a conviction for unlawful act manslaughter was upheld after Cato had consensually injected the deceased with morphine. This was taken a stage further in *Kennedy* (1999) where the Court of Appeal held that the victim's self-injection constituted an unlawful act, and the defendant's assistance and encouragement amounted to aiding and abetting the offence. The criticism of *Kennedy* (Smith 1999) appears to have been heeded in *Dias* below where the Court of Appeal quashed a manslaughter conviction on the basis that since there was no offence of injecting oneself with a prohibited drug, there could be no secondary liability. Nevertheless, it recognised that a jury may be directed that supplying heroin could constitute a dangerous act causing death, although the chain of causation is likely to be broken where the deceased has volunarily taken the drug (see **section IV.c.** below). Prompted by the government's criminal justice White Paper (2001c), the Law Commission has returned to work on codification of general principles, including causation.

R v Dias [2001] EWCA Crim 2986

Lord Justice Keene.

This appeal raises a short but important point about the offence of manslaughter by an unlawful and dangerous act. ... [T]he appellant was convicted by a majority verdict of ten to two of manslaughter, for which he was sentenced to three years' imprisonment. ...

The facts of the case are not complicated or, sadly, uncommon. On 27 August 2000, Edward Escott died as a result of an injection of heroin. The only person with him was the appellant. They were both vagrants. They did not know each other well, but in July and August of that year they were living in, or associated with, a night shelter at Northampton. Mr Escott regularly abused drugs. Drugs other than heroin were found in his body, as was alcohol. However, although he smoked heroin, no one had seen him inject it. The appellant was a heroin addict who did inject the drug. The appellant did not give evidence at trial. When interviewed by the police he had said that he and Escott had agreed to put £5 each into a kitty. The appellant then contacted his dealer and bought a £10 bag of heroin. He and Escott then found a suitable place on the stairway of a block of flats. Using his own "kit", the appellant prepared the heroin injection by putting the powder into a spoon, adding the citric acid and water, heating it up and drawing it into the syringe. He then handed the syringe to Escott. Escott removed the belt from his own trousers, used it as a tourniquet and injected the heroin into himself. The appellant washed the syringe and injected the heroin into himself. By the time the appellant had recovered from the effects of the heroin, Escott was dying. The appellant arranged for a passer-by to call an ambulance and then left the scene. Escott was taken to hospital but died.

The prosecution did not originally accept this version of events. They argued that there was evidence from which it could properly be inferred that the appellant had injected Escott. However, the judge took the view that that was not sufficiently supported by the evidence and would be "guesswork". He left the case to the jury on the basis that Escott had injected himself with the heroin.

Although there were several possible bases relied on by the Crown for the manslaughter charge, the possibilities were narrowed down by the time the matter was left to the jury. The Crown had been running manslaughter by gross negligence, but the judge was not prepared to leave such a verdict open to the jury. The Crown had also relied on section 23 of the Offences against the Person Act 1861 which insofar as material provides:

> "Whosoever shall unlawfully and maliciously administer to, or cause to be administered to or taken by any other person any poison, or other destructive or noxious thing, so as thereby to endanger the life of such person ... shall be guilty of an offence ..."

The argument was that if the appellant's actions came within the terms of that section then they were unlawful and would support a verdict of unlawful and dangerous act manslaughter. However, the judge did not direct the jury that they should consider whether the appellant had "caused" the heroin to be administered to or taken by Escott or had otherwise administered it to him, and so it seems that the judge was not persuaded by the legal argument which had been advanced by the Crown to that effect. The direction actually given to the jury was in the following terms:

> " ... manslaughter, is proved in this particular case if the prosecution satisfy you so that you are sure that the defendant assisted and deliberately encouraged Mr Escott to take the heroin."
>
> ...

So far as causation in concerned, Mr Coker reminds us that the prosecution does not have to prove that the acts of the appellant were the sole cause of the death of Escott, but simply that they amounted to a substantial cause. The appellant's assistance and encouragement, as found by the jury, could amount to a contributory cause of death. However, it is accepted by Mr Coker that the judge here did not direct the jury to consider whether the appellant's acts caused the death of Escott. That is in some contrast to what happened at trial in Kennedy. Our attention has been drawn to page 11 of the transcript in that case where the questions left to the jury in a formal sense are set out. It is to be noted that the fourth of those questions reads as follows:

> "Are we sure that the defendant's act was a significant cause of death?"

Mr Coker draws our attention also to the following passage from the decision in Kennedy where part of the summing-up by the trial judge is quoted. The judge in that case said:

> "Preparing the heroin mixture that he brought into the room and handing the heroin mixture in a syringe to Bosque for immediate injection is capable of amounting to a significant cause of death."

It is argued that, if the unlawful act is the supply and the handing of the mixture in a syringe to the victim, one can find manslaughter properly based on the facts of the case such as the present. In Kennedy the jury had found that there was an unlawful supply of drugs and that that, plus the encouragement given by Kennedy, caused the death of the victim. That was a dangerous act because the encouragement carried with it the risk of harm. In the present case it is suggested that the jury's findings that the appellant's acts assisted and encouraged Escott must be sufficient to show causation.

... In Dalby the appellant had supplied the deceased with a class A drug (Diconal) in tablet form and both had then injected themselves intravenously. It was not contended that the act of self-injection was unlawful. The supply of the tablets clearly was, and the case turned on the issue of causation. But the end result was that the conviction for manslaughter was quashed. ...

[I]t is not easy to see on what basis the court [in Kennedy] concluded that the act of self-injection was unlawful because there is no real elaboration of this point. It is not surprising that the Crown in this present appeal finds it difficult to uphold that particular sentence in the report. The decision on this aspect has been criticised in both Archbold 2002 at paragraph 19–100 and in Smith and Hogan (9th ed) page 432. If Kennedy is rightly decided on this aspect, then it would seem that Dalby should have had a different result since on the facts there seems to have been a comparable degree of assistance and encouragement by the appellant in the latter case to that which took place in Kennedy. There is no offence under the Misuse of Drugs Act 1971, or other statute, or at common law, of injecting oneself with a prohibited drug.

There is the offence of possession of such a drug, and that offence was committed by Escott, the deceased. We have considered, therefore, whether that renders the act of injection unlawful for these purposes, but we find it difficult to see that it can do so. The causative act (the act causing death) was essentially the injection of the heroin rather than the possession of it. Self-injection undoubtedly requires unlawful possession in a case such as this, but it is not in itself a separate offence. No one could be charged with injecting himself with heroin, only with the possession of it. The deceased was in possession of the heroin before he injected it and also after he had injected it. Such possession amounted to an offence, but the act of injecting was not itself part of the offence. It was merely made possible by the unlawful possession of the heroin.

...

There is a further problem about the basis of the present conviction, given the direction by the trial judge. The case was not left to the jury on the footing that the appellant might have caused the death of Escott, and that is perhaps understandable since the act of self-injection was seen by the judge as a voluntary act of an adult not labouring under any mistake as to what he was doing. The judge seems to have taken the view that the chain of causation would have been broken by Escott's own action. It follows from that that the appellant could only have been guilty of manslaughter as a secondary party and not as a principal. But in that case who is the principal guilty of manslaughter? As there is no offence of self-manslaughter, it is difficult to see how the appellant could be guilty of that offence as a secondary party because of his encouragement or assistance to Escott over the injection of the drug.

We accept that there may be situations where a jury could find manslaughter in cases such as this, so long as they were satisfied so as to be sure that the chain of causation was not broken. That is not this case because causation here was not left to the jury. The argument advanced by Mr Coker that the jury found assistance and encouragement on the part of the appellant will not, in our judgment, suffice. Assistance and encouragement is not to be automatically equated with causation. Causation raises questions of fact and degree. The recipient does not have to inject the drug which he is encouraged and assisted to take. He has a choice. It may be that in some circumstances the causative chain will still remain. That is a matter for the jury to decide. The Crown's current approach as argued on this appeal hearing, namely that the supply of heroin is unlawful and can be a dangerous act causing death, is sound. The most obvious case is where the supply takes the form of one person injecting the other who then dies. The position is more difficult where the victim injects himself, but there may possibly be situations where the chain of causation could be established. It is, however, important that that issue be left to the jury to determine, as happened at the trial in Kennedy.

The trial judge in a case such as this, after identifying the unlawful act on the part of the defendant relied upon, must direct the jury to ask whether they are sure that that act was at least a substantive cause of the victim's death, as well as being dangerous. That did not happen here, and we cannot see that the jury's finding can be seen as establishing causation between unlawful supply on the one hand and death on the other. That is not how the matter was left to them. It may seem to some that there is morally not a great deal between this situation where A hands B a syringe containing a drug such as heroin, with death resulting, and that where A injects B with his consent with the contents of the syringe. But the vital difference (and this is why causation cannot be assumed) is that the former situation involves an act of B's taken voluntarily and leading to his death. We do not wish to suggest that there may not sometimes be cases where, on somewhat different facts, manslaughter by way of gross negligence may arise if a duty of care can be established, or where section 23 may be relied on so long as the chain of causation is not broken.

But for the reasons already given this conviction cannot be regarded as safe and it follows that it will be quashed. This appeal is allowed.

III.e.   Who can be killed?

This section has already shown that the edges of medical practice and criminal law are blurred or, to put it another way, that the determination of many critical questions about the definition of unlawful homicide is complicated and sometimes compromised by issues relating to contemporary medical practice. If we think about our stereotypes of murder or manslaughter, then these 'edge' issues do not concern us – we imagine a violent encounter between strangers, or perhaps a domestic argument taken too far. It is when law attempts to capture the huge variety of human behaviour in the fragility of definitions that those stereotypes are exposed. At the beginning of this section, we took the example of handicapped newborn babies and the decisions which are made in relation to their survival as an example of how arguments might be framed to authorise practices which appear to contravene homicide laws. More immediately, we have been discussing the circumstances in which caring for patients and reducing their pain may be regarded as lawfully acceptable despite contravention of the prohibition against causing the death of another human being. This led to a consideration of when life ends. Now we turn to a related issue – when does criminal law regard life as beginning – when do we become a 'person' for the purposes of homicide law?

Homicide is the killing of another human being. When do we become a human being? And what are we before that in the eyes of the law? It is sometimes assumed that, because foetuses do not have legal personality, they do not have rights or interests which are recognised by law. This is a serious mis-statement of their position in English law. Foetal interests are protected in many ways, whether from injury by the woman carrying them or from third parties. As we saw in **Chapter 5.IV.a.**, criminal laws regulate women who are pregnant, thus providing foetuses with some protection from conception to birth. The death of an unborn foetus cannot amount to homicide: the victim of homicide must be a human being, a person who has breathed independently of its mother. The relationship between the foetus and homicide offences can nonetheless give rise to difficulty. In *Tait* (1990) the Court of Appeal rejected an argument that a threat to kill a foetus was a threat to kill a person (under s 16 of the Offences Against the Person Act 1861). Yet it is an offence to threaten to kill – should it perhaps also be an offence to threaten to kill a foetus? A different question is raised by pre-natal injury leading to post-natal death. In *A-G's Reference (No 3 of 1994)*, below, the House of Lords ruled that a pre-natal injury leading to post-natal death could amount to unlawful homicide. There is no requirement in homicide that the person who dies needs to be a person in being at the time the death-causing injury is inflicted.

This case ranges widely over the law of murder and manslaughter and we use the following extracts from Lord Mustill's speech to introduce the core issues in relation to the culpability element which marks murder from manslaughter, in addition to the intrinsic question about when, as human beings, we come under the protection of the law.

A-G's Reference No 3 of 1994 [1997] 3 All ER 936, HL

Lord Mustill.

Murder is widely thought to be the gravest of crimes. One could expect a developed system to embody a law of murder clear enough to yield an unequivocal result on a given set of facts, a result which conforms with apparent justice and has a sound intellectual base. This is not so in England, where the law of homicide is permeated by anomaly, fiction, misnomer and obsolete reasoning. One conspicuous anomaly is the rule which identifies the malice aforethought; (a doubly misleading expression) required for the crime of murder not only with a conscious intention to kill but also with an intention to cause grievous bodily harm. It is, therefore, possible to commit a murder not only without wishing the death of the victim but without the least thought that this might be the result of the assault. Many would doubt the justice of this rule, which is not the popular conception of murder and (as I shall suggest) no longer rests on any intellectual foundation. The law of Scotland does very well without it, and England could perhaps do the same ...

As will appear, the events which founder the appeal were never conclusively proved at the trial, but are assumed to have been as follows. At the time in question a young woman, M, was pregnant, with between 22 and 24 weeks of gestation. According to the present state of medical knowledge if her baby had been born after 22 weeks it would not have had any significant prospect of survival. Two further weeks would have increased the chance to about 10 per cent. The pregnancy was, however, proceeding normally, and the risk that it would fail to continue to full term and be followed by an uneventful birth was very small indeed. Sadly, however, the natural father B quarrelled with M and stabbed her in the face, back and abdomen with a long-bladed kitchen knife in circumstances raising a prima facie inference that he intended to do her grievous bodily harm. M was admitted to hospital for surgical treatment and was later discharged in an apparently satisfactory state, still carrying the baby. Unfortunately, some 17 days after the incident M went into premature labour. The baby, named S, was born alive. The birth was still grossly premature, although by that time the chance that the baby would survive had increased to 50 per cent. Thereafter S lived for 121 days, when she succumbed to broncho-pulmonary dysplasia from the effects of premature birth. After her birth it was discovered that one of the knife cuts had penetrated her lower abdomen. The wound needed surgical repair, but it is agreed that this 'made no provable contribution to her death'.

The case for the Crown at the trial of B was that the wounding of M by B had set in train the events which caused the premature birth of S and hence her failure to achieve the normal prospect of survival which she would have had if the pregnancy had proceeded to full term. In this sense, therefore, we must assume that the wounding of M, at a time when S was a barely viable foetus, was the reason why she later died when she did.

Meanwhile, B had been prosecuted for an offence of wounding the mother with intent to cause her grievous bodily harm, had pleaded guilty and had been sentenced to a term of four years' imprisonment. After S died he was charged again, this time with the murder of S, to which he pleaded not guilty. At his trial a submission was advanced that on the evidence no criminal offence relating to S was proved. In a considered ruling the trial judge upheld that submission, as regards the offences of both murder and manslaughter ... The gist of the ruling lay in the law, and was to the effect that both the physical and the mental elements of murder were absent. There was no relevant actus reus, for the foetus was not a live person; and the cause of the death was the wounding of the mother, not of S. As to mens rea again there was none. When B stabbed the mother he had no intent to kill or do serious harm to any live person other than the mother, or to do any harm at all to the foetus. The Crown could not make good this deficiency by reliance on the concept of transferred malice, for this operates only where the mens rea of one crime causes the actus reus of the same crime, albeit the result is in some respects unintended. Here, the intent to stab the mother (a live person) could not be transferred to the foetus (not a live person), an organism which could not be the victim of a crime of murder.

As to the alternative verdict of manslaughter the judge was at first exercised by the possibility that since the stabbing of M was an unlawful and dangerous act which led to the death of S a conviction could be sustained even though the act was not aimed at the ultimate victim: see *R v Mitchell* [1983] QB 741. In the end, however, he was persuaded that this approach could not be sustained where there was at the material time no victim capable of dying as a direct and immediate result.

Accordingly, the trial judge directed the jury to acquit the defendant.

Considering that this ruling should be reviewed the Attorney-General referred the matter to the opinion of the Court of Appeal under s 36 of the Criminal Justice Act 1972. The point of law referred was as follows:

1. Subject to the proof by the prosecution of the requisite intent in either case: whether the crimes of murder or manslaughter can be committed where unlawful injury is deliberately inflicted: (i) to a child in utero (ii) to a mother carrying a child in utero where the child is

subsequently born alive, enjoys an existence independent of the mother, thereafter dies and the injuries inflicted while in utero either caused or made a substantial contribution to the death.

2.   Whether the fact that the death of the child is caused solely as a consequence of injury to the mother rather than as a consequence of direct injury to the foetus can negative any liability for murder or manslaughter in the circumstances set out in question 1 ...

In the result, the court answered the first of the referred questions in the affirmative, adding ...

the requisite intent to be proved in the case of murder is an intention to kill or cause really serious bodily injury to the mother, the foetus before birth being viewed as an integral part of the mother. Such intention is appropriately modified in the case of manslaughter.

The court answered the second question in the negative, provided the jury is satisfied that causation is proved. The accused person now brings the matter before this House, and maintains that the answers given to both questions were wrong, and that the ruling of the trial judge was right.

I. Murder

The first of the questions referred involves a number of alternative assumptions of fact concerning both the act of the defendant and the intent with which it was done ... [O]n the hypothesis that the unlawful injury was directed to the mother alone, with the intention of hurting the mother alone ... I will begin by considering the issue of murder ...

I perceive the established rules to be as follows.

1.   It is sufficient to raise a prima facie case of murder (subject to entire or partial excuses such as self-defence or provocation) for it to be proved that the defendant did the act which caused the death intending to kill the victim or to cause him at least grievous bodily harm ...

2.   If the defendant does an act with the intention of causing a particular kind of harm to B, and unintentionally does that kind of harm to V, then the intent to harm B may be added to the harm actually done to V in deciding whether the defendant has committed a crime towards V ...

3.   Except under statute an embryo or foetus in utero cannot be the victim of a crime of violence. In particular, violence to the foetus which causes its death in utero is not a murder ...

4.   The existence of an interval of time between the doing of an act by the defendant with the necessary wrongful intent and its impact on the victim in a manner which leads to death does not in itself prevent the intent, the act and the death from together amounting to murder, so long as there is an unbroken causal connection between the act and the death ...

5. Violence towards a foetus which results in harm suffered after the baby has been born alive can give rise to criminal responsibility even if the harm would not have been criminal (apart from statute) if it had been suffered in utero ...

Two arguments for the Crown

1. The first argument: the foetus identified with the mother
   The decision of the Court of Appeal founded on the proposition that the foetus is part of the mother, so that an intention to cause really serious bodily injury to the mother is equivalent to the same intent directed towards the foetus. This intent could be added to the actus reus ... Obviously, nobody would assert that once the mother had been delivered of S, the baby and her mother were in any sense 'the same'. Not only were they physically separate, but they were each unique human beings, though no doubt with many features of resemblance. The reason for the uniqueness of S was that the development of her own special characteristics had been enabled and bounded by the collection of genes handed down not only by M but also by the natural father. This collection was different from the genes which had enabled and bounded the development of M, for these had been handed down by her own mother and natural father. S and her mother were closely related but, even apart from differing environmental influences, they were not, had not been, and in the future never would be 'the same'. There was, of course, an intimate bond between the foetus and the mother, created by the total dependence of the foetus on the protective physical environment furnished by the mother, and on the supply by the mother through the physical linkage between them of the nutriments, oxygen and other substances essential to foetal life and development. The emotional bond between the mother and her unborn child was also of a very special kind. But the relationship was one of bond, not of identity. The mother and the foetus were two distinct organisms, living symbiotically, not a single organism with two aspects. The mother's leg was part of the mother; the foetus was not ...

2. The second argument: the foetus as a separate organism
   I would, therefore, reject the reasoning which assumes that since (in the eyes of English law) the foetus does not have the attributes which make it a 'person' it must be an adjunct of the mother. Eschewing all religious and political debate, I would say that the foetus is neither. It is a unique organism. To apply to such an organism, the principles of a law evolved in relation to autonomous beings is bound to mislead. I prefer, so far as binding authority permits, to start afresh, and to do so by reference to the second of the arguments advanced by the Attorney General. This builds on the rules stated above by the following stages.

If D struck X intending to cause her serious harm, and the blow, in fact, caused her death, that would be murder (rule 1). If she had been nursing a baby Y which was accidentally struck by the blow and consequently died, that would also be murder (rules 1 and 2). So, also, if an evil-doer had intended to cause harm but not death to X by giving her a poisoned substance and the substance was, in fact, passed on by X to the baby, which consumed it and died as a result (rules, 1, 2 and 3). Again it would have been murder if the foetus had been injured in utero and had succumbed to the wound after being born alive (rules 1, 2, 4 and 5). It is only a short step to make a new rule, adding together the malice towards the mother, the contemporaneous starting of a train of events, and the coming to fruition of those events in the death of the baby after being born alive.

My Lords, the attractions of this argument are plain, not least its simplicity. But for my part I find it too dependent on the piling up of old fictions, and too little on the reasons why the law takes its present shape ... [S]ince the original concepts are no longer available to explain why an intent to cause grievous bodily harm will found a conviction for murder, the reason must be sought elsewhere: for reason, in regard to such a grave crime, there must surely be. The obvious recourse is to ascribe this doctrine to the last vestiges of the murder/felony rule, and to see in it a strong example of that rule, for unlike the more extravagant early manifestations it offers at least some resemblance in nature and degree between the intended act and its unintended consequences. It would follow, therefore, that when the murder/felony rule was expressly abolished by s 1 of the 1957 Act the only surviving justification for the 'grievous harm' rule fell away, with nothing left. [A decisive answer was given by the House in *R v Cunningham* [1981] 2 All ER 863.] The 'grievous harm' rule had survived the abolition of the murder/felony principle ...

My Lords, in a system based on binding precedent there could be no ground for doubting a long course of existing law, and certainly none which could now permit this House even to contemplate such a fundamental change as to abolish the grievous harm rule: and counsel rightly hinted at no such idea. But when asked to strike out into new territory it is, I think, right to recognise that the grievous harm rule is an outcropping of old law from which the surrounding strata of rationalisations have weathered away. It survives but exemplifies no principle which can be applied to a new situation ...

To make any sense of [transferred malice] there must, as it seems to me, be some compatibility between the original intention and the actual occurrence, and this is, indeed, what one finds in the cases. There is no such compatibility here. The defendant intended to commit and did commit an immediate crime of violence to the mother. He committed no relevant violence to the foetus, which was not a person, either at the time or in the future, and intended no harm to the foetus or to the human person which it would become. If fictions are useful, as they can be, they are only damaged by straining them beyond their limits. I would not overstrain the idea of transferred malice by trying to make it fit the present case ...

All that is needed, once causation is established, is an act creating a risk to anyone; and such a risk is obviously established in the case of any violent assault by the risk to the person of the victim herself (or himself). In a case such as the present, therefore, responsibility for manslaughter would automatically be established even if (which cannot have been the case here) the attacker had no idea that the woman was pregnant. On a broader canvas, the proposition involves that manslaughter can be established against someone who does any wrongful act leading to death, in circumstances where it was foreseeable that it might hurt anyone at all; and that this is so even if the victim does not fall into any category of persons whom a reasonable person in the position of the defendant might have envisaged as being within the area of potential risk. This is strong doctrine, the more so since it might be said with some force that it recognises a concept of general malice (that those who do wrong must suffer the consequences of a resulting death, whether or not the death was intended or could have been foreseen) uncomfortably similar to the one rejected more than 150 years ago by the courts and commentators in the context of murder; and one which, it is proper to add, I have proposed in the first part of this speech, should be rejected once again in that context.

It is this feature which has caused me to hesitate long in joining the remainder of your Lordships to hold that a verdict of manslaughter can be available in circumstances as broad as this. I am, however, entirely convinced by the speech of Lord Hope that this is the present state of English law. To look for consistency between and within the very different crimes of murder and manslaughter is, I believe, hoping for too much. Once can, however, look for a result which does substantial justice, and this is what I believe verdicts that B was not guilty of murder and guilty of manslaughter would have achieved.

Lord Mustill's speech is explicitly an exercise in damage limitation thought necessary because murder can be based on an intention to cause grievous bodily harm and is not limited to intention to kill. Not only is this seen as unacceptably broad but also as a 'fiction'. In the same way, 'transferred malice' is regarded as a route to constructive crime. This is puzzling. Why should a defendant's culpability vary according to whether her victim is the intended Mr X, or the unfortunate Ms Y? Why should an 'intention' (in the sense in which the term is used in criminal law, see below) to cause injury to a person need to be specific in relation to the victim's identity? Furthermore, if transferred malice does involve a fiction, is it not somewhat arbitrary to resurrect the fiction again so that a manslaughter charge could be supported in these circumstances? As a result of Lord Mustill's preoccupation with the house of murder, the opportunity to consider the criminal law's response to a pregnant woman's interest in her foetus, has been lost (see Wells and Morgan 1991).

FURTHER READING

Huxtable, Richard (2002) 'Separation of Conjoined Twins: Where Next for English Law?' Crim LR 459.

Lee, Robert and Morgan, Derek (eds) (1994) *Death Rites: Law and Ethics at the End of Life* (Routledge).

Magnet, Joseph and Kluge, Eike-Henner (1985) *Withholding Treatment from Defective Newborn Children* (Brown Legal Publications).

Medical Law Review (2001) Special Edition: *The Conjoined Twins Case* 9 Med LR 201–98.

Wells, Celia (1989) 'Otherwise Kill Me: Marginal Children and Ethics at the Edges of Existence' in Robert Lee and Derek Morgan (eds) *Birthrights: Law and Ethics at the Beginnings of Life* (Routledge).

Wells, Celia and Morgan, Derek (1991) 'Whose Foetus Is It?' 18 Journal of Law and Society 431.

IV. Murder and manslaughter

The offences of murder and manslaughter are built on the moral and conceptual foundations discussed in the previous section. We have seen that, in terms of the conduct elements, for murder and manslaughter the prosecution has to prove that the defendant unlawfully caused the death of a person. For murder, the prosecution must also prove that the defendant intended to kill or to cause grievous bodily harm. Absent this, a homicide may still be regarded as unlawful if it comes within the recognised categories of 'involuntary manslaughter', that is, unlawful act and gross negligence manslaughter. Even where there is the appropriate intention, murder may be reduced to manslaughter on account of diminished responsibility or provocation. Both murder and manslaughter may be regarded as 'lawful' if committed in self-defence or the prevention of crime. Gender is an ever-present, though often hidden, element in constructions of murder and manslaughter. In the last 10 years, the relevance of the history of violence in a relationship has featured more overtly, both in scholarly discussions and in judicial explorations of the partial defences of diminished responsibility and provocation and in self-defence.

Linking this basic account with the discussion in the last section, we can summarise in the following way: a person who causes the death of another with intention to kill or with intention to cause grievous bodily harm commits murder unless:

(a) the person is in persistent vegetative state (PVS) and satisfies the *Bland* criteria and death is brought about through withdrawal of treatment; or

(b) the defendant is acting in self-defence or prevention of crime; or

(c) the act was justified on the basis of necessity (see discussion of *Re A (Conjoined twins* 2000 above in **Chapter 4.II.f.** and below at **section IV.f.**).

In these circumstances the homicide is lawful.

Or unless:

(d) the defendant was provoked; or

(e) the defendant was suffering from diminished responsibility.

In these last two cases the offence will be one of ('voluntary') manslaughter.

There are also two specific forms of homicide which are treated as neither murder nor manslaughter, although the deaths occur in circumstances which would otherwise indicate a finding of murder or manslaughter: these are infanticide and killing in pursuance of a suicide pact (see **Chapter 5.V.**).

IV.a.   The penalty for murder

The punishment for murder has had a significant impact on the delineation between murder and manslaughter.

Murder (Abolition of Death Penalty) Act 1965, s 1

(1) No person shall suffer death for murder, and a person convicted of murder shall ... be sentenced to imprisonment for life.

(2) On sentencing any person convicted of murder to imprisonment for life the Court may at the same time declare the period which it recommends to the Secretary of State as a minimum period which in its view should elapse before the Secretary of State orders the release of that person on licence under section 27 of the Prison Act 1952 or section 21 of the Prisons (Scotland) Act 1952.

Capital punishment remains a matter of contemporary political debate, although the European Court of Human Right's ruling in *Ocalan* (2003) sends a clear message that the death penalty cannot be accommodated as an exception to Article 2. The Court said that

[C]apital punishment in peacetime has come to be regarded as an unacceptable, if not inhuman, form of punishment, which is no longer permissible under Art 2.

Turkey has followed many other signatory states in abolishing the death penalty in peacetime under the Protocol 6 procedure. By 2003, all European states had signed the protocol, with only Turkey, Armenia and Russia yet to ratify it (see Gray NLJ 2003: 620; and Hood 2002).

Tom Sorrell, *Moral Theory and Capital Punishment* (Blackwells, 1987) pp 32ff

On 11 May 1982, the British House of Commons debated clauses in the Criminal Justice Bill that, if approved, would have reintroduced the death penalty for certain categories of crime in England and Wales ... Vivian Bendall ... opened the debate. Speaking first to the catch-all clause concerning murder, he said that the death penalty would act as a deterrent. A would-be murderer will think twice before taking a life if he knows that he may well forfeit his own ... If one examines the homicides that have been reported to the police since 1964, the year the death penalty was done away with on a trial basis, one sees that the figure for murders in 1964 was 296. In 1980, the figure was 620. The number has more than doubled. [23 Official Report (*Hansard*) (5th series) col 610.]

Later in his speech Bendall gave statistics for murders of police officers. 'In the seventeen years prior to the death penalty being abolished', he said, 'eleven police officers were murdered. In the seventeen years since the death penalty was abolished, twenty-seven have been murdered. That is another doubling of the figure. The figures speak for themselves' [col 612].

Do the figures speak for themselves? The fact that murders increased after the abolition of the death penalty does not show that murders increased because of the abolition of the death penalty. But unless this causal claim is demonstrated, it is hard to show that the death penalty would prevent or reduce the numbers of murders ...

The increase in the number of murders was evidence for Bendall's claim that the abolition of the death penalty encouraged an increase in the rate of homicide. The point is, it was weak evidence: other things besides the abolition of the death penalty could have led to more murders, for example a growing belief, independent of the penalty, that the rate of successful detection of murder was going down. Or, to cite a very different possibility, if many murders were due to tensions within families, then an increase in factors creating such tensions, factors as diverse as adultery and unemployment could have increased the murder rate ...

The deterrent effect of capital punishment was not the only ground offered for its reintroduction in the new clauses of the Criminal Justice Bill. Vivian Bendall ... cited then recent soundings of public opinion ... He went on to suggest that a vote for the return of capital punishment was 'needed if democracy was to be upheld'.

Suppose the opinion polls that Bendall cited were accurate and three-quarters of the British people were in favour of capital punishment. Does the fact that a majority supports it make the death penalty right? Does the fact that a majority supports it mean that a vote by an MP against capital punishment is anti-democratic? Several speakers gave reasons for answering 'No' to the second question. One of these was Edward Heath, who quoted

Edmund Bruce on the duty of a representative of the people: 'Your representative owes you, not his industry only, but his judgment; and he betrays instead of serving you if he sacrifices it to your opinion.' ...

It is possible to hold that in a democracy the laws should reflect the views of the majority right or wrong. But it seems to me that whether this position is reasonable depends on what the views of the majority are about, and also on the purpose of a liberal democracy. If a liberal democracy exists to enable each of the many to pursue his own ends, and exists also to promote positively the ends most of the many share, then the fact that many people in a democracy want a particular thing is by itself a strong argument for legislating in favour of it ...

But at this point it is important to distinguish between ways in which something can be wanted. It is possible to want capital punishment for murder as a means of getting something else that is desirable, say a situation in which there are fewer murders. It is also possible to want capital punishment for murder and want it for its own sake, for example in the belief that that crime and that punishment are made for one another. Now if capital punishment for murder were wanted for its own sake by many people in a democracy, a good case would exist for making it legal ... On the other hand, if capital punishment for murder were desired for its supposed power of reducing the number of murders, and it actually had no such effect, or it was doubtful that it had such an effect, then the argument in favour of capital punishment legislation would be weak. Similarly if capital punishment did have the desired effect but the means of inflicting the death penalty were found extremely repellent by most people. At best there would be an argument for legislating in favour of whatever palatable measures in fact reduced the rate of murder ...

R Hood, *The Death Penalty – A Worldwide Perspective* (Clarendon Press, 2002) pp 181–190. Reprinted by permission of Oxford University Press.

Even though some states may justify their use of the death penalty on simple retributive grounds, the most common political justification is the belief that it has a unique general deterrent capacity to save further innocent lives or reduce significantly other capital offences. If it does not have such a utility – or if it does not control crime through incapacitation of the criminal – beyond what can be achieved by life imprisonment, it would be, in the words of the United States Supreme Court in *Coker v George*, 'nothing more than the purposeless and needless imposition of pain and suffering' – and thus, in that Court's view, an unconstitutional punishment.

The deterrent justification has been voiced by many retentionist countries – by China, Japan, Singapore, by most of the countries of the former USSR, by many nations in the Middle East and by some in Africa, and by the Justice Department and Supreme Court of the United States of America ...

The argument that the threat of death must deter more than any other punishment has been based on what appears to be the self-evident intuition that people would find the prospect of death more painful than life imprisonment. Yet intuition also suggests that the policy of deterrence is only likely to have any impact if it is enforced with a high degree of certainty against a group of persons for which the punishment of death is both morally and politically acceptable and who, in the course of their conduct, correctly calculate the probable penal consequences. It has for example, frequently been pointed out that these consequences are often far more remote than being killed by a victim or by the police. The assumption upon which guided discretionary statutes rest is that the death sentence will be applied to those from whom society needs the greatest protection. Thus, the prime aggravating circumstance which leads to a death sentence is that the murder was committed during the commission of another felony, the assumption being that these are the actions of rational 'calculating criminals', not those which have arisen from emotional outbursts amongst the ordinary population. Any study of deterrence should seek to test this specific hypothesis because the threat of death is not made to the generality of potential murderers. Furthermore, several of the aggravating circumstances, which make a person liable for the death penalty in many jurisdictions relate to crimes which intuitively do not seem likely to be affected by rational calculation of the marginally increased probability of execution. The murders which are described as 'especially heinous, atrocious or cruel' are likely to be carried out by psychopathic personalities or persons who have lost control of their normal inhibitions ...

It is obvious that any change in the use of the death penalty may itself be associated with social changes and changes in penal practice which affect the rate of crime ... Nevertheless, the fact that all the evidence continues to point in the same direction is persuasive *a priori* evidence that countries need not fear sudden and serious changes in the curve of crime if they reduce their reliance on the death penalty. In Australia, for example, where the last executions took place in the mid-1960s, the reported homicide rate ... has fallen, and the murder rate has changed very little ...

The number of homicides has risen in the United Kingdom since the abolition of the death penalty – the recorded homicides being 60 per cent higher in the twenty years 1966 to 1985 than in the twenty years 1946 to 1965. But the increase has been far less than in serious violent offences, which over the same two periods rose by over 160 per cent. Furthermore, while the number of recorded homicides was lower in 1993 than in 1986, the number of recorded serious woundings was over 60 per cent higher. In other abolitionist countries which have been experiencing a rise in crime, homicide rates have also lagged a long way behind increases in violent offences in general.

By retaining a mandatory penalty for murder but replacing the death penalty with imprisonment for life, it is argued that the symbolic denunciation of murder is preserved. Life imprisonment is itself a subject which generates much controversy because of its indeterminacy. What we therefore have is the certainty of a mandatory sentence combined with the executive discretion attaching to the decision as to release from life imprisonment. Life imprisonment is also a discretionary sentence for, amongst other offences, manslaughter. The following case discusses the roles of the Home Secretary and the trial judge in determining the decision to release on licence:

Doody v Secretary of State for the Home Department [1993] 3 All ER 92, HL

[*The four appellants had all been convicted of murder and applied for judicial review of the Home Office procedure for the release of mandatory life prisoners on licence. The Divisional Court refused the application. The Court of Appeal allowed the appeal in part, endorsing the Home Secretary's right to set the 'penal' element of the sentence, but confirming a prisoner's right to make representations in respect of the timing of the first review by the Parole Board. The Home Secretary appealed and the appellants cross-appealed.*]

Lord Mustill.

[T]he sentencing of a convicted murderer according to English law is a unique formality ... in this sense, that the task of the judge is entirely mechanical. Once a verdict of guilty is returned the outcome is preordained ...

... The sentence of life imprisonment is also unique in that the words which the judge is required to pronounce do not mean what they say ... Whilst in a very small minority of cases the prisoner is in the event confined for the rest of his natural life, this is not the usual nor the intended effect of a sentence of life imprisonment ... [A]lthough everyone knows what the words do not mean, nobody knows what they do mean, since the duration of the prisoner's detention depends on a series of recommendations to, and executive decisions by, the Home Secretary, some made at an early stage and others much later, none of which can be accurately forecast at the time when the offender is sent to prison.

There is, however, another form of life sentence, of which the philosophy, statutory framework and executive practice are quite different even though the words pronounced by the judge are the same. This is the discretionary life sentence ... Where the criteria [for imposing the sentence] ... are satisfied the judge has a choice between two very different procedures. He may decide to focus on the offence, passing a sentence appropriate to its gravity by the familiar process of identifying the range of sentences established through decisions of the Court of Appeal as being in general apposite to an offence of the kind in question, and then placing the individual offence within (or exceptionally, outside) the range by reference to circumstances of mitigation or aggravation. The judge may however think it right to adopt a different approach, and to concentrate on the offender rather than the offence, imposing a sentence of life imprisonment to reflect his appraisal that even a long fixed term of years may not adequately protect the public against the risk that when the term has been served the prisoner will continue to be a danger to the public. Such a sentence ensures that the prisoner will be kept in custody until it is thought safe to release him.

The discretionary life sentence may thus be regarded as the sum of two sentences, to be served consecutively. First, a determinate number of years appropriate to the nature and gravity of the offence. This is often called the 'tariff' element of the sentence. For my part, although I recognise that this is not inappropriate in the context of a discretionary life sentence, I consider that for reasons which I will later develop it is illogical and mis-leading when the usage is transferred to a mandatory sentence. I therefore prefer to avoid this terminology and will instead call the first component of the life sentence the 'penal element'. The second component is an indeter-minate period, which the offender begins to serve when the penal element is exhausted. I will call this the 'risk element' [discretionary life sentences are governed by the Crime (Sentences) Act 1997, s 28].

In the past there was no need for the sentencer to give separate attention to these two components. Having once decided that a determinate sentence at the general level suggested by the nature of the offence would not adequately reflect the degree of risk, he would proceed directly to the imposition of a life sentence, and would have no reason to identify with precision, or to publish, the fixed term which he would have passed if he had chosen the alternative course. As will appear, the law and practice have more recently developed in a way which attaches great importance to the composite nature of the discretionary life sentence, and now requires that in the great majority of cases the judge will quantify and announce the penal element and will thereby fix directly the minimum period in custody which the offender must serve, before the question whether it is safe to release him becomes decisive. Although it is a comparative novelty this regime conforms very well with the rationale of the discretionary life sentence and, as it appears to me, is fair, practical in operation and easy to comprehend.

The same cannot I believe be said of the situation created by the minis-terial decision, some ten years ago, to import the concept of a penal element into the theory and practice governing the release on licence of prisoners serving mandatory life sentences for murder ... [T]he current practice, established by executive changes of policy rather than by Act of Parliament, now requires the division of the sentence into penal and risk elements, and entails that the ascertainment by the Home Secretary of the penal element fixes, at one remove, the minimum period for which the convicted murderer will be detained. It is to this element that the present appeal is directed.

The respondents to the appeal ... were each convicted of murder and sentenced to life imprisonment on various occasions between 1985 and 1987. It is possible to deduce from the dates fixed by the Home Secretary for the first review of their cases by the Parole Board (and in the case of Pierson from correspondence with the Home Office) that the penal elements of these life sentences fixed by the Home Secretary were respectively 15 years, not more than 20 years, 12 years and 11 years. So much each prisoner knows, but what he does not know is why the particular term was selected, and he is now trying to find out, partly from an obvious human desire to be told the reason for a decision so gravely affecting his future and partly because he hopes that once the information is obtained he may be able to point out errors of fact or reasoning and thereby persuade the Home Secretary to change his mind, or if he fails in this to challenge the decision in the courts. Since the Home Secretary has declined to furnish the information the respondents have set out to obtain it by applications for judicial review.

(1) Until the enactment of the Homicide Act 1957 the mandatory sentence for murder was death. This was mitigated by an executive power to commute the sentence to one of penal servitude (later imprisonment) for life, which in turn was subject to an executive power to release the prisoner on licence. There was a long-established practice whereby the trial judge wrote privately to the Home Secretary drawing attention to any features of the case which he considered relevant to the anxious decision on whether or not to commute.

(2) When the 1957 Act created the category of non-capital murder it prescribed a mandatory sentence of imprisonment for life. Eight years later, at the time when the abolition of the death penalty for murder was before Parliament it was proposed that the previous mandatory sentences of death and life imprisonment should be replaced by a discretionary sentence of life imprisonment, but Parliament did not agree and a sentence of life imprisonment was made mandatory for all murders; see the Murder (Abolition of Death Penalty) Act 1965, s 1(1). At the same time two statutory concessions were made to those who feared excessive leniency by the Executive in the treatment of convicted murderers. First, by s 1(2) the trial judge was given power to recommend to the Home Secretary the minimum period which should elapse before the release of the prisoner under the statutory power to release on licence which had been created by the Prison Act 1952. Second, it was stipulated that no person convicted of murder would be released on licence unless the Home

Secretary had previously consulted the Lord Chief Justice and the trial judge, if available: s 2.

[In 1983] in response to pressure of public opinion the Home Secretary (the Rt Hon Leon Brittan QC) announced a series of radical changes in the existing policies relating to the release of prisoners on parole and licence ... [including] the creation of a completely new philosophy and practice for the release of life prisoners on licence ... This practice was to have the following features: (i) the joint Home Office/Parole Board committee, which had been established to recommend the date for the first review by the Parole Board was disbanded; (ii) instead, the Home Secretary would himself, after consulting the judges 'on the requirements of retribution and deterrence', fix the date for the first review; (iii) the review would normally take place three years before the expiry of the 'period necessary to meet the requirements of retribution and deterrence'. This would give sufficient time for preparations for release, if the Parole Board were to recommend it; (iv) subject to exceptional circumstances the first review would in fact take place on the date so fixed; (v) meanwhile the progress of the prisoner would be kept under regular review by the Home Office; (vi) the consultation with the judges required by s 61 of the Criminal Justice Act 1967 would take place when release was an actual possibility; (vii) in the case of certain types of murder the prisoner would not normally be released until 20 years or even longer had been served.

Equally important were the changes in philosophy underlying the new practice. The first was tacit, but obvious. Whereas at the outset the power of the trial judge to recommend a minimum term, and the duty of the Home Secretary to consult the judges before release had been a protection against a foreseen risk of excessive leniency by the Executive, the new regime was intended to forestall risk of excessive leniency by the judges, or the Parole Board, or both.

My Lords, I believe that this summary has shown how, in contrast with the position as regards discretionary life sentences, the theory and the practice for convicted murderers are out of tune. The theory ... [is] that murder is an offence so grave that the proper 'tariff' sentence is invariably detention for life, although as a measure of leniency it may be mitigated by release on licence. Yet the practice established by Mr. Brittan in 1983 and still in force founds on the proposition that there is concealed within the life term a fixed period of years, apt to reflect not only the requirements of deterrence, but also the moral quality of the individual act (retribution). These two philosophies of sentencing are inconsistent. Either may be defensible, but they cannot both be applied at the same time.

As it seems to me, the only possible choice is the regime installed by Mr. Brittan, as later modified. This is the regime by which successive Home Secretaries have chosen to exercise the wide powers conferred by Parliament, and the arguments have throughout assumed that the regime is firmly in place, and that the task of the courts is to decide what the elements of fairness demand as to the working out of that regime, in the light of the sentencing philosophy which is expressed to underlie it.

...

The respondents' second argument is an appeal to symmetry. Mandatory and discretionary sentences are now each divided into the two elements. Under both regimes the judges play a part in fixing the penal element, and the Parole Board in fixing the risk element. At the stage of the Parole Board review the practice as to the disclosure of materials and reasons is now the same under the two regimes. Given that the post-*Handscomb* practice, embodied in s 34 of the 1991 Act, now gives a direct effect to the trial judge's opinion, it is irrational (so the argument runs) for the Home Secretary not to have brought into alignment the two methods of fixing the penal element.

Whilst there is an important grain of truth in this argument, I believe it to be overstated. The discretionary and mandatory life sentences, having in the past grown apart, may now be converging. Nevertheless, on the statutory framework, the underlying theory and the current practice there remains a substantial gap between them. It may be – I express no opinion – that the time is approaching when the effect of the two types of life sentence should be further assimilated. But this is a task for Parliament, and I think it quite impossible for the courts to introduce a fundamental change in the relationship between the convicted murderer and the state, through the medium of judicial review.

Lord Mustill concluded that mandatory life prisoners were entitled to the following rights in respect of the Home Secretary's decision in fixing the penal element: (1) the right to put forward reasons for fixing a lower rather than higher term; (2) the right to know what factors the Home Secretary would take into account; (3) the right to be given reasons for any departure from the judge's recommendation. This does not include the right to access to any documents in which the judge's opinion was given.

There seems little doubt that one result of the abolition of the death penalty has been an increase in the amount of time spent in prison by all convicted murderers, including those who would not have been hanged.

Ian Cameron 'Life in the Balance: The Case of Frank Marritt' in P Scraton and P Gordon (eds) *Causes for Concern* (Penguin, 1984) p 257

[U]nder the Homicide Act 1957 there were five categories of murder which were capital. These were considered by Parliament to be the most grave types of murder. They were murder in the course or furtherance of theft; murder by shooting or by causing an explosion; murder in the course of resisting arrest or escaping from lawful custody; murder of police officers in the execution of their duty, and persons assisting them; and murder by prisoners of prison officers in the execution of their duty, and the persons assisting them.

Those convicted of capital offences were sentenced to death and the Home Secretary then considered all such cases to see if there were grounds for granting a reprieve. [On average 45% were reprieved.] The penalty for non-capital murder under the Homicide Act 1957 was a mandatory life sentence. Reprieved capital murderers were made to serve life sentences ... [T]he Murder (Abolition of Death Penalty) Act 1965 ... removed the earlier distinctions drawn by the Homicide Act ... Parliament intended that this power [to make a minimum recommendation] could be used by judges to make 'low tariff' minimum recommendations (for example in mercy killing cases) but this has not happened. Indeed, judges have limited the use of this power to making recommendations of twelve years or longer ... Furthermore the range of cases in which the power has been used includes a considerable number which, under the Homicide Act 1957 criteria, would have been non-capital. The result has been that among the life-prisoner population during the last seventeen years are persons variously convicted of capital- and non-capital-murder offences as well as others, convicted after the 1965 Act, who have received 'minimum recommendations' for offences which would previously have been capital and non-capital ...

A Select Committee of the House of Lords (1989) has recommended that the mandatory penalty should be replaced, but governments have shown little inclination to introduce any changes. Some experience with a discretionary sentence for murder has been gained in New South Wales, where the mandatory penalty was abolished in 1982. The amendment to the Crimes Act 1900 (NSW) has the effect of retaining life as the penalty 'unless it appears to the Judge that the person's culpability for the crime is significantly diminished by mitigating circumstances, whether disclosed by the evidence in the trial or otherwise' (s 19) (see Yeo 1987).

Recently, in a number of high-profile cases, convicted killers have sought to challenge the Home Secretary's role in the tariff system. The first of these involved an appeal brought by Robert Thompson and John Venables, two 10-year-old boys convicted of killing two-year-old James Bulger, by repeated acts of violence in 1993.

R v Secretary of State for the Home Department ex p Venables, ex p Thompson [1997] 3 All ER 97

[The trial judge imposed the mandatory sentence of detention during Her Majesty's pleasure provided for by s 53(1) of the Children and Young Persons Act 1933 and in his report to the Home Secretary recommended that the 'tariff' *period of their sentence be eight years' detention. The tariff was increased to 10 years, on the advice of the Lord Chief Justice, and to 15 years by a Home Secretary swayed by a public petition containing some 278,300 signatures, a high-profile newspaper campaign, and over 5000 letters, all demanding that the applicants should remain in detention for life. This was an exercise of his discretion under s 35 of the Criminal Justice Act 1991. The applicants succeeded in their judicial review proceedings at the Divisional Court, which quashed the Home Secretary's decision. The Home Secretary appealed to the Court of Appeal, which accepted his argument that he was entitled to set a tariff but dismissed his appeal on the grounds, inter alia, that he had wrongly taken into account the public petition and media campaign in setting the tariff and therefore there had been procedural unfairness in reaching the decision. The Home Secretary appealed to the House of Lords. The applicants cross-appealed against the Court of Appeal's decision that the Home Secretary was entitled to impose the tariff.*]

Lord Steyn.

The Home Secretary treated two sentences for murder as exactly alike, namely (1) a mandatory sentence of life imprisonment passed on an adult convicted of murder and (2) a mandatory sentence of detention during Her Majesty's pleasure passed on a child or young person convicted of murder. He emphasised that in a policy statement to the House of Commons of 27 July 1993 (229 HC Official Report (6th series) written answers cols 861–864) in the following words:

'Everything that I have said about the practice of the Secretary of State in relation to mandatory life sentence prisoners applies equally to persons who are, or will be, detained during Her Majesty's Pleasure under s 53(1) ... '

In the same policy statement he contrasted the position of a prisoner subject to a mandatory life sentence with that of a prisoner subject to a discretionary life sentence. Once the minimum period fixed for retribution and deterrence has been satisfied, and provided that he is no longer a risk, a prisoner serving a discretionary life sentence is entitled to be released: s 34 of the Criminal Justice Act 1991. But a more severe regime applies to prisoners convicted of murder who are subject to mandatory life sentences. The Home Secretary indorsed the 'practice' that an adult prisoner subject to mandatory life sentence has forfeited his liberty to the state for the rest of his days. He said that the 'presumption' is that such a prisoner should remain in custody until the Home Secretary concludes that the public interest would be better served by the prisoner's release than by his continued detention. This is how the Home Secretary also viewed the nature of a sentence of detention during Her Majesty's pleasure under s 53(1).

It is now necessary to examine the correctness of the Home Secretary's view of a s 53(1) sentence. In order to understand the nature of a sentence of detention during Her Majesty's pleasure it is necessary to start with the position before the 1908 Act was enacted. For this purpose I gratefully draw on a report prepared by Professor A W B Simpson, the distinguished legal historian, and submitted to the European Court of Human Rights in *Singh v UK* (1996) 1 BHRC 119. Until the 1908 Act the formal law (as opposed to Home Office practice) made no special provision for children or young persons convicted of murder. In strict law youthful convicted murderers could be executed. But it became the practice not to execute murderers who were under the age of 18 years. It is probable that whenever a convicted murderer was reprieved on account of youth, a life sentence of penal servitude would have been imposed, and the individual would only have been released after serving a conventional period of 20 years unless he was then thought to be still dangerous. This practice was consistent with the notion that if children were criminally responsible they were amenable to exactly the same punishments as adults. Gradually, that policy fell into disfavour: the view gained ground that all juvenile offenders formed a distinct category of offenders for whom special arrangements for disposal should be made. The 1908 Act was a reforming measure which throughout reflected this change in attitude to young offenders. Thus it abolished the use of prisons for offenders under 14; it abolished penal servitude for those under it; and it permitted imprisonment for those between 14 and 16 only exceptionally. Section 103 formally abolished a sentence of death against a child or young person. That left the important question of the substitute penalty. Following previous practice regarding the punishment of children convicted of murder Parliament could have provided for a sentence of life imprisonment, or for detention for life. But Parliament chose not to do so. Instead, the 1908 Act provided that the new sentence to be imposed on children (those between 8 and 14) and young persons (those between 14 and 16) would be detention during His Majesty's pleasure. And the statute provided that, if so sentenced, the child or young person would be liable to be detained in such place and under such conditions as the Secretary of State directed.

...

Subsequently, Parliament revisited this subject. Section 53(1) of the 1933 Act re-enacted s 103 in respect of persons under 18 convicted of murder.

...

It was, of course, possible for Parliament subsequently to reverse the policy adopted in 1908 and repeatedly reaffirmed. Counsel for the Home Secretary said that Parliament did so by provisions in the 1991 Act. Carefully distancing himself from the view that a s 53(1) sentence 'is the same' as a sentence of life imprisonment, counsel for the Home Secretary said that the 1991 Act shows that Parliament was satisfied that a s 53(1) sentence had sufficient similarities to a mandatory life sentence imposed on an adult murderer to make it appropriate to deal with the question of release on life licence of prisoners in both categories under the same provisions. As I understood the argument it involves saying that Parliament in effect assimilated the two sentences and that in fixing a tariff for Venables and Thompson the Home Secretary was entitled to proceed on the basis that, like adults serving mandatory life sentences, they had forfeited the rest of their lives to the state. This argument crucially depends on two sections in the 1991 Act. Section 43(2) of the 1991 Act provides that the provisions for release apply to s 53(1) sentences. This is a reference to s 35(2) which provides that if the Parole Board so recommends, the Home Secretary may, after consulting the Lord Chief Justice and the trial judge, release on life licence a life prisoner who is not a discretionary life prisoner. By s 35(2) 'life prisoner' includes a child or young person sentenced under s 53(1). These provisions are perfectly consistent with the policy that a sentence of detention during Her Majesty's pleasure is a sentence different in conception from a sentence of mandatory life imprisonment. These are procedural provisions which do not alter the nature of the s 53(1) sentence. It is true that there is similarity between a s 53(1) sentence and a sentence of life imprisonment in the sense that all persons released on licence shall remain in force until their death: s 37(3) of the 1991 Act. That is unremarkable. It tells us nothing about the nature of a s 53(1) sentence.

It is necessary to put counsel's arguments in context. It postulates that in 1991 Parliament reversed the policy it had adopted in 1908, and reaffirmed subsequently, by assimilating the sentences of children and young persons convicted of murder with adults convicted of murder. Given that no dissatisfaction with the conception of a sentence of detention during Her Majesty's pleasure ever became public such a change of direction would have been surprising. The merits of such a radical change, contrary to the long standing policy of differentiating between the sentences of adults and children, were never debated in public or in Parliament.

...

If his argument were to be accepted it would amount to legislation by stealth. But the truth is that the argument that in 1991 Parliament intended to assimilate s 53(1) sentences and mandatory life sentences is misconceived.

It follows that in making his decisions the Home Secretary wrongly equated the sentences of Venables and Thompson with that applicable to adults convicted of murder. I will assume that the Home Secretary was entitled to apply a 'practice' that a prisoner serving a mandatory life sentence has forfeited his life to the state and that the 'presumption' must be that the prisoner will spend the rest of his days in prison. But in my judgment this practice is plainly not legitimate in respect of the different sentence of detention during Her Majesty's pleasure. Section 53(1) is based on the premise that, to some extent, children are less accountable for their actions than adults. Subject to continued detention for reasons of risk, s 53(1) was intended to be a more merciful punishment than life imprisonment ... The Home Secretary misunderstood the legal nature of the sentence in respect of which he was called upon to exercise a discretion. He did take the ages of Venables and Thompson into account. But he misinterpreted the sentence prescribed by law for children convicted of murder. He did so to the detriment of Venables and Thompson. The Home Secretary's decisions were therefore unlawful. For the same reasons his policy statement of 27 July 1993 to the House of Commons was unlawful so far as it related to s 53(1) sentences.

[*Lord Steyn proceeded to consider the legality of increasing the tariff by the Home Secretary, particularly in view of the public clamour in the form of a petition and a tabloid newspaper campaign.*]

The Home Secretary regarded 'the public concern about this case' as evidenced by the 'petitions and other correspondence' as evidence in favour of increasing the tariff ... The Home Secretary in fixing a tariff may, like a sentencing judge, take into account the general consideration of public confidence in the criminal justice system. He may also take into account a more specific feature such as public concern about the severity, or lack of severity, of sentences imposed on children for crimes of violence. But may the Home Secretary take into account public clamour about the tariff to be fixed in a particular case? May he treat as relevant a newspaper campaign to obtain an increase in the tariff? May he take into account a demonstration in Queen Anne's Gate to protest about the tariff to be imposed?

For my part the matter can be decided on a twofold basis. First, the material in fact taken into account by the Home Secretary was worthless and incapable of informing him in a meaningful way of the true state of informed public opinion in respect of the tariff to be set in the cases of Venables and Thompson. By 'informed public opinion' I mean public opinion formed in the knowledge of all the material facts of the case. Plainly, the 'evidence' to which the Home Secretary referred did not measure up to his standard. It was therefore irrelevant. But the Home Secretary was influenced by it. He gave weight to it. On this ground his decision is unlawful. But the objection to the course adopted by the Home Secretary is more fundamental. The starting-point must be to inquire into the nature of the power to fix a tariff which the Home Secretary exercised. Writing on behalf of the Home Secretary the Home Office explained in correspondence placed before us that: '[The Home Secretary] must ensure that, at all times, he acts with the same dispassionate sense of fairness as a sentencing judge.'

The comparison between the position of the Home Secretary, when he fixes a tariff representing the punitive element of the sentence, and the position of a sentencing judge is correct. In fixing a tariff the Home Secretary is carrying out, contrary to the constitutional principle of separation of powers, a classic judicial function ... Parliament entrusted the underlying statutory power, which entailed a discretion to adopt a policy of fixing a tariff, to the Home Secretary. But the power to fix a tariff is nevertheless equivalent to a judge's sentencing power. Parliament must be assumed to have entrusted the power to the Home Secretary on the supposition that, like a sentencing judge, the Home Secretary would not act contrary to fundamental principles governing the administration of justice. Plainly a sentencing judge must ignore a newspaper campaign designed to encourage him to increase a particular sentence. It would be an abdication of the rule of law for a judge to take into account such matters. The same reasoning must apply to the Home Secretary when he is exercising a sentencing function. He ought to concentrate on the facts of the case and balance considerations of public interest against the dictates of justice. Like a judge the Home Secretary ought not to be guided by a disposition to consult how popular a particular decision might be. He ought to ignore the high-voltage atmosphere of a newspaper campaign. The power given to him requires, above all, a detached approach. I would therefore hold that public protests about the level of a tariff to be fixed in a particular case are legally irrelevant and may not be taken into account by the Home Secretary in fixing the tariff. I conclude that the Home Secretary misdirected himself in giving weight to irrelevant considerations. It influenced his decisions. And it did so to the detriment of Venables and Thompson.

For this further reason I conclude that his decisions were unlawful.

A majority of the House of Lords held that the decision of the Home Secretary was unlawful for two reasons: first, for failing to distinguish between mandatory sentences for adults and the detention imposed here on children, and second, because tariff fixing was a power equivalent to a judge's sentencing power, it ought to have remained detached from the pressure of public opinion. The applicants also successfully persuaded the European Court of Human Rights that the Home Secretary's role in tariff setting represented a violation of Article 6 (*V v UK* (2000)).

In *Anderson* (2002), a seven-panel House of Lords confidently declared that the Home Secretary should play no part in fixing the tariff of a convicted murderer. In a powerful rejection of this 'striking anomaly' (Lord Steyn at para 51), the House was helped by two recent decisions of the European Court of Human Rights (*Stafford v UK* and *Benjamin v UK* (2002)). The decision in *Anderson* both confirms and rejects predictions made by Lord Mustill in *Doody* (1993). It confirms the suggested assimilated approach towards discretionary and mandatory life sentences. However, it also rejects the proposition that the courts cannot alter the relationship between the convicted murderer and the state. In this context, Article 6 of the ECHR has emerged as a powerful tool for the judiciary to chip away at executive discretion in relation to tariff setting.

R (on the application of Anderson) v Secretary of State for the Home Dept [2002] 4 All ER 1089

Lord Steyn.

My Lords, the question is whether decisions about the term of imprisonment to be served by convicted murderers, sentenced to mandatory life imprisonment, should be made by the Secretary of State for the Home Department, a member of the executive, or by independent courts or tribunals.

The Home Secretary's power to control the release of mandatory life sentence prisoners derives from s 29 of the Crime (Sentences) Act 1997. It reads:

> '(1) If recommended to do so by the Parole Board, the Secretary of State may, after consultation with the Lord Chief Justice together with the trial judge if available, release on licence a life prisoner who is not one to whom section 28 above applies.
>
> (2) The Parole Board shall not make a recommendation under subsection (1) above unless the Secretary of State has referred the particular case, or the class of case to which that case belongs, to the Board for its advice.'

Given that the primary focus of this case is the Home Secretary's power of fixing the tariff, it is of some relevance to set out how the system worked and still works. On 17 July 1995 the Home Secretary explained the position to the House of Commons. He said (263 HC Official Report 6th series col 1353):

> 'In every case where an offender is convicted of murder, the trial judge completes a detailed report on the background to the case. Whether or not he has made a formal recommendation in open court, the judge sets out his advice on the minimum period that should be served for retribution and deterrence. This report goes first to the Lord Chief Justice, who adds his own comments and then forwards the report to me. All this normally happens within two or three weeks of the conviction. The whole of the report, apart from opinions about future risk, is disclosed to the prisoner, together with any other relevant papers, such as details of previous convictions, which will be put to Ministers in due course. This means that in practice, the prisoner sees everything that is relevant to the setting of the tariff. The prisoner is given the opportunity to make any representations he wishes on the judicial recommendations and the other contents of the report. It is, however, made clear to him that the judicial views are

advisory and that the tariff will be set by the Secretary of State. The prisoner's representations, along with the judicial report, are then submitted to Ministers, who make the decision on tariff. This is communicated to the prisoner. If, after considering the judicial advice and the prisoner's representations, I decide that a tariff higher than that recommended by the trial judge is required for deterrence and retribution, the prisoner is given detailed reasons for that decision and these reasons are, of course, open to scrutiny by the courts by way of judicial review. To summarise, the prisoner is aware of the judicial view and has the opportunity to make representations. He is then told of the tariff set. If there is any departure from the judicial advice, he is given detailed reasons. Once the prisoner has been informed of the tariff, we are prepared to disclose both the tariff and the judicial recommendation in individual cases to anyone who asks. The process cannot therefore be described as secretive – it could hardly be more open.'

There have been subsequent ministerial statements on this subject but as far as the executive is concerned the 1995 statement is still controlling. It is to be noted that within the institutional constraints of a decision taken by a member of the executive, a concerted attempt was made to model the fixing of the tariff on a quasi-judicial procedure. The procedure highlights the analogy between the role of the Home Secretary, when he fixes a tariff representing the punitive element of the sentence, and the role of a sentencing judge.

In a series of decisions since *Doody*'s case ... the House of Lords has described the Home Secretary's role in determining the tariff period to be served by a convicted murderer as punishment akin to a sentencing exercise ... While a series of House of Lords decisions have revealed concerns about the compatibility of the operation of the system with the rule of law, the lawfulness in principle of the Home Secretary's role was not in doubt.

The question is now whether the Home Secretary's decision-making power over the terms to be served by mandatory life sentence prisoners is compatible with a later statute enacted by Parliament, namely that by which Parliament incorporated the European Convention for the Protection of Human Rights and Fundamental Freedoms 1950 into the law of the United Kingdom. Article 6(1) of the convention, so far as it is material, provides:

'In the determination of his civil rights and obligations or of any criminal charge against him, everyone is entitled to a fair and public hearing within a reasonable time by an independent and impartial tribunal established by law.'

Article 6(1) requires effective separation between the courts and the executive, and further requires that what can, in shorthand, be called judicial functions may only be discharged by the courts ...

The relevant developments for present purposes include the following. First, as a result of a decision of the European Court of Human Rights in *Thynne v UK* (1991) 13 EHRR 666, Parliament made the judiciary and the Parole Board alone responsible for decisions about the release of discretionary life sentence prisoners. The Home Secretary was not perceived to be independent. Parliament reformed the law by enacting s 34 of the Criminal Justice Act 1991. In the result, the Home Secretary no longer controls release of a category of life-sentence prisoners which includes some of the most dangerous prisoners in our prisons. Secondly, a parallel development followed in respect of young persons sentenced to detention during Her Majesty's pleasure. As a result of the decision of the European Court in *V v UK* (2000) 30 EHRR 121, the tariff system in respect of juveniles had to be reorganised. Ministers lost their power to set the tariff [He referred to Practice Statements *2000 and 2002*]. Again, the reason for this development was that the Home Secretary could no longer be regarded as independent for the purposes of performing this function.

Thirdly, the coming into force in 1999 of the Scotland Act 1998 to which was scheduled the Human Rights Act 1998 led to legislation by the Scottish Parliament effectively to eliminate the role of the executive in Scotland in fixing terms to be served by mandatory life sentence prisoners: Convention Rights (Compliance) (Scotland) Act 2001. The reason for this legislation was the apprehension that the executive's role would be in conflict with art 6(1) ... For the same reason the role of the executive in controlling the periods to be served by mandatory life-sentence prisoners in Northern Ireland was brought to an end ... These developments have increased the doubts about the Home Secretary's remaining role in England and Wales about the one class of life-sentence prisoners over whom he still exercises control.

Until recently, however, there was a justification in European jurisprudence for the Home Secretary's retention of the power to fix the tariff in respect of mandatory life sentence prisoners. It derived from the ruling in *Wynne v UK* (1995) ... As a result of two recent decisions of the European Court this prop of the Home Secretary's position has now, in terms of European jurisprudence, been knocked out.

In *Stafford v UK* (2002) 13 BHRC 260 at 279 (para 78), the Grand Chamber of the European Court reviewed developments which in its view led to the conclusion that–

'the continuing role of the Secretary of State in fixing the tariff and in deciding on a prisoner's release following its expiry, has become increasingly difficult to reconcile with the notion of separation of powers between the executive and the judiciary, a notion which has assumed growing importance in the case law of the Court ... '

Referring to the judgment in *Wynne v UK* the court observed ((2002) 13 BHRC 260 at 279):

'The court considers that it may now be regarded as established in domestic law that there is no distinction between mandatory life prisoners, discretionary life prisoners and juvenile murderers as regards the nature of tariff-fixing. It is a sentencing exercise. The mandatory life sentence does not impose imprisonment for life as a punishment. The tariff, which reflects the individual circumstances of the offence and the offender, represents the element of punishment. The court concludes that the finding in *Wynne v UK* [(1995) 19 EHRR 333] that the mandatory life sentence constituted punishment for life can no longer be regarded as reflecting the real position in the domestic criminal justice system of the mandatory life prisoner.' ...

The House of Lords concluded that s 29 of the 1997 Act and the Home Secretary's tariff setting practice were incompatible with Article 6(1), and issued a declaration of incompatibility pursuant to s 4 of the 1998 Act. This was in line with reforms introduced in Scotland and Northern Ireland. The UK Government responded by amending the Criminal Justice Bill 2003 during its passage through Parliament. This introduces a three-tier classification for murder sentencing. A 15-year starting-point will be doubled to 30 for the murder of police or prison officers, witnesses and for sadistic and sexual murders. This higher sentence will also form the starting-point for murders committed for gain, such as robbery, and for those involving guns or explosives. Most controversial is the direction for 'whole life tariffs' for premeditated multiple murder and child murder following abduction or sadistic or sexual conduct, terrorist murders and for repeat offenders. A whole life tariff satisfies the oft-voiced call that 'life should mean life', that is incarceration for the whole of the prisoner's natural life. In allowing for judges to vary such starting-points with reference to mitigating factors, it remains to be seen whether these proposals allow sufficient room for manoeuvre in terms of their compatibility with Article 6.

Somewhat ironic (and fortunate for the Home Secretary) was the death of Myra Hindley, serving her 37th year in prison following her role in the notorious Moors Murders, a few days before the ruling in *Anderson* (2002). She was convicted in 1966 along with Ian Brady for the sadistic killing of three children. The Lord Chief Justice recommended a tariff of 25 years, but after she had admitted to a further two killings, successive Home Secretaries confirmed a 'whole life' tariff. In 2000, the House of Lords dismissed Hindley's appeal against her tariff (*R v Secretary of State for the Home Dept ex p Hindley*, 2000). Although the decision in *Anderson* might have opened the door for Hindley's release, as the extract from Lord Steyn below makes clear, the capacity to ensure that 'life means life' is preserved:

R (on the application of Anderson) v Secretary of State for the Home Dept [2002] 4 All ER 1089

Lord Steyn.

This appeal raises the question whether the period of imprisonment to be served by a mandatory life sentence prisoner as punishment should be determined by the executive or the judiciary. It does not concern the question how individual cases should be approached. On the hypothesis, however, that the appeal in this case succeeds, it is important to guard against misunderstanding in one respect. If the role of the executive in setting the tariff should cease it does not follow that life imprisonment for murder may never, even in the worst cases imaginable, literally mean detention for life. In the Divisional Court in *R v Secretary of State for the Home Dept, ex p Hindley* ... Lord Bingham of Cornhill CJ observed that he could–

'see no reason, *in principle*, why a crime or crimes, if sufficiently heinous, should not be regarded as deserving lifelong incarceration for purposes of pure punishment.'

On appeal to the House of Lords, ... I expressed myself in similar terms: The following passage is part of the ratio of that case:

'The last submission is that the policy of imposing whole life tariffs is inconsistent with the notion of a tariff which requires expression in a term of years. This is an appeal to legal logic. But there is nothing logically inconsistent with the concept of a tariff by saying that there are cases where the crimes are so wicked that even if the prisoner is detained until he or she dies it will not exhaust the requirements of retribution and deterrence.'

In *Stafford v UK* (2002) 13 BHRC 260 at 279–280 (para 79) the European Court observed 'that a whole life tariff may, in exceptional cases, be imposed where justified by the gravity of the particular offence'. If in future the judiciary and the Parole Board are given the sole responsibility for the system there may still be cases where the requirements of retribution and deterrence will require lifelong detention.

The crimes of other infamous lifers such as Rosemary West and Harold Shipman would presumably represent such 'exceptional cases'. In two other appeals heard alongside *Anderson*, s 1(1) of the 1965 Act survived a challenge that it was arbitrary and disproportionate in requiring the same life sentence to be passed on all murderers. In *Lichniak, Pyrah* (2002), the House of Lords dismissed the claim that it was incompatible with Articles 3 and 5 of the Convention (prohibition on inhuman and degrading treatment and the right to liberty, respectively).

The mandatory penalty contributes to, although does not completely account for, the need to make a distinction between murder and manslaughter. The differentiation between the two types of homicide emerged in the early sixteenth century in statutes and legal writings and remained of fundamental importance in the eighteenth century because manslaughter was clergyable, and thus non-capital. Before that, juries achieved a rough-and-ready distinction by distorting the law:

Thomas Andrew Green, *Verdict According to Conscience* (University of Chicago Press, 1985) pp 30–32

[The extension of royal jurisdiction in the twelfth century to encompass the entire area of homicide had two revolutionary effects: many homicides that formerly had not resulted in capital punishment were now made capital under the law; and strict and largely unenforceable requirements were introduced into a law of self-defence.] The following study attempts to demonstrate that from late Anglo-Saxon times to the end of the Middle Ages there existed a widespread societal distinction between 'murder', i.e., homicide perpetrated through stealth, and 'simple' homicide, roughly what a later legal age termed manslaughter. This distinction, which was imposed upon the courts through the instrument of the trial jury, was fundamentally at odds with the letter of the law.

In the early twelfth century, the Crown took exclusive jurisdiction over all homicides and defined them as (1) culpable and thereby capital, (2) excusable and thereby pardonable, (3) justifiable and thereby deserving of acquittal. The last class at first incorporated the slaying of manifest felons (e.g., 'hand-having thieves') and outlaws who resisted capture. By the middle of the fourteenth century it came to include the killing of housebreakers and robbers caught in the act, though it was not until the sixteenth century that a statute turned this policy into firm law. Pardonable homicides were those committed by the insane, those committed in self-defense, and those committed unintentionally. The rules of self-defense were rigorous throughout the entire medieval period. The slayer had to have made every possible attempt to escape his attacker, must have reached a point beyond which he could not retreat, and must have retaliated out of literally vital necessity. All other intentional homicides, those deliberate but of a sudden, as well as those planned and stealthily perpetrated, fell into the large category of culpable homicide. According to the rules of the law, there were to be no distinctions made among them. The classification remained intact until the late sixteenth century, when the judicial distinction between murder and manslaughter finally emerged ...

[T]he early history of criminal liability, especially for the period just preceding the imposition of royal jurisdiction in all homicides, suggests that from their very inception the official rules ran counter to and never really became a part of social practice. This argument, admittedly speculative, takes the following form. During the Anglo-Saxon period only those who committed homicide through secrecy or stealth – murder – had to pay for their act with their life. The new, twelfth-century practice subjected to the death penalty not only 'murderers' but the large class of open slayers formerly allowed to compensate for their act by payment of the wergild. The community resisted this harsh extension of capital punishment and subsequently found means – acquittals and verdicts of self-defense – to impose upon the courts their long-held notions of justice, a process that becomes visible to us only in the fourteenth century. Thus the societal distinction between murder and simple homicide had its source deep in the English past. The introduction of novel and strict official rules of liability did away with the traditional means of dispute settlement in simple homicide, but it did not erase traditional social attitudes about liability. Nor did the imposition of a new scheme of criminal administration prevent society from acting, within the context of that scheme, in accordance with its traditional attitudes.

Throughout the medieval period for which written records are extant, the great majority of defendants who stood trial for homicide were acquitted. While today many are acquitted, one must take into account the fact that most suspects do not now stand trial; the vast majority of them plead guilty. In the Middle Ages few pleaded guilty to any felony since the penalty was invariably capital ... Though malicious prosecution and honestly moved but mistaken indictments may account in part for the high rate of acquittals, other factors must also have been at work. It is contended here that, for the most part, those few who were condemned had especially offended against the standards of the community. By discriminating between them and the many who committed homicides of a less serious nature, the jurors were creating a de facto classification roughly similar to the later legal distinction between murder and manslaughter ...

The evidence as to jury attitudes in the fourteenth century may aid in understanding social attitudes towards criminal liability in the entire period from late Anglo-Saxon times to the end of the Middle Ages. If so, the argument would run as follows. Originally, the Anglo-Saxons practised the feud in homicide cases. The kin of the slain took vengeance upon the slayer or one of his kin, who were jointly liable for their kinsman's act. Whether the mental element was taken into account is unknown. Secret homicide was a matter for the king, but all other homicides were emendable; failure to pay the wergild rendered the slayer and his kin liable to vendetta, though reduction of the amount of compensation by agreement was probably common. By the tenth century, the laws restricted liability to vendetta to the actual slayer. They also mandated a reduction of wergild compensation where there had been mitigating circumstances. In such cases, where the slayer had acted in self-defense or through accident, the king relinquished the writ. While the kin of the slain might have taken a narrow view of such mitigating circumstances, society at large took a broader view of the matter, having nothing to gain from feud or compensation, and in a day when fights began easily and led often to death or sepsis or other results of poor medical techniques. In its eyes, secret homicide or especially malicious attacks justified punishment by death. Simple homicides were seen as requiring compensation, with mitigation if the act was unintentional or to some extent provoked. When all homicides were drawn within the sphere of royal jurisdiction and made, unless excusable, punishable by death, the community was forced to choose between presentment of the slayer and payment of the murdrum, a fine imposed for an unexplained homicide. Before 1215, persons presented for homicide were forced to undergo the ordeal, so that if the community desired to absolve a slayer it had to fail to present him in the first place ... By the third decade of the thirteenth century, however, this tension had been relieved: once the slayer had been presented, it was left to the trial jury to state whether he was guilty or not.

This provided them with an opportunity to acquit or adduce circumstances of pardonable homicide.

Clear modern examples of juries attempting in their decision-making to assert attitudes running counter to the law can be seen in the discussion of the *Herald of Free Enterprise* disaster (see **section II.c.iii.**), in the acquittals of doctors Arthur and Adams (see **section III.b.**), and in the *Sutcliffe* case below.

In the same way that in earlier periods juries were influenced by the capital consequences of some of their decisions, in modern times the existence of the mandatory life sentence for murder has helped to sustain the distinction between the two offences. This has been institutionalised through the manipulation of the mental element in murder, as well as through a number of excuse devices, for example provocation and diminished responsibility. But the distinction was and is more than procedure – or sentence-orientated. Although often obscured by the conceptual apparatus of the law with its use of mental elements as a means of delineation, a moral judgment is also being made. As can be seen in the extracts from the series of cases below, *DPP v Smith* (1961) to *Moloney* (1985), *Hancock* (1986), *Nedrick* (1986) and *Woollin* (1998) there is an ever-more desperate search for a magic formula whereby the murderer can be distinguished from the manslaughterer through the use of the notion of intention. Lord Goff's suggestion (see below) is that the concept of wicked recklessness used in Scotland might be of assistance in making the distinction. The moral factor becomes clearer when provocation and diminished responsibility are examined. They are fascinating examples of the way law denies the relevance of factors beyond the cognitive mental elements, and provide a mechanism through which motive and other legally 'irrelevant' considerations can be reflected (Norrie 2000).

IV.b.   The mental element in murder

Murder requires proof of intention to kill or to cause grievous bodily harm. The interaction of the two sides of this requirement – the meaning of 'intention' and its extension to grievous bodily harm – causes much judicial angst. On the second there has been more certainty than the first. Courts have been consistent in upholding this aspect of the law of murder (*Cunningham*, 1982). Law reform bodies and commentators have been less sure about the appropriateness of the grievous bodily harm rule and, as we have seen, Lord Mustill was strongly critical of it in *A-G's Reference (No 3 of 1994)* when he endorsed the following comments by Lord Steyn in *Powell/English* (1997):

R v Powell, R v English [1997] 4 All ER 545

Lord Steyn.

… That brings me to the qualification which I have foreshadowed. In English law a defendant may be convicted of murder who is in no ordinary sense a murderer. It is sufficient if it is established that the defendant had an intent to cause really serious bodily injury. This rule turns murder into a constructive crime. The fault element does not correspond to the conduct leading to the charge, ie the causing of death. A person is liable to conviction for a more serious crime than he foresaw or contemplated … This is a point of considerable importance. The Home Office records show that in the last three years for which statistics are available mandatory life sentences for murder were imposed in 192 cases in 1994; in 214 cases in 1995; and in 257 cases in 1996. Lord Windlesham, writing with great Home Office experience, has said that a minority of defendants convicted of murder have been convicted on the basis that they had an intent to kill: *Responses to Crime* vol 3 (1996) at 342, n 29. That assessment does not sur- prise me. What is the justification for this position? There is an argument that, given the unpredictability whether a serious injury will result in death, an offender who intended to cause serious bodily injury cannot complain of a conviction of murder in the event of a death. But this argument is outweighed by the practical consideration that immediately below murder there is the crime of manslaughter for which the court may impose a discretionary life sentence or a very long period of imprisonment. Accepting the need for a mandatory life sentence for murder, the problem is one of classification. The present definition of the mental element of murder results in defendants being classified as murderers who are not in truth murderers. It happens both in cases where only one offender is involved and in cases resulting from joint criminal enterprises. It results in the imposition of mandatory life sentences when neither justice nor the needs of society require the classification of the case as murder and the imposition of a mandatory life sentence.

The observations which I have made about the mental element required for murder were not directly in issue in the appeals under consideration. But in the context of murder the application of the accessory principle, and the definition of murder, are inextricably linked. For that reason I have felt at liberty to mention a problem which was not addressed in argument. That counsel did not embark on such an argument is not altogether surprising. After all, in *R v Cunningham* [1982] AC 566 the House of Lords declined to rationalise and modernise the law on this point. Only Lord Edmund-Davies expressed the hope that the legislature would undertake reform (at 583). In my view the problem ought to be addressed. There is available a precise and sensible solution, namely, that a killing should be classified as murder if there is an intention to kill or an intention to cause really serious bodily harm coupled with awareness of the risk of death: 14th Report of the Law Revision Committee, (1980) para 31, adopted in the Criminal Code, for England and Wales (Law Com No 177) (1986) cl 54(1). This solution was supported by the House of Lords Select Committee on Murder and Life Imprisonment, HL Paper 78–1, 1989, para 68.

The extracts below consider whether intention should be subjectively determined and what it might mean to 'intend' a result:

DPP v Smith [1961] AC 290

[*The appellant was driving a car containing some stolen property when a policeman told him to draw into the kerb. Instead, he accelerated and the constable clung on to the side of the car. The policeman fell off in front of another car and was killed. At trial Donovan J directed the jury: 'if you are satisfied that … he must, as a reasonable man, have contemplated that grievous bodily harm was likely to result to that officer … and that such harm did happen and the officer died in consequence, then the accused is guilty of capital murder.' The jury convicted. The Court of Criminal Appeal quashed the conviction. The House of Lords restored it.*]

Viscount Kilmuir LC.

… The main complaint is that the learned judge was there applying what is referred to as an objective test, namely the test of what a reasonable man would contemplate as the probable result of his acts, and, therefore, would intend, whereas the question for the jury, it is said, was what the respondent himself intended …

The jury must of course in such a case as the present make up their minds on the evidence whether the accused was unlawfully and voluntarily doing something to someone. The unlawful and voluntary act must clearly be aimed at someone in order to eliminate cases of negligence or of careless or dangerous driving. Once, however, the jury are satisfied as to that, it matters not what the accused in fact contemplated as the probable result, or whether he ever contemplated at all, provided he was in law responsible and accountable for his actions, ie was a man capable of forming an intent, not insane within the M'Naghten Rules and not suffering from diminished responsibility. On the assumption that he is so accountable for his actions, the sole question is whether the unlawful and voluntary act was of such a kind that grievous bodily harm was the natural and probable result ...

[T]here seems to be no ground on which the approach by the trial judge in the present case can be criticised ... My only doubt concerns the use of the expression 'a reasonable man', since this to lawyers connotes the man on the Clapham omnibus by reference to whom a standard of care in civil cases is ascertained. In judging of intent, however, it really denotes an ordinary man capable of reasoning who is responsible and accountable for his actions, and this would be the sense in which it would be understood by a jury.

Another criticism of the summing-up and one which found favour in the Court of Criminal Appeal concerned the manner in which the trial judge dealt with the presumption that a man intends the natural and probable consequences of his acts. I will cite the passage again:

> The intention with which a man did something can usually be deter-mined by a jury only by inference from the surrounding circumstances including the presumption of law that a man intends the natural and probable consequences of his acts.

It is said that the reference to this being a presumption of law without explaining that it was rebuttable amounted to a misdirection. Whether the presumption is one of law or of fact or, as has been said, of common sense, matters not for this purpose.

The real question is whether the jury should have been told that it was rebuttable. In truth, however, as I see it, this is merely another way of applying the test of the reasonable man. Provided that the presumption is applied, once the accused's knowledge of the circumstances and the nature of his acts have been ascertained, the only thing that could rebut the presumption would be proof of incapacity to form an intent, insanity or diminished responsibility. In the present case, therefore, there was no need to explain that the presumption was rebuttable ...

The objective test endorsed in *Smith* was effectively abolished by s 8 of the Criminal Justice Act 1967. Although the appellate courts have found great difficulty in finding a universal formula for the 'mens rea' of murder, there has been no sign of a move to depart from a 'subjective' test. The subjective test itself has, however, been subjected to both stretching and contraction. There has been considerable judicial wavering on the question of what is meant by intention itself, or whether indeed intention is what is needed. In *Hyam v DPP* (1975) the House of Lords considered the correctness of a jury direction in terms of foresight of death or grievous bodily harm as highly probable. The defendant, who was jealous of another woman, had poured petrol through the rival's letter-box followed by newspaper which she lit. She did not know whether the house was occupied but she had checked that her lover was not there. Two children died. Although the case is notoriously unclear, her conviction for murder was upheld on a 3:2 majority. Eleven years later, an appeal against conviction for murder was allowed in an almost identical case. The same direction to the jury in *Nedrick* (1986) in terms of foresight of death or grievous bodily harm as highly probable was held by the Court of Appeal to be wrong and the conviction was quashed. Those impressed by the doctrine of a strict adherence to precedent will wonder how this could occur. The clue(s) lie in two intervening House of Lords' cases, *Moloney* (1985) and *Hancock* (1986), extracts from which are given below:

R v Moloney [1985] AC 905

[Moloney was convicted of the murder of his stepfather, whom he shot at close range as the result of a drunken contest as to which of them could load and draw a shotgun the fastest. The Crown had refused a plea of guilty to a charge of manslaughter. The Court of Appeal dismissed his appeal but certified the following point of general public importance: Is malice aforethought in the crime of murder established by proof that when doing the act which causes the death of another the accused either: (a) intends to kill or do serious harm; or (b) foresees that death or serious harm will probably occur, whether or not he desires either of those consequences?]

Lord Bridge.

The true and only basis of the appellant's defence that he was guilty not of murder but of manslaughter was encapsulated in the two sentences in his statement: 'I didn't aim the gun. I just pulled the trigger and he was dead.' The appellant amplified this defence in two crucial passages in his evidence. He said: 'I never deliberately aimed at him and fired at him intending to hurt him or to aim close to him intending to frighten him.' A little later he said he had no idea in discharging the gun that it would injure his father: 'In my state of mind I never considered that the probable consequence of what I might do might result in injury to my father. I never conceived that what I was doing might cause injury to anybody. It was just a lark.'

This being the evidence, the issue for the jury was a short and simple one. If they were sure that, at the moment of pulling the trigger which discharged the live cartridge, the appellant realised that the gun was pointing straight at his stepfather's head, they were bound to convict him of murder. If, on the other hand, they thought it might be true that, in the appellant's drunken condition and in the context of this ridiculous challenge, it never entered the appellant's head when he pulled the trigger that the gun was pointing at his father, he should have been acquitted of murder and convicted of manslaughter.

The judge correctly directed the jury that, in order to prove the appellant guilty of murder, 'the prosecution have to prove that he intended either to kill his stepfather or to cause him some really serious bodily injury'. But he had earlier given the following direction on intent:

> When the law requires that something must be proved to have been done with a particular intent, it means this: a man intends the consequences of his voluntary act (a) when he desires it to happen, whether or not he foresees that it probably will happen, and (b) when he foresees that it will probably happen, whether he desires it or not.

[I]t is necessary to examine two later passages in the summing up and a supplementary direction given to the jury in answer to a question which they asked. The judge, when he came to set out the case for the defence, quoted what I have described above as the two crucial passages in the appellant's evidence amplifying the sentence in his statement: 'I didn't aim the gun.' The judge did not relate these passages to his direction on intent, as many judges, I think, might have done, by saying to the jury: 'Members of the jury, if you believe that may be true, you should acquit of murder and convict of manslaughter.' Moreover, only a few sentences further on he quoted an answer given by the appellant under cross-examination as follows:

> There is no doubt that when I fired that gun it was pointing at my father's head at a distance of about six feet, and at this distance there is no doubt it would cause death. It is a lethal weapon.

It is clear that this answer must have been intended to acknowledge what the appellant recognised to be the fact with hindsight; it cannot have been intended as an admission of his state of mind at the time of the shooting ...

... The fact that, when the appellant fired the gun, the gun was pointing directly at his stepfather's head at a range of about six feet was not, and could not be, disputed. The sole issue was whether, when he pressed the trigger, this fact and its inevitable consequences were present to the appellant's mind. If they were, the inference was inescapable, using words in their ordinary, everyday meaning, that he intended to kill his stepfather. The undisputed facts that the appellant loved his stepfather and that there was no premeditation or rational motivation could not, as any reasonable juror would understand, rebut this inference. If, on the other hand, as the appellant was in substance asserting, it never crossed his mind, in his more or less intoxicated condition and when suddenly confronted by his stepfather's absurd challenge, that by pulling the trigger he might injure, let alone kill, his stepfather, no question of foresight of consequence arose for consideration. Whatever his state of mind, the appellant was undoubtedly guilty of a high degree of recklessness. But, so far as I know, no one has yet suggested that recklessness can furnish the necessary element in the crime of murder.

... If the jury had not demonstrated, by the question they asked after four hours of deliberation, that the issue of intent was one they did not understand, there might be room for further argument as to the outcome of this appeal. As it is, the jury's question, the terms of the judge's further direction and the jury's decision, just over an hour later, to return a unanimous verdict of guilty of murder leave me in no doubt, with every respect to the trial judge, and the Court of Appeal, that this was an unsafe and unsatisfactory verdict ...

... I am firmly of opinion that foresight of consequences, as an element bearing on the issue of intention in murder, or indeed any other crime of specific intent, belongs not to the substantive law but to the law of evidence. Here again I am happy to find myself aligned with Lord Hailsham in *Hyam v DPP* [1974] 2 All ER 41 at 43; where he said: 'Knowledge or foresight is at the best material which entitles or compels a jury to draw the necessary inference as to intention.' A rule of evidence which judges for more than a century found of the utmost utility in directing juries was expressed in the maxim, 'A man is presumed to intend the natural and probable consequences of his acts.' In *DPP v Smith* (1961) your Lordships' House, by treating this rule of evidence as creating an irrebuttable presumption and thus elevating it, in effect, to the status of a rule of substantive law, predictably provoked the intervention of Parliament by s 8 of the Criminal Justice Act 1967 to put the issue of intention back where it belonged, viz in the hands of the jury, 'drawing such inferences from the evidence as appear proper in the circumstances'. I do not by any means take the conjunction of the verbs 'intended or foresaw' and 'intend or forese' in that section as an indication that Parliament treated them as synonymous; on the contrary, two verbs were needed to connote two different states of mind.

I think we should now no longer speak of presumptions in this context but rather of inferences. In the old presumption that a man intends the natural and probable consequences of his acts the important word is 'natural'. This word conveys the idea that in the ordinary course of events a certain act will lead to a certain consequence unless something unexpected supervenes to prevent it. One might almost say that, if a consequence is natural, it is really otiose to speak of it as also being probable.

... In the rare cases in which it is necessary to direct a jury by reference to foresight of consequences, I do not believe it is necessary for the judge to do more than invite the jury to consider two questions. First, was death or really serious injury in a murder case (or whatever relevant consequence must be proved to have been intended in any other case) a natural consequence of the defendant's voluntary act? Second, did the defendant foresee that consequence as being a natural consequence of his act? The jury should then be told that if they answer Yes to both questions it is a proper inference for them to draw that he intended that consequence. [Lord Hailsham, Lord Fraser, Lord Edmund-Davies and Lord Keith concurred.]

The last paragraph contains the (in)famous '*Moloney*' guidelines which were soon reconsidered by the House of Lords:

R v Hancock [1986] 2 WLR 357

[*The two defendants caused the death of a taxi driver when they pushed two concrete slabs from a bridge which crossed the road on which the taxi was travelling. The deaths occurred during the 1984–1985 miners' strike. The defendants were on strike; the taxi was carrying a non-striking miner to work. Both denied intending death or serious bodily harm. Although the Court of Appeal allowed their appeals against convictions for murder, the prosecution, unusually and unsuccessfully, appealed to the House of Lords. Lord Lane CJ, in the Court of Appeal, had suggested that the following guidelines be substituted for those of Lord Bridge in Moloney:*

> *In cases in which the defendant's motive or purpose was not primarily to kill or injure, the judge should ask the jury to consider some such questions as these. (a) Are you sure that the defendant did the act which caused death, knowing what he was doing and intending to do it? If No, you must find him not guilty of both murder and manslaughter. If Yes, go on to consider the next question. (b) Are you sure that the defendant's act was of a kind which was highly likely to cause death or really serious bodily injury? If No, you must find him not guilty of murder, but he may be guilty of manslaughter. If Yes, go on to consider the next question. (c) On the evidence considered as a whole, which will of course include the defendant's evidence and that of his witnesses, are you sure that the defendant appreciated that what he did was highly likely to cause death or really serious bodily injury? If your answer is No, you must not find him guilty of murder, but he may be guilty of manslaughter. If your answer is Yes, there is evidence before you from which you can infer that the defendant intended to cause death or really serious bodily injury, but you must not find him guilty of murder unless you feel sure that he so intended. If however you are sure, the fact that he may not have desired that result is irrelevant. Desire and intent are two different things.*]

Lord Scarman.

The appeal is brought to secure a ruling from the House on the refusal of the Court of Appeal to accept as sound the guidelines formulated by this House in ... *R v Moloney* ... The Court of Appeal quashed the convictions on the ground that the judge's guidance [which was based on the *Moloney* guidelines] may well have misled the jury. The court refused leave to appeal but certified the following point of general public importance:

'Do the questions to be considered by a jury set out in the speech of Lord Bridge in *R v Moloney* as a model direction require amplification?'

It will be observed that the questions which it was suggested in *Moloney*'s case that the jury should ask themselves refer to a 'natural' consequence, not a 'natural and probable' consequence. The Crown now appeals with the leave of the House.

The appeal is of importance for two reasons. First, of course, there is the need to settle a point of difference between this House and the Court of Appeal. The *Moloney* guidance was intended to be authoritative in the sense that it was given to be followed by judges in appropriate cases, ie those 'exceptional' cases, as the House thought, where the foreseeability of death or serious bodily harm may be relevant to a decision as to the intent underlying the act of violence. The House realised and declared, however, that the guidance was no part of the ratio decidendi in the case ... The guidance was offered as an attempt in a practical way to clarify and simplify the task of the jury. It was not intended to prevent judges from expressing in other language, if they should deem it wise in a particular case, guidance designed to assist the jury to reach a conclusion on the facts in evidence.

The dangers inherent in general guidance for the assistance of juries in determining a question of fact lead me to the second reason for the importance of the appeal, namely that the cases to which the guidance was expressly limited by the House in *Moloney*'s case, i.e. the 'rare cases' in which it is necessary to direct a jury by reference to foresight of consequences, are unlikely to be so rare or so exceptional as the House believed. As the House then recognised, the guidelines as formulated are applicable to cases of any crime of specific intent, and not merely murder. But further and disturbingly crimes of violence where the purpose is by open violence to protest, demonstrate, obstruct or frighten are on the increase. Violence is used by some as a means of public communication. Inevitably there will be casualties; and inevitably death will on occasions result. If death results, is the perpetrator of the violent act guilty of murder? It will depend on his intent. How is the specific intent to kill or to inflict serious harm proved? Did he foresee the result of his action? Did he foresee it as probable? Did he foresee it as highly probable? If he did, is he guilty of murder? How is a jury to weigh up the evidence and reach a proper conclusion amidst these perplexities? The best guidance that can be given to a trial judge is to stick to his traditional function, i.e. to limit his direction to the applicable rule (or rules) of law, to emphasise the incidence and burden of proof, to remind the jury that they are the judges of fact and against that background of law to discuss the particular questions of fact which the jury have to decide, indicating the inferences which they may draw if they think it proper from the facts which they find established. Should not appellate guidance emphasise the importance of particular facts and avoid generalisation? This is a question to be considered. The facts of this case would appear to indicate an affirmative answer.

... Lord Bridge ... omitted any reference in his guidelines to probability. He did so because he included probability in the meaning which he attributed to 'natural'. My Lords, I very much doubt whether a jury without further explanation would think that 'probable' added nothing to 'natural'. I agree with the Court of Appeal that the probability of a consequence is a factor of sufficient importance to be drawn specifically to the attention of the jury and to be explained. In a murder case where it is necessary to direct a jury on the issue of intent by reference to foresight of consequences the probability of death or serious injury resulting from the act done may be critically important. Its importance will depend on the degree of probability: if the likelihood that death or serious injury will result is high, the probability of that result may, as Lord Bridge noted and Lord Lane CJ emphasised, be seen as overwhelming evidence of the existence of the intent to kill or injure. Failure to explain the relevance of probability may, therefore, mislead a jury into thinking that it is of little or no importance and into concentrating exclusively on the causal link between the act and its consequence. In framing his guidelines Lord Bridge emphasised that he did not believe it necessary to do more than to invite the jury to consider his two questions [see [1985] AC 905 at 929]. Neither question makes any reference (beyond the use of the word 'natural') to probability. I am not surprised that when in this case the judge faithfully followed this guidance the jury found themselves perplexed and unsure. In my judgment, therefore, the *Moloney* guidelines as they stand are unsafe and misleading. They require a reference to probability. They also require an explanation that the greater the probability of a consequence the more likely it is that the consequence was foreseen and that if that consequence was foreseen the greater the probability is that that consequence was also intended. But juries also require to be reminded that the decision is theirs to be reached on a consideration of all the evidence.

Accordingly, I accept the view of the Court of Appeal that the *Moloney* guidelines are defective. I am, however, not persuaded that guidelines of general application, albeit within a limited class of case, are wise or desirable. Lord Lane CJ formulated in this case guidelines for the assistance of juries but, for the reason which follows, I would not advise their use by trial judges when summing up to a jury.

I fear that their elaborate structure may well create difficulty. Juries are not chosen for their understanding of a logical and phased process leading by question and answer to a conclusion but are expected to exercise practical common sense. They want help on the practical problems encountered in evaluating the evidence of a particular case and reaching a conclusion. It is better, I suggest, notwithstanding my respect for the comprehensive formulation of the Court of Appeal's guidelines, that the trial judge should follow the traditional course of a summing up. [The judge] … should make certain that the jury understand that whereas the law is for him the facts are for them to decide. Guidelines, if given, are not to be treated as rules of law but as a guide indicating the sort of approach the jury may properly adopt to the evidence when coming to their decision on the facts.

In a case where foresight of a consequence is part of the evidence supporting a prosecution submission that the accused intended the consequence, the judge, if he thinks some general observations would help the jury, could well, having in mind s 8 of the Criminal Justice Act 1967, emphasise that the probability, however high, of a consequence is only a factor, though it may in some cases be a very significant factor, to be considered with all the other evidence in determining whether the accused intended to bring it about. The distinction between the offence and the evidence relied on to prove it is vital. Lord Bridge's speech in *Moloney*'s case made the distinction crystal clear; it would be a disservice to the law to allow his guidelines to mislead a jury into overlooking it. [Lord Keith, Lord Roskill, Lord Brightman and Lord Griffiths concurred.]

R v Nedrick [1986] 1 WLR 1025, Court of Appeal

[*The appellant poured paraffin through the letterbox of a woman against whom he bore a grudge and set it alight. The woman's child died. He claimed that he merely wanted to frighten the woman. He was convicted after a Hyam direction that the appellant was guilty of murder if he knew that it was highly probable that his act would result in death or serious bodily injury. Lord Lane delivered the judgment of the court, allowing the appeal and substituting a conviction of manslaughter:*]

What then do a jury have to decide so far as the mental element in murder is concerned? They simply have to decide whether the defendant intended to kill or do serious bodily harm. In order to reach that decision the jury must pay regard to all the relevant circumstances, including what the defendant himself said and did.

In the great majority of cases a direction to that effect will be enough, particularly where the defendant's actions amounted to a direct attack on his victim, because in such cases the evidence relating to the defendant's desire or motive will be clear and his intent will have been the same as his desire or motive. But in some cases, of which this is one, the defendant does an act which is manifestly dangerous and as a result someone dies. The primary desire or motive of the defendant may not have been to harm that person, or indeed anyone. In that situation what further directions should a jury be given as to the mental state which they must find to exist in the defendant if murder is to be proved?

We have endeavoured to crystallise the effect of their Lordships' speeches in *R v Moloney* and *R v Hancock* in a way which we hope may be helpful to judges who have to handle this type of case. It may be advisable first of all to explain to the jury that a man may intend to achieve a certain result whilst at the same time not desiring it to come about. In *R v Moloney* [1985] AC 905 at 926 Lord Bridge gave an illustration of the distinction:

> A man who, at London Airport, boards a plane which he knows to be bound for Manchester, clearly intends to travel to Manchester, even though Manchester is the last place he wants to be and his motive for boarding the plane is simply to escape pursuit.

The man who knowingly boards the Manchester aircraft wants to go there in the sense that boarding it is a voluntary act. His desire to leave London predominates over his desire not to go to Manchester. When he decides to board the aircraft, if not before, he forms the intention to travel to Manchester.

In *R v Hancock* the House decided that the *R v Moloney* guidelines require a reference to probability. Lord Scarman said ([1986] AC 455 at 473):

> They also require an explanation that the greater the probability of a consequence the more likely it is that the consequence was foreseen and that if that consequence was foreseen the greater the probability is that that consequence was also intended.

When determining whether the defendant had the necessary intent, it may therefore be helpful for a jury to ask themselves two questions. (1) How probable was the consequence which resulted from the defendant's voluntary act? (2) Did he foresee that consequence?

If he did not appreciate that death or serious harm was likely to result from his act, he cannot have intended to bring it about. If he did, but thought that the risk to which he was exposing the person killed was only slight, then it may be easy for the jury to conclude that he did not intend to bring about that result. On the other hand, if the jury are satisfied that at the material time the defendant recognised that death or serious harm would be virtually certain (barring some unforeseen intervention) to result from his voluntary act, then that is a fact from which they may find it easy to infer that he intended to kill or do serious bodily harm, even though he may not have had any desire to achieve that result.

As Lord Bridge said in *R v Moloney* [1985] AC 905 at 925: ' ... the probability of the consequence taken to have been foreseen must be little short of overwhelming before it will suffice to establish the necessary intent.'

Later he uses the expression 'moral certainty' ([1985] AC 905 at 926) and says, 'will lead to a certain consequence unless something unexpected supervenes to prevent it' (at 929).

Where the charge is murder and in the rare cases where the simple direction is not enough, the jury should be directed that they are not entitled to infer the necessary intention unless they feel sure that death or serious bodily harm was a virtual certainty (barring some unforeseen intervention) as a result of the defendant's actions and that the defendant appreciated that such was the case. Where a man realises that it is for all practical purposes inevitable that his actions will result in death or serious harm, the inference may be irresistible that he intended that result, however little he may have desired or wished it to happen. The decision is one for the jury to be reached on a consideration of all the evidence.

Nedrick left unclear what it is that the jury should be looking for in inferring intention. *Woollin* (1998) afforded yet another opportunity for the House of Lords to pin down intention. Woollin was convicted of murdering his three-month-old son after losing his temper and throwing him onto a hard surface. It was accepted that he had no direct intention to kill his son, but the prosecution alleged that he indirectly intended to cause him grievous bodily harm. He appealed against the trial judge's use in his summing up of the phrase 'substantial risk that he would cause serious injury', arguing that this unacceptably broadened the boundaries of murder. In allowing his appeal, and substituting a verdict of manslaughter, the House of Lords approved the *Nedrick* direction, albeit with three minor 'jury friendly' modifications:

> Where the charge is murder and in the rare cases where the simple direction is not enough, the jury should be directed that they are not entitled to find the necessary intention unless they feel sure that death or serious bodily harm was a virtual certainty (barring some unforeseen intervention) as a result of the defendant's actions and that the defendant appreciated that such was the case. The decision is one for the jury to be reached on a consideration of all the evidence.

First, Lord Steyn and Lord Hope dispensed with the two questions posed in the first part of the *Nedrick* direction ('How probable was the consequence which resulted from the defendant's voluntary act? Did he foresee that consequence?'). Second, they substituted the words 'to infer' intention with 'to find', and thirdly they tidied up the final part of the direction. However, this gives little assistance on what 'intention' might connote, a question which the judgment in *Nedrick* also skilfully avoided answering. The extract below reflects on the underlying assumptions which inform the debates about intention:

Nicola Lacey, 'A Clear Concept of Intention: Elusive or Illusory?' (1993) 56 MLR 621, 623

In considering recent discussions of the concept of intention in criminal law, it will be useful to distinguish between those which emphasise the importance of conceptual analysis, and those which give greater emphasis to the claims of 'ordinary usage.'

 ... The role of conceptual analysis in debates about the meanings of legal terms such as intention is widely regarded as simply inevitable: since concepts are the basic currency of the intellect, human practices are constructed and carried on in terms of conceptual frameworks which it is incumbent upon us to analyse. Yet conceptual analysis is further motivated by some very familiar and widely held political commitments. These are beliefs associated with the rule of law and indeed the 'principle of mens rea' which forms a central part of criminal law doctrine. Most importantly, they include the idea that criminal law, which imposes significant burdens and risks on citizens, should be as clear, certain, consistent and coherent as possible, so as to enable us to plan our lives around its proscriptions (an idea which depends upon the assumption of a rationalist, anti-determinist conception of human behaviour). Conceptual analysis can contribute to this ideal, so the argument goes, by fixing or explicating our legal concepts as clearly as possible and hence by promoting certainty and predictability.

... At the other end of the spectrum, we have the resort in the face of difficulties of definition to 'ordinary usage'. It should be noted that ordinary usage is itself something of a chimera. For just as 'legal usage' is arguably a relatively specific and autonomous area of discourse, many other areas of linguistic usage develop particular, local and technical meanings for 'ordinary words'. And even within these local areas, usage is fluid and often contested. This notwithstanding, the report to the 'common usage' or the 'ordinary person's understanding' of a particular term is a familiar technique in criminal law – perhaps most famously debated in recent years in the context of the concept of dishonesty under the Theft Act 1968. On the view which appeals to 'ordinary usage,' the attempt to articulate and fix particular conceptual analyses in legislative or judicial form is both unnecessary and misguided. It is unnecessary because, in the case of concepts such as intention, dishonesty, violence and so on, 'ordinary people' have a clear if unarticulated sense of what these terms mean. So it can simply be left to the jury or the lay magistrate to apply those ordinary understandings to the case at hand. And it is misguided, because part of the function of criminal laws which employ those terms is precisely to bring to bear on the alleged offender the standards of judgment thought to be buried within and reflected by 'ordinary usage': the thought behind the legal proscription in question is the application of a general rather than a technical standard in this respect. The 'ordinary language' view is therefore motivated by at least two concerns: the investment of mens rea terms with 'ordinary' or 'common sense' meanings, and the delegation of decision-making power in Crown Court cases to jury rather than to judge.

In the cases of *Moloney*, *Hancock*, *Shankland* and *Nedrick*, the Court of Appeal and the House of Lords engaged in an extended and somewhat tortuous analysis of the idea of intention in the context of murder: their reasoning expressly applies, however, to intention generally in criminal law. Because of the facts of these particular cases, and because of the last major House of Lords decision in the area – the case of *Hyam* – the main practical and conceptual question which arose was how the concept of intention related to that of foresight. In particular, the cases concern whether foresight of consequences as virtually or 'morally' certain constitutes an intent to bring those consequences about. On this basic conceptual issue, as is well known, the three successive cases of *Moloney*, *Hancock* and *Nedrick* failed to take up a clear stance, judicial analysis veering between implicit inclusions and exclusions of 'oblique intent' as a species of intention, often in the space of as little as a few phrases. The really important and interesting feature of the cases from my point of view is, however, not their resounding failure in this respect. It is rather the source of that failure and, more generally, the judicial methodology which led to what I have called the compromise strategy.

Whilst the combined strategy of partial conceptual stipulation and appeal to ordinary usage is on one level confused and contradictory, on another it can be seen as logical and effective. To put it colloquially, it is part of a complex strategy which allows criminal law to keep various balls of different shapes and colours in the air at once: to be a system of imposed social control; a system based on reciprocity of obligations and the recognition of certain universally held rights and interests; a system which reproduces and reinforces certain shared meanings; a system which manages or suppresses certain kinds of social conflict; and many other things besides. Thus, what from one point of view looks like judicial contradictoriness from another looks both astute and highly ideologically effective.

Let us now pursue the implications of this argument for the issue of how we should approach the study of criminal law, and relate the approach implicit in the analysis so far and approaches sometimes labelled 'critical legal studies' and represented by the work of, among others, Mark Kelman, David Nelken and Alan Norrie. The particular debate over appeals to ordinary usage versus conceptual stipulation provides a promising area in which to consider some of the questions raised by critical approaches to criminal law. Typically such approaches reject the claim that criminal law is characterised by some fundamental coherent, if inchoately realised, set of rationalising principles. They thus reject what I take to be the orthodox approach to criminal law scholarship: that is, to see it as the enterprise of eliciting, articulating and, where necessary, prescribing the proper principles informing criminal law, ironing out and rationalising apparent contradictions and exceptions, and paving the way for a clear, consistent and coherent theory and practice of criminal law on the basis of a loosely speaking liberal set of principles. The critical scholar sees this approach as both limited and ultimately distorting in terms of the image of criminal justice which it purveys. In particular, a certain degree of conceptual incoherence and contradiction is argued to be endemic to criminal law and criminal justice, and part of the role of the criminal law scholar is to confront and attempt to come to grips with this apparent incoherence. Secondly, the conflicts and inconsistencies which arise at the level of criminal law practice and doctrine are seen as symptomatic of deeper, substantive political questions which cannot be effectively submerged by doctrinal rationalisation or by formal conceptual analysis – that which focuses on the clear definition or delineation of terms without addressing itself to underlying political questions. If we are to confront apparent incoherence adequately, we have to go beyond not just the enterprise of the stipulative analyst but also that of the moral analyst; for we cannot assume that all the political issues relevant to an understanding of how criminal law definitions are applied in practice can be explicated in terms of an analysis of the substantive values underlying the concepts in terms of which those definitions are constructed. This means, thirdly, as at least some critical scholars acknowledge, that we have to come to terms with the diversity of roles and meanings which criminal justice has in our society if we are to come anywhere near understanding the significance of a whole range of practical problems which it throws up. These problems range from inconsistencies of enforcement through to what seem on the surface to be conceptual arguments at the level of criminal law doctrine. Not least, we have to come to terms with the ideological and symbolic aspects of criminal law as well as its instrumental functions as one powerful system of social ordering if we are to appreciate both the real significance of these various criminal justice issues and how they relate to one another.

    ... In analysing the recent cases, my main emphasis was on an interesting and logically problematic combination of appeals to conceptual stipulation and ordinary usage. The argument was that problems with either approach constantly pushed judges back towards the other, in a kind of endless dialectic. At the doctrinal level, this looks incoherent. But once we step back and think about the broader context within which criminal law operates, it begins to look like a rather meaningful strategy which contributes quite directly and comprehensibly to the perceived legitimacy of criminal law. The judges are seen to desist from behaving like legislators; they appeal to common usage in a way which suppresses the extent to which criminal laws are imposed by an exercise of power, emphasising the reciprocity of the system.

The passage below shows the (unconscious) slippage between conceptual and 'ordinary meaning' analysis:

Lord Goff, 'The Mental Element in the Crime of Murder' (1988) 104 LQR 30, 43

[I]t is plain that, just as intention can exist without desire, although they frequently coincide, so also intention can exist without foresight of the relevant consequence, although again they frequently coincide. Let us not forget that there can be intention to achieve the relevant result even though that is most unlikely to occur and so cannot be said to have been foreseen ... The idea that intention and foresight of consequences, or probability, necessarily coexist was, if not hit for six, at least hit into the rough by Lord Reid ...

In fact people often intend something quite different from what they know to be the natural and probable result of what they are doing. To take a trivial example, if I say I intend to reach the green, people will believe me although we all know that the odds are ten to one against my succeeding; and no one but a lawyer would say that I must be presumed to have intended to put my ball in the bunker because that was the natural and probable result of my shot.

So there can be intention without foresight that the relevant consequence was likely to occur. Conversely, there can be foresight of consequences without intention. To take an example given to me by a friend: when Field Marshal Montgomery invaded France on D-Day, he foresaw that many of the troops under his command would be killed on that very day. Obviously, however, he did not intend that any of them should be killed. But, of course, frequently intention to kill and foresight of consequences do go hand-in-hand ...

The narrowing down of the mental element in murder to the concept of 'intention' has generally been welcomed by jurists. But they are discovering that some cases, which they feel ought to be embraced within the crime of murder, do not quite fit within the concept of intention; and so they are embarking on the enterprise of illegitimately expanding the concept of intention to include these cases. The classic example of this technique is to be found in the idea of 'oblique' intention as expounded by Professor Glanville Williams in his textbook of Criminal Law ...

... To take a hypothetical case: suppose that a villain ... sends an insured parcel on an aircraft, and includes in it a time-bomb by which he intends to bring down the plane and consequently to destroy the parcel. His immediate intention is merely to collect on the insurance. He does not care whether the people on board live or die, but he knows that success in his scheme will inevitably involve their deaths as a side-effect. On the theoretical point, common sense suggests that the notion of intention should be extended to this situation; it should not merely be regarded as a case of recklessness. A consequence should normally be taken as intended although it was not desired, if it was foreseen by the actor as the virtually certain accompaniment of what he intended. This is not the same as saying that any consequence foreseen as probable is intended.

... [T]he trouble with this kind of approach is that it has distorted the plain meaning of the word. To the question – did the defendant mean to destroy the parcel? The answer is, of course, yes, he did. But to the question – did the defendant mean to kill the pilot? The answer is, no, he didn't. Indeed, if he saw the pilot land safely by parachute, he would no doubt be delighted; and so it is absurd to say that he meant to kill him.

The question of intention also arose in the context of the legality of separating conjoined twins Mary and Jodie (*Re A (Conjoined Twins)*, 2000): see **Chapter 4.II.f.** and **section III.a.** above. As Norrie explains, the Court of Appeal's approach offers a good example of orthodox subjectivism being manipulated to satisfy the moral context of the case.

Alan Norrie, 'From Criminal to Legal Theory: The Mysterious Case of the Reasonable Glue Sniffer' (2002) 65 Modern Law Review 538

This narrowing of the law of intention to exclude its indirect form (foresight of the criminal result as a virtual certainty) was recently rejected in a case involving conjoined twins. There it was held that doctors separating Mary and Jodie knowing that Mary would die would intend to kill Mary, their only refuge against a charge of murder being a defence of necessity, or perhaps self defence. Yet necessity, their favoured solution, had not been available on a murder charge for over a hundred years. When, however, it came to dealing with the Human Rights Act 1998, under which everyone has the right not to be *intentionally* deprived of a right to life [Article 2], the judges held that no doctor could be said to kill intentionally … Intention under the Human Rights Act was given precisely the meaning they had *rejected* when considering intention under the law of murder. In this case, one can say that the judges first reject, then accept, the existence of a contextual *moral threshold* concerning how intention is to be judged. They alternate their definition of intention to achieve the desired moral result, that the doctors can operate to save Jodie. The underlying problem is that the legal concept of intention is really out of phase with the intuited moral result. One might say here, rephrasing the old saw, that truly the road to legal hell is paved with good intentions.

Nearly all jurisdictions have a ladder of homicide offences. The debate about intention is largely a debate about which culpable killings should be at the most serious end of that ladder. Many civil law jurisdictions, as well as those derived from the common law, rely on more rungs than the two (murder and manslaughter) surviving in England and Wales. It is not uncommon for the most serious offence to involve either pre-meditation or an aggravating factor, such as use of firearms. On the other hand, many jurisdictions allow broader and more objective culpability tests than 'intention'. The felony murder rule still operates in many US states, for example. Under Scots law indifference is given a more central role.

Cawthorne v HM Advocate 1968 JC 32

[*The defendant fired shots from a rifle at random into a room in which four people had barricaded themselves. He was charged with attempted murder.*]

Lord Avonside (presiding).

In our law the crime of murder is committed when the person who brings about the death of another acted deliberately with intent to kill, or acted with intent to do bodily harm, or, and this is the third leg, acted with utter and wicked recklessness as to the consequences of his act upon his victim.

Lord Justice-General (Clyde).

In our law murder is constituted by any wilful act causing the destruction of life. Mens rea may be intention to kill ... or by satisfactory evidence of such wicked recklessness as to imply a disposition depraved enough to be regardless of consequences. The reason for this alternative being allowed in our law is that in many cases it may not be possible to prove what was in the accused's mind at the time, but the degree of recklessness in his actings, as proved by what he did, may be sufficient to establish proof of the wilful act on his part which caused the loss of life.

The Criminal Law Revision Committee in its Fourteenth Report (1980) did not refer directly to Scots law, but was rather dismissive of such a formula. In discussing the American Law Institute's Model Penal Code, s 210.2, which makes murder any killing committed recklessly in circumstances manifesting 'extreme indifference to the value of human life', the report (para 26) concludes that: 'apart from the adjective "extreme", this formula merely restates a require-ment of recklessness as to causing death in somewhat emotive terms' (cf Duff 1990).

See **Chapter 3.II.e.** for the Law Commission's proposed definition of 'intentionally', although there appear to be no plans to extend this to murder.

IV.c. Involuntary manslaughter

The category of homicide known as 'manslaughter' has been used to mop up killings which are not perceived, for one reason or another, as sufficiently heinous to deserve the label 'murder'. The foregoing section has already shown how reliance on the concept of intention has caused much difficulty in the delineation of murder. Manslaughter comprises both those unlawful killings where that intention is lacking, which we consider here, and those intentional killings for which there is a defence such as provocation or diminished responsi-bility: these are known as 'voluntary' manslaughters and are considered in the following sections.

Manslaughters of the type where the intention for murder is lacking are sometimes referred to as 'involuntary' manslaughters. What is needed to con-vert these non-intentional killings into manslaughter is extraordinarily vague and potentially far-reaching. These requirements have already been touched on in the discussion of corporate liability (see **section II.c.** above). There are currently two different routes to this type of manslaughter. The first is via an unlawful act: if the death is the result of a crime, and if that crime is one which carries with it the objective risk of physical harm of any kind, then this will be sufficient for manslaughter. The other route does not require an initial unlawful act and is satisfied by proof of gross negligence. Returning to a simple formulation, after an interregnum influenced by the *Caldwell* (1982) definition of recklessness (via *Lawrence*, 1982 and *Seymour*, 1983) in *Adomako* (1995), Lord Mackay summed up the test in this way: 'The jury will have to decide whether the extent to which the defendant's conduct departed from the proper standard of care incumbent upon him ... was such that it should be judged criminal.'

We have chosen to use involuntary manslaughter as an area in which to illustrate and discuss the Law Commission's proposed Criminal Code. This represents the aspirations for codification which underpin many of the ideological values (the rule of law, certainty, consistency, etc) central to criminal law doctrine (cf **Chapter 1.I.b.i.** and **Chapter 4.II.a.ii.**). The background to this Code is explained in the following extract:

Law Commission Report No 177, *A Criminal Code for England and Wales* (HMSO, 1989) paras 1.3, 1.4, 2.1, 2.2, 3.30, 3.31, 3.34

1.3 English criminal law is derived from a mixture of common law and statute. Most of the general principles of liability are still to be found in the common law, though some, for example the law relating to conspiracy and attempts to commit crime, have recently been defined in Acts of Parliament. The great majority of crimes are now defined by statute but there are important exceptions. Murder, manslaughter and assault are still offences at common law, though affected in various ways by statute. There is no system in the relative roles of common law and legislation ... Whether an offence is defined by statute has almost always been a matter of historical accident rather than systematic organisation ... The legislation in force extends over a very long period of time. It is true that only a very small amount of significant legislation is earlier than the mid-nineteenth century, but that is quite long enough for the language of the criminal law and the style of drafting to have undergone substantial changes.

1.4 There has been a steady flow of reform of the criminal law in recent years but it has been accomplished in somewhat piecemeal fashion. Some of it is derived from our own reports, where in recent years we have been pursuing the policy of putting common law offences into statutory form, and some from reports of the Criminal Law Revision Committee and committees, like the Heilbron Committee, appointed to deal with particular problems. Other reforms have resulted from the initiative of Ministers or private Members of Parliament in introducing Bills. As there is no authoritative statement of general principles of liability or of terminology to which we or these other bodies, or their draftsmen, can turn it would be surprising if there were not some inconsistencies and incongruities in the substance and language of the measures which are proposed and which become law ... This Report addresses the question whether it is desirable to replace the existing fluctuating mix of legislation and common law by one codifying statute.

[*The Code was prepared for the Law Commission by a team drawn from members of the Society of Public Teachers of Law from whom the initiative came in 1981.*]

2.1 The Code team identified the aims of codification at the present time as being to make the criminal law more accessible, comprehensible, consistent and certain ... We believe, however, that there are also fundamental constitutional arguments of principle in favour of codification which we consider first ...

2.2 ... 'Due notice' or 'fair warning' – by which is meant the idea that the law should be known in advance to those accused of violating it – should clearly be regarded as a principle of major importance in our criminal justice system. While there is room for argument as to how much or how little of the content of the criminal law should be left to be developed by the common law, codification provides the opportunity for ensuring that this principle is followed over a substantial part of the criminal law. Moreover, since the criminal law is arguably the most direct expression of the relationship between a State and its citizens, it is right as a matter of constitutional principle that the relationship should be clearly stated in a criminal code the terms of which have been deliberated upon by a democratically elected legislature.

3.30 A substantial part of the draft Bill appended to this Report limits itself to a restatement of existing principles. The Code team's assertion that '[t]he fundamental principles of the law are well settled and it would be neither politically feasible nor desirable to depart from them' is, in our view, correct. As they argued, however, there are several reasons why the proposed Code Bill cannot be a mere restatement and the draft clauses embody a substantial body of proposed reform.

3.31 The Code cannot reproduce inconsistencies. Where the inconsistency represents a conflict of policies, a choice has to be made to produce a coherent law ...

3.34 More importantly, we have thought it right, as the Code team did, to incorporate into the Code recommendations for the reform of the law made in recent years by official bodies such as the Criminal Law Revision Committee and ourselves, and ad hoc committees such as the Butler Committee on Mentally Abnormal Offenders, which have not yet been implemented by legislation ...

Neither codification nor law reform is an unproblematic exercise. There are some questions which need to be asked before it is possible to consider whether the proposals are good ones. As we argue in **Chapter 1**, the liberal ideology which underlies most representations of criminal law makes various assumptions about the socio-economic-political world in which it operates. In order to assess the draft Code we need criteria by which to judge it. Although the Report gives some, such as certainty, consistency and accessibility, these are procedural rather than substantive values. On the Report's own admission, they cannot be achieved without entering the territory of law reform. Yet the Report is keen to deny that any political choices have been made in the process of restatement, rationalisation and systematisation. The Report fails to acknowledge that the status quo is a political choice or that general principles are not nearly so well established as it is keen to assert. The Report appears to say that insofar as the Commission agrees with the current state of the law it is well settled but when it disagrees it can dub that part inconsistent with the rest.

In the search for accessibility and certainty, the Report has a particular view of the power of the written word (see the discussion of codification of theft in **Chapter 4.II.a.ii.**). It is certainly difficult to justify the present chaotic state of sources of law in the classic common law system. But it would be a mistake to believe that codification would suddenly transform law into a readily accessible form. It may improve accessibility for lawyers, and it may be an improvement, but that is very far from claiming accessibility. The form is a charade. Similarly, the notion of certainty is a firmly entrenched one in the legal tradition. The history of the codification of particular offence areas, such as theft and criminal damage (see the critique of 'ordinary language' legislation in **Chapter 4.II.a.ii.**), itself bears witness to the malleability of language. Words lack 'self-evident reference' and law, whether enshrined in a code or not, is available for exploitation by those with power.

The (re)statement of the law of involuntary manslaughter below involves the eradication of unlawful act manslaughter as well as a subjectivising of gross negligence/reckless manslaughter. We have already seen (above, **section II.c.iv.**), that the recommended additional offence of corporate killing is likely to be introduced in the 2003/2004 Parliamentary Session.

> **Law Commission Report No 237, *Involuntary Manslaughter* (HMSO, 1996) paras 1.22, 2.1, 2.3–2.8, 2.14, 2.16, 2.22, 2.23, 2.26, 2.27, 3.1, 4.2–4.6, 4.11, 4.12–4.14, 4.17–4.20, 4.43, 5.6, 5.13, 5.16, 5.17, 5.34, 5.45, 5.69**
>
> 1.22 In 1989 we published our report on a Criminal Code for England and Wales. This represented the culmination of eight years of work which had the central purpose of making the criminal law more accessible, comprehensible, consistent and certain.
>
> ...

2.1 As we have observed, 'involuntary manslaughter' is the name given to those unintentional killings that are criminal at common law: causing death in the course of doing an unlawful act, and causing death by gross negligence or recklessness. 'Involuntary manslaughter' is not recognised as a separate crime in its own right: it is simply a label used to describe certain ways of committing the very broad common law crime of manslaughter.

[*The Report considered unlawful act manslaughter first. See also Dias in* **section III.d.**. *above.*]

2.3 The basis of this type of manslaughter is that the defendant caused the death of another by or in the course of performing an act which would have been unlawful whether or not death was caused. As Lord Parker CJ put it:

A man is guilty of involuntary manslaughter when he intends an unlawful act and one likely to do harm, to the person and death results which was neither foreseen nor intended. It is the accident of death resulting which makes him guilty of manslaughter as opposed to some lesser offence.

2.4 The alternative name of this type of crime, 'constructive manslaughter', draws attention to the fact that although the accused did not intend to cause serious harm or foresee the risk of doing so, and although an objective observer would not necessarily have predicted that serious harm would result, the accused's responsibility for causing death is 'constructed' from her fault in committing a quite unconnected and possibly minor unlawful act. Because of this feature of the offence, the accused's mental state is not assessed with reference to the death that she has accidentally caused, but only in relation to her unlawful act.

2.5 Over the years judges have tried in various ways to limit the scope of unlawful act manslaughter. Two ways in which they attempted to restrict liability were, first, by imposing stricter tests of causation than the test normally applied in criminal law, and, secondly, by requiring that the accused's act must have been 'directed at' the deceased. Neither of these two approaches, however, has been consistently applied. A more lasting modification was the rule that the accused must have committed a crime of some sort in order to incur liability; at one time it was thought that the commission of a tort, if it caused death, was sufficient. In 1937 the House of Lords restricted the offence still further by holding that negligent acts, even those that were capable of constituting statutory criminal offences (such as dangerous driving), would not automatically be sufficient to found a conviction for manslaughter where death was caused. Instead, it became necessary to prove that the defendant's negligence had been of a very high level. In such a case the prosecution would have to proceed under the second head of involuntary manslaughter, gross negligence manslaughter.

2.6 Another rule that judges have introduced relatively recently to limit the width of unlawful act manslaughter is the rule that the act that causes the death, in addition to being unlawful, must also have been 'dangerous', in the sense that 'all sober and reasonable people would inevitably recognise [that it] must subject the other person to, at least the risk of some harm resulting therefrom, albeit not serious harm'. When applying this test, the 'sober and reasonable person' is accredited with any special knowledge that would have been available to the defendant, but no more. However, the reasonable observer will not have attributed to her any mistaken belief held by the accused.

2.7 It is unlawful manslaughter, then, if D slaps V in the face, V loses her balance, falls to the ground and dies as a result of brain injury caused by hitting her head on the pavement; if D breaks into a house with intent to steal, and terrifies the occupant into a heart attack; or if D unlawfully carries a knife for self-defence, with which she accidentally stabs V. It is, of course, possible to think of numerous other examples.

[*The Report then moved on to consider the second sub-type of involuntary manslaughter:*]

2.8 Where a person causes death through extreme carelessness or incompetence, the law of gross negligence manslaughter is applied. Frequently the defendants in such cases are people carrying out jobs that require special skills or care, such as doctors, police or prison officers, ships' captains or electricians, who fail to meet the standard which could be expected from them and cause death; however, an ordinary person who carries out a lawful activity, such as hunting or driving, without due caution, or who fails properly to look after a dependent person in her care, may be the subject of such a charge. The categories of unlawful act and gross negligence manslaughter are not mutually exclusive; for example, a defendant who unlawfully shoots at a trespasser may be guilty on both counts.

2.14 ... [In *Adomako*], which was decided after the publication of Consultation Paper No.135, the accused, an anaesthetist, was acting as such during an eye operation which involved paralysing the patient. A tube became disconnected from the ventilator, the accused failed to notice the warning signs and the patient suffered a cardiac arrest and died. The House was asked to answer the following certified question: in cases of manslaughter by criminal negligence not involving driving but involving a breach of duty is it a sufficient direction to the jury to adopt the gross negligence test set out in the Court of Appeal in

[*Prentice*] ... without reference to the test of ... [*Caldwell* recklessness] or as adapted to the circumstances of the case?

2.16 This decision resolved the principal uncertainty in the law – whether the test of *Bateman* gross negligence or of *Caldwell* recklessness should be applied. It also restored to the law the flexibility of the *Bateman* gross negligence test, which allowed the jury to consider the accused's conduct in all the surrounding circumstances, and only punished her if her negligence was very serious. There are, however, still some remaining difficulties, which we consider in Part III below.

2.22 It is clearly established that the crime of involuntary manslaughter can be committed by omission, but only where the accused owes the deceased a duty to act. The circumstances in which a positive duty to act arises are uncertain, but we set out the common law position, so far as we were able to determine it, in Consultation Paper No.135, and no-one on consultation dissented from our view, which we summarise in the paragraphs that follow.

2.23 There is no general rule in the criminal law imposing a duty to act. However, in the law of manslaughter a number of discrete cases have become established in which there is a duty to act; if the duty is neglected and the person to whom it is owed dies, the person subject to the duty may be guilty of manslaughter. First, there is a duty to care for certain defined classes of helpless relatives: for example, spouses must take care of each other, and parents must look after their dependent children. A duty to act can also arise as a result of a contract, and a contractual duty can give rise to criminal liability if persons outside the contractual relationship, who are nonetheless likely to be injured by any failure to perform the contractual duty, are killed.

2.26 Apart from unlawful act manslaughter and gross negligence manslaughter, there is one further way in which manslaughter may now be committed in the absence of intention to kill or cause serious injury. This arises when the accused is aware that her conduct involves a risk of causing death (or, probably, serious injury) and she unreasonably takes that risk. This combination of awareness of risk and unreasonable risk-taking is called 'subjective' recklessness. Again, this type of mental state does not exclude liability for gross negligence or unlawful act manslaughter; a defendant may be guilty on all three counts.

2.27 Until ten years ago many cases of this type were treated as falling within the definition of murder. However, in a murder case in 1985 the House of Lords held that cases in which the defendant may have foreseen that death or really serious injury were highly probable to result from her act, without intending such consequences, would no longer constitute murder. These cases must then have fallen, by default, into the scope of the offence of manslaughter. There is little or no separate authority, however, about this type of manslaughter, since such cases are dealt within practice as cases of unlawful manslaughter, and the accused's awareness of the risk is taken into account only as an aggravating factor when it comes to sentencing.

[The Commission proceeded to discuss the principles which should inform any reform of this area:]

3.1 We now turn to consider the problems created by the present law. The two major problems relate to the very wide range of conduct falling within the scope of involuntary manslaughter. As we explained in Part II, the offence encompasses, first, cases involving conduct that falls only just short of murder, where the accused was aware of a risk of causing death or serious injury, although he did not intend to cause either; second, cases where the accused is a professional person who makes a very minor mistake that results in death; and third, cases where a relatively minor assault ends in death. This leads to problems in sentencing and labelling, including the fundamental problem that many cases currently amounting to unlawful manslaughter involve only minor fault on the part of the perpetrator, and therefore ought not, perhaps, to be described as manslaughter at all. There are also a number of more specific problems which we consider below.

...

4.2 The extent to which a person is responsible for the unintended results of her actions is a question that has puzzled legal philosophers for years. We have had to consider this question again because we believe that it is essential that any new law of involuntary manslaughter that we may propose should be founded on just, coherent and logical principles.

4.3 We are also aware that our proposed new homicide offences ought, in time, to form part of a complete criminal code. It is evident that, in the interests of justice, logic and consistency, the same fundamental principles should, so far as possible, influence all the parts of this growing code. In this part, then, we begin by describing the philosophy that this Commission has traditionally applied in our criminal law reform work; it is known as 'subjectivist legal theory'. We will then consider how this philosophy has shaped the work we have already done on the reform and codification of the law of offences against the person. Finally, we undertake a thorough examination of this philosophy, in order to decide whether it should apply in the present subject.

4.4 The legal philosophy traditionally applied in mainstream English criminal law and by this Commission is known as 'subjectivist theory'. It rests on the principle that moral guilt, and hence criminal liability, should be imposed only on people who can be said to have chosen to behave in a certain way or to cause or risk causing certain consequences. The roots of subjectivism lie in a liberal philosophy that regards individuals as autonomous beings, capable of choice, and each deserving of individual respect. It is called 'subjectivism' because of the significance it accords to the individual's state of mind at the time of the prohibited conduct.

4.5 Three principles have been identified as inherent in this basis of liability. The first of these is the 'mens rea' principle, which imposes liability only for outcomes which were intended or knowingly risked by the alleged wrongdoer. The second principle, the 'belief principle', judges a defendant according only to what she believed she was doing or risking. Thirdly, according to the 'principle of correspondence', subjectivists insist that the fault element of a crime correspond to the conduct element; for example, if the conduct element is 'causing serious injury', the fault element ought to be 'intention or recklessness' as to causing serious injury. This ensures that the defendant is punished only for causing a harm which she chose to risk or bring about.

4.6 Subjectivist philosophy applies widely in the criminal law today. A man cannot be convicted of rape, for example, if he genuinely believed, albeit unreasonably, that his victim consented to sexual intercourse, because this belief would be incompatible with the intention to have intercourse with a woman without her consent, or recklessness as to that possibility, which are the mental states required for rape *[although see now **Chapter 5.II.b.IV.**]*.

...

4.11 The difficult question is whether, and in what circumstances, a person should be held criminally liable for causing death unintentionally when she was not aware that her conduct created such a risk. We consider this question in the following paragraphs.

4.12 Orthodox subjectivist theory, then, requires the defendant to have been, at least, aware of the risk of causing the prohibited harm. However, there is a body of criticism, from very distinguished commentators, of the orthodox subjectivist mens rea principle. One ground of criticism is that it is based on a simplistic view of what constitutes knowledge or awareness of risk:

... while we do indeed sometimes make our knowledge of what we are doing explicit to ourselves in ... silent mental reports, it is absurd to suggest that such knowledge can be actual only if it is made this explicit. When I drive my car, my driving is guided by my (actual) knowledge of my car and of the context in which I am driving: but my driving is not accompanied by a constant silent monologue in which I tell myself what to do next, what the road conditions are, whether I am driving safely or not, and all the other facts of which I am certainly aware while I am driving ... The occurrence or the non-occurrence of certain explicit thoughts is irrelevant to whether I am actually aware of what I am doing: my actions can manifest my awareness even if no explicit thoughts about the relevant facts pass through my mind at the time [Duff 1990: 160].

4.13 On this view of what constitutes a mental state, the contrast between awareness and lack of awareness of risk is not as stark as in conventional subjectivist accounts, and it is less clear why inadvertence ought not to be classified as mens rea in certain circumstances.

4.14 The main argument in favour of criminalising some forms of inadvertent risk-taking, however, is that in some circumstances a person is at fault in failing to consider the consequences that might be caused by her conduct. The example given by R.A. Duff is that of a bridegroom who misses his wedding because it slipped his mind when he was in the pub. An orthodox subjectivist would point to his lack of intention or awareness, and deem him consequently less culpable. The bride, however, would rightly condemn him, because it is plain from his conduct that he did not care, and this attitude is sufficient to make him blameworthy. Duff argues that this account retains a subjective element, because attitudes are subjective.

...

4.17 In all the sources cited in paragraphs 4.12–4.16, the view is taken that it may be justifiable to impose criminal liability for the unforeseen consequences of a person's acts, at any rate where the harm risked is great and the actor's failure to advert to this risk is culpable. We are persuaded by this reasoning. In the following paragraphs, therefore, we consider the criteria by which culpable inadvertence should be judged if it is to attract the sanctions of the criminal law when death results.

4.18 The first criterion of culpability upon which we must insist is that the harm to which the accused failed to advert was at least foreseeable, if not strikingly foreseeable or obvious. If the accused is an ordinary person, she cannot be blamed for failing to take notice of a risk if it would not have been apparent to an average person in her position, because the criminal law cannot require an exceptional standard of perception or awareness from her. If the accused held herself out as an expert of some kind, however, a higher standard can be expected from her; if she is a doctor, for example, she will be at fault if she fails to advert to a risk that would have been obvious to the average doctor in her position.

4.19 As a matter of strict principle, the accused ought only to be held liable for causing death if the risk to which she culpably failed to advert was a risk of death. In practice, however, there is a very thin line between behaviour that risks serious injury and behaviour that risks death, because it is frequently a matter of chance, depending on such factors as the availability of medical treatment, whether serious injury leads to death. Admittedly it is possible for conduct to involve a risk of serious injury (such as a broken limb) though not a risk of death; but intention to cause serious injury constitutes the mens rea of murder although the actus reus is the causing of death, and we see no compelling reason to distinguish between murder and manslaughter in this respect. We consider, therefore, that it would not be wrong in principle if a person were to be held responsible for causing death through failing to advert to a clear risk of causing death or serious injury – subject of course to a second criterion, to which we now turn.

4.20 The second criterion of culpability which we consider to be essential is that the accused herself would have been capable of perceiving the risk in question, had she directed her mind to it. Since the fault of the accused lies in her failure to consider a risk, she cannot be punished for this failure if the risk in question would never have been apparent to her, no matter how hard she thought about the potential consequences of her conduct. If this criterion is not insisted upon, the accused will, in essence, be punished for being less intelligent, mature or capable than the average person.

...

[And, finally, the Report proposed the following tier of offences to replace the existing sub-types:]

4.43 In conclusion, we consider, as a matter of principle, that the criminal law ought to hold a person responsible for unintentionally causing death only in the following circumstances:

(1) when she unreasonably and advertently takes a risk of causing death or serious injury; or

(2) when she unreasonably and inadvertently takes a risk of causing death or serious injury, where her failure to advert to the risk is culpable because

(a) the risk is obviously foreseeable, and

(b) she has the capacity to advert to the risk.

...

5.6 The first of our proposed new offences, set out in clause 1 of the attached Involuntary Homicide Bill, is 'reckless killing'. This offence shares the same concept of 'recklessness' as the non-fatal offences in Law Com. No.218, and is drafted as follows:

A person who by his conduct causes the death of another is guilty of reckless killing if–

(a) he is aware of a risk that his conduct will cause death or serious injury; and

(b) it is unreasonable for him to take that risk having regard to the circumstances as he knows or believes them to be.

...

5.13 We recommend the creation of a new offence of reckless killing, which would be committed if

(1) a person by his or her conduct causes the death of another;

(2) he or she is aware of a risk that his or her conduct will cause death or serious injury; and

(3) it is unreasonable for him or her to take that risk, having regard to the circumstances as he or she knows or believed them to be. (Recommendation 2)

...

5.16 For this reason we recommend the abolition of unlawful act manslaughter in its present form. This would not of course mean that all those who would be convicted under the present law of unlawful act manslaughter would escape criminal liability altogether. The overwhelming majority of such cases would fall within one of the offences that we do propose: even if the defendant was not aware of the risk of death or serious injury (in which case he would be guilty of reckless killing) it would usually be possible to say that that risk was obvious and that he should have been aware of it – in which case he would be guilty of the offence of killing by gross carelessness that we propose below. In the minority of cases where this is not so, he could be prosecuted for the appropriate non-fatal offence. (Recommendation 3)

5.17 The second new offence which we recommend ought to be created is 'killing by gross carelessness'. This offence is set out in clause 2(1) of the attached Bill.

...

5.34 For all these reasons, we recommend the creation of a new offence of killing by gross carelessness, which would be committed if

(1) a person by his or her conduct causes the death of another;

(2) a risk that his or her conduct will cause death or serious injury would be obvious to a reasonable person in his or her position;

(3) he or she is capable of appreciating that risk at the material time; and

(4) either

(a) his or her conduct falls far below what can reasonably be expected of him or her in the circumstances, or

(b) he or she intends by his or her conduct to cause some injury, or is aware of, and unreasonably takes, the risk that it may do so, and the conduct causing (or intending to cause) the injury constitutes an offence. (Recommendation 4)

...

5.45 We have therefore reluctantly adopted the third option, and we recommend that the duty to act continue to be governed by the common law for the purposes of involuntary manslaughter for the time being. This was also the course we adopted in Law Com. No.218. (Recommendation 5)

...

5.69 We recommend that no change should be made to the offences of causing death by bad driving, and that it should also be possible, where appropriate, to prosecute such cases as reckless killing or killing by gross carelessness. (Recommendation 10)

The more serious of the two offences, reckless killing, relies on a subjective recklessness test, but the Commission betrayed its previous adherence to subjective tests in proposing a second offence of killing by gross carelessness. The Government at one stage indicated that it intended to legislate all of these proposals but appeared unwilling to abandon unlawful act manslaughter altogether (Home Office 2000e). The only area in which the Government has displayed enthusiasm to use Parliamentary time to introduce partial codifications is that of sexual offences. The draft Bills on non-fatal offences against the person and on involuntary manslaughter (save corporate killing) are gathering dust.

In the meantime, the number of cases of gross negligence manslaughter appears to be rising. The breadth of this sub-type, coupled with mounting public pressure for prosecution helps explain the increase of such cases. The rise of manslaughter prosecutions against healthcare professionals is a notable example of this (see Childs 1999). The ability of the duty of care concept to embrace a wide range of conduct is evident in the next two cases. In *Sinclair and Johnson* (1998), the Court of Appeal were prepared to recognise a duty of care where a drug addict fails to look after a fellow addict who has overdosed:

R v Sinclair [1998] NLJR 1353

[*At trial, the judge ruled that it was for the jury to decide whether the defendants had voluntarily assumed a duty of care to him, and that there was sufficient evidence on causation (omission to seek medical attention) to be left to the jury. Although ultimately considering that the evidence on causation was unsafe to leave to the jury, nevertheless, the court recognised the possibility of a duty of care.*]

Sinclair was in a different position. The evidence was that he was a close friend of the deceased for many years and the two had lived together almost as brothers. It was Sinclair who paid for and supplied the deceased with the first dose of methadone and helped him to obtain the second dose. He knew that the deceased was not an addict. He remained with the deceased throughout the period of his unconsciousness and, for a substantial period, was the only person with him. In the light of this evidence, there was in our judgment material on which the jury properly directed, could have found that Sinclair owed the deceased a legal duty of care. The judge was therefore correct to leave Sinclair's case to the jury on this aspect. We do accept however, that there is force in Mr Carter's [counsel for the appellant] submission that, in the law of manslaughter, it is important to distinguish between acts of commission and omission and that, even if it is appropriate, in criminal as well as in civil law, for the circumstances in which a duty of care exists to expand incrementally, it is undesirable there should be such elasticity in that expansion that potential defendants are unaware until after the event whether their conduct is capable of being regarded as criminal. We say this by reference to the circumstances in which a duty of care should arise in criminal law: we do not seek to deviate from the observations of Lord Mackay in Adomako that it is for the jury to determine whether an accused's conduct is so grossly negligent as to be criminal. We are inclined to the view that Mr Cassell's submission, that Lord Mackay's speech in Adomako was not concerned with whether a duty of care exists, is correct. But for the purposes of the present appeal it is unnecessary to say anything further on this aspect of the case.

It was for these reasons that we allowed the appeals of Sinclair and Johnson and quashed their convictions.

The malleability of gross negligence manslaughter was also reflected in the different context of the deaths of illegal immigrants during their transportation into the UK. The extracts below illustrate the refusal to allow the use of other legal concepts (in this case joint illegal enterprise) to prevent a manslaughter conviction.

R v Wacker [2003] 1 Cr App R 22

[*The appellant was stopped driving a lorry disembarking from a ferry at Dover. The bodies of 58 illegal immigrants were found in the trailer together with two surviving illegal immigrants. They suffered death by suffocation following inadequate ventilation in the lorry. The appellant was convicted of conspiracy to facilitate the entry into the UK of illegal immigrants and 58 offences of manslaughter on the basis of gross negligence, and sentenced to 14 years' imprisonment. He appealed against the convictions for manslaughter. It was submitted on his behalf that because the deceased illegal immigrants shared the same illegal purpose as the appellant, namely to gain entry for the illegal immigrants into the UK, there was no duty of care owed by the appellant to the deceased; and that the principle that the law of negligence does not recognise the relationship between those involved in a criminal enterprise as giving rise to a duty of care owed by one participant to another (ex turpi causa non oritur actio) applied.*]

There are occasions when it is helpful when considering questions of law for the court to take a step back and to look at an issue of law that arises without first turning to, and becoming embroiled in, the technicalities of the law. This is such a case. We venture to suggest that all right minded people would be astonished if the propositions being advanced on behalf of the appellant correctly represented the law of the land. The concept that one person could be responsible for the death of another in circumstances such as these without the criminal law being able to hold him to account for that death even if he had shown not the slightest regard for the welfare and life of the other is one that would be unacceptable in civilised society. Taking this perspective of the case causes one immediately to question whether the whole approach adopted by both counsel and the judge in the court below can be correct, and we must, therefore, examine this matter.

In other situations, it is clear that the criminal law adopts a different approach to the civil law in this regard. A person who sold a harmless substance to another pretending that it was an unlawful dangerous drug could not be the subject of a successful civil claim by the purchasers for the return of the purchase price. However the criminal law would, arising out of the same transaction, hold that he was guilty of the offence of obtaining property by deception. Many other similar examples readily come to mind.

Why is there, therefore, this distinction between the approach of the civil law and the criminal law? The answer is that the very same public policy that causes the civil courts to refuse the claim points in a quite different direction in considering a criminal offence. The criminal law has as its function the protection of citizens and gives effect to the state's duty to try those who have deprived citizens of their rights of life, limb or property. It may very well step in at the precise moment when civil courts withdraw because of this very different function. The withdrawal of a civil remedy has nothing to do with whether as a matter of public policy the criminal law applies. The criminal law should not be disapplied just because the civil law is disapplied. It has its own public policy aim which may require a different approach to the involvement of the law.

Further the criminal law will not hesitate to act to prevent serious injury or death even when the persons subjected to such injury or death may have consented to or willingly accepted the risk of actual injury or death. By way of illustration, the criminal law makes the assisting another to commit suicide a criminal offence and denies a defence of consent where significant injury is deliberately caused to another in a sexual context (*Brown* (1993) [*above* **Chapter 5.III.a.II.**]). The state in such circumstances has a overriding duty to act to prevent such consequences.

The next question which is posed is whether it is right to say in this case that no duty of care can arise because it is impossible or inappropriate to determine the extent of that duty. We do not accept this proposition. If at the moment when the vent was shut, one of the Chinese had said "you will make sure that we have enough air to survive", the appellant would have had no difficulty understanding the proposition and clearly by continuing with the unlawful enterprise in the way that he did, he would have been shouldering the duty to take care for their safety in this regard. The question was such an obvious one that it did not need to be posed and we have no difficulty in concluding that in these circumstances the appellant did voluntarily assume the duty of care for the Chinese in this regard. He was aware that no one's actions other than his own could realistically prevent the Chinese from suffocating to death and if he failed to act reasonably in fulfilling this duty to an extent that could be characterised as criminal, he was guilty of manslaughter if death resulted.

One further issue merits consideration, namely is it any answer to a charge of manslaughter for a defendant to say "we were jointly engaged in a criminal enterprise and weighing the risk of injury or death against our joint desire to achieve our unlawful objective, we collectively thought that it was a risk worth taking". In our judgment it is not. The duty to take care cannot, as a matter of public policy, be permitted to be affected by the countervailing demands of the criminal enterprise. Thus, in this case, the fact that keeping the vent shut increased the chances of the Chinese succeeding in entering the United Kingdom without detection was not a factor to be taken into account in deciding whether the appellant had acted reasonably or not.

In the next section we move on to consider partial defences to murder which may result in a verdict of manslaughter. Defences usefully illustrate a number of the questions and issues we have sought to raise throughout the book. The contextual reality of criminal law, often contingent as it is on circumstance and chance, is played out in the operation of defences. This includes the curiously hidden yet obvious issues of plea at trial, interpretation of evidence, and the (prejudiced?) perception of particular roles. Stories emerge as cases unfold and 'legal lines' prompt as well as dictate such stories. Even this brief insight into the reality of defences exposes the common call for a coherence or rationalisation of defences as somewhat unrealistic.

IV.d. Voluntary manslaughter

Sometimes a homicide has the hallmark of murder as far as the mental element goes but is regarded as mitigated in some way. With most other offences there is, at least on the surface, a strict division between factors which are taken as affecting the category of offence in which to place the defendant's conduct, and circumstances of mitigation which affect sentence. Sometimes the relevant factor is gravity of harm. For example, assault occasioning *actual* bodily harm is less serious than assault causing *grievous* bodily harm. Or mental states may reflect degrees of culpability, as in, for example, the two offences of maliciously inflicting grievous bodily harm and causing grievous bodily harm with intent.

Since any distinction between murder and manslaughter cannot depend on gravity of harm (death is death), and since post-conviction mitigation is ruled out by the mandatory penalty, two partial defences have developed to circumvent the rigidity which dependence on the mental element imposes:

these are (i) diminished responsibility and (ii) provocation. They reduce what would otherwise be murder to manslaughter.

IV.d.i.   Diminished responsibility

In this section we examine *diminished responsibility* and compare it with *infanticide*.

Until 1957, mentally disordered persons charged with murder had to rely on the general defence of insanity. This was not an attractive option, since it carried with it mandatory admission to a Special Hospital. Disposal is now discretionary under the Insanity (Criminal Procedure) Act 1964, as amended by the Criminal Procedure (Insanity and Unfitness to Plead) Act 1991. The insanity defence is also unduly restrictive, given its emphasis on defects in cognitive abilities such as reasoning and knowledge. The M'Naghten Rules require a defendant to have been suffering from a 'defect of reason from disease of the mind' resulting in her not realising the nature and quality of her act or in her failure to realise that it was wrong. This does not allow for the psychiatrically recognised emotive disorders, nor those involving lack of self-control. The vast majority of mentally disordered persons accused of murder will continue to rely on diminished responsibility.

Homicide Act 1957, s 2(1)

Where a person kills or is a party to the killing of another, he shall not be convicted of murder if he was suffering from such abnormality of mind (whether arising from a condition of arrested or retarded development of mind or any inherent causes or induced by disease or injury) as substantially impaired his mental responsibility for his acts and omissions in doing or being a party to the killing.

Although the Home Office's general policy is to encourage diversion of mentally disordered offenders from the criminal justice system (Home Office Circular 66/90), those who commit homicide are unlikely to benefit from this. The introduction of a mandatory life sentence for a second serious offence in s 2 of the Crime (Sentences) Act 1997 sits awkwardly with this policy (see now the Powers of Criminal Courts (Sentencing) Act 2000, s 109). The 1997 Act also contains a provision to allow courts to combine a prison sentence with an immediate direction that the offender be detained in hospital and thus subject to Mental Health Act restrictions (s 46, inserting s 45A in the Mental Health Act 1983). The Criminal Justice Act 1991 imposes a duty on a court to obtain and consider a medical report before passing any custodial sentence on a person who appears to be mentally disordered (s 4). Despite this, a large proportion of the prison population suffers from mental disturbance. In relation to sentencing in diminished responsibility cases there is, as Ashworth points out, 'a clear compromise between punishment and treatment' with the sentence reflecting the responsibility element once the mental abnormality is discounted (Ashworth 2000: 110).

The number of convictions for manslaughter by reason of diminished responsibility has decreased in recent years: in 2000/2001 there were 20 convictions, compared with 262 for murder (Home Office 2003f: Table 1.08). Ashworth here gives an indication of the disposal of diminished responsibility offenders:

Andrew Ashworth, *Principles of Criminal Law* (4th edn, Oxford University Press, 2003) pp 284–285

In the three years from 1997–8 to 1999–2000 there were some 108 such cases, of which some 60% were dealt with by a hospital order under the Mental Health Act 1983 (with or without restrictions). Ten per cent received life imprisonment, 14 per cent were given determinate prison sentences of between four and ten years, 5 per cent were given prison sentences of four years or less, and some 12 per cent were given community rehabilitation orders (with or without a condition of psychiatric treatment). These figures show the diversity of cases dealt with under section 2, and reveal a 70/30 split between treatment-based orders and prison disposals ...

Should the qualified defence of diminished responsibility be retained? In answering this question, one has to contend with two muddles in English law: a general muddle about mental disorder and criminal responsibility, and a specific muddle about murder and manslaughter ... [I]n principle, a person whose conduct was caused by mental disorder should not be liable to criminal conviction at all, but in practice the narrow and antiquated defence of insanity is rarely invoked in England ... [If] a broader mental disorder defence [as proposed by the Butler Committee in 1975] ... were available in murder cases ... the case for a separate doctrine of diminished responsibility would be weak. However, some of the cases now brought within section 2 result in prison sentences, and the courts might be reluctant to accept a verdict that made any punitive disposal impossible.

Even where the prosecution accepts the defence of diminished responsibility, the trial judge may insist on the pursuit of the murder charge, as occurred in the trial of Peter Sutcliffe. Shortly after his conviction for murder he was transferred to a Special Hospital because of his mental disorder.

Lucy Bland, 'The Case of the Yorkshire Ripper: Mad, Bad, Beast or Male?' in P Scraton and P Gordon (eds) *Causes for Concern* (Pelican, 1984) p 184

The case was set up in terms of whether Peter Sutcliffe was a lunatic or a liar; whether the doctors were correct in believing that he was a paranoid schizophrenic who felt he had a 'divine mission' to kill prostitutes, or whether he 'was a clever, callous murderer who had tried to feign insanity'.

To back his argument that he was a liar ... [the prosecution] initially pointed to three different kinds of evidence: first, that Sutcliffe had never mentioned the 'divine mission' during his hours of police interrogation; second, that while in custody, one prison officer had heard Sutcliffe plan to feign madness, while Sutcliffe had told another prison officer how amusing it was that the doctors thought him mad; third, that the last six women killed by Sutcliffe were not prostitutes but 'absolutely respectable' women, thus refuting Sutcliffe's claim of a 'divine mission' ...

The prosecution ... developed two further arguments to substantiate its claim that Sutcliffe was not suffering from diminished responsibility: first, that Sutcliffe's killings were 'understandable' in terms of rational, reasonable motives; second, that there was a sexual component to six of the attacks. The latter contradicted the divine-mission argument ... and offered a reason for the attacks (sexual provocation) ...

One disturbing aspect of the trial was the way in which the prosecution developed its argument that Sutcliffe's killings were 'understandable' in terms of rational motive and motivation ... in the case of Sutcliffe, as in many other cases of male violence against women, the language of law and psychiatry met in a common 'understanding' of Sutcliffe's acts, in terms of female precipitation.

Both the prosecution and the defence, despite different objectives (the one to establish Sutcliffe's 'reason', the other to establish his 'diminished responsibility'), took the actions of certain women in Sutcliffe's life as the key to understanding and explaining his behaviour ... For the prosecution, Sutcliffe was responsible for his actions in the sense of having rationally responded to the behaviour of ... a prostitute who 'cheated' him of £5, his wife ... and, to a certain extent, his mother. The fact that these women had acted to precipitate his behaviour, however, effectively removed his responsibility. For the defence, Sutcliffe was not responsible for his actions because he was acting under a 'divine mission'. To the psychiatrists, this mission was 'understandable' in terms of the behaviour of certain women (again the cheating prostitute, [his wife] and his mother) ...

Given that the trial of Sutcliffe turned out to be more a trial of prostitutes ... and of psychiatry, would it have been better if Judge Boreham had accepted a plea of diminished responsibility, thereby curtailing the length of the trial? Sutcliffe may or may not be a paranoid schizophrenic; I do not and cannot know. I would argue, however, that the greatest cause for concern in the conduct of the trial was not the ultimate verdict, but the means by which that verdict was arrived at.

Assumptions about gender differences infuse the conduct and outcome of trials in which diminished responsibility is raised, as discussed in depth by Hilary

Allen (1987). She argues broadly that while mental disorder is seen as abnormal in men, it is assumed to underlie the criminal (and other) behaviour of women, who are thought 'by nature' not to be rational. She concludes that this is unfair to both: women are unduly pathologised, while men are treated punitively when they are genuinely mentally ill.

Criminal trials involve a construction of fact and law which may not accord at all with other readings. *Tandy* (1989) is a good example. The defendant appealed unsuccessfully against her conviction for murder, arguing that she should have been allowed a defence of diminished responsibility. The 'legal' significance of the case is that alcoholism cannot amount to diminished responsibility unless the first drink of the day was involuntary. The report of the case tells us something of the social context of the murder, but the legal construction ignores this. The victim was the defendant's 11-year-old daughter. Shortly before she was killed, the daughter had told her mother that she was being sexually abused. Although she refused to name the abuser, the mother suspected her husband, the child's stepfather. The post-mortem confirmed recent and persistent anal abuse. The mother was an alcoholic and during the day on which she killed her daughter had drunk almost a bottle of vodka. Evidence of her intoxication would have been admissible, yet the jury's verdict suggests that they were satisfied that she formed the intent for murder. The case highlights dramatically the effect of the artificial construction of fact in legal trials and appeals which, together with assumptions about appropriate gender behaviour, denied a defence to murder. Presumably, Tandy's defence counsel chose a particular strategy, that of arguing that her responsibility was diminished; this forced a concentration on her weaknesses rather than on the absent villain's (the abuser's) responsibility. If counsel had pursued a provocation line, that might have been no more successful. The alcoholism would then be an obstruction, as would the application of the actually gendered, but formalistically neutered, concept of the 'reasonable man'. Would a reasonable mother (probably not an alcoholic) have lost her self-control?

Tandy shows how the partial defences to murder are of limited assistance to women who act in response to male violence. It would be interesting to compare the legally constructed 'biographies' of Moloney (see **section IV.b.** above) and Tandy. The House of Lords was clearly able to identify with the mess which Moloney, a soldier, had got himself into while drunk, while the Court of Appeal shows no understanding of the emotional trauma Tandy must have experienced when she discovered her husband had abused her daughter.

Confusion arises when abnormal behaviour may be caused by a combination of diminished responsibility and intoxication. In *Dietschmann* (2003) the House of Lords have sought to clarify the appropriate jury direction. Here the defendant killed a man whilst suffering from a mental abnormality, namely depressed grief reaction to a bereavement. He was also at the time heavily intoxicated. The trial judge directed the jury that such a defence could only succeed if the defendant could establish, on a balance of probabilities, two things: first, that he would have killed even if he was not intoxicated, and secondly that he would have been under diminished responsibility when doing so. The jury convicted and this was upheld by the Court of Appeal. In holding that there was no requirement to satisfy the first issue, to what extent have the House broadened the scope of diminished responsibility?

R v Dietschmann [2003] 1 All ER 897

Lord Hutton.

In a case where the defendant suffered from an abnormality of mind of the nature described in s 2(1) and had also taken alcohol before the killing and where (as the Court of Appeal held in this case) there was no evidence capable of establishing alcohol dependence syndrome as being an abnormality of mind within the subsection, the meaning to be given to the subsection would appear on first consideration to be reasonably clear. I would read the subsection to mean that if the defendant satisfies the jury that, notwithstanding the alcohol he had consumed and its effect on him, his abnormality of mind substantially impaired his mental responsibility for his acts in doing the killing, the jury should find him not guilty of murder but (under sub-s 3) guilty of manslaughter. I take this view because I think that in referring to substantial impairment of mental responsibility the subsection does not require the abnormality of mind to be the sole cause of the defendant's acts in doing the killing. In my opinion, even if the defendant would not have killed if he had not taken drink, the causative effect of the drink does not necessarily prevent an abnormality of mind suffered by the defendant from substantially impairing his mental responsibility for his fatal acts.

Where a defendant suffers from an abnormality of mind arising from arrested or retarded development of mind or inherent causes or induced by disease or injury and has also taken drink before the killing, the abnormality of mind and the effect of the drink may each play a part in impairing the defendant's mental responsibility for the killing. (ii) Therefore the task for the jury is to decide whether, despite the disinhibiting effect of the drink on the defendant's mind, the abnormality of mind arising from a cause specified in sub-s 2(1) nevertheless substantially impaired his mental responsibility for his fatal acts. (iii) Accordingly it is not correct for the judge to direct the jury that unless they are satisfied that if the defendant had not taken drink he would have killed, the defence of diminished responsibility must fail. Such a direction is incorrect because it fails to recognise that the abnormality of mind arising from a cause specified in the subsection and the effect of the drink may each play a part in impairing the defendant's mental responsibility for the killing.

In his submissions on behalf of the Crown Mr Perry submitted that it was the policy of the criminal law that self-induced intoxication did not constitute a defence to a criminal charge, and that if the appellant's submissions were correct an intoxicated disinhibited killer would be excused. I am unable to accept this argument. The policy of the criminal law in respect of persons suffering from mental abnormality is to be found in the words of s 2, and the section provides that if a person suffers from such abnormality of mind as substantially impairs his mental responsibility, he should not be convicted of murder but of manslaughter. As my noble and learned friend, Lord Rodger of Earlsferry, observed in the course of Mr Perry's submissions, a brain-damaged person who is intoxicated and who commits a killing is not in the same position as a person who is intoxicated, but not brain-damaged, and who commits a killing.

Therefore I would answer the first part of the certified question in the negative. As regards the second part of the question, without attempting to lay down a precise form of words as the judge's directions are bound to depend to some extent on the facts of the case before him, I consider that the jury should be directed along the following lines:

> 'Assuming that the defence have established that the defendant was suffering from mental abnormality as described in s 2, the important question is: did that abnormality substantially impair his mental responsibility for his acts in doing the killing? You know that before he carried out the killing the defendant had had a lot to drink. Drink cannot be taken into account as something which contributed to his mental abnormality and to any impairment of mental responsibility arising from that abnormality. But you may take the view that both the defendant's mental abnormality and drink played a part in impairing his mental responsibility for the killing and that he might not have killed if he had not taken drink. If you take that view, then the question for you to decide is this: has the defendant satisfied you that, despite the drink, his mental abnormality substantially impaired his mental responsibility for his fatal acts, or has he failed to satisfy you of that? If he has satisfied you of that, you will find him not guilty of murder but you may find him guilty of manslaughter. If he has not satisfied you of that, the defence of diminished responsibility is not available to him.'

The House remitted the case to the Court of Appeal for it to decide whether to allow the appeal, quash the conviction and order new trial, or substitute a verdict of manslaughter. This more generous view of the defence echoes the similarly expansive approach to provocation (see below).

The legal categorisation of defences to murder fails in a number of ways to accommodate women defendants. Or, to put it another way, insofar as they cater for anyone they cater for men. One difficult dilemma has been the extent to which women should argue that pre-menstrual tension (PMT), usually known as pre-menstrual syndrome (PMS), should be pursued as an excusing factor. The only legal category of defence into which it can be fitted is diminished responsibility, but this has unfortunate overtones in relation to the way women offenders may be too readily seen as psychiatric cases (see *Ahluwalia*, 1992 below).

Provocation more closely resembles the nature of a PMS defence but, as we see below, the reference to the reasonable man is not very helpful. A successful defence of diminished responsibility stemming from PMS was pleaded in *Smith* (1982). Smith had been sentenced 30 times before for criminal activity, ranging from theft to trespass to arson and assault. She was sentenced to probation after she persuaded the court that PMS turned her into a 'raging animal each month and forced her to act out of character'. A year later she was charged with threatening to kill a police officer, for which a defence of diminished responsibility is not of course available. Evidence of PMS led to a mitigation of her sentence to one of probation.

The attempt to define PMS in medical terms began in 1931 when Frank (1931: 1053–1057) described 15 cases of the syndrome. The primary symptom was described as 'a feeling of indescribable tension from seven to ten days preceding menstruation which in most instances continues until the menstrual flow occurs'. Since then the medical profession has been divided on whether the syndrome is a psychiatric disorder. The syndrome does appear to be separate from other forms of psycho-pathologies. In terms of its use as a criminal defence it may be better to view it as a category of its own rather than as a form of diminished responsibility or a type of provocation. But this would have its own dangers – rather like the offence of infanticide, it would over-pathologise and obscure the effects of socio-economic and structural difference between men and women.

Infanticide

The creation of the offence/defence of infanticide provides a good example of the construction of a legal category from a socially created expectation about women's role as carers of babies:

Infanticide Act 1938, s 1(1)

Where a woman by any wilful act or omission causes the death of her child being a child under the age of twelve months, but at the time of the act or omission the balance of her mind was disturbed by reason of her not having fully recovered from the effect of giving birth to the child or by reason of the effect of lactation consequent upon the birth of the child, then, notwithstanding that the circumstances were such that but for this Act the offence would have amounted to murder, she shall be guilty of felony, to wit of infanticide, and may for such offence be dealt with and punished as if she had been guilty of the offence of manslaughter of the child.

In any year, there are rarely more than half a dozen convictions for this offence (in 2000 there were two):

Elaine Showalter, *Women, Madness and English Culture 1830–1980* (Virago, 1987) p 58

It was during the nineteenth century that the infanticidal woman first became the subject of psychiatric as well as legal discourse. Her crime was the worst that could be imagined by a society that exalted maternity; medical theory struggled to account for it in a way that maintained the mythology of motherhood and the maternal instinct. The psychiatric explanation of puerperal insanity was that after childbirth a woman's mind was abnormally weak, her constitution depleted, and her control over her behaviour diminished. In fact, infanticide did not appear randomly in the population; in middle class households, where there were nurses and servants to help with child care, puerperal insanity rarely ended in infanticide. As we would expect, child murder was much more likely to occur in conjunction with illegitimacy, poverty, and brutality. These factors, whether or not they were considered by medical specialists, were certainly taken into account by Victorian judges and juries, who were reluctant to sentence infanticidal women to death, and who responded compassionately to the insanity defence generally used in their behalf. Infanticidal women who were committed for life to Bethlem or Broadmoor were also more likely to be released by order of the Home Secretary than any other group of the criminally insane.

Humanitarian in its legal effects, the psychiatric definition of puerperal violence nonetheless ignored both the social problems of unmarried, abused, and destitute mothers and the shocks, adjustments, and psychological traumas of the maternal role. Rather than looking at the social meaning of infanticide and at its contexts, doctors, lawyers, and judges categorized it as an isolated and biologically determined phenomenon, an unfortunate product of woman's 'nature'.

Hilary Allen, *Justice Unbalanced: Gender, Psychiatry and Judicial Decisions* (Open University Press, 1987) pp 27–28

As a chargeable offence, infanticide is unique in several ways. First, it is the only offence in which mental abnormality is a positive precondition for conviction ... and not, as elsewhere, a defence or partial defence against conviction. Infanticide is thus an offence that can only be committed by an abnormal subject. Second, the exemption from full responsibility is unique in that it does not seem to depend on the usual logic of criminal responsibility. As the wording stands, the reduction of the offence does not require that killing of the child is actually related to the imbalance of mind. Finally this legislation is unique in the very obvious links that it makes between female biology and legal pathology. It implies that the normal conditions of childbirth and lactation are inherently disruptive of the rational subjectivity that the law requires ...

It is tempting, of course, to make much of the infanticide provisions. Their interlinking of femininity and psychopathology is so transparent and their presentation of female pathology as essentially debilitating to legal subjectivity so accessible. They seem to promise an illustration par excellence of the psychiatrisation of female crime ...

The criminal law is quite capable of generating discrepancies of gender without recourse to any 'special provisions' ... The analysis of those cases leaves the important question unanswered: how is it that legal discourse allows sexual divisions to arise so pervasively within the law despite the stated neutrality of the legal subject, and the legislation's declared indifference to the gender of legal subjects?

The answer is, in one sense, perfectly simple. The normal centrality of mens rea as a necessary component of any offence requires the agents of the law to 'look into the mind' of the defendants whom they judge, and to make their own assessment of what mental state must have accompanied the alleged offence ... [I]n looking into the mind of the defendant, the agents of the law quite routinely – one might almost say inevitably – make commonsense assumptions about human nature and motivation which are powerfully influenced by preconceptions of sexual differences. Commonsense tells us that there are no ungendered neutral subjects ... Yet this is not the whole of the story. In addition to underlining the ways in which legal agents do in fact take gender considerations into account when making decisions about legal culpability, I want to make a rather stronger point: that despite its claims to the contrary, judicial discourse actually requires them to do so.

This line of argument is continued in the discussion of the concept of the 'reasonable man' in the context of provocation.

IV.d.ii.   Provocation

Provocation, like diminished responsibility, is a partial defence to murder. Homicide is sometimes justified on the grounds of self-defence. There is much similarity in the way laws of provocation and self-defence have developed. Both use the notion of reasonableness, a concept which is apparently gender-neutral but in reality discriminates against women who are provoked and/or attempt to defend themselves against persistent male violence or indeed anyone who is physically vulnerable. Thus we deal with them together. Two points need to be emphasised, however: (1) self-defence, unlike provocation (and diminished responsibility), is not confined to homicide – it can also justify lesser forms of violence; and (2) self-defence, unlike provocation (and diminished responsibility), is a complete defence; when invoked successfully it results in acquittal.

Female victims are far more likely to have known their killer: 72% of female victims knew the suspect at the time of the offence, with 46% being killed by their partner or ex-partner. This compared with 40% of males who knew the main suspect and only 5% who were killed by their partner or ex-partner (Home Office 2003f: Fig 1.3).

In the case of partner killings there has nearly always been a history of marital discord and violence, particularly male violence. However, this does not mean that the killings represent an incident of 'normal' violence gone wrong. One characteristic of the male killers is that they are often separated from their partner and the killings arise from disputes about exclusivity and child custody. Women, on the other hand, do not usually kill from jealousy or following the termination of a relationship. When they kill, there has usually been a high degree of violence within an ongoing relationship (Wallace 1986; Ewing 1990).

Fiona Brookman and Mike Maguire, 'Reducing homicide: Summary of a Review of the Possibilities' RDS Occasional Paper No 84 (Home Office 2003)

Researchers have consistently found that a high proportion of female victims of domestic homicide have previously experienced domestic violence. It has therefore been suggested that one important avenue for reducing domestic homicide is to identify and intervene with female victims of domestic violence. However, in practice the proportion of reported cases of domestic violence which ultimately result in a homicide is very small. Researchers have therefore focused on identifying those groups of domestic violence victims which appear to be associated with fatal outcomes. From the available evidence, much of which emanates from North America, a number of indicators can be identified as most appropriate to assessing risk of homicide within the domestic setting. The following list, which is adapted from Campbell (1995:111), includes some which are undoubtedly more applicable to the US than the UK, such as access to guns. Most are likely to be as important in the UK context as in the US, although this cannot be confirmed without further research.

- Access to/ownership of guns
- Displaying weapons such as knives within the household
- Threats with weapons
- Threats to kill
- Serious injury in prior abusive incident

- Threats of suicide by male partner (in response to female partner's threats to leave)
- Drug and alcohol abuse by male partner
- Forced sex of female partner
- Obsessiveness/extensive jealousy, extensive dominance
From other research, we might add to this list:
- Women's (survivors') predictions of future risk and its likely severity
- Evidence of stalking
- Recent ending of a relationship instigated by female partner

The research findings suggest that predictions of serious domestic violence can be refined to a sufficient extent to allow targeted interventions, but that the scope for predicting domestic homicide – and hence for specific interventions – seems much more limited. Even so, there is evidence of some links between the two, suggesting that a significant reduction in the overall frequency of domestic violence (especially that involving serious and repeated assaults) would be accompanied by at least a small reduction in the number of homicides. The research literature on reducing levels of domestic violence has tended to advocate changes within the criminal justice system (e.g. through encouraging prosecutions and specific pieces of legislation, for instance to deter stalking), and effective joint working with other agencies such as the police, probation service, social services and voluntary sector providers. If these approaches are informed by a better understanding of the risk factors associated with serious harm within a domestic setting, they would appear to be the most effective means of achieving these double aims.

The partial defence of provocation existed at common law but is now partially defined by statute, which makes clear that there are two separate questions – did the provocation cause the defendant to lose her self-control (the subjective element) and was the provocation such that a reasonable person would have acted similarly (the objective element).

Homicide Act 1957, s 3

Where on a charge of murder there is evidence on which the jury can find that the person charged was provoked (whether by things done or by things said or by both together) to lose his self-control, the question whether the provocation was enough to make a reasonable man do as he did shall be left to be determined by the jury; and in determining that question the jury shall take into account everything both done and said according to the effect which, in their opinion, it would have on a reasonable man.

Section 3 supplements rather than replaces the common law of provocation, and this hybrid construction has contributed to the uncertainty surrounding its operation. As Norrie explains, provocation:

has both a factual and regulative aspect. The factual aspect concerns whether the accused in fact lost his self-control ... [and] the regulative aspect is the requirement that what was said or done should have been enough to make the reasonable person do as the accused did [Norrie 2002].

Two contentious questions are thus posed. First, does the loss of self-control have to be sudden? Secondly, who is the reasonable person against whom the defendant's actions have to be compared? Debate has surrounded Lord Diplock's suggested direction in *Camplin* (1978) that the reasonable man is 'a person having the power of self-control to be expected of an ordinary person of the sex and age of the accused, but on other respects sharing such of the accused's characteristics as they think would affect the gravity of the provocation to him'. Some have doubted whether these two issues of 'provocability' (one's self-control) and 'provocativeness' (the gravity of the provocation) are susceptible to such neat separation (Norrie 2002).

The discussion below focuses on the gendered nature of the defence, but it should be noted that the intense debate about provocation, which these arguments have set in train, has touched a raw nerve in the delicate balance between sense and nonsense on which the defence rests.

Through a series of high-profile cases in the 1980s, appellate courts struggled to accommodate the newly-discovered social reality of domestic violence, including the fact that women sometimes kill their abusive partners, and of the gendered basis of legal constructions of provocation as a partial defence. Contemporary understanding of the phenomenon of domestic violence has been influenced by the emergence of Battered Wife Syndrome (BWS). This was developed by a psychologist to map the stages through which a woman subjected to long-term physical abuse within a relationship might pass (Walker 1984). The syndrome postulates that, after repeated violence, a woman is likely to become immobilised, passive and unable to act to escape the oppression of her situation. It is often remarked that a woman should leave a violent relationship rather than endure it; BWS offers one explanation as to why she might not. The advantage of BWS is that it is a medicalised specialist term and as such might be admitted as expert evidence. It is difficult otherwise to bring before a court generalised evidence about domestic violence or social and economic disadvantage – courts are assumed to need no help in understanding the 'normal' world. Yet the acceptance of evidence of BWS carries with it all sorts of problems. For example, by rendering matters into the rarefied sphere of the expert, domestic violence is seen as unusual; the woman's own experiences are taken over by the expectations of others; the issue is driven towards the 'psychological/iatric' professions and discourses and thus may appear more suitable for diminished responsibility with all the unfortunate associations of 'only women who are mad commit offences'; the approach is internally inconsistent because BWS at once speaks of the woman's helplessness while explaining the fact that she has killed; and it distracts attention from all sorts of other valid reasons why a woman might stay in a violent relationship, or ignore the fact that she might well have made many attempts to leave (Sheehy, Stubbs and Tolmie 1992).

Evidence of a woman's mental state, including that she was suffering from BWS, is admissible in order to assess both the 'subjective' and 'objective' aspects of the provocation defence. In other words, the evidence can be used to help support the claim that she lost her self-control and that a reasonable woman would have also lost hers in the circumstances (*Ahluwalia*, 1992).

Most commentators agree that the provocation defence is applied inconsistently by juries and judges (Ashworth 2003: 272; McColgan 1993: 509, amongst many). Nicolson analyses (below) the way the Court of Appeal represented the 'stories' of Sara Thornton and Kiranjit Ahluwalia, whose cases dominated the debate about battered women who kill in the UK. The article was written before Sara Thornton's second appeal (1996), which was allowed on the grounds that fresh medical evidence of personality disorder and BWS would have led to different directions to the jury. A retrial was ordered and a verdict of manslaughter was returned. Apart from the observations that Nicolson makes, the *Thornton* and *Ahluwalia* cases underline the difficult choices facing defence lawyers as to whether to concentrate on diminished responsibility (as in Thornton's first trial) or on provocation. If diminished responsibility is not raised by the defence, no direction will be given to the jury, whereas a judge is obliged to direct the jury on provocation if there is evidence on which to base such a verdict. New rules on disclosure both restrict the prosecution's duty of disclosure and introduce for the first time a defence duty to disclose (Criminal Procedure and Investigations Act 1996, ss 3 and 5). This may relieve the prosecution of a duty to disclose evidence relevant to provocation where the defence has indicated a different line of defence (Grieve 1997). The Act compounds the difficulties already faced in choosing the line of defence on which to concentrate. Going for a full defence, such as alibi or self-defence, might undermine a claim of provocation. The 1996 Act allows adverse inferences to be drawn where the defence fails to satisfy the disclosure duty in one of the following ways: by defaulting altogether; by setting out inconsistent defences; or by putting forward a different defence at trial (s 11) (see Sprack 1997).

Donald Nicolson [the following material originally appeared in 'Telling Tales: Gender Discrimination, Gender Construction and Battered Women Who Kill' Feminist Legal Studies III/2 (1995), 185–206 at 185–196, and is here reprinted by permission of Deborah Charles Publications]

For some time now the inaccessibility of criminal law defences to battered women who kill their batterers has received much attention. This inaccessibility has been shown to stem from two forms of gender discrimination.

In terms of 'double standard' discrimination, women are expected to conform to standards of behaviour not expected of men. More subtly, 'formal equality' discrimination involves the application of standards of behaviour which, albeit formally gender neutral, are premised upon the experiences and behavioural patterns of men.

Recently feminist analysis has also begun to focus on the legal construction of women. Even when not directly discriminatory, law, and its personnel are said to disseminate frequently sexist and oppressive ideas of what it means to be a 'real woman', how she behaves and what social role she performs. These constructs are reinforced by rewarding women who match them and punishing those who do not. This educative process helps to shape the thoughts and actions of women, if not to construct their very being.

[The cases of] Sara Thornton and Kiranjit Ahluwalia ... illustrate the complex relationship between gender construction and gender discrimination: how discrimination may flow from and reinforce gender constructions; and how the eradication of gender neutral bias may be replaced by a subtle process of gender construction in which female experiences and differences are considered, but in the form of sexist stereotypes which reinforce the oppression and control of women in general.

[Their] stories are sufficiently similar to justify comparison. Both suffered numerous beatings and death threats from jealous and possessive husbands, although Kiranjit's ordeal lasted much longer, and included rape and sexual abuse ... Deepak Ahluwalia had started an affair and was about to leave Kiranjit. Malcolm Thornton, on the other hand, was a chronic alcoholic. Both women killed their husbands following provocative conduct. Sara stabbed Malcolm after he had made wounding remarks, threatened to kill her and taunted her with her own helplessness. Kiranjit set Deepak alight a few hours after he had declared their marriage to be over, threatened to beat her and placed a hot iron against her face.

At both murder trials, their defences alleging no mens rea, provocation and diminished responsibility were rejected. On appeal, both appellants attacked the law on provocation, which requires that defendants actually lose their self-control – the subjective condition – and that a reasonable person sharing the defendant's age, sex, and any other characteristics relevant to the type of provocation would have done so – the objective condition. In particular, both appeals alleged that the *Duffy* [1949] interpretation of the subjective condition, which required a 'sudden and temporary loss of self-control' and barred the defence whenever there is 'time for cooling' between provocation and the killing, discriminates against battered women since they rarely act instantaneously following provocation, but after a 'slow burn' of fear and desperation.

But there the similarities between the two cases end. Whereas, in *Thornton* the Court of Appeal upheld the *Duffy* interpretation as authoritative and comprehensible to a jury, in *Ahluwalia* it subtly and surreptitiously rendered the law more amenable to battered women by holding, albeit *obiter*, that a 'cooling time' was no longer an absolute legal bar to the defence, merely evidence that self-control had not been suddenly lost. In addition, the *Ahluwalia* court also amended – again *obiter* – the objective condition of provocation so as to include the perspective of defendants suffering from so-called battered woman syndrome.

Both reforms are limited. Nevertheless, the *Ahluwalia* decision stands in stark contrast to the unsympathetic *Thornton* judgment ... By contrast Kiranjit Ahluwalia's appeal was upheld on the grounds of fresh evidence of diminished responsibility ... [and at] her retrial she was freed.

... [A]n important factor in the two courts' differing sympathies ... was their judgments of Sara Thornton and Kiranjit Ahluwalia as women.

The dominant societal standard against which women are judged can be termed that of 'appropriate femininity' ... [which] is constructed by a number of disparate discourses clustered around three core ideas: domesticity, sexuality and pathology, each of which is defined not so much in the abstract, but in contrast to their masculine corollaries ... [T]hese binary oppositions involve hierarchies, with the masculine side constructed as superior and as the norm against which femininity is measured, thus rendering the 'normal' woman always already abnormal.

The notion of domesticity requires women to be good and caring mothers, loyal and supportive wives, competent housewives and to remain in the private domain of the nuclear family, economically and emotionally dependent upon their husbands who bestride the public sphere of society. Feminine sexuality is neither promiscuous nor frigid. The single woman is chaste and demure. On marriage, her sexuality is unlocked by her husband upon whom her sexual fulfilment depends. Unlike male sexuality which is driven by physical needs, female sexuality is constructed in terms of love, marriage, the family and children. Finally, there are a number of disparate discourses united by the idea of women as the pathological Other. By contrast to men who are rational and whose minds control their bodies, women are portrayed as powerfully subject to the control of nature via their reproductive cycle and role, and their 'raging hormones'. Consequently, they are emotional, irrational, compulsive, unstable, fickle and contrary. Moreover, women are weak, neurotic and prone to illness, both physical and mental. But they can also be calculating and deceitful when they wish ...

The Court of Appeal's judgments of Sara Thornton and Kiranjit Ahluwalia as women emerge from its descriptions of 'the facts' of their cases. These 'facts' did not exist pre-packaged for judicial recital. 'Reality' is unbounded ... multi-faceted, and subject to varying interpretations. Facts have to be selected, interpreted and communicated. This process is neither mechanical nor neutral, but is aimed at persuading the reader of the legal and emotional force of the judge's decision in much the same way that advocates persuade courts ...

The tone of the two stories are clearly set by their opening sentences. The detached listing of Sara Thornton's personal details anticipates the court's lack of sympathy for her ... Beldam LJ distanced himself from the emotive aspects of the case ... This attempt at objectivity is markedly absent in the *Ahluwalia* judgment. Its opening words 'This is a tragic case ...' portend the sympathy for Kiranjit which pervades the judgment ...

The intimation that Sara ungratefully threw away a promising start to life is expanded into the more damning suggestion that she was responsible for her battered experience. Thus we are told that her previous husband drank and was violent, and that '[f]rom the start she realised that [Malcolm] was a heavy drinker and was jealous and possessive.' This echoes both the idea that sexual offence victims 'ask for it', and the equally absurd 'women who love too much' thesis, which portrays battered women as pathologically needing and even enjoying male violence ...

The most striking and significant aspect of the judgment is that it drastically downplayed the single most important feature of the case: Sara's experience as a battered woman. Whereas a total of 161 lines were devoted to describing 'the facts' which led to the deceased's death, only five dealt with his violence and abusive behaviour ...

By contrast 41 out of 100 lines describing Kiranjit Ahluwalia's story were devoted to her 'many years of violence and humiliation' ...

[U]nlike Sara Thornton's, [her story] was not told in the classical dramaturgic tradition, in terms of which the tragedy stems from the protagonist's own character flaws. Kiranjit's tragedy was presented as that of a passive victim of harsh fate ...

Throughout ... the focus is on what was done to Kiranjit rather than on her own actions ... The caring mother theme was most effectively used by immediately following the description of the killing with the sentence: 'She then went to dress her son'. The picture of passive femininity disrupted by Kiranjit's violence is thus partly restored by an image of domesticity and caring.

... The appellants' agency in the killing could not be denied. Nor could the jury findings that they intended to kill be challenged. What was relevant on appeal was whether they had acted rationally and in cold-blood (murder) or irrationally due to a sudden and temporary loss of self-control (provocation) or to impaired mental responsibility (diminished responsibility) ...

The *Thornton* and *Ahluwalia* cases illustrate the long-standing tendency for the prosecution of women to be transformed into trial of their character, with their perceived conformity or non-conformity with the standards of appropriate femininity determining their treatment. Having been perceived as unfeminine, Sara Thornton's biography and actions were presented so as to construct her as having rejected demure sexuality and submissive domesticity, and as aggressive, fickle and devious. As such she was shown no sympathy. Her experience as a battered woman was down-played almost to the point of invisibility, while her agency and intention was highlighted. By contrast, Kiranjit Ahluwalia's conformity with women's allotted role as passive and submissive wives and mothers appeared to encourage the Court of Appeal to give due regard to her role as victim of conjugal violence and to erase her agency in killing ...

The construction of women who kill as either pathologically mad or doubly bad pushes the battered female defendant towards the option of mental abnormality. Otherwise she risks being reconstructed as an evil woman taking revenge. As neither image comes close to matching their experiences, battered women tend either to receive mandatory life sentences for murder or to be regarded as mentally ill following a finding of diminished responsibility ...

Nicolson's powerful analysis of these two cases emphasises the unpredictability and contradiction inherent in the constructions of 'woman' which infuse legal standards. Women, as defendants and as victims, always seem to be caught at the wrong end of the swing between excuse and justification. For example, the difficulties referred to earlier with the use of provocation as a vehicle for a PMS defence can now be seen more clearly. The question whether a 'reasonable woman' with pre-menstrual tension would have lost her self-control would be even more difficult to apply than the 'reasonable man' test often is. If what lies behind the 'reasonable man' test is an attempt to limit the scope of the defence to those situations where the loss of self-control was understandable or even deserving of sympathy, then pre-menstrual tension could be relevant. However, outside the issue of taking PMS specifically into account there is nonetheless a failure to accommodate women in the very way provocation is conceived:

L J Taylor, 'Provoked Reason in Men and Women: Heat of Passion, Manslaughter and Imperfect Self-Defense' (1986) UCLA LR 1679, 1689–1697

In the debate over its usefulness and the proper level of its subjectivity, one glaring effect – the male orientation of the reasonable man standard – has been minimised or ignored. Women rarely have been defendants in the history of voluntary manslaughter law. One exception is the woman whose plea that her pregnancy should be considered in her reaction to provoca-tion was held 'a ground to which we are unable to attach any importance' [*R v Smith* (1914)]. The neutrality of the modern term 'reasonable person' masks a profoundly gender-based and sex-specific standard. Catharine MacKinnon has warned of the danger inherent here: 'When [the state] is most ruthlessly neutral, it will be most male; when it is most sex-blind, it will be most blind to the sex of the standard being applied.' There is not a single common-law reference to a 'reasonable woman' … Rather than developing a separate standard for women, criminal law has held and continues to hold female defendants to a male standard of reasonableness. Nevertheless the notion that women are beyond the pale of reasonable action retains some currency. As recently as 1981, one writer wondered 'as to what law might be involved in the law of the reasonable woman, we follow precedent and venture no opinion … leaving open the question of whether conjoining "reasonable" and "woman" creates a contradiction in terms.'

The historical development of the standard reveals its male bias, but the language of the standard reveals more. Linguistic theory has confirmed that women have been present in official language only as the 'other', and experience proves that the use of male pronouns effectively excludes a woman's perspective and experience. In short, 'man' does not include 'woman', nor are the terms interchangeable. Asking a woman to behave as a reasonable man places her violent behaviour – when it does not comport with a male norm – outside the boundaries of reason.

Although women's use of violence scarcely figured in the definition of the 'reasonable man' in provocation, women have been present as victims or provokers of homicide. Women are almost always killed by men, often by those with whom they have had an intimate relationship. Therefore, it is not surprising that in heat-of-passion killings of women, the passion often is connected to the victim's sexuality. Many defendants in the early English cases that define voluntary manslaughter were men who had killed their wives or their wives' lovers upon discovering them in the act of adultery … While the law sympathised with the jealous rage of men, it assumed that wives did not experience similar rage. In 1946, 275 years after a court first announced the defence of provocation, an English court finally stated that wives who killed their husbands or their husbands' lovers could also avail themselves of the defence [*Holmes v DPP* (1946)].

The law of provocation endorses men's ownership of women's sexuality by expressly sanctioning violent reactions by husbands to their wives' infidelity. Although the defence of provocation upon the discovery of adultery now applies to women as well as to men, it is a shallow concession to equality that bears little legitimacy or meaning. Cases and social studies show that women rarely react to their husband's infidelity with deadly violence. In contrast, men who kill their wives or lovers frequently act after accusing them of infidelity. Female homicide defendants may be exceptional because they are rare, but they may not be exceptional women; they may be ordinary women pushed to extremes. Yet the law has never incorporated these 'ordinary' women into its standards for assessing the degree of criminality in homicide, as it has done with 'ordinary' men.

The study of violent crime and homicide in particular must confront the two cultures in which men and women live, acknowledge that criminal law has been the product of a dominant male culture, and work towards an understanding of how the law might change through an integration of women's experience – an integration crucial to the analysis of intersexual homicide.

The debate surrounding provocation has been driven by cases involving killings by women who have been subjected to long-term abuse by their husbands or partners. These cases have brought to the fore the 'hidden gender' in the development of the provocation defence. Attempts to explain some women's responses through the use of the psychological construct 'Battered Wife Syndrome' have disrupted previous understandings. Notably, appeal courts have struggled to contain the 'reasonable man', veering between a version which all but emasculates him as he merges into the defendant and rebuilding him into the 'straight citizen'. Two sets of cases thus sat either side of the interpretation of *Camplin*. *Morhall* (1995) and a majority of the Privy Council in *Luc Thiet Thuan* (1997) favouring the restrictive objective approach, with *Humphreys* (1995), *Thornton* (1996) and *Dryden* (1995) exemplifying the broader approach. This division reached its climax in *Smith* (2000), where a majority of the House of Lords preferred the more personalised approach to provocation.

R v Smith (Morgan) [2000] 4 All ER 289

[*Smith was charged with murder after fatally stabbing the deceased. At trial he sought to rely on the defence of provocation and adduced psychiatric evidence that he was suffering from clinical depression which reduced his powers of self-control. The trial judge directed the jury that his mental state was a characteristic relevant in considering the gravity of the provocation (provocativeness) but was not relevant to loss of self-control (provocability). He was convicted of murder but the Court of Appeal allowed his appeal, substituting a manslaughter conviction. The Crown appealed after the Court of Appeal certified the following question of general public importance:*

'*Are characteristics other than age and sex, attributable to a reasonable man, for the purpose of section 3 of the Homicide Act 1957, relevant not only to the gravity of the provocation to him but also to the standard of self-control to be expected?*'

By a 3 to 2 majority, the House dismissed the appeal holding that all of the particular defendant's characteristics were relevant to both whether he was in fact provoked and to the issue of self-control.]

Lord Hoffmann.

My Lords, it is impossible to read even a selection of the extensive modern literature on provocation without coming to the conclusion that the concept has serious logical and moral flaws. But your Lordships must take the law as it stands. Whatever your decision in this case, the result is not likely to be wholly satisfactory. The doctrine of provocation has always been described as a concession to human frailty and the law illustrates Kant's dictum that, from the crooked timber of humanity, nothing completely straight can be made. Nevertheless, I shall suggest to your Lordships that this appeal offers an opportunity, within the constraints imposed by history and by Parliament, to make some serviceable improvements.

[*Lord Hoffmann went on to interpret Lord Diplock's judgment in Camplin.*]

But the actual facts in *Camplin*'s case were not primarily concerned with a characteristic with affected the gravity of the provocation. It is true that the gravity of the alleged taunts and sexual abuse may have been affected by the accused's consciousness of his physical and intellectual inferiority in relation to the deceased. But the main case for the defence was that a 15-year-old boy could not be expected to have the same powers of self-control as an adult. Lord Diplock acknowledged that–

> 'in strict logic there is a transition between treating age as a character-
> istic that may be taken into account in assessing the gravity of the
> provocation addressed to the accused and treating it as a characteristic
> to be taken into account in determining what is the degree of
> self-control to be expected of the ordinary person with whom the
> accused's conduct is to be compared. But to require old heads on
> young shoulders is inconsistent with the law's compassion of human
> infirmity to which Sir Michael Foster ascribed the doctrine of
> provocation more than two centuries ago. The distinction as to the
> purposes for which it is legitimate to take the age of the accused into
> account involves considerations of too great nicety to warrant a place
> in deciding a matter of opinion, which is no longer one to be decided
> by a judge trained in logical reasoning but by a jury drawing on their
> experience of how ordinary human beings behave in real life.'

This is a most important passage and I invite your Lordships' attention to the following points.

(1) Lord Diplock says that youth may be taken into account because the principle of compassion to human infirmity, as a jury drawing on their experience may apply it, requires one to do so. He does say that the same principle of compassion is incapable of applying to any other characteristics which a jury might on similar grounds think should be taken into account. It would have been easy for him to have said that youth was for this purpose unique.

(2) Lord Diplock expressly rejects the distinction between the effect of age on the gravity of the provocation and on the power of self-control on the grounds that it is 'of too great nicety' for application by a jury. Again, there is nothing to suggest that this comment is not equally true of other characteristics. Since *Camplin*'s case, there is a great deal of material which demonstrates that Lord Diplock's scepticism about

whether the distinction could be made to work in practice was well founded.

(3) If age were to be the only case in which a particular characteristic could be taken into account as relevant to the expected power of self-control, it would be necessary to explain why it should be so singled out. The High Court of Australia, in *Stingel v R* (1990) 171 CLR 312 at 330, said that it was because age is a normal characteristic 'the process of development from childhood to maturity is something which, being common to us all, is an aspect of ordinariness'. This explanation was embraced by Lord Goff of Chieveley in *Luc Thiet Thuan v R* [1996]. It had, as I have said, been relied upon in *Camplin*'s case by the Court of Appeal to distinguish *Bedder*'s case. But the distinction between normal and abnormal characteristics was expressly rejected by Lord Diplock. He said that:

'The reasoning in *Bedder* would, I think, permit of this distinction between normal and abnormal characteristics, which may affect the powers of self-control of the accused; but for reasons that I have already mentioned the proposition stated in *Bedder* requires qualification as a consequence of the changes in the law effected by the 1957 Act. To try to salve what can remain of it without conflict with the Act could in my view only lead to unnecessary and unsatisfactory complexity in a question which has now become a question for the jury alone.'

[This passage in Lord Diplock's speech] provides in my view no support for the theory, widely advanced in the literature, that he was making a clear distinction between characteristics relevant to the gravity of the provocation and characteristics relevant to the power of self-control, with age (and possibly sex) as arbitrary exceptions which could be taken into account for the latter purpose.

This, in my view, goes to the heart of the matter and is in accordance with the analysis of the effect of s 3 which I have made earlier in my speech. The jury is entitled to act upon its own opinion of whether the objective element of provocation has been satisfied and the judge is not entitled to tell them that for this purpose the law requires them to exclude from consideration any of the circumstances or characteristics of the accused.

The difficulty about the practical application of this distinction in the law of provocation is that in many cases the two forms of claim are inextricably muddled up with each other. A good example is the recent New Zealand case of *R v Rongonui* (13 April 2000, unreported). The accused was a woman with a history of violence against her, suffering from post-traumatic stress disorder. The alleged provocation was that a neighbour she was visiting to ask for help in babysitting her children had produced a knife – not in a threatening way, but sufficient to make her lose control of herself, seize the knife and stab the neighbour to death. The Court of Appeal agreed that it was very difficult in such a case to distinguish between the gravity of the provocation (the accused's previous experience of violence making the mere production of a knife a graver provocation than it would be to someone who had led a more sheltered life) and the accused's capacity for self-control which had been affected by the psychological stress of the violence she had suffered. Tipping J, giving one of the majority judgments which held that the New Zealand statute on provocation (s 169 of the Crimes Act 1961) mandated the application of the distinction, said that it required 'mental gymnastics'. Thomas J, who thought that the statute did not have to be construed so rigidly, said that most trial judges had seen–

> 'the glazed look in the jurors' eyes as, immediately after instructing them that it is open to them to have regard to the accused's alleged characteristic in assessing the gravity of the provocation, they are then advised that they must revert to the test of the ordinary person and disregard that characteristic when determining the sufficiency of the accused's loss of self-control.'

Professor Stanley Yeo, in his recent book *Unrestrained Killings and the Law* (1998), points out (at p 61) that the reason why jurors find the distinction so difficult is that it–

> 'bears no conceivable relationship with the underlying rationales of the defence of provocation. The defence has been variously regarded as premised upon the contributory fault of the victim and, alternatively, upon the fact that the accused was not fully in control of his or her behaviour when the homicide was committed. Neither of these premises requires the distinction to be made between characteristics of the accused affecting the gravity of the provocation from those concerned with the power of self-control.'

There is however one really serious argument in favour of the distinction between characteristics affecting the gravity of the provocation and characteristics affecting the power of self-control. This is the claim that, despite all its difficulties of application, it is the only way to hold the line against complete erosion of the objective element in provocation. The purpose of the objective element in provocation is to mark the distinction between (partially) excusable and inexcusable loss of self-control. As Lord Diplock said in *Camplin* ... the conduct of the accused should be measured against 'such powers of self-control as everyone is entitled to expect that his fellow citizens will exercise in society as it is today'. If there is no limit to the characteristics which can be taken into account, the fact that the accused lost self-control will show that he is a person liable in such circumstances to lose his self-control. The objective element will have disappeared completely.

My Lords, I share the concern that this should not happen. For the protection of the public, the law should continue to insist that people must exercise self-control. A person who flies into a murderous rage when he is crossed, thwarted or disappointed in the vicissitudes of life should not be able to rely upon his anti-social propensity as even a partial excuse for killing. In *R v Stingel* (1990) 171 CLR 312, for example, the accused was obsessively infatuated with a woman who had terminated their relationship. He became a stalker, following her about. She obtained a court order restraining him from approaching her. One evening after a party he found the woman in a car with another man. According to his own account, they were having sex. He went back to his own car, fetched a butcher's knife and came back and killed the man. His evidence conformed to the standard narrative which the legal requirement of 'loss of control' imposes on such defences:

'I was all worked up and feeling funny. It was like I was in a rage, almost to the stage where I felt dazed. It was like I really didn't know what happened until the knife went into him.'

The High Court of Australia held that the judge was right to withdraw the issue of provocation from the jury on the ground that such conduct could not raise even a reasonable doubt as to whether the objective element in the defence had been satisfied. I respectfully agree. Male possessiveness and jealousy should not today be an acceptable reason for loss of self-control leading to homicide, whether inflicted upon the woman herself or her new lover. In Australia the judge was able to give effect to this policy by withdrawing the issue from the jury. But s 3 prevents an English judge from doing so. So, it is suggested, a direction that characteristics such as jealousy and obsession should be ignored in relation to the objective element is the best way to ensure that people like Stingel cannot rely upon the defence.

My Lords, I do emphasise that what has been rendered unworkable is not the principle of objectivity which (subject to the changes noted in *Camplin* case) s 3 was plainly intended to preserve, but a particular way of explaining it. I am not suggesting that your Lordships should in any way depart from the legal principle embodied in s 3 but only that the principle should be expounded in clear language rather than by the use of an opaque formula.

In my opinion, therefore, judges should not be required to describe the objective element in the provocation defence by reference to a reasonable man, with or without attribution of personal characteristics. They may instead find it more helpful to explain in simple language the principles of the doctrine of provocation. First, it requires that the accused should have killed while he had lost self-control and that something should have caused him to lose self-control. For better or for worse, s 3 left this part of the law untouched. Secondly, the fact that something caused him to lose self-control is not enough. The law expects people to exercise control over their emotions. A tendency to violent rages or childish tantrums is a defect in character rather than an excuse. The jury must think that the circumstances were such as to make the loss of self-control sufficiently *excusable* to reduce the gravity of the offence from murder to manslaughter. This is entirely a question for the jury. In deciding what should count as a sufficient excuse, they have to apply what they consider to be appropriate standards of behaviour; on the one hand making allowance for human nature and the power of the emotions but, on the other hand, not allowing someone to rely upon his own violent disposition. In applying these standards of behaviour, the jury represent the community and decide, as Lord Diplock said in *Camplin*'s ... what degree of self-control 'everyone is entitled to expect that his fellow citizens will exercise in society as it is today'. The maintenance of such standards is important. As Viscount Simon LC said more than 50 years ago in *Holmes v DPP* ... , 'as society advances, it ought to call for a higher measure of self-control'.

The general principle is that the same standards of behaviour are expected of everyone, regardless of their individual psychological make-up. In most cases, nothing more will need to be said. But the jury should in an appropriate case be told, in whatever language will best convey the distinction, that this is a principle and not a rigid rule. It may sometimes have to yield to a more important principle, which is to do justice in the particular case. So the jury may think that there was some characteristic of the accused, whether temporary or permanent, which affected the degree of control which society could reasonably have expected of *him* and which it would be unjust not to take into account. If the jury take this view, they are at liberty to give effect to it.

Lord Hoffmann notes the flawed basis of provocation, and this is reflected in the sharp division within the House, with Lords Millett and Hobhouse dissenting. The latter criticised the majority for introducing a variable standard of self-control which subverted the moral basis of the defence. That such a schism surrounding provocation presents itself a mere six years after the unanimity in *Morhall* arguably provides another reason for its abolition. In March 2003 it was reported that the Government were considering the possibility of such an abolition (*Independent*, 3 March 2003).

Celia Wells, 'Provocation: The Case for Abolition' in Andrew Ashworth and Barry Mitchell (eds) *Rethinking English Homicide Law* (Oxford University Press, 2000) pp 85–106. Reprinted by permission of Oxford University Press.

The objective requirement, that a reasonable man would have done as the defendant did, was released from some of its common-law restrictions much earlier by the House of Lords in *Camplin* in 1978. But it continues to cause conceptual difficulties and it is the main impediment to achieving any semblance of coherence in the provocation defence. For over half a century the reasonable man was the primary mechanism for containing the defence. It was one thing to say that provocation was a concession to human frailty, another to admit individual weaknesses or abnormality. The development of the defence is partly testimony to the cultural (and historical) relativity of perceptions of normality. This also was a powerful reason (or motive) for law to adopt a strict approach to the reasonable man, and to refuse to endow him with characteristics of gender, age, race, impotence, mental instability, or irascibility. It wasn't that he had no identity. It was that giving him explicit identity would expose his implicit identification with a certain kind of manhood. *Camplin* was an easy case in which to challenge this. The defendant was a 15-year-old boy. The victim, and provoker, a middle-aged homosexual. And what was more he was Pakistani – a description that is gratuitously added in Lord Diplock's speech and repeated in some accounts of the case. Neither the strict, homogeneous, imperialistic version of the reasonable man, nor the personalized version, has proved manageable. In most common-law jurisdictions the defendant's characteristics clothe the reasonable man (or ordinary person) in assessing the gravity of the provocation, but the question that causes huge difficulty is how to construct the reasonable man for the purposes of assessing the standard of self-control ...

Provocation's concession to human frailty sits uncomfortably in a criminal law which is premised on the denial of explanations based on individual circumstances. Provocation therefore never knows quite where to place itself in the turmoil of competing realities and tensions. It tends to function as a distorting echo of contemporary fears and concerns ...

If there is to be an ordinary person, there is some argument for taking account of age. We expect to make allowances for the level of toleration of a 13-year-old compared with that of a 17-year-old, and possibly that of a 20-year-old compared with someone who is 30. But we should not make allowances on grounds of gender or race. We should ask a jury to imagine an ordinary person of the same sort of age as the defendant. This of course is an entirely different question from taking into account 'characteristics' which affect the gravity of the provocation – being called a stupid woman is a different insult if you are a woman, being called a 'stupid nigger' is a different insult if you are black, and so on. Otherwise we are in danger of adopting an 'essentialised view of race and ethnicity, that is, the notion that there is one authentic experience of an ethnic identity for each ethnic group.' Such an approach could actually endorse racism.

The debates about the characteristics of the ordinary person lead to the inexorable conclusion that it is the nature of the provocation defence which needs questioning, not its finer contours. It is precisely because assessments of provocativeness are culturally relative, and the need to have regard for 'equality' for the victim as well as equity for the accused, that we need to move beyond provocation as an organizing concept in excusing or mitigating homicide.

Much has been written about the mixed message which provocation seeks to carry. On the one hand it is a concession to human frailty, on the other it is based on wrongdoing by the victim, or someone other than the defendant. The moral equation that the circumstances arose from another's wrongdoing is attractive at an intuitive level. But beyond the superficial the cracks appear. Excuses such as provocation can be accommodated at a general level because they respond to particularized events rather than general conditions, such that the empirical question of whether others would succumb can be incorporated in the defence itself, into a prescriptive inquiry as to whether a person of reasonable firmness would have acted similarly.

It is full of internal contradiction – the loss of self-control posited against the reasonable man, ordinary person test. There are three broad options: clarify the objective standard, abandon the objective standard, or abolish the defence altogether. Attempts to take account of specific characteristics which might affect either the provocation itself or the reaction to it have proved problematic, as has the accommodation of hitherto ignored differences, such as gender, race, and sexuality ...

Smith (2000) has also been criticised for institutionalising roles such as 'battered wives' and for blurring the distinction between provocation and diminished responsibility:

Timothy Macklem and John Gardner, 'Provocation and Pluralism' (2001) 64 Modern Law Review 815

Is it possible to extend this point to the predicament, say, of battered women, whether their predicament is expressed as a syndrome or simply as a terrible history? The answer depends on whether there is such a thing as a set of special standards for being a good or adequate battered woman, such that this adds up to a role in the sense in which we have been using the term. Even if there are such special standards, is this a role that the criminal law should institutionalize? Both of these subsidiary questions are hard to answer. We tend to think that if there is a distinct role of being a battered woman, with its own distinctively lowered standards of self-control, it should not be institutionalized. This is not simply because the standards are lower, for lower standards should sometimes be upheld, when they are constitutive of worthwhile roles. It is because the role of a battered woman should not exist and its unwarranted existence in our society should not be given the stamp of legal approval. To draw a dramatic parallel, it is possible for people to be good slaves, not just in the sense of being good at performing the tasks of slaves, but also in the sense of being temperamentally and dispositionally well suited to slavery. In an attenuated sense such a people can be 'self-respecting slaves', for they live up to the standards of the role that they are forced to play. Nevertheless the role is foul and its standards should not be institutionalized in law. If a slave is provoked to the point of killing someone, be it his master or some other person, in circumstances where a freeman would not be so provoked, the slave's response should be judged by the standard appropriate to freemen, not the lesser standard of a lesser being. That is where real self-respect lies.

Of course this – the lowering of standards to fit the role – is not the argument that many campaigners make or wish to make with respect to battered women. The argument that many wish to make is an argument that abandons standards altogether. For them there is no question of *judging* the reactions of battered women, of seeing whether they are up to scratch, of assessing them as reasonable. It is a matter of making the space to 'excuse' them by accommodating the reactions that they have been reduced to by their batterers. This is, of course, quite literally to diminish their responsibility by abandoning any claim that they are people who can be judged by standards, in this case by standards of self-control. This makes the whole exercise of accommodation self-defeating, however, since the whole point of pleading provocation rather that diminished responsibility is to garner the respect and self-respect that flows from being judged by the proper standards. The plea of provocation then becomes merely euphemistic: It is really a defence of diminished responsibility by another name, with a more positive public relations spin. Nor should one imagine that the spin is *all* positive. Those who use violence in domestic settings are often systematic torturers. Part of the evil of what they do lies in its tendency gradually to brutalize and dehumanize its victims. It is one thing for the law to admire the resilience of those who survive this torture and manage to maintain their reasonableness. It is quite another for the law to pretend that the torture is never successful, that it never does brutalise and dehumanize its victims to the point at which they no longer react reasonably so that their responsibility is diminished. To pretend that such torture is never successful by rebranding genuine diminished responsibility cases as provocation cases is to understate the evil of the torturer.

An increased awareness of the problems of domestic violence led to a reform of the law relating to provocation in New South Wales. The Crimes (Homicide) Amendment Act 1982 (NSW) removed the emphasis from the events immediately prior to the killing and allows any past conduct of the deceased towards the defendant to be the basis for provocation. There are dangers here too, however. In the same way that the ease with which the provocation defence is available to men who lose their tempers and kill women deflects attention from the seriousness and prevalence of male violence against women (Edwards 1987), so also allowing women who respond to domestic violence to plead provocation would leave them with blame for their own victimisation. Since its conceptual basis is fundamentally unsound, any expansion of the provocation defence should then be treated with caution. It is argued below that women who retaliate in the face of domestic violence should be able more easily to use self-defence, which is a complete defence when successful.

IV.e.   Self-defence

Self-defence goes to an essential element in the definition of crime. Murder and manslaughter involve the *unlawful* killing of another person. A successful plea of self-defence leads to an acquittal because it renders the defendant's actions lawful. In pleading self-defence, the defendant is arguing that her action was entirely appropriate in the circumstances. Self-defence covers both the common law right to defend oneself against invasion of person and property, and the public right to use reasonable force in the prevention of crime. In most cases of course the two will overlap.

> **Criminal Law Act 1967, s 3**
> (1) A person may use such force as is reasonable in the circumstances in the prevention of crime, or in effecting or assisting in the lawful arrest of offenders or suspected offenders or of persons unlawfully at large.
> (2) Subsection (1) above shall replace the rules of the common law on the question when force used for a purpose mentioned in the subsection is justified by that purpose.

The decision whether force is required is a subjective question, whereas the reasonableness of the response, as with the loss of self-control in provocation, is entirely a matter for the jury (*A-G for Northern Ireland's Reference (No 1 of 1975)* (1977)). But the judge will indicate factors to be taken into account in determining whether the retaliation was necessary, such as the imminence of the attack. In addition, the force used is expected to be proportional to that used in the attack. However, it has been said that:

> If a jury thought that in a moment of unexpected anguish a person attacked had only done what he honestly and instinctively thought was necessary that would be most potent evidence that only reasonable defensive action had been taken [Lord Morris in *Palmer* [1971] 1 All ER 1077 at 1078].

Mistaken belief in relation to acting in self-defence is subjectively assessed. In *Beckford* (1987) the Privy Council approved the following passage from the judgment of Lord Lane CJ in *R v Williams* (Gladstone) (1987) as correctly stating the law of self-defence:

> The reasonableness or unreasonableness of the defendant's belief is material to the question of whether the belief was held by the defendant at

all. If the belief was in fact held, its unreasonableness, so far as guilt or innocence is concerned, is neither here nor there. It is irrelevant ... In a case of self-defence, where self-defence or the prevention of crime is concerned, if the jury come to the conclusion that the defendant believed or may have believed, that he was being attacked or that a crime was being committed, and that force was necessary to protect himself or to prevent crime, then the prosecution have not proved their case ... Even if the jury come to the conclusion that the mistake was an unreasonable one, if the defendant may genuinely have been labouring under it, he is entitled to rely on it.

In *Scarlett* (1993) a mistake as to the circumstances leading to the use of more force than necessary was tolerated. However, in *Owino* (1996) the Court of Appeal has re-affirmed that the question of the appropriate degree of force used is objectively evaluated. None of this applies to a defendant whose mistake, whether as to the need for self-defence or as to the amount of force required, was caused by self-induced intoxication (*O'Grady*, 1987).

The trial and appeal of Tony Martin, convicted of murder and wounding with intent after shooting two burglars who had broken into his farmhouse, offers an interesting insight into the procedural and substantive operation of defences. The intruders were retreating when Martin open fired with an unlicensed pump action shotgun, killing one and injuring the other. At trial, his defence lawyers failed to persuade the jury that his acts were justified as self-defence. The case re-opened the public debate about the appropriateness of using violence in defending one's person and property, and there was no shortage of populist sympathy for Martin. It also provides an insight into the context and circumstance that surround defences, as well as the interplay between complete and partial defences. On appeal, a newly instructed legal team adduced fresh evidence suggesting that Martin suffered from a paranoid personality disorder and depression which heightened his sense of fear of threats. Something of a scatter-gun strategy was adopted of using this evidence in relation to both self-defence and diminished responsibility. Counsel also sought to persuade the court that the more personalised approach to provocation confirmed in *Smith* (2000) also applied to self-defence.

R v Martin (Anthony) [2002] 1 Cr App R 27

Lord Woolf.

There are policy reasons for distinguishing provocation from self-defence. Provocation only applies to murder, but self-defence applies to all assaults. In addition, provocation does not provide a complete defence; it only reduces the offence from murder to manslaughter. There is also the undoubted fact that self-defence is raised in a great many cases resulting from minor assaults and it would be wholly disproportionate to encourage medical disputes in cases of that sort. Lord Hobhouse in his dissenting speech in Smith recognised that in relation to self-defence, too generous an approach as to what is reasonable could result in an "exorbitant defence". Lord Hoffmann also appeared conscious of this. As a matter of principle we would reject the suggestion that the approach of the majority in Smith in relation to provocation should be applied directly to the different issue of self-defence.

We would accept that the jury are entitled to take into account in relation to self-defence the physical characteristics of the defendant. However, we would not agree that it is appropriate, except in exceptional circumstances which would make the evidence especially probative, in deciding whether excessive force has been used to take into account whether the defendant is suffering from some psychiatric condition.

Martin's appeal against his murder conviction was allowed, and was substituted by a verdict of manslaughter by reason of diminished responsibility. A few noteworthy points arise from the case. On one level, the rejection of self-defence seems inconsistent with the accepted law on mistaken self-defence (see above). The Court of Appeal appear to be making a distinction between cases of mistaken facts (*Beckford* and *Williams (Glanville)*) and those where the mistake lies in over-estimating the dangerousness of threats (*Martin (Anthony)*). Whilst belief in facts are judged subjectively, objectivity is allowed to creep in to the risk assessments based on such facts. To what extent are such artificial distinctions explained by the underlying notion of moral contextualism (see Norrie 2002)? In this case, perhaps a strong sense that Martin had taken the law into his own hands and ought not be afforded an acquittal that successful self-defence would bring. The final outcome also illustrates the interplay between defences, with diminished responsibility on hand to step in and partially excuse Martin's violence.

In *Re A* (2000) the Court of Appeal turned to self-defence in the unlikely context of conjoined twins in order to justify the killing of one of the twins, Mary (see **section III.a.** above). Ward LJ reasoned that Mary was killing the other twin, Jodie, by draining her life-blood and that the doctors would be justified in removing this threat of fatal harm. However, this elasticity is probably not enough on its own to ensure that self-defence is available to the battered woman who eventually retaliates. An image underlying all discussions of self-defence is that these are one-off occurrences which can be responded to or repelled. It is important to consider more closely how the notions of necessary and proportional force should apply to the long-term battered wife. Part of the requirement that the force used has to be necessary is the (so-called) duty to retreat (*Bird*, 1985). A woman who has been battered will probably have retreated time and time again. Should she be required to go on retreating forever? Should we not take into account on the one occasion when she does not retreat that she has indeed retreated before?

Another strategy which could be used on her behalf would be to recall the right of the property owner to repel an intruder. The right to 'stand fast' in defending one's home is itself a qualification of the duty to retreat (Ashworth 1975: 294). By analogy, should not a woman be able to defend her right to occupy her home without fear of attack? Where she eventually does retaliate, the jury could be encouraged to take into account that it is not only her physical integrity which has been threatened by the violence, but also her right to peaceful occupation of her home.

Similarly, she could benefit from the decision in *Field* (1972). This was a case in which the Court of Appeal rejected the argument that a victim had to avoid places where he knew, because of threats and previous experience, that he might be attacked. Although we might share Ashworth's caution about this and require a prima facie duty to inform the police (1975: 296), it might nonetheless be invoked by women. She may have attempted to get police help in the past. Even if she had not sought police help it would seem wrong to blame her for having absorbed so well the social message that this is really a private matter. In any case, the place she would be being asked to avoid is her own home. By combining the right to remain on one's own property with the *Field* principle, she would have a better chance of arguing that the force was necessary. At a wider level, the prevalence of domestic violence makes something of a nonsense of the idea that she can be expected to avoid it!

The requirement of proportionality could also be rethought in terms of its applicability to the battered wife situation. The argument for proportionality is based on what Ashworth calls the 'human rights' approach – that is, respect for the attacker's right to life and physical security (1975: 296, 297). The problem lies in knowing where that balance should be struck in a situation where lethal force is used to prevent persistent, but not lethal, physical bullying and violence.

McColgan argues that the Canadian decision of *Lavallee* could be used as a model:

Aileen McColgan, 'In Defence of Battered Women Who Kill' (1993) 13 OJLS 508, 510 [by permission of Oxford University Press]

A movement towards the use of self-defence ... started about ten years ago in the United States ... In some respects the current UK law of self-defence avails itself more readily to such an application than does the law in Canada or in many US jurisdictions ... An attempt will be made here to transpose some of the Canadian and US reasoning into the UK context ...

Research suggests that many battered women kill in order to escape the threat of death or serious injury, or to protect their children. Insofar as this is the case, they should be afforded the same defence as is available to men who kill for the same reasons although, given their relative safety in the private sphere and the greater likelihood of physical parity with potential attackers, in different circumstances ...

Even where women kill in the course of a violent attack on them, defence lawyers and the courts are apparently blind to the possibilities of a self-defence plea ...

Given the current model of self-defence, it is clear that attention has to be drawn to its inequitable application to women who kill to protect themselves ... In the absence of challenges to the common assumptions about when force is necessary in response to actual or threatened violence, and about the level of force which a woman might reasonably use against an unarmed man, such women will be unable to successfully plead self-defence. Judicial resistance ... is evident from US cases such as *State v Stewart* [243 Kan 639 (1988)] where the court ruled that, as a matter of law, the defendant could not plead self-defence when she killed her sleeping husband, taking the view that to allow such a plea would be to 'leap into the abyss of anarchy' ... [T]he reluctance of the courts to categorize women's killings as self-defence is rooted partly in the ideology of family life ...

It was not until 1991 that the English courts ... removed husbands' freedom to rape their wives, and the financial dependency historically forced upon women by their husbands' automatic ownership of their goods still finds its existence in women's loss of entitlement upon cohabitation or marriage to most social security benefits. It is therefore essential, where women kill in response to a perceived threat from an abusive partner to their life or the lives of their children, that juries are made aware of the circumstances of the case, including the history of violence and its effects on the woman's perceptions of the threat of violence, as well as to the effect of the relative disadvantages of many women in terms of passive socialization and physical size, strength and training. This approach would not afford women defendants favourable legal treatment; it would, rather, go some way to addressing the prejudice against them that is built into the system by virtue of its development through typically male cases of self-defence. In the context of self-defence, then, the male standards of necessity and proportionality, together with the current failure adequately to address the reality of extreme violence under which many women exist, must be recognized and compensated for in the application of the self-defence standard to battered women who kill ... Early US theorists such as Elizabeth Schneider argued that evidence of the psychological effects of repeated assaults could be utilized, together with lay evidence about the history of defendant and deceased, in order to combat the prejudice inherent in the traditionally male model of self-defence and to allow the question of reasonableness to be assessed in the light of all the circumstances relevant to the defendant. In the event, however, decisions about whether or not to admit such evidence have often been based on the courts' assessment of the reasonableness of the defendant's actions, testimony often being excluded in the non-traditional confrontation cases on the basis that the battered woman's behaviour was unreasonable ... [E]xpert evidence on the effects of prolonged abuse ... has frequently been used to construct a stereotypical battered woman ... When women failed to fit the stereotype (here for example they had fought back before) the evidence would often then be put to one side and their conduct judged against the standard of the 'reasonable man' without consideration of the fact that a woman's, especially a battered woman's, perceptions of danger might reasonably differ from those of a man ...

English law creates no duty in the defendant to avoid places where she may lawfully be, and she may arm herself against an anticipated attack ... [I]t is inappropriate that a woman's failure to leave her own home should be used to cast doubt on her plea of self-defence. This was explicitly recognized by the Supreme Court of Canada in *Lavalee*, where Wilson J, delivering the unanimous decision of the court, stated [1990] 1 SCR 852:

> it is not for the jury to pass judgment on the fact that an accused battered woman stayed in the relationship. Still less is it entitled to conclude that she forfeited her right to self-defence for having done so ... the traditional self-defence doctrine does not require a person to retreat from her home instead of defending herself ...

One argument that could be raised against allowing women to benefit from self-defence in this way is that self-defence is the paradigm justification. It is said that no offence is committed because in the circumstances it was the right act. This way of conceptualising it is difficult to sustain, however, in the light of recent developments which extend the defence to cover situations where the defendant mistakenly believed (whether reasonably or not) that she was under attack (see below).

Any argument for a qualified defence where excessive force was used would also encounter the 'right act' analysis (Dressler 1984). The Australian High Court adopted an excessive defence solution for a time, but later abandoned it (*Zecevic*, 1987). The House of Lords has confirmed that no such half-way house exists in English law, but gave the proposal its strong support (*Clegg*, 1995). Once again, the argument was connected with the continuation of the mandatory penalty for murder. While superficially attractive, the notion that all the problems associated with distinguishing murder from manslaughter or lawful homicides from unlawful homicides would be solved by the introduction of a discretionary penalty for murder, needs careful thought. One argument against the partial defence is that, rather than giving an option to those caught by the severity of the current all-or-nothing self-defence doctrine, it would bring back into the criminal frame those who would otherwise have been acquitted. It is easy to imagine women who kill their violent partners being caught this way. Just as at present they appear to be deprived of self-defence and, through defence tactics or ignorance, led to a choice between murder and manslaughter by diminished responsibility or provocation, so the availability of a partial self-defence would tend to reinforce their culpability. The subjectivising of self-defence described below may be a far more useful development although its application to women in these situations has yet to be exploited. In its review of partial defences the Law Commission is set to consider whether self-defence with excessive force should be added. A report is expected by spring 2004 (*The Guardian*, 3 July 2003).

We have shown in this chapter how a seemingly straightforward concept such as violence is deceptively complex. Our conception of violence is a product of social and legal construction. Legal definitions do not capture neatly the areas over which the net of legal enforcement is cast. Social and cultural forces exercise at least as strong and pervasive an influence. Family violence is a good example of this thesis. The increased emphasis on corporate liability for conventional crime is a development highlighting the fluidity of legal constructions of crime which have been stressed throughout this book.

But it is not just the landscape over which criminal law ranges, not just the nature of the behaviour that might be regarded as included in criminal proscription, that is subject to shifts over time. This does change at a formal level of course, as we have seen in the abolition of offences of buggery, as well as at the constructed level, as changing attitudes both to domestic violence and road safety demonstrate. Social forces also affect 'internal' legal conceptions as well. We have seen clearly in the last two chapters how the tectonic plates of 'mens rea' are moving in different directions. The patterns of this movement are not uniform: it is not all in the direction of subjectivisation or individualisation. In relation to sexual offences, a clear line is being drawn between the ideals of subjective 'mens rea' and of acceptable behaviour and respect for others. At the same time, there has been a move towards individualising the partial defence of provocation and a willingness to develop other defences such as necessity and self-defence.

FURTHER READING

Alldridge, Peter (2000) *Relocating Criminal Law* (Ashgate).

Ashworth, Andrew and Mitchell, Barry (eds) (2000) *Rethinking English Homicide Law* (Oxford University Press).

Downs, Donald (1996) *More than Victims: Battered Women, The Syndrome Society, and the Law* (University of Chicago Press).

Dressler, Joshua (1988) 'Provocation: Partial Justification or Partial Excuse?' 51 MLR 467.

Gardner, John and Macklem, Timothy (2001) 'Compassion without Respect? Nine Fallacies in R v Smith' Crim LR 623.

Horder, Jeremy (1992) *Provocation and Responsibility* (Clarendon Press).

Lacey, Nicola (1993b) 'A Clear Concept of Intention: Elusive or Illusory?' 56 MLR 621.

Norrie, Alan (1999) 'After *Woollin*' Crim LR 532.

Peay, Jill (2002) 'Mentally Disordered Offenders' in Maguire et al (eds) *Oxford Handbook of Criminology* (Oxford University Press) 749.

Rogers, J (2001) 'Necessity, Private Defence and the Killing of Mary' Crim LR 515.

Schneider, E (2002) *Battered Women and Feminist Lawmaking* (Yale University Press).

Valier, Claire (2003) 'Minimum Terms of Imprisonment in Murder, Just Deserts and the Sentencing Guidelines' Crim LR 326.

Wasik, Martin (1982) 'Cumulative Provocation and Domestic Killing' Crim LR 29.

Wilczynski, A and Morris, A (1993) 'Parents who Kill their Children' Crim LR 31.

Bibliography

Abramson, Jeffrey (1994) *We the Jury: The Jury System and the Ideal of Democracy* (New York: Basic Books).

Adler, Zsuzsanna (1987) *Rape on Trial* (Routledge).

Akdenis Y, Taylor, N and Walker, C (2001) 'Regulation of Investigatory Powers Act 2000: Big Brother.co.uk: State Surveillance in the Age of Information and Rights' Crim LR 73.

Alexander, Priscilla (1997) 'Feminism, Sex Workers, and Human Rights' in J Nagle (ed) *Whores and Other Feminists* (Routledge).

Alldridge, Peter (1983) 'The Coherence of Defences' Crim LR 665.

— (1989) 'Duress, Duress of Circumstances and Necessity' 139 NLJ 911.

— (1997) 'The Sexual Offences (Conspiracy and Incitement) Act 1996' Crim LR 30.

— (2000) *Relocating Criminal Law* (Ashgate).

Alldridge, Peter and Belsey, Catherine (1989) 'Murder under Duress: Terrorism and the Criminal Law' 2 International Journal for the Semiotics of Law 223.

Allen, C K (1931) *Legal Duties and Other Essays in Jurisprudence* (Oxford University Press).

Allen, Hilary (1987) *Justice Unbalanced* (Open University Press).

— (1988) 'One Law for All Reasonable Persons?' 16 International Journal of Sociology and Law 419.

Andreano, R and Siegfried, J (eds) (1980) *The Economics of Crime* (Wiley).

Andrews, Lori B (1988) 'Surrogate Motherhood: The Challenge for Feminists' 16 Law, Medicine and Health Care 72.

Armstrong, G and Hobbs, D (1994) *Tackled from Behind* in R Giulianotti, N Bonney and M Hepworth (eds) *Football Violence and Social Identity*.

Ashworth, Andrew (1975) 'Self-Defence and the Right to Life' 34 CLJ 282.
— (1987a) 'Defining Offences Without Harm' in P Smith (ed) *Criminal Law: Essays in Honour of J C Smith* (Butterworths).
— (1987b) 'The "Public Interest" Element in Prosecutions' Crim LR 595.
— (1989) 'The Scope of Criminal Liability for Omissions' LQR 424.
— (1998) *The Criminal Process: An Evaluative Study* (Oxford University Press).
— (2000a) 'The Human Rights Act: A Non-Minimalist View' Crim LR 564.
— (2000b) *Sentencing and Criminal Justice* (3rd edn, Butterworths).
— (2001) 'Criminal Proceedings After the Human Rights Act The First Year' Crim LR 855.
— (2002) *Human Rights, Serious Crime and Criminal Procedure* (Sweet & Maxwell).
— (2003) *Principles of Criminal Law* (4th edn, Oxford University Press).
Ashworth, A and Blake, M (1996) 'The Presumption of Innocence in English Criminal Law' Crim LR 306.
Ashworth, A and Fionda, J (1994) 'The New Code for Crown Prosecutors: Prosecution: Accountability and the Public Interest' Crim LR 894.
Ashworth, A and Mitchell, B (2000) *Rethinking English Homicide Law* (Oxford University Press).
Atkins, Susan and Hoggett, Brenda (1984) *Women and the Law* (Blackwell Publishers).
Aubrey, C (1981) *Who's Watching You?: Britain's Security Services and the Official Secrets Act* (Penguin).
Auld Report (2001) *Review of the Criminal Courts in England and Wales* (Stationery Office).
Aust, R et al (2002) *Prevalence of drug use: key findings from the 2001/2002 British Crime Survey*, Home Office Findings 182 (Home Office).
Bailey, V and Blackburn, S (1979) 'The Punishment of Incest Act 1908: A Case Study in Law Creation' Crim LR 708.
Bailey, V and McCabe, S (1979) 'Reforming the Law of Incest' Crim LR 757.
Baldwin, J and McConville, M (1977) *Negotiated Justice* (Martin Robertson).
— (1979) *Jury Trials* (Clarendon Press).
Banton, M (1985) *Investigating Robbery* (Gower).
Barendt, Eric (1985) *Freedom of Speech* (Clarendon Press).
Barnard, Catherine and Hare, Ivan (1997) 'The Right to Protest and the Right to Export: Police Discretion and the Free Movement of Goods' 60 Mod LR 394.
Barrett, Michele and McIntosh, Mary (1982) *The Anti-Social Family* (Verso).
Barrington Moore Jr (1967) *Social Origins of Dictatorship and Democracy* (Penguin).

Bassen, Paul 'Present Stakes and Future Prospects: The Status of Early Abortion' 11 Philosophy and Public Affairs 315 (© 1982 by Princeton University Press).

Bayley, D and Shearing, Clifford (1996) 'The Future of Policing' 30 Law and Society Review 586.

Bean, Philip (1975) *The Social Control of Drugs* (Martin Robertson).

Beatson, Jack and Simester, Andrew (1999) 'Stealing One's Own Property' 115 Law Quarterly Review 115.

Beattie, J M (1986) *Crime and the Courts in England, 1660–1800* (Oxford University Press).

— (1987) 'Crime and the Courts in Surrey 1736–1753' in J S Cockburn (ed) *Crime and Society in England 1550–1800*.

Beck, Ulrich (1992) *Risk Society: Towards a New Modernity* (translated by Mark Ritter, Sage).

Becker, Howard (1963) *Outsiders* (New York: Free Press).

Becker, L (1977) *Property Rights* (Routledge).

Bedford, Sybille (1989) *The Best We Can Do* (Penguin).

Beier, A L (1985) *Masterless Men* (Methuen).

Bell, C and Fox, M (1996) 'Telling Stories of Women who Kill' Soc and Leg Studies 427.

Bellamy, J (1973) *Crime and Public Order in England in the Later Middle Ages* (Routledge).

Bennett, W L and Feldman, M S (1981) *Reconstructing Reality in the Courtroom* (Tavistock).

Bentham, J (1853) *Works IV* (ed Bowring).

Bentley, Lionel and Flynn, Leo (eds) (1996) *Law and the Senses* (Pluto Press).

Benyon, J (1987) 'Interpretations of Civil Disorder' in J Benyon and J Solomos (eds) *The Roots of Urban Unrest*.

Benyon, J and Solomos, J (eds) (1987) *The Roots of Urban Unrest* (Pergamon Press).

Bequai, A (1978a) *Computer Crime* (Lexington Books).

— (1978b) *White Collar Crime* (Lexington Books).

— (1979) *Organised Crime* (Lexington Books).

Bergman, David (1990) 'A Killing in the Boardroom' 140 NLJ 1496.

Bibbings, Lois and Alldridge, Peter (1993) 'Sexual Expression, Body Alteration and the Defence of Consent' 20 Journal of Law and Society 356.

Blackstone, William (1765) *Commentaries on the Laws of England* vol IV (Clarendon Press).

Blake, N (1985) 'Picketing, Justice and the Law' in B Fine and R Millar (eds) *Policing the Miners' Strike* (Lawrence & Wishart).

Bland, Lucy (1985a) 'Cleansing the Portals of Life' in Centre for Contemporary Cultural Studies (ed) *Crisis of Hegemony: Transformations in the British State, 1890–1920* (Hutchinson).

Bland, Lucy (1985b) 'In the Name of Protection: the Policing of Women in the First World War' in J Brophy and C Smart (eds) *Women in Law: Explorations in Law, Family and Sexuality*.

— (1985c) 'The Case of the Yorkshire Ripper: Mad, Bad, Beast or Male?' in P Scraton and P Gordon (eds) *Causes for Concern*.

Block, A (1980) *East Side, West Side* (University College Cardiff Press).

Block, B (2000) 'Taking Liberties' 164 Justice of the Peace 580–582.

Blom Cooper, L (1981) *Blasphemy: An Ancient Wrong or a Modern Right?* (Essex Hall Centre).

Bondeson, W et al (eds) (1983) *Abortion and the Status of the Fetus* (Reidel).

Bottomley, A K (1973) *Decisions in the Penal Process* (Martin Robertson).

Bottomley, A K and Pease, K (1986) *Crime and Punishment: Interpreting the Data* (Open University Press).

Bottoms, A E (1983) 'Some Neglected Features of Contemporary Penal Systems' in D Garland and P Young (eds) *The Power to Punish*.

Bowling, Ben and Foster, Janet (2002) 'Policing and Police' in Maguire et al (eds) *The Oxford Handbook of Criminology*, p 980.

Box, Steven (1983) *Power, Crime and Mystification* (Routledge Tavistock).

— (1987) *Recession, Crime and Punishment* (Macmillan).

Boyle, K, Hadden, T and Hillyard, P (1975) *Law and the State: the Case of Northern Ireland* (Martin Robertson).

— (1980) *Ten Years on in Northern Ireland* (Cobden Trust).

Braggins, J (1997) *Tackling Drugs Together: One Year On* (ISTD).

Braithwaite, John (1979) 'Transnational Corporations and Corruption: Towards some International Solutions' 7 International Journal of the Sociology of Law 125.

— (1989) *Crime, Shame and Reintegration* (Cambridge University Press).

— (2002) *Restorative Justice and Responsive Regulation* (New York: Oxford University Press).

Brantingham, P J and Kness, J M (1979) *Structure, Law & Power* (Sage).

Brazier, M (1998) *Surrogacy: Review for Health Ministers of Current Arrangements for Payments and Regulation*, Cm4068 (HMSO).

— (1999) 'Regulating the Reproduction Business?' Medical Law Review 166–193.

Brearley, N and King, M (1996) 'Policing Social Protest: Some Indicators of Change' in Critcher and Waddington, *Policing Public Order: Theoretical and Practical Issues*.

Breed, B (1979) *White Collar Bird* (John Clare).

Brewer, J and Styles, J (eds) (1980) *An Ungovernable People* (Hutchinson).

British Medical Association (1988) *Euthanasia* (Report of the Working Party to Review the British Medical Association's Guidance on Euthanasia).

Brod, Harry (1988) 'Pornography and the Alienation of Male Sexuality' 15 Social Theory and Practice 265.

Bronitt, Simon (1992) 'Rape and Lack of Consent' 16 Crim LJ 289.
— (1994) 'Spreading Disease and the Criminal Law' Crim LR 21.
— (1996) '"No Records No Time No Reason"; Protecting Rape Victims' Privacy and the Fair Trial' 8 Current Issues in Criminal Justice 131.
Bronitt, Simon and McSherry, Bernadette (2001) *Principles of Criminal Law* (Sydney: Law Book Company).
Brookman, F and Maguire, M (2003) *Reducing homicide: Summary of a review of the possibilities*, RDS Occasional Paper No 84 (Home Office).
Brophy, Julia and Smart, Carol (eds) (1985) *Women in Law: Explorations in Law, Family and Sexuality* (Routledge).
Brown, A (1994) 'Football Fans and Civil Liberties' Journal of Sport and Law 22.
Brown, Beverley (1998) *Legal Spectacles* (Athlone Press).
Brown, Beverley, Burman, Michele and Jamieson, Lynn (1993) *Sex Crimes on Trial* (Edinburgh University Press).
Brown, D and Ellis, T (1994) *Policing Low-level Disorder: Police Use of section 5 of the POA 1986*, Home Office Research Study 135 (Home Office).
Bucke, T and James, Z (1998) *Trespass and Protest*, Home Office Research Study 190 (Home Office).
Budd, T and Mattinson, J (2000) *The Extent and Nature of Stalking: Findings from the 1998 British Crime Survey*, Home Office Research Study 210 (Home Office).
Burney, Elizabeth (2002) 'Talking Tough, Acting Coy: What Happened to the Anti Social Behaviour Order?' 41 Howard Jnl 469.
Burney, Elizabeth and Rose, Gerry (2002) *Racist Offences– how is the law working?* Home Office Research Study 244 (Home Office).
Burr, A (1986) *Shooting Up* (Sydney: Hale and Ironmonger).
Burris, C A and Jaffe, P (1983) 'Wife Abuse as a Crime: the Impact of Police Laying Charges' 25 Canadian Journal of Criminology 30.
Burrows, J (1986) *Investigating Burglary: the Measurement of Police Performance*, Home Office Research Study 88 (Home Office).
Burton, M (2003) 'Criminalising Breaches of Civil Orders for Protection from Domestic Violence' Crim LR 301.
Butler Committee (1975) *Report of the Committee on Abnormal Offenders*, Cmnd 6254 (HMSO).
Butler, Judith (1997) *Excitable Speech* (Routledge).
Butler-Sloss, Lord Justice (1988) *Report of the Inquiry into Child Abuse in Cleveland 1987*, Cm 412 (HMSO).
Buxton, Richard (2000) 'The Human Rights Act and the Substantive Criminal Law' Crim LR 331.
Byrne P (ed) (1986) *Rights and Wrongs in Medicine* (Oxford University Press).
Cadoppi, Alberto (1993) 'Failure to Rescue and the Continental Criminal Law' in M Menlowe and A McCall Smith (eds) *The Duty to Rescue*.

Cain, Maureen (ed) (1990) *Growing Up Good* (Sage).

Cameron, Deborah and Frazer, Elizabeth (1988) *The Lust to Kill* (Blackwell Publishers).

Cameron, I (1984) 'Life in the Balance: The Case of Frank Marritt' in P Scraton and P Gordon (eds) *Causes for Concern*.

Campbell, A (1981) *Girl Delinquents* (Blackwell).

Campbell, Beatrix (1988) *Unofficial Secrets, Child Sexual Abuse: The Cleveland Case* (Virago).

— (1993) *Goliath: Britain's Dangerous Places* (Methuen).

Campbell, D and Connor, S (1986) *On the Record: Surveillance Computers and Privacy* (Michael Joseph).

Campbell, J (1995), 'Prediction of Homicide of and by Battered Women' in J C Campbell (ed) *Assessing Dangerousness: Violence by Sexual Offenders, Batterers and Child Abusers* (Sage).

Campbell, Robert and Collinson, Diane (1988) *Ending Lives* (Basil Blackwell).

Campbell, Siobhan (2002) *A Review of Anti-Social Behaviour Orders*, Home Office Research Study 236 (Home Office).

Campbell, Sue (1995) 'Gypsies: The Criminalisation of a Way of Life?' Crim LR 28.

Campbell, T, Ewing, K and Tomkins, A (2001) *Sceptical Essays on Human Rights* (Oxford University Press).

Card, R (1987) *Public Order: The New Law* (Butterworths).

Carlen, P (1976) *Magistrates' Justice* (Martin Robertson).

— (2002) *Women and Punishment: The Struggle for Justice* (Willan Publishing).

Carlen, P and Morgan, R (eds) (1999) *Crime Unlimited? Questions for the 21st Century* (Macmillian Press).

Carlen, P and Worrall, A (eds) (1987) *Gender, Crime and Justice* (Open University Press).

Carlen, P, Hicks, J, O'Dwyer, J, Christina, D and Tchaikovsky, C (1985) *Criminal Women* (Polity).

Carlen, Pat and Cook, Dee (eds) (1989) *Paying for Crime* (Open University Press).

Carlisle, Lord (1988) *The Parole System in England and Wales*, Report of the Review Committee, Cm 532 (HMSO).

Carson, W G (1970) 'White-collar Crime and the Enforcement of Factory Legislation' 10 Br J Crim 383.

— (1979) 'The Conventionalization of Early Factory Crime' 1 International Journal of the Sociology of Law 37.

— (1980) 'White-collar Crime and the Institutionalization of Ambiguity: the Case of the Early Factory Acts' in G Geis and E Stotland (eds) *White-Collar Crime*.

— (1982) *The Other Price of Britain's Oil* (Martin Robertson).

Carter, R and Hill, K (1979) *The Criminal's Image of the City* (Pergamon Press).

Cavadino, Michael and Dignan, James (2002) *The Penal System: An Introduction* (3rd edn, Sage).

Centre for Corporate Accountability (1999) 'The Health and Safety Executive', Memorandum to the House of Commons' Environment Sub Committee of the Select Committee on Environment, Transport and Regional Affairs HC 828.

Chadwick, Kathryn and Little, Catherine (1987) 'The Criminalization of Women' in P Scraton (ed) *Law, Order and the Authoritarian State.*

Chambers, G and Millar, A (1987) 'Proving Sexual Assault: Prosecuting the Offender or Persecuting the Victim?' in P Carlen and A Worrall (eds) *Gender, Crime and Justice.*

Chambliss, W J (1978) *On the Take: From Petty Crooks to Presidents* (Indiana University Press).

Chambliss, W and Seidman, R (1982) *Law, Order & Power* (2nd edn, Addison Wesley).

Chibnall, S (1977) *Law-and-Order News* (Tavistock).

Childs, M (1999) 'Medical manslaughter and corporate liability' 19 Legal Studies 316.

Childs, M and Ellison, L (eds) (2000) *Feminist Perspectives on Evidence* (Cavendish).

Christian, L (1985) 'Restriction without Conviction: The Role of the Courts in Legitimising Police Control in Nottinghamshire' in B Fine and R Millar (eds) *Policing the Miners' Strike.*

Christina, Diana and Carlen, Pat (1985) 'Christina: In Her Own Time' in P Carlen et al (eds) *Criminal Women.*

Clark, Alan (2002) *The Last Diaries* (Weidenfeld & Nicolson).

Clark, Anna (1987) *Women's Silence, Men's Violence: Sexual Assault in England 1770–1845* (Pandora).

Clark, Lorenne and Lewis, Debra (1977) *Rape, the Price of Coercive Sexuality* (Toronto Women's Press).

Clarke, R G V and Mayhew, P (1980) *Designing Out Crime*, Home Office Research Unit (Home Office).

Clarke, Ronald V (ed) (1997) *Situational Crime Prevention: successful case studies* (Harrow and Heston, Perpetuity Press).

Clarkson, C and Keating, H (1994) *Criminal Law: Text and Materials* (3rd edn, Sweet & Maxwell).

Clarkson, C, Cretney, A, Davis, G and Shephard, J (1994) 'Assaults, the Relationship between Seriousness, Criminalisation and Punishment' Crim LR 4.

Cleveland Inquiry: *see* Butler-Sloss (1988).

Closen, Michael L, Bobinski, Mary-Anne, Hermann, Donald H J, Hernandez, John F, Schultz, Gene P and Strader, J Kelly (1994) 'Discussion: Criminalization of an Epidemic: HIV-AIDS and Criminal Exposure Laws' 46 Arkansas LR 921.

Cobley, Cathy (1997) 'Keeping Track of Sex Offenders – Part I of the Sex Offenders Act (1997)' 60 Mod LR 690.

Cockburn, J S (1977) 'The Nature and Incidence of Crime in England 1559–1625: a Preliminary Survey' in Cockburn (ed) *Crime and Society in England 1550–1800*.

Cockburn, J S (ed) (1977) *Crime and Society in England 1550–1800* (Methuen & Co).

Cohen, Stanley (1972) *Folk Devils and Moral Panics* (St Martin's Press).

— (1985) *Visions of Social Control* (Polity).

Cohen, S and Scull, A (1983) *Social Control and the State* (Blackwell).

Cohen, S and Young, J (1973) *The Manufacture of News* (Constable).

Collier, Richard (1994) *Masculinity, Law and the Family* (Routledge).

— (1998) *Masculinities, Crime and Criminology* (London, Sage).

Collins, Hugh (1982) *Marxism and Law* (Clarendon Press).

Comer, M J (1985) *Corporate Fraud* (2nd edn, McGraw-Hill).

Cook, Dee (1989) *Rich Law, Poor Law: Different Responses to Tax and Supplementary Benefit Fraud* (Open University Press).

Cook, Dee and Hudson, Barbara (eds) (1993) *Racism and Criminology* (Sage).

Cook, Judith (1989) *An Accident Waiting to Happen* (Unwin).

Cooper, Jo (2003) 'Public Order Review' Legal Action, 18 Feb.

Corker, David (2002) 'Trying Fraud Cases without Juries' Crim LR 272.

Cornell, Drucilla (1995) *The Imaginary Domain: Abortion, Pornography and Sexual Harassment* (Routledge).

Cotta, Sergio (1985) *Why Violence?* (University of Florida Press).

Cowell, D, Jones, T and Young, J (1982) *Policing the Riots* (Junction Books).

Crawford, A, Jones, T and Woodhouse, T (1990) *The Second Islington Crime Survey* (Middlesex Polytechnic).

Crawford, A and Newburn, T (2002) 'Recent Developments in Restorative Justice for Young People in England and Wales' 42 British Journal of Criminology 476.

Cressey, D R (1973) *Other People's Money: A Study in the Social Psychology of Embezzlement* (Patterson Smith).

Cretney, A and Davis, G (1997) 'Prosecuting Domestic Assault: Victims Failing Courts, or Courts Failing Victims?' 36 Howard Journal of Criminal Justice 146.

Criminal Injuries Compensation Authority (2001) *Guide to the Criminal Injuries Compensation Scheme 2001* (CICA).

Criminal Law Revision Committee (1980) Fourteenth Report *Offences Against the Person*, Cmnd 7844 (HMSO).

— (1984a) Fifteenth Report *Sexual Offences*, Cmnd 9213 (HMSO).

— (1984b) Sixteenth Report *Prostitution in the Street*, Cmnd 9329 (HMSO).

— (1985) Seventeenth Report *Prostitution: Off-Street Activities*, Cmnd 9688 (HMSO).

— (1986) Eighteenth Report *Conspiracy to Defraud*, Cmnd 9873 (HMSO).

Critcher, C (1996) 'On the Waterfront: Applying the Flashpoints Model to Protests against Live Animal Exports' in Critcher and Waddington (eds) *Policing Public Order: Theoretical and Practical Issues*.

Critcher, C and Waddington, D (eds) (1996) *Policing Public Order: Theoretical and Practical Issues* (Ashgate).

Croall, Hazel (1988) 'Mistakes, Accidents and Someone Else's Fault: The Trading Offender in Court' 15 Journal of Law and Society 293.

Cullen, F et al (1984) 'The Ford Pinto Case and Beyond: Corporate Crime, Moral Boundaries and the Criminal Sanction' in E Hochstedler (ed) *Corporations as Criminals*.

Cunningham, S (2001) 'The Reality of Vehicular Homicides: Convictions for Murder, Manslaughter and Causing Death by Dangerous Driving' Crim LR 679.

Cusine, Douglas (1988) *New Reproductive Techniques: A Legal Perspective* (Gower).

Dahrendorf, R (1985) *Law and Order* (Stevens).

Dallon, K (1980) 'Cyclic Criminal Acts in Pre-Menstrual Syndrome' The Lancet 1970.

Daly, Kathleen (2002) 'Restorative Justice: The Real Story' 4 Punishment and Society 55–79.

Darbyshire, P (1991) 'The Lamp that Shows that Freedom Lives – Is it Worth the Candle' Crim LR 740.

— (1997) 'An Essay on the Importance and the Neglect of the Magistracy' Crim LR 627.

Darbyshire, Penny, Maughan, Andy and Stewart, Angus (2001) 'What Can We Learn from Jury Research?' Crim LR 970.

Davies, Margaret and Naffine, Ngaire (2001) *Are Persons Property? Legal Debates about Property and Personality* (Ashgate).

Davies, M and Tyrer, J (2003) 'Filling the Gaps: A Study of Judicial Culture' Crim LR 243–265.

Davis, Nancy (1984) 'Abortion and Self-Defence' 13 Philosophy and Public Affairs 175.

Davis, Nanette J (1988) 'Battered Women: Implications for Social Control' Contemporary Crises 345.

De Gama, Katherine (1993) 'A Brave New World? Rights Discourse and the Politics of Reproductive Autonomy' 20 Journal of Law and Society 114.

Deards, E (2002) 'Human Rights for Football Hooligans' 27 ELR 206.

Dell, Susanne (1982) 'Diminished Responsibility Reconsidered' Crim LR 809.
— (1984) *Murder into Manslaughter* (Oxford University Press).
Dennis, Ian (ed) (1987) *Criminal Law and Justice* (Sweet & Maxwell).
— (1997) 'The Critical Condition of Criminal Law' Current Legal Problems 213.
— (1999) *The Law of Evidence* (London, Sweet & Maxwell).
Devlin, Patrick (1965) *The Enforcement of Morals* (Oxford University Press).
— (1985) *Easing the Passing* (Bodley Head).
Diamantides, Marinos (1995) 'Ethics in Law: Death Marks on a "Still Life"' VI Law and Critique 209.
Dickinson, D T (1968) 'Bureaucracy and Morality: An Organisational Perspective on a Moral Crusade' 16 Social Problems 143–156.
Dingwall, R and Eekelaar, J (1988) 'Families and the State: An Historical Perspective on the Public Regulation of Private Conduct' 10 Law and Policy 341.
Ditton, J (1977) *Part Time Crime: An Ethnology of Fiddling and Pilfering* (Macmillan).
Dobash, R E and Dobash, R P (1979) *Violence against Wives* (Free Press, New York).
— (1992) *Women, Violence and Social Change* (Routledge).
— (eds) (1998) *Rethinking Violence Against Women* (Sage).
— (1998) 'Violent Men and Violent Contexts' in Dobash and Dobash (eds) *Rethinking Violence Against Women*.
Dobash, R E, Dobash, R P and Gutteridge, S (1986) *The Imprisonment of Women* (Blackwell).
Dobash, R E, Dobash, R P and Noaks, L (eds) (1995) *Gender and Crime* (University of Wales Press).
Donson, F (2000) *Legal Intimidation* (Free Association Books).
Donzelot, Jacques (1980) *The Policing of Families* (Hutchinson).
Downes, D (1983) *Law and Order: Theft of an Issue* (Fabian Society).
Downs, Donald (1996) *More than Victims: Battered Women, The Syndrome Society, and the Law* (University of Chicago Press).
Drakeford, Mark and Butler, Ian (1998) 'Curfews for Children: Testing a Policy Proposal in Practice' 62 Youth and Policy 1–14.
Drakeford, M and Vanstone, M (2000) *Social Exclusion and the Politics of Criminal Justice: A Tale of Two Administrations* 39 Howard Journal 369–381.
Dressler, Joshua (1984) 'New Thoughts about the Concept of Justification: A Critique of Fletcher's Thinking and Rethinking' 32 University of California LR 61.
— (1987) *Understanding Criminal Law* (New York: Bender).
— (1988) 'Provocation: Partial Justification or Partial Excuse?' 51 Mod LR 467.

Dripps, Donald A (1992) 'Beyond Rape: An Essay on the Difference Between the Presence of Force and the Absence of Consent' 92 Columbia LR 1780.

Duff, Peter (1987) 'Criminal Injuries Compensation and "Violent" Crime' Crim LR 219.

Duff, R A (1980) 'Recklessness' Crim LR 282.

— (1983) 'Caldwell and Lawrence: the Retreat from Subjectivism', 3 OJLS 77.

— (1987) 'Codifying Criminal Fault' in I Dennis (ed) *Criminal Law and Justice*.

— (1990) *Intention, Agency and Criminal Liability: Philosophy of Action and the Criminal Law* (Blackwell).

— (1996) *Criminal Attempts* (Clarendon Press).

— (1998) *Philosophy and the Criminal Law: Principle and Critique* (Cambridge University Press).

— (2001) *Punishment, Communication and Community* (Oxford University Press).

Duff, Raymond and Campbell, A G M (1973) 'Moral and Ethical Dilemmas in the Special Care Nursery' 289 New England Journal of Medicine 890.

Duncan, Sheila (1995) 'Law's Sexual Discipline: Visibility, Violence and Consent' 22 Journal of Law and Society 326.

Dunning, E, Murphy, P and Williams, J (1984) *Hooligans Abroad* (Routledge).

— (1988) *The Roots of Football Hooliganism* (Routledge).

Dupont, I R, Goldstein, A and O'Donnell, J (eds) (1979) *A Handbook on Drug Abuse* (National Institute on Drug Abuse).

Duster, Troy (1970) *The Legislation of Morality* (Free Press).

Dworkin, Andrea (1981) *Pornography: Men Possessing Women* (Women's Press).

— (1983) *Right Wing Women* (Women's Press).

Dworkin, Gerald (1972) 'Paternalism' The Monist 56.

Dworkin, R M (1981a) 'Is there a Right to Pornography?' 1 OJLS 177.

— (1981b) 'What is Equality?' 10 Philosophy and Public Affairs 185.

— (1993) *Life's Dominion: An Argument about Abortion and Euthanasia* (HarperCollins).

Easton, Susan (1994) *The Problem of Pornography* (Routledge).

Eaton, Mary (1986) *Justice For Women?* (Open University Press).

Eckersley, Robyn (1987) 'Whither the Feminist Campaign? An Evaluation of Feminist Critiques of Pornography' 15 International Journal of the Sociology of Law 149.

Edelhertz, H and Rogovin, C (1980) *A National Strategy for Containing White Collar Crime* (Lexington Books).

Editorial (1994) 'Charging Standards: Offences against the Person' Crim LR 777.

Edwards, Anne (1987) 'Male Violence in Feminist Theory: An Analysis of the Changing Conceptions of Sex/Gender Violence and Male Dominance' in J Hanmer and M Maynard (eds) *Women, Violence and Social Control*.

Edwards, Ian (2002) 'The Place of Victims' Preferences in the Sentencing of "Their" Offender' Crim LR 689.

Edwards, Susan (1984) *Women on Trial* (Manchester University Press).

— (1986) 'Police Attitudes and Dispositions in Domestic Disputes: the London Study' Police Journal 230–241.

— (1986) 'The Police Response to Domestic Violence in London' Central London Polytechnic.

— (1987) 'Prostitutes: Victims of Law, Social Policy and Organised Crime' in P Carlen and A Worrall (eds) *Gender, Crime and Justice*.

— (1989) *Policing 'Domestic' Violence* (Sage).

Ellickson, Robert C (1991) *Order Without Law: How Neighbours Settle Disputes* (Harvard University Press).

Elliott, I D L (1986) 'Heroin in Australia: The Costs and Consequences of Prohibition' 16 Journal of Drug Issues 131.

Emsley, Clive (1996) *Crime and Society in England 1750–1900* (2nd edn, Longman, New York).

— (2002) 'The History of Crime and Crime Control Institutions' in Maguire et al (eds) *The Oxford Handbook of Criminology*.

Ennew, Judith (1986) *The Sexual Exploitation of Children* (Polity).

Ericson, Richard and Haggerty, K (1997) *Policing the Risk Society* (Oxford University Press).

Ericson, R V, Baranek, P M and Chan, J B L (1987) *Visualising Deviance* (Open University Press).

Estrich, Susan (1987) *Real Rape* (Harvard University Press).

European Commission (1996) *Euthanasia and Assisted Suicide in the Netherlands and in Europe*, Directorate-General XII, Luxembourg, OOPEC.

Everywoman (1988) *Pornography and Sexual Violence Evidence of the Links* (Everywoman).

Ewing, J (1990) 'Psychological Self-defence: A Proposed Justification for Battered Women' 14 Law and Behaviour 579.

Farmer, Lindsay (1996) 'The Obsession with Definition: The Nature of Crime and Critical Legal Theory' 5 Social and Legal Studies 57.

— (1997) *Criminal Law, Tradition and Legal Order: Crime and the Genius of Scots Law* (Cambridge University Press).

Feeley, Malcom (1979) *The Process is the Punishment* (Russell Sage Foundation).

Feeley, Malcom and Simon, Jonathan (1994) 'Actuarial Justice: The Emerging New Criminal Law' in D Nelken (ed) *The Futures of Criminology*.

Fegan, Eileen V (1996) 'Father's Foetuses and Abortion Decision-making: The Reproduction of Maternal Ideology in Canadian Judicial Discourse' 5 Social and Legal Studies 75.

Feinberg, Joel (1970) *Doing and Deserving* (Princeton University Press).

— (1979) 'Pornography and the Criminal Law' 40 U Pitt LR 567.

— (1980) 'Abortion' in T Regan et al (eds) *Matters off Life and Death: New Introductory Essays in Moral Philosophy*.

— (1983) 'The Models of Responsibility' 2 Law and Philosophy 371.

— (1984–88) *The Moral Limits of Criminal Law: Harm to Others; Offense to Others; Harm to Self; Harmless Wrongdoing* (Oxford University Press Inc).

Feldman, David (1988) 'Binding-over Powers: The Royal Prerogative and Public Order' CLJ 101.

— (2002) *Civil Liberties and Human Rights in England and Wales* (Oxford University Press).

Fennell, Phil (1991) 'Diversion of Mentally Disordered Offenders from Custody' Crim LR 333.

Fennell Report (1988) *Investigation into the King's Cross Underground Fire*, Cm 499 (HMSO).

Fenwick, H and Phillipson, G (2000) 'Public Protest, the Human Rights Act and Judicial Responses to Political Expression' Public Law 627.

Fenwick, Helen (1997) 'Procedural "Rights" of Victims of Crime: Public or Private Ordering of the Criminal Justice Process' 60 Mod LR 317.

Ferrajoli, L and Zolo, D (1985) 'Marxism and the Criminal Question' 4 Law and Philosophy 71.

Field, S and Southgate, P (1982a) *Public Disorder*, Home Office Research Study 72 (Home Office).

Field, Stewart and Roberts, Pauline (2002) 'Racism and Police Investigations' 22 Legal Studies 493.

Field, Stewart and Thomas, Phil (eds) (1994) *Justice and Efficiency* (Journal of Law and Society).

Finch, Emily (2002a) 'Stalking the perfect Stalking Law: An Evaluation of the Efficacy of the Protection from Harassment Act 1997' Crim LR 703.

— (2002b) *Stalking: A violent Crime or a Crime of Violence?* 41 Howard Journal 422.

Findlay, Mark and Hogg, Russell (eds) (1988) *Understanding Crime and Criminal Justice* (Sydney: Law Book Co).

Fine, B and Millar, R (eds) (1985) *Policing the Miners' Strike* (Lawrence & Wishart).

Fine, Bob (ed) (1979) *Capitalism and the Rule of Law* (Hutchinson).

Fionda, J (1995) *Public Prosecutors and Discretion* (Clarendon Press).

— (1999) 'New Labour, Old Hat: Youth Justice and the Crime and Disorder Act 1998' Crim LR 36.

Firth, Alison (1995) 'The Criminalisation of Offences against Intellectual Property' in Loveland (ed) *Frontiers of Criminality*.

Fishwick, Elaine (1968) 'Sexual Assault and Criminal Justice: A Comparative Perspective on Legislation, Policing and Research' in M Findlay and R Hogg (eds) *Understanding Crime and Criminal Justice*.

Fisse, Brent and Braithwaite, John (1983) *The Impact of Publicity on Corporate Offenders* (State University of New York Press).

— (1988a) 'Accountability and the Control of Corporate Crime: Making the Buck Stop' in M Findlay and R Hogg (eds) *Understanding Crime and Criminal Justice*.

— (1988b) 'The Allocation of Responsibility for Corporate Crime; Individualism, Collectivism and Accountability' 11 Sydney LR 468.

Fitzgerald, M (1999) *Searches in London under section 1 of the Police and Criminal Evidence Act* (Metropolitan Police).

Fitzgerald, M and Hale, C (1996) *Ethnic Minorities: Victimisation and Racial Harassment*, Home Office Research Study 154 (Home Office).

Fitzgerald, P J (1962) *Criminal Law and Punishment* (Clarendon Press).

Fitzpatrick, Peter (1987) 'Racism and the Innocence of Law' 14 Journal of Law and Society 119.

Fletcher, G (1978) *Rethinking Criminal Law* (Little, Brown).

Foucault, M (1976) *The History of Sexuality: An Introduction* (Peregrine translation).

— (1977) *Discipline and Punish* (Penguin, translation A Sheridan).

— (1988) 'The Dangerous Individual' in L Kritzman (ed) *Michel Foucault*.

Frank, R T (1931) 'The Hormonal Causes of Pre-Menstrual Tension' 26 Archives of Neurological Psychiatry 1053.

Freeman, M D A (1989) 'Is Surrogacy Exploitative?' in S McLean (ed) *Legal Issues in Human Reproduction*.

— (2002) 'Denying Death its Dominion: Thoughts on the Dianne Pretty Case' 10 Med LR 245.

Friedland, M L (ed) (1990) *Securing Compliance: Seven Case Studies* (University of Toronto Press).

Frigon, Sylvie (1995) 'A Genealogy of Women's Madness' in Dobash, Dobash and Noaks (eds) *Gender and Crime*.

Frohock, Fred (1986) *Special Care: Medical Decisions at the Beginning of Life* (University of Chicago Press).

Galligan, D (1981) 'Guidelines and Just Deserts' Crim LR 297.

Gardiner, S (2000) 'Keeping Football Hooliganism in Check', 4 July, Solicitors Journal 1655–1656.

Gardner, John (1998) 'The Gist of Excuses' 1 Buffalo Criminal Law Review 575.

Gardner, John and Jung, Heike (1991) 'Making Sense of Mens Rea: Antony Duff's Account' 11 OJLS 559.

Gardner, John and Macklem, Tim (2001) 'Compassion without Respect? Nine Fallacies in R v Smith' Crim LR 623.

Gardner, S (1991) 'Reckless and Inconsiderate Rape' Crim LR 172.

— (1994) 'The Importance of Majewski' 14 OJLS 279.

Garland, David (1985) *Punishment and Welfare* (Gower).

— (1990) *Punishment and Modern Society* (Oxford University Press).

— (2001) *The Culture of Control* (Oxford University Press).

Garland, D and Young, P (eds) (1983) *The Power to Punish* (Heinemann).

Garry, Ann (1983) 'Abortion: Models of Responsibility' 2 Law and Philosophy 371.

Garton, Stephen (1988) 'The State, Labour Markets and Incarceration: A Critique' in M Findlay and R Hogg (eds) *Understanding Crime and Criminal Justice*.

Gatrell, V A C (1994) *The Hanging Tree: Execution and the English People 1770–1868* (Oxford University Press).

Gatrell, V A C, Lenman, B and Parker, G (1980) *Crime and The Law, The Social History of Crime in Western Europe since 1500* (Europa Publications).

Geary, R (1985) *Policing Industrial Disputes: 1893 to 1985* (Cambridge University Press).

Geis, G (1972) *Not the Law's Business* (National Institute of Mental Health, Washington).

Geis, G and Meier, R F (1977) *White-Collar Crime* (Free Press).

Geis, G and Stotland, E (eds) (1980) *White-Collar Crime* (Sage).

Gelsthorpe, Lorraine (2002) 'Feminism and Criminology', in Maguire et al (eds) *The Oxford Handbook of Criminology*.

Genders, Elaine (1999) 'Reform of the Offences against the Person Act: Lessons from the Law in Action' Crim LR 689.

Gibson, E and Klein, S (1969) *Murder 1957–68* (HMSO).

Giddens, A (1990) *The Consequences of Modernity* (Polity Press).

— (1991) *Modernity and Self-Identity* (Polity Press).

Gifford, Lord (1986) *The Broadwater Farm Inquiry* (Kavia Press).

Giles, Marianne (1992) 'Judicial Law-Making in the Criminal Courts: the Case of Marital Rape' Crim LR 407.

Gilling, Daniel (1997) *Crime Prevention: Theory, Policy and Politics* (University College London Press).

Giulianotti, M, Bonney, R and Hepworth, M (eds) (1994) *Football Violence and Social Identity* (Routledge).

Glasgow Media Group (1976) *Bad News* (Routledge).

— (1985) *War and Peace News* (Open University Press).

Glazebrook, P (ed) (1978) *Reshaping the Criminal Law* (Stevens).

Glendon, Mary Ann (1987) *Abortion and Divorce in Western Law* (Harvard University Press).

Glover, Jonathan (1977) *Causing Death and Saving Lives* (Penguin).

Gobert, J (1989) 'The Peremptory Challenge: An Obituary' Crim LR 528.
— (1994a) 'Corporate Criminality: Four Models of Fault' 14 Legal Studies 393.
— (1994b) 'New Crimes for the Times' Crim LR 722.
Gobert, J and Punch M (2003) *Rethinking Corporate Crime* (Butterworths).
Goff, Lord (1988) 'The Mental Element in Murder' 104 LQR 30.
Goode, Erich and Nachman, Ben-Yahuda (1994) *Moral Panics* (Blackwell).
Goode, M (1995) 'Stalking: A Crime of the Nineties?' Crim LJ 21.
Gordon, P (1987) 'Community Policing: Towards the Local Police State?' in Scraton (ed) *Law, Order and the Authoritarian State*.
Gostin, Larry (ed) (1988) *Civil Liberties in Conflict* (Routledge).
Grace, S (1995) *Policing Domestic Violence in the 1990s*, Home Office Research Study 139 (Home Office).
— (1996) *Obscenity: an International Comparison of Laws and Controls Relating to Obscene Material*, Home Office Research Study 157 (Home Office).
Gray, J (2003) 'Is complete abolition of the death penalty on the legal horizon?' 153 NLJ 620.
Graycar, Regina (ed) (1990) *Dissenting Opinions* (Sydney: Allen & Unwin).
Green, T A (1985) *Verdict According to Conscience* (University of Chicago Press).
Greenberg, David F (1988) *The Construction of Homosexuality* (University of Chicago Press).
Greenfield, S and Osborn, G (1995) 'Criminalising Football Supporters: Tickets, Touts and the CJPOA 1994' Journal of Sport & Law 36.
— (1996) 'After the Act: The (Re)construction and Regulation of Football Fandom' Journal of Civil Liberties 7.
— (2000) 'The Football (Offences and Disorder) Act 1999: Amending s 3 of the Football Offences Act 1991' Journal of Civil Liberties 55.
Grieve, M (1997) 'Stacking the Odds against the Defence' 29 April, The Lawyer 16.
Griew, Edward (1995) *The Theft Acts* (7th edn, Sweet & Maxwell).
Griffith, J (1985) *The Politics of the Judiciary* (3rd edn, Fontana).
Gross, H (1979) *A Theory of Criminal Justice* (Oxford University Press).
Grubb, A (1991) 'The New Law of Abortion: Clarification or Ambiguity?' Crim LR 659.
— (2002) 'Commentary' 10 Med LR 100.
Gunningham, Neil (1974) *Pollution, Social Interest and the Law* (Martin Robertson).
— (1987) 'Negotiated Non-Compliance: A Case Study of Regulatory Failure' 9 Law and Policy 69.
Gunningham, Neil and Johnstone, Richard (1999) *Regulating Workplace Safety: Systems and Sanctions* (Oxford University Press).
Gurr, T (1976) *Rogues, Rebels and Reformers* (Sage).

Gusfield, J (1968) 'Moral Passage: The Symbolic Process in Designations of Deviance' 15 Social Problems 175.

Hair, P E H (1971) 'Deaths from Violence in Britain: A Tentative Secular Survey' 25 Population Studies 5.

Hall, J (1952) *Theft, Law and Society* (2nd edn, Bobbs-Merrill).

— (1982) *Law, Social Science and Criminal Theory* (Rothman, Colorado).

Hall, S (1980) *Drifting into a Law and Order Society* (Cobden Trust).

Hall, S, Critcher, C, Jefferson, T, Clarke, J and Roberts, B (1978) *Policing the Crisis: Mugging, the State, and Law and Order* (Macmillan Press Ltd).

Halpin, Andrew (1996) 'The Test for Dishonesty' Crim LR 286.

Hanmer, J and Maynard, M (eds) (1987) *Women, Violence and Social Control* (Macmillan).

Harding, C and Koffman, L (1987) *Sentencing and the Penal System* (Sweet & Maxwell).

Harris, J and Grace, S (1999) *A Question of Evidence? Investigating and Prosecuting Rape in the 1990s*, Home Office Research Study 196 (Home Office).

Harris, John (1980) *Violence and Responsibility* (Routledge).

Hart, H L A (1961) *The Concept of Law* (Oxford University Press).

— (1963) *Law, Liberty and Morality* (Oxford University Press).

— (1968) *Punishment and Responsibility* (Oxford University Press).

Hart, H L A and Honoré, A M (1985) *Causation in the Law* (2nd edn, Oxford University Press).

Haste, Cate (1992) *Rules of Desire: Sex in Britain, World War I to the Present* (Pimlico).

Hawkins, Keith (1983) *Environment and Enforcement* (Clarendon Press).

— (2002) *Law as Last Resort: Prosecution Decision-Making in a Regulatory Agency* (Oxford University Press).

Hay, D (1975) 'Property, Authority and the Criminal Law' in D Hay, P Linebaugh, E P Thompson and C Winslow (eds) *Albion's Fatal Tree*.

Hay, D, Linebaugh, P, Thompson, E P and Winslow, C (eds) (1975) *Albion's Fatal Tree* (Penguin).

Hazell, R (1974) *Conspiracy and Civil Liberties* (National Council for Civil Liberties, Cobden Trust).

Heal, K and Laycock, G (1986a) *Situational Crime Prevention*, Home Office Research & Planning Unit (Home Office).

Health and Safety Executive (1988) *Deadly Maintenance* (HMSO).

— (2003) *Health and Safety Offences and Penalties 2001/2002* (HMSO).

Heidensohn, Frances (1985) *Women and Crime* (Macmillan).

— (2002) 'Gender and Crime' in Maguire et al (eds) *The Oxford Handbook of Criminology*.

Heilbron Report (1976) *Report of the Advisory Group on the Law of Rape*, Cmnd 6352 (HMSO).

Henham, Ralph (1994) 'Attorney-Generals' References and Sentencing Policy' Crim LR 499.

Henry, S (1978) *The Hidden Economy* (Martin Robertson).

— (1983) *Private Justice* (Routledge).

Hillyard, Paddy (1987) 'The Normalisation of Special Powers' in Scraton (ed) *Law, Order and the Authoritarian State*.

— (1993) *Suspect Community: People's Experiences of the Prevention of Terrorism Acts in Britain* (Pluto Press).

Hillyard, Paddy and Gordon, D (1999) 'Arresting Statistics: The Drift to Informal Justice in England and Wales' 26 Journal of Law and Society 502.

Hillyard, Paddy, Gordon, Dave and Pantazis, Chris (forthcoming, January 2004) *An Atlas of Crime and Justice* (Willan Publishing).

HM Crown Prosecution Service Inspectorate (2002) *A Report on the Joint Investigation and Prosecution of Cases Involving Allegations of Rape* (HMSO).

HM Inspectorate of Constabulary (1999) *Keeping the Peace: Policing Disorder* (HMSO).

Hochstedler, E (ed) (1984) *Corporations as Criminals* (Sage).

Hodge, J (1993) 'Alcohol and Violence' in P Taylor (ed) *Violence in Society*.

Hodgson, D (1984) *Profits of Crime and Their Recovery* (Heinemann).

Hogarth, J (1971) *Sentencing as a Human Process* (University of Toronto Press).

Home Affairs Committee (1981) Third Report, *Vagrancy Offences* (HMSO).

Home Office (1983) *Review of the Operation of the Prevention of Terrorism (Temporary Provisions) Act 1976*, Cmnd 8803 (HMSO).

— (1988) *Practical Ways to Crack Crime* (Home Office).

— (1990) Circular No 66/90, *Provision for Mentally Disordered Offenders* (Home Office).

— (1995) *Tackling Drugs Together: A Strategy for England 1995–8* (Home Office).

— (1996) *Criminal Statistics for England and Wales 1995*, Cm 3421 (Stationery Office).

— (2000a) *The Prison Population in 2000: a statistical review*, Home Office Findings 154 (Home Office).

— (2000b) *Statistics on Race and the Criminal Justice System* (Home Office).

— (2000c) *Statistics on Women and the Criminal Justice System* (Home Office).

— (2000d) *Setting the Boundaries: Reforming the Law on Sex Offences* (Home Office).

— (2000e) *Reforming the Law of Involuntary Manslaughter: The Government's Proposals* (Home Office).

— (2000f) *Consultation Paper on the Regulation of R18 Videos* (Home Office).

— (2001a) *Recorded Crime in England and Wales*, Statistical Bulletin 12/01(Home Office).

— (2001b) *Criminal Statistics England and Wales 2000*, Cm 5312 (HMSO).

— (2001c) *Criminal Justice: The Way Ahead*, Cm 5074 (HMSO).

— (2002a) *Protecting the Public: Strengthening Protection against Sex Offenders and Reforming the Law on Sexual Offences*, Cm 5668 (HMSO).

— (2002b) *Justice for All*, Cm 5563 (HMSO).

— (2002c) *Arrests for Notifiable Offences and the Operation of Certain Police Powers under PACE*, Statistical Bulletin 12/02 (Home Office).

— (2002d) *Projections of Long Term Trends in the Prison Population*, Statistical Bulletin 14/02 (Home Office).

— (2002e) *Statistics on Women and the Criminal Justice System 2002* (Home Office).

— (2002f) *Statistics on Race and the Criminal Justice System* (Home Office).

— (2002g) *Crime in England and Wales 2001–2*, 7/02 (Home Office).

— (2002h) *Statistics on Football-Related Arrests and Banning Orders, Season 2001–2* (previously published by NCIS) (Home Office).

— (2002i) *Action Plan to Implement the Recommendations of the HMCPSI/HMIC Joint Investigation into the Investigation and Prosecution of Cases Involving Allegations of Rape* (Home Office).

— (2002j) *Criminal Statistics England and Wales 2001*, Cm 5696 (HMSO).

— (2002k) *Bail Conditions Circular 61/2002* (Home Office).

— (2003a) *Prison Statistics 2001*, Cm 5743 (HMSO).

— (2003b)*Tackling alcohol related crime, disorder and nuisance*, reference: 041/2003 (Home Office).

— (2003c) *Bind-Overs – A Power for the 21st Century*, Consultation Document (Home Office).

— (2003d) *Respect and Responsibility – Taking a Stand against Anti Social Behaviour*, Cm 5778 (HMSO).

— (2003e) *Offences Relating to Motor Vehicles*, Supplementary Tables (Home Office).

— (2003f) *Crime in England and Wales 2001/2*, Supplementary Volume (Home Office).

— (2003g) *Safety and Justice: The Government's Proposals on Domestic Violence* (Home Office).

Hood, R (1992) *Race and Sentencing* (Clarendon Press).

— (2002) *The Death Penalty – A Worldwide Perspective* (Clarendon Press).

Hopkins, J (ed) (1984) *Perspectives on Rape and Sexual Assault* (Harper & Row).

Horder, Jeremy (1987) 'The Problem of Provocative Children' Crim LR 655.

— (1989) 'Sex, Violence and Sentencing in Domestic Provocation Cases' Crim LR 546.

— (1992) *Provocation and Responsibility* (Clarendon Press).

— (1994) 'Rethinking Non-Fatal Offences against the Person' 14 OxJLS 335.

— (1995) 'A Critique of the Correspondence Principle in Criminal Law' Crim LR 759.

— (1997) 'Two Histories and Four Hidden Principles of Mens Rea' 113 LQR 95.

— (1998) 'Reconsidering Psychic Assault' Crim LR 392.

— (2001) 'How Culpability Can and Cannot Be Denied in Under-Age Sex Crimes' Crim LR 15.

— (2002) 'Strict Liability, Statutory Construction and the Spirit of Liberty' 118 LQR 458.

Horder, Jeremy and Mitchell, Barry (1999) 'On the Correspondence Principle' Crim LR 894.

Hough, J M and Mayhew, P (1983) *The British Crime Survey*, Home Office Research Study 76 (Home Office).

Hough, Michael (1995) *Anxiety about Crime: Findings from the 1994 British Crime Survey*, Home Office Research Study 147 (Home Office).

House of Commons (1974–5) *Select Committee on Violence in Marriage*, HC 248.

House of Lords (1989) *Report of the Select Committee on Murder and Life Imprisonment*, HL Paper 78 (HMSO).

— (1993–4) *Report of the Select Committee on Medical Ethics*, HL Paper 21I.

Hoyle, Carolyn (1998) *Negotiating Domestic Violence: Police, Criminal Justice, and Victims* (Clarendon).

Hoyle, C and Sanders, A (2000) 'Police response to Domestic Violence: From Victim Choice to Victim Empowerment' BJ Crim 40.

Hunt, A (1999) *Governing Morals* (Cambridge University Press).

Hunter, C and Nixon, J (2001) 'Taking the Blame and Losing the Home: Women and Anti-Social Behaviour' 23 JSWFL 395.

Hunter, Rosemary (1996) 'Gender in Evidence: Masculine Norms vs Feminist Reforms' 19 Harv Women's LJ 127.

Husak, Douglas (2002) *Legalize This! The Case for Decriminalizing Drugs* (Verso).

Huxtable, R (2001) 'Logical Separation? Conjoined Twins, Slippery Slopes and Resource Allocation' 23 Journal of Social Welfare and Family Law 459.

Idriss, M M (2002) 'Religion and the Anti-Terrorism, Crime and Security Act 2001' Crim LR 890.

Ignatieff, M (1989) *A Just Measure of Pain* (Penguin).

Inciardi, J A and Chambers, C D (eds) (1974) *Drugs and the Criminal Justice System* (Sage).

Institute of Race Relations (1979) *Police Against Black People*.

Irwin, S and Glasson, J (1997) 'Declaration of Life and Death – Part 2' 147 NLJ 1432.

Itzin, Catherine (ed) (1992) *Pornography: Women, Violence and Civil Liberties* (Oxford University Press).

Ivison, D, Patton, P and Sanders, W (2001) *Political Theory and the Rights of Indigenous Peoples* (Cambridge University Press).

Jackson, Emily (1997) 'Fractured Values: Law, Ideology and the Family' in A Sarat and S Silbey (eds) *Studies in Law, Politics and Society* (vol 17).

Jackson, John (2002) 'Modes of Trial' Crim LR 249.

Jackson, John and Doran, Sean (1997) 'Judge and Jury: Towards a New Division of Labour in Criminal Trials' 60 Mod LR 759.

Jaffe, H H (1979) 'The Swinging Pendulum: The Treatment of Drug Users in America' in Dupont et al (eds) *A Handbook on Drug Abuse*.

Johnston, Les (1992) *The Rebirth of Private Policing* (Routledge).

Johnstone, Gerry (2002), *Restorative Justice: Ideas, Values, Debates* (Willan Publishing).

Jones, Helen and Sagar, Tracey (2001) 'Crime and Disorder Act 1998: Prostitution and the Anti-Social Behaviour Order' Crim LR 873.

Jones, J, MacLean, B and Young, J (1986) *The Islington Crime Survey: Crimes, Victimisation and Policing in Inner-City London* (Gower).

Jones, K (1982) *Law and Economy: The Legal Regulation of Corporate Capital* (Academic Press).

Jones, K B (1987) 'On Authority: Or Why Women Are Not Entitled to Speak' in J R Pennock and J M Chapman (eds) *Authority Revisited*.

Jones, S and Levi, M (1987) 'Law and Order and the Causes of Crime: Some Police and Public Perspectives' 26 Howard Journal 1.

Jordan, J (2001) 'Worlds Apart? Women, Rape and the Police Reporting Process' 41 British Journal of Criminology, 679–706.

— (1998) 'The Art of Necessity: The Subversive Imagination of Anti-Road Protest and Reclaim the Streets', in McKay (ed) *DIY Culture – Party and Protest in Nineties Britain*.

Joshua, H and Wallace, T with Booth, H (1983) *To Ride the Storm: the 1980 Bristol 'Riot' and the State* (Heinemann).

Jowell, R, Brook, L, Prior, G and Taylor, B (1992) *British Social Attitudes, Ninth Report* (Dartmouth).

Jowell, R, Curtice, J, Park, A, Brook, L and Thomson, K (1996) *British Social Attitudes, Eleventh Report* (Dartmouth).

Jowell, R, Witherspoon, S and Brook, L (1986) *British Social Attitudes, Third Report* (Gower).

— (1988) *British Social Attitudes, Fifth Report* (Gower).

Justice (Report) (1984) *Fraud Trials*.

Kaplan, J (1983) *The Hardest Drug: Heroin and Public Policy* (University of Chicago Press).

Kappeler, Susanne (1986) *The Pornography of Representation* (Polity Press).

Kaye, J M (1967) 'The Early History of Murder and Manslaughter' 83 LQR 365 and 569.

Kelly, Liz (1988) *Surviving Sexual Violence* (Polity Press, Blackwell Publishers).

— (1999) *Domestic Violence Matters*, Home Office Research Study No 193 (Home Office).

Kelly, Liz and Radford, Jill (1987) 'The Problem of Men: Feminist Perspectives on Sexual Violence' in Scraton (ed) *Law, Order and the Authoritarian State*.

Kelman, Mark (1981) 'Interpretive Construction in the Substantive Criminal Law' 33 Stanford LR 591.

— (1987) *A Guide to Critical Legal Studies* (Harvard University Press).

Kennedy, Helena (1992) *Eve Was Framed: Women and British Justice* (Chatto & Windus).

Kennedy, Ian (1988) *Treat Me Right* (Oxford University Press).

Kennedy, Ian and Grubb, Andrew (2000) *Medical Law: Text and Materials* (3rd edn, Butterworths).

Keown, John (1988) *Abortion, Doctors and the Law* (Cambridge University Press).

— (2002) *Euthanasia, Ethics and Public Policy: An Argument Against Legalisation* (Cambridge University Press).

Kerrigan, K (1997) 'Breach of the Peace and Binding Over – Continuing Confusion' Journal of Civil Liberties 30.

Kershaw, C, Chivite-Matthews, N, Thomas, C and Aust, R (2001) *The 2001 British Crime Survey*, Statistical Bulletin 18/01 (Home Office).

Kettle, M (1985) 'The National Reporting Centre and the 1984 Miners' Strike' in B Fine and R Millar (eds) *Policing the Miners' Strike*.

Kilvington, J, Day, S and Ward, H (2001) 'Prostitution Policy in Europe: A Time of Change' 67 Feminist Review 79–83.

King, M (1989) 'Social Crime Prevention à la Thatcher' 28 Howard Journal 291.

King, M and Brearley, N (1996) *Public Order Policing – Contemporary Perspectives on Strategy and Tactics* (Perpetuity Press).

King, Michael and Piper, Christine (1995) *How the Law Thinks about Children* (2nd edn, Arena).

Kingdom, Elizabeth (1985) 'Consent, Coercion and Consortium: The Sexual Politics of Sterilisation' 12 Journal of Law and Society 19.

Kinsey, R, Lea, J and Young, J (1986) *Losing the Fight Against Crime* (Blackwell).

Kritzman, L (ed) (1988) *Michel Foucault: Politics, Philosophy and Culture, Interviews and Other Writings* (Routledge).

Kuhse, Helga and Singer, Peter (1985) *Should the Baby Live?* (Oxford University Press).

Lacey, N (1985) 'The Territory of the Criminal Law' 5 OJLS 453.
— (1986) 'Responsibility: Law, Medicine or Morals?' in P Byrne (ed) *Rights and Wrongs in Medicine*.
— (1987) 'Discretion and Due Process in Criminal Justice' in I Dennis (ed) *Criminal Law and Justice*.
— (1988) *State Punishment: Political Principles and Community Values* (Routledge).
— (1993a) 'Theory into Practice? Pornography and the Public/Private Dichotomy' 20 Journal of Law and Society 93.
— (1993b) 'A Clear Concept of Intention: Elusive or Illusory?' 56 Mod LR 621.
— (1994a) 'Making Sense of Criminal Justice' in N Lacey (ed) *A Reader in Criminal Justice*.
— (1994b) 'Government as Manager, Citizen as Consumer: the Case of the Criminal Justice Act 1991' 57 Mod LR 534.
— (1994c) 'Abstraction in Context' 14 OJLS 255.
— (ed) (1994d) *A Reader in Criminal Justice* (Clarendon Press).
— (1995) 'Contingency and Criminalisation' in I Loveland (ed) *Frontiers of Criminality*.
— (1998a) 'Unspeakable Subjects, Impossible Rights: Integrity, Sexuality and Criminal Law' Canadian Journal of Jurisprudence (reprinted in N Lacey, *Unspeakable Subjects*).
— (1998b) 'Contingency, Coherence and Conceptualism: Reflections on an Encounter between "Critique" and "Philosophy" of the Criminal Law' in A Duff (ed) *Philosophy and the Criminal Law*.
— (1998c) *Unspeakable Subjects* (Hart Publishing).
— (2001a) 'Criminal Responsibility and Modernity' 9 Journal of Political Philosophy 1.
— (2001b) 'In Search of the Responsible Subject' 64 Mod LR 350.
— (2001c) 'Beset By Boundaries: The Home Office Review of Sex Offences' Crim LR 3.
— (2002) 'Legal Constructions of Crime' in Maguire et al (eds) *The Oxford Handbook of Criminology*.
Lacey, Nicola and Zedner, Lucia (1995) 'Discourses of Community in Criminal Justice' Journal of Law and Society 301.
Lamb, David (1985) *Death, Brain Death and Ethics* (Croom Helm).
— (1988) 'The Death of Reason in Intensive Care' The Times Higher Education Supplement, 25 March.
Lambert, J (1984) 'The Policing Crisis' in P Norton (ed) *Law and Order in British Politics*.
Lane Report (1972) *Committee on the Working of the Abortion Act*, Cmnd 5579 (HMSO).

Langbein, John H (1987) 'The Criminal Trial Before the Lawyers' 45 University of Chicago LR 263.

Lanham, David (1988) 'Death of a Qualified Defence' 104 LQR 239.

Lasch, C (1979) *Haven in a Heartless World: The Family Besieged* (Basic Books).

Law Commission (1974) *Offences of Entering and Remaining on Property*, Report No 54 (HMSO).

— (1976) *Criminal Law: Conspiracy and Criminal Law Reform*, Report No 76 (HMSO).

— (1979) *The Mental Element in Crime*, Report No 89 (HMSO).

— (1983) *Offences against Public Order*, Report No 123 (HMSO).

— (1985a) *Criminal Law: Codification of the Criminal Law*, Report No 143 (HMSO).

— (1985b) *Criminal Law: Offences against Religion and Public Worship*, Report No 145 (HMSO).

— (1985c) *Criminal Libel*, Report No 149 (HMSO).

— (1987a) *Binding Over*, Working Paper No 103 (HMSO).

— (1987b) *Conspiracy to Defraud*, Working Paper No 104 (HMSO).

— (1988a) *Attempt, and Impossibility in Relation to Attempt, Conspiracy and Incitement*, Consultation Paper No 102 (HMSO).

— (1988b) *Computer Misuse*, Working Paper No 110 (HMSO).

— (1989a) *A Criminal Code for England and Wales*, Report No 177 (HMSO).

— (1989b) *Computer Misuse*, Report No 186 (HMSO).

— (1992) *Legislating the Criminal Code: Offences Against the Person and General Principles*, Consultation Paper No 122 (HMSO).

— (1993) *Legislating the Criminal Code, Offences against the Person and General Principles*, Report No 218, Cm 2370 (HMSO).

— (1994a) *Bind Overs*, Report No 222 (HMSO).

— (1994b) *Consent and Offences Against the Person*, Consultation Paper No 134 (HMSO).

— (1994c) *Conspiracy to Defraud*, Report No 228 (HMSO).

— (1995a) *Consent in the Criminal Law*, Consultation Paper No 139 (HMSO).

— (1995b) *Legislating the Criminal Code: Intoxication and Criminal Liability*, Report No 229 (HMSO).

— (1999) *Legislating the Criminal Code: Fraud and Deception*, Consultation Paper 155.

— (2001) *Bail and the Human Rights Act 1998*, Report No 269 HC 7 (HMSO).

— (2002) *Fraud*, Report No 276, Cm 5560 (HMSO).

Law Reform Commission of Canada (1989) *Crimes Against the Foetus*, Working Paper No 58.

Law Reform Commission of Western Australia (1988) *Medical Treatment for the Dying*, Report No 84.

Law Reform Commission, Ireland (1988) *Rape*, Report No 24.

Lee, R G and Morgan, D (1989a) 'A Lesser Sacrifice: Sterilisation and Mental Handicap' in R G Lee and D Morgan (eds) *Birthrights*.

— (eds) (1989b) *Birthrights: Law and Ethics at the Beginnings of Life* (Routledge).

— (eds) (1994) *Death rites: Law and Ethics at the End of Life* (Routledge).

Lees, Sue (1996) *Carnal Knowledge: Rape on Trial* (Hamish Hamilton).

Leigh, L H (1982) *The Control of Commercial Fraud* (Heinemann).

— (1988) 'Territorial Jurisdiction and Fraud' Crim LR 280.

Leng, R (1982) 'R. v. Malcherek, R. v. Steel' 45 Mod LR 206.

— (1994) 'Consent and Offences against the Person: Law Commission Consultation Paper no 134' Crim LR 480.

Levi, M (1987) *Regulating Fraud: White-Collar Crime and the Criminal Process* (Routledge).

— (1989) 'Suite justice: Sentencing for Fraud' Crim LR 420.

Lewis, Jane (1984) *Women in England 1870–1950* (Wheatsheaf Books).

Lewis, Jane and Cannell, Fenella (1986) 'The Politics of Motherhood in the 1980s' 13 Journal of Law and Society 321.

Lidstone, K W (1987) 'Social Control and the Criminal Law' 27 Br J Crim 31.

Lloyd, C and Walmsley, R (1989) *Changes in Rape Offences and Sentencing*, Home Office Research Study 105 (Home Office).

Loader, I and Sparks, R (2002) 'Contemporary Landscapes of Crime, Order and Control' in Maguire et al (eds) *The Oxford Handbook of Criminology*.

Loveland, Ian (ed) (1995) *Frontiers of Criminality* (Sweet & Maxwell).

Lukes, S (1987) 'Perspectives on Authority' in J R Pennock and J M Chapman (eds) *Authority Revisited*.

Lustgarten, L (1986) *The Governance of Police* (Sweet & Maxwell).

— (1987) 'The Police and the Substantive Criminal Law' Br J Crim 24.

— (2002) 'The Future of Stop and Search' Crim LR 603.

MacFarlane, A (1981) *The Justice and the Mare's Ale* (Blackwell).

MacKinnon, Catharine (1983) 'Feminism, Marxism, Method and the State: an Agenda for Theory' 7 Signs: Journal of Women in Culture and Society 635.

— (1987) *Feminism Unmodified* (Harvard University Press).

— (1989) *Toward a Feminist Theory of the State* (Harvard University Press).

— (1993) *Only Words* (Harvard University Press).

Macklem, T and Gardner, J (2001) 'Provocation and Pluralism' 64 Mod LR 815.

MacMillan, Elizabeth (1978) 'Birth Defective Infants' 30 Stanford LR 620.

MacPherson Report (1999) *The Stephen Lawrence Inquiry*, Cm 4262 (London, HMSO).

MacPherson, C B (1978) *Property: Mainstream and Critical Positions* (Toronto University Press).

Magnet, Joseph and Kluge, Eike-Henner (1985) *Withholding Treatment from Defective Newborn Children* (Canada: Brown Leg Publications).

Magnusson, R (2002) *Angels of Death: Exploring the Euthanasia Underground* (Melbourne University Press).

Maguire, Mike (2002) 'Crime Statistics, The "Data Explosion" and Its Implications' in Maguire et al (eds) *The Oxford Handbook of Criminology*.

Maguire, M and Bennett, J (1982) *Burglary in a Dwelling* (Heinemann).

— (eds) (1988) *Victims of Crime: A New Deal?* (Open University Press).

Maguire, M, Morgan, R and Reiner, R (eds) (2002) *The Oxford Handbook of Criminology* (3rd edn, Oxford University Press).

Maguire, Sara (1988) '"Sorry Love" – Violence Against Women in the Home and the State Response' 8 Critical Social Policy 34.

Malik, M (1999) '"Racist Crime": Racially Aggravated Offences in the Crime and Disorder Act 1998, Part II' 62 Mod LR 409.

Malleson, Kate (1998) *The New Judiciary* (Ashgate).

Malleson, Kate and Roberts, Stephanie (2002) 'Streamlining and Clarifying the Criminal Process' Crim LR 272.

Manning, P (1987) *Police Work* (MIT Press).

Mansfield, G and Peay, J (1987) *The Director of Public Prosecutions: Principles and Practices for the Crown Prosecutor* (Tavistock).

Mars, G (1982) *Cheats at Work: An Anthropology of Workplace Crime* (Unwin Paperbacks).

Marsh, P, Rosser, E and Harré, R (1978) *The Rules of Disorder* (Routledge).

Marston, J and Tain, P (2001), *Public Order: The Criminal Law* (Callow).

Mason, J K and Meyers, D (1986) 'Parental Choice and Selective Non-Treatment' 12 Journal of Medical Ethics 67.

Matsuda, M, Lawrence III, C, Delgado, R and Williams Crenshaw, K (1993) *Words that Wound: Critical Race Theory, Assaultive Words and the First Amendment* (Westview Press).

Matthiesen, T (1983) 'The Future of Control Systems – the Case of Norway' in D Garland and P Young (eds) *The Power to Punish*.

Mawby, R I and Walklate, S (1994) *Critical Victimology* (Sage).

Mayhew, P, Maung, N A and Mirrlees-Black, C (1993) *The 1992 British Crime Survey*, Home Office Research Study 132 (Home Office).

McBarnet, D (1981) *Conviction: Law, the State and the Construction of Justice* (Macmillan Press Ltd).

McBride, D C and McCoy, C B (1981) 'Crime and Drug Use: Using Behaviour – An Area Analysis' 19 Criminology 281–302.

McColgan, Aileen (1993) 'In Defence of Battered Women Who Kill' 13 OJLS 508.

McConville, M (1998) 'Plea Bargaining: Ethics and Politics' 25 Journal of Law and Society 562.

McConville, M, Hodgson, J, Bridges, L and Pavlovic, A (1994) *Standing Accused: The Organisation and Practices of Defence Lawyers in Britain* (Clarendon Press).

McConville, Mike, Sanders, Andrew and Leng, Roger (1991) *The Case for the Prosecution* (Routledge).

McConville, Mike and Shepherd, Dan (1992) *Watching Police, Watching Communities* (Routledge).

McCoy, A W (1980) *Drug Traffic: Narcotics and Organised Crime in Australia* (Harper & Row).

McGillivray, A (1987) 'Battered Women: Definition, Models and Prosecutorial Policy' 6 Canada Journal of Family Law 15.

McHugh, Paul (1980) *Prostitution and Victorian Social Reform* (Croom Helm).

McIntosh, M (1975) *The Organisation of Crime* (Macmillan).

McKay G (1998) *DIY Culture. Party and Protest in Nineties Britain* (Verso).

McKee, Grant and Franey, Ros (1988) *Time-Bomb: Irish Bombers, English Justice and the Guildford Four* (Bloomsbury).

McLean, Sheila (ed) (1989) *Legal Issues in Human Reproduction* (Gower).

McMillan, J L (1987) 'Crime, Law and Order in Early Modern England' 27 Br J Crim 252.

McNeill, Sandra (1987) 'Flashing: Its Effect on Women' in J Hanmer and M Maynard (eds) *Women, Violence and Social Control* (Macmillan Press Ltd).

Mead, D (1998a) 'Will Peaceful Protestors Be Foxed by the Divisional Court Decision in *Capon v. DPP*' Crim LR 870.
— (1998b) 'The Human Rights Act – A Panacea for Peaceful Public Protest' Journal of Civil Liberties 206 (Part 2, 1999, J Civ Lib 7).

Medical Law Review (2001) Special Edition: *The Conjoined Twins Case* 9 Med LR 201–98.

Menlowe, Michael and McCall Smith, Alexander (eds) (1993) *The Duty to Rescue* (Dartmouth).

Metropolitan Police (1987) *Public Order Review: Civil Disturbances 1981–1985*.

Miers, David (1997) *State Compensation for Criminal Injuries* (Oxford University Press).

Mill, J S (1974) *On Liberty 1859* (Penguin).

Millett, Kate (1976) *The Prostitution Papers* (Ballantine Books).

Mirfield, P (1988) 'The Legacy of *Hunt*' Crim LR 19.

Mirrlees-Black, C (1999) *Domestic Violence: Findings from a new British Crime Survey self-completion questionnaire*, Home Office Research Study No 191 (Home Office).

Mirrlees-Black, C, Mayhew, P and Percy, A (1996) *The 1996 British Crime Survey*, Home Office Statistical Bulletin 19/96 (Home Office).

Mitra, Charlotte (1987) 'Judicial Discourse in Father–Daughter Incest Appeal Cases' 15 International Journal of the Sociology of Law 121.

Moonman, E and Bradley, P (1984) 'Football as a Political Arena' in Centre for Contemporary Studies *Football as a Form for Disorder*.

Moran, Leslie J (1995) 'Violence and the Law: The Case of Sado-Masochism' 4 Social and Legal Studies 225.

— (1996) *The Homosexual(ity) of Law* (Routledge).

Morgan, Derek (1986) 'Who to Be or Not to Be: The Surrogacy Story' 49 Mod LR 358.

Morgan, Rod (2002) 'Imprisonment' in Maguire et al (eds) *The Oxford Handbook of Criminology*.

Morgan, J (1987) *Conflict and Order* (Clarendon Press).

Morgan, Jane and Zedner, Lucia (1992) *Child Victims: Crime, Impact and Criminal Justice* (Oxford University Press).

Morgan, P A (1978) 'The Legislation of Drug Law' 8 Journal of Drug Issues 53–62.

Morison, J (1987) 'New Strategies in the Politics of Law and Order' 26 Howard Journal 203.

Morris, A (1987) *Women, Crime and Criminal Justice* (Blackwell Publishers).

Morris, Allison and Gelsthorpe, Lorraine (2000) 'Re-visioning Men's Violence against Female Partners' 39 Howard Journal 412.

Morris, Gillian S (2002) 'Extending the Police Family: Issues and Anomalies' Public Law 670.

Mort, Frank (1987) *Dangerous Sexualities: Medico-Moral Politics in England Since 1830* (Routledge).

Mullen, Paul E and Pathe, Michele (2002) 'Stalking' in Tonry (ed) *Crime and Justice: A Review of Research*, vol 29 (University of Chicago Press).

Murphy, D J (1986) *Customers and Thieves, An Ethnography of Shoplifting* (Gower).

Musto, D F (1973) *The American Disease: Origins of Narcotic Control* (Yale University Press).

Myhill, A and Allen, J (2002h) *Rape and Sexual Assault of Women: The Extent and Nature of the Problem*, Home Office Research Study 237 (Home Office).

Naffine, Ngaire (1994) 'Possession: Erotic Love in the Law of Rape' 57 Mod LR 10.

— (1997a) 'The Body Bag' in N Naffine and R Owens (eds) *Sexing the Subject of Law*.

— (1997b) *Feminism and Criminology* (Polity Press).

Naffine, Ngaire and Owens, Rosemary (eds) (1997) *Sexing the Subject of Law* (The Law Book Company).

National Council for Civil Liberties (1980) *Unofficial Committee of Inquiry, Report: Southall, 23 April 1979*.

— (1986) *Stonehenge: A Report into the Civil Liberties Implications of Events Relating to the Convoys of Summer 1985 and 1986* (Yale Press).

Nelken, David (1987a) 'Critical Criminal Law' 14 Journal of Law and Society 105.

— (1987b) 'Criminal Law and Criminal Justice: Some Notes on their Irrelation' in I Dennis (ed) *Criminal Law and Justice* (Sweet & Maxwell).

— (ed) (1994) *The Futures of Criminology* (Sage).

— (2002) 'White-Collar Crime' in Maguire et al (eds) *The Oxford Handbook of Criminology*.

Nelli, H S (1976) *The Business of Crime* (Oxford University Press, New York).

Nellis, Mike (2003) 'News Media, Popular Culture and the Electronic Monitoring of Offenders in England and Wales' 42 Howard Journal 1–31.

Newburn, Tim (2002) *Young People, Crime, and Youth Justice* in Maguire et al (eds) *The Oxford Handbook of Criminology*, p 531.

Nicolson, Donald (1995) 'Telling Tales: Gender Discrimination, Gender Construction and Battered Women Who Kill' III Feminist Legal Studies 185.

Nicolson, Donald and Bibbings, Lois (2000) *Feminist Perspectives on Criminal Law* (Cavendish).

Nobles, Richard and Schiff, David (2000) *Understanding Miscarriages of Justice* (Oxford University Press).

Nolan, Jacqueline (1976) 'Defective Children, Their Parents and the Death Decision' 4 Journal of Legal Medicine 9.

Norrie, Alan (1983) 'Freewill, Determinism and Criminal Justice' 3 Legal Studies 60.

— (1989) 'Oblique Intention and Legal Politics' Crim LR 793.

— (1991) *Law, Ideology and Punishment* (Kluwer).

— (1999) 'After *Woollin*' Crim LR 532.

— (2000) *Punishment, Responsibility and Justice* (Oxford University Press).

— (2001a) 'Criminal Justice, Judicial Interpretation, Legal Right: On Being Sceptical about the Human Rights Act 1998' in Campbell T, Ewing K and Tomkins A *Sceptical Essays on Human Rights*.

— (2001b) 'The Structure of Provocation' *Current Legal Problems*, vol 54 (Oxford University Press).

— (2001c) *Crime Reason and History* (2nd edn, Butterworths).

— (2002) 'From Criminal Law to Legal Theory: The Mysterious Case of the Reasonable Glue Sniffer' 65 Mod LR 538.

Norrie, Kenneth McK (1985) 'Abortion in Great Britain: One Act, Two Laws' Crim LR 475.

North Report (1988) *Road Traffic Law Review Report* (HMSO).

Norton, P (ed) (1984) *Law and Order in British Politics* (Gower).

Note (1987) 'Getting Away With Murder: Federal OSHA Pre-emption of State Criminal Prosecutions for Industrial Accidents' 101 Harv LR 535.

Nozick, R (1974) *Anarchy, State and Utopia* (Blackwell).

Nussbaum, Martha (1999) *Sex and Social Justice* (Oxford University Press).

O'Connell Davidson, Julia *Prostitution, Power and Freedom* (Polity).

O'Donovan, Katherine (1984) 'The Medicalisation of Infanticide' Crim LR 259.

— (1985) *Sexual Divisions in Law* (Weidenfeld & Nicolson).

— (1989) 'Engendering Justice: Women's Perspectives and the Rule of Law' 39 University of Toronto LJ 127.

— (1993) *Family Law Matters* (Pluto Press).

O'Neill, O (2002) *A Question of Trust: the BBC Reith Lectures 2002* (Cambridge University Press).

OECD (1986) *Computer-related Crime* (OECD Publications, Paris).

Orchard, G (1993) 'Surviving without Majewski' Crim LR 426.

Ormerod, David (1999) 'A Bit of a Con? The Law Commission's Consultation Paper on Fraud' Crim LR 789.

Ormerod, D and Roberts, A (2003) 'The Police Reform Act 2002 – Increasing Centralisation, Maintaining Confidence and Contracting Out Crime' Crim LR 141.

Ormerod, D C and Gunn, M J (1996) 'Consent – a Second Bash' Crim LR 694.

Orth, J (1987) 'The English Combination Acts Reconsidered' in F Snyder and D Hay (eds) *Labour, Law and Crime*.

Orwell, George (1970) 'Decline of the English Murder' in *The Collected Essays, Journalism and Letters of George Orwell*, vol V (Penguin).

Osufsky, Howard and Blumenthal, Susan (1985) *Pre-Menstrual Syndrome: Current Findings and Future Directions* (Am Psych Press).

Otlowski Margaret (1997) *Voluntary Euthanasia and the Common Law* (Clarendon Press).

Pace, P J (1983) 'Sexuality, Identity and the Criminal Law' Crim LR 317.

Packer, H (1968) *The Limits of the Criminal Sanction* (Stanford University Press).

Padfield, Nicola (1992) 'Duress, Necessity and the Law Commission' Crim LR 778.

— (2000) *Text and Materials on the Criminal Justice Process* (Butterworths).

Pahl, Jan (1985) *Private Violence and Public Policy* (Routledge).

Painter, K and Farrington, D (1998) 'Marital Violence in Great Britain and its Relationship to Marital and Non-Marital Rape' International Review of Victimology, Vol 5.

Palmer, Stephanie (1997) 'Rape in Marriage and the European Convention on Human Rights: *CR v UK, SW v UK*' V Feminist Legal Studies 91.

Park et al (2002) *British Social Attitudes, Nineteenth Report* (Sage).

Parker, D B (1976) *Crime by Computer* (Charles Scribeners).

Parker, H (1997) 'Adolescent Drugs Pathways in the 1990s' in J Braggins *Tackling Drugs Together: One Year On.*

Parker, Howard (1999) 'Illegal Leisure: Alcohol, Drugs and the Regulation of Modern Youth' in Carlen and Morgan (eds) *Crime Unlimited? Questions for the 21st Century.*

Pateman, Carole (1988) *The Sexual Contract* (Polity Press, Blackwell Publishers).

Paton, E (1995) 'Reformulating the Intoxication Rules: The Law Commission's Report' Crim LR 382.

Patten Report (1999) *A New Beginning: Policing in Northern Ireland – Report of the Independent Commission on Policing for NI* (HMSO).

Pattenden, R (1982) *The Judge, Discretion and the Criminal Trial* (Clarendon Press).

— (1989) *Judicial Discretion and Criminal Litigation* (Clarendon Press).

Paulus, Ingeborg (1975) *The Search for Pure Food* (Martin Robertson).

— (1978) 'Strict Liability: Its Place in Public Welfare Offences' 21 Crim LQ 445.

Pearce L, Knowles, J, Davies, G P, Buttress, S and TRL Limited (2002) *Road Safety Research Report No. 26 Dangerous Driving and the Law* (Department for Transport).

Pearce, F (1978) *Crimes of the Powerful: Marxism, Crime and Deviance* (Pluto Press).

Pearson, Geoffrey (1983) *Hooligan: A History of Respectable Fears* (Macmillan Press Ltd).

— (1998) 'The English Disease? – The Socio-Legal Construction of Football Hooliganism' 60 Youth Policy 1.

Pease, Ken (2002) 'Crime Reduction' in Maguire et al (eds) *The Oxford Handbook of Criminology.*

Peay, Jill (2002) 'Mentally Disordered Offenders, Mental Health and Crime' in Maguire et al (eds) *The Oxford Handbook of Criminology.*

Pennock, J R and Chapman, J M (eds) (1987) *Authority Revisited* Nomos XXIX (New York University Press).

Percy, Smith J and Hillyard, P (1985) 'Miners in the Arms of the Law: A Statistical Analysis' 12 Journal of Law and Society 345.

Petchesky, Rosalind Pollack (1986) *Abortion and Woman's Choice* (Verso).

Phillips, Coretta and Bowling, Ben (2002) 'Racism, Ethnicity, Crime and Criminal Justice' in Maguire et al (eds) *The Oxford Handbook of Criminology.*

Picardie, J and Wade, D (1985) *Heroin: Chasing the Dragon* (Penguin).

Plumer, Ken (1995) *Telling Sexual Stories: Power, Change and Social Worlds* (Routledge).

Policy Advisory Committee (1981) *Report on the Age of Consent in Relation to Sexual Offences*, Cmnd 8216.

Posner, Richard (1987) *The Economic Structure of Tort Law* (Harvard University Press).

Prescott-Clarke, P (1982) *Public Attitudes Towards Industrial Work Related and Other Risks* (SCPR).

President's Commission for the Study of Ethical Problems in Medicine (1981) *Defining Death* (Washington).

Price, David (1988) 'Selective Reduction and Feticide: The Parameters of Abortion' Crim LR 199.

Pudney, Stephen (2002) *The Road to Ruin? Sequences of Initiation into Drug Use and Offending by Young People in Britain*, Home Office Research Study 253 (Home Office).

Purvis, R N (1979) *Corporate Crime* (Butterworths, Sydney).

Quinn, Warren (1971) 'Abortion: Identity and Loss' 1 Philosophy and Public Affairs 24.

Quinney, R (1970) *The Social Reality of Crime* (Little, Brown).

Rachels, James (1986) 'Euthanasia' in T Regan et al (eds) *Matters of Life and Death*.

Radcliffe Richards, Janet (1982) *The Sceptical Feminist* (Penguin).

Raphael, D D (1988) 'Handicapped Infants: Medical Ethics and the Law' Journal of Medical Ethics 5.

Rawls, R (1972) *A Theory of Justice* (Oxford University Press).

Reasons, C et al (1981) *Assault on the Worker* (Butterworths, Canada).

Reeve, A (1986) *Property* (Macmillan).

Regan, Tom et al (eds) (1986) *Matters of Life and Death: New Introductory Essays in Moral Philosophy* (Random House).

Reich, C (1964) 'The New Property' 73 Yale LJ 733.

Reiner, Robert (2000) *The Politics of the Police* (3rd edn, Oxford University Press).

— (2002) 'Media-made Criminality' in Maguire et al (eds) *The Oxford Handbook of Criminology*.

Report (1928) *Committee on Street Offences*, Cmnd 3231 (HMSO).

Report of the Special Committee on Pornography and Prostitution (1985) *Pornography and Prostitution in Canada*.

Rich, Adrienne (1976) *Of Woman Born: Motherhood as Experience and Institution* (Norton).

Richardson, Genevra (1993) *Law, Process and Custody: Prisoners and Patients* (Butterworths).

— (1987) 'Strict Liability for Regulatory Crime: the Empirical Research' Crim LR 295.

Roberts, Paul (1995) 'Taking the Burden of Proof Seriously' Crim LR 783.

Robertshaw, Paul (1994) 'Sentencing Rapists: First Tier Courts in 1991–92' Crim LR 343.

Robertson, Geoffrey (1974) *Whose Conspiracy?* (National Council for Civil Liberties).
— (1993) *Freedom, the Individual and the Law* (7th edn, Penguin).
— (2002) *Media Law* (Penguin).
Robertson, John A (1975) 'Involuntary Euthanasia of Defective Newborns' 27 Stanford LR 217.
Robinson, Paul (1993) 'Should the Criminal Law abandon the Actus Reus–Mens Rea distinction?' in S Shute, J Gardner and J Horder (eds) *Action and Value in Criminal Law*.
— (1997) *Structure and Function in Criminal Law* (Clarendon Press).
Roche, Declan (2003) *Accountability in Restorative Justice* (Oxford University Press).
Rock, Paul (1993) *The Social World of an English Crown Court* (Clarendon Press).
— (2002) 'Sociological Theories of Crime' in Maguire et al (eds) *The Oxford Handbook of Criminology*.
Rona, Epstein and Wise, Ian (2003) 'Children Behind Bars' 153 New Law Journal 263.
Rose, A (1995) '1995 Australian Criminal Code Act: Corporate Criminal Provisions' 6 Criminal Law Forum 129.
Rose, G (2000) *The Criminal Histories of Road Traffic Offenders*, Home Office Research Study 206 (Home Office).
Rose, Nikolas (1987) 'Beyond the Public/Private Division: Law, Power and the Family' 14 Journal of Law and Society 61.
Rose, Nikolas (1999) *Powers of Freedom* (Cambridge University Press).
Rosen, Catherine Jo (1986) 'The Excuse of Self Defence: Correcting a Historical Accident on Behalf of Battered Women who Kill' 36 American University LR 11.
Roskill, Lord (1986) *Report of the Fraud Trials Committee* (HMSO).
Rowan-Robinson, J, Watchman, P and Barker, C R (1988) 'Crime and Regulation' Crim LR 211.
Royal College of Paediatrics and Child Health (1997) 'Withholding or Withdrawing Lifesaving Treatment in Children: A Framework for Practice'.
Royal Commission (Runciman) (1993) *Criminal Justice*, Cm 2263 (HMSO).
Rubin, G R (1987) *War, Law and Labour* (Clarendon Press).
Rubin, G R and Sugarman, D (1984) *Law, Economy & Society* (Professional Books).
Rudé, G (1978) *Protest and Punishment* (Clarendon Press).
— (1985) *Criminal and Victim: Crime and Society in Early Nineteenth-Century England* (Clarendon Press).
Rumney, P (1999) 'When Rape Isn't Rape: Court of Appeal Sentencing Practice in Cases of Marital and Relationship Rape' OJLS 243.
Ryan, A (1984) *Property and Political Theory* (Blackwell).

Sanders, A (1987) 'Constructing the Case for the Prosecution' 14 Journal of Law and Society 229.

— (1988) 'Personal Violence and Public Order' 16 International Journal of the Sociology of Law 359.

Sanders, Andrew and Young, Richard (2000) *Criminal Justice* (2nd edn, Butterworths).

— (2002). 'From Suspect to Trial' in Maguire et al (eds) *The Oxford Handbook of Criminology*.

Sarat, A and Silbey, S (eds) (1997) *Studies in Law, Politics and Society*, vol 17 (JAI).

Scambler, G and Scambler, A (eds) (1997) *Rethinking Prostitution: Purchasing Sex in the 1990s* (Routledge).

Scarman, Lord (1982) *The Scarman Report: The Brixton Disorders* (Pelican).

Schneider, Elizabeth (1980) 'Equal Rights to Trial for Women: Sex Bias in the Law of Self-Defense' 15 Harvard Civil Rights–Civil Liberties LR 623.

— (2002) *Battered Women and Feminist Lawmaking* (Yale University Press).

Schulhofer, Stephen (1998) *Unwanted Sex: The Culture of Intimidation and the Failure of Law* (Harvard University Press).

Scraton, P (1987a) 'Unreasonable Force: Policing, Punishment and Marginalization' in P Scraton (ed) *Law, Order and the Authoritarian State*.

— (ed) (1987b) *Law, Order and the Authoritarian State* (Open University Press).

Scraton, P and Gordon, P (eds) (1984) *Causes for Concern* (Penguin).

Sebba, Leslie (1980) 'Is Mens Rea a Component of Perceived Offence Seriousness?' 71 Journal of Criminal Law and Criminology 127.

Segal, Lynne and McIntosh, Mary (1993) *Sex Exposed: Sexuality and the Pornography Debate* (Rutgers University Press).

Seymour, John (2000) *Childbirth and the Law* (Oxford University Press).

Shapland, J, Wilmore, J and Duff, P (1985) *Victims in the Criminal Justice System* (Gower).

Sheehy, E, Stubbs, J and Tolmie, J (1992) 'Defending Battered Women on Trial: The Battered Women Syndrome and its Limitations' Crim LJ 369.

Sheen Report (1987) *MV Herald of Free Enterprise, Report of the Court No 8074*, Department of Transport.

Sheldon, Sally (1997) *Beyond Control: Medical Power and Abortion Law* (Pluto).

Sheldon, S and Thomson, M (eds) (1998) *Feminist Perspectives on Health Care Law* (Cavendish Publishing).

Sherr, A (1989) *Freedom of Protest, Public Order and the Law* (Blackwell).

Shover, N (1980) 'The Criminalization of Corporate Federal Surface Coal Mining' in Geis and Stotland (eds) *White-Collar Crime*.

Showalter, Elaine (1987) *The Female Malady: Women, Madness and English Culture 1830–1890* (Virago).

Shute, S (1994) 'Prosecution Appeals against Sentence: the First Five Years' 57 Mod LR 745.

— (1996) 'Something Old, Something New, Something Borrowed: Three Aspects of the Project' Crim LR 684.

— (1999) 'Who Passes Unduly Lenient Sentences? A Survey of Attorney-General's Reference Cases, 1989–97' Crim LR 603.

— (2002) 'Appropriation and the Law of Theft' Crim LR 445.

Shute, S, Gardner, J and Horder, J (eds) (1993) *Action and Value in Criminal Law* (Clarendon Press).

Sieh, E H (1987) 'Garment Workers: Perceptions of Inequality and Employee Theft' 27 Br J Crim 174.

Sim, J, Scraton, P and Gordon, P (1987) 'Introduction: Crime, the State and Critical Analysis' in P Scraton (ed) *Law, Order and the Authoritarian State*.

Simester, Andrew and Sullivan, G R (2000) *Criminal Law: Theory and Doctrine* (Hart Publishing).

Simmons, M (2002) 'Drugs: the Facts' 20 Howard League Magazine No 3, 6.

Simpson, A W B (1983) *Pornography and Politics: The Williams Committee in Retrospect* (Waterlow Publishers).

— (1984) 'Legal Liability for Bursting Reservoirs: The Historical Context of *Rylands v Fletcher*' 13 Journal of Legal Studies 209.

Sims, M (1986) 'Informed Dissent: the Views of Some Mothers of Severely Mentally Handicapped Children' 12 Journal of Medical Ethics 72.

Singer, Peter (2002) 'Ms B and Diane Pretty: a commentary' 28 Journal of Medical Ethics 234.

Singer, Richard G (1989) 'The Resurgence of Mens Rea: III – The Rise and Fall of Strict Criminal Liability' 30 Boston College LR 337.

Skolnick, J (1968) 'Coercion to Virtue: The Enforcement of Morals' 41 Southern California LR 588.

Slapper, G (1998) 'A Deniable Success' 148 NLJ 586.

Smart, Carol (1976) *Women, Crime and Criminology* (Routledge).

— (1985) 'Legal Subjects and Sexual Objects: Ideology, Law and Female Sexuality' in J Brophy and C Smart (eds) *Women in Law* (Routledge).

— (1986) 'Feminism and Law: Some Problems of Analysis and Strategy' 14 International Journal of the Sociology of Law 109.

— (1989) *Feminism and the Power of Law* (Routledge).

— (1990) 'Law's Truth, Women's Experience' in R Graycar (ed) *Dissenting Opinions* (Sydney: Allen & Unwin Pty Ltd).

— (1995) *Law, Crime and Sexuality* (Sage).

Smith, A T H (1987) *Offences Against Public Order* (Sweet & Maxwell).

— (1988) 'Conspiracy to Defraud: The Law Commission's Working Paper' Crim LR 508.

— (1994) *Property Offences* (Sweet & Maxwell).

— (1995) 'The Criminal Justice and Public Order Act 1994: The Public Order Elements' Crim LR 19.

Smith, D J and Gray, J (1983) *Police and People in London, Vol IV: The Police in Action* (Policy Studies Institute).

Smith, J C (1989) *Justification and Excuse in Criminal Law* (Sweet & Maxwell).

— (1993) *The Law of Theft* (7th edn, Butterworths).

— (1995) 'Conspiracy to Defraud: Some Comments on the Law Commission's Report' Crim LR 209.

— (1998) 'Offences against the Person: The Home Office Consultation Paper' Crim LR 317.

— (1999) 'Commentary' Crim LR 100.

Smith, J C and Gunn, M J (1985) 'Arthur's Case and the Right to Life of a Down's Syndrome Child' Crim LR 705.

Smith, J P and Hillyard, P (1985) 'Miners in the Arms of the Law: A Statistical Analysis' 12 Journal of Law and Society 319.

Smith, K J M (1983a) 'Assisting in Suicide – The Attorney-General and the Voluntary Euthanasia Society' Crim LR 579.

— (1983b) 'Liability for Endangerment: English Ad Hoc Pragmatism and American Innovation' Crim LR 127.

— (1989) 'Must Heroes Behave Heroically?' Crim LR 622.

— (1991a) 'Sexual Etiquette, Public Interest and the Criminal Law' 42 Northern Ireland LQ 309.

— (1991b) *A Modern Treatise on the Law of Complicity* (Clarendon Press).

— (1994) 'The Law Commission Consultation Paper on Complicity: A Blueprint for Rationalisation' Crim LR 239.

— (2001) 'Withdrawal in Complicity; a Restatement of Principles' Crim LR 769.

Smith, L (1989a) *Concerns About Rape*, Home Office Research Study 106 (Home Office).

— (1989b) *Domestic Violence*, Home Office Research Study No 108 (Home Office).

Smith, L J F and Burrows, J (1986) 'Nobbling the Fraudster: Crime Prevention through Administrative Change' 25 Howard Journal of Criminal Justice 13.

Smith, P (ed) (1987) *Criminal Law: Essays in Honour of J C Smith* (Butterworths).

Smith, Roger (1981) *Trial By Medicine* (Edinburgh).

Smith, S (1986) *Crime, Space and Society* (Cambridge University Press).

Snider, Laureen (1987) 'Towards a Political Economy of Reform: Regulation and Corporate Crime' 9 Law and Policy 37.

Snyder, F and Hay, D (eds) (1987) *Labour, Law and Crime* (Tavistock).

Society of Conservative Lawyers (1970) *Public Order* (Conservative Political Centre, London).

Somerville, Margaret (2001) *Death Talk: The Case Against Euthanasia and Physician-Assisted Suicide* (McGill–Queen's University Press).

Soothill, K and Francis, B (1997) 'Sexual Reconvictions and the Sex Offenders Act 1997' 147 NLJ 1285.

Sorell, Tom (1987) *Moral Theory and Capital Punishment* (Blackwell Publishers).

South, Nigel (2002) 'Drugs: Use, Crime and Control' in Maguire et al (eds) *The Oxford Handbook of Criminology*.

Sparks, Richard (1994) *Television and the Drama of Crime* (Open University Press).

Spencer, J R (1985) 'Motor Vehicles as Weapons of Offence' Crim LR 29.

— (1988) 'Road Traffic Law: A Review of the North Report' Crim LR 707.

— (1988) 'Child Witnesses, Video Technology and the Law of Evidence' Crim LR 76.

— (1999) 'The European Convention and the Rules of Criminal Procedure and Evidence in England' in Centre for Public Law, the University of Cambridge, *The Human Rights Act and the Criminal Justice and Regulatory Process* (Hart).

Spencer, Shaun (1986) 'Assault with Intent to Rape – Dead or Alive?' Crim LR 110.

Spicer, R (1981) *Conspiracy: Law, Class and Society* (Lawrence & Wishart).

Sprack, John (1997) 'The Criminal Procedure and Investigations Act 1996: The Duty of Disclosure' Crim LR 308.

Stedman Jones, G (1984) *Outcast London* (2nd edn, Penguin).

Steinbock, Bonnie (1988) 'Surrogate Motherhood as Pre-Natal Adoption' 16 Law, Medicine and Health Care 44.

Stephen, James F (1883) *A History of the Criminal Law of England* (Burt Franklin, 1973).

Stevens, P and Willis, C F (1979) *Race, Crime and Arrests*, Home Office Research Study 58 (Home Office).

Stinson, Robert and Peggy (1981) 'On the Death of a Baby' 7 Journal of Medical Ethics 5.

Stychin, Carl (1996) *Law's Desire: Sexuality and the Limits of Justice* (Routledge).

— (1998) 'Body-Talk: Rethinking Autonomy, Commodification and the Embodied Legal Self' in Sheldon and Thomson, *Feminist Perspectives on Health Care Law*.

Sugarman, D (ed) (1983) *Legality, Ideology and the State* (Academic Press).

Sullivan, G R (1989) 'The Need for a Crime of Sexual Assault' Crim LR 351.

— (1994) 'Fault Elements and Joint Enterprise' Crim LR 252.

Sumner, Colin (1987a) '"Political Hooliganism" and "Rampaging Mobs"; The national press coverage of the Toxteth "Riots"' in C Sumner (ed) *Crime, Justice and the Mass Media*.

— (ed) (1987b) *Crime, Justice and the Mass Media*, Cropwood Conference Series No 14.

— (1994) *The Sociology of Deviance: An Obituary* (Open University Press).

Sunstein, Cass (1988) 'Pornography, Sex Discrimination and Free Speech' in L Gostin (ed) *Civil Liberties in Conflict* (Routledge).

Sutherland, E H (1937) *The Professional Thief* (University of Chicago Press).
— (1983) *White Collar Crime* (Yale University Press).
Swigert, P and Farrell, D (1970) *Deviance and Social Control* (Little, Brown).
Tadros, Victor (2002) 'The System of the Criminal Law' 22 Legal Studies 448.
Taylor, Chris (2000) 'Advance Disclosures: Reflections on the Criminal Procedure and Investigations Act 1996' Howard Journal 114.
Taylor, Ian (1983) *Crime, Capitalism and Community* (Butterworths, Toronto).
— (1997) 'The Political Economy of Crime' in Maguire et al (eds) *The Oxford Handbook of Criminology*.
Taylor, Laurie J (1986) 'Provoked Reason in Men and Women: Heat of Passion, Manslaughter and Imperfect Self Defense' 33 University of California LR 1679.
Taylor, P (ed) (1993) *Violence in Society* (Royal College of Physicians).
Teff, H (1975) *Drugs, Society and the Law* (Lexington Books).
Temkin, Jennifer (1986) 'Pre-Natal Injury, Homicide and the Draft Criminal Code' 45 CLJ 414.
— (1993) 'Sexual History Evidence: the Ravishment of Section 2' Crim LR 3.
— (ed) (1995) *Rape and the Criminal Justice System* (Dartmouth).
— (1996) 'Doctors, rape and criminal justice' 35 Howard Journal 1.
— (1997) 'Plus ca Change: Reporting Rape in the 1990s' 37 B J Crim 507.
— (1998) 'Criminal law Medical Evidence in Rape cases: a Continuing Problem for Criminal Justice' 61 Mod LR 821.
— (2000) 'Criminal Procedure Prosecuting and Defending Rape: Perspectives from the Bar' 27 J Law & Soc 219.
— (2002) *Rape and the Legal Process* (Oxford University Press).
— (2003) 'Sexual History Evidence – Beware the Backlash' Crim LR 217.
Thomas, D A (1978) 'Form and Function in Criminal Law' in Glazebrook (ed) *Reshaping the Criminal Law*.
Thomas, D (1998) 'Right of Peaceful Protest Preserved', Legal Action (April) 10.
Thomas, Keith (1978) *Religion and the Decline of Magic* (Peregrine Books).
Thompson, E P (1975) *Whigs and Hunters* (Penguin).
— (1989) 'Property in Land: the Case of the Mohegan Indians in the Privy Council' James Ford Lecture.
Thompson, Kenneth (1998) *Moral Panics* (Routledge).
Thomson, Judith Jarvis (1971) 'A Defense of Abortion' 1 Philosophy and Public Affairs 47.
Thornton, Margaret (1995) 'Embodying the Citizen' in Thornton (ed) *Public and Private: Feminist Legal Debates* (Oxford University Press Australia) 198.
Tieman, C R (1981) 'From Victims to Criminals to Victims: A Review of the Issues' in J A Inciardi and C D Chambers (eds) *Drugs and the Criminal Justice System*.

Tooley, Michael (1983) *Abortion and Infanticide* (Clarendon Press).

Travis, Alan (2000) *Bound and Gagged, A Secret History of Obscenity in Britain* (Profile).

Trebach, A S (1982) *The Heroin Solution* (Yale University Press).

Tunkel, Victor (1985) 'Late Abortions and the Crime of Child Destruction' Crim LR 133.

Tur, Richard (2003) 'Legislative Technique and Human Rights: The Sad Case of Assisted Suicide' Crim LR 3.

Uglow, S (2002) *Criminal Justice* (Sweet & Maxwell).

Valier, C (2003) 'Minimum Terms of Imprisonment in Murder, Just Deserts and the Sentencing Guidelines' Crim LR 326.

Valverde, Mariana (1998) *Diseases of the Will* (Cambridge University Press).

Vandervort, L (1987) 'Social Justice in the Modern Regulatory State; Duress, Necessity and the Consensual Model in Law' 6 Law and Philosophy 205.

Veatch, Robert M (1976) *Death, Dying and the Biological Revolution* (Yale University Press).

— (1988) 'Justice and the Economics of Terminal Illness' 18 Hastings Center Report 34.

Vega, Judith (1988) 'Coercion and Consent: Classic Liberal Concepts in Texts on Sexual Violence' 16 International Journal of the Sociology of Law 75.

von Hirsch, Andrew (1976) *Doing Justice* (Hill & Wang).

— (1993) *Censure and Sanctions* (Oxford University Press).

von Hirsch, Andrew, Bottoms, A E, Burney, E and Wikstrom, P-O (1999) *Criminal Deterrence: an Analysis of Recent Research* (Hart Publishing).

von Hirsch, A, Garland, D and Wakefield, A (2000) *Ethical and Social Perspectives on Situational Crime Prevention* (Hart Publishing).

Waddington, D (1992) *Contemporary Issues in Public Disorder* (Routledge).

Waddington, P A J (1991) *The Strong Arm of the Law: Armed and Public Order Policing* (Clarendon Press).

— (2000) 'Public Order Policing: citizenship and moral ambiguity' in F Leishman, B Loveday and S Savage (eds) *Core Issues in Policing* (Pearson).

Waldron, J (1988) *The Right to Private Property* (Clarendon Press).

Walker, C (1986) *The Prevention of Terrorism in British Law* (Manchester University Press).

— (2002) *The Anti-Terrorism Legislation* (Oxford University Press).

Walker, L (1984) *The Battered Woman Syndrome* (Springer Publishing Co).

Walker, N (1985) *Sentencing: Theory, Law and Practice* (Butterworths).

Walkowitz, Judith (1980) *Prostitution in Victorian Society* (Cambridge University Press).

Wallace, A (1986) *Homicide: The Social Reality*, Research Study No 5, NSW Attorney-General's Department.

Walmsley, Roy (1986) *Personal Violence* (Home Office).

Walsh, D P (1978) *Shoplifting: Controlling a Major Crime* (Macmillan).

Walter, J (1980) 'Grain riots and popular attitudes to the law: Maldon and the Crisis of 1629' in J Brewer and J Styles (eds) *An Ungovernable People*.

Ward, P and Dobinson, I (1988) 'Heroin: A Considered Response?' in M Findlay and R Hogg (eds) *Understanding Crime and Criminal Justice*.

Warnock, Mary (1985) *A Question of Life?* (Blackwell).

Warnock Report (1984) *Report of the Committee of Inquiry into Human Fertilisation and Embryology*, Cmnd 9314 (HMSO).

Wasik, M (1982) 'Cumulative Provocation and Domestic Killing' Crim LR 22.

— (1983) 'Criminal Injuries Compensation and Family Violence' Journal of Social Welfare Law 100.

— (1989) 'Law Reform Proposals on Computer Misuse' Crim LR 257.

— (1991) *Crime and the Computer* (Oxford University Press).

— (2001) 'Legislating in the Shadow of the Human Rights Act: The Criminal Justice and Police Act 2001' [2001] Crim LR 931.

Wasik, M and Pease, K (1987) *Sentencing Reform: Guidance or Guidelines?* (Manchester University Press).

Wasik, Martin and Taylor, Richard (1995) *Criminal Justice and Public Order Act 1994* (Blackstone Press).

Weait, Matthew (1995) 'The Serious Fraud Office: Nightmares (and Pipe Dreams) on Elm Street' in I Loveland (ed) *Frontiers of Criminality*.

— (1996) 'Fleshing it Out' in L Bentley and L Flynn (eds) *Law and the Senses*.

Weeks, Jeffrey (1985) *Sexuality and its Discontents: Meanings, Myths and Modern Sexualities* (Routledge).

Weinberger, B (1987) 'Police perceptions of labour in the inter-war period: the case of the unemployed and of miners on strike' in F Snyder and D Hay (eds) *Labour, Law and Crime*.

Weir, Robert (1984) *Selective Non-Treatment of Handicapped Newborns: Moral Dilemmas in Neonatal Medicine* (Oxford University Press Inc).

— (ed) (1986) *Ethical Issues in Death and Dying* (2nd edn, Columbia University Press).

Wells, Celia (1982) 'Swatting the Subjectivist Bug' Crim LR 209.

— (1986a) 'Codification of the Criminal Law: Restatement or Reform?' Crim LR 314.

— (1989b) 'Otherwise Kill Me; Marginal Children and Ethics at the Edges of Existence' in R Lee and D Morgan (eds) *Birthrights*.

— (1995a) 'Corporate Manslaughter: A Cultural and Legal Form' 6 Criminal Law Forum 45.

— (1995b) 'A Quiet Revolution in Corporate Liability for Crime' 145 New Law Journal 1326.

— (1996) 'Law Commission Report 237, The Corporate Manslaughter Proposals: Paradox, Pragmatism and Peninsularity' Crim LR 545.

— (1997) 'Stalking: The Criminal Law Response' Crim LR 463.

— (1998a) 'I Blame the Parents: Fitting New Genes in Old Criminal Laws' 61 Mod LR 724.

— (1998b) 'On the outside looking in: Perspectives on Enforced Caesareans' in Sheldon and Thomson eds *Feminist Perspectives on Health Care Law*.

— (2000a) 'Girls Gangs and Fears' in Nicolson and Bibbings, *Feminist Perspectives on Criminal Law*.

— (2000b) 'Prosecuting Safety – A Cautionary Tale' 150 New Law Journal 1648.

— (2001) *Corporations and Criminal Responsibility* (Clarendon Press).

Wells, Celia and Morgan, Derek (1991) 'Whose Foetus Is It?' 18 Journal of Law and Society 431.

Welsh, B and Farrington, D (2002*) Crime Prevention Effects of Closed Circuit Television: A Systematic Review*, Home Office Research Study 252 (Home Office).

West, D (1984) 'The Victim's Contribution to Sexual Offences' in J Hopkins (ed) *Perspectives on Rape and Sexual Assault*.

Whitaker, Ben (1987) *The Global Connection: The Crisis of Drug Addiction* (Jonathan Cape).

Whitbeck, Caroline (1983) 'The Moral Implications of Regarding Women as People: New Perspectives on Pregnancy and Personhood' in W Bondeson et al (eds) *Abortion and the Status of the Fetus*.

Whitelaw, Andrew (1986) 'Death as an Option in Neonatal Intensive Care' 9 August, The Lancet 328.

Whitty, N, Murphy, T and Livingstone, S (2001) *Civil Liberties Law: The Human Rights Act Era* (Butterworths).

Wiener, Martin (1990) *Reconstructing the Criminal: culture, law and policy in England, 1830–1914* (Cambridge University Press).

Wilczynski, A and Morris, A (1993) 'Parents who Kill their Children' Crim LR 31.

Williams, B (1979) *Home Office Departmental Committee, Obscenity and Film Censorship*, Cmnd 7772 (HMSO).

Williams, D G T (1965) *Not in the Public Interest* (Hutchinson).

— (1967) *Keeping the Peace* (Hutchinson).

Williams, Glanville (1955) 'The Definition of Crime' 8 Current Legal Problems 107.

— (1958) *The Sanctity of Life and the Criminal Law* (Stevens).

— (1983) *A Textbook of Criminal Law* (2nd edn, Sweet & Maxwell).

— (1987a) 'Oblique Intentions' CLJ 417.

— (1987b) 'The Logic of "Exceptions"' CLJ 261.

Williams, S (1984) 'The Classic Rape: When do Victims Report?' 31 Social Problems 459.

Wilson, William (1998) *Criminal Law* (Longmans).

Winchester, S and Jackson, H (1982b) *Residential Burglary: the Limits of Prevention*, Home Office Research Study 74 (Home Office).

Windlesham, Lord (1989) 'Life Sentences: The Paradox of Uncertainty' Crim LR 244.

Wolfenden Report (1957) *Homosexual Offences and Prostitution*, Cmnd 247 (HMSO).

Wolfram, Sybil (1983) 'Eugenics and the Punishment of Incest Act 1908' Crim LR 308.

Wood, J (1989) 'The Serious Fraud Office' Crim LR 175.

Wootton, B (1963) *Crime and the Criminal Law* (2nd edn, 1981, Stevens).

Worrall, A and Pease, K (1982) 'Personal Crime against Women: Evidence from the British Crime Survey' 25 Howard Journal 118.

Wright, H and Sagar, T (2000) 'Out of Sight, Out of Mind' 150 New Law Journal, 1792.

Young, Alison (1990) *Femininity in Dissent* (Routledge).

— (1996) *Imagining Crime: Textual Outlaws and Criminal Conversations* (Sage).

Young, Jock (1971) *The Drugtakers: The Social Meaning of Drug Use* (Paladin).

— (1999) *The Exclusive Society* (London, Sage).

— (2002) 'Crime and Social Exclusion' in Maguire et al (eds) *The Oxford Handbook of Criminology*.

Young, T and Kettle, M (1976) *Incitement to Disaffection* (Cobden Trust).

Zedner, Lucia (1994) 'Reparation and Retribution: Are They Reconcilable?' 57 Mod LR 228.

— (1995) 'Regulating Sexual Offences within the Home' in I Loveland (ed) *Frontiers of Criminality*.

— (2002a) 'Dangers of Dystopia in Penal Theory' Ox JLS 341.

— (2002b) 'Victims' in Maguire et al (eds) *The Oxford Handbook of Criminology*.

— (2003) 'The Concept of Security: an agenda for comparative analysis' 23 Legal Studies 153.

Index